D0225453

SIPRI Yearbook 2000
Armaments, Disarmament and International Security

sipri

Stockholm International Peace Research Institute

SIPRI is an independent international institute for research into problems of peace and conflict, especially those of arms control and disarmament. It was established in 1966 to commemorate Sweden's 150 years of unbroken peace.

The Institute is financed mainly by the Swedish Parliament. The staff and the Governing Board are international. The Institute also has an Advisory Committee as an international consultative body.

The Governing Board is not responsible for the views expressed in the publications of the Institute.

Governing Board

Professor Daniel Tarschys, Chairman (Sweden)
Dr Oscar Arias Sánchez (Costa Rica)
Dr Willem F. van Eekelen (Netherlands)
Sir Marrack Goulding (United Kingdom)
Professor Helga Haftendorn (Germany)
Dr Catherine Kelleher (United States)
Professor Ronald G. Sutherland (Canada)
Dr Abdullah Toukan (Jordan)
The Director

Director

Dr Adam Daniel Rotfeld (Poland)

Adam Daniel Rotfeld, Director, *Yearbook Editor and Publisher*
Connie Wall, *Managing Editor*
Coordinators
Taylor B. Seybolt, Elisabeth Sköns, Jean Pascal Zanders
Editors
Billie Bielckus, Jetta Gilligan Borg, Eve Johansson
Editorial Assistant
Anna Lundeborg

sipri

Stockholm International Peace Research Institute

Signalistgatan 9, SE-169 70 Solna, Sweden
Cable: SIPRI
Telephone: 46 8/655 97 00
Telefax: 46 8/655 97 33
E-mail: sipri@sipri.se
Internet URL: http://www.sipri.se

SIPRI Yearbook 2000

Armaments, Disarmament and International Security

Stockholm International Peace Research Institute

OXFORD UNIVERSITY PRESS
2000

OXFORD

UNIVERSITY PRESS

Great Clarendon Street, Oxford OX2 6DP

Oxford University Press is a department of the University of Oxford.
It furthers the University's objective of excellence in research, scholarship,
and education by publishing worldwide in

Oxford New York

Athens Auckland Bangkok Bogotá Buenos Aires Calcutta
Cape Town Chennai Dar es Salaam Delhi Florence Hong Kong Istanbul
Karachi Kuala Lumpur Madrid Melbourne Mexico City Mumbai
Nairobi Paris São Paulo Singapore Taipei Tokyo Toronto Warsaw
and associated companies in Berlin Ibadan

Oxford is a registered trade mark of Oxford University Press
in the UK and certain other countries

Published in the United States
by Oxford University Press Inc., New York

© *SIPRI 2000*

*Yearbooks before 1987 published under title
'World Armaments and Disarmament:
SIPRI Yearbook [year of publication]'*

All rights reserved. No part of this publication may be reproduced,
stored in a retrieval system, or transmitted, in any form or by any means,
without the prior permission in writing of SIPRI or as expressly permitted by law,
or under terms agreed with the appropriate reprographics rights organizations.
Enquiries concerning reproduction outside the scope of the above should be sent to
SIPRI, Signalistgatan 9, SE-169 70 Solna, Sweden

You must not circulate this book in any other binding or cover
and you must impose the same condition on any acquirer

British Library Cataloguing in Publication Data

Data available
ISSN 0953–0282
ISBN 0-19-924162-7

Library of Congress Cataloging in Publication Data

Data available
ISSN 0953–0282
ISBN 0-19-924162-7

Typeset and originated by Stockholm International Peace Research Institute
Printed and bound in Great Britain by
Biddles Ltd., Guildford and King's Lynn

Contents

Part II. Military spending and armaments, 1999

Part III. Non-proliferation, arms control and disarmament, 1999

Annexes

To
Frank Blackaby
1921–2000
First Editor of the SIPRI Yearbook
Director of SIPRI 1981–1986
Contributor to SIPRI's work,
and source of inspiration

Preface

SIPRI's objective in publishing the Yearbook remains unchanged: the presentation of facts, data and analyses is intended to encourage openness and transparency in the field of arms control, disarmament and international security.

In its analyses, SIPRI research focuses on three clusters of issues: conflicts, conflict prevention and regional security; military spending, arms production and arms transfers; and weapons of mass destruction, non-proliferation, arms control and disarmament. The findings in these three areas for 1999 are reflected in the respective parts of this Yearbook.

The data contained in the Yearbook continue to be regarded as reliable and competently verified, in the United Nations and other international organizations as well as by the governments of numerous states. SIPRI data have also been referred to in UN Secretary-General Kofi Annan's report on the role of the United Nations in the 21st century, prepared for the UN Millennium Summit to be held in the autumn of 2000.

The Institute's promotion of transparency has resulted in two particular achievements. Since 1993 the Institute of World Economy and International Relations (IMEMO) of the Russian Academy of Sciences has published a Russian edition of the Yearbook, and in 2000 the China Institute of International Studies (CIIS), Beijing, published the first Chinese edition.

All the chapters in this Yearbook reflect the results of the research conducted at SIPRI. I would like to thank the external experts who contributed several of the appendices in this volume: Peter Wallensteen, Margareta Sollenberg and others at the Uppsala Conflict Data Project, William M. Arkin, Edvard Karlsson, Milton Leitenberg, Lena Melin, Robert S. Norris, Erik Näslund and Lennart Thaning.

The production of a volume of this size and complexity requires the diligent work and support of the entire SIPRI staff, to whom I am grateful. I would like in particular to acknowledge the professional work and advice of Connie Wall and the Yearbook editorial team—Billie Bielckus, Jetta Gilligan Borg, Eve Johansson and Anna Lundeborg, editorial assistant. My thanks also go to Gunnel von Döbeln, Christine-Charlotte Bodell and the other SIPRI librarians; Billie Bielckus, cartographer; Gerd Hagmayer-Gaverus, information technology manager; and Peter Rea, indexer.

Adam Daniel Rotfeld
Director of SIPRI
May 2000

Acronyms

ABACC	Brazilian–Argentine Agency for Accounting and Control of Nuclear Materials
ABM	Anti-ballistic missile
ACM	Advanced cruise missile
ACRI	African Crisis Response Initiative
ACV	Armoured combat vehicle
ADF	Allied Democratic Forces
ADFL	Alliance of Democratic Forces for the Liberation of Congo
ADM	Atomic demolition munition
AEW	Airborne early-warning
AFRC	Armed Forces Revolutionary Council
AG	Australia Group
AIAM	Annual Implementation Assessment Meeting
AIFV	Armoured infantry fighting vehicle
AIS	Armée Islamique du Salut
ALCM	Air-launched cruise missile
AMRAAM	Advanced medium-range air-to-air missile
AMU	Arab Maghreb Union
APC	Armoured personnel carrier
APEC	Asia Pacific Economic Cooperation
APF	Alliance of Palestinian Forces
APM	Anti-personnel mine
ARF	ASEAN Regional Forum
ARV	Armoured recovery vehicle
ASEAN	Association of South-East Asian Nations
ASEAN–PMC	ASEAN Post Ministerial Conference

ATAP	Alternative Technologies and Approaches Program
ATBM	Anti-tactical ballistic missile
ATC	Armoured troop carrier
ATTU	Atlantic-to-the-Urals (zone)
AUD	Autodefensas Unidas de Colombia
AWACS	Airborne warning and control system
BIC	Bilateral Implementation Commission
BMD	Ballistic missile defence
BTWC	Biological and Toxin Weapons Convention
BW	Biological weapon/warfare
C&E	Customs and Excise
CBM	Confidence-building measure
CBW	Chemical and biological weapon/warfare
CCW	Certain Conventional Weapons (Convention)
CD	Conference on Disarmament
CEE	Central and Eastern Europe
CEI	Central European Initiative
CESDP	Common European Security and Defence Policy
CFE	Conventional Armed Forces in Europe (Treaty)
CFSP	Common Foreign and Security Policy
CIA	Central Intelligence Agency
CICA	Conference on Interaction and Confidence-Building Measures in Asia
CIO	Chairman-in-Office
CIS	Commonwealth of Independent States
CJTF	Combined Joint Task Forces

CNDD	Conseil National pour la Défense de la Démocratie	ECOWAS	Economic Community of West African States
CPC	Conflict Prevention Centre	EFTA	European Free Trade Association
CPI	Consumer price index		
CSBM	Confidence- and security-building measure	EIPCP	Enhanced International Peacekeeping Capabilities Program
CSCAP	Council for Security Cooperation in the Asia Pacific	ELN	Ejército de Liberación Nacional
CSP	Conference of States Parties	Enmod	Environmental modification
CTBT	Comprehensive Nuclear Test-Ban Treaty	EPRDF	Ethiopian People's Revolutionary Democratic Front
CTBTO	Comprehensive Nuclear Test-Ban Treaty Organization	ESDI	European Security and Defence Identity
CTR	Cooperative Threat Reduction	ESDP	European Security and Defence Policy
CW	Chemical weapon/warfare	ETA	Euzkadi Ta Azkatasuna
CWC	Chemical Weapons Convention	EU	European Union
		Euratom	European Atomic Energy Community (EAEC)
DCI	Defence Capabilities Initiative	FAR	Forces Armées Rwandaises
DGA	Délégation Générale d'Armements	FARC	Fuerzas Armadas Revolu-cionarias Colombianas
DOD	Department of Defense	FDD	Forces pour la Défense de la Démocratie
DOE	Department of Energy		
DOP	Declaration of Principles	FIS	Front Islamique du Salut
DPA	Department of Political Affairs	FMT	Fissile Material Treaty
		FOA	Swedish Defence Research Establishment
DPKO	Department of Peacekeeping Operations	FROG	Free rocket over ground
DPSS	Designated permanent storage sites	FROLINA	Front pour la Libération Nationale
DRC	Democratic Republic of Congo	FRY	Federal Republic of Yugoslavia
EAEC	European Atomic Energy Community (Euratom)	FSC	Forum for Security Co-operation
EAPC	Euro-Atlantic Partnership Council	FUNA	Former Ugandan National Army
ECOMOG	ECOWAS Monitoring Group	FY	Fiscal year
		FYDP	Future Years Defense Program (USA)
ECOSOC	Economic and Social Council		

FYROM	Former Yugoslav Republic of Macedonia	IMF	International Monetary Fund
G-21	Group of 21	INF	Intermediate-range nuclear forces
G7	Group of Seven		
G8	Group of Eight	INTERFET	International Force for East Timor
GAM	Gerakan Aceh Merdeka	IPP	Initiatives for Proliferation Prevention
GAO	General Accounting Office		
GCC	Gulf Cooperation Council	IPTF	International Police Task Force
GDP	Gross domestic product		
GIA	Groupe Islamique Armé	IRA	Irish Republican Army
GLCM	Ground-launched cruise missile	IRBM	Intermediate-range ballistic missile
GNP	Gross national product	ISTC	International Science and Technology Centre
GUUAM	Georgia–Ukraine–Uzbekistan–Azerbaijan–Moldova	JACADS	Johnston Atoll Chemical Agent Disposal System
HACV	Heavy armoured combat vehicle	JACO	Joint Armaments Cooperation Organization
HCNM	High Commissioner on National Minorities	JCC	Joint Consultative Commission
HEU	Highly enriched uranium	JCC	Joint Coordinating Committee
HLTF	High Level Task Force	JCG	Joint Consultative Group
IAEA	International Atomic Energy Agency	JCIC	Joint Compliance and Inspection Commission
ICBL	International Campaign to Ban Landmines	JKLF	Jammu and Kashmir Liberation Front
ICBM	Intercontinental ballistic missile	JMC	Joint Military Commission
ICC	International Criminal Court	KEDO	Korean Peninsula Energy Development Organization
ICG	International Crisis Group		
ICJ	International Court of Justice	KFOR	Kosovo Force
		KLA	Kosovo Liberation Army
ICTR	International Criminal Tribunal for Rwanda	KNU	Karen National Union
		KPC	Kosovo Protection Corps
ICTY	International Criminal Tribunal for the Former Yugoslavia	KTC	Kosovo Transitional Council
IDC	International Data Centre	KVM	Kosovo Verification Mission
IFOR	Implementation Force	LCA	Light Combat Aircraft
IFV	Infantry fighting vehicle	LEU	Low enriched uranium
IGAD	Intergovernmental Authority on Development	LOC	Line of Control

LRA	Lord's Resistance Army	NATO	North Atlantic Treaty Organization
LTTE	Liberation Tigers of Tamil Eelam	NBC	Nuclear, biological and chemical (weapons)
MANPADS	Man-portable air defence systems	NC	National ceiling
MBT	Main battle tank	NCI	Nuclear Cities Initiative
MD	Military District	NDA	National Democratic Alliance
MERCOSUR	Mercado Común del Sur		
MFO	Multinational Force and Observers in the Sinai	NDFB	National Democratic Front of Bodoland
MICIVIH	International Civilian Mission in Haiti	NGO	Non-governmental organization
MIK	Mission in Kosovo	NIE	National Intelligence Estimate
MINUGUA	UN Mission for the Verification of Human Rights in Guatemala	NLD	National League for Democracy
MIRV	Multiple independently targetable re-entry vehicle	NMD	National missile defence
		NNWS	Non-nuclear weapon state
MKO	Mujahideen e-Khalq Organization	NPA	New People's Army
		NPT	Non-Proliferation Treaty
MNLH	Maximum National Levels for Holdings	NSG	Nuclear Suppliers Group
MOD	Ministry of Defence	NSIP	NATO Security Investment Programme
MOMEP	Military Observer Mission to Ecuador/Peru	NTM	National technical means (of verification)
MONUC	UN Observer Mission in the Democratic Republic of Congo	NWFZ	Nuclear weapon-free zone
		NWS	Nuclear weapon state
MOU	Memorandum of understanding	O&M	Operation and maintenance
MOUS	Memorandum of Understanding on Succession	OAS	Organization of American States
		OAU	Organization of African Unity
MSF	Médecins sans Frontières	OCCAR	Organisme Conjoint de Coopération en Matière d'Armement
MTCR	Missile Technology Control Regime		
MTM	Multinational technical means (of verification)	ODIHR	Office for Democratic Institutions and Human Rights
NAC	North Atlantic Council		
NACC	North Atlantic Cooperation Council	OECD	Organisation for Economic Co-operation and Development
NAM	Non-Aligned Movement	OIC	Organization of the Islamic Conference

OMV	Ongoing Monitoring and Verification	RDT&E	Research, development, testing and evaluation
OOV	Object(s) of verification	REACT	Rapid Expert Assistance and Cooperation Teams
OPANAL	Agency for the Prohibition of Nuclear Weapons in Latin America and the Caribbean	RECAMP	Renforcement des Capacités Africaines de Maintien de la Paix
OPBTW	Organization for the Prohibition of Bacteriological (Biological) and Toxin Weapons	RPV	Remotely piloted vehicle
		RUF	Revolutionary United Front
		RV	Re-entry vehicle
OPCW	Organisation for the Prohibition of Chemical Weapons	SADC	Southern African Development Community
		SAIRI	Supreme Assembly for the Islamic Revolution in Iraq
OSCC	Open Skies Consultative Commission	SAM	Surface-to-air missile
OSCE	Organization for Security and Co-operation in Europe	SANDF	South African National Defence Forces
P5	Permanent Five (members of the UN Security Council)	SCC	Standing Consultative Commission
PA	Palestinian Authority	SCCC	Common System of Accounting and Control of Nuclear Materials
PAROS	Prevention of an Arms Race in Outer Space		
PFDJ	People's Front for Democracy and Justice	SDR	Strategic Defence Review
		SEEMNF	South-Eastern Europe Multi-National Force
PFP	Partnership for Peace	SFOR	Stabilization Force
PJC	Permanent Joint Council	SLBM	Submarine-launched ballistic missile
PKK	Partiya Karkeren Kurdistan		
PLO	Palestine Liberation Organization	SLCM	Sea-launched cruise missile
PMG	Peace Monitoring Group	SLV	Space launch vehicle
PNE	Peaceful nuclear explosion	SNDV	Strategic nuclear delivery vehicle
PPP	Purchasing power parity		
PTB(T)	Partial Test Ban (Treaty)	SNF	Short-range nuclear forces
R&D	Research and development	SOAE	Strategic Offensive Arms Elimination
RCG	Rassemblement Congolais pour la Démocratie	SPLA	Sudanese People's Liberation Army
RCG–G	Rassemblement Congolais pour la Démocratie–Goma	SPLM	Sudanese People's Liberation Movement
RCG–ML	Rassemblement Congolais pour la Démocratie–Mouvement de Libération	SRAM	Short-range attack missile
		SRBM	Short-range ballistic missile

SRCC	Sub-Regional Consultative Commission
SSBN	Nuclear-powered, ballistic-missile submarine
SSM	Surface-to-surface missile
START	Strategic Arms Reduction Treaty
SWAPO	South West Africa People's Organisation
TC	Territorial ceiling
THAAD	Theater High-Altitude Area Defense
TIPH	Temporary International Presence in Hebron
TLE	Treaty-limited equipment
TMD	Theatre missile defence
TNF	Theatre nuclear forces
TS	Technical Secretariat
UAV	Unmanned aerial vehicle
UCK	Ushtria Clirimtare e Kosoves
UIFSA	United Islamic Front for the Salvation of Afghanistan
ULFA	United Liberation Front of Assam
UN	United Nations
UNAMET	UN Mission in East Timor
UNAMSIL	UN Mission in Sierra Leone
UNCIIM	UN Commission on Investigation, Inspection and Monitoring
UNCIM	UN Special Commission on Inspection and Monitoring
UNDP	UN Development Programme
UNHCHR	UN High Commissioner for Human Rights
UNHCR	UN High Commissioner for Refugees
UNIFIL	UN Interim Force in Lebanon
UNITA	União Nacional Para a Independência Total de Angola
UNMIC	UN Monitoring and Inspection Commission
UNMIK	UN Interim Administration Mission in Kosovo
UNMOT	UN Mission of Observers in Tajikistan
UNMOVIC	UN Monitoring, Verification and Inspection Commission
UNOA	UN Office in Angola
UNOGBIS	UN Peace-Building Support Office
UNRF II	Ugandan Rescue Front II
UNROCA	UN Register of Conventional Arms
UNSCOM	UN Special Commission on Iraq
UNTAET	UN Transitional Administration in East Timor
UTO	United Tajik Opposition
WA	Wassenaar Arrangement
WEAG	Western European Armaments Group
WEAO	Western European Armaments Organization
WEU	Western European Union
WMD	Weapon of mass destruction
WNBF	West Nile Bank Front
WTO	Warsaw Treaty Organization (Warsaw Pact)
WTO	World Trade Organization

Glossary

RAGNHILD FERM, CONNIE WALL and
CHRISTER BERGGREN

The main terms and organizations discussed in this Yearbook are defined in the glossary. For acronyms that appear in the definitions, see page xviii; for the arms control and disarmament agreements mentioned in the glossary, see annexe A.

Agency for the Prohibition of Nuclear Weapons in Latin America and the Caribbean (OPANAL)	Established by the 1967 Treaty of Tlatelolco to resolve, together with the IAEA, questions of compliance with the treaty.
Anti-ballistic missile (ABM) system	*See* Ballistic missile defence and National missile defence.
Anti-personnel mine (APM)	A landmine designed to be exploded by the presence, proximity or contact of a person and that will incapacitate, injure or kill one or more persons.
Arab League	The League of Arab States, established in 1945, with Permanent Headquarters in Cairo. Its principal objective is to form closer union among Arab states and foster political and economic cooperation. An agreement for collective defence and economic cooperation among the members was signed in 1950. *See* the list of members.
Arab Maghreb Union (AMU)	Established in 1989 among five North African states to ensure regional stability, enhance policy coordination and promote common defence. *See* the list of members.
Asia–Pacific region	The Pacific rim states of Asia, North and South America, and Oceania. It is defined differently by the membership of different Asia–Pacific organizations.
Association of South-East Asian Nations (ASEAN)	Established in 1967 to promote economic, social and cultural development as well as regional peace and security in South-East Asia. The seat of the Secretariat is in Jakarta. The ASEAN Regional Forum (ARF) was established in 1993 to address security issues. The ASEAN Post Ministerial Conference (ASEAN–PMC) was established in 1979 as a forum for discussions of political and security issues with Dialogue Partners. *See* the lists of the members of ASEAN, ARF and ASEAN–PMC.
Atlantic-to-the-Urals (ATTU) zone	Zone of application of the 1990 CFE Treaty, the 1992 CFE-1A Agreement and the 1999 Agreement on Adaptation of the CFE Treaty, stretching from the Atlantic Ocean to the Ural Mountains. It covers the entire land territory of the European states parties (excluding part of Turkey) and the territory of Russia and Kazakhstan west of the Ural River.

Australia Group (AG)

Group of states, formed in 1985, which meets informally each year to monitor the proliferation of chemical and biological products and to discuss chemical and biological weapon-related items which should be subject to national regulatory measures. *See* the list of members.

Balkan states

States in south-eastern Europe bounded by the Adriatic, Aegean and Black seas: Albania, Bosnia and Herzegovina, Bulgaria, Croatia, Greece, the Former Yugoslav Republic of Macedonia, Romania, Slovenia, Turkey and the Federal Republic of Yugoslavia.

Ballistic missile

Missile which follows a ballistic trajectory (part of which may be outside the earth's atmosphere) when thrust is terminated.

Ballistic missile defence (BMD)

Weapon system designed to defend against a ballistic missile attack by intercepting and destroying ballistic missiles or their warheads in flight.

Baltic states

Estonia, Latvia and Lithuania, three Baltic Sea littoral states in north-eastern Europe.

Binary chemical weapon

A shell or other device filled with two chemicals of relatively low toxicity which mix and react while the device is being delivered to the target, the reaction product being a super-toxic chemical warfare agent, such as a nerve agent.

Biological weapon (BW)

Weapon containing infectious agents or living organisms, or infective material derived from them, when used or intended to cause disease or death in humans, animals or plants, as well as their means of delivery.

Brazilian–Argentine Agency for Accounting and Control of Nuclear Materials (ABACC)

Established by a 1991 agreement between Brazil and Argentina to promote the exclusively peaceful use of nuclear energy. It administers the Common System of Accounting and Control of Nuclear Materials.

Central and Eastern Europe (CEE)

Bulgaria, the Czech Republic, Hungary, Poland, Romania, Slovakia and Slovenia. The term is sometimes also taken to include Armenia, Azerbaijan, Belarus, Georgia, Moldova, the European part of Russia and Ukraine—and sometimes also the Baltic states.

Central Asia

Kazakhstan, Kyrgyzstan, Tajikistan, Turkmenistan and Uzbekistan.

Central European Initiative (CEI)

Established in 1989 to promote cooperation among members in the political and economic spheres. It provides support to its non-EU members in their process of accession to the EU. The seat of the Executive Secretariat is in Trieste, Italy. *See* the list of members.

Chemical weapon (CW)

Chemical substances—whether gaseous, liquid or solid—when used or intended for use in weapons because of their direct toxic effects on humans, animals or plants, as well as their means of delivery.

Combined Joint Task Forces (CJTF)

Concept launched in 1993, endorsed in 1994 and approved in 1996 for a multinational force to facilitate NATO contingency operations, including the use of 'separable but not separate' military capabilities in operations which might in future be led by the European Union/Western European Union with the participation of states outside the NATO alliance. *See also* European Security and Defence Identity.

Common European Security and Defence Policy (CESDP)

See European Security and Defence Policy.

Common Foreign and Security Policy (CFSP)

Institutional framework, established by the 1992 Maastricht Treaty, for consultation and development of common positions and joint action on European foreign and security policy. It constitutes the second of the three 'pillars' of the European Union. The CFSP was further elaborated in the 1997 Amsterdam Treaty and at the December 1999 Helsinki European Council meeting as the European Security and Defence Policy (ESDP). *See also* European Union and European Security and Defence Policy.

Commonwealth of Independent States (CIS)

Established in 1991 as a framework for multilateral cooperation among former Soviet republics. *See* the list of members.

Comprehensive Nuclear Test-Ban Treaty Organization (CTBTO)

Established by the 1996 CTBT to resolve questions of compliance with the treaty and as a forum for consultation and cooperation among the states parties. Its seat is in Vienna.

Conference on Disarmament (CD)

A multilateral arms control negotiating body, set up in 1961 as the Eighteen-Nation Committee on Disarmament; it has been enlarged and renamed several times and has been called the Conference on Disarmament since 1984. The CD is based in Geneva and is today composed of states representing all the regions of the world, including the permanent members of the UN Security Council. It reports to the UN General Assembly. *See* the list of members under United Nations.

Conference on Interaction and Confidence-Building Measures in Asia (CICA)

Initiated in 1992, and established by the 1999 Declaration on the Principles Guiding Relations among the CICA Member States, as a forum to enhance security cooperation and confidence-building measures among the member states. It also promotes economic, social and cultural cooperation. *See* the list of members.

Confidence- and security-building measure (CSBM)

Measure undertaken by states to promote confidence and security through military transparency, openness, constraints and cooperation. CSBMs are militarily significant, politically binding, verifiable and, as a rule, reciprocal.

Confidence-building measure (CBM)

Measure undertaken by states to help reduce the danger of armed conflict and of misunderstanding or miscalculation of military activities.

Conventional weapon

Weapon not having mass destruction effects. *See also* Weapon of mass destruction.

Conversion	Term used to describe the reallocation of resources from military to civilian use. It usually refers to the conversion of industry from military to civilian production but may also include the reorientation of research and development activities, the reintegration of military personnel into civilian life, the redevelopment of military bases and facilities for other purposes, and the dismantling, scrapping or reusing of surplus weapons.
Council for Security Cooperation in the Asia Pacific (CSCAP)	Established in 1993 as an informal, non-governmental process for regional confidence building and security cooperation through dialogue, consultation and cooperation in Asia–Pacific security matters. *See* the list of members.
Council of Europe	Established in 1949, with its seat in Strasbourg, France. The Council is open to membership of all the European states that accept the principle of the rule of law and guarantee their citizens human rights and fundamental freedoms. Among its organs is the European Court of Human Rights. *See* the list of members.
Counter-proliferation	Measures or policies to prevent the proliferation or enforce the non-proliferation of weapons of mass destruction.
Cruise missile	Guided weapon-delivery vehicle which sustains flight at subsonic or supersonic speeds through aerodynamic lift, generally flying at very low altitudes to avoid radar detection, sometimes following the contours of the terrain. It can be air-, ground- or sea-launched (ALCM, GLCM and SLCM, respectively) and carry a conventional, nuclear, chemical or biological warhead.
Dual-capable	Term that refers to a weapon system or platform that can carry either conventional or non-conventional explosives.
Dual-use technology	Technology that can be used for both civilian and military applications.
Economic Community of West African States (ECOWAS)	A regional organization established in 1975, with its Executive Secretariat in Lagos, Nigeria, to promote trade and cooperation and contribute to development in West Africa. In 1981 it adopted the Protocol on Mutual Assistance in Defence Matters. The ECOWAS Cease-fire Monitoring Group (ECOMOG) was established in 1990. *See* the list of members.
Euro-Atlantic Partnership Council (EAPC)	Established in 1997, the EAPC provides the overarching framework for cooperation between NATO and its PFP partners, with an expanded political dimension. *See* the list of members under North Atlantic Treaty Organization.
European Atomic Energy Community (Euratom or EAEC)	Established by the 1957 Treaty Establishing the European Atomic Energy Community (Euratom Treaty) to promote the development of nuclear energy for peaceful purposes and to administer the multinational regional safeguards system covering the EU member states. Euratom is located in Brussels.

European Security and
Defence Identity (ESDI)
    Concept aimed at strengthening the European pillar of NATO while reinforcing the transatlantic link. Militarily coherent and effective forces, capable of conducting operations led by the European Union/Western European Union, are to be created.

European Security and
Defence Policy (ESDP)
    Concept initiated at the June 1999 Cologne European Council meeting and launched at the December 1999 Helsinki European Council meeting. Several interim bodies, including a political and security committee, were set in place on 1 March 2000. An EU military force of up to 60 000 troops, to be deployed within 60 days and for at least one year, will be established by 2003. *See also* Common Foreign and Security Policy.

European Union (EU)
    Organization of European states, with its headquarters in Brussels. The 1992 Treaty on European Union (Maastricht Treaty), which created the EU, entered into force in 1993. The 1997 Treaty of Amsterdam Amending the Treaty on European Union (Amsterdam Treaty), which entered into force on 1 May 1999, strengthens the political dimension of the EU and prepares it for enlargement. At the June 1999 Cologne European Council meeting, the General Affairs Council was tasked with preparing the conditions and measures for transferring from the WEU to the EU those functions related to the Petersberg tasks. The three EU pillars are: cooperation in economic and monetary affairs and Euratom; the Common Foreign and Security Policy (CFSP); and cooperation in justice and home affairs. *See also* Petersberg tasks, Common Foreign and Security Policy and *see* the list of members.

Fissile material
    Material composed of atoms which can be split by either fast or slow (thermal) neutrons. Uranium-235 and plutonium-239 are the most common fissile materials.

Georgia–Ukraine–
Uzbekistan–Azerbaijan–
Moldova (GUUAM)
    An organization formed as a response by Azerbaijan, Georgia and Ukraine to the creation of the Russia–Belarus Union in 1996. Moldova joined in 1997, when it was called the GUAM. Uzbekistan formally joined in 1999. The GUUAM acts on matters of common interest in the CIS, notably issues related to oil transport routes.

Great Lakes Region
(Africa)
    Region around lakes Victoria, Tanganyika, Kivu, Edward and Albert, consisting of Burundi, the Democratic Republic of Congo, Kenya, Rwanda, Tanzania and Uganda.

Group of Seven/Eight
(G7/G8)
    Group of the seven leading industrialized nations which have met informally, at the level of heads of state or government, since the 1970s; from 1997 Russia has participated with the G7 in meetings of the G8. *See* the list of members.

Group of 21 (G-21)
    Originally 21, now over 30, non-aligned CD member states which act together on proposals of common interest.

Intercontinental ballistic
missile (ICBM)
    Ground-launched ballistic missile with a range greater than 5500 km.

Intergovernmental Authority on Development (IGAD)	Established in 1996 to promote peace and stability in the Horn of Africa and to create mechanisms for conflict prevention, management and resolution. Its Secretariat is in Djibouti. *See* the list of members.
Intermediate-range nuclear forces (INF)	Non-strategic nuclear forces with a range of 1000–5550 km.
International Atomic Energy Agency (IAEA)	An intergovernmental organization within the UN system, with headquarters in Vienna. The IAEA is endowed by its Statute, which entered into force in 1957, to promote the peaceful uses of atomic energy and ensure that nuclear activities are not used to further any military purpose. It has cooperated with UNSCOM (and is requested in UN Security Council Resolution 1284 (1999) to assist UNMOVIC) in carrying out the removal of nuclear weapon-usable material from Iraq. Under the NPT and the nuclear weapon-free zone treaties, non-nuclear weapon states must accept IAEA nuclear safeguards to demonstrate the fulfilment of their obligation not to manufacture nuclear weapons. *See* the list of IAEA members under United Nations.
International Court of Justice (ICJ)	The principal juridical organ of the United Nations, set up in 1945 and located in The Hague. It settles legal disputes submitted to it by states and gives advisory opinions on legal questions referred to it by international organs and agencies.
International Criminal Court (ICC)	The Rome Statute of the International Criminal Court was adopted by the UN on 17 July 1998; it has not entered into force. The ICC is intended to be a permanent court, with jurisdiction over persons who have committed crimes of genocide, crimes against humanity, war crimes and crimes of aggression, as defined in the statute. It will assume jurisdiction over national systems only after it determines that they are unwilling or unable to prosecute. The seat of the court will be in The Hague.
International Criminal Tribunal for the Former Yugoslavia (ICTY)	The international tribunal, with its seat in The Hague, established in 1993 to prosecute persons responsible for war crimes committed since 1991 in the former Yugoslavia.
International Criminal Tribunal for Rwanda (ICTR)	The international tribunal, with its seat in Arusha, Tanzania, established to prosecute persons responsible for crimes of genocide committed in 1994 in Rwanda or by Rwandan citizens in neighbouring states.
Joint Consultative Group (JCG)	Established by the 1990 CFE Treaty to promote the objectives and implementation of the treaty by reconciling ambiguities of interpretation and implementation. Under the 1999 Agreement on Adaptation of the CFE Treaty the JCG will also address issues arising from the intentions of states to revise their TLE ceilings, consider cooperative measures to enhance the verification regime, consider requests to accede to the treaty and conduct any further negotiations.

Joint Compliance and Inspection Commission (JCIC)

The forum to resolve questions of compliance, clarify ambiguities and discuss ways to improve implementation of the 1991 START I and 1993 START II treaties. It convenes at the request of at least one of the parties.

Landmine

An anti-personnel or anti-vehicle mine, emplaced on land.

Maghreb

An Arabic term for north-western Africa, referring to the areas of Algeria, Morocco and Tunisia that lie between the Atlas Mountains and the Mediterranean Sea. *See also* Arab Maghreb Union.

Mine

A munition placed under, on or near the ground or other surface area, designed to be detonated or exploded by the presence, proximity or contact of a person or vehicle. A mine may be directly emplaced or remotely delivered (by artillery, rocket, mortar or similar means or dropped from an aircraft).

Minsk Group

Group of states created in 1992 which act together in the OSCE for political settlement of the conflict in the Armenian enclave of Nagorno-Karabakh in Azerbaijan. *See* the list of members under Organization for Security and Co-operation in Europe.

Missile Technology Control Regime (MTCR)

An informal military-related export control regime, established in 1987, which produced the Guidelines for Sensitive Missile-Relevant Transfers. Its goal is to limit the spread of weapons of mass destruction by controlling ballistic missile delivery systems. *See* the list of members.

Multiple independently targetable re-entry vehicles (MIRVs)

Re-entry vehicles, carried by a single ballistic missile, which can be directed to separate targets along separate trajectories.

National missile defence (NMD)

An anti-ballistic missile system, prohibited under the ABM Treaty, that is capable of defending a state's national territory. The US National Missile Defense Act of 1999 commits the USA to deploy 'as soon as is technologically possible' an NMD system capable of defending the territory of the USA against limited ballistic missile attack.

National technical means (NTM) of verification

Technical means of intelligence, under the national control of a state, which are used to monitor compliance with an arms control treaty to which the state is a party.

NATO–Russia Permanent Joint Council (PJC)

Established by the 1997 NATO–Russia Founding Act on Mutual Relations, Cooperation and Security for regular exchanges of information, consultation and cooperation.

NATO–Ukraine Commission

Established by the 1997 NATO–Ukraine Charter on a Distinctive Partnership, the commission meets for consultations on political and security issues, conflict prevention and resolution, non-proliferation, arms exports and technology transfers, and other subjects of common concern.

Non-Aligned Movement (NAM)	Group established in 1961, sometimes referred to as the Movement of Non-Aligned Countries. The NAM is a forum for consultations and coordination of positions on political and economic issues. The Coordinating Bureau of the Non-Aligned Countries (also called the Conference of Non-Aligned Countries) is the forum in which the NAM coordinates its actions within the UN. *See* the list of members.
Non-conventional weapon	*See* Weapon of mass destruction.
Non-governmental organization (NGO)	A national or international organization of individuals or organizations whose aim is to provide advice and present positions to national and international bodies, to inform the public about specific issues or to provide practical assistance and services in the field. Some NGOs are accredited by international organizations such as the UN and the OSCE, which seek their advice and assistance.
Non-strategic nuclear weapon	Nuclear weapon with a range up to and including 5500 km. Also referred to as a tactical nuclear weapon.
North Atlantic Treaty Organization (NATO)	Established in 1949 by the North Atlantic Treaty (Washington Treaty) as a defence alliance. Article 5 of the treaty defines the members' commitment to respond to an armed attack on any party. The 1999 NATO Strategic Concept states that the alliance will seek to prevent conflict or, should a crisis arise, to contribute to its effective management, consistent with international law, including through the possibility of conducting non-Article 5 crisis response operations. Its headquarters are in Brussels. *See* the list of members.
Nuclear Suppliers Group (NSG)	Also known as the London Club and established in 1975, the NSG coordinates multilateral export controls on nuclear materials. In 1977 it agreed the Guidelines for Nuclear Transfers (London Guidelines, subsequently revised), which contain a 'trigger list' of materials that should trigger IAEA safeguards when exported for peaceful purposes to any non-nuclear weapon state. In 1992 the NSG agreed the Guidelines for Transfers of Nuclear-Related Dual-Use Equipment, Material and Related Technology (Warsaw Guidelines, subsequently revised). *See* the list of members.
Open Skies Consultative Commission (OSCC)	Established by the 1992 Open Skies Treaty to resolve questions of compliance with the treaty.
Organisation for Economic Co-operation and Development (OECD)	Established in 1961, its objectives are to promote economic and social welfare by coordinating policies among the member states. Its headquarters are in Paris. *See* the list of members.
Organisation for the Prohibition of Chemical Weapons (OPCW)	Established by the 1993 Chemical Weapons Convention as a body for the parties to oversee implementation of the convention and resolve questions of compliance. Its seat is in The Hague.

Organisme Conjoint de Coopération en Matière d'Armement (OCCAR)	Established in 1996 as a management structure for international cooperative armaments programmes between France, Germany, Italy and the UK. It is also known as the Joint Armaments Cooperation Organization (JACO).
Organization for Security and Co-operation in Europe (OSCE)	Initiated in 1973 as the Conference on Security and Co-operation in Europe (CSCE), which adopted the Helsinki Final Act in 1975. The 1990 Charter of Paris for a New Europe set up several standing institutions and regular summit meetings. The new mandate included the implementation of human rights, pluralistic democracy (election monitoring), and economic and environmental security. In 1995 it was renamed the OSCE and transformed into an organization, as a primary instrument for early warning, conflict prevention and crisis management. Its Forum for Security Co-operation (FSC) deals with arms control and CSBMs. The OSCE comprises several institutions, all located in Europe. *See* the list of members.
Organization of African Unity (OAU)	A union of African states established in 1963 to promote African international cooperation and harmonization of *inter alia* defence policies. The seat of the Secretary-General is in Addis Ababa. *See* the list of members.
Organization of American States (OAS)	Group of states in the Americas which adopted a charter in 1948, with the objective of strengthening peace and security in the western hemisphere. The General Secretariat is in Washington, DC. *See* the list of members.
Organization of the Islamic Conference (OIC)	Established in 1971 by Islamic states to promote cooperation among the members and to support peace, security and the struggle of the people of Palestine and all Muslim people. Its Secretariat is in Jedda, Saudi Arabia. *See* the list of members.
Pact on Stability in Europe	The French proposal presented in 1993 as part of the cooperation in the framework of the EU Common Foreign and Security Policy (CFSP). Its objective is to contribute to stability by preventing tension and potential conflicts connected with border and minorities issues. The Pact on Stability was adopted in 1995, and the instruments and procedures were handed over to the OSCE.
Partnership for Peace (PFP)	Launched in 1994, the PFP is the programme for political and military cooperation between NATO and its partner states within the framework of the EAPC. It is open to all OSCE states able to contribute to the programme. The Enhanced PFP programme, adopted in 1997, is intended to strengthen political consultation, develop a more operational role, and provide for greater involvement of partners in PFP decision making and planning. *See* the list of members under North Atlantic Treaty Organization.
Peaceful nuclear explosion (PNE)	A nuclear explosion for non-military purposes, such as digging canals or harbours or creating underground cavities. The USA terminated its PNE programme in 1973. The USSR conducted its last PNE in 1988.

Petersberg tasks	Tasks emanating from the 1992 meeting of the WEU Council at Petersberg, Germany. WEU members declared themselves prepared to support the CSCE (from 1995 the OSCE) or the UN Security Council on a case-by-case basis by engaging in humanitarian and rescue tasks, peacekeeping tasks and tasks of combat forces in crisis management, including peacemaking. The 1997 Amsterdam Treaty provides the EU with access to an operational capability in the context of the Petersberg tasks. At the June 1999 Cologne European Council meeting it was decided that the Petersberg tasks should be transferred to the EU. *See also* European Union and Western European Union.
Re-entry vehicle (RV)	The part of a ballistic missile which carries a nuclear warhead and penetration aids to the target. It re-enters the earth's atmosphere and is destroyed in the final phase of the missile's trajectory. A missile can have one or several RVs and each RV contains a warhead.
Safeguards agreements	*See* International Atomic Energy Agency.
Southern African Development Community (SADC)	Established in 1992 to promote regional economic development and fundamental principles of sovereignty, peace and security, human rights and democracy. The Secretariat is in Gaborone, Botswana. *See* the list of members.
Stability Pact for South Eastern Europe	Initiated by the EU at the Conference on South Eastern Europe, convened in Cologne, Germany, on 10 June 1999 and placed under OSCE auspices on 1 July. The facilitating states, organizations and institutions endorsed the Stability Pact through the Sarajevo Summit Declaration on 30 July 1999. The Stability Pact is to promote political and economic reforms, development and enhanced security; and facilitate the integration of south-east European countries into the Euro-Atlantic structures. Its activities are coordinated by the South Eastern Europe Regional Table, chaired by the Special Coordinator of the Stability Pact, appointed by the EU after consultations with the OSCE Chairman-in-Office. The Special Coordinator is seated in Brussels. *See* the list of participants.
Standing Consultative Commission (SCC)	Established by the 1972 Anti-Ballistic Missile (ABM) Treaty to which parties may refer issues regarding implementation of the treaty.
Strategic nuclear weapons	ICBMs and SLBMs with a range usually of over 5500 km, as well as bombs and missiles carried on aircraft of intercontinental range.
Subcritical experiments	Experiments in which the configuration and quantities of explosives and nuclear materials used do not produce a critical mass, i.e., there is no self-sustaining nuclear fission chain reaction.
Submarine-launched ballistic missile (SLBM)	A ballistic missile launched from a submarine, usually with a range in excess of 5500 km.

Sub-Regional Consultative Commission (SRCC)	Established by the 1996 Agreement on Sub-Regional Arms Control (Florence Agreement) as a forum for the parties to resolve questions of compliance with the agreement.
Tactical nuclear weapon	*See* Non-strategic nuclear weapon.
Theatre missile defence (TMD)	Weapon systems designed to defend against non-strategic nuclear missiles by intercepting and destroying them in flight.
Toxins	Poisonous substances which are products of organisms but are not living or capable of reproducing themselves, as well as chemically created variants of such substances.
Treaty-limited equipment (TLE)	Five categories of equipment on which numerical limits are established by the 1990 CFE Treaty and the 1999 Agreement on Adaptation of the CFE Treaty: battle tanks, armoured combat vehicles, artillery, combat aircraft and attack helicopters.
United Nations	The world intergovernmental organization, open to membership of all states, with headquarters in New York, founded in 1945 through the adoption of its Charter at San Francisco, California. Its six principal organs are the General Assembly, the Security Council, the Economic and Social Council (ECOSOC), the Trusteeship Council, the International Court of Justice (ICJ) and the Secretariat. It also has a great number of specialized agencies and other autonomous bodies. *See* the list of members.
United Nations Monitoring, Verification and Inspection Commission (UNMOVIC)	Established in UN Security Council Resolution 1284 (1999) to undertake responsibilities previously mandated to UNSCOM with regard to the verification of compliance by Iraq with Resolution 687 (1991). It will report to the Security Council through the Secretary-General.
United Nations Register of Conventional Arms (UNROCA)	A voluntary reporting mechanism set up in 1992 for UN member states to report annually their imports and exports of seven categories of weapons or systems: battle tanks, armoured combat vehicles, large-calibre artillery systems, attack helicopters, combat aircraft, warships, and missiles and missile launchers.
Visegrad Group	Group of states comprising the Czech Republic, Hungary, Poland and Slovakia, formed in 1991 with the aim of intensifying subregional cooperation in political, economic and military areas and coordinating relations with multilateral European institutions.
Warhead	The part of a weapon which contains the explosive or other material intended to inflict damage.

Warsaw Treaty Organization (WTO)	The WTO, or Warsaw Pact, was established in 1955 by the Treaty of Friendship, Cooperation and Mutual Assistance between eight countries: Albania (withdrew in 1968), Bulgaria, Czechoslovakia, the German Democratic Republic, Hungary, Poland, Romania and the USSR. The Warsaw Pact was dissolved in 1991.
Wassenaar Arrangement (WA)	The Wassenaar Arrangement on Export Controls for Conventional Arms and Dual-Use Goods and Technologies was formally established in 1996. It aims to prevent the acquisition of armaments and sensitive dual-use goods and technologies for military uses by states whose behaviour is cause for concern to the member states. *See* the list of members.
Weapon of mass destruction	Nuclear weapon and any other weapon, such as chemical and biological weapons, which may produce comparable types of destructive effect.
Western European Union (WEU)	Established by the 1954 Protocols to the 1948 Brussels Treaty. The seat of the WEU is in Brussels. In 1992 it undertook to engage in humanitarian and rescue tasks, peacekeeping tasks and tasks of combat forces in crisis management including peacemaking (Petersberg tasks). At the June 1999 Cologne European Council meeting a decision was taken that the Petersberg tasks were to be dealt with by the EU within the Common Foreign and Security Policy (CFSP). *See also* European Union, and *see* the list of members.
Yield	Energy released in a nuclear explosion measured in kilotons or megatons of trinitrotoluene (TNT).
Zangger Committee	Established in 1971, the Nuclear Exporters Committee, called the Zangger Committee after its first chairman, is a group of nuclear supplier countries that meets informally twice a year to coordinate export controls on nuclear materials. *See* the list of members.

Membership of international organizations

The UN member states and organizations within the UN system are listed first, followed by all other organizations in alphabetical order. Note that not all members of the organizations are UN member states.

United Nations members (188) and year of membership

Afghanistan, 1946
Albania, 1955
Algeria, 1962
Andorra, 1993
Angola, 1976
Antigua and Barbuda, 1981
Argentina, 1945
Armenia, 1992
Australia, 1945
Austria, 1955
Azerbaijan, 1992
Bahamas, 1973
Bahrain, 1971
Bangladesh, 1974
Barbados, 1966
Belarus, 1945
Belgium, 1945
Belize, 1981
Benin, 1960
Bhutan, 1971
Bolivia, 1945
Bosnia and Herzegovina, 1992
Botswana, 1966
Brazil, 1945
Brunei Darussalam, 1984
Bulgaria, 1955
Burkina Faso, 1960
Burundi, 1962
Cambodia, 1955
Cameroon, 1960
Canada, 1945
Cape Verde, 1975
Central African Republic, 1960
Chad, 1960
Chile, 1945
China, 1945
Colombia, 1945
Comoros, 1975
Congo, Republic of (Congo-
    Brazzaville), 1960
Congo, Democratic Republic of
    (DRC), 1960
Costa Rica, 1945
Côte d'Ivoire, 1960
Croatia, 1992
Cuba, 1945
Cyprus, 1960
Czech Republic, 1993
Denmark, 1945
Djibouti, 1977

Dominica, 1978
Dominican Republic, 1945
Ecuador, 1945
Egypt, 1945
El Salvador, 1945
Equatorial Guinea, 1968
Eritrea, 1993
Estonia, 1991
Ethiopia, 1945
Fiji, 1970
Finland, 1955
France, 1945
Gabon, 1960
Gambia, 1965
Georgia, 1992
Germany, 1973
Ghana, 1957
Greece, 1945
Grenada, 1974
Guatemala, 1945
Guinea, 1958
Guinea-Bissau, 1974
Guyana, 1966
Haiti, 1945
Honduras, 1945
Hungary, 1955
Iceland, 1946
India, 1945
Indonesia, 1950
Iran, 1945
Iraq, 1945
Ireland, 1955
Israel, 1949
Italy, 1955
Jamaica, 1962
Japan, 1956
Jordan, 1955
Kazakhstan, 1992
Kenya, 1963
Kiribati, 1999
Korea, Democratic People's
    Republic of (North Korea),
    1991
Korea, Republic of (South
    Korea), 1991
Kuwait, 1963
Kyrgyzstan, 1992
Lao People's Democratic
    Republic, 1955
Latvia, 1991

Lebanon, 1945
Lesotho, 1966
Liberia, 1945
Libya, 1955
Liechtenstein, 1990
Lithuania, 1991
Luxembourg, 1945
Macedonia, Former Yugoslav
    Republic of (FYROM), 1993
Madagascar, 1960
Malawi, 1964
Malaysia, 1957
Maldives, 1965
Mali, 1960
Malta, 1964
Marshall Islands, 1991
Mauritania, 1961
Mauritius, 1968
Mexico, 1945
Micronesia, 1991
Moldova, 1992
Monaco, 1993
Mongolia, 1961
Morocco, 1956
Mozambique, 1975
Myanmar (Burma), 1948
Namibia, 1990
Nauru, 1999
Nepal, 1955
Netherlands, 1945
New Zealand, 1945
Nicaragua, 1945
Niger, 1960
Nigeria, 1960
Norway, 1945
Oman, 1971
Pakistan, 1947
Palau, 1994
Panama, 1945
Papua New Guinea, 1975
Paraguay, 1945
Peru, 1945
Philippines, 1945
Poland, 1945
Portugal, 1955
Qatar, 1971
Romania, 1955
Russia, 1945[a]
Rwanda, 1962
Saint Kitts and Nevis, 1983

Saint Lucia, 1979
Saint Vincent and the
  Grenadines, 1980
Samoa, Western, 1976
San Marino, 1992
Sao Tome and Principe, 1975
Saudi Arabia, 1945
Senegal, 1960
Seychelles, 1976
Sierra Leone, 1961
Singapore, 1965
Slovakia, 1993
Slovenia, 1992
Solomon Islands, 1978
Somalia, 1960
South Africa, 1945

Spain, 1955
Sri Lanka, 1955
Sudan, 1956
Suriname, 1975
Swaziland, 1968
Sweden, 1946
Syria, 1945
Tajikistan, 1992
Tanzania, 1961
Thailand, 1946
Togo, 1960
Tonga, 1999
Trinidad and Tobago, 1962
Tunisia, 1956
Turkey, 1945
Turkmenistan, 1992

Uganda, 1962
UK, 1945
Ukraine, 1945
United Arab Emirates, 1971
Uruguay, 1945
USA, 1945
Uzbekistan, 1992
Vanuatu, 1981
Venezuela, 1945
Viet Nam, 1977
Yemen, 1947
Yugoslavia, Federal Republic of
  (FRY), 1945[b]
Zambia, 1964
Zimbabwe, 1980

[a] In Dec. 1991 Russia informed the UN Secretary-General that it was continuing the membership of the USSR in the Security Council and all other UN bodies.

[b] A claim by the Federal Republic of Yugoslavia in 1992 to continue automatically the membership of the Socialist Federal Republic of Yugoslavia was not accepted by the UN General Assembly. It was decided that the FRY should apply for membership, which it had not done by 1 Jan. 2000. It may not participate in the work of the General Assembly, its subsidiary organs, or the conferences and meetings it convenes.

UN Security Council

Permanent members (the P5): China, France, Russia, UK, USA

Non-permanent members in 1999 (elected by the UN General Assembly for two-year terms; the year in brackets is the year at the end of which the term expires): Argentina (2000), Bahrain (1999), Brazil (1999), Canada (2000), Gabon (1999), Gambia (1999), Malaysia (2000), Namibia (2000), Netherlands (2000), Slovenia (1999)

Note: Bangladesh, Jamaica, Mali, Tunisia and Ukraine were elected non-permanent members for 2000–2001.

Conference on Disarmament (CD)

Members: Algeria, Argentina, Australia, Austria, Bangladesh, Belarus, Belgium, Brazil, Bulgaria, Cameroon, Canada, Chile, China, Colombia, Congo (Democratic Republic of), Cuba, Ecuador, Egypt, Ethiopia, Finland, France, Germany, Hungary, India, Indonesia, Iran, Iraq, Ireland, Israel, Italy, Japan, Kazakhstan, Kenya, Korea (North), Korea (South), Malaysia, Mexico, Mongolia, Morocco, Myanmar (Burma), Netherlands, New Zealand, Nigeria, Norway, Pakistan, Peru, Poland, Romania, Russia, Senegal, Slovakia, South Africa, Spain, Sri Lanka, Sweden, Switzerland, Syria, Tunisia, Turkey, UK, Ukraine, USA, Venezuela, Viet Nam, Yugoslavia,* Zimbabwe

* The Federal Republic of Yugoslavia has been suspended since 1992.

International Atomic Energy Agency (IAEA)

Members: Afghanistan, Albania, Algeria, Angola, Argentina, Armenia, Australia, Austria, Bangladesh, Belarus, Belgium, Bolivia, Bosnia and Herzegovina, Brazil, Bulgaria, Burkina Faso, Cambodia, Cameroon, Canada, Chile, China, Colombia, Congo (Democratic Republic of), Costa Rica, Côte d'Ivoire, Croatia, Cuba, Cyprus, Czech Republic, Denmark, Dominican Republic, Ecuador, Egypt, El Salvador, Estonia, Ethiopia, Finland, France, Gabon, Georgia, Germany, Ghana, Greece, Guatemala, Haiti, Holy See, Hungary, Iceland, India, Indonesia, Iran, Iraq, Ireland, Israel, Italy, Jamaica, Japan, Jordan, Kazakhstan, Kenya, Korea (South), Kuwait, Latvia, Lebanon, Liberia, Libya, Liechtenstein, Lithuania, Luxembourg, Macedonia (Former Yugoslav Republic of), Madagascar, Malaysia, Mali, Malta, Marshall Islands, Mauritius, Mexico, Moldova, Monaco, Mongolia, Morocco, Myanmar (Burma), Namibia, Netherlands, New Zealand, Nicaragua, Niger, Nigeria, Norway, Pakistan, Panama, Paraguay, Peru, Philippines,

Poland, Portugal, Qatar, Romania, Russia, Saudi Arabia, Senegal, Sierra Leone, Singapore, Slovakia, Slovenia, South Africa, Spain, Sri Lanka, Sudan, Sweden, Switzerland, Syria, Tanzania, Thailand, Tunisia, Turkey, Uganda, UK, Ukraine, United Arab Emirates, Uruguay, USA, Uzbekistan, Venezuela, Viet Nam, Yemen, Yugoslavia,* Zambia, Zimbabwe

* The Federal Republic of Yugoslavia has been suspended since 1992. It is deprived of the right to participate in the IAEA General Conference and the Board of Governors' meetings but is assessed for its contribution to the budget of the IAEA.

Note: North Korea was a member of the IAEA until Sep. 1994.

Arab League

Members: Algeria, Bahrain, Comoros, Djibouti, Egypt, Iraq, Jordan, Kuwait, Lebanon, Libya, Mauritania, Morocco, Oman, Palestine, Qatar, Saudi Arabia, Somalia, Sudan, Syria, Tunisia, United Arab Emirates, Yemen

Arab Maghreb Union (AMU)

Members: Algeria, Libya, Mauritania, Morocco, Tunisia

Association of South-East Asian Nations (ASEAN)

Members: Brunei, Cambodia, Indonesia, Laos, Malaysia, Myanmar (Burma), Philippines, Singapore, Thailand, Viet Nam

ASEAN Regional Forum (ARF)

Members: The ASEAN states plus Australia, Canada, China, European Union (EU), India, Japan, Korea (South), Mongolia, New Zealand, Papua New Guinea, Russia, USA

ASEAN Post Ministerial Conference (ASEAN–PMC)

Members: The ASEAN states plus Australia, Canada, China, European Union (EU), India, Japan, Korea (South), New Zealand, Russia, USA

Australia Group (AG)

Members: Argentina, Australia, Austria, Belgium, Canada, Czech Republic, Denmark, Finland, France, Germany, Greece, Hungary, Iceland, Ireland, Italy, Japan, Korea (South), Luxembourg, Netherlands, New Zealand, Norway, Poland, Portugal, Romania, Slovakia, Spain, Sweden, Switzerland, UK, USA

Observer: European Commission

Central European Initiative (CEI)

Members: Albania, Austria, Belarus, Bosnia and Herzegovina, Bulgaria, Croatia, Czech Republic, Hungary, Italy, Macedonia (Former Yugoslav Republic of), Moldova, Poland, Romania, Slovakia, Slovenia, Ukraine

Commonwealth of Independent States (CIS)

Members: Armenia, Azerbaijan, Belarus, Georgia, Kazakhstan, Kyrgyzstan, Moldova, Russia, Tajikistan, Turkmenistan, Ukraine, Uzbekistan

Conference on Interaction and Confidence-Building Measures in Asia (CICA)

Members: Afghanistan, Azerbaijan, China, Egypt, India, Iran, Israel, Kazakhstan, Kyrgyzstan, Pakistan, Palestinian Authority, Russia, Tajikistan, Turkey, Uzbekistan

Council for Security Cooperation in the Asia Pacific (CSCAP)

Members: Australia, Canada, China, European Union (EU), Indonesia, Japan, Korea (North), Korea (South), Malaysia, Mongolia, New Zealand, Philippines, Russia, Singapore, Thailand, USA, Viet Nam

Associate member: India

Council of Europe

Members: Albania, Andorra, Austria, Belgium, Bulgaria, Croatia, Cyprus, Czech Republic, Denmark, Estonia, Finland, France, Germany, Georgia, Greece, Hungary, Iceland, Ireland, Italy, Latvia, Liechtenstein, Lithuania, Luxembourg, Macedonia (Former Yugoslav Republic of), Malta, Moldova, Netherlands, Norway, Poland, Portugal, Romania, Russia, San Marino, Slovakia, Slovenia, Spain, Sweden, Switzerland, Turkey, UK, Ukraine

Observers: Canada, Holy See, Japan, Mexico, USA

Economic Community of West African States (ECOWAS)

Members: Benin, Burkina Faso, Cape Verde, Côte d'Ivoire, Gambia, Ghana, Guinea, Guinea-Bissau, Liberia, Mali, Mauritania, Niger, Nigeria, Senegal, Sierra Leone, Togo

European Union (EU)

Members: Austria, Belgium, Denmark, Finland, France, Germany, Greece, Ireland, Italy, Luxembourg, Netherlands, Portugal, Spain, Sweden, UK

Group of Seven/Eight (G7/G8)

Members: Canada, France, Germany, Italy, Japan, UK, USA. As the G8, the members of the G7 plus Russia.

Intergovernmental Authority on Development (IGAD)

Members: Djibouti, Eritrea, Ethiopia, Kenya, Somalia, Sudan, Uganda

Missile Technology Control Regime (MTCR)

Members: Argentina, Australia, Austria, Belgium, Brazil, Canada, Czech Republic, Denmark, Finland, France, Germany, Greece, Hungary, Iceland, Ireland, Italy, Japan, Luxembourg, Netherlands, New Zealand, Norway, Poland, Portugal, Russia, South Africa, Spain, Sweden, Switzerland, Turkey, UK, Ukraine, USA

Non-Aligned Movement (NAM)

Members: Afghanistan, Algeria, Angola, Bahamas, Bahrain, Bangladesh, Barbados, Belarus, Belize, Benin, Bhutan, Bolivia, Botswana, Brunei, Burkina Faso, Burundi, Cambodia, Cameroon, Cape Verde, Central African Republic, Chad, Chile, Colombia, Comoros, Congo (Democratic Republic of), Congo (Republic of), Côte d'Ivoire, Cuba, Cyprus, Djibouti, Ecuador, Egypt, Equatorial Guinea, Eritrea, Ethiopia, Gabon, Gambia, Ghana, Grenada, Guatemala, Guinea, Guinea-Bissau, Guyana, Honduras, India, Indonesia, Iran, Iraq, Jamaica, Jordan, Kenya, Korea (North), Kuwait, Laos, Lebanon, Lesotho, Liberia, Libya, Madagascar, Malawi, Malaysia, Maldives, Mali, Malta, Mauritania, Mauritius, Mongolia, Morocco, Mozambique, Myanmar (Burma), Namibia, Nepal, Nicaragua, Niger, Nigeria, Oman, Pakistan, Palestine, Panama, Papua New Guinea, Peru, Philippines, Qatar, Rwanda, Saint Lucia, Sao Tome and Principe, Saudi Arabia, Senegal, Seychelles, Sierra Leone, Singapore, Somalia, South Africa, Sri Lanka, Sudan, Suriname, Swaziland, Syria, Tanzania, Thailand, Togo, Trinidad and Tobago, Tunisia, Turkmenistan, Uganda, United Arab Emirates, Uzbekistan, Vanuatu, Venezuela, Viet Nam, Yemen, Yugoslavia,* Zambia, Zimbabwe

* The Federal Republic of Yugoslavia has not been permitted to participate in NAM activities since 1992.

North Atlantic Treaty Organization (NATO)

Members: Belgium, Canada, Czech Republic, Denmark, France,* Germany, Greece, Hungary, Iceland, Italy, Luxembourg, Netherlands, Norway, Poland, Portugal, Spain, Turkey, UK, USA

* France is not in the integrated military structures of NATO.

Euro-Atlantic Partnership Council (EAPC)

Members: The NATO states plus Albania, Armenia, Austria, Azerbaijan, Belarus, Bulgaria, Estonia, Finland, Georgia, Kazakhstan, Kyrgyzstan, Latvia, Lithuania, Macedonia (Former Yugoslav Republic of), Moldova, Romania, Russia, Slovakia, Slovenia, Sweden, Switzerland, Tajikistan, Turkmenistan, Ukraine, Uzbekistan

Partnership for Peace (PFP)

Partner states: Albania, Armenia, Austria, Azerbaijan, Belarus, Bulgaria, Estonia, Finland, Georgia, Kazakhstan, Kyrgyzstan, Latvia, Lithuania, Macedonia (Former Yugoslav Republic of), Moldova, Romania, Russia, Slovakia, Slovenia, Sweden, Switzerland, Turkmenistan, Ukraine, Uzbekistan

Nuclear Suppliers Group (NSG)

Members: Argentina, Australia, Austria, Belgium, Brazil, Bulgaria, Canada, Czech Republic, Denmark, Finland, France, Germany, Greece, Hungary, Ireland, Italy, Japan, Korea (South), Latvia, Luxembourg, Netherlands, New Zealand, Norway, Poland, Portugal, Romania, Russia, Slovakia, South Africa, Spain, Sweden, Switzerland, UK, Ukraine, USA

Organisation for Economic Co-operation and Development (OECD)

Members: Australia, Austria, Belgium, Canada, Czech Republic, Denmark, Finland, France, Germany, Greece, Hungary, Iceland, Ireland, Italy, Japan, Korea (South), Luxembourg, Mexico, Netherlands, New Zealand, Norway, Poland, Portugal, Spain, Sweden, Switzerland, Turkey, UK, USA

The European Commission participates in the work of the OECD.

Organization for Security and Co-operation in Europe (OSCE)

Members: Albania, Andorra, Armenia, Austria, Azerbaijan, Belarus, Belgium, Bosnia and Herzegovina, Bulgaria, Canada, Croatia, Cyprus, Czech Republic, Denmark, Estonia, Finland, France, Georgia, Germany, Greece, Holy See, Hungary, Iceland, Ireland, Italy, Kazakhstan, Kyrgyzstan, Latvia, Liechtenstein, Lithuania, Luxembourg, Macedonia (Former Yugoslav Republic of), Malta, Moldova, Monaco, Netherlands, Norway, Poland, Portugal, Romania, Russia, San Marino, Slovakia, Slovenia, Spain, Sweden, Switzerland, Tajikistan, Turkey, Turkmenistan, UK, Ukraine, USA, Uzbekistan, Yugoslavia*

* The Federal Republic of Yugoslavia has been suspended since 1992.

Members of the Minsk Group in 1999: Armenia, Austria, Azerbaijan, Belarus, Finland, France, Germany, Italy, Norway, Russia, Sweden, Turkey, USA

Partners for Co-operation: Algeria, Egypt, Israel, Japan, Jordan, Korea (South), Morocco, Tunisia

Organization of African Unity (OAU)

Members: Algeria, Angola, Benin, Botswana, Burkina Faso, Burundi, Cameroon, Cape Verde, Central African Republic, Chad, Comoros, Congo (Democratic Republic of), Congo (Republic of), Côte d'Ivoire, Djibouti, Egypt, Equatorial Guinea, Eritrea, Ethiopia, Gabon, Gambia, Ghana, Guinea, Guinea-Bissau, Kenya, Lesotho, Liberia, Libya, Madagascar, Malawi, Mali, Mauritania, Mauritius, Mozambique, Namibia, Niger, Nigeria, Rwanda, Western Sahara (Saharawi Arab Democratic Republic, SADR*), Sao Tome and Principe, Senegal, Seychelles, Sierra Leone, Somalia, South Africa, Sudan, Swaziland, Tanzania, Togo, Tunisia, Uganda, Zambia, Zimbabwe

* The Western Sahara was admitted in 1982, but its membership was disputed by Morocco and other states. Morocco withdrew from the OAU in 1985.

Organization of American States (OAS)

Members: Antigua and Barbuda, Argentina, Bahamas, Barbados, Belize, Bolivia, Brazil, Canada, Chile, Colombia, Costa Rica, Cuba,* Dominica, Dominican Republic, Ecuador, El Salvador, Grenada, Guatemala, Guyana, Haiti, Honduras, Jamaica, Mexico, Nicaragua, Panama, Paraguay, Peru, Saint Kitts and Nevis, Saint Lucia, Saint Vincent and the Grenadines, Suriname, Trinidad and Tobago, Uruguay, USA, Venezuela

* Cuba has been excluded from participation since 1962.

Permanent observers: Algeria, Angola, Austria, Belgium, Bosnia and Herzegovina, Bulgaria, Croatia, Cyprus, Czech Republic, Egypt, Equatorial Guinea, European Union (EU), Finland, France, Germany, Ghana, Greece, Holy See, Hungary, India, Israel, Italy, Japan, Kazakhstan, Korea (South), Latvia, Lebanon, Morocco, Netherlands, Pakistan, Philippines, Poland, Portugal, Romania, Russia, Saudi Arabia, Spain, Sri Lanka, Sweden, Switzerland, Thailand, Tunisia, Turkey, UK, Ukraine, Yemen

Organization of the Islamic Conference (OIC)

Members: Afghanistan, Albania, Algeria, Azerbaijan, Bahrain, Bangladesh, Benin, Brunei, Burkina Faso, Cameroon, Chad, Comoros, Djibouti, Egypt, Gabon, Gambia, Guinea, Guinea-Bissau, Indonesia, Iran, Iraq, Jordan, Kazakhstan, Kuwait, Kyrgyzstan, Lebanon, Libya, Malaysia, Maldives, Mali, Mauritania, Morocco, Mozambique, Niger, Nigeria, Oman, Pakistan, Palestine, Qatar, Saudi Arabia, Senegal, Sierra Leone, Somalia, Sudan, Suriname, Syria, Tajikistan, Togo, Tunisia, Turkey, Turkmenistan, Uganda, United Arab Emirates, Uzbekistan, Yemen

Observers: Bosnia and Herzegovina, Central African Republic

Southern African Development Community (SADC)

Members: Angola, Botswana, Congo (Democratic Republic of), Lesotho, Malawi, Mauritius, Mozambique, Namibia, Seychelles, South Africa, Swaziland, Tanzania, Zambia, Zimbabwe

Stability Pact for South Eastern Europe

Participants: All EU member states (Austria, Belgium, Denmark, Finland, France, Germany, Greece, Ireland, Italy, Luxembourg, Netherlands, Portugal, Spain, Sweden, UK), Albania, Bosnia and Herzegovina, Bulgaria, Croatia, Hungary, Macedonia (Former Yugoslav Republic of), Romania, Russia, Slovenia, Turkey, USA, European Commission, Organization for Security and Co-operation in Europe Chairman-in-Office, Council of Europe

Facilitators and regional initiatives: Canada, Japan, United Nations, UN High Commissioner for Refugees, North Atlantic Treaty Organization, Organisation for Economic Co-operation and Development, Western European Union, International Monetary Fund, World Bank, European Investment Bank, European Bank for Reconstruction and Development, Royaumont Process, Black Sea Economic Cooperation, Central European Initiative, South East Europe Cooperation Initiative, South Eastern Europe Cooperation Process

Wassenaar Arrangement (WA)

Members: Argentina, Australia, Austria, Belgium, Bulgaria, Canada, Czech Republic, Denmark, Finland, France, Germany, Greece, Hungary, Ireland, Italy, Japan, Korea (South), Luxembourg, Netherlands, New Zealand, Norway, Poland, Portugal, Romania, Russia, Slovakia, Spain, Sweden, Switzerland, Turkey, UK, Ukraine, USA

Western European Union (WEU)

Members: Belgium, France, Germany, Greece, Italy, Luxembourg, Netherlands, Portugal, Spain, UK
Associate Members: Czech Republic, Hungary, Iceland, Norway, Poland, Turkey
Associate Partners: Bulgaria, Estonia, Latvia, Lithuania, Romania, Slovakia, Slovenia
Observers: Austria, Denmark, Finland, Ireland, Sweden
Members of WEAG and WEAO: Belgium, Denmark, France, Germany, Greece, Italy, Luxembourg, Netherlands, Norway, Portugal, Spain, Turkey, UK

Zangger Committee

Members: Argentina, Australia, Austria, Belgium, Bulgaria, Canada, China, Czech Republic, Denmark, Finland, France, Germany, Greece, Hungary, Ireland, Italy, Japan, Korea (South), Luxembourg, Netherlands, Norway, Poland, Portugal, Romania, Russia, Slovakia, South Africa, Spain, Sweden, Switzerland, Turkey, UK, Ukraine, USA

Conventions

. .	Data not available or not applicable
–	Nil or a negligible figure
( )	Uncertain data
b.	Billion (thousand million)
km	Kilometre (1000 metres)
kt	Kiloton (1000 tonnes)
m.	Million
Mt	Megaton (1 million tonnes)
th.	Thousand
tr.	Trillion (million million)
$	US dollars, unless otherwise indicated

Introduction
In search of a global security system for the 21st century

ADAM DANIEL ROTFELD

The end of the 20th century and the beginning of the third millennium provide an occasion to consider the ongoing changes and the expectations and requirements that a new world security system should meet.

I. The key emerging trends

In his report to the United Nations General Assembly on the UN Millennium Summit, to be held in the autumn of 2000, UN Secretary-General Kofi Annan addressed the role of the world organization in the 21st century. The report identifies several challenges and proposes a number of priorities to be considered by the gathering of the heads of state and government of all the UN member states. In the Secretary-General's view, the central challenge is 'to ensure that globalization becomes a positive force for all the world's people, instead of leaving billions of them behind in squalor'.[1] Meeting this challenge of inclusive globalization requires both 'the great enabling force of the market' and 'a broader effort to create a shared future. . . . That in turn requires that we think afresh about how we manage our joint activities and our shared interests, for many challenges that we confront today are beyond the reach of any state to meet on its own.'[2] Similar thoughts were contained in the message of Pope John Paul II for the World Day of Peace, 1 January 2000: '[T]here will be peace only to the extent that humanity as a whole rediscovers its fundamental calling to be one family, a family in which the dignity and rights of individuals—whatever their status, race or religion—are accepted as prior and superior to any kind of difference or distinction'.[3] Globalization, for all its risks, also offers exceptional and promising opportunities if it is built on the values of justice, equity and solidarity, as noted by these two prominent world figures.

A less optimistic view of globalization is presented in a report prepared by the US Institute for National Strategic Studies of the National Defense University. Unlike the forecasts of the early 1990s, in which stability and greater integration were predicted to prevail, the key trends of 1999 indicate that 'the

[1] Annan, K. A., Millennium Report of the Secretary-General of the United Nations, We, the Peoples, The Role of the United Nations in the 21st Century, UN document A/54/2000, 3 Apr. 2000, pp. 5–6, available at URL <http://www.un.org/millennium/sg/report/>.
[2] Annan (note 1), p. 7.
[3] Message of His Holiness Pope John Paul II for the celebration of the World Day of Peace, Holy See, 8 Dec. 1999, para. 5, available at URL <http://www.vatican.va>.

world is becoming murkier and more dangerous'.[4] This assessment is influenced by such adverse tendencies and phenomena as the Asian economic crisis, the increased assertiveness of Iraq and North Korea, the tensions between China and Taiwan, the conflict in Chechnya, the failed reforms in Russia, Ukraine and other former Soviet republics (with the exception of the three Baltic states Estonia, Latvia and Lithuania), the nuclear and missile tests by India and Pakistan, the mounting fear of nuclear proliferation elsewhere and—last but not least—the wars in the Balkans. The conclusion drawn by the US security analysts is that the future can be influenced 'in major ways' by how the USA and its allies act. It was along this line of reasoning that the leaders of the North Atlantic Treaty Organization (NATO) took the decision to intervene militarily in Kosovo, a province of the Federal Republic of Yugoslavia. This was done under the alliance's new strategic concept, which defined a new role for NATO in addressing 'regional and ethnic conflicts beyond the territory of NATO members'.[5]

A comprehensive review of the main trends and uncertainties brought the US analysts to the conclusion that within about a decade from today developments may have unfolded in one of three different ways, each posing particular challenges. The first scenario, one of continuity, assumes that 'the United States and its allies act effectively'; 'the overall magnitude of danger and opportunity might be similar to now'. The second scenario is that of 'a rapid plunge into global turmoil in which the overall level of instability and danger increases greatly'. The third is the most optimistic scenario—'rapid progress toward greater stability and peace'.[6] As desirable as this scenario is, it is also the least likely one. Attempts to translate complex realities into simple projections are, however, as a rule, neither illuminating nor very inspiring.

II. Divergent concepts of the world structure

The novelty of the situation today is that globalization generates interdependence and cooperation.[7]

With the collapse of the bipolar structure after nearly half a century, concepts have emerged of how the new amorphous, unstable and fragmented

---

[4] *Strategic Assessment 1999: Priorities for a Turbulent World* (National Defense University, Institute for National Strategic Studies: Washington, DC, 1999), p. xi.

[5] United States Information Service (USIS), 'Clinton says NATO may intervene beyond its borders', The White House, Office of the Press Secretary, 24 Apr. 1999, *European Washington File* (US Embassy: Stockholm, 24 Apr. 1999). A year later, NATO Secretary General Lord Robertson stated: 'Kosovo did not mark NATO's mutation into a crusader for universal values'; it 'represented a unique circumstance' and 'did not set a precedent for the Alliance'. Lord Robertson, 'Law, morality and the use of force', Speech to the Institut de Relations Internationales et Stratégiques (IRIS), Paris, 16 May 2000. In the USA, NATO's intervention in Kosovo was met with strong criticism on the part of both lawyers and security analysts. See the editorial comments published in *American Journal of International Law*, vol. 93, not. 4 (Oct. 1999), pp. 824–62. See also Mandelbaum, M., 'A perfect failure: NATO's war against Yugoslavia', *Foreign Affairs*, Sep./Oct. 1999, pp. 2–8.

[6] *Strategic Assessment 1999* (note 4).

[7] 'In contrast to the past, the existing distribution of capabilities generates incentives for cooperation.' Wohlforth, W. C., 'The stability of a unipolar world', *International Security*, vol. 24, no. 1 (summer 1999), p. 38.

reality could be managed under a new global organizing principle of either a unipolar or a multipolar world. US officials tend to speak of the United States as a 'leader' or 'indispensable nation' because they consider any new grand strategy designed to 'preserve unipolarity by preventing the emergence of a global rival' as 'quixotic and dangerous'.[8] However, most politicians and analysts, irrespective of their assessments, share the view that the USA today occupies an exceptional position because of the unprecedented concentration of power, which constitutes a new quality in international relations. Unipolarity, in the view of some analysts, is 'a deeply embedded material condition of world politics that has the potential to last for many decades'.[9]

Understandably, analyses published in China and Russia reject, on political grounds, a unipolar vision of the world in which the United States is to play the role of an empire or leader.[10] The assessments in these publications see a unipolar security system as legitimizing US hegemony. The idea of 'a new multipolar world' is presented in China as 'a historical necessity as well as a realistic existence'.[11] The new Russian military doctrine defines, among the main external threats to Russia, 'attempts to ignore (infringe) the Russian Federation's interests in resolving international security problems, and to oppose its strengthening as one influential centre in a multipolar world'.[12] This reasoning embodies a dual simplification. First, it assumes that security in the new international environment will be based on balance-of-power politics. Second, it assumes that interstate relations do not change, failing to take into account the new correlation of forces and distribution of power and the fact that the processes of globalization are without precedent. The new, powerful position of the USA in the world is a fact.

This does not mean, however, that it will carry out an imperialist policy or a policy guided by the pursuit of hegemony, such as that of the European powers over the course of the past three centuries.

US analysts have written that the USA faces the following type of dilemma: 'If China integrates into the Western community, regional stability will be enhanced. If not, China could become a major security problem and eventual military threat in ways that affect the entire region, as well as US relationships with key allies'.[13] Naturally, this type of understanding of world leadership provokes negative reactions in China.[14]

[8] Wohlforth (note 7), p. 5.

[9] Wohlforth (note 7), p. 37.

[10] Huang Zhengji, 'There is unlikely such thing as a unipolar world', *International Strategic Studies* (China Institute for International Strategic Studies), no. 1, serial no. 55 (Jan. 2000), pp. 21–28. See also the report published by the Institute of World Economy and International Relations (IMEMO), Russian Academy of Sciences: *Rossiya i zapad: krizis otnosheniy v sfere bezopastnosti i problema kontrola nad vooruzheniyami* [Russia and the West: the crisis of relations in the sphere of security and arms control issues] (IMEMO: Moscow, 1999), pp. 16–21.

[11] Huang Zhengji (note 10), p. 22.

[12] The new Russian military doctrine was formally approved by President Vladimir Putin in his decree of 21 Apr. 2000. The full text is published in *Nezavisimaya Gazeta*, 22 Apr. 2000, p. 5. An unofficial English translation was released by BBC Monitoring on 22 Apr. 2000.

[13] *Strategic Assessment 1999* (note 4), p. xiii.

[14] Huang Zhengji (note 10), pp. 25–27.

The question is not whether China, Russia and the rest of the world should be incorporated into the Western community; on the contrary, the international security system should be inclusive and security cooperation and mutual reassurance should replace mutual deterrence, associated with balance-of-power politics. Multinational security structures would then increasingly be able to take national security interests into account. However, so far, with the exception of those in Europe, regional security institutions are either weak or non-existent.

III. Regional developments

The most stable and predictable region of the world is Europe. Its southern Balkan periphery notwithstanding, the European system is based on democratic pluralism, human rights and market economy within states, and well-developed multinational security institutions—NATO, the European Union (EU), the Organization for Security and Co-operation in Europe (OSCE) and the Council of Europe. The Eurasian post-Soviet region—comprising Russia and essentially all the former Soviet republics except the three Baltic states—is less stable. In Russia, failed economic reform, widespread crime and the war in Chechnya have led to a search for a strong autocratic power with an anti-Western, nationalist orientation rather than democratic arrangements. The economic breakdown in Ukraine puts at risk its future political orientation and the form of its independent statehood. The Central Asian states often distance themselves from Russia in their external policies, while substituting domestic authoritarian regimes based on ethnic nationalism and religious identity for the old totalitarian Soviet communist ideology. In the Caucasus, tensions and hostilities prevail as a result of the unsettled conflicts: that between Azerbaijan and Armenia over Nagorno-Karabakh; the separatist movements in Abkhazia and South Ossetia in Georgia; and, in Russia's North Caucasus region, the bloody war in Chechnya, where the Russian military victory, war crimes, mass violations of human rights and destruction failed to bring any prospect of a lasting political solution.

The most unpredictable developments of all are those in Asia. The situations on the Korean Peninsula, across the Taiwan Strait and on the Indian subcontinent, which can easily get out of control, are potential sources of serious conflict. The financial crisis in Asia led to political and economic upheaval in Indonesia, Malaysia and other countries of the region. However, Sino-Japanese–US relations are of key importance.[15]

A priority matter for the international community is the situation in Africa. An estimated 44 per cent of Africans, and 51 per cent of those in sub-Saharan Africa, are living in abject poverty. Of the 30 million people infected by the

---

[15] 'In the long term, the emergence of China as a world power and the reactions of Japan and other countries will be key.' *Strategic Assessment 1999* (note 4), p. xiii.

human immunodeficiency virus/acquired immunodeficiency syndrome (HIV/AIDS) in the world, 23 million live in the sub-Saharan belt.[16]

It would be wrong to ascribe the main, or the sole, cause of armed conflict in Africa to poverty and economic decline. The underlying cause of conflict is inequality. As the UN Secretary-General rightly noted, inequality 'tends to be reflected in unequal access to political power that too often forecloses paths to peaceful change'.[17] In broader terms, poverty, lack of prospects, economic decline, inequalities and poor governance all lead to wars triggered by the deliberate mobilization of grievances, especially in the failed states. Better-organized states, more legitimate governments and more effective prevention strategies would help the international community to stop or more effectively contain most armed conflicts. However, a caveat is required here: since conflicts and wars cannot be explained by any single cause, there is no simple solution that is applicable to each situation in every corner of the world.

IV. A functional and pragmatic approach

Pre-World War I industrialization brought the development of new weapon systems and rapid modernization of transport and communications; similarly, after World War II, as a result of scientific developments and the arms race within the bipolar framework, the great powers came into possession of huge arsenals of nuclear warheads and missiles. In the wake of the cold war, future military potentials are likely to be determined by the so-called Revolution in Military Affairs (development of, e.g., precision-guided munitions; new information technologies; advanced intelligence, surveillance and reconnaissance; and advanced command, control, communications and intelligence). Information technologies in particular will propel the processes of both globalization and fragmentation of the world.

In the view of some security analysts, the dominant world trends—globalization, democratization, fragmentation and proliferation of weapons of mass destruction—tend to lead the major powers to base their relations on a new bipolarity. This time, the polarization would be an outcome not of ideological antagonism but of a clash of interests.[18] The new dividing line in the era of information technology would be the degree of technological advancement. While the authors of this vision make the reservation that a new bipolar world is not inevitable, they add that 'current trends are leading us in that direction'.[19] Such reasoning seeks to conceptualize the new reality according to the categories and formulae of the past.

---

[16] UN, Annual Report of the Secretary-General on the work of the Organization, UN document A/54/1, supplement no. 1, 31 Aug. 1999, para. 172.

[17] UN (note 16), para. 17.

[18] 'The United States and its allies could face an informal coalition of Russia, China, and rogue states made more dangerous by the rogues' ties to these two major powers. . . . This coalition might be more difficult to deal with and deter than our Cold war foes.' Binnendijk, H., with Henrikson, A., 'Back to bipolarity?', *Strategic Forum* (National Defense University, Institute for National Strategic Studies), no. 161 (May 1999), p. 4.

[19] Binnendijk and Henrikson (note 18).

In the search for a new security system, the ways of effectively resolving specific problems are much more important than the creation of grand regimes and new structures based on theoretical concepts.[20] In this context it is worth noting that, despite numerous pessimistic forecasts, many potential and real conflicts in various parts of the world have been either settled or extinguished, or, at least, contacts have been established between the main antagonists. In the Middle East, the peace process has been renewed and contacts between Israel and Syria have opened up. US–North Korean relations have improved, and a summit meeting between North Korea and South Korea to start normalizing relations on the Korean Peninsula has been scheduled for June 2000.[21] Chinese–Taiwanese relations as well as those in the whole region of South-East Asia and the Pacific are characterized by reduced tension. With the election of Vladimir Putin as President of Russia, a new opening has taken place in relations between Russia and NATO and the European Union, and new political solutions to the Chechnya conflict are being sought. The list of such positive changes in the world is long. Regrettably, however, it does not include all the regions and problems that constitute a real or potential threat to international peace and security.

A complex and pragmatic approach is required not only to the prevention and resolution of domestic and interstate conflicts but also to the effective prevention of situations where the proliferation of armaments is out of control. In the cold war era, arms control was in the focus of attention of politicians and the public. Although other problems of international security have claimed priority in the post-cold war period, a number of arms control and disarmament agreements have been reached. Some of these agreements have not entered into force, while others are encountering considerable obstacles to implementation. The Review Conference of the 1968 Treaty on the Non-Proliferation of Nuclear Weapons (Non-Proliferation Treaty, NPT), convened in April–May 2000, faced a number of serious problems. The United States had announced plans that would require a revision of the 1972 Anti-Ballistic Missile (ABM) Treaty. The US Senate had rejected ratification of the 1996 Comprehensive Nuclear Test-Ban Treaty (CTBT), which was negotiated and signed after years of US diplomacy efforts. Russia had renounced its 'no first use' policy and decided to rely more heavily on its nuclear weapons under the new Russian military doctrine, approved by President Putin.[22] For seven years, the Russian State Duma rejected ratification of the 1993 Treaty on Further Reductions and Limitation of Strategic Offensive Arms (START II Treaty).[23] Russia and the USA continue to maintain nuclear launchers on 'hair-trigger

---

[20] Jervis, R., 'Realism, neoliberalism and cooperation: understanding the debate', *International Security*, vol. 24, no. 1 (summer 1999), pp. 42–63.

[21] Resolving the question of North Korean nuclear and missile capabilities is seen as an integral part of the normalization of relations on the Korean Peninsula. See chapter 11 in this volume.

[22] 'The Russian Federation reserves the right to use nuclear weapons in response to the use of nuclear and other types of weapons of mass destruction against it and/or its allies as well as in response to large-scale aggression using conventional weapons in situations critical to the national security of the Russian Federation'. The new Russian military doctrine (note 12), para 9.

[23] The START II Treaty was finally ratified by the Duma on 14 Apr. 2000.

alert', and India and Pakistan carried out nuclear tests in 1998.[24] Two non-nuclear-weapon states parties to the NPT (Iraq and North Korea) have carried out clandestine nuclear weapon programmes.

These and other developments are a challenge for the international community. It remains an open question whether such issues can or even should be resolved in the established institutions and with the procedures elaborated within the bipolar framework after World War II or whether they call for a functional and innovative approach that takes into account the new premises and the new international security environment.

V. The Stockholm Agenda for Arms Control

The question is what has to be done in practice to forestall adverse developments and a situation in which arms control and disarmament evolve from a bad to a worse condition. It is often claimed that, since the end of the cold war, arms control and disarmament have lost their significance as a priority matter in the security policies of the major powers because the threat of a global war has receded dramatically. Non-military aspects of security have come to the fore. In defining a new agenda, arms control should not be seen as an artificial process in which producing an agreement is a value per se. With the intention to contribute to a serious political and intellectual debate, SIPRI organized the 1999 Nobel Symposium on A Future Arms Control Agenda. It was convened to contribute to building a common and cooperative security system of which arms control is an important pillar. The debate at the symposium provided the inspiration for *The Stockholm Agenda for Arms Control*, which stresses that unconventional problems call for unconventional solutions. To create the strategic conditions in which arms control can succeed, the following six objectives were suggested.

• To initiate a focused dialogue on the political and strategic context in which arms control is being carried out
• To revitalize the institutional framework for making and implementing arms control policy without assuming the primacy of any single institution
• To organize the relations between major powers in ways that minimize the risk of war
• To engage the USA in the international system on the basis of responsible leadership within a common framework
• To manage relations with the few states outside the normative framework for nuclear, biological and chemical weapons-related arms control and disarmament
• To establish a rule-based agreed framework for the legitimate use of force in the new security environment.[25]

---

[24] In the view of some observers, this poses a real risk of a nuclear war in the region. Taylor, P. D., 'Nuclear war between India and Pakistan is a real possibility', *International Herald Tribune*, 14 Mar. 2000, p. 6.

[25] *The Stockholm Agenda for Arms Control. Report based on the Rapporteur's Statement at the Nobel Symposium on A Future Arms Control Agenda, 1–2 October 1999* (SIPRI: Stockholm, Nov. 1999), p. 1; and SIPRI, *Proceedings of Nobel Symposium no. 118, 1999: A Future Arms Control Agenda* (Oxford University Press: Oxford, forthcoming 2000).

The Stockholm Agenda proposed a pragmatic approach to realizing these objectives through the establishment of an informal World Forum on Security and Arms Control. In his Millennium Report, UN Secretary-General Annan called on the Millennium Summit to consider 'convening a major international conference that would help to identify ways of eliminating nuclear dangers'.[26]

VI. SIPRI findings

The main conclusions from the original data, facts and analyses of developments in 1999 presented in this volume are the following.

Conflicts.[27] In 1999 there were 27 major armed conflicts in 25 countries throughout the world. More than 1000 people died in 14 of the conflicts; such a high incidence of intensive conflict occurred in only two other years of the past decade. Africa is the only region of the world in which there has been a significant increase in the number of major armed conflicts since 1995. Foreign military intervention remains the exception and is not becoming the rule.

Conflict prevention, management and resolution.[28] Lack of agreement among the five permanent members of the UN Security Council led to the ending of the UN's first preventive operation, in the Former Yugoslav Republic of Macedonia, even as stability in the Balkans became more fragile. NATO's armed intervention in Kosovo lacked UN approval and the UN was only a subsidiary actor in mediation to bring the conflict to an end. In post-referendum East Timor, moreover, peace was restored by an ad hoc multinational coalition of forces. The most likely scenario for peacekeeping in the future is intense practical cooperation between the UN and regional organizations. The complex nature of modern peace operations was demonstrated in 1999. Peace-building operations, in particular, are long, arduous and expensive, and in 1999 the international community was made increasingly aware of the commitment necessary for peace operations.

Russia.[29] Separatist movements are seen in Russia as one of the most serious threats to its national security and territorial integrity. In 1999 the Russian federal forces intervened militarily with the aim of re-establishing control over Chechnya. As the conflict in Chechnya caused numerous casualties and a massive refugee problem among its civilian population, the Russian Government came under strong criticism from the West.

Europe.[30] The 1999 NATO and EU summit meetings imparted a new quality to the transatlantic agenda: the EU gained recognition at the NATO Washington summit meeting as a partner on defence matters, although it may take a long time for the EU's politico-military dimension to be complemented with a

---

[26] Annan (note 1), p. 53. Among the various initiatives, in this context should also be mentioned the New Agenda Coalition (Brazil, Egypt, Ireland, Mexico, New Zealand, Slovenia, South Africa and Sweden), which has tried to 'move the nuclear disarmament debate towards middle ground'. Salander, H., 'Special comment', *Disarmament Forum* (UNIDIR, Geneva), no. 1 (2000), p. 3.

[27] See chapter 1 and appendices 1A and 1B in this volume.

[28] See chapter 2 in this volume.

[29] See chapter 3 in this volume.

[30] See chapter 4 in this volume.

Defence Union. The future of transatlantic relations is dependent on how the differing interests of the United States and Europe on three inseparable planes—economic, political and military—can be resolved. The OSCE Charter for European Security codified a set of arrangements for closer cooperation between all security-related international institutions existing in Europe.

Military expenditure.[31] World military expenditure increased by more than 2 per cent in real terms and amounted to roughly $780 billion (in current prices) in 1999. While it is almost one-third less than 10 years earlier, it still represents a significant share of world economic resources: 2.6 per cent of world gross national product. The consistent annual decline in world military spending since 1988 came to an end in 1996 and expenditure has since then fluctuated. However, behind this fluctuation is a general slight rise in military spending in most regions. The fall in world military expenditure in 1998 was due primarily to significant cuts in Russian and continued reductions in US expenditure, while both these countries increased their military spending in 1999. The rise in world military expenditure in 1999 is accounted for primarily by a few major spender countries, including the USA (36 per cent of the world total), France (7 per cent), and Russia and China (3 per cent each).

Military expenditure in Africa.[32] Military expenditure in Africa has been increasing since 1997, after a relatively long period of decline. The increase is due primarily to the involvement of many countries in the region in armed conflict either directly or indirectly. The costs and methods of financing armed conflict vary but usually include resource absorption outside the official defence budget, making accurate reporting of the amount of economic resources committed to military activities difficult. While African military expenditure represents a small share of the world total, it constitutes a heavy economic burden in many African countries where many social needs are competing for scarce economic resources.

Arms production.[33] There are no firm statistics on global arms production. SIPRI data on the 100 largest arms-producing companies in the Organisation for Economic Co-operation and Development countries and the developing countries, apart from China, show that the combined arms sales of these companies ($154.5 billion in 1998), roughly three-quarters of the total amount of world arms production, declined by 29 per cent in real terms between 1990 and 1995 but by only 3 per cent between 1995 and 1998. The dramatic decline in Russian arms production was halted. In 1999 there was a significant increase for the first time since the disintegration of the Soviet Union. The military output of the Russian defence complex increased by 37 per cent in real terms in 1999, but still amounted to only 14 per cent of Soviet arms production in 1991.

Transfers of major conventional weapons.[34] Transparency concerning transfers of major conventional weapons has increased significantly in recent years

---

[31] See chapter 5 in this volume.
[32] See appendix 5D in this volume.
[33] See chapter 6 in this volume.
[34] See chapter 7 in this volume.

and the governments of most of the major arms suppliers now report details of their arms trade. By aggregating these data SIPRI has been able to estimate the financial value of the arms trade for the first time. The global financial value of the legal international arms trade in 1998 is estimated at $35–49 billion. The volume of the transfers of major conventional weapons as measured by the SIPRI trend-indicator has been fairly stable since 1995, at about one-half of the 1987 peak value. The USA was by far the largest supplier during the period 1995–99, delivering almost as much as all other suppliers combined. While Russia was the second largest supplier in this period, its deliveries amounted to only 27 per cent of those of the USA. The other major suppliers were France, the UK and Germany. The main recipients of major conventional weapons in 1995–99 were Taiwan, Saudi Arabia, Turkey, South Korea and Egypt. In 1999 Taiwan ranked as the largest recipient for the third consecutive year. A number of the leading recipients of weapons from the major supplier countries were involved in armed conflicts during 1999.

Nuclear arms control.[35] In 1999 the controversy over ballistic missile defence and the future of the ABM Treaty moved to the fore of the nuclear arms control agenda. In the USA there was an emergent consensus in favour of developing a limited NMD system designed to protect the US territory against attack by a small number of ballistic missiles launched by a 'rogue state'. Russian officials warned that the deployment of any NMD system would lead to the collapse of the entire US–Russian nuclear arms control framework, including a Russian withdrawal from existing nuclear arms reduction treaties. China also expressed concern about the implications of a US NMD system for its nuclear deterrent. The US Senate's vote in October 1999 to reject ratification of the CTBT marked a setback for efforts to bring that treaty into force, but the US Administration reaffirmed its intention to observe its nuclear testing moratorium.

IAEA safeguards.[36] The adoption in 1997 of the strengthened safeguards system by the International Atomic Energy Agency (IAEA) Board of Governors was a fundamental step towards limiting the spread of nuclear weapons and enhancing international security. Universal acceptance and full implementation of the new scheme are imperative for guaranteeing the political assurances necessary for advancing the non-proliferation and disarmament agenda.

CBW developments.[37] The proliferation of chemical and biological weapons (CBW) remained a major concern in 1999. Agreement on a range of technical matters ensured the steady advancement of the 1993 Chemical Weapons Convention (CWC) treaty-building process and the negotiation of the new protocol to the 1972 Biological and Toxin Weapons Convention (BTWC). The internal political, social and economic turmoil in Russia raised questions about the country's ability to meet or domestically enforce its treaty obligations. It was the only declared possessor state not to have started the destruction of its CW stockpile, and serious international concern persisted that it still has illegal

---

[35] See chapter 8 in this volume.
[36] See appendix 8B in this volume.
[37] See chapter 9 in this volume.

BW programmes. The USA was increasingly perceived to be less than fully committed to multilateral disarmament: it was in technical non-compliance with the CWC regarding initial industry declarations and it resists strong compliance mechanisms for the future BTWC regime.

Terrorism.[38] In the 1990s terrorism became a major security concern and several international efforts were launched. Governments face threats of CB terrorism, but the most catastrophic scenarios involving mass casualties are not likely to occur. Balanced policies are needed. Overreaction can create an atmosphere in which hoaxes may become as efficient as attacks with CBW.

UNSCOM.[39] In 1999 the UN Special Commission on Iraq (UNSCOM) was disbanded after Iraq had obstructed inspections and exploited the political disagreement in the Security Council. No inspections or monitoring have been conducted in Iraq since December 1998. UNSCOM was replaced by the UN Monitoring, Verification and Inspection Commission (UNMOVIC), which Iraq has so far rejected. UNMOVIC will have to redo the work of UNSCOM because Iraq has moved relevant materials, equipment and files.

Conventional arms control.[40] The conventional arms control regime in Europe was strengthened in 1999 when negotiations were finalized on the Agreement on Adaptation of the Treaty on Conventional Armed Forces in Europe and on the Vienna Document 1999 on Confidence- and Security-Building Measures (CSBMs). Both documents were signed at the Istanbul Summit Meeting of the OSCE. The most important modernization of the Vienna Document is the introduction of voluntary political and legally binding measures tailored to regional needs. While there was generally little progress in conventional arms control outside Europe, after two years of intense consultations by Brazil and the United States on a regional transparency regime, the Organization of American States approved an Inter-American Convention on Transparency in Conventional Weapons Acquisitions. Although the 1997 Convention on the Prohibition of the Use, Stockpiling, Production and Transfer of Anti-Personnel Mines and on their Destruction (the APM Convention) entered into force on 1 March, the main producers and exporters of landmines—China, India, Pakistan, Russia and the USA—as well as many user countries involved in conflicts around the world, have not signed the convention.

The North Korean ballistic missile programme.[41] In the 1990s North Korea accelerated the development of intercontinental-range missiles. It has not met its obligations under bilateral safeguards agreements with the IAEA, strengthening the suspicion that it has a clandestine nuclear weapon programme. Given the continued state of high tension on the Korean Peninsula, regional states in particular have cause for concern about the impact of North Korean missile programmes on regional and international security. In the current international security environment new types of political response to weapon

---

[38] See appendix 9A in this volume.
[39] See appendix 9B in this volume.
[40] See chapter 10 and appendix 10A in this volume.
[41] See chapter 11 and appendix 11A in this volume.

development programmes of concern are supplementing traditional forms of arms control. Elements of this 'new' arms control include the application of sanctions, offering of incentives and coordination of political responses outside the framework of international organizations.

VII. Conclusions

Many factors will determine the further development of the international security system. While the cold war era was characterized by bipolarity and ideological clarity, today the world has no clear-cut dividing lines or overriding threat. A critical element of the shaping of a new international system is the ever growing recognition of democratic principles, respect for human rights and the rule of law, and market economy as the common values. Indeed, these values are recognized in most parts of the world and have been laid down in legal norms and instruments. The priority in the world today is not only to agree on new rules and set up new institutions but also to guarantee the practical application of these norms and 'ensure that governments are accountable for the rights of all those within their jurisdiction'.[42] Attempts to mechanically implant the transatlantic and European solutions in other regions have not suceeded; imposing them from outside, against the will of the states directly concerned, may result in the most undesirable effects. Regional and subregional systems should be designed according to regional needs and traditions so that they can respond to specific challenges and threats.

One of the main questions in shaping a new global security system is how the USA should accommodate the interests of other actors on the international scene. The USA is often criticized as an excessively interventionist power.[43] However, one cannot ignore the fact that US interventionism is frequently a response to the expectations of the international community, represented by various international organizations or groups of states. Two other currents in US policy may become more dangerous than the United States' involvement in world and regional security: looming neo-isolationism, and a propensity to ignore international structures and commitments while acting according to self-proclaimed rules as a 'lone sheriff'.

International structures, organizations and institutions should be seen as forums in which national security interests can be addressed. This means that the new international system will function only when states find that it ensures their security more effectively than exclusive reliance on national strategies. Treaties and institutions provide the organizational and regulatory framework, provided they both reflect the interests of the participating states and promote political will and active security cooperation. In other words, the international security system of the 21st century should respond to the concrete new needs and challenges that face individual states and regions of the world.

---

[42] Robinson, M., *Human Rights: Challenges for the 21st Century*, The Dag Hammarskjöld Lecture 1998 (Dag Hammarskjöld Foundation: Uppsala, 1998), p. 20.

[43] 'Critics note that the United States is far more interventionist than any previous system leader.' Wohlforth (note 7), p. 39.

Part I. Security and conflicts, 1999

Chapter 1. Major armed conflicts

Chapter 2. Armed conflict prevention, management and resolution

Chapter 3. Russia: separatism and conflicts in the North Caucasus

Chapter 4. Europe: the new transatlantic agenda

1. Major armed conflicts

TAYLOR B. SEYBOLT
in collaboration with the UPPSALA CONFLICT DATA PROJECT*

I. Introduction

Major armed conflicts in 1999 exhibited the following quantitative patterns. There were 27 major armed conflicts in 25 countries throughout the world. Only two of the conflicts were interstate. There was no change from the previous year in the number of conflicts, but the number of countries with a major armed conflict decreased by one.

More than 1000 people died in each of 14 of the conflicts in 1999—7 in Africa, 1 in South America, 4 in Asia and 2 in Europe.[1] Only twice in the past decade, in 1992 and 1993, was there such a high incidence of intensive conflict. In 1994, 1996 and 1997, 7 conflicts accounted for over 1000 deaths and in the remaining four years of the decade between 9 and 13 conflicts. In 1999 nearly 1000 people were killed in 3 conflicts, while far fewer died as a result of 10 of the conflicts.[2] The conflicts in 1999, their locations and the death tolls are presented in the table in appendix 1A, compiled by the Uppsala Conflict Data Project, led by Margareta Sollenberg and Peter Wallensteen.

A 'major armed conflict' is defined as the use of armed force between the military forces of two or more governments,[3] or of one government and at least one organized armed group, resulting in the battle-related deaths of at least 1000 people in any single year and in which the incompatibility concerns control of government and/or territory. This definition differs somewhat from the one applied in previous SIPRI Yearbook chapters on major armed conflicts. The requirement that a conflict must cause 1000 or more battle-related

---

[1] These 14 conflicts are Afghanistan, Algeria, Angola, Colombia, the Democratic Republic of Congo, the Republic of Congo, Eritrea–Ethiopia, India (Kashmiri separatists), India–Pakistan, Russia (Chechnya), Sierra Leone, Sri Lanka, Sudan and the Federal Republic of Yugoslavia (Kosovo).

[2] The conflicts with nearly 1000 deaths in 1999 are Burundi, Guinea-Bissau and Somalia; those with far below 1000 deaths are India (Assam), Indonesia (Aceh), Indonesia (East Timor), Iran, Israel, Myanmar, Peru, the Philippines, Rwanda and Turkey. These 13 conflicts are included in tables 1.1 and 1A because they crossed the threshold of 1000 deaths in some year in their history and the continued use of force related to control of territory or government resulted in at least a few deaths in 1999.

[3] The government of a state is that party which is generally regarded as being in central control even by those organizations seeking to assume power. If this criterion is not applicable, the government is the party which controls the capital. In most cases where there is a government, the 2 criteria coincide.

* The definitions of terms and the criteria that apply to the conflict statistics in this chapter and appendix 1A have been developed by the Uppsala Conflict Data Project of the Department of Peace and Conflict Research, Uppsala University, Sweden. For detailed descriptions of the Uppsala Conflict Data Project criteria, see appendix 1A and Heldt, B. (ed.), *States in Armed Conflict 1990–91* (Department of Peace and Conflict Research, Uppsala University: Uppsala, 1992), chapter 3. The Uppsala Conflict Data Project also contributed table 1.1 in this chapter.

Table 1.1. Regional distribution, number and types of major armed conflicts, 1990–99[a]

Region[a]	1990 G	1990 T	1991 G	1991 T	1992 G	1992 T	1993 G	1993 T	1994 G	1994 T	1995 G	1995 T	1996 G	1996 T	1997 G	1997 T	1998 G	1998 T	1999 G	1999 T
Africa	8	3	8	3	6	1	6	1	5	1	4	1	2	1	4	–	10	1	10	1
America, South	4	–	4	–	3	–	3	–	3	–	3	–	3	–	2	–	2	–	2	–
Asia	4	9	3	8	4	8	4	6	4	6	4	7	4	6	3	6	3	6	2	7
Europe	–	–	–	1	–	3	–	5	–	4	–	3	–	1	–	–	–	1	–	2
Middle East	1	3	2	4	2	3	2	4	2	4	2	4	2	4	2	2	2	2	1	2
Total	**17**	**15**	**17**	**16**	**15**	**15**	**15**	**16**	**14**	**15**	**13**	**15**	**11**	**12**	**11**	**8**	**17**	**10**	**15**	**12**
Total	**32**		**33**		**30**		**31**		**29**		**28**		**23**		**19**		**27**		**27**	

G = government and T = territory, the two types of incompatibility.

[a] The total annual number of conflicts does not necessarily correspond to the number of conflict locations in table 1A, appendix 1A, since there may be more than 1 major armed conflict in each country. Retroactive adjustments to reflect the new definition of major armed conflict have been made to the figures for all the years appearing in the table above.

Source: Uppsala Conflict Data Project.

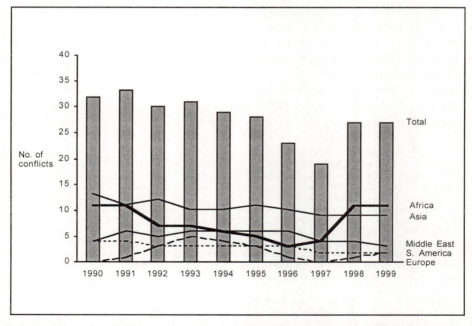

Figure 1.1. Regional distribution and total number of major armed conflicts, 1990–99

deaths in a single year ensures that only conflicts that reach a high level of violence are included.[4] Once a conflict has reached that threshold it continues to appear in the data until it ends or goes into remission, even if the level of violence decreases significantly. The use of armed force does not have to have occurred over a prolonged period of time, as stipulated in past years.

The vast majority of the major armed conflicts in 1999 were in Africa and Asia; there were 11 in Africa, 9 in Asia, 3 in the Middle East, 2 in Europe and 2 in South America. Table 1.1 presents the regional distribution, number and types of incompatibility for the major armed conflicts in the 10-year period 1990–99.[5] Figure 1.1 shows the regional distribution and total number of conflicts for each year in this period. In Africa, 10 of the conflicts concerned control of government. Africa has the highest incidence of new conflicts—nine of the conflicts began after 1990—and is the only region of the world in which there has been a significant increase in the number of major armed conflicts since 1995. Two of the conflicts have been active for over 10 years. Seven of the nine conflicts in Asia were over territory, and all of them began at least 10 years ago. In the Middle East, two conflicts concerned territory and have been active for 25 years or more; one concerned government and has been active for eight years. In Europe, both conflicts concerned territory and have been active for no longer than two years. In South America, both conflicts concerned control of government and have been active for at least 19 years. Of the 25 intra-state conflicts, 15 concerned control over government and 10 control over territory. Both of the interstate wars were over the latter.[6]

The fact that the total number of conflicts was the same in 1999 as in 1998 obscures three changes. First, the conflicts in Cambodia and Iraq do not appear in the table for 1999: the Cambodian conflict was resolved with the

---

[4] It should be noted that the figures given in this chapter for the deaths caused by the conflicts do not always agree with those in table 1A. The reasons are definitional and methodological. The Uppsala Conflict Data Project registers only 'battle-related' deaths, which excludes from the data in the appendix those deaths caused by political violence that are not attributable to one of the identified 'warring parties'. The present author counts all deaths directly caused by the conflict in question, including deaths caused by ethnic expulsion and militia violence. The Uppsala Conflict Data Project compiles data through a comprehensive review of reports of individual violent incidents in each conflict; the author of this chapter uses aggregate numbers and cites specific sources that he judges to be reliable. The numbers presented by the Uppsala Project are used to determine which conflicts are classified as 'major armed conflicts'.

[5] Retroactive adjustments to table 1.1 reflect the revised definition of a major armed conflict. Four conflicts have been entirely excluded from the data because they never resulted in 1000 or more battle-related deaths in a single year. They previously appeared for the years given in parentheses: Bangladesh (1990–97), Senegal (1997–98), Uganda (1996–98) and the United Kingdom (1990–97). Three conflicts still appear in the data but did not reach the casualty threshold immediately. They no longer appear for the years given in parentheses but do appear in later years: Burundi (1997), Sierra Leone (1994–97) and Turkey (1990–91). Other revisions were made on the basis of new information: Laos was excluded in 1990 and 1992, and Nicaragua in 1990. The Republic of Congo and Somalia were included in 1998. Margareta Sollenberg, Uppsala Conflict Data Project.

[6] The term 'war' is used sparingly in this chapter in reference to the most intense conflicts of 1999, although according to the definition it is synonymous with the term 'major armed conflict'. The Uppsala Conflict Data Project defines a war as a conflict with more than 1000 battle-related deaths in a single year. Wallensteen, P. and Sollenberg, M., 'Armed conflict, 1989–98', *Journal of Peace Research*, vol. 36, no. 5 (Sep. 1999), p. 595. Since this is also a necessary criterion for a major armed conflict according to the revised definition, all the conflicts named here were wars at some point, even if they were active at a low level in 1999.

demise of the Khmer Rouge, and the Iraqi Government's contest with the Supreme Assembly for the Islamic Revolution in Iraq (SAIRI) appeared to be in remission.[7] The conflicts in the Russian republic of Chechnya and in the Indonesian province of Aceh are included for 1999 after several years in which they did not cause any battle-related deaths. Second, two conflicts are included for 1999 that, upon re-examination of the data, should also have been included in the table for 1998. Fighting in the Republic of Congo (Congo-Brazzaville) crossed the intensity threshold in 1998. Somalia is registered as a conflict in 1999 because there is ample evidence that the warring parties are fighting over governmental power, even though none of them can be considered to be the government of the state. Third, the conflicts in Senegal and Uganda are not registered for 1999 because of the temporal limit introduced into the definition: there were not 1000 or more battle-related deaths in any single year of these two conflicts.

Section II describes the interstate conflicts between Eritrea and Ethiopia and between India and Pakistan and section III the conflicts within states. The latter are categorized by whether or not there was foreign military intervention in 1999. The five conflicts with foreign military intervention receive considerable attention, while the reviews of the 20 conflicts in which there was no significant foreign military intervention are brief. Section IV notes a few broad topics that deserve continued research and policy attention in the light of this review of the current major armed conflicts.

II. Major armed conflicts between states

An interstate conflict occurs between the armed forces of two or more recognized states, at least one of which attempts to change the government or the status of a specified territory of the other state. The only two interstate conflicts in 1999 were those that pitted Eritrea against Ethiopia and India against Pakistan.[8] The incompatibility in both conflicts was over territory.

Eritrea–Ethiopia

Eritrea and Ethiopia fought the world's deadliest battles of 1999, with tens of thousands of soldiers killed. It is one of the very few interstate armed conflicts that have occurred in Africa in the post-colonial period. Cross-border violence broke out in May 1998, surprising most observers. It occurred between states that had had friendly relations and was over land with little economic or

---

[7] The SAIRI claimed to have engaged in some violent activity in 1999 but, since the claims could not be confirmed, Iraq is not included in the table in appendix 1A.

[8] It should be noted that the conflict between North and South Korea is not included because the parties to a conflict must perceive that they are acting on a current and active incompatibility that has resulted in a major armed conflict. The Uppsala Conflict Data Project argues that none of the events on the Korean peninsula since 1953 has been of that kind. The border incidents are instead the result of their poor relations and normal security concerns.

strategic value.[9] The governing parties of the two countries—the Ethiopian People's Revolutionary Democratic Front (EPRDF) and the People's Front for Democracy and Justice (PFDJ) in Eritrea—had been allies in a rebellion against the Ethiopian regime of Mengistu Haile Mariam. The 1000-km line separating the two states was not fully surveyed when Eritrea gained independence from Ethiopia in 1993.

Tensions over who would administer the border areas were at a low level until 1997, when the border served as a focus for antagonism between the two states as a result of their divergent economic policies. Ethiopia, fearing the vulnerability of its industry to the import of cheap Eritrean products, imposed high tariffs. Eritrea stopped using the Ethiopian currency, believing it to be overvalued for its exports. Ethiopia refused to trade with Eritrea's new currency, ruining commerce between them. The antagonism worsened when Ethiopia began to deport thousands of ethnic Eritreans whose families had for generations lived on the disputed land.[10] The disagreement came to a head when an Eritrean Army unit crossed the border to negotiate on behalf of Eritrean farmers who had been expelled from their land. It is unclear who fired first, but a clash resulted in Eritrean soldiers seizing the border town of Badme in May 1998. After a series of bloody battles and a Rwandan–US peace initiative that brought a lull in the fighting but no peace agreement, in June 1998 the Organization of African Unity (OAU) drew up a peace plan in a Framework Agreement. Ethiopia accepted it, while Eritrea asked for clarification of a number of points.[11]

Serious fighting resumed in February 1999, when Ethiopian troops dislodged Eritrean units that were dug into trenches at Badme and drove deep into Eritrea. After suffering severe casualties and setbacks on the battlefield, Eritrea accepted the Framework Agreement in principle, but the fighting continued because the two sides disagreed over implementation of the peace plan.[12] Intense but geographically limited clashes continued throughout the spring and early summer.[13] The OAU presented a document containing 'Modalities' to clarify the terms for implementation of the Framework Agreement in July 1999. A month later it introduced a document on the 'Technical

---

[9] It can be argued, however, that Eritrea's territory is so narrow that any loss of land deprives it of strategic depth.

[10] Smythe, F., 'Eritrea stakes its claim', *Jane's Intelligence Review*, vol. 11, no. 2 (Feb. 1999), pp. 45–46; Masland, T., 'Was this war necessary?', Interview with Yemane Ghebreab, *Newsweek*, 8 Mar. 1999, p. 66; 'Africa's forgotten war', *The Economist*, 8 May 1999, p. 45; and Jenkins, C., 'Ethiopia's Eritreans lose their homeland', BBC News Online, 22 July 1999, URL <http://news.bbc.co.uk/hi/english/special_report/1999/07/99/battle_in_the_horn/newsid_396000/396203.stm>.

[11] 'Proposals for a Framework Agreement for a peaceful settlement of the dispute between Ethiopia and Eritrea', annex to UN, Letter dated 24 December 1998 from the Permanent Representative of Ethiopia to the United Nations addressed to the President of the Security Council, UN document S/1998/1223, 28 Dec. 1998, para. 33; Smythe (note 10), pp. 47–48; and Plaut, M. and Gilkes, P., 'Conflict in the Horn: why Eritrea and Ethiopia are at war', Royal Institute of International Affairs (RIIA), Briefing paper, New series no. 1, Mar. 1999, URL <www.riia.org/briefingpapers/bpn1.html>.

[12] Masland (note 10).

[13] Tadesse, T., 'Eritrean–Ethiopian conflict', *Horn of Africa Bulletin*, vol. 11, no. 3 (May/June 1999), p. 7; 'Battling for Badme', *Africa Confidential*, vol. 40, no. 22 (5 Nov. 1999), p. 2; and Last, A., 'Reggae and tea as shells fall', BBC News Online, 23 July 1999, URL <http://news.bbc.co.uk/english/special_report/1999/07/99/battle_in_the_horn/newsid_394000/394640.stm>.

Arrangements', intended to facilitate implementation.[14] Eritrea accepted all three documents. Ethiopia objected to the Technical Arrangements because they did not guarantee a return to the status quo ante and because it claimed that they threatened its sovereignty by calling for a UN peacekeeping operation rather than an unarmed OAU observer mission. At the end of 1999 there was no fighting but each country publicly questioned the other's commitment to peace and warned of an impending return to war.[15]

The war encouraged Ethiopia to establish ties with the Sudanese Government, hoping to build an alliance with the Eritrean dissidents residing there. This forced Eritrea also to establish relations with Sudan. In addition, Eritrea allied with Somali warlord Hussein Aideed and materially supported the Oromo Liberation Front (OLF) in northern Kenya and the Ogaden National Liberation Front (ONLF) in western Somalia, both of which are fighting in Ethiopia to overthrow the government. Ethiopia tried to counter this tactic by supporting various factions in Somalia opposed to Aideed.[16]

The cost to both sides was enormous.[17] Estimates of the number of people killed are in the range of 50 000–100 000. At least 30 000 died in 1999.[18] At the end of the year internally displaced Eritreans numbered at least 258 300[19] and Ethiopia had deported over 67 000 ethnic Eritreans.[20] The number of displaced Ethiopians was in the range of 315 000–385 000.[21] In 1998 about one-third of Eritrea's gross domestic product (GDP) went to defence spending, economic growth slowed, and the main port operated at one-third of its capacity. With an economy eight times the size of Eritrea's, Ethiopia spent about 3.5 per cent of its GDP on defence in 1998, requiring a reduction in other gov-

---

[14] 'Modalities for the implementation of the OAU Framework Agreement on the settlement of the dispute between Ethiopia and Eritrea', Annex III to UN, Letter dated 16 July 1999 from the permanent representative of Eritrea to the United Nations addressed to the President of the Security Council, UN document S/1999/794, 16 July 1999; and 'Technical Arrangements for the implementation of the OAU Framework Agreement and its Modalities', on file at SIPRI.

[15] 'Cease-fire under threat', *Africa Confidential*, vol. 40, no. 22 (5 Nov. 1999), p. 1; United Nations Office for the Coordination of Humanitarian Affairs (OCHA), Integrated Regional Information Network–Central and Eastern Africa (IRIN-CEA), 'Ethiopia: peace process in danger—Meles' and 'Eritrea: Ethiopia "poised for war"', IRIN-CEA weekly round-up 49, 4–10 Dec. 1999; and IRIN-CEA, 'Ethiopia–Eritrea: fighting flares up as peace envoys visit', 24 Feb. 2000. News items from all the IRIN offices—Central and Eastern Africa (Nairobi, Kenya), Western Africa (Abidjan, Côte d'Ivoire) and Southern Africa (Johannesburg, South Africa)—are archived on ReliefWeb, URL <http://www.reliefweb.int/IRIN/index.phtml>.

[16] 'Africa's forgotten war' (note 10); and Gilkes, P., 'The Somali connection', BBC News Online, 23 July 1999, URL <http://news.bbc.co.uk/hi/english/special_report/1999/07/99/battle_in_the_horn/newsid_399898.stm>.

[17] For a general discussion of the costs and financing of wars, see section III of chapter 5 in this volume; for a discussion of military spending in the countries of Africa, see appendix 5D.

[18] Fisher, I., 'Peace deal may be near for Ethiopia and Eritrea', *New York Times* (Internet edn), 23 Aug. 1999, URL <http://www.nytimes.com/library/world/africa/082399eritrea-ethiopia.html>; 'Battling for Badme' (note 13); and 'Africa's forgotten war' (note 10).

[19] Oxfam estimated the number of displaced Eritreans to be as high as 500 000. Oxfam, 'Africa's forgotten crises: people in peril: Angola, Ethiopia, Eritrea, Sierra Leone, Congo', 9 Sep. 1999, available on ReliefWeb, URL <http://www.reliefweb.int/w/rwb.nsf/437a83f9fa966c40c12564f2004fde87/63c9ca5ceca7c68f852567e7006e82e6?OpenDocument>.

[20] 'Eritrea: update on figures of displaced, deported', IRIN-CEA weekly round-up 3, 21 Jan. 2000.

[21] US Agency for International Development (USAID), Bureau for Humanitarian Response, Office of Foreign Disaster Assistance (OFDA), 'Ethiopia—drought/border conflict, factsheet #2, fiscal year 1999', 22 Sep. 1999, p. 1; and Oxfam (note 19).

ernment expenditures and exacerbating severe food shortages caused by drought.[22]

India–Pakistan

Hopes for a rapprochement between India and Pakistan after their 1998 nuclear explosions faded when fighting flared in Kashmir in early May 1999.[23] The 'Kargil war' was the heaviest fighting between the two countries since 1971, when they fought a full-scale war.[24] Between 700 and 1000 Kashmiri Mujahideen militants based in Pakistan crossed the Line of Control (LOC)—the de facto boundary between the two countries—near the town of Kargil and occupied positions overlooking a key Indian supply route.[25] Pakistani Army soldiers crossed into India to support the Mujahideen, although Pakistan initially denied this.[26] The fighting rapidly escalated to the use of artillery and helicopters on both sides and massive air strikes by India.[27] Both India and Pakistan raised the state of readiness for some heavy units, increasing the possibility of a wider war.[28]

On 20 June 1999 the Group of Eight (G8) called for an immediate ceasefire and restoration of the LOC.[29] Most governments rejected Pakistan's claim that it had no control over the militants and accepted Indian's position that the well-organized and -supplied offensive could only have been executed with Pakistan's support.[30] Diplomatic pressure on Pakistan increased when China called for resolution of the conflict through dialogue. In a 4 July meeting with US President Bill Clinton, Pakistani Prime Minister Nawaz Sharif agreed to restore the LOC. Two weeks later most of the forces were disengaged.[31] Low-level clashes continued until the end of the year, despite a pledge to reduce tensions made by General Pervez Musharraf after he seized control of Pakistan in a coup in October.[32] Indian and Pakistani claims about the number of com-

[22] 'Africa's forgotten war' (note 10); 'Cease-fire under threat' (note 15); Oxfam (note 19); and Smythe (note 10).

[23] For further information see Widmalm, S., 'The Kashmir conflict', *SIPRI Yearbook 1999: Armaments, Disarmament and International Security* (Oxford University Press: Oxford, 1999), pp. 34–46; and Arnett, E., 'Nuclear tests by India and Pakistan', *SIPRI Yearbook 1999*, pp. 371–86.

[24] LePoer, B. L., *Recent Developments in Kashmir and US Concerns*, CRS Report for Congress, 26 July 1999 (US Government Printing Office: Washington, DC, 1999), p. 1.

[25] Bedi, R., 'Pakistan–Indian peace hopes crushed', *Jane's Defence Weekly*, vol. 32, no. 7 (18 Aug. 1999), p. 3; and LePoer (note 24).

[26] Kazmin, A. L., 'Pakistan says its troops crossed over Kashmir line', *Financial Times*, 17–18 July 1999, p. 4.

[27] Bedi, R., 'India vows Kashmir strikes will continue', *Jane's Defence Weekly*, vol. 31, no. 22 (2 June 1999), p. 3.

[28] Lancaster, J., 'Kashmir crisis took both sides to a dangerous brink', *International Herald Tribune*, 27 July 1999, pp. 1, 4.

[29] For the members of the Group of Eight industrialized countries, see the glossary in this volume.

[30] Dhume, S. and Rashid, A., 'On higher ground', *Far Eastern Economic Review*, 8 July 1999, p. 10.

[31] Constable, P., 'U.S. makes breakthrough in India–Pakistan conflict', *International Herald Tribune*, 6 July 1999, pp. 1, 5; and 'Indians resume gunfire on intruders', *International Herald Tribune*, 22 July 1999, p. 7.

[32] Bearak, B., 'India shoots down Pakistani aircraft', *International Herald Tribune*, 11 Aug. 1999, pp. 1, 8; and 'India and Pakistan clash in Kashmir', BBC News Online, 10 Nov. 1999, URL <http://news2.thls.bbc.uk/hi/english/world/south_asia/newsid_513000/513810.stm>.

batant deaths diverged widely, but the total appears to have been about 1100.[33] About 70 000 people fled the conflict zone during the fighting.[34]

III. Major armed conflicts within states

An intra-state conflict takes place within a single state and involves control over the government and/or territory of that state. The definition includes secessionist conflicts. Internal conflicts frequently have international attributes and sometimes become interstate conflicts. On the 'input' side, one or more parties to the conflict can attract the support of other states or non-state actors. Efforts to find a negotiated settlement usually involve other states and international organizations. On the 'output' side, intra-state conflicts spill over state borders in the forms of refugee flows, actions by military units, arms transfers and so on. The distinction between intra-state and interstate conflicts is not always clear in practice. For example, the conflict in the Kosovo province of the Yugoslav Republic of Serbia is internal, but most of the fighting in 1999 was between the Federal Republic of Yugoslavia (FRY) and the NATO member states.

This section distinguishes between intra-state conflicts that involved foreign military intervention in 1999 and those that did not. Foreign military intervention is defined as the use of foreign troops for the purpose of affecting the outcome or consequences of an armed conflict in another country to which at least one of the primary belligerents does not give its consent.[35] Many definitions of military intervention specify only the consent of the legally recognized government. This definition allows the use of the term where there is no recognized government. Where there is a recognized government, it reflects the understanding that the non-governmental side is equally important to the outcome of the conflict. The definition does not include the provision of equipment and training. Rebels operating from a base in a neighbouring state are not intervention forces. Traditional peacekeeping is not foreign military intervention but part of a consensual peace process.

Conflicts that involved foreign military intervention

There was foreign military intervention in only 5 of the 25 intra-state conflicts in 1999. Nevertheless, foreign intervention and the challenge it poses to the principles of state sovereignty are spread across Africa, Europe and South-

---

[33] Clifton, T., 'Militants on the march', *Newsweek*, 23 Aug. 1999, p. 39; Bedi, R., 'India sets up Kashmir committee', *Jane's Defence Weekly*, vol. 32, no. 5 (4 Aug. 1999), p. 13; Bedi, R., 'India to step up Kashmir guard', *Jane's Defence Weekly*, vol. 32, no. 4 (28 July 1999), p. 12; and Associated Press (AP), 'India, Pakistan clash in Kashmir', *New York Times* (Internet edn), 21 July 1999, URL <http://www.nytimes.com/apoline/i/AP-India-Pakistan. html>.

[34] Sanctuary, C., 'Thousands displaced by Kashmir fighting', BBC News Online, 15 July 1999, URL <http://news2.thls.bbc.co.uk/hi/english/world/south_asia/newsid_369000/369984.stm>.

[35] This definition of 'foreign military intervention' was developed by the present author. It does not correspond exactly to the Uppsala Conflict Data Project's terminology of the 'contribution of regular troops of another state to one of the warring parties in a conflict', which implies that the intervening state shares the goals of the party to which it contributes troops.

East Asia. The interventions involved more than one state except in the Republic of Congo. In the Republic of Congo and the Democratic Republic of Congo (DRC), the intervenors were neighbouring states. Regional powers led multilateral interventions in Sierra Leone (Nigeria) and East Timor (Australia); NATO led the intervention in Kosovo. International organizations sanctioned two of the interventions: the Economic Community of West African States (ECOWAS) in Sierra Leone and the United Nations in East Timor. Neither in the Republic of Congo nor in the DRC was the intervention internationally sanctioned, and the NATO operation in Kosovo was only tacitly sanctioned. In Kosovo and East Timor, the intervening organizations claimed humanitarian motives. All the UN-commanded operations authorized in 1999 were peacekeeping missions.[36]

The Democratic Republic of Congo

The continued fighting in the DRC was one of the three conflicts in Africa in which neighbouring states intervened.[37] Large-scale violence broke out in eastern Kivu province in August 1998, after only 14 months of relative peace following the military defeat of President Mobutu Sese Seko in May 1997.[38] It began after the new leader, Laurent-Désiré Kabila, parted ways with his former allies in Rwanda and Uganda over their security concerns and his assertion of independence. Rwanda and Uganda portray the fighting as an internal rebellion that they support to secure their own borders, but the vast majority of the DRC population does not support the revolt.[39] The DRC Government consistently argues that it is the victim of external aggression by Rwanda and Uganda.[40]

A year of fighting led to a stalemate in mid-1999 between the government, backed by troops from Angola, Namibia, Zimbabwe and several militia groups, on the one side, and three Congolese rebel groups, backed by troops from Rwanda and Uganda, on the other side.[41] The Ugandan-backed Mouvement de Libération Congolais (MLC, Congolese Liberation Movement) and the Rassemblement Congolais pour la Démocratie–Mouvement de Libération

[36] The UN Observer Mission in the Democratic Republic of Congo (MONUC) has the consent of the warring parties in principle, but troops have been slow to deploy partly because the environment is hostile; see appendix 1B. For a review of UN peace operations in 1999 see chapter 2 in this volume.
[37] For a detailed account of the conflict and the peace process in the DRC see appendix 1B.
[38] When Kabila replaced Mobutu as president, he changed the country's name from Zaire to the Democratic Republic of Congo.
[39] Fisher, I., 'Congolese rebels gain territory but not support of the people', *International Herald Tribune*, 14–15 Aug. 1999, p. 4; McNulty, M., 'The collapse of Zaire: implosion, revolution or external sabotage?', *Journal of Modern African Studies*, vol. 37, no. 1 (1999), pp. 78–79; Shearer, D., 'Africa's great war', *Survival*, vol. 41, no. 2 (summer 1999), pp. 93–96; and International Crisis Group (ICG), *How Kabila Lost his Way*, ICG Democratic Republic of Congo report no. 3, 21 May 1999, URL <http://www.intl-crisis-group.org/projects/cafrica/reports/ca06main.htm>.
[40] In June 1999 the DRC Government instituted proceedings in the International Court of Justice against Rwanda, Uganda and Burundi for 'acts of armed aggression'. Report of the International Court of Justice, General Assembly, 54th session, 1 Aug. 1998–31 July 1999, section III, A 25–27, reproduced at URL <http://www.icj-cij.org/icjwww/igeneralinformation/igeninf_Annual_Reports/iICJ_Annual_Report _1998-1999.htm>.
[41] Chad had sent about 2000 troops to assist the DRC Government but withdrew them in May 1999.

(RCD-ML, Congolese Rally for Democracy–Liberation Movement) stalled in the north. The Rwandan-backed Rassemblement Congolais pour la Démocratie–Goma (RCD-G, Congolese Rally for Democracy–Goma) could not reach the diamond-mining town of Mbuji-Mayi, strategically located in the south-east.[42]

This stand-off helped to bring progress in peace talks that were mediated by Zambian President Frederick Chiluba on behalf of the Southern African Development Community (SADC).[43] The six states still involved in the conflict signed the Lusaka Ceasefire Agreement on 10 July; the MLC signed it on 1 August; and on 31 August, after intense diplomatic pressure, all 50 founding members of the fractious RCD signed it.[44]

Fighting characterized by ethnic expulsions, mass killings, rape and destruction of property continued to take its toll after the Lusaka Agreement was signed.[45] Estimates of the number of internally displaced persons stood at about 960 000 people in eight of the 11 provinces at the end of 1999. About 10.5 million people, of a country-wide population of almost 50 million, faced moderate to critical food shortages.[46] The UN Special Rapporteur on Human Rights in the DRC estimated that 6000 people were killed from August 1998 to August 1999, many of them civilians.[47] Other estimates are much higher.[48] Almost all economic activity in the east stopped. UN humanitarian aid appeals for $81 million were funded to less than 25 per cent by the end of the year.[49]

The Republic of Congo

The Republic of Congo lies on the north-western border of the DRC. It suffered a devastating civil war in 1993 and another in late 1997 that killed 10 000 people when Denis Sassou Nguesso toppled former President Pascal

---

[42] 'The blue helmets return', *Africa Confidential*, vol. 40, no. 24 (3 Dec. 1999), p. 3; IRIN-CEA weekly round-up 49, 4–10 Dec. 1999; Simpson, C., 'DR Congo: what price peace?', BBC News Online, 23 June 1999, URL <http://news2.thls.bbc.co.uk/hi/english/world/africa/newsid_376000/376633.stm>; and 'Congo city engulfed by Rwanda–Uganda fighting', *International Herald Tribune*, 17 Aug. 1999, p. 2.

[43] Statement of the President of the Security Council, UN document S/PRST/1999/17, 24 June 1999. For the members of the SADC, see the glossary in this volume.

[44] The Lusaka Ceasefire Agreement is contained in UN, Letter dated 23 July 1999 from the permanent representative of Zambia to the United Nations addressed to the President of the Security Council, UN document S/1999/815, 23 July 1999. For more on the Lusaka Agreement, see appendix 1B.

[45] 'Precious little peace', *Africa Confidential*, vol. 40, no. 22 (5 Nov. 1999), pp. 3–5; and 'DRCongo: heavy fighting said resumes in northwest', 30 Nov. 1999, in Foreign Broadcast Information Service, *Daily Report–Sub-Saharan Africa (FBIS-AFR)*, FBIS-AFR-1999-1130, 1 Dec. 1999.

[46] UN, Report of the Secretary-General on the United Nations Organization Mission in the Democratic Republic of Congo, UN document S/2000/30, 17 Jan. 2000, para. 24.

[47] 'DRC: Some 6,000 deaths in war's first year', IRIN-CEA weekly round-up 44, 30 Oct.–5 Nov. 1999. The Zimbabwean force has experienced a 10–15% casualty rate, mostly from disease. IRIN-CEA, 'Harare to wait before DRC withdrawal', 26 Aug. 1999.

[48] Fisher, I. *et al.*, 'Rival armies ravage Congo in Africa's "world war"', *International Herald Tribune*, 7 Feb. 2000, pp. 1, 2.

[49] 'Displacement surge in affected populations', IRIN-CEA weekly round-up 52, 25–30 Dec. 1999; UN, Second report of the Secretary-General on the United Nations preliminary deployment in the Democratic Republic of Congo, UN document S/1999/1116, 1 Nov. 1999, paras 22–24; Amnesty International (AI), 'Democratic Republic of Congo: massacres of civilians continue unabated in the east', AI document AFR 62/04/00, 17 Jan. 2000; and Oxfam (note 19).

Lissouba with the help of the Angolan military.[50] Fighting broke out again in December 1998 and January 1999 around the capital, Brazzaville, between President Nguesso's government troops and Cobra militia and former Prime Minister Bernard Kolelas' Ninja militia. Fighting also occurred throughout the year between government forces and Lissouba's Cocoyes militia in the south-western Pool region.[51] Government and opposition fighters regularly kill, rape and loot civilians.[52] The violence forced 250 000–350 000 people, out of a total population of 2.5 million, to flee their homes.[53] By the end of September about two-thirds of them had returned.[54] The country's economy hardly functioned; death from malnutrition waas rampant.[55]

Both Lissouba and Kolelas are in exile and belong to the Congolese opposition group in exile, the Republican Forum for the Defence of Democracy and National Unity.[56] President Nguesso continues to receive support from several thousand Angolan troops in the country.[57] Lissouba and Kolelas have close ties to the Angolan rebel movement União Nacional Para a Independência Total de Angola (UNITA, National Union for the Total Independence of Angola). Prospects for a political settlement in 'Africa's forgotten war' are uncertain at best. In September members of Lissouba's former government presented President Nguesso with a peace initiative.[58] The government released some political prisoners and signed a peace agreement with several senior rebel figures in November, but Lissouba and Kolelas, who were excluded, immediately denounced the signatories.[59] The agreement included an amnesty under which militiamen began to hand in their weapons in December.[60]

Sierra Leone

The eight-year civil war in Sierra Leone has caused the death of about 20 000 people, most of them civilians. An unstable peace collapsed in December 1998, when the Revolutionary United Front (RUF) and members of the former national army, the Armed Forces Revolutionary Council (AFRC), captured a string of northern towns and then entered the capital Freetown on 6 January

[50] Panafrican News Agency (PANA), 'Hard times as Congo marks 2nd anniversary of civil war', 5 June 1999, URL <www.africanews.org/PANA/index.html>.

[51] PANA, 'The army shells northern suburb of Brazzaville', 5 Jan. 1999; and PANA, 'Rebels seize dam in Congo-Brazzaville', 13 Jan. 1999.

[52] All Africa News Agency, 'Forgotten war takes toll on population', 12 July 1999, URL <http://www.africanews.org/central/congo/stories/19990712_feat1.html>.

[53] Hule, J., 'UN official urges world to remember Congo's crisis', PANA, 15 May 1999; and 'Duel to the death', The Economist, 10 Apr. 1999, p. 42.

[54] 'Humanitarian situation "much worse" than thought', IRIN-CEA weekly round-up 39, 25 Sep.–1 Oct. 1999.

[55] 'Survey reveals high death rate', Republic of Congo: IRIN news briefs, 15 Oct. 1999.

[56] Paris Radio France International, 'Congo—Ex-minister hails rebel moves, denies UNITA ties', 4 Feb. 1999, in FBIS-AFR-1999-0204, 5 Feb. 1999.

[57] All Africa News Agency (note 52).

[58] 'Peace initiative launched for Congo Brazzaville', BBC News Online, 1 Sep. 1999, URL <http://news.bbc.co.uk/hi/english/wolrd/africa/newsid_519000/519778.stm>.

[59] 'Army and rebels sign truce', IRIN-CEA weekly round-up 46, 13–19 Nov. 1999.

[60] 'Hardcore militiamen warned to lay down their weapons', Republic of Congo: IRIN news briefs, 22 Dec. 1999.

1999.[61] Their military success came from the element of surprise, material support from Liberia and mercenaries paid from the diamond wealth.[62] The RUF and the AFRC have 20 000–45 000 fighters, many of them children, who are known for maiming, raping and torturing civilians.[63] The ECOWAS Monitoring Group (ECOMOG) peacekeeping force of 15 000 in Freetown, in place since May 1997, drove the insurgents out after three weeks of fighting.[64] Battles continued outside the capital, and the rebels controlled about two-thirds of the country until a ceasefire was agreed on 18 May. An estimated 5000 people were killed and 700 000 to 1 million displaced, out of a total population of about 4.5 million.[65] President Ahmed Tejan Kabbah and the RUF leaders signed the Lomé Peace Agreement on 7 July, giving the rebels a large role in the government.[66] A tenuous peace held until the end of the year, when the first of 6000 peacekeeping troops of the United Nations Mission in Sierra Leone (UNAMSIL) arrived to relieve ECOMOG.[67]

East Timor, Indonesia

In January 1999 Indonesian President B. J. Habibie promised the East Timorese a referendum on independence, after 24 years of conflict that killed 200 000–250 000 people, most of them civilians.[68] Indonesia had forcibly annexed East Timor in 1975 after Portugal relinquished colonial control. The United Nations and most of the province's population never accepted Jakarta's rule.[69] The United Nations established the UN Mission in East Timor (UNAMET) in June to organize and oversee the vote.[70] The Indonesian Government was responsible for security. A paramilitary campaign of violence and killing, clandestinely supported by Indonesian Army units, attempted to persuade the population to vote for continued rule by the government in Jakarta. The tactic did not work and 79 per cent of the people who voted on 30 August chose independence, with the results announced on 3 September.[71] In an apparent attempt to punish the population or override the referendum results,

---

[61] Mabry, M., 'War with no rules', *Newsweek*, 29 Mar. 1999, p. 44; and USAID, OFDA, 'Sierra Leone, fact sheet #1, FY 2000', 7 Oct. 1999.

[62] Alao, A., 'ECOMOG presence fails to stem the violence in Sierra Leone', *Jane's Intelligence Review*, vol. 11, no. 4 (Apr. 1999), pp. 40–41.

[63] Devenport, M., 'UN force for Sierra Leone', BBC News Online, 28 Sep. 1999, URL <http://news.bbc.co.uk/hi/english/world/africa/newsid_459000/459490.stm>; and Mabry (note 61).

[64] Adeyemi, S., 'ECOMOG in crisis', *Jane's Defence Weekly*, vol. 31, no. 3 (20 Jan. 1999), p. 27.

[65] USAID, OFDA (note 61).

[66] 'Peace agreement between the Government of Sierra Leone and the Revolutionary United Front for Sierra Leone', 7 July 1999, available at URL <http://www.sierra-leone.org/documents.html>.

[67] For information on the UNAMSIL and ECOMOG operations, see chapter 2 in this volume.

[68] 'Terror in Timor', *The Economist*, 1 May 1999, p. 15; Richberg, K., 'Peace or war in East Timor? views form opposing sides', *International Herald Tribune*, 26 Aug. 1999, p. 6; and Chomsky, N., 'U.S. complicity in the atrocities', *Press for Conversion!*, no. 38 (Sep. 1999), p. 20.

[69] The violence in East Timor is treated as an intra-state conflict because Jakarta exercised de facto jurisdiction over the territory from 1975 and there was no separate, recognized East Timorese government.

[70] UN Security Council Resolution 1246, 11 June 1999.

[71] Haseman, J., 'Security implications for an independent East Timor', *Jane's Defence Weekly*, vol. 32, no. 11 (15 Sep. 1999), p. 57; and Mufson, S. and Lynch, C., 'East Timor failure puts U.N. in dock', *Guardian Weekly*, 30 Sep.–6 Oct. 1999, p. 31.

the paramilitary and army attacked virtually every settlement in East Timor. Foreigners were evacuated, including all but a few members of UNAMET.[72]

The Indonesian Government declared martial law as the UN and individual member states put diplomatic and economic pressure on Jakarta to consent to the deployment of a multinational force to restore peace. President Habibie reluctantly agreed to this on 12 September.[73] The Security Council unanimously passed Resolution 1264 on 15 September, authorizing under Chapter VII of the UN Charter an International Force for East Timor (INTERFET) to restore peace, protect UNAMET personnel and assist humanitarian operations.[74] Under Australian command, INTERFET troops began to arrive in East Timor on 20 September.[75]

During the rampage by militiamen and soldiers, outsiders feared that the number of deaths was in the thousands.[76] In retrospect, it appears that of a population of 890 000 the militiamen and soldiers killed hundreds of people and drove 520 000–620 000 from their homes, of whom 150 000–250 000 fled to West Timor.[77] Damage to property was extensive, with up to 50 per cent of the homes in some areas damaged, livestock killed, crops destroyed, and stores and hospitals looted.[78] Even after the arrival of foreign troops, militiamen continued to attack refugees in West Timor.[79]

There were about 26 000 Indonesian troops on the island of Timor, 16 000 of them in East Timor, when the multinational force arrived.[80] The USA estimated that at the time of the referendum 10 000 militiamen were also there.[81]

---

[72] 'The violent reaction to East Timor's voice', *The Economist*, 4 Sep. 1999, p. 58.

[73] From a legal point of view the international military presence in East Timor was not a military intervention, since the Indonesian Government gave its reluctant consent. INTERFET is categorized here as an intervention because the author considers the militia to be independent from direct government control. Militiamen were responsible for most of the violence; they did not give their consent to the presence of an international military force. In addition, the Australian component of INTERFET acted like an aggressive intervention force, in accordance with its mandate under Chapter VII of the UN Charter.

[74] UN Security Council Resolution 1264, 15 Sep. 1999.

[75] Moore, J., 'East Timor and Australia's security', Speech by the Australian Minister for Defence to the House of Representatives, 21 Sep. 1999, URL <http://www.minister.defence.government.au/1999/28499.html>; and Robinson, G., 'E. Timor peacekeepers unopposed', *Financial Times*, 21 Sep. 1999, p. 6.

[76] The UN Food and Agriculture Organization (FAO) estimated in early Sep. 1999 that over 7000 persons were killed. 'Grave humanitarian and food crisis developing in East Timor, FAO warns', UN Press Release SAG/56, 14 Sep. 1999.

[77] Richberg, K., 'East Timor mass grave may hold 50 victims', *International Herald Tribune*, 21 Dec. 1999, p. 8; Donnan, S. and Robinson, G., 'Mass grave find adds to pressure for Timor probe', *Financial Times*, 20 Oct. 1999, p. 6; UN Office for the Coordination of Humanitarian Affairs (OCHA), 'United Nations inter-agency and non-governmental organization preliminary assessment of needs for humanitarian assistance for East Timorese, September 1999–February 2000', Oct. 1999, section 2.1 and annex 1, para. A; and Schork, K., 'UN says 400,000 missing Timorese in mountains', Reuters, 13 Oct. 1999, available at URL <http://wwww.reliefweb.int/w/rwb.nsf/f303799b16d2074285256830007fb33f/c44f3eb347ba1630c125680900368446?OpenDocument>. The Uppsala Conflict Data Project does not register deaths caused by the militia as battle-related deaths attributable to a recognized warring party and therefore records a low number of deaths in the East Timor conflict in table 1A.

[78] OCHA (note 77), annex 1, para. D.

[79] There were press reports of 50 East Timorese killed in West Timor by Indonesian troops and the militia. USAID, OFDA, 'East Timor crisis, fact sheet #11, FY2000', 18 Oct. 1999.

[80] 'Armed with U.N. approval, Australia prepares for East Timor mission', CNN Online, 16 Sep. 1999, URL <http://cnn.com/ASIANOW/southeast/9909/15/e.timor.03/>; and 'US timidity', *Financial Times*, 27 Sep. 1999, p. 17.

[81] Mufson and Lynch (note 71).

INTERFET initially deployed 2000 Australian troops; the number of international troops increased to 9400 by the end of November, of whom 4500 were Australian.[82] The force secured the capital, Dili, in a few days and then sent small units to the countryside.[83] Talks between Australian and Indonesian military commanders and their civilian superiors enabled the sides to avoid violent confrontations, but the relationship between them was tense. Continued low-level militia activity, on the other hand, led to aggressive patrolling by Australian units under permissive rules of engagement. They raided strongholds and conducted border patrols, resulting in the death of several militiamen.[84] In early October INTERFET increased the number of troops on the West Timor border to 3000, at a time when its total strength was 6500, to prevent militia incursions.[85] Indonesia and other states in South-East Asia expressed strong concern over the Australian actions. Australia responded by pressing the United Nations for rapid deployment of the follow-on UN Transitional Administration in East Timor (UNTAET).[86]

Kosovo, Federal Republic of Yugoslavia

In February and March 1999 the Contact Group of France, Germany, Italy Russia, the UK and the USA[87] brought the FRY Government and the Ushtria Clirimtare e Kosoves (UCK—Kosovo Liberation Army, KLA) to Rambouillet Manor outside Paris for two rounds of talks to secure a three-year interim agreement on autonomy.[88] In late March the talks failed, foreign personnel were withdrawn from Kosovo, Belgrade launched a major offensive to drive out Kosovar Albanians and disable the KLA, and NATO decided to bomb Yugoslavia. NATO's stated objectives were to avert a humanitarian disaster, preserve regional stability and maintain the alliance's credibility.[89]

NATO aircraft first struck on 24 March. The air campaign focused on Kosovo and Belgrade but attacked sites throughout the FRY. It escalated

[82] Robinson, G., 'Peacekeeping force prepares to spread out from Dili', *Financial Times*, 22 Sep. 1999, p. 6; Robinson, G., 'Canberra disquiet on role in E Timor', *Financial Times*, 4 Oct. 1999, p. 5; and Australian Ministry of Defence, 'INTERFET Weekly Operational Update', 19 Nov. 1999, URL <http://203.46.183.231/EASTTIMOR>.

[83] For an assessment of the advantages of a multilateral military operation compared to those of a UN-led operation, see chapter 2 in this volume.

[84] Robinson, 'Canberra disquiet on role in E Timor' (note 82); Mack, A., 'Intervention in East Timor—from the ground', *RUSI Journal*, vol. 144, no. 6 (Dec. 1999), p. 22; USAID, OFDA, 'East Timor crisis, fact sheet #7, FY2000', 28 Sep. 1999; USAID, OFDA (note 79); and 'The stakes were raised', *Aviation Week & Space Technology*, 11 Oct. 1999, p. 25.

[85] Shenon, P., 'U.N. to triple its border forces in East Timor', *New York Times* (Internet edn), 11 Oct. 1999, URL <http://www.nytimes.com/library/world/asia/101199timor-un.html>.

[86] Robinson, 'Canberra disquiet on role in E Timor' (note 82). For information on UNTAET see chapter 2 in this volume.

[87] Italy joined the Contact Group for the Kosovo conflict, although it was not a member when the informal group formed in 1994 to address the conflict in Bosnia and Herzegovina.

[88] The text of the Interim Agreement for Peace and Self-Government in Kosovo is available in *International Peacekeeping*, Jan.–Apr. 1999, pp. 51–65. For information on the Rambouillet talks see chapter 2 in this volume, and for events in Kosovo in 1998 see Troebst, S., 'The Kosovo conflict', *SIPRI Yearbook 1999* (note 23), pp. 47–62.

[89] US Department of State, 'U.S. and NATO objectives and interests in Kosovo', Fact sheet, 26 Mar. 1999, available in *International Peacekeeping*, Jan.–Apr. 1999, pp. 49–50.

gradually, reaching the maximum daily intensity in late May.[90] Extensive use of precision-guided munitions enabled pilots to destroy oil depots, disable the electric power grid and severely damage transport infrastructure with little damage to the surrounding area in most cases. Damage to Yugoslav military equipment was far less serious. The FRY fielded regular army troops, internal security forces, police and paramilitary units in Kosovo, totalling about 40 000.[91] According to revised NATO estimates the FRY had about 350 tanks, 440 armoured personnel carriers, and 750 artillery pieces, mortars and anti-aircraft artillery committed to the Kosovo conflict.[92] Belgrade claimed to have lost only 13 tanks.[93] A NATO report released figures that were much higher— 93 'successful strikes' against tanks, 153 against armoured personnel carriers, 339 against military vehicles, and 389 against artillery and mortars[94]—but it has been criticized by analysts in NATO military and intelligence organizations. An unpublished US Air Force analysis reportedly claimed that the numbers of mobile targets that were verifiably destroyed were 14 tanks, 18 armoured personnel carriers and 20 artillery pieces.[95]

On 9 June the FRY signed an agreement that called for NATO to suspend its air operations; for all Serb forces to withdraw from Kosovo within 11 days, after which the air campaign would formally end; and for the entry into Kosovo of an international force.[96] On 10 June NATO suspended its air strikes. UN Security Council Resolution 1244 welcomed the agreement and mandated a NATO-led multinational force of 50 000, the Kosovo Force (KFOR).[97] The first NATO troops entered Kosovo on 12 June. By 20 June all the Yugoslav military and police forces had left Kosovo and NATO formally ended its air campaign.[98] On 24 June the FRY Parliament voted to put out of force all regulations adopted when it declared the country to be in a 'state of war' in late March.[99]

The air campaign was notable for at least six reasons.

1. It was NATO's only combat experience in its 50-year history. There was some question whether all 19 members would give their consent for action, as

[90] Sokut, S. and Kedrov, I., 'Analysis: BDA of NATO Kosovo campaign', *Nezavisimoye Voyennoye Obozreniye*, no. 25 (2–8 July 1999), p. 3, in Foreign Broadcast Information Service, *Daily Report– Central Eurasia (FBIS-SOV)*, FBIS-SOV-1999-9709, 2 July 1999.

[91] Sokut and Kedrov (note 90); and Meyers, S. L., 'Serb troops complete their pullout from Kosovo', *New York Times* (Internet edn), 21 June 1999, URL <http://www.nytimes.com/library/world/europe/062199kosovo-rdp.html>.

[92] Clark, W. K. (Gen.) and Corley, J. (Gen.), 'Press conference on the Kosovo strike assessment', NATO Headquarters, 16 Sep. 1999.

[93] Ripley, T., 'Kosovo: a bomb damage assessment', *Jane's Intelligence Review*, vol. 11, no. 9 (Sep. 1999), p. 10.

[94] Clark and Corley (note 92).

[95] Barry, J. and Thomas, E., 'The Kosovo cover-up', *Newsweek*, 15 May 2000, pp. 23–28.

[96] Rogers, M. and Deen, T., 'First NATO force of peacekeepers move on Kosovo', *Jane's Defence Weekly*, vol. 31, no. 24 (16 June 1999), p. 4.

[97] UN Security Council Resolution 1244, 10 June 1999. For information on KFOR and the UN Interim Administration Mission in Kosovo (UNMIK), a civil operation, see chapter 2 in this volume.

[98] Kozaryn, L. D., 'U.S., allied troops flow into Kosovo', American Forces Information Service, URL <http://www.defenselink.mil/news/Jul1999/n07011999_9907014.html>.

[99] Federal Republic of Yugoslavia, Federal Ministry of Foreign Affairs, 'Yugoslav Government puts all state of war regulations out of force', *Yugoslav Daily Survey*, morning edn, Belgrade, 24 June 1999.

required by the NATO Charter. Greece was especially reluctant but maintained its support. Defence of NATO's credibility, and by extension preservation of the alliance, was one of the primary reasons cited for the need to prevail.[100] The air operation tested alliance interoperability. National forces managed to work fairly well together despite some difficulties, but a French Ministry of Defence report claimed that the USA sometimes operated outside the NATO framework.[101] In addition, the technological dominance of the United States meant that US aircraft and pilots flew the majority of the strike missions and released about 80 per cent of the ordnance used.[102] As a result, government officials in the USA and some of the European NATO member states called for increased European defence spending.[103]

2. NATO did not seek UN approval as China and Russia would have vetoed a resolution in the Security Council, had one come up for a vote. Many observers deplored NATO's decision, arguing that under international law only the UN can authorize the use of force against a state other than in self-defence.[104] NATO's political leaders countered that the alliance had the authority to respond to threats to international peace and security within its area. The Security Council gave its tacit approval when it rejected by a vote of 3 to 12 a draft resolution put forth by Russia that called for the cessation of the use of force against the FRY.[105]

3. The attempt 'to prevent more human suffering and more repression and violence against the civilian population of Kosovo'[106] revived the humanitarian rationale for military intervention. Critics contended that bombing, particularly from high altitudes—a practice followed to avoid anti-aircraft fire from the ground—was not a humanitarian means of intervention. It did not stop the expulsion of Albanians by Serb troops, police and militia and might even have accelerated the process. The bombing killed civilians in Kosovo and the rest of the FRY and destroyed infrastructure necessary for economic activity.[107] It is true that NATO action did not prevent a humanitarian disaster, but it is equally

---

[100] Prescott, J., 'Kosovo: the Deputy Prime Minister, John Prescott, made a statement to the House of Commons on 24 March about the NATO air strikes against Yugoslavia', *Survey of Current Affairs*, Apr. 1999, p. 123.

[101] Clark, C., 'Campaign in Kosovo highlights allied interoperability shortfalls', *Defence News*, 16 Aug. 1999, p. 6; and Whitney, C., 'U.S. military acted outside NATO framework during Kosovo conflict, France says', *New York Times* (Internet edn), 11 Nov. 1999, URL <http://www.nytimes.com/library/world/europe/111199france-kosovo.html>.

[102] Sokut and Kedrov (note 90).

[103] Kozaryn, L. D., 'Cohen "previews" Kosovo lessons learned', American Forces Information Service, URL <http://www.defenselink.mil/news/Sep1999/n09131999_9909135.html>.

[104] Henkin, L., 'Kosovo and the law of "humanitarian intervention"' (pp. 824–28), Charney, J. I., 'Anticipatory humanitarian intervention in Kosovo' (pp. 834–41), and Chinkin, C. M., 'Kosovo: a "good" or a "bad" war?' (pp. 841–47), *American Journal of International Law*, vol. 93, no. 4 (Oct. 1999); and Zarchi, M. J. A., 'A review of some aspects of the Kosovo crisis', *Iranian Journal of International Affairs*, vol. 11, no. 2 (summer 1999), pp. 146–60.

[105] 'Security Council rejects demand for cessation of use of force against Federal Republic of Yugoslavia', UN Press Release SC/6659, 26 Mar. 1999.

[106] Solana, J., 'Press statement by Dr. Javier Solana, Secretary General of NATO', NATO Press Release (1999) 040, 23 Mar. 1999, available in *International Peacekeeping*, Jan.–Apr. 1999, p. 49.

[107] Human Rights Watch, *Civilian Deaths in the NATO Air Campaign*, Human Rights Watch Reports, vol. 12, no. 1 (D), (Feb. 2000); and Evans, D. M., 'Dark victory', *U.S. Naval Institute Proceedings*, vol. 125, no. 9 (Sep. 1999), pp. 33–37.

true that the return home of the refugees so soon after their flight was unprecedented.[108]

4. The amount of credit the air campaign deserves for forcing the withdrawal of Serb forces from Kosovo is a matter of controversy. The evidence appears to support the advocates of air power in the long-running debate about the ability of air operations alone to force political concessions from an adversary. There was no ground operation, after all.[109] Sceptics concede the dominant role of bombing but point to several other important factors. The first was the threat of a ground attack. The KLA had begun to strike at Serb forces in the western part of Kosovo, and FRY officers claimed that most of their casualties came from those battles.[110] In late May NATO members decided to prepare a ground force of 50 000 troops on Kosovo's borders.[111] More important were two diplomatic events. On 6 May the G8 agreed on principles for a peace settlement. The agreement marked the first time Russia publicly accepted the idea of a strong international security presence in Kosovo.[112] On 2 June Russia agreed to NATO's terms for ending the air strikes.[113] President Slobodan Milosevic accepted the agreement the next day.[114]

5. Despite the Russian decision to join NATO in opposing Belgrade, the conflict hurt relations between Russia and the West. NATO's action on the heels of its eastward expansion marginalized and threatened Russia, which froze political and military contacts with the alliance.[115] The Russian Government expressed its frustration on 11 June, when it sent 200 troops from Bosnia and Herzegovina to rapidly take up position at Pristina airport and prevent British troops from entering to prepare the airfield for operations. The dispute was settled within a week,[116] but a more confrontational approach to the West was reflected in the new Russian military doctrine and Acting President Vladimir Putin's revision of the National Security Concept.[117]

---

[108] UN High Commissioner for Refugees (UNHCR), 'Kosovo statistics', *Refugees*, vol. 3, no. 116 (1999), p. 11.

[109] McPeak, M. A., 'The Kosovo result: the facts speak for themselves', *Armed Forces Journal International*, Sep. 1999, pp. 62–63.

[110] Ripley (note 93), p. 13.

[111] The decision was in anticipation of a future peacekeeping operation, but the strength of the proposed force also increased pressure on Belgrade. 'Troops boost for NATO', BBC News Online, 26 May 1999, URL <http://news.bbc.co.uk/hi/english/world/europe/newsid_352000/352426.stm>.

[112] Drosdiak, W., 'Russia and the G-7 draft Kosovo plan', *International Herald Tribune*, 7 May 1999, pp. 1, 5.

[113] Cohen, R., 'Russia set to back NATO's terms', *International Herald Tribune*, 3 June 1999, pp. 1, 9.

[114] Erlanger, S., 'Milosevic accepts plan, but NATO is cautious', *International Herald Tribune*, 4 June 1999, pp. 1, 4.

[115] Sokut and Kedrov (note 90).

[116] US Office of the Assistant Secretary of Defense, 'News release: agreement on Russian participation in KFOR', no. 301-99 (18 June 1999).

[117] A draft of the new military doctrine was published in *Krasnaya Zvezda*, 9 Oct. 1999, pp. 3–4. The final version, as approved by President Putin on 21 Apr. 2000, was published in *Nezavisimaya Gazeta*, 22 Apr. 2000. An unofficial English translation was released by BBC Monitoring on 22 Apr. 2000. The National Security Concept was revised by Presidential Decree no. 24 on 10 Jan. 2000. The decree and the full text of the National Security Concept were published in *Krasnaya Zvezda*, 20 Jan. 2000. An English translation is available in *Military News Bulletin*, vol. 9, no. 2 (Feb. 2000), pp. 1–12; excerpts appear in *Arms Control Today*, Jan./Feb. 2000, pp. 15–20.

6. The costs of the conflict were substantial. NATO gave no official estimate of the number of FRY troops killed but unofficially claimed that it was over 5000.[118] The FRY military stated that NATO bombs and engagements with the KLA killed 524 soldiers and 114 policemen and wounded 2000 and that a number of paramilitary were also killed.[119] According to Human Rights Watch, NATO bombing killed 489–528 civilians in 90 separate incidents. NATO did not officially estimate the number of civilians killed, although it admitted 20–30 incidents of 'collateral damage' and a top US officer unofficially estimated 'less than 1500 dead'. FRY Government sources claimed that at least 1200 civilians were killed and possibly as many as 5700.[120] In monetary terms, the air operation cost up to $4 billion. The European Union estimates the cost of rebuilding Kosovo at $30 billion. A Belgrade research team estimates that it will cost $50–150 billion and take decades of effort to rebuild the FRY.[121] Destroyed bridges that block commerce on the Danube River continue to cost countries in Central and Eastern Europe hundreds of millions of dollars.[122]

A November 1999 report by the International Criminal Tribunal for the Former Yugoslavia on atrocities committed by Serbs in Kosovo stated that 2108 bodies had been exhumed from approximately one-third of the known mass graves.[123] This number is far lower than Western officials' claims during the war that Serb forces had killed 10 000–100 000 people and the US contention in December that 10 000 Kosovar Albanians had been killed in 1999.[124] An estimated 848 100 people fled Kosovo to neighbouring countries, the republic of Montenegro and other parts of Serbia.[125] Serb forces and militia drove nearly all of them out by burning their homes, raping women and killing people. Belgrade contends that people fled because of the NATO bombing.[126] By September 770 000 people had returned to Kosovo.[127] Since the return of Albanian refugees and the KLA under NATO protection, about 200 000 Serbs, Montenegrins and Roma have fled, leaving 51 per cent of the 1998 Serb population and 43 per cent of the population of other minorities.[128] The number of

[118] Clark and Corley (note 92); and Ripley (note 93), p. 12.

[119] 'New figures for Yugoslav losses', *Jane's Defence Weekly*, vol. 33, no. 2 (12 Jan. 2000), p. 6; and Ripley (note 93), p. 12.

[120] Human Rights Watch (note 1067.

[121] Zakarai, F., 'What price victory', *Newsweek*, 14 June 1999, p. 26.

[122] Finn, P., 'Anger growing in East Europe over NATO-blocked Danube', *International Herald Tribune*, 7 Feb. 2000, p. 5.

[123] 'Prosecutor for former Yugoslavia, Rwanda tribunals briefs Security Council, emphasises need for cooperation from states', UN Press Release SC/6749, 10 Nov. 1999; Erlanger, S. and Wren, C. S., 'Early count hints at fewer Kosovo deaths', *New York Times* (Internet edn), 11 Nov. 1999, URL <http://www.nytimes.com/library/world/europe/111199kosovo-un.html>; and Partos, G., 'Q & A: counting Kosovo's dead', BBC News Online, 12 Nov. 1999, URL <http://news.bbc.co.uk/hi/english/world/europe/newsid_517000/517168.stm>.

[124] 'Grisly math: the atrocity count falls', *Newsweek*, 22 Nov. 1999, p. 28; and Shenon, P., 'U.S. puts Kosovar Albanian deaths at 10,000', *International Herald Tribune*, 11–12 Dec. 1999, p. 4.

[125] UNHCR (note 108).

[126] 'High Commissioner Mary Robinson briefs Commission on Human Rights on situation of Kosovar refugees', UN Press Release HR/CN/905, 9 Apr. 1999.

[127] UNHCR, 'Country profiles—Federal Republic of Yugoslavia', URL <http://www.unhcr.ch/world/euro/fryugo.htm>.

[128] UNHCR (note 127); and USAID, OFDA, 'Kosovo crisis, fact sheet #114', 10 Sep. 1999.

deaths in Kosovo in October was similar to the number before the NATO action, when an average of about 30 people per week were killed.[129] NATO reported that from the start of the KFOR activities until November about 400 people, one-half of this number Serbs, had been killed.[130]

Conflicts without foreign military intervention

Algeria

Events in Algeria in 1999 offered hope of a transformation to peace after seven years of violence in which about 100 000 people were killed. About 1000 people were killed in 1999, in contrast to several thousand per year in previous years. The military junta has conducted a counter-insurgency campaign against the Armée Islamique du Salut (AIS, Islamic Salvation Army)—the armed wing of the Front Islamique du Salut (FIS, Islamic Salvation Front)—the Groupe Islamique Armé (GIA, Armed Islamic Group) and other insurgents since it denied the FIS an election victory by forcibly taking power in 1992.[131] In September 1998 President Liamine Zeroual called an election for February 1999, one year early. (The election was later rescheduled for April in order to allow more time for preparation.) Convinced they would serve only as 'window dressing' in a rigged election, all the candidates but one withdrew in protest.[132] The remaining candidate, Abdelaziz Bouteflika, a retired general and the army's choice, won the election. Contrary to expectations, he fulfilled his campaign promises to crack down on corruption and promote a national reconciliation process that included many of the government's Islamic opponents. The Algerian Parliament approved an amnesty for all the rebels who put down their arms by 13 January 2000. Many fighters from the AIS surrendered, but GIA members stood fast. The government reported in early January 2000 that nearly 80 per cent of the country's militants had surrendered their arms under the amnesty offer, including the entire AIS, which disbanded. The government responded with force against the GIA and others who rejected the amnesty offer.[133]

---

[129] ICG, *Violence in Kosovo: Who's Killing Whom?*, ICG Balkans Report no. 78 (International Crisis Group: Pristina, London, Washington, DC, 2 Nov. 1999), pp. 1–2.

[130] 'Belgrade "sceptical" on Kosovo death toll', BBC News Online, 11 Nov. 1999, URL <http://news.bbc.co.uk/hi/english/world/europe/newsid_515000/515350.stm>.

[131] Labarre, F., 'Algeria at a crossroad', *Peacekeeping and International Relations*, vol. 28, no. 2 (Mar./Apr. 1999), p. 5; Pfaff, W., 'Here is a referendum to patch Algeria back together', *International Herald Tribune* (Internet edn), 16 Sep. 1999, URL <http://www.iht.com/IHT/WP/99/wp091699.html>; 'Civil war to reconciliation? Ten years of conflict', *Le Monde Diplomatique*, Sep. 1999, URL <http://www.monde-diplomatique.fr/en/1999/09/?c=05algeria>; and 'Algeria bomb kills 17', BBC News Online, 22 Aug. 1999, URL <http://news2.thls.bbc.co.uk/hi/english/world/middle%5Feast/newsid%5F427000/427070.stm>.

[132] Labarre (note 131); and 'The power and the vote', *The Economist*, 9 Jan. 1999, pp. 38–39.

[133] Burns, J. F., 'Campaign to end Algerian civil war sets off fierce fighting', *International Herald Tribune*, 26 Jan. 2000, p. 2.

Angola

The civil war in Angola recommenced in December 1998 after four years of relative peace after the November 1994 signing of the Lusaka Protocol between the government of President Eduardo dos Santos and Jonas Savimbi's UNITA.[134] Rather than disarm and turn over the areas under its control in exchange for a role in a coalition government, as stipulated in the peace agreement, UNITA rearmed itself and launched a broad offensive in the central and northern provinces, apparently in order to create a new power base in the central part of the country.[135] The action was condemned by the UN and the OAU.[136] The rebels were thought to have 30 000–60 000 troops under arms in the first half of 1999.[137] Although total government forces numbered about 80 000, they were surprised by the force of the UNITA attack and gave ground quickly.[138] UNITA had apparently reorganized its forces so as to more effectively use its tanks, armoured fighting vehicles, missiles and long-range artillery.[139] By mid-1999 rebels controlled nearly three-quarters of the country but were unable to take the strategic central highland towns of Huambo and Cuito.[140] In five months of fighting about 6000 soldiers and 4000 civilians were killed.[141]

After two abortive attempts to counter rebel advances, the government launched a mid-September offensive that caused UNITA's military capacity to crumble.[142] The army bombed rebel strongholds heavily before advancing on the ground to capture UNITA's headquarters at Andulo and a string of towns in the northern, central and eastern provinces.[143] The rebels retreated to border areas in the east and north without putting up serious resistance.[144] At the end of 1999 the government occupied nearly all Angolan territory.[145] It claimed to have destroyed 80 per cent of UNITA's conventional military capability.[146]

[134] 'Lusaka Protocol', 15 Nov. 1994, available at URL <http://www.incore.ulst.ac.uk/cds/agreements/lusaka.html>.

[135] Human Rights Watch, *Angola Unravels: The Rise and Fall of the Lusaka Peace Process* (Human Rights Watch: New York, Sep. 1999), available at URL <http://www.hrw.org/reports/1999/angola/>; 'Angola: snapping the backbone', *The Economist*, 30 Oct. 1999, p. 54; and Gordon, C., 'UNITA launches new offensive', *Jane's Intelligence Review*, vol. 11, no. 2 (Feb. 1999), p. 7.

[136] Action for Southern Africa, 'OAU condemns Savimbi', *Angola Peace Monitor*, vol. 5, no. 7 (Mar. 1999), URL <http://www.anc.organization.za/angola/apm0507.html>.

[137] The high estimate was made by a top Angolan military officer. Shearer (note 39), p. 97; and Action for Southern Africa, 'Dry-season escalation in fighting expected', *Angola Peace Monitor*, vol. 5, no. 9 (May 1999), URL <http://www.anc.org.za/angola/apm0509.html>.

[138] Gordon (note 135).

[139] Gordon (note 135). UNITA did not acquire new heavy weapons in 1999. See also chapter 7 in this volume.

[140] Action for Southern Africa, 'Military situation', *Angola Peace Monitor*, vol. 5, no. 7 (Mar. 1999), URL <http://www.anc.organization.za/angola/apm0507.html>; and Jeter, J., 'Rebel setbacks give Angolans some hope of an end to war', *International Herald Tribune*, 7 Dec. 1999, p. 1.

[141] 'Angolan statistics', *Jane's Intelligence Review*, vol. 11, no. 5 (May 1999), p. 5.

[142] 'Angola: battling, in the rain', *The Economist*, 9 Oct. 1999, p. 60.

[143] 'Angola: battling, in the rain' (note 142); and 'Angola: snapping the backbone' (note 135).

[144] 'Angola: snapping the backbone' (note 135).

[145] Integrated Regional Information Network–Southern Africa (IRIN-SA), 'Angola: army surrounds enclave', IRIN-SA weekly round-up 45, 6–12 Nov. 1999.

[146] Pawson, L., '"End of war in sight"—Angolan general', BBC News Online, 16 Nov. 1999, URL <http://news.bbc.co.uk/hi/english/world/africa/newsid_522000/522695.stm>.

Defections by key UNITA military officers and long-overdue, energetic enforcement of UN sanctions against UNITA's diamond trade gave the Angolan Government further reason to stand by dos Santos' early 1999 vow never again to engage in talks with Savimbi.[147] However, conventional wisdom held that the government could not militarily eliminate the rebel's guerrilla capability and a political solution would have to be found.[148] It was unlikely that the 25-year conflict that had killed thousands, displaced 1–2 million and caused one of the worst humanitarian crises in the world would be resolved.[149]

Burundi

Fighting continued in Burundi between the government of General Pierre Buyoya and the Tutsi militia, on the one side, and three Hutu armed groups, on the other side, which are not party to the ongoing peace talks—Conseil National pour la Défense de la Démocratie–Forces pour la Défense de la Démocratie (CNDD–FDD, National Council for the Defence of Democracy–Forces for Defence of Democracy), the Parti pour la Libération du Peuple Hutu (Palipehutu, Party for the Liberation of the Hutu People) and the Front pour la Libération Nationale (FROLINA, National Liberation Front).[150] Inter-ethnic violence since 1993 is believed to have cost the lives of more than 200 000 people and created about 300 000 refugees and over 600 000 inter-nally displaced people out of a population of about 8 million.[151] Most of the killing has not directly involved the army or the three rebel groups fighting for control of the government. Instead, most people have been killed by loose groupings of civilians. Among the 20 or so political and military groups in Burundi, the militarily active groups recruited soldiers heavily from Rwandan Hutu refugees and the extremists who committed genocide in 1994.[152] During the early months of 1999 rebels increased the number of their ambushes and civilian massacres in the south and around the capital, Bujumbura.[153] Govern-ment forces responded with harsh counter-insurgency operations.[154] On 1 July the rebels escalated their activities with an attack on the capital, killing a large

[147] Action for Southern Africa, 'UNITA defections', *Angola Peace Monitor*, vol. 6, no. 3 (Nov. 1999); 'Angola: diamonds—arms for UNITA', *Africa Research Bulletin*, 16 Apr.–15 May 1999, p. 13869; and 'Angola: De Beers stops all Angolan diamond purchases', IRIN-SA daily report, 6 Oct. 1999.

[148] 'Angola: conflict moves east', IRIN-Southern Africa daily update, 18 Oct. 1999.

[149] 'Angolan statistics' (note 141); and USAID, OFDA, 'Angola situation report #1, fiscal year 2000', 8 Oct. 1999.

[150] While they share the objective of overthrowing the current government, Palipehutu and FROLINA are quick to distance themselves from the CNDD–FDD. IRIN-CEA, 'Burundi: IRIN focus on rebel movements', 13 Oct. 1999.

[151] UNHCR, 'Africa fact sheet', Nov. 1999; IRIN-CEA, 'Great Lakes: humanitarian situation worsens significantly', 30 Aug. 1999; McGreal C., '800,000 Hutus held in Burundi camps', *Guardian Weekly*, 16–22 Dec. 1999, p. 3; and 'Hutu rebels kill 40 in Burundi', *Jane's Defence Weekly*, vol. 31, no. 15 (14 Apr. 1999), p. 19.

[152] Cornwell, R. and de Beer, H., 'Burundi: the politics of intolerance', *African Security Review*, vol. 8, no. 6 (1999), p. 89 and table 1, p. 92.

[153] Mthembu-Salter, G., *An Assessment of Sanctions Against Burundi* (Action Aid: London, May 1999), p. 6.

[154] Prendergast, J. and Smock, D., *Postgenocidal Reconstruction: Building Peace in Rwanda and Burundi*, Special report (United States Institute of Peace: Washington, DC, Sep. 1999), p. 4.

number of Tutsi civilians in the outlying areas. Tutsi militia took revenge on the Hutu population.[155] The government responded by forcing about 350 000 Hutu civilians into squalid 'regroupment' camps, resulting in a 28 per cent increase in the number of displaced persons from August to December.[156] Earlier regroupment in the north and east of the country was relatively successful in separating the rebels from the population, but thousands of civilians in the camps died of disease and hunger. Regroupment camps held about 800 000 Hutus at the end of 1999.[157]

Guinea-Bissau

In Guinea-Bissau, General Ansumane Mane led a mutiny in June 1998 with about 6000 soldiers against the forces loyal to President João Bernardo Vieira. Fighting went on until July but did not dislodge the president.[158] Senegalese and Guinean troops sent to secure Senegal's border and support the president began to withdraw in January 1999, but not quickly enough to satisfy the junta.[159] Despite the Abuja Agreement, signed on 1 November 1998, fighting broke out in February 1999, causing up to 100 deaths and delaying slightly the planned deployment of ECOMOG troops.[160] All the parties had consented to the deployment of an ECOMOG military mission to coincide with the withdrawal of Senegalese and Guinean troops.[161] The violence quickly subsided and a Government of National Unity was sworn in on 20 February with President Vieira at its head. The 600 unarmed ECOMOG soldiers in Guinea-Bissau were not mandated to protect the government, and the president was overthrown on 7 May in a coup led by General Mane. Of the population of about 1 million, hundreds were killed and thousands fled their homes in 1999.[162] However, the prospects for peace were promising: successful presidential and legislative elections were held in November 1999, and the presidential run-off in January 2000 elected Kumba Yalla over the military's chosen candidate.[163]

---

[155] McGreal (note 151).
[156] 'Great Lakes: displacement surge in affected populations', IRIN-CEA weekly round-up 52, 25–30 Dec. 1999; and Fisher, I., 'Crackdown on Burundi rebels forces 350,000 Hutu into camps', *International Herald Tribune*, 28 Dec. 1999, p. 1.
[157] McGreal (note 151).
[158] Agence France Presse (AFP) (World Service), 'Senegal—further on troop deployment to Guinea-Bissau', 6 Feb. 1999, in FBIS-AFR [no number], 6 Feb. 1999.
[159] PANA, 'Senegal withdraws troops from Bissau', 14 Jan. 1999; and AFP, 'French ship to transport ECOMOG troops to Guinea-Bissau', 26 Jan. 1999, in FBIS-AFR-99-027, 27 Jan. 1999.
[160] AFP (World Service), 2 Feb. 1999, in 'Guinea-Bissau: Guinea-Bissau—rebels fall back, reject cease-fire', FBIS-AFR-99-033, 2 Feb. 1999. The agreement, signed in Abuja, Nigeria, established plans for a government of national unity and elections to be held in Mar. 1999.
[161] 'Agreement between the government of Guinea-Bissau and the self-proclaimed military junta', African Society of International and Comparative Law, document 38 I.L.M. 28 (1999), 1 Nov. 1998.
[162] UN, Report of the Secretary-General pursuant to Security Council Resolution 1216 (1998) relative to the situation in Guinea-Bissau, UN document S/1999/294, 17 Mar. 1999; PANA, 'OAU condemns coup in Guinea Bissau', 10 May 1999; and 'Guinea-Bissau: one war ends', *The Economist*, 15 May 1999, p. 49.
[163] UN, Report of the Secretary-General on developments in Guinea-Bissau and on the activities of the United Nations peace-building support office in that country, UN document S/1999/1276, 23 Dec. 1999; and 'Guinea Bissau's new president', BBC News Online, 22 Jan. 2000, URL <http://news2.thls.bbc.co.uk/hi/english/world/africa/newsid_614000/614541.stm>.

Rwanda

There was very little political violence in Rwanda in 1999 because of the effectiveness of a 1995–98 counter-insurgency campaign in the north-western part of the country and the elimination of militants' rear bases in the DRC in the course of the war there. The only sizeable incident was an attack on a camp for displaced persons by a group from the DRC calling itself the Armée de Libération du Rwanda in which 20 people were killed.[164] In effect, the conflict between the Rwandan Government and Hutu rebels has been trans-ferred to the DRC's territory, where the two sides support different parties in that country's civil war. Violence in the DRC and peace in Rwanda also induced 30 000 refugees who had fled after the 1994 genocide to return to Rwanda in 1999.[165]

Somalia

Southern Somalia continued to suffer endemic violence between rival war-lords in the absence of a political settlement or a dominant military force. Vio-lence and drought caused a full-blown humanitarian crisis for about 4.3 million people. The lack of physical security made it impossible for humanitarian agencies to reach about one-third of them.[166] The Eritrean–Ethiopian war spilled over into Somalia and intensified inter-clan rivalries as both countries gave military support to rival Somali factions because of those factions' support for Eritrean and Ethiopian insurgencies. Ethiopian troops also participated directly in military operations that cost the lives of dozens of civilians.[167] In November 1999 the Intergovernmental Authority on Develop-ment (IGAD) endorsed a new peace plan that sought to strengthen the position of leaders seeking peaceful solutions rather than focus on the warlords, as was done in the past.[168] The situation in Somaliland in the north-east and Puntland in the north-west, both of which operate as independent territories but are not internationally unrecognized states, was relatively stable and peaceful.[169]

[164] 'Rwanda: Interahamwe militia strikes in Gisenyi', IRIN-CEA weekly round-up 52, 25–30 Dec. 1999.

[165] 'Rwanda: returnee flow from eastern DRC continues', IRIN-CEA weekly round-up 52, 25–30 Dec. 1999.

[166] OCHA, 'A snapshot of the consolidated appeal for Somalia in 2000', 22 Nov. 1999, available on ReliefWeb, URL <http://wwww.reliefweb.int/w/rwb.nsf/s/83023C65CE136A4DC12568310053D8B3>; and 'Somalia: MSF suspends activities in Kismayo', IRIN-CEA weekly round-up 47, 20–26 Nov. 1999.

[167] Russell, R., 'Somalia under pressure', *Horn of Africa Bulletin*, vol. 11, no. 3 (May/June 1999), p. 8; and 'Ethiopia: famine of biblical proportions', *Africa Research Bulletin*, vol. 36, no. 7 (16 July–15 Aug. 1999), p. 13986. Hussein Aideed supported the Oromo Liberation Front (OLF) against the Ethiopian authorities but disarmed them at the end of the year after talks with the Ethiopian Government. 'Somalia–Ethiopia: Aideed shuts down Oromo Liberation Front in Mogadishu', IRIN-CEA weekly round-up 48, 29 Nov.–3 Dec. 1999.

[168] 'Somalia: IGAD summit endorses Guelleh plan', IRIN-CEA weekly round-up 48, 29 Nov.– 3 Dec. 1999.

[169] Bertholet, J., 'A return to Somalia', *Newsweek*, 1 Nov. 1999, pp. 36–43.

Sudan

After 11 years of peace following a civil war in 1956–72, a separate civil war between the Sudanese Government and the Sudanese People's Liberation Movement/Army (SPLM/A)[170] began in 1983 when the south protested against the imposition of Islamic law and demanded greater autonomy. Both sides, but particularly the government, use scorched-earth tactics. SPLM/A factions began to fight each other in 1991.[171] The human cost has been the highest in the world in the past 15 years. At least 1.9 million people have died from violence, famine and disease since 1983, and 4.5 million have been displaced.[172] Much of the southern population is kept alive by Operation Lifeline Sudan, run by UN aid agencies operating out of Kenya. During 1999 the government and rebels declared and then violated several ceasefires intended to facilitate the delivery of humanitarian aid.[173] In August President Omar Hassan al-Bashir accepted a peace initiative sponsored by Egypt and Libya but SPLM/A leader John Garang rejected it in favour of one put forward by the IGAD, which al-Bashir then also endorsed.[174] In November the USA made the controversial decision to provide non-military aid directly to southern Sudan rather than through the government in Khartoum, which the US Government accuses of sponsoring terrorism. The Sudanese Government and others predicted that the action would undermine the SPLM/A's incentive to participate in the IGAD peace initiative.[175] In December Sudan and Uganda agreed to re-establish diplomatic ties and promised to stop harbouring each other's rebels. SPLM/A leader Garang said that this would not affect his insurgency because he had no bases in Uganda.[176] At the end of 1999 President al-Bashir declared a state of emergency and dissolved parliament, causing northern opposition leaders to warn of a return to violence.[177]

Colombia

In 1999 the Colombian Government's decades-long conflict with an estimated 20 000 leftist guerrillas appeared intractable, even with the infusion of

[170] The SPLA is a member of the National Democratic Alliance (NDA), a umbrella organization of disparate northern and southern opposition groups.

[171] van de Veen, H., 'Who has the will for peace?', eds M. Mekenkamp, P. van Tongeren and H. van de Veen, *Searching for Peace in Africa* (European Platform for Conflict Prevention and Transformation: Utrecht, 1999), p. 168.

[172] Burr, M., *Quantifying Genocide in Southern Sudan and the Nuba Mountains, 1983–1998* (US Committee for Refugees: Washington, DC, Dec. 1998), p. 3, available at URL <http://www.regufees.organization/news/crisis/sudan.pdf>.

[173] USAID, OFDA, 'Sudan fact sheet #1, FY 2000', 2 Dec. 1999, ReliefWeb, URL <http://wwww.reliefweb.int/w/rwb.nsf/s/6983CC767F3EC9E7C125683C003FE42e>.

[174] USAID, OFDA (note 173); and 'Through the looking glass', *The Economist*, 30 Oct. 1999, p. 53.

[175] Al-Sharq Al-Awsat, 'Sudanese FM on US aid to rebels, others', 10 Dec. 1999, in FBIS-AFR-1999-1212, 13 Dec. 1999.

[176] AFP (World Service), 'Uganda: Sudan rebel Garang says accord not to affect war', 11 Dec. 1999, in FBIS-AFR-1999-1212, 13 Dec. 1999.

[177] Osman, M., 'President declares state of emergency in Sudan', *Guardian Weekly*, 16–22 Dec. 1999, p. 4; and AFP (World Service), 'Sudanese opposition leader Mahdi warns of new civil war', 14 Dec. 1999, in FBIS-AFR-1999-1214, 14 Dec. 1999. The 1956–72 war was fought between rivals in the north of Sudan.

$300 million in military aid to the government by the USA during the year.[178] The rebels finance their struggle largely through drug trafficking. The USA's support for the Colombian Government stems from its determination to see the government prevail in its 'drug war'.[179] The Marxist Fuerzas Armadas Revolucionarias Colombianas (FARC, Revolutionary Armed Forces of Colombia) number about 15 000 and have fought for 40 years to take over the government, at a cost of about 35 000 lives and 1 million displaced people.[180] Right-wing death squads of about 5000 in a group called the Autodefensas Unidas de Colombia (AUD, United Self-Defence Forces of Colombia)—financed by drug traffickers, ranchers and mining companies—have waged a counter-insurgency campaign that copies the guerrillas' tactics. The AUC reportedly has ties to parts of the Colombian military but is outside the control of President Andrés Pastrana.[181] He staked his leadership on the peace talks with FARC that began in January 1999. Even as FARC participated in talks with the government, it carried out offensive operations, apparently to strengthen its negotiating hand.[182] At the end of 1999 the government also explored talks with the second largest guerrilla group, the Ejército de Liberación Nacional (ELN, National Liberation Army), as fighting continued.[183] As the government lost territory to the guerrillas and to coca cultivation, the USA promised even more military aid.[184]

Peru

The Peruvian Government's 19-year battle with the Maoist Sendero Luminoso (Shining Path) guerrillas has cost the lives of over 30 000 people. After it captured rebel leader Abimael Guzman in 1992, the death toll dropped to a few hundred a year. In July 1999 the government dealt another hard blow when it captured the new Shining Path leader, Oscar Ramirez Durand. The

---

[178] 'Colombia: a new war', *The Economist*, 15 Jan. 2000, p. 58.

[179] It is difficult to separate in practical terms the 'war on drugs' from the war against the guerrillas because coca is grown in rebel-controlled areas and some FARC revenue comes from interaction with people involved in drug production. US involvement borders on military intervention. In July a US communications intelligence-gathering aircraft crashed in Colombia with 2 Colombians and 5 US soldiers on board. 'Colombia loses its secret weapon against the FARC', *Defence Systems Daily*, 29 July 1999, URL <http://defence-data.com/current/page4922.htm>.

[180] 'Colombia talks peace in the long shadow of war', *The Economist*, 9 Jan. 1999, pp. 47–48.

[181] 'Colombia: the butchers strike back', *The Economist*, 16 Jan. 1999, p. 50.

[182] 'Violence escalates as Bogota peace talks near', *International Herald Tribune*, 10–11 July 1999, p. 5; Thompson, A., 'Many die in fresh Colombia fighting', *Financial Times*, 13 July 1999, p. 5; AFP, 'Colombian government, FARC conclude fourth meeting', 2 Dec. 1999, in Foreign Broadcast Information Service, *Daily Report–Latin America (FBIS-LAT)*, FBIS-LAT-1999-1203, 3 Dec. 1999; AFP, 'Navy commander admits FARC delivered tough blow', 14 Dec. 1999, in FBIS-LAT-1999-1214, 14 Dec. 1999.

[183] AFP, 'Ricardo reports meeting ELN to discuss peace process', 23 Dec. 1999, in FBIS-LAT-1999-1223, 23 Dec. 1999; and AFP, 'Troops reportedly kill at least 30 ELN rebels', 28 Dec. 1999, in FBIS-LAT-1999-1228, 28 Dec. 1999.

[184] Golden, T. and Myers, S. L., 'U.S. plans big aid package to rally a reeling Colombia', *New York Times* (Internet edn), 15 Sep. 1999, URL <http://www.nytimes.com/library/world/americas/091599 Colombia-us-drugs.html>.

number of rebel fighters is estimated to be fewer than 1000, down from 10 000 in the early 1990s.[185]

Afghanistan

Afghanistan has been wracked by violence since the coup of 1978. Seemingly unending offensives and counter-offensives continued in 1999. Most of the current parties came into conflict with each other when the Soviet-backed regime fell in 1992. The Taleban appeared in 1994 and now control the capital city of Kabul and 80–90 per cent of the country. They call themselves the Islamic Emirate of Afghanistan but are not recognized by the United Nations.[186] The United Islamic Front for the Salvation of Afghanistan (UIFSA, also called the Northern Alliance) opposes them.[187] The Taleban field 45 000–50 000 men, of whom about 8000 are volunteers from Pakistan and other Arab countries. They have the support of Pakistan, Saudi Arabia and the United Arab Emirates.[188] The UIFSA maintains 7000–15 000 men under arms and receives support from Iran, Tajikistan and Uzbekistan.[189]

There was some hope of progress towards peace when the Taleban and the UIFSA concluded talks in Ashkhabad, Turkmenistan, on 15 March. They agreed to a ceasefire and political power sharing. However, both sides lapsed into public recriminations and engaged in a series of inconclusive battles during April and May.[190] Foreign diplomats led peace talks again in July, but the Taleban rejected a ceasefire and on 28 July launched a scorched-earth offensive, using 10 000–15 000 troops, that yielded substantial territorial gains.[191] The UIFSA quickly regained most of the land in a surprise counter-offensive. In the two weeks of fighting about 1200 Taleban, 600 UIFSA soldiers and reportedly up to 1000 civilians were killed. More than 100 000 people fled their homes.[192] Sporadic fighting continued throughout the year. Continued but

---

[185] 'Lima troops arrest last Shining Path rebel leader', *International Herald Tribune*, 15 July 1999, p. 3; and 'Peru captures guerrilla leader', *New York Times* (Internet edn), 14 July 1999, URL <http://www.nytimes.com/yr/mo/day/world/index-americas.html>.

[186] 'Taliban pushed back', *Jane's Intelligence Review*, vol. 11, no. 3 (Mar. 1999), p. 5; Pour, A. B., 'UN sees little hope for Afghan peace', *Guardian Weekly*, 28 Feb. 1999, p. 13; and UN Security Council Resolution 1267, 15 Oct. 1999.

[187] This military alliance was formed in 1996 under the name Supreme Council for the Defence of Afghanistan (SCDA), renamed the UIFSA in 1997. It consists of the regime deposed by the Taleban (still recognized in the UN General Assembly) and the Jamiat-i-Islami, Hezb-i-Islami, Hezb-i-Wahdat, Ittehad-i-Islami, Jumbesh-i-Milli and Harakat-i-Enqilab-i-Islami.

[188] Davis, A., 'Pakistan's war by proxy in Afghanistan loses its deniability', *Jane's Intelligence Review*, vol. 11, no. 10 (Oct. 1999), pp. 32–34; 'Back to war in Afghanistan', *The Economist*, 31 July 1999, p. 53; and Bearak, B., 'Afghan "Lion" fights Taliban with rifle and fax machine', *New York Times* (Internet edn), 9 Nov. 1999, URL <http://www.nytimes.com/library/world/asia/110999afghan-taliban.html>.

[189] Davis, A., 'Summer season in Afghanistan may see Taliban complete their conquest', *Jane's Intelligence Review*, vol. 11, no. 8 (Aug. 1999), p. 2; Bearak (note 32); 'Back to war in Afghanistan' (note 188); and 'Living with the Taliban', *The Economist*, 24 July 1999, p. 60.

[190] UN, The situation in Afghanistan and its implications for International Peace and Security, Report of the UN Secretary-General, UN document A/53/1002 S/1999/698, 21 June 1999.

[191] Rashid, A., 'Final offensive?', *Far Eastern Economic Review*, 5 Aug. 1999, p. 12; and Davis, A., 'Taliban summer push is bloodiest in years', *Jane's Defence Weekly*, vol. 32, no. 6 (11 Aug. 1999), p. 3.

[192] 'Security Council, in Presidential statement, condemns Afghanistan's Taliban for July military offensive, sheltering terrorists', UN Press Release SC/6743, 22 Oct. 1999; Bearak, B., 'Onslaught by

fruitless peace efforts by the UN and the 'six plus two' group were made from August until the end of October.[193]

Assam, India

In India, separatists of the United Liberation Front of Assam (ULFA) and the National Democratic Front of Bodoland (NDFB) continued fighting government troops and police in the north-eastern state of Assam. The militants continued to have links with Pakistan's Inter-Service Intelligence, but Bhutan pressed the rebels to leave the border camps on its territory.[194] There were no signs of an end to the conflict, which would require the Indian Government to strike an agreement with the ULFA, the NDFB and several other insurgent groups in Assam which oppose the government and sometimes also fight among themselves.[195]

Kashmir, India

Groups in the Indian state of Jammu and Kashmir have fought a 10-year insurgency that has killed 24 000–40 000 people and displaced over 300 000.[196] Some want an independent state, while others want to join Pakistan. The latter's actions are closely linked to India's border war with Pakistan, as demonstrated by the fighting near Kargil in 1999. Although the insurgency began as an indigenous movement, Pakistan now helps to fund and train at least three militant groups active in the Kashmir valley: Lashkar-e-Toiba, with about 300 fighters; Hisbul Mujahideen, with 500–800 fighters; and Harkat-ul-Ansar, with about 350 fighters. India claims that there are about 3500 insurgents on its territory. The government relies on 125 000 paramilitary and state police units, reserving its 200 000 soldiers in the area to guard against a Pakistani attack. There is no sign of a political resolution to the conflict aside from a ceasefire proclaimed by the Jammu and Kashmir Liberation Front (JKLF) since 1994.[197]

Taliban leaves many Afghans dead or homeless', *New York Times* (Internet edn), URL <http://www.nytimes.com/library/world/asia/101899afghan-massacre.html>; and Davis (note 189).

[193] The 'six plus two' group consists of China, Iran, Pakistan, Tajikistan, Turkmenistan and Uzbekistan, plus Russia and the United States. *Islamabad News* (Internet edn), 17 Sep. 1999, in Foreign Broadcast Information Service, *Daily Report–Near East and South Asia* (FBIS-NES), FBIS-NES-1999-0917; and 'High-level meeting of "six plus two" group on Afghanistan', UN Press Release SG/SM/7144 AFG/108, 23 Sep. 1999.

[194] 'Indian soldiers are shelled in Kashmir', *International Herald Tribune*, 9 Aug. 1999, p. 4; and 'Bhutan govt holds talks with ULFA', *Assam Tribune* (Internet edn), 23 July 1999, URL <http://assamtribune.com/jul2399/at03.html>.

[195] '102 ultras lay down arms', *Assam Tribune* (Internet edn), 26 May 1999, URL <http://assamtribune.com/may2699/at02.html>.

[196] The low estimate is the Indian Government's official count. Bearak, B., 'For India and Pakistan, an endless cycle of violence', *International Herald Tribune*, 13 Aug. 1999, p. 2. The Indian Army has killed about 8300 militants since 1990. Bedi, R., 'Clashes in Kashmir stretch Indian CI operations', *Jane's Intelligence Review*, vol. 11, no. 8 (Aug. 1999), pp. 31–32. For a detailed review of the fighting in Kashmir in 1998, see Widmalm (note 23).

[197] 'Kashmir's main militant groups', *Jane's Intelligence Review*, vol. 11, no. 8 (Aug. 1999), p. 32; and Bearak (note 32).

Aceh, Indonesia

The 'special territory' of Aceh, in the north of the Indonesian island of Sumatra, gained considerable autonomy in 1959.[198] The Gerakan Aceh Merdeka (GAM, Free Aceh Movement) has sought an independent Islamic state since 1976.[199] The Indonesian Government imposed martial law in 1989–98 while the army attempted to crush the movement.[200] On 4 November 1999 President Abdurrahman Wahid offered the Acehnese the possibility of a June 2000 referendum on the degree of central government control over the territory. He promised to remove the armed forces responsible for past abuses and to give the province 75 per cent of the revenues generated by its rich natural resources.[201] He later made several modified statements that led to some confusion about his intentions. The announcements led to large demonstrations for total independence, but the Indonesian military was adamant that the republic remain a part of Indonesia and President Wahid ruled out independence as an option.[202] At the end of November 1999, 900 national riot police arrived in Aceh to oppose the popular uprising.[203] The renewed violence killed several hundred people and displaced about 150 000 out of a population of about 3.75 million.[204]

Myanmar

The Karen National Union (KNU), located along the eastern border of Myanmar (formerly Burma), has been fighting for its own state for 40 years. It is the only major armed ethnic group in the country that has not signed a ceasefire agreement with the ruling military junta.[205] Government troops launched a dry-season offensive in February 1999 that the KNU claimed caused the death of thousands of civilians and displaced 300 000. The Thai military increased

---

[198] In addition to Aceh and East Timor, the Indonesian province of Moluccas (Malaku) was the site of violence that killed 700–2000 people in 1999. Muslims and Christians fought over sectarian differences and because they feared each other. Since the conflict does not concern territory or governance, it would not appear in the table of major armed conflicts even if the number of people killed exceeded 1000. 'More troops sent to Malaku as religious clashes persist', *International Herald Tribune*, 24–26 Dec. 1999, p. 4; and 'Megawati launches Moluccas mission', BBC News Online, 24 Jan. 1999, URL <http://news2.thls.bbc.co.uk/hi/english/world/asia%2Dpacific/newsid%5F616000/616133.stm>.

[199] Mydans, S., 'Indonesia's many faces reflect one nation, divisible', *New York Times*, 5 Sep. 1999, section E, p. 5; and AFP, 'Exiled Aceh leader agrees to talks with Wahid', 6 Nov. 1999, in Foreign Broadcast Information Service, *Daily Report–East Asia (FBIS-EAS)*, FBIS-EAS-1999-1106, 6 Nov. 1999.

[200] Head, J., 'Indonesian Army to withdraw from Aceh', BBC News Online, 3 Nov. 1999, URL <http://news2.thls.bbc.co.uk/hi/english/world/asia%2Dpacific/newsid%5F503000/503826.stm>.

[201] AFP, 'Exiled Aceh leader agrees to talks with Wahid', 6 Nov. 1999, in FBIS-EAS-1999-1106, 6 Nov. 1999; and AFP, 'Aceh referendum offer causes heated debate on federalism', 17 Nov. 1999, in FBIS-EAS-1999-1116, 17 Nov. 1999.

[202] Firdaus, I., '1m people in Aceh rally for freedom', *Guardian Weekly*, 11–17 Nov. 1999, p. 2.

[203] Ford, M., 'At the breaking point', *Newsweek*, 6 Dec. 1999, p. 64.

[204] Head (note 200). Estimates of the number killed range from over 300 (by early Dec. 1999) to over 500 (by late Nov. 1999). Ford (note 203), p. 67; and AFP, 'Exiled Aceh leader agrees to talks with Wahid', 6 Nov. 1999, in FBIS-EAS-1999-1106, 6 Nov. 1999.

[205] 'Possible preparations for attack on refugee camps', *The Nation* (Bangkok, Internet edn), 10 Oct. 1999, in 'Rangoon masses troops near border to attack refugee camps', FBIS-EAS-1999-1010, 11 Oct. 1999.

security on its border with Myanmar because Karen refugee camps in Thailand have been used as rear bases by the rebels.[206] The KNU has suffered setbacks on the battlefield since 1995 and now has an estimated fighting strength of less than 6000. Factions within the KNU reportedly favour a ceasefire agreement with the government, and the Thai military put great pressure on hard-liners to cease military operations.[207]

The Philippines

In March 1999 Philippine President Joseph Estrada suspended the government's long-running talks with the New People's Army (NPA) after it captured several policemen and soldiers.[208] Popular support for the NPA, which promised a better standard of living, waned after end of the cold war and with the gradual reduction of poverty in the Philippines. Support for the rebels increased again in 1999 as the economic gains did not meet expectations. Although it is far below its mid-1980s peak strength of 25 000, the 30-year-old group has about 8000 members but only 6000 firearms, according to a statement by the chief of the armed forces, General Angelo Reyes.[209] Small encounters took place during the remainder of the year after talks collapsed completely in May.[210]

Sri Lanka

The Liberation Tigers of Tamil Eelam (LTTE) have fought for an independent Tamil state in the north-eastern part of the island state of Sri Lanka since the mid-1970s. Full-scale civil war broke out in 1983.[211] The conflict has caused at least 53 000 deaths.[212] The LTTE claim that 14 355 of their fighters were killed, 9558 of them in the course of a May 1997–December 1998 government campaign during the first administration of President Chandrika Kumaratunga, who was re-elected in December 1999. Over 3500 government soldiers lost their lives during the same period.[213] Since then the separatists have dramatically increased their firepower by acquiring surface-to-air missiles, multiple

---

[206] Brooke, M., 'Myanmar's armed forces and their ongoing campaigns', *Asian Defence Journal*, Mar. 1999, pp. 12–13; and 'Thai Army on alert as fighting mounts', *Jane's Defence Weekly*, vol. 31, no. 9 (3 Mar. 1999), p. 17.

[207] 'Rebel groups under pressure to surrender', *Asian Defence Journal*, July 1999, p. 40.

[208] 'The Philippines: a red army strikes', *The Economist*, 13 Mar. 1999, pp. 73–74.

[209] Roxas, F. M., 'Army brass say new NPA recruits are ill-equipped and uneducated', Balita News, BALITA-L Digest–11 Apr. 1999–Special issue (#1999-394), 11 Apr. 1999, Official Balita Web Archive, URL <http://www.balita.org>; and 'Communists growing in size but falling in quality', Balita News, BALITA-L Digest –29 July to 30 July 1999–(#1999-635), 30 July 1999.

[210] 'Army presses offensive vs. NPA in Davao', Balita News, BALITA-L Digest—1 July 1999–Special issue (#1999-592), 1 July 1999.

[211] Philipson, L., 'Sri Lanka's trials', *New Routes*, Jan. 1999, pp. 22–23.

[212] Some sources claim that 55 000 people have been killed since 1972. Jayasinghe, A., 'Kumaratunga wins second term in office', *Financial Times*, 23 Dec. 1999, p. 3; and AFP, 'Fierce fighting rages in northern Sri Lanka', 26 Dec. 1999, in FBIS-NES-1999-1226, 26 Dec. 1999. Another source gives contradictory estimates: 53 000 since 1983 and 58 000 since 1983. 'Sri Lankan troops kill rebels', *Jane's Defence Weekly*, vol. 32, no. 4 (28 July 1999), p. 13; and 'Troops kill 20 rebels in jungle fighting', *Jane's Defence Weekly*, vol. 31, no. 25 (23 June 1999), p. 17.

[213] Athas, I., 'Sri Lanka's endless war', *Jane's Defence Weekly*, vol. 33, no. 2 (12 Jan. 2000), p. 20.

rocket launchers, artillery and anti-tank guided missiles.[214] During the first 10 months of 1999 government offensives led to battles that killed many hundreds but changed little on the ground.[215] A surprise offensive by the LTTE in November and December overran government-held positions on the Jaffna peninsula and in the Vanni region. By late December the rebels had retaken about 1000 square kilometres of territory that government forces had secured during two years of hard fighting in 1995–97. The fighting killed a number of civilians and displaced thousands.[216] The government admitted that 300 troops were either killed or missing in action. At the end of the year the battle for the Elephant Pass continued, with the goal being control of the Jaffna peninsula, where the LTTE ran a de facto state for several years.[217]

Chechnya, Russia

The war in the Russian republic of Chechnya between the federal government and separatist rebels was one of the more notable cases of non-intervention in 1999.[218] In August Islamic militants from Chechnya occupied several towns in the neighbouring republic of Dagestan. Together with four terrorist bombings in Russia that killed hundreds of people—attributed by the government to Chechen terrorists—the action prompted a severe military response from Moscow. Soldiers drove the militants out of Dagestan and then pursued them in Chechnya, with the objective of wiping them out and retaking control of the republic from the Chechen government, which has controlled the republic since the Chechen war of 1994–96. They met little resistance as they swept through the northern third of Chechnya but resistance stiffened in towns around the capital, Grozny, the site of a long and vicious battle.

Russia had over 90 000 soldiers in Chechnya in 1999, according to the chief of the General Staff.[219] Arrayed against them were 12 000–15 000 Chechen fighters, according to Russian estimates.[220] Wary of losing thousands of soldiers in close combat, as it had in the war of 1994–96, the Russian military used aircraft and artillery to bombard Grozny for weeks before attempting a ground assault on the lightly armed but entrenched guerrilla force.[221] Western politicians and international human rights organizations criticized the govern-

[214] Athas (note 213). See also chapter 7 in this volume.

[215] AFP, 'Defence Ministry: renewed Sri Lanka fighting kills 80', 18 Feb. 1999, in FBIS-NES-1999-0218, 18 Feb. 1999; and AFP, 'Toll in Sri Lanka fighting at 48 killed, over 200 injured', 13 Sep. 1999, in FBIS-NES-1999-0913, 13 Sep. 1999.

[216] AFP, 'Sri Lanka Tigers attack Kanakarayankulam military base', 3 Nov. 1999, in FBIS-NES-1999-1103, 20 Nov. 1999; and 'Growing fears for Sri Lanka's civilians', BBC News Online, 24 Nov. 1999, URL <http://news.bbc.co.uk/hi/english/world/south_asia/newsid_534000/534712.stm>.

[217] AFP (note 216); AFP, 'Sri Lanka Tamil Tigers claim capture of key military base', 12 Dec. 1999, in FBIS-NES-1999-1212, 13 Dec. 1999; Athas (note 213); and AFP (note 212).

[218] For an analysis of the 1999 Chechen war, see chapter 3 in this volume.

[219] Voronov, V., 'The price of "conquering" Chechnya', *New Times*, Dec. 1999, p. 15.

[220] Hoffman, D., 'Russia, pressing offensive, rejects Chechen leader's plea for talks', *International Herald Tribune*, 16 Dec. 1999, p. 8.

[221] Gordon, M., 'Russia uses a sledgehammer in Chechen war this time', *New York Times* (Internet edn), 8 Dec. 1999, URL <http://www.nytimes.com/library/world/europe/120899russia-chechnya.html>; and Williams, D., 'Fierce Chechen resistance slows Russian onslaught', *International Herald Tribune*, 28 Dec. 1999, p. 1.

ment harshly for its disregard for civilians and the indiscriminate nature of Russian tactics. Russia insisted that it was not killing civilians and did not alter its strategy.[222] Federal troops captured Grozny in early February 2000, and the war appeared to be entering a protracted counter-insurgency phase.[223]

About 200 000 refugees, out of the Chechen population of 350 000, fled to Ingushetia.[224] A small number of them returned to Russian-held territory.[225] The number of Russian soldiers killed was highly sensitive for domestic political reasons. The Russian Ministry of Defence reported combined military and Interior Ministry losses at 1173 killed, 3487 wounded and 53 missing in Dagestan and Chechnya from August to the end of January 2000.[226] The independent Association of Soldiers' Mothers protest group estimated that 3000 soldiers had been killed.[227] No casualty figures were available for the Chechens who fought on the Russian side, but the number was almost certainly higher than that for the regular army. The rebels offered no figures for their own dead, but the Russian Ministry of Defence said that more than 10 000 militants had been killed by the end of January 2000.[228]

Iran

The conflict between the Iranian Government and the Mujahideen e-Khalq Organization (MKO) continued at a very low level in 1999. The rebels are based in Iraq, where their presence since 1986 has been a major obstacle to diplomatic relations between the two countries.[229] Violence during the year took the form of cross-border hit-and-run attacks by the MKO on government security forces.[230] Iraq and the MKO claim that Iran makes frequent clandestine strikes on MKO bases in Iraq. The Iranian Government denies the

---

[222] Hoffman, D., 'Russia brushes off western criticism', *International Herald Tribune*, 8 Dec. 1999, p. 1.

[223] Thornhill, J., 'Putin declares victory in Chechnya', *Financial Times*, 7 Feb. 2000, p. 2.

[224] Most Chechens had left the region during and after the previous war. ITAR-TASS, 'Russia: FMs says 202,313 people have left Chechnya', 12 Nov. 1999, in FBIS-SOV-1999-1112, 20 Nov. 1999.

[225] ITAR-TASS, 'Over 40,000 Chechen refugees leave Ingushetia', 10 Dec. 1999, in FBIS-SOV-1999-1211, 10 Dec. 1999; Islamic Relief, 'Overcrowding and disease feared in Chechen refugee camps', 27 Jan. 2000, available on ReliefWeb, URL <http://www.reliefweb.int/w/rwb.nsf/480fa8736b88bbc 3c12564f6004c8ad5/f8f974e2ee3c18de85256873007d3db2>; and UNHCR, 'North Caucasus Update: Aid operation continues', 21 Jan. 2000, URL <http://www.unhcr.ch/news/media/chechnya/latest.htm>.

[226] Interfax, 'Russia admits over 1,000 killed in North Caucasus', 25 Jan. 2000, in FBIS-SOV-2000-0125, 25 Jan. 2000. One day earlier slightly lower unofficial figures appeared in the Russian press. Interfax, 'Russian losses in Chechnya 1,152 dead, 3, 246 injured', 24 Jan. 2000, in FBIS-SOV-2000-1224, 24 Jan. 2000.

[227] 'Russians "concealing casualties"', BBC News Online, 24 Jan. 2000, URL <http://news.bbc. co.uk/hi/english/wolrd/europe.newsid_616000/616663.stm>.

[228] Over 2500 were reportedly killed during the fighting in Dagestan and over 7500 were killed in Chechnya by late Jan. 2000, before Grozny fell to the Russian forces. Moscow Interfax in Russian, 'Russian general claims over 10,000 rebels dead', 25 Jan. 2000, in FBIS-SOV-2000-0125, 25 Jan. 2000. A report that appeared a day earlier cited 'various sources' that estimated rebel losses as between 4000 and 7000. 'Russian losses in Chechnya . . .' (note 226).

[229] AFP (North Europe Service), 'Iraqi killed in attack on Mojahedin-e Khalq base', 11 May 1999, in FBIS-NES-1999-0511, 11 May 1999.

[230] AFP (North Europe Service), 'MKO denies Shirazi killers arrested in Iran', 22 June 1999, in FBIS-NES-1999-0622, 22 June 1999; and AFP (North Europe Service), 'AFP receives Iran opposition statement claiming attacks', 11 Dec. 1999, in FBIS-NES-1999-1211, 11 Dec. 1999.

charges.[231] The government claimed that the MKO was involved in the July 1999 student riots, which were the largest and most turbulent since the Islamic revolution of 1979.[232] There is no evidence to support the claim, however.

Israel

Israel continued to engage in violent clashes with non-Palestine Liberation Organization (PLO) groups such as Hamas, Hizbollah and Amal. Fighting with the latter two groups was over the 'security zone' in southern Lebanon which Israel has occupied since 1985. The government of Ehud Barak announced its intention to withdraw from Lebanon by mid-2000. The move was favoured by the majority of Israelis in the face of the continued killing of soldiers followed by Israeli retaliatory strikes against guerrilla locations. Withdrawal from Lebanon would fulfil Hizbollah's primary objective. The most significant step towards peace was the initiation of talks between Israel and Syria in December 1999.[233] The Syrian Government has long held a hard line against Israel and also acts as power broker in Lebanon. A breakthrough in Arab–Israeli relations looked possible if Syria could guarantee Israel that it would prevent militants based in Lebanon from entering Israel in exchange for Israel's withdrawal from the Golan Heights, which it captured from Syria in 1967. Israel continued to have good relations with Jordan after Abdullah II became king following the death of his father, King Hussein, in February 1999. The Israeli Government's interaction with the Palestinian Authority continued to be tense but peaceful.[234]

Turkey

The most significant development in the 15-year confrontation between the Turkish Government and the Partiya Karkeren Kurdistan (PKK, Kurdish Workers' Party) was the capture in February 1999 and subsequent trial of PKK leader Abdullah Öcalan. He was found guilty of treason in May and sentenced to death in June. The sentence was widely criticized internationally

[231] Republic of Iraq Radio Network, 'Official Iraqi spokesman on attack on MKO in south', 3 Nov. 1999, in FBIS-NES-1999-1103, 3 Nov. 1999; Islamic Republic News Agency (IRNA), '"Mo'aredhin" claims responsibility for MKO blast', 3 Nov. 1999, in FBIS-NES-1999-1103, 3 Nov. 1999; and AFP (North Europe Service), 'Opposition blames Tehran for car bomb in Iraq', 14 Nov. 1999, in FBIS-NES-1999-1114, 14 Nov. 1999.

[232] AP, 'Iran arrests alleged protest leader', *New York Times* (Internet edn), 19 July 1999, URL <http://www.nytimes.com/aponline/i/AP-Iran-Protests.html>.

[233] For an assessment of the multilateral tracks of negotiations between Israel, the Palestinian Authority, Syria, Jordan and Lebanon, see Jones, P. and Jägerskog, A., 'The Middle East', *SIPRI Yearbook 1999* (note 23), pp. 169–95. For information on the Israeli negotiations with the Palestinian Authority, Syria and Lebanon, see chapter 2 in this volume.

[234] Matthews, R. and Gerdner, D., 'Between Israel's might and Arab suspicions', *Financial Times*, 8 Feb. 1999, p. 3; Dempsey, J., 'Jordanians crack down on Hamas', *Financial Times*, 23 Sep. 1999, p. 6; Schofield, J., 'Lebanon cautious over Syrian talks with Israel', *Financial Times*, 10 Dec. 1999, p. 6; Khalaf, R. and Dempsey, J., 'The long, hard road to Damascus', *Financial Times*, 10 Dec. 1999, p. 15; 'A Syrian–Israeli peace?', *The Economist*, 8 Jan. 2000, p. 16; and Dempsey, J., 'Pressure mounts on Barak as another Israeli soldier is killed', *Financial Times*, 12–13 Feb. 2000, p. 24.

and not carried out in 1999.[235] Öcalan's surprising response during and after the trial was to instruct the PKK to surrender arms and adopt peaceful political tactics. Despite continued Turkish military operations, some Kurdish fighters surrendered while others continued to train new recruits. The government remained unbending towards Kurdish autonomy, arresting the fighters who turned themselves in. Disillusionment within the PKK led to reports in November of a split within the tightly run organization.[236] The rebels' estimated strength inside Turkey was about 1000, down from a peak of 10 000 in 1992, with additional rebels located outside the country. The fighters who remained outside the country lost critical bases in Iran, Iraq and Syria. On the other hand, the organization has gained increased support in some European political circles.[237] The conflict is estimated to have cost about 30 000 lives.[238]

IV. Conclusions

The introduction to this chapter identified patterns in the major armed conflicts in 1999 in terms of their number, intensity, geographical distribution and type of incompatibility. The reviews of each conflict show that they are too diverse to yield a typical profile but, taken as a group, they reveal several common characteristics. These characteristics point to issues that deserve continued research and policy attention.

1. The vast majority of the contemporary major armed conflicts occur within a single state, as frequently noted. Few governments, at present, appear to be interested in changing the borders of other states. The reasons for this observation are a point of strong disagreement between scholars of the realist and liberal traditions. Realists emphasize that strong states have an interest in maintaining the international status quo and the capability to enforce that interest. Weak states lack the capacity to challenge national borders (when they believe such action would be in their interest). In addition, the weakest states lack the capacity to control their own territory, which permits armed opposition to arise and persist. Liberals, on the other hand, emphasize normative and economic changes. They argue that governments do not challenge state borders because normative prohibitions against such challenges have become embedded in the international system through institutionalization of conflict resolution mechanisms. In addition, direct control over raw materials is no longer necessary for economic gain. In the age of telecommunications and cheap transport, economic advantage comes from cooperation rather than conquest.

---

[235] Zaman, A., 'A ray of hope in the Kurdish conflict', *International Herald Tribune*, 27 Aug. 1999, pp. 1, 4.
[236] Scott, R., 'PKK guerrillas "surrender" to Turks', *Jane's Intelligence Review*, vol. 11, no. 2 (Dec. 1999), p. 7.
[237] 'Turkey's Kurds: still on their feet', *The Economist*, 23 Oct. 1999, pp. 41–42; and Radu, M., 'Is the PKK in Turkey on the ropes?', *Foreign Policy Research Institute E-Notes*, 28 Sep. 1999, Foreign Policy Research Institute, fpri@aol.com.
[238] Dennis, M. and Seibert, S., 'A Kurdish inferno', *Newsweek*, 1 Mar. 1999, pp. 12–17.

2. Most of the major armed conflicts registered for 1999 are protracted (17 have been active for at least eight years) or recurrent (4 conflicts).[239] Historically, it appears that in conflicts based on ethnic divisions outright victory by one side has led to lasting peace more often than has negotiated settlement, although the proposition needs further investigation.[240] (Ethnic identity is a strong defining characteristic in over one-half of the major armed conflicts in 1999.) Yet in most conflicts a purely military solution is not feasible because none of the belligerents is able to eliminate the other(s). Physical elimination is particularly difficult when one side uses guerrilla tactics. In this situation the belligerents may seek to strengthen themselves through alliances with outsiders or to find a solution through negotiation. They often pursue both at the same time. In the vast majority of cases, outside allies are either unwilling or unable to supply enough assistance for that side to achieve a victory. In such cases conflicts become protracted when belligerents refuse to negotiate or when they negotiate but cannot reach a mutually satisfactory agreement.[241]

3. Foreign military intervention occurred in only 5 of the 27 conflicts waged in 1999, even though the persistence of many conflicts suggests that there is a 'market' for such intervention where the belligerents are looking for external help. There are several reasons why foreign military intervention is not more common, including norms against the practice, states' calculation that the costs would outweigh the benefits, and states' lack of capability in cases where they believe that the benefits would outweigh the costs. Foreign military intervention without the express consent of the UN Security Council, most notably in 1999 in Kosovo, has led to a concern that the norm of nonintervention is eroding and with it the foundation of a stable international system. Similarly, humanitarian intervention justified on the ground that state sovereignty is contingent on how a government treats its residents has heightened the fears of weaker states that they are increasingly vulnerable to invasion. The concerns deserve serious consideration, but the record indicates that foreign military intervention remains the exception and is not becoming the rule. In three of the five cases in 1999—the FRY (Kosovo), Indonesia (East Timor) and Sierra Leone—multilateral coalitions were sanctioned by a regional body or the United Nations. Only in the Republic of Congo and the DRC was foreign military intervention entirely unauthorized.

In short, states and non-state actors concerned with the occurrence of violent conflict face a two-pronged dilemma—persistent intra-state conflicts and the continual eruption of new ones (six of the conflicts in 1999 have been waged

[239] The 17 protracted conflicts are Afghanistan, Angola, Colombia, India (Assam), India (Kashmiri separatists), India–Pakistan, Indonesia (East Timor), Iran, Israel, Myanmar, Peru, the Philippines, Sierra Leone, Somalia, Sri Lanka, Sudan and Turkey. The 4 recurrent conflicts are Republic of Congo, Democratic Republic of Congo, Indonesia (Aceh) and Russia (Chechnya).

[240] Licklider, R. (ed.), *Stopping the Killing: How Civil Wars End* (New York University Press: New York, 1993).

[241] Stedman, S., 'Spoiler problems in peace processes', *International Security*, vol. 22, no. 2 (fall 1997), pp. 5–53; and Zartman, I., *Ripe for Resolution: Conflict and Intervention in Africa* (Oxford University Press: New York, 1989).

for two years or less),[242] combined with their own well-justified reluctance to intervene militarily. There are occasions when a military response by outside actors is justified.[243] In these cases, external actors can pursue several objectives, including those of preventing a conflict from spreading, helping one side to win, creating a stalemate as a step towards negotiations and/or minimizing humanitarian costs. They often pursue more than one objective simultaneously but do not clearly distinguish between them. Policies and people may suffer as a consequence.

Non-military responses to conflict are always preferable to military responses. They offer the possibility of achieving solutions to the underlying causes of a conflict, although it is notoriously difficult to find a mutually agreed, long-term compromise. They are usually less costly in terms of money and lives, with some notable exceptions. In many cases non-military responses are the only ones that outsiders will consider making.[244] Nevertheless, there are circumstances in which a military response is the only remaining option. When diplomatic efforts and sanctions have been exhausted and the conflict or threat to international security remains unresolved, the use of international military force must be considered. In conflicts involving genocide, ethnic expulsion or massive abuse of human rights, the decision whether or not to use force should be made quickly.

The ideal way to cope with a conflict is to prevent it from becoming violent or, if it is already militarized, to prevent it from escalating into a major armed conflict. The major armed conflicts which were active in 1999 indicate that there is vast room for improvement in both reactive and preventive action.

[242] These 6 conflicts are the Republic of Congo, the DRC, Ethiopia–Eritrea, Guinea-Bissau, Russia (Chechnya) and the FRY (Kosovo).
[243] The debate about when to intervene has run for a long time and is not likely ever to reach a consensus. The objective upon which there is the broadest agreement in theory is the termination of genocide. The 1994 genocide in Rwanda shows that even that objective is not consistently pursued in practice.
[244] Chapter 2 in this volume discusses the variety of ways in which international organizations, states and individuals seek to prevent, manage and resolve conflicts without resort to force.

Appendix 1A. Major armed conflicts, 1999

MARGARETA SOLLENBERG, STAFFAN ÅNGMAN, YLVA
BLONDEL, ANN-SOFI JAKOBSSON HATAY, ANDRÉS JATO,
THOMAS OHLSON and PETER WALLENSTEEN*

The following notes and sources apply to table 1A. Note that, although some countries are also the location of minor armed conflicts, the table lists only the major armed conflicts in those countries. Reference to the tables of major armed conflicts in previous SIPRI Yearbooks is given in the list of sources.

[a] The stated general incompatible positions. 'Govt' and 'Territory' refer to contested incompatibilities concerning government (type of political system, a change of central government or in its composition) and territory (control of territory [interstate conflict], secession or autonomy), respectively. Each location may have one or more incompatibilities over territory if the disputed territories are different entities. There can be only one incompatibility over government in each location as, by definition, there can be only one government in each location. Each incompatibility may have more than two parties.

[b] 'Year formed' is the year in which the incompatibility was stated. 'Year joined' is the year in which use of armed force began or recommenced.

[c] The non-governmental warring parties are listed by the name of the parties using armed force. Only those parties and alliances which were active during 1999 are listed in this column. Alliances are indicated by a comma between the names of the warring parties.

[d] The figures for 'No. of troops in 1999' are for total armed forces (rather than for army forces, as in the *SIPRI Yearbooks 1988–1990*) of the government warring party (i.e., the government of the conflict location) and for non-government parties from the conflict location. For government and non-government parties from outside the location, the figures in this column are for total armed forces within the country that is the location of the armed conflict. Deviations from this method are indicated by a note (*) and explained.

[e] The figures for deaths refer to total battle-related deaths, that is, those deaths that were caused by the warring parties and which can be directly connected to the incompatibility, during the conflict. 'Mil.' and 'civ.' refer, where figures are available, to *military* and *civilian* deaths, respectively; where there is no such indication, the figure refers to total military and civilian battle-related deaths in the period or year given. Information which covers a calendar year is necessarily more tentative for the last months of the year. Experience has also shown that the reliability of figures improves over time; they are therefore revised each year.

* S. Ångman was responsible for the conflict locations Colombia, Peru, Russia, Sri Lanka, Sudan, Turkey and the Federal Republic of Yugoslavia; Y. Blondel for Algeria; A.-S. Jakobsson Hatay for Israel; A. Jato for Guinea-Bissau; and T. Ohlson for Sierra Leone. M. Sollenberg was responsible for the remaining conflict locations.

f The 'change from 1998' is measured as the increase or decrease in the number of battle-related deaths in 1999 compared with the number of battle-related deaths in 1998. Although based on data that cannot be considered totally reliable, the symbols represent the following changes:

+ +   increase in battle deaths of > 50%
+   increase in battle deaths of > 10 to 50%
0   stable rate of battle deaths (± 10%)
−   decrease in battle deaths of > 10 to 50%
− −   decrease in battle deaths of > 50%
n.a. not applicable, since the major armed conflict was not recorded for 1998.

Note: In the last three columns ('Total deaths', 'Deaths in 1999' and 'Change from 1998'), '. .' indicates that no reliable figures, or no reliable disaggregated figures, were given in the sources consulted.

Sources: For additional information on these conflicts, see the chapters on major armed conflicts in the *SIPRI Yearbooks 1987–1999*.

Reference literature and other information available at the Department of Peace and Conflict Research, at SIPRI and on the official Internet sites of governments and opposition organizations were used as sources.

In addition, the following journals, newspapers and news agencies were consulted: *Africa Confidential* (London); *Africa Events* (London); *Africa Reporter* (New York); *Africa Research Bulletin* (Oxford); Agence France Presse (Paris); *AIM Newsletter* (London); *Asiaweek* (Hong Kong); *Asian Defence Journal* (Kuala Lumpur); *Asian Recorder* (New Delhi); *Balkan War Report* (London); *Burma Focus* (Oslo); British Broadcasting Corporation (BBC) Monitoring Service (Reading); *Burma Issues* (Bangkok); *Conflict International* (Edgware); *Dagens Nyheter* (Stockholm); Dialog Information Services Inc. (Palo Alto); *The Economist* (London); *Facts and Reports* (Amsterdam); *Far Eastern Economic Review* (Hong Kong); *Financial Times* (Frankfurt); *Fortnight Magazine* (Belfast); *The Guardian* (London); *Horn of Africa Bulletin* (Uppsala); *Jane's Defence Weekly* (Coulsdon, Surrey); *Jane's Intelligence Review* (Coulsdon, Surrey); *The Independent* (London); the Integrated Regional Information Networks (IRIN), URL <http://www.reliefweb.int/IRIN/index.phtml>; *International Herald Tribune* (Paris); *Kayhan International* (Teheran); *Keesing's Contemporary Archives* (Harlow, Essex); *Latin America Weekly Report* (London); *Le Monde Diplomatique* (Paris); *Mexico and Central America Report* (London); *Middle East International* (London); *Moscow News* (Moscow); *New African* (London); *New Times* (Moscow); *New York Times* (New York); *Newsweek* (New York); *OMRI (Open Media Research Institute) Daily Digest* (Prague); *Pacific Report* (Canberra); *Pacific Research* (Canberra); *Reuters Business Briefing* (London); *Prism* (Washington, DC); *RFE/RL (Radio Free Europe/Radio Liberty) Research Report* (Munich); *S.A. Barometer* (Johannesburg); *Selections from Regional Press* (Institute of Regional Studies: Islamabad); *Southern African Economist* (Harare); *Southern Africa Political & Economic Monthly* (Harare); *SouthScan* (London); *Sri Lanka Monitor* (London); *The Statesman* (Calcutta); *Sudan Update* (London); *Svenska Dagbladet* (Stockholm); *Tehran Times* (Teheran); *The Times* (London); *Transition* (Prague); and *World Aerospace & Defense Intelligence* (Newtown, Conn.).

Table 1A. Table of conflict locations with at least one major armed conflict in 1999

Location	Incompatibility[a]	Year formed/year joined[b]	Warring parties[c]	No. of troops in 1999[d]	Total deaths[e] (incl. 1999)	Deaths in 1999	Change from 1998[f]
Africa							
Algeria	Govt	1993/1993	Govt of Algeria vs. GIA	300 000* ..	40 000– 100 000**	> 1 000	– –

GIA: Groupe Islamique Armé (Armed Islamic Group).
* Including the Gendarmerie, the National Security Forces and Legitimate Defence Groups (local militias).
** Note that these figures include deaths in the fighting since 1992 in which other parties than those listed above also participated, notably the Front Islamique du Salut (FIS), or Islamic Salvation Front.

Angola	Govt	1975/1998	Govt of Angola vs. UNITA	110 000 50 000–60 000	..	> 10 000	+ +

UNITA: União Nacional Para a Independência Total de Angola (National Union for the Total Independence of Angola)

Burundi	Govt	1998/1998 ../..	Govt of Burundi vs. CNDD–FDD vs. Palipehutu	40 000 10 000 2 000	> 3 000*	> 600	–

CNDD–FDD: Conseil National pour la Défense de la Démocratie–Forces pour la Défense de la Démocratie (National Council for the Defence of Democracy–Forces for Defence of Democracy)
Palipehutu: Parti pour la Libération du Peuple Hutu (Party for the Liberation of the Hutu People)
* Political violence in Burundi since 1993, involving other groups than the CNDD–FDD, has claimed a total of at least 100 000 lives.

Congo, Republic of	Govt	1998/1998	Govt of Rep. of Congo, Angola vs. Opposition militias*	10 000	> 2 000	> 1 000	n.a.

* The Ninja militia, representing Bernard Kolélas of the Mouvement Congolais pour la Démocratie et le Développement Intégral (Congolese Movement for Democracy and Integral Development) and the Cocoye (formerly Zoulou) militia representing Pascal Lissouba of the Union panafricaine pour la Démocratie Sociale (Pan-African Union for Social Democracy).

Location			Warring parties		Total deaths	Deaths in year	Change
Congo, Democratic Republic of			Govt of Dem. Rep. of Congo,	55 000	>4 000***	>2 000***	0
			Angola,	500–2 500			
			Namibia,	800–2 000			
			Zimbabwe,	8 000–12 000			
			Chad	1 000			
	Govt	1998/1998	vs. RCD,*	50 000			
			Rwanda,	10 000–20 000			
			Uganda	.**			
			vs. MLC,	10 000			
			Uganda	.**			
Eritrea–Ethiopia	Territory	1998/1998	Govt of Eritrea	150 000–250 000*	50 000–100 000	>30 000	+
			vs. Govt of Ethiopia	250 000–300 000*			
Guinea-Bissau			Govt of Guinea-Bissau,	600–1 000	>1 000	700–1 000	–
			Senegal,	3 500			
			Guinea	1 500			
	Govt	1998/1998	vs. Military faction	10 000			
Rwanda			Govt of Rwanda	40 000–60 000	..	..	..
	Govt	1994/1994	vs. Opposition alliance*	30 000–50 000			

RCD: Rassemblement Congolais pour la Démocratie (Congolese Rally for Democracy)
MLC: Mouvement de Libération Congolais (Congolese Liberation Movement)

* The RCD split into 2 factions in May 1999, 1 supported by Rwanda and 1 supported by Uganda.
** The total number of Ugandan troops was c. 15 000. It is unclear how many of these troops supported the RCD and the MLC, respectively.
*** These death figures serve only as an indication of the absolute minimum number of battle-related deaths; the real figures may be much higher.

* Including all the mobilized forces and militias.

Location	Incompat-ibility[a]	Year formed/ year joined[b]	Warring parties[c]	No. of troops in 1999[d]	Total deaths[e] (incl. 1999)	Deaths in 1999	Change from 1998[f]
Sierra Leone			Govt of Sierra Leone, ECOMOG	15 000–20 000* 12 000	..	> 6 000	+ +
	Govt	1991/1991	vs. RUF, AFRC	45 000**			
Somalia	Govt*	1991/1991	RRA SNF faction (Buraleh) DSF SPM USC faction (Bood) USC–PM Ethiopia USC faction (Aideed) USC (Mahdi) SNF**	.. ..	..	> 600	n.a.

* Consisting of former government troops of the Forces Armées Rwandaises (the former Rwandan Armed Forces, ex-FAR) and the Interahamwe militia. There are contradictory reports on whether the alliance is identical to the Peuples en armes pour la libération du Rwanda (People in Arms for the Liberation of Rwanda).

ECOMOG: ECOWAS (Economic Community of West African States) Monitoring Group
RUF: Revolutionary United Front
AFRC: Armed Forces Revolutionary Council
* Mainly local civil defence forces, including the Kamajors militia.
** A minority are trained RUF/AFRC soldiers; the vast majority are armed ad hoc rebels.

RRA: Rahanweyne Resistance Army
SNF: Somali National Front
DSF: Digil Salvation Front
SPM: Somali Patriotic Movement
USC: United Somali Congress
USC–PM: United Somali Congress–Patriotic Movement

* No party is listed as the Government of Somalia since no such party can be identified or said to exist. The criterion that at least one party is the government of a state is thus not met. However, since the case of Somalia is unique and there is ample evidence that the warring parties are fighting over governmental power in all or part of Somalia, it is included in the table.

** The RRA, the DSF, the SNF faction (Buraleh), the SPM and the USC faction (Bood) received support from Ethiopia in 1999, although no formal military alliance exists. Ethiopia contributed regular troops to support at least the RRA and the DSF. The remaining organizations/parties also cooperate loosely and receive material support from Eritrea. There is no evidence that Eritrea has contributed regular troops. In addition to the parties listed above, a multitude of smaller factions and militias are active in Somalia, but they cannot be identified as fighting for governmental power.

| Sudan | Govt | 1980/1983 | Govt of Sudan vs. NDA** | 110 000* 30 000–50 000 | 37 000– 40 000 (mil.)*** >1 000 | – |

NDA: National Democratic Alliance

* Including paramilitary forces.

** The June 1995 Asmara Declaration forms the basis for the political and military activities of the NDA. The NDA is an alliance of several southern and northern opposition organizations, of which the SPLM (Sudan People's Liberation Movement) is the largest, with 30 000–50 000 troops. SPLM leader John Garang is also the leader of the NDA.

*** Figure for up to 1991.

America, South

| Colombia | Govt | 1949/1978 1965/1978 | Govt of Colombia vs. FARC vs. ELN | 230 000* 10 000–17 000 5 000 | ..** | >1 000 | 0 |

FARC: Fuerzas Armadas Revolucionarias Colombianas (Revolutionary Armed Forces of Colombia)
ELN: Ejército de Liberación Nacional (National Liberation Army)

* Including paramilitary forces.

** In the past 3 decades the civil wars of Colombia have claimed a total of > 30 000 battle-related deaths.

| Peru | Govt | 1980/1981 | Govt of Peru vs. Sendero Luminoso | 190 000* 500–1 000 | >28 000 | 50–100 | 0 |

Sendero Luminoso: Shining Path

* Including paramilitary forces.

Location	Incompatibility[a]	Year formed/ year joined[b]	Warring parties[c]	No. of troops in 1999[d]	Total deaths[e] (incl. 1999)	Deaths in 1999	Change from 1998[f]
Asia							
Afghanistan	Govt	1992/1992	Govt of Afghanistan vs. UIFSA*	25 000–50 000 ..	..	>2 000	0

UIFSA: United Islamic Front for the Salvation of Afghanistan
* A military alliance, the SCDA (Supreme Council for the Defence of Afghanistan), was formed in Oct. 1996 by the Jamiat-i-Islami, Hezb-i-Wahdat and Jumbish-i Milli-ye Islami. The SCDA changed its name to the UIFSA in June 1997.

Location	Incompatibility[a]	Year formed/ year joined[b]	Warring parties[c]	No. of troops in 1999[d]	Total deaths[e] (incl. 1999)	Deaths in 1999	Change from 1998[f]
India	Territory (Kashmir)	../1989	Govt of India vs. Kashmiri insurgents*	1 175 000 ..	>20 000	>1 200	+
	Territory (Assam)	1982/1988	vs. ULFA	..			
	..	../1986	vs. NDFB	..	..	>100	

ULFA: United Liberation Front of Assam
NDFB: National Democratic Front of Bodoland
* Several groups are active, some of the most important of which are the Jammu and Kashmir Liberation Front (JKLF), the Hizb-ul-Mujahideen, the Harkat-ul-Ansar and the Lashkar-e-Toiba.

Location	Incompatibility[a]	Year formed/ year joined[b]	Warring parties[c]	No. of troops in 1999[d]	Total deaths[e] (incl. 1999)	Deaths in 1999	Change from 1998[f]
India–Pakistan	Territory	1947/1996	Govt of India vs. Govt of Pakistan	1 175 000 590 000	..	1 000–1 500 (mil.)	++

Location	Incompatibility[a]	Year formed/ year joined[b]	Warring parties[c]	No. of troops in 1999[d]	Total deaths[e] (incl. 1999)	Deaths in 1999	Change from 1998[f]
Indonesia	Territory (East Timor)	1975/1975	Govt of Indonesia vs. Fretilin	500 000* 200–600	15 000– 16 000 (mil.)	<50	0
	Territory (Aceh)	1976/1989	vs. GAM	200–600		50–200	

Fretilin: Frente Revolucionária do Timor Leste Independente (Revolutionary Front of Independent East Timor)

GAM: Gerakan Aceh Merdeka (Free Aceh Movement)

* Including paramilitary forces. Some 20 000 troops were used in East Timor and 10 000 in Aceh.

| Myanmar | Territory | 1948/1948 | Govt of Myanmar vs. KNU | 400 000* 2 000–4 000 | 1948–50: 8 000 1981–88: 5 000–8 000 | .. |

KNU: Karen National Union

* Including paramilitary forces.

| Philippines | Govt | 1968/1968 | Govt of the Philippines vs. NPA | 110 000 7 000–9 000 | 21 000–25 000 | < 100 | 0 |

NPA: New People's Army

| Sri Lanka | Territory | 1976/1983 | Govt of Sri Lanka vs. LTTE | 110 000–115 000 6 000–7 000 | > 45 000 | > 3 500 | 0 |

LTTE: Liberation Tigers of Tamil Eelam

Europe

| Russia | Territory | 1991/1999 | Govt of Russia vs. Republic of Chechnya | 1 000 000* 8 000–25 000 | 30 000–60 000 | > 4 000 | n.a. |

* Some 100 000–150 000 troops, including paramilitary forces, were used in Chechnya.

Location	Incompatibility[a]	Year formed/ year joined[b]	Warring parties[c]	No. of troops in 1999[d]	Total deaths[e] (incl. 1999)	Deaths in 1999	Change from 1998[f]
Yugoslavia, Federal Republic of	Territory	1997/1998 1999/1999	Govt of Yugoslavia vs. UCK vs. NATO forces**	110 000* 15 000–17 000 30 000–40 000	2 000–5 000	1 000–3 000	0

UCK: Ushtria Cliirimtare e Kosoves (Kosovo Liberation Army, KLA)
NATO: North Atlantic Treaty Organization
* Approximately 40 000 troops, including paramilitary forces, were used in Kosovo.
** NATO forces comprised troops from 13 of the 19 NATO member states: Belgium, Canada, Denmark, France, Germany, Italy, the Netherlands, Norway, Portugal, Spain, Turkey, the UK and the USA.

Middle East

Location	Incompatibility[a]	Year formed/ year joined[b]	Warring parties[c]	No. of troops in 1999[d]	Total deaths[e] (incl. 1999)	Deaths in 1999	Change from 1998[f]
Iran	Govt	1970/1991	Govt of Iran vs. Mujahideen e-Khalq	500 000–550 000* ..	..	..	..

* Including the Revolutionary Guard.

Location	Incompatibility[a]	Year formed/ year joined[b]	Warring parties[c]	No. of troops in 1999[d]	Total deaths[e] (incl. 1999)	Deaths in 1999	Change from 1998[f]
Israel	Territory	1964/1964	Govt of Israel vs. Non-PLO groups*	170 000–180 000 ..	1948–: >13 000	25 (civ.) 75 (mil.)	—

PLO: Palestine Liberation Organization
* Examples of these groups are Amal, Hamas, Hizbollah and Islamic Jihad.

Location	Incompatibility[a]	Year formed/ year joined[b]	Warring parties[c]	No. of troops in 1999[d]	Total deaths[e] (incl. 1999)	Deaths in 1999	Change from 1998[f]
Turkey	Territory	1974/1984	Govt of Turkey vs. PKK	800 000* 5 000	>30 000	300–600	—

PKK: Partiya Karkeren Kurdistan, Kurdish Workers' Party, or Apocus
* Including the Gendarmerie/National Guard. Some 10 000 troops were used against the PKK.

Appendix 1B. The war in the Democratic Republic of Congo

TAYLOR B. SEYBOLT

I. Introduction

The Democratic Republic of Congo (DRC) is the site of one of the world's most complicated wars.[1] Since 1998 the armed forces of nine states and at least nine rebel groups have fought in the DRC for control of the DRC Government; control of the governments in Angola, Burundi, Rwanda and Uganda; exploitation of the DRC's mineral wealth; and because of ethnic hatred. (Figure 1B shows the territory held by each rebel group at the end of 1999.) The current conflict began after strong disagreements arose between the governments of the DRC, Rwanda and Uganda, which had been allies in the 1996–97 civil war that ended the long rule of dictator Mobutu Sese Seko and brought Laurent-Désiré Kabila to power. A critical antecedent to the civil war was the presence of hundreds of thousands of Rwandans in the eastern DRC after the 1994 genocide and civil war in Rwanda.

The intertwined involvement of governments, insurgents and refugees from countries in the African Great Lakes region and to the west and south also makes the war in the DRC one of the world's most troubling.[2] The course of the war and its outcome will strongly influence political stability and economic development throughout central and southern Africa for years to come. In 1999 most of the warring parties signed a peace accord, the Lusaka Ceasefire Agreement,[3] after intense diplomatic efforts, but its successful implementation is in doubt. Continuation of the war would inhibit efforts to establish a stable peace in neighbouring states. It also could lay waste to one

---

[1] The DRC (area c. 2 million square kilometres, population c. 51 million), formerly called Zaire, is a dictatorship in which President Laurent-Désiré Kabila holds legislative, executive and military powers and rules by decree. There are no legal opposition parties. The Congo gained its independence from Belgium in 1960 and war immediately ensued. Belgium intervened unilaterally to restore order, Katanga province declared independence, Belgium withdrew, and the United Nations Security Council authorized its first complex peacekeeping operation. When the UN withdrew in 1964, after Katanga ended its secessionist fight, Cyrille Aduola became prime minister. In 1965 Mobutu Sese Seko seized power, named the country Zaire and ruled until 1996, when he was overthrown by Kabila. Mobutu was supported by the USA during the cold war and by France in the late 1980s and early 1990s. After the 1994 genocide in Rwanda c. 1 million Rwandan Hutus entered the country. In 1996 their presence helped spark a Tutsi-led rebellion that led to Mobutu's removal from power by Kabila's Alliance of Democratic Forces for the Liberation of Congo, with the assistance of Rwandan and Ugandan troops. In 1998 disagreements between Kabila and his former allies led to a new rebellion in the east which continued throughout 1999. Turner, B. (ed.), *The Statesman's Yearbook 2000* (Macmillan Reference Limited: London, 2000), pp. 483–87; 'Democratic Republic of Congo', *Military Technology*, Jan. 1999, pp. 238–39; and 'United Nations operation in the Congo (ONUC)', *The Blue Helmets: A Review of United Nations Peacekeeping*, 3rd edn (United Nations Department of Public Information: New York, 1996), pp. 175–99.

[2] The Uppsala Conflict Data Project defines a war as a conflict over territory or government with more than 1000 battle-related deaths in a given year. Wallensteen, P. and Sollenberg, M., 'Armed conflict, 1989–98', *Journal of Peace Research*, vol. 36, no. 5 (Sep. 1999), p. 595. A list of the countries in the region is given in the glossary in this volume.

[3] The Lusaka Ceasefire Agreement is contained in UN, Letter dated 23 July 1999 from the permanent representative of Zambia to the United Nations addressed to the President of the Security Council, UN

Figure 1B. Map of the Democratic Republic of Congo showing territory held by each rebel group as of December 1999

Sources: The approximate location of the front line and the borders between rebel areas is based on 'Timeline: the conflict in the DR Congo', 20 Dec. 1999, BBC News Online, URL <http://news2.thls.bbc.co.uk/hi/english/world/africa/newsid%5F573000/ 573051.stm>; and Fisher, I. *et al.*, 'Rival armies ravage Congo in Africa's "world war"', *International Herald Tribune*, 7 Feb. 2000, pp. 1, 2.

of the most densely populated and mineral-rich regions of the continent. The direct and indirect costs of the war have been devastating: tens of thousands of people have died; hundreds of thousands have fled their homes, placing a burden on neighbouring countries; the collapse of the DRC's economy that began under former President Mobutu has continued; and capital investments are virtually non-existent.[4]

document S/1999/815, 23 July 1999. It can be retrieved via UN Website Search at URL <http://www.un. org/search/>.
  [4] Fisher, I. *et al.*, 'Rival armies ravage Congo in Africa's "world war"', *International Herald Tribune*, 7 Feb. 2000, pp. 1, 2; US Committee for Refugees, 'Country report: Congo-Kinshasa', URL <http:// www.refugees.org/world/countryrpt/africa/congokinshasa.htm>; and 'Democratic Republic of Congo: war stifles economy', *Africa Research Bulletin*, 10 May 1999, pp. 13835–36.

This appendix offers an account of the war in the DRC from its outbreak on 2 August 1998 to the end of 1999. Section II explains why the fighting began and details events during the first three months, when the rebels advanced dramatically and all the warring parties became engaged. It identifies the parties to the conflict, their motives and their alliances. Section III recounts the continuation of war from November 1998 to the nearly stalemated military situation of late 1999. Section IV reviews the Lusaka Ceasefire Agreement and its implementation. Section V discusses the war's regional context and the prospects for peace. Section VI offers a brief summary.

II. The outbreak of war in 1998

Underlying and immediate causes

The causes of the civil war that began in 1998 include poverty, misrule and the tension between ethnic groups that has existed in the Great Lakes region for over 100 years. In particular, disputes between Tutsis and other ethnic groups in the northern and southern parts of the province of Kivu arose over access to land. People of Tutsi extraction never received full citizenship (and thus land rights) from the Belgian colonial administration nor from the Mobutu Government.[5] Mobutu worsened the situation by engaging in extensive governmental corruption and by the use of a 'divide and rule' strategy designed to maintain control over the vast undeveloped country. Violence flared up after the 1994 Hutu genocide of Tutsis in Rwanda and the victory of the Tutsi rebels in the simultaneous civil war, after which over 1 million Hutus crossed into Zaire, as the DRC was then called. In addition to legitimate refugees the mass exodus included tens of thousands of armed Hutu extremists who had committed genocide. In 1995 and 1996 these extremists massacred Zairean Tutsis in the northern part of Kivu province.

The civil war of 1996–97 toppled Mobutu and brought Kabila to power as the head of the Alliance des Forces Démocratiques pour la Libération du Congo-Zaïre (ADFL, Alliance of Democratic Forces for the Liberation of Congo).[6] The war began in the southern part of Kivu province (on the border with Rwanda and Burundi) when the governor threatened to expel all Tutsis, no matter how long they had lived in the country, because they were not Congolese citizens. The Banyamulenge (Congolese Tutsis from Kivu province) rebelled to protect themselves from massacre by displaced Rwandan Hutus and local Mayi-Mayi militiamen. The Rwandan Government provided military support to the ADFL in an effort to secure its borders from incursions by genocidal Hutu Interahamwe militia and former Rwandan Army Forces (FAR, Forces Armée Rwandaises), the ex-FAR. That objective was largely achieved within weeks as rebels and Rwandan troops forcibly evacuated refugee camps, caus-

[5] Breytenbach, W. *et al.*, 'Conflicts in the Congo: from Kivu to Kabila', *African Security Review*, vol. 8. no. 5 (1999), pp. 33–36.

[6] Kabila first fought the national government as a Katangan separatist from 1960 to 1964. Between 1964 and 1996 he remained an ineffective guerrilla fighter in eastern Zaire. Kabila is not a Banyamulenge. He comes from northern Katanga and belongs to the Baluba ethnic group, although his mother was a Lunda from southern Katanga. For many years he was a Marxist opponent of the Mobutu Government whose guerrilla campaign met little success. In 1995 he outflanked other potential leaders of the ADFL to become the leader of the country. International Crisis Group, 'Congo at war: a briefing on the internal and external players in the Central African conflict', 17 Nov. 1998, section 2. B., URL <http://www.intl-crisis-group.org/projects/cafrica/reports/ca04main1.htm>.

ing most residents to return to Rwanda and depriving the 'genocidaires' of their bases. The Rwandan military pursued Hutu extremists and civilians through the Zairean jungle killing those they could intercept. With additional assistance from Uganda, the ADFL captured the capital Kinshasa in May 1997 after seven months of steadily advancing across Zaire against the national army that fled more often than it fought.

President Kabila continued to rely heavily on Rwandan military support after he took power. His chief of staff was a Rwandan officer and the presidential guard was composed of Rwandan troops. However, the alliance of convenience soon cracked. Kabila's leadership disappointed the Rwandan and Ugandan governments, which disapproved of his economic policies, exclusionary political tactics and, most importantly, inability or unwillingness to prevent Rwandan and Ugandan rebel groups from using DRC territory to launch cross-border attacks.[7] Kabila began to court popular support through ethnically charged politics, particularly playing on the traditional dislike of the Banyamulenge, whom many people believed received undue attention from the new government.[8]

The second civil war was precipitated by Kabila's announcement on 27 July, days after firing his Rwandan Tutsi military commander, that all foreign troops had to leave the country. The few hundred Rwandan soldiers who remained in Kinshasa left the next day.[9] On 2 August an armed rebellion began, once again in the southern part of Kivu province. The Kinshasa Government immediately accused Rwanda and Uganda of military invasion.[10]

Uganda admitted that it had troops in the DRC but claimed that they were only engaged in operations along the border between the DRC and Uganda against Ugandan rebels.[11] Rwanda denied that it was involved, despite reports of Rwandan military units crossing into the DRC.[12] After a meeting in November with South African President Nelson Mandela, Rwandan Vice-President and military leader Paul Kagame admitted that Rwandan forces played a central role. By then the substantial Ugandan involvement had also become public knowledge.[13]

Motives of the rebels and their allies

The rebel group the Rassemblement Congolais pour la Démocratie (RCD, Congolese Rally for Democracy) is Congolese, with a distinct regional and ethnic composition. The RCD came into being in August 1998 when army soldiers based in the east, who had not been paid for months, rebelled under the leadership of Congolese Major Jean

---

[7] International Crisis Group (note 6).

[8] Breytenbach *et al.* (note 5), p. 39.

[9] 'Congo's bloody-go-round', *The Economist*, 15 Aug. 1998, pp. 31–32; and International Crisis Group (note 6), section 2. A.

[10] 'Rebels seize port', *Africa Research Bulletin*, 9 Sep. 1998, p. 13537. In June 1999 the DRC Government brought charges in the International Court of Justice against Burundi, Rwanda and Uganda for violating its sovereignty and for 'acts of armed aggression'. Report of the International Court of Justice, General Assembly, 54th session, 1 Aug. 1998–31 July 1999, section III, A 25–27, reproduced at URL <http://www.icj-cij.org/icjwww/igeneralinformation/igeninf_Annual_Reports/iICJ_Annual_Report_1998-1999.htm>.

[11] Heitman, H., 'Loyalty split remains as Congo fighting intensifies', *Jane's Defence Weekly*, vol. 30, no. 9 (2 Sep. 1998), p. 19.

[12] Heitman (note 11).

[13] Duke, L., 'Rwanda admits its troops are in Congo', *International Herald Tribune*, 7–8 Nov. 1998, p. 1.

Pierre Ondekane, who became its military commander.[14] The civilian leaders of the RCD are primarily former allies of Kabila and former members of the Mobutu Government. The Banyamulenge and former ADFL fighters who no longer supported Kabila joined the new rebel alliance. Its stated objective is to establish a new government in Kinshasa that will bring about elections, education reform and fair ethnic representation.[15]

Rwanda's overriding objective in the DRC is to secure its western border from incursions by genocidaires who have received arms from the Kabila Government.[16] The Rwandan Government had laid the groundwork for a revolt before the final break in relations, when it realized that Kabila would neither eliminate the Hutu extremists nor allow Rwandan military officers to retrain the DRC Army. A secondary (undeclared) motive is to secure economic gains from natural resources and trade routes in the eastern DRC.[17] Military officers reportedly steal diamonds which are then sold through agencies in Kigali and Nairobi.[18] Rwanda is not a diamond-producing country although, according to the Belgian Diamond Office, it exported 1500 carats worth of diamonds in the first half of 1999.[19]

Uganda was motivated to enter the war by security concerns, a tacit alliance with the Rwandan Government, economic interests and, probably, by miscalculation. A number of Ugandan rebel movements (most of them small) have bases in the eastern DRC which Ugandan troops have attacked. The leaders of Rwanda and Uganda helped to bring each other to power through military means and were close allies before differences arose over actions in the DRC.[20] Ugandan military and government officials are involved in exploiting the area's mineral wealth.[21] Like Rwanda, Uganda is not a diamond-producing country, but it exported 11 000 carats worth of diamonds in the first half of 1999 according to the Belgian Diamond Office.[22] Uganda might also have miscalculated the cost of helping to overthrow a neighbouring government, believing that victory would be as swift as it was in Rwanda in 1994 and in Zaire in 1996–97. Despite the miscalculation, continuing economic gains by military and government officials appear to be the primary reason for Ugandan troops to remain in the DRC. Congolese diamond and gold deposits are almost entirely alluvial and mined by artisanal methods at many small sites, which means that they can be exploited without a large commercial investment.[23]

[14] Breytenbach et al. (note 5), p. 40; and International Crisis Group (note 6), section 2. A.

[15] Fisher, I., 'Rebels share only a goal: oust Kabila', International Herald Tribune, 3 Nov. 1998, p. 4; and International Crisis Group (note 6), sections 1. A., 2. A.

[16] 'Rwandan troops to stay in DRC', Jane's Defence Weekly, vol. 31, no. 22 (2 June 1999), p. 16.

[17] 'War turns commercial', The Economist, 24 Oct. 1998, pp. 54–55.

[18] 'Mineral, general: Democratic Republic of Congo', Africa Research Bulletin, 5 July 1999, pp. 13925–26.

[19] Mutume, G., 'The economics of financing war in Africa', Daily Mail and Guardian, 20 Oct. 1999, URL <http://www.mg.co.za/mg/news/99oct2/20oct-war.html>.

[20] Rwandan Tutsis exiled in Uganda fought for Museveni in the conflict that brought him to power in 1986. Museveni supported these same fighters during the 1990–94 civil war in Rwanda that brought the present government to power.

[21] 'War turns commercial' (note 17); and 'Gambling on the war', The Economist, 7 Nov. 1998, p. 56.

[22] Mutume (note 19).

[23] 'Democratic Republic of Congo: neighborly economic colonialism?', Africa Research Bulletin, 8 Nov. 1999, p. 14058.

Rebel advances and the entrance of government allies

In the eastern provinces of Kivu and Orientale[24] the RCD gained ground quickly as many government army units switched sides. Within four days, by 6 August 1998, the rebels had taken the key towns of Bukavu and Goma, bordering on Rwanda, and Uvira on Lake Tanganyika.[25] On 13 August the rebels captured Bunia, 360 kilometres north of Goma near the border with Uganda. Sympathetic army forces had also rebelled in Kisangani, the country's third largest city, located at the juncture of several roads, a railway line and the Congo River. By the end of August they controlled Kisangani.[26] The government's loss of the city meant that it could not be used for a counter-offensive.

In a dramatic and nearly successful bid for sudden victory the rebels flew across the country in a hijacked Boeing 737 cargo aeroplane on 6 August to directly threaten the capital. More rebels followed in other aircraft, landing at Moanda on the Atlantic coast. One week later the RCD controlled the country's main port at Matadi and the Inga hydroelectric plant that served the capital and the copper-mining region in the south-east. With the national army in disarray, the rebels advanced as far as the airport outside Kinshasa.[27] Kabila fled to Katanga province, most foreigners left the city, and humanitarian aid agencies warned of impending catastrophe as the supply of electricity and water became sporadic.[28]

The RCD was within days of taking the capital when Angola, Namibia and Zimbabwe came to the government's rescue. The Kabila Government had recently become a member of the Southern African Development Community (SADC), and Kabila appealed to its members for assistance. The SADC gave its diplomatic support to Kabila in the interest of preserving state sovereignty and territorial integrity.[29] Most member states, however, refused the request for military assistance. Angola and Zimbabwe quickly deployed aircraft and artillery around the capital and along the Congo River towards the Atlantic Ocean.[30] The RCD pulled its troops back to safer territory in the east by the beginning of September.[31]

In contrast to its retreat from the western DRC, in early September 1998 rebel spokesmen stated that the RCD was moving into Equateur province in the north-west

---

[24] Orientale was called Haut-Zaire under Mobutu and was renamed Ituri by the rebels.

[25] 'Rebels seize port' (note 10).

[26] 'Rebels seize port' (note 10); 'Congo's bloody-go-round' (note 9); and 'Friends, ex-friends and rebels', *The Economist*, 29 Aug. 1998, p. 42.

[27] 'Rebels seize port' (note 10); Mabry, M., 'Old friends, new enemies', *Newsweek*, 24 Aug. 1998, p. 18; 'Friends, ex-friends and rebels' (note 26); and Heitman (note 11).

[28] United Nations Office for the Coordination of Humanitarian Affairs (OCHA), Integrated Regional Information Network (IRIN), 'DRC: Kinshasa plunged into darkness as rebels take power plant', 14 Aug. 1998; and IRIN-CEA, 'Democratic Republic of Congo: aid workers confirm abuses against Tutsis in Kinshasa', IRIN-CEA weekly round-up 34-98, 14–20 Aug. 1998. News items from all the IRIN offices—Central and Eastern Africa (CEA, Nairobi, Kenya), Western Africa (WA, Abidjan, Côte d'Ivoire) and Southern Africa (SA, Johannesburg, South Africa)—are archived at URL <http://www.reliefweb.int/IRIN/index.phtml>.

[29] IRIN-CEA, 'SADC pledges support for Kabila, government ready to meet rebels', IRIN-CEA weekly round-up 12, 20–26 Mar. 1999. A list of the members of the SADC is given in the glossary in this volume.

[30] Gordon, C., 'Pointer: Africa's wars all becoming one', *Jane's Intelligence Review*, vol. 11, no. 10 (Oct. 1998), p. 12; 'War turns commercial' (note 17); and Heitman (note 11).

[31] 'PM Live', SAFM Radio Network (Johannesburg), 10 Sep. 1998, in 'DRCongo rebel spokesman discusses conflict, peace talks', Foreign Broadcast Information Service, *Daily Report–Sub-Saharan Africa* (*FBIS-AFR*), FBIS-AFR-98-253.

and advancing towards the middle of Katanga province in the south-east.[32] If the rebels could control the mineral mines of Katanga province they would gain huge wealth with which to fund their war and deny it to the government. On 12 October the RCD seized the city of Kindu in the Maniema region of Kivu. The loss was a severe blow to the government, which had planned to launch a counter-offensive from there. The airfield at Kindu would have allowed aircraft to strike at most of the territory held by the rebels.[33] Conversely, for the RCD Kindu was an essential stepping stone towards the diamond-mining town of Mbuji-Mayi. By late October 1998 the RCD claimed to control one-third of the territory of the DRC.[34]

A major escalation of the conflict began on 21 October 1998 when Angola, Namibia and Zimbabwe decided to fight the rebels in the east, in response to unrelenting government losses. They were especially concerned that Mbuji-Mayi should not fall.[35] Zimbabwe sent 2000 troops to join the 3000 soldiers it already had in the DRC.[36] Eventually, the number of Zimbabwean troops reached 7000–11 000.[37] The number of Namibian troops in the DRC increased from 200 to approximately 2000 men.[38] An undetermined number of Angolan troops moved north and east from the border between Angola and the DRC.

Several other parties also entered the conflict at this point. Chad sent soldiers to fight for Kabila.[39] Sudan occasionally used its bombers against the rebels and their backers, although it denied any military involvement.[40] The Hutu Interahamwe and the ex-FAR fought troops from the RCD, Rwanda and Uganda. Zimbabwe reportedly supplied arms to the extremist Hutus but it denies the allegation.[41] The Kabila Government also forged an alliance with the Mayi-Mayi militia, who were fighting the RCD in southern Kivu province. In addition, both sides recruited small numbers of mercenaries.[42] Table 1B summarizes information about the armed parties in the DRC.

Motives of the government's allies

Zimbabwean President Robert Mugabe has claimed that his military is fighting in the DRC to uphold the principle of state sovereignty in the face of foreign invasion, as

---

[32] 'DRCongo rebel spokesman discusses conflict, peace talks' (note 31).

[33] 'War turns commercial' (note 17).

[34] Duke, L., 'Rebels accuse Kabila of provoking conflict', *International Herald Tribune*, 28 Oct. 1998, p. 7.

[35] South African Press Agency (Johannesburg), 22 Oct. 1998, in 'Analysts "stunned" by Zimbabwe's intervention in DRCongo', FBIS-AFR-98-295, 23 Oct. 1998; and Fisher (note 15).

[36] Bartlett, L., Agence France-Presse (AFP), (Paris, World Service), 22 Oct. 1998, in 'Congo-Kinshasa: AFP reports Zimbabwe starts troop build-up in DRCongo', FBIS-AFR-98-295, 23 Oct. 1998.

[37] Most estimates are at the high end of the range. Fisher *et al.* (note 4); 'DRC rebels seize more towns', *Jane's Defence Weekly*, vol. 31, no. 17 (28 Apr. 1999), p. 17; Ferrett, G., 'Mugabe's unpopular war', BBC News Online, 2 Dec. 1998, URL <http://news.bbc.co.uk/hi/english/special_report/1998/12/98/zimbabwe/newsid_225000/225562.stm>; and 'Zimbabwe: cabinet pay rises as war destroys economy', *Africa Research Bulletin*, 4 Oct. 1999, p. 14015.

[38] Gordon (note 30), p. 12; and Fisher *et al.* (note 4).

[39] Chadian troops were reportedly deployed in northern DRC beginning in Sep. 1998. IRIN-WA, 'DR Congo: Chad troops return home', 31 May 1999.

[40] Fisher *et al.* (note 4).

[41] Final report of the International Commission of Inquiry (Rwanda), annexe to UN, Letter dated 18 November 1998 from the Secretary-General addressed to the President of the Security Council, UN document S/1998/1096, 18 Nov. 1998, para. 51.

[42] The mercenaries reportedly came from Bosnia and Herzegovina, France, Germany, Serbia, South Africa, Ukraine and elsewhere. Venter, A., 'Out-of-state and non-state actors keep Africa down', *Jane's Intelligence Review*, vol. 11, no. 5 (May 1999), p. 46.

Table 1B. Armed parties in the Democratic Republic of Congo, as of 1999

Parties	Estimated number of troops	Comments
Government side		
DRC Govt	50 000–70 000	Army is poorly trained; with allies it controls capital and roughly western and southern parts of the DRC
Angolan Govt	2 000–7 000	Mainly interested in preventing UNITA use of DRC territory; active on DRC/Angola border
Chadian Govt	2 000	Withdrew at the end of May 1999 after the Sirte Agreement.
Namibian Govt	2 000–3 000	Historical alliance with Angola from apartheid era; no direct interests; active in north-west
Sudanese Govt	Bombing	Allied with Kabila apparently because he is opposed by Uganda
Zimbabwean Govt	7 000–11 000	Extracting minerals; President Robert Mugabe's rivalry with Ugandan President Yoweri Museveni; active on front line from the north-west to the south
Interahamwe and Ex-FAR	5 000–25 000	Responsible for Rwandan genocide; motivated by hatred of Tutsis; active near Mbuji-Mayi and in Kivu
Mayi-Mayi militia	Unknown	Shifting loyalties, allied with Kabila and Hutu extremists because they hate Tutsis; active in Kivu
Rebel side		
RCD-G rebels	10 000–15 000	Appeared 2 Aug. 1998; Emile Ilunga new leader May 1999; allied with Rwanda; located in east and south
RCD-ML rebels	< 3500	Established by Ernest Wamba dia Wamba Oct. 1999; allied with Uganda; located in north-east
MLC rebels	< 10 000–20 000	Jean-Pierre Bemba leader; appeared Nov. 1998; allied with Uganda; located in north-west
Rwandan Govt	10 000	Main concern is its own security against Hutu extremists; mineral extraction; active in central east
Ugandan Govt	8 000–10 000	Counter-insurgency; mineral extraction; active in north-east and north-west
Not contesting DRC		
Burundian Govt	..	Fighting its own Hutu rebels in DRC
Burundian rebels (CNDD–FDD)	..	Use DRC territory for rear bases; allied with Rwandan Hutu extremists
Ugandan rebels (ADF, FUNA, LRA, UNRF II, WNBF)	..	Use DRC territory for rear bases
Angolan rebels (UNITA)	..	Use DRC territory for rear bases and supply routes

Notes: Ex-FAR = former Rwandan Army Forces (Forces Armée Rwandaises); RCD-G = Rassemblement Congolais pour la Démocratie–Goma (Congolese Rally for Democracy–Goma); RCD-ML = Rassemblement Congolais pour la Démocratie–Mouvement de Libération (Congolese Rally for Democracy–Liberation Movement); MLC = Mouvement de Libération Congolais (Congolese Liberation Movement); CNDD–FDD = Conseil National pour la Défense de la Démocratie–Forces pour la Défense de la Démocratie (National Council for the Defence of Democracy–Forces for Defence of Democracy); ADF = Allied Democratic Forces;

FUNA = Former Ugandan National Army; LRA = Lord's Resistance Army; UNRF II = Ugandan National Rescue Front II; WNBF = West Nile Bank Front; UNITA = União Nacional Para a Independência Total de Angola (National Union for the Total Independence of Angola).

Sources: Fisher, I. *et al.*, 'Rival armies ravage Congo in Africa's "world war"', *International Herald Tribune*, 7 Feb. 2000, pp. 1, 2; '3000 Namibian troops in DRC', *Jane's Defence Weekly*, vol. 32, no. 24 (15 Dec. 1999), p. 19; 'Namibia in "state of emergency" after rebel raids', *Jane's Defence Weekly*, vol. 32, no. 7 (18 Aug. 1999), p. 18; 'Congo tension rises', *AirForces Monthly*, Oct. 1999, p. 5; Heitman, H., 'DRC chief threatens to "attack Bujumbura"', *Jane's Defence Weekly*, vol. 31, no. 23 (9 June 1999), p. 51; 'Ex-Rwandan soldiers killed in DRC', *Jane's Defence Weekly*, vol. 31, no. 23 (9 June 1999), p. 46; 'DRC rebels seize more towns', *Jane's Defence Weekly*, vol. 31, no. 17 (28 Apr. 1999), p. 17; Ferrett, G., 'Mugabe's unpopular war', BBC News Online, 2 Dec. 1998, URL <http://news.bbc.co.uk/hi/english/special_report/1998/12/98/zimbabwe/newsid_225000/22556 2.stm>; 'Zimbabwe: cabinet pay rises as war destroys economy', *Africa Research Bulletin*, 4 Oct. 1999, p. 14015; 'Gambling on the war', *The Economist*, 7 Nov. 1998, p. 56; South African Press Agency (Johannesburg), 22 Oct. 1998, in 'Analysts "stunned" by Zimbabwe's intervention in DRCongo', Foreign Broadcast Information Service, *Daily Report–Sub-Saharan Africa (FBIS-AFR)*, FBIS-AFR-98-295, 23 Oct. 1998; 'Renewed danger in the Congo', *Strategic Comments*, vol. 4, no. 6 (July 1998), p. 1; 'The blue helmets return', *Africa Confidential*, vol. 40, no. 24 (3 Dec. 1999), p. 3; and 'Democratic Republic of Congo', *Military Technology*, Jan. 1999, p. 239.

determined by the SADC. There appear to be other motives as well. One is the likelihood that Mugabe, like President Yoweri Museveni of Uganda, underestimated the length of the conflict when he first sent troops.[43] A second factor is Mugabe's personal desire to be recognized as one of sub-Saharan Africa's foremost leaders. He reportedly sees his competition as Nelson Mandela and Museveni.[44] As president of South Africa, Mandela was head of the SADC in 1998 and did not support military aid to Kabila. Despite this, Mugabe was able to act in the SADC's name because of Zimbabwe's position as chair of the Organ for Politics, Defence and Security within the SADC. A third motive for top government and military officials is access to the DRC's minerals. The DRC and Zimbabwean defence forces established a joint company to exploit Congolese natural resources, from which some proceeds are meant to reimburse the Zimbabwean Government for the cost of its intervention.[45] According to the Belgian Diamond Office, Zimbabwe exported 19 000 carats worth of diamonds in early 1999, even though it is not a diamond-producing country.[46] The Zimbabwe national railway company built a new line to export copper ore from the DRC for processing in Zimbabwe.[47] In addition, Zimbabwe has obtained the use of more than 500 000 hectares of agricultural land in the DRC. None of the wealth appears to have entered Zimbabwe's economy.[48] As Mugabe's regime rapidly loses domestic and international support he appears to be using the DRC's natural resources to maintain the loyalty of his top supporters.

---

[43] 'Zimbabwe: cabinet pay rises as war destroys economy' (note 37).

[44] Fisher *et al.* (note 4).

[45] Mutume (note 19); and 'Democratic Republic of Congo: neighborly economic colonialism?' (note 23). See also appendix 5D in this volume.

[46] Mutume (note 19).

[47] 'Democratic Republic of Congo: neighborly economic colonialism?' (note 23).

[48] 'War turns commercial' (note 17); and 'Democratic Republic of Congo: neighborly economic colonialism?' (note 23).

Angola's main concern is to deny supply routes and rear bases to its own União Nacional Para a Independência Total de Angola (UNITA, National Union for the Total Independence of Angola) rebel movement.[49] Mobutu had allowed UNITA to ship diamonds out of, and weapons into, Angola over the border shared by Angola and Zaire. The need to control UNITA's activities in the DRC became urgent when UNITA recommenced the civil war in Angola in contravention of the November 1994 Lusaka Protocol.[50] The Angolan Government is also protecting commercial interests. Its troops control all of the oil-producing towns along the Atlantic coast and the governments of Angola and the DRC have formed a joint oil-exploration company.[51]

Namibia supports Angola in an alliance that was established when Namibia's ruling party, the South West Africa People's Organisation (SWAPO), was a rebel group and the apartheid government in South Africa used South-West Africa (former name of Namibia) as a buffer while it supported UNITA. Namibia now faces a small secessionist movement in the Caprivi Strip, a narrow wedge of land between Angola and Botswana, and fears that UNITA forces will move in and further destabilize the area.[52]

The Government of Chad had no strong motive to become involved in the war in the DRC and probably underestimated the length of time that the conflict would last when it did so. It withdrew its 2000 troops in May 1999.[53] The Government of Sudan appears to support Kabila on the principle that 'my enemy's enemy is my friend'. Sudan and Uganda have long been at odds, each accusing the other of supporting rebels in their respective countries. Since Uganda opposes Kabila, Sudan supports him.[54] The Interahamwe and the ex-FAR are motivated by their desire to overthrow the Rwandan Government. They need bases and supply routes in the east, close to the border with Rwanda. The Mayi-Mayi seem to be motivated largely by ethnic antipathy for the Banyamulenge.

Other armed forces are active in the DRC but are not directly engaged in the civil war. Burundian Hutu rebels belonging to the Conseil National pour la Défense de la Démocratie–Forces pour la Défense de la Démocratie (CNDD–FDD, National Council for the Defence of Democracy–Forces for Defence of Democracy) have bases in the southern part of Kivu province.[55] Burundian Army units have entered the DRC to attack those rebels. The DRC Government has claimed that Burundi actively supports the forces arrayed against it.[56] Also using DRC territory to fight their own governments are Angolan UNITA rebels and several Ugandan groups: the Allied Democratic Forces (ADF), the Lord's Resistance Army (LRA), the West Nile Bank Front (WNBF), the Ugandan National Rescue Front II (UNRF II) and the Former Ugandan National Army (FUNA).[57]

---

[49] Gordon (note 30).

[50] Lusaka Protocol: Lusaka, Zambia, 15 Nov. 1994, URL <http://www.incore.ulst.ac.uk/cds/agreements/lusaka.html>.

[51] 'War turns commercial' (note 17).

[52] Gordon (note 30).

[53] IRIN-WA (note 39).

[54] Uganda and Sudan re-established diplomatic contact in Dec. 1999 and promised not to support each other's rebels.

[55] In late 1999 they reportedly began to coordinate some military operations with the Interahamwe and the ex-FAR, as well as with the Mayi-Mayi militia. UN, Report of the Secretary-General on the United Nations Organization Mission in the Democratic Republic of the Congo, UN document S/2000/30, 17 Jan. 2000, para. 11.

[56] Heitman, H., 'DRC chief threatens to "attack Bujumbura"', Jane's Defence Weekly, vol. 31, no. 23 (9 June 1999), p. 51.

[57] Lusaka Ceasefire Agreement (note 3); and Fisher et al. (note 4).

III. Stalemate

The escalation of external assistance to the Government of the DRC appeared as if it might turn the tide against the rebels. At the end of November 1998 Zimbabwean aircraft bombed rebel positions on the shore of Lake Tanganyika.[58] In mid-January 1999 the formerly secure rebel town of Bukavu came under attack from Burundian and Rwandan Hutus and Mayi-Mayi militia.[59] However, DRC and allied forces proved unable to push the rebels back, succeeding instead in dramatically slowing the rebels' advance. After capturing one-third of the territory of the DRC from August to the end of October 1998, rebel forces held about one-half of the country 14 months later, at the end of 1999.[60]

The most dramatic changes in this 14-month period were political. By the end of 1999 there were three distinct rebel groups fighting the government, Ugandan and Rwandan military forces came close to parting ways, and most of the warring parties had signed a peace accord.

The first new rebel group appeared in November 1998 in the western part of northeastern Orientale province.[61] The Mouvement de Libération Congolais (MLC, Congolese Liberation Movement) was led by businessman Jean-Pierre Bemba, whose father had been a business associate of Mobutu. Despite the fact that Bemba had no political experience and little military training he soon announced the capture of two towns held by Chadian troops. By the end of November he reportedly commanded over 2000 troops and enjoyed strong public support in a limited area.[62] It soon became known that Uganda backed the MLC, and Rwanda accused the Ugandan military officers of being more interested in striking business deals than pursuing war. Uganda contended that its support for Bemba was an attempt to popularize an unpopular war.[63]

The RCD had little choice but to accept the MLC, which shared the goal of overthrowing Kabila and had managed to establish its own area of control in the north.[64] The rebel groups appear to be only loosely coordinated with each other. They occupy separate territories and are supported by different states. The relations between their backers, Rwanda and Uganda, have deteriorated to the point of armed clashes. Both the RCD and the MLC signed the Lusaka Ceasefire Agreement with the Government of the DRC but at different times. The deterioration of relations between Rwanda and Uganda and the Lusaka Agreement are discussed below.

The new alliance benefited the rebels on the battlefield. Ugandan and MLC units clashed heavily with Angolan troops in northern Equateur province in December 1998, causing Angola to withdraw its troops from the front.[65] In mid-February 1999 the rebels announced a multi-pronged offensive in which the MLC attacked Gemena in the north and the RCD attacked Kabalo and Moba in Katanga province to the

---

[58] 'Congo rebels acknowledge attack', *International Herald Tribune*, 26 Nov. 1998, p. 12.

[59] 'Attacks on Bukavu', *Jane's Defence Weekly*, vol. 31, no. 4 (27 Jan. 1999), p. 20.

[60] Fisher *et al.* (note 4).

[61] 'New rebel forces reported in Zaire', *International Herald Tribune*, 11 Nov. 1998.

[62] 'A hard war to stop—or win', *The Economist*, 5 Dec. 1998, pp. 51–52.

[63] 'A hard war to stop—or win' (note 62).

[64] Goujon, E., AFP, 'DR Congo rebels pull together', 11 Mar. 1999, URL <http://www.reliefweb.int/w/rwb.nst>.

[65] Borzello, A., AFP, 'Uganda welcomes Rwandan cessation of hostilities in DR Congo', 29 May 1999, URL <http://www.reliefweb.int/w/rwb.nsf>.

south.[66] The rebels claimed gains in both areas. The movement of up to 10 000 refugees from Equateur into the Republic of Congo (Congo-Brazzaville) in late February and another 10 000 from Katanga into Zambia in mid-March attested to the brutality of the fighting.[67] In mid-April the RCD continued to advance slowly towards Mbuji-Mayi.[68] The government suffered another blow when some Angolan forces withdrew in May to cope with a strong UNITA challenge in Angola.[69]

However, it became apparent in May 1999 that the RCD was losing its advantage. On 11 May the strongholds of Goma and Uvira were bombed for the first time.[70] In May the government claimed to have recaptured the Kalemie railhead on Lake Tanganyika, retaken land near Mbuji-Mayi, and erased other rebel gains in Katanga province and the southern part of Kivu province.[71]

More important, RCD leader Ernest Wamba dia Wamba was deposed on 16 May and replaced by Emile Ilunga three days later after a special congress of the RCD's 50 founding members and 22 military commanders. According to rebel officials, the move resolved a power struggle that had intensified in March.[72] The split occurred at a time when SADC-mediated peace negotiations were beginning to make progress, as discussed in section IV. The government claimed that Ilunga was a puppet of hardline invader Rwanda and viewed the change in leadership as a setback for the prospect of peace.[73] It is not possible to judge the impact on the peace negotiations at the time, but the depiction of Ilunga as Rwanda's choice was indirectly confirmed over the course of 1999.

The factional split in the RCD was reflected in continually worsening relations between Rwanda and Uganda, which reportedly disagreed over how the war should be fought. After Wamba was removed as leader of the RCD, Uganda pulled troops and equipment out of areas where they had been deployed to support Rwandan troops.[74] Wamba and a small number of followers moved from Goma to Kisangani, where the Ugandan military had its headquarters. A clash between the rival RCD factions in Kisangani on 9 August led Rwandan and Ugandan forces to exchange heavy fire in the city several days later. As many as 2000–4000 soldiers and civilians died.[75] The factional fighting apparently was an attempt by the new leader Ilunga's supporters to prevent a visit to Kisangani by a Zambian delegation in order to decide who should represent the RCD at the signing of the Lusaka Ceasefire Agreement, which had recently been agreed upon by the states involved in the war. Deposed leader Wamba had enjoyed an upsurge in popular support after advocating negotiations with

[66] 'Congo rebels launch major offensive', BBC News Online, 16 Feb. 1999, URL <http://news2.thls.bbc.co.uk/hi/english/world/africa/newsid%5F280000/280278.stm>.

[67] Panafrican News Agency (PANA), 'Around 10 000 refugees from DRC', 26 Feb. 1999, URL <http://www.africanews.org/PANA/news>; Goujon, E., AFP, 'DR Congo rebels claim gains, refugees on the move', 11 Mar. 1999, URL <http://www.reliefweb.int/w/rwb.nsf>; and 'Congo's family at war', BBC News Online, 15 Mar. 1999, URL <http://news2.thls.bbc.co.uk/hi/english/world/africa/newsid_297000/297252.stm>.

[68] 'DRC rebels seize more towns' (note 37).

[69] Venter (note 42).

[70] 'Kabila "bombs rebel towns"', BBC News Online, 12 May 1999, URL <http://news2.thls.bbc.co.uk/hi/english/world/africa/newsid_341000/341458.stm>.

[71] Bosongo, B., AFP, 'Government troops claim major victory in DR Congo war', 21 May 1999, URL <http://www.reliefweb.int/w/rwb.nsf>.

[72] IRIN-CEA, 'Ilunga new RCD leader', IRIN Update no. 675 for Central and Eastern Africa, 20 May 1999.

[73] IRIN-CEA (note 72).

[74] Borzello (note 65).

[75] AFP (Paris, World Service), 11 Sep. 1999, in 'Ugandan-backed DRCongo rebel faction moves HQ to Bunia', FBIS-AFR-1999-0911, 13 Sep. 1999.

Kabila.[76] The fighting ended when Ugandan President Museveni and Rwandan Vice-President Kagame met to agree on a ceasefire, redeployment of troops from the city and a joint report on the circumstances of the clash.[77] Uganda relocated its headquarters from Kisangani to Gbadolite in the north-west. Wamba and his still unnamed RCD faction moved to Bunia, near the border with Uganda.[78]

Wamba reaffirmed his refusal to leave the political stage on 1 October when he established a separate faction called the Rassemblement Congolais pour la Démocratie–Mouvement de Libération (RCD-ML, Congolese Rally for Democracy–Liberation Movement).[79] The main RCD faction then became known by the location of its headquarters: the Rassemblement Congolais pour la Démocratie–Goma (RCD-G, Congolese Rally for Democracy–Goma). Uganda supported the RCD-ML, which was militarily weak and more inclined to negotiate with the government. Rwanda supported the stronger RCD-G, which was more inclined to fight.

IV. The Lusaka Ceasefire Agreement

From the time the second civil war began politicians and diplomats outside the DRC tried to establish a ceasefire and begin peace negotiations. The presidents of South Africa, Tanzania and Zambia negotiated on behalf of the SADC from August to October 1998.[80] In November France and the United Nations tried to broker a ceasefire at the Franco-African summit meeting.[81] High-level diplomats from the United States and the United Kingdom travelled to the region in October and November 1998 and February 1999, respectively.[82] None of the efforts was successful. Three factors stood in the way: talks did not involve the rebels; Rwanda refused for months to admit that it was involved; and President Kabila insisted that Ugandan and Rwandan 'invaders' had to leave the DRC before he would negotiate.[83]

Temporary hope of a settlement came on 18 April 1999, when presidents Kabila and Museveni signed an accord in Sirte, Libya, under the guidance of President Muammar Qadhafi. The 10-point agreement called among other things for a ceasefire; African peacekeeping troops to deploy in areas occupied by Burundian, Rwandan and Ugandan soldiers; and dialogue between the DRC Government and the

---

[76] Russell, R., Reuters, 'Congo rebels fire on each other, terrorise town', 9 Aug. 1999, URL <http://www.reliefweb.int/w/rwb.nsf>.

[77] AFP, 'Rwandans, Ugandans reach ceasefire in DR Congo city', 17 Aug. 1999, URL <http://www.reliefweb.int>.

[78] AFP (Paris, World Service), 14 Sep. 1999, in 'Uganda to move military HQ from Kisangani to Gbadolite', FBIS-AFR-1999-0914, 15 Sep. 1999.

[79] IRIN-CEA, 'Wamba renames rebel group', IRIN-CEA weekly round-up 40, 2–8 Oct. 1999.

[80] 'War turns commercial' (note 17); and 'Fighting in DRC despite talks', *Jane's Defence Weekly*, vol. 30, no. 17 (28 Oct. 1998), p. 14.

[81] Lewis, J. A. C., 'Ceasefire accord will decide DRC future', *Jane's Defence Weekly*, vol. 30, no. 23 (9 Dec. 1998), p. 18.

[82] US Department of State, 'Assistant Secretary Susan Rices's trip to Africa', *Press Statement*, 26 Oct. 1998, URL <http://secretary.state.gov/www/briefings/statements/1998/ps981026.html>; and Press Association (London), 20 Feb. 1999, in 'UK premier sends minister in bid to end Congo war', Foreign Broadcast Information Service, *Daily Report–West Europe* (*FBIS-WEU*), FBIS-WEU-1999-0220, 22 Feb. 1999.

[83] 'DRCongo rebel spokesman discusses conflict, peace talks' (note 31); Phiri, R., *The Post* (Lusaka, Internet edn), 1 Sep. 1998, in 'Zimbabwe: Kabila says S. Africa sending arms to Rwanda', FBIS-AFR-98-245; and PANA, 'Congo spells out terms for a possible truce', PANA, 16 Dec. 1998, URL <http://www.africanews.org/PANA/news>.

rebels.[84] A number of central and west African countries supported the Sirte Agreement, and Chad took the opportunity to withdraw its troops from the DRC. However, the rebels and Rwanda immediately rejected the agreement, causing Uganda to declare that it was no more than 'a statement of our desires'.[85]

When Zambian President Frederick Chiluba succeeded Mandela as chairman of the SADC he led negotiations, in cooperation with the Organization of African Unity (OAU), that resulted in the Lusaka Ceasefire Agreement. The agreement was signed in Lusaka, Zambia, by the governments of Angola, the DRC, Namibia, Rwanda, Uganda and Zimbabwe on 10 July, by the MLC on 1 August, and by 50 people representing both factions of the RCD on 31 August.[86] The agreement stipulated a ceasefire within 24 hours; release of prisoners and exchange of prisoners of war; free movement of people throughout the country; creation of conditions to facilitate the delivery of humanitarian assistance; a request to the UN Security Council for an OAU–UN military force mandated under Chapter VII of the UN Charter to ensure implementation of the agreement and to disarm all armed groups in the DRC, with the assistance of the agreement's signatories; the formation of a Joint Military Commission (JMC) by the parties to the agreement to implement the agreement prior to deployment of a UN force; the withdrawal of all foreign forces from the DRC; equal rights and protection for all ethnic groups in the DRC; control of national borders, including arms trafficking and infiltration of armed groups; re-establishment of state administration in all parts of the DRC; open national dialogue between the government, the RCD, the MLC and unarmed opposition groups leading to elections and a new constitution; and integration of rebel forces into a restructured national army.[87]

Initial steps towards implementation included Security Council authorization of the UN Observer Mission in the Democratic Republic of Congo (MONUC) under Chapter VI of the UN Charter on 6 August 1999, to consist of 90 military liaison officers and additional civilian personnel.[88] The mission was intended to assist the joint military and political commissions named in the Lusaka Agreement and to lead to a larger peacekeeping operation after the rebels signed the agreement.[89] In October the JMC agreed on locations for UN troop deployment.[90] In November the OAU appointed as mediator former President of Botswana Ketumile Masire, and the UN Secretary-General named Kamel Morjane of Tunisia as Special Envoy.[91]

However, the parties to the agreement did not appear committed to its objectives, much less the timetable that envisioned the completion of all tasks within one year. Low-level fighting continued in a number of locations from September through December. In November Kabila stated that he would lead a liberation mission against Rwandan occupation. The RCD-G maintained its encirclement of 2000–3000

[84] Peace Agreement, signed in Sirte, Libya, on 18 April 1999, text provided by Embassy of the Democratic Republic of Congo, Stockholm.

[85] PANA, 'Syrte peace agreement to end Congo war gets a boost', 14 May 1999, URL <http://www.reliefweb.int>; and Borzello (note 65).

[86] McNeil, D. G., Jr, 'Congo truce signed amid miscues', *International Herald Tribune*, 12 July 1999, p. 4.

[87] Lusaka Ceasefire Agreement (note 3).

[88] For more information on MONUC, see chapter 2 in this volume.

[89] UN Security Council Resolution 1258, 6 Aug. 1999.

[90] Kalyegira, T., 'DRC peace deployment', *Jane's Defence Weekly*, vol. 32, no. 16 (20 Oct. 1999), p. 18. By 31 Jan. 2000 only 79 military and 24 civilian personnel had been deployed. United Nations Department of Public Information, 'Current peacekeeping operations', UN Department of Public Information document DPI/1634 Rev.12, 1 Feb. 2000.

[91] IRIN-CEA, 'Democratic Republic of Congo: Masire asked to mediate', 15 Dec. 1999; and 'The blue helmets return', *Africa Confidential*, vol. 40, no. 24 (3 Dec. 1999), p. 3.

Namibian and Zimbabwean soldiers at Ikela. The MLC made small territorial gains, and MLC leader Bemba announced in November that owing to government attacks on his forces he considered the ceasefire to be 'null and void'. A December report to the UN Security Council identified numerous ceasefire violations and blamed most of them on the government.[92] The United Nations, for its part, has been unwilling to deploy military observers or peacekeepers until all parties to the Lusaka Agreement guarantee their safety and demonstrate their commitment to the ceasefire.

Implementation of the agreement is hampered by more than just uncooperative participants. Completion of all of the tasks identified in the agreement is necessary to settle the conflict, but there is little reason to expect attainment of the more difficult objectives. Disarmament of armed groups is one example. The Lusaka Agreement names nine groups on DRC territory that did not sign the agreement: the Rwandan ex-FAR and the Interahamwe; the Angolan UNITA; the Ugandan ADF, LRA, WNBF, UNRF II and FUNA; and the Burundian CNDD–FDD. It requires their members to be disarmed and, if appropriate, arrested for war crimes.[93] The negotiations leading to the Lusaka Agreement did not include the named groups, and the agreement does not give their members an incentive to disarm. Indeed, the threat of prosecution for war crimes is a strong disincentive. Paradoxically, in the unlikely event that UN troops or national armies attempt forced disarmament, they would disrupt the little peace that has been achieved. The Burundian and Ugandan rebel groups are weak and would probably flee in the face of a direct assault, but the Angolan and Rwandan rebels are formidable armed groups that would fight for their lives. Furthermore, the DRC's dense jungles would almost surely prevent forced disarmament from succeeding, as Rwanda discovered in 1996–97 when its troops marched across the country and did not eliminate the Hutu extremists.

V. The regional context

The key to settling the DRC conflict is to simultaneously settle the security concerns of Angola, Rwanda, Uganda and Burundi (which is not a signatory to the Lusaka Agreement).[94] Until these countries feel secure they will continue to be militarily active in the DRC. As long as they support opposing sides in the DRC, the government and the rebels will be able to carry on the war.

Important pieces of the puzzle are in place for a regional solution. First, the Lusaka Ceasefire Agreement is commendable for the explicit attention it gives to the security concerns of all the state signatories. It is a welcome departure from the agreements and negotiations in Angola, Burundi, Rwanda and Uganda that failed to recognize the regional dimension of conflicts in those countries. Second, because the envoys from the SADC, the OAU and the UN have regional mandates they have the potential to

---

[92] IRIN-CEA, 'Accusations of ceasefire violations rife', IRIN-CEA weekly round-up 40, 2–8 Oct. 1999; 'Precious little peace', *Africa Confidential*, vol. 40, no. 22 (5 Nov. 1999), p. 3; AFP (Paris, World Service), 25 Nov. 1999, in 'DRCongo: heavy fighting reportedly continues in northwest', FBIS-AFR-1999-1125, 26 Nov. 1999; AFP (Paris, World Service), 5 Dec. 1999, in 'DRC rebel chief Bemba to move headquarters to seized town', FBIS-AFR-1999-1205, 6 Dec. 1999; AFP (Paris, World Service), 27 Nov. 1999, in 'DRC rebel Bemba presents list of cease-fire violations', FBIS-AFR-1999-1127, 29 Nov. 1999; Heitman, H., 'Ineffective DRC ceasefire hailed as "null and void"', *Jane's Defence Weekly*, vol. 32, no. 20 (17 Nov. 1999), p. 20; and 'More rumblings', *Africa Confidential*, vol. 41, no. 1 (7 Jan. 2000), p. 5.

[93] Lusaka Ceasefire Agreement (note 3), annex A, section 9.1.

[94] Shearer, D., 'Africa's great war', *Survival*, vol. 40, no. 2 (summer 1999), p. 90.

address violence in the region as a whole, rather than on a country-by-country basis. Third, the governments with troops in the DRC are not traditional enemies. In fact, they have been allies in the past. They have the potential to negotiate directly with one another about withdrawing support from the DRC Government and rebels. If they do so, they can make it difficult for each other's rebels to operate. The complicating factor here is that the Kabila Government and the regimes in Rwanda and Uganda truly are enemies.

There are also individual reasons for foreign forces to withdraw. First, the war is not popular in Uganda or Zimbabwe. Second, it is a financial burden on all of the countries. The practice of mineral extraction noted above benefits individuals but does not alleviate the burden of war on the national economies. Recent international loans to Rwanda and Uganda have been accompanied by admonishments to limit military spending.[95] Zimbabwe is deeply in debt and its economy is so distorted by military expenditures that the International Monetary Fund (IMF) and the European Union have publicly expressed concern. President Mugabe castigated the IMF after the international lending institution alleged that his government had misled it about the costs of its involvement in the DRC.[96] Third, since September 1999 Angolan military operations have severely weakened UNITA. Together with recent enforcement of international sanctions against the rebel organization, this opens the possibility that Angola will feel less need to maintain troops in the DRC. Fourth, negotiations to resolve the conflict in Burundi resumed when Nelson Mandela was appointed as the new mediator in December 1999.

Nonetheless, critical impediments to peace remain. President Kabila, the MLC's Bemba and the RCD-G's Ilunga will not talk to each other. Without dialogue there is little choice other than to fight. Further, Angola, the DRC and the Republic of Congo signed a pact in December 1999 to assist each other in national security matters.[97] It appears that Angola remains interested in maintaining troops outside its own borders. Rwanda is steadfast in its refusal to withdraw from the DRC until it is assured that the ex-FAR and the Interahamwe are no longer a threat. As noted above, the armed parties which did not sign the Lusaka Agreement have no incentive to seek peace. Finally, the agreement calls for equal rights and protection for all ethnic groups, open elections and a new constitution, but those steps can be taken only after the above concerns are addressed. Even then it is an open question whether the steps will address land disputes and ethnic animosities in Kivu that have sparked violence in the DRC twice since 1996.

VI. Conclusions

Peace in the Democratic Republic of Congo depends on assistance from the SADC, the OAU, the UN and concerned national governments. African leaders came to this conclusion soon after the fighting began and made a concerted effort to stop the

---

[95] 'Uganda gets $12m from IMF', BBC News Online, 11 Dec. 1999, URL <http://news2.thls.bbc.co.uk/hi/english/world/africa/newsid%5F559000/559680.stm; and 'EU resumes aid to Rwanda', BBC News Online, 9 Mar. 2000, URL <http://news2.thls.bbc.co.uk/hi/english/world/africa/newsid%5F671000/671636.stm>.

[96] 'Zimbabwe "misled IMF" over Congo', BBC News Online, 4 Oct. 1999, URL <http://news2.thls.bbc.co.uk/hi/english/world/africa/newsid%5F464000/464344.stm>; IRIN-SA, 'Zimbabwe: donors concerned at cost of DRC intervention', 25 Oct. 1999; and IRIN-SA, 'Zimbabwe: IMF should "shut up"—Mugabe', 29 Oct. 1999.

[97] 'Three sign defence pact', *Jane's Defence Weekly*, vol. 32, no. 24 (15 Dec. 1999), p. 19.

conflict through negotiation. The Lusaka Ceasefire Agreement attests to the success of this effort, at least on paper. The question now is who is responsible for ensuring that the signatories to the agreement follow through on their commitment.

The United Nations is criticized in some quarters for not being more forceful in its effort to facilitate implementation of the agreement. The UN Secretariat has been reluctant to deploy even the small number of military personnel authorized by the Security Council, despite verbal assurances of protection by the parties to the Lusaka Agreement. There is no possibility of ending a large and complex conflict, the argument goes, without a large and ambitious peace operation. The counter-argument is that caution is warranted. Several disastrous peacekeeping operations in the 1990s made it painfully clear that peacekeeping can only be effective when all the warring parties are interested in peace. The multitude of clashes since the Lusaka Agreement was signed, President Kabila's refusal to talk directly to the rebel leaders and the continued presence of thousands of foreign troops in the DRC indicate how far the parties are from ending their confrontation. Furthermore, the exclusion of UNITA, the Interahamwe and the ex-FAR from the agreement, while probably necessary to produce the agreement, ensures that they will play a spoiler role. Political stability is not in the interest of people determined to come to power though violence.

The Lusaka Agreement attempts to address these problems by calling for an ambitious peace enforcement mission to ensure and verify the steps to which the signatories committed themselves. Yet a peacekeeping operation is the most that can be expected. The UN Security Council held a special session on the DRC conflict in January 2000 during which it reviewed the prospects for peace, urged the belligerents to abide by the Lusaka Ceasefire Agreement, and considered the Secretary-General's request for 5500 UN troops, possibly to be followed by a larger and more complex peacekeeping operation. The presidents of a number of African states made it clear that they regard this as a litmus test of UN resolve to settle the conflicts in Africa.[98] It appears that they will be disappointed. No state with the capability to launch a peace enforcement operation is interested in doing so.[99]

The war in the DRC will not end until the belligerents themselves make it happen. The main parties to the dispute—the DRC Government and the Congolese rebels—are not the most important players in this regard. Both sides depend heavily on their external allies. It is the external parties who hold the keys to success. Considerable progress towards peace could be made if Angola, Rwanda, Uganda and Zimbabwe agreed among themselves to a reciprocal withdrawal of their troops and pledged not to support each other's insurgents in any way. An obstacle to this approach is the belief on the part of the Angolan, Rwandan and Ugandan governments that they can only control the infiltration of insurgents across their borders by maintaining soldiers in the DRC. Another obstacle is the inevitable loss of proprietary access to mineral wealth by high-level military and government officials in all four countries. At present, peace in the DRC appears to be a distant hope owing to the fear and greed of the outside parties combined with the refusal of the main parties to talk to each other.

---

[98] IRIN-CEA, 'IRIN focus on UN response to conflict', 16 Dec. 1999; and 'African leaders demand UN deployment', BBC News Online, 24 Jan. 2000, URL <http://news.bbc.co.uk/english/africa/newsid_616000/616516.stm>.

[99] France, which frequently intervened in African states in the past, has decided it will no longer do so. Lewis (note 81). The USA, which held the Security Council presidency during the Jan. 2000 special session, announced that it will only provide logistical support for a future operation. It is unlikely that any European soldiers would be sent. Crosette, B., 'US formally calls for UN Congo force', *International Herald Tribune*, 10 Feb. 2000, p. 2.

2. Armed conflict prevention, management and resolution

RENATA DWAN

I. Introduction

The states and international organizations that dominate the international community have traditionally reacted cautiously to intra-state conflict. Respect for the principle of sovereignty, lack of interest in other states' domestic affairs and the perception that the greatest threat to international stability is interstate conflict contribute to a culture of non-intervention. Changing patterns of conflict, increased penetration of the state, politically, economically and socially, and the heightened international visibility of war have challenged the supremacy of the state in the management of armed conflict.

International actors are responding to this new environment of conflict in a variety of ways. States have demonstrated increased willingness to intervene in intra-state conflict on behalf of the international community through international organizations, in some cases with force. This was particularly marked in 1999, when the greatest increase of new UN operations since the beginning of the decade was seen. The growing role played by ad hoc multinational coalitions of states in conflict management was reinforced in conflicts such as those in Afghanistan, Kosovo in the Federal Republic of Yugoslavia (FRY) and East Timor in Indonesia. Powerful individual states continued to lead peace efforts in a wide range of inter- and intra-state conflicts.

Events in 1999 underscored the limitations of this proactive approach to conflict, however. External intervention, threatened or actual, failed to prevent or resolve violent conflict in Africa, Asia and Europe. Successful interventions in 1999 have yet to demonstrate their ability to manage long-term conflict resolution. Even as the unconditionality of sovereignty is questioned, there is increased recognition of the significance of the state for international peace and security.

This chapter describes efforts undertaken by a range of international actors to prevent, manage, resolve and contain violent conflict in 1999. The list is inevitably selective, with an emphasis on states and intergovernmental organizations. It is impossible to identify all actions aimed at addressing potential or ongoing conflict, much less to measure their impact. The chapter therefore focuses more on peacekeeping and conflict resolution than on prevention and long-term peace building and does not analyse the impact of these activities on current or threatened conflicts. Section II surveys the main peace and conflict activities of the UN system during 1999. Section III describes the parallel efforts undertaken by the principal regional organizations in this regard, sometimes separately, sometimes in coordination with the UN, while section IV examines a number of multinational ad hoc coalitions that addressed conflicts in 1999. Section V explores the role played by other significant actors in peace promotion and conflict resolution: states, individuals and select non-governmental actors. The final section offers some brief conclusions on dominant trends in conflict prevention, management and resolution.

II. The United Nations

The Secretary-General and the Secretariat

The Secretariat has three departments dealing directly with conflict prevention, management and resolution tasks: the Political Affairs and Peacekeeping Operations departments and the Office for the Coordination of Humanitarian Affairs. The Department of Political Affairs (DPA), as convener of the Executive Committee on Peace and Security, is the focal point for post-conflict peace building.

Conflict mediation and prevention activities are less institutionalized, although Secretary-General Kofi Annan has sought to make full use of his personal offices in these regards. Annan, supporting efforts undertaken by then South African President Nelson Mandela and Saudi Arabian officials, mediated successfully in the long-running dispute between Libya and the UN concerning the extradition of two Libyan agents accused of the 1988 bombing of Pan Am Flight 103 over the Scottish town of Lockerbie.[1] On 5 April 1999, Libya handed over the suspects to the UN for trial by a Scottish court in the Netherlands, in response to which the UN Security Council suspended sanctions in place since 1992. In his report 90 days later the Secretary-General confirmed that Libya would pay compensation to families of the 270 people killed if the accused were found guilty.[2]

The Secretary-General continued to exploit the practice of appointing special representatives to underscore UN concern for particular states or issues; 48 individuals were carrying out specific functions on his behalf and the Secretary-General's annual report for 1999 drew attention to the role a skilled representative may play in preventing the escalation of tensions.[3] The appointment of such individuals also serves as a means of demonstrating UN support for mediation and resolution efforts by other actors. Thus Annan dispatched a Special Envoy, Kamel Morjane of Tunisia, to the Democratic Republic of Congo (DRC) in November to support the diplomatic solution to the conflict there put forward by the Southern African Development Community (SADC).[4] Similarly, Special Envoy Mohammed Sahnoun of Algeria

---

[1] Black, I., 'Libya delivers Lockerbie bomb suspects to Scots', *Guardian Weekly*, 11 Apr. 1999, p. 1.

[2] UN, Letter of the Secretary-General to the Security Council, UN document S/1999/378, 5 Apr. 1999; and UN, Report of the Secretary-General, UN document S/1999/726, 30 June 1999.

[3] UN, Annual Report of the Secretary-General on the work of the Organization, UN document A/54/1, 31 Aug. 1999.

[4] 'The Blue Helmets return', *Africa Confidential*, vol. 40, no. 24 (3 Dec. 1999), p. 3. For the members of SADC see the glossary in this volume.

assists Organization of African Unity (OAU) mediation efforts in the conflict between Eritrea and Ethiopia. Sweden's Carl Bildt was appointed Special Envoy to the Balkans in May 1999 and represents the UN in the work of the Stability Pact for South Eastern Europe.[5] An advantage of this mechanism is that it does not require the formal agreement of the Security Council and the special representatives can therefore be deployed at relatively short notice.[6]

Formal strategic coordination with UN agencies is another mechanism by which the Secretary-General has sought to address prevention and post-conflict peace-building tasks. In cases of multidimensional operations a 'lead agency' is appointed to coordinate cooperation between the various UN bodies involved. In El Salvador, it is the United Nations Development Programme (UNDP) that is responsible for assisting implementation of the country's peace accord, although overall charge of the UN presence remains with the DPA. The United Nations High Commissioner for Refugees (UNHCR) takes the lead in managing refugee returns within UN operations. The United Nations High Commissioner for Human Rights (UNHCHR), meanwhile, continued to play a significant role in post-conflict monitoring missions, particularly the International Civilian Mission in Haiti (MICIVIH) and the UN Mission for the Verification of Human Rights in Guatemala (MINUGUA).

The high profile of the UNHCR and the UNHCHR in 1999, however, was primarily a consequence of their efforts to negotiate the massive humanitarian and refugee crises brought about by the conflicts in Chechnya, Kosovo and East Timor. The UNHCR was one of the few international actors permitted by the Russian authorities to visit Russia's southern borders where the conflict in Chechnya displaced over 202 000 people, the majority to the neighbouring republic of Ingushetia.[7] Once the International Force for East Timor (INTERFET) in Indonesia had brought the violence in East Timor under control, the UNHCR coordinated the return of over 55 000 refugees from West Timor. The High Commissioner for Human Rights, Mary Robinson, incurred the ire of a number of states following her forceful criticism of human rights abuses in the province. This notwithstanding, a special session of the UN Human Rights Commission on 27 September, only the fourth of its kind in 40 years, voted to establish an enquiry into alleged atrocities in East Timor (similar decisions preceded the Yugoslav and Rwanda tribunals). The decision was contentious, with nine Asian nations, including China and India, opposing the enquiry. It began investigations in mid-November and one month later produced a report indicating evidence of serious violations.[8]

[5] UN Press Release SG/SM/7175, 13 Oct. 1999.

[6] Hume, C., 'The Secretary-General's representatives', *SAIS Review*, vol. 15, no. 2 (summer–fall 1995), pp. 75–90.

[7] ITAR-TASS (Moscow), 'Russia: FMs says 202,313 people have left Chechnya', 12 Nov. 1999, in Foreign Broadcast Information Service, *Daily Report–Central Eurasia (FBIS-SOV)*, FBIS-SOV-1999-1112, 20 Nov. 1999. See also chapter 3 in this volume.

[8] Murphy, D. and McBeth, J., 'Days of reckoning', *Far Eastern Economic Review*, vol. 162, no. 40 (7 Oct. 1999), p. 18; 'HR investigation commission starts work in East Timor', *Kompas* (Jakarta), 19 Nov. 1999, in Foreign Broadcast Information Service, *Daily Report–East Asia (FBIS-EAS)*, FBIS-EAS-1999-1119, 23 Nov. 1999; and UN, Note by the Secretary-General, Situation of human rights in East Timor, UN document A/54/660, 10 Dec. 1999.

Cooperation with regional organizations was also emphasized by the Secretary-General. In 1999 Annan attended meetings of the Organization for Security and Co-operation in Europe (OSCE), the OAU, NATO, the Western European Union (WEU) and the European Union (EU), and underscored his support for regional efforts in crisis prevention and resolution, as well as peace enforcement. His February report on the enhancement of African peacekeeping capacity focused on ways in which the UN could assist regional and sub-regional peacekeeping initiatives on that continent while at the same time cautioning against such measures being used to justify a reduction in the international community's engagement in Africa.[9] In the wake of NATO's non-UN sanctioned attack on the FRY, the Secretary-General's statements increasingly stressed the need for regional security operations to have a UN mandate if they were to have any international legal standing.[10]

The overall theme dominating the Secretary-General's statements in 1999 could be paraphrased as 'people-centric globalism'. It was particularly evident in his emphasis on humanitarian assistance, protection of civilians in armed conflict and support for humanitarian intervention. Annan argued that abuse of human rights, poverty and deprivation are the root causes of conflict and drew attention to the 'war-proneness' of societies afflicted by inequality, lack of economic development and weak infrastructures. The link between security and development necessitated greater preventive action on the part of the international community. Prevention, according to the Secretary-General, is the 'primary purpose' of the UN (under Article 1.1 of the UN Charter) and must be the focus of UN reform and orientation.[11] The need for stronger links between the security and development communities continued to be stressed as an important element in a prevention-oriented approach. In this spirit, the UNDP and the UNHCR began a series of discussions with the World Bank and a number of governments on the establishment of coordination and funding mechanisms to facilitate the transition from humanitarian to development aid.[12] The Secretary-General, meanwhile, launched a new initiative at the World Economic Forum in Davos, Switzerland, in February, calling for a global compact of universal values between the UN system and the business community.[13]

Civilian suffering in conflict through direct attack, starvation or displacement was underscored particularly during 1999—the 50th anniversary of the Geneva Conventions. In September the Secretary-General submitted a wide-ranging report to the Security Council on the protection of civilians in armed conflict. Arguing that 'the main thrust of policy must be to minimize the con-

---

[9] UN, Report of the Secretary-General, Enhancement of African peacekeeping capacity, UN document S/1999/171, 12 Feb. 1999, p. 2.

[10] UN Secretary-General address to the UN General Assembly, 20 Sep. 1999, reproduced in *Towards a Culture of Prevention: Statements by the Secretary-General of the United Nations* (Carnegie Commission on Preventing Deadly Conflict: Washington, DC, Dec. 1999).

[11] UN (note 3).

[12] 'Secretary-General's address to the World Bank', UN Press Release SG/SM/7187, 19 Oct. 1999; and Statement by the UNHCR, Sadako Ogata, to the General Assembly's Third Committee, 12 Nov. 1999, URL <http://www.unhcr.ch/refworld/unhcr/hcspeech/991112.htm>.

[13] UN Press Release SG/T/2168, 2 Feb. 1999.

sequences of violence for civilian populations', Annan called for greater consideration of the civilian impact of conflict by states.[14] The plight of children was singled out for special attention by the Secretariat. Olara Otunnu, the Secretary-General's Special Representative for Children in Armed Conflict, reported that, since 1989, 2 million children had been killed in conflict, 1 million orphaned, 6 million seriously injured and over 10 million left with severe psychological trauma. Currently 300 000 children are serving as soldiers or guerrillas or in support roles in over 30 states. A Security Council resolution passed in August recommended that governments prosecute those who recruit children to fight and proposed the incorporation of child protection and welfare measures in peace negotiations and peacekeeping operations. Efforts in 1999 to raise the legal age limit for the recruitment of national armed forces from 15 to 18 years failed, however, after opposition led by the USA.[15]

Attention was also drawn to increased attacks on humanitarian workers. In 1998 casualties among UN civilian relief workers exceeded for the first time those of military peacekeeping missions, a grim continuing trend. Since 1992, 184 UN agency civilian staff have been killed, with 292 violent incidents in 1999 alone.[16] Although the 1994 Convention on the Safety of United Nations and Associated Personnel, making it an international crime to abduct or kill a UN worker, came into force in January 1999, it is limited to workers on missions mandated by the Security Council and ratification has been slow.[17] The Secretariat called on member states to take a more energetic approach to the investigation of crimes against UN staff and to devote greater resources to the Trust Fund for the Security of Personnel of the United Nations.[18]

By way of demonstrating the UN's own responsibilities for civilian protection, the Secretary-General formally committed UN forces to observance of international humanitarian law and declared that minimizing the consequences of conflict for civilians necessitates a comprehensive approach to peacekeeping.[19] Some critical self-assessment also took place: Kofi Annan presented a report on the 1995 massacre in Srebrenica, Bosnia and Herzegovina, acknowledging that the UN bore responsibility for the Serb attack on the former UN 'safe area'. 'The cardinal lesson of Srebrenica is that a deliberate

---

[14] UN, Report of the Secretary-General to the Security Council on the protection of civilians in armed conflict, UN document S/1999/957, 8 Sep. 1999.

[15] UN Security Council Resolution 1261, 25 Aug. 1999; and United Nations Office for the Coordination of Humanitarian Affairs (OCHA), Integrated Regional Information Network (IRIN), 'Africa: New UN resolution on child soldiers', 26 Aug. 1999. News items from all the IRIN offices—Central and Eastern Africa (Nairobi, Kenya), Western Africa (Abidjan, Côte d'Ivoire) and Southern Africa (Johannesburg, South Africa)—are archived at URL <http://www.reliefweb.int/IRIN/index.phtml>.

[16] Statement by the executive director of the World Food Programme (WFP) in UN Press Release SC/6803, 9 Feb. 2000. There were 17 fatalities among UN peacekeepers in 1999. Information provided by UN–DPKO (Department of Peacekeeping Operations) Situation Centre, 24 Feb. 2000.

[17] UN General Assembly Resolution 49/59, 9 Dec. 1994. By the end of 1999, 29 states had ratified the convention. UN Press Release SC/6803, 9 Feb. 1999.

[18] 'Action to improve security of staff asked of member states, Deputy Secretary-General tells General Assembly', UN Press Release DSG/SM/71 GA/9636, 14 Oct. 1999.

[19] UN Secretary-General's Bulletin, Observance by United Nations forces of international humanitarian law, ST/SGB/1999/13, 6 Aug. 1999; and UN (note 3), para. 93, p. 11.

and systematic attempt to terrorize, expel or murder an entire people must be met decisively with all necessary means and with the political will to carry the policy through to its logical conclusion'.[20] An independent inquiry into the UN's role in Rwanda before and after the 1994 genocide of 800 000 Tutsis delivered an even more damning report in December.[21] It concluded that senior UN staff, including Annan (then head of peacekeeping) had failed to respond to advance warnings from the mission in Kigali, and Security Council members refused to authorize the expansion of the mission's mandate. The withdrawal of UN peacekeepers further facilitated massacres by the Hutu army and Interahamwe militia.[22]

The Secretary-General's robust assertion of the grounds for international intervention in humanitarian crises was based on civilian concerns. At the General Assembly in September, Annan argued that a state is an instrument of its people and that state sovereignty must therefore be understood in relation to the rights of the population concerned. He noted that nothing in the UN Charter precludes the recognition of rights beyond borders, and called for a new commitment to humanitarian action. The expansion of the concept of intervention beyond the use of military force and a broader definition of national interest were key elements in this.[23] At the same time, the Secretary-General continued to insist that this wider concept could only be achieved through collective action in the UN, the guarantor of international legitimacy. A new consensus within the organization was therefore necessary if the UN's authority and ability to act were to be maintained.

The Security Council and the General Assembly

Under the UN Charter the Security Council has primary responsibility for the maintenance of international peace and security. It is mandated to negotiate pacific settlement of disputes and take action with respect to threats or to breaches of peace and acts of aggression. The General Assembly may discuss any matter within the scope of the UN Charter but has little recommendatory power in matters of international peace and security.[24]

The greatest challenge to the authority of the Security Council in the first post-cold war decade was the decision by NATO states not to seek UN endorsement for the air strikes launched against the FRY on 24 March 1999. This circumvention was directly related to divisions among the five permanent members of the Council on the use of force to resolve the *Kosovo* crisis and

[20] Report of the Secretary-General pursuant to General Assembly Resolution 53/35 (1998), Srebrenica Report, UN document A/54/549, 15 Nov. 1999, chapter XI, para. 502.
[21] OCHA, Integrated Regional Information Network–Central and Eastern Africa (IRIN-CEA) weekly round-up, 28 Aug–3 Sep. 1999.
[22] Report of the independent inquiry into the actions of the United Nations during the 1994 genocide in Rwanda, 15 Dec. 1999, p. 17, United Nations Internet site, URL <http://www.un.org/News/ossg/rwanda_report.htm>; and McGreal, C., 'We couldn't believe the UN was going to let us die', *Guardian Weekly*, 23–29 Dec. 1999, p. 4.
[23] Annan, K., 'Two concepts of sovereignty', *The Economist*, 18 Sep. 1999, pp. 49–50.
[24] Chapter IV, Article 12 of the UN Charter prohibits the Assembly from making recommendations in any dispute of which the Security Council is seized.

the commitment of China and Russia to veto military intervention there. The fact that the elaboration of a political solution to end the war did not take place in the Security Council, but rather in the Group of Eight (G8) industrialized countries forum,[25] further undermined the Council's position as the principal actor in the management of international peace.

China demonstrated its willingness to use its UN veto power in February when it rejected the Secretary-General's request to extend the mandate of the UN's first preventive deployment operation in the Former Yugoslav Republic of Macedonia (FYROM)—the UN Preventive Deployment Force, (UNPREDEP).[26] The mission, based along the contested FRY–FYROM border since 1995, had been generally recognized to have contributed substantially to maintaining stability in the ethnically diverse state and had the support of the FYROM Government. Although China argued that the situation in the country was stabilized and that UNPREDEP's presence was no longer needed, most observers saw the decision as a response to the FYROM's official recognition of Taiwan one month earlier.[27]

These events inevitably prompted widespread discussion of the need for reform of the Security Council, in terms of both its size and composition and the continued use of the veto. African leaders again drew attention to the lack of permanent representation of developing countries, arguing that Council reform constituted one of 'the most important components in the efforts to strengthen, revitalize and democratize the United Nations'.[28] German Foreign Minster Joschka Fischer proposed that states which cast a veto in the Security Council be required to explain their reasons before the General Assembly.[29] Council reform remains a distant prospect, however, given the reluctance of the current permanent members to cede authority and the need to secure the support of at least two-thirds of the member states for any decision.

The Security Council continued to address specific conflicts in its meetings, particularly through regular updates on UN missions, most of which require mandate renewal every six months. The deterioration of the situation in Kosovo was the principal focus of attention throughout the spring. The Council was swift to condemn the massacre of 45 civilians by Serb security forces in Racak, Kosovo, in January and called for a full investigation by the International Criminal Tribunal for the Former Yugoslavia (ICTY).[30] It monitored the efforts of the Contact Group,[31] particularly the negotiations in Rambouillet, France, in February, to obtain a political settlement between the

---

[25] For the members of the G8, see the glossary in this volume.

[26] UN Press Release SC/6648, 25 Feb. 1999.

[27] Koiwai, M., 'Veto ends UN mission in Macedonia', *Peacekeeping and International Relations*, vol. 28, no. 2 (1999), p. 11.

[28] Namibian President Sam Nujoma's speech to UN General Assembly, 20 Sep. 1999; and 'South Africa: Mbeki calls for UN reform', OCHA, Integrated Regional Information Network–Southern Africa (IRIN-SA) weekly round-up 38, 18–24 Sep. 1999.

[29] UN Press Release GA/9601, 22 Sep. 1999.

[30] UN Press Release SC/6628, 19 Jan. 1999; and UN Press Release S/PRST/1999/2, 19 Jan. 1999.

[31] The Contact Group consists of France, Germany, Russia, the UK and the USA. Italy joined the group for the Kosovo conflict, although it was not a member when the informal group formed in 1994 to address the conflict in Bosnia and Herzegovina.

FRY Government and Kosovar Albanians on an autonomy arrangement for the province. The accord, largely drafted by US Ambassador Christopher Hill, provided for the re-establishment of a substantial degree of Kosovo's pre-1989 autonomy and the deployment of a NATO-led force of 28 000 to the province. An international conference was envisaged after three years to determine a mechanism for the final settlement on Kosovo.[32] Despite Western pressure on both sides, the 23 February deadline produced no agreement, the most significant obstacle being FRY opposition to the deployment of a NATO force on its territory. By the time talks resumed three weeks later and the Kosovar Albanian delegation agreed to sign the Rambouillet accord, the likelihood of NATO fulfilling its threat to carry out air strikes against the FRY appeared almost inevitable. The build-up of Serb security forces in Kosovo and the closure of the OSCE's observer mission on 20 March merely confirmed this inevitability.

Although the Council continued to express concern at the gravity of the political and humanitarian situation in Kosovo, intervention in a sovereign state remained a fundamental point of dissension. The launch of NATO air strikes on 24 March thus elicited strong reactions from Russia and China. Russia convened meetings on 24 and 26 March to discuss the action, at which NATO members defended their position by pointing to FRY violation of Security Council resolutions 1199 and 1203 and citing Chapter VII of the UN Charter.[33] A Russian-sponsored resolution identifying the NATO action as a threat to international peace and security and calling for an immediate end to the use of force garnered support only from China and Namibia. Following the bombing of its Belgrade embassy on 7 May, China requested that a Security Council meeting be convened to issue a formal protest to the NATO action. It abstained, along with Russia, from the Council's resolution to instruct the UNHCR and other relief organizations to provide assistance to refugees as well as from the 10 June resolution marking the end of the conflict and the establishment of a UN interim administration in Kosovo.[34]

Engagement in *East Timor* was less controversial given that the UN had never recognized Indonesia's seizure of the former Portuguese colony in 1975. The Council welcomed an agreement in May between Indonesia and Portugal in which the former agreed to the holding of a referendum on autonomy or independence for the province. Under the terms of the agreement the UN would be responsible for running the elections.[35] Resolution 1246 on 11 June established the UN Mission in East Timor (UNAMET) to organize and conduct the 'popular consultation' for 8 August (later delayed until 30 August). The violence that erupted after the vote, and the justifiable blame placed on UNAMET's underestimation of the threat to security in East Timor, prompted

[32] Interim Agreement for Peace and Self-Government in Kosovo, Chapter 8, Article I, 23 Feb. 1999, published in *International Peacekeeping*, Jan.–Apr. 1999, pp. 51–65.

[33] UN Press Release SC/6657, 24 Mar. 1999; UN Security Council Resolution 1199, 23 Sep. 1998; and UN Security Council Resolution 1203, 24 Oct. 1998.

[34] Statement by the President of the Security Council, UN document S/PRST/1999/12, 14 May 1999; UN Security Council Resolution 1239, 14 May 1999; and UN Security Council Resolution 1244, 10 June 1999.

[35] UN Security Council Resolution 1236, 7 May 1999.

the Security Council to quickly dispatch a delegation to solicit reluctant Indonesian consent to outside intervention.[36] On 15 September the Council passed a unanimous resolution giving a non-UN multinational peacekeeping force, INTERFET, authority under Chapter VII of the Charter to 'ease the humanitarian crisis and restore order to the province'.[37] Bypassing normal procedures for the creation of a UN operation enabled the speedy deployment of troops led by Australia.[38] A resolution one month later gave the UN Transitional Administration in East Timor (UNTAET) a mandate to succeed INTERFET, provide security and humanitarian assistance in the province, and establish an effective administration to support capacity building for self-government.[39]

Sanctions continued to be an issue of serious dissension within the Council. *Iraq* occupied the largest part of meetings for the first quarter of the year following its suspension of cooperation with the UN Special Commission on Iraq (UNSCOM) investigating and destroying Iraqi weapons of mass destruction and the subsequent launch of US and British air strikes against the country in December 1998.[40] In January the Council established three separate panels on Iraq in an effort to facilitate some agreement on the different aspects of Iraq's obligations set out in Council resolutions.[41] Discussion of an Anglo-Dutch proposal to revive UN monitoring of Iraq's heavy weapons arsenals and weapon programmes in return for the lifting of sanctions on imports failed, however, to achieve Security Council consensus.[42] Although Chinese, French and Russian abstention in December permitted the establishment of a new UN Monitoring, Verification and Inspection Commission (UNMOVIC), the Council failed to agree on who should lead the agency.[43]

Sanctions were imposed on *Afghanistan* on 15 October, following the Taleban's refusal to expel the indicted terrorist Usama bin Laden.[44] The USA, which claims that bin Laden is responsible for the 1998 bombings of its embassies in Kenya and Tanzania, had lobbied hard for Security Council support for its position. News of the decision, which freezes Afghanistan's overseas assets and restricts the national airline, prompted demonstrations against UN offices in the capital, Kabul.[45]

Despite the April suspension of embargoes against *Libya*, the Council did not formally lift the sanctions that freeze Libyan funds abroad and prohibit the sale of equipment for oil refining and transport. The USA, in particular,

---

[36] UN, Report of the Security Council mission to Jakarta and Dili, UN document S/1999/976, 14 Sep. 1999.

[37] UN Security Council Resolution 1264, 15 Sep. 1999.

[38] Previously authorized multinational operations under Chapter VII include those in Kuwait (UN Security Council Resolution, SCR, 678, 29 Nov. 1990), Rwanda (SCR 929, 22 June 1994), Haiti (SCR 940, 31 July 1994) and Albania (SCR 1101, 16 Aug. 1995).

[39] UN Security Council Resolution 1272, 25 Oct. 1999.

[40] For a detailed account of UNSCOM activities see appendix 9B in this volume.

[41] 'Diplomatic attempts begin to resuscitate Iraq–UN cooperation', *Disarmament Diplomacy*, no. 34 (Feb. 1999), pp. 44–46.

[42] Littlejohns, M., 'UN struggles to find Iraq sanctions accord', *Financial Times*, 24 Sep. 1999, p. 6.

[43] UN Security Council Resolution 1284, 17 Dec. 1999. Malaysia also abstained.

[44] UN Press Release SC/6756, 15 Nov. 1999.

[45] Burke, J., 'Afghans storm UN offices over sanctions', *Guardian Weekly*, 18–24 Nov. 1999, p. 1.

argued that Libya must demonstrate complete compliance with its UN obligations by the opening of the trial in February 2000.[46]

The Security Council continued its trend of increased thematic discussions in 1999. It held a two-day meeting on the protection of civilians in armed conflict in September in response to the Secretary-General's report on the subject, passing a resolution that condemned the deliberate targeting of civilians and underlined the violation of international law it represented. Members expressed their willingness to respond to conflict situations in which civilians are targeted or humanitarian assistance deliberately obstructed.[47] In keeping with the UN's state-centric basis, however, most of the proposals outlined, like the August resolution on children in armed conflict, call for action on the part of national governments in ratification of, implementation of and compliance with international humanitarian law. In November the Council held a two-day debate on its role in prevention of armed conflict intended to develop what the Secretary-General described as a 'culture of prevention'.[48]

In the General Assembly, the Special Committee on Peacekeeping Operations, established in 1965 and comprising member states that have contributed personnel to UN peacekeeping operations, continued its regular review processes.

New UN peace operations

In 1999 the UN initiated five new peace operations (two in East Timor, and one each in the Democratic Republic of Congo, Kosovo and Sierra Leone), two of which represented a massive expansion of an existing UN mission. The Council endorsed the Secretary-General's recommendation in February to end all but the human rights activities of the UN Observer Mission in *Angola* (MONUA) following the country's descent into war and the shooting down of two UN-chartered aircraft.[49] Concern at the country's humanitarian situation prompted the Council in October to authorize the establishment of the UN Office in Angola (UNOA) to facilitate humanitarian assistance as well as human rights and the exploration of 'effective measures for restoring peace'.[50] The Angolan Government, however, permitted the 30-member office to be set up only on the condition that its activity be restricted to humanitarian aid.[51]

The vague wording of Security Council Resolution 1244 on *Kosovo* revealed the fragility of consensus regarding the authority of the UN in the post-conflict peace operation. Although the decision authorized the deployment of an international presence, including a security presence of relevant international organizations, the UN Special Representative to Kosovo, Bernard

---

[46] UN, Statement by the President of the Security Council, UN document S/PRST/1999/22, 9 July 1999.

[47] UN Security Council Resolution 1265, 17 Sep. 1999.

[48] UN Press Release SC/6759, 29 Nov. 1999.

[49] UN Security Council Resolution 1229, 26 Feb. 1999.

[50] UN Security Council Resolution 1268, 15 Oct. 1999.

[51] 'Angola: Government stresses humanitarian role for new UN mission', IRIN-SA weekly round-up 44, 30 Oct.–5 Nov. 1999.

Kouchner, was given specific control only over the civil presence. His relationship with the NATO-led security presence (KFOR) is described as one of close coordination 'to ensure that both presences operated towards the same goals and in a mutually supportive manner'.[52] The UN Interim Administration Mission in Kosovo (UNMIK) of over 1500 personnel coordinates the rehabilitation and civil administration of the province.

Humanitarian aid was the first priority, with the UNHCR serving as the lead agency in the effort to assist over 810 000 refugees to return to the province.[53] Attacks on Kosovar Serb and Roma minorities by the Albanian majority complicated this task and put greater pressure on UNMIK, in cooperation with KFOR, to accomplish the demilitarization of the Ushtria Clirimtare e Kosoves (UCK—Kosovo Liberation Army, KLA) and the establishment of functioning police services. The murder of an UNMIK staff member on 11 October heightened the precariousness of the security situation in the province. With KFOR directing the KLA's transition to a civilian emergency force, the Kosovo Protection Corps (KPC, see section III), UNMIK focused on the deployment of international police officers to fulfil its executive policing mandate. Kouchner publicly criticized the poor international response to his request for 6000 police officers: by mid-December UNMIK police totalled a mere 1817.[54] The lack of capacity constrained UNMIK's ability to take over law-enforcement responsibilities from KFOR and forced the mission to begin recruitment of former Kosovar police officers expelled by the Federal Government in 1989–90.[55]

The Kosovo Transitional Council (KTC) was set up, under the leadership of the Special Representative, to bring representatives of all the political parties and ethnic groups together and facilitate the gradual assumption of responsibility by the population of Kosovo for the administration of the province. The withdrawal of Serb representatives (in protest at the establishment of the KPC) and subsequently of former leaders of the KLA severely undermined the KTC's status. A second body, the Kosovo–UNMIK Joint Interim Administrative Structure, was initiated in December with the support of the leading political parties to serve as the main framework for UNMIK's interaction with Kosovo's emerging political elite.[56] The process of economic rehabilitation began with UNMIK's establishment of the Deutschmark as Kosovo's currency and is the primary responsibility of the EU. UNMIK turned its attention to the development of a judiciary for the province and, in response to the views of the local judicial community, established UNMIK regulations, as well as the pre-1989 law, as the applicable law. In practice this significantly limits the use of federal law in Kosovo. Institution-building tasks, including elections, are

[52] UN Security Council Resolution 1244, 10 June 1999.
[53] Of the 810 000 estimated to have returned, only 110 000 did so in an organized manner. UN, Report of the Secretary-General on the United Nations Interim Administration Mission in Kosovo, UN document S/1999/1250, 23 Dec. 1999.
[54] 'Désillusion au Kosovo, cinq mois après la fin de la guerre' [Disillusion in Kosovo, five months after the end of the war], Le Monde, 2 Nov. 1999, p. 2.
[55] UN (note 53).
[56] The KTC will remain, in an enlarged capacity, as a consultative forum.

being coordinated with the OSCE. By the end of 1999 UNMIK had established comprehensive authority in all aspects of Kosovar society with an annual budget of over $427 million.[57] The significance of its elaboration of a civil administration for the future status of Kosovo remains to be negotiated.

The UN expressed its support for efforts by the Economic Community of West African States (ECOWAS) to negotiate a peace agreement between the Government of *Sierra Leone* and the Revolutionary United Front (RUF) rebel movement.[58] A ceasefire agreement in May paved the way for peace negotiations between the two sides in the Togolese capital, Lomé, and culminated in the Lomé Peace Agreement on 7 July.[59] It provided for the disarmament and demobilization of the RUF and its entry into a power-sharing government of national unity. The amnesty for war crimes committed by both sides provided in the agreement was roundly criticized by many human rights organizations, and the Secretary-General's Special Representative, Francis Okelo, added a disclaimer when he signed the treaty on behalf of the UN.[60] In October the Security Council agreed to the establishment of the United Nations Mission in Sierra Leone (UNAMSIL) as set out in the Lomé Peace Agreement.[61] The force of up to 6000 military personnel, replacing the observer mission, UNOMSIL, is intended to facilitate implementation of the peace, concentrating on the disarmament, demobilization and reintegration aspects of the peace process. An advance party of military observers was forced to confront challenges to UN authority in November as fighting continued between rebel groups, while the first deployment of UNAMSIL troops later that month confronted very poor responses to the disarmament, demobilization and reintegration programme established in October.[62] The civilian component of UNAMSIL, meanwhile, began work with the UNHCHR on the establishment of Truth and Reconciliation and Human Rights commissions in Sierra Leone.

A similar commitment to deploy a peacekeeping force to support the peace process was undertaken in the *Democratic Republic of Congo*, this time in collaboration with the OAU.[63] The UN, like the OAU, is a full participant in the two bodies established by the Lusaka Ceasefire Agreement in July to supervise the country's political rehabilitation and demilitarization, the Political Committee and the Joint Military Commission (JMC).[64] The first stage of the projected UN Observer Mission in the Democratic Republic of Congo (MONUC) was the deployment in August of up to 90 military liaison personnel to under-

[57] Sum approved by the General Assembly's Fifth Committee, UN Press Release GA/AB/3353, 15 Dec. 1999.

[58] UN Security Council Resolution 1231, 11 Mar. 1999.

[59] 'Peace agreement between the Government of Sierra Leone and the Revolutionary United Front for Sierra Leone', 7 July 1999, available at URL <http://www.sierra-leone.org/documents.html>.

[60] Lewis, P., 'Sierra Leone's amnesty plan assailed', *International Herald Tribune*, 27 July 1999, p. 4.

[61] UN Security Council Resolution 1270, 22 Oct. 1999.

[62] 'UN warns warring Sierra Leone rebels', BBC News Online, 3 Nov. 1999, URL <http://news.bbc. co.uk/hi/english/world/africa/newsid_503000/503725.stm>; and UN, First report on the United Nations mission in Sierra Leone (UNAMSIL), UN document S/1999/1223, 6 Dec. 1999.

[63] UN, Report of the Secretary-General on the United Nations preliminary deployment in the Democratic Republic of the Congo, UN document S/1999/790, 15 July 1999.

[64] See chapter 1 and appendix 1B in this volume.

take technical surveys and evaluations in preparation for the force authorized by the Security Council on 30 November.[65] The deployment of up to 500 military observers, the eventual participation of formed units to protect them and the participation of civilian staff covering humanitarian, human rights and child protection issues in the UN operation are envisaged.[66]

The slow pace prompted the Political Committee to express its concern in October, noting that similar situations in other regions 'normally receive more prompt and appropriate response'.[67] For its part, the UN criticized the DRC Government for continuing to impose conditions and restrictions on the written security guarantees demanded from all parties to the peace agreement.[68] UN personnel would not be deployed outside the capital, Kinshasa, until satisfactory guarantees had been received. Although the UN finally accepted the government's conditional guarantees at the start of November, sporadic fighting between rebel groups further hampered the work of the preliminary UN presence.[69] The Secretary-General, meanwhile, warned that MONUC could be a large, expensive and difficult operation, realization of which contributed to the Security Council's approval of a phased approach to MONUC's elaboration.[70]

Although the mandate of UNAMET, the first UN mission in *East Timor*, permitted the deployment of up to 280 (unarmed) civilian police officers and 50 military liaison officers in an advisory capacity, responsibility for the maintenance of security and order during the August referendum lay with the Indonesian armed forces. The UN's acquiescence to this demand, and its subsequent failure to take action to force Indonesia to curb anti-independence militia, became the subject of severe criticism when violence erupted after the results of the vote were announced (78.5 per cent of the 99 per cent registered voter turnout voted for independence).[71] The timing of the UNAMET operation so soon after the war in Kosovo and the perceived need to maintain a cooperative relationship with the Indonesian Government undoubtedly influenced the UN's slowness to react. The capacity of the UN to deploy armed peacekeepers in a short space of time was another inhibiting factor. The tragic outcome saw a population rewarded for their response to the UN call to vote with savage violence. It was this sense of responsibility that led a number of UNAMET staff to refuse to leave the mission's headquarters without the

---

[65] UN Security Council Resolution 1258, 6 Aug 1999; and UN Security Council Resolution 1279, 3 Nov. 1999. By the end of the year there were 76 liaison officers in the field.

[66] UN, Second report of the Secretary-General on the United Nations preliminary deployment in the Democratic Republic of Congo, UN document S/1999/1116, 1 Nov. 1999.

[67] Quoted in the Secretary-General's second report (note 66).

[68] 'DR Congo: UN observers denied access to Katanga, Kasai', Radio France Internationale (Paris), 28 Oct. 1999, in Foreign Broadcast Information Service, *Daily Report–Sub-Saharan Africa (FBIS-AFR)*, FBIS-AFR-1999-1029, 20 Nov. 1999.

[69] 'DRC: UN accepts conditional DRC security guarantees', IRIN-CEA weekly round-up 44, 30 Oct.–5 Nov. 1999; and 'DRC: Rebel RCD claims Kabila troops attacking positions', AFP (Paris), 12 Nov. 1999, in FBIS-AFR-1999-1112, 20 Nov. 1999.

[70] UN Security Council Resolution 1279, 30 Nov. 1999.

[71] Mufson, S. and Lynch, C., 'East Timor failure puts UN in dock', *Guardian Weekly*, 30 Sep.–6 Oct. 1999, p. 31.

1000 or so refugees sheltering in the compound.[72] The evacuation of all but 12 personnel finally took place on 14 September and staff did not return until two weeks later, to assist in the delivery of humanitarian assistance, refugee return and preparation for UNTAET.[73] UNTAET, mandated to replace the Australian-led INTERFET force, contained a substantial security component of up to 8950 troops, 200 military observers and 1640 civilian police.[74] The first military observers were deployed in November to liaise with INTERFET before the scheduled transition in February 2000.[75]

The presidential elections in September marked the culmination of the peace process facilitated by the UN Mission in the *Central African Republic* (MINURCA). In October the Security Council extended the mission's mandate a further three months to enable its gradual withdrawal and the establishment of a UN peace-building office in the country.[76] The transfer of the mission's functions to local security and police forces was the principal task in this, and so MINURCA stepped up its police training efforts.[77]

The UN's third peace-building office was established in *Guinea-Bissau* (UN Peace-Building Support Office, UNOGBIS) in March to support the peace accord of November 1998 and the establishment of a Government of National Unity on 20 February.[78] The principal purpose of the office was to provide a framework for coordinating UN activities in the country and facilitate stability in the lead-up to the November national elections.[79] The UN presence also signalled support for the peacekeeping role of the ECOWAS Monitoring Group (ECOMOG).[80] It became even more significant after the ousting of the country's president on 7 May and the subsequent withdrawal of ECOMOG forces.[81] The UN remained there after assurances by the coup leaders that elections would go ahead as scheduled. In September it responded to the transitional government's request for international military observers to monitor borders with Guinea and Senegal by dispatching a team to examine the situation. Despite the latter's recommendation that 200 military observers be deployed, the Secretary-General decided not to expand the UN's activities beyond UNOGBIS.[82] Following the successful holding of elections in November

[72] 'Militia invade UN compound', BBC News Online, 10 Sep. 1999, URL <http://news.bbc.co.uk/hi/english/world/asia-pacfic/newsid_443000/443456.stm>.

[73] UN Press Briefing by the Secretary-General's Special Representative for East Timor, 28 Sep. 1999.

[74] UN Security Council Resolution 1272, 25 Oct. 1999.

[75] UN Press Release SC/6776, 22 Dec. 1999.

[76] UN Press Release SG/SM/7190, 22 Oct. 1999.

[77] UN Security Council Resolution 1271, 22 Oct. 1999; and IRIN news briefs, 12 Oct. 1999.

[78] UN, Report of the Secretary-General pursuant to Security Council Resolution 1216 (1998) relative to the situation in Guinea-Bissau, UN document S/1999/294, 17 Mar. 1999. Peace-building offices, which are not under Chapters VI and VII of the UN Charter, already exist in Liberia and Bougainville.

[79] UN Security Council Resolution 1233, 6 Apr. 1999.

[80] UN Press Release SC/6663, 6 Apr. 1999.

[81] UN, Report of the Secretary-General submitted pursuant to Security Council Resolution 1233 (1999) relative to the situation in Guinea-Bissau, UN document S/1999/741, 1 July 1999.

[82] UN, Letter dated 13 October to Security Council, UN document S/1999/1091, 26 Oct. 1999.

1999, the UNOGBIS mandate was extended into 2000 to facilitate stability during negotiations for the formation of a new government.[83]

International legal mechanisms

The International Court of Justice (ICJ) is the judicial organ of the United Nations, seated at The Hague. Its 15 judges, elected by the General Assembly and the Security Council, hear cases brought by UN signatory states in accordance with international law. To the extent that it facilitates the negotiated settlement of disputes, the ICJ can be seen as a useful preventive tool.

The caseload in 1999 reflected the increased attention paid by states to asserting the legality of their position in cases of conflict. As the Eritrean–Ethiopian conflict escalated, Eritrea filed proceedings against Ethiopia over alleged violation of its diplomatic mission's premises and staff in Addis Ababa.[84] On 29 April the FRY instituted separate proceedings against 10 states, claiming that in launching a NATO attack on FRY territory they had violated the obligation not to use force against another state. The FRY also requested the court, in the interim, to order the 10 states to immediately cease their actions.[85] The court rejected the request by 12 votes to 3 on 2 June.[86]

The DRC brought cases against Burundi, Rwanda and Uganda for violation of its sovereignty and acts of armed aggression in breach of the UN and OAU charters in June. Croatia's July claim against the FRY was more retroactive, based on alleged violations during 1991–95 of the 1948 Convention on the Prevention and Punishment of the Crime of Genocide. Croatia maintains that the FRY has an obligation to pay reparations for damages to persons and property during that period.[87] Pakistan instituted proceedings against India on 21 September concerning the shooting down of a Pakistani aircraft by the Indian Air Force on 10 August 1999.[88]

The *International Criminal Tribunal for the Former Yugoslavia*, established by the Security Council in May 1993, continued its groundbreaking work in investigating gross violations of international law on human rights by individuals in the former Yugoslavia. Fourteen judges under the overall supervision of a prosecutor (who also serves in the same capacity on the Tribunal for Rwanda) heard cases in three trial chambers in The Hague. In August, the Security Council accepted the Secretary-General's nomination of former Swiss Attorney General Carla del Ponte to replace the first prosecutor, Canadian Louise Arbour.[89]

---

[83] UN, Report of the Secretary-General on Developments in Guinea-Bissau and on the activities of the United Nations Peace-Building Support Office in that country, UN document S/1999/1276, 23 Dec. 1999.

[84] ICJ Press Communiqué 99/4, 16 Feb. 1999.

[85] The states were Belgium, Canada, France, Germany, Italy, the Netherlands, Portugal, Spain, the UK and the USA. ICJ Press Communiqué 99/17, 29 Apr. 1999.

[86] ICJ Press Release ICJ/582, 3 June 1999.

[87] ICJ Press Communiqué 99/41, 16 Sep. 1999.

[88] ICJ Press Release ICJ/589, 22 Sep. 1999.

[89] UN Security Council Resolution 1259, 11 Aug. 1999.

The ICTY continued to pursue the strategy initiated in 1997 of indicting only high-level offenders and avoiding making new indictments public.[90] This led to the capture of a number of prominent figures in the Republika Srpska, including General Momir Talic, Chief of Staff of the Bosnian Serb Army, while he was in Vienna for a conference sponsored in part by the OSCE on 25 August. His arrest marked the first time a war crimes suspect was arrested outside the territory of the former Yugoslavia and signalled the increased willingness of national judiciaries to actively assist the ICTY in its work.[91] Only a small number of states, however, have expressed willingness to enforce the prison sentences of the tribunal by incarcerating those convicted.[92]

There are now 36 Bosnian Serbs awaiting trial, with nine so far convicted of war crimes. No conviction for genocide has yet been registered.[93] Apart from the conduct of trials, the tribunal continued its field investigations into mass grave sites, collecting documents and interviewing witnesses in Bosnia and Herzegovina. It issued a formal complaint against Croatia in August for its refusal to cooperate with investigations.[94]

A significant step was taken on 27 May when an indictment was issued for President Slobodan Milosevic and four other senior FRY officials for crimes against humanity and violations of the laws of war. This set a legal precedent: it was the first time a head of state was charged with gross violation of international humanitarian law during armed conflict. Although the failure to indict Milosevic for war crimes during the Bosnian conflict had been severely criticized in the past, the timing of this indictment led some to attack the ICTY as a tool of the NATO states.[95] The new prosecutor asserted that the investigation and prosecution of the five FRY leaders would be the primary focus of her office and that evidence from Kosovo for the relevant time period would be used in the prosecution.[96]

Belgrade's policy of non-compliance with the tribunal hindered the investigation of violations in Kosovo well before the launch of NATO attacks. Although three Security Council resolutions in 1998 supported the prosecutor's position that the tribunal's jurisdiction covers crimes committed in Kosovo, the ICTY attempt to investigate the Racak massacre was hampered by the FRY refusal to allow Prosecutor Arbour into the country. The resolution ending the Kosovo conflict, calling for full cooperation by all parties, including the international security presence, in the pursuit and apprehension of indicted war criminals, demonstrated UN determination to sustain the

---

[90] Murphy, S. D., 'Progress and jurisprudence of the International Criminal Tribunal for the Former Yugoslavia', *American Journal of International Law*, vol. 93, no. 43 (1999), p. 59.

[91] Trueheart, C., 'Bosnian Serb General is arrested in Vienna', *International Herald Tribune*, 26 Aug. 1999, p. 1. Germany previously initiated 2 war crime prosecutions within its national judicial system.

[92] The states were Austria, Finland, Italy, Norway and Sweden. The UN has no permanent jail facilities.

[93] ICTY, Fact Sheet on ICTY Proceedings, 28 Dec. 1999, URL <http://www.un.org/icty/glance/fact.htm>.

[94] ICTY Press Release CC/P.I.S./433-E, 25 Aug. 1999.

[95] Murphy (note 90), p. 95.

[96] ICTY Press Release PR/PIS/437-E, 29 Sep. 1999.

tribunal's proactive approach.[97] ICTY ground investigations in Kosovo began rapidly with a number of Western states pledged to provide experts to assist the process.[98] The relative speed and efficiency of the tribunal in Kosovo were at least partly explained by the desire of NATO states to prove that the scale of atrocities justified extensive air strikes against Serb forces. Awareness that the process could serve as a model for future International Criminal Court investigations was also an important motivating factor.[99]

The *International Criminal Tribunal for Rwanda* (ICTR), established in 1994 and based in Arusha, Tanzania, also attempted to accelerate progress by grouping several indicted individuals in a single trial for conspiracy to commit genocide.[100] Although hampered by lack of resources and the legacy of previous mismanagement, it has had more success than its Yugoslav counterpart in bringing to trial individuals who were in charge of the country at the time of the genocide.[101] The willingness of states to arrest indicted criminals on their territory and to assist witnesses to travel to and from the court has played a part in this.[102] A number of states have also agreed to incarcerate persons convicted by the tribunal.[103] The fact that indictees are no longer in government is perhaps the most important reason for this cooperation. A memorandum of understanding between the UN and Rwanda signed in June was followed by the latter's appointment of a special representative to the tribunal.[104] However, Rwanda's fury at the court's release on procedural grounds of a former government official accused of genocide, Jean-Bosco Barayagwiza, provoked it to suspend cooperation with the tribunal in November and prompted efforts to launch a review of the decision.[105]

A third trial chamber began work in February, with a total of nine judges serving on the tribunal.[106] In June Judge Navanthem Pillay of South Africa was elected as the tribunal's president, replacing Laity Kama of Senegal. At the end of 1999 there were 39 detainees in the tribunal's detention facility in Arusha. Six judgements have so far been delivered to seven people, including three convictions of genocide and crimes against humanity.[107]

The statute agreeing the establishment of the *International Criminal Court* (ICC) was adopted by 120 states at the Rome Conference in July 1998.[108] The

---

[97] UN Security Council Resolution 1244, 10 June 1999.

[98] ICTY Press Release CC/P.I.S.424-E, 20 July 1999.

[99] A point made by Mirko Klarin in Institute for War and Peace Reporting (IWPR) Tribunal Update 145, 27 Sep.–2 Oct. 1999.

[100] 'Group trials', *The Economist*, vol. 352, no. 8132 (14 Aug. 1999), p. 36.

[101] Okali, A. U., 'Blazing a trail', *UN Chronicle*, vol. 36, no. 2 (1999), p. 59.

[102] UN, 'President of UN war crimes tribunal for Rwanda urges ratification of treaty on International Criminal Court', *Daily Highlights* (UN Department of Public Information), 14 Sep. 1999, URL <http://www.un.org/news/dh>.

[103] Mali and Benin signed agreements on cooperation with the tribunal in 1999; Belgium, Denmark, Norway and some other African countries have also indicated willingness to assist in this regard. ICTR Fact Sheet no. 6, Jan. 1999.

[104] ICTR Press Release ICTR/INFO-9-2-206.EN, 13 Oct. 1999.

[105] 'Advantage, Kigali', *Africa Confidential*, vol. 40, no. 25 (17 Dec. 1999), pp. 6–7; and ICTR Press Release ICTR/INFO-9-2-215.EN, 2 Dec. 1999.

[106] UN Security Council Resolution 1165, 24 Feb. 1999.

[107] Information provided by Tom Kennedy, UN Press Office, New York, Feb. 2000.

[108] Rome Statute of the International Criminal Court, UN document A/CONF.183/9, 17 July 1998.

court will be responsible for ruling on crimes against humanity, war crimes and acts of genocide wherever they are committed. Its mandate, however, is restricted to nationals of states that have accepted its jurisdiction or persons whose acts were committed in a signatory state. It will assume jurisdiction over national systems only after it determines that they are unwilling or unable to prosecute. In order for the ICC to be established, 60 ratifications are required. By the end of 1999 only six had been obtained.[109] A Preparatory Commission held three sessions in 1999 to work on rules of procedure and evidence and on elements of crimes. The definition of a 'crime of aggression' has been a dominant concern of the commission, which is due to conclude by 30 June 2000.[110]

Peacekeeping reform and finance

Institutional reforms

The structure of the Department of Peacekeeping Operations was revised in 1999, resulting in the consolidation of all military expertise in a new Military and Civilian Police Division and the integration of the Policy Analysis and Lessons Learned units under the direct authority of the Under Secretary-General. Gratis personnel seconded from national governments were phased out over the course of the year, leading to calls for additional staff, particularly with expertise in civil administrative affairs.[111] The continued emphasis on downsizing and reform hampered the Secretary-General's efforts to establish the Rapidly Deployable Mission Headquarters, intended to enable newly mandated peacekeeping operations to start up quickly.[112] Standby arrangements for UN peacekeeping did make some progress by December 1999: 87 countries had expressed willingness to participate in the mechanism. However, only 32 of these countries had signed the memorandum of understanding with the UN that can be used by national authorities to expedite approval for deployment of personnel, equipment and services in a UN operation, and the provision of detailed planning data continues to be slow. From data received so far 147 500 personnel could be made available to the UN at short notice.[113] The two mission 'start-up kits' held at the UN Logistics Base at Brindisi, Italy,

---

[109] ICC, Ratification status, 27 Dec. 1999, URL <http://www.un.org/law/icc/index.him>. The USA did not sign the statute.

[110] UN Press Release L/2933, 13 Aug. 1999.

[111] UN, Report of the Secretary-General on the support account for peacekeeping operations, UN document A/54/648, 3 Dec. 1999. Pakistan had insisted on an end to the use of gratis personnel, claiming they disrupted the geographical balance of the department.

[112] UN, Progress report of the Secretary-General on standby arrangements for peacekeeping, UN document S/1999/361, 20 Mar. 1999, p. 3; and UN, Support account for peacekeeping operations, Report of the Advisory Committee on Administrative and Budgetary Questions, UN document A/53/901, 6 Apr. 1999, pp. 2–3.

[113] UN Department of Peacekeeping Operations, UN Standby Arrangements Status Report as of 1 December 1999, URL <http://www.un.org/Depts/dpko/rapid/str.htm>.

demonstrated their value in facilitating rapid deployment of new missions in 1999, but by the end of the year replenishment was urgently needed.[114]

Sufficient peacekeeping training is a precondition for a swift response to crises. The UN Training Unit continued to hold exercises in the field and undertook pre-deployment training for UNAMSIL and UNTAET. Cooperation with regional organizations, particularly African, was emphasized in 1999 and the UN provided training personnel and support to the OAU as well as seminars with SADC and ECOWAS, and specific workshops and 'train-the-trainer' activities. These efforts complement initiatives by Western states to improve African and Asian participatory capacities. The US Enhanced International Peacekeeping Capabilities Program (EIPCP) provided funding to Bangladesh for the construction of a regional peacekeeping training centre as well as to Nepal for a regional peacekeeping exercise.[115] The US African Crisis Response Initiative (ACRI) provided $8.1 million in grants to 39 African states for military education and training while a parallel French programme, Renforcement des Capacités Africaines de Maintien de la Paix (RECAMP, Reinforcement of Capabilities of African Missions of Peacekeeping), operates training projects through subregional organizations such as the SADC and ECOWAS. A French-sponsored peacekeeping school in the Côte d'Ivoire was opened in July.[116]

The growing role of civilian police in UN operations led to calls for greater attention to be paid to the selection, training and operating procedures for civilian police activities.[117] The Civilian Police Unit was expanded during the year and has begun preparation of standardized operating procedures for police in peace operations. The division of labour between military and police, particularly in operations that provide for an executive policing role, continues to be the subject of discussion in the UN.[118]

Finance

The rise in UN peacekeeping operations in 1999 meant that budget estimates were revised from $650 million to over $2 billion for fiscal year July 1999–June 2000.[119] The peacekeeping budget is supplemented by Inter-Agency Consolidated Appeals and trust funds for specific countries. The disparities of donations that can result from this were a cause of concern for the UN, which

---

[114] UN, Implementation of the recommendations of the Special Committee on Peacekeeping Operations, Report of the Secretary-General, UN document A/54/670, 6 Jan. 2000.

[115] Karniol, R., 'Bangladesh and Nepal to support peacekeeping bid', *Jane's Defence Weekly*, vol. 31, no. 10 (10 Mar. 1999), p. 34.

[116] Deen, T., 'Africa progressing with plan for regional force of peacekeepers', *Jane's Defence Weekly*, vol. 31, no. 14 (7 Apr. 1999), p. 8; and Fisher-Thompson, J., 'French General details renewed commitment to Africa', United States Information Service (USIS), *Washington File*, 3 June 1999, United States European Command, URL <http://www.eucom.mil/programs/acri/>.

[117] UN, Financing of the United Nations peacekeeping operations, Report of the Advisory Committee on Administrative and Budgetary Questions, UN document A/53/895, 1 Apr. 1999, p. 4; and UN, Report of the Special Committee on Peacekeeping Operations, UN document A/54/87, 23 June 1999.

[118] UN document A/54/670 (note 114).

[119] UN document A/54/648 (note 111).

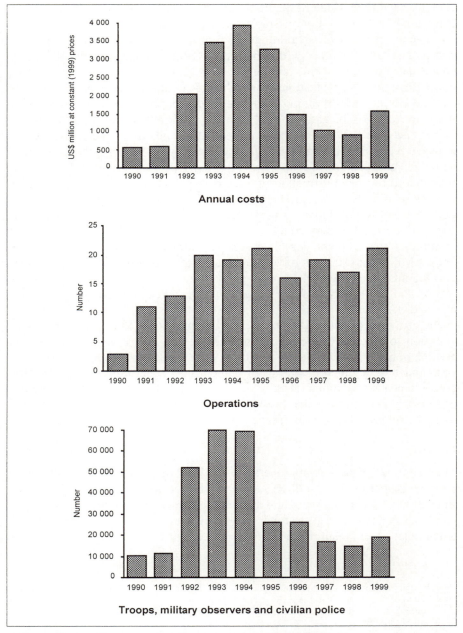

Figure 2.1. Statistics on UN peacekeeping operations in 1990–99

Source: Based on information from the UN Department of Peacekeeping Operations, New York, 1999. Cost figures are approximate and based on annualized costs of UN operations.

expressed concern in the summer that the focus on Kosovo would divert aid from crisis situations elsewhere. Contributions to UN relief programmes for the region were estimated to be around 50 per cent greater than for other regions.[120]

The ongoing battle between the US Administration and Congress over the payment of nearly $1 billion of UN arrears took on greater urgency in 1999 given that the USA faced the threat of automatic loss of its General Assembly vote at the end of the year. Republicans in the Congress continued to demand that payment be linked to the restriction of US assistance to international family planning programmes, despite appeals by the administration that the latter was not a national security matter and should not be treated as such.[121] A compromise was reached in November, when the White House accepted the inclusion of language linking dues payments to the introduction of restrictions on abortion advocacy. The new legislation authorizes payment of $926 million during 1999–2002.[122] The first payment of $51.2 million arrived on 31 December 1999.[123]

III. Regional organizations

Chapter VIII of the UN Charter provides for the contribution of regional organizations to the maintenance of international peace and security under UN primacy and/or utilization.[124] The assumption of greater preventive, peace-keeping and peace-enforcing tasks by regional organizations, with or without official Security Council approval, was one of the most significant trends of the first post-cold war decade. 1999 marked a new climax for region-led peace operations both in number and in intensity. It was, arguably, also the nadir, as the weaknesses and limitations of regional peacekeeping were increasingly revealed.

Europe

The Organization for Security and Co-operation in Europe

The OSCE stresses its role as a primary instrument for early warning, conflict prevention, conflict management and post-conflict rehabilitation.[125] OSCE mission and field activities in Central and Eastern Europe, South-Eastern Europe, the Caucasus and Central Asia concentrate on institution and democracy building as well as human rights. The Secretariat's Conflict Prevention Centre (CPC) is intended to serve as the focal point for OSCE prevention and peace-building activities, supplemented by the Office for Democratic Institutions and Human Rights (ODIHR), the High Commissioner on National

---

[120] Associated Press (AP), 'UN pleads for more crisis aid', *New York Times* (Internet edn), 22 July 1999, URL <http://www.nytimes.com/apongline/i/AP-UN-Appeals.html>.

[121] Dewar, H., 'Dispute threatens U.S. vote at UN', *Guardian Weekly*, 4–10 Nov. 1999, p. 31.

[122] Pianin, E. and Harris, J., 'Deal on U.S. dues to UN is reached', *International Herald Tribune*, 16 Nov. 1999, p. 1; and 'Don't ask for more Mr Annan', *The Economist*, 20 Nov. 1999, p. 57.

[123] 'In brief', *Guardian Weekly*, 6–12 Jan. 2000, p. 2.

[124] UN Charter, Chapter VIII, Article 53 (1).

[125] OSCE Secretary General, *Annual Report 1999 on OSCE Activities (1 December 1998–31 October 1999)*, SEC.DOC/2/99, Vienna, 17 Nov. 1999, Introduction.

Minorities and the Representative on Freedom of the Media. The OSCE's role in Kosovo, first through the Kosovo Verification Mission and subsequently through the OSCE Mission in Kosovo (OSCE MIK), expanded the organization's activities into a number of new domains in 1999, notably police, judicial and administrative personnel training.[126] Institutional changes reflect the broadening agenda: an ad hoc Coordination and Planning Group was set up in the Secretariat to facilitate preparations for the establishment of new missions at short notice. A 24-hour 'situation room' was also established to improve communication between the Secretariat and OSCE missions.

There was also increased emphasis on the need for mission personnel training in 1999. This was taken further at the OSCE Summit Meeting in Istanbul in November with the US-led proposal for the establishment of an international team of experts—Rapid Expert Assistance and Cooperation Teams (REACT)—permanently on call. REACT is intended to provide the OSCE with the capability to mobilize police, judicial and relevant civilian personnel for conflict prevention, crisis management and post-conflict rehabilitation tasks. Although the concept was included in the OSCE Charter for European Security[127] and a CPC Task Force was set up to develop a plan for REACT's implementation by June 2000, many questions, such as potential duplication with EU activities, remain to be settled.[128]

The OSCE continued to serve as the principal framework for peace negotiations in Moldova and Nagorno-Karabakh, as well as the principal international actor in the Georgian–Ossetian conflict. In July, the post-conflict rehabilitation programme initiated in June by the EU, the Stability Pact for South Eastern Europe, was placed under OSCE auspices. There was some progress in the *Nagorno-Karabakh* conflict under the OSCE Minsk Group[129] and its co-chairs France, Russia and the USA. A new mood of moderation among the presidents of Armenia and Azerbaijan, Robert Kocharian and Heidar Aliyev, respectively, led to four rounds of unmediated talks between them in the second half of 1999.[130] The number of skirmishes along the border between the two states, meanwhile, was reported to have fallen.[131] Progress was facilitated by active US mediation, including visits by the deputy secretary of state to both countries, which in turn led to the resumption of shuttle diplomacy by OSCE negotiators in the region. The substance of the meetings remains highly secret, but it is widely believed to centre on the proposal of the OSCE peace plan that Azerbaijan and Nagorno-Karabakh form a common state and whether repre-

---

[126] OSCE (note 125).
[127] For details of the Charter for European Security, signed at Istanbul on 19 Nov. 1999, see chapter 4 in this volume. Excerpts of the text are reproduced in appendix 4A.
[128] OSCE Permanent Council, 261st Plenary Meeting, Decision no. 326, PC.DEC/326, 9 Dec. 1999; and Smith, J., 'OSCE to adopt new civilian response capability at summit', *BASIC Reports*, no. 72 (15 Nov. 1999).
[129] For a list of Minsk Group member states in 1999 see the glossary in this volume.
[130] Radio Free Europe/Radio Liberty (RFE/RL), *RFE/RL Caucasus Report*, vol. 2, no. 34 (26 Aug. 1999), and no. 45 (11 Nov. 1999).
[131] 'Armenian president views Karabakh accord', Snark (Yerevan), 18 Oct. 1999, in FBIS-SOV-1999-1018, 18 Oct. 1999.

sentatives of the latter should be represented at the peace talks. In September Russia and the USA separately signalled support for Karabakh participation.[132]

Domestic difficulties in the two Caucasian states, however, blocked any breakthrough. Azerbaijani opposition parties organized public protests against President Aliyev's alleged softening on a political status for the Armenian enclave and in October the Azerbaijani peace process negotiator, Vafa Guluzade, announced his resignation, followed by that of Foreign Minister Tofiq Zulfugarov.[133] In the same month Armenia was rocked by a terrorist attack on the parliament and the shooting of the prime minister, the speaker of the parliament and four other legislators. It took the personal negotiation of President Kocharian to bring an end to the siege, which the gunmen claimed was in protest against the government's failure to improve the country's economic situation. Although commentators did not view the political turmoil in either republic as directly linked to the Karabakh conflict, it constrained both leaders' freedom of manoeuvre and halted further substantive negotiations on a peace deal.[134] The OSCE Istanbul Summit Declaration mentioned the dispute but, unlike the 1996 Lisbon Summit Declaration, did not contain any reference to Azerbaijan's territorial integrity.[135]

The OSCE continued to mediate, along with Russia and Ukraine, in the conflict between the breakaway region of *Trans-Dniester* and Moldova, and the OSCE mission there continued its efforts to find an acceptable special status for Trans-Dniester within Moldova. The OSCE convinced Russia to withdraw the former 14th Army from the region by 2002.[136] In return it agreed to consider the creation of a voluntary international fund to assist the weapon withdrawal and destruction process.[137]

Some progress was also made in one of Georgia's two secessionist conflicts—the OSCE assisted with the resumption of meetings between the principal parties to the conflict in *South Ossetia* after a break of 18 months.[138] No proposals for the political status of the region have yet reached the negotiating table, however.

Russia's support for OSCE engagement in conflicts on the territory of the Commonwealth of Independent States (CIS) did not extend to its own breakaway republic of *Chechnya*. A delegation of OSCE observers cut short its visit to the region after being prevented from entering Chechnya on 11 November.[139] The Norwegian Chairman-in-Office made a return trip on

---

[132] Giragosian, R., *Transcaucasus Chronology*, vol. 8, no. 10 (Oct 1999), URL <http://www.soros.org/caucasus/0075.html>.

[133] *Transcaucasus Chronology*, vol. 8, no. 11 (Nov. 1999).

[134] Williams, S., *IWPR Caucasus Report*, no. 6 (12 Nov. 1999); and Fuller, L., *RFE/RL Caucasus Report*, vol. 2, no. 45 (11 Nov. 1999).

[135] OSCE, Istanbul Summit Declaration, SUM.DOC/2/99, Istanbul, 19 Nov. 1999, para. 20, URL <http://www.osce.org/e/docs/summits/istadec/99e.htm>.

[136] Russian peacekeeping forces in Moldova and South Ossetia operate under bilateral and not CIS agreement. Joint Control Commissions, made up of the parties to the conflict and Russia, provide the principal security frameworks within each.

[137] 'Russia to withdraw army property from Transdnestria', Interfax (Moscow), 24 July 1999, in FBIS-SOV-1999-0724, 24 July 1999; and OSCE (note 135), para. 19. See chapter 10 in this volume.

[138] OSCE (note 125), chapter II, section 1.1.13.

[139] Jack, A., 'OSCE kept from Chechen refugees', *Financial Times*, 12 Nov. 1999, p. 4.

14–15 December, and on the request of the Georgian Government the OSCE agreed to expand the mandate of its mission in Georgia to include monitoring of the Georgian–Chechen border. Up to 20 additional unarmed personnel were to be deployed in early 2000.[140]

The North Atlantic Treaty Organization

NATO's 11-week attack on the *Federal Republic of Yugoslavia* made its post-cold war identity—as humanitarian defender, peace-enforcer or aggressive warmonger—the subject of bitter international controversy during its 50th anniversary year. Many sympathetic to the operation expressed reservations at NATO's failure to solicit UN Security Council authorization and, even after the end of the former Yugoslavia's latest war, the relationship between the UN and NATO remains ambiguous.

NATO provided back-up to the OSCE Kosovo Verification Mission during the first three months of 1999 in the form of verification flights (Operation Eagle Eye) and the NATO Extraction Force based in FYROM. Both operations terminated with the halt of the OSCE mission in March, although the Extraction Force subsequently formed the basis for the establishment of KFOR in June.[141] The NATO-led international force, made up of troops from 28 countries, had almost reached its full strength of 50 000 troops (49 412) by the end of September.[142] The effect of such a large force on the NATO operation in Bosnia and Herzegovina was apparent by October when the North Atlantic Council agreed to reduce the Stabilization Force (SFOR) by over one-third, from 32 000 to 20 000, in six months.[143] NATO Secretary General Javier Solana argued that SFOR was carrying out its stabilization tasks successfully and that what Bosnia now most needed was civil policing rather than an extensive military presence.[144] The NATO force deployed to Albania (A-For) to assist with the Kosovar refugee influx during the war was replaced in September by an Italian-led contingent of 2400.[145] Further efforts to rationalize the NATO Balkan presence included measures for shared resources and cross-border tasking between the two operations.

KFOR's establishment began dramatically with the seizure on 12 June of Pristina airport by 583 Russian troops stationed in Bosnia and Herzegovina.[146] Despite on-site discussions led by British commander General Michael Jackson, the stand-off was not resolved until 9 July, when Russia agreed to deploy over 3500 troops in four of the five multinational divisional sectors

[140] OSCE Permanent Council Decision no. 334, PC.Jour/267, 15 Dec. 1999.

[141] Allied Forces Southern Europe, 'Operation Determined Guarantor', URL <http://www.afsouth.nato.int/operations/operations.htm>.

[142] Of these, 42 500 are based in Kosovo, with the remainder in Albania, Greece and Macedonia. UN, Letter dated 15 October 1999 from the Secretary-General addressed to the Security Council, UN document S/1999/1062, 15 Oct. 1999.

[143] *Atlantic News*, no. 3141 (24 Sep. 1999), p. 1.

[144] Nicoll, A., 'NATO set to reduce Bosnia peacekeepers', *Financial Times*, 22 Sep. 1999, p. 2.

[145] *Keesing's Record of World Events*, vol. 45, no. 9 (Sep. 1999), p. 43171.

[146] Radio Rossii Network (Moscow), 9 July 1999, in 'Sergeyev: Russia, NATO troops in Kosovo simultaneously', FBIS-SOV-1999-0709, 12 July 1999; and Interfax (Moscow), 9 July 1999, in 'Russia: Commander says 583 paratroops in Slatina', FBIS-SOV-1999-0709, 12 July 1999.

under British, French, German, Italian and US command.[147] Russian peace-keepers, moreover, encountered significant local hostility: entry by a column deployed to the city of Orahovac was initially blockaded by Albanian civilians, who claimed Russian peacekeepers would be biased towards the city's Serb minority and would fail to arrest suspected war criminals.[148] This violence was extended to other national forces as KFOR moved to prevent Albanians from attacking Serbs and Serb-dominated areas of the province.[149]

KFOR quickly achieved its initial task of securing Kosovo's borders and initiated mine-clearing and disarmament programmes. The demobilization of the KLA and its transformation into the core of an unarmed, multi-ethnic civil emergency force, the KPC, set out in the undertaking on demilitarization and transformation signed by the KLA and KFOR on 21 June, was a more difficult challenge.[150] Although the KLA leadership declared its commitment to the proposed transition, its disagreement with NATO over the symbols and defensive capacity of the force delayed its establishment until 20 September.[151] The KPC's mandate includes humanitarian, demining and reconstruction assistance, as well as civil emergency support under the authority of the UN Special Representative. KFOR provides day-to-day direction for the KPC and undertook training over a 60-day transition phase. When this ended on 21 November, no Serb applications to join the envisaged force of 3000 active and 2000 reserve members and only a small number of applications from other minorities had been received.[152] Criminal activity by former KLA/future KPC personnel also continued to be a problem despite the screening and application process carried out by the International Organization for Migration (IOM). KFOR initiated a crackdown and pressed the provisional commander of the new force and last KLA military leader, General Agim Ceku, to publicly condemn the wrongdoing.[153]

Public law and order provided the greatest problem for KFOR. Violent revenge attacks on Kosovar Serbs and other ethnic groups, particularly Roma, by the Albanian majority in the province began immediately after the end of the conflict, with estimates of 135–170 Serbs killed in the first four months of the peace and 200 000 non-Albanians having fled by the end of 1999.[154] The high incidence of crime and violence delayed the transition of responsibility for public security from KFOR to UNMIK until the end of the year. Even then

[147] 'Transfer of Russian troops to Kosovo to last through July', Interfax (Moscow), 16 July 1999, in FBIS-SOV-1999-0716, 19 July 1999.
[148] Gall, C., 'Kosovo Albanians blocking Russian troops from a city', New York Times (Internet edn), 24 Aug. 1999, URL <htttp://www.nytimes.com/library/world/europe/082499Kosovo-russians.html>.
[149] 'French troops feel anger of Albanian Kosovars', International Herald Tribune, 9 Aug. 1999, p. 5.
[150] 'Undertaking of demilitarization and transformation by the UCK', New New York Times (Internet edn), 21 June 1999, URL <http://www2.uclick.com/client/nyt/jf/>.
[151] Kusovac, Z., 'Disbanded KLA to transform in 60 days', Jane's Defence Weekly, vol. 32, no. 13 (29 Sep. 1999), p. 5.
[152] UN, Letter dated 17 December 1999 from the Secretary-General addressed to the President of the Security Council (Monthly report to the UN on KFOR operations), UN document S/1999/1266, 20 Dec. 1999.
[153] UN document S/1999/1250 (note 53).
[154] International Crisis Group, Violence in Kosovo: Who's Killing Whom?, Brussels, Nov. 1999, p. 1; KFOR press update, Pristina, 10 Nov. 1999; and UNHCR, FRY Information Bulletin, Jan. 2000.

KFOR continued to provide troops for joint KFOR–UNMIK patrols in urban areas and remained the principal security force in the Kosovo countryside.[155] At the end of December approximately 750 patrols, 550 static guard posts and 200 checkpoints were in operation.[156]

SFOR's peace stabilization operation in *Bosnia and Herzegovina* entered its third year in 1999. The NATO-led force of 25 states provides security and oversees implementation of the military provisions of the 1995 General Framework Agreement for Peace in Bosnia and Herzegovina (the Dayton Agreement) through three multinational divisions. SFOR troops monitoring the border with the FRY were reinforced during the Kosovo conflict to enforce the 1998 embargo on the transfer of weapons into Serbia.[157] A demining campaign took place in the summer and weapon storage site inspections continued throughout the year. Isolated violent attacks were reported over the course of the year but Bosnia and Herzegovina remained stable overall, even during the Kosovo conflict and following the arrest of suspected war criminal General Momir Talic.[158]

Civilian implementation tasks occupied most of SFOR's attention in 1999.[159] These usually took the form of provision of assistance to international organizations: SFOR continued to provide security support to the International Police Task Force (IPTF) in developing a police force and establishing law and order in the country. It was also active in the UNHCR's ongoing refugee return programmes as well as in the apprehension of suspected war criminals, detaining six indictees in 1999.[160] The issuance of the annex to the final arbitration award on the district of Brcko in August paved the way for the establishment of a demilitarized district to be held in condominium by resident Serb and Croat communities and the end of the international supervisory authority.[161] The development of joint institutions among the three entities of Bosnia and Herzegovina remained slow, although SFOR continued its efforts in regular meetings of the Standing Committee on Military Matters which agreed, in July, to establish a Permanent Secretariat.[162]

NATO continued to redefine its strategic purpose with emphasis on its capability to undertake conflict prevention and active crisis management, including crisis response operations within and outside its borders.[163] The

---

[155] UN (note 152).

[156] KFOR press update, Pristina, 18 Jan. 2000.

[157] UN, Letter from the Secretary-General addressed to the President of the Security Council (Monthly report on SFOR operations), UN document S/1999/1041, 8 Oct. 1999.

[158] UN, Letter from the Secretary-General addressed to the Security Council (Monthly report on SFOR operations), UN document S/1999/1237, 13 Dec. 1999.

[159] News Briefing on Bosnia by General Wesley Clark, US Office of the Assistant Secretary of Defense, 9 Dec. 1999.

[160] Information provided by Paul Hubbard, SFOR Spokesman, 25 Jan. 2000.

[161] Statement by Javier Solana on the Brcko arbitration, NATO press release 28, 5 Mar. 1999; and UN, Report of the Secretary-General on the UN mission in Bosnia and Herzegovina, UN document S/1999/989, 17 Sep. 1999.

[162] Joint OHR, SFOR and OSCE Press Release, 16 July 1999, URL <http://www.ohr.int/press/p990716a.htm>.

[163] 'Washington Summit Communiqué', *NATO Review*, vol. 47, no. 2 (24 Apr. 1999). See also chapter 4 in this volume and excerpts from the communiqué in appendix 4A.

Partnership for Peace (PFP) programme, established in 1994, has become an important element in this, assisted by the Euro-Atlantic Partnership Council (EAPC), created in 1997. A range of regionally coordinated peacekeeping, civil disaster, and humanitarian aid planning and exercises take place regularly under the aegis of the PFP, intended to facilitate cooperation between participating states. A feature of the PFP has been the establishment of multinational peacekeeping battalions for deployment in UN, and usually NATO, peace operations. One of the most significant of these is the South-Eastern Europe Multi-National Force (SEEMNF), a brigade of up to 4000 troops from seven countries which became operational in September 1999.[164] In the same month Denmark, Germany and Poland inaugurated the Multinational Corps North-East, based in the Baltic port of Szczecin. In addition to joint defence the force will participate in humanitarian and peacekeeping operations.[165]

The European Union/Western European Union

The EU has traditionally focused on economic tools, especially the provision of technical, financial and humanitarian assistance, for conflict prevention, conflict management and post-conflict rehabilitation tasks within and outside Europe. The EU has lead responsibility for economic reconstruction within the UN interim administration in Kosovo. Together with the World Bank it drew up an economic recovery programme for the province focusing on the restoration of public services, the establishment of financial, customs and tax systems in the province and private-sector development.[166] The EU and the World Bank also led the drive for international funding through two donor conferences in July and November. Over half the $1 billion pledged for Kosovo's reconstruction programme is to be provided by the Union.[167]

On 10 June the EU initiated its largest single rehabilitation project to date, the Stability Pact for South Eastern Europe.[168] This multilateral programme, modelled on the 1994 Pact on Stability in Europe, aims to assist regional stabilization and development by offering states of the former Yugoslavia (including the FRY) the perspective of integration into the EU. The potential of membership is seen as one of the most important incentives to encourage sustainable economic and political transition in the countries involved. Under the pact three working tables have been established on democratization and human rights, economic reconstruction and development, and security issues, including justice and home affairs, with a number of EU member states desig-

---

[164] Albania, Bulgaria, Greece, Italy, Macedonia, Romania and Turkey. *Defence News Analysis*, Issue 99/34 (13 Sep. 1999), p. 2.

[165] *Atlantic News*, no. 3144 (6 Oct. 1999), p. 2.

[166] European Union and World Bank, Toward stability and prosperity: a programme for reconstruction and recovery in Kosovo, 3 Nov. 1999, URL <http://www.seerecon.org/Calendar/SDC/ecwb-kosovo.pdf>.

[167] 'Kosovo's $1bn rescue package', BBC News Online, 18 Nov. 1999 URL <http://news2.thls.bbc.co.uk/hi/english/world/europe/newsid%5f525000/525602.stm>.

[168] Stability Pact for South Eastern Europe, Cologne, 10 June 1999. URL <http://europa.eu.int/comm/external_relations/see/stapact/10_june_99.htm>. On the Stability Pact for South Eastern Europe see chapter 4 in this volume. The Stability Pact is reproduced (without the Annex) in appendix 4A.

nated lead actors for specific areas therein. Although the EU estimates contributing 5.5 billion euros to the Pact between 2000 and 2006, the initiative has been criticized as slow and lacking in substance.[169]

There were significant breakthroughs in 1999 in EU efforts to develop political and military capabilities for conflict prevention and crisis management. The commitment to strengthen the Union's defence identity, which began with the British–French Joint Declaration on European Defence (the St Malo Declaration) in December 1998,[170] continued to propel the Union towards the development of an independent peacekeeping capability. It was given further impetus by the Kosovo conflict, where Europe's inability to deploy significant forces rapidly, much less lead a crisis management operation, was evident. At the European Council meeting in Cologne in June, EU leaders declared their intention to incorporate the crisis management and peacekeeping tasks performed at its request by the WEU into the Union and to merge the two organizations by the end of 2000.[171] It was agreed that Eurocorps, the multinational force established in 1993 by Germany and France and later joined by Belgium, Luxembourg and Spain, should become a European rapid reaction force.[172] Plans were further elaborated at the December European Council meeting in Helsinki, at which EU leaders moved to establish, by the end of 2003, a rapid deployment force of up to 60 000 troops.[173]

In October, former NATO Secretary General Javier Solana was appointed High Representative for the EU's Common Foreign and Security Policy. The Policy Planning and Early Warning Unit envisaged in the 1997 Treaty of Amsterdam also came into existence and is intended to provide support and proposals to the High Representative.[174] One month later, WEU foreign ministers designated Solana Secretary General of their organization, thereby facilitating its incorporation into the EU.[175] The WEU is already undertaking two operations at the request of the EU. The Multinational Advisory Police Element (MAPE) provides police training, assistance and advice in Albania as part of the EU's contribution to the re-establishment of a viable police force.[176] In May the WEU embarked on a 12-month demining assistance mission in Croatia, providing nine military experts to give technical and training support to the Croatian Mine Action Centre.[177]

[169] 'Commission proposes new funding for Kosovo: political priorities in a framework of budgetary discipline', EU Commission Press Release, DN IP/99/819, 3 Nov. 1999.

[170] For the text of the declaration see *SIPRI Yearbook 1999: Armaments, Disarmament and International Security* (Oxford University Press: Oxford, 1999), p. 265.

[171] EU, Cologne European Council, Presidency Conclusions, 3–4 June 1999, Annexe III, European Council Declaration on strengthening the common European policy on security and defence. See also chapter 4 in this volume; the text of Annexe III is available in appendix 4A.

[172] *Atlantic News*, no. 3115 (9 June 1999), p. 4.

[173] EU, Helsinki European Council, Presidency Conclusions, 10–11 Dec. 1999, URL <http://europa. eu.int/council/off/conclu/dec99/dec99_en.htm>. For excerpts see appendix 4A in this volume.

[174] Cottey, A., *The European Union and Conflict Prevention: The Role of the High Representative and the Policy Planning and Early Warning Unit* (Saferworld/International Alert: London, Dec. 1998).

[175] Norman, P., 'EU goes forward with plan for peace force', *Financial Times*, 16 Nov. 1999, p. 2.

[176] 'Monitoring the situation in the Balkans', WEU Assembly Report, 45th Session, Document 1653, 10 June 1999.

[177] Joint WEU–EU Press Statement, 10 May 1999, URL <http://www.weu.int/eng/press/ p990510a.htm>.

The EU continued to maintain its small civilian monitoring mission in the western Balkans (the European Community Monitoring Mission, ECMM). Other peace-building instruments include EU special envoys to the Middle East peace process and the African Great Lakes region, and the Euro-Mediterranean partnership designed to enhance stability among littoral countries. The EU's approach in conflict-prone areas is generally regional in nature, directed towards the encouragement of trade, development and social cooperation, as well as political dialogue, among the states concerned.[178]

The Council of Europe

The Council of Europe joined the panoply of organizations participating in the UNMIK-led operation in Kosovo as well as the Stability Pact for South Eastern Europe. Its office in Pristina, which opened in August, provides training in law and human (particularly minority) rights and encourages the establishment of non-judicial machinery for rights' protection.[179]

The Commonwealth of Independent States

The capacity of the CIS as an actor in the field of crisis management and peacekeeping was further eroded in 1999 following the withdrawal of Azerbaijan, Georgia and Uzbekistan from the 1992 CIS Collective Security Treaty in April.[180] Terrorist attacks by Islamic militants in *Dagestan* and *Kyrgyzstan* in August and September, however, restored some degree of CIS coordination. On 2 October Armenia, Belarus, Russia, Kazakhstan, Kyrgyzstan, Tajikistan and Uzbekistan signed an agreement on the provision of multilateral assistance to Kyrgyzstan in its efforts against Islamist rebels who had crossed into its southern territory from *Tajikistan*. The additional decision by the four Central Asian states and Russia to establish a headquarters for coordination of military cooperation in Central Asia was as much a reflection of their desire to prevent the insurgents creating conflict between themselves as of their desire to successfully negotiate terrorist threats.[181] The potential for conflict was clearly demonstrated on 15 August, when Uzbek aircraft bombed Tajik territory. Although Uzbekistan first denied and then defended its action as part of a joint Uzbek–Kyrgyz effort to defeat the militants, the incident exacerbated tensions in Tajikistan and Uzbekistan.[182] CIS foreign ministers held a special meeting

[178] Lund, M., 'Solidarity without cooperation', ed. M. Mekenkamp *et al., Searching for Peace in Africa: An Overview of Conflict Prevention and Management Activities* (European Platform for Conflict Prevention and Transformation: Utrecht, 1999), pp. 74–80.

[179] Press Communiqué of the 105th session of the Committee of Ministers, Council of Europe, 4 Nov. 1999, URL <http://www.coe.fr/cp/99/616a.htm>.

[180] 'Azerbaijan to pull out of CIS collective security pact', BBC News Online, 10 Feb. 1999, URL <http://news2.thls.bbc.co.uk/hi/english/world/asia%2dpacific/newsid%5f276000/276991.stm>. Moldova, Turkmenistan and Ukraine were not party to the treaty, the former 2 for reasons of neutrality.

[181] Lamyr, A., 'Kyrgyzstan signs decision on Central Asian situation', ITAR-TASS (Moscow), 2 Oct. 1999, in FBIS-SOV-1999-1002, 4 Oct. 1999.

[182] David, A., 'Tensions in Central Asia', *Jane's Defence Weekly*, vol. 32, no. 9 (1 Sep. 1999), p. 20.

on the margins of the CIS summit meeting in early October to discuss joint measures for combating terrorism.[183]

The instability in Central Asia indirectly encouraged support for the continued presence of the CIS peacekeeping force in Tajikistan and the 8000-strong contingent of Russian border guards along the Tajik–Afghan border.[184] It is the only multinational CIS peacekeeping operation, comprising the Russian 201st Motorized Division and a small Kazakh battalion serving alongside the Russian border guards.[185] The force continued to liaise with the UN Mission of Observers in Tajikistan (UNMOT) as well as the OSCE mission in facilitating continued implementation of the 1997 General Agreement on Peace and National Accord.[186] The disbandment of the armed forces of the United Tajik Opposition (UTO) enabled the UTO to contest the country's first post-conflict presidential elections on 6 November, although it claimed that President Imomali Rakhmonov's Government had effectively blocked all opposition candidates from the ballot.[187] Parliamentary elections in 2000 mark the last phase of the transition period set out in the General Agreement, at which point an assessment of future international involvement in the country is expected. An electoral observation role is envisaged for UNMOT, which it did not have in the November presidential elections.[188]

The CIS meeting in Yalta in October also discussed the conflict in *Abkhazia*, where up to 2500 Russian peacekeepers continue to patrol the conflict zone between Georgia and the breakaway region.[189] The situation on the ground remained volatile throughout the year, with little progress in the UN-led negotiations on the future status of Abkhazia within Georgia, and two hostage-taking incidents, albeit short-lived, in July and October. Tensions further increased when elections, deemed illegal by the UN, were held in the province and resulted in the re-election of Vladislav Ardzinba as president.[190] One week later the Abkhaz Parliament passed a state independence act, even as Abkhaz leaders maintained their readiness to continue talks with Georgia for a political settlement.[191] The agreement reached between Georgia and Russia at the

[183] Reuters, 'CIS premiers to devise anti-terror blueprint at regional summit', *Russia Today*, 7 Oct. 1999, European Internet Network, URL <http://www.centraleurope/com/search.php3?method= all&format=builtin-long&exclude=&restrict=.&words=CIS>.

[184] David, A., 'Russia battles drug smugglers on Tajikistan border', *Jane's Defence Weekly*, vol. 32, no. 4 (28 July 1999), p. 13; and Zviagelskaya, I., 'The Tajikistan conflict', *SIPRI Yearbook 1999* (note 170), p. 74.

[185] UN, Report of the Secretary-General on the situation in Tajikistan, UN document S/1999/514, 6 May 1999.

[186] Clayton, A., 'Uzbekistan plans to quit CIS Treaty', *Jane's Defence Weekly*, vol. 31, no. 6 (10 Feb. 1999), p. 6.

[187] UN Press Release SC/6750, 12 Nov. 1999; and Human Rights Watch statement, 28 Oct. 1999, URL <http://www.hrw.org>.

[188] ITAR-TASS (Moscow), 4 Nov. 1999, 'UN Envoys in Tajikistan not to observe elections', in FBIS-SOV-1999-1104, 20 Nov. 1999.

[189] ITAR-TASS (Moscow), 6 Oct. 1999, in 'Yalta forum to discuss Abkhazia, CIS reform', FBIS-SOV-1999-1007, 7 Oct 1999; and Stern, D., AFP, 3 Oct. 1999, in 'AFP Previews Election in Abkhazia', FBIS-SOV-1999-1003, 4 Oct. 1999.

[190] UN Security Council Resolution 1255, 5 Oct. 1999; and UN Press Release SC/6751, 12 Nov. 1999.

[191] ITAR-TASS (Sukhumi), 12 Oct. 1999, in 'Georgia: Abkhazian Parliament passes independence Act', FBIS-SOV-1999-1012, 12 Oct. 1999.

OSCE Summit Meeting in November to close down two of the four Russian bases in Georgia by 2001 created some uncertainty as to the future of Russian peacekeepers in the conflict, given that one of the designated bases is located in Abkhazia. Some senior Georgian officials, however, have declared their support for the maintenance of Russian peacekeepers in the province.[192]

Africa

Africa outranks all other regions in the number and scope of institutions addressing the prevention, management and resolution of conflicts, and the international community continues to emphasize the need to further develop these capacities. Conflicts in 1999, however, illustrated the difficulty of this task, particularly the constraints imposed by a lack of resources, raising further questions about the capacity of regional organizations for more than limited, reactive responses to conflict.

The Organization of African Unity

The OAU, the only pan-African institution, continued as the primary regional forum and main partner to the UN on the continent. A new tone of self-criticism was evident in 1999 in the face of continued conflict and humanitarian crises among its members. Africa's marginalization was a dominant theme at the 35th OAU summit meeting in July and encouraged participants to demonstrate a renewed sense of responsibility.[193] For the first time, the OAU committed itself to refuse membership to countries whose leaders come to power illegally.[194] Its instruments for conflict management, however, including the Mechanism for Conflict Prevention, Management and Resolution and the OAU Peace Fund, remained hampered by financial constraints. A new programme of institutional restructuring was set in motion, which includes the suspension of member states in arrears.[195]

The OAU saw its efforts to broker peace in the Indian Ocean island state of *Comoros* rise and fall in 1999. An OAU Framework Agreement signed in April, which granted separatist Anjouan broad autonomy under a unified federal government, was undermined some weeks later by a military coup. In response, the OAU withdrew its mission of 20 observers deployed since January 1998.[196] Prospects for settlement were further diminished by the Anjouanese separatists' refusal to sign the April accord, despite repeated mediation efforts by the OAU Special Envoy to the Comoros.[197]

[192] ITAR-TASS (Moscow), 6 Oct. 1999, in 'Georgia wants Russian peacekeepers to stay in Abkhazia', FBIS-SOV-1999-1006, 6 Oct. 1999.

[193] 'Une Afrique lucide' [A lucid Africa], *Le Monde*, 15 July 1999, p. 12.

[194] Gaye, S., 'What lies ahead for OAU under President Bouteflika?', Panafrican News Agency (PANA), 20 July 1999, URL <http://www.africanews.org/PANA/news>.

[195] *Africa Research Bulletin*, 16 June–15 July 1999, p. 13944.

[196] 'OAU withdraws from Comoros Islands', *Jane's Defence Weekly*, vol. 31, no. 25 (23 June 1999), p. 19.

[197] Communiqué of the 60th Ordinary Session of the Central Organ for the OAU Mechanism for Conflict Prevention, Management and Resolution, Central Organ/MEC/AMB/Comm.(LX), Addis

The organization continued to exert considerable effort in the conflict raging between *Ethiopia* and *Eritrea*, serving as the lead mediator in the tripartite (OAU–UN–US) effort to facilitate resolution of a war that has resulted in at least 70 000 deaths and 500 000 displaced people since May 1998.[198] In February Eritrea signalled its acceptance of the 1998 Framework Agreement drafted by the OAU, but fighting continued until July when the states committed themselves to implement the settlement set out in a 'Modalities' document.[199] Violence along their shared border has not ended, however, and Ethiopia continues to raise objections to the OAU's subsequent 'Technical Arrangements' for implementation of the agreement. Plans were being put in place for the deployment of a team of 110 OAU liaison officers/observers, to provide interim support before the arrival of a UN peacekeeping mission, once the agreement is signed.[200] The prospects for this looked increasingly bleak by the end of 1999, however, with both sides preparing for more fighting, despite repeated missions by the OAU Special Envoy.[201]

The OAU was one of many actors trying to facilitate a viable settlement of the conflict in the *Democratic Republic of Congo*. It supported the SADC-led regional peace process that resulted in the signing of the Lusaka Ceasefire Agreement.[202] The agreement envisages close collaboration between the OAU and the UN in the establishment of a peacekeeping force to ensure implementation of the ceasefire. The OAU was charged with appointing a neutral head of the Joint Military Commission responsible for monitoring the ceasefire and facilitating the withdrawal of foreign forces before the deployment of the UN force and on 20 July nominated General Rachid Lallali of Algeria.[203] Lallali undertook an immediate tour of the region and began meetings with UN military officers on the commission's operationalization.[204] The JMC headquarters is located in Zambia with an initial four local offices in the DRC, to be staffed by 48 OAU military observers (trained by the UN) as well as a representative from each party to the peace agreement. Deployment was slow,

Ababa, 19 Nov. 1999, p. 1; and 'OAU envoy ends Comoros mission', BBC News Online, 31 Oct. 1999, URL <http://news2.thls.bbc.co.uk/hi/english/world/africa/newsid%5F500000/500585.stm>.

[198] 'Battling for Badme, *Africa Confidential*, vol. 40, no. 22 (5 Nov. 1999), p. 2; and UN Security Council statement quoted in the *Horn of Africa Bulletin*, vol. 11, no. 2 (May–June 1999), p. 10.

[199] 'Ethiopia–Eritrea: Fighting flares up as peace envoys visit', IRIN-CEA special report, 24 Feb. 2000; and 'Proposals for a Framework Agreement for a peaceful settlement of the dispute between Ethiopia and Eritrea', annex to UN, Letter dated 24 December 1998 from the Permanent Representative of Ethiopia to the United Nations addressed to the President of the Security Council, UN document S/1998/1223, 28 Dec. 1998, para. 33.

[200] 'Modalities for the implementation of the OAU Framework Agreement on the settlement of the dispute between Ethiopia and Eritrea', Annex III to UN, Letter dated 16 July 1999 from the permanent representative of Eritrea to the United Nations addressed to the President of the Security Council, UN document S/1999/794, 16 July 1999; and 'Technical Arrangements for the implementation of the OAU Framework Agreement and its Modalities', on file at SIPRI.

[201] 'Ceasefire under threat', *Africa Confidential*, vol. 40, no. 22 (5 Nov. 1999), p. 2.

[202] The Lusaka Ceasefire Agreement is contained in UN, Letter dated 23 July 1999 from the permanent representative of Zambia to the United Nations addressed to the President of the Security Council, UN document S/1999/815, 23 July 1999.

[203] UN, Report of the Secretary-General on the United Nations preliminary deployment in the Democratic Republic of Congo, UN document S/1999/790, 15 July 1999.

[204] Report of the OAU Secretary-General on the DRC peace process, Central Organ/MEC/AMB/3 (LIX), Addis Ababa, 23 Sep. 1999.

however, with the first 12 observers (from Algeria, Malawi and Senegal) arriving only in mid-November.[205] Financing for the operation has been difficult, with funds pledged from the EU, the USA and other Western states as well as states of the region slow to arrive. The question of financial support for the OAU role in the DRC conflict has been a major element in coordination planning between the UN and the OAU.[206]

The Economic Community of West African States

Since its inception in 1975, the 16-member Economic Community of West African States has had a much wider brief than its name suggests. Its conflict management profile was dominated in 1999 by the operations of the ECOWAS Monitoring Group (ECOMOG) in Guinea-Bissau, Liberia and Sierra Leone. Approximately 600 ECOMOG troops were deployed to *Guinea-Bissau* in February to support the ceasefire and re-establishment of the government after the military putsch of June 1998. Peace was short-lived, however, and in May army rebels, led by Army Chief of Staff General Ansumane Mane, overthrew the president.[207] In response, and in spite of the new regime's request for their retention, ECOMOG withdrew its troops.[208] In keeping with ECOWAS practice Guinea-Bissau was not expelled from the organization, and the coup leaders kept their promise to hold legislative and presidential elections in November.[209]

Most of the ECOWAS peace efforts centred on *Sierra Leone*, where an ECOMOG force of around 15 000 troops was the main defence against a rebel takeover of the entire country.[210] Although ECOMOG received significant external funding, particularly from the UK, the military and human cost of the peace-enforcement operation continued to weigh on participating states. As early as January, Nigeria, whose 12 000 troops provided the bulk of the force, signalled its desire to conclude the operation.[211] This consideration lent further urgency to ECOWAS efforts to bring the government and rebel parties to the negotiating table under the mediation of Togo, then ECOWAS chair. It also influenced the attitude of the Sierra Leone Government, which was completely

---

[205] 'OAU observers in Congo', BBC News Online, 19 Nov. 1999, URL <http://news.bbc.co.uki/hi/english/world/africa/newsid_527000/527470.stm>; and PANA, 'OAU deploys first investigators to DR Congo', 16 Nov. 1999, URL <http://www.africanews.org/PANA/news/>.

[206] UN document S/1999/1116 (note 66). The OAU is also committed to opening a liaison office in Kinshasa. Communiqué of the 59th Ordinary Session of the Central Organ of the OAU Mechanism for Conflict Prevention, Management and Resolution at Ambassadorial Level, Central Organ/MEC/AMB/(LIX), Addis Ababa, p. 3.

[207] 'OAU condemns coup in Guinea Bissau', 10 May 1999, PANA, URL <http://search.nando.net/plweb-cgi/fastweb?getdoc+pana_archive+pana_archive+37104+9++>.

[208] Final Communiqué, Meeting of ECOWAS Ministers of Foreign Affairs, 24–25 May 1999, URL <http://www.sierra-leone.org/ecowas052599.html>.

[209] UN, Report of the Secretary-General on developments in Guinea-Bissau and on the activities of the United Nations peace-building support office in that country, UN document S/1999/1276, 23 Dec. 1999. For the ECOWAS members see the glossary in this volume.

[210] Deen, T., 'UN appeals for help to preserve ECOMOG force', *Jane's Defence Weekly*, vol. 31, no. 11 (17 Mar. 1999), p. 6.

[211] Adeyemi, S., 'ECOMOG in crisis', *Jane's Defence Weekly*, vol. 31, no. 3 (20 Jan. 1999), p. 27.

dependent on ECOMOG for its survival.[212] A ceasefire negotiated in May provided the breakthrough for comprehensive peace talks that culminated in the July Lomé Peace Accord. One month later Nigeria began the first phase of a staged withdrawal from Sierra Leone, causing much international consternation, given that ECOMOG remained responsible for security in the fragile post-conflict environment.[213] The UN Secretary-General, who had earlier in the year expressed concern at reports of summary executions and mistreatment of civilians by ECOMOG soldiers, called for international support for the ECOMOG operation.[214] The USA, in response, pledged an additional $11 million to the force.[215] Meanwhile, around 2500 of the remaining 9000 Nigerian troops deployed in Sierra Leone were incorporated into the UN peacekeeping force in December.[216] ECOMOG remains responsible for ensuring the security of Freetown and protecting the government.[217]

Between January and October Nigeria also withdrew from the ECOMOG force in *Liberia*, an action widely seen as a response to alleged Liberian support to rebels in neighbouring Sierra Leone.[218] The action effectively ended the nine-year ECOMOG operation that, since the 1995 Abuja Accord, had concentrated on peace monitoring and disarmament. ECOWAS remained concerned at ongoing rebel activity in the country, however, particularly when Liberia and Guinea accused each other of destabilization activities along their mutual border. Prompted by fears that the dispute could wreck the fragile regional peace established by the Lomé Peace Accord, ECOWAS convened a mini-summit meeting in September to discuss the crisis.[219]

The international significance accorded to the role of ECOWAS in peace and security in West Africa was reflected in the EU decision to provide $2.03 million for the planned establishment of an ECOWAS mechanism for conflict prevention and resolution, which will include a stand-by force as well as mediation and judicial instruments.[220]

---

[212] Onishi, N., 'Foes agree on ending civil war in Sierra Leone', *International Herald Tribune*, 8 July 1999, pp. 1, 5.

[213] 'Nigeria: 2,000 troops pulling out', OCHA, Integrated Regional Information Network–West Africa (IRIN-WA) weekly round-up 35, 28 Aug.–3 Sep. 1999.

[214] The ECOMOG High Command promised to investigate allegations of human rights abuses, UN, Sixth report of the Secretary-General on the United Nations Observer Mission in Sierra Leone, UN document S/1999/645, 4 June 1999.

[215] 'Sierra Leone: Albright promises help if peace prevails', IRIN-WA weekly round-up 42, 16–22 Oct. 1999; and UN Press Release SC/6742, 22 Oct. 1999.

[216] 'UN troops arrive in Sierra Leone', BBC News Online, 30 Nov. 1999, URL <http://news.bbc.co.uk/hi/english/world/africa/newsid_543000/543292.stm>.

[217] UN, Eighth report of the Secretary-General on the United Nations Observer Mission in Sierra Leone, UN document S/1999/1003, 28 Sep. 1999.

[218] Adeyemi, S., 'Nigerian monitoring troops leave Liberia', *Jane's Defence Weekly*, vol. 31, no. 4 (27 Jan. 1999), p. 19; and 'Nigeria: Obasanjo counts the cost of ECOMOG', IRIN-WA weekly round-up 43, 23–29 Oct. 1999.

[219] PANA, 'ECOWAS leaders meet on Liberia, Guinea crisis', 14 Sep. 1999, Africa News Online, URL <http://www.africanews.org/africa.html>.

[220] Ikeh, G., 'EU to fund ECOWAS conflict prevention and resolution mechanism', PANA, 21 July 1999, URL <http://www.africanews.org/PANA/news/>.

The Intergovernmental Authority on Development

The Intergovernmental Authority on Development (IGAD), established in 1996, unites East African states in a similar economic integration initiative. Its seven members have been slow to develop a conflict prevention and management capacity, but the elaboration of a strategy for action is under discussion. IGAD has taken initiatives in the civil wars in Sudan and Somalia, establishing a subcommittee for each conflict that in turn liaises with non-African states and international organizations through IGAD Partners Forums.

The effort to resolve *Sudan's* 16-year civil war made progress in July when the Islamist government and opposition Sudan People's Liberation Movement/ Army (SPLM/A) agreed to IGAD's Declaration of Principles (DOP) as the basis for the initiation of peace talks. The DOP acknowledges the southern rebels' right of self-determination and envisages a four-year transition period followed by a referendum on unity in the south of the country. IGAD placed a Special Envoy (Daniel Mboya) and Secretariat in Nairobi, Kenya, to mediate in the negotiations.[221] The IGAD initiative was constrained by the presence of a parallel Egyptian–Libyan mediation effort, which won the support of the opposition in the north of the country, primarily through the umbrella National Democratic Alliance (NDA), and was accepted by the government in August.[222] Although Khartoum declared a ceasefire in the south, progress was hampered by rebel divisions and the government's questionable commitment to peace.[223] The UN and Western states, particularly the USA, accused government troops of aerial bombings and civilian massacres around oilfields in the south, as part of Khartoum's strategy to exploit the country's energy potential in its war against the rebels.[224] The NDA, meanwhile, was further divided when one of its senior figures met with Sudanese President Omar Hassan al-Bashir at the IGAD summit meeting in November and agreed to support the IGAD peace initiative.[225] President Bashir's declaration of a national state of emergency on 12 December, in order to oust his main political rival, the parliamentary speaker, marked a dramatic turn in events.[226] IGAD negotiators were undaunted and arrived in Khartoum a few days later to discuss the possibility of government–SPLM/A peace talks in January 2000.[227]

---

[221] Communiqué of the IGAD Ministerial Sub-committee meeting on the conflict in Sudan, 23 July 1999, URL <http://www.IGAD.org/press08.htm>; and IGAD Secretariat, Press Release on the Sudan Peace Process, 27 Oct. 1999, URL <http://www.IGAD.org/press14.htm>.

[222] 'Cairo meeting discusses Sudan peace plan', BBC News Online, 24 Oct. 1999, URL <http://news.bbc.co.uk/hi/english/world/middle_east/newsid_483000/483147.stm>; and US Agency For International Development (USAID), 'Sudan: complex emergency', Situation Report no. 1 (FY 2000), 5 Jan. 2000, URL <http://www.info.usaid.gov/ofda/sudan_sr1_fy00.html>.

[223] 'Through the looking glass', *The Economist*, vol. 353, no. 8143 (30 Oct. 1999), p. 53; and Prendergast, J., *Building for Peace in the Horn of Africa: Diplomacy and Beyond* (United States Institute of Peace Report, Washington, DC, 28 June 1999).

[224] Venter, A., 'Sudan in strife: a catalyst for conflict', *Jane's Intelligence Review*, Dec. 1999, pp. 36–37; and 'Human rights rapporteur says situation worsening', Sudan: IRIN news briefs, 15 Nov. 1999.

[225] Umma party leader, Sadiq al-Mahdi, 'Sudan: Rubin condemns deal with Umma', IRIN-CEA weekly round-up 48, 29 Nov.–3 Dec. 1999.

[226] 'SPLA welcomes "the Bashir coup"', Sudan: IRIN news briefs, 20 Dec. 1999.

[227] 'IGAD team visits Khartoum to discuss peace talks', Sudan: IRIN news briefs, 20 Dec. 1999.

The IGAD's attempt to halt continued factional fighting in *Somalia* appeared unconvincing for much of the year given Ethiopia's position as the lead IGAD country in the mediation process. Both Ethiopia and Eritrea are widely accused of arming the rival Somali factions that have driven the country into a state of violent anarchy.[228] In November the organization adopted a new peace proposal by then IGAD Chairman, Djiboutian President Ismail Omar Gelleh, which focuses on civil society development rather than negotiations with various warlords as the basis for the restoration of the Somalian state.[229] However, Eritrea and Uganda did not attend the summit meeting, the former claiming that Djibouti supported Ethiopia in their current conflict and the latter that its unpaid dues would prevent it from speaking.[230] The UN Security Council has voiced its support for the initiative and its concern at the serious humanitarian crisis in Somalia.[231]

The Southern African Development Community

The SADC experienced its most difficult year since its formation in 1992, riven by divisions over the conflict in one of its member states, the *Democratic Republic of Congo*. Intervention by Angola, Namibia and Zimbabwe to support President Laurent-Désiré Kabila's Government under the framework of the SADC Allied Forces was roundly criticized by South Africa, which was sympathetic to Rwanda's claim that the DRC was sheltering exiled rebel Hutus responsible for the 1994 genocide.[232] Relations between South African President Nelson Mandela, several times a mediator in Congolese conflicts, and his Zimbabwean counterpart, President Robert Mugabe, cooled considerably and it was not until the former's departure, in June, that the two governments managed to set their differences aside. This gave a new impetus to the SADC's ongoing efforts, assisted by the OAU, to broker a settlement in the DRC. President Frederick Chiluba of Zambia continued to lead the complex negotiations that culminated, after a month's postponement, in the signing of the Lusaka Ceasefire Agreement in Zambia on 10 July.[233] It took another month to persuade the rival rebel factions to resolve their dispute over whose signature should represent them, but on 2 September 50 rebel leaders finally marked their agreement to end the war.[234] Although the SADC was given responsibility for the selection of the neutral facilitator provided in the agreement

---

[228] Adeba, B., 'Yet another war in a troubled region', *Africa News*, vol. 4, no. 8 (15 Aug. 1999), p. 9.

[229] Declaration of 7th IGAD summit of heads of states and government, 26 Nov. 1999, URL <http://www.IGAD.org/sum7dec.htm>; and Gidley-Kitchin, V., 'Organization amid chaos in Somalia', BBC News Online, 25 Nov. 1999, URL <http://news2.thls.bbc.co.uk/hi/english/world/africa/newsid%5F536000/536634.stm>.

[230] 'Somalia: IGAD summit endorses Guelleh plan', Horn of Africa: IRIN news briefs, 1 Dec. 1999. Somalia has not participated in IGAD since its collapse in 1991.

[231] UN Press Release SC/6752, 12 Nov. 1999.

[232] International Crisis Group (ICG), 'Africa's seven-nation war', 21 May 1999, pp. 7–8.

[233] Kayaya, M., 'DRC ceasefire summit postponed', PANA, 26 June 1999; and 'Congo draft ceasefire agreed', BBC News Online, 7 July 1999, URL <http://news2.thls.bbc.co.uk/hi/english/world/africa/newsid_388000/388642.stm>; and UN (note 202). On the Lusaka Ceasefire Agreement see appendix 1B in this volume.

[234] Fisher, I., 'A shaky start in Congo', *International Herald Tribune*, 2 Sep. 1999, p. 4.

to support the national reconciliation, this task was increasingly taken over by the OAU, following the rebels' rejection of the first nominations.[235]

The DRC debacle was the second unauthorized military operation in the name of the SADC, Botswana and South Africa having invoked the organization in their 1998 intervention in Lesotho. The SADC forum for conflict management, the Organ for Politics, Defence and Security, finally moved to address the institutional separation between it and the organization proper that has permitted groups of SADC states to deploy troops without the prior consensus of all members. An extraordinary meeting of SADC foreign, defence and security ministers in October agreed on a new structure incorporating the organ into the main organization and to develop a protocol governing the SADC's reaction to conflict situations.[236] In November SADC leaders agreed to provide increased humanitarian assistance to the Angolan Government in its war against the rebel movement União Nacional Para a Independência Total de Angola (UNITA, National Union for the Total Independence of Angola).[237]

The SADC made some progress in operationalizing its capabilities with its first peacekeeping exercise in South Africa in April. 'Exercise Blue Crane', comprising a military and civilian component, was the largest of its kind ever held in the continent and involved Western states as well as UN, OAU and non-governmental organization (NGO) actors.[238] A SADC Regional Peace Training Centre opened in Harare, Zimbabwe in June.[239]

Asia

The unity of the Association of South-East Asian Nations (ASEAN), already weakened by the 1997 financial crisis and domestic instability within its member states, was thrown into further disarray by the conflict in *East Timor*. Although ASEAN leaders met at the annual Asia Pacific Economic Cooperation (APEC) summit meeting in September, they were unable to agree on a common position that would permit an ASEAN presence in either the Australian-led multinational force or the subsequent UN peacekeeping operation in East Timor.[240] In a belated gesture in November ASEAN expressed support for East Timor's future accession to the organization.[241]

The ASEAN Regional Forum (ARF) debated a range of regional security concerns during the year, but progress from confidence building towards the

---

[235] 'Congo peace plan: the main points', BBC News Online, 8 July 1999, URL <http://news.bbc.co.uk/hi/english/world/africa/newsid_389000/389119.stm>.

[236] 'New dawn for SADC', IRIN-SA weekly round up 35, 28 Aug–3 Sep. 1999; and Editorial, *African Security Review*, vol. 8, no. 6 (1999).

[237] 'SADC to "speed up" program to aid Angola against UNITA', SAPA (Johannesburg), 15 Nov. 1999, in FBIS-AFR-1999-1115, 20 Nov. 1999.

[238] Neethling, T., 'Exercise Blue Crane: Forward with peacekeeping in Southern Africa?', University of Pretoria, Institute for Strategic Studies, *ISSUP Bulletin*, no. 5 (1999).

[239] UN document A/54/670 (note 114).

[240] Vatikiotis, M. *et al.*, 'Missing in action', *Far Eastern Economic Review*, vol. 162, no. 39 (30 Sep. 1999), pp. 14–15; and 'Thai daily says 'ASEAN has invited Howard's bravado', *Bangkok Post*, 24 Sep. 1999, in '"Howard Doctrine" worries ASEAN members', FBIS-EAS-1999-0924, 27 Sep. 1999.

[241] 'Indonesian president wants Timor in ASEAN', BBC News Online, 7 Nov. 1999, URL <http://news2.thls.bbc.co.uk/hi/english/world/asia%2dpacfic/newsid%5F508000/508682.stm>.

envisaged goal of preventive diplomacy remained slow.[242] A similar goal is shared by the so-called 'second-track' Council for Security Cooperation in the Asia Pacific (CSCAP), whose working groups continued regular discussions on cooperative security issues.[243] The CSCAP Working Group on Confidence- and Security-Building Measures (CSBMs) held a workshop on preventive diplomacy just prior to the ARF Bangkok meeting in March.[244]

The Middle East

Few regional security mechanisms exist in the Middle East. The six-member state Gulf Cooperation Council (GCC) carried out joint military exercises in the Persian Gulf in February and October.[245] The GCC expressed concern at the territorial dispute between Iran and the United Arab Emirates (UAE) over the Abu Musa and Tunba islands in the Persian Gulf and in August established a tripartite (Oman–Qatar–Saudi Arabia) committee to monitor the dispute. Both Iran and the UAE subsequently declared their willingness to have the committee involved, but Iran continued to stress that bilateral negotiations between the two parties were the best way to resolve tensions.[246]

Latin America

The Organization of American States (OAS) is the principal regional organization in the Americas undertaking peace and security activities. It concentrates on democracy and human rights promotion and dispatched 15 electoral observation missions in the region in 1999.[247] Its Committee on Hemispheric Security addresses non-military confidence- and security-building measures.[248] Practical security activity has been confined to post-conflict operations through the OAS demining programme in Central America and the joint UN–OAS International Civil Mission in Haiti (MICIVIH). Financial constraints, however, forced the organization to practically terminate its participation in MICIVIH during 1999: on 30 June all but one of the 35 OAS mission members were withdrawn and, as a consequence, five of the nine regional MICIVIH offices on the island were closed.[249] In December the OAS

---

[242] David, A., 'ASEAN forum discusses regional tensions', *Jane's Defence Weekly*, vol. 32, no. 5 (4 Aug. 1999), p. 6. For a list of ARF member states see the glossary in this volume.

[243] For a list of CSCAP member states see the glossary in this volume.

[244] 'Australia and security cooperation in the Asia Pacific', *AUS–CSCAP Newsletter*, no. 8 (Apr. 1999), URL <http://www.coombs.anu.edu.au/Depts/RSPAS/AUSCSCAP/8(1).html#CSBM>.

[245] 'Signing of Gulf common defense agreement postponed', ArabicNews.com, 19 Nov. 1999, URL <http://www.arabicnews.com/ansub/Daily/Day/991119/1999111905.html>.

[246] Joint communiqué, EU-GCC Ministerial Meeting and 9th Joint Council, CE-GOLFE 3502/99, 2 Nov. 1999; 'Iranian FM conveys a message to Saudi crown prince', ArabicNews.com, 22 July 1999, URL <http://www.arabicnews.com/ansub/Daily/Day/990722/1999072223.html>; and 'UAE expresses readiness for dialogue with Iran over islands', ArabicNews.com, 31 Aug. 1999, URL <http://www.arabicnews.com/ansub/Daily/Day/990831/1999083110.html>.

[247] OAS Press Release E-077/99ie, 21 July 1999.

[248] OAS Permanent Council, Report of the Committee on Hemispheric Security 1999, OAS document OEA/Ser.G, 19 May 1999.

[249] UN General Assembly, 54th Assembly, 'Situation of human rights in Haiti', UN document A/54/366, 20 Sep. 1999.

was called to mediate a dispute between Honduras and Nicaragua after approval by the Honduran Congress of a maritime delimitation treaty with Colombia.[250] An OAS envoy met with both sides, and on 30 December the two agreed to establish a military exclusion zone in the Caribbean and to undertake specific tension-reducing measures.

IV. Multinational coalitions

The establishment of ad hoc multinational coalitions to manage or mediate in internal crises is widely regarded as an important trend in peacekeeping. Coalitions of interested states, acting under their own initiative but with the support of the UN and regional organizations, are usually capable of swifter and more flexible action in a given conflict than bureaucratic, financially constrained institutions. The political sensitivities of the potential host country may encourage it to regard this type of intervention as more acceptable than a formal UN operation. Factors determining state engagement in multinational activities usually include proximity to the conflict; perceived security, political and economic interests; capacity for action; and international stature. Against the potential advantages of multinational coalitions the risk of partisanship, lack of transparency and national agendas that might contribute to further intensification of conflict have to be considered. All of these issues resonated during 1999, which saw Asia's largest multinational force operation take place in East Timor.

Europe

One of the most powerful non-institutionalized groupings is the *Group of Eight* industrialized states. Although the G8 has neither an international legal basis nor an institutional framework its annual summit meeting has come to play a significant role in addressing political, as well as economic, issues of the day.[251] In 1999 it provided the framework for the elaboration of the Kosovo peace agreement.

It was Russia, on 1 April, that first proposed a special meeting of the G8 to discuss the conflict. It did not materialize, however, although the six-nation Contact Group on Yugoslavia did meet for the first time since the start of the war a week later.[252] In the second half of April, NATO and Russia each presented peace plans which differed on the extent of a Yugoslav withdrawal from Kosovo (Russia proposed that 'the greatest part' of the military forces be withdrawn; Western states insisted on full withdrawal).[253] The nature of the

---

[250] 'OAS envoy meets with Nicaraguan, Honduran representatives', OAU Press Release E-/199, 10 Dec. 1999, OAU Communiqué, 30 Dec. 1999.

[251] Hajnal, P., *The G7/G8 System: Evolution, Role and Documentation* (Ashgate: Aldershot, 1999).

[252] 'Yeltsin demands G8 Kosovo meeting', BBC News Online, 1 Apr. 1999, URL <http://news2.thls.bbc.co.uk/hi/english/world/europe/newsid%5F309000/309592.stm>.

[253] Ivanov, I., 'Du problème kosovar à la tragédie yougoslave' [From the Kosovo problem to the Yugoslav tragedy], *Le Monde*, 22 Apr. 1999, pp. 1, 19; and NATO Summit Statement on Kosovo, Press Release S-1(99)62, 23 Apr. 1999.

post-conflict force was also disputed, with NATO's insistence on a NATO-led force in contrast to the UN force proposed by Russia. Germany, as President of the European Council, led the European effort to find a compromise and following meetings in Moscow, Bonn and Rome, Russian Special Envoy Viktor Chernomyrdin travelled to Belgrade to urge Milosevic to accept an international presence in Kosovo. German officials, for their part, reiterated Moscow's call for a meeting of the G8 to discuss formulation of a UN resolution outlining a political and military settlement.[254]

The G8 foreign ministers' statement in Bonn on 6 May 1999 on general principles on the political solution to the Kosovo crisis substantially narrowed the gap between Russian and Western positions. The statement called for the deployment of an effective international civil and security presence, 'endorsed and adopted by the United Nations', a UN interim administration and a political settlement providing substantial self-government for the province.[255]

It took intense shuttle diplomacy between Chernomyrdin, US Deputy Secretary of State Strobe Talbott and EU envoy Finnish President Martti Ahtisaari during May before the details of a common peace deal for President Milosevic were worked out. After tense negotiations in Germany on 1–2 June, the three agreed on a deal that proposed an end to NATO bombing and a UN-authorized international force with an 'essential NATO participation' upon the 'verifiable withdrawal' of all Serb forces from Kosovo.[256] The FRY Parliament accepted the plan the next day. There was further disagreement among the G8 as to when NATO would cease its attacks, and discussions with China, also critical of the lack of an immediate ceasefire. It was thus not until 8 June that the G8 foreign ministers, meeting in Germany, agreed on a draft UN Security Council resolution, which in turn permitted agreement between NATO and the FRY on the phased withdrawal of all FRY forces from Kosovo on 9 June 1999.[257] The Security Council approved the G8 text the next day.

Asia

The multinational initiatives taking place in Asia reflect, in part, the lack of effectiveness of institutional frameworks for peace and security in that region. Australia's leadership of an international peacekeeping force in *East Timor* in September provided the most striking example of this. The *INTERFET* operation was distinct in a number of important ways. The Security Council approved the deployment of this force on 15 September to restore peace and security and provide humanitarian assistance to East Timor after anti-independence militia began violent rampages in protest at the results of the UN-organized referendum on the future of the province. INTERFET was

---

[254] Congressional Research Service (CRS) report for Congress, *Kosovo Situation Reports*, RL30156, Library of Congress, Washington, DC, May 1999, p. 4.

[255] For the text of the statement see *Disarmament Diplomacy*, June 1999, pp. 31–32.

[256] Cited in CRS report for Congress, *Kosovo Situation Reports*, RL30191, Library of Congress, Washington, DC, June 1999, p. 5.

[257] Atkins, R., 'G8 ministers agree Kosovo resolution', *Financial Times*, 9 June 1999, p. 1.

authorized, under Chapter VII of the UN Charter, to take all necessary measures to fulfil its mandate, which included protection of UNAMET.[258] The decision to approve a multinational rather than a UN force was partly in response to Indonesia's reluctance to hand over responsibility for security in East Timor to the UN (given long-standing UN condemnation of the Indonesian takeover of the province) and partly out of the need for a rapid response to the crisis. Such an operation was also a way of side-stepping the need for US congressional approval and financial support.[259]

Australia's willingness to lead the multinational operation was another crucial determinant in INTERFET's speedy deployment. On 20 September the first 2000 Australian troops arrived in East Timor, under the command of Major General Peter Cosgrove. By December, INTERFET had become much more than a coalition of regional actors, with 19 states contributing to a total force of 9400, of whom 4500 were Australian.[260]

This efficiency, combined with its robust mandate, enabled INTERFET to engage and disarm anti-independence militia groups relatively swiftly, so that by mid-October order had largely been restored to East Timor.[261] The border with West Timor remained a source of unrest, however, with pro-Jakarta militia using the latter as a staging post for cross-border attacks and prompting INTERFET to move half of its troops to the area.[262] The action was controversial: the Indonesian Government refused to grant INTERFET authorization to pursue the militia into West Timor and accused the Australian command of bias and over-aggression, an opinion allegedly shared by Asian members of the coalition force.[263] The memorandum of technical understanding on border management signed by INTERFET, the UN mission and the Indonesian armed forces on 22 November marked a significant improvement in relations between the security forces on the island. INTERFET also assisted humanitarian operations and the repatriation of over 110 000 refugees to East Timor.[264]

The diplomatic tensions that INTERFET leadership created for Australia's regional relations and the financial commitment involved made Australia eager to initiate the UN successor mission as rapidly as possible.[265] Although the Security Council voted on 25 October to establish a UN Transitional Administration (UNTAET) to assist East Timor's transition to independence,

[258] UN Security Council Resolution 1264, 15 Sep. 1999, para. 3.
[259] Crossette, B., 'UN moving ahead to organize force for Eastern Timor', *New York Times*, 14 Sep. 1999, p. 1.
[260] Australian Ministry of Defence, INTERFET Weekly Operational Update, 19 Nov. 1999, URL <http://203.46.183.231/EASTTIMOR>.
[261] Bostock, I., 'New UN ROE's key to Timor success or failure', *Jane's Defence Weekly*, vol. 32, no. 13 (29 Sep. 1999), p. 4.
[262] 'Peacekeepers dispute with Jakarta on clash', *International Herald Tribune*, 12 Oct. 1999, p. 7; and Shenon, P., 'UN to triple its border forces in East Timor, *New York Times* (Internet edn), 11 Oct. 1999, URL <http://www.nytimes.com/library/world/asia/101199timor-un.html>.
[263] 'World news round up', *Aviation Week & Space Technology*, 11 Oct. 1999, p. 25; and Robinson, G., 'Canberra disquiet on role in East Timor', *Financial Times*, 4 Oct. 1999, p. 5.
[264] Fifth periodic report to the UN on the operations of the International Force, East Timor, 11 Nov.–9 Dec 1999, Appendix to Letter from the Secretary-General to the President of the Security Council, UN document S/1999/1248, 14 Dec. 1999.
[265] Richardson, M., 'Australia presses UN to send Timor Force', *International Herald Tribune*, 5 Oct. 1999, p. 5.

the appointment of a force commander was contentious. East Timorese leaders vetoed proposals for a representative of an ASEAN state, and no states outside the region appeared keen to play a leading role. Agreement was finally reached on a Filipino commander, Major General Jaime de los Santos.[266] UNTAET will consist of up to 8950 troops, 200 military observers and 1640 officers. Its deployment was not envisaged before February 2000. With the envisaged transfer of many current INTERFET troops to the UN operation, the responsibility for preparing a transition plan was placed with Australia.[267]

A number of informal groupings continue to serve as facilitators for peace processes. In Afghanistan the *'six plus two'* group of China, Iran, Pakistan, Tajikistan, Turkmenistan and Uzbekistan along with the USA and Russia continued its efforts to engage the Taleban and the northern-based United Islamic Front for the Salvation of Afghanistan (UIFSA, also called the Northern Alliance) opposition in peace talks. A meeting held by the group in Uzbekistan in July failed to secure any agreement between the warring parties, and one week later the Taleban launched a major new offensive against the United Front.[268] The group did succeed in signing a declaration that commits participating states not to provide military support to the combatants.[269] Although the 'six plus two' group reiterated this agreement at the UN in September, Kofi Annan criticized unspecified members for continued support to various sides in the conflict.[270] Pakistan, despite government denials, is widely regarded as the main external source of Taleban support in terms of volunteers (up to 8000 men according to some estimates) and logistic support and advice from Pakistani military intelligence.[271] The potential significance of the group for a future peace initiative increased with the freezing of the UN special envoy's efforts in Afghanistan and Security Council imposition of economic sanctions on the country in November.[272]

The South Pacific and Australia

The South Pacific proved a more congenial environment for Australian-led multinational forces. A combined operation of 295 Australian, Fijian, New Zealand and Vanuatun troops monitors implementation of the Lincoln Agreement on Peace, Security and Development, signed at Lincoln University, New

---

[266] UN Security Council Resolution 1272, UN Press Release SC/6745, 25 Oct. 1999; Richardson, M., 'East Timor leaders oppose a Malaysian-led force', *International Herald Tribune*, 3 Nov. 1999, p. 5; and UN Press Release SG/A/718, 29 Dec. 1999.

[267] UN document S/1999/1248 (note 264).

[268] UN, Report of the Secretary-General, The situation in Afghanistan and its implications for international peace and security, UN document S/1999/994, 21 Sep. 1999.

[269] Davis, A., 'Taliban's summer attack kills latest peace talks', *Jane's Defence Weekly*, vol. 32, no. 5 (4 Aug. 1999), p. 13.

[270] UN Press Release SG/SM/7144, AFG/108, 23 Sep. 1999; and 'Afghan brokers criticized over peace efforts', BBC News Online, 28 Sep. 1999, URL <http://news.bbc.co.uk/hi/english/world/south_asia/newsid_458000/458700.stm>.

[271] Davis, A., 'Pakistan's war by proxy in Afghanistan loses its deniability', *Jane's Intelligence Review*, vol. 11, no. 10 (Oct. 1999), pp. 32–34; and 'Pavement pals', *The Economist*, vol. 352, no. 8130 (31 July 1999), p. 53.

[272] UN, Office of Spokesman for Secretary-General, Daily Press Briefing, 29 Nov. 1999.

Zealand in January 1998 between the government and secessionists on the Papua New Guinean island of Bougainville.[273] The mandate of the *Peace Monitoring Group* (PMG) includes the creation and training of a police force and a significant peace-building component to facilitate the restoration of civilian authority on the island. Australia has established a five-year AUS$100 million ($75 million) programme as part of this rehabilitation effort.[274] The PMG supports the UN Political Office in Bougainville supervising the disarmament of former combatants. The office also began developing a plan for weapons disposal during the year.[275]

The Middle East

The *Temporary International Presence in Hebron* (TIPH) continued to monitor Israeli–Palestinian relations in the West Bank town that remains one of the flashpoints of the conflict between the two sides. The 180 observers from Denmark, Italy, Norway, Sweden, Switzerland and Turkey are intended to provide reassurance to the Palestinians in the city and have been increasingly criticized by Israeli officials for bias.[276] The five-nation *Monitoring Group* observing the Israeli–Lebanon ceasefire in south Lebanon since 1996 met regularly during the year to consider complaints of violation from both sides of the 1996 understanding banning attacks on civilians.[277] The *Multinational Force and Observers in the Sinai* (MFO) continues to monitor military activities along their common border in accordance with the 1979 Treaty of Peace between Egypt and Israel. During 1999, 1844 personnel from 11 countries served in the force, with additional funding from Germany, Japan and Switzerland.[278]

Latin America

The *Military Observer Mission to Ecuador/Peru* (MOMEP), established in 1995 by Argentina, Brazil, Chile and the USA, was formally ended in June. The mission to verify the ceasefire between Ecuador and Peru facilitated resolution of the century-old border dispute with the formal demarcation of the border in May.[279]

---

[273] UN, Statement by the President of the Security Council, UN document S/PRST/1998/10, 22 Apr. 1998.

[274] Information provided by the Australian Embassy, Stockholm, 10 Dec. 1999; and Australian Agency for International Development, Press Release AA27, 30 Apr. 1998.

[275] UN Press Release SC/6697, 8 July 1999.

[276] Agreement on the Temporary International Presence in Hebron (TIPH), 21 Jan. 1999; and 'Mandate of International Presence in Hebron Extended', Israel Foreign Ministry Statement, 2 Aug. 1999, URL <http://www.israel.org/mfa/go.asp?MFAH0dga0>.

[277] US Department of State, Office of the Spokesman, Press Statements on Behalf of the Chairman of the Monitoring Group, 15 Apr., 20 Apr. and 23 Sep. 1999.

[278] Annual Report of the Director General of the Multinational Force and Observers, Rome, Jan. 1999.

[279] US Department of Defense, News Release, no. 298–99, 17 June 1999, URL <http://www.defenselink.mil/news/Jun1999/b06171999_bt298-99.html>.

V. Other players

Unilateral action by states

Third-party efforts

The leading role played by the *USA* in practically every significant conflict in the world during 1999 testified to the multifaceted nature of its relative power. It was also a reflection of US preferences for unilateral foreign policy action and the particular reluctance of its legislators to work through UN channels.

The USA led the international community's efforts to prevent India and Pakistan's clash over the disputed territory of Kashmir escalating into general war in May–July 1999. The imperative for restraint in this long-running conflict became more urgent in the light of both sides' testing of nuclear devices in 1998 but is hampered by India's traditional reluctance to permit international mediation in the Himalayan region. The UN and the G8 responded to the incursion by Pakistan-backed militants across the Line of Control (LOC) into the Indian-administered part of Kashmir in May with calls for bilateral resolution of the dispute. Although there was concern at India's refusal to begin talks before the withdrawal of all foreign troops from its territory, international opinion was sceptical of Pakistan's initial insistence that it had no control over the militants (Pakistan's army chief later admitted that his country's troops had crossed the LOC).[280] On 15 June, three days after an unsuccessful bilateral meeting, President Bill Clinton telephoned Pakistani Prime Minister Nawaz Sharif and requested him to withdraw his troops behind the LOC. He also contacted the Indian Prime Minister, A. B. Vajpayee, to express US appreciation of India's restraint in ordering its troops not to cross the LOC.[281] US officials followed this up with visits to both countries urging a return to bilateral negotiations.

A breakthrough in the conflict came in a meeting between President Clinton and Prime Minister Sharif in Washington on 4 July where Sharif agreed to the withdrawal of Pakistani forces and the restoration of the LOC. A joint statement called for bilateral dialogue and promised that the US president 'would take a personal interest in encouraging an expeditious resumption and intensification of those bilateral efforts, once the sanctity of the Line of Control has been fully restored'.[282] Although Pakistani Army forces completed their withdrawal from Indian territory by mid-July, the situation between the two states remained uneasy, with Islamic militants still undertaking rebel attacks across the LOC and sporadic clashes between Indian and Pakistani

---

[280] 'India rejects Pak talks offer', *Assam Tribune*, 26 June 1999, URL <http://www.assamtribune. com/jun2699/at03.html>; Dhume, S. and Rashid A., 'On higher ground', *Far Eastern Economic Review*, vol. 162, no. 27 (8 July 1999), pp. 10–11; and Kazmin, A. L. 'Pakistan says its troops crossed over Kashmir line', *Financial Times*, 17–18 July 1999, p. 4.

[281] 'Clinton asks Sharif to pull out forces', *Assam Tribune*, 16 June 1999, URL <http://www. assamtribune.com/jun1699/at01.html>; and Leitch LePoer, B., *Recent Developments in Kashmir and US Concerns*, CRS Report for Congress, RS20277 (Library of Congress: Washington, DC, 26 July 1999).

[282] Text of the joint statement issued by US President Bill Clinton and Pakistani Prime Minister Nawaz Sharif, 4 July 1999, *Disarmament Diplomacy*, no. 38 (June 1999), pp. 35–36.

troops. At the end of 1999 negotiations between New Delhi and Islamabad on the dispute had not resumed.[283]

The USA put new energy into its brokerage of the deadlocked Middle East peace process in the second half of 1999, with President Clinton declaring it his top priority for the remainder of his administration. The defeat of the confrontational Benjamin Netanyahu by the leader of the Israeli Labour Party, Ehud Barak, in May's national elections gave new impetus to the resumption of discussions on the implementation of the 1998 Wye River Memorandum.[284] Barak pledged to proceed with Israeli withdrawal from southern Lebanon and the West Bank and to review the status of Palestinian territories.[285] A peace administration was established in the Prime Minister's Office to manage negotiations with Lebanon, the Palestinian Authority and Syria, with the first meetings initiated prior to a four-day US–Israeli summit meeting in July.[286]

Subsequent Israeli and Palestinian discussions addressed the difficult issues of the safe passage of Palestinians, the release of prisoners by both sides and the withdrawal of Israeli troops. US and Egyptian facilitation was necessary before the two sides signed the Sharm el-Sheikh Memorandum on 4 September, which outlines a timetable for the implementation of the final peace accord by September 2000 including the transfer of 40 per cent of the West Bank to full or partial Palestinian control.[287] Agreement on a plan for safe passage of Palestinians between the West Bank and the Gaza Strip was reached one month later, as were arrangements for the handover of prisoners between the two sides. Talks on the final status of Jerusalem and the borders of the Palestine state, as well as the fate of Palestinian refugees and Jewish West Bank settlers, continued to the end of the year. Progress was blighted by Israel's decision to delay its planned 5 per cent withdrawal from the West Bank and led to Palestinian threats to call off negotiations.

The standoff in Israeli–Palestinian talks coincided with the renewal of contact between Israel and Syria for the first time since 1996. Syria's president of 30 years, Hafez al-Assad, demonstrated willingness to meet Barak half-way when he ordered the factions of the Alliance of Palestinian Forces (APF) under Syria's patronage to lay down arms.[288] US Secretary of State Madeleine Albright visited Damascus during her tour of the region in September, paving the way for intense telephone diplomacy between Clinton and Assad and Barak that culminated in Syrian–Israeli preliminary talks in Washington on 15 December. The core issue is Israeli withdrawal from the Golan Heights. Syria insists that the late Israeli Prime Minister, Yitzhak Rabin, agreed in prin-

---

[283] 'India and Pakistan clash in Kashmir', BBC News Online, 10 Nov. 1999, URL <http://news2.thls.bbc.co.uk/hi/english/world/south_asia/newsid_513000/513810.stm>.

[284] For the text of the Wye River Memorandum, see *SIPRI Yearbook 1999* (note 170), appendix 3A.

[285] 'Barak pledges to unite Israel', BBC News Online, 18 May 1999, URL <http://news2.thls.bbc.co.uk/hi/english/world/middle%5Feast/newsid%5F346000/346512.stm>.

[286] Eshel, D., 'New teams set to manage Israel's security issues', *Jane's Defence Weekly*, vol. 31, no. 25 (23 June 1999), p. 19.

[287] For the text of the Sharm el-Sheikh Memorandum see URL <http://www.monde-diplomatique.fr/focus/mideast/charm99-en>.

[288] Strindberg, A., 'Palestinian alliance prepares for peace', *Jane's Intelligence Review*, vol. 11, no. 10 (Oct. 1999), pp. 23–26.

ciple to withdrawal to the pre-1967 frontier prior to his assassination in 1995. Israel, however, denies that any definite agreement was reached.[289]

Israeli–Syrian developments are closely linked to the third strand of the Arab–Israeli peace process: relations between Israel and Lebanon. Although Barak promised the withdrawal of army forces from southern Lebanon by July 2000, Israeli negotiators were unwilling to contemplate this step before the Islamic resistance group active in the area, Hizbollah, was brought under control. Syria, as Lebanon's principal power broker, has been a source of support for Hizbollah in the past and, given its 30 000 troops deployed in Lebanon, the only actor that could conceivably rein in the militants.[290] Syria insists that Israel's withdrawal from southern Lebanon, the last militarily active frontier of the Arab–Israeli conflict, must be part of any regional peace agreement.

The USA was far from the only actor involved in the steps towards reconciliation between Greek and Turkish Cypriots during 1999, the 25th anniversary of the Turkish invasion of the northern third of Cyprus. Its renewed engagement, however, provided the crucial boost in the complex hexagonale of Greece, Turkey, Greek and Turkish Cypriots, the EU and the UN. Grounds for the resumption of talks between Greek and Turkish Cypriot leaders, frozen since 1997, were laid by the UN Secretary-General in June, when he outlined his intention to invite both sides to negotiations.[291] The proposed framework for a political settlement remained that of a loose federation of two semi-autonomous communities, an unacceptable arrangement for Turkish Cypriot leader Rauf Denktash, who insists on international recognition of northern Cyprus as a sovereign state. The growing thaw in Greek–Turkish relations after the disastrous earthquake in Turkey in August, however, and the consequent resumption of high-level contact between Turkey and the EU in September, offered hope that the two countries might persuade their respective Cypriot partners to modify their positions. The USA capitalized on the improved political climate to raise the issue with Turkish Prime Minister Bülent Ecevit during his visit in September and appointed a Special Envoy, Alfred Moses, to Cyprus.[292] Clinton's statement that there could be no return to the pre-1974 status of the island was regarded as a significant breakthrough by Turkey and the first step on the way to achieving some way of satisfying northern Cyprus' demand for recognition short of statehood.[293] Clinton's visit to Greece and Turkey in November coincided with the agreement of Greek

[289] Hirst, D., 'What price an honourable peace?', *Guardian Weekly*, 23–29 Dec. 1999, p. 6.

[290] Kahwaji, R., 'Syria expects "swift but tough" talks with Israel', *Jane's Defence Weekly*, vol. 32, no. 25 (22 Dec. 1999), p. 21.

[291] UN Press Release SC/6694, 29 June 1999; and UN Security Council Resolution 1251, 29 June 1999.

[292] Boulton, L., 'Clinton renews effort to settle Cyprus dispute', *Financial Times*, 20 Sep. 1999, p. 3; and 'Clinton calls for Cyprus deal', BBC News Online, 29 Sep. 1999, URL <http://news2.thls.bbc.co.uk/hi/english/world/europe/newsid_460000/460408.stm>.

[293] Anadolu Agency, News in English, 2 Oct. 1999, point 17, URL <http://www.hri.org/news/turkey/anadolu/1999/99-10-02.anadolu.html#17>; and Boulton, L., 'Settlement sought to end "myth" of a single Cyprus', *Financial Times*, 18 Oct. 1999, p. 2.

and Turkish Cypriots to begin so-called 'proximity talks' at the UN on 3 December.[294]

Mediation between Turkey and the EU was another element in the US strategy. The USA continued to press the EU to satisfy Turkey's long-standing EU ambitions, an effort that contributed to a breakthrough at the Helsinki European Council meeting when Greece set aside its reservations to enable the EU to offer Turkey formal status as a candidate for membership. The EU proposal is linked to a political settlement on Cyprus, reflecting members' concern at incorporating a divided island into the Union, and also calls on Greece and Turkey to bring their disputes to international arbitration. Turkey's hesitation towards a conditional offer necessitated Clinton's personal intervention to urge its acceptance of the proposed EU terms.[295]

The on-again off-again diplomacy between North and South Korea and the USA continued throughout 1999.[296] There was initial optimism that South Korea's 1998 'sunshine' policy stressing peaceful coexistence could be the key to facilitating North Korean cooperation on a range of issues, including missile testing and security on the peninsula.[297] The visit of US Presidential Envoy William Perry to Pyongyang in May signalled US support for this new engagement and encouraged hopes for the resumption of US–North Korean relations, formally frozen since the Korean War.[298] An armed clash between North and South Korean navies in the fishing ground that spans their disputed maritime border two weeks later, however, put hopes of a rapprochement once again on hold.[299] Talks between generals from the US-led UN Command and North Korea on 21 July failed to reach agreement on ways of avoiding future incidents and North Korea subsequently declared that it wanted to deal directly with the US Administration.[300] In August North Korean President Kim Jong II indicated his willingness to negotiate the possible suspension of long-range missile tests. Such statements are widely interpreted as an attempt to use the missile threat as a way of extracting international economic assistance to alleviate famine in the country.[301]

Domestic efforts

States are commonly reluctant to involve outside actors in internal conflicts, partly because external intervention is perceived to demonstrate weakness, partly for fear that outside involvement may bestow legitimacy on an opposi-

[294] Boulton, L. and Fidler, S., 'Turkey, Greece urged to continue talking', *Financial Times*, 16 Nov. 1999, p. 2.

[295] Peel, Q. and Boulton, L., 'Solana tries to clear Turkey's path to EU candidacy', *Financial Times*, 11 Dec. 1999, p. 1.

[296] See also chapters 8 and 11 in this volume.

[297] For an outline of this policy see Hong, S., 'Thawing Korea's cold war: the path to peace on the Korean Peninsula', *Foreign Affairs*, vol. 78, no. 3 (May–June 1999), pp. 8–12.

[298] Wehrfritz, G., 'Behind the closed door, a deal is born', *Newsweek*, 7 June 1999, p. 53.

[299] Hollingsbee, T., 'Koreans clash in the Yellow Sea', *Jane's Intelligence Review*, vol. 11, no. 7 (July 1999), p. 2.

[300] AP, 'Generals from UN Command, North Korea fail to reach agreement', 21 July 1999.

[301] Sims, C., 'North Korea offers to negotiate on missile tests, easing crisis', *New York Times* (Internet edn), 19 Aug. 1999, URL <http://www.nytimes.com/library/world/asia/081999nkorea-missile.html/>.

tion movement and partly out of unwillingness to have constraints imposed on their handling of disputes. The principle of state sovereignty has traditionally provided strong justification for non-interference. In 1999, a significant number of states attempted unilateral negotiation of their own intra-state conflicts. International approbation, or at least tolerance, of such efforts is determined as much by considerations of the relative power of the state in question and the potential of the conflict for spreading as by the efficacy and legitimacy of its policies. Russia's operations in Chechnya amply illustrated these issues in 1999.[302]

The ceasefire declared by the *Basque* guerrilla group Euzkadi Ta Azkatasuna (ETA, Basque Homeland and Liberty) in September 1998 raised the prospect of an end to the 30-year conflict between the Spanish Government and Basque separatists. Progress was fitful, however, with street violence rife in the region and the continued crackdown by Spanish and French police forces on ETA guerrillas. Although the government of President José María Aznar declared itself willing to begin peace talks, Spain refused to discuss recognition of a Basque right of self-determination.[303] The ETA and its political arm Euskal Herritarrok (formerly Herri Batasuna), meanwhile, refuse to consider a permanent ceasefire until provisions are made to give the Basques a right to decide on their status.[304] With such entrenched positions little headway was made in a round of secret talks between the two sides held outside the country in May.[305] An ETA offer of new talks in October received little response and was instrumental in the group's announcement, one month later, that it would suspend its ceasefire on 3 December.[306] The ETA blamed the Spanish and French governments for their lack of effort and moderate Basque nationalists for reneging on a 1998 secret accord to cooperate in seeking independence (an agreement since renewed).[307] Thousands of people throughout Spain marked 3 December with street protests against the ETA decision.

The election, albeit uncontested, of Abdelaziz Bouteflika as president of *Algeria* in April increased hopes for a settlement to the conflict waged since 1992 between the Algerian Army and military supporters of the banned Armée Islamique du Salut (AIS, Islamic Salvation Army). Although falling well short of a peace process, Bouteflika's call for national reconciliation, his release of thousands of jailed Islamic militants in July and a publicly endorsed amnesty plan for Islamic rebels in September represented the most significant breakthrough in the civil conflict since the AIS suspended active operations in 1997.[308] The government remained adamant, however, that the AIS would not

---

[302] The conflict in Chechnya is addressed in chapter 3 of this volume.

[303] Such a concession would require the revision of the 1978 Spanish Constitution and, in theory, could pave the way for Basque secession.

[304] 'No permanent Basque ceasefire without independence—ETA', BBC News Online, 29 Mar. 1999, URL <http://news2.thls.bbc.co.uk/hi/english/world/europe/newsid%5F307000/307389.stm>.

[305] 'Spain and the Basques, more talks', *The Economist*, vol. 351, no. 8124 (19 June 1999), p. 34.

[306] 'Basque separatists offer peace talks', BBC News Online, 24 Oct. 1999, URL <http://news2.thls.bbc.co.uk/hi/english/world/europe/newsid%5F483000/483925.stm>.

[307] White, D., 'ETA to end truce after 14 months', *Financial Times*, 29 Nov. 1999, p. 3.

[308] Cooley, J., 'Light at last in Algerian darkness', *International Herald Tribune*, 15 July 1999, p. 8.

be permitted to return to national politics, prompting its jailed leader, Abassi Madani, to renounce in December his initial support of the peace initiative.[309]

The accession of King Mohammed VI to the throne vacated with the death of his father, King Hassan II, in July marked the initiation of a programme of domestic political liberalization in *Morocco*. King Mohammed's promising start also extended to Western Sahara, where a UN-brokered 1991 ceasefire maintains an uneasy peace between the Moroccan regime and the Western Saharan Independence Movement, the Popular Front for the Liberation of the Saguia el Hamra and Rio de Oro (the Polisario Front). The promised UN-sponsored referendum on the future of Western Sahara continues to be delayed by differences between the two sides on voter eligibility. Mohammed's speech on the 24th anniversary of his country's occupation of the territory, on 6 November, appeared to indicate the likelihood of a more cooperative Moroccan approach. The king promised a 'new vision' for the territory and the extension of a degree of self-government to Western Sahara.[310] Even as the king promised reform, however, Moroccan police used heavy force to break up pro-independence demonstrations in the territory.[311] Morocco's continued insistence on a comprehensive appeal process for a provisional voter list make the prospects of a referendum before 2002 remote.[312]

Fighting between government troops and the Liberation Tigers of Tamil Eelam (LTTE) in *Sri Lanka* intensified during 1999 after the army launched major offensives in June and September to unseat the separatist Tamil movement's dominance in the north and east of the island. A Tamil offensive in November led to the worst fighting in over a year.[313] Resumption of the stalled 1995 peace process was further blocked by the continued failure of the ruling alliance and opposition to establish a bipartisan consensus over a proposed constitutional reform plan that would grant significant autonomy to Tamil-majority areas. Presidential elections on 21 December increased opposition criticism of the government's dual strategy of defeating the LTTE militarily while proposing negotiated autonomy arrangements.[314] Colombo's political elite remained united in its opposition to the LTTE demand for international mediation in the conflict.[315] LTTE leaders insist on full independence, with continued assassinations of leaders of the moderate Tamil United Liberation

---

[309] 'Call to end Algeria truce', BBC News Online, 7 Dec. 1999, URL <http://news2.thls.bbc.co.uk/hi/english/world/middle%5Feast/newsid%5F553000/553691.stm>.

[310] Excerpts of King's speech, World mediawatch/BBC Monitoring, BBC News Online, 8 Nov. 1999, URL <http://news2.thls.bbc.co.uk/hi/english/world/monitoring/newsid%5F508000/508675.stm>.

[311] Pelham, N., 'King proposes Western Sahara council', BBC News Online, 14 Dec. 1999, URL <http://news2.thls.bbc.co.uk/hi/english/world/africa/newsid%5F508000/508335.stm>.

[312] UN, Report of the Secretary-General on the situation concerning Western Sahara, UN document S/1999/1219, 6 Dec. 1999.

[313] 'Sri Lanka rebels seize two bases', *International Herald Tribune*, 4 Nov. 1999, p. 4.

[314] Kainikara, S., 'The Tamil insurrection in Sri Lanka: an unwinnable war', *Asia–Pacific Defence Reporter*, Feb.–Mar. 1999, pp. 44–45.

[315] 'Tigers attack government-held town', BBC News Online, 18 Nov. 1999, URL <http://news.bbc.co.uk/hi/english/world/south_asia/newsid_526000/526216.stm>; and AFP (Colombo), 'Lankan troops kill four LTTE terrorists', 28 Sep. 1999, in 'Sri Lanka Tigers call for "international mediation"', FBIS-NES-1999-0930, 30 Sep. 1999.

Front underscoring a hardline approach.[316] The re-election of President Chandrika Kumaratunga, after an election campaign marked by violent LTTE attacks, made the prospect of a resolution to the war that is estimated to cost 5 per cent of Sri Lanka's annual gross domestic product gloomy.[317]

In *Myanmar* (Burma) fighting between the military junta government and rebels from the ethnic independence movement, the Karen National Union (KNU), continued along the Thai–Burmese frontier during the year, forcing the Thai Army to step up border security.[318] Pro-democracy student activists intensified their campaign against the regime: on 1 October five gunmen stormed the Burmese embassy in Bangkok in protest at the junta's continued refusal to enter talks with the National League for Democracy (NLD), which won the 1990 election. Although the ensuing hostage crisis ended peacefully, Myanmar criticized the Thai Government's handling of the affair, notably its negotiation of the release of the gunmen in exchange for the 38 captives, and closed its border with Thailand. This prompted fears for the 150 000 Burmese refugees mainly located in refugee camps along the frontier.[319] The imposition of tighter security controls in Myanmar in September prompted the cancellation of UN Assistant Secretary-General Alvaro de Soto's scheduled visit to Rangoon, and international sanctions against the regime's policies continue.[320] So far, however, they have failed to persuade military rulers to begin talks with the NLD leader, Nobel peace laureate Aung San Suu Kyi.

The way was cleared for the start of peace talks between *Colombia's* most powerful leftist guerrilla group, the Fuerzas Armadas Revolucionarias Colombianas (FARC, Revolutionary Armed Forces of Colombia) and the government in late 1998, when President Andres Pastrana agreed to establish a demilitarized zone in the south of the country. Nevertheless FARC continued to demand significant proof that the government was clamping down on right-wing parliamentary groups that it alleges have strong contacts with security forces, before entering talks.[321] Dissension among senior military figures over the government's strategy and worsening violence, particularly by the second

---

[316] Dugger, C., 'Sri Lanka peacemaker's high-risk life, and death', *New York Times*, 24 Aug. 1999, URL <http://www.nytimes.com/library/world/asia/082499lanka-terror.html>.

[317] Chipauz, F., 'Sympathy vote seals president's victory', *Guardian Weekly*, 6–12 Jan. 2000, p. 26.

[318] 'Thai army on alert and fighting mounts', In brief, *Jane's Defence Weekly*, vol. 31, no. 9 (3 Mar. 1999), p. 63; and 'Rebels attack government troops', In brief, *Jane's Defence Weekly*, vol. 31, no. 26 (30 June 1999).

[319] 'AFP: Gunmen release hostages, flee to Thai–Burma border', AFP, 2 Oct. 1999, in FBIS-EAS-1999-1002, 4 Oct. 1999; 'Burmese gunmen release Thai minister', AFP (Hong Kong), 2 Oct. 1999, in 'Thai-Burmese border "tense" after embassy siege', FBIS-EAS-1999-1003, 4 Oct. 1999; 'AFP: Possible preparations for attack on refugee camps', *The Nation* (Bangkok), 11 Oct. 1999, in 'Rangoon masses troops near border to attack refugee camps', FBIS-EAS-1999-1010, 12 Oct. 1999; and 'Thailand wants Burmese students sent to third country', *Bangkok Post* (Bangkok), 10 Oct. 1999, in 'Thai official proposes UNHCR–Rangoon meeting on refugees', FBIS-EAS-1999-1010, 12 Oct. 1999.

[320] 'Senior UN Envoy's visit to Burma postponed', AFP (Hong Kong), 10 Sep. 1999, in FBIS-EAS-1999-0910, 13 Sep. 1999; and 'EU extends sanctions on Burma for six months', AFP (Paris), 11 Oct. 1999, in Foreign Broadcast Information Service, *Daily Report–West Europe (FBIS-WEU)*, FBIS-WEU-1999-1011, 12 Oct. 1999.

[321] 'Colombia talks peace in the long shadow of war', *The Economist*, vol. 350, no. 8101 (9 Jan. 1999), pp. 47–48; and 'Colombians dream of peace', *The Economist*, vol. 351, no. 8119 (15 May 1999), pp. 61–62.

left-wing guerrilla group, the Ejército de Liberación Nacional (ELN, National Liberation Army), whose demand for a demilitarized zone was rejected, hampered progress still further. In July FARC refused the government's proposal for the deployment of international observers in the demilitarized zone as a confidence-building measure and continue to run the area as a 'mini-state'.[322] Peace talks finally opened in the demilitarized zone on 24 October, alongside country-wide public demonstrations for peace. A 12-point agenda on political, economic and social reforms for the country, including FARC's long-standing demand for agrarian reform, is under discussion. A ceasefire agreement is not currently part of the negotiations.[323] In November the government agreed to reopen separate negotiations with the ELN after a number of secret meetings in Cuba and Venezuela.[324]

The regional implications of Latin America's longest-running conflict became an increasing source of concern during the year. Colombia is now the third largest recipient of US military aid as part of the US battle against drug trafficking, the source of most guerrilla funding.[325] US support to Colombia's counter-insurgency efforts has led to fears of full-scale military intervention, while the spillover of violence prompted Colombia's neighbours—Brazil, Ecuador, Peru and Venezuela—to mobilize troops along their borders in 1999.[326] In August Venezuela's new president, Hugo Chavez, announced that he would hold talks with Colombia's left-wing guerrilla groups in an effort to facilitate peace, a proposal that prompted immediate rebuke from Colombia. Although Colombian authorities are not categorically opposed to external mediation, it remains an option of last resort only if current internal negotiations fail.[327]

Individuals

A number of individuals played important roles as instigators, mediators and/or facilitators in peace processes during 1999. The influence of a particular individual may derive from his/her relationship with one or more of the parties in a conflict or from his/her status as an informal representative of a significant third party. Personal stature may also enable individuals to serve as authoritative independent actors in a conflict.

---

[322] 'Colombia's trembling peace', *The Economist*, vol. 351, no. 8123 (12 June 1999), pp. 57–58; and Reuters, 'Gunmen kill ex-Colombian peace commissioner', *New York Times* (Internet edn), 16 Sep. 1999, URL <http://www.nytimes.com/reuters/international/international-colombi.html>.

[323] 'Colombia: no more!', *The Economist*, vol. 353, no. 8143 (30 Oct. 1999), p. 68.

[324] 'Narco-terrorism rears its head again', *Latin American Weekly Report*, WR-99-45, 16 Nov. 1999, p. 532.

[325] US aid to Colombia totalled $1.6 billion over the past 2-year period. Dudley, S., 'Albright brings anti-drug aid and support for Colombia', *Guardian Weekly*, 20–26 Jan. 2000, p. 32.

[326] Leongómez, E. P., 'Clouds over Colombia', *NACLA Report on the Americas*, vol. 33, no. 2 (Sep.–Oct. 1999), pp. 6–9; and 'Brazil orders troop mobilisation to contain Colombian "spillover"', *Latin American Weekly Report*, WR-99-44, 9 Nov. 1999, p. 517.

[327] AFP, 'Pastrana reaffirms Colombia not regional threat', 18 Aug. 1999, in Foreign Broadcast Information Service, *Daily Report–Latin America (FBIS-LAT)*, FBIS-LAT-1999-0818, 18 Aug. 1999; and *O Globo* (Rio de Janeiro), 'FARC guerrillas willing to accept Brazilian mediation', 25 Aug. 1999, in FBIS-LAT-1999-0825, 25 Aug 1999.

The former Tanzanian President, *Julius Nyerere*, who died in October, was representative of the latter. His energetic efforts to facilitate a political settlement in Burundi led to the initiation of peace talks between the Burundi Government and opposition forces in Arusha, Tanzania, in mid-1998. The Nyerere Foundation was established to raise funds and general support for the negotiations, aimed at bringing an end to the conflict that has resulted in one of Africa's worst humanitarian plights.[328] In January Nyerere succeeded in convincing Burundi's neighbours to suspend economic sanctions imposed on the country after the 1996 military coup, in order to encourage the cooperation of the Burundian regime led by General Pierre Buyoya.[329] Three rounds of talks took place between January and September, but even before Nyerere's death in October violence between Hutu rebels and the Tutsi-dominated army had spiralled upward while doubts were being expressed as to the commitment to peace of the 18 parties involved.[330] The lack of participation of the principal armed opposition groups, the Conseil National pour la Défense de la Démocratie–Forces pour la Défense de la Démocratie (CNDD–FDD, National Council for the Defence of Democracy–Forces for Defence of Democracy) and the Parti pour la Libération du Peuple Hutu (Palipehutu, Party for the Liberation of the Hutu People), on Nyerere's own insistence, was also seen as a significant obstacle to a viable agreement.[331] The personalized nature of the Arusha peace process made the search for a new mediator particularly challenging.[332] At the Great Lakes regional summit on Burundi in December, *Nelson Mandela* was appointed to take over the process.[333] Mandela's first statements indicated his desire to bring all sides of the conflict into the talks, garnering rebel opposition support for his mediation.

Mandela's stature made him a prominent figure in conflicts throughout the world in 1999 and, with his retirement in June, he declared himself open to consider requests for mediation.[334] His long-running efforts for Libya's international rehabilitation came to fruition in April when the USA and the UK accepted his 1995 proposal that the trial of Libyan suspects of the Lockerbie aircraft bombing take place in a third country. Mandela's help was solicited in the Kosovo conflict and, although he declined to mediate there, he did assist Australia to secure the release of three Australian aid workers arrested by Serb authorities.[335] In a historic trip to the Middle East in October he visited Iran, Israel, Jordan, Syria and the Palestinian territories, but his offer to facilitate

[328] Kimani, M., 'Nyerere: end of the peace talks?', *Africa News*, vol. 5, no. 10 (15 Oct. 1999), p. 4.

[329] UN Press Release SG/SM/8671, AFR/128, 25 Jan. 1999.

[330] 'Burundi: December deadline for peace accord', IRIN-CEA weekly round-up 37, 11–17 Sep. 1999.

[331] Prendergast, J. and Smock, D., *Postgenocidal Reconstruction: Building Peace in Rwanda and Burundi*, Special report (United States Institute of Peace: Washington, DC, Sep. 1999), p. 9.

[332] Kimani, N., 'Nyerere: End of the peace talks?', *Africa News*, vol. 5, no. 10 (15 Oct. 1999), pp. 3–4.

[333] 'Burundi: Mandela succeeds Nyerere as peace facilitator', IRIN-CEA weekly round-up 48, 29 Nov.–3 Dec. 1999.

[334] Moyahi, G., 'Mandela continues to receive invitations for mediator role', SAPA (Johannesburg), 23 Nov. 1999, in 'RSA: Mandela still receives requests for mediation in DRC', FBIS-AFR-1124, 26 Nov. 1999.

[335] 'Mandela working on release of jailed Australians', SAPA (Johannesburg), 30 May 1999, in 'Mandela "working" on release of Australians jailed in FRY', FBIS-AFR-1999-0530, 1 June 1999.

progress in ongoing peace efforts was downplayed by the lead mediator, the USA.[336] Mandela claimed that his involvement in this region was the main reason for his reluctance to mediate in the DRC conflict, where he is the preferred candidate of the rebel opposition groups.[337]

Former US Senator *George Mitchell* renewed his brokerage of the Northern Ireland peace process in 1999. The April 1998 Good Friday Agreement between Republicans and Unionists provided for self-government for the province through the creation of a Northern Ireland Assembly and a 12-member cabinet, as well as the decommissioning of all paramilitary arms by May 2000.[338] The two sides, however, remained locked in disagreement over the timing of the process. Unionists, led by David Trimble of the Ulster Unionist Party, insisted that a prior start had to be made in the disarmament of the Irish Republican Army (IRA), while Republicans refused to contemplate handing over guns before the formation of a Northern Ireland government.[339] On 2 July, after intense negotiation efforts failed to produce agreement, the prime ministers of Britain and Ireland, Tony Blair and Bertie Ahern, presented the two sides with a joint devolution timetable. The strategy backfired as the Unionists maintained their steadfast refusal to participate in the new assembly while the discovery of continued IRA arms smuggling brought relations between the two sides to a new nadir.

George Mitchell agreed to a request by the two governments to undertake a review of the stalled peace process and, on 27 October, began a final round of talks. Mitchell's insistence on a media blackout, his quiet mediation style, and the trust he enjoys from both sides facilitated a breakthrough in mid-November when Unionists agreed to participate in a devolved government prior to IRA decommissioning. The IRA responded with a declaration stating its unequivocal support for the agreement. An independent disarmament commission, led by retired Canadian General John de Chastelain, is to oversee the decommissioning process.[340] The agreement paved the way for significant progress in the implementation of the 1998 agreement with the appointment of a cross-party cabinet for Northern Ireland on 29 November. The formal devolution of power from Westminister to the Northern Ireland Assembly followed two days later, while on 2 December the government of the Irish Republic amended Articles 2 and 3 of its Constitution. The new versions remove the

[336] US Department of State, International Information Programs, Public Diplomacy Query (PDQ), Transcript: State Department Noon Briefing, 29 Nov. 1999, PDQ Internet site, URL <http://pdq.state.gov/pdqhome.html>.

[337] 'Mandela declines mediation role in DRC conflict', PANA, 24 Nov. 1999, in 'RSA: Mandela "reluctant to mediate" in DRC conflict', FBIS-AFR-1999-1127, 29 Nov. 1999.

[338] Anthony, I., 'The Northern Ireland Good Friday Agreement', *SIPRI Yearbook 1999* (note 170), pp. 159–68.

[339] Schulze, K. and Smith, M. L. R., 'Arms issue plagues Ulster peace deal', *Jane's Intelligence Review*, vol. 11, no. 9 (Sep. 1999), pp. 18–22.

[340] Hoge, W., 'IRA endorses Ulster accord "unequivocally"', *International Herald Tribune*, 18 Nov. 1999, p. 4; and 'Positive signs of movement', *Irish Times* (Internet edn), 16 Nov. 1999, URL <http://www.ireland.com/newspaper/opinion/1999/1116/edi1.htm>.

territorial claim of the Republic on Northern Ireland and state that a united Ireland can only come about by consent.[341]

Former US President *Jimmy Carter* continued his conflict resolution activities through the International Negotiation Network established by his institute, the Carter Center. In December Carter brokered an agreement between Ugandan President Yoweri Museveni and President Bashir of Sudan to re-establish bilateral relations. The 11-point agreement calls for the formation of a Joint Ministerial Committee to establish a timetable for implementation.[342] Other individuals who played significant mediation and facilitation roles in 1999 include President *Hosni Mubarak* of Eygpt and Libyan leader Colonel *Muammar Qadhafi*.

Non-governmental organizations and financial actors

Although NGOs are central to the prevention, management and resolution of certain conflicts, their activities usually focus on civil society and emphasize long-term transformation of the conditions for conflict within and between societies. Humanitarian organizations such as the *International Committee of the Red Cross* and 1999 Nobel peace prize winners *Médecins sans Frontières* (MSF) operate under principles of strict neutrality or impartiality that inhibit their mediation in conflicts or peace processes. Such independence can incur the wrath of host countries, as MSF discovered in July when it was expelled from Afghanistan for criticizing the Taleban regime's treatment of women.[343]

Lobbying organizations work to bring international attention to a conflict or to offer potential peace proposals. In September the New York-based *Human Rights Watch* released an influential report on the failed Angolan peace process which criticized the UN and US failure to speak out against violations of the peace accord as a major cause of the return to war in Angola.[344] The *International Crisis Group* (ICG), based in Brussels, continued to provide authoritative analyses of the conflicts in the African Great Lakes region and the Balkans.[345] *Amnesty International*, meanwhile, continued to campaign actively for the establishment of the International Criminal Court.

The *Comunita di Sant'Egidio* is a public association of Christian laypeople based in Rome. It became active in conflict resolution in Mozambique's civil war in 1992 and since then has played a discreet but significant role in many conflict zones.[346] In 1999 it was active in peace initiatives in Burundi, the DRC and Sudan. In the DRC it was one of the actors initially nominated by the

---

[341] Rafter, K. and de Bréadún, D., 'Historic ceremonies to put seal on new era', *Irish Times*, 2 Dec. 1999, p. 1.

[342] 'Presidents of Sudan and Uganda take steps to restore diplomatic relations, cease rebel support', Carter Center press release, 8 Dec. 1999, URL <http://www.cartercenter.org/NEWS/RLS99/prsudanuganda.html>.

[343] Pilling, D., 'Doctors without fear or favour', *Financial Times*, 16–17 Oct. 1999, p. 9.

[344] Human Rights Watch, 'Angola unravels: the rise and fall of the Lusaka peace process', Sep. 1999, URL <http://www.hrw.org/reports/1999/angola>.

[345] IGC publications are available on the ICG Internet site, URL <http://www.crisisweb.org>.

[346] The Comunita di Sant'Egidio's Internet site is located at URL <http://www.santegidio.org>.

OAU to facilitate the national reconciliation process set out in the Lusaka Ceasefire Agreement.[347]

The *World Bank* leads international financial institutions in increasing awareness of the impact of development policies on conflict and the potential for conflict.[348] Its effort to elaborate a strategic approach to post-conflict reconstruction led to the establishment in 1997 of a Post-Conflict Unit within its Social Development Department. The Bank defines its role as a facilitator in 'the transition to sustainable peace' through support in infrastructure rehabilitation, advice on economic policy, aid coordination, institution building and social sector investment.[349] This was demonstrated particularly in its involvement in the Stability Pact for South Eastern Europe. The Bank's decision to award a $100 million loan to Russia on 28 December, despite the conflict in Chechnya, elicited criticism from some human rights activists.[350]

Private business has not been immune from articulation of the need for greater responsibility. The South African diamond firm De Beers bowed to international pressure in October and placed a worldwide embargo on the purchase of diamonds from Angola. The company also promised to review its buying operations in West and Central Africa after an NGO campaign, supported by the UN Sanctions Committee, brought public attention to the diamond trade as a major funding source for African conflicts.[351]

VI. Conclusions

There were mixed signals from the states, international organizations and other actors that constitute the international community regarding the resolution of armed conflict during 1999. Increased emphasis on the need to view the causes and consequences of conflict more comprehensively and greater willingness for critical self-assessment were some of the positive signs that emerged. These were paralleled, however, by a tendency to regard conflict as 'endemic' in some parts of the world and subsequent reluctance to provide the resources and support necessary to break cycles of conflict.

Perhaps the most significant lesson reinforced in 1999 is that the unity of the international community in negotiating violent conflict remains a fragile and rare commodity. This was most starkly demonstrated in the attempt by the UN Secretary-General to articulate a new norm of sovereignty which foundered on the opposition of many, predominantly African and Asian, states, to further

---

[347] UN document S/1999/1116 (note 66). The International Organization of La Francophonie was the other proposed facilitator.

[348] The World Bank is a group comprising the International Bank for Reconstruction and Development, the International Development Association and the International Financial Corporation as well as associated organizations. Although it is a specialized agency of the UN, like all such bodies it is a separate autonomous organization established by intergovernmental agreement.

[349] Annual Report of the World Bank, 1999, pp. 4–5, URL <http://www.worldbank.org/html/extpb/annrep/over/htm>.

[350] Jack, A., 'Russia receives $100m loan in spite of Chechen conflict', *Financial Times*, 29 Dec. 1999, p. 10.

[351] 'Angola: De Beers stops all Angolan diamond purchases', IRIN-SA weekly round-up 40, 2–8 Oct. 1999.

erosion of the principles of the equality of states and of non-intervention. The gulf between these states and those, mainly Western, countries keen to adapt the norms of the international system in an interventionist direction will provide a serious challenge to international cooperation in future conflict prevention, management and resolution.

Conflict prevention

The growing respectability of the concept of conflict prevention, illustrated by the UN Security Council's two-day debate on the issue in November, is one consequence of the change in patterns of international conflict. The contemporary dominance of internal conflict has encouraged the perception that the roots of organized violence—poverty, socio-economic disparities and absence of good governance—can be identified and addressed by internal and external actors. The conflicts in the DRC, Kosovo and East Timor forcefully demonstrated that the international community is not in need of early warning to prevent conflict but rather of sufficient political will and the appropriate tools. In response, discussion has moved further in the direction of assessing the cost of failure to prevent conflict and the means by which the international community can actively tackle prevention in the short, medium and long term. The challenge now is to elaborate concrete preventive policies for international and regional organizations that are specific and measurable in application. A number of Western states have already begun this process at the national level. Awareness of the need for greater critical assessment of the impact of arms transfers and development aid on the potential for conflict in the recipient state, and greater coordination between national security and development policies, are two significant consequences of this rethinking.

Peacekeeping and peace enforcement

The concept of peacekeeping was stretched perilously thin in 1999. External intervention in the name of humanitarian, peace-making or peacekeeping purposes, principally by regional organizations and multinational coalitions of states, continued to rise as a consequence of the dominance of intra-state conflict. The increasing primacy of these actors in international peace operations has at least three important consequences. First, it has enabled peacekeeping operations to be launched with greater speed and, often, efficiency. This is an important criterion for the achievement of an operation's goals, as INTERFET's deployment in East Timor illustrated. Second, regional peace operations have contributed to an increased willingness to employ robust rules of engagement and to enforce peace on the ground, particularly in defence of a legitimate government under attack from opposition forces (the rationale for ECOMOG's intervention in Sierra Leone). The often chaotic violence involved in intra-state conflict and the refusal of warring parties to respect the security of external peacekeepers have highlighted the need for peacekeepers to have the means, and the mandate, to adequately defend themselves and carry out their appointed tasks.

Peace enforcement also indicates that there is an external agenda beyond the separation of warring parties. The degree of impartiality with which foreign forces are perceived, therefore, is closely linked to the kind of peace being enforced. The NATO intervention in Kosovo amply illustrates this tension and points to the third important consequence of increased regional peacekeeping, namely, the challenge to the legitimacy and transparency of peace operations. Peace operations in the name of the international community, even with the explicit approval of the UN, are fraught with ambiguity. The potential for an operation to become identified with the national agenda of one or more states, as ECOMOG operations in Sierra Leone and Guinea-Bissau testify, is closely linked to the leadership role played by key states. The limited ability of the international community to monitor the day-to-day activities of a peace operation is an impediment to transparency.

The UN has in recent years moved from a focus on expanding its own capacities for peacekeeping to increased coordination and supervision of regional peace operations. Events in 1999 underscored renewed interest in the practical modalities for cooperation between the UN and regional organizations, both in general and specific cases, such as the UN–OAU liaison in peacekeeping in the DRC conflict. Training constitutes an important element in UN efforts to improve regional peacekeeping capacities, particularly in Africa.

Paradoxically, it was demonstrated in 1999 that the international legitimacy conferred by the UN is crucial for successful peace operations. Resolution of the Kosovo conflict came about only when the UN's legal and practical authority in the post-conflict operation was established. The lessons of this were quickly apparent in the negotiation of subsequent peacekeeping missions. Financial considerations are also significant for the reassertion of UN primacy because small groups of states are unable or unwilling to support an extensive operation. It is the UN, in most cases, that is saddled with the costly tasks of reconstruction and post-conflict rehabilitation.

Peace building

Ultimately, the evolving nature of peace operations is forcing a return to UN-centred operations. Peace operations in contemporary conflicts have become enormous, complex undertakings, in which the distinction between keeping, enforcing and building peace is ever more blurred. In most cases, the reconstruction and rehabilitation of society are the central tasks. In some, it involves the constitution of a state, as in East Timor and, arguably, Kosovo. The fact that the demand for civilian police and personnel in 1999 far outweighed that for troops is merely one indication of these developments. The UN system of specialized agencies and networks is arguably the only framework currently able to provide the diverse expertise and experience necessary for comprehensive peace operations. The trend towards inter-agency UNcoordinated operations, which incorporate regional organizations and international financial institutions, advanced significantly in 1999.

This development, however, creates a host of new problems and exacerbates old ones. Bureaucratic wrangling, different organizational cultures and rivalry over resource allocation are inevitable and may significantly impede, if not prevent, peace implementation. Although the UN-administered mission in Kosovo has sought to build on the lessons learned in Bosnia and Herzegovina, the difficulties inherent in a multi-agency peace-building operation are apparent there. The UN, with adequate financial and technical resources and sufficient political direction, may well manage oversight of such operations. The likelihood of it obtaining such resources, however, is less than slight. In the meantime, two consequences of complex peace operations are evident: first, the discrepancy in resources provided by the international community to different peace missions is likely to continue, if not increase. Second, peace operations are likely to evolve in character, composition and substance over the course of their life-cycle. The days of protracted, relatively static peace operations (e.g., the UN Interim Force in Lebanon, UNIFIL) are gone.

Conflict resolution

Conflict resolution can no longer be seen as a discrete activity culminating in a peace agreement but as a process that accompanies, if not follows, successful peace building. Events in 1999 demonstrated, yet again, the statist, top–down nature of most international resolution activity, with the UN continuing to serve more as a facilitator than as an initiator of resolution strategies. To some extent, this is a realistic reflection of its limited coercive or conducive abilities; yet it reinforces selective resolution by powerful external actors often concentrated on short-term opportunism and bargaining among political elites to the detriment of long-term resolution. During 1999, lack of international coordination and even rivalry in some cases contributed to ongoing conflict. There is a strong case to be made for greater international coordination of top–down conflict resolution and more substantive attention to long-term bottom–up strategies. The activities of NGOs and individuals provide innovative paths for the UN and states to follow.

Appendix 2A. Multilateral peace missions, 1999

RENATA DWAN, THOMAS PAPWORTH, MARTA REUTER and HENRY WATHEN

Table 2A lists multilateral peace missions (conflict prevention, observer, peace-keeping, peace-building and combined peacekeeping and peace-enforcement operations) initiated, ongoing or terminated in 1999. The missions are grouped principally by organization, either sole or lead, and listed chronologically within these groups. The first group, covering UN missions, is divided into three sections: 21 operations run by the Department of Peacekeeping Operations; 3 missions not properly defined as peacekeeping (under Chapters VI and VII of the UN Charter) and coordinated by the Department of Political Affairs; and 1 mission initiated by UN authority but carried out at UN request by an ad hoc coalition of member states. The next six groups cover missions conducted or led by regional organizations: 13 by the Organization for Security and Co-operation in Europe (OSCE); 4 by the North Atlantic Treaty Organization (NATO); 3 by the European Union (EU)/Western European Union (WEU); 3 by the Organization of African Unity (OAU); and 3 by the Economic Community of West African States (ECOWAS) Monitoring Group (ECOMOG). The section covering peace missions of the Commonwealth of Independent States (CIS) includes 2 missions carried out by Russia under bilateral arrangements. A final group lists missions led by other organizations or ad hoc coalitions of states recognized by the UN. Peace missions comprising non-resident individuals or teams of negotiators or sub-regional operations with ambiguous mandates, such as the interventions in the Democratic Republic of Congo, are not included.

Missions initiated in 1999, or new participating states in a mission, are listed in bold text; operations and participation ending in 1999 are in italics. Legal instruments underlying the establishment of an operation—UN Security Council resolutions or formal decisions by regional organizations—are cited in the first column.

Personnel numbers given for each operation are inevitably approximate, given regular staff rotation and temporary responses to on-the-ground situations. Numbers of personnel do not usually include civilian observers or civilian staff, either local or international. The main exception is for observers in OSCE missions, who are usually civilian. More detailed information on personnel, where available, is given in the endnotes. Mission fatalities are recorded from the beginning of the mission until the last reported date for 1999 and as a total for 1999. UN data on total mission fatalities are for all UN missions since 1948.

The annual cost of the missions, as well as any reported outstanding contributions to the operation at the close of the 1999 budget period (the date of which varies according to operation and institution) is approximate. Unless otherwise stated UN mission figures are as of 31 December 1999. Budget figures are given in millions of US dollars. Conversion from budgets set in other currencies is based on the rate of exchange on the date of the cited budget statement. In these cases, the original currency is included in the relevant endnote.

Table 2A. Multilateral peace missions

Acronym/(Legal instrument[a]) Name	Location	Start date	Countries contributing troops, military observers (mil. obs) and/or civilian police (CivPol) in 1999	Troops/ Mil. obs/ CivPol	Deaths: To date/ In 1999	Cost: Yearly/ Unpaid
United Nations peacekeeping operations (21 operations) (UN Charter, Chapters VI and VII)				12 768[1] 1 256[2] 4 436[3]	1 597 17[4]	1 700[5] 1 453.7[6]
UNTSO (SCR 50)[7] UN Truce Supervision Organization	Egypt/Israel/ Lebanon/Syria	June 1948	Argentina, Australia, Austria, Belgium, Canada, Chile, China, Denmark, Estonia, Finland, France, Ireland, Italy, Netherlands, New Zealand, Norway, Russia, Slovakia, Slovenia, Sweden, Switzerland, USA	– 78[8] –	38 –	.. ..
UNMOGIP (SCR 91)[9] UN Military Observer Group in India and Pakistan	India/Pakistan (Kashmir)	Jan. 1949	Belgium, Chile, Denmark, Finland, Italy, South Korea, Sweden, Uruguay	– 46[10] –	9 –	8.3[11]
UNFICYP (SCR 186)[12] UN Peacekeeping Force in Cyprus	Cyprus	Mar. 1964	Argentina, Austria, Canada, Finland, Hungary, Ireland, Netherlands, Slovenia, UK[13]	1 219[14] – 35[15]	169 1	45.6[16] 19.1[17]
UNDOF (SCR 350)[18] UN Disengagement Observer Force	Syria (Golan Heights)	June 1974	Austria, Canada, Japan, Poland, Slovakia	1 053[19] –[20] –	39 –	35.4[21] 53.8[22]
UNIFIL (SCR 425, 426)[23] UN Interim Force in Lebanon	Lebanon (southern)	Mar. 1978	Fiji, Finland, France, Ghana, India, Ireland, Italy, Nepal, Poland	4 504[24] –[25] –	235[26] 8[27]	148.9[28] 108.7[29]
UNIKOM (SCR 689)[30] UN Iraq–Kuwait Observation Mission	Iraq/Kuwait (Khawr 'Abd Allah water-way and UN DMZ)	Apr. 1991	Argentina, Austria, Bangladesh, Canada, China, Denmark, Fiji, Finland, France, Germany, Ghana, Greece, Hungary, India, Indonesia, Ireland, Italy, Kenya, Malaysia, Nigeria, Pakistan, Poland, Romania, Russia, Senegal, Singapore, Sweden, Thailand, Turkey, UK, USA, Uruguay, Venezuela	1 094[31] ..[32] –	13 –	54[33] 13.2[34]

Acronym (SCR)	Name	Location	Date	Contributing countries							
MINURSO (SCR 690)[35]	UN Mission for the Referendum in Western Sahara	Western Sahara	Sep. 1991	Argentina, Austria, Bangladesh, **Belgium**, *Canada*, China, Egypt, El Salvador, France, Ghana, Greece, Guinea, Honduras, **Hungary**, India, Ireland, Italy, Kenya, Malaysia, Nigeria, Norway, Pakistan, Poland, Portugal, Russia, **Senegal**, South Korea, Sweden, USA, Uruguay, Venezuela	27[36] 203[37] 81[38]			10 1		54.1[39] ..	
UNOMIG (SCR 849, 858)[40]	UN Observer Mission in Georgia	Georgia (Abkhazia)	Aug. 1993	Albania, Austria, Bangladesh, Czech Rep., Denmark, Egypt, France, Germany, Greece, Hungary, Indonesia, Jordan, Pakistan, Poland, Russia, South Korea Sweden, Switzerland, Turkey, UK, USA, Uruguay[41]	– 101[42] –			3 –		31[43] 8.8[44]	
UNMOT (SCR 968)[45]	UN Mission of Observers in Tajikistan	Tajikistan	Dec. 1994	Austria, Bangladesh, Bulgaria, Czech Rep., Denmark, Ghana, Indonesia, Jordan, Nepal, Nigeria, Poland, Switzerland, Ukraine, Uruguay	– 36[46] 3[47]			7 –		18.7[48] ..	
UNPREDEP (SCR 983)[49]	*UN Preventive Deployment Force*	*Macedonia*	*Mar. 1995*	*Argentina, Bangladesh, Belgium, Brazil, Canada, Czech Rep., Denmark, Egypt, Finland, Ghana, Indonesia, Ireland, Jordan, Kenya, Nepal, New Zealand, Nigeria, Norway, Pakistan, Poland, Portugal, Russia, Sweden, Switzerland, Turkey, Ukraine, USA*	1 049[50] 35 26			4 –		50[51] 20.3[52]	
UNMIBH (SCR 1035)[53]	UN Mission in Bosnia and Herzegovina	Bosnia and Herzegovina	Dec. 1995	Argentina, Austria, Bangladesh, Bulgaria, Canada, Chile, Denmark, Egypt, Estonia, Fiji, Finland, France, Germany, Ghana, Greece, Hungary, Iceland, India, Indonesia, Ireland, Italy, Jordan, Kenya, Lithuania, Malaysia, Nepal, Netherlands, Nigeria, Norway, Pakistan, Poland, Portugal, Romania, Russia, Senegal, Spain, Sweden, Switzerland, Thailand, Tunisia, Turkey, UK, Ukraine, USA	– – 1 795[54]			6 1		167.6[55] ..	
UNMOP (SCR 1038)[56]	UN Mission of Observers in Prevlaka	Croatia	Jan. 1996	Argentina, Bangladesh, Belgium, Brazil, Canada, Czech Rep., Denmark, Egypt, Finland, Ghana, Indonesia, Ireland, Jordan, Kenya, Nepal, New Zealand, Nigeria, Norway, Pakistan, Poland, Portugal, Russia, Sweden, Switzerland, Ukraine	– 27[57] –			– –		See UNMIBH[58]	
MONUA (SCR 1118)[59]	*UN Observer Mission in Angola*	*Angola*	*July 1997*	*Argentina, Bangladesh, Brazil, Bulgaria, Congo, Egypt, France, Gambia, Ghana, Guinea-Bissau, Hungary, India, Jordan, Kenya, Malaysia, Mali, Namibia, New Zealand, Nigeria, Norway, Pakistan, Poland, Portugal, Romania, Russia, Senegal, Slovakia, Spain, Sweden, Tanzania, Ukraine, Uruguay, Zambia, Zimbabwe*	589[60] 86[61] 309[62]			17 3		130.8[63] 101.2[64]	

Acronym/ (Legal instrument[a])	Name	Location	Start date	Countries contributing troops, military observers (mil. obs) and/or civilian police (CivPol) in 1999	Troops/ Mil. obs/ CivPol	Deaths: To date/ In 1999	Cost: Yearly/ Unpaid
MIPONUH (SCR 1141)[65]	UN Civilian Police Mission in Haiti	Haiti	Nov. 1997	Argentina, Benin, Canada, France, *India*, Mali, Niger, Senegal, Togo, Tunisia, USA	– / – / 242[66]	– / –	18.6[67] / ..
MINURCA (SCR 1159)[68]	UN Mission in the Central African Republic	Central African Republic	Apr. 1998	Benin, *Burkina Faso*, **Cameroon**, *Canada*, Chad, Côte d'Ivoire, Egypt, France, Gabon, Mali, *Portugal*, Senegal, *Togo*, Tunisia	762[69] / 37[70] / 16[71]	2 / –	33.4[72] / 36.9[73]
UNOMSIL (SCR 1181)[74]	*UN Observer Mission in Sierra Leone*	Sierra Leone	*July 1998*	*Bangladesh, Bolivia, China, Egypt, France, Gambia, India, Jordan, Kenya, Kyrgyzstan, Malaysia, Nepal, New Zealand, Norway, Pakistan, Russia, Slovakia, Sweden, Tanzania, UK, and Zambia*[75]	– / 105[76] / –	– / –	40.7[77] / 4.5[78]
UNMIK (SCR 1244)[79]	**UN Interim Administration Mission in Kosovo**	Kosovo (FRY)	June 1999	**Argentina, Austria, Bangladesh, Belgium, Bulgaria, Canada, Czech Rep., Denmark, Egypt, Estonia, Fiji, Finland, France, Germany, Ghana, Hungary, Iceland, Italy, Jordan, Kenya, Kyrgyzstan, Lithuania, Malaysia, Netherlands, Nigeria, Pakistan, Philippines, Poland, Romania, Russia, Senegal, Spain, Sweden, Tunisia, Turkey, Ukraine, UK, USA, Zambia, Zimbabwe**	– / – / 1 817[80]	1 / 1[81]	66.3[82] / ..
UNAMET (SCR 1246)[83]	*UN Mission in East Timor*	*East Timor*	*June 1999*	..	– / 36[84] / 16[85]	5 / 5[86]	54.4[87] / ..
UNAMSIL (SCR 1270)[88]	**UN Mission in Sierra Leone**	Sierra Leone	Oct. 1999	**Bangladesh, Bolivia, Canada, China, Croatia, Czech Republic, Denmark, Egypt, France, Gambia, Ghana, India, Indonesia, Jordan, Kenya, Kyrgyzstan, Malaysia, Namibia, Nepal, New Zealand, Nigeria, Norway, Pakistan, Russia, Slovakia, Sweden, Thailand, UK, Tanzania, Uruguay and Zambia**	4 600[89] / 220[90] / 4[91]	– / –	265.8[92] / ..

Mission	Location	Start	Participating states							
UNTAET (SCR 1272)[93] UN Transitional Administration in East Timor	East Timor	Oct. 1999	**Argentina, Australia, Austria, Bangladesh, Bolivia, Brazil, Canada, Denmark, Egypt, France, Ghana, Ireland, Japan, Jordan, Malaysia, Mozambique, Nepal, New Zealand, Pakistan, Philipines, Russia, Senegal, Spain, Sweden, Thailand, USA, UK, Uruguay, Zimbabwe[94]**	8 950[95] 200[96] 1 640[97]	— —		386.3[98] ..
MONUC (SCR 1279)[99] UN Observer Mission in the Democratic Republic of Congo	Democratic Republic of Congo	Nov. 1999	**Algeria, Bangladesh, Benin, Bolivia, Canada, Egypt, France, Ghana, India, Italy, Kenya, Libya, Mali, Nepal, Pakistan, Poland, Romania, Russia, Senegal, South Africa, Sweden, Tanzania, United Kingdom, Uruguay, Zambia**	— 79[100] —	— —		..[101] ..

Other UN operations[102] (3 operations)

Mission	Location	Start	Participating states							
MICIVIH (A/RES/47/20B)[103] International Civilian Mission in Haiti	Haiti	Feb. 1993	Argentina, Barbados, **Benin**, *Brazil*, Canada, Cap Verde, *Colombia*, **Cote d'Ivoire**, Chile, El Salvador, **France**, *Grenada*, **Italy**, *Jamaica, Mexico, Nicaragua, Paraguay, Peru*, **Rwanda**, *Saint Lucia*, **Senegal**, **Spain**, Trinidad and Tobago, UK, USA	.. 35[104] ..	— —		2.8[105] ..
UNSMA (A/RES 48/208)[106] UN Special Mission to Afghanistan	Afghanistan/Pakistan	Mar. 1994	France, **Germany**, Japan, **Spain**, UK[107]	— 7[108] —	1[109] —		3.0[110] ..
MINUGUA (A/RES 48/267)[111] UN Verification Mission in Guatemala	Guatemala	Oct. 1994	Argentina, **Bolivia**, Brazil, Canada, Colombia, El Salvador, **France**, Italy, Norway, Portugal, Spain, Sweden, Uruguay, Venezuela	— 20[112] 50[113]	6[114] —		30.1[115] ..

Multinational Missions Tasked and Authorized by the UN (1 operation)

Mission	Location	Start	Participating states							
INTERFET (SCR 1264)[116] *International Force for East Timor*	*East Timor*	*Sep. 1999*	*Australia, Brazil, Canada, Denmark, Egypt, Fiji, France, Germany, Ireland, Italy, Jordan, Kenya, Malaysia, New Zealand, Norway, Philippines, Portugal, Singapore, South Korea, Thailand, UK, USA[117]*	9 900[118] — —	2 2[119]		..[120] ..

Organization for Security and Co-operation in Europe (OSCE)[121] (13 operations)

Mission	Location	Start	Participating states							
— OSCE Spillover Mission to Skopje (CSO 18 Sep. 1992)[122]	Former Yugoslav Rep. of Macedonia	Sep. 1992	Germany, Italy, Norway, *Poland*, Slovakia, *Sweden*, UK, USA[123]	— 8[124] —	— —		0.6[125] ..

Acronym/ (Legal instrument[a])	Name	Location	Start date	Countries contributing troops, military observers (mil. obs) and/or civilian police (CivPol) in 1999	Troops/ Mil. obs/ CivPol	Deaths: To date/ In 1999	Cost: Yearly/ Unpaid
(CSO 6 Nov. 1992)[126]	OSCE Mission to Georgia	Georgia[127]	Dec. 1992	Austria, Bulgaria, Czech Rep., Denmark, France, Germany, Hungary, Ireland, Moldova, Norway, Poland, Romania, Slovakia, Spain, Sweden, Switzerland, Ukraine, USA	– 18 –	– –	1.4 ..
(CSO 13 Dec. 1992)[128]	OSCE Mission to Estonia	Estonia	Feb. 1993	Canada, Denmark, Finland, Germany, Sweden	– 6[129] –	– –	0.5[130] ..
(CSO 4 Feb. 1993)[131]	OSCE Mission to Moldova	Moldova	Apr. 1993	Finland, France, Germany, Lithuania, Netherlands, Poland, Slovakia, USA	– 8 –	– –	0.6 ..
(CSO 23 Sep. 1993)[132]	OSCE Mission to Latvia	Latvia	Nov. 1993	Finland, Germany, Norway, Poland, UK	5[133]	– –	0.6[134] ..
(1 Dec. 1993)[135]	OSCE Mission to Tajikistan	Tajikistan	Feb. 1994	Austria, France, Italy, Norway, Romania, Russia. USA	– 9[136] –	– –	0.1[137] ..
(PC 11 Apr. 1995)[138]	OSCE Assistance Group to Chechnya	Chechnya	Apr. 1995	Czech. Rep., Germany, Moldova, Norway, Poland, Romania	– 5[139] –	– –	1.4 ..
(10 Aug. 1995)[140]	Personal Representative of the Chairman-in-Office on the Conflict Dealt with by the OSCE Minsk Conference	Azerbaijan (Nagorno-Karabakh)[141]	Aug. 1995	Czech Rep., Germany, Hungary, Poland, Ukraine	– 5	– –	1.3 ..
(MC/5/DEC/1 8 Dec. 1995)[142]	OSCE Mission to Bosnia and Herzegovina	Bosnia and Herzegovina	Dec. 1995	Austria, Belarus, Belgium, Bulgaria, Canada, Czech Rep., Denmark, Finland, France, Georgia, Germany, Greece, Hungary, Ireland, Italy, Netherlands, Norway, Poland, Portugal, Romania, Russia, Spain, Sweden, Switzerland, Turkey, Ukraine, UK, USA	196	– –	37.4[143] ..

Reference	Mission	Location	Date	Participating States			
(PC/DEC 112, 18 Apr. 1996)[144]	OSCE Mission to Croatia	Croatia	July 1996	**Albania**, Armenia, Austria, Belarus, Belgium, Bulgaria, Canada, Czech Rep., Denmark, Finland, Former Yugoslav Republic of Macedonia, France, Georgia, Germany, Greece, **Hungary**, Ireland, Italy, Japan, Lithuania, **Moldova,** Netherlands, Norway, Poland, Portugal, Romania, Russia, Spain, Sweden, Switzerland, Turkey, Ukraine, UK, USA	205[145] / 98[146]	– / –	24.1[147] / ..
(PC/DEC 160, 27 Mar. 1997)[148]	OSCE Presence in Albania	Albania	Apr. 1997	Austria, *Bulgaria,* **Canada, Czech Rep., Denmark, France,** *Georgia,* Germany, Ireland, Italy, **Kazakhstan,** *Lithuania,* **Luxembourg,** Netherlands, Norway, *Poland,* Sweden, Switzerland, **Tajikistan,** UK, USA	38 / –	– / –	3.4 / ..
KVM (PC/DEC 263, 15 Oct. 1998)[149]	*Kosovo Verification Mission*	*Kosovo, FRY*	*Oct. 1998*	*Belgium, Canada, Denmark, Finland, France, Germany, Greece, Hungary, Italy, Kazakhstan, Lithuania, Norway, Poland, Romania, Russia, Sweden, Switzerland, Turkey, Ukraine, UK, USA*	1 400[150] / –	– / –	See OSCE Mission in Kosovo / –
(PC/DEC 305, 1 July 1999)[151]	**OSCE Mission in Kosovo**	**Kosovo**	**July 1999**	**Austria, Azerbaijan, Belarus, Belgium, Bulgaria, Canada, Czech Rep., Denmark, Estonia, Finland, France, Georgia, Germany, Greece, Hungary, Iceland ,Italy, Kazakhstan, Kyrgyzstan, Lithuania, Malta, Moldova, Netherlands, Norway, Poland, Portugal, Romania, Russia, Slovakia, Slovenia, Spain, Sweden, Switzerland, Tajikistan, Turkey, Ukraine, UK, USA**	481[152] / ..	– / –	81.2[153] / ..

North Atlantic Treaty Organization (NATO) and NATO led operations (4 operations)

Reference	Mission	Location	Date	Participating States			
SFOR (SCR 1088)[154]	NATO Stabilization Force	Bosnia and Herzegovina	Dec. 1996	Albania, Argentina, **Australia,** Austria, Belgium, Bulgaria, Canada, Czech Rep., Denmark, Estonia, Finland, France, Germany, Greece, Hungary, Iceland, Ireland, Italy, Latvia, Lithuania, Luxembourg, Morocco, Netherlands, **New Zealand,** Norway, Poland, Portugal, Romania, Russia, Slovakia, Slovenia, Spain, Sweden, Turkey, UK, *Ukraine,* USA[155]	24 500[156] / –	666 / –	.. / ..
KVM (SCR 1203)[157]	*NATO Kosovo Verification Mission*	*Kosovo, FRY*	*Oct. 1998*	*France, Germany, Italy, Netherlands, UK, USA*[158]	.. / ..	– / –	.. / ..

Acronym/(Legal instrument[a])	Name	Location	Start date	Countries contributing troops, military observers (mil. obs) and/or civilian police (CivPol) in 1999	Troops/Mil. obs/CivPol	Deaths: To date/In 1999	Cost: Yearly/Unpaid
XFOR (SCR 1203)[159]	NATO Extraction Force	Former Yugoslav Republic of Macedonia	Dec. 1998	France, Germany, Italy, Netherlands, UK	2 300[160] / – / –	– / –	.. / ..
KFOR (SCR 1244)[161]	NATO Kosovo Force	Kosovo, FRY	June 1999	Argentina, Austria, Azerbaijan, Belgium, Canada, Czech Rep., Denmark, Finland, France, Georgia, Germany, Greece, Hungary, Ireland, Italy, Jordan, Lithuania, Morocco, Netherlands, Norway, Poland, Portugal, Russia, Slovakia, Spain, Sweden, Switzerland, Turkey, UAE, UK, USA, Ukraine[162]	42 500[163] / .. / –	2[164] / 2[165]	.. / ..
European Union / Western European Union (3 operations)							
ECMM (Brioni Agreement)[166]	European Community Monitoring Mission	Former Yugoslavia/Albania	July 1991	Austria, Belgium, Denmark, Finland, France, Germany, Greece, Ireland, Italy, Netherlands, Norway, Portugal, Slovakia, Spain, Sweden, UK	– / 280[167] / –	7 / 1[168]	10.5[169] / ..
MAPE (WEU Council, 2 May 1997)[170]	Multinational Advisory Police Element for Albania	Albania	May 1997	Austria, Belgium, Czech Rep, Denmark, Estonia, Finland, France, Germany, Greece, Hungary, Italy, Luxembourg, Netherlands, Norway, Poland, Portugal, Romania, Slovenia, Spain, Sweden, Turkey, UK	144[171]	– / –	4.9[172]
WEUDAM (10 May 1999)[173]	**Western European Union Demining Assistance Mission in Croatia**	**Croatia**	**May 1999**	**Austria, Belgium, Bulgaria, Finland, France, Germany, Italy, Sweden**[174]	9[175] / – / –	– / –	0.5[176]
Russian and Commonwealth of Independent States (CIS) missions (4 operations)							
– (Bilat, 24 June 1992)[177]	South Ossetia Joint Force	Georgia (S. Ossetia)	July 1992	Georgia, Russia, South Ossetia	1 700[178] / .. / ..	.. / ..	.. / ..
– (Bilat, 21 July 1992)[179]	Joint Control Commission Peace-keeping Force	Moldova (Trans-Dniestr)	July 1992	Moldova, Russia, Trans-Dniesteria, Ukraine	1 590[180] / 38[181] / ..	3 / –	2.5[182] / ..

– (CIS 24 Sep. 1993)[183]	CIS Collective Peacekeeping Force	Tajikistan	Aug. 1993	Kazakhstan, *Kyrgyzstan*, Russia, Tajikistan	14 000[184]	–	>100	1[185]	.. ..
– (CIS 15 Apr. 1994)[186]	CIS Peacekeeping Forces in Georgia	Georgia (Abkhazia)	June 1994	Russia	1 600[187]	–	65	8[188]	.. ..

Organization of African Unity (OAU) (3 operations)

OMIB (OAU, 7 Dec. 1993)[189]	OAU Mission in Burundi	Burundi	Dec. 1993	..	3[190]	–	..	–	0.3[191] ..
OMIC (OAU, 6 Nov. 1997)[192]	OAU Observer Mission in the Comoros	Comoros	Nov. 1997	*Egypt, Niger, Senegal, Tunisia*	2[193]	–	..	–	0.6[194] ..
JMC (OAU, 3 Sep. 1999)[195]	Joint Military Commission	Democratic Republic of Congo	Sep. 1999	Algeria, Malawi, Nigeria, Senegal[196]	33	–	–	–	[197] .. ..

Economic Community of West African States Monitoring Group (ECOMOG) (3 operations)

ECOMOG (ECOWAS, 7 Aug. 1990)[198]	ECOWAS Monitoring Group	Liberia	Aug. 1990	*Ghana, Nigeria*[199]	–	–	+500	–	..
ECOMOG (OAU, 4 June 1997)[200]	ECOWAS Monitoring Group	Sierra Leone	May 1997	Ghana, Guinea, Mali, Nigeria	9 000[201]	–	..	..	202 .. ..
ECOMOG (Abuja Peace Agreement, 1 Nov. 1998)[203]	ECOWAS Cease-fire Monitoring Group in Guinea-Bissau	Guinea-Bissau	Dec. 1998	*Benin, Gambia, Niger, Togo*[204]	600[205]	–	..	–	.. ..

Other [206] (6 operations)

Acronym/ (Legal instrument[a])/ Name	Location	Start date	Countries contributing troops, military observers (mil. obs) and/or civilian police (CivPol) in 1999	Troops/ Mil. obs/ CivPol	Deaths: To date/ In 1999	Cost: Yearly/ Unpaid
NNSC (Armistice Agreement)[207] — Neutral Nations Supervisory Commission	North Korea/ South Korea	July 1953	Sweden, Switzerland, (Poland)[208]	– 10[209] –	– –	.. ..
MFO (Protocol to treaty)[210] — Multinational Force and Observers in the Sinai	Egypt (Sinai)	Apr. 1982	Australia, Canada, Colombia, Fiji, France, Hungary, Italy, New Zealand, Norway, Uruguay, USA	1 844[211] –	42 3[212]	49.4[213] –
MOMEP (Decl. of Itamaraty)[214] — Mission of Military Observers Ecuador/ Peru	Ecuador/Peru	Mar. 1995	Argentina, Brazil, Chile, Ecuador, Peru, USA	110[215] 34[216] –	– –	.. ..
TIPH 2 (Hebron Protocol)[217] — Temporary International Presence in Hebron	Hebron	Jan. 1997	Denmark, Italy, Norway, Sweden, Switzerland, Turkey	– 80[218] –	– –	2.3[219] ..
PMG (Lincoln Agt 1998)[220] — Bougainville Peace Monitoring Group	Papua New Guinea	May 1998	Australia, Fiji, New Zealand, Vanuatu[221]	295[222] .. –	– –	10.8[223] ..
CPDTF (Edinburgh Summit, Oct. 1997)[224] — Commonwealth Police Development Task Force	Sierra Leone	July 1998	Canada, **Malaysia**, Sri Lanka, UK, *Zimbabwe*	– – 6[225]	– –	.. ..

Notes for table 2A

[a] A/RES = UN General Assembly Resolution; Bilat = Bilateral; CSO = OSCE Committee of Senior Officials (now the Senior Council); DMZ = Demilitarized Zone; FY = Fiscal Year; GA = UN General Assembly; MC = Ministerial Council; MOU = Memorandum of Understanding; SC = UN Security Council; SCR = UN Security Council Resolution; PC.DEC = OSCE Permanent Council Decision.

[1] Information from Lt-Gen. Luigi Fraticelli, Military Adviser, UN Department of Peacekeeping Operations, 22 Feb. 2000.
[2] Fraticelli (note 1).
[3] Fraticelli (note 1).

4 Unless otherwise indicated information on fatalities in 1999 is from Tom Hojbjerg, UN Department of Peacekeeping Operations, Situation Centre, 24 Feb. 2000.

5 Total outstanding assessed contributions for all UN peacekeeping operations as of Nov. 1999. Report of the Secretary-General on the UN Operation in Cyprus, UN document S/1999/1203, 29 Nov. 1999.

6 As of 1 Jan. 2000. UN Status of Outstanding Contributions to the regular Budget, International Tribunals and Peacekeeping Operations as at 31 January 2000, UN Information Centre for the Nordic Countries, Copenhagen, 2000.

7 UNTSO was established in May 1948 to assist the Mediator and the Truce Commission in supervising the observance of the truce in Palestine after the Arab–Israeli War that followed the creation of the state of Israel. The mandate was maintained during 1999.

8 Report of the Secretary-General on the United Nations Disengagement Observer Force (UNDOF), UN document S/1999/1175, 15 Nov. 1999; and UN Press Release SC/6758, 24 Nov. 1999.

9 UNMOGIP was established in Mar. 1951 to replace the United Nations Commission for India and Pakistan, UNCIP (SCR 91). Its task mission was to supervise the ceasefire in Kashmir under the July 1949 Karachi Agreement. UNMOGIP Internet site, URL <www.un.org/Depts/DPKO/Missions/unmogip.htm>.

10 United Nations Peacekeeping Operations (UNPKO), Background Note, 1 Feb. 2000, UN Department of Public Information, New York, Peace and Security Section.

11 Appropriated for 2000. See note 10.

12 UNFICYP was established by the SC in Mar. 1964 through SCR 186 (1964) to prevent fighting between the Greek Cypriot and Turkish Cypriot communities and to contribute to the maintenance and restoration of law and order. Since 1974 UNFICYP's mandate has included monitoring the ceasefire and maintaining a buffer zone between the 2 sides. In Dec. 1999 the mandate was extended until 15 June 2000. SCR 1283, 15 Dec. 1999.

13 The Argentinian contingent also included soldiers from Bolivia, Brazil, Paraguay and Uruguay. UN document S/1999/1203 (note 5).

14 Military personnel as of Nov. 1999. UN document S/1999/1203 (note 5).

15 CivPol were provided by Austria and Ireland. UN document S/1999/1203 (note 5).

16 Appropriated amount for 1 July 1999 to 30 June 2000. A/RES/53/231, 8 June 1999.

17 From 16 June 1993 to 31 Dec. 1999. UN document S/1999/1203 (note 5).

18 UNDOF was established after the 1973 Middle East War under the Agreement on Disengagement and SCR 350 (1974), to maintain the ceasefire between Israel and Syria and to supervise the disengagement of Israeli and Syrian forces. In Nov. 1999 the mandate was extended until 30 May 2000. SCR 1276, 24 Nov. 1999.

19 Austria (368), Canada (189), Japan (45), Poland (358) and Slovakia (93). UN document S/1999/1175 (note 8).

20 UNDOF was assisted by 78 UNTSO military observers. UN document S/1999/1175 (note 8); and UN Press Release SC/6758, 24 Nov. 1999.

21 Appropriated amount for 1 July 1999 to 30 June 2000. UN document S/1999/1175 (note 8).

22 Unpaid assessments to the Special Account for UNDOF as of 31 Oct. 1999. UN document S/1999/1175 (note 8).

23 UNIFIL was established in Mar. 1978 through SCR 425 to confirm the withdrawal of Israeli forces from southern Lebanon, and to assist the Government of Lebanon in ensuring the return of its effective authority in the area. The force was prevented from fulfilling its mandate by the 1982 Israeli invasion of Lebanon, and its role is limited to providing protection and humanitarian assistance to the local population. In Jan. 2000 the mandate was extended until July 2000.

24 Fiji (600), Finland (494), France (245), Ghana (653), India (619), Ireland (612), Italy (46), Nepal (604) and Poland (631). Report of the Secretary-General on the United Nations Interim Force in Lebanon, UN document S/2000/28, 17 Jan. 2000.

25 UNIFIL was assisted by 51 UNTSO military observers. UN document S/2000/28 (note 24); and UN Press Release SC/6758, 24 Nov. 1999

26 The Secretary-General's report in Jan. 2000 only accounts for 2 fatalities during 1999 and 229 since the inception of the mission. Of these 229, 77 resulted from firings or bomb explosions, 94 from accidents and 58 from other causes. UN document S/2000/28 (note 24).

27 One Irish soldier was killed in a traffic accident and a Fijian soldier died of natural causes. UN document S/2000/28 (note 24).

28 Appropriated amount for 1 July 1999 to 30 June 2000. UN document S/2000/28 (note 24).

29 Unpaid assessments to the Special Account for as of 31 Dec. 1999. UN document S/2000/28 (note 24).

30 UNIKOM was established in Apr. 1991 through SCR 689 as an unarmed observation mission with the mandate to monitor the Khawr 'Abd Allah and the demilitarized zone and to observe any hostile actions between the two states. In Feb. 1993 the mandate was expanded with an infantry battalion by SCR 806 (1993) to prevent small-scale violations of the DMZ and the borders. UNIKOM's mandate does not have to be renewed but can only be terminated by a SC decision. SCR 687, 3 Apr. 1991.

31 Troops and military observers. UNPKO (note 10).

32 UNPKO (note 10).

33 $34.7 m. are paid by Kuwait. UNPKO (note 10).

34 As of 28 Feb. 1999. Report of the Secretary-General on the United Nations Iraq–Kuwait Observation Mission, UN document S/1999/330, 25 Mar. 1999.

35 MINURSO was established in 1991 to monitor the ceasefire between Frente Polisario and the Moroccan Government, verify the reduction of Moroccan troops in Western Sahara and organize a free and fair referendum. In Dec. MINURSO's mandate was extended until 29 Feb. 2000 (SCR 1282, 14 Dec. 1999).

36 Report of the Secretary-General on the situation concerning Western Sahara, UN document S/1999/1219, 6 Dec. 1999.

37 UN document S/1999/1219 (note 36).

38 UN document S/1999/1219 (note 36).

39 Appropriated for July 1999 to June 2000. UNPKO (note 10).

40 UNOMIG was established on 24 Aug. 1993. Its tasks included verifying compliance with the ceasefire agreement between the Government of Georgia and the Abkhaz authorities in Georgia, and to investigate ceasefire violations. The mission's original mandate was invalidated by resumed fighting in Abkhazia in Sep. 1993, and UNOMIG was given an interim mandate to maintain contacts with both sides to the conflict and with Russian military contingents, and to monitor and report on the situation. In 1996 a human rights office was established in Sukhumi as part of UNOMIG (SCR 1077, 26 Oct. 1996). UNOMIG's mandate was extended throughout 1999 and until 31 July 2000. SCR 1287, 31 Jan. 2000.

41 On 13 Oct. 1999, 7 members of the UNOMIG personnel were abducted by unidentified gunmen in Abkhazia. They were released on 15 Oct. after talks with Georgian officials. BBC News Online, 15 Oct. 1999, URL <http://news2.thls.bbc.co.uk/hi/english/world/europe/newsid%5F475000/475050.stm>.

42 Report of the Secretary-General concerning the situation in Abkhazia, Georgia, UN document S/2000/39, 19 Jan. 2000.

43 Appropriated amount for 1 July 1999 to 30 June 2000. UN document S/2000/39 (note 42).

44 Unpaid assessments to the Special Account for UNOMIG as of 31 Dec. 1999. UN document S/2000/39 (note 42).

45 UNMOT was established in Dec. 1994 to monitor the implementation of the Agreement on temporary ceasefire, investigate ceasefire violations and maintain contact with all the parties involved. In Nov. 1997 the mandate was expanded by SCR 1138 to include participation in the work of the Contact Group of guarantor states and organizations, monitoring the disarmament and demobilization of United Tajik Opposition (UTO) fighters, and coordination of UN assistance to Tajikistan during the transition period. In July 1998 UNMOT suspended all its field activities after the killing of 4 UN personnel. At the end of May 1999 UNMOT re-established the first of 4 field stations in the country. Interview with Brig.-Gen. John Hvidegaard, Chief Military Observer for UNMOT, *Jane's Defence Weekly*, vol. 32, no. 1 (21 July 1999), p. 32. The mission's observers resumed their activities in Oct. 1999. ITAR-TASS (Moscow), 15 Oct. 1999, in 'UN military observers return to Tajikistan', Foreign Broadcast Information Service, *Daily Report–Central Eurasia (FBIS-SOV)*, FBIS-SOV-1999-1016, 15 Oct. 1999. UNMOT's mandate was extended throughout 1999 and until 15 May 2000. SCR 1274, 12 Nov. 1999.

46 UNPKO (note 10).

47 UNPKO (note 10).

48 Appropriated amount for July 1999 to June 2000. UNPKO (note 10).

49 UNPREDEP was the first UN mission with a preventive mandate. Its main task was to monitor and report any developments in the border areas which could undermine confidence and stability in the Former Yugoslav Republic of Macedonia and threaten its territory. On 25 Feb. 1999 the SC failed to extend the mandate of UNPREDEP after a veto from China. UN Press Release SC/6648, 25 Feb. 1999.

[50] As of Feb. 1999. Report of the Secretary-General on the United Nations Preventive Deployment Force Pursuant to SCR 1186 (1998), UN document S/1999/161, 12 Feb. 1999.

[51] $21 m. were appropriated for 1 July 1998 to 30 June 1999 by A/RES/54/245, Finance of United Nations Interim Administration Mission in Kosovo, 26 June 1998. An additional $29 m. were appropriated for the same period by A/RES/53/20, 2 Nov. 1998.

[52] UN document S/1999/161 (note 50).

[53] The International Police Task Force (IPTF) was authorized in accordance with Annex 11 of the 1995 General Framework Agreement for Peace in Bosnia and Herzegovina, the Dayton Agreement (SCR 1035, 21 Dec. 1995), together with a civilian mission proposed by the Secretary-General in Dec. 1995. Report of the Secretary-General on Former Yugoslavia, UN document S/1995/1031, 13 Dec. 1995. The mission was later given the name UNMIBH. On 18 June 1999 its mandate was extended until 21 June 2000.

[54] The IPTF has an authorized strength of 2057. Many IPTF officers were re-deployed to Kosovo to reinforce UNMIK. Report of the Secretary-General on the United Nations Mission in Bosnia-Herzegovina, UN document S/1999/1260, 17 Dec. 1999.

[55] Appropriated amount for 1 July 1999 to 30 June 2000. Report of the Secretary-General on the United Nations Mission of Observers in Prevlaka, UN document S/1999/1302, 31 Dec. 1999.

[56] UNMOP was established in 1996 to monitor the demilitarization of the Prevlaka peninsula, hitherto carried out by UNPROFOR and UNCRO. SCR 1038, 15 Jan. 1996. UNMOP's mandate was extended throughout 1999 and until 15 July 2000. SCR 1285, 13 Jan. 2000.

[57] UN document S/1999/1302 (note 55).

[58] For administrative and budgetary purposes UNMOP is treated as part of UNMIBH. UN document S/1999/1302 (note 55).

[59] MONUA (Missao de Observação das Nações Unidas em Angola) was established in 1997 as a follow-on mission to UNAVEM III. SCR 1118, 30 June 1997. In Dec. 1998 all MONUA personnel were withdrawn from UNITA-held areas for safety reasons. Report of the Secretary-General on the United Nations Observer Mission in Angola, UN document S/1999/49, 17 Jan. 1999. In Feb. 1999 the mission mandate expired and peacekeepers withdrew over 6 months. SCR 1229, 25 Feb. 1999; and Koiwai, M., 'UN Mission in Angola cancelled', *Peacekeeping and International Relations*, vol. 28, no. 2 (1999), p. 10.

[60] As of 18 Jan. 1999. UN document S/1999/49 (note 59). About 30 officers and 12 CivPols would remain in Angola for 2–3 months after the end of the mandate. Report of the Secretary General on the United Nations Observer Mission in Angola (MONUA). UN document S/1999/202, 24 Feb. 1999.

[61] As of 18 Jan. 1999. UN document S/1999/49 (note 59).

[62] As of 18 Jan. 1999. UN document S/1999/49 (note 59).

[63] Appropriated amount for 1 July 1998 to 30 June 1999. UN document S/1999/202 (note 60).

[64] Unpaid assessments to the Special Account for MONUA as of 31 Dec. 1998. UN document S/1999/202 (note 60).

[65] MIPONUH (Mission de Police Civile des Nations Unies en Haiti) was established in Nov. 1997 to replace the UN Transitional Mission in Haiti, UNTMIH (SCR 1141, 28 Nov. 1997). SCR 1277, 30 Nov. 1999, extended MIPONUH's mandate until 15 Mar. 2000 and called for the establishment of an International Civilian Support Mission to Haiti (MICAH), to replace both MIPONUH and MICIVIH. UN Press Release SC/6763, 30 Nov. 1999.

[66] UNPKO (note 10).

[67] Appropriated amount for the year ending 30 June 2000. UN Press Release SC/6763, 30 Nov. 1999.

[68] MINURCA (Mission des Nations Unies en République centrafricaine) was established on 27 Mar. 1998 to replace the Inter-African Mission to Monitor the Implementation of the Bangui Agreements (MISAB), with an initial mandate including assistance in maintaining security, supervision of the collection and destruction of arms and training police. The mandate was later expanded to include support for the conduct of legislative elections. SCR 1201, 15 Oct. 1998. The mission's mandate was extended twice in 1999, but was scheduled to terminate after 15 Feb. 2000. SCR 1271, 22 Oct. 1999.

[69] Chad (114 troops), Côte d'Ivoire (224 troops and support units), Egypt (304 troops and support units), Gabon (1 soldier) and Senegal (119 troops). Ninth Report of the Secretary-General on the United Nations Mission in the Central African Republic, UN document S/2000/24, 14 Jan. 2000.

[70] Chad (6), Cote d'Ivoire (10), Egypt (8), Gabon (4) and Senegal (9). UN document S/2000/24 (note 69).

[71] Benin (2), Cameroon (1), France (2), Mali (6), Senegal (3) and Tunisia (2). UN document S/2000/24 (note 69).

[72] Appropriated amount for 1 July 1999 to 30 June 2000. UN document S/2000/24 (note 69).

[73] Unpaid assessments to the Special Account for MINURCA as of Dec. 1999. UN document S/2000/24 (note 69).

[74] UNOMSIL was established on 13 July 1998 with a mandate to monitor the security and military situation in Sierra Leone, monitor ECOMOG in its role of providing security, and collect and destroy arms. In Aug. UNOMSIL's mandate was expanded to 210 military observers. SCR 1269, 20 Aug. 1999. In Oct. the SC voted to establish a peacekeeping mission, the United Nations Mission in Sierra Leone (UNAMSIL), to take over the substantive civilian and military functions of UNOMSIL as well as its assets. SCR 1270, 22 Oct. 1999.

[75] On 4 Aug. a group of UNOMSIL personnel along with Nigerian ECOMOG soldiers and local journalists were abducted by an armed Sierra Leonian group. They were released after a few days. UN Press Releases SG/SM/7089, 5 Aug. 1999 and SG/SM/7093, 10 Aug. 1999.

[76] Plus 2 medical personnel. Eighth Report of the Secretary-General on the UNOMSIL, UN document S/1999/1003, 28 Sep. 1999.

[77] Estimated budget for 1 July 1999 to 30 June 2000. UNOMSIL Internet site, URL <http://www.un.org/Depts/DPKO/Missions/unosil_p.htm>. This figure became invalid when UNOMSIL's mandate expanded. SCR 1269, 20 Aug. 1999.

[78] UN document S/1999/1003 (note 76).

[79] UNMIK was established on 10 June 1999 for an initial period of 12 months. Its main tasks are: promoting the establishment of substantial autonomy and self-government in Kosovo; civilian administrative functions; maintaining law and order; promoting human rights; and assuring the safe return of all refugees and displaced persons. SCR 1244, 10 June 1999.

[80] Of whom 78 were transferred from UNMIBH. Report of the Secretary-General on the United Nations Interim Administration Mission in Kosovo, UN document S/1999/1250, 23 Dec. 1999.

[81] A UN international staff member was shot and killed on 11 Oct. 1999. UN document S/1999/1250 (note 80), para. 15.

[82] DM125 m. ($66.25 m.) Budget for 1999 as set out in UNMIK regulation no. 17, 6 Nov. 1999. Cited in UN document S/1999/1250 (note 80).

[83] UNAMET was established on 11 June 1999 with the task of organizing and conducting a referendum on independence in the territory. Violence erupted following the 4 Sep. referendum, prompting the evacuation of all UNAMET personnel except for a small team which remained in the Dili headquarters. As INTERFET began to deploy on 20 Sep., UNAMET personnel began to return to East Timor. UN General Assembly, Agenda item 96: Question of East-Timor, Progress Report of the Secretary-General, UN document A/54/654, 13 Dec. 1999. The mandate was subsequently extended until 30 Nov. (SCR 1262, 27 Aug. 1999), when INTERFET was replaced by UNTAET. SCR 1272, 25 Oct. 1999.

[84] Report of the Secretary-General on the Situation in East Timor, UN document S/1999/1024, 4 Oct. 1999, refers to 36 military liaison officers. The initial mandate authorized up to 280 CivPols and 50 military liaison officers. SCR 1246, 11 June 1999. In Aug. the SC extended this to 460 CivPols and 300 military liaison officers. SCR 1262, 27 Aug. 1999.

[85] See note 84.

[86] Five local UNAMET staff members were killed in the post-ballot violence and 2 others remain missing. UN document A/54/654 (note 83).

[87] Appropriated amount for 5 May 1999 to 30 Sep. 1999. A/RES/54/20, 22 Nov. 1999.

[88] UNAMSIL was established on 22 Oct. 1999 following the signature of the Lomé Peace Agreement between the Government of Sierra Leone and the Revolutionary United Front (RUF) on 7 July 1999. The tasks of the mission were to include, among others, assisting in the implementation of the Lomé Agreement, monitoring adherence to the ceasefire, encouraging the parties to create confidence-building mechanisms, supporting the anticipated elections and ensuring the security and freedom of movement of UN personnel. SCR 1270, 22 Oct. 1999.

[89] Ghana (780), India (1428), Kenya (832) and Nigeria (1560) as of 10 Jan. 2000. Second Report of the Secretary-General Pursuant to Security Council Resolution

1270 (1999) on the United Nations Mission in Sierra Leone, UN document S/2000/13, 11 Jan. 2000.

90 As of 10 Jan. 2000. UN document S/2000/13 (note 89).

91 As of 10 Jan. 2000, from Namibia, Ghana, Kenya and Norway. UN document S/2000/13 (note 89).

92 Proposed expanded budget: \$310.8 m. (gross). UNPKO (note 10). UN, Fifth Committee discusses Sierra Leone Peacekeeping Finance, approves test calling for \$4.56 million for Angola Office, UN document GA/AB/3369, 11 May 2000.

93 UNTAET was established on 25 Oct. 1999 for an initial period until 31 Jan. 2001. The mission was endowed with overall responsibility for the administration of East Timor and empowered to exercise all legislative and executive authority, including the administration of justice. The military component of UNTAET replaces INTERFET. SCR 1272, 25 Oct. 1999; and 'Statement by the Prime Minister the Hon. John W. Howard MP on East Timor', 23 Nov. 1999, URL <http://www.pm.gov.au/media/pressrel/1999/easttimor2311.htm>.

94 As of Jan. 2000, contributors were still being determined. 185 military observers were deployed by 24 Jan. A force of c. 8500 troops and military observers from 27 countries is planned. Report of the Secretary-General on the United Nations Transitional Administration in East Timor, UN document S/2000/53, 26 Jan. 2000.

95 Authorized strength. UNPKO (note 10).

96 UNPKO (note 10).

97 Authorized strength. As of 31 Jan. 2000, UNTAET had deployed 480 CivPols. UNPKO (note 10).

98 \$386.3 m. for 1 Dec. 1999–30 June 2000. 'East Timor–UNTAET: Facts and figures', UN Department of Public Information, 1999 URL <http://www.un.org/peace/etimor/UntaetF.htm>.

99 In Aug. 1999 the SC authorized the deployment of 90 UN military liaison personnel to the capitals of the states signatories to the Ceasefire Agreement for the Democratic Republic of the Congo in preparation for a future mission. SCR 1258, 6 Aug. 1999. In Nov. 1999 MONUC was established. SCR 1297, 30 Nov. 1999. The mandate of the force was extended until 31 Aug. 2000 by SCR 1291, 24 Feb. 2000. Up to 5537 military personnel, including 500 military observers, may be deployed. Second Report of the Secretary-General on the United Nations Preliminary Deployment in the Democratic Republic of Congo, UN document S/1999/1116, 1 Nov. 1999.

100 Military liaison personnel deployed under SCR 1258 and incorporated into MONUC after 30 Nov. This figure is as of 12 Jan. 2000. Report of the Secretary-General on the United Nations Organization Mission in the Democratic Republic of the Congo, UN document S/2000/30, 17 Jan. 2000.

101 To be determined.

102 UN peace operations not deployed under chapter VI or VII of the UN Charter, administered by the UN Department of Political Affairs (UNDPA).

103 MICIVIH (Mission Civile Internationale en Haiti) was established in 1993 as a joint mission of the OAS and the UN, charged with monitoring, verifying and strengthening human rights conditions in Haiti. In June 1999 the OAS announced that because of financial constraints it would have to reduce its contribution to MICIVIH and withdrew all but one of its staff. Letter dated 6 Aug. 1999 from the Secretary-General addressed to the President of the General Assembly, UN document A/54/211, 10 Aug. 1999. MICIVIH was scheduled to close 15 Mar. 2000: see MIPONUH.

104 'Staff' of 34 UN and 1 OAS personnel. E-mail from darnet@un.org, 9 Mar. 2000.

105 UN document A/54/211 (note 103).

106 In Apr. 1999, UNSMA military advisers returned to Kabul for the first time since late Aug. 1998, when all UN staff were withdrawn from Afghanistan after the killing of 2 local UN staff and a military adviser. Report of the Secretary-General on the Situation in Afghanistan, UN document S/1999/698, 20 June 1999. Since Apr., UNSMA has kept a rotational presence in Kabul. It also began the recruitment of civil affairs officers to be included in the new Civil Affairs Unit. Report of the Secretary-General on the situation in Afghanistan and its implications for international peace and security, UN document A/54/378, S/1999/994, 21 Sep. 1999.

107 Information from Horst Heitmann, UNDPA, personal contact 9 and 10 Mar. 2000.

108 Head of Mission, 3 political officers and 3 military advisers. Information from Kiyotaka Kawabata, Asia and the Pacific Division, UNDPA, 17 Dec. 1999.

109 'Secretary-General expresses condolences to Italian Government over shooting death in Afghanistan of Lt-Col Carmine Calo, of UN Special Mission', UN Press Release

SG/SM/6681/AFG/83, 24 Aug. 1999.

110 Approximate amount. Information from Kawabata (note 108).

111 MINUGUA (Misíon de Verificacion de las Naciones Unidas en Guatemala) had until 1997 been limited to verifying the Comprehensive Agreement on Human Rights and the human rights aspects of the Agreement on Identity and Rights of Indigenous Peoples. In 1997 the parties to the agreement requested that MINUGUA expand its functions to verify all the signed agreements, and that the mission's functions should also comprise good offices, advisory and support services and public information. In 1999 MINUGUA's mandate was extended until 31 Dec. 2000. A/RES/54/99, 17 Dec. 1999.

112 Information from Bertrand de la Grange, MINUGUA Public Information Office, 23 Feb. 2000.

113 Information from de la Grange (note 112).

114 Information from de la Grange (note 112).

115 Appropriated amount for 2000. This will be supplemented by bilateral contributions from various countries. Information from de la Grange (note 112).

116 INTERFET was authorized by the SC on 15 Sep. 1999 following the violence in the aftermath of the referendum on independence in East Timor. Its tasks included restoring peace and security to East Timor, protecting and supporting UNAMET, and facilitating humanitarian assistance operations. Australia was appointed lead nation. SCR 1264, 15 Sep. 1999. The transition from INTERFET to UNTAET began 1 Feb. 2000. Information from Andrea Gleason, Second Secretary, Australian Embassy in Sweden.

117 Information from Gleason (note 116). See also: 'Statement by the Prime Minister the Hon. John W. Howard MP on East Timor', 23 Nov. 1999, URL <http://www.pm.gov.au/media/pressrel/1999/easttimor2311.htm>.

118 At the peak of deployment in Nov.–Dec. 1999. The total number of personnel was closer to 12 600 if maritime and air support from troop-contributing nations is included. Information from Gleason (note 116).

119 A New Zealander died in a traffic accident and an Australian soldier died of natural causes. Information from Gleason (note 116).

120 To be determined. The cost for Australia's contribution may be as high as $2.5 b. (AUD 4 b.). 'East Timor drains Australian budgets', *AirForces Monthly*, no. 144, Mar. 2000, p. 4.

121 OSCE missions and field activities differ widely in mandate and size. In general, however, they are directed at facilitating political processes aimed at the prevention or settlement of conflict. In addition to the operations listed, a number of OSCE field offices have been established in Central Asia, the Caucasus and Eastern Europe. Unless otherwise indicated, mandates have been extended until 30 June 2000 and information regarding the mandates is taken from OSCE Secretariat, Conflict Prevention Centre, *Survey of OSCE Long-Term Missions and other OSCE Field Activities*, SEC.INF/32/00, Vienna, 17 Jan. 2000.

122 Decision to establish the mission taken at 16th CSO meeting, 18 Sep. 1992, Journal no. 3, Annex 1. Authorized by the Government of the Former Yugoslav Republic of Macedonia (FYROM) through Articles of Understanding agreed by exchange of letters, 7 Nov. 1992. The mission's tasks include assessing the level of stability and the possibility of conflict and unrest.

123 Unless otherwise indicated, information on which countries contribute personnel to each OSCE mission is from the OSCE Secretariat, Conflict Prevention Centre (CPC) factsheet: 'Overview of deployment (by mission) as of 31-Dec-1999'.

124 Information from Robin Seaword, Deputy Head of Mission, 8 Dec. 1999. Unless otherwise indicated the number of personnel refers only to the international staff, as stated in OSCE Secretariat (note 123). The OSCE overview does not distinguish type of personnel deployed.

125 Information from Seaword (note 124). Unless otherwise indicated, all OSCE budget figures are from Labib Sahab, Chief of Budgets, OSCE Secretariat, 3 Feb. 2000.

126 Decision to establish the mission taken at 17th CSO meeting, 6 Nov. 1992, Journal no. 2, Annex 2. Authorized by Government of Georgia through MOU, 23 Jan. 1993, and by South Ossetia's leaders by exchange of letters on 1 Mar. 1993. Initially the objective of the mission was to promote negotiations between the conflicting parties. The mandate was expanded on 29 Mar. 1994 to include *inter alia* monitoring of the Joint Peacekeeping Forces in South Ossetia. On 15 Dec. 1999 the mission's tasks were further expanded to include monitoring Georgia's border with Chechnya, and an additional 20 personnel deployed for the purpose. OSCE Permanent Council Decision no. 334, PC.Jour/267, 15 Dec. 1999.

127 The mission is based in Tbilisi. In Apr. 1997, a branch office in Tskhinvali became operational.

128 Decision to establish the mission taken at the 18th CSO meeting, 13 Dec. 1992, Journal no. 3, Annex 2. Authorized by Estonian Government through MOU, 15 Feb. 1993. The mission's tasks include assisting in the recreation of civil society and collecting information relating to the status and rights of the communities in Estonia.

129 The actual number may be smaller in connection with rotation. As of Dec. 1999 there were 4 monitors. Information from C. Bistrup, Acting Head of OSCE Mission to Estonia, 7 Dec. 1999.

130 Information from Bistrup (note 129).

131 Decision to establish the mission taken at the 19th CSO meeting, 4 Feb. 1993, Journal no. 3, Annex 3. Authorized by the Government of Moldova through MOU, 7 May 1993. The mission's tasks include assisting the parties in pursuing negotiations on a lasting political settlement to the conflict as well as gathering and providing information on the situation.

132 Decision to establish the mission taken at the 23rd CSO meeting, 23 Sep. 1993, Journal no. 3, Annex 3. Authorized by Government of Latvia through MOU, 13 Dec. 1993. The tasks of the mission include addressing citizenship issues, providing information, advice on these issues and reporting on the implementation of OSCE norms.

133 Civilian mission members. Information from Undine Bollow, Deputy Head of OSCE Mission to Latvia, 8 Dec. 1999.

134 Information from Bollow (note 133).

135 Decision to establish the mission taken at 4th meeting of the Council, Rome (CSCE/4-C/Dec. 1), Decision I.4, 1 Dec. 1993. No bilateral MOU signed. The tasks of the mission include facilitating dialogue, promoting human rights and informing the OSCE about further developments.

136 Information from Regina Tauschek, Administrative Officer, OSCE Mission to Tajikistan, 11 Dec. 1999.

137 Annual budget of the mission. The mission also implements a wide range of projects funded separately by different governments and international donors. Project expenditures in 1999 amounted to c. US $255 000. Information from Tauschek (note 136).

138 Decision to establish the mission taken at 16th meeting of the PC, 11 Apr. 1995, Decision (a). No bilateral MOU signed. The mission's tasks include promoting respect for human rights and a peaceful resolution to the crisis, facilitating delivery of humanitarian aid and ensuring the return of refugees and displaced persons. All international staff of the mission withdrew from Chechnya in Dec. 1998, but members visited Grozny 3 times during the period Jan.–Mar. 1999. The worsening security situation prompted the mission to halt visits in Mar. since then the Assistance Group has operated from the Norwegian Embassy in Moscow. In Sep. the mission began to relocate local personnel and property to Ingushetia. OSCE Secretary General, *Annual Report 1999 on OSCE Activities (1 December 1998–31 October 1999)*, SEC.DOC/2/99, Vienna, 17 Nov. 1999, p. 35.

139 Authorized mission strength is 12. URL <http://www.osce.org/e/f-che.htm>.

140 In Aug. 1995 the OSCE Chairman-in-Office appointed a Personal Representative (PR) on the conflict dealt with by the OSCE Minsk Conference. The Minsk Conference, planned for since 1992 by the Minsk Group (Armenia, Azerbaijan, Austria, Belarus, Finland, France, Germany, Italy, Norway, Russia, Sweden, Turkey and the USA) with the purpose of negotiating a peaceful settlement to the Nagorno-Karabakh conflict, has not been held because the conflicting parties cannot agree about it. However, the Minsk Group has continued to hold meetings. The PR's mandate consists of assisting the Minsk Group in planning possible peacekeeping operations, assisting the parties in confidence-building measures and in humanitarian matters, and cooperating with other international organizations. The PR together with his field assistants is responsible for monitoring the ceasefire. OSCE (note 121), p. 61.

141 The headquarters for the PR is in Tbilisi, with regional offices in Baku, Stepanakert and Yerevan. OSCE (note 121), p. 61.

142 Decision to establish the mission taken at 5th meeting, Ministerial Council, Budapest, 8 Dec. 1995 (MC(5).DEC/1) in accordance with Annex 6 of the Dayton Agreement. The tasks of the mission include assisting the parties in regional stabilization measures and democracy building. The mandate has been extended until 31 Dec. 2000. 260th PC meeting, PC.DEC/319, 2 Dec. 1999.

143 34 617 620 euros ($ 37 387 030). Budget for 1999, as of 19 Oct. 1999. OSCE (note 138), p. 105.

144 Decision to establish the mission taken by the PC, 18 Apr. 1996, Journal no. 65 (PC.DEC/112). Adjustment of the mandate by the PC, 26 June 1997, Journal no. 121, PC.DEC/176, and 25 June 1998, Journal no. 174, PC/DEC/239. The mission's tasks include assisting and monitoring the return of refugees and displaced persons as well as the

protection of national minorities. The mandate has been extended until 31 Mar. 2000. PC/DEC/327, 9 Dec. 1999.

145 Including CivPol.

146 Police monitors in the Croatian Danube Region, as of 25 Nov. 1999. Information from Antonio Ortiz, Mission Liaison Officer, Conflict Prevention Centre, the OSCE Secretariat, 7 Dec. 1999.

147 22 289 111 euros (\$ 24 072 240). Budget for 1999, as of 19 Oct. 1999. OSCE (note 138), p. 104.

148 Decision to establish the mission taken at 108th meeting of the PC, 27 Mar. 1997, PC.DEC/160. Mandate adjusted on 11 Dec. 1997. Journal no. 193, PC.DEC/206. The mandate was temporarily widened in Mar. 1998 to include monitoring the border with Kosovo. PC.DEC/218, 11 Mar. 1998.

149 Decision to establish the KVM taken by the PC, 25 Oct. 1998, PC.DEC/263, after endorsement by SCR 1203, 24 Oct. 1998. On 16 Oct. the OSCE and FRY signed an agreement on the creation of the KVM for 1 year. Its mandate was to verify FRY compliance with SCR 1160, 31 Mar. 1998 and SCR 1199, 23 Sep. 1998 with an envisaged staff of 2000. The Kosovo Diplomatic Observer Mission (KDOM) was included in the KVM. 'Tense Christmas in Kosovo', *OSCE Newsletter*, vol. 5, no. 12 (Dec. 1998). The KVM was withdrawn on 24 Mar. 1999, 4 days before the commencement of NATO air strikes on Kosovo. OSCE (note 138), pp. 26–27.

150 Strength of the KVM at the time of withdrawal. OSCE Press Release no. 24/99, URL <http://www.osce.org/docs/presrel/pr24-99-htm>.

151 On 1 July 1999 the PC established the OSCE Mission in Kosovo for an initial period until 10 June 2000, to replace the transitional OSCE Kosovo Task Force established on 8 June 1999 (PC.DEC/296). The tasks of OSCE Mission to Kosovo include training police, judicial personnel and civil administrators, and monitoring and promoting human rights. The initial mandate runs until 10 June 2000.

152 In addition, the mission employs 1049 local staff, as of 31 Jan. 2000. Internet site of the OSCE mission in Kosovo, URL <http://www.osce.org/kosovo/update.htm>.

153 75 146 086 euros (\$ 81 157 773). Budget for 1999, as per 19 Oct. 1999. OSCE (note 138), p. 105. This amount also covers KVM.

154 SFOR was established in Dec. 1996 to replace the NATO Implementation Force (IFOR), created to implement the military aspects of the Dayton Agreement. SCR 1088, 12 Dec. 1996. In June 1999 the SC authorized NATO to extend the mandate of SFOR for another 12 months. SCR 1247, 18 June 1999.

155 As of 31 Dec. 1999. Information from Lt-Comm. Paul Hubbard, Spokesman, SFOR Public Information Office, Sarajevo, 2 Feb. 2000.

156 As of 31 Dec. 1999. About 1000 of these are based in support centres in Croatia. Countries providing major contingents in Bosnia and Herzegovina include: Canada (1200), France (3000), Germany (1600), Italy (1600), Spain (1100), Turkey (1600), UK (3200), USA (5000) and Russia (1300) Information from Hubbard (note 155).

157 KVM—Operation Eagle Eye—was activated on 30 Oct. 1998 by the North Atlantic Council, after the adoption of SCR 1203 endorsing both OSCE and NATO verification missions. Among other things the task of the mission was to verify the activities of security forces, respect of the ceasefire, free movement of civilians, ground monitors and humanitarian organizations, and compliance or non-compliance with SCR 1199, 23 Sep. 1998. Operation Eagle Eye flights ceased on 24 Mar. 1999 as a result of the withdrawal of OSCE monitors from Kosovo. 'Operation Eagle Eye', AFSOUTH Internet site <http://www.afsouth.nato.int>.

158 Countries providing air assets. Personnel from Belgium, Canada and Norway also participated in coordinating KVM from Kumanovo, Macedonia. 'Operation Eagle Eye', AFSOUTH Internet site (note 157).

159 On 4 Dec. 1998 the North Atlantic Council authorized the activation of XFOR—a contingency force to extract OSCE and other designated personnel from the FRY. As a result of the withdrawal of OSCE monitors from Kosovo the operation was cancelled. Allied Forces Southern Europe, 'Operation Determined Guarantor', AFSOUTH Internet site (note 157).

160 Allied Forces Southern Europe, 'Operation Determined Guarantor', AFSOUTH Internet site (note 157).

161 KFOR received its mandate from the SC on 10 June 1999. Its tasks include deterring renewed hostilities, ensuring the withdrawal and preventing the return of the FRY military and police forces, demilitarizing the KLA, establishing a secure environment, supporting UNMIK and monitoring borders. SCR 1244, 10 June 1999.

162 KFOR Internet site, URL <http://www.kforonline.com/kfor/nations/belgium.htm>.

163 An additional 7500 provide support from Albania, Greece and Macedonia. KFOR Internet site, URL <http://www.kforonline.com/kfor/kfor_hq.htm>.

164 Polish officer, 11 Dec. 1999. KFOR Press Update, 12 Dec. 1999.

165 US soldier, 15 Dec. 1999. KFOR Press Update, 16 Dec 1999.

166 Mission established by the Brioni Agreement, signed at Brioni (Croatia), 7 July 1991 by representatives of the European Community (EC) and the governments of Croatia, Slovenia and the FRY. An MOU signed with the Government of Albania in 1997 was later extended. On 21 Dec. 1998 a new MOU was signed with Croatia. Information from Sven Linder, Former Head of the Swedish delegation to the ECMM, Sarajevo. The ECMM withdrew from the FRY when NATO air strikes against Kosovo began. Letter from Ambassador Jorma Inki, Head of ECMM, to Bernard Kouchner, Special Representative of the Secretary-General and Head of UNMIK, 19 Aug. 1999.

167 280 civilian monitors and 180 local staff. Information from Gunnar Hultner, Head of the Swedish Delegation to the ECMM, Sarajevo. 22 of the monitors were deployed to Kosovo as of 19 Aug 1999. Letter from Inki (note 166).

168 Death from natural causes. Information from Hultner (note 167).

169 Information from Hultner (note 167).

170 Established under the authority of the Western European Union (WEU) Council, 2 May 1997. On 24 June 1997 an MOU between the Government of Albania and the WEU was signed, enabling MAPE's deployment by early July 1997. MAPE's mission is to rebuild and gradually hand over training responsibilities to the Albanian police. WEU Fact Sheet, no 1/98, 12 Nov. 1998. On 2 Feb. 1999 the WEU Council approved an enhanced MAPE mandate. Training and advice are now given throughout the country and down to police unit level. The new phase of the mission started formally in July 1999 with a mandate until Apr. 2000. Information from Myriam Sochacki, Head of Press and Information, WEU Secretariat- General, 2 Dec 1999.

171 According to the operation plan, the strength will be built up to 170 police officers. Information from Sochacki (note 170).

172 The budget allocated for support to the Albanian police during the year 1998/99 under the EU PHARE programme. Information from Sochacki (note 170).

173 The Western European Union Demining Assistance Mission (WEUDAM) became operational on 10 May 1999, following a request by the EU, on the basis of Article J 4.2 of the Treaty on European Union. The mission provides advice, technical expertise and training support to the Croatian Mine Action Centre (CROMAC). WEUDAM Internet site, URL <http://www.weu.int/eng/info/weudam.htm>.

174 Sweden is the lead nation.

175 WEUDAM Internet site (note 173).

176 424 197 euros ($386 026) allocated by the EU. In addition, Norway has contributed 61 652 euros ($56 130), WEUDAM Internet site (note 173).

177 Agreement on the Principles Governing the Peaceful Settlement of the Conflict in South Ossetia, signed in Dagomys, 24 June 1992, by Georgia and Russia. Implementation of the agreement was to be monitored by a Joint Monitoring Commission with representatives of Russia, Georgia and South Ossetia (an autonomous district within Georgia whose local leadership announced its secession from Georgia and union with the North Ossetian Autonomous Republic in Russia in 1991. The Dagomys Agreement was finalized at another meeting between Yeltsin and Shevardnadze in Helsinki on 9 July 1992 during the CSCE summit meeting. Baev, P., *The Russian Army in a Time of Troubles* (Sage: London, 1996), p. 117; and Jonson, L., *Keeping the Peace in the CIS: The Evolution of Russian Policy*, Royal Institute of International Affairs Discussion Paper 81 (RIIA: London, 1999), pp. 3, 10.

178 International Institute for Strategic Studies (IISS), *The Military Balance 1999–2000* (Oxford University Press: Oxford, 1999), p. 117.

179 The Agreement on Principles Governing the Peaceful Settlement of the Armed Conflict in the Trans-Dniester Region, signed in Moscow, 21 July 1992 by the presidents of Moldova and Russia, established a peacekeeping force consisting of 5 Russian battalions and 3 each from Moldova and the self-proclaimed Trans-Dniester Republic. Baev (note 177), p. 106; and Jonson (note 177), p. 10. No changes in mandate in 1999. Information from Gen. Roman Harmoza, Deputy Head of the OSCE Mission to Moldova, 16 Dec. 1999.

180 Russian, Moldovian and Trans-Dniestrian contingents. Military observers included. Information from Harmoza (note 179).

181 Russia (9), Trans-Dniestr (9), Moldova (10), Ukraine (10). Information from General Harmoza (note 179).

182 Approximate annual cost. Russia: $998 000; Trans-Dniestr: $1 150 512; Moldova: $387 939. Information from Harmoza (note 179).

183 The CIS Agreement on the Collective Peacekeeping Forces (CPF), signed in Moscow, 24 Sep. 1993, by Kazakhstan, Kyrgyzstan, Russia, Tajikistan and Uzbekistan,

authorizes the CPF to implement decisions taken by their heads of state and formally establishes a joint command. Although the agreement was occasioned by the conflict in Tajikistan it could be interpreted to apply to the CIS in general. Baev (note 177), p. 12; and Jonson (note 177), p. 11. Uzbekistan and Kyrgyzstan withdrew their peacekeepers in Tajikistan. Radio Free Europe/Radio Liberty, *RFE/RL Newsline*, 19 Apr. 1999, URL <http://www.rferl.org/newsline/1999/04/2-tca-190499.html>.

Nov. 1998 and Feb. 1999, respectively. ITAR-TASS, 'Uzbekistan: Uzbek peacekeepers leave deployment position in Tajikistan', 17 Nov. 1998, in Foreign Broadcast Information Service, *Daily Report–Central Eurasia: Military Affairs (FBIS-UMA)*, FBIS-UMA-98-321, 17 Nov. 1998; and Interfax (Moscow), 'Kyrgyz official justifies border reinforcement', 11 Mar. 1999, FBIS-SOV-1999-0311, 11 Mar. 1999. In Apr. 1999 the defence ministers of Russia and Tajikistan signed a bilateral treaty allowing Russia formally to establish military bases on the sites where the Russian troops are currently stationed. The treaty does not envisage an increase in the number of Russian troops in

[184] 8000 border guards as of July 1999, and an additional 6000 (201st Motor Rifle Division) in the interior, as of Nov. 1998. Davis, A. 'Russia battles drug smugglers on Tajikistan border', *Jane's Defence Weekly*, vol. 32, no. 4 (28 July 1999); and *Sodruzhestvo* (supplement to *Nezavisimaya Gazeta*), no. 10 (Nov. 1998), p. 6. Russian troops in Tajikistan number 22 700—8200 Army and 14 500 border guards. IISS (note 178), p. 169.

[185] Shot off-duty, 25 Nov. 1999. ITAR-TASS, 'Russian officer shot dead in Tajikistan', 25 Nov. 1999, in FBIS-SOV-1999-1125, 26 Nov. 1999.

[186] Georgia and the self-proclaimed Republic of Abkhazia signed a ceasefire agreement on 14 May 1994. In June Russian troops began to deploy along the ceasefire line. The force's mandate was approved by the CIS Council of Collective Security, 21 Oct. 1994, and endorsed by the UN through SCR 937, 21 July 1994. Baev (note 177), p. 120. The force continues to perform its tasks while the extension is awaiting formal approval at the next CIS summit meeting. ITAR-TASS, 'Georgia wants Russian peacekeepers to stay in Abkhazia', 6 Oct. 1999, in FBIS-SOV-1999-1006, 6 Oct. 1999; and *Transcaucasus: A Chronology*, vol. 7, no. 10 (Sep. 1999).

[187] Information from Maj. Mark Jones, Senior Liaison Officer, UNOMIG, 2 Mar. 2000.

[188] Information from Jones (note 187).

[189] OMIB (or MIOB, Mission de l'OUA au Burundi) was established on 7 Dec. 1993 by the Central Organ of the OAU Mechanism for Conflict Prevention, Resolution and Management. The mission's mandate, to promote dialogue between military and government leaders, was endorsed by a treaty between the OAU and Burundi, 8 Apr. 1994. Ognimba, E., 'Connaissance de la Mission de l'OUA au Burundi' [Briefing on the OAU Mission in Burundi], *Resolving Conflicts*, Feb.–Mar. 1996, p. 10.

[190] The military component of the mission was withdrawn following the 26 July 1996 military putsch in Burundi. Only civilian staff are currently in place. Information from Sam Ibok, Director of the Department of Political Affairs, OAU, 28 Dec. 1999.

[191] Information from Ibok (note 190).

[192] OMIC (La Mission d'Observation Militaire aux Comores) was established by decisions of the OAU at its 39th and 40th Ordinary Sessions at Ambassadorial Level in Addis Ababa, Ethiopia, 24 Oct. and 6 Nov. 1997. The tasks of the force include monitoring the situation on the Comoros and creating a climate of trust. De Matha, J. (Lt-Col, Logistics Officer, OMIC), 'La Mission d'Observation Militaire aux Comores', *Resolving Conflicts*, May–June 1998, pp. 25–26.

[193] At the beginning of 1999 the mission had 18 military observers. These were withdrawn on 25 May 1999 after the military takeover in Comoros and only 2 civilian officers remain. Information from Ibok (note 190).

[194] Information from Ibok (note 190).

[195] The JMC was formally established on 3 Sep. 1999 with a mandate to monitor compliance with the provisions of the July Lusaka Ceasefire Agreement and to investigate violations. The JMC consists of 1 central and 3 regional commissions. Information from Ibok (note 190); and OAU, 'Report of the Secretary-General on the DRC Peace Process', Central organ/MEC/AMB/3, 23 Sep. 1999.

[196] These countries provide neutral investigators to the JMC. In addition the commissions include representatives from the belligerents, Zambia and the UN. Information from Ibok (note 190).

[197] $246.474 were spent from 10 Nov. to 14 Dec. 1999. Information from Ibok (note 190).

[198] Decision A/DEC.1/8/90 on the ceasefire and establishment of an Economic Community of West African States (ECOWAS) Monitoring Group (ECOMOG) for Liberia,

Economic Community of West African States, First Session of the Community Standing Mediation Committee, Banjul, 6–7 Aug. 1990. ECOMOG's tasks included assisting the government in providing security in the country, maintaining law and order, and restructuring the army and police. ECOMOG troops began to withdraw in Jan. 1999 and by Oct. all had left Liberia. BBC News Online, 'World: Africa ECOMOG quits Liberia', 17 Jan. 1999, URL <http://news2.thls.bbc.co.uk/hi/english/world/africa/newsid%5F256000/256740.stm>; and United Nations Office for the Coordination of Humanitarian Affairs (OCHA), Integrated Regional Information Network–West Africa (IRIN-WA), IRIN-WA weekly round-up, 16–22 Oct 1999, URL <http://www.reliefweb.int/IRIN>.

199 BBC News Online, 'World: Africa ECOMOG completes Liberia withdrawal', 17 Jan. 1999, URL <http://news2.thls.bbc.co.uk/hi/english/world/africa/newsid_483000/483469.stm>; and AFP (Paris), 'Liberia: AFP reports Nigerian ECOMOG troops leave Liberia', 15 Jan. 1999, in Foreign Broadcast Information Service, Daily Report–Sub-Saharan Africa (FBIS-AFR), FBIS-AFR-99-015, 20 Jan 1999.

200 ECOMOG peacekeeping forces intervened in Sierra Leone on 2 June 1997 after a military coup on 25 May 1997. The OAU approved the intervention the same day. SAPA (Johannesburg), 'Zimbabwe: OAU gives "green light" to use force in Sierra Leone', 3 June 1997, in FBIS-AFR-97-155, 4 June 1997. It was also supported by the SC and by the Secretary General of the Commonwealth. 'The situation in Sierra Leone', UN document S/PRST/1997/36, 11 July 1997; and 'ECOMOG forces seize Freetown', Pointer, Apr. 1998. Following the signature of the Peace Agreement in Lomé on 7 July 1999, ECOWAS adopted a new mandate for ECOMOG on 25 Aug. 1999. The tasks of the force include providing protection for UN and other international staff involved in the peace process, disarming all fighters of the RUF and other armed groups and assisting in the destruction of recovered arms and ammunition. The ECOMOG troops, together with observers from UNOMSIL, are to constitute the new UNAMSIL peacekeeping mission in Sierra Leone. UN document S/1999/1003 (note 76).

201 Approximate strength of the Nigerian contingent, which accounts for most of the force. BBC News Online, 'World: Africa Nigerian troops announce Sierra Leone pull-out', 21 Oct. 1999, URL <http://news.bbc.co.uk>.

202 The Nigerian contingent is estimated to cost $1 m. per day. BBC News Online (note 201).

203 According to the Abuja Peace Agreement of 1 Nov. 1998 negotiated by ECOWAS, ECOMOG's role was to guarantee security along the Guinea-Bissau–Senegal border, separate the parties in the conflict and guarantee access for humanitarian organizations. The deployment of ECOMOG was endorsed by SCR 1216, 21 Dec. 1998. However, following the ousting of Guinea-Bissau's President João Bernado Veira from office by opposition forces on 7 May 1999, ECOWAS withdrew its troops from Guinea-Bissau. Report of the Secretary-General submitted pursuant to Security Council Resolution 1233 (1999) relative to the situation in Guinea-Bissau, UN document S/1999/741, 1 July 1999; and BBC News Online, 'World: Africa, First ECOMOG troops to leave Guinea-Bissau', 29 May 1999, URL <http://news2.thls.bbc.co.uk/hi/english/world/africa/newsid%5F356000/356123.stm>.

204 As of 17 Mar. 1999. Report of the Secretary-General submitted pursuant to Security Council Resolution 1216 (1998) relative to the situation in Guinea-Bissau, UN document S/1999/294, 17 Mar. 1999.

205 BBC News Online (note 203).

206 Multinational missions not established by the UN or other recognized organizations, but which have the support of international organizations.

207 Agreement concerning a military armistice in Korea, signed at Panmunjom on 27 July 1953 by the Commander-in-Chief, UN Command; the Supreme Commander of the Korean People's Army; and the Commander of the Chinese People's Volunteers. Entered into force on 27 July 1953.

208 The NNSC entrusted to oversee the armistice agreement originally consisted of representatives from Czechoslovakia, Poland, Sweden and Switzerland. The Czech delegation was forced to leave in Apr. 1993 and the Polish delegation in Feb. 1995. Poland, however, remains an NNSC member, maintaining an office in Warsaw, and participating in regular NNSC meetings. Information from Lena von Sydow, Swedish Foreign Ministry, Department of Global Security, 18 Feb. 2000.

209 Information from von Sydow (note 208).

210 The Multinational Force and Observers was established on 3 Aug. 1981 by the Protocol to the Treaty of Peace between Egypt and Israel, signed 26 Mar. 1979. Deployment began 20 Mar. 1982, following the withdrawal of Israeli forces from Sinai. 'The Multinational Force and Observers', Report from the Office of Personnel and Publications, MFO, Rome, June 1993, MFO Internet site, URL <http://www.mfo.org/S_of_Peace/history.htm>.

211 The force also includes 15 civilian observers. 'FY 1999 operations', MFO Annual Report, Jan. 2000, p. 4, 11, URL <http://www.mfo.org/Annual_R/fy.htm>.

212 Deaths due to illness and a traffic accident. Information from Mary Cordis, MFO. Regarding the traffic accident see 'Safety programmes', MFO Annual Report (note 211), p. 2. URL <http://www.mfo.org/Annual_R/safeprog.htm>.

213 Expenditures for FY 1999. MFO Annual Report (note 211), p. 29.

214 MOMEP was created by Argentina, Brazil, Chile and the USA in 1995, to verify compliance with ceasefire agreements in disputed areas following a border conflict between Ecuador and Peru. After the signing of a peace accord by the 2 countries in Oct. 1998 and the formal demarcation of border regions in May 1999, MOMEP was closed on 17 June 1999. US Department of Defense, Press Release no. 298–99, 17 June 1999. The last US personnel were withdrawn by 30 June 1999. Information from US Embassy in Lima, 1 Feb. 2000.

215 Logistical support personnel. Information from Ambassador Dennis C. Jett, US Embassy in Lima, 1998.

216 Information from Jett (note 215).

217 Protocol Concerning the Redeployment in Hebron, signed 15 Jan. 1997. In May 1996, a group of Norwegian observers were sent to Hebron. After Israel and the Palestinian Authority signed and implemented the Hebron Protocol in Jan. 1997, the mission was expanded to include observers from 5 additional countries. Information from Ambassador Mona Juul, Norwegian Ministry of Foreign Affairs, Oslo, 3 Dec. 1999.

218 Information from Juul (note 217).

219 Information from Juul (note 217).

220 The PMG was established on 30 Apr. 1998 in accordance with the Lincoln Agreement signed by the Government of Papua New Guinea and the Bougainville parties in Lincoln, New Zealand, 19–23 Jan. 1998. The PMG mandate included monitoring the ceasefire, promoting confidence, providing information to the local population, and assisting in the democratization and development process in accordance with the agreement. Information from Second Secretary Matthew Broadhead, Embassy of New Zealand to Sweden, 6 Dec. 1999.

221 The PMG is headed by Australia.

222 PMG personnel are both military and civilian. Information from Broadhead (note 220).

223 Information from Andrea Gleason, Second Secretary, Australian Embassy to Sweden, 10 Dec. 1999.

224 The CPDTF was established by the Commonwealth Secretary-General following the Sierra Leone President's request to the Commonwealth Ministerial Action Group (CMAG). The aim of the Task Force is to develop a strategic plan for the reorganization of the Sierra Leone Police Force in cooperation with the UN and other international agencies. Initial deployment began in July 1998 but came to an abrupt halt when rebels attacked Freetown in Jan. 1999. Task Force members were evacuated and the project was formally suspended. In Aug. 1999, the Task Force was reconstituted for a period of 6 months. Information from Chief Programme Officer Sandra Pepera, Commonwealth Political Affairs Division, 21 Feb. 2000.

225 Information from Pepera (note 224).

3. Russia: separatism and conflicts in the North Caucasus

GENNADY CHUFRIN

I. Introduction

Of the various threats to its national security and territorial integrity which Russia is now facing, one of the most prominent is that of separatism, which could result in the Russian Federation being transformed into a loose confederation or even the disintegration of the Russian state.

Separatist forces are particularly strong in the North Caucasus, often acting under the guise of ethnic or religious movements. The security situation in the region, which has remained tense and conflict-prone throughout the post-Soviet period, culminating in the 1994–96 war in Chechnya, became seriously destabilized again in 1999. The instability escalated dramatically in the second half of the year, initially with the separatist armed rebellion in Dagestan, initiated in and actively supported from neighbouring Chechnya, and then with the war in Chechnya itself between Russian federal forces and Chechen separatists. Strong separatist tendencies also developed in some other North Caucasus republics, including Karachaevo-Cherkessia, which until then had been relatively calm and stable.[1]

This chapter explores the major conflicts in the North Caucasus and the role of separatist forces in their build-up. Section II analyses the conflict in Karachaevo-Cherkessia against the backdrop of growing inter-ethnic tensions in the North Caucasus. Section III explores the Chechen-led armed rebellion in Dagestan, the events that preceded it, and the subsequent escalation of the Russian–Chechen conflict. Section IV deals with the implications of the current conflict situation in the North Caucasus for Russia's national security and territorial integrity and draws conclusions as to the significance of events in the region for security and stability in a larger international context.

II. Separatism on ethnic grounds

One of the instruments most actively exploited by the leaders of separatist forces in the North Caucasus is the tensions, of which the origins often date back to pre-Soviet times, between more than 30 ethnic groups and communities in the region. In the Soviet period these tensions were exacerbated by the mass deportations and then resettlement of the Chechens, Ingush, Karachais and Balkars; by the creation of republics with a double, and therefore

---

[1] Developments in the North Caucasus have been covered in successive chapters of the SIPRI Yearbook since 1993.

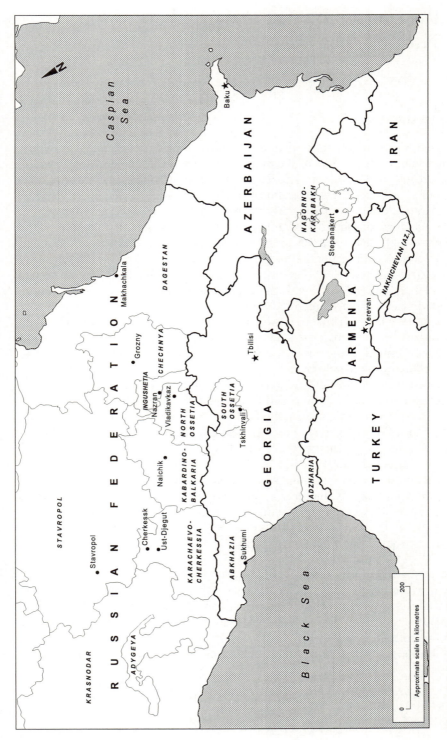

Figure 3.1. Map of the Caucasus

potentially conflictual, national tutelage (Checheno-Ingushetia, Karachaevo-Cherkessia and Kabardino-Balkaria); and by the imposition of arbitrary administrative borders in the region. As a consequence, when the Soviet Union began to fall apart, some of these ethnic conflicts assumed a new, ethno-nationalistic dimension, feeding separatist sentiments. Additional impulse was given by the bitter dissatisfaction of the local populations with the rapid impoverishment they have suffered in the post-Soviet period. Most other regions of the Russian Federation were also struggling with deep socio-economic crisis, but the North Caucasus was even worse affected, becoming one of the poorest regions in the country.[2]

Among these conflicts, that between North Ossetia and Ingushetia, which brought the two republics to armed confrontation in 1992, remains one of the most serious.[3] Although hostilities were stopped in the same year, profound tensions in inter-ethnic relations between the two republics have not been reconciled since. In March 1999 a major explosion in the central market of Vladikavkaz, the North Ossetian capital, which cost the lives of 60 people and was blamed on Ingush terrorists, seriously exacerbated these tensions.[4] It was only thanks to timely political and security measures undertaken in a coordinated manner by the federal and North Ossetian authorities that the situation was contained and a new open Ingush–Osset conflict avoided.

In Karachaevo-Cherkessia, relations between the two major (although not the largest) ethnic communities there—the Cherkess and Karachai[5]—deteriorated dramatically following the presidential elections there in May 1999. Victory in the second round of the elections was claimed by General Vladimir Semenov, a former Russian Army ground troops commander and a Karachai by nationality. According to the results announced, Semenov received over 70 per cent of the vote. His main rival, Stanislav Derev, mayor of Cherkessk, the capital of the republic, a Cherkess and leader of the Cherkess community, refused to accept defeat, claiming that the election results were rigged, and called on his supporters to stage mass protests. The conflict escalated further when Derev appealed against the election result and the republican election committee failed to reach a decision: 50 per cent of the committee members accepted the results as valid while the other 50 per cent considered them to have been rigged.[6] The tensions did not subside even after the republican Supreme Court ruled that they were valid.

---

[2] According to the available data the annual per capita gross regional product in the North Caucasus republics of Adygeya, Dagestan, Ingushetia and North Ossetia was in 1996 on average one-third or less that of the 10 most affluent regions of Russia. For more detail, see Nicholson, M., *Towards a Russia of the Regions*, Adelphi Paper no. 330 (International Institute for Strategic Studies: London, 1999).

[3] For an analysis of ethno-nationalism in post-Soviet Russia and a description of the Ingush–Osset conflict in 1992, see Baranovsky, V., 'Post-Soviet conflict heritage and risks', *SIPRI Yearbook 1993: World Armaments and Disarmament* (Oxford University Press: Oxford, 1993), pp. 140–43, 146–47. See also SIPRI, 'Crisis in Russia: facts and figures, people and data', Fact sheet, Oct. 1993.

[4] Radio Free Europe/Radio Liberty, *RFE/RL Newsline*, vol. 3, no. 56, Part 1 (22 Mar. 1999).

[5] The share of the Karachai in the population in the republic is estimated to be 30%; that of the Abazins and Cherkess, who are ethnically close to them, *c.* 17%. The largest ethnic community in the republic is represented by Russians at over 43% of the population.

[6] Rotar, I., 'Mir v Karachaevo-Cherkessii pod ugrozoy' [Peace is under threat in Karachaevo-Cherkessia], *Nezavisimaya Gazeta*, 23 July 1999.

Refusing to recognize this ruling, Derev's supporters appealed to the Supreme Court of the Russian Federation, which on 23 July annulled the decision of the Karachaevo-Cherkessia Supreme Court and instructed it to review the case. In another move intended to defuse the situation and give the conflicting parties time to reach a compromise, then Russian President Boris Yeltsin appointed Valentin Vlasov, a Russian, a Yeltsin loyalist and veteran expert on North Caucasus affairs, as acting president of Karachaevo-Cherkessia.[7]

Whatever Moscow's intentions in doing this were, they were interpreted by both sides in the conflict as a refusal or inability to take a clear stand on the issue and did little to reduce tensions in the republic. Moreover, not only Derev's supporters but also Semenov's now began staging mass protests. They condemned the decision to appoint Vlasov acting president as unconstitutional and even threatened to resort to arms.[8]

Nor did Derev and other leaders of the Cherkess community find much comfort in the ambivalent position of Moscow. They rejected the compromise proposal made by the Russian Presidential Administration to Derev to take the post of Prime Minister of Karachaevo-Cherkessia.[9] After the republican Supreme Court ruled again at the end of August in support of the May election results,[10] Derev and his followers threatened to restore the Cherkess autonomy which had been abolished in 1957 and secede from Karachaevo-Cherkessia.[11] Although Derev himself said that this did not mean the secession of Cherkessia from the Russian Federation, other and more radical Cherkess leaders did not exclude that possibility; in fact they began to promote it actively. Most prominent among these radicals were Boris Akbashev, Murat Khatukaev and Muhammed Kilba, leaders and activists in the International Cherkess Association, an organization set up in 1989 in the Netherlands by members of the Cherkess diaspora resident in Jordan, Syria and Turkey. The goals of the organization were not only the partition of Karachaevo-Cherkessia along ethnic lines but also the establishment—by force if necessary—of an independent state, Great Cherkessia.[12] Another group of Cherkess separatists meanwhile pursued a plan, first put forward in 1991–92 and also very threatening for the security of the Russian Federation, to unite the Cherkess and Abazins with the Adygeys and Kabardins in the neighbouring republic of Kabardino-Balkaria, who are ethnically close to them.[13] If realized, these plans would undermine peace and stability in Kabardino-Balkaria as well.

[7] Rotar, I., 'Pered opasnym pretsedentom' [On the verge of a dangerous precedent], *Nezavisimaya Gazeta*, 27 July 1999.

[8] Konstantinova, N., 'Situatsiya v Karachaevo-Cherkessii ostayotsya slozhnoy' [Situation in Karachaevo-Cherkessia remains tense], *Nezavisimaya Gazeta*, 27 July 1999.

[9] ITAR-TASS, 7 Sep. 1999, in 'Voloshin, Karachaevo-Cherkessia head discuss stand-off', Foreign Broadcast Information Service, *Daily Report–Central Eurasia (FBIS-SOV)*, FBIS-SOV-1999-0907, 7 Sep. 1999.

[10] *RFE/RL Newsline*, vol. 3, no. 170, Part I (1 Sep. 1999).

[11] ITAR-TASS, 5 Sep. 1999, in 'Rally in Cherkessk insists on cancelling poll results', FBIS-SOV-1999-0905, 5 Sep. 1999.

[12] Panov, V., 'Dremlushchiy vulkan na yuge Rossii' [Slumbering volcano in the south of Russia], *Nezavisimaya Gazeta*, 10 July 1999.

[13] Yazkova, A., 'Vozmozhna li "balkanizatsiya" Severnogo Kavkaza?' [Is the Balkanization of the North Caucasus possible?], *Krasnaya Zvezda*, 17 Sep. 1999.

Threats of partition contributed, predictably, to further escalation of the conflict in Karachaevo-Cherkessia. The Russian ethnic community, the largest in the republic, now also decided to take an active stand in defence of its interests. In early September 1999 representatives of the Russian population formed an action committee, which claimed to enjoy the overwhelming support of the Russian community. It called on the federal authorities to recognize the May election results as valid and not to allow partition of the republic, which would inevitably lead to an escalation of conflict in the ethnically heterogeneous society. It also demanded that the ethnic composition of the governing structures in the republic should reflect the relative sizes of the ethnic communities there and that the historical name Batalpashinsk be restored to Cherkessk. (The name was changed in the 1950s.)[14]

Amid these rapidly growing ethnic tensions, and against the express advice of the federal authorities, President-elect Semenov decided to assume office formally and to use his presidential powers to prevent the situation in the republic getting out of control. His decision was helped by plans of his supporters to organize a 150 000-strong protest march on Cherkessk. Since by that time there had already been repeated violent ethnic clashes in the republic, resulting in several deaths, such mass action could easily have provoked further violence. His inauguration ceremony, held on 14 September (in Ust-Djegut, the second-largest town after Cherkessk, as the security situation did not allow it to be staged in the capital[15]), was attended by many republican officials, including members of the government and city mayors, and by representatives of the Karachai, Russian, Cossack and other ethnic communities in the republic. Conspicuously absent were the leaders of the Cherkess and Abazins, who continued to defy Semenov's authority. On 16 September they held an extraordinary congress attended by 900 delegates representing them and the minority part of the Russian community. They voted in favour of restoring a Cherkess Autonomous Region (*rayon*) as part of the neighbouring Stavropol territory (*krai*) and named Derev as head of administration in the new autonomous formation.[16]

Confronted with these new developments, the federal authorities finally chose to support Semenov. He promised to restore law and order, appealed for harmony and tolerance between the republic's ethnic groups, and said that the issue of partition should be put to a referendum.[17] In mid-October the People's Assembly, the main legislative body of Karachaevo-Cherkessia, endorsed Semenov's proposals of Vasiliy Neshchadinov, a Russian by nationality, as the new prime minister and of Akham Sochiev and Fatima Khunizheva, who were ethnic Karachai and Abazin, respectively, as deputy prime ministers. The two

---

[14] ITAR-TASS, 6 Sep. 1999, in 'Russia: Committee opposes Karachay-Cherkessia division', FBIS-SOV-1999-0907, 6 Sep. 1999.

[15] Bondarenko, M., 'General prinyos prisyagu' [General sworn in], *Nezavisimaya Gazeta*, 15 Sep. 1999.

[16] *RFE/RL Newsline*, vol. 3, no. 182, Part 1 (17 Sep. 1999); and Bondarenko, M., 'Karachaevo-Cherkessia razdelyaetsya' [Karachaevo-Cherkessia is divided], *Nezavisimaya Gazeta*, 17 Sep. 1999.

[17] Bondarenko, M., 'Cherez chetyre mesyatsa posle vyborov' [Four months after the elections], *Nezavisimaya Gazeta*, 23 Sep. 1999.

remaining deputy prime minister posts, which were to go to a Cherkess and a Nogai, remained vacant. In another move aimed at establishing representation of different ethnic groups in the governing bodies of the republic, Semenov appointed a Cossack *ataman*, Major-General (ret.) Yuriy Antonov, to head the newly created Security Council of Karachaevo-Cherkessia.[18]

These decisions failed to mollify the political opponents of Semenov in the Cherkess community. They boycotted the People's Assembly, continued to demand the reversal of the Karachaevo-Cherkessia Supreme Court's ruling recognizing Semenov as the legally elected president, and persisted in their demands for the partition of Karachaevo-Cherkessia.

In late October Semenov and Derev were persuaded by then Russian Prime Minister Vladimir Putin to reach a political compromise in order to defuse the tension in the republic. Under the agreement reached, Semenov was given one year to run the republic and thereafter was to hold a popular vote of confidence.[19] Explaining the terms of the agreement at a press conference in Moscow, he said: 'I will stay if the people decide that I'm doing my job properly. Otherwise new elections will be called'.[20] Derev turned down Semenov's offer to become his prime minister as part of the deal but urged his supporters to work with the new government. The reaction among the Cherkess and Abazin communities to the agreement between Semenov and Derev was mixed. Some accepted the need for compromise and were prepared to give Semenov time to put the negotiated agreement into effect; the radicals, led by Boris Akbashev, refused to accept it and continued to demand the division of Karachaevo-Cherkessia.[21]

III. The Chechen conflict[22]

The conflict between Russia and Chechnya continued to be the most destabilizing in the North Caucasus in 1999. Although the war between them was officially stopped in August 1996 with the signing of the Khasaviurt agreement,[23] contradictions remained between the federal authorities and the government of the Chechen Republic which had to be resolved if meaningful and sustainable cooperation between them was to be possible.

---

[18] *RFE/RL Newsline*, vol. 3, no. 201, Part I (14 Oct. 1999).

[19] *RFE/RL Newsline*, vol. 3, no. 208, Part 1 (25 Oct. 1999).

[20] Interfax (Moscow), 24 Oct. 1999, in 'Parties in Karachaevo-Cherkessia reach compromise', FBIS-SOV-1999-1024, 24 Oct. 1999.

[21] *RFE/RL Newsline*, vol. 3, no. 221, Part 1 (12 Nov. 1999).

[22] On the Chechen conflict, see also chapter 1, section III in this volume.

[23] The Agreement on the Principles for Clarifying the Basis for Mutual Relations between the Russian Federation and the Chechen Republic. On the Khasaviurt agreement, see Baranovsky, V., 'Russia: conflicts and its security environment', *SIPRI Yearbook 1997: Armaments, Disarmament and International Security* (Oxford University Press: Oxford, 1997), pp. 108–10. For the text of the agreement, see *Nezavisimaya Gazeta*, 3 Sep. 1996, p. 3.

The imbroglio over the Khasaviurt agreement

In the years that followed the Khasaviurt agreement, Moscow and Grozny had failed, in spite of numerous pledges to the contrary, to achieve any substantial and mutually acceptable results on most of the issues negotiated, including economic ones. They also proved unable to cooperate effectively on fighting the drug trafficking, money laundering, illegal arms trading or kidnapping of people carried out by numerous Chechen gangs inside Chechnya itself as well as in neighbouring areas.[24] Each side accused the other of not meeting its commitments under the Khasaviurt agreement. Most significantly, Moscow and Grozny remained diametrically opposed on the final definition of the status of the Chechen Republic, decision on which was deferred until 2001 by the agreement. The federal authorities continued to regard Chechnya as an integral part of the Russian Federation while the Government of Chechnya regarded it as a sovereign state which had de facto gained independence as a result of the 1994–96 war with Russia. Differences and disagreements in relations between them continued to mount. Vladimir Zorin, Chairman of the Russian Duma Committee on Nationalities, stated in August 1999 that 'the Khasaviurt agreement exhausted itself strategically and tactically'.[25]

This imbroglio in Russo-Chechen relations was already contributing to a serious deterioration of the security situation around Chechnya in the first half of 1999. In response the federal authorities stepped up security measures in the North Caucasus. In April 1999 Sergey Stepashin, then Russian Interior Minister, ordered the 'effective closure' of the administrative border between the Stavropol Region and Chechnya and continuous patrols by helicopter gunships, and issued instructions for a police regiment to be formed, manned by locals.[26] In June the Interior Ministry troops and police of the adjacent Republic of Dagestan were put on heightened alert. Controls were tightened at all crossing-points on the administrative border between Dagestan and Chechnya and security around industrial enterprises, bridges, communication centres, schools and hospitals was intensified.[27] In July the federal authorities took additional security measures to protect the federal Caucasus Highway, the railway linking the North Caucasus with the Transcaucasus, and the main Baku–Novorossiysk oil pipeline.[28]

The security of this 1411-km long pipeline, part of which runs through Chechnya, was considered especially important by the federal authorities. Russia began to experience serious problems with its use in 1999. In the first

---

[24] The Russian Interior Ministry reported that more than 60 armed Chechen gangs had kidnapped nearly 1300 people, including 63 foreigners, since the end of the 1994–96 war. Dolgov, A., 'Russia: 1300 kidnapped in Chechnya', Yahoo news, 11 Oct. 1999. Yahoo news reports are archived at URL <http://dailynews.yahoo.com>.

[25] 'Russia: MP urges fundamentally new North Caucasus policy', FBIS-SOV-1999-0901, 30 Aug. 1999.

[26] Interfax (Moscow), 'Russia "effectively" closes border with Chechnya', FBIS-SOV-1999-0426, 26 Apr. 1999.

[27] ITAR-TASS, 26 Apr. 1999, in 'Situation on Dagestan–Chechen border deteriorates', in FBIS-SOV-1999-0615, 15 June 1999.

[28] ITAR-TASS, 19 July 1999, in 'Russian security units in Caucasus on heightened alert', FBIS-SOV-1999-0719, 19 July 1999.

six months of the year the operation of the pipeline was stopped for 95 days as a result of numerous accidents, which raised legitimate complaints from Azerbaijan and reduced its interest in continuing cooperation with Russia. That cooperation was already at a very low ebb after the commissioning of an alternative oil route from Baku to Supsa (Georgia) at the beginning of 1999.[29]

The reasons for these stoppages were not only technical but increasingly of a security nature, in particular where the pipeline crossed Chechnya. According to an agreement reached between Moscow and Grozny in 1997, protection of this section of the pipeline against theft of oil and technical damage was entrusted to the Chechen National Guard, which failed to fulfil its commitments.[30] The Russian Government therefore decided at the end of June to shut down indefinitely the transit of oil through the Chechen section of the pipeline and find alternative routes.[31] Russia began to bypass Chechnya in early July by shipping oil via pipeline only up to Dagestan and from there by train to Novorossiysk.[32] This caused dissatisfaction in Baku and especially in Grozny—in the former case mainly because it significantly reduced the capacity of Russia to transport Azerbaijani oil (to about 50 per cent of the planned amount of 120 000 tonnes per month),[33] but in the case of Grozny because it amounted to the Chechen Government's losing almost its only reliable source of revenue. Inevitably it led to political relations between Moscow and Grozny cooling further, probably to their coolest since the end of the Chechen war in 1996.

Meanwhile the social and economic situation in Chechnya also continued to deteriorate rapidly. The living standards of the majority of its population fell below the poverty level. Unemployment was massive and with no prospects of a reduction, while the social infrastructure, education and the medical services broke down completely. Seriously discredited, the government of President Aslan Maskhadov was rapidly losing the public support which it had enjoyed in the wake of the war with Russia and, as a consequence, its ability to control the political and security situation in the republic.

The opposition to Maskhadov continued to gain ground in the republic. It began to defy his authority openly and resort to violence, including several attempts on his life, the latest in March 1999.[34] With the weakening of his political influence, whatever chances might still exist of a negotiated settlement with the federal authorities were quickly fading, while the Chechen Government's stand vis-à-vis Moscow grew increasingly intransigent under the

---

[29] Interfax (Moscow), 9 July 1999, in 'Azerbaijan unhappy over problems in Russian pipeline', FBIS-SOV-1999-0709, 9 July 1999. On the oil transport routes, see Chufrin, G., 'The Caspian Sea Basin: the security dimensions', *SIPRI Yearbook 1999: Armaments, Disarmament and International Security* (Oxford University Press: Oxford, 1999), pp. 217–23.

[30] ITAR-TASS, 24 May 1999, in '"Accident" in Chechnya halts Azeri oil pipeline', FBIS-SOV-1999-0524, 24 May 1999; and ITAR-TASS, 17 June 1999, in 'Azerbaijan–Russia oil pipeline plagued at Chechnya leg', FBIS-SOV-1999-0617, 17 June 1999.

[31] Interfax (Moscow), 16 June 1999, in 'Minister: Russia should shut Baku–Novorossiysk pipeline', FBIS-SOV-1999-0616, 16 June 1999.

[32] 'Azerbaijanskaya neft' poshla v obkhod Chechni' [Azeri oil began to bypass Chechnya], *Nezavisimaya Gazeta*, 10 July 1999.

[33] *RFE/RL Newsline*, vol. 2, no. 160, Part 1 (18 Aug. 1999).

[34] *RFE/RL Newsline*, vol. 3, no. 56, Part 1 (22 Mar. 1999).

influence of the radical opposition. In the course of 1999 the opposition was building up its own armed forces and expanding direct control over various regions, including parts of Grozny itself. At the head of the opposition stood radical Chechen leaders and field commanders who started to use the growing social tension and dissatisfaction among ordinary people for their own political aims.

The principal aim of the opposition was the creation of a unified Islamic state in the North Caucasus that would comprise, besides Chechnya, Dagestan, Ingushetia, Kabardino-Balkaria and Karachaevo-Cherkessia. The inclusion of Dagestan was particularly important as it would give landlocked Chechnya an outlet to the Caspian Sea. With this aim in mind a Congress of Chechen and Dagestani Peoples was set up in April 1998. Shamil Basaev, former Acting Prime Minister of Chechnya and one of the most radical field commanders, became its chairman. In February 1999 he was also elected by the Islamic Shura (Council) of Chechnya, the main opposition body, as its formal leader.[35]

The role of Wahhabism

To create a large base of devoted followers who would be prepared to fight fanatically for an Islamic state, the allied opposition leaders began in the 1990s to exploit Wahhabism, a form of Islamic teaching based on austere puritanical principles. An official school of Islam in Saudi Arabia, Wahhabism was previously unknown in the North Caucasus, but with financial support from abroad, mainly from private organizations in Saudi Arabia,[36] it had begun to be increasingly popular, particularly among those sectors of local society that had suffered most from adverse economic conditions, widespread unemployment and political turmoil.

As a result Chechnya was turned into a hotbed of Wahhabism in the North Caucasus. Wahhabism also projected its influence to neighbouring regions, Dagestan in particular. The first signs of the political impact of the spread of Wahhabism to Dagestan were felt as early as 1997, when members of Dzhammat, a pro-Wahhabi organization, established control over several villages in Buinaksk District, only 80 km south of Makhachkala, the Dagestani capital, after driving the local authorities out. In August 1998 residents of three villages in that district declared them 'an independent Islamic territory'.[37] The Russian Federal Ministry of Nationalities tried at the time to play down the incident, saying that only three villages were involved and that it was a local problem.[38] This judgement proved tragically wrong and cost dearly in human life and material loss only one year later. The Wahhabites, entrenched in the Buinaksk District villages, although formally retracting their proclama-

---

[35] *RFE/RL Newsline*, vol. 3, no. 36, Part 1 (22 Feb. 1999).

[36] Influential private sources in Saudi Arabia were accused of financing the Wahhabi movement in Chechnya by Russian politicians and by President Maskhadov, who expressed deep concern about these activities and their political consequences. Interfax (Moscow), 2 Oct. 1998, in 'Russia: Chechnya's Maskhadov sees US–Saudi Caucasus intervention', FBIS-SOV-98-275, 2 Oct. 1998.

[37] *RFE/RL Newsline*, vol. 2, no. 158, Part 1 (18 Aug. 1998).

[38] *RFE/RL Newsline*, vol. 2, no. 161, Part 1 (21 Aug. 1998).

tion of independence, continued to build up a military stronghold with active outside assistance, and when an armed rebellion led by Chechens broke out in Dagestan in August 1999 they joined it.

The spread of Wahhabism in Dagestan, as well as Adygeya, Ingushetia, Karachaevo-Cherkessia and Kabardino-Balkaria, could not be attributed solely to the activities of its proselytes in Chechnya. The major centres of Wahhabite teaching were located after all not in Chechnya but in Afghanistan, Pakistan, Saudi Arabia and Turkey where, according to press reports, over 1500 young Dagestanis and 2500 residents of other North Caucasus republics underwent intensive indoctrination and training.[39] However, the role of Chechnya in the proliferation of Wahhabism in the North Caucasus was very prominent, if only because, with the ongoing introduction of the norms and rules of Islamic law into its legal practice and everyday life, Chechnya was rapidly losing its secular status and becoming an Islamic state itself. This process received a boost when in February 1999 Aslan Maskhadov signed decrees suspending the legislative functions of the Chechen Parliament and ordering a transition to Shariah law throughout Chechnya.[40] This enabled radical Islamists such as the Wahhabites to operate quite openly in the republic and to use its territory as a base for carrying their activities to other regions and as a safe haven when chased out of other North Caucasus republics. Wahhabism was by now a well-established force in Chechnya, even though formally the number of its followers was estimated at not more than 10 per cent of the Chechen population.[41]

The Wahhabite movement was not the only one planning to establish an Islamic state in the North Caucasus. Analysis of the political landscape there shows that there were many other radical organizations and political groups in Chechnya, Dagestan and elsewhere with similar ideas, although some were opposed to Wahhabism on theological grounds—Kavkazskiy Dom (Caucasian Home), for example, whose leaders included Nadirshakh Khachilaev, Chairman of the Union of Muslims of Russia and a former member of the Russian Duma; his brother Magomed Khachilaev, leader of the Lak national minority in Dagestan; and the notorious Chechen field commander Salman Raduev. However, of the many Muslim groups supporting the cause of an Islamic state in the North Caucasus, the Wahhabi organizations proved most persistent and aggressive in the pursuit of that idea.

The jihad in Dagestan

On 7 August 1999 several hundred Islamic militants invaded Dagestan from neighbouring Chechnya and established a stronghold in its mountainous Botlikh District. Three days later the self-proclaimed Islamic Shura of Dages-

---

[39] Nikulin, A., 'Severo-Kavkazskiy uzel' [North Caucasus knot], *Nezavisimaya Gazeta*, 7 May 1998; and Varisov, M.-Z., 'Na yuge Rossii nagnetaetsya napryazhennost' [Tension builds up in the south of Russia], *Nezavisimaya Gazeta*, 26 Aug. 1998.

[40] *RFE/RL Newsline*, vol. 3, no. 24, Part 1 (4 Feb. 1999).

[41] Interview with Federal Minister Ramazan Abdulatipov, *Krasnaya Zvezda*, 26 Aug. 1999.

tan declared the establishment of an independent Islamic state in this southern republic of the Russian Federation. The decision to start the jihad (holy war) in Dagestan was reportedly taken at an extraordinary meeting of the Congress of Chechen and Dagestani Peoples in Grozny on 24 July, chaired by Shamil Basaev. According to Movladi Udugov, Deputy Chairman of the Congress and member of the Chechen National Security Council, the meeting adopted 'concrete decisions on Dagestan of a classified nature'.[42] After the invasion began, Basaev was proclaimed the emir (ruler) of the new 'Islamic state of Dagestan'.[43]

Federal armed forces started an intensive military operation using artillery and air power widely against the intruders. Two weeks after the incursion of the Islamic rebels into Botlikh District, the federal forces succeeded in driving them out from the area. By the end of August it seemed that military victory over the rebels was within reach. The Russian Defence Ministry hastened to announce that the militants were defeated and were trying to retreat to the territory of Chechnya in small groups.[44] It was even announced that the army units that had taken part were to be withdrawn from Botlikh District[45] and that what remained to be done was a 'mopping-up' operation by the local police and law enforcement authorities to encircle and eliminate the remaining groups of militants.

However, military success took more time and effort than originally anticipated. At the beginning of September Islamic militants launched a new wave of hostilities in Dagestan, this time in Novolaksky District on the western border with Chechnya. The new assault by the rebels followed a bomb attack by Islamic extremists on a Russian military settlement in the town of Buinaksk, killing 64 Russian servicemen and members of their families.[46] In Novolaksky District the rebels succeeded in seizing several villages and the town of Novolaksk. Another flashpoint in the renewed fighting with separatists developed in central Dagestan, where heavily armed Wahhabites in the villages of Karamakhy and Chabanmakhy in Buinaksk District not only refused to disarm but put up stiff resistance, destroying several government armoured vehicles and even shooting down a Su-25 ground-attack aircraft.[47]

There were several reasons for the rebels' military successes. First, not only were they well armed, but they had also undergone intensive training in guerrilla warfare in special camps in Chechnya, such as those in Vedeno,

[42] Radio Rossii (Moscow), 24 July 1999, in 'Chechen–Dagestan Congress discusses regional issues', FBIS-SOV-1999-0724, 24 July 1999.

[43] Paukov, V. and Lefko, E., '"Allah's warriors" zero in on Caucasus', *Moscow News*, 8–14 Sep. 1999.

[44] Russian Defence Ministry, Press Service, 'Summary of operations in the Republic of Dagestan', *Krasnaya Zvezda*, 28 Aug. 1999.

[45] Russian Defence Ministry, Press Service, 'Summary of operations in the Republic of Dagestan', *Krasnaya Zvezda*, 31 Aug. 1999.

[46] Paukov, V., 'Nash kavkazskiy dom' [Our Caucasus home], *Vremya*, 6 Sep. 1999.

[47] Fatullaev, M., 'Na vtorom etape operatsii v Dagestane stali razoruzhat' boevikov v Karamakhy i Chabanmakhy' [At the second stage of the operation in Dagestan militants began to be disarmed in Karamakhy and Chabanmakhy], *Nezavisimaya Gazeta*, 31 Aug. 1999; and Aleksin, V., 'Gibel' shturmovika SU-25 v Dagestane' [Su-25 jet fighter lost in Dagestan], *Nezavisimaya Gazeta*, 11 Sep. 1999.

Serzhen-Yurt and Nozhai-Yurt, in preparation for the jihad.[48] Second, they received large-scale financial support from a number of international extremist organizations, such as the Islamic Action Front in Jordan and the Muslim Brotherhood in Egypt.[49] Russian Government officials claimed that among those financing the separatists in Chechnya and Dagestan were Usama bin Laden, a Saudi millionaire and terrorist wanted worldwide, and international drug cartels.[50] Large sums of money were also transferred to Chechnya by members of the influential Chechen business community operating inside Russia, either as voluntary contributions or extorted by Chechen criminal gangs.[51] Third, using this money, many veteran mercenaries from Afghanistan, Jordan, Pakistan, Saudi Arabia and some other Arab countries were employed.[52] In other words the jihad in Dagestan was well-prepared and -planned, with a wide variety of local as well as international political, economic and downright criminal interests behind it.

As a result, instead of the planned routine, low-key mopping-up operation, the government forces found themselves drawn into a serious conflict, the largest Russia had faced since the 1994–96 war in Chechnya. The fierce fighting that followed the incursions into Dagestan caused massive destruction of villages occupied by rebels, large-scale flows of civilian refugees, mostly women and children, and heavy loss of life among the combatants. By mid-September federal forces, making the most of their air and fire superiority, took over the villages of Karamakhy and Chabanmakhy and forced the militants out of Novolaksky District, from where they returned to Chechnya.[53]

In spite of this success the conflict was far from over. It escalated rapidly after Chechen militants were accused of organizing acts of terrorism against the civilian population in Russian cities. In Moscow a series of powerful bomb explosions which killed 277 people was blamed on them. The first of these took place in an underground shopping centre near the Kremlin on 31 August 1999 and the next two in a residential area in the south-eastern part of the city in early September.[54] Following the explosions, the Russian Government

[48] Interfax (Moscow), 5 Sep. 1999, in 'Bin Laden said in Chechnya before Dagestan incursion', FBIS-SOV-1999-0905, 5 Sep. 1999.

[49] According to the Russian Defence Ministry, the amount of money received by Islamic militants from abroad to finance preparation for the rebellion was not less than $50 million. *Krasnaya Zvezda*, 29 Sep. 1999.

[50] *Der Spiegel*, 23 Aug. 1999, in 'Deputy Interior Minister views Dagestan conflict', FBIS-SOV-1999-0823, 23 Aug. 1999.

[51] The amount of such transfers is unknown, but they were undoubtedly very large. When a relatively small Moscow-based bank, Trustkreditbank, was raided by police in early 2000, it was discovered that its managers were implicated in cash transfers to Chechen militants to the amount of $180 000 daily. According to the Russian Federal Security Service, this bank was only part of a widespread network of banking organizations specially set up in Russia for this purpose. Litvinov, A., 'Boeviki poluchali pomoshch' iz Moskvy' [Militants received aid from Moscow], *Nezavisimaya Gazeta*, 23 Mar. 2000.

[52] Krutikov, Ye., 'V Dagestane voevali inostrannye nayomniki' [Foreign mercenaries fought in Dagestan], *Izvestiya*, 28 Aug. 1999.

[53] *RFE/RL Newsline*, vol. 3, no. 179, Part 1 (14 Sep. 1999).

[54] Petrov, K. and Soldatenko, B., 'Vzryv v tsentre Moskvy' [Explosion in the centre of Moscow], *Krasnaya Zvezda*, 2 Sep. 1999; and Novoselskaya, A., Nikitina, S. and Bronzova, M., 'Vzryv zhilogo doma v Moskve polozhil konets spokoystviyu v stolitse' [Explosion in an apartment house in Moscow puts an end to complacency in the capital], *Nezavisimaya Gazeta*, 10 Sep. 1999.

began a massive national anti-terrorist campaign, Operation Whirlwind, not only to protect the civilian population but also to safeguard industrial installations, electric and nuclear power plants, airports and railway stations. These measures failed, however, to prevent another terrorist attack on civilians: on 16 September a bomb outside an apartment block in the town of Volgodonsk, 1200 km south of Moscow, killed 17 people.[55] The fears of the civilian population were exacerbated with the announcement by Basaev that a 'death squad' had been formed of his fanatical followers prepared to carry out suicide missions inside Russia.[56]

Even so, in spite of their ruthless determination, the extremists failed to achieve their goals in Dagestan. This happened for several reasons, ranging from political to military to psychological and cultural.

First, the uprising did not succeed because its leaders either seriously misinterpreted or ignored the prevailing views of Dagestani society. In preparing for the uprising they clearly overestimated the advantages presented by the availability of military bases, training camps and Wahhabi ideological centres on the territory of Chechnya. Basaev, Movladi Udugov, Jordanian-born Khattab, other radicals and their followers believed the Chechen connection to be all-important for the success of the rebellion. However, they seriously underestimated the popular distrust of their declared goals and general aversion to the methods by which those goals were to be achieved. The majority of the population of Dagestan, receiving news of the rebellion, interpreted it not as a war of national liberation but as an act of aggression from Chechnya against their republic—even though there were local Dagestani residents among the rebels.[57] Numerous meetings were held in Makhachkala and other towns and villages in Dagestan at which representatives of various local nationalities and of different political parties joined in condemning the invasion, thus frustrating the rebel leaders' hopes of local support.

Mistrust of and opposition to the rebels were increased by their belonging to the Wahhabi movement. In the eyes of the majority of the Muslim population of Dagestan, this made them reactionary sectarians waging a fratricidal war.[58] Consequently, instead of supporting the rebels, thousands of Dagestani citizens volunteered to fight them and took an active part in combat operations against the intruders, cooperating closely with the army and police.[59] This cooperation proved effective, in no small degree because Dagestani self-defence units helped the regular army and police fighting in the mountainous terrain, thus largely offsetting the rebels' training advantages.

[55] *RFE/RL Newsline*, vol. 3, no. 182, Part 1 (17 Sep. 1999).
[56] *RFE/RL Newsline*, vol. 3, no. 184, Part 1 (21 Sep. 1999).
[57] It was estmated that *c.* 2000–4000 Dagestanis took part in the armed rebellion on the side of the rebels. *Krasnaya Zvezda*, 26 Aug. 1999.
[58] Plotnikov, N., 'Narody Dagestana splotilis' pered litsom obshchey opasnosti' [Dagestan peoples unite to face a common threat], *Nezavisimaya Gazeta*, 13 Aug. 1999.
[59] After hostilities began in Novolaksky District, according to the Chairman of the Dagestan Security Council, Ahmednabi Magdigadjiev, at least 25 000 volunteers expressed their intention to fight the militants. ITAR-TASS, 6 Sep. 1999, in 'At least 25 000 Dagestanis ready to fight militants', FBIS-SOV-1999-0906, 6 Sep. 1999.

Basaev, Khattab and their emissaries also failed to mobilize public support in other North Caucasus republics, such as Ingushetia, where the population was largely sympathetic to Chechnya when it fought the federal forces in 1994–96. This time neither ordinary citizens of Ingushetia nor the Ingush elders showed any intention to back up the Chechen extremist leaders. Reflecting this mood, Ruslan Aushev, President of Ingushetia, joined his counterpart in North Ossetia, Aleksandr Dzasokhov, in an appeal to the people of both republics and especially to those in the areas bordering Chechnya not to give in to provocation and to exhibit 'watchfulness, restraint and courage'.[60]

Second, in contrast to the time of the 1994–96 Chechen war, Russian society was basically united on the need to crush the rebellion in the most effective way and within the shortest time possible, preserve the integrity of the Russian state and support the army in fighting the separatists. The ferocity of terrorist acts against civilians only strengthened this resolve, added to public indignation with the Islamic militants and increased demands for them to be brought to justice. These public attitudes were rightly understood by all major political parties in the country. As a result the federal government received practically unanimous support in both chambers of the Federal Assembly (the Russian Parliament) in its campaign against the rebels. In mid-September the Assembly, meeting in closed session, endorsed Prime Minister Putin's tough measures in dealing with Chechnya, fighting the mutiny in Dagestan and stepping up security in Russian cities. Addressing the Assembly, Putin said that in his opinion the Khasaviurt agreement was a mistake. He proposed to effectively seal all administrative borders with Chechnya and to introduce a 'special economic regime' in dealing with it. This meant, among other things, tight economic sanctions against the breakaway republic. He also proposed to provide political support to 'respected members of the Chechen diaspora who had to take residence now outside their republic' in forming what amounted to a Chechen government-in-exile.[61]

With these changes in public opinion and with elections forthcoming, even the most radical politicians in Russia refrained from criticizing the counter-insurgency operation in Dagestan as they had done only a few years before during the 1994–96 Chechen war.

Finally, the Russian military had learned, if only partly, their lessons from the disastrous 1994–96 war in Chechnya. In order to minimize Russian casualties the military command used its unquestionable superiority in air- and fire-power more widely and efficiently before starting ground operations. The Russian Air Force established several units armed with Mi-24 gunships and Mi-8 cargo helicopters specially fitted for operations against guerrillas.[62] When regular air operations began, An-30 and Su-24MR aircraft conducted

---

[60] *Vremya,* 19 Aug. 1999, p. 2, in 'Tensions on Ingush–Ossete border', FBIS-SOV-1999-0820, 19 Aug. 1999.
[61] Rodin, I., 'Putin predlagaet novy plan Chechenskogo uregulirovaniya' [Putin proposes a new plan for Chechen settlement], *Nezavisimaya Gazeta,* 15 Sep. 1999; *RFE/RL Newsline,* vol. 3, no. 180, Part 1 (15 Sep. 1999); and Tropkina, O., 'Vystuplenie Putina ponravilos' [Putin's address well received], *Nezavisimaya Gazeta,* 17 Sep. 1999.
[62] *RFE/RL Newsline,* vol. 3, no. 171, Part 1 (2 Sep. 1999).

reconnaissance missions while Su-25 attack aircraft performed air strikes. The federal forces carried out daily massive bombing raids and artillery attacks on the positions held by the rebels in Dagestan, inflicting losses at comparatively low risk to their own troops. In response to domestic criticism and demands the share of recruits among the front-line troops was greatly reduced in favour of better-trained servicemen. In order to maintain domestic support, tight control was also established over information coming from the conflict zone.

The second Chechen war

In the second half of September 1999 the conflict escalated further when, as part of the continuing anti-insurgency operation, the Russian Air Force was ordered to bomb guerrilla bases inside Chechnya so as to dislodge the Islamic militants, disrupt and destroy their lines of command, communication and supply, and prevent new incursions into Dagestan. As part of this air campaign Russian aircraft started to raid Chechen targets regularly, hitting suspected guerrilla bases in the districts of Gudermes, Nozhai-Yurt, Vedeno and Shelkovsky.[63] On 23 September Grozny was attacked for the first time since 1996, and its airport and an arms depot and a radar station there were destroyed.[64]

As a result the situation inside Chechnya was seriously aggravated. Not only were its communication centres, oil and industrial enterprises and transport facilities destroyed or severely damaged by the air strikes, but tens of thousands of refugees began to flee to the neighbouring regions of the North Caucasus, mostly to Ingushetia, fearing a new escalation of hostilities.[65]

Trying to avert large-scale war with Russia that would deal a mortal blow to the self-proclaimed sovereignty of Chechnya, President Maskhadov appealed for urgent talks with Yeltsin. The Russian Government responded by saying that such a meeting could take place only 'under appropriate conditions'. As Prime Minister Putin explained, this meant a condemnation of terrorism 'in explicit and definite terms' by the Chechen Government and the immediate extradition of the terrorist leaders from Chechnya to Russia.[66]

As Maskhadov refused to meet these demands, the Russian military continued to encircle Chechnya and attack guerrilla-related targets inside the republic. They also started the long-expected ground operation, moving gradually to occupy Chechnya's low-lying northern districts as far as the Terek river. By the beginning of October they had succeeded in taking control of roughly one-third of the Chechen territory north of the Terek and established a

[63] *RFE/RL Newsline*, vol. 3, no. 183, Part 1 (20 Sep. 1999).

[64] Golotyuk, Yu., 'Aviaudar po Groznomu' [Airstrike at Grozny], *Izvestiya*, 24 Sep. 1999.

[65] According to the Russian Ministry of Emergency Situations, at the beginning of Oct. the total number of Chechen refugees had reached 155 000, including 112 000 in Ingushetia, and their number was continuing to rise. *Krasnaya Zvezda*, 9 Oct. 1999, p. 1, and 12 Oct. 1999, p. 1.

[66] Williams, D., 'Moscow sets its terms for ending raids on Chechnya', *International Herald Tribune*, 30 Sep. 1999.

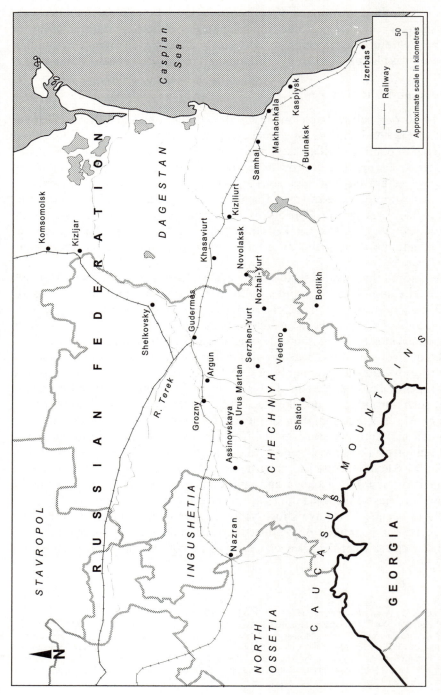

Figure 3.2. Map of Chechnya

'security zone' there.[67] At the same time Putin made a statement in support of the earlier, pro-Moscow, Chechen Parliament which was dissolved in 1996, declaring it 'the only legitimate governing body in Chechnya'.[68] His statement fell short of a formal de-recognition of Maskhadov as legitimate President of Chechnya. However, it indicated clearly enough that the federal authorities were no longer prepared to confine their goals in the conflict to a mere counter-insurgency operation but were aiming at a fundamental revision of the results of the 1994–96 war by crushing Chechen separatism and reimposing federal rule in the republic.

President Maskhadov then declared martial law in Chechnya and called for a jihad against Russia.[69] In an attempt to consolidate all anti-Russian forces in the republic he also officially put Basaev, Ruslan Gelaev and Khattab in command of the resistance forces,[70] defying Russian demands for them to be extradited as terrorists. However, in contrast to the situation in 1994–96, Maskhadov did not succeed in uniting the population of Chechnya behind him, deeply divided as it was—along *teip* (clan) lines, between the pro- and anti-Wahhabite sections of the population, and between the lowland and mountainous areas of the country. The call for a jihad received a muted response, even among the senior clergy of the republic, the most notable being the refusal of the Chief Mufti (head of Muslims) of Chechnya, Akhmed-khadji Kadyrov, to support Maskhadov.[71]

Meanwhile the conflict was turning into another full-scale war in Chechnya, only three years after the end of the first. Russian troops continued to expand their control over the territory of the republic south of the Terek river. They relied heavily on aviation and artillery, keeping ground fighting, which could be costly in terms of Russian casualties, to the minimum, and established a tight semi-circle in the east, west and north of Chechnya which pushed the Chechen fighters to the south into the mountains. They closed in on Grozny, although delaying entering it in order to avoid repeating the painful experience of house-to-house fighting of the previous military campaign. In their advance the federal forces, apart from using sheer military power, were also capitalizing on the civilian population's weariness of the prolonged and devastating conflict and the divisions in Chechen society. These tactics allowed them to take control of Gudermes, the second largest city of the republic, and several other towns and villages, meeting little or no resistance there after reaching agreement with local elders. Moreover, some of the Chechen *teip* leaders and their followers (such as Beslan Gantimirov, a former mayor of Grozny) fought readily on the side of the federal forces.

---

[67] *RFE/RL Newsline*, vol. 3, no. 193, Part 1 (4 Oct. 1999).
[68] Kasaev, A. and Maksakov, I., 'Neverny shag v pravil'nom napravlenii' [A wrong step in the right direction], *Nezavisimaya Gazeta*, 2 Oct. 1999.
[69] *RFE/RL Newsline*, vol. 3, no. 195, Part 1 (6 Oct. 1999).
[70] Russian Defence Ministry, Press Service, [Situation in the North Caucasus region], *Krasnaya Zvezda*, 28 Oct. 1999.
[71] Shermatova, S., 'Russian lotto: the game's not up yet', *Moscow News*, 13–19 Oct. 1999.

The international reaction

As part of its campaign in Chechnya, which was still officially termed anti-terrorist, the Russian Government also tightened border controls and imposed travel restrictions in the whole North Caucasus region. At the beginning of November it closed the border crossings with Azerbaijan and Georgia for all except citizens of the member states of the Commonwealth of Independent States (CIS); suspended air flights between southern Russia and Azerbaijan, Georgia, Turkey, Pakistan, Iran and Arab countries; and intensified searches of ships entering the port of Makhachkala in Dagestan.[72] Russia received assurances of support from Azerbaijan and Georgia in its fight against Chechen separatists and in tightening border security for that purpose,[73] but the actual arrangements they made apparently did not work well. Russia lodged official complaints to both, claiming that neither was doing enough to intercept the transport of arms and mercenaries across its territory to Chechnya.

Since the situation did not improve, and Georgia, the only country having a common border with Chechnya, refused to agree to Russian and Georgian joint patrolling of this 80 km-long border, the Russian Government threatened in November to impose visa requirements from January 2000 for Azerbaijani and Georgian citizens wishing to enter Russia.[74] If implemented this would have meant heavy economic losses for Azerbaijan and Georgia. The threat thus made their already strained relations with Russia more tense. It could have negative consequences for the CIS, of which all three countries are members. A clear indication of that was given by Georgia when it expressed official concern at Russia's exceeding its quotas for heavy military equipment in the North Caucasus under the 1990 Treaty on Conventional Armed Forces in Europe (the CFE Treaty)[75] and threatened to intensify its campaign for NATO membership, while President Eduard Shevardnadze cancelled a planned visit of Russian Defence Minister Igor Sergeyev to Tbilisi.[76]

Georgia was not the only country to express concern over Russia's violations of the CFE ceilings, although Russia officially notified other signatories to the treaty that these violations and the deployment of a reported 90 000 federal troops in Chechnya, three times the number of Russian soldiers deployed there during the 1994–96 war,[77] were temporary and required by the anti-

---

[72] *RFE/RL Newsline*, vol. 3, no. 219, Part 1 (10 Nov. 1999).

[73] ITAR-TASS, 28 Sep. 1999, in 'Russia: Transcaucasian state ministers sign statement', FBIS-SOV-1999-0928, 28 Sep. 1999.

[74] Babaeva, S. and Krutikov, Ye., 'Rossiya nastaivaet na vvedenii vizovogo rezhima s Gruziey' [Russia insists on introduction of visa regime with Georgia], *Izvestiya*, 5 Nov. 1999; and Olegov, F., 'Konets bezvizovogo rezhima v SNG?' [End of visa-free regime in the CIS?], *Nezavisimaya Gazeta*, 5 Nov. 1999.

[75] See chapter 10, section II in this volume.

[76] Andreev, N., 'Tbilisi vedyot opasnuyu igru' [Tbilisi plays a dangerous game], *Nezavisimaya Gazeta*, 3 Nov. 1999.

[77] AFP (Moscow), 21 Oct. 1999, in 'Defense Ministry: 90 000 troops deployed in Chechnya', FBIS-SOV-1999-1021, 21 Oct. 1999. According to the government spokesman, there were 93 000 Russian troops in Chechnya by the end of Jan. 2000—57 000 from the armed forces and 36 000 from the Interior Ministry. *Krasnaya Zvezda*, 29 Jan. 2000, p. 1.

terrorist operation.[78] At the Summit Meeting of the Organization for Security and Co-operation in Europe (OSCE) held in Istanbul on 18–19 November similar criticism was made by the USA and a number of European countries. Even more concern was expressed by them about the plight of civilian refugees in Chechnya, whose number continued to increase.[79] Although recognizing the sovereign right of Russia to fight terrorism on its territory, Western leaders urged Russia to find a political resolution of the conflict.

Even before the Istanbul meeting, Finnish Prime Minister Paavo Lipponen, whose country held the European Union (EU) presidency at the time, called on Russia to reach a political settlement.[80] Meeting Putin in Oslo at the beginning of November, US President Bill Clinton also urged Russia to seek a political solution, possibly through mediation.[81] On 4 November the Council of Europe adopted a resolution calling on Russia to stop hostilities in Chechnya and open negotiations with President Maskhadov.[82] It was at Istanbul, however, that Russia was subjected to the most severe criticism over the humanitarian aspects of the conflict: Western leaders termed its use of force in Chechnya indiscriminate and disproportionate and called for a political resolution. Calls for international financial aid to Russia to be withheld began to be widespread, not only in the US and European media but also as an important part of the unfolding US presidential campaign.[83] In the wake of the OSCE's Istanbul meeting, the Managing Director of the International Monetary Fund (IMF), Michel Camdessus, warned Russia that future IMF financial aid might be linked to Russia's military operation in Chechnya.[84]

The Russian response

These attempts to influence Russia made little impact on its stand in Chechnya. Enjoying solid domestic support, the Russian Government refused to yield to Western pressure, reaffirming that Russia was entitled to act freely in Chechnya as it was its internal affair. In a statement at the end of October on the situation in Chechnya, the Russian Government underlined that its highest priority was to combat terrorism and 'achieve complete restoration of law and order on the whole territory of the Chechen Republic'.[85] Even though

[78] Interfax (Moscow), 12 Oct. 1999, in 'Implications of North Caucasus operations for CFE Treaty', FBIS-SOV-1999-1012, 12 Oct. 1999.

[79] Even according to Russian official sources, by the beginning of Nov. there were over 195 000 refugees. *Krasnaya Zvezda*, 4 Nov. 1999.

[80] *RFE/RL Newsline*, vol. 3, no. 208, Part 1 (25 Oct. 1999).

[81] McCullough, E., 'US asks Russia to back off Chechnya', Yahoo news, 2 Nov. 1999.

[82] *RFE/RL Newsline*, vol. 3, no. 216, Part 1 (5 Nov. 1999).

[83] See, e.g., 'Russia's brutal folly', *The Economist*, 13 Nov. 1999, p. 14; 'US can't stay silent as Russia bullies Chechens', *USA Today*, 19 Nov. 1999); and statements by US presidential campaigners George W. Bush, Bill Bradley and John McCain.

[84] Denisov, A. and Kozlovsky, V., 'IMF plays the Chechnya card', *Moscow News*, 1–7 Dec. 1999. Russia was indeed refused a long-expected loan by the IMF in Dec. 1999, although the reasons for this decision were presented as purely technical.

[85] 'Zayavlenie pravitelstva RF o situatsii v Chechenskoy Respublike i merakh po ego ureguliro-vaniyu' [Russian Government statement on the situation in the Chechen Republic and measures to resolve it], *Krasnaya Zvezda*, 23 Oct. 1999.

it indicated its readiness to open a political dialogue to resolve the political issues, Moscow had earlier made it clear that such a dialogue would be possible only with those political forces there that were ready

to comply with the Constitution of the Russian Federation and the sovereignty and territorial integrity of Russia; to denounce terrorism in all its manifestations; to disarm illegal armed formations and hand over to the federal authorities persons guilty of terrorist acts, hostage-taking and banditry; to free all hostages on the territory of Chechnya; to guarantee respect for human rights and fundamental freedoms; to create conditions for the safe return of people who had been forced to leave their homes.[86]

Russia left no room for doubt as to its intention to re-establish full control over Chechnya, even at the risk of exacerbating the cooling down of relations with the West that had begun earlier in the year over the Kosovo crisis.[87] At a major meeting with senior Russian military commanders in Moscow in mid-November, in the presence of Putin, Defence Minister Sergeyev not only flatly rejected any outside interference in the Chechen conflict but also accused the USA and NATO of using the crisis to 'weaken Russia's international position and oust it from strategically important regions of the world, above all the Caspian region, the Transcaucasus and Central Asia'.[88] This hard-line approach was reiterated by Yeltsin himself at the Istanbul Summit Meeting when he refused to accept the right of the West to criticize Russia's anti-terrorist campaign in Chechnya and pledged to continue it unabated.[89]

On the concluding day of the Summit Meeting Russia agreed to invite an OSCE fact-finding mission to visit the North Caucasus, but it continued to maintain that it would welcome only humanitarian international aid. (The Istanbul Summit Declaration states that 'A political solution is essential, and that the assistance of the OSCE would contribute to achieving this goal'.[90]) Russia rejected reports in the Western press about the 'disastrous humanitarian situation' in the conflict zone. In this it was encouraged by the statement made by the UN High Commissioner for Refugees, Sadako Ogata, who after visiting refugee camps in Ingushetia in November refused to qualify the situation there as a humanitarian catastrophe, although she described it as very serious.[91]

Disagreement between Russia and the West on how to handle the Chechen conflict was further exacerbated after the Russian armed forces completed the encirclement of Grozny at the beginning of December and the Russian military command issued an ultimatum to those still remaining in the city either to leave it through a safe passage or to risk being killed 'as terrorists and

[86] 'Zayavlenie pravitelstva RF o situatsii v Chechenskoy Respublike . . .' (note 85).

[87] On the Kosovo crisis, see also chapter 1, section III and chapter 2, section III in this volume.

[88] Ermolin, V., 'U Rossii vnov' poyavilsya veroyatny protivnik' [Russia gets a potential enemy again], *Izvestiya*, 13 Nov. 1999.

[89] Pankov, Yu., 'Rossii nuzhen dialog a ne nravoucheniya' [Russia needs dialogue, not moralizing], *Krasnaya Zvezda*, 19 Nov. 1999.

[90] OSCE, Istanbul Summit Declaration, SUM.DOC/2/99, 19 Nov. 1999, para. 23, URL <http://www.osce.org/e/docs/summits/istadec/99e.htm>

[91] Ryurikov, K., 'Gumanitarnoy katastrofy net' [There is no humanitarian catastrophe], *Nezavisimaya Gazeta*, 20 Nov. 1999.

bandits'.[92] The ultimatum drew strong condemnation from Western leaders. Clinton warned Russia that it would 'pay a heavy price for these actions'[93] while the EU Council of Ministers adopted a statement saying that 'the present campaign and the unacceptable threat to the people of Grozny can only perpetuate, not break, the cycle of violence in the northern Caucasus'.[94]

The Russian response to these criticisms was a mixed one. On the one hand its military command hastened to clarify that the ultimatum was addressed only to Chechen fighters and not to the civilian population.[95] On the other had, seeking international support for Russia's tough stand on Chechnya, Yeltsin immediately travelled to China to meet his Chinese counterpart, President Jiang Zemin. The Chinese and Russian leaders issued a joint statement stressing their determination to allow no country to 'interfere in another sovereign country's fight against domestic terrorism' or to use the issue of human rights for that purpose.[96]

As tensions between Western countries and Russia over the Chechen conflict continued to escalate, the EU leaders issued a statement at the European Council meeting in Helsinki (10 and 11 December) describing Russia's campaign in Chechnya as 'totally unacceptable' and urging the Russian Government to end the 'indiscriminate use of force' against civilians. Although they stopped short of calling for immediate sanctions, they threatened to review the EU's economic and trade relationship with Russia if it continued the war in Chechnya.[97] A similar position was taken by NATO foreign ministers, meeting in Brussels in mid-December, and then a few days later by the foreign ministers of the Western members of the Group of Eight (G8) industrialized countries, meeting in Berlin.[98] OSCE Chairman Knut Vollebaeck, who addressed the G8 meeting after coming back from the North Caucasus, where he had been on the invitation of the Russian Government, proposed his own plan for resolving the conflict in Chechnya. The main points of this plan included: (*a*) the declaration of a ceasefire; (*b*) an international conference on Chechnya; and (*c*) a political role for the OSCE in resolving the conflict.[99]

Russia's stand on the conflict remained unchanged. It pointed out that any ceasefire would only help the terrorists to regroup and continued to decline all offers of mediation. In its hard-line stand the government was greatly encouraged by results of the national parliamentary elections held on 19 December. Indeed, even though Russia continued to face a range of serious

[92] Williams, D., 'In ultimatum Russia warns civilians to flee Grozny', *International Herald Tribune*, 7 Dec. 1999.

[93] Williams (note 92).

[94] European Union, General Affairs Council, Brussels, 6–7 Dec. 1999, EU document Conseil/99/390, URL <http://europa.eu.int/comm/external_relations/news/12_99/pres_99_390.htm>.

[95] *RFE/RL Newsline*, vol. 30, no. 237, Part 1 (8 Dec. 1999).

[96] 'Sovmestnoye rossiysko-kitayskoye zayavlenie' [Joint Russian–Chinese statement], *Diplomaticheskiy Vestnik*, no. 1 (Jan. 2000), pp. 8–11.

[97] [European Union], Helsinki European Council, Presidency Conclusions, 10–11 Dec. 1999, Doc/99/17, Annexe II, para. 7, URL <http://europa.eu.int//comm/external_relations/news/12_99/doc_99_16.htm>.

[98] On the G8, see the glossary in this volume.

[99] Gornostaev, D., '"Semyorka" osudila "vosmogo"' [The 'seven' condemn the eighth], *Nezavisimaya Gazeta*, 18 Dec. 1999.

political, social and economic problems, they were relegated to the back stage as the issue of fighting Chechen terrorism and separatism became the central one on the domestic political agenda. The popularity of political parties and individual politicians in large measure reflected their attitudes to the Chechen conflict. As it transpired, those political parties and blocs, such as Yedinstvo (Unity), which were associated in the public mind with an uncompromising stand on the conflict fared well in the elections, while those like Yabloko (Apple) which were critical of the government on the issue lost heavily.

Popular approval of the campaign in Chechnya resulted in another major political event. On 31 December President Yeltsin announced his resignation from office six months ahead of the expiry of his term and elevated Prime Minister Putin, widely acclaimed for his policies on Chechnya, to the position of acting president in order to give him a head start in the coming presidential elections.[100]

Appraising the results of the four-month campaign in Chechnya, the Russian military high command claimed that by the end of December federal forces had succeeded in liberating 122 out of a total of 199 towns and villages in the republic and in establishing control over the territory where over 90 per cent of the population lived. It was also stated that over 70 000 Chechen refugees had returned safely to their homes, while the federal authorities were taking active steps to restore electricity, heating, water and the normal functioning of schools and hospitals.[101] Serious doubt was cast on these successes when the separatists, outnumbered and outgunned, not only repulsed the Russian offensive in Grozny but also staged a successful counter-offensive in the first week of January 2000, inflicting heavy losses on the federal troops.[102] Even though this counter-offensive was rebuffed and Grozny taken by Russian troops at the beginning of February 2000, the Russian military command was forced to admit that the attainment of a decisive military victory in Chechnya would be a painful and long-drawn out process.[103] While it was still unclear when the military stage of the conflict would be finished, a political resolution seemed to be even more remote.

IV. Conclusions

Two principal groups of factors are being used by the leaders of the separatist movements and conflicts in the North Caucasus. The first is based on the widespread public discontent which derives from the current profound social and economic crisis and the breakdown of law in the region. The second is connected with ethnic differences in the region, manipulated by separatist leaders into major ethnic conflicts—for instance, in Karachaevo-Cherkessia, with a tendency to seriously destabilize security there.

[100] *RFE/RL Newsline*, vol. 4, no. 1, Part 1 (3 Jan. 2000).
[101] Russian Defence Ministry, Press Service [Summary of operations in the Republic of Chechnya], quoted in *Krasnaya Zvezda*, 29 Dec. and 30 Dec. 1999.
[102] *RFE/RL Newsline*, vol. 4, no. 6, Part 1 (10 Jan. 2000).
[103] *RFE/RL Newsline*, vol. 4, no. 7, Part 1 (11 Jan. 2000).

Contrary to widespread expectations, attempts by leaders of separatist forces to use the green banner of Islam for their ends have so far met with little success in the North Caucasus. The exception is Chechnya, and even there the conflict with the Russian federal authorities was of a political rather than of a religious nature. Not only did the Muslim leaders of the North Caucasus refuse to support the establishment of an Islamic state in Dagestan in August 1999; they also condemned the activities of the rebels using religious slogans as incompatible with the ideas of Islam. It is obvious, however, that unless there is a visible improvement in the socio-economic situation in the North Caucasus and existing ethnic grievances are properly addressed and resolved the 'Islamic factor' is bound to become increasingly important there, feeding separatist tendencies and seriously challenging the state of security in the region.

Although there are many conflicts of a separatist nature at different stages of development and intensity in the North Caucasus, the main one is still undoubtedly the Chechen conflict. It creates a very unstable and dangerous security situation in the whole region, as events there and in Dagestan have shown beyond any doubt. Unless the Chechen problem is resolved Russia cannot expect to ensure its national security and territorial integrity. The use of force by Russia against the Chechen-led rebellion in Dagestan or against Chechen terrorists and separatists has been unavoidable, but it cannot help resolve the larger political, social, economic and other problems in the Russian–Chechen relationship in the long run. Clearly, as the conflict is a political one, it can only be resolved by political means, which include the establishment of a Russian–Chechen political dialogue.

It will be difficult to achieve this dialogue in practice since the existing political institutions in Chechnya, including the presidency, are very weak and ineffective. Moreover, the logic of the expanding military operation—originally aimed at fighting terrorism but then targeted against Chechen separatism as well—makes political dialogue between the federal authorities and Aslan Maskhadov, leader of the separatist forces, increasingly difficult. If it proves impossible, this will leave the Russian Government only one option—to find alternative dialogue partners among Chechen politicians, including those now living outside Chechnya, who command sufficient respect and influence, both among the powerful 500 000-strong Chechen diaspora in Russia and especially among the population of Chechnya itself. If a political resolution, the focal point of which would be the determination of the future status of Chechnya, is not found the confrontation in Chechnya may end in deadlock, causing new suffering to its civilian population and a continuing strain on Russian resources.

The separatist conflicts in the North Caucasus are basically rooted in domestic causes, the threat they pose is primarily to Russia's national security and integrity, and their resolution is unquestionably a prime concern and duty of the Russian federal authorities. However, these conflicts (or at least some of them) have also acquired serious international aspects.

In Moscow, the linkage between the domestic conflicts in Chechnya and Dagestan and such external threats to Russia's security as the illegal arms trade, drug trafficking and international terrorism has been openly recognized. According to Putin, these conflicts were 'nothing less than a war declared against Russia by international terrorism with the aim of seizing a number of its areas rich in natural resources'[104] and were initiated with strong backing from extremist forces in a number of Muslim states.

The conflicts in Chechnya and Dagestan could not but invite reaction in the outside world as well. Some countries, such as China, offered firm support for Russia's anti-terrorist and anti-separatist operation there. The countries of the Muslim world and the Organization of Islamic Countries (OIC) adopted a remarkably muted tone on the issue, at least officially, recognizing these conflicts as an internal affair of Russia, although urging it to exercise maximum restraint in their resolution.

In the USA and the EU countries the attitude to the Russian campaign in the North Caucasus, and in Chechnya in particular, was highly critical and was forcefully expressed, individually and collectively. This response was justified in Western capitals by concern over the humanitarian aspects of the operation.

Nonetheless, these disagreements, although a major irritant in relations between Russia and the West, are unlikely to affect the central issues of their relationship, such as their interaction on global security issues.

---

[104] ITAR-TASS, 24 Sep. 1999, in 'Putin: International terrorism escalating Caucasus war', FBIS-SOV-1999-0924, 24 Sep. 1999.

4. Europe: the new transatlantic agenda

ADAM DANIEL ROTFELD

I. Introduction

In 1999 European security developments were dominated by the NATO intervention in Kosovo, a province of the Republic of Serbia in the Federal Republic of Yugoslavia (FRY), and the war waged by Russian federal forces against Chechnya, a part of the Russian Federation.[1] The debate on European security in the context of transatlantic security and defence cooperation was crowned with the decisions adopted: within NATO by the North Atlantic Council (NAC) meeting in Washington on 23–24 April 1999;[2] within the European Union (EU) by the European Council at its meetings in Cologne on 3–4 June 1999 and in Helsinki on 10–11 December 1999;[3] and within the Organization for Security and Co-operation in Europe (OSCE) at its Summit Meeting in Istanbul on 18–19 November 1999.[4] In response to the developments in South-Eastern Europe, a ministerial conference representing 36 governments and 11 international institutions, meeting in Cologne, adopted the Stability Pact for South Eastern Europe on 10 June 1999.[5] The Pact was launched on the initiative of the EU and placed under OSCE auspices on 1 July 1999.

[1] These conflicts are analysed in chapters 1, 2 and 3 in this volume.
[2] The 6 documents approved by the meeting are: (a) the Washington Declaration, Press Release NAC-S(99)63, 23 Apr. 1999; (b) Statement on Kosovo, Press Release S-1(99)62, 23 Apr. 1999; (c) the Washington Summit Communiqué, 'An alliance for the 21st century', Press Release NAC-S(99)64, 24 Apr. 1999; (d) the Membership Action Plan, Press Release NAC-S(99)66, 24 Apr. 1999; (e) the Alliance's Strategic Concept approved by the Heads of States and Government participating in the meeting of the North Atlantic Council in Washington, DC, 23–24 Apr. 1999, Press Release NAC-S(99)65, 24 Apr. 1999; and (f) the Defence Capabilities Initiative, Press Release NAC-S(99)69, 25 Apr. 1999. All are published in *NATO Review*, summer 1999, Documentation, URL <http://www.nato.int/docu/review/1999/9902-toc.htm>. Excerpts from the Washington Summit Communiqué are reproduced in appendix 4A.
[3] [European Union], Cologne European Council, Presidency Conclusions, 3–4 June 1999, SN 150/99, pp. D1–D16, URL <http://europa.eu.int/council/off/conclu/june99/june99_en.htm>; and [European Union], Helsinki European Council, Presidency Conclusions, 10–11 Dec. 1999, SN 300/99 and Annexes, URL <http://europa.eu.int/council/off/conclu/dec99/dec99_en.htm>. Excerpts from both documents are reproduced in appendix 4A.
[4] The Istanbul Summit Meeting adopted, among others, 4 documents: (a) the Vienna Document 1999 of the Negotiations on Confidence- and Security-Building Measures, FSC.DOC/1/99, 16 Nov. 1999, URL <http://www.osce.org/htdig/search.html>; (b) the Istanbul Summit Declaration, SUM.DOC/2/99, 19 Nov. 1999, URL <http://www.osce.org/e/docs/summits/istadec/99e.htm>; (c) the Charter for European Security, SUM.DOC/1/99, 19 Nov. 1999, URL <http://www.osce.org/indexe-da.htm>; and (d) the Final Act of the Conference of the States Parties to the CFE Treaty, CFE.DOC/2/99, 19 Nov. 1999, URL <http://www.osce.org/htdig/search.html>. Excerpts from the Charter for European Security are reproduced in appendix 4A. Excerpts from the Vienna Document 1999 are reproduced in appendix 10B.
[5] European Union, European Commission, 'Stability Pact for South Eastern Europe, Cologne, 10 June 1999, URL <http://europa.eu.int/comm/external_relations/see/stapact/10_june_99.htm>; and Sarajevo Summit Declaration of the Heads of State and Government of the participating and facilitating countries of the Stability Pact and the Principals of participating and facilitating international organizations and agencies and regional initiatives, Sarajevo, 30 July 1999, URL <http://www.stabilitypact.org/summit.htm>. The Stability Pact is reproduced (without the Annex) in appendix 4A.

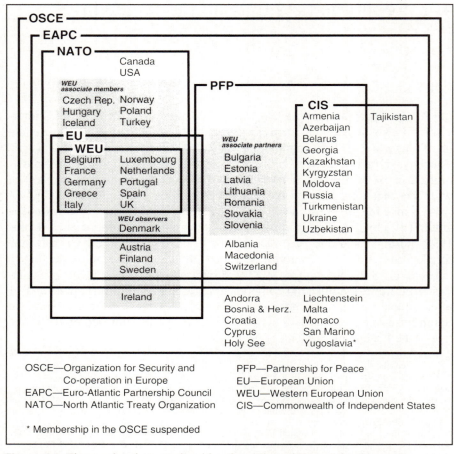

Figure 4.1. The overlapping membership of multilateral Euro-Atlantic security organizations, as of 1 January 2000

All these documents are of both an operational and a conceptual character. The decisions reached in Washington, Cologne, Helsinki and Istanbul were all future-oriented, but they were also influenced by the US and European reactions to developments in the former Yugoslavia and to NATO's intervention in Kosovo in particular. The documents adopted have determined the political and strategic framework of, and shown how Europe and the United States intend to put into effect, the agreed new ideas and norms aimed at strengthening security and stability in the entire transatlantic region. Aspects of security in relations between NATO and the EU and between NATO and Russia were also redefined; this was reflected in the new military doctrine adopted by Russia.[6]

---

[6] A draft of the new doctrine was published by *Krasnaya Zvezda* on 9 Oct. 1999, pp. 3–4. The final version as approved by President Vladimir Putin on 21 Apr. 2000 was published in *Nezavisimaya*

This chapter reviews the main developments in the European security structures. Section II examines transatlantic relations, new NATO strategies, and the European Security and Defence Identity (ESDI) within NATO. Section III presents the decision to strengthen the EU Common Foreign and Security Policy (CFSP), the new common European Security and Defence Policy (ESDP) announced at the Helsinki meeting.[7] Section IV reviews the activities of and new decisions taken by the OSCE and the Stability Pact for South Eastern Europe. Section V presents the conclusions.

II. NATO in 1999: new strategies, old structures

In order to understand the new role for NATO in Europe, the question must be asked whether before July 1990 and the London Declaration[8] the North Atlantic alliance could have decided on and carried out a military intervention outside the territory of its member states, as it did in Bosnia and Herzegovina and Kosovo. The answer is evident: it did not take and could not have taken such a decision during the cold war. At that time, the basis for global and European security was the bipolar system.

NATO's mandate and the Kosovo intervention

According to Article 5 of the 1949 North Atlantic Treaty (the Washington Treaty), if

an armed attack against one or more of [the parties to the Treaty] in Europe or North America . . . occurs, each of them, in exercise of the right of individual or collective self-defence recognized by Article 51 of the Charter of the United Nations, will assist the Party or Parties so attacked by taking forthwith, individually, and in concert with the other Parties, such actions it deems necessary, including the use of armed force, to restore and maintain the security of the North Atlantic area.[9]

In neither Bosnia and Herzegovina nor Kosovo did this definition of a *casus belli* apply. The armed intervention in Kosovo in late March 1999 without UN authorization[10] opened up a new chapter in NATO's history, legally, politically and militarily. It implies the principle that human rights and the rights

---

Gazeta, 22 Apr. 2000. An unofficial translation into English was released by BBC Monitoring on 22 Apr. 2000.

[7] The Cologne and Helsinki Presidency Conclusions (note 3) also refer to a Common European Security and Defence Policy (CESDP) of which the aim would be 'to strengthen the CFSP by the development of a common European policy on security and defence'. See, e.g., Helsinki European Council, Presidency Conclusions (note 3), annex 1 to Annex IV. The term ESDP has been used increasingly since then, e.g., in speeches by the European Commissioner for External Relations, Chris Patten, and is adopted here.

[8] NATO, London Declaration on a Transformed North Atlantic Alliance, issued by the Heads of State and Government participating in the meeting of the North Atlantic Council, London, 5–6 July 1990, Press Communiqué S-1(90)36, reproduced in Rotfeld, A. D. and Stützle, W., *Germany and Europe in Transition* (Oxford University Press: Oxford, 1991), pp. 150–52.

[9] *NATO Handbook*, 50th Anniversary edn (NATO: Brussels, 1998), p. 396.

[10] The 1994 enforcement of the 'no-fly' zone in Bosnia by NATO and the subsequent implementation of the 1995 Dayton Agreement (the General Framework Agreement for Peace in Bosnia and Herzegovina) were legitimized by UN Security Council decisions.

of minorities are equal in law to the sovereignty of states. States use the argument that the principle of non-intervention in their internal affairs gives them the absolute right to prevent international intervention in cases of gross violations of human and minority rights. As a rule decisions on such intervention should be taken by the UN Security Council. The Kosovo intervention therefore cannot set a precedent for the future.[11]

The Kosovo intervention produced critically differing judgements. Some leading US and other NATO security analysts argued that the war was ill-conceived, had put NATO at risk and undermined its relations with China and Russia,[12] and it was claimed that the political consequences of the war were the 'opposite of what NATO's political leaders intended'.[13] The arguments of the opponents may be summarized under three points. First, NATO abandoned its mandate and definition of itself as 'a strictly defensive coalition and insisted on the right to occupy a province of a state with which it was not at war'.[14] Second, the intervention was 'the unintended consequence of a gross error in political judgement' and the people of the Balkans emerged from the war 'considerably worse off than they had been before'.[15] Third, the doctrine of 'humanitarian intervention' is incompatible with the notion of a defensive alliance (in Henry Kissinger's view, 'probably with the notion of alliance altogether'[16]) and illegal.[17]

An opposite position was taken by the leaders of the NATO member states, especially the USA, the UK and Germany, and the then NATO Secretary General, Javier Solana. In their view the Kosovo operation was motivated by moral and political factors, was warranted from the legal and military points of view, and demonstrated the role and place of the Atlantic alliance after the end of the cold war. Italian Foreign Minister Lamberto Dini noted that the Kosovo crisis demonstrated 'the primacy of human rights in international politics'.[18] For the first time, Solana argued, NATO, a defensive alliance, 'launched a military campaign to avoid a humanitarian tragedy outside its own borders'; it fought in Kosovo not to conquer or preserve territory, but to protect the values on which the alliance was founded.[19] The intervention in Kosovo was a major challenge for NATO's political and military cohesion. It was a test of its capacity not only to elaborate a common strategy with a view to agreeing on

---

[11] 'Rede vor der 54. Generalversammlung der Vereinten Nationen . . . des Bundesministers des Auswärtigen Joschka Fischer, 22 Sep. 1999' [Speech of the German Minister for Foreign Affairs, Joschka Fischer, before the 54th UN General Assembly, 22 Sep. 1999], URL <http://www.auswaertiges-amt.government.de/6_archiv/2/r/r990922a.htm>.

[12] Kissinger, H., 'New world disorder', *Newsweek*, 31 May 1999.

[13] Mandelbaum, M., 'A perfect failure: NATO's war against Yugoslavia', *Foreign Affairs*, Sep./Oct. 1999, p. 2.

[14] Kissinger, H., 'The end of NATO as we know it?', *Los Angeles Times Syndicate*, 15 Aug. 1999, p. B07.

[15] Mandelbaum (note 13).

[16] Kissinger (note 14).

[17] In Mandelbaum's view, 'humanitarian intervention' is 'by the established standards of proper international conduct, illegal. The basic precept of international law is the prohibition against interference in the internal affairs of other sovereign states. Without this rule there would be no basis for international order of any kind'. Mandelbaum (note 13), p. 5.

[18] Dini, L., 'Taking responsibility for Balkan security', *NATO Review*, no. 3 (autumn 1999), p. 4.

[19] Solana, J., 'NATO's success in Kosovo', *Foreign Affairs*, Nov./Dec. 1999, pp. 114–20.

decisions but also to put its decisions into effect on the battlefield. Politically, the action in Kosovo provided a partial and ambiguous answer to the question whether interventions of this kind can promote durable peace solutions.

NATO, the USA and the European allies

The Kosovo intervention demonstrated that NATO is capable of acting. However, it also showed: (*a*) that there is a clear disproportion between the burdens borne by the United States and its European allies with respect to financial resources, technological input and military commitments; (*b*) that the role of the USA in Europe's defence and security was once again a live issue; and (*c*) that following the campaign in Kosovo there is a need to redefine the alliance's mandate and establish whether in the light of Article 5 of the Washington Treaty it is still a collective self-defence alliance or a Euro-Atlantic collective security system *in statu nascendi*. In this context, a debate is going on about the ESDI within NATO and about the ESDP within the EU.[20] Analysing the official declarations, one might conclude that things continue undisturbed: NATO accepts the ESDI; its multinational command structure does, in fact, work; the 19 member nations maintain cohesion and political unity within the alliance framework; and the new technologies, such as precision-guided munitions, unmanned aerial vehicles and cargo transport, have proved to be valuable investments.[21]

However, the experience gained in Kosovo has led many politicians to be critical of the practical operation of the alliance. At the February 2000 Munich Conference on Security Policy, US Defense Secretary William Cohen told his European allies: 'We simply cannot continue with a posture in which one member of NATO conducts virtually two thirds of all air support sorties and half of all air combat missions; in which only a handful of countries have precision munitions that can operate in all kinds of weather; and in which some pilots had to communicate over open frequencies in a hostile environment'.[22] The USA's public criticism was wide-ranging. Fewer than half of the countries which had agreed to do so had contributed fully to logistical support; fewer than half of the countries asked to contribute to an advanced intelligence network had provided their full share; fewer than half of the countries asked had provided deployable command-and-control modules; the European provision of air-to-air refuelling was poor; and among the European allies

---

[20] On the ESDI, see Bailes, A. J. K., 'NATO's European pillar: the European Security and Defence Identity', *Defence Analysis*, vol. 15, no. 3 (1999), pp. 305–22. The debate, which began many years ago, took on greater political weight after the Franco-British St Malo Declaration on 4 Dec. 1998. Rotfeld, A. D., 'Europe: the institutionalized security process', *SIPRI Yearbook 1999: Armaments, Disarmament and International Security* (Oxford University Press: Oxford, 1999), pp. 240–41. The 1999 NAC meeting in Washington and European Council meetings in Cologne and Helsinki ushered in a new stage of the debate. See also Mathiopoulos, M. and Gyarmati, I., 'Saint Malo and beyond: toward European defense', *Washington Quarterly*, vol. 22, no. 4 (autumn 1999), pp. 65–76.

[21] '36th Munich Conference on Security Policy: Remarks as prepared by Secretary of Defense William S. Cohen on "European Security and Defense Identity"', 5 Feb. 2000, URL <http://www.defenselink.mil:80/speeches/2000/s20000205-secdef2.html>.

[22] See note 21; and Drozdiak, W., 'US seems increasingly uncomfortable with EU defense plan', *International Herald Tribune*, 6 Mar. 2000, p. 8.

assigned to work on a deployable headquarters that can withstand biological and chemical weapon attacks only one will meet the goal in 2000. In this context Cohen referred to the view expressed succinctly by the German Minister of Defence, Rudolf Scharping: 'The problem in NATO is not too much America, but too little Europe'.[23] Indeed, relations between Europe and the United States are the main issue.

The decisions adopted by the NAC at its April 1999 meeting in Washington determined NATO's strategy for action in this regard.

The Washington NAC meeting: transatlantic partnership

The Washington Declaration, signed by the heads of state and government participating in the meeting of the NAC to mark the 50th anniversary of NATO and to set forth a vision of an alliance for the 21st century, stated: 'NATO embodies the vital partnership between Europe and North America. We welcome the further impetus that has been given to the strengthening of European defence capabilities to enable the European Allies to act more effectively together, thus reinforcing the transatlantic partnership'.[24] Defining the approach to security in the 21st century, the NATO Strategic Concept adopted at Washington recognized the security of Europe and that of North America as 'indivisible' and their commitment to 'the indispensable transatlantic link and the collective defence of its members fundamental to its credibility and to the security and stability of the Euro-Atlantic area'.[25]

What does this mean in practice? There was no doubt until the end of 1998 that the concept of the ESDI was the concept of a European pillar of NATO and that it could be developed only within the alliance framework.[26] This meant that the USA's approval was needed. For many years the United States strongly endorsed the 'ESDI within the alliance' position. US officials began to demonstrate a more cautious approach after the Franco-British St Malo Declaration of 4 December 1998: at the NAC meeting on 8 December 1998 US Secretary of State Madeleine Albright warned the European allies against de-linking the ESDI from NATO, against duplicating existing efforts and against discriminating against non-EU members.[27] US fears mounted after the entry into force of the Amsterdam Treaty in May 1999[28] and the launching by the EU of the work of giving the CFSP an operational dimension. EU policy did not, however, envisage responsibility for a defence policy. Nor has the 'ESDI within NATO' concept ever been intended to create a separate European defence capability.

[23] See note 21; and Rede des Bundesministers der Verteidigung, Rudolf Scharping, anlässlich der 36 Internationalen Konferenz für Sicherheitspolitik am 5 Feb. 2000 in München [Speech of Federal Defence Minister Rudolf Scharping at the 36th International Conference on Security Policy, Munich, 5 Feb. 2000], URL <http://www.bundesregierung.de/05/0513/19/fischer.html>.

[24] 'Washington Declaration', *NATO Review*, summer 1999, Documentation (note 2), p. D1.

[25] 'The Alliance's Strategic Concept' (note 2), p. D9.

[26] Bailes (note 20), pp. 305–22. See also Mathiopoulos and Gyarmati (note 20), p. 66.

[27] For more detail, see Rotfeld (note 20), pp. 240–41. The text of the declaration is reproduced in *SIPRI Yearbook 1999* (note 20), p. 265.

[28] See section III of this chapter.

NATO, the WEU and the European Union

The Western European Union (WEU) was considered a *sui generis* bridge between NATO and the EU states. The NAC meeting in Berlin in June 1996 proposed the use of 'separable but not separate' military assets in WEU-led operations.[29] The Washington NAC meeting reaffirmed the three fundamental objectives as defined at Berlin.[30] The ESDI will: (*a*) enable all the European allies to make a more coherent and effective contribution to the missions and activities of the alliance as 'an expression of their shared responsibilities'; (*b*) reinforce the transatlantic partnership; and (*c*) help the European allies to act by themselves through the readiness of NATO, on a case-by-case basis and by consensus, to make its assets and capabilities available for operations in which it is not engaged militarily. These military actions may be conducted under the political control and strategic direction either of the WEU or as otherwise agreed, 'taking into account the full participation of all European Allies if they were so to choose'.[31] In fact, the signatories of the 1999 NATO Strategic Concept wished both to secure the existing central role of NATO in the Euro-Atlantic security structure and to acknowledge the developments and changes that have taken place in the security sphere since the 1991 Strategic Concept was adopted.[32]

The crucial point is that the Berlin decisions of 1996 addressed to the WEU referred to missions and roles for the WEU as defined by the Petersberg Declaration of 1992—conflict prevention, crisis management, peacekeeping, and humanitarian and rescue work.[33] The military role NATO envisaged for the WEU was limited to humanitarian assistance in peacetime and did not include a defence and security role as such.

The debate initiated by the St Malo Declaration centres around the new role which can and should be played by the European Union in matters of security and defence. This is not a new idea. The Brussels Treaty of 1948 and the WEU, created in 1954, included a plan for common defence.[34] It was assumed

---

[29] For more detail, see Rotfeld, A. D., 'Europe: in search of cooperative security', *SIPRI Yearbook 1997: Armaments, Disarmament and International Security* (Oxford University Press: Oxford, 1997), pp. 130–32.

[30] The 1999 Strategic Concept affirms: 'On the basis of decisions taken by the Alliance, in Berlin in 1996 and subsequently, the European Security and Defence Identity will continue to be developed within NATO. This process will require close cooperation between NATO, the WEU and, if and when appropriate, the European Union'. *NATO Review*, summer 1999, Documentation (note 2), p. D9.

[31] 'The Alliance's Strategic Concept' (note 2), para. 30. The WEU and NATO organized a crisis management exercise involving joint staff work as an expression of the development of the ESDI, CMX/CRISEX2000, 17–23 Feb. 2000.

[32] The Strategic Concept of 1991, agreed by the heads of state and government in the meeting of the NAC in Rome on 7–8 Nov. 1991, is published in *The Transformation of An Alliance: The Decisions of NATO's Heads of State and Government* (NATO Secretariat: Rome, 1991), pp. 29–54.

[33] On the Petersberg tasks, see the glossary in this volume.

[34] The signatories of the Brussels Treaty were Belgium, France, Luxembourg, the Netherlands and the UK. The WEU was created by the protocols to the Brussels Treaty signed in Paris in Oct. 1954. A treaty to create the European Defence Community was signed in 1952 but never entered into force because the French National Assembly failed to ratify it, and the WEU was set up following the failure of the idea. For further detail, see Deighton, A. (ed.) *Western European Union 1954–1997: Defence, Security, Integration* (St Anthony's College: Oxford, 1997); and Deighton, A. and Remade, E. (eds), 'The

that the WEU and NATO would be connected, but the parties to the Brussels Treaty would not in practice build up any military cooperation separate from or competing with NATO.[35] In practice the WEU's activities were of a marginal character, less military than involving customs assistance (Sanctions Assistance Missions during the Bosnian crisis), police training, advice and advisory missions (the Multinational Advisory Police Element for Albania, MAPE, launched in May 1997).

The 1999 Washington Communiqué reflected to some degree the new situation signalled by the St Malo Declaration.[36] In practice it meant NATO acceptance that the EU can have the capacity for autonomous action, take decisions and approve military action where the alliance as a whole is not engaged, and that cooperation between NATO and the EU will be based on the mechanisms that exist between NATO and the WEU. NATO's support for an autonomous EU force and military capability is qualified. It is not support for an independent European defence but for the European allies taking steps to strengthen their defence capabilities, to be addressed to new missions and avoiding unnecessary duplication with NATO.[37]

In response to fears of possible discrimination against the states that are not EU members, the EU committed itself at Cologne to ensure the fullest possible involvement of non-EU NATO members in EU-led crisis-response operations.[38] Eight NATO states belong to this category—Canada, the Czech Republic, Hungary, Iceland, Norway, Poland, Turkey and the United States. In this context, further development was also recommended of the concept of WEU-led operations elaborated at the 1996 Berlin NAC meeting. NATO also declared its readiness 'to define and adopt the necessary arrangements for ready access by the European Union to the collective assets and capabilities of the Alliance, for operations in which the Alliance as a whole is not engaged militarily as an Alliance'.[39] To put it simply, the alliance recommended that the EU should tackle the problems which NATO does not wish to or cannot handle. The EU's role in defence matters or broader military issues is seen by NATO as marginal.

The 1999 Strategic Concept

In July 1997 the Madrid NATO meeting of heads of state and government decided to re-examine the 1991 Strategic Concept in order to reflect the changes that had taken place in Europe since it was adopted. The 1999 Stra-

Western European Union, 1948–1998: from the Brussels Treaty to the Treaty of Amsterdam', *Studia Diplomatica* (Brussels), nos. 1–2 (1998).

[35] Bailes (note 20), p. 306.

[36] The Washington Summit Communiqué, para. 9, declared: 'We welcome the new impetus given to the strengthening of a common European policy in security and defence by the Amsterdam Treaty and the reflections launched since then in the WEU and—following the St Malo Declaration—in the EU, including the Vienna European Council Conclusions'. Washington Summit Communiqué (note 2).

[37] Washington Summit Communiqué (note 2), para. 9(c), p. D4.

[38] Cologne European Council, Presidency Conclusions (note 3), Annexe III, 'Presidency report on strengthening of the common European policy on security and defence', para. 5, URL <http://europa. eu.int/council/off/conclu/june99/annexe_en.htm#3>.

[39] Washington Summit Communiqué (note 2), para. 10, p. D4.

tegic Concept approved in Washington describes the purpose and tasks of the alliance, examines its strategic perspectives in the light of the evolving strategic environment, security challenges and risks, and presents NATO's approach to security in the 21st century. It embodies the same new qualities as the 1991 Strategic Concept in that it emphasized cooperation with former adversaries and it was published.[40] The principle of strategic equilibrium has disappeared from the Strategic Concept: discussion of Russia has been moved from the section on risks and challenges, where it was placed in the 1991 document, to the section on partnership, cooperation and dialogue.[41] All the alliance strategies in the past, such as 'massive retaliation' in the 1950s and 'flexible response' in the late 1960s, were set out in classified documents and, as a reflection of cold war realities, were not made public.[42]

The 1999 Strategic Concept, like all NATO's basic documents, required consensus on both the substance and the language. Three elements in it are fundamental: confirmation of the commitment to collective defence; the transatlantic link; and ensuring that NATO strategy is fully adapted to the challenges of the next century. It set out a role for NATO in fighting religious and ethnic rivalries and conflicts, preventing regional instability, combating terrorism and organized crime, and preventing the proliferation of weapons of mass destruction. The representatives of the three new NATO members—the Czech Republic, Hungary and Poland—were included in the last stage of the intensive work on preparing the Washington decisions.

The Membership Action Plan

Under Article 10 of the North Atlantic Treaty, the alliance may admit new members.[43] The process of NATO enlargement initiated by the January 1994 Brussels summit meeting was meant to extend the zone of security and stability and overcome the division of Europe. The 1997 NATO Madrid documents declared a new 'open door policy' and promised to review the enlargement process at the next summit meeting, in Washington in 1999.[44] The Membership Action Plan (MAP) issued at the Washington NAC meeting was intended to help the aspiring countries meet NATO criteria and standards. The MAP is addressed to the European states which have declared that they wish to join the alliance.[45]

---

[40] See note 32.

[41] 'The Alliance's Strategic Concept' (note 2), para. 32.

[42] Greater openness began with the 1967 Harmel Report. See, e.g., NATO, 'The Harmel Report : full reports by the rapporteurs on the future tasks of the alliance', May 1999, URL <http://www.nato.int/archives/harmel.htm>.

[43] 'The Parties may by unanimous agreement invite any other European state in a position to further the principles of this Treaty and to contribute to the security of the North Atlantic area to accede to this treaty.' *NATO Handbook* (note 9), p. 398.

[44] For more detail, see Rotfeld, A. D., 'Europe: the transition to inclusive security', *SIPRI Yearbook 1998: Armaments, Disarmament and International Security* (Oxford University Press: Oxford, 1998), pp. 149–53; and Rotfeld (note 20), pp. 247–50.

[45] These states are: Romania, Slovenia and Slovakia; Albania, Bulgaria and Macedonia; and the 3 Baltic states, Estonia, Latvia and Lithuania. See Rotfeld (note 20), pp. 247–50.

Participation in the MAP is based on self-selection and self-differentiation. The MAP consists of five chapters dealing with political and economic, defence and military, resource, security and legal issues. Each aspiring country is asked to draw up an annual national programme of preparations for possible future membership which would provide a basis for NATO to keep track of progress made by candidates and to provide feedback. Evaluation will be done in the '19 + 1' format (that is, at meetings of all the 19 NATO members and each individual applicant). Every year NATO will draw up for individual aspirant states a report giving feedback on progress made in their respective programmes.[46] Countries aspiring to join NATO are expected to continue active participation in the Euro-Atlantic Partnership Council (EAPC) and the Partnership for Peace (PFP).[47] The MAP does not provide a checklist for countries to fulfil; neither does it prejudge any eventual NATO decision on inviting the country concerned to accession negotiations. Such decisions will be made only on a case-by-case basis with the consent of all NATO members.

In short, the concept of the MAP is to keep the door open for aspirants without any binding commitments. This approach is motivated by the intentions not to 'water down' the alliance before new members are properly prepared and not to alienate Russia.

Partnership activities

NATO's partnership activities are reflected in the PFP and the EAPC, in special relations with Russia and Ukraine, and in the Mediterranean dialogue.

An important framework for a more operational partnership is the PFP, established in 1994. Its basic aims include: increasing transparency in national defence planning and military budgeting; democratic civilian control over national armed forces; and the development of military and security cooperation between PFP and NATO partners. The biennial programme in which NATO members and their partners participate has included more than 2000 activities covering virtually all areas of NATO's work, including military exercises. The enhanced and more operational PFP as decided at the Washington NAC meeting is built on three elements: a political–military framework for NATO-led PFP operations; an expanded and adapted Planning and Review Process (PARP); and enhanced military and defence-related cooperation.[48]

The EAPC, set up in 1997 to replace the North Atlantic Cooperation Council (NACC), brings together the 19 NATO members and 25 partners in a forum established for regular consultation and cooperation. A summit meeting

---

[46] This document will be the basis for discussion at a meeting of the NAC with the aspirant country. *NATO Review*, summer 1999, Documentation (note 2), pp. D13–16.

[47] In the assessment of the Washington NAC meeting, the EAPC and the PFP 'have transformed political–military relations across the continent and have become the instruments of choice when the Alliance and its Partners consult and act together in the pursuit of peace and security'. Washington Summit Communiqué (note 2), para. 22, p. D5. For the membership of the PFP and the EAPC, see the glossary in this volume.

[48] *The Reader's Guide to the NATO Summit in Washington, 23–25 April 1999* (NATO Office of Information and Press: Brussels, 1999), pp. 93–94, URL <http://www.nato.int/docu/rdr-gde/rdrgde-e.pdf>.

of the 44 partners in Washington on 25 April 1999 focused mainly on the situation in Kosovo. Its decisions were reflected in two documents. The first, the 'Political–military framework for NATO-led PFP operations', addressed the involvement of the partner states in political consultation, decision making, operational planning and command arrangements for future operations led by the alliance, in which they will participate. The other, 'Towards a partnership for the 21st century: the enhanced and more operational partnership', outlines the main elements for making the PFP more operational.[49]

Following Russia's proposal of June 1998, the EAPC established a Euro-Atlantic Disaster Response Coordination Centre (EADRCC) at NATO headquarters. The centre was called on to support the UN High Commissioner for Refugees in relief efforts in Albania for people fleeing from Kosovo. It also coordinated humanitarian assistance from NATO and partner countries in response to the growing refugee crisis after the intervention in Kosovo.[50]

NATO and Russia

As a result of NATO's air campaign against the FRY, Russia suspended cooperation with the alliance.[51] Russia's response to NATO's military intervention was dual: strong government-inspired public protests and statements by politicians and commentators were accompanied by a more businesslike approach, particularly with respect to military contacts in Kosovo.[52] On several occasions during the Kosovo crisis, high representatives of NATO and Russia met in extraordinary sessions of the Permanent Joint Council (PJC) at various levels. They were not able to agree on how to bring about a political solution to the conflict, although Russia and NATO agreed that such a solution should be based on broad autonomy for Kosovo, short of independence. The tension in Russia–NATO relations thus had little to do with the real essence of the Kosovo dispute. Not only did Russia participate in the various negotiations that were carried out by NATO and the FRY up until the collapse of the Rambouillet talks in February 1999; then Russian Prime Minister Yevgeniy Primakov and former Prime Minister Viktor Chernomyrdin as special envoy of President Boris Yeltsin also played a mediating role. The NATO states for

---

[49] Chairman's Summary of the Euro-Atlantic Partnership Council at Summit Level, Washington DC, 25 Apr. 1999, in *Reader's Guide* (note 48), pp. 87–88. Almost all the non-NATO partners have established diplomatic missions accredited to NATO. One form of fostering practical regional security cooperation is the organization of topical regional seminars within the EAPC action plan: these have taken place in Georgia (1998) and in Lithuania, Slovakia, Bulgaria and Uzbekistan (1999).

[50] The EAPC has also explored some other initiatives, including a joint action against landmines and ways of controlling the transfer of small arms.

[51] At the Conference on Strengthening of Security in Europe/Eurasia in Moscow on 15 Nov. 1999, organized by the George C. Marshall European Center for Security Studies and the Diplomatic Academy of the Russian Foreign Ministry, in his paper on 'Russia–NATO: Perspectives of re-establishing mutual relations', V. P. Kozin of the Russian Foreign Ministry stated that 20 of the 22 projects prepared for 1999 under the 1997 NATO–Russia Founding Act were suspended.

[52] It is telling that the 2 platforms of cooperation between NATO and Russia that were not frozen were military contact within the framework of peace forces in Kosovo and Bosnia guided by the Russia–NATO Permanent Joint Council and the Standing Military Committee. Kozin (note 51).

their part were interested in keeping the businesslike spirit of relations and cooperation with Russia after the crisis erupted.[53]

Russia presented the crisis in Kosovo and the NATO intervention as a challenge to world peace comparable with the 1949 Berlin blockade or the 1961 Cuban missile crisis. However, much suggests that the virulence of its response to the NATO intervention was motivated by its domestic situation and the consequent need to identify an external enemy, and, arguably more critical, its refusal to reconcile itself with NATO enlargement to the east and readiness to use force out-of-area, disregarding the limitations envisaged in Article 5 of the Washington Treaty and without UN Security Council approval.[54] From the Russian perspective, the crisis ushered in a qualitative change not only on a European scale but also in the global security system.[55]

The more cataclysmic forecasts presented by Russian commentators in the wake of the bombardment of the FRY predicted that the Russian communists would win the forthcoming parliamentary and presidential elections; that the conflict would spill over into large-scale war; that the conflict would mark the beginning of the end of the 'US global empire'; that Europe would decline as a major actor on the world stage; and that NATO would shut the door to its eastward enlargement.[56] None of this happened. Nor did the Balkan crisis bring the favourable effects for Russia that it expected—the reconstruction in a limited measure of a Russia federated with the Slavic countries of the former USSR (Belarus and Ukraine) and the 'consolidation of the Russian society vis-à-vis the NATO aggression'.[57] Paradoxically, however, NATO's military action gave the Russian military and political leadership the pretext to use force against rebellious Chechnya.

While preparing its new military doctrine and new national security concept,[58] Russia proceeded from the assumption that, the lack of direct military threat notwithstanding, there is an increased threat to its external and domestic security. Commenting on the new military doctrine, the Chief of the Russian General Staff, General Anatoliy Kvashnin, presented a long catalogue of new risks and challenges, in addition to ill-defined territorial issues, attempts to interfere in Russia's internal affairs and the escalation of armed conflicts in the

[53] NATO foreign ministers, meeting in Brussels on 12 Apr. 1999 to discuss the Kosovo crisis, noted that 'the Alliance shares a common interest with Russia in reaching a political solution to the crisis in Kosovo, and wants to work constructively with Russia, in the spirit of the Founding Act, to this end'. *Reader's Guide* (note 48), p. 96.

[54] Antonenko, O., 'Russia, NATO and European security after Kosovo', *Survival*, vol. 41, no. 4 (winter 1999/2000), p. 124.

[55] Tretyakov, V., 'Imperativy dlya Rossii [Imperatives for Russia]', *Nezavisimaya Gazeta*, 25 Mar. 1999, pp. 1–3; and Arbatov, A., 'NATO glavnaya problema dlya yevropeyskoy bezopastnosti' [NATO, the main problem for European security], *Nezavisimaya Gazeta*, 16 Apr. 1999.

[56] 'This organization [NATO] has clearly reached the limits of its expansion, beyond which there remains only thing—step by step or rapid self-destruction.' Tretyakov (note 55), pp. 1–3.

[57] Tretyakov (note 55), p. 3. See also Rodman, P. W., 'The fallout from Kosovo', *Foreign Affairs*, July/Aug. 1999, pp. 45–51.

[58] For the new military doctrine, see note 6. The National Security Concept was revised by Presidential Decree no. 24 on 10 Jan. 2000. The decree and the full text of the National Security Concept were published in *Krasnaya Zvezda*, 20 Jan. 2000. An English translation is available in *Military News Bulletin*, vol. 9, no. 2 (Feb. 2000), pp. 1–12; and excerpts in English were published in *Arms Control Today*, Jan.–Feb. 2000, pp. 15–20.

vicinity of its borders. He pointed to the change in the balance of forces consequent on an increased military presence in territories bordering on Russia and its allies; the enlargement of military alliances; and the introduction without UN Security Council approval of foreign forces into the territories of states friendly to Russia. In his view, NATO enlargement has changed the ratio of military forces in Europe. As a result of the admission of three new members, 'the radius of NATO's zone of responsibility has increased by 650–750 km eastward, which has critically reduced the strategic warning time for the Russian Federation'.[59] It has done harm, Kvashnin went on, to Russia's political, military and economic interests. The second phase of enlarging NATO by admitting other Central and East European states 'will be considered by [Russia] as a challenge to our national security'.[60] Even so, despite the confrontational criticism voiced by many political and military representatives of Russia, it was symptomatic that both NATO and Russia left the door to the resumption of good relations and security cooperation ajar.

In Russia's perception, cooperation with NATO should be based on NATO agreeing with Moscow the decisions it adopts and the way to implement them. NATO stresses the significance of consultation and exchange of information within the procedures and mechanisms of the PJC and collaboration in the EAPC and the PFP. In its declarations Russia has as a rule emphasized the central role of the OSCE: all other organizations, structures and alliances in Europe should be subordinated to the OSCE or at least guided by the principles it has laid down. This approach reflects the concept of a multipolar world as opposed to the emerging security system where the central place is occupied by the United States and NATO.[61]

Both Russia and NATO assume that there is no reasonable alternative to cooperation, the framework and scope of which were set out in the 1997 NATO–Russia Founding Act.[62] The differences between them in 1999 concerned not only the scope and forms of cooperation but also the whole approach to what is commonly termed the architecture of European security. The main cause of the difference in perceptions of the present and future security system, however, is Russia's domestic weakness and sense of loss of its superpower status. Its enormous nuclear potential, irrelevant to its real defence needs, lost much of its political leverage after the end of the cold war and has instead become a burdensome liability. In parallel with the collapse of its economic and social development in the 1990s, Russia's self-perception suffered from a kind of dissociation which impedes its ability to shape relations with the outside world in general, and NATO in particular, rationally.

[59] Paper presented by A.V. Kvashnin, Chief of the General Staff of the Russian Armed Forces at the Conference on Strengthening of Security in Europe/Eurasia (note 51).

[60] Kvashnin (note 59).

[61] Antonenko (note 54), p. 126; Clark, W. K., 'The United States and NATO: the way ahead', *Parameters*, vol. 29, no. 4 (winter 1999/2000), pp. 2–14; and Wohlforth, W. C., 'The stability of a unipolar world', *International Security*, vol. 24, no. 1 (summer 1999), pp. 5–41.

[62] Kvashnin (note 59); and 'Final Communiqué–Ministerial Meeting of the NAC held at NATO Headquarters, Brussels, 15 Dec. 1999', Press Release M-NAC2(99)166, 15 Dec. 1999. The NATO–Russia Founding Act is reproduced in *SIPRI Yearbook 1998* (note 44), pp. 168–73.

The pragmatic approach signalled by Vladimir Putin when acting president of Russia, accompanied by efforts to explain and resolve problems of domestic development in a rational manner and to determine policy vis-à-vis NATO in the same spirit, has thus helped a gradual return to normal relations between NATO and Russia.[63]

The most disquieting element in those relations in 1999 was the growing awareness that neither the USA nor the EU can do much to make Russia's policy more predictable and transparent.[64] Particular concern arose during the year from Russia's emphasis on and readiness to use its nuclear weapons, expressed in the new military doctrine and national security concept.[65]

A certain thaw in Russia–NATO relations came about with Yeltsin's resignation from the presidency on 31 December 1999 and handover to Prime Minister Putin until the presidential election in March 2000.[66] In February 2000 after talks with Putin in Moscow, NATO Secretary General Lord Robertson stated: 'I think we have moved from the permafrost into slightly softer ground'.[67] All this opens up prospects for a return to the pursuit of the goals set out in the NATO–Russia Founding Act: 'The shared objective of NATO and Russia is to identify and pursue as many opportunities for joint action as possible'.[68] Among the major complex issues in relations between Russia, on the one hand, and the USA and NATO, on the other, are the further enlargement of NATO, the 1972 Anti-Ballistic Missile (ABM) Treaty, ratification of the 1993 Treaty on Further Reduction and Limitation of Strategic Offensive Arms (START II Treaty) by the Russian State Duma, and the beginning of the associated START III negotiations.[69]

These issues apart, of key importance for the future of the security system in Europe are relations between the United States and Europe.

---

[63] From this point of view, a telling article was published by Russian Acting President Vladimir Putin: 'Rossiya na rubezhe tysyacheletii' [Russia on the threshold of the millennium], *Nezavisimaya Gazeta*, 30 Dec. 1999, p. 4. Putin writes that it would take 15 years at an annual growth rate of 8% for Russia's gross national product (GNP) per capita to equal those of contemporary Portugal or Spain, neither of which is among the leading world economies. 'In the world today [Putin says] might does not express itself in military power terms.'

[64] Mirsky, G., 'Rossiya w sovremennom mire: vzglyady amerikanskikh politikov i uchyenykh' [Russia in the contemporary world: views of American politicians and researchers], *Mirovaya Ekonomika i Mezhdunarodnye Otnosheniya*, no. 12 (1999), p. 12.

[65] See notes 6 and 58.

[66] In a lecture delivered on 21 Jan. 2000 at All Souls College, Oxford University, the US Deputy Secretary of State, Strobe Talbott, noted that Putin told him that he wanted to see Russia as part of the West. 'Talbott observations on Russia's future', *USIS Washington File* (United States Information Agency), 2 Jan. 2000.

[67] 'NATO and Russia agree on a thaw', *International Herald Tribune*, 17 Feb. 2000, p. 1. A joint statement issued at the end of the talks said, 'NATO and Russia will work to intensify their dialogue in the Permanent Joint Council. They agreed that Russia and NATO would pursue a vigorous dialogue on a wide range of security issues that will enable NATO and Russia to address the challenges that lie ahead and to make their mutual cooperation a cornerstone of European security'. Joint statement on the occasion of the visit of the Secretary General of NATO, Lord Robertson, to Moscow on 16 Feb. 2000, URL <http://www.nato.int/docu/pr/2000/p000216e.htm>.

[68] NATO–Russia Founding Act (note 62), p. 170.

[69] See also chapter 8 in this volume.

III. The European Union: a common security and defence policy

The essence of the process initiated by the 1998 St Malo Declaration was to seek a new role for Europe in its alliance relations with the United States. The objective was set out in the 1991 Treaty on European Union (the Maastricht Treaty), which provided for the CFSP to be established. According to Article J.4, the CFSP 'shall include all questions related to the security of the Union, including the eventual framing of a common defence policy, which might in time lead to a common defence'.[70] A later stage in developing the CFSP was the 1997 Amsterdam Treaty, which entered into force on 1 May 1999 after being ratified by all 15 members.[71]

Since then a number of decisions have been made which have borne witness to the EU's ambitions rather than giving those ambitions more practical substance. Experts and security analysts[72] and EU officials[73] have been critical of this. The decisions taken at the meetings of the European Council, the highest body of the EU, in Cologne and Helsinki in 1999 were the first real attempt to hammer general declarations into an operational act.

This was made possible by the profound change that has taken place in the premises of European states' security. First, none of the EU member states is any longer in a zone of immediate threat. During the cold war transatlantic relations were dominated by the overriding priority for collective defence. This warranted not only the involvement but also the dominant role of the United States in European security.[74] Second, the policies of the EU members have changed. The British Government of Prime Minister Tony Blair is much more pro-European than previous governments; France has become less anti-US; unified Germany under the Social Democratic–Green coalition led by Chancellor Gerhard Schröder and Foreign Minister Joschka Fischer is demonstrating commitment to NATO and the ability to take independent decisions; and the non-aligned members—Austria, Finland, Ireland and Sweden—

---

[70] Treaty on European Union (Maastricht Treaty), Dec. 1991, *SIPRI Yearbook 1994* (Oxford University Press: Oxford, 1994), p. 253. At the NATO summit meeting in Brussels on 10–11 Jan. 1994 and the Ministerial Meeting of the NAC in Istanbul on 9 June 1994 the alliance confirmed its commitment 'to a strong transatlantic partnership between North America and Europe developing a Common Foreign and Security Policy and taking on greater responsibility on defence matters'. NATO, Press Communiqué M-NAC-1(94)46, 9 June 1994.

[71] Treaty of Amsterdam amending the Treaty on European Union, 2 Oct. 1997. For excerpts, see *SIPRI Yearbook 1998* (note 44), pp. 177–81. See also the analysis in Rotfeld (note 44), pp. 154–60.

[72] Herolf, G., 'The security and defence policy of the EU—the Intergovernmental Conference and beyond', Conference Papers no. 21 (Swedish Institute of International Affairs: Stockholm, 1997); and Zielonka, J., *Explaining Euro-Paralysis: Why Europe is Unable to Act in International Politics* (St Anthony's College, Oxford and Macmillan: London, 1998), pp. 2–8.

[73] European Union, European Commission, 'Report on the operation of the Treaty on European Union', SEC(95), Brussels, 10 May 1995, p. 5; and van den Broek, H., 'The view of the European Commission' and Loriga, J. D., 'CFSP: the view of the Council of the European Union', both eds S. A. Pappas and S. Vonhoonacker, *The European Union's Common Foreign and Security Policy: The Challenges for the Future* (European Institute of Public Administration: Maastricht, 1996), pp. 25–31.

[74] van Eekelen, W., 'Report for NATO Parliamentary Assembly on EU, WEU and NATO: Towards a European security and defence identity', doc. DSC/DC(99)7 in 'Amsterdam reports adopted in 1999', 45th Annual Session (Amsterdam: Nov. 1999), p. AS257.

are less oriented to their traditional interpretation of neutrality.[75] Third, the process towards a European identity in matters of security and defence was accelerated by the experience of allied decision making during NATO's intervention in Kosovo. For all the US official representatives' repeated calls on the European allies to take on a share of the military burden that is commensurate with the USA's, the United States was not eager to translate the transatlantic partnership into sharing its leadership with Europe. The US message to the European allies is rather that they should 'halt the reduction of resources dedicated to defense—the so-called peace dividend—and face up to the reality that in this still dangerous world security never comes cheap'.[76]

The Cologne European Council decisions

The Cologne meeting of the European Council on 3–4 June 1999 concluded with the adoption of several major decisions on a common foreign policy and security. Specifically, they concerned EU enlargement, the elaboration of an EU Charter of Fundamental Rights, a position on the Balkans, the Stability Pact for South Eastern Europe,[77] and a common strategy vis-à-vis Russia, Ukraine, the Middle East and other regions. With regard to the future transatlantic framework, of key significance was the Declaration on Strengthening the Common European Policy on Security and Defence.[78] In this context, the decision to designate former NATO Secretary General Solana for the new post of Secretary General of the European Council and the High Representative for the Common Foreign and Security Policy testified to the fact that the CFSP was gradually being given an operational form.

Two meetings convened later at the summit level between the EU and Canada (17 June) and the EU and the USA (21 June) were significant. The main aim of both those meetings was to prevent disputes over trade and broader economic issues from disturbing transatlantic relations in general and security matters in particular.

The most important decision at Cologne, however, was that 'the Union must have the capacity for autonomous action backed by credible military forces, the means to decide to use them, and a readiness to do so, in order to respond to international crises without prejudice to actions by NATO'.[79] In accordance with this decision, the mandate for such forces will be limited to the Petersberg tasks. However, they will not collide with possible NATO military action. A commitment was adopted at Cologne to develop more effective European military capabilities on the basis of existing national, bi-national and multinational capabilities. Here the Cologne documents referred to the NATO Washington decisions of April 1999. The EU will take over the functions of

---

[75] Dörfer, I., 'Ett europeiskt försvar?' [A European defence?], *Svenska Dagbladet*, 24 and 25 Feb. 2000.

[76] Clark, W. K., 'The United States and NATO: the way ahead', *Parameters* (US Army College Quarterly), vol. 29, no. 4 (winter 1999/2000), p. 5.

[77] The Stability Pact is discussed further in section IV of this chapter.

[78] Cologne European Council, Presidency Conclusions (note 3), Annex III.

[79] Cologne European Council, Presidency Conclusions (note 3), Annex III, para. 1.

the WEU by the end of 2000 and the WEU will cease to exist. The relevant NATO and EU documents are in agreement that the CFSP should be compatible with the 'common security and defence policy established within the framework of the Washington Treaty'.[80]

The process initiated by the St Malo Declaration and continued in Cologne is intended to achieve 'more complementarity, cooperation and synergy' between NATO and the EU.[81] If a common European policy on security and defence is to be taken seriously it will require the building up of credible military capabilities and the establishment within the EU of appropriate decision-making bodies. The EU members are aware that NATO has such military capabilities. In fact, a common European policy on security and defence is not an alternative to NATO. The debate initiated and recommendations adopted at Cologne set in motion a process which is to lead not to the EU replacing NATO in Europe but to the development of effective 'consultation, cooperation and transparency' between the EU and NATO.

The paradox is that, although all the EU states except Austria, Finland, Ireland and Sweden belong to NATO, still no institutional arrangements or formal contacts exist between the two security structures. Here the decisions adopted by NATO and the EU at Cologne can be seen as qualitatively new.

One caveat is in order here. It will take a long time to create European military capabilities, including shared intelligence, strategic transport and command and control networks, even for more limited humanitarian tasks. This means that in the foreseeable future EU-led military operations will be possible only when NATO assets and capabilities are placed at the EU's disposal.

The Helsinki European Council meeting

The Finnish Presidency (July–December 1999) responded to the mandate given it by the Cologne European Council meeting to strengthen the common European policy on security and defence.[82] The main decisions of the Helsinki meeting of 10–11 December 1999 in this respect may be summarized as follows. First, the EU must be able by 2003 to deploy within 60 days and sustain for at least one year military forces of up to 50 000–60 000 troops capable of carrying out the full range of Petersberg tasks. (Allowing for the need to rotate military personnel, this will in fact require 200 000 troops.) Second,

---

[80] Cologne European Council, Presidency Conclusions (note 3), Annex III, 'Presidency report on strengthening the common European policy on security and defence', sect. 1. On 14 Feb. 2000 the Council of Ministers of the EU decided to set up an Interim Political and Security Committee (Council Decision 2000/143/CFSP) and an Interim Military Body (Council Decision 2000/144/CFSP) and to second national experts in the military field to the General Secretariat of the Council during an interim period (Council Decision 2000/145/CFSP). All 3 decisions were published in the *Official Journal of the European Communities*, ser. L. no. 049 (22 Feb. 2000), pp. 1–3.

[81] Cologne European Council, Presidency Conclusions (note 3), Annexe III, 'Presidency Report on Strengthening of the common European policy on security and defence', sect. 1. The subject was also discussed by the EU foreign ministers at an informal meeting in Reinhartshausen on 13–14 Mar. 1999; at the General Affairs Council on 17 May 1999; and by the WEU Ministerial Council on 10–11 May 1999.

[82] Helsinki European Council, Presidency Conclusions (note 3), Annex IV.

'new political and military bodies and structures will be established to enable the Union to ensure the necessary political guidance and strategic direction to such operations, while respecting the single institutional framework'.[83] Third, modalities will be developed for full consultation, cooperation and transparency between the EU and NATO. Fourth, 'appropriate arrangements will be defined that would allow, while respecting the Union's decision-making autonomy', the six NATO member countries which are not yet EU members—the Czech Republic, Hungary, Iceland, Norway, Poland and Turkey—and 'other interested states' to contribute to EU military crisis management.[84]

The decisions of the Cologne and Helsinki European Council meetings thus provide for the EU to have an autonomous capacity to launch, lead and conduct military operations in response to international crises; but it is understood that this can only be done if NATO as a whole is neither engaged nor interested in being involved in such operations.

The new common objectives and capabilities

The entry into force of the Amsterdam Treaty re-emphasized the need to move from words to deeds in the realm of a common European security and defence policy. There are two questions here: what is needed? and can it be done?

On the first, should the EU create an autonomous armed force and what kind of mission such a force could carry out? Political and military ambitions cannot be defined in an abstract way but should respond to concrete needs. 'New common objectives' have now been defined in the Cologne and Helsinki documents. They concern not the defence of the territories of the European states—after the end of the cold war and for the foreseeable future threat to territory no longer looms—but the Petersberg tasks.

On the second, there is a fairly common view that the USA's European allies are not capable of carrying out operations independently. Here two aspects are relevant—their military capabilities and their political will.

There were widespread critical comments in the USA to the effect that its European allies, with over 2 million persons under arms, had difficulty in fielding 40 000 soldiers for peacekeeping duty in the Balkans.[85] Since the mandate of the force to be set up is defined in the Petersberg tasks, the operations for which it would be used—peace support operations—are certainly not beyond the European allies' capabilities. New burdens will therefore not be imposed on the European states, increasing their military expenditure; rather a restructuring of their expenditures is needed—'funds will have to be transferred from one area to another'.[86] European capabilities measured by troop

---

[83] Helsinki European Council, Presidency Conclusions (note 3), para. 28.

[84] See note 83. The Portuguese Presidency (Jan.–June 2000) was invited to draw up a 1st progress report for the Lisbon European Council meeting (June 2000) and an overall report is to be presented to the Feira European Council meeting (Dec. 2000) with an indication whether it is necessary to amend the Amsterdam Treaty.

[85] Drozdiak (note 22).

[86] van Eekelen rightly wrote: 'For all members of the Alliance, priority should be given to changing allocations in defence budgets to make their forces more relevant to their new missions'. van Eekelen

numbers are in fact much larger than those of the USA.[87] These forces, however, belong to the individual EU member states, not to the EU itself.

The greatest difficulty in overcoming traditional thinking does not stem, as often presented, from military considerations, but is political.[88] The failure hitherto to create a European armed force either within the WEU or within the EU cannot be blamed on NATO or the United States. It happened because there was no political will on the part of Europe. The decisions adopted in 1999 are the first step towards a major change in this regard. In the new European security environment, the European states deem it desirable, possible and realistic to take the initiative and play in the future on the European continent a role commensurate with that played in the past by the United States. EU political integration has reached a level that enables it to develop a collective European capability for crisis management operations. Multinational planning and harmonization of military requirements and procurement will furthermore increasingly encourage thinking in broader common European terms instead of narrow, national security interests.

The question now arises whether a European security and defence policy as decided at Cologne and Helsinki will strengthen or weaken the EU–NATO relationship and in a broader sense the transatlantic relationship. Four practical steps necessary to implement the new transatlantic agenda have been suggested: the WEU should be abolished and its functions divided between the EU and NATO; the European militaries must enhance their capability for projecting and sustaining power; NATO's military structure should be adapted to incorporate French command within NATO- or EU-led reaction forces; and the USA and Europe must 'establish better patterns for managing inevitable transatlantic disagreements over such crises as Bosnia and Iraq'.[89] The authors of this article postulated that in order to preserve transatlantic cooperation NATO needs a new bargain 'that shares more equitably the responsibilities of common interests, and is codified in reformed institutional structures'.

This reasoning stems from two assumptions: first, that having greater capability will give the EU more confidence to act; and, second, that it will make Europe a more attractive partner for the USA 'in areas of common interest, and a potential challenger when interests conflict'.[90]

The Secretary General of the European Council and High Representative for the CFSP, Javier Solana, firmly believes that the ESDP will consolidate European–US relations. To support this, he has put forward several arguments: the new agenda will reassure the North American allies that Europe is doing 'what they have urged us to do for decades'; there will be no duplication, since

(note 74), p. AS257. On the increases in procurement spending among NATO member countries, see also chapter 5 in this volume.

[87] Depending on what is included, the number of permanent personnel under arms is *c.* 2 million in Europe and 1.4 million in the USA. van Eekelen (note 74), p. AS257.

[88] Schake, K., Bloch-Lainé, A. and Grant, C., 'Building a European defence capability', *Survival*, vol. 41, no. 1 (spring 1999), pp. 20–40.

[89] Schake *et al.* (note 88) p. 21. Kosovo is not mentioned because the article was written before the NATO intervention.

[90] Schake *et al.* (note 88), p. 21.

the role of NATO is collective defence and that of the EU crisis management; the Defence Capabilities Initiative adopted in Washington[91] and the EU's objectives are complementary; and they have the same aims—'greater modernisation, professionalisation, strict resource priorities, closer cooperation among leading nations in each sector, interoperability, intra-European burden-sharing and perhaps some task specialisation'.[92]

Finally, the Cologne and Helsinki decisions herald significant changes in the organization of Europe's armed forces, moving from monolithic standing armies towards the creation of a rapid-reaction capability. This, however, is a matter for the distant future. The goal for the foreseeable future is not to create a European army but to improve existing national forces and multinational units and formations. At present the aim is to organize not collective defence within the EU but arrangements for a common European policy on security and defence. The new European military capability should also, and probably will, be complemented by the development of a civilian capacity. In crisis resolution the civilian component is as important as, if not more important than, military capabilities. Here the roles of the EU and the OSCE are crucial.

The Kosovo crisis brought the three main security structures—NATO, the EU and the OSCE—together. It was also a test of the effectiveness of the procedures, forms and tools in practice and of the realization of an inclusive European security architecture.[93]

The enlargement process

For Europe's security, the enlargement of the EU is as important as, if not more important than, hammering out the questions of NATO–EU relations and the establishment of a European force.[94] The accession process now involves 13 candidate states whose applications to join are being handled in a single framework. The European Council at Cologne evaluated positively the work undertaken and progress achieved in negotiations with Cyprus, the Czech Republic, Estonia, Hungary, Poland and Slovenia. At Helsinki the decision was taken to convene bilateral conferences in February 2000 to begin negotiations with Bulgaria, Latvia, Lithuania, Malta, Romania and Slovakia on the conditions for their joining the EU and the ensuing adjustments to the Amsterdam Treaty. The main motive in broadening the list of candidates is 'to lend a positive contribution to security and stability on the European continent'.[95]

---

[91] See note 2.

[92] 'Speech by Dr J. Solana, Secretary-General of the Council and High Representative for the EU Common Foreign and Security Policy', 36th Munich Wehrkunde Conference on Security Policy, 5 Feb. 2000, URL <http://www.bundesregierung.de/05/0513/19/solana.html>. Solana stated at the same conference: 'We no longer face the threat of massive conventional and non-conventional attack. There are new challenges. They may not threaten our existence. But they threaten our way of life, our values and interests'.

[93] The concept of inclusive security—proclaimed by NATO in the 1990 London Declaration on a Transformed North Atlantic Alliance (see note 8) and its successive documents of 17–18 Dec. 1990, the Madrid Declaration on Euro-Atlantic Security and Cooperation of 8 July 1997—was confirmed in the 1999 Washington Summit Communiqué, 'An alliance for the 21st Century (note 2), para. 17.

[94] Helsinki European Council, Presidency Conclusions (note 3), para. 4.

[95] Helsinki European Council, Presidency Conclusions (note 3), para. 10.

A new element in 1999 was the invitation to Turkey to enter accession negotiations; this reflected the EU's reaction to 'recent positive developments' there. Turkey has embarked on a process of reform that will bring it closer to compliance with the Copenhagen criteria.[96] In its case, the criteria it has to meet concern mainly respect for human rights and the rights of minorities in the context of its internal conflict with the Kurd population.[97] Since December 1999 Turkey has thus been a candidate for membership of the EU on the basis of the same criteria as apply to other states.[98] In this way, the crisis in EU–Turkish relations over the admission of Cyprus to the EU was defused.

IV. The OSCE: managing change in the new century

The documents adopted at the 1999 Istanbul Summit Meeting summed up an important stage of the evolution of the OSCE after the end of the cold war and determined the directions of its further development. The Conference on Security and Co-operation in Europe (CSCE) Helsinki Final Act of 1975 proclaimed the norms, procedures and framework which were to promote a transformation in Central and Eastern Europe and the Soviet Union. The Helsinki process facilitated the peaceful move from totalitarian one-party regimes to democratic states based on the rule of law and respect for political pluralism, human rights and the rights of minorities. The new stage was marked by the 1990 Charter of Paris for a New Europe, which defined a system of shared values that should guide the signatory states in their mutual relations. Three successive summit meetings, at Helsinki (1992), Budapest (1994) and Lisbon (1996), consolidated the new rules of conduct, giving them an institutional and operational character.[99] The Helsinki process was initially a conference in permanence; in time it became an operational organization. NATO acknowledged the OSCE as the most inclusive Europe-wide security organization.[100] Indeed, it is the only European security structure that includes Russia, other former Soviet republics and the United States. Without their active political involvement, the OSCE would never have played the growing

---

[96] For the 'Copenhagen criteria', agreed by the European Council in Copenhagen in June 1993 and endorsed by the European Council in Essen in Dec. 1994, see European Union, European Commission, 'What is Phare?', URL <http://europa.eu.int/comm/enlargement/pas/phare/wip/copenhagen.htm>.

[97] See also chapter 2 in this volume.

[98] This means that Turkey will have the same opportunity as the other candidates to participate in EU programmes. A programme to scrutinize Turkey's compliance with the *acquis communautaire* will speed up the harmonization of Turkish law with EU law. Helsinki European Council, Presidency Conclusions (note 3), para 12.

[99] The basic decisions were reflected in the summit documents—the 1992 Helsinki Document, *The Challenges of Change*, Helsinki, July 1992; the Budapest Document 1994, partly reproduced in *SIPRI Yearbook 1995: Armaments, Disarmament and International Security* (Oxford University Press: Oxford, 1995), pp. 309–13; and the 1996 Lisbon Declaration on a Common and Comprehensive Security Model for Europe for the 21st Century, partly reproduced in *SIPRI Yearbook 1997* (note 29), pp. 153–55. See also Rotfeld, A. D., 'Prescriptions for improving OSCE effectiveness in responding to the risks and challenges of the 21st century', eds V.-Y. Ghebali and D. Warner, *The OSCE and Preventive Diplomacy*, Study of International Organizations at Geneva University, PSIO Occasional Papers no. 1 (PSIO: Geneva, 1999), pp. 51–70.

[100] NATO, 'Madrid Declaration on Euro-atlantic security and cooperation', *NATO Review*, July–Aug. 1997, p. 3. Excerpts from the declaration are reproduced in *SIPRI Yearbook 1998* (note 44), pp. 175–77.

role which it does play in resolving difficult problems in various regions of Europe and Central Asia.

In 1999 the OSCE expanded its operations considerably and strengthened its role as a primary instrument for early warning, conflict prevention, conflict management and post-conflict rehabilitation. New tasks were taken up in Central Asia, the Caucasus and South-Eastern Europe. In total, OSCE permanent missions and other forms of field activities encompassed 25 different operations,[101] supplemented by the work of such OSCE institutions as the High Commissioner on National Minorities (HCNM), the Office for Democratic Institutions and Human Rights (in Warsaw), the OSCE Representative on Freedom of the Media, the OSCE Regional Strategy and the Stability Pact for South Eastern Europe.

A test of the OSCE's capabilities and limitations in 1999 was its role in the Balkans, in Kosovo in particular.[102] In early 1999 it finished the building of the Kosovo Verification Mission (KVM), which was established by the Permanent Council on 25 October 1998—to a great extent as a result of the efforts of US Special Envoy Richard Holbrooke. By far the largest OSCE operation, it was withdrawn from Kosovo on 20 March 1999 because of the grave deterioration of the security situation and the erosion of its ability to discharge its tasks. The brief history of the KVM demonstrated that the OSCE can play a key role only if it has the strong support of the major powers and the major European multilateral security institutions.

Following UN Security Council Resolution 1244 of 1 July 1999, a new OSCE mission was established within the UN Interim Administration (UNMIK).[103] This mission has taken a leading role in the institution- and democracy-building process and human rights.[104] Its responsibilities are unprecedented within the OSCE. Its work covers, among other things, the training of a new police service and judicial and administrative personnel.

In Kosovo, the OSCE interacted closely with the UN, NATO, the EU and the Council of Europe. Its experience in 1999 in the Balkans confirmed the tendency towards a gradual expansion of its security role. This was also demonstrated in the OSCE Regional Strategy and the Stability Pact for South Eastern Europe.

---

[101] The OSCE missions and other field activities take different forms: the OSCE Presence in Albania; 2 missions in Bosnia and Herzegovina; Croatia; the Long Duration Mission in Kosovo, Sandjak and Vojvodina; the Spillover Monitor Mission to Skopje (Macedonia); 2 missions to Estonia and Latvia; the Advisory and Monitoring Group in Belarus; the Assistance Group to Chechnya (Russia); the Personal Representative of the Chairman-in-Office on the Nagorno-Karabakh conflict dealt with by the Minsk Conference; the OSCE Offices and Missions to Armenia, Georgia, Moldova, Tajikistan; the OSCE Liaison Office in Central Asia (Uzbekistan); the OSCE Centres in Almaty (Kazakhstan), Ashkhabad (Turkmenistan) and Bishkek (Kyrgyzstan); the OSCE Project Coordinator in Ukraine; 3 types of activity in Kosovo—the KVM, the Task Force for Kosovo and the Mission in Kosovo; and 2 specific activities in Estonia—on Military Pensioners and the Joint Committee on the Skrunda Radar Station. For more detail, see OSCE, Secretary General, *Annual Report 1999 on OSCE Activities* (1 Dec. 1998–31 Oct. 1999) (OSCE: Vienna, 1999).

[102] See chapters 1 and 2 in this volume.

[103] On UNMIK, see chapter 2, section III in this volume.

[104] *Annual Report 1999 on OSCE Activities* (note 101).

The Stability Pact for South Eastern Europe

The initiative to launch a Stability Pact in the aftermath of the Kosovo crisis reflects an integrated, comprehensive and coherent approach to the entire region.[105] The concept of the Stability Pact was (a) to isolate and limit the Kosovo crisis, and (b) to develop in a more coordinated way a political framework for promoting stability in South-Eastern Europe. The concept is innovative, although in its essence it is reminiscent of the Marshall Plan offered to post-war Europe by the United States in 1947. Operating under the auspices of the OSCE, in the long term the Stability Pact offers those countries in the region which seek integration in the Euro-Atlantic structures a prospect of achieving this, especially in the context of their aspirations to join the EU.

The FRY is not a participant. Bodo Hombach (Germany), appointed in July 1999 as Special Coordinator of the Stability Pact, noted that it remains a central problem and challenge: '[as] soon as Yugoslavia has solved its political problems, it can and should become a participant in the Stability Pact with full rights. Until then, the Stability Pact will reach out to the democratic forces in Serbia and Montenegro'.[106] He pointed out that the process launched with the signing of the Pact is not directed against the people of the FRY; what is more, it opens up a prospect of their future integration into the Euro-Atlantic structures as full partners.

The decision-making bodies of the Stability Pact consist of a system of three Working Tables addressing issues similar to the 'baskets' of the Helsinki process established 25 years before: (a) democratization and the promotion of civil societies; (b) economic development; and (c) internal and external security. The results of the Working Tables are brought together at the Regional Table. The members of the Working Tables are the states which are participants in the Stability Pact and other institutions such as non-governmental organizations (NGOs) and financial institutions by invitation. A novelty of the Stability Pact process is that all the members of the Working Tables enjoy full equality. The Pact did not create any new organization or structure but made it possible for all interested states and international organizations to collaborate under OSCE auspices. Some progress has already been noted in the work of all the Working Tables.[107]

The Sarajevo Summit Declaration of heads of state and government, issued on 30 July, confirmed the commitments undertaken under the Stability Pact. Two aspects of the process initiated in Cologne and endorsed in Sarajevo are central: (a) promoting political and economic reforms, development and enhanced security; and (b) facilitating the integration of South-East European

---

[105] See note 5. On the Stability Pact, see the glossary in this volume; and URL <http://www.stabilitypact.org/Foreign%Ministries.htm>.

[106] Hombach, B., 'The Stability Pact: breaking new ground in the Balkans', *NATO Review*, winter 1999, p. 20.

[107] Hombach (note 106), p. 22. Hombach reported that on the defence side progress had been made on such matters as improved military-to-military contacts similar to confidence-building measures, control of arms sales, reducing the transfer of small arms, and non-proliferation of weapons of mass destruction. The question of resources for many of the projects to be implemented will be decided at a regional financing conference to be held in 2000.

countries into the Euro-Atlantic structures. The Sarajevo Declaration contained a message addressed to the people of the FRY 'to embrace democratic change and work actively for regional reconciliation'. With this intention, the participants at the Sarajevo Summit decided to 'consider ways of making the Republic of Montenegro an early beneficiary of the pact' and reaffirmed their support to all democratic forces.[108]

The philosophy reflected in both the Stability Pact and the Sarajevo Declaration is to engage the countries of the region in security cooperation and in the democratic transformation and reconstruction of South-Eastern Europe. They bear the main responsibility for its stabilization and their actions are of critical importance. The other state signatories of both documents undertook to support these actions in order 'to accelerate the transition in the region to stable democracies, prosperous market economies and open and pluralistic societies in which human rights and fundamental freedoms, including the rights of persons belonging to natural minorities, are respected, as an important step in their integration into euro-atlantic and global institutions'.[109]

The main challenge for all European security institutions is to build in Kosovo and other countries of the region a multi-ethnic society on the basis of substantial autonomy while still respecting the sovereignty and territorial integrity of existing states, including the FRY. The decisions taken in 1999 by NATO, the EU and the OSCE demonstrated the need for a broader view of the region: regional cooperation should be a catalyst for the integration of the South-East European countries into broader structures. The Istanbul Summit Declaration states that the OSCE 'has a key role to play in contributing to [the Stability Pact's] success'.[110] In fact, the problems that face the signatories of the documents adopted in Cologne and Sarajevo—ensuring democratic development, political pluralism and respect for the rights of individuals and minorities within states as well as the integrity of those states—concern almost all conflict situations. They are the very problems the OSCE was set up to deal with and, although often associated with developments in the area of the former Yugoslavia, they are also the main cause of instability in the former Soviet space.

The Istanbul Summit Meeting

The Istanbul Summit Declaration reaffirmed several essential elements that make up a new type of security system in Europe. First, except for the dispute which has lasted for more than 10 years between Armenia and Azerbaijan over Nagorno-Karabakh, all the conflicts the OSCE has dealt with are essentially of a domestic character. Even so, none of the states concerned, including Belarus, Croatia, Georgia, Macedonia, Moldova and Ukraine, has questioned the legitimacy or role of the OSCE in seeking peaceful solutions. Russia at Istanbul accepted that the assistance of the OSCE in Chechnya would contribute to

---

[108] Sarajevo Summit Declaration (note 5), para. 4.
[109] Sarajevo Summit Declaration (note 5), para. 7.
[110] Istanbul Summit Declaration (note 4), para. 11.

achieving a political solution to the problem there.[111] The second aspect is the commitment to apply in practice the acknowledged principles and norms, including respect for human rights and the rights of minorities, condemnation and rejection of 'ethnic cleansing', and support for the unconditional and safe return of refugees and internally displaced persons. The third element, which is of key importance for ensuring stability in the OSCE area, is overall support for a policy of tolerance and for a multi-ethnic society 'where the rights of all citizens and the rule of law are respected'[112] but there is no intention to undermine or call into question the sovereignty and territorial integrity of the states to whom decisions of the international community are addressed.

The meeting at Istanbul faced the question of Russia's use of force on a mass scale in Chechnya. The use of violence and terror against the civilian population as a whole and recourse to the rule of 'collective responsibility'—holding the population at large answerable for the crimes of the few, as has been seen in Chechnya—cannot be equated with combating terrorism. Russia's reaction to the criticism of the international community in the period up to the Istanbul Summit Meeting came close to jeopardizing the successful conclusion of the meeting,[113] but it was not broken off and several important documents were adopted. However, the price of this 'moderate success' was the application of a double standard: the OSCE in practice made greater demands of the small and medium-sized states and was more lenient towards the major powers, especially Russia, regarding violations of their international commitments.[114] The result was seriously to erode the OSCE's authority and demonstrate its limits in enforcing its principles.

In the confrontation between principles and practice, the latter won. Since OSCE decisions are taken by consensus, the documents adopted reflect the balance of interests. In effect, a political compromise made it possible to agree on several essential new steps which are to facilitate the implementation of OSCE principles and norms and make more effective its decisions aimed at preventing the outbreak of violent conflict wherever possible.

The Charter for European Security

The decision to prepare a Common and Comprehensive Security Model for Europe for the 21st Century was taken at the Budapest Summit Meeting of the OSCE in December 1994.[115] It stemmed from the twin needs *(a)* to give

[111] Istanbul Summit Declaration (note 4), para. 23.

[112] Sarajevo Summit Declaration (note 5), para. 4.

[113] 'The conflict in Chechnya shows clearly the limitations of the OSCE. In times of serious crises, it is too weak to be able to enforce its principles.' *Süddeutsche Zeitung*, 19 Nov. 1999, translated in *OSCE Newsletter*, vol. 6 (Nov./Dec. 1999), pp. 16–18.

[114] 'The OSCE is an Organization with great ambitions but little power to act.' *La Stampa*, 20 Nov. 1999. 'The OSCE meeting in Istanbul will go down in history as "the Chechnya meeting" . . . Russia was at the centre of attention—Russia with the bleeding issue of Chechnya.' *Izvestiya*, 20 Nov. 1999. See also *Frankfurter Allgemeine Zeitung*, 20 Nov. 1999. All 3 reports are translated in *OSCE Newsletter* (note 113).

[115] CSCE, Budapest Document 1994, Budapest, 6 Dec. 1994, chapter VII, p. 20; and 'Decision on a common and comprehensive security model for Europe for the 21st century: a new concept for a new

expression to fundamental changes and define the new risks and challenges, and (*b*) to develop new instruments which would be not only expedients but also part of a broader system and mechanism of conflict prevention.[116] Over more than five years of negotiations since then, hundreds of proposals have been made which reflect differing visions of a European security system and different concepts of the OSCE's role in such a system. Russia demanded a hierarchical and normative order which would reaffirm legal and international treaty commitments. The EU states, differences among them notwithstanding, were inclined towards more pragmatic solutions.[117]

The Charter for European Security, signed at Istanbul on 19 November 1999 by 54 OSCE heads of states and government (excluding the FRY), reflects the experience and the crises of recent years and adapts the OSCE principles and norms to the new needs. The main new elements in it are new steps, means and mechanisms to enhance the role of the OSCE as a key instrument for early warning, conflict prevention, crisis management and post-conflict rehabilitation; it does not seek yet again to determine new or reinterpret old principles.

Agreement was reached on six new types of activity: (*a*) a Platform for Cooperative Security, the aim of which is to strengthen cooperation between the OSCE and other international organizations and institutions and thus make better use of the resources of the international community; (*b*) the development of the OSCE's role in peacekeeping operations; (*c*) the creation of Rapid Expert Assistance and Co-operation Teams (REACT) to enable the OSCE to respond quickly to requests for assistance, to offer civilian and police expertise in conflict situations, to deploy the civilian component of peacekeeping operations quickly and to address problems before they become crises; (*d*) the expansion of the OSCE's ability to do police-related work, including police monitoring, training and assisting in maintaining the primacy of law; (*e*) the establishment of an Operation Centre at the OSCE Secretariat in Vienna to facilitate preparation, planning and rapid deployment of OSCE field operations; and (*f*) the establishment of a Preparatory Committee under the OSCE Permanent Council to strengthen the consultation process.[118]

The Charter is designed much more for operational tasks than was originally assumed or expected. It reaffirms states' duty to respect human rights and fundamental freedoms, including 'the rights of persons belonging to national minorities'.[119] This is not an innovative provision: such commitments were contained in numerous documents and conventions adopted within the UN system, in the Council of Europe, in the 1975 Helsinki Final Act and in the 1990 Charter of Paris for a New Europe. A new provision, however, is that international security and peace must be enhanced through a dual approach:

century', Budapest, 8 Dec. 1995, reproduced in *SIPRI Yearbook 1996: Armaments, Disarmament and International Security* (Oxford University Press: Oxford, 1996), pp. 320–21.

[116] 'To find comprehensive solutions and not just "quick fixes", we must look beyond these immediate needs', stated Wilhelm Höynck, OSCE Secretary General. See also Rotfeld, A. D., 'Europe: towards new security arrangements', *SIPRI Yearbook 1996* (note 115), p. 303.

[117] On the main opening positions see Rotfeld (note 116), pp. 303–06.

[118] Charter for European Security (note 4), para. 1.

[119] Charter for European Security (note 4), para. 3.

'we must build confidence among people within States and strengthen co-operation between States'.[120]

Also new are the instruments and mechanisms to assist and consolidate state bodies in activities that would traditionally be seen as falling within the competence and discretionary power of the individual state. In their security policies, states should be guided by 'equal partnership, solidarity and transparency'. An essential element of the Charter for European Security is an elaborate code of conduct of the OSCE in its cooperation with other organizations.[121] It recognizes the integrating role that the OSCE can play, without creating a hierarchy of organizations or a permanent division of labour among them. The Platform for Co-operative Security, adopted within the Charter, can be considered a new stage in the development of the concept reflected in the Code of Conduct on Politico-Military Aspects of Security contained in the 1994 Budapest Document.[122]

Two follow-up conferences, in 1997 and 1999, confirmed states' adherence to the 1994 Code of Conduct and the principle of democratic control of armed forces which it emphasized. A suggestion was raised at the OSCE Review Conference in June 1999 that the issue of corruption in defence spending should be addressed. To promote transparency, it was suggested that information exchanges based on national responses to the questionnaire on implementation of countries' OSCE commitments could be made public on an Internet site.[123] The Charter for European Security reaffirmed the validity of the 1994 Code of Conduct and declared that the signatory states will consult promptly 'with a participating State seeking assistance in realizing its right to individual or collective defence in the event that its sovereignty, territorial integrity and political independence are threatened'.[124] In other words, the Charter reflects a new political commitment to consider jointly the nature of threats and actions that may be required in defence of common values.

The Charter on European Security should be evaluated in the context of the general political situation and in particular the Russian military action in Chechnya. They account for its character of an operational document rather than a code of principles and norms guiding the relations between the OSCE member states.

---

[120] Charter for European Security (note 4), para. 3.
[121] This code of conduct is reflected in the Platform for Co-operative Security set out as an 'operational document' attached to the Charter for European Security. It defines the rules, commitments and modalities of cooperation. Charter for European Security (note 4), pp. 14–16.
[122] Budapest Decisions, in Budapest Document 1994 (note 115), chapter IV, pp. 9–13.
[123] For more detail, see Review of the Implementation of all OSCE Principles and Commitments, OSCE Review Conference, RC(99).JOUR/10, Vienna, 1 Oct. 1999. Several proposals have been made with the aim of ensuring proper implementation and further development of the 1994 Code of Conduct. See also Reports of the Second Follow-up Conference on the Code of Conduct, FSC.DEL/221/99, 30 June 1999, FSC.DEL/235/99 and FSC.DEL/236/99, 1 July 1999; and Chairman's report, FSC./DEL/252/99, 7 July 1999 and FSC/GAL/84/99/Rev. 1, 19 July 1999.
[124] Charter for European Security (note 4), para. 16.

V. Conclusions

Ten years after the end of the cold war, the realities that determine the transatlantic agenda are completely changed. The decisions adopted by and arrangements made within NATO, the EU and the OSCE have taken these changes into account and set out a new conceptual framework for the further shaping of the security system in Europe. These three security-related structures are adapting internally; NATO and the EU have initiated the process of enlargement eastwards. The OSCE Charter for European Security codified a set of arrangements for closer cooperation between all security-related international institutions existing in Europe. The NATO intervention in Kosovo and the bloody conflict in Chechnya in 1999 were the litmus test of the effectiveness and, at the same time, of the limitations which these multilateral security institutions have encountered in their attempts to prevent and resolve conflicts.

The NATO, EU and OSCE documents are the expression of the new role played by the multinational security organizations and reflect the process of redefining national interests.[125] The decisions regarding security adopted in 1999 give expression to the concept that political and operational coherence is possible if it is based on common values and in close cooperation between all the bodies dealing with transatlantic security.

The future of transatlantic relations is dependent on how the differing interests of the United States and Europe on three planes—economic, political and military—can be resolved. In essence, they are inseparable.[126] The dilemma which the states of Europe now face can be boiled down to the question how they are to secure the United States' politico-military commitment and leading role without acquiescing in US domination of and hegemony in Europe. The US dilemma is different: it concerns how the USA can help to consolidate the European Union's independent capability to act in the field of security and defence policy without undermining NATO and its own leading role. The 1999 Washington NATO summit meeting and the Cologne and Helsinki EU summit meetings gave a new quality to the transatlantic agenda: the EU gained recognition in Washington as a partner on defence matters, although it may take a long time before the EU's politico-military dimension is complemented with a Defence Union.

For regional and global security, the renationalization of security policies and too-slow progress in shaping a common European security and defence policy are much greater threats than too-rapid change.[127]

---

[125] Nye, J. S., 'Redefining the national interest', *Foreign Affairs*, July/Aug. 1999, pp. 22–35.
[126] Drozdiak (note 22).
[127] Nye, J. S., 'The US and Europe: continental drift?', *International Affairs,* Jan. 2000, p. 58.

Appendix 4A. Documents on European security

NATO WASHINGTON SUMMIT COMMUNIQUÉ

Issued by the Heads of State and Government participating in the meeting of the North Atlantic Council in Washington, DC on 24 April 1999

Excerpts

An Alliance for the 21st Century

1. We, the Heads of State and Government of the member countries of the North Atlantic Alliance, have gathered in Washington to celebrate the 50th anniversary of NATO and to set forth our vision of the Alliance of the 21st century. The North Atlantic Alliance, founded on the principles of democracy, individual liberty and the rule of law, remains the basis of our collective defence; it embodies the transatlantic link that binds North America and Europe in a unique defence and security partnership.

2. Fifty years ago, the North Atlantic Alliance was founded in troubled and uncertain times. It has withstood the test of five decades and allowed the citizens of Allied countries to enjoy an unprecedented period of peace, freedom and prosperity. Here in Washington, we have paid tribute to the achievements of the past and we have shaped a new Alliance to meet the challenges of the future. This new Alliance will be larger, more capable and more flexible, committed to collective defence and able to undertake new missions including contributing to effective conflict prevention and engaging actively in crisis management, including crisis response operations. The Alliance will work with other nations and organisations to advance security, prosperity and democracy throughout the Euro-Atlantic region. The presence today of three new Allies—the Czech Republic, Hungary and Poland—demonstrates that we have overcome the division of Europe.

3. The Alliance takes the opportunity of this 50th anniversary to recognise and express its heartfelt appreciation for the commitment, sacrifice, resolve and loyalty of the servicemen and women of all Allies to the cause of freedom. The Alliance salutes these active and reserve forces' essential contributions, which for 50 years have guaranteed freedom and safeguarded trans-Atlantic security. Our nations and our Alliance are in their debt and offer them profound thanks.

4. The NATO of the 21st century starts today—a NATO which retains the strengths of the past and has new missions, new members and new partnerships. To this end, we have:

– approved an updated Strategic Concept;

– reaffirmed our commitment to the enlargement process of the Alliance and approved a Membership Action Plan for countries wishing to join;

– completed the work on key elements of the Berlin Decisions on building the European Security and Defence Identity within the Alliance and decided to further enhance its effectiveness;

– launched the Defence Capabilities Initiative;

– intensified our relations with Partners through an enhanced and more operational Partnership for Peace and strengthened our consultations and co-operation within the Euro-Atlantic Partnership Council;

– enhanced the Mediterranean Dialogue; and

– decided to increase Alliance efforts against weapons of mass destruction and their means of delivery.

5. As part of the Alliance's adaptation to the new security challenges, we have updated our Strategic Concept to make it fully consistent with the Alliance's new security environment. The updated Concept reaffirms our commitment to collective defence and the transatlantic link; takes account of the challenges the Alliance now faces; presents an Alliance ready and with a full range of capabilities to enhance the security and stability of the Euro-Atlantic area; reaffirms our commitment to building the ESDI within the Alliance; highlights the enhanced role of partnership and dialogue; underlines the need to develop defence capabilities to their full potential to meet the spectrum of Alliance missions, including forces which are more deployable, sustainable, survivable and able to engage effectively; and provides guidance to the NATO Military Authorities to this end.

6. To achieve its essential purpose, as an Alliance of nations committed to the Wash-

ington Treaty and the United Nations Charter, the Alliance performs the following fundamental security tasks:

Security: To provide one of the indispensable foundations for a stable Euro-Atlantic security environment, based on the growth of democratic institutions and commitment to the peaceful resolution of disputes, in which no country would be able to intimidate or coerce any other through the threat or use of force.

Consultation: To serve, as provided for in Article 4 of the North Atlantic Treaty, as an essential transatlantic forum for Allied consultations on any issues that affect their vital interests, including possible developments posing risks for members' security, and for appropriate co-ordination of their efforts in fields of common concern.

Deterrence and Defence: To deter and defend against any threat of aggression against any NATO member state as provided for in Articles 5 and 6 of the Washington Treaty.

And in order to enhance the security and stability of the Euro-Atlantic area:

– *Crisis Management*: To stand ready, case-by-case and by consensus, in conformity with Article 7 of the Washington Treaty, to contribute to effective conflict prevention and to engage actively in crisis management, including crisis response operations.

– *Partnership*: To promote wide-ranging partnership, cooperation, and dialogue with other countries in the Euro-Atlantic area, with the aim of increasing transparency, mutual confidence and the capacity for joint action with the Alliance.

7. We warmly welcome the participation of the three new Allies—the Czech Republic, Hungary and Poland—in their first Alliance Summit meeting. Their accession to the North Atlantic Treaty opens a new chapter in the history of the Atlantic Alliance.

We reaffirm today our commitment to the openness of the Alliance under Article 10 of the North Atlantic Treaty and in accordance with Paragraph 8 of the Madrid Summit Declaration. We pledge that NATO will continue to welcome new members in a position to further the principles of the Treaty and contribute to peace and security in the Euro-Atlantic area. This is part of an evolutionary process that takes into account political and security developments in the whole of Europe. Our commitment to enlargement is part of a broader strategy of projecting stability and working together with our Partners to build a Europe whole and free. The ongoing enlargement process strengthens the Alliance and enhances the security and stability of the Euro-Atlantic region. The three new members will not be the last.

At the Summit in Madrid we recognised the progress made by a number of countries aspiring to join the Alliance in meeting the responsibilities and obligations for possible membership.

Today we recognise and welcome the continuing efforts and progress in both Romania and Slovenia. We also recognise and welcome continuing efforts and progress in Estonia, Latvia and Lithuania. Since the Madrid Summit, we note and welcome positive developments in Bulgaria. We also note and welcome recent positive developments in Slovakia. We are grateful for the co-operation of the former Yugoslav Republic of Macedonia[1] with NATO in the present crisis and welcome its progress on reforms. We welcome Albania's co-operation with the Alliance in the present crisis and encourage its reform efforts.

We welcome the efforts and progress aspiring members have made, since we last met, to advance political, military and economic reforms. We appreciate the results achieved, and look forward to further progress by these countries in strengthening their democratic institutions and in restructuring their economies and militaries. We take account of the efforts of these aspiring members, together with a number of other Partner countries, to improve relations with neighbours and contribute to security and stability of the Euro-Atlantic region. We look forward to further deepening our co-operation with aspiring countries and to increasing their political and military involvement in the work of the Alliance.

The Alliance expects to extend further invitations in coming years to nations willing and able to assume the responsibilities and obligations of membership, and as NATO determines that the inclusion of these nations would serve the overall political and strategic interests of the Alliance and that the inclusion would enhance overall European security and stability. To give substance to this commitment, NATO will maintain an active relationship with those nations that have expressed an interest in NATO membership as well as those who may wish to seek membership in

[1] Turkey recognises the Republic of Macedonia with its constitutional name.

the future. Those nations that have expressed an interest in becoming NATO members will remain under active consideration for future membership. No European democratic country whose admission would fulfil the objectives of the Treaty will be excluded from consideration, regardless of its geographic location, each being considered on its own merits. All states have the inherent right to choose the means to ensure their own security. Furthermore, in order to enhance overall security and stability in Europe, further steps in the ongoing enlargement process of the Alliance should balance the security concerns of all Allies.

We welcome the aspirations of the nine countries currently interested in joining the Alliance. Accordingly, we are ready to provide advice, assistance and practical support. To this end, we approve today a Membership Action Plan which includes the following elements:

– the submission by aspiring members of individual annual national programmes on their preparations for possible future membership, covering political, economic, defence, resource, security and legal aspects;
– a focused and candid feedback mechanism on aspirant countries' progress on their programmes that includes both political and technical advice, as well as annual 19+1 meetings at Council level to assess progress;
– a clearinghouse to help co-ordinate assistance by NATO and by member states to aspirant countries in the defence/military field;
– a defence planning approach for aspirants which includes elaboration and review of agreed planning targets.

We direct that NATO Foreign Ministers keep the enlargement process, including the implementation of the Membership Action Plan, under continual review and report to us. We will review the process at our next Summit meeting which will be held no later than 2002.

8. We reaffirm our commitment to preserve the transatlantic link, including our readiness to pursue common security objectives through the Alliance wherever possible. We are pleased with the progress achieved in implementing the Berlin decisions and reaffirm our strong commitment to pursue the process of reinforcing the European pillar of the Alliance on the basis of our Brussels Declaration of 1994 and of the principles agreed at Berlin in 1996. We note with satisfaction that the key elements of the Berlin decisions are being put in place. These include flexible options for the selection of a European NATO Commander and NATO Headquarters for WEU-led operations, as well as specific terms of reference for DSACEUR and an adapted CJTF concept. Close linkages between the two organisations have been established, including planning, exercises (in particular a joint crisis management exercise in 2000) and consultation, as well as a framework for the release and return of Alliance assets and capabilities.

9. We welcome the new impetus given to the strengthening of a common European policy in security and defence by the Amsterdam Treaty and the reflections launched since then in the WEU and—following the St Malo Declaration—in the EU, including the Vienna European Council Conclusions. This is a process which has implications for all Allies. We confirm that a stronger European role will help contribute to the vitality of our Alliance for the 21st century, which is the foundation of the collective defence of its members. In this regard:

a. We acknowledge the resolve of the European Union to have the capacity for autonomous action so that it can take decisions and approve military action where the Alliance as a whole is not engaged;

b. As this process goes forward, NATO and the EU should ensure the development of effective mutual consultation, co-operation and transparency, building on the mechanisms existing between NATO and the WEU;

c. We applaud the determination of both EU members and other European Allies to take the necessary steps to strengthen their defence capabilities, especially for new missions, avoiding unnecessary duplication;

d. We attach the utmost importance to ensuring the fullest possible involvement of non-EU European Allies in EU-led crisis response operations, building on existing consultation arrangements within the WEU. We also note Canada's interest in participating in such operations under appropriate modalities.

e. We are determined that the decisions taken in Berlin in 1996, including the concept of using separable but not separate NATO assets and capabilities for WEU-led operations, should be further developed.

10. On the basis of the above principles and building on the Berlin decisions, we therefore stand ready to define and adopt the necessary arrangements for ready access by the European Union to the collective assets and capa-

bilities of the Alliance, for operations in which the Alliance as a whole is not engaged militarily as an Alliance. The Council in Permanent Session will approve these arrangements, which will respect the requirements of NATO operations and the coherence of its command structure, and should address:

a. Assured EU access to NATO planning capabilities able to contribute to military planning for EU-led operations;

b. The presumption of availability to the EU of pre-identified NATO capabilities and common assets for use in EU-led operations;

c. Identification of a range of European command options for EU-led operations, further developing the role of DSACEUR in order for him to assume fully and effectively his European responsibilities;

d. The further adaptation of NATO's defence planning system to incorporate more comprehensively the availability of forces for EU-led operations.

We task the Council in Permanent Session to address these measures on an ongoing basis, taking into account the evolution of relevant arrangements in the EU. The Council will make recommendations to the next Ministerial meeting for its consideration.

. . .

39. Co-operation and co-ordination between the Alliance and the Organisation for Security and Co-operation in Europe has expanded considerably in the light of the support we have provided to the OSCE-led Kosovo Verification Missions. We hope to make use of these important bridges between our two organisations to work together in conflict prevention, peacekeeping, crisis management and post-conflict rehabilitation, in the spirit of the OSCE's Common Concept for the Development of Co-operation between Mutually Reinforcing Institutions. We continue to support the efforts of the OSCE to develop a Document-Charter on European Security, worthy of adoption at the OSCE Istanbul Summit in November 1999.

40. The Alliance and the European Union share common strategic interests. Our respective efforts in building peace in the former Yugoslavia are complementary. Both organisations make decisive contributions to peace and stability on the European continent. Co-operation between the two organisations on topics of common concern, to be decided on a case-by-case basis, could be developed when it enhances the effectiveness of action by NATO and the EU.

41. The Alliance, in order to adapt its structures to better prepare it to meet future challenges, launched a comprehensive programme including the continuing adaptation of NATO's command structure. Accordingly, Allies welcome the activation decision of the implementation phase of the Alliance's new command structure. This will ensure NATO's ability to carry out the whole range of its missions more effectively and flexibly; support an enlarged Alliance and our more operational relationship with Partners; and provide, as part of the development of the ESDI within NATO, for European command arrangements able to prepare, support, command and conduct WEU-led operations. After successful trials, we have embarked on the full implementation of the CJTF concept, giving us an important new tool for crisis management in the next century. Allies also welcome the full integration of Spain into NATO's military structure from January this year, another significant milestone for the Alliance.

42. Terrorism constitutes a serious threat to peace, security and stability that can threaten the territorial integrity of States. We reiterate our condemnation of terrorism and reaffirm our determination to combat it in accordance with our international commitments and national legislation. The terrorist threat against deployed NATO forces and NATO installations requires the consideration and development of appropriate measures for their continued protection, taking full account of host nation responsibilities.

43. NATO Heads of State and Government believe that a key to the future success of the North Atlantic Alliance is the efficient production and availability of advanced weapons and technology in support of security for all its members. We also believe that viable defence industries on both sides of the Atlantic are critical to the efficient functioning of NATO military forces. To that end, we welcome continued transatlantic defence industrial co-operation to help ensure interoperability, economies of scale, competition and innovation. We will seek to ensure that NATO's armament activities meet the Alliance's evolving military needs.

. . .

Source: NATO Press Release NAC-S(99)64, 24 Apr. 1999, URL <http://www.nato.int/docu/pr/1999/p99-063e.htm>.

PRESIDENCY CONCLUSIONS
COLOGNE EUROPEAN COUNCIL

3–4 June 1999

Excerpts

I. Introduction

1. The European Council met in Cologne on 3 and 4 June 1999 to consider major issues for the future following the entry into force of the Amsterdam Treaty.

2. The European Council involved the President designate of the Commission, Mr Romano Prodi, in its proceedings in order to discuss with him basic questions concerning European Union policy over the next few years. It welcomed Mr Prodi's presentation outlining the future Commission's work and reform programme. In that context, the European Council confirms that it would like to see the appointment procedure for the new Commission continued swiftly and completed as soon as possible after the European Parliament elections.

3. At the start of the proceedings an exchange of views was also conducted with the President of the European Parliament, Mr José María Gil-Robles, on the main topics for discussion.

II. Staffing decisions

4. The European Council took several major staffing decisions. Pursuant to the Amsterdam Treaty, it designated Mr Javier Solana Madariaga for the new post of Secretary-General of the Council and High Representative for the Common Foreign and Security Policy. It designated Mr Pierre de Boissieu as Deputy Secretary-General.

. . .

ANNEX III. European Council Declaration on strengthening the common European policy on security and defence

1. We, the members of the European Council, are resolved that the European Union shall play its full role on the international stage. To that end, we intend to give the European Union the necessary means and capabilities to assume its responsibilities regarding a common European policy on security and defence. The work undertaken on the initiative of the German Presidency and the entry into force of the Treaty of Amsterdam permit us today to take a decisive step forward.

In pursuit of our Common Foreign and Security Policy objectives and the progressive framing of a common defence policy, we are convinced that the Council should have the ability to take decisions on the full range of conflict prevention and crisis management tasks defined in the Treaty on European Union, the 'Petersberg tasks'. To this end, the Union must have the capacity for autonomous action, backed up by credible military forces, the means to decide to use them, and a readiness to do so, in order to respond to international crises without prejudice to actions by NATO. The EU will thereby increase its ability to contribute to international peace and security in accordance with the principles of the UN Charter.

2. We are convinced that to fully assume its tasks in the field of conflict prevention and crisis management the European Union must have at its disposal the appropriate capabilities and instruments. We therefore commit ourselves to further develop more effective European military capabilities from the basis of existing national, bi-national and multi-national capabilities and to strengthen our own capabilities for that purpose. This requires the maintenance of a sustained defence effort, the implementation of the necessary adaptations and notably the reinforcement of our capabilities in the field of intelligence, strategic transport, command and control. This also requires efforts to adapt, exercise and bring together national and multinational European forces.

We also recognise the need to undertake sustained efforts to strengthen the industrial and technological defence base, which we want to be competitive and dynamic. We are determined to foster the restructuring of the European defence industries amongst those States involved. With industry we will therefore work towards closer and more efficient defence industry collaboration. We will seek further progress in the harmonisation of military requirements and the planning and procurement of arms, as Member States consider appropriate.

3. We welcome the results of the NATO Washington summit as regards NATO support for the process launched by the EU and its confirmation that a more effective role for the European Union in conflict prevention and crisis management will contribute to the vitality of a renewed Alliance. In implementing this process launched by the EU, we shall ensure the development of effective mutual consultation, cooperation and transparency between the European Union and NATO.

We want to develop an effective EU-led crisis management in which NATO members, as well as neutral and non-allied members, of the EU can participate fully and on an equal footing in the EU operations.

We will put in place arrangements that allow non-EU European allies and partners to take part to the fullest possible extent in this endeavour.

4. We therefore approve and adopt the report prepared by the German Presidency, which reflects the consensus among the Member States.

5. We are now determined to launch a new step in the construction of the European Union. To this end we task the General Affairs Council to prepare the conditions and the measures necessary to achieve these objectives, including the definition of the modalities for the inclusion of those functions of the WEU which will be necessary for the EU to fulfil its new responsibilities in the area of the Petersberg tasks. In this regard, our aim is to take the necessary decisions by the end of the year 2000. In that event, the WEU as an organisation would have completed its purpose. The different status of Member States with regard to collective defence guarantees will not be affected. The Alliance remains the foundation of the collective defence of its Member States.

We therefore invite the Finnish Presidency to take the work forward within the General Affairs Council on the basis of this declaration and the report of the Presidency to the European Council meeting in Cologne . . . [*Presidency report on strengthening of the common European policy on security and defence not reproduced here.*]

Source: European Union, Cologne European Council, Presidency Conclusions, 3–4 June 1999, SN 150/99, URL <http://europa.eu.int/council/off/conclu/june99/annexe_en.htm>.

STABILITY PACT FOR SOUTH EASTERN EUROPE

Cologne, 10 June 1999

I. Participants, description of situation

1. We, the Foreign Ministers of the Member States of the European Union, the Euro-

pean Commission, the Foreign Ministers of Albania, Bosnia and Herzegovina, Bulgaria, Croatia, Hungary, Romania, the Russian Federation, Slovenia, the former Yugoslav Republic of Macedonia, Turkey, the United States of America, the OSCE Chairman in Office and the Representative of the Council of Europe representing the participants in today's Conference on South Eastern Europe; and the Foreign Ministers of Canada and Japan, Representatives of the United Nations, UNHCR, NATO, OECD, WEU, International Monetary Fund, the World Bank, the European Investment Bank and the European Bank for Reconstruction and Development, acting within their competences, representing the facilitating States, Organisations and Institutions of today's Conference, as well as the Representatives of the Royaumont process, BSEC, CEI, SECI and SEECP, have met in Cologne on 10 June 1999, in response to the European Union's call to adopt a Stability Pact for South Eastern Europe.

2. The countries of South Eastern Europe recognize their responsibility to work within the international community to develop a shared strategy for stability and growth of the region and to cooperate with each other and major donors to implement that strategy. Seizing the opportunity to address structural shortfalls and unresolved issues will accelerate democratic and economic development in the region.

3. We will strive to achieve the objective of lasting peace, prosperity and stability for South Eastern Europe. We will reach this objective through a comprehensive and coherent approach to the region involving the EU, the OSCE, the Council of Europe, the UN, NATO, the OECD, the WEU, the IFIs and the regional initiatives. We welcome the fact that the European Union and the United States have made support for the Stability Pact a priority in their New Transatlantic Agenda, as well as the fact that the European Union and the Russian Federation have made the Stability Pact a priority in their political dialogue.

4. A settlement of the Kosovo conflict is critical to our ability to reach fully the objectives of the Stability Pact and to work towards permanent, long term measures for a future of peace and inter-ethnic harmony without fear of the resurgence of war.

II. Principles and norms

5. We solemnly reaffirm our commitment to all the principles and norms enshrined in the UN Charter, the Helsinki Final Act, the

Charter of Paris, the 1990 Copenhagen Document and other OSCE documents, and, as applicable, to the full implementation of relevant UN Security Council Resolutions, the relevant conventions of the Council of Europe and the General Framework Agreement for Peace in Bosnia and Herzegovina, with a view to promoting good neighbourly relations.

6. In our endeavours, we will build upon bilateral and multilateral agreements on good neighbourly relations concluded by States in the region participating in the Pact, and will seek the conclusion of such agreements where they do not exist. They will form an essential element of the Stability Pact.

7. We reaffirm that we are accountable to our citizens and responsible to one another for respect for OSCE norms and principles and for the implementation of our commitments. We also reaffirm that commitments with respect to the human dimension undertaken through our membership in the OSCE are matters of direct and legitimate concern to all States participating in the Stability Pact, and do not belong exclusively to the internal affairs of the State concerned. Respect for these commitments constitutes one of the foundations of international order, to which we intend to make a substantial contribution.

8. We take note that countries in the region participating in the Stability Pact commit themselves to continued democratic and economic reforms, as elaborated in paragraph 10, as well as bilateral and regional cooperation amongst themselves to advance their integration, on an individual basis, into Euro-Atlantic structures. The EU Member States and other participating countries and international organisations and institutions commit themselves to making every effort to assist them to make speedy and measurable progress along this road. We reaffirm the inherent right of each and every participating State to be free to choose or change its security arrangements, including treaties of alliance as they evolve. Each participating State will respect the rights of all others in this regard. They will not strengthen their security at the expense of the security of other States.

III. Objectives

9. The Stability Pact aims at strengthening countries in South Eastern Europe in their efforts to foster peace, democracy, respect for human rights and economic prosperity, in order to achieve stability in the whole region. Those countries in the region who seek integration into Euro-Atlantic structures, alongside a number of other participants in the Pact, strongly believe that the implementation of this process will facilitate their objective.

10. To that end we pledge to cooperate towards:

– preventing and putting an end to tensions and crises as a prerequisite for lasting stability. This includes concluding and implementing among ourselves multilateral and bilateral agreements and taking domestic measures to overcome the existing potential for conflict;

– bringing about mature democratic political processes, based on free and fair elections, grounded in the rule of law and full respect for human rights and fundamental freedoms, including the rights of persons belonging to national minorities, the right to free and independent media, legislative branches accountable to their constituents, independent judiciaries, combating corruption, deepening and strengthening of civil society;

– creating peaceful and good-neighbourly relations in the region through strict observance of the principles of the Helsinki Final Act, confidence building and reconciliation, encouraging work in the OSCE and other fora on regional confidence building measures and mechanisms for security cooperation;

– preserving the multinational and multiethnic diversity of countries in the region, and protecting minorities;

– creating vibrant market economies based on sound macro policies, markets open to greatly expanded foreign trade and private sector investment, effective and transparent customs and commercial/regulatory regimes, developing strong capital markets and diversified ownership, including privatisation, leading to a widening circle of prosperity for all our citizens;

– fostering economic cooperation in the region and between the region and the rest of Europe and the world, including free trade areas;

– promoting unimpeded contacts among citizens;

– combatting organised crime, corruption and terrorism and all criminal and illegal activities;

– preventing forced population displacement caused by war, persecution and civil strife as well as migration generated by poverty;

– ensuring the safe and free return of all refugees and displaced persons to their homes, while assisting the countries in the region by sharing the burden imposed upon them;

– creating the conditions, for countries of South Eastern Europe, for full integration into political, economic and security structures of their choice.

11. Lasting peace and stability in South Eastern Europe will only become possible when democratic principles and values, which are already actively promoted by many countries in the region, have taken root throughout, including in the Federal Republic of Yugoslavia. International efforts must focus on consolidating and linking areas of stability in the region to lay a firm foundation for the transition of the region as a whole to a peaceful and democratic future.

We declare that the Federal Republic of Yugoslavia will be welcome as a full and equal participant in the Stability Pact, following the political settlement of the Kosovo crisis on the basis of the principles agreed by G8 Foreign Ministers and taking into account the need for respect by all participants for the principles and objectives of this Pact.

In order to draw the Federal Republic of Yugoslavia closer to this goal, respecting its sovereignty and territorial integrity, we will consider ways of making the Republic of Montenegro an early beneficiary of the Pact. In this context, we welcome involvement in our meetings of representatives of Montenegro, as a constituent Republic of the Federal Republic of Yugoslavia. We also note the intention of the European Union and other interested participants to continue to work closely with its democratically elected government.

IV. Mechanisms of the Stability Pact

12. To reach the objectives we have set for ourselves, we have agreed to set up a South Eastern Europe Regional Table. The South Eastern Europe Regional Table will review progress under the Stability Pact, carry it forward and provide guidance for advancing its objectives.

13. The Stability Pact will have a Special Coordinator, who will be appointed by the European Union, after consultation with the OSCE Chairman in Office and other participants, and endorsed by the OSCE Chairman in Office. The Special Coordinator will chair the South Eastern Europe Regional Table and will be responsible for promoting achievement of the Pact's objectives within and between the individual countries, supported by appropriate structures tailored to need, in close cooperation with the governments and relevant institutions of the countries, in particular other interested associated countries of the European Union, as well as relevant international organisations and institutions concerned. The Special Coordinator will provide periodic progress reports to the OSCE, according to its procedures, on behalf of the South Eastern Europe Regional Table.

14. The South Eastern Europe Regional Table will ensure coordination of activities of and among the following Working Tables, which will build upon existing expertise, institutions and initiatives and could be divided into sub-tables:

– Working Table on democratisation and human rights;

– Working Table on economic reconstruction, development and cooperation;

– Working Table on security issues.

15. Responsibilities for these Working Tables are referred to in the Annex to this document. The Working Tables will address and facilitate the resolution of the issues entrusted to them by arrangements to be agreed at each table.

16. The South Eastern Europe Regional Table and the Working Tables will consist of the participants of the Stability Pact. The facilitator States, Organisations and Institutions as well as the regional initiatives referred to in paragraph 1 of this document are entitled to participate in the Working Tables and in the South Eastern Europe Regional Table if they so wish. Neighbouring and other countries, in particular other interested associated countries of the EU, as well as relevant international organisations and institutions may be invited as participants or observers, as appropriate, and without any ensuing commitment to the future, to the South Eastern Europe Regional Table and/or the Working Tables, in order to contribute to the objectives of the Stability Pact.

V. Roles of and cooperation between participants

17. Work in the Stability Pact should take into account the diversity of the situation of participants. To achieve the objectives of this Pact, we will provide for effective coordination between the participating and facilitating States, international and regional Organisations and Institutions, which have unique knowledge and expertise to contribute to the common endeavour. We look to the active and creative participation by all concerned to bring about the conditions which will enable

the countries in the region to seize the opportunity represented by this Pact. Each of the participants will endeavour to ensure that the objectives of the Stability Pact are furthered in their own participation in all relevant international Organisations and Institutions.

Role of the EU

18. We welcome the European Union's initiative in launching the Stability Pact and the leading role the EU is playing, in cooperation with other participating and facilitating States, international Organisations and Institutions. The launching of the Pact will give a firm European anchorage to the region. The ultimate success of the Pact will depend largely on the efforts of the States concerned to fulfil the objectives of the Pact and to develop regional cooperation through multilateral and bilateral agreements.

19. We warmly welcome the European Union's readiness to actively support the countries in the region and to enable them to achieve the objectives of the Stability Pact. We welcome the EU's activity to strengthen democratic and economic institutions in the region through a number of relevant programmes. We note progress towards the establishment and development of contractual relations, on an individual basis and within the framework of its Regional Approach, between the EU and countries of the region. We take note that, on the basis of the Vienna European Council Conclusions, the EU will prepare a 'Common Strategy towards the Western Balkans', as a fundamental initiative.

20. The EU will draw the region closer to the perspective of full integration of these countries into its structures. In case of countries which have not yet concluded association agreements with the EU, this will be done through a new kind of contractual relationship taking fully into account the individual situations of each country with the perspective of EU membership, on the basis of the Amsterdam Treaty and once the Copenhagen criteria have been met. We note the European Union's willingness that, while deciding autonomously, it will consider the achievement of the objectives of the Stability Pact, in particular progress in developing regional cooperation, among the important elements in evaluating the merits of such a perspective.

Role of countries in the region

21. We highly appreciate the contribution and the solidarity of the countries in the region with the efforts of the international community for reaching a peaceful solution on Kosovo. We welcome the efforts so far deployed and results achieved by countries in South Eastern Europe towards democratisation, economic reform and regional cooperation and stability. These countries will be the main beneficiaries of the Pact and recognise that its successful implementation, and the advance towards Euro-Atlantic structures for those seeking it depend decisively on their commitment to implement the objectives of the Pact, in particular on their willingness to cooperate on a bilateral and multilateral level and to promote the objectives of the Pact within their own respective national structures.

Role of the OSCE

22. We welcome the OSCE's intention, as the only pan-European security organisation and as a regional arrangement under Chapter VIII of the UN Charter and a primary instrument for early warning, conflict prevention, crisis management and post-conflict rehabilitation, to make a significant contribution to the efforts undertaken through the Stability Pact. We reaffirm that the OSCE has a key role to play in fostering all dimensions of security and stability. Accordingly, we request that the Stability Pact be placed under the auspices of the OSCE, and will rely fully on the OSCE to work for compliance with the provisions of the Stability Pact by the participating States, in accordance with its procedures and established principles.

23. We will rely on the OSCE institutions and instruments and their expertise to contribute to the proceedings of the South Eastern Europe Regional Table and of the Working Tables, in particular the Working Table on Democratisation and Human Rights. Their unique competences will be much needed in furthering the aims and objectives of the Stability Pact. We express our intention, in cases requiring OSCE involvement with regard to the observance of OSCE principles in the implementation of the Stability Pact, to resort, where appropriate, to the instruments and procedures of the OSCE, including those concerning conflict prevention, the peaceful settlement of disputes and the human dimension. States parties to the Convention establishing the Court of Conciliation and Arbitration may also refer to the Court possible disputes and ask for the non-binding opinion of the Court.

Role of the Council of Europe

24. We welcome the Council of Europe's readiness to integrate all countries in the region into full membership on the basis of the principles of pluralist democracy, human rights and the rule of law. The Council of Europe can make an important contribution to the objectives of the Pact through its parliamentary and intergovernmental organs and institutions, its European norms embodied in relevant legally-binding Conventions, primarily the European Convention of Human Rights (and the Court), its instruments and assistance programmes in the fields of democratic institutions, human rights, law, justice and education, as well as its strong links with civil society. In this context, we take note with great interest of the Council of Europe's Stability Programme for South East Europe to be implemented together and in close coordination with the countries concerned and other international and regional organisations active in the field.

Role of the UN, including UNHCR

25. We underline the UN's central role in the region for peace and security and for lasting political normalisation, as well as for humanitarian efforts and economic rehabilitation. We strongly support UNHCR's lead agency function in all refugee-related questions, in particular the protection and return of refugees and displaced persons and the crucial role undertaken by WFP, UNICEF, WHO, UNDP, UNHCHR and other members of the UN system. We look forward to the active involvement of relevant UN agencies in the South Eastern Europe Regional Table. We note that the UN Economic Commission for Europe has expertise which can usefully contribute to the proceedings of the Working Tables of the Stability Pact.

Role of NATO

26. We note NATO's decision to increase cooperation with the countries of South Eastern Europe and its commitment to openness, as well as the intention of NATO, the Euro-Atlantic Partnership Council and the Partnership for Peace to work in cooperation with other Euro-Atlantic structures, to contribute to stability and security and to maintain and increase consultations with the countries of the region. We call for their engagement, in conformity with the objectives of the Pact, in regional security cooperation and conflict prevention and management. We welcome these stabilization activities aimed at promoting the objectives of this Pact. The enhanced use of NATO's consultative fora and mechanisms, the development of an EAPC cooperative mechanism and the increased use of Partnership for Peace programmes will serve the objectives of overall stability, cooperation and good-neighbourliness envisaged in the Pact.

27. The members of NATO and a substantial number of other participants underscore that the Alliance has an important role to play in achieving the objectives of the Pact, noting in particular NATO's recent decisions to reach out to countries of the region.

Role of the United States of America

28. Having worked closely with the European Union to launch this Pact, the United States of America will continue to play a leading role in the development and implementation of the Pact, in cooperation with other participants and facilitators. We believe that the active role of the United States underscores the vital importance attached by countries of the region to their integration into Euro-Atlantic structures.

We note the United States' readiness to support this objective, as these countries work to become as strong candidates as possible for eventual membership in Euro-Atlantic institutions. We welcome the ongoing contribution of the United States, including through economic and technical assistance programmes, and through its shared leadership in International financial Institutions, to the States of South Eastern Europe. The United States will coordinate and cooperate with the other donors to ensure the maximum effectiveness of assistance to the region.

Role of the Russian Federation

29. Russia has played and continues to play a key role in the region. Russian efforts and contribution to achieving a peaceful solution of conflicts there, in particular of the Kosovo crisis, are appreciated. Having been involved at an early stage in the launching of this Pact, the Russian Federation will continue to play a leading and constructive role in development and implementation of the Pact, in cooperation with the EU, the UN, the OSCE, the Council of Europe, international economic and financial organisations and institutions, as well as regional initiatives and individual states. The Russian Federation can make a valuable contribution to activities aimed at promoting peace, security and post-conflict cooperation.

Role of the IFIs

30. The IMF, the World Bank, the EBRD and the EIB, as the European Union financing institution, have a most important role to play, in accordance with their specific mandates, in supporting the countries in the region in achieving economic stabilisation, reform, and development of the region. We rely on them to develop a coherent international assistance strategy for the region and to promote sound macro-economic and structural policies by the countries concerned. We call on these International Financial Institutions to take an active part in the South Eastern Europe Regional Table and the relevant Working Tables.

Role of the OECD

31. We note the OECD's unique strength as a forum for dialogue on medium-term structural policy and best practices. We rely on the OECD in consideration of its well-known competence in dealing with economies in transition and its open dialogue with the countries of South Eastern Europe, to take an active part in the South Eastern Europe Regional Table and to assist in the process of economic reconstruction, the strengthening of good governance and administrative capacities and the further integration of affected States into the European and global economy.

Role of the WEU

32. We welcome the role which the WEU plays in promoting stability in the region. We note in this respect the contribution to security the WEU makes, at the request of the European Union, through its missions in countries in the region.

VI. Regional initiatives and organisations

33. We stress our interest in viable regional initiatives and organisations which foster friendly cooperation between neighbouring States. We welcome sub-regional cooperation schemes between participating countries. We will endeavour to ensure cooperation and coordination between these initiatives and the Stability Pact, which will be mutually reinforcing. We will build on their relevant achievements.

34. We note that the Royaumont process has already established a dynamic framework for cooperation in the area of democracy and civil society. Therefore, Royaumont has a key role to play in this area, particularly within the framework of the first Working Table of the Stability Pact.

35. We note the role of the Organization of the Black Sea Economic Cooperation in promoting mutual understanding, improving the overall political climate and fostering economic development in the Black Sea region. Welcoming its engagement to peace, security and stability through economic cooperation, we invite the BSEC to contribute to the implementation of the Stability Pact for South Eastern Europe.

36. We note that the Central European Initiative has established, with countries in the region, a stable and integrated framework of dialogue, coordination and cooperation in the political, economic, cultural and parliamentary fields. On the basis of its experience, it has an important role to play in the framework of the South Eastern Europe Regional Table.

37. We note that the South East Europe Cooperation Initiative (SECI) has developed an innovative approach to economic and infrastructure related cooperation in the region by facilitating joint decision-making by the South Eastern European countries in its areas of activity. As such, it has a key role to play concerning regional economic issues, in particular the removal of disincentives to private investment in the region, in the framework of the Stability Pact.

38. We commend the South Eastern Europe Cooperation Process as a further successful regional cooperation scheme. We encourage its further development and institutionalisation, including the finalisation of its charter on good-neighbourly relations and cooperation.

39. We note the contribution in the security dimension of the South Eastern European Defence Ministers (SEDM) group, which has brought the countries of the region and other nations into a variety of cooperative activities which enhance transparency and mutual confidence, such as the new Multinational Peace-Keeping Force for South East Europe.

40. We expect the proposed Conference on the Adriatic and Ionian Sea region to provide a positive contribution to the region.

VII. International donor mobilisation and coordination process

41. We reaffirm our strong commitment to support reconstruction, stabilisation and integration for the region, and call upon the international donor community to participate generously. We welcome the progress made by the World Bank and the European Union, through the European Commission, towards

establishing a donor coordination process. This process will closely interact with the relevant Working Table, and will identify appropriate modalities to administer and channel international assistance. The World Bank and the European Commission will also be responsible for coordinating a comprehensive approach for regional development and the necessary donors conferences.

VIII. Implementation and review mechanisms

42. Effective implementation of this Pact will depend on the development and the strengthening of administrative and institutional capacity as well as civil society in the countries concerned—both at national and local level—in order to reinforce the consolidation of democratic structures and have longer-term benefits for effective administration and absorption of international assistance for the region.

43. The South Eastern Europe Regional Table and the Working Tables will be convened for their inaugural meetings at the earliest possible opportunity at the invitation of the Presidency of the European Union. They will work to achieve concrete results according to agreed timelines, in conformity with the objectives of the Stability Pact. The South Eastern Europe Regional Table will meet periodically, at a level to be determined, to review progress made by the Working Tables. The South Eastern Europe Regional Table will provide guidance to the Working Tables.

Source: European Union, European Commission, 'Stability Pact for South-Eastern Europe', Cologne, 10 June 1999, URL <http://europa.eu.int/comm/dg1a/see/stapact/10_june_99.htm>.

OSCE CHARTER FOR EUROPEAN SECURITY

Agreed by the Heads of State and Government of the OSCE participating states at Istanbul, 19 November 1999

Excerpts

1. At the dawn of the 21st century we, the Heads of State or Government of the OSCE participating States, declare our firm commit-

ment to a free, democratic and more integrated OSCE area where participating States are at peace with each other, and individuals and communities live in freedom, prosperity and security. To implement this commitment, we have decided to take a number of new steps. We have agreed to:

– Adopt the Platform for Co-operative Security, in order to strengthen co-operation between the OSCE and other international organizations and institutions, thereby making better use of the resources of the international community;

– Develop the OSCE's role in peacekeeping, thereby better reflecting the Organization's comprehensive approach to security;

– Create Rapid Expert Assistance and Co-operation Teams (REACT), thereby enabling the OSCE to respond quickly to demands for assistance and for large civilian field operations;

– Expand our ability to carry out police-related activities in order to assist in maintaining the primacy of law;

– Establish an Operation Centre, in order to plan and deploy OSCE field operations;

– Strengthen the consultation process within the OSCE by establishing the Preparatory Committee under the OSCE Permanent Council.

We are committed to preventing the outbreak of violent conflicts wherever possible. The steps we have agreed to take in this Charter will strengthen the OSCE's ability in this respect as well as its capacity to settle conflicts and to rehabilitate societies ravaged by war and destruction. The Charter will contribute to the formation of a common and indivisible security space. It will advance the creation of an OSCE area free of dividing lines and zones with different levels of security.

. . .

III. Our common response

Co-operation with other organizations: the Platform for Co-operative Security

12. The risks and challenges we face today cannot be met by a single State or organization. Over the last decade, we have taken important steps to forge new co-operation between the OSCE and other international organizations. In order to make full use of the resources of the international community, we are committed to even closer co-operation among international organizations.

We pledge ourselves, through the Platform for Co-operative Security, which is hereby adopted as an essential element of this Charter, to further strengthen and develop co-operation with competent organizations on the basis of equality and in a spirit of partnership. The principles of the Platform for Co-operative Security, as set out in the operational document attached to this Charter, apply to any organization or institution whose members individually and collectively decide to adhere to them. They apply across all dimensions of security; politico-military, human and economic. Through this Platform we seek to develop and maintain political and operational coherence, on the basis of shared values, among all the various bodies dealing with security both in responding to specific crises and in formulating responses to new risks and challenges. Recognizing the key integrating role that the OSCE can play, we offer the OSCE, when appropriate, as a flexible co-ordinating framework to foster co-operation, through which various organizations can reinforce each other drawing on their particular strengths. We do not intend to create a hierarchy of organizations or a permanent division of labour among them.

We are ready in principle to deploy the resources of international organizations and institutions of which we are members in support of the OSCE's work, subject to the necessary policy decisions as cases arise.

13. Subregional co-operation has become an important element in enhancing security across the OSCE area. Processes such as the Stability Pact for South-Eastern Europe, which has been placed under the auspices of the OSCE, help to promote our common values. They contribute to improved security not just in the subregion in question but throughout the OSCE area. We offer the OSCE, in accordance with the Platform for Co-operative Security, as a forum for subregional co-operation. In this respect, and in accordance with the modalities in the operational document, the OSCE will facilitate the exchange of information and experience between subregional groups and may, if so requested, receive and keep their mutual accords and agreements.

Solidarity and partnership

14. Peace and security in our region is best guaranteed by the willingness and ability of each participating State to uphold democracy, the rule of law and respect for human rights. We individually confirm our willingness to comply fully with our commitments. We also have a joint responsibility to uphold OSCE principles. We are therefore determined to co-operate within the OSCE and with its institutions and representatives and stand ready to use OSCE instruments, tools and mechanisms. We will co-operate in a spirit of solidarity and partnership in a continuing review of implementation. Today we commit ourselves to joint measures based on co-operation, both in the OSCE and through those organizations of which we are members, in order to offer assistance to participating States to enhance their compliance with OSCE principles and commitments. We will strengthen existing co-operative instruments and develop new ones in order to respond efficiently to requests for assistance from participating States. We will explore ways to further increase the effectiveness of the Organization to deal with cases of clear, gross and continuing violations of those principles and commitments.

15. We are determined to consider ways of helping participating States requesting assistance in cases of internal breakdown of law and order. We will jointly examine the nature of the situation and possible ways and means of providing support to the State in question.

16. We reaffirm the validity of the Code of Conduct on Politico-Military Aspects of Security. We will consult promptly, in conformity with our OSCE responsibilities, with a participating State seeking assistance in realizing its right to individual or collective self-defence in the event that its sovereignty, territorial integrity and political independence are threatened. We will consider jointly the nature of the threat and actions that may be required in defence of our common values.

Our institutions

17. The Parliamentary Assembly has developed into one of the most important OSCE institutions continuously providing new ideas and proposals. We welcome this increasing role, particularly in the field of democratic development and election monitoring. We call on the Parliamentary Assembly to develop its activities further as a key component in our efforts to promote democracy, prosperity and increased confidence within and between participating States.

18. The Office for Democratic Institutions and Human Rights (ODIHR), the High Commissioner on National Minorities (HCNM) and the Representative on Freedom of the Media are essential instruments in ensuring respect for human rights, democracy and the

rule of law. The OSCE Secretariat provides vital assistance to the Chairman-in-Office and to the activities of our Organization, especially in the field. We will also strengthen further the operational capacities of the OSCE Secretariat to enable it to face the expansion of our activities and to ensure that field operations function effectively and in accordance with the mandates and guidance given to them.

We commit ourselves to giving the OSCE institutions our full support. We emphasize the importance of close co-ordination among the OSCE institutions, as well as our field operations, in order to make optimal use of our common resources. We will take into account the need for geographic diversity and gender balance when recruiting personnel to OSCE institutions and field operations.

We acknowledge the tremendous developments and diversification of OSCE activities. We recognize that a large number of OSCE participating States have not been able to implement the 1993 decision of the Rome Ministerial Council, and that difficulties can arise from the absence of a legal capacity of the Organization. We will seek to improve the situation.

The human dimension

19. We reaffirm that respect for human rights and fundamental freedoms, democracy and the rule of law is at the core of the OSCE's comprehensive concept of security. We commit ourselves to counter such threats to security as violations of human rights and fundamental freedoms, including the freedom of thought, conscience, religion or belief and manifestations of intolerance, aggressive nationalism, racism, chauvinism, xenophobia and anti-semitism.

The protection and promotion of the rights of persons belonging to national minorities are essential factors for democracy, peace, justice and stability within, and between, participating States. In this respect we reaffirm our commitments, in particular under the relevant provisions of the Copenhagen 1990 Human Dimension Document, and recall the Report of the Geneva 1991 Meeting of Experts on National Minorities. Full respect for human rights, including the rights of persons belonging to national minorities, besides being an end in itself, may not undermine, but strengthen territorial integrity and sovereignty. Various concepts of autonomy as well as other approaches outlined in the above-mentioned documents, which are in line with

OSCE principles, constitute ways to preserve and promote the ethnic, cultural, linguistic and religious identity of national minorities within an existing State. We condemn violence against any minority. We pledge to take measures to promote tolerance and to build pluralistic societies where all, regardless of their ethnic origin, enjoy full equality of opportunity. We emphasize that questions relating to national minorities can only be satisfactorily resolved in a democratic political framework based on the rule of law.

We reaffirm our recognition that everyone has the right to a nationality and that no one should be deprived of his or her nationality arbitrarily. We commit ourselves to continue our efforts to ensure that everyone can exercise this right. We also commit ourselves to further the international protection of stateless persons.

20. We recognize the particular difficulties faced by Roma and Sinti and the need to undertake effective measures in order to achieve full equality of opportunity, consistent with OSCE commitments, for persons belonging to Roma and Sinti. We will reinforce our efforts to ensure that Roma and Sinti are able to play a full and equal part in our societies, and to eradicate discrimination against them.

21. We are committed to eradicating torture and cruel, inhumane or degrading treatment or punishment throughout the OSCE area.

To this end, we will promote legislation to provide procedural and substantive safeguards and remedies to combat these practices.

We will assist victims and co-operate with relevant international organizations and non-governmental organizations, as appropriate.

22. We reject any policy of ethnic cleansing or mass expulsion. We reaffirm our commitment to respect the right to seek asylum and to ensure the international protection of refugees as set out in the 1951 Convention Relating to the Status of Refugees and its 1967 Protocol, as well as to facilitate the voluntary return of refugees and internally displaced persons in dignity and safety. We will pursue without discrimination the reintegration of refugees and internally displaced persons in their places of origin.

In order to enhance the protection of civilians in times of conflict, we will seek ways of reinforcing the application of international humanitarian law.

. . .

The politico-military dimension

28. The politico-military aspects of security remain vital to the interests of participating States. They constitute a core element of the OSCE's concept of comprehensive security. Disarmament, arms control and confidence- and security-building measures (CSBMs) are important parts of the overall effort to enhance security by fostering stability, transparency and predictability in the military field. Full implementation, timely adaptation and, when required, further development of arms control agreements and CSBMs are key contributions to our political and military stability.

29. The Treaty on Conventional Armed Forces in Europe (CFE) must continue to serve as a cornerstone of European security. It has dramatically reduced equipment levels. It provides a fundamental contribution to a more secure and integrated Europe. The States Parties to this Treaty are taking a critical step forward. The Treaty is being strengthened by adapting its provisions to ensure enhanced stability, predictability and transparency amidst changing circumstances. A number of States Parties will reduce further their equipment levels. The adapted Treaty, upon its entry into force, will be open to voluntary accession by other OSCE participating States in the area between the Atlantic Ocean and the Ural Mountains and thereby will provide an important additional contribution to European stability and security.

30. The OSCE Vienna Document 1999, together with other documents adopted by the Forum for Security Co-operation (FSC) on politico-military aspects of security, provide valuable tools for all OSCE participating States in building greater mutual confidence and military transparency. We will continue to make regular use of and fully implement all OSCE instruments in this field and seek their timely adaptation in order to ensure adequate response to security needs in the OSCE area. We remain committed to the principles contained in the Code of Conduct on politico-military aspects of security. We are determined to make further efforts within the FSC in order to jointly address common security concerns of participating States and to pursue the OSCE's concept of comprehensive and indivisible security so far as the politico-military dimension is concerned. We will continue a substantial security dialogue and task our representatives to conduct this dialogue in the framework of the FSC.

. . .

Rule of law and fight against corruption

33. We reaffirm our commitment to the rule of law. We recognize that corruption poses a great threat to the OSCE's shared values. It generates instability and reaches into many aspects of the security, economic and human dimensions. Participating States pledge to strengthen their efforts to combat corruption and the conditions that foster it, and to promote a positive framework for good government practices and public integrity. They will make better use of existing international instruments and assist each other in their fight against corruption. As part of its work to promote the rule of law, the OSCE will work with NGOs that are committed to a strong public and business consensus against corrupt practices.

IV. Our common instruments

Enhancing our dialogue

34. We are determined to broaden and strengthen our dialogue concerning developments related to all aspects of security in the OSCE area. We charge the Permanent Council and the FSC within their respective areas of competence to address in greater depth security concerns of the participating States and to pursue the OSCE's concept of comprehensive and indivisible security.

35. The Permanent Council, being the regular body for political consultations and decision-making, will address the full range of conceptual issues as well as the day-to-day operational work of the Organization. To assist in its deliberations and decision-making and to strengthen the process of political consultations and transparency within the Organization, we will establish a Preparatory Committee under the Permanent Council's direction. This open-ended Committee will normally meet in informal format and will be tasked by the Council, or its Chairman, to deliberate and to report back to the Council.

36. Reflecting our spirit of solidarity and partnership, we will also enhance our political dialogue in order to offer assistance to participating States, thereby ensuring compliance with OSCE commitments. To encourage this dialogue, we have decided, in accordance with established rules and practices, to make increased use of OSCE instruments, including:

– Dispatching delegations from the OSCE institutions, with the participation of other relevant international organizations, when appropriate, to provide advice and expertise for reform of legislation and practices;

– Dispatching Personal Representatives of the Chairman-in-Office, after consultations with the State concerned, for fact-finding or advisory missions;

– Bringing together representatives of the OSCE and States concerned in order to address questions regarding compliance with OSCE commitments;

– Organizing training programmes aimed at improving standards and practices, *inter alia*, within the fields of human rights, democratization and the rule of law;

– Addressing matters regarding compliance with OSCE commitments at OSCE review meetings and conferences as well as in the Economic Forum;

– Submitting such matters for consideration by the Permanent Council, *inter alia*, on the basis of recommendations by the OSCE institutions within their respective mandates or by Personal Representatives of the Chairman-in-Office;

– Convening meetings of the Permanent Council in a special or reinforced format in order to discuss matters of non-compliance with OSCE commitments and to decide on appropriate courses of action;

– Establishing field operations with the consent of the State concerned.

OSCE field operations

37. The Permanent Council will establish field operations. It will decide on their mandates and budgets. On this basis, the Permanent Council and the Chairman-in-Office will provide guidance to such operations.

38. The development of OSCE field operations represents a major transformation of the Organization that has enabled the OSCE to play a more prominent role in promoting peace, security and compliance with OSCE commitments. Based on the experience we have acquired, we will develop and strengthen this instrument further in order to carry out tasks according to their respective mandates, which may, *inter alia*, include the following:

– Providing assistance and advice or formulating recommendations in areas agreed by the OSCE and the host country;

– Observing compliance with OSCE commitments and providing advice or recommendations for improved compliance;

– Assisting in the organization and monitoring of elections;

– Providing support for the primacy of law and democratic institutions and for the maintenance and restoration of law and order;

– Helping to create conditions for negotiation or other measures that could facilitate the peaceful settlement of conflicts;

– Verifying and/or assisting in fulfilling agreements on the peaceful settlement of conflicts;

– Providing support in the rehabilitation and reconstruction of various aspects of society.

39. Recruitment to field operations must ensure that qualified personnel are made available by participating States. The training of personnel is an important aspect of enhancing the effectiveness of the OSCE and its field operations and will therefore be improved. Existing training facilities in OSCE participating States and training activities of the OSCE could play an active role in achieving this aim in co-operation, where appropriate, with other organizations and institutions.

40. In accordance with the Platform for Co-operative Security, co-operation between OSCE and other international organizations in performing field operations will be enhanced. This will be done, *inter alia*, by carrying out common projects with other partners, in particular the Council of Europe, allowing the OSCE to benefit from their expertise while respecting the identity and decision-making procedures of each organization involved.

41. The host country of an OSCE field operation should, when appropriate, be assisted in building its own capacity and expertise within the area of responsibility. This would facilitate an efficient transfer of the tasks of the operation to the host country, and consequently the closure of the field operation.

Rapid Response (REACT)

42. We recognize that the ability to deploy rapidly civilian and police expertise is essential to effective conflict prevention, crisis management and post-conflict rehabilitation. We are committed to developing a capability within the participating States and the OSCE to set up Rapid Expert Assistance and Co-operation Teams (REACT) that will be at the disposal of the OSCE. This will enable OSCE bodies and institutions, acting in accordance with their respective procedures, to offer experts quickly to OSCE participating States

to provide assistance, in compliance with OSCE norms, in conflict prevention, crisis management and post-conflict rehabilitation. This rapidly deployable capability will cover a wide range of civilian expertise. It will give us the ability to address problems before they become crises and to deploy quickly the civilian component of a peacekeeping operation when needed. These Teams could also be used as surge capacity to assist the OSCE with the rapid deployment of large-scale or specialized operations. We expect REACT to develop and evolve, along with other OSCE capabilities, to meet the needs of the Organization.

Operation Centre

43. Rapid deployment is important for the OSCE's effectiveness in contributing to our conflict prevention, crisis management and post-conflict rehabilitation efforts and depends on effective preparation and planning. To facilitate this, we decide to set up an Operation Centre within the Conflict Prevention Centre with a small core staff, having expertise relevant for all kinds of OSCE operations, which can be expanded rapidly when required. Its role will be to plan and deploy field operations, including those involving REACT resources. It will liaise with other international organizations and institutions as appropriate in accordance with the Platform for Co-operative Security. The Centre's core staff will, to the extent possible, be drawn from personnel with appropriate expertise seconded by participating States and from existing Secretariat resources. This core will provide the basis for rapid expansion, to deal with new tasks as they arise. The precise arrangements will be decided in accordance with existing procedures.

Police-related activities

44. We will work to enhance the OSCE's role in civilian police-related activities as an integral part of the Organization's efforts in conflict prevention, crisis management and post-conflict rehabilitation. Such activities may comprise:

– Police monitoring, including with the aim of preventing police from carrying out such activities as discrimination based on religious and ethnic identity;
– Police training, which could, *inter alia*, include the following tasks:
• Improving the operational and tactical capabilities of local police services and reforming paramilitary forces;

• Providing new and modern policing skills, such as community policing, and anti-drug, anti-corruption and anti-terrorist capacities;
• Creating a police service with a multi-ethnic and/or multi-religious composition that can enjoy the confidence of the entire population;
• Promoting respect for human rights and fundamental freedoms in general.

We will encourage the provision of modern equipment appropriate to police services that receive training in such new skills.

In addition, the OSCE will examine options and conditions for a role in law enforcement.

45. We shall also promote the development of independent judicial systems that play a key role in providing remedies for human rights violations as well as providing advice and assistance for prison system reforms. The OSCE will also work with other international organizations in the creation of political and legal frameworks within which the police can perform its tasks in accordance with democratic principles and the rule of law.

Peacekeeping

46. We remain committed to reinforcing the OSCE's key role in maintaining peace and stability throughout our area. The OSCE's most effective contributions to regional security have been in areas such as field operations, post-conflict rehabilitation, democratization, and human rights and election monitoring. We have decided to explore options for a potentially greater and wider role for the OSCE in peacekeeping. Reaffirming our rights and obligations under the Charter of the United Nations, and on the basis of our existing deision, we confirm that the OSCE can, on a case-by-case basis and by consensus, decide to play a role in peacekeeping, including a leading role when participating States judge it to be the most effective and appropriate organization. In this regard, it could also decide to provide the mandate covering peacekeeping by others and seek the support of participating States as well as other organizations to provide resources and expertise. In accordance with the Platform for Co-operative Security, it could also provide a co-ordinating framework for such efforts.

The Court of Conciliation and Arbitration

47. We reiterate that the principle of the peaceful settlement of disputes is at the core of OSCE commitments. The Court of Conciliation and Arbitration, in this respect,

remains a tool available to those, a large number of participating States, which have become parties to the 1992 Convention of Stockholm. We encourage them to use this instrument to resolve disputes between them, as well as with other participating States which voluntarily submit to the jurisdiction of the Court. We also encourage those participating States which have not yet done so to consider joining the Convention.

. . .

Source: OSCE, SUM.DOC/1/99, URL <http://www.osce.org/e/docs/summits/istachrt 99e.htm#Anchor-I-. O-21028>.

EU PRESIDENCY CONCLUSIONS HELSINKI EUROPEAN COUNCIL

10–11 December 1999

Excerpts

Introduction

1. The European Council met in Helsinki on 10 and 11 December 1999. It adopted the Millennium Declaration. It has taken a number of decisions marking a new stage in the enlargement process. Steps have also been taken to ensure that the Union itself will have effective, reformed institutions, a strengthened common security and defence policy and a competitive, job-generating, sustainable economy.

2. At the start of proceedings, the European Council and the President of the European Parliament, Mrs Nicole Fontaine, exchanged views on the main items under discussion, in particular enlargement, institutional reform and employment.

I. Preparing for enlargement

The enlargement process

3. The European Council confirms the importance of the enlargement process launched in Luxembourg in December 1997 for the stability and prosperity for the entire European continent. An efficient and credible enlargement process must be sustained.

4. The European Council reaffirms the inclusive nature of the accession process, which now comprises 13 candidate States within a single framework. The candidate States are participating in the accession pro-

cess on an equal footing. They must share the values and objectives of the European Union as set out in the Treaties. In this respect the European Council stresses the principle of peaceful settlement of disputes in accordance with the United Nations Charter and urges candidate States to make every effort to resolve any outstanding border disputes and other related issues. Failing this they should within a reasonable time bring the dispute to the International Court of Justice. The European Council will review the situation relating to any outstanding disputes, in particular concerning the repercussions on the accession process and in order to promote their settlement through the International Court of Justice, at the latest by the end of 2004. Moreover, the European Council recalls that compliance with the political criteria laid down at the Copenhagen European Council is a prerequisite for the opening of accession negotiations and that compliance with all the Copenhagen criteria is the basis for accession to the Union.

5. The Union has made a firm political commitment to make every effort to complete the Intergovernmental Conference on institutional reform by December 2000, to be followed by ratification. After ratification of the results of that Conference the Union should be in a position to welcome new Member States from the end of 2002 as soon as they have demonstrated their ability to assume the obligations of membership and once the negotiating process has been successfully completed.

6. The Commission has made a new detailed assessment of progress in the candidate States. This assessment shows progress towards fulfilling the accession criteria. At the same time, given that difficulties remain in certain sectors, candidate States are encouraged to continue and step up their efforts to comply with the accession criteria. It emerges that some candidates will not be in a position to meet all the Copenhagen criteria in the medium term. The Commission's intention is to report in early 2000 to the Council on progress by certain candidate States on fulfilling the Copenhagen economic criteria. The next regular progress reports will be presented in good time before the European Council in December 2000.

7. The European Council recalls the importance of high standards of nuclear safety in Central and Eastern Europe. It calls on the Council to consider how to address the issue of nuclear safety in the framework of the

enlargement process in accordance with the relevant Council conclusions.

8. The European Council notes with satisfaction the substantive work undertaken and progress which has been achieved in accession negotiations with Cyprus, Hungary, Poland, Estonia, the Czech Republic and Slovenia.

9. (a) The European Council welcomes the launch of the talks aiming at a comprehensive settlement of the Cyprus problem on 3 December in New York and expresses its strong support for the UN Secretary-General's efforts to bring the process to a successful conclusion.

(b) The European Council underlines that a political settlement will facilitate the accession of Cyprus to the European Union. If no settlement has been reached by the completion of accession negotiations, the Council's decision on accession will be made without the above being a precondition. In this the Council will take account of all relevant factors.

10. Determined to lend a positive contribution to security and stability on the European continent and in the light of recent developments as well as the Commission's reports, the European Council has decided to convene bilateral intergovernmental conferences in February 2000 to begin negotiations with Romania, Slovakia, Latvia, Lithuania, Bulgaria and Malta on the conditions for their entry into the Union and the ensuing Treaty adjustments.

11. In the negotiations, each candidate State will be judged on its own merits. This principle will apply both to opening of the various negotiating chapters and to the conduct of the negotiations. In order to maintain momentum in the negotiations, cumbersome procedures should be avoided. Candidate States which have now been brought into the negotiating process will have the possibility to catch up within a reasonable period of time with those already in negotiations if they have made sufficient progress in their preparations. Progress in negotiations must go hand in hand with progress in incorporating the *acquis* into legislation and actually implementing and enforcing it.

12. The European Council welcomes recent positive developments in Turkey as noted in the Commission's progress report, as well as its intention to continue its reforms towards complying with the Copenhagen criteria. Turkey is a candidate State destined to join the Union on the basis of the same criteria as applied to the other candidate States. Building on the existing European strategy, Turkey, like other candidate States, will benefit from a pre-accession strategy to stimulate and support its reforms. This will include enhanced political dialogue, with emphasis on progressing towards fulfilling the political criteria for accession with particular reference to the issue of human rights, as well as on the issues referred to in paragraphs 4 and 9(a). Turkey will also have the opportunity to participate in Community programmes and agencies and in meetings between candidate States and the Union in the context of the accession process. An accession partnership [*sic*] will be drawn up on the basis of previous European Council conclusions while containing priorities on which accession preparations must concentrate in the light of the political and economic criteria and the obligations of a Member State, combined with a national programme for the adoption of the *acquis*. Appropriate monitoring mechanisms will be established. With a view to intensifying the harmonisation of Turkey's legislation and practice with the *acquis*, the Commission is invited to prepare a process of analytical examination of the *acquis*. The European Council asks the Commission to present a single framework for coordinating all sources of European Union financial assistance for pre-accession.

13. The future of the European Conference will be reviewed in the light of the evolving situation and the decisions on the accession process taken at Helsinki. The forthcoming French Presidency has announced its intention to convene a meeting of the conference in the second half of 2000.

. . .

II. Common European policy on security and defence

25. The European Council adopts the two Presidency progress reports (see Annex IV) on developing the Union's military and non-military crisis management capability as part of a strengthened common European policy on security and defence.

26. The Union will contribute to international peace and security in accordance with the principles of the United Nations Charter. The Union recognises the primary responsibility of the United Nations Security Council for the maintenance of international peace and security.

27. The European Council underlines its determination to develop an autonomous capacity to take decisions and, where NATO as a whole is not engaged, to launch and conduct EU-led military operations in response to international crises. This process will avoid unnecessary duplication and does not imply the creation of a European army.

28. Building on the guidelines established at the Cologne European Council and on the basis of the Presidency's reports, the European Council has agreed in particular the following:

– cooperating voluntarily in EU-led operations, Member States must be able, by 2003, to deploy within 60 days and sustain for at least 1 year military forces of up to 50 000–60 000 persons capable of the full range of Petersberg tasks;

– new political and military bodies and structures will be established within the Council to enable the Union to ensure the necessary political guidance and strategic direction to such operations, while respecting the single institutional framework;

– modalities will be developed for full consultation, cooperation and transparency between the EU and NATO, taking into account the needs of all EU Member States;

– appropriate arrangements will be defined that would allow, while respecting the Union's decision-making autonomy, non-EU European NATO members and other interested States to contribute to EU military crisis management;

– a non-military crisis management mechanism will be established to coordinate and make more effective the various civilian means and resources, in parallel with the military ones, at the disposal of the Union and the Member States.

29. The European Council asks the incoming Presidency, together with the Secretary-General/High Representative, to carry work forward in the General Affairs Council on all aspects of the reports as a matter of priority, including conflict prevention and a committee for civilian crisis management. The incoming Presidency is invited to draw up a first progress report to the Lisbon European Council and an overall report to be presented to the Feira European Council containing appropriate recommendations and proposals, as well as an indication of whether or not Treaty amendment is judged necessary. The General Affairs Council is invited to begin implementing these decisions by establishing as of March 2000 the agreed interim bodies and arrangements within the Council, in accordance with the current Treaty provisions.

_____

Source: European Union, Helsinki European Council, Presidency Conclusions, 10–11 Dec. 1999, SN 300/99 and Annexes, URL <http://europa.eu.int/council/off/conclu/dec99/dec99_en.htm>.

Part II. Military spending and armaments, 1999

Chapter 5. Military expenditure

Chapter 6. Arms production

Chapter 7. Transfers of major conventional weapons

5. Military expenditure

ELISABETH SKÖNS, EVAMARIA LOOSE-WEINTRAUB,
WUYI OMITOOGUN and PETTER STÅLENHEIM

I. Introduction

World military expenditure in 1999, according to SIPRI estimates, amounted to $719 billion at constant 1995 prices and exchange rates—approximately $780 billion in current prices,[1] and $130 per capita.[2] This represented an increase of 2.1 per cent in real terms over the previous year. The post-cold war decline in world military expenditure, which began in 1988, was interrupted in 1996 and over the period 1996–99 world military expenditure has fluctuated. The increase in 1999 is likely to be followed by further increases if current expenditure plans are implemented, but whether world military expenditure has passed its low point and will now enter a period of long-term increase is still subject to political decision.

The main reason for the overall increase in 1999 is the rise in the military expenditure of some of the major spenders, including the USA, France, Russia, China, Brazil and Turkey. The continuing increase in South Asia and other West European countries has also contributed to the rise in the world total. The rise in African military spending in 1999 does not have a significant impact on the world total, because of its small relative size, but has a great social and economic impact in the region.

Global military expenditure is highly concentrated on a few countries. The 10 major spenders account for almost three-quarters. However, they are not generally the countries where the military sector constitutes the heaviest economic burden. The latter are generally poor countries, those in armed conflict or those located in areas of tension.

Expenditure on arms procurement is rising more rapidly than overall military expenditure. The US procurement budget proposed for fiscal year (FY) 2001, at $60 billion, is 29 per cent higher in real terms than that for FY 1998 and 9 per cent higher than that for FY 2000, and further increases are planned for the five-year period FY 2001–05 (table 5.11). The European NATO countries began to increase their expenditure on military equipment in 1996 (appendix 5B). In early 2000 Russia announced a 50 per cent increase in its procurement budget for 2000, a target which is likely to be more nearly met than previous budgets. In several countries in East Asia, arms procurement is also taking a larger slice of total military expenditure. One explanation for these disproportionate increases in arms procurement is the wish to support

---

[1] This estimate in current dollars is derived by applying the US inflation rate between 1995 and 1999 (8.6% over 4 years) to the figure in constant (1995) prices.
[2] World population passed the 6 billion mark in 1999. US Bureau of the Census, URL <http://www.census.gov/ipc/www/world.html>.

domestic arms industries in a difficult period of adjustment and increased competition on world markets.[3]

The trends in and pattern of world and regional military expenditure are summarized in section II of this chapter, while the subsequent sections provide further detail on the development of military expenditure in specific regions and countries.

The costs of military activities are greater than shown in official government expenditure figures. Some of the additional costs are paid via hidden accounts in the government budget and some are financed outside the official budgets. While some of the costs of war and the means of financing them can be described, their magnitude is impossible to measure and difficult to assess. This is particularly true during conditions of war. These difficulties are illustrated in appendix 5D on African military expenditure.

The chapter is based on the data on military expenditure presented in appendix 5A. Table 5A.2 of this appendix shows military expenditure by region and country in local currency and current prices. These are the original data as provided by countries or as calculated by SIPRI, converted to calendar year for those countries whose fiscal year is not the calendar year. Table 5A.3 shows military expenditure in constant US dollars, which is used to establish changes in military expenditure in real terms, that is, after adjusting for inflation. Table 5A.4 provides figures on military expenditure as a share of gross domestic product (GDP), which is a rough measure of the economic burden of military expenditure.

II. Global and regional trends and patterns

On the basis of provisional figures for 1999, world military expenditure increased by 2.1 per cent in real terms in that year to $719 billion in constant (1995) prices (table 5.1). While the SIPRI military expenditure figures for recent years are normally subject to significant subsequent revision, it appears clear that the post-cold war decline in military expenditure has ceased, at least temporarily. Over the entire decade of the 1990s, world military expenditure has declined by 29 per cent, or at an average annual rate of 3.7 per cent. The decline began in 1988 and continued until 1996. During the period 1996–99 world military expenditure has fluctuated. Behind this fluctuation is a general slight rise in military expenditure in most regions. There are, however, great regional and national variations in trend. The sharp fall in 1998 was due primarily to significant cuts in Russian and US military expenditure in that year, in both cases followed by major increases in 1999.

The SIPRI estimate of total world military expenditure understates the true level because there are gaps in its coverage. There are three main reasons for this: (a) data are not available at all for some countries because of a policy of secrecy in some—Afghanistan, Iraq, Libya, North Korea and Qatar—and in others because the economy is so distorted, by war or for other reasons, that economic data are meaningless or at best unreliable—Angola, the Democratic

---

[3] See chapter 6 in this volume.

Republic of Congo (DRC) and Somalia; (*b*) not all government expenditure on military activities is possible to trace, because it is outside the official defence budget or even outside the ordinary budget; and (*c*) there is no reporting of military expenditure by non-government forces. For some regions this lack of data makes a big difference.

Military expenditure data are rough indicators of the economic resources devoted to military activities. However, they are by no means indisputable. The SIPRI figures are based on official government data as reported by governments, either directly to SIPRI or to other organizations—primarily the International Monetary Fund (IMF) and the UN—or as reported in national official publications or to the media directly. Efforts are made to include systematically military expenditure items (according to SIPRI's definition: see appendix 5C) that are included in other budget accounts than those categorized as military expenditure by the different governments. However, SIPRI does not make estimates based on other indicators, such as economic growth or growth in total central government expenditure, or by extrapolation from previous trends, since this would introduce assumptions into the figures for national military expenditures.[4]

Regional military expenditure

The trend in African military expenditure is similar to the world trend in that the decline ended in 1996 (table 5.1). Since then military expenditure has increased in North Africa and remained constant in Sub-Saharan Africa. The estimate for 1999, which by end-1999 was still rather unreliable because of lack of information, indicates a strong increase, and in reality the increase may have been even greater because of the hidden cost of wars in Africa (appendix 5D).

The increase in total military expenditure in the Americas in 1999 reflects primarily the rise in the USA—by 1.5 per cent in 1999 (table 5.2). In Latin America military expenditures have tended to increase since 1996, but adequate data are not available for recent years, except for Brazil.

In East Asia the long-term increase in military expenditure was interrupted in 1998 as a result of the 1997 financial crisis in the region.[5] The resulting fall in military expenditure continued in 1999 in most East Asian countries, but the overall trend was still increasing because China's military expenditure was rising. That of the other major spender in region, Japan, remained constant.

---

[4] Some country data also include an element of estimation. Thus, the figures for China and Russia include estimates for some items of their military expenditure. The bases for these estimates are explained in previous SIPRI Yearbooks. Cooper, J., 'The military expenditure of the USSR and the Russian Federation, 1987–97', *SIPRI Yearbook 1998: Armaments, Disarmament and International Security* (Oxford University Press: Oxford, 1998), pp. 243–59; and Shaoguang Wang, 'The military expenditure of China, 1989–98', *SIPRI Yearbook 1999: Armaments, Disarmament and International Security* (Oxford University Press: Oxford, 1999), pp. 334–49. Estimation is also required when calculating regional trends. When data are not available for all countries in a region, it is assumed that the military expenditures of these countries change in the same way as the average for the region. These estimates are used only for the regional total and are not included in the country tables.

[5] See section VI in this chapter.

Table 5.1. Regional military expenditure estimates, 1990–99

Figures are in US $b., at constant 1995 prices and exchange rates. Figures do not always add up to totals because of the conventions of rounding.

Region[a]	1990	1991	1992	1993	1994	1995	1996	1997	1998	1999	% change 1990–99
Africa[b]	11.9	11.1	9.9	9.9	10.0	9.4	8.9	9.3	[9.5]	[10.6]	– 11
North	2.4	2.5	2.7	2.9	3.4	3.1	3.2	[3.5]	[3.7]	..	+ 54[c]
Sub-Sahara[b]	9.5	8.7	7.2	7.0	6.6	6.3	5.8	5.8	5.8	[6.6]	– 30
Americas	386	339	359	343	326	312	294	294	[287]	[294]	– 24
North	369	325	343	325	308	290	274	272	266	269	– 27
Central	0.8	0.6	0.6	0.5	0.5	0.5	0.5	0.4	..	..	– 50[d]
South	16.3	13.5	15.6	17.8	17.5	21.3	19.5	22.1	..	..	+ 36[d]
Asia/Oceania	115	118	124	126	127	130	134	137	137	139	+21
Central	..	..	1.1	1.4	0.9	1.0	1.0	1.2	..	..	+ 9[e]
East	95.1	97.9	103	104	105	108	111	114	113	114	+ 20
South	11.6	11.4	11.4	12.4	12.3	12.8	13.0	13.4	13.6	14.5	+ 25
Oceania	8.2	8.2	8.6	8.9	8.8	8.5	8.4	8.6	8.9	9.3	+13
Middle East	[51.7]	[69.1]	50.0	48.0	47.2	44.9	45.5	50.3	49.5	49.4	– 5
Europe	442	..	275	260	253	228	226	227	221	226	– 49
CEE	[213]	..	[59.9]	[52.6]	[52.0]	[36.8]	[34.3]	[36.1]	[29.2]	[33.0]	– 85
CIS Europe	0	..	[49.3]	[43.6]	[43.2]	[28.0]	[25.6]	[27.3]	[20.4]	[24.6]	– 50[f]
West	229	225	215	207	201	192	192	191	192	194	– 16
World	**1 007**	**..**	**818**	**787**	**763**	**724**	**708**	**718**	**[704]**	**[719]**	**– 28.6**
Change (%)	*– 4.6*	*..*	*– 18.8[g]*	*– 3.8*	*– 3.0*	*– 5.1*	*– 2.2*	*+ 1.4*	*– 1.9*	*+ 2.1*	*– 3.7*

[a] For the country coverage of the regions, see appendix 5A, table 5A.1 in this volume. Some countries are excluded because of lack of consistent time-series data. Africa here excludes Angola, the Republic of Congo (Congo-Brazzaville), the Democratic Republic of Congo (DRC), Libya and Somalia; Asia excludes Afghanistan; and the Middle East excludes Iraq and Qatar. World totals exclude all these countries. CIS = Commonwealth of Independent States.

[b] Because some countries are excluded, total military expenditure in Africa is understated in this table. Because of the effect of war on its economy, it is impossible to make a time series in constant dollars for Angola. Its official military expenditure may have been as high as $5–6 billion in 1996–97, which would mean that total Sub-Saharan military expenditure was twice the figure shown here.

[c] Change over the period 1990–98.

[d] Change over the period 1990–97.

[e] Change over the period 1992–97.

[f] Change over the period 1992–99.

[g] Change over the period 1990–92.

Source: Appendix 5A, table 5A.1.

The main factor behind the rise in European military expenditure in 1999 is the rise in Russian military expenditure.[6] However, most of the major spending countries in Western Europe also increased their military expenditure in 1999, including France, Germany, Italy, Spain, and Sweden. Two, Finland and the UK, cut theirs substantially. The most significant trend in Western Europe is

[6] See section VII in this chapter.

the increasing share of equipment purchases in total military expenditure. This is shown in the NATO statistics, which are the only standardized data available on such purchases. While the European NATO countries' total military expenditure increased by 1 per cent in real terms over the period 1995–99, expenditure on equipment increased by 14 per cent (appendix 5B).

In the Middle East there has been a fairly general decline in official military expenditure since 1997 in all the Persian Gulf countries. The trend is different in the countries involved in the Arab–Israeli conflict—Egypt, Israel, Jordan, Lebanon and Syria—which have all increased their military expenditure since 1997. Although the fall in oil prices in late 1997 and early 1998 affected most of the countries in the region because they are heavily dependent on oil revenues, their priorities have remained unchanged. Saudi Arabia, the region's main spender, continues to spend about one-third of its revenue on military activities and did not cancel any major arms contract even at the worst stage of the drop in oil price; rather it slowed down the rate of delivery. Kuwait's military expenditure has declined since 1996, but this was from a peak resulting from the 1991 Persian Gulf War, after which Kuwait's defence was rebuilt and the NATO countries reimbursed for their military intervention. Nevertheless, close to 20 per cent of its total annual government expenditure still goes to defence. Egypt's military expenditure continues its steady increase—in 1999 by 6 per cent in real terms. Israel's military expenditure, which has been increasing over the past couple of years, is set to be cut by about $300 million in FY 2000.

The major spenders

The global distribution of military expenditure corresponds by and large to the global economic and political structure. The greater part of military spending takes place in the richer regions. In 1999 the member countries of the Organisation for Economic Co-operation and Development (OECD) accounted for 77 per cent of the world total, while all the African and Latin American countries together accounted for less than 5 per cent.

The greater part of world military expenditure is accounted for by a small number of countries: three-fifths by the five major spender countries and four-fifths by the 15 major spenders (table 5.2). By the end of the 1990s the USA, by far the largest spender, accounted for one-third of the total. The military expenditure of Japan, the second in ranking, was only one-fifth that of the USA; the combined total for the five major West European countries corresponded to three-fifths that of the USA; and Russia's was less than one-tenth that of the USA. Many of the other major spenders listed in table 5.2 are regional powers, which dominate the military expenditure pattern of their respective regions. Thus, Japan accounted for 45 per cent of East Asian military expenditure on average during the period 1995–99, Brazil for 55 per cent of South American, India for 66 per cent of South Asian and Saudi Arabia for 31 per cent of Middle East military expenditure.

Table 5.2. The fifteen major spenders in 1999

Figures are in US $b., at constant 1995 prices and exchange rates. Figures in italics are percentages.

		Military expenditure					Share (%) of world mil. exp. 1999
Rank	Country	1995	1996	1997	1998	1999	
1	USA	278.9	263.7	262.2	256.1	259.9	*36*
2	Japan	50.1	51.1	51.3	51.3	51.2	*7*
3	France	47.8	46.6	46.8	45.5	46.8	*7*
4	Germany	41.2	40.3	38.9	39.0	39.5	*5*
5	UK	33.8	34.4	32.3	32.6	31.8	*4*
Sub-total top 5						**429.2**	*60*
6	Italy	19.4	21.4	22.4	23.1	23.5	*3*
7	Russia	25.7	23.4	24.9	18.1	22.4	*3*
8	China	12.5	13.7	14.9	16.9	18.4	*3*
9	South Korea	14.4	15.5	15.6	15.2	15.0	*2*
10	Saudi Arabia	13.2	13.2	17.9	16.4	14.5	*2*
Sub-total top 10						**523.0**	*73*
11	Brazil	10.9	9.4	11.5	10.9	14.3	*2*
12	India	8.0	8.2	8.9	9.3	10.2	*1*
13	Turkey	6.6	7.4	7.7	8.1	9.6	*1*
14	Taiwan	9.9	10.2	10.5	10.6	9.3	*1*
15	Spain	8.7	8.5	8.5	8.4	8.7	*1*
Sub-total top 15						**575.1**	*80*
World total		**724**	**708**	**718**	**[704]**	**[719]**	**100.0**

Source: Appendix 5A (tables 5A.1 and 5A.3).

III. The economic burden of military expenditure

One estimate of the economic burden of military expenditure on a country is its share in the total output of the country measured by its GDP or gross national product (GNP). It is not an entirely faultless measure since in poor countries a large part of GDP is accounted for by subsistence production, which is not easily available for spending on military activities. Thus, the military expenditure/GDP measure would understate the actual economic burden of the military in poor countries. On the other hand, the measure could show an absurdly high ratio if a state receives external support for defence, as Kuwait did during the Persian Gulf War. Nevertheless, the measure is the best available and the standard measure for comparison of the economic burden of government expenditure.

The share of military expenditure in world output is estimated as 2.6 per cent in 1999.[7] The relative priorities given to military and social expenditure, such as health and education, are shown by comparing their shares in national

---

[7] This share is based on an estimate for 1999 world GDP of $30 186 billion as provided by the International Monetary Fund in *World Economic Outlook* (IMF: Washington, DC, Oct. 1999), p. 169.

Table 5.3. The economic burden of military and social expenditure, 1995–96
Figures are percentages.

Country aggregates	Education/GNP 1996	Health/GDP 1995	Milex/GDP 1996
Developing countries	3.6	1.8	2.3
Eastern Europe and CIS	4.6	4.5	3.2
Industrial countries	5.1	6.3	2.3
World	**4.8**	**5.5**	**2.4**

Note: CIS = Commonwealth of Independent States.

Source: United Nations Development Programme (UNDP), *Human Development Report 1999* (Oxford University Press: New York and Oxford, 1999), appendix table 13, pp. 188–91.

product. Such comparisons are difficult because of the differences between countries in the extent of private financing of social expenditures, and comprehensive data exist only for public expenditure on health and education. However, using aggregate data for large groups of countries a comparison does say something about the relative economic burden and national priorities. Table 5.3 shows a comparison for 1995 and 1996, the most recent years for which data are available. According to these data, the world average in 1996 for the share of military expenditure in GDP (2.4 per cent) was half the share of public expenditure on education in GNP in 1996 and 44 per cent of that of health in GDP in 1995 (table 5.3). However, these shares were very different for different groups of countries. For example, in the developing countries military activities were a heavier economic burden than public health expenditure, while in industrial countries the share of military expenditure was only one-third of the share of public health expenditure in GDP.

There is also great variation between countries in the share of military expenditure in GDP. Those with the highest shares in 1995–98 are shown in table 5.4. They have some characteristics in common, the most striking being their involvement in conflict. Most of them have been engaged in armed conflict at some point during the period 1995–98 or are located in a region dominated by conflict. Some of the countries in the table—especially those in Europe, the Middle East and to some extent Asia—belong either to the high or to the upper-middle income group. In these countries a high military expenditure : GDP ratio does not have the same striking economic impact on the population as it does in poorer countries. This is particularly the case with the oil-rich countries of the Middle East, whose military expenditure shares continue to be among the highest in the world. In poorer countries in Africa and Southern Africa where resources are scarce and social needs are great the same ratio can mean a significant economic burden on the population.

Table 5.4. Military expenditures as a share of GDP, select countries,[a] 1990–98
Figures are percentages of gross domestic product (GDP).

Country	Income group[b]	1990	1991	1992	1993	1994	1995	1996	1997	1998
Africa										
Angola	Low	5.8	6.8	12.0	12.4	19.8	17.0	19.2	(23.9)	14.9
Burundi	Low	3.4	3.8	3.6	3.2	4.0	3.6	5.5	5.8	..
Eritrea	Low	..	..	..	21.4	13.0	19.9	22.8	13.5	..
Morocco	Middle	4.1	4.1	4.3	4.4	4.9	4.7	3.9	..	..
Mozambique	Low	10.1	8.7	8.3	7.6	8.8	3.9	3.6	3.7	(4.2)
Rwanda	Low	3.7	5.5	4.4	4.5	3.5	4.2	5.3	4.1	4.3
Asia and Oceania										
Brunei	High	..	[6.7]	[6.5]	[6.0]	[6.3]	[5.7]	6.2	6.9	7.6
Cambodia	Low	..	..	..	[3.0]	[4.9]	4.2	3.6	3.3	2.7
Pakistan	Low	5.7	5.8	6.1	5.7	5.2	5.2	5.1	4.6	4.2
Singapore	High	4.8	4.6	4.8	4.3	4.0	4.4	4.5	4.6	[5.1]
Sri Lanka	Low	2.1	2.8	3.0	3.1	3.4	5.3	5.0	4.2	4.2
Taiwan	Upper-middle	4.9	4.7	4.5	4.3	4.0	3.8	3.7	3.5	3.5
Turkmenistan	Middle	..	..	..	..	1.1	1.4	2.1	4.2	3.6
Europe										
Armenia	Low	..	..	..	2.1	..	4.1	3.3	3.8	3.6
Croatia	Upper-middle	..	..	7.3	8.2	8.4	9.8	7.5	6.2	6.2
Greece	Upper-middle	4.7	4.3	4.5	4.4	4.4	4.4	4.5	4.6	4.8
Russia	Middle	[12.3]	..	[5.5]	[5.3]	[5.9]	[4.1]	[3.8]	[4.2]	[3.2]
Yugoslavia (Federal Rep.)	Middle	..	..	..	..	5.8	4.2	(6.0)	(7.2)	(5.4)
Middle East										
Bahrain	Upper-middle	5.1	5.3	5.3	5.0	4.8	5.0	5.0	4.8	5.0
Israel	High	12.3	11.0	10.5	9.4	8.8	8.5	8.7	8.6	8.7
Jordan	Middle	9.6	9.5	7.7	7.8	8.2	8.5	9.1	9.3	9.6
Kuwait	High	48.5	116.1	30.8	12.0	13.1	13.9	10.6	8.1	[9.3]
Lebanon	Middle	5.0	3.4	5.2	4.0	4.6	4.4	3.7	3.0	[3.2]
Oman	Upper-middle	18.3	14.7	16.2	15.4	15.7	14.6	12.5	11.5	(12.8)
S. Arabia	Upper-middle	[12.8]	[22.6]	11.7	13.9	11.9	10.3	9.5	12.4	[12.8]
Syria	Middle	6.9	10.4	9.0	7.2	7.4	7.1	6.0	5.9	[6.3]
Turkey	Middle	3.5	3.7	3.7	3.8	4.1	3.9	4.1	4.1	4.4
UAE	High	4.7	4.7	4.5	4.5	4.3	4.1	[3.7]	3.4	3.3
Yemen	Low	8.4	9.1	9.2	9.0	11.3	8.0	6.9	7.4	6.5

[a] Countries have been selected on the criterion that the share of their military expenditure was higher than 4.0% in any of the years 1995–98.
[b] Based on GNP per capita 1995.

Source: Appendix 5A, table 5A.4.

The cost and financing of wars

Wars consume a considerable amount of resources. Exactly how much is impossible to say. First, there is the conceptual issue of what to measure; second, it is difficult to assess these costs in practice; and, third, it is not always clear how costs of various types are financed. The main components which could be considered in a cost assessment of an armed conflict are: (*a*) the direct cost of the military activities of the war-fighting parties; (*b*) the economic impact of the war, for instance, in terms of humanitarian and physical damage, refugee camps, and disruption of production and trade; (*c*) the cost of peace operations after fighting has ended; and (*d*) the cost of economic reconstruction. If only military activities are considered, only two of these are relevant (*a* and *c*). Even so, there are conceptual difficulties. The costs of war-fighting are sometimes expressed in terms of the incremental cost, which is often small because training in peacetime is expensive. Thus, the incremental cost often covers only transport to the location of conflict, munitions and losses of equipment.

The practical exercise of cost assessment is difficult without access to detailed information, which is seldom available. Therefore, most assessments are based on a series of assumptions. In addition, budget information is not always tailored to costs. For example, the wear and tear on equipment used during war may not be reflected in military budgets until several years after the fighting.

During 1999 there were two large-scale armed conflicts in Europe—in the Federal Republic of Yugoslavia (FRY) and in Russia. As regards the cost to the Russian Government of the Chechnya war, the only information available is a statement by then Deputy Prime Minister Mikhail Kasyanov in January 2000 to the effect that the costs during 1999 amounted to about 5 billion roubles ($176 million at the official exchange rate of 28 roubles : $1), more than the expected 3.5 billion roubles.[8]

There is not much more information available on the costs of the conflict in the Kosovo province of the FRY, which during 1999 led to an 11-week bombing campaign by NATO forces—Operation Allied Force—followed by the deployment of a peacekeeping force—the Kosovo Force (KFOR) of 50 000 troops from NATO and other countries. While there are no good estimates available on the cost of the war to the FRY or to the UCK (Kosovo Liberation Army, KLA), some preliminary estimates have been made of the cost of the military intervention and KFOR. One rough estimate is that the NATO bombing campaign cost $2.3–4.0 billion.[9] The cost of KFOR has been estimated at approximately $2.0–3.5 billion annually for a US contingent of 7000 troops.[10] Assuming the same average cost per soldier for all countries, this would imply a total annual cost for KFOR of $14–25 billion.

---

[8] 'Government says Chechnya operation costing more than expected', Radio Free Europe/Radio Liberty, *RFE/RL Newsline*, 25 Jan. 2000, URL <http://www.rferl.org/newslink/>.

[9] Kosiak, S., 'Total cost of Allied Force air campaign', Center for Strategic and Budgetary Assessments (CSBA), Washington, DC, 10 June 1999, URL <http://users.erols.com/csba/Publications/Preliminary%20Total%20Cost%20of%20Allied%20Force%20Air%20Campaign.htm>. This estimate is based on an estimate of $1.8–3.0 billion for the US part of the air operation, extrapolated to the other NATO allies on the basis of their relative contributions to the operation.

[10] Kosiak, S., 'After the war: Kosovo peacekeeping operations could cost US $2–3.5 billion a year', Center for Strategic and Budgetary Assessments (CSBA), Washington, DC, 7 June 1999, URL <http://users.erols.com/csba/Publications/After%20the%20War%20Kosovo%20Peacekeeping%20Costs.htm>.

In principle, the military activities of government armed forces should be financed via defence budgets and thus be included in the officially reported military expenditures. However, it is unclear whether this always is the case. Thus, in the UK there was disagreement between the Treasury and the Ministry of Defence over which department should pay for the UK's participation in the NATO air campaign against the FRY, the Ministry of Defence arguing that the Treasury should pay because it was an unexpected expenditure. Furthermore, it is not always the participating country which pays the final bill for its activities; there may be various types of burden-sharing arrangement to share the costs after completion of an intervention.

The fact that the great majority of armed conflicts are currently internal conflicts means that at least one of the parties is a non-state actor using non-government forces. The financing of such military groups and their armaments and activities is not reported anywhere. Furthermore, since these parties seldom have access to sufficient funds for their activities, they often resort to illegal means for the financing of their forces. This is one of the reasons why wars result in catastrophic economic deterioration and completely distort economic relationships, as has happened in some African countries.[11]

IV. Central America

Military expenditure in Central America, according to SIPRI estimates, has been halved over the eight-year period 1990–97. Trends for the period up to 1999 are difficult to discern because of the scarcity of data for some countries in the region. El Salvador, Guatemala and Nicaragua all cut their military expenditure substantially during 1990–99: Nicaragua's declined dramatically by 89 per cent.

This fall shows that substantial economic resources have been released by the demilitarization process in Central America. However, it is social unrest, the drug traffic and crime rather than politically inspired armed conflict that are inflicting casualties on the civilian population in Central America. In El Salvador both the armed forces and former guerrilla groups have yet to adjust to the post-conflict situation. In Guatemala the process of demobilizing and integrating forces continues. Furthermore, the economic development of Central America is impeded by the consequences of natural disaster.

As the process of democratization grows stronger throughout Central America, public institutions become increasingly representative of civil society. Security policy making and transparency in the defence budget process should take into account the public interest and its priorities, as has also been manifested in a declaration within the Organization of American States (OAS): at a regional conference in El Salvador in 1998 it adopted the Declaration of San Salvador on Confidence- and Security-Building Measures, which among other measures recommended 'studies for establishing a

---

[11] As described in Kaldor, M., *New and Old Wars: Organized Violence in a Global Era* (Polity Press: Cambridge, 1999). See also appendix 5D.

common methodology in order to facilitate the comparison of military expenditure in the region'.[12]

New data on the military and internal security expenditure of the Central American countries were presented during 1999 by a project carried out by the UNESCO Chair of Peace and Human Rights of the University of Barcelona. This was a first step towards more transparency in the region and may serve to stimulate continued efforts to release data on military expenditure in a region with previously very little transparency in military matters. Some of its findings are summarized below. The report provides data for six countries in the region—Costa Rica, El Salvador, Guatemala, Honduras, Nicaragua and Panama—on total security expenditure, defined to include both military and internal security.[13] The level of detail varied and only one country— Nicaragua—reported a full time series for the period 1992–99. The data for 1999 are presented in table 5.5. They differ from SIPRI figures, as presented in appendix 5A, (a) because the SIPRI series are consistent over time, and the data obtained in the UNESCO project are for one single year only, and (b) because it has not been possible to reconcile the UNESCO data with other official data reported by the countries themselves to SIPRI and elsewhere.

Table 5.5 shows the type and scale of security expenditure in the region, and includes the UNESCO study's assessment of which parts of total security expenditure can be regarded as military expenditure. Two countries—*Costa Rica* and *Panama*—have abolished their regular military forces altogether. Costa Rica dissolved its armed forces in 1948; Panama disbanded its in 1990 and created a National Guard consisting of the national police and the maritime and air services, as they are called. For these two countries, military expenditure was estimated on the basis of the functions of these respective services. The services classified as military or paramilitary in Costa Rica are the border guards and the maritime and air surveillance services, which are responsible for guarding the borders, customs, search and rescue, fighting drug trafficking and illegal emigration, and the protection of coastlines; in the case of Panama they are the national maritime and air services. According to these estimates, military expenditure accounted for 19 and 10 per cent, respectively, of Costa Rica's and Panama's total security expenditure in 1999.

All countries reported data for 1999 disaggregated by type of cost for 1999. However, items are not uniformly defined, so a strict comparison is difficult to make. El Salvador has the highest proportion in the region for personnel costs—81 per cent of the total. In Guatemala, personnel costs account for 69 per cent of the total, about half of which is for commissioned officers.

[12] Organization of American States Conference on Confidence- and Security-Building Measures (CSBMs), San Salvador, 25–27 Feb. 1998; and Inter-American Convention on Transparency in Conventional Weapons Acquisitions, approved by the General Assembly of the OAS, 7 June 1999. Conference on Disarmament document CD/1591, re-issued, 26 Aug. 1999.

[13] The findings are reported in Fisas, V., 'Los gastos de defensa en Centroamérica: la transparencia, como medida de confianza' [Military expenditure in Central America: transparency as a confidence-building measure], Universidad Autonóma de Barcelona, Cátedra UNESCO sobre Paz y Derechos Humanos [Autonomous University of Barcelona, UNESCO Chair of Peace and Human Rights], Nov. 1999, pp. 1–20.

Table 5.5. Central America: military expenditure and other security expenditure, 1999

Unless otherwise stated, figures are in local currency and current prices. Figures in italics are percentages.

	Costa Rica (m. colones)	El Salvador (m. colones)	Guatemala (m. quetzales)	Honduras (m. lempiras)	Nicaragua (m. córdobas)	Panama (m. balboas)
Military expenditure						
Armed forces	..	963	827	429	290	..
National air service	729					7
National maritime service	656					5
Border guards	2 821					
Military expenditure (in local currency)	**(4 206)**	**963**	**827**	**429**	**290**	**(12)**
Military expenditure (in constant 1995 US $m.)	**(14)**	**93**	**105**	**24**	**25**	**(12)**
Internal security expenditure						
Civil guards	9 671					
Public security	3 285	1 454	895	502	234	108
Other departments	4 487					
Internal security expenditure	**17 443**	**1 454**	**895**	**502**	**234**	**108**
Total security exp. (in local currency)	**21 649**	**2 417**	**1 722**	**931**	**524**	**120**
Total security exp. (in constant 1995 US $m.)	**74**	**233**	**219**	**53**	**45**	**115**
Military as a share of total security expenditure	*19*	*40*	*48*	*46*	*55*	*(10)*
Disaggregated military expenditure (items as % of total military expenditure)						
Personnel: salaries and remuneration	*78.9*	*81.2*	*69.3*	*37.6*	*46.6*	*66.4*
Running cost (incl. operations and maintenance)	*2.0*	*3.6*	*1.9*	*1.1*	*18.3*	*14.4*
Matériel and supply	*7.3*	*3.0*	*13.5*	*28.0*	*30.1*	*12.3*
Arms imports	*0.7*	*3.1*	*1.5*	*5.6*	*0.2*	*6.2*
Construction	*0.1*	*1.2*	*0.7*	*2.7*	*0.0*	*0.8*
Other expenditures[a]	*11.0*	*7.9*	*13.1*	*24.9*	*4.8*	*0.0*

Notes: These figures have not been used as a source for the SIPRI military expenditure figures in appendix 5A since comparable data are not available for previous years.

[a] Other expenditures include compensation as part of the demilitarization process, military health and education expenditure, and transfers.

Source: Fisas, V., 'Los gastos de defensa en Centroamérica: la transparencia, como medida de confianza' [Military expenditure in Central America: transparency as a confidence-building measure], Universidad Autonóma de Barcelona, Cátedra UNESCO sobre Paz y Derechos Humanos [Autonomous University of Barcelona, UNESCO Chair of Peace and Human Rights], Nov. 1999, pp. 9–10, 17.

Honduras devotes only 38 per cent of the total to personnel. It has experienced a profound transformation in its defence policy during recent years: a civilian president is now commander-in-chief of the armed forces and compulsory military service has been abolished.[14] In Nicaragua the share of military expenditure devoted to 'running costs' (operations and maintenance (O&M), electricity, water and telecommunications), at about 18 per cent, is significant compared to the other countries in the region, while Nicaragua's share of 30 per cent for '*matériel* and supply' (including food, fuel and clothing) is the highest for Central America.

V. South Asia

In spite of growing poverty in South Asia after two decades of improving conditions for the poor,[15] military expenditures continued to grow during 1999. The increase is due primarily to rising defence budgets in India and Pakistan, which dominate military spending in the region.

India's military expenditure, which has been rising since 1992, increased even faster after the nuclear tests in May 1998, as was announced immediately after the tests.[16] The defence budget adopted for FY 1999/2000, which amounted to 457 billion rupees ($6.3 billion), represents a real increase of around 6 per cent over the previous year. In reality India's military expenditure is higher, since the official defence budget does not include all military expenditure items. The items financed under other budget headings are primarily those related to India's nuclear weapon programme[17] and its paramilitary forces.[18] In spite of its high level, India's military expenditure will probably be insufficient to finance its extensive modernization plans.[19] Its defence budget is therefore likely to continue to increase in the near future. During 1999 the armed conflict in Kashmir generated requests for supplementary allocations. On top of the original budget for FY 1999/2000, an emergency grant of 6 billion rupees ($140 million) was adopted for extraordinary procurement requirements because of the armed conflict in Kashmir.[20] This brought the increase over 1998/99 to 10 per cent in real terms. The army had requested an increase 10 times greater, claiming that the cost of the increased

---

[14] Fisas (note 13), p. 13.

[15] 'Defence bills fuel South Asia poverty: report', *Air Letter*, no. 14328 (17 Sep. 1999), p. 5 (citing 'Human development in South Asia, 1999', Human Development Centre, Islamabad).

[16] Sköns, E. *et al.*, 'Military expenditure', *SIPRI Yearbook 1999* (note 4), p. 283.

[17] Arnett, E., 'Military research and development', *SIPRI Yearbook 1999* (note 4), p. 356.

[18] Ghosh, A. K., *India's Defence Budget and Expenditure Management in a Wider Context* (Lancer Publishers Ltd: New Delhi, 1996), p. 16.

[19] 'Indian budget fall may affect modernisation', *Jane's Defence Weekly*, vol. 31, no. 10 (10 Mar. 1999), p. 29.

[20] *Asian Age* (New Delhi), 16 June 1999, pp. 1–2, in 'Report reveals Indian arms shopping list', Foreign Broadcast Information Service, *Daily Report–Near East and South Asia (FBIS-NES)*, FBIS-NES-1999-0616, 17 June 1999.

guard along the disputed border between India and Pakistan in the province of Kashmir was 100–150 million rupees daily.[21]

In *Pakistan*, where military expenditure has been falling since 1996, it increased in real terms in 1999. However, the increase in military expenditure announced shortly after the nuclear tests in 1998 has been smaller than planned because of economic hardship. In FY 1998/99 actual military expenditure was 13 per cent less than budgeted.[22] The defence budget adopted for FY 1999/2000 (ending 30 June 2000) was for 142 billion rupees, an increase of 7 per cent in real terms over the previous fiscal year.[23] However, the new military regime of General Pervez Musharraf, which took over power in October 1999, decided to reduce the defence budget by 5 per cent as part of an economic recovery plan.[24] The direct cost of Pakistan's support for incursions in the Indian part of Kashmir requires considerable investment.[25] The nuclear programme, the exact size of which is not known, reportedly accounts for a substantial part of expenditure.[26] As economic constraints are likely to set further limits to Pakistan's military expenditure, and thereby limit the possibilities of conventional deterrence, there is a risk that its response to India's conventional military build-up may be a lowering of the nuclear threshold.[27]

VI. East Asia

After a small decline in 1998 in the combined military expenditure of the East Asian countries, the long-term increase was resumed in 1999. China, Malaysia and Myanmar (Burma) increased their military expenditure significantly, and the size of their increases was enough to outweigh the cuts in the rest of the region. The countries with the sharpest cuts in their military expenditure in 1999 were Taiwan and Thailand.

Japan, which has the highest military expenditure in the region (45 per cent of the total for East Asia in 1999), has kept its level of military expenditure roughly constant since 1996. Its defence budget for FY 2000, adopted by the cabinet on 17 January 2000, implies a continuation of this trend: at 4936 billion yen ($48 billion) it represents an increase of only 0.1 per cent in

---

[21] Bedi, R., 'India goes arms shopping', BBC News Online, 17 Nov. 1999, URL <http://news2.thls.bbc.co.uk/hi/english/world/south_asia/newsid_524000/524819.stm>; and 'India to step up Kashmir guard', *Jane's Defence Weekly*, vol. 32, no. 4 (28 July 1999).

[22] 'Pakistani budget set at $2.7 b.', *Jane's Defence Weekly*, vol. 31, no. 25 (23 June 1999), p. 17.

[23] *Khabrain* (Islamabad), 15 June 1999, p. 10, in 'Daily view Indian threats, increase in defence budget', FBIS-NES-1999-0617, 18 June 1999; and *The Pioneer* (Delhi), 6 Mar. 1999, p. 9, in 'Defence budget said inadequate for forces', FBIS-NES-1999-0306, 8 Mar. 1999.

[24] Address to the Nation by Chief Executive of Pakistan General Pervez Musharraf, 15 Dec. 1999, URL <http://www.pak.gov.pk/public/govt/reports/address_dec15.htm>; and '"Painful" measures for Pakistan', BBC News Online, 16 Dec. 1999, URL <http://news.bbc.co.uk/hi/english/world/south_asia/newsid_566000/566654.stm>.

[25] 'A problem for the generals', *Far Eastern Economic Review*, 21 Oct. 1999, p. 71.

[26] 'Pakistan armed forces seek 11 per cent increase in budget', *Pakistan Observer*, 16 May 1999, in FBIS-NES-1999-0517, 18 May 1999.

[27] Boharin, F., 'Pakistan declines to enter arms race with arch-enemy', *Financial Times,* 8 Mar. 2000, p. 7.

real terms.[28] This is much lower than the 1.6 per cent increase requested by the Japan Defense Agency.[29] Allocations for arms procurement will decrease by 34.4 billion yen, while funding for research on ballistic missile defence in cooperation with the USA will almost double by 1.1 billion yen to 2 billion yen in FY 2000.[30]

China's military expenditure has been increasing at an average annual rate of 10 per cent in real terms since 1995. It is still not a heavy economic burden: because of China's strong economic growth the share of military expenditure in GDP did not rise until 1997. The official budget for national defence in 1999, as proposed to the National People's Congress (NPC) in March 1999, amounted to 104.65 billion yuan—a 12.6 per cent increase in nominal terms compared with the actual expenditure for 1998. The increase was officially motivated by economic arguments—that it was affordable and was smaller than the increase in total government expenditure—and by the compensation to the armed forces, the People's Liberation Army (PLA), for their loss of revenues consequent on the government's decision in August 1998 to ban their commercial activities.[31]

The banning of PLA business activities makes it difficult to estimate Chinese military expenditure for 1999, since the SIPRI estimates for previous years include estimated PLA revenues.[32] Until it is known how effective the implementation of this decision is, the SIPRI estimate assumes a significant reduction in these revenues (table 5.6). If this is true, then the Chinese military budget increased by 9 per cent in real terms in 1999. During 1999 there were demands from the military for higher military expenditure. In June, prior to the convening of the NPC, a number of generals signed a request for higher funding levels—reportedly the first time that the military in China had exerted pressure on the central government. A proposal was subsequently submitted to the NPC arguing that 'Given the crisis in national security, unification, and military construction, and facing the threat of US military hegemony and the revival of Japanese militarism, defence spending for China's military is seriously inadequate, and has been hidden peril for a long time'.[33]

Taiwan did not increase its military expenditure during 1999, in spite of increased tension with China in that year. Its defence budget for 1999 actually fell by 12 per cent in real terms, and the defence burden fell from 3.5 to 2.9 per cent of GDP. While the government recognizes a need for increased

---

[28] Ebata, K., 'Japan reveals FY00 defence spending', *Jane's Defence Weekly*, vol. 33, no. 2 (12 Jan. 2000), p. 4; and 'Japan drafts its largest-ever budget', *St Petersburg Times*, 21 Jan. 2000, p. 16.

[29] 'Japan seeks bigger defence budget', *Air Letter*, 2 Sep. 1999, p. 4. The Japan Defense Agency (JDA) is the Japanese equivalent of a ministry of defence.

[30] See also chapter 8, section II in this volume.

[31] 'PLA wins budget boost for business ban', *Air Letter*, 5 Mar. 1999, p. 4; Xinhua Hong Kong Service, 8 Mar. 1999, in 'PLA General defends 1999 military budget', Foreign Broadcast Information Service, *Daily Report–China (FBIS-CHI)*, FBIS-CHI-1999-0310, 8 Mar. 1999; Zhongguo Xinwen She, 15 Jan. 1999, 1002 GMT, in 'China: armed forces' budget increased after commercial ban', FBIS-CHI-99-018, 20 Jan. 1999; and *Ta Kung Pao* (Hong Kong), 6 Dec. 1998, p. A2, in 'Hu Angang on military spending, reform', FBIS-CHI-98-350, 21 Dec. 1998.

[32] Wang (note 4).

[33] 'Mainland military expenditures show sustained increase', *Inside China Mainland* (Taipei), June 1999, p. 41.

Table 5.6. Chinese military expenditure, 1995–99

Figures in italics are percentages.

Item	1995	1996	1997	1998	1999B
'National defence' (official, b. yuan, current)	63.67	72.01	81.26	92.86	104.65
'National defence' (US $b., current)	7.6	8.7	9.8	11.2	12.6
Other military expenditure (b. yuan):					
People's Armed Police, PAP	7.39	9.02	10.90	13.17	..
Off-budget military expenditure	26.8	30.0	33.8	38.1	..
of which commercial earnings	7.6	8.6	9.8	9.9	2.2
Arms imports (extra-budgetary)	6.1	12.5	12.5	12.5	..
PLA revenues from arms exports	0.5	0.5	0.2	0.1	..
SIPRI estimates:					
Military expenditure (b. yuan, current)	104.5	124.0	138.7	155.6	166.3
Military exp. (constant 1995 US $b.)	12.5	13.7	14.9	16.9	18.4
Military expenditure/GDP (%)	*1.8*	*1.8*	*1.9*	*1.9*	*[2.0]*

Notes: Figures show actual expenditure except where otherwise indicated. B = budget. The SIPRI estimate for total military expenditure in 1999 is derived by applying the percentage change (12.7%) in the official figure for 'national defence' to the SIPRI estimate of total military expenditure in 1998, taking account of the reduction in commercial earnings, as shown in the table. GDP for 1999 is estimated on the basis of the first 9 months.

Sources: Shaoguang Wang, 'The military expenditure of China, 1989–98', *SIPRI Yearbook 1999: Armaments, Disarmament and International Security* (Oxford University Press: Oxford, 1999), pp. 334–49; and Xinhua (Hong Kong), 8 Mar. 1999, 0926 GMT, 'PLA general defends 1999 military budget', Foreign Broadcast Information Service, *Daily Report–China (FBIS-CHI)*, FBIS-CHI-99-0310, 11 Mar. 1999.

military expenditure, it also acknowledges the limitations of the budget. Therefore, according to Prime Minister Vincent Siew, the 2000 defence budget should remain at the same level as that for 1999, but the aim is to achieve more with less economic resources. However, the realism of this policy has been questioned, among others by the prime minister himself.[34]

Military expenditure in the industrializing countries in East Asia has historically been related to economic growth. In 1999 the East Asian economies began to grow again. While there was no immediate correlation with their military expenditure, as can be seen in the declining shares of military expenditure in GDP for South Korea, the Philippines and Thailand (table 5.7), *Malaysia* increased its 1999 defence budget by considerably more than its economic growth during the year, by a full 39 per cent in real terms—a rate of increase five times higher than that of the total government budget, resulting in a significantly increased share of military expenditure in GDP. Almost the entire increase in the defence budget was allocated to 'development expenditure', roughly the same as capital expenditure, which has been declining since 1995 and was cut by almost 50 per cent in the aftermath of the financial

[34] Taiwan Central News Agency WWW, 19 Oct. 1999, in 'Premier urges no more cuts in defence budget', FBIS-CHI-1999-1019, 20 Oct. 1999.

Table 5.7. East Asia: military expenditure in five countries, 1990–99

Figures are in US $b., at constant 1995 prices and exchange rates. Figures in italics are percentage changes over previous year.

	1990	1991	1992	1993	1994	1995	1996	1997	1998	1999
Military expenditure										
East Asia	95.1	97.9	103	104	105	108	111	114	113	114
% change	*2.9*	*2.9*	*5.1*	*0.5*	*1.1*	*2.8*	*3.6*	*2.6*	*−0.7*	*0.1*
Indonesia	2.15	2.19	2.35	2.26	2.50	2.51	2.77	3.63	2.39	[2.32]
% change	*10.6*	*1.7*	*7.6*	*−4.0*	*10.5*	*0.6*	*10.3*	*31.1*	*−34.3*	*−2.9*
Korea, South	11.7	12.6	13.1	13.0	13.6	14.4	15.5	15.6	15.2	15.0
% change	*3.7*	*8.3*	*3.9*	*−1.0*	*4.8*	*5.9*	*7.3*	*0.5*	*−2.5*	*−1.1*
Malaysia	1.50	2.04	2.03	2.16	2.34	2.44	2.35	2.21	1.61	2.24
% change	*7.4*	*36.1*	*−0.6*	*6.3*	*8.3*	*4.5*	*−3.9*	*−6.0*	*−27.1*	*39.1*
Philippines	0.94	0.85	0.85	0.96	1.03	1.19	1.15	1.26	1.18	[1.05]
% change	*−19.0*	*−9.0*	*−0.5*	*13.2*	*6.5*	*15.8*	*−3.0*	*9.5*	*−6.4*	*−10.5*
Thailand	2.48	2.66	3.00	3.29	3.32	3.57	3.56	3.51	3.27	2.65
% change	*2.9*	*7.5*	*12.5*	*9.8*	*1.0*	*7.5*	*−0.2*	*−1.5*	*−6.8*	*−18.9*
Military expenditure as share of GDP (%)										
Indonesia	1.6	1.4	1.4	1.3	1.3	1.2	1.3	1.5	1.0	[1.0]
Korea, South	3.7	3.7	3.5	3.3	3.1	2.9	3.0	2.9	3.1	2.9
Malaysia	2.6	3.3	3.0	3.0	2.9	2.8	2.4	2.1	1.7	2.3
Philippines	1.4	1.3	1.3	1.4	1.4	1.6	1.5	1.5	1.4	[1.3]
Thailand	2.2	2.2	2.3	2.3	2.2	2.1	2.0	2.1	2.1	1.7

Source: Appendix 5A, tables 5A.3 and 5A.4; and the SIPRI military expenditure database.

crisis.[35] Priority was given to development expenditure in order to enable Malaysia to resume some of the procurement programmes that were cancelled or postponed during the budget reductions of 1998.[36]

South Korea has cut its military budget by 3.5 per cent in real terms since 1997 for economic reasons. In order to avoid the cancellation of arms procurement programmes, significant reallocations are being made within the defence budget. Over the five years 2000–2004 the proportion of allocations for 'force improvement programmes'—primarily for 'import of high-cost weapons'—will be raised at the expense of allocations for O&M.[37]

The decline in *Myanmar's* military expenditure over the three-year period 1996–98 was broken in 1999, with an increase of 11 per cent in real terms in order to build up the capability of its armed forces. It was argued that the equipment left after its long civil war is too old for the maintenance of its

[35] Malaysian Treasury, 'Economic report 1999/2000', URL <http://www2.treasury.gov.my/er992k/report.htm>, and 'Economic report 1998/1999', URL <http://www2.treasury.gov.my/er9899/er9899.htm>; and 'Exclusive interview with Malaysia's Defence Minister', *Asian Defence Journal*, no. 9 (1998), pp. 18, 20.

[36] Sengupta, P. K., 'Malaysia's force modernisation plans back on stream', *Asian Defence Journal*, Dec. 1999, pp. 14–17.

[37] South Korean Ministry of National Defense, *Defense White Paper 1998/99* (Ministry of National Defense: [Seoul, 1999]), chapters on 'Mid-term defense program and 1999 defense budget' and 'Force improvement programs for advanced weapon systems', pp. 133–39 and 140–55, respectively.

national security.[38] While military expenditure in Myanmar constitutes a fairly typical share of GDP (about 3 per cent), its share in government expenditure is high (about 30 per cent), in particular in comparison with expenditure on education and health, which were allocated 10 and 2.5 per cent, respectively, for FY 1998/99.[39]

The long-term rising trend in East Asia is likely to continue. Major procurement plans remain in place in several countries. Related not to short-term changes in regional security but to long-term defence plans, they were only suspended by the financial crisis of 1997–98 and are still awaiting implementation in countries such as Malaysia, Taiwan and Thailand.[40]

VII. Russia

The military expenditure of the Russian Federation, which has been declining rapidly since the disintegration of the Soviet Union, increased in 1999. This was due partly to supplementary allocations to finance the Russian forces in KFOR and cover the costs of the war in Chechnya, but mainly to improved economic performance, which made possible a much higher rate of budget implementation than previously. The budget adopted for 2000 includes allocations for 'national defence' at an unchanged level in real terms and is likely to be more fully implemented than the budgets for previous years.

Implementation of the defence budget for 1999

Total Russian military expenditure, according to the SIPRI definition, rose by 24 per cent in real terms in 1999 (table 5.8).[41] The increase in the official 'national defence' budget head was somewhat greater.[42] In contrast to previous years, actual expenditure exceeded budget by 25 per cent (table 5.8). For the five years 1994–98 actual military expenditure was far short of budget, as can be seen by comparing tables 5.8 and 5.9. Military expenditure has been set to grow in each budget, but because of economic difficulties the budget has been far from fully implemented, resulting in a sharp decline in actual military expenditure. In 1999, however, allocations were exceeded in most categories of military expenditure—in some more than others: expenditure for military pensions exceeded budget by 41 per cent and the military expenditure of the Ministry for Atomic Energy (Minatom) was 93 per cent over budget (3728 million rather than 1933 million roubles) in 1999.

[38] AFP (Hong Kong), 19 May 1999, 0135 GMT, in 'Official: Burma completes military buildup', Foreign Broadcast Information Service, *Daily Report–East Asia (FBIS-EAS)*, FBIS-EAS-1999-0518, 20 May 1999.

[39] IMF Country Report no. 99/134 (International Monetary Fund: Washington, DC, Nov. 1999).

[40] *East Asian Strategic Review 1998/99* (National Institute for Defense Studies Japan: Tokyo, 1999), pp. 33–35.

[41] It almost doubled in nominal terms, from 85.6 billion roubles in 1998 to 171.1 billion roubles in 1999. Applying inflation as measured by the annual average change in the GDP deflator over the year, of 61%, this results in a 24% real increase. Using instead the inflation rate most commonly used in the Russian budget process, of 36.5% Dec. 1998–Dec. 1999, the 1999 rise in Russian military expenditure is 46% in real terms.

[42] It more than doubled in nominal terms from 56.7 billion roubles in 1998 to 116.3 billion roubles in 1999. Applying inflation as measured by the GDP deflator, this was a 27% real increase.

Table 5.8. The Russian Federation: military expenditure, 1992–2000

Figures in italics are percentages.

	National defence[a] (m. current roubles)	Total military expenditure[b] (m. current roubles)	Total military expenditure[b] (constant 1995 US $m.)[c]	GDP (b. current roubles)	National defence as % of GDP	Total military expenditure as % of GDP
1992	855	1 049	47.5	19.1	*4.5*	*5.5*
1993	7 213	9 037	41.9	171.5	*4.2*	*5.3*
1994	28 500	35 890	40.5	610.7	*4.7*	*5.9*
1995	49 600	63 220	25.7	1 540.5	*3.2*	*4.1*
1996	63 891	82 485	23.4	2 145.7	*3.0*	*3.8*
1997B	[104 318]	[133 562]	..	[2 725.0]	*[3.8]*	*[4.9]*
1997	79 692	105 034	24.9	2 521.9	*3.2*	*4.2*
1998B[d]	[81 765]	..	..	[2 840.0]	*[2.9]*	..
1998B[e]	[92 763]	[116 802]	..	[2 840.0]	*[3.3]*	*[4.1]*
1998[d]	56 704	..	..	2 684.5	*2.1*	..
1998[e]	68 004	85 574	18.1	2 684.5	*2.5*	*3.2*
1999B[d]	[93 703]	..	..	[4 000.0]	*[2.3]*	..
1999B[e]	[107 083]	[136 696]	..	[4 000.0]	*[2.7]*	*[3.4]*
1999[d]	116 297	..	..	4 476.0	*2.6*	..
1999[e]	135 116	171 096	22.4	4 476.0	*3.0*	*3.8*
2000B[d]	[140 852]	..	..	[5 350.0]	*[2.6]*	..
2000B[e]	[161 134]	[212 025]	[23.3]	[5 350.0]	*[3.0]*	*[4.0]*

Notes: Figures show actual expenditure if not otherwise indicated. B = budget as first adopted and signed into law.

[a] Military pensions were included in the budget chapter 'national defence' before 1998. From 1998 this table also provides a figure for national defence including pensions.

[b] Total military expenditure (the SIPRI figure) includes military pensions and military-related items under other budget chapters, such as expenditures for paramilitary forces and military research and development (R&D).

[c] Constant dollar figures are in PPP terms with 1995 as the base year.

[d] Excluding military pensions.

[e] Including military pensions.

Sources: Professor Julian Cooper, using: **1992–96 and 1997B**: Cooper, J., 'The military expenditure of the USSR and the Russian Federation, 1987–97', *SIPRI Yearbook 1998: Armaments, Disarmament and International Security* (Oxford University Press: Oxford, 1998), appendix 6D; **1997 (actual expenditure)**: Russian Ministry of Finance, URL <http://www.minfin.ru/isp/3.htm>; **1998B**: *Rossiyskaya Gazeta,* 31 Mar. 1998; **1998 (actual)**: Russian Ministry of Finance report on budget execution, URL <http://www.minfin.ru/isp/>; **1999B**: *Sobraniye Zakonodatelstva Rossiyskoy Federatsii* [Collection of legislation of the Russian Federation], no. 9 (1999), article 1093 (budget as adopted 22 Feb. 1999); **1999 (actual)**: Russian Ministry of Finance, 'On the preliminary results of the execution of the federal budget of the Russian Federation for 1999' (in Russian), URL <http://www.minfin.ru/budjet99.htm>, 24 Feb. 2000; **2000B**, see table 5.9. PPP rate for 1995: *World Bank Atlas 1997* (World Bank: Washington, DC, 1997), p. 37.

Table 5.9. The Russian Federation defence budgets, disaggregated, 1995–2000

Figures are in m. current roubles. Figures in italics are percentages.

	1994	1995	1996	1997	1998	1999	2000
'National defence':							
Ministry of Defence (MOD)							
Personnel/O&M	22 105	31 881	41 120	48 661	46 160	59 064	..
Investment:	15 653	21 349	27 324	39 679	29 246	32 556	..
Procurement	8 442	10 275	13 213	20 963	15 146	..	..
R&D	2 433	4 936	6 474	11 575	10 800	..	..
Construction	4 778	6 138	7 637	7 141	3 300	..	..
Military reform	0	0	0	0	3 995	0	0
Total MOD	**37 758**	**53 230**	**68 444**	**88 340**	**79 401**	**91 620**	**137 780**
Military items of the Ministry for Atomic Energy (Minatom)	874	1 017	1 512	2 095	2 095	1 933	2 909
Total MOD+Minatom	**38 632**	**54 247**	**69 956**	**90 435**	**81 496**	**93 553**	**140 689**
Other items	70	265	330	24	267	150	163
National defence	**38 702**	**54 512**	**70 286**	**90 459**	**81 763**	**93 703**	**140 852**
Military pensions	1 994	4 867	9 899	13 859	11 000	13 380	20 282
'National defence' including pensions	**40 696**	**59 379**	**80 185**	**104 318**	**92 763**	**107 083**	**161 134**
Additional exp. to MOD:							
Fund for military reform	0	0	0	0	0	2 475	0
From Federal Road Fund	0	0	0	0	0	0	5 500
Total additional	**0**	**0**	**0**	**0**	**0**	**2 475**	**5 500**
Other military expenditure:							
Paramilitary forces	5 059	7 852	12 382	16 842	14 626	17 494	25 716
Interior troops	1 129	1 798	3 252	4 147	3 714	4 043	5 787
Border troops	1 800	2 901	3 988	5 765	3 943	5 402	7 727
Security services	2 130	3 153	5 142	6 930	6 969	8 049	12 202
Peacekeeping operations[a]	0	0	0	0	0	443	1 625

Military-related R&D[c]	(1 683)	(2 485)	(3 855)	(5 086)	(3 719)	(4 654)	(6 371)
Closed towns/Baikonur[d]	583	(1 239)	2 653	3317	3000	2 361	9 125
Mobilization preparation	70	68	81	888	772	450	484
Total other	**(8 232)**	**(11 644)**	**(22 295)**	**(29 244)**	**(24 039)**	**(27 138)**	**(45 391)**
Total military exp.	**(48 928)**	**(71 023)**	**(102 480)**	**(133 562)**	**(116 802)**	**(136 696)**	**(212 025)**
From 1% income tax	0	0	0	0	0	8 403	0
Total gov. exp.	194 495	284 778	435 750	529 765	499 945	575 047	855 073
Mil. exp./total government exp. (%)	25.2	24.9	23.5	25.2	23.4	25.8	24.8
GDP according to budget ($b.)	7 250	1 650	2 300	2 725	2 848	4 000	5 350
Military exp./GDP (%)	6.7	4.3	4.5	4.9	4.1	3.4	4.0

Notes: The data in this table refer to the budget as adopted. Actual expenditures differed from these figures, in some years significantly. See table 5.8. The figures for 'national defence' are the official Russian figures on military expenditure.

[a] Russian participation in peacekeeping in Bosnia and Herzegovina and Kosovo.

[b] Allocations for the destruction of weapon systems and for other measures to fulfil international arms control agreements, in so far as they are allocated to organizations of the MOD.

[c] Military R&D estimated as one-third of the total budget on science for the years 1992–97. For the 3 years 1998–2000 this share was increased to 40% to compensate for the removal of space research to a separate budget head.

[d] Subsidies to closed towns and expenditures for the Baikonur space centre.

Source: Professor Julian Cooper, using: **1994:** *Sobraniye Zakonodatelstva Rossiyskoy Federatsii*, no. 10 (1994), art. 1108 (budget as adopted, 1 July 1994); and *Proekt, Federalny Byudzhet Rossiyskoy Federatsii na 1995 god*, Moscow, Oct. 1994; **1995:** *Rossiyskaya Gazeta*, 4 Jan. 1996 (final version of 1995 budget, adopted 27 Dec. 1995). Note: the initial version, adopted 31 Mar. 1995, included an allocation to national defence of 48 577 billion roubles (*Rossiyskaya Gazeta*, 7 Apr. 1995); revised again on 12 Aug. 1995 to 50 854 billion roubles (*Sobraniye Zakonodatelstva RF*, no. 35 (1995), art. 3502); **1996:** *Rossiyskaya Gazeta*, 10 Jan. 1996 (budget as adopted 31 Dec. 1995). This budget was not revised; **1997:** *Rossiyskaya Gazeta*, 4 Mar. 1997 (budget as adopted 26 Feb. 1997). Note: the budget was revised on 30 Apr. 1997, with the approval of a law on sequestration: national defence reduced to 83 177 billion roubles (*Sobraniye Zakonodatelstva RF*, no. 35 (1997), art. 3502); **1998:** *Rossiyskaya Gazeta*, 31 Mar. 1998 (budget as adopted, 26 Mar. 1998); **1999:** *Sobraniye Zakonodatelstva RF*, no. 9 (1999), art. 1093 (budget as adopted 22 Feb. 1999); **2000:** budget as adopted, 31 Dec. 1999, <URL http://www.rg.ru/official/federal_zakon>, accessed 20 Jan. 2000. **GDP estimates** are those on which the federal budgets are based: **1994:** Sinelnikov, S., *Byudzhetny Krizis v Rossii: 1985–1995 Gody* (Evraziya: Moscow, 1995), pp. 110, 152; **1995–99:** calculated from sources for budget data, as above.

The defence budget debate in the Russian Federation has been focused on the target set by President Boris Yeltsin in July 1998 of defence expenditure of 3.5 per cent of GDP.[43] As can be seen in table 5.8, this target was not met for 'national defence' in 1999. However, total military expenditure corresponded to 3.8 per cent of GDP in 1999.

The budget adopted for 2000

The budget for 2000 was signed into law by Yeltsin on 31 December 1999 (his last day in office). This was earlier than has been the practice: only once before has the budget of the Russian Federation been adopted before the beginning of the financial year. In contrast to previous years, the defence budget for 2000 does not provide for an increase in real terms. Expenditure for 'national defence' was budgeted to rise by roughly the same rate as inflation (21 per cent over actual expenditure in 1999: forecast inflation for 2000 in the federal budget is 18–20 per cent). The share of the defence budget in total federal expenditure is also roughly the same as in that for 1999—16 per cent for national defence and 25 per cent for total military expenditure (table 5.9).

The main difference in the defence budget for 2000 appears to lie in its shift of priorities, shown in higher-than-average increases for arms procurement, military research and development (R&D), paramilitary forces and peace-keeping operations. The increases in the two latter can be seen in table 5.9. The two former cannot be seen there because the level of disaggregation is insufficient but can be inferred from the announcements about the large increases in the state defence order for 2000, adopted in January 2000, which received extensive press coverage. The state defence order—government orders to industry and elsewhere—is based on the state budget and includes orders for arms procurement and military R&D, not only for the armed forces but also for the Ministry of the Interior security forces. The state defence order for 2000, at 62 billion roubles, was 50 per cent higher than that for 1999[44] and included a significant increase in the allocation for 'scientific research and experimental designing'. The structure of the order was also revised to reveal more information, changing from a division into four main segments (purchase of armaments, purchases of *matériel*, repairs and construction) to 50 budget categories within the 'fundamental economic law'. The highest-priority sector was reportedly military aerospace.[45]

Considering the weakness of the link between budgeted and actual expenditure in Russia in the past, a relevant question is whether the defence budget

[43] This target is provided for in 'The basics (concept) of the state policy of the Russian Federation on military development until the year 2005', Presidential directive no. 1068-Pr, 30 July 1998 (unpublished). Arbatov, A., 'Russia: military reform', *SIPRI Yearbook 1999* (note 4), p. 197.

[44] ITAR-TASS, 14 Jan. 2000, in 'Russian defence orders seen working more effectively', Foreign Broadcast Information Service, *Daily Report–Central Eurasia (FBIS-SOV)*, FBIS-SOV-2000-0114, 18 Jan. 2000; 'Putin vows to beef up military as troops struggle in Grozny', *International Herald Tribune*, 28 Jan. 2000, p. 5; and 'Putin to double Russian arms spending', *Guardian Weekly*, 28 Jan. 2000.

[45] Statement by Deputy Prime Minister Ilya Klebanov. ITAR-TASS, 23 Nov. 1999, in 'Russia defense budget to be rearranged', FBIS-SOV-1999-1123, 24 Nov. 1999.

for 2000 will actually be implemented. The government itself is confident that it will be: this is illustrated in its resolution of January 2000 stipulating that there should be full implementation of all budget expenditure.[46] How far this expectation is realized will depend both on the performance of the Russian economy and, in the shorter term, on the development of the Russian foreign debt, budget deficit and prospects of renewing the agreements with Western creditors after the suspension of foreign economic aid in October 1999. The economy appears to be recovering. Most economic indicators showed an improvement in early or mid-1999.[47] Although the inflation forecast for 2000 may be somewhat exceeded, at the time the budget was adopted the excess was not expected to be large. The prospects of easing the debt burden also seemed relatively good. While a final solution to the problem of the debt inherited from the Soviet Union, amounting to over $100 billion—including $42 billion to government (Paris Club) creditors and $32 billion to commercial (London Club) creditors[48]—was not expected to be achieved, the Russian Government assumed that 35–40 per cent of these debts would be written off during the year 2000 and that payment of the remaining debt would be post-poned for 30 years.[49] The government has also committed itself to a repayment schedule to the IMF, amounting to $3.6 billion during 2000 on a total debt to the IMF of $15.2 billion as of January 2000.[50] While the federal budget for 2000 provides for revenues from the IMF to help finance debt repayment, by early February 2000 there was still no agreement on new loans with the inter-national credit organizations and negotiations were not expected to resume until May 2000, after the Russian presidential elections and the installation of a new director for the IMF; however, the IMF mission to Russia in January 2000 came to very positive conclusions and, although no formal new credit arrangement could be established, there were no objections to further IMF loans.[51] The meeting between the Russian Government and the London Club creditors in mid-February also gave positive results.[52]

[46] Interfax (Moscow), 25 Jan. 2000, in 'Khristenko: Russia's 2000 budget not to be sequestered', FBIS-SOV-2000-0125, 27 Jan. 2000.

[47] *Russian Economic Trends, Monthly Update* (Russian–European Centre for Economic Policy, RECEP, in cooperation with the Working Centre for Economic Reform, Government of the Russian Federation), Feb. 2000.

[48] Ware, R., 'The prospects for Russia', House of Commons Research Paper 99/87, London, 8 Nov. 1999.

[49] This was reported by First Deputy Finance Minister Aleksey Kudrin at a meeting of the Russian Ministry of the Economy. *Rossiyskaya Gazeta*, 11 Feb. 2000, in '"Final solution" seen unlikely in Russia–London Club talks', FBIS-SOV-2000-0211, 14 Feb. 2000.

[50] ITAR-TASS (Moscow), 18 Jan. 2000, in 'Russia repays $249 million of IMF debt in Jan.', FBIS-SOV-2000-0118, 19 Jan. 2000.

[51] ITAR-TASS (Moscow), 4 Feb. 2000, in 'IMF mission agreed on budget policy for 2000', FBIS-SOV-2000-0204, 7 Feb. 2000.

[52] Interfax (Moscow), 15 Feb. 2000, in 'Putin satisfied with talks with London Club', FBIS-SOV-0215, 16 Feb. 2000.

Table 5.10. Military and arms procurement expenditure in the Czech Republic, Hungary and Poland, 1995–99

	1995	1996	1997	1998	1999
Czech Republic					
Total military expenditure					
(m. current korunas)	22 275	30 509	31 328	37 643	41 484
(US $m., 1995 prices and exchange rates)	839	1 057	1 000	1 086	1 175
Procurement (m. current korunas)	2 978	3 739	3 072	3 765	7 933
(US $m., 1995 prices and exchange rates)	112	129	98	109	225
Procurement as % of total military expenditure	*13.4*	*12.3*	*9.8*	*10.0*	*19.1*
GDP (m. current korunas)	1 381 100	1 572 300	1 680 000	1 820 700	1 806 639
Military expenditure as % of GDP	*1.6*	*1.9*	*1.9*	*2.1*	*2.3*
Hungary					
Total military expenditure					
(m. current forints)	76 937	85 954	96 814	134 570	164 051
(US $m., 1995 prices and exchange rates)	612	554	527	641	715
Procurement (m. current forints)	1 319	1 907	1 994	1 852	2 791
(US $m., 1995 prices and exchange rates)	10	12	11	9	12
Procurement as % of total military expenditure	*1.7*	*2.2*	*2.1*	*1.4*	*1.7*
GDP (m. current forints)	5 561 900	6 823 300	8 461 600	10 162 600	11 442 000
Military expenditure as % of GDP	*1.4*	*1.3*	*1.1*	*1.3*	*1.4*
Poland					
Total military expenditure					
(m. current zlotys)	6 595	8 313	10 077	11 687	12 587
(US $m., 1995 prices and exchange rates)	2 720	2 852	2 983	3 097	3 144
Procurement (m. current zlotys)	712	701	1 557	1 817	1 902
(US $m., 1995 prices and exchange rates)	294	240	461	482	475
Procurement as % of total military expenditure	*10.8*	*8.4*	*15.5*	*15.5*	*15.1*
GDP (m. current zlotys)	306 318	385 448	469 372	550 930	611 307
Military expenditure as % of GDP	*2.2*	*2.2*	*2.1*	*2.1*	*2.1*

Source: SIPRI questionnaires. Responses: Czech Republic, 28 June 1999; Hungary, 20 May 1999; Poland, 10 June 1999.

VIII. Central and Eastern Europe

Combined military expenditure for Central and Eastern Europe (excluding the members of the Commonwealth of Independent States, CIS) fell by 16 per cent in real terms over the 10-year period 1990–99. Most of the countries of the region cut their military expenditure sharply: Albania, Bulgaria and Romania more than halved theirs over these 10 years. The three Baltic states have had a flat or increasing trend in their military expenditure since they gained independence in 1991, while at least three of the four states which emerged from the former Yugoslavia—Croatia, Macedonia and Slovenia—have not increased their military expenditure since independence. The Kosovo war had a major impact on the economies of the Balkan region, especially the countries around the war zone—Albania, Bosnia, Bulgaria, Croatia, Macedonia and Romania.

In 1999 the largest decline in military expenditure in the region was experienced in *Croatia*—by about 25 per cent in real terms. This fall was partly due to shortcomings in state revenue collection and partly to the adverse overall economic situation as a consequence of the war against the FRY, which has held up the economic development of Croatia.[53] In *Slovenia,* which hopes to join NATO in the medium term, military expenditure has been roughly constant since 1992, the year the country came into existence. However, Slovenia plans to increase military expenditure from the present level of 1.5 per cent to 2.3 per cent of GDP by 2010.[54]

In the Baltic states there is also much interest in joining NATO at some stage and large increases in defence budgets are planned. *Estonia's* current long-term defence plans call for spending to be increased from the present 1.2 per cent to 2 per cent of GDP; in order to ensure accession *Latvia* and *Lithuania* have committed themselves to increase their military expenditure as a share of GDP from their present 0.7 and 1.3 per cent, respectively, to at least 2 per cent.[55]

The challenge for the new NATO members—the *Czech Republic, Hungary* and *Poland*—is to modernize and restructure their armed forces and work towards interoperability with NATO forces. The shift of priorities this implies within military budgets is difficult. Personnel costs represent a large share of defence spending in most countries, at the expense of, for example, procurement.

---

[53] Zunec, O., 'Revised military expenditure in Croatia 1999', Zagreb, 30 Oct. 1999; data based on 'State budget of the Republic of Croatia for 1999', Dec. 1999; 'Revisions and amendments of the state budget of the Republic of Croatia for 1999', 7 July 1999; and (for military pensions) 'Jutarnji list', Zagreb, 3 Apr. 1999, unpublished papers prepared for SIPRI.

[54] 'Slovenia to up defence spending to 2.3% of GDP', *Air Letter*, 28 June 1999, p. 5.

[55] Woehrel, S., Kim, J. and Ek, C., *NATO Applicant States: a Status Report*, CRS Report for Congress (Congressional Research Service, Library of Congress: Washington, DC, 11 May 1999), pp. CRS-11, CRS-15, CRS-18-19; and 'Baltic states must firm defence budgets for NATO', *New Europe, The Baltics*, 26 July–1 Aug. 1999, p. 29.

In 1999 the three countries reported their military expenditures to NATO for the first time, this being the year of their accession. It is difficult to compare the figures reported to NATO with those which SIPRI has received from their respective governments because NATO and national definitions differ and it is not known exactly how they differ. NATO disaggregated figures diverge considerably from those reported to SIPRI by these countries. They also include a residual category called 'other expenditure', accounting for roughly 30 per cent of total military expenditure in these countries, without defining what is included under this heading.[56]

All three increased their military expenditure in real terms between 1995 and 1999 (table 5.10). Procurement expenditure increased over the same period, given their objective of developing their armed forces to meet their new commitments in NATO. They all plan to modernize their air forces with advanced combat aircraft but decisions have had to be deferred, mainly for financial reasons. However, the Czech Republic in 1997 ordered 72 L-159 light combat aircraft; deliveries began in 1999. The whole programme is estimated to cost about $1 billion.[57] In the case of Hungary, out-of-area deployments, particularly in Kosovo, have required significant budget resources that are to be paid out of the military budget. Hungary spent about 4 billion forints ($17 million) for its KFOR mission in 1999 and this expenditure will rise to about 5.5 billion forints ($23 million) in 2000.[58] It plans to increase its defence budget by 43 per cent in nominal terms over the next five years, to reach 287.9 billion forints by the year 2004.[59] Poland's total military expenditure will rise by about 14 per cent in 2000, but no further increase in procurement expenditure is planned.[60] Polish Deputy Defence Minister Romuald Szeremietiew expects the Parliament and the Ministry of Finance to secure extra financing of $1.5–3 billion for planned acquisitions of combat aircraft.[61]

IX. The USA

The downward trend in US post-cold war military expenditure ended in 1998. In 1999 US military expenditure increased by 1.5 per cent in real terms according to the NATO standardized data used by SIPRI (table 5.2). During the six-year period FY 2000–2005, planned military expenditure will remain roughly

[56] 'Financial and economic data relating to NATO defence, 1975–1999', *Atlantic News*, no. 3162 (Annex), 8 Dec. 1999, pp. 1–7.

[57] *Jane's All the World's Aircraft, 1999–2000* (Jane's Information Ltd: Coulsdon, 1999), pp. 86–87.

[58] 'Der Ungarische beitrag bei der KFOR' [The Hungarian contribution to KFOR], *Allgemeine Schweizerische Militärzeitschrift*, vol. 165, no. 10 (Oct. 1999), p. 46; and *Vilaggazdasag*, 17 June 1999, reported by MTI (Budapest), 17 June 1999, 0933 GMT, in 'Defence budget deficit to reach 10 billion forints', Foreign Broadcast Information Service, *Daily Report–East Europe (FBIS-EEU)*, FBIS-EEU-1999-0617, 18 June 1999, p. 1.

[59] *Magyar Hirlap* (Budapest), 21 July 1999, in 'Government decree on army review to go public today', FBIS-EEU-1999-0721 (22 July 1999), pp. 1–2; and 'Hungary announces budget increase', *Jane's Defence Weekly*, vol. 32, no. 13 (29 Sep. 1999), p. 14.

[60] Reply to SIPRI questionnaire by the Polish Ministry of Defence, 10 June 1999; and *Rzeczpospolita*, 27 Oct. 1999, p. A2, in 'Polish Deputy MOD on purchases', FBIS-EEU-1999-1029, 20 Nov. 1999, pp. 1–2.

[61] 'Financial constraints delay Polish fighter deal', *Air Letter*, 28 Oct. 1999, p. 1.

constant in real terms with a slight increase in FY 2001. While slight expenditure reductions are planned for personnel and O&M, the plan provides for large increases in arms procurement, which already received a significant increase in FY 2000. Although the US Government in 1999 decided to add $112 billion for the period FY 2000–2005 in planned military spending[62] (as provided in the 2000 Future Years Defense Program, FYDP), it is still unclear whether this is sufficient to finance currently planned requirements.

The adoption of the defence budget for FY 2000

During the congressional decision-making process on the FY 2000 defence budget, Congress added significant amounts under some of the headings to the budget proposed by the administration of President Bill Clinton. It also introduced several major changes to the defence budget during 1999 in supplementary allocations to the budget already adopted for FY 1999 (1 October 1998–30 September 1999) and to the proposed defence budget for FY 2000.

The administration budget request for FY 2000, as presented in February 1999, included $280.8 billion for national defence.[63] Preceded by a wide-ranging debate about the deteriorating conditions in the US armed forces, it responded to complaints by proposing improvement in three priority areas: readiness, quality of life and modernization. The budget proposal therefore included significant increases in the allocations for personnel, O&M and procurement. These increases were the main motivation for the increase in the overall defence budget and accounted for over 90 per cent of the total increase of $50.8 billion over the previous year.[64]

While Congress did not change the total size of the defence budget, significant changes were made to its structure. The largest were the additions for research, development, testing and evaluation (RDT&E) (+ $3.0 billion) and for construction (+ $2.5 billion).[65] At the same time major cuts were made in the administration's request for O&M and some cuts in personnel expenditure. This illustrates the difference between Congress and the administration in the prioritization of functions within the defence budget. However, through the technique of 'emergency funding', in November 1999 Congress provided an additional allocation of $7.2 billion to the FY 2000 defence budget.

Emergency funding is a technique to get around the balanced budget agreement of 1997, by which ceilings or caps were defined for all discretionary spending. Discretionary spending is programmes for which appropriations must be approved every year. They account for about one-third of the federal budget, half of which is for defence and the other half for education, transport,

[62] US Department of Defense, 'Department of Defense budget for FY2001', News release, Office of the Assistant Secretary of Defense (Public Affairs), Washington, DC, 7 Feb. 2000, URL <http://www. dtic.mil/comptroller/fy2001budget/>.

[63] Sköns, E. et al., 'Military expenditure', *SIPRI Yearbook 1999* (note 4), p. 281.

[64] US General Accounting Office, 'Future years defense program: funding increase and planned saving in fiscal year 2000 program are at risk', GAO/NSIAD-00-11, Nov. 1999, p. 5.

[65] Kosiak, S. M. and Heeter, E. E., 'FY 2000 defense budget wrap-up and prospects for the coming year', Center for Strategic and Budgetary Assessments, Washington, DC, Dec. 1999, p. 3.

Table 5.11. US military expenditure, budget authority by function, FY 2000–05

Figures are in US $b. Figures in italics are percentages. Figures do not always add up because of the conventions of rounding.

	Adopted 2000	Request 2001	Planned				% change 2000–2005[a]
			2002	2003	2004	2005	
Constant (FY 2001) prices:							
Department of Defense (DOD):							
Personnel	76.1	75.8	76.0	75.7	76.0	76.0	*± 0.0*
O&M	108.7	109.3	105.5	105.0	105.4	105.3	*– 3.2*
Procurement	55.1	60.3	62.0	64.4	64.0	65.8	*+ 19.5*
RDT&E	39.0	37.9	37.7	36.3	35.4	33.7	*– 13.8*
Construction	4.9	4.5	4.2	3.7	4.3	5.0	*+ 1.5*
Family housing	3.7	3.5	3.7	3.7	3.8	3.8	*+ 3.7*
Total DOD	**287.9**	**291.1**	**288.6**	**288.2**	**288.3**	**288.9**	*+ 0.3*
Annual change (%)	*– 1.6*	*+ 1.1*	*– 0.9*	*– 0.1*	*+ 0.0*	*+ 0.2*	*+ 0.3*
National defence	**301.6**	**305.4**	**302.7**	**302.2**	**302.4**	**302.8**	*+ 0.4*
Annual change (%)	*– 1.7*	*+ 1.3*	*– 0.9*	*– 0.2*	*+ 0.1*	*+ 0.1*	*+ 0.4*
Current prices:							
Total DOD	279.9	291.1	294.8	300.9	308.3	316.4	
National defence	293.3	305.4	309.2	315.6	323.4	331.7	

[a] Changes are calculated before rounding from US $m. to US $b.

Sources: US Department of Defense, Office of the Under Secretary of Defense (Comptroller), 'National Defense Budget Estimates for FY 2001', Washington, DC, Mar. 2000, pp. 102, 109; and US Department of Defense, Office of the Assistant Secretary of Defense, 'Department of Defense budget for FY 2001', News release, Washington, DC, 7 Feb. 2000, both on URL <http://www.dtic.mil/comptroller/fy2001budget/>.

health research, foreign aid and environmental protection. Spending desig-nated 'emergency' is not subject to the spending caps.[66] The technique was used when Congress decided in May 1999 on supplementary appropriations of $9 billion for military expenditure for FY 1999 and of $1.8 billion for FY 2000 to finance the US part of the military intervention in Kosovo.

In May 1999 Congress adopted a supplementary appropriation to finance US military intervention in Kosovo, which added $9 billion to military expen-diture for FY 1999 and $1.8 billion for FY 2000. Additional emergency fund-ing of $7.2 billion was added to the FY 2000 defence budget in November 1999.

The defence budget request for FY 2001

The budget for FY 2001 (October 2000–September 2001) as proposed by the administration on 7 February 2000 included $291.1 billion in budget authority

[66] Kosiak and Heeter (note 65), p. 8.

for the Department of Defense (DOD) and $305.4 billion for national defence (which includes the military expenditure of the Department of Energy (DOE) for nuclear weapons and some military-related activities of other ministries: see table 5.11). This represented an increase of 1 per cent in real terms over the previous year.[67] The two priority areas in this defence budget were 'quality of life' and arms procurement. The emphasis on improved conditions for military personnel included a pay rise of 3.7 per cent—slightly over the forecast rate of growth in civilian wages—a major increase in housing allowance, and improved health care for military personnel and their families.

The allocation for arms procurement was proposed to increase by 9 per cent in real terms to $60.3 billion. This was the third major increase in three consecutive years in procurement; in all procurement funding was set to increase by 29 per cent over the level of FY 1998.

Funding requested for continued development of a national missile defence (NMD) system to protect US territory against intercontinental ballistic missiles amounted to $1.9 billion for FY 2001.[68] The planned total for NMD for the period FY 2001–2005 was $10.4 billion—$2.3 billion more than the plan for that period of one year before. This includes funding for system deployment with initial capability in 2005 if the president decides on deployment later in the year 2000.

The $60 billion level for arms procurement funding is in line with the recommendations of the DOD's 1997 Quadrennial Defense Review (QDR), which analysed US military strategy, force structure, readiness, modernization and infrastructure and constitutes the basis for current US force planning and defence budgeting. Planning for 4–6 years ahead is done through the FYDP. In 2000 the administration added $4.8 billion to its FYDP compared with the previous FYDP, primarily for operations in Bosnia and Kosovo and for higher fuel costs. In 1999 the addition was significantly higher: $50 billion was added for the years FY 2000–03. The addition has been reviewed by the US General Accounting Office in order to assess how realistic it is. The conclusion of this review was that the implementation of the programme 'was at risk', meaning that the DOD may not receive all the funds it expects.[69]

---

[67] US Department of Defense (note 62).
[68] See also chapter 8, section II in this volume.
[69] US General Accounting Office (note 64), pp. 5–7 provides a summary of these results.

Appendix 5A. Tables of military expenditure

ELISABETH SKÖNS, EVAMARIA LOOSE-WEINTRAUB, WUYI OMITOOGUN and PETTER STÅLENHEIM[1]

Sources and methods are explained in appendix 5C. Notes and explanations of the conventions used appear below table 5A.4. Data in this appendix should not be combined with those in previous SIPRI Yearbooks because of revision.[2]

Table 5A.1. Military expenditure by region, in constant US dollars, 1990–99

Figures are in US $b., at constant 1995 prices and exchange rates. Figures do not always add up to totals because of the conventions of rounding.[3]

	1990	1991	1992	1993	1994	1995	1996	1997	1998	1999
World total	**1 007**	..	**818**	**787**	**763**	**724**	**708**	**718**	**[704]**	**[719]**
Geographical regions										
Africa	..	11.1	9.9	9.9	10.0	9.4	8.9	9.3	[9.5]	[10.6]
North Africa	2.4	2.5	2.7	2.9	3.4	3.1	3.2	[3.5]	[3.7]	..
Sub-Saharan Africa	9.5	8.7	7.2	7.0	6.6	6.3	5.8	5.8	5.8	[6.6]
Americas	386	339	359	343	326	312	294	294	[287]	[294]
North America	369	325	343	325	308	290	274	272	266	269
Central America	0.8	0.6	0.6	0.5	0.5	0.5	0.5	0.4	..	..
South America	16.3	13.5	15.6	17.8	17.5	21.3	19.5	22.1	..	..
Asia and Oceania	115	118	124	126	127	130	134	137	137	139
Central Asia	..	..	1.1	1.4	0.9	1.0	1.0	1.2	..	..
East Asia	95.1	97.9	103	104	105	108	111	114	113	114
South Asia	11.6	11.4	11.4	12.4	12.3	12.8	13.0	13.4	13.6	14.5
Oceania	8.2	8.2	8.6	8.9	8.8	8.5	8.4	8.6	8.9	9.3
Europe	442	..	275	260	253	228	226	227	221	226
Central and Eastern Europe	[213]	..	[59.9]	[52.6]	[52.0]	[36.8]	[34.3]	[36.1]	[29.2]	[33.0]
CIS Europe	0	..	[49.3]	[43.6]	[43.2]	[28.0]	[25.6]	[27.3]	[20.4]	[24.6]
Western Europe	229	225	215	207	201	192	192	191	192	194
Middle East	[51.7]	[69.1]	50.0	48.0	47.2	44.9	45.5	50.3	49.5	49.4

Organizations

ASEAN	10.0	10.8	11.5	11.9	12.6	14.2	14.7	19.5	17.0	17.2
CIS	. .	. .	[50.3]	[45.0]	[44.1]	[29.0]	[26.6]	[28.5]	[21.5]	[25.6]
EU	209	206	195	188	183	184	184	183	184	186
NATO	585	538	546	522	498	472	458	454	449	456
OECD	657	610	619	595	572	547	552	550	545	552
OPEC	34.0	50.3	30.5	30.3	28.8	26.6	26.2	31.9	29.2	28.0
OSCE	816	. .	623	590	566	523	506	505	493	504
Income group (GNP/cap. 1995)										
Low (≤ $765)	33.9	33.4	36.3	36.4	35.6	36.3	37.4	39.2	40.6	44.1
Middle ($766–3100)	237	. .	84.3	79.9	80.5	65.2	63.9	68.9	60.4	65.9
Upper-middle ($3101–9385)	54.6	65.4	56.3	58.6	56.8	58.2	56.4	63.1	60.8	61.3
High (≥ $9386)	682	638	641	612	590	564	550	547	542	547

Notes:

Africa: Algeria, Angola, Benin, Botswana, Burkina Faso, Burundi, Cameroon, Cape Verde, Central African Republic, Chad, Comoros, Congo (Republic of), Congo (Democratic Republic of Congo), Côte d'Ivoire, Djibouti, Equatorial Guinea, Eritrea, Ethiopia, Gabon, Gambia, Ghana, Guinea, Guinea-Bissau, Kenya, Lesotho, Liberia, Libya, Madagascar, Malawi, Mali, Mauritania, Mauritius, Morocco, Mozambique, Namibia, Niger, Nigeria, Rwanda, Senegal, Seychelles, Sierra Leone, Somalia, South Africa, Sudan, Swaziland, Tanzania, Togo, Tunisia, Uganda, Zambia, Zimbabwe.

North Africa: Algeria, Libya, Morocco, Tunisia.

Sub-Saharan Africa: Angola, Benin, Botswana, Burkina Faso, Burundi, Cameroon, Cape Verde, Central African Republic, Chad, Congo (Rep. of), Congo (DRC), Côte d'Ivoire, Djibouti, Equatorial Guinea, Eritrea, Ethiopia, Gabon, Gambia, Ghana, Guinea, Guinea-Bissau, Kenya, Lesotho, Liberia, Madagascar, Malawi, Mali, Mauritania, Mauritius, Mozambique, Namibia, Niger, Nigeria, Rwanda, Senegal, Seychelles, Sierra Leone, Somalia, South Africa, Sudan, Swaziland, Tanzania, Togo, Uganda, Zambia, Zimbabwe.

Americas: Argentina, Belize, Bolivia, Brazil, Canada, Chile, Colombia, Costa Rica, Ecuador, El Salvador, Guatemala, Guyana, Honduras, Mexico, Nicaragua, Panama, Paraguay, Peru, Uruguay, USA, Venezuela.

North America: Canada, USA.

Central America: Belize, Costa Rica, El Salvador, Guatemala, Honduras, Mexico, Nicaragua, Panama.

South America: Argentina, Bolivia, Brazil, Chile, Colombia, Ecuador, Guyana, Paraguay, Peru, Uruguay, Venezuela.

Asia: Afghanistan, Bangladesh, Brunei, Cambodia, China, India, Indonesia, Japan, Kazakhstan (1992–), North Korea, South Korea, Kyrgyzstan (1992–), Laos, Malaysia, Mongolia, Myanmar (Burma), Nepal, Pakistan, Philippines, Singapore, Sri Lanka, Taiwan, Tajikistan (1992–), Thailand, Turkmenistan (1992–), Uzbekistan (1992–), Viet Nam.

Central Asia: Kazakhstan (1992–), Kyrgyzstan (1992–), Tajikistan (1992–), Turkmenistan (1992–), Uzbekistan (1992–).

East Asia: Brunei, Cambodia, China, Indonesia, Japan, North Korea, South Korea, Laos, Malaysia, Myanmar (Burma), Philippines, Singapore, Taiwan, Thailand, Viet Nam.

South Asia: Afghanistan, Bangladesh, India, Nepal, Pakistan, Sri Lanka.

Europe: Albania, Armenia (1992–), Austria, Azerbaijan (1992–), Belarus (1992–), Belgium, Bosnia and Herzegovina (1992–), Bulgaria, Croatia (1992–), Cyprus, Czechoslovakia (–1992), Czech Republic (1993–), Denmark, Estonia (1991–), Finland, France, Georgia (1992–), German Democratic Republic (–1990), Germany, Greece, Hungary, Ireland, Italy, Latvia (1991–), Lithuania (1991–), Luxembourg, Macedonia (1992–), Malta, Moldova (1992–), Netherlands, Norway, Poland, Portugal, Romania, Russia (1992–), Slovakia (1993–), Slovenia (1992–), Spain, Sweden, Switzerland, UK, Ukraine (1992–), USSR (–1991), Yugoslavia (former, –1991), Yugoslavia (Serbia and Montenegro, 1992–).

Central and Eastern Europe: Albania, Armenia (1992–), Azerbaijan (1992–), Belarus (1992–), Bosnia and Herzegovina (1992–), Bulgaria, Croatia (1992–), Czechoslovakia (–1992), Czech Republic (–1993), Estonia (1991–), Georgia (1991–), German DR (–1990), Latvia (1991–), Lithuania (1991–), Macedonia (1992–), Moldova (1992–), Poland, Romania, Russia (1992–), Slovakia (1992–), Slovenia (1992–), Ukraine (1992–), USSR (–1991), Yugoslavia (former, –1991), Yugoslavia (Serbia and Montenegro, 1992–).

Commonwealth of Independent States (CIS) Europe: Armenia, Azerbaijan, Belarus, Georgia (1993–), Moldova, Russia, Ukraine.

Western Europe: Austria, Belgium, Cyprus, Denmark, Finland, France, Germany, Greece, Ireland, Italy, Luxembourg, Malta, Netherlands, Norway, Portugal, Spain, Sweden, Switzerland, UK.

Middle East: Bahrain, Egypt, Iran, Iraq, Israel, Jordan, Kuwait, Lebanon, Oman, Qatar, Saudi Arabia, Syria, Turkey, United Arab Emirates, North Yemen (–1990), South Yemen (–1990), Yemen (1991–).

Oceania: Australia, Fiji, New Zealand, Papua New Guinea.

Association of South-East Asian Nations (ASEAN): Brunei, Indonesia, Laos (1997–), Malaysia, Myanmar (Burma) (1997–), the Philippines, Singapore, Thailand, Viet Nam (1995–).

Organization for Security and Co-operation in Europe (OSCE)/Conference on Security and Co-operation in Europe (CSCE): Albania (1991–), Andorra, Armenia (1992–), Austria, Azerbaijan (1992–), Belarus (1992–), Belgium, Bosnia and Herzegovina (1992–), Bulgaria, Canada, Croatia (1992–), Cyprus, Czechoslovakia (–1992), Czech Republic (1993–), Denmark, Estonia (1991–), Finland, France, Georgia (1992–), German Democratic Republic (–1990), Germany, Greece, Holy See, Hungary, Iceland, Ireland, Italy, Kazakhstan (1992–), Kyrgyzstan (1992–), Latvia (1991–), Liechtenstein, Lithuania (1991–), Luxembourg, Macedonia (1995–), Malta, Moldova (1992–), Monaco, Netherlands, Norway, Poland, Portugal, Romania, Russia (1992–), San Marino, Slovakia (1992–), Slovenia (1992–), Spain, Sweden, Switzerland, Tajikistan (1992–), Turkey, Turkmenistan (1992–), UK, Ukraine (1992–), USA, USSR (–1992), Uzbekistan (1992–), Yugoslavia (former, –1991), Yugoslavia (Serbia and Montenegro, suspended since 1992).

Commonwealth of Independent States (CIS): Armenia, Azerbaijan, Belarus, Georgia (1993–), Kazakhstan, Kyrgyzstan, Moldova, Russia, Tajikistan, Turkmenistan, Ukraine, Uzbekistan.

European Union (EU): Austria (1995–), Belgium, Denmark, Finland (1995–), France, Germany, Greece, Ireland, Italy, Luxembourg, Netherlands, Portugal, Spain, Sweden (1995–), UK.

NATO: Belgium, Canada, Czech Republic (1999–), Denmark, France, Germany, Greece, Hungary (1999–), Iceland, Italy, Luxembourg, Netherlands, Norway, Poland (1999–), Portugal, Spain, Turkey, UK, USA.

Organization of the Petroleum-Exporting Countries (OPEC): Algeria, Ecuador (–1992), Gabon (–1995), Indonesia, Iran, Iraq, Kuwait, Libya, Nigeria, Qatar, Saudi Arabia, United Arab Emirates and Venezuela.

Organisation for Economic Co-operation and Development (OECD): Australia, Austria, Belgium, Canada, Czech Republic (1995–), Denmark, Finland, France, Germany, Greece, Hungary (1996–), Iceland, Ireland, Italy, Japan, South Korea (1996–), Luxembourg, Mexico (1994–), Netherlands, New Zealand, Norway, Poland (1996–), Portugal, Spain, Sweden, Switzerland, Turkey, UK, USA.

The country coverage of income groups is based on figures of 1995 GNP per capita as calculated by the World Bank and presented in its *World Development Report 1997* (International Bank for Reconstruction and Development and Oxford University Press: Washington, DC and New York, June 1997).

Totals for geographical regions add up to the world total and subregional totals add up to regional totals. Totals for regions and income groups cover the same group of countries for all years, while totals for organizations cover only the member countries in the year given.

The world total and the totals for regions, organizations and income groups in table 5A.1 are estimates, based on data in table 5A.3. When military expenditure data for a country are missing for a few years, estimates are made, most often on the assumption that the rate of change in that country's military expenditure is the same as that for the subregion to which it belongs. When no estimates can be made, countries are excluded from the totals. The countries excluded from all totals in table 5A.1 are: Afghanistan, Angola, the Republic of Congo (Congo Brazzaville), the Democratic Republic of Congo (DRC), Iraq, Libya, Qatar and Somalia.

Table 5A.2. Military expenditure by region and country, in local currency, 1990–99

Figures are in local currency, current prices.

State	Currency	1990	1991	1992	1993	1994	1995	1996	1997	1998	1999
Africa											
North Africa											
Algeria	m. dinars	[8 470]	10 439	[20 125]	29 810	46 800	58 847	79 519	101 126	112 248	121 600
Libya	m. dinars									..	..
Morocco	m. dirhams	8 816	10 002	10 488	11 071	13 557	13 245	12 602	..	..	..
Tunisia	m. dinars	287	315	319	347	364	326	343	369	398	..
Sub-Saharan											
Angola[4]	m./b./tr. kwanzas	52.0	102	438	| 3.5	130	2 469	| 162	(356)	389	..
Benin	m. francs	8 935									
Botswana	m. pulas	291	348	376	450	457	460	467	596	811	855
Burkina Faso	m. francs	22 997	19 608	18 824	17 200	16 800	18 400	19 000	22 500	23 100	..
Burundi	m. francs	6 782	7 760	8 121	8 579	10 126	11 010	14 630	20 019	..	(28 500)
Cameroon	m. francs	[55 891]	[51 277]	[48 300]	48 300	53 100	57 850	57 550	..	..	..
Cape Verde	m. escudos				220	281	477	352	382	443	..
Central Afr. Rep.	m. francs		6 093	6 137	5 421	5 935	6 496	6 239			
Chad	m. francs				11 085	12 333	10 000	12 681	9 700	9 500	
Congo, Rep.	m. francs										
Congo, Dem. Rep.[5]	new zaïres										
Côte d'Ivoire	m. francs	39 199	40 671	41 503	42 088	46 677		52 516	54 588		
Djibouti	m. francs			5 089	4 702	4 648	4 481	3 712	4 019	4 013	
Equatorial Guinea	m. francs					1 321	1 721				
Eritrea[6]	m. birr				539	439	771	968	634		
Ethiopia[7]	m. birr	1 744	1 140	658	672	700	755	804	1 463	1 695	2 400
Gabon	m. francs									9 000	
Gambia	m. dalasis	27.3	34.9	31.2	23.3	22.2	27.6	38.5	42.6	40.8	..
Ghana	m. cedis	9 006	15 230	18 201	26 600	36 147	58 823	72 644	93 148	133 000	158 000

Country	Unit										
Guinea	m. francs	..	..	..	..	..	..	..	..	..	..
Guinea-Bissau[8]	m. francs	..	..	54 100	50 200	42 000	44 800	770	615	..	..
Kenya	m. shillings	6 438	6 034	5 052	5 047	6 344	8 203	[11 500]	[13 470]	[16 055]	[19 985]
Lesotho	m. maloti	62.5	62.4	60.1	62.4	81.9	95.1	107	135	156	..
Liberia[9]	m. dollars	28.3	21.7	23.6	37.3	41.3	..	..	..	..	8.1
Madagascar	b. francs	56.7	63.7	68.9	72.4	84.6	116	201	267	..	..
Malawi	m. kwachas	66.3	66.5	90.9	118	151	225	317	328	287	..
Mali	b. francs	14.2	..	15.7	20.7	24.7	25.3	26.6	..	..	28.8
Mauritania	m. ouguiyas	3 239	3 232	3 427	3 640	3 640	3 640	3 680	3 660	..	..
Mauritius	m. rupees	137	164	178	190	213	234	233	206	181	..
Mozambique[10]	b. meticais	136	178	259	417	762	522	704	830	(1 040)	..
Namibia[11]	m. dollars	..	400	355	229	202	248	286	386	436	660
Niger	m. francs	12 315	..	..	..	..	..	..	..	..	..
Nigeria[12]	m. naira	1 745	(3 783)	(3 004)	[6 790]	(7 032)	14 000	15 350	17 920	23 100	..
Rwanda[13]	m. francs	7 963	13 184	11 863	12 900	5 700	14 700	22 600	23 300	27 340	45 400
Senegal[14]	m. francs	31 300	29 928	29 056	33 962	36 725	40 389	40 809	41 324	40 300	[27 000]
Seychelles	m. rupees	79.2	87.6	105	67.1	60.1	55.2	52.4	57.3	61.7	62.5
Sierra Leone	m. leones	1 369	4 792	10 081	13 244	15 546	18 898	17 119	9 315	..	..
Somalia	shillings	..	..	..	..	..	..	..	..	..	..
South Africa	m. rand	10 982	10 699	10 724	10 713	12 352	11 942	11 143	11 124	10 535	10 589
Sudan	m. pounds	[5 340]	8 460	15 760	35 265	59 390	80 600	95 200	163 000	..	..
Swaziland	m. emalangeni	34.7	41.7	54.9	72.5	80.8	96.3	118	143	..	..
Tanzania	b. shillings	21.2	21.2	25.8	21.3	26.7	44.0	52.8	61.2	[78.0]	[90.5]
Togo	m. francs	13 817	(12 950)	13 000	14 200	14 100	15 400	..	..	..	..
Uganda	m./b. shillings	39 625	48 675	56 904	72 174	[81 050]	[87.7]	116	134	181	204
Zambia	b. kwachas	4.2	5.6	16.8	22.0	39.0	65.8	56.9	90.8	114	73.7
Zimbabwe[15]	m. dollars	954	1 116	1 269	1 439	1 826	2 214	2 742	3 393	3 613	7 200
America											
Central America											
Belize	th. dollars	9 538	9 466	10 584	12 261	15 799	16 106	15 932	18 790	..	..
Costa Rica[16]	m. colones	[1 973]	[2 310]	[2 651]	[3 449]	[4 424]	[7 901]	[12 485]	[14 379]	..	..

State	Currency	1990	1991	1992	1993	1994	1995	1996	1997	1998	1999
El Salvador	m. colones	975	1 011	975	888	829	849	843	853	908	963
Guatemala	m. quetzals	502	661	785	869	1 008	(837)	(817)	(729)	(798)	(845)
Honduras	m. lempiras	276	252	280	263	(385)	445	530	548	(580)	..
Mexico	m. new pesos	[3 138]	[4 247]	[5 430]	[6 514]	[8 694]	10 368	14 637	18 306	20 950	23 200
Nicaragua[17]	m. gold córdobas	(32.2)	211	211	224	232	235	240	245	265	302
Panama[18]	m. balboas	74.1	80.1	86.7	94.6	98.7	96.8	101	118	..	..
North America											
Canada[19]	m. dollars	13 473	12 830	13 111	13 293	13 008	12 457	11 511	10 801	11 168	11 048
USA[19]	m. dollars	306 170	280 292	305 141	297 637	288 059	278 856	271 417	276 324	274 278	283 096
South America											
Argentina[20]	m. pesos	[877]	[2 555]	[3 280]	[3 830]	4 021	4 361	4 136	4 016	4 056	3 987
Bolivia	m. bolivianos	357	440	473	537	569	612	682	768	828	762
Brazil[20]	th./m. reais	(142)	(448)	7 018	| 188	4 108	10 008	9 994	13 114	12 743	17 546
Chile	b. pesos	[220]	[280]	330	370	408	492	530	588	628	526
Colombia	b. pesos	[520]	[652]	[882]	1 104	1 296	1 775	2 500	3 376	3 109	3 547
Ecuador	b. sucres	156	273	532	841	982	893	1 260	..	..	..
Guyana	m. dollars	142	227	453	562	759	801	780	[1 000]	..	..
Paraguay	m./b. guaranies	79 883	| 137	154	167	(202)	[240]	[266]	..	..	..
Peru[17]	m. new soles	130	480	1 001	(1 390)	(1 778)	[1 878]	[2 000]	2 638	..	..
Uruguay	m. pesos	233	363	813	974	2 083	1 816	2 228	2 638	..	..
Venezuela	m. bolivares	(45 379)	45 269	54 994	94 995	110 940	196 841	240 576	473 388	(685 000)	(859 000)
Asia											
Central Asia											
Kazakhstan[21]	b. tenge	..	..	..	(0.3)	(3.8)	10.8	15.0	17.9	18.9	17.3
Kyrgyzstan[21]	m. soms	..	..	..	38.8	105	251	314	482	491	..
Tajikistan[21]	m. roubles	..	..	(2.6)	(243)	(347)	(713)	(3 977)	(7 240)	..	..
Turkmenistan[21]	b. manats	..	..	..	..	1.5	15.1	158	440	461	582
Uzbekistan[21]	m. soms	..	..	(11.7)	(164)	(991)	(3 355)	(6 900)	[13 700]	..	..

East Asia

	Unit										
Brunei[22]	m. dollars	[439]	[444]	[430]	[398]	[420]	[425]	474	555	614	(500)
Cambodia	b. riels	..	..	..	[165]	[302]	302	298	305	298	[300]
China, P. R.[23]	b. yuan	[49.3]	[53.7]	[69.2]	[73.1]	[87.2]	[105]	[124]	[139]	[156]	[166]
Indonesia	b. rupiahs	3 156	3 512	4 066	4 281	5 135	5 652	6 734	9 401	9 740	[11 399]
Japan	b. yen	4 130	4 329	4 510	4 618	4 673	4 714	4 815	4 917	4 932	4 922
Korea, North	b. won	(4.3)	(4.5)	(4.6)	(4.7)	(4.8)	..	..	..	..	..
Korea, South	b. won	6 665	7 892	8 709	9 040	10 057	11 125	12 533	13 160	13 800	13 749
Laos	b. kip	..	..	..	..	..	..	49.2	53.5	..	..
Malaysia	m. ringgits	3 043	4 323	4 500	4 951	5 565	6 121	6 091	5 878	4 545	6 511
Mongolia	m. tugriks	592	888	1 184	4 795	7 017	9 547	11 850	14 778	[18 130]	[19 070]
Myanmar	b. kyats	5.2	5.9	8.4	12.7	16.7	22.3	24.3	28.8	34.6	[44.3]
Philippines	m. pesos	14 707	15 898	17 462	21 132	24 401	30 510	32 269	37 405	38 412	[36 520]
Singapore	m. dollars	3 266	3 495	3 799	4 010	4 273	5 206	5 782	6 618	[7 161]	(7 290)
Taiwan	b. dollars	211	227	239	253	255	261	277	288	298	265
Thailand	m. baht	48 846	55 502	64 961	73 708	78 300	88 983	93 959	97 783	98 461	80 008
Viet Nam	b. dong	3 319	4 292	3 730	3 168	4 730	..	..	..	..	..

South Asia

	Unit										
Afghanistan	m. afghanis	..	..	..	..	..	..	..	..	..	..
Bangladesh	m. taka	11 965	13 980	16 095	17 290	18 080	19 110	21 376	24 921	27 610	29 374
India	b. rupees	153	163	174	209	229	260	288	338	397	450
Nepal[24]	m. rupees	988	1 114	1 320	1 607	1 801	1 940	2 066	2 244	2 989	3 323
Pakistan	m. rupees	58 122	69 683	81 604	89 608	98 144	112 085	123 550	126 323	126 603	135 000
Sri Lanka	b. rupees	6.7	10.3	12.9	15.4	19.4	35.2	38.1	37.1	42.5	35.6

Europe

	Unit										
Albania	m. leks	990	..	2 368	3 837	4 412	4 922	4 401	4 928	5 100	5 400
Armenia[21]	b. dram	..	..	1.3	17.9	..	21.2	21.7	30.5	33.3	[46.0]
Austria	m. shillings	(18 700)	(19 400)	19 600	20 500	21 200	21 500	21 690	22 050	22 280	22 340
Azerbaijan[21]	b. manats	..	..	0.8	7.9	85.6	248	305	353	463	472
Belarus[21]	b. roubles	..	..	1.5	17.7	365	1 723	2 231	5 051	6 448	19 935
Belgium	m. francs	155 205	157 919	132 819	129 602	131 955	131 156	131 334	131 796	133 007	136 393

State	Currency	1990	1991	1992	1993	1994	1995	1996	1997	1998	1999
Bosnia and Herz.[25]	m. marks	..	..	..	..	(335)	(462)	(189)	(254)	230	400
Bulgaria	m. leva	1.6	4.4	5.7	8.1	12.9	21.8	37.3	399	541	634
Croatia[26]	m. kuna	..	..	200	3 422	7 149	9 282	7 760	7 000	7 500	5 798
Cyprus	m. pounds	127	131	191	90.0	99.0	91.0	141	(200)	(205)	(168)
Czech Rep.[27]	m. korunas	..	43 037	48 503	[26 230]	27 008	22 275	30 509	31 328	37 643	41 484
Czechoslovakia[28]	m. korunas	41 900	..	..	..	..	..	..	..	..	..
Denmark	m. kroner	16 399	17 091	17 129	17 390	17 293	17 468	17 896	18 521	19 079	19 577
Estonia[29]	m. kroons	..	..	(64.0)	174	327	427	546	750	854	994
Finland	m. markkaa	[8 190]	8 903	9 298	9 225	9 175	8 594	9 776	9 246	10 194	8 715
France	m. francs	231 911	240 936	238 874	241 199	246 469	238 432	237 375	241 103	236 226	244 026
Georgia[30]	th./m. lari	..	..	3.5	200	[40.0]	[55.0]	77.0	95.0	[69.0]	[67.0]
German DR[31]	marks	..	..	..	..	..	..	..	..	..	..
Germany[32]	m. marks	68 376	65 579	65 536	61 529	58 957	58 986	58 671	57 602	58 327	59 730
Greece	m./b. drachmas	612 344	693 846	835 458	932 995	1 053	1 171	1 343	1 511	1 725	1 853
Hungary	m. forints	52 367	53 999	61 216	67 492	67 996	76 937	85 954	96 814	134 570	164 051
Ireland	m. pounds	355	362	376	385	412	426	456	485	506	581
Italy	b. lire	28 007	30 191	30 813	32 364	32 835	31 561	36 170	38 701	40 763	41 888
Latvia[33]	m. lats	..	..	..	12.0	19.0	23.0	21.0	22.1	24.8	32.9
Lithuania[34]	m. litas	..	..	..	85.4	79.3	115	169	302	537	715
Luxembourg	m. francs	3 233	3 681	3 963	3 740	4 214	4 194	4 380	4 797	5 197	5 460
Macedonia[35]	m. denars	..	..	..	..	..	..	5 223	4 163	4 302	4 733
Malta	th. liri	6 722	7 029	8 513	9 419	10 533	10 996	12 002	11 996	11 297	11 257
Moldova[21]	m. lei	..	..	..	9.7	36.7	60.0	70.7	(80.5)	57.0	[60.0]
Netherlands	m. guilders	13 513	13 548	13 900	13 103	12 990	12 864	13 199	13 345	13 561	13 676
Norway	m. kroner	21 251	21 313	23 638	22 528	24 019	22 224	22 813	23 010	25 087	25 074
Poland	m. zlotys	1 495	1 830	2 624	3 980	5 117	6 595	8 313	10 077	11 687	12 587
Portugal	m. escudos	267 299	305 643	341 904	352 504	360 811	403 478	401 165	418 772	420 654	448 690
Romania	b. lei	30.0	80.0	196	420	1 170	1 538	1 957	5 370	7 342	8 547
Russia[36]	m. roubles	[123]	..	[1 049]	[9 037]	[35 890]	[63 220]	[82 485]	[105 034]	[85 574]	[171 100]

Country	Unit										
Slovak Rep.[37]	m. korunas	..	..	..	8 211	9 614	13 588	13 412	13 901	14 628	13 836
Slovenia[38]	m. tolars	..	..	[24 290]	[27 690]	[32 540]	[42 110]	[47 420]	49 301	50 030	56 207
Spain	b. pesetas	923	947	928	1 055	995	1 079	1 091	1 123	1 124	1 186
Sweden	m. kronor	[34 999]	[35 552]	[35 769]	36 992	37 182	33 194	28 847	38 825	40 034	42 088
Switzerland	m. francs	5 797	5 936	6 014	5 524	5 723	5 011	4 782	4 634	4 532	4 491
UK[19]	m. pounds	22 287	24 380	22 850	22 686	22 490	21 439	22 330	21 612	22 551	22 283
Ukraine[21]	m. hryvnias	..	..	..	8.0	337	1 665	2 833	3 428	3 712	3 875
Yugoslavia (FRY)[39]	m. dinars	..	..	..	678	1 200	1 611	(4 210)	(6 500)	(6 550)	(6 550)
Yugoslavia (former)[40]	m. new dinars	5 180	..	..	..	..	..	..	..	..	..
Middle East											
Bahrain	m. dinars	81.0	89.0	95.0	94.0	96.3	103	109	109	111	..
Egypt	m. pounds	3 855	4 646	5 265	5 723	6 142	6 682	7 164	7 557	8 026	[8 756]
Iran	b. rials	1 011	1 235	1 482	2 255	4 023	4 457	6 499	8 540	10 050	..
Iraq	m. dinars	..	..	..	..	..	..	..	..	..	..
Israel	m. new shekels	12 940	14 776	16 919	17 539	19 836	22 216	26 489	29 257	32 258	[33 720]
Jordan	m. dinars	255	270	273	300	348	387	429	458	502	530
Kuwait	m. dinars	2 585	3 637	1 792	871	970	1 100	971	745	[716]	[710]
Lebanon	b. pounds	97.9	140	499	518	704	795	760	702	[811]	..
Oman	m. riyals	742	643	778	738	779	776	737	702	(698)	[620]
Qatar	m. dinars	..	..	..	..	..	..	..	..	..	..
Saudi Arabia	m. riyals	[50 000]	[100 000]	54 000	61 636	53 549	49 501	50 025	67 975	[62 000]	[54 000]
Syria	m. pounds	18 429	32 483	33 412	29 948	37 270	40 500	40 746	42 842	[44 850]	..
Turkey	b./tr. liras	13 866	23 657	42 320	77 717	| 157	303	612	1 183	2 289	4 368
UAE[41]	m. dirhams	5 827	5 827	5 827	5 827	5 827	6 027	[6 027]	6 027	6 027	6 027
Yemen[42]	m. rials	10 382	13 227	16 812	19 752	30 273	35 897	44 964	55 104	53 824	58 311
Oceania											
Australia	m. dollars	8 522	8 945	9 584	10 201	10 326	10 472	10 608	10 761	11 298	[11 750]
Fiji	m. dollars	45.2	47.9	45.9	49.4	49.3	48.8	51.2	48.0	47.7	53.9
New Zealand	m. dollars	[1 300]	1 210	1 097	1 050	1 015	1 004	1 023	1 159	1 239	1 140
Papua New Guinea	m. kina	65.6	50.1	56.5	67.1	54.3	60.0	68.0	92.6	86.0	80.0

Table 5A.3. Military expenditure by region and country, in constant US dollars, 1990–99

Figures are in US $m., at constant 1995 prices and exchange rates.[3]

State	1990	1991	1992	1993	1994	1995	1996	1997	1998	1999
Africa										
North Africa										
Algeria	[606]	593	[869]	1 067	1 297	1 235	1 371	1 680	1 828	1 881
Libya	. .	. .	. .	. .	. .	. .	. .	. .	. .	. .
Morocco	1 383	1 453	1 441	1 446	1 684	1 551	1 433	. .	. .	. .
Tunisia	402	407	390	409	409	345	349	363	380	. .
Sub-Saharan										
Angola[4]	. .	. .	. .	. .	. .	. .	. .	. .	. .	. .
Benin	30.8	. .	. .	. .	. .	. .	. .	. .	. .	. .
Botswana	190	204	189	198	182	166	153	180	230	226
Burkina Faso	62.6	52.0	51.0	46.3	36.1	36.9	35.8	41.5	40.5	. .
Burundi	45.3	47.5	48.8	47.0	48.3	44.1	46.3	48.3	. .	(61.6)
Cameroon	[167]	[153]	[144]	149	121	116	110	. .	. .	. .
Cape Verde	. .	. .	. .	3.1	3.9	6.2	4.3	4.3	4.8	. .
Central Afr. Rep.	. .	17.4	17.7	16.1	14.2	13.0	12.0	. .	14.3	. .
Chad	. .	. .	. .	34.0	26.9	20.0	22.6	16.4	. .	. .
Congo, Rep.	. .	. .	. .	. .	. .	. .	. .	. .	. .	. .
Congo, Dem. Rep.[5]	. .	. .	. .	. .	. .	. .	. .	. .	. .	. .
Côte d'Ivoire	123	125	122	121	107	. .	103	103	. .	. .
Djibouti	. .	. .	33.4	29.6	27.4	25.2	20.0	21.2	21.1	. .
Equatorial Guinea	. .	. .	. .	. .	3.0	3.4	. .	. .	. .	. .
Eritrea[6]	. .	. .	. .	98.5	76.6	122	141	89.8	. .	. .
Ethiopia[7]	521	251	131	129	125	123	137	260	285	. .
Gabon	. .	. .	. .	. .	. .	. .	. .	. .	16.2	. .
Gambia	3.9	4.6	3.8	2.7	2.5	2.9	4.0	4.3	4.1	. .
Ghana	26.5	38.0	41.2	48.2	52.5	49.0	45.1	45.3	56.4	60.9

Guinea	..	74.9	59.6	46.6	47.7	..	..	..	..	..
Guinea-Bissau[8]	..	..	..	..	2.1	2.2	1.8	..	..	..
Kenya	368	288	186	128	124	159	[206]	[215]	[242]	[294]
Lesotho	31.8	27.0	22.2	20.4	24.7	26.2	26.9	32.0	34.2	..
Liberia[9]	28.3	21.7	23.6	37.3	41.3	27.2	39.3	50.1	50.7	8.1
Madagascar	37.7	39.0	36.8	35.1	29.6	..	..	..	..	..
Malawi	17.7	15.8	17.6	19.1	18.1	14.7	15.1	14.3	..	..
Mali	37.8	33.3	32.1	43.9	47.0	49.5	47.4	50.2	52.1	..
Mauritania	35.2	..	..	31.1	29.9	28.1	27.1	25.8	..	..
Mauritius	11.1	12.4	12.9	12.5	13.0	13.4	12.6	10.4	12.7	..
Mozambique[10]	104	103	103	116	130	..	..	..	..	..
Namibia[11]	32.3	..	..	..	..	57.8	53.8	60.1	(75.3)	..
Niger	555	356	269	160	127	141	151	187	199	278
Nigeria[12]	..	(1 066)	(585)	[842]	(555)	639	542	585	684	1 240
Rwanda[13]	102	141	116	112	30.1	56.1	78.9	69.9	87.3	[83.5]
Senegal[14]	87.3	85.0	82.6	97.0	79.3	80.9	79.5	79.1	76.3	..
Seychelles	18.0	19.5	22.7	14.3	12.6	11.6	11.1	12.1	12.7	..
Sierra Leone	11.6	20.1	25.5	27.4	25.9	25.0	18.4	8.7	..	12.2
Somalia	..	..	..	..	..	..	..	..	..	..
South Africa	5 162	4 362	3 839	3 497	3 698	3 292	2 859	2 632	2 332	2 230
Sudan	[327]	231	198	220	172	139	70.4	82.2	..	..
Swaziland	16.0	17.7	21.7	25.5	25.0	26.5	30.6	34.5	..	..
Tanzania	..	97.3	96.1	63.3	59.5	76.6	75.9	75.8	[85.6]	[91.9]
Togo	44.1	..	40.8	44.5	32.7	30.9	..	..	..	..
Uganda	101	96.9	74.4	88.9	[91.0]	[90.5]	112	120	163	175
Zambia	151	103	116	52.5	60.6	76.1	45.0	57.6	57.9	25.0
Zimbabwe[15]	369	350	280	249	259	256	261	273	220	343
America										
Central America										
Belize	5.3	5.2	5.7	6.5	8.1	8.1	7.5	8.7	..	..
Costa Rica[16]	[26.4]	[24.0]	[22.6]	[26.8]	[30.3]	[44.0]	[59.1]	[60.1]	..	..

State	1990	1991	1992	1993	1994	1995	1996	1997	1998	1999
El Salvador	204	185	161	123	104	97.0	87.7	84.9	88.2	93.0
Guatemala	170	168	182	180	188	(144)	(127)	(103)	(106)	(107)
Honduras	74.1	50.5	51.6	43.8	(52.6)	47.0	45.2	38.9	(36.2)	..
Mexico	[1 097]	[1 210]	[1 340]	[1 465]	[1 828]	1 615	1 697	1 759	1 737	1 668
Nicaragua[17]	(229)	49.3	39.8	35.1	34.1	31.1	28.5	26.6	25.5	25.7
Panama[18]	78.5	83.7	89.1	96.7	99.6	96.8	99.9	115	..	..
North America										
Canada[19]	10 976	9 897	9 963	9 917	9 686	9 077	8 262	7 625	7 809	7 640
USA[19]	356 994	313 647	331 280	313 784	296 188	278 856	263 727	262 159	256 051	259 913
South America										
Argentina[20]	[3 544]	[3 796]	[3 910]	[4 127]	4 156	4 362	4 127	3 987	3 978	3 959
Bolivia	131	133	127	133	131	127	126	136	136	123
Brazil[20]	(6 360)	(4 005)	5 605	7 402	7 431	10 906	9 408	11 545	10 877	14 294
Chile	[1 059]	[1 105]	1 127	1 127	1 110	1 240	1 245	1 298	1 316	1 071
Colombia	[1 733]	[1 666]	[1 775]	1 811	1 717	1 945	2 278	2 595	1 980	2 042
Ecuador	317	373	471	514	471	348	395	..	..	..
Guyana	3.7	2.9	4.5	5.0	6.0	5.6	5.1	[6.3]	..	..
Paraguay	93.8	129	126	116	[116]	[122]	[123]	..	..	..
Peru[17]	1 042	754	908	(848)	(877)	(834)	[796]	..	..	..
Uruguay	396	306	406	316	467	286	273	270	..	..
Venezuela	(1 608)	1 195	1 104	1 382	1 003	1 113	681	893	(951)	(987)
Asia										
Central Asia										
Kazakhstan[21]	..	..	..	(609)	(390)	401	401	407	401	346
Kyrgyzstan[21]	..	..	..	46.4	38.3	59.7	55.5	67.4	60.4	..
Tajikistan[21]	..	..	..	(144)	(82.2)	(59.1)	(72.4)	(70.2)	..	..
Turkmenistan[21]	..	..	..	..	(167)	(148)	(143)	(216)	(193)	(192)
Uzbekistan[21]	..	..	(133)	(431)	(189)	(294)	(369)	[429]	..	..

East Asia										
Brunei[22]	[361]	[359]	[344]	[305]	[314]	[300]	328	378	418	..
Cambodia	..	..	..	[70.9]	[125]	123	110	109	93.3	[95.3]
China, P. R.[23]	[10 800]	[11 400]	[13 800]	[12 700]	[12 200]	[12 500]	[13 700]	[14 900]	[16 900]	[18 400]
Indonesia	2 150	2 187	2 354	2 261	2 499	2 513	2 772	3 633	2 386	[2 317]
Japan	46 984	47 676	48 819	49 377	49 632	50 112	51 092	51 319	51 285	51 184
Korea, North	(1 988)	(2 058)	(2 112)	(2 162)	(2 220)	..	..	..	..	..
Korea, South	11 666	12 638	13 130	13 002	13 625	14 424	15 481	15 564	15 182	15 022
Laos	..	..	..	..	..	..	54.1	46.1	..	..
Malaysia	1 502	2 044	2 032	2 159	2 339	2 444	2 349	2 208	1 610	2 239
Mongolia	52.2	39.3	28.7	31.4	24.5	21.3	17.7	16.1	[18.1]	[17.4]
Myanmar	3 007	2 610	3 023	3 480	3 699	3 932	3 681	3 364	2 668	[2 969]
Philippines	938	854	850	962	1 025	1 187	1 151	1 260	1 179	[1 055]
Singapore	2 615	2 706	2 875	2 967	3 068	3 673	4 026	4 518	[4 901]	(4 972)
Taiwan	9 584	9 952	10 023	10 324	9 996	9 858	10 163	10 471	10 620	9 324
Thailand	2 478	2 664	2 996	3 289	3 321	3 571	3 563	3 511	3 271	2 653
Viet Nam	884	625	462	373	486	..	..	..	..	..
South Asia										
Afghanistan	..	..	..	..	..	..	..	..	..	..
Bangladesh	391	426	471	491	487	474	510	565	578	593
India	7 750	7 249	6 939	7 832	7 795	8 004	8 165	8 935	9 264	10 174
Nepal[24]	32.3	31.5	31.9	36.1	37.3	37.4	36.4	38.1	46.1	48.3
Pakistan	3 195	3 426	3 664	3 659	3 565	3 624	3 620	3 324	3 134	3 229
Sri Lanka	214	293	328	351	408	687	642	569	597	478
Europe										
Albania	85.4	..	203	54.7	51.3	53.1	42.1	35.4	30.4	31.7
Armenia[21]	..	..	..	..	..	..	..	..	..	..
Austria	(2 176)	(2 185)	2 121	2 141	2 151	2 133	2 114	2 120	2 120	2 131
Azerbaijan[21]	..	..	611	490	302	171	175	195	258	277
Belarus[21]	..	..	671	614	545	318	270	373	275	400
Belgium	5 939	5 855	4 808	4 566	4 540	4 449	4 362	4 385	4 350	4 386

State	1990	1991	1992	1993	1994	1995	1996	1997	1998	1999
Bosnia and Herz.[25]	..	..	..	..	(164)	(236)	(129)	(152)	131	227
Bulgaria[26]	1 098	695	470	383	312	325	249	225	250	285
Croatia[26]	..	..	1 305	1 410	1 421	1 775	1 422	1 232	1 240	926
Cyprus	354	348	476	214	226	201	303	(414)	(415)	(338)
Czech Rep.[27]	..	..	..	[1 186]	1 110	839	1 057	1 000	1 086	1 175
Czechoslovakia[28]	2 334	2 398	2 702	..	..	..	..	..	..	..
Denmark	3 226	3 283	3 224	3 230	3 150	3 118	3 126	3 168	3 205	3 223
Estonia[29]	..	..	(20.1)	28.9	36.7	37.2	38.7	48.1	50.6	57.1
Finland	[2 087]	2 180	2 219	2 155	2 120	1 968	2 225	2 078	2 259	1 913
France	51 851	52 198	50 527	49 979	50 233	47 768	46 596	46 793	45 531	46 792
Georgia[30]	..	..	127	215	[273]	[143]	144	166	[116]	[92.2]
German DR[31]	..	..	..	..	..	..	..	..	..	..
Germany[32]	56 760	52 533	49 951	44 930	41 906	41 160	40 343	38 906	39 001	39 543
Greece	5 059	4 797	4 987	4 866	4 950	5 056	5 359	5 712	6 222	6 543
Hungary	1 284	987	910	819	694	612	554	527	641	715
Ireland	645	637	642	648	678	683	719	754	768	871
Italy	21 974	22 283	21 643	21 758	21 220	19 376	21 369	22 409	23 125	23 458
Latvia[33]	..	..	..	38.6	45.0	43.6	33.8	32.8	35.2	45.7
Lithuania[34]	..	..	..	51.3	27.7	28.8	33.9	55.7	94.2	124
Luxembourg	126	..	..	..	146	142	147	158	170	177
Macedonia[35]	..	139	145	132	..	..	134	106	109	117
Malta	22.4	22.8	27.2	28.9	31.0	31.2	33.2	32.2	29.6	29.0
Moldova[21]	..	..	..	31.8	20.6	30.0	29.3	(30.8)	20.5	[15.4]
Netherlands	9 627	9 362	9 308	8 549	8 249	8 011	8 058	7 976	7 945	7 851
Norway	3 774	3 660	3 968	3 697	3 885	3 508	3 554	3 495	3 728	3 650
Poland	3 661	2 536	2 502	2 773	2 675	2 720	2 852	2 983	3 097	3 144
Portugal	2 503	2 569	2 639	2 547	2 486	2 670	2 573	2 632	2 571	2 685
Romania	1 401	1 362	1 072	647	761	756	693	747	642	541
Russia[36]	[203 000]	..	[47 500]	[41 900]	[40 500]	[25 700]	[23 400]	[24 900]	[18 100]	[22 400]

Slovak Rep.[37]	. .	. .	. .	345	356	457	427	417	411	357
Slovenia[38]	. .	. .	[365]	[315]	[309]	[355]	[365]	348	325	345
Spain	9 517	9 224	8 529	9 275	8 347	8 651	8 451	8 529	8 389	8 675
Sweden	[6 035]	[5 624]	[5 507]	5 452	5 343	4 653	4 044	5 399	5 540	5 714
Switzerland	5 726	5 542	5 395	4 795	4 928	4 238	4 010	3 869	3 778	3 718
UK[19]	41 583	42 954	38 828	37 962	36 712	33 841	34 404	32 285	32 566	31 810
Ukraine[21]	. .	. .	. .	376	1 608	1 665	1 572	1 641	1 607	1 380
Yugoslavia (FRY)[39]	. .	. .	. .	. .	774	597	(807)	(1 052)	(817)	(545)
Yugoslavia (former)[40]	460	. .	. .	. .	. .	. .	. .	. .	. .	. .
Middle East										
Bahrain	230	251	268	259	263	273	289	287	294	. .
Egypt	2 171	2 185	2 178	2 113	2 096	1 971	1 971	1 988	2 027	[2 151]
Iran	2 030	2 118	2 022	2 539	3 444	2 550	2 884	3 235	3 189	. .
Iraq	. .	. .	. .	. .	. .	. .	. .	. .	. .	. .
Israel	7 851	7 533	7 706	7 200	7 250	7 378	7 905	8 010	8 375	[8 364]
Jordan	448	439	426	454	508	552	575	596	625	647
Kuwait	9 928	12 801	6 341	3 070	3 338	3 685	3 140	2 395	[2 298]	[2 259]
Lebanon	300	283	458	382	480	490	428	376	[414]	. .
Oman	2 022	1 675	2 008	1 889	2 001	2 018	1 915	1 812	(1 828)	[1 614]
Qatar	. .	. .	. .	. .	. .	. .	. .	. .	. .	. .
Saudi Arabia	[14 913]	[28 433]	15 369	17 360	14 997	13 218	13 204	17 926	[16 409]	[14 523]
Syria	2 801	4 529	4 197	3 322	3 585	3 608	3 353	3 445	[3 653]	. .
Turkey	5 502	5 655	5 948	6 578	6 442	6 606	7 396	7 706	8 074	9 588
UAE[41]	2 149	1 905	1 815	1 729	1 663	1 642	[1 589]	1 522	1 476	1 420
Yemen[42]	1 365	1 279	1 256	1 101	1 157	879	846	983	885	871
Oceania										
Australia	7 153	7 275	7 720	8 070	8 018	7 765	7 669	7 760	8 085	[8 300]
Fiji	38.9	38.7	35.3	36.1	35.8	34.7	35.3	32.0	30.1	33.1
New Zealand	[952]	864	776	732	691	659	656	735	776	715
Papua New Guinea	72.6	51.8	56.0	63.4	49.9	47.0	47.7	62.5	51.1	39.7

Table 5A.4. Military expenditure by region and country, as percentage of gross domestic product, 1990–99

State	1990	1991	1992	1993	1994	1995	1996	1997	1998
Africa									
North Africa									
Algeria	[1.5]	1.2	[1.9]	2.6	3.2	3.0	3.3	3.9	3.9
Libya	..	..	..	..	..	..	..	..	..
Morocco	4.1	4.1	4.3	4.4	4.9	4.7	3.9	..	..
Tunisia	2.7	2.6	2.3	2.4	2.3	1.9	1.8	1.8	1.8
Sub-Saharan									
Angola[4]	5.8	6.8	12.0	12.4	19.8	17.0	19.2	(23.9)	14.9
Benin	1.8	..	..	..	..	..	..	..	..
Botswana	3.9	4.2	4.1	4.0	3.6	3.1	2.6	2.9	3.5
Burkina Faso	3.0	2.4	2.3	2.1	1.6	1.6	1.5	1.7	1.5
Burundi	3.4	3.8	3.6	3.2	4.0	3.6	5.5	5.8	..
Cameroon	[1.7]	[1.6]	[1.5]	1.4	1.3	1.3	1.1	0.8	..
Cape Verde	..	..	..	0.8	0.8	1.3	0.9	0.8	0.9
Central Afr. Rep.	..	1.6	1.6	1.5	1.3	1.2	1.2	..	..
Chad	..	..	..	3.8	2.7	2.0	2.2	1.6	1.4
Congo, Rep.	..	..	..	..	..	..	..	..	..
Congo, Dem. Rep.[5]	..	..	..	..	..	..	..	..	..
Côte d'Ivoire	1.5	1.4	1.4	1.4	1.1	..	0.9	0.9	..
Djibouti	..	..	6.1	5.6	5.4	5.1	4.2	4.5	4.4
Equatorial Guinea	..	..	..	..	2.3	2.2	..	..	..
Eritrea[6]	..	..	..	21.4	13.0	19.9	22.8	13.5	..
Ethiopia[7]	9.1	5.5	2.5	2.4	2.1	2.0	1.9	3.2	3.5
Gabon	1.1	1.3	1.1	0.9	0.8	0.9	..	..	0.3
Gambia	..	..	..	..	..	..	1.2	1.2	1.1
Ghana	0.4	0.6	0.6	0.7	0.7	0.8	0.7	0.7	0.8
Guinea	..	2.4	1.7	1.3	1.3	..	..	..	..

Guinea-Bissau[8]	..	..	..	..	0.3	0.5	0.6	..	..
Kenya	3.3	2.7	1.9	1.5	1.6	1.8	[2.2]	[2.1]	[2.3]
Lesotho	4.1	3.4	2.6	2.3	2.8	2.8	2.6	2.9	3.2
Liberia[9]	..	..	..	..	..	..	..	..	..
Madagascar	1.2	1.3	1.2	1.1	0.9	0.9	1.2	1.5	1.4
Malawi	1.3	1.1	1.4	1.3	1.5	1.0	0.9	0.8	..
Mali	2.1	..	..	2.2	2.1	2.1	1.9	1.9	1.9
Mauritania	3.8	3.6	3.5	3.2	2.9	2.7	2.5	2.3	..
Mauritius	0.3	0.4	0.4	0.3	0.3	0.3	0.3	0.2	..
Mozambique[10]	10.1	8.7	8.3	7.6	8.8	3.9	3.6	3.7	(4.2)
Namibia[11]	..	5.7	4.3	2.6	1.8	2.0	2.1	2.5	2.6
Niger	1.9	..	..	..	..	..	..	..	..
Nigeria[12]	0.7	(1.2)	(0.5)	[0.7]	(0.6)	0.7	0.5	0.6	0.7
Rwanda[13]	3.7	5.5	4.4	4.5	3.5	4.2	5.3	4.1	4.3
Senegal[14]	2.0	1.9	1.8	2.2	1.8	1.8	1.7	1.6	1.4
Seychelles	4.0	4.4	4.7	2.8	2.5	2.3	2.1	2.0	2.0
Sierra Leone	0.7	1.5	2.2	2.4	2.2	2.2	1.8	0.8	..
Somalia	..	..	..	..	..	..	..	..	..
South Africa	4.0	3.5	3.1	2.8	2.9	2.5	2.1	1.9	1.6
Sudan	[3.5]	2.8	2.5	2.8	2.5	1.7	0.9	1.0	..
Swaziland	1.6	1.7	1.9	1.8	2.0	2.2	2.2	2.4	..
Tanzania	..	2.0	1.9	1.2	1.2	1.5	1.4	1.3	[1.4]
Togo	3.2	(3.1)	2.9	4.0	2.6	2.4	..	..	..
Uganda	2.5	2.2	1.5	1.8	[1.6]	[1.5]	1.8	1.8	2.2
Zambia	3.7	2.6	3.0	1.5	1.7	2.2	1.4	1.8	1.8
Zimbabwe[15]	4.5	3.8	3.7	3.4	3.3	3.6	3.2	3.4	2.6
America									
Central America									
Belize	1.2	1.1	1.1	1.2	1.4	1.4	1.3	1.5	..
Costa Rica[16]	0.4	0.3	0.3	0.3	0.3	0.5	0.7	0.6	..

State	1990	1991	1992	1993	1994	1995	1996	1997	1998
El Salvador	2.7	2.4	2.0	1.5	1.2	1.0	0.9	0.9	0.9
Guatemala	1.5	1.4	1.5	1.4	1.4	(1.0)	(0.9)	(0.7)	(0.7)
Honduras	2.2	1.5	1.5	1.2	(1.3)	1.2	1.1	0.9	(0.8)
Mexico	[0.5]	[0.4]	[0.5]	[0.5]	[0.6]	0.6	0.6	0.6	0.6
Nicaragua[17]	(2.1)	2.8	2.3	2.0	1.9	1.6	1.4	1.3	1.2
Panama[18]	1.4	1.4	1.3	1.3	1.3	1.2	1.2	1.4	..
North America									
Canada[19]	2.0	1.9	1.9	1.9	1.7	1.6	1.4	1.3	1.3
USA[19]	5.3	4.7	4.9	4.5	4.1	3.8	3.5	3.4	3.2
South America									
Argentina[20]	[1.3]	[1.4]	[1.4]	[1.6]	1.6	1.7	1.5	1.4	1.4
Bolivia	2.3	2.3	2.1	2.2	2.1	1.9	1.8	1.8	1.8
Brazil[20]	(1.3)	(0.7)	1.1	1.3	1.2	1.5	1.3	1.5	1.4
Chile	[2.4]	[2.3]	2.2	2.1	1.9	1.9	1.9	1.9	1.9
Colombia	[2.6]	[2.5]	[2.6]	2.5	2.2	2.4	2.8	3.3	2.6
Ecuador	1.9	2.2	2.7	3.1	2.7	1.9	2.1	..	..
Guyana	0.9	0.6	1.0	1.0	1.0	0.9	0.8	..	..
Paraguay	1.2	1.6	1.6	1.4	[1.4]	[1.4]	[1.3]	[0.9]	..
Peru[17]	2.0	1.5	1.9	(1.7)	(1.6)	[1.4]	[1.3]	..	..
Uruguay	2.4	1.8	2.3	1.8	2.5	1.6	1.5	1.4	..
Venezuela	(2.0)	1.5	1.3	1.7	1.3	1.4	0.8	1.1	(1.3)
Asia									
Central Asia									
Kazakhstan[21]	..	..	..	(1.0)	(0.9)	1.1	1.1	1.1	1.0
Kyrgyzstan[21]	..	..	..	0.7	0.9	1.6	1.4	1.6	1.4
Tajikistan[21]	..	..	(0.4)	(3.9)	(2.0)	(1.1)	(1.3)	(1.2)	..
Turkmenistan[21]	..	..	..	..	1.1	1.4	2.1	4.2	3.6
Uzbekistan[21]	..	..	(2.6)	(3.2)	(1.5)	(1.1)	(1.2)	[1.4]	..

East Asia									
Brunei[22]	..	[6.7]	[6.5]	[6.0]	[6.3]	[5.7]	6.2	6.9	7.6
Cambodia	[2.7]	..	[2.7]	[3.0]	[4.9]	4.2	3.6	3.3	2.7
China, P. R.[23]	[2.7]	[2.5]	[2.7]	[2.1]	[1.9]	[1.8]	[1.8]	[1.9]	[1.9]
Indonesia	1.6	1.4	1.4	1.3	1.3	1.2	1.3	1.5	1.0
Japan	1.0	0.9	1.0	1.0	1.0	1.0	1.0	1.0	1.0
Korea, North	..	..	..	..	..	..	..	..	..
Korea, South	3.7	3.7	3.5	3.3	3.1	2.9	3.0	2.9	3.1
Laos	..	..	..	..	..	..	..	2.4	..
Malaysia	2.6	3.3	3.0	3.0	2.9	2.8	2.9	2.1	1.7
Mongolia	5.7	4.7	2.5	2.9	2.5	2.2	2.4	2.0	[2.2]
Myanmar	4.1	3.9	4.5	5.1	4.6	4.7	4.0	3.6	3.1
Philippines	1.4	1.3	1.3	1.4	1.4	1.6	1.5	1.5	1.4
Singapore	4.8	4.6	4.8	4.3	4.0	4.4	4.5	4.6	[5.1]
Taiwan	4.9	4.7	4.5	4.3	4.0	3.8	3.7	3.5	3.5
Thailand	2.2	2.2	2.3	2.3	2.2	2.1	2.0	2.1	2.1
Viet Nam	8.7	6.1	3.4	2.3	2.8	..	..	..	..
South Asia									
Afghanistan	..	..	..	..	..	..	..	..	..
Bangladesh	1.4	1.5	1.7	1.7	1.5	1.5	1.5	1.6	1.6
India	2.9	2.6	2.5	2.4	2.2	2.1	2.0	2.2	2.1
Nepal[24]	0.8	0.7	0.8	0.8	0.8	0.8	0.7	0.8	0.9
Pakistan	5.7	5.8	6.1	5.7	5.2	5.2	5.1	4.6	4.2
Sri Lanka	2.1	2.8	3.0	3.1	3.4	5.3	5.0	4.2	4.2
Europe									
Albania	..	..	4.4	3.1	2.3	2.2	1.6	1.4	1.1
Armenia[21]	(1.0)	..	..	2.1	..	4.1	3.3	3.8	3.6
Austria	(1.0)	(1.0)	1.0	1.0	0.9	0.9	0.9	0.9	0.8
Azerbaijan[21]	..	..	3.3	5.0	4.6	2.3	2.2	2.3	2.7
Belarus[21]	..	..	1.6	1.8	2.0	1.4	1.2	1.4	1.0
Belgium	2.4	2.3	1.8	1.7	1.7	1.6	1.6	1.5	1.5

State	1990	1991	1992	1993	1994	1995	1996	1997	1998
Bosnia and Herz.[25]	..	..	..	..	..	..	..	..	..
Bulgaria	4.5	3.3	2.9	2.7	2.5	2.5	2.1	2.3	2.5
Croatia[26]	..	4.9	7.3	8.2	8.4	9.8	7.5	6.2	6.2
Cyprus	5.0	..	6.2	2.7	2.7	2.3	3.4	(4.6)	(4.4)
Czech Rep.[27]	..	..	..	[2.6]	2.3	1.6	1.9	1.9	2.1
Czechoslovakia[28]	2.1	2.0	1.9	..	..	..	..	..	..
Denmark	..	2.0	1.9	1.9	1.8	1.7	1.7	1.7	1.6
Estonia[29]	..	..	(0.5)	0.8	1.1	1.0	1.0	1.2	1.2
Finland	[1.6]	1.8	1.9	1.9	1.8	1.5	1.7	1.5	1.5
France	3.6	3.6	3.4	3.4	3.3	3.1	3.0	2.9	2.8
Georgia[30]	..	..	..	1.2	[2.9]	[1.5]	1.4	1.4	[1.0]
German DR[31]	..	..	..	..	..	..	..	..	..
Germany[32]	2.8	2.3	2.1	2.0	1.8	1.7	1.6	1.6	1.5
Greece	4.7	4.3	4.5	4.4	4.4	4.4	4.5	4.6	4.8
Hungary	2.5	2.2	2.1	1.9	1.6	1.4	1.3	1.1	1.3
Ireland	1.3	1.2	1.2	1.1	1.1	1.0	1.0	0.9	0.8
Italy	2.1	2.1	2.1	2.1	2.0	1.8	1.9	2.0	2.0
Latvia[33]	..	..	..	0.7	0.5	0.5	0.5	0.8	0.7
Lithuania[34]	..	..	0.9	0.8	0.8	0.8	0.8	0.8	1.3
Luxembourg	0.9	0.9	0.9	0.8	0.8	0.8	0.8	0.8	0.8
Macedonia[35]	..	..	..	1.0	1.0	1.0	3.3	2.5	2.4
Malta	0.9	0.9	1.0	0.5	0.8	0.9	1.0	0.9	0.8
Moldova[21]	..	..	..	..	0.8	0.9	0.9	(0.9)	0.6
Netherlands	2.6	2.5	2.5	2.3	2.1	2.0	2.0	1.9	1.8
Norway	2.9	2.8	3.0	2.6	2.8	2.4	2.2	2.1	2.3
Poland	2.7	2.3	2.3	2.6	2.3	2.2	2.2	2.1	2.1
Portugal	2.7	2.7	2.7	2.6	2.5	2.6	2.4	2.3	2.2
Romania	3.5	3.6	3.3	2.1	2.4	2.1	1.8	2.1	2.2
Russia[36]	[12.3]	..	[5.5]	[5.3]	[5.9]	[4.1]	[3.8]	[4.2]	[3.2]

Slovak Rep.[37]	:	:	:	2.2	2.2	2.6	2.3	2.1	2.0
Slovenia[38]	:	:	[2.4]	[1.9]	[1.8]	[1.9]	[1.9]	1.7	1.5
Spain	1.8	1.7	1.6	1.7	1.5	1.5	1.5	1.4	1.4
Sweden	[2.6]	[2.5]	[2.5]	2.6	2.4	2.0	1.7	2.2	2.2
Switzerland	1.8	1.8	1.8	1.6	1.6	1.4	1.3	1.2	1.2
UK[19]	4.0	4.2	3.8	3.6	3.4	3.0	3.0	2.7	2.7
Ukraine[21]	:	:	:	0.5	2.8	3.1	3.5	3.7	3.6
Yugoslavia (FRY)[39]	:	:	:	:	5.8	4.2	(6.0)	(7.2)	(5.4)
Yugoslavia (former)[40]	:	:	:	:	:	:	:	:	:
Middle East									
Bahrain	5.1	5.3	5.3	5.0	4.8	5.0	5.0	4.8	5.0
Egypt	3.5	3.3	3.3	3.3	3.0	2.9	2.8	2.7	2.6
Iran	2.8	2.5	2.2	2.4	3.1	2.5	2.8	3.1	3.1
Iraq	:	:	:	:	:	:	:	:	:
Israel	12.3	11.0	10.5	9.4	8.8	8.5	8.7	8.6	8.7
Jordan	9.6	9.5	7.7	7.8	8.2	8.5	9.1	9.3	9.6
Kuwait	48.5	116.1	30.8	12.0	13.1	13.9	10.6	8.1	[9.3]
Lebanon	5.0	3.4	5.2	4.0	4.6	4.4	3.7	3.0	[3.2]
Oman	18.3	14.7	16.2	15.4	15.7	14.6	12.5	11.5	(12.8)
Qatar	[12.8]	[22.6]	:	:	:	:	:	:	:
Saudi Arabia	6.9	10.4	11.7	13.9	11.9	10.3	9.5	12.4	[12.8]
Syria	3.5	3.7	9.0	7.2	7.4	7.1	6.0	5.9	[6.3]
Turkey	3.5	3.7	3.7	3.8	4.1	3.9	4.1	4.1	4.4
UAE[41]	4.7	4.7	4.5	4.5	4.3	4.1	[3.7]	3.4	3.3
Yemen[42]	8.4	9.1	9.2	9.0	11.3	8.0	6.9	7.4	6.5
Oceania									
Australia	2.2	2.2	2.3	2.3	2.2	2.1	2.0	2.0	1.9
Fiji	2.2	2.3	2.0	1.9	1.8	1.7	1.7	1.5	1.4
New Zealand	[1.8]	1.7	1.5	1.3	1.2	1.1	1.1	1.2	1.3
Papua New Guinea	2.1	1.4	1.3	1.4	1.0	1.0	1.0	1.3	1.0

Conventions:

( ) Uncertain figure.

[ ] SIPRI estimate.

| Change of currency unit.

Notes:

[1] Contributions of military expenditure data, estimates and advice are gratefully acknowledged from: Julian Cooper (CREES, University of Birmingham) for Russia and the newly independent states in Europe, Dimitar Dimitrov (University of National and World Economy, Sofia) for Bulgaria, Paul Dunne (Middlesex Business University, London), Ivan Hostnik (Centre for Strategic Studies, Slovenia), Thomas Scheetz (Buenos Aires) for Argentina, Ron Smith (Birkbeck College, London), Shaoguang Wang (Chinese University of Hong Kong) for China and Ozren Zunec (University of Zagreb) for Croatia.

[2] Military expenditure data from different volumes of the SIPRI Yearbook should not be combined because of data revision between volumes. Revisions can be significant, for instance, when a better time series has become available, when the entire SIPRI series is revised accordingly.

[3] Figures in constant dollars are converted using the market exchange rate for all countries except Armenia, Azerbaijan, Belarus, Georgia, Kazakhstan, Kyrgyzstan, Moldova, Russia, Tajikistan, Turkmenistan, Ukraine and Uzbekistan. For these countries conversion to dollars has been made using the purchasing power parity (PPP) rates as derived from GNP per capita data of the World Bank and the European Bank for Reconstruction and Development (EBRD).

[4] The official figure for Angola in 1999 of 345 615 trillion kwanzas is not included in the table. This level of expenditure would imply that Angola's military expenditure increased approximately 250 times in real terms in 1999—an unrealistic representation of actual trends also bearing in mind the effect of war on the Angolan economy.

[5] Formerly Zaire.

[6] Eritrea became independent from Ethiopia in May 1993. Figures for 1995 include expenditure for demobilization.

[7] The figure for Ethiopia in 1999 includes an allocation of 1 billion birr in addition to the original defence budget.

[8] Figures in local currency are in Communauté financière africaine (CFA) francs. Up to and including the *SIPRI Yearbook 1998*, data were expressed in pesos. The peso was replaced in 1997 at the rate of 65 pesos per CFA franc.

[9] Figures in the table for constant dollars are in current prices and 1995 exchange rate. The figure for Liberian military expenditure in 1999 is for security which represents 13% of total government expenditure of $64 million.

[10] Figures include expenditure for the demobilization of government and RENAMO soldiers and the formation of a new unified army from 1994 onwards.

[11] Namibia became independent on 21 Mar. 1990. During the period 1990/91–1992/93 military construction accounted for more than half of Namibian military expenditure. Figures for 1999 refer to the budget of the Ministry of Defence only. In addition to this the 1999 budget of the Ministry of Finance includes a contingency provision of 104 million ND for the Namibian military presence in the Democratic Republic of Congo (DRC).

[12] Figures for Nigeria before 1999 are understated because of the use by the military of a favourable specific dollar exchange rate.

[13] Figures for Rwanda in 1997 do not include a demobilization allowance of 1.0 billion francs. The figure for 1998 is the official defence budget. According to the International Monetary Fund (IMF) there are additional sources of funding for military activities, both within budget and extra-budgetary. Alternative estimates put Rwanda's military expenditure at twice the official figure.

[14] Figures for Senegal do not include expenditure for paramilitary forces, which in 1998 amounted to 21 100 million francs.

[15] The figure for Zimbabwe in 1999 includes a supplementary allocation of 1800 million ZD.

[16] Figures are official figures from the Costa Rican Ministry for Internal Security.

[17] This state has changed currency during the period. All figures have been converted to the most recent currency.

[18] The Panamanian defence forces were disbanded in 1990 and replaced by the national guard, consisting of the national police and the air and maritime services.

[19] Figures are for fiscal year rather than calendar year.

[20] Figures are uncertain because of very rapid inflation and a change in the currency. All figures have been converted to the most recent currency.

[21] Became independent after the disintegration of the Soviet Union in Dec. 1991. Figures are converted to dollars using the PPP.

[22] Figures for Brunei are current expenditure on the Royal Brunei Armed Forces.

[23] Figures are for estimated total military expenditures. On the estimates in local currency and as a share of GDP, see Shaoguang Wang, 'The military expenditure of China, 1989–98', *SIPRI Yearbook 1999: Armaments, Disarmament and International Security* (Oxford University Press: Oxford, 1999), pp. 334–49. Dollar figures are converted using the market exchange rate.

[24] Figures for Nepal do not include expenditures on paramilitary forces, which in fiscal year 1998/99 amounted to 3315 million taka.

[25] Bosnia and Herzegovina declared its independence from the former Yugoslavia in Mar. 1992 and was recognized by the European Community and the USA in Apr. 1992. The local currency since Jan. 1998 is the convertible mark, set at 1 convertible mark = 1 Deutsche Mark. Figures in US$ are at 1998 prices and exchange rates.

[26] Croatia declared its independence from the former Yugoslavia in June 1991 and was recognized by the European Community in Jan. 1992 and by the United Nations in May 1992.

[27] The Czech Republic was formed on 1 Jan. 1993 after the break-up of Czechoslovakia.

[28] Czechoslovakia was divided into the Czech Republic and the Republic of Slovakia on 1 Jan. 1993. Figures in the table for constant dollars are in current prices and 1990 exchange rate.

[29] Estonia became independent in Sep. 1991. Figures do not include expenditures for paramilitary forces.

[30] Georgia became independent after the disintegration of the Soviet Union in Dec. 1991. Figures are converted to dollars using the PPP. Figures probably do not include the military aid received from Turkey of $7.2 million in 1998 and $3.7 million in 1999.

[31] The German Democratic Republic (East Germany) ceased to exist in Oct. 1990 when it was unified with the Federal Republic of Germany (West Germany).

[32] Figures up to and including 1990 refer to the former Federal Republic of Germany (West Germany).

[33] Latvia became independent in Sep. 1991. Figures do not include: (*a*) allocations for military pensions paid by Russia, which averaged 27 million lats per year over the three years 1996–98; or (*b*) expenditure on paramilitary forces, which amounted to 98.5 million lats in 1999.

[34] Lithuania became independent in Sep. 1991.

[35] Macedonia declared its independence from the former Yugoslavia in Nov. 1992 and was admitted to the United Nations in Apr. 1993.

[36] Figures up to and including 1991 are for the Soviet Union. For sources and methods of the military expenditure figures for the USSR and Russia, see Cooper, J., 'The military expenditure of the USSR and the Russian Federation, 1987–97', *SIPRI Yearbook 1998: Armaments, Disarmament and International Security* (Oxford University Press: Oxford, 1998), appendix 6D, pp. 243–59. Dollar figures are converted using the PPP.

[37] The Slovak Republic was formed on 1 Jan. 1993 after the break-up of Czechoslovakia. Figures do not include expenditure on paramilitary forces. These amounted to 400 million korunas in 1998 and 458 million in 1999.

[38] Slovenia declared its independence from the former Yugoslavia in June 1991 and was recognized by the European Community in Jan. 1992 and by the United Nations in May 1992. Figures have been revised according to the NATO definition, as provided to SIPRI by Slovenia for the years 1997–99.

[39] Serbia and Montenegro announced the creation of the Federal Republic of Yugoslavia in Apr. 1992. Figures do not include revenues from the special defence tax introduced in 1998.

[40] Former Yugoslavia, including Croatia, Macedonia and Slovenia, has a separate entry up to and including the year 1991. Figures in the table for constant dollars are in constant 1990 prices and exchange rate.

[41] Figures for UAE exclude local military expenditure by each of the 7 emirates that form the United Arab Emirates.

[42] The Republic of Yemen was formed in May 1990 by the merger of the People's Democratic Republic of Yemen (South Yemen) and the Yemen Arab Republic (North Yemen).

Source: SIPRI military expenditure database.

Appendix 5B. Table of NATO military expenditure

Table 5B. NATO distribution of military expenditure by category, 1990–99

Figures are in US $m. at 1995 prices and exchange rates. Figures in italics are percentage changes from previous year.

State	Item	1990	1991	1992	1993	1994	1995	1996	1997	1998	1999
North America											
Canada	Personnel	5 488	4 889	4 972	4 730	4 979	4 336	3 793	3 249	3 374	3 523
	Person. change	*4.5*	*–10.9*	*1.7*	*–4.9*	*5.3*	*–12.9*	*–12.5*	*–14.3*	*3.9*	*4.4*
	Equipment	1 866	1 791	1 853	1 904	1 685	1 682	1 286	986	860	1 123
	Equip. change	*–7.5*	*–4.0*	*3.4*	*2.7*	*–11.5*	*–0.2*	*–23.5*	*–23.3*	*–12.8*	*30.7*
USA	Personnel	130 660	135 496	130 193	121 748	115 513	111 038	102 334	102 568	99 803	100 234
	Person. change	*–8.5*	*3.7*	*–3.9*	*–6.5*	*–5.1*	*–3.9*	*–7.8*	*0.2*	*–2.7*	*0.4*
	Equipment	88 535	85 626	75 863	69 032	86 487	77 253	70 812	68 100	65 482	63 527
	Equip. change	*–6.3*	*–3.3*	*–11.4*	*–9.0*	*25.3*	*–10.7*	*–8.3*	*–3.8*	*–3.8*	*–3.0*
Europe											
Belgium	Personnel	4 062	4 034	3 140	3 178	3 147	3 163	3 012	3 041	2 979	2 976
	Person. change	*0.0*	*–0.7*	*–22.2*	*1.2*	*–1.0*	*0.5*	*–4.8*	*1.0*	*–2.0*	*–0.1*
	Equipment	469	480	394	320	354	239	231	272	256	248
	Equip. change	*–21.7*	*2.3*	*–17.9*	*–18.9*	*10.8*	*–32.5*	*–3.3*	*18.1*	*–6.0*	*–3.2*
Czech Rep.	Personnel										549
	Equipment										187
Denmark	Personnel	1 884	1 878	1 828	1 835	1 849	1 887	1 867	1 864	1 924	1 937
	Person. change	*–2.3*	*–0.3*	*–2.7*	*0.4*	*0.8*	*2.1*	*–1.1*	*–0.2*	*3.3*	*0.7*
	Equipment	481	519	574	472	501	389	391	435	444	450
	Equip. change	*13.8*	*7.9*	*10.6*	*–17.8*	*6.2*	*–22.4*	*0.4*	*11.2*	*2.0*	*1.4*
Germany	Personnel	29 572	29 734	29 271	26 689	25 479	25 374	25 042	24 396	23 854	23 748
	Person. change	*7.5*	*0.5*	*–1.6*	*–8.8*	*–4.5*	*–0.4*	*–1.3*	*–2.6*	*–2.2*	*–0.4*
	Equipment	10 047	8 195	6 643	4 987	4 568	4 686	4 474	4 189	4 949	5 395
	Equip. change	*–1.8*	*–18.4*	*–18.9*	*–24.9*	*–8.4*	*2.6*	*–4.5*	*–6.4*	*–6.0*	*9.0*

State	Item	1990	1991	1992	1993	1994	1995	1996	1997	1998	1999
Greece	Personnel	3 243	3 089	3 062	3 027	3 119	3 202	3 278	3 556	3 759	4 017
	Person. change	5.4	-4.7	-0.9	-1.2	3.0	2.7	2.4	8.5	5.7	6.9
	Equipment	1 083	974	1 167	1 202	1 208	1 002	1 132	1 109	1 284	1 267
	Equip. change	-1.2	-10.1	19.8	3.0	0.5	-17.1	13.0	-2.1	15.8	-1.3
Hungary	Personnel										381
	Equipment										153
Italy	Personnel	13 536	14 284	13 787	13 686	13 921	13 056	14 797	16 888	16 960	17 115
	Person. change	0.9	5.5	-3.5	-0.7	1.7	-6.2	13.3	14.1	0.4	0.9
	Equipment	3 845	3 632	3 246	3 742	3 289	2 904	3 064	2 543	2 875	2 861
	Equip. change	-17.9	-5.5	-10.6	15.3	-12.1	-11.7	5.5	-17.0	13.0	-0.5
Luxembourg	Personnel	100	98	110	102	114	115	121	125	131	136
	Person. change	7.4	-2.1	12.0	-7.1	11.6	0.9	5.1	3.1	5.0	3.8
	Equipment	4	8	7	4	3	3	6	6	11	6
	Equip. change	-12.4	86.4	-11.1	-44.5	-17.3	0.0	79.1	-8.8	100.6	-44.9
Netherlands	Personnel	5 189	5 168	5 352	5 078	4 809	4 805	4 488	4 460	4 153	4 013
	Person. change	-2.5	-0.4	3.6	-5.1	-5.3	-0.1	-6.6	-0.6	-6.9	-3.4
	Equipment	1 723	1 461	1 322	1 197	1 386	1 246	1 506	1 255	1 219	1 260
	Equip. change	-1.2	-15.3	-9.5	-9.4	15.8	-10.1	20.9	-16.7	-2.8	3.4
Norway	Personnel	1 634	1 695	1 738	1 331	1 356	1 310	1 332	1 345	1 406	1 484
	Person. change	2.4	3.7	2.5	-23.4	1.9	-3.4	1.7	1.0	4.5	5.6
	Equipment	853	805	968	1 020	1 107	890	896	860	932	859
	Equip. change	-8.2	-5.6	20.2	5.4	8.5	-19.6	0.6	-3.9	8.3	-7.8
Poland	Personnel										1 977
	Equipment										309
Portugal	Personnel	1 830	1 924	2 125	2 032	1 956	2 076	2 076	2 104	2 131	2 121
	Person. change	5.2	5.2	10.4	-4.3	-3.7	6.1	0.0	1.4	1.3	-0.5
	Equipment	258	218	58	183	104	157	162	216	98	253
	Equip. change	-11.0	-15.3	-73.4	215.8	-43.1	51.0	2.8	33.9	-54.6	157.6

Spain Personnel	5 901	5 968	5 928	5 778	5 526	5 685	5 690	5 641	5 660	5 778
Person. change	1.3	1.1	−0.7	−2.5	−4.4	2.9	0.1	−0.9	0.3	2.1
Equipment	1 209	1 190	930	1 252	1 018	1 178	1 130	1 160	1 005	1 038
Equip. change	−35.0	−1.6	−21.9	34.7	−18.7	15.7	−4.0	2.6	−13.3	3.3
Turkey Personnel	2 657	2 743	2 897	3 585	3 280	3 363	3 418	3 733	3 912	4 426
Person. change	26.6	3.2	5.6	23.8	−8.5	2.4	1.6	9.2	4.8	13.1
Equipment	1 100	1 284	1 475	1 506	1 884	1 961	2 282	2 082	1 667	2 833
Equip. change	40.6	16.7	14.9	2.1	25.1	3.9	16.4	−8.8	−19.9	70.0
UK Personnel	16 883	17 912	17 007	16 513	15 199	14 013	13 709	12 577	12 247	12 307
Person. change	−0.2	6.1	−5.1	−2.9	−8.0	−7.8	−2.2	−8.3	−2.6	0.5
Equipment	7 443	8 333	7 028	9 870	9 141	7 379	8 141	7 970	8 527	8 629
Equip. change	−20.7	12.0	−15.7	40.4	−7.4	−19.3	10.3	−2.1	7.0	1.2
NATO Western Europe Personnel	86 408	88 655	86 243	82 835	79 759	78 049	78 829	79 729	79 116	80 058
Person. change	3.5	2.6	−2.7	−4.0	−3.7	−2.1	1.0	1.1	−0.8	1.2
Equipment	28 515	27 098	23 812	25 756	24 567	22 034	23 415	22 097	23 267	25 099
Equip. change	−10.9	−5.0	−12.1	8.2	−4.6	−10.3	6.3	−5.6	5.3	7.9
NATO total Personnel	222 555	229 040	221 408	209 313	200 251	193 423	184 956	185 546	182 293	183 816
Person. change	−3.9	2.9	−3.3	−5.5	−4.3	−3.4	−4.4	0.3	−1.8	0.8
Equipment	118 915	114 515	101 529	96 692	112 740	100 969	95 514	91 183	89 608	89 749
Equip. change	−7.5	−3.7	−11.3	−4.8	16.6	−10.4	−5.4	−4.5	−1.7	0.2

Note: The NATO data show percentage shares; the dollar figures have been calculated using these percentages and the total expenditures shown in table 7A.3. France does not return figures giving this breakdown to NATO.

Sources: NATO, *Financial and Economic Data Relating to NATO Defence*, Press release M-DPC-2 (1999)152, 2 Dec. 1999, URL <http://www.nato.int/docu/pr/1999/p99-152e.htm>, version current on 2 Dec. 1999; and NATO Press releases M-DPC-2(97)147 (2 Dec. 1997), M-DPC-2(96)168 (17 Dec. 1996), M-DPC-2(96)168 (17 Dec. 1996), M-DPC-2(95)115 (29 Nov. 1995) and M-DPC-2(93)76 (8 Dec. 1993).

Appendix 5C. Sources and methods for military expenditure data

This appendix provides only the most basic information.[1] The military expenditure tables in appendix 5A cover 161 countries for the 10-year period 1990–99. These data cannot be combined with the series for earlier years as published in previous SIPRI Yearbooks, since these are updated each year and the revisions can be extensive—not only are significant changes made in figures which were previously estimates, but entire series are revised when new and better sources come to light. As a result there is sometimes considerable variation between data sets for individual countries in different Yearbooks.

I. Purpose of the data

The main purpose of the data on military expenditures is to provide an easily identifiable measure of the scale of resources absorbed by the military. Military expenditure is an input measure which is not directly related to the output of military activities, such as military capability or military security. Long-term trends in military expenditure and sudden changes in trend may be signs of a change in military output, but such interpretations should be made with caution.

Military expenditure data as measured in constant dollars (table 5A.3) are an indicator of the trend in the volume of resources used for military activities with the purpose of allowing comparisons over time for individual countries and comparisons between countries. The share of gross domestic product (GDP—table 5A.4) is a rough indicator of the proportion of national resources used for military activities, and therefore of the economic burden imposed on the national economy.

II. Sources

The sources for military expenditure data are, in order of priority: (*a*) primary sources, that is, official data provided by national governments, either in their official publications or in response to questionnaires; (*b*) secondary sources which quote primary data; and (*c*) other secondary sources.

The first group consists of national budget documents, defence white papers and public finance statistics published by ministries of finance and of defence, central banks and national statistical offices. It also includes government responses to questionnaires about military expenditure sent out by SIPRI, the United Nations or the Organization for Security and Co-operation in Europe (OSCE).

The second group includes international statistics, such as those of NATO and the International Monetary Fund (IMF). Data for NATO countries are taken from NATO defence expenditure statistics as published in a number of NATO sources. Data for many developing countries are taken from the IMF's *Government Financial Statistics Yearbook*, which provides a defence line for most of its member countries. This group also includes publications of other organizations which provide proper references to

---

[1] For an overview of the conceptual problems and sources of uncertainty involved in the compilation of military expenditure data, the reader is referred to Brzoska, M., 'World military expenditures', eds K. Hartley and T. Sandler, *Handbook of Defense Economics*, vol. 1 (Elsevier: Amsterdam, 1995).

the primary sources used. The three main sources in this category are the *Europa Yearbook* (Europa Publications Ltd, London), the *Country Reports* of the Economist Intelligence Unit (London), and the *Country Reports* by IMF staff.

The third group of sources consists of specialist journals and newspapers.

III. Methods

Definition of military expenditure

Although the lack of sufficiently detailed data makes it difficult to apply a common definition of military expenditure on a worldwide basis, SIPRI has adopted a definition, based on the NATO definition, as a guideline. Where possible, SIPRI military expenditure data include all current and capital expenditure on: (*a*) the armed forces, including peacekeeping forces; (*b*) defence ministries and other government agencies engaged in defence projects; (*c*) paramilitary forces, when judged to be trained and equipped for military operations; and (*d*) military space activities. Such expenditures should include: (*a*) military and civil personnel, including retirement pensions of military personnel and social services for personnel; (*b*) operations and maintenance; (*c*) procurement; (*d*) military research and development; and (*e*) military aid (in the military expenditure of the donor country). Excluded are civil defence and current expenditures for previous military activities, such as for veterans' benefits, demobilization, conversion and weapon destruction.

In practice it is not possible to apply this definition for all countries, since this would require much more detailed information than is available about what is included in military budgets and off-budget military expenditure items. In many cases SIPRI cannot make independent estimates but is confined to using the national data provided. Priority is then given to the choice of a uniform definition over time for each country to achieve consistency over time, rather than to adjusting the figures for single years according to a common definition. In cases where it is impossible to use the same source and definition for all years, the percentage change between years in the deviant source is applied to the existing series in order to make the trend as correct as possible. In the light of these difficulties, military expenditure data are not suitable for close comparison between individual countries and are more appropriately used for comparisons over time.

Estimates and the use of brackets

SIPRI data reflect the official data reported by governments. As a general rule, SIPRI assumes national data to be accurate until there is convincing information to the contrary. Estimates are made primarily when the coverage of official data does not correspond to the SIPRI definition or when there is no consistent time series available. In the first case, estimates are made on the basis of an analysis of official government budget and expenditure accounts. The most comprehensive estimates, for China and Russia, have been presented in detail in previous Yearbooks. In the second case, differing time series are linked together. In order not to introduce assumptions into the military expenditure statistics, estimates are always based on empirical evidence and never based on assumptions nor extrapolations. Thus, no estimates are made for countries which do not release any official data, but these countries are displayed without figures.

SIPRI estimates are presented in square brackets in the tables. Round brackets are used when data are uncertain for other reasons, such as the reliability of the source or because of the economic context. Figures are more unreliable when inflation is rapid and unpredictable. Supplementary allocations made during the course of the year to cover losses in purchasing power often go unreported and recent military expenditure can appear to be falling in real terms when it is in fact increasing.

Data for the most recent years include two types of estimate which apply to all countries: (a) figures for the most recent years are for adopted budget, budget estimates or revised estimates, and are thus more often than not revised in subsequent years; and (b) the deflator used for the last year in the series is an estimate. Unless exceptional uncertainty is involved in these estimates, they are not bracketed.

Calculations

The SIPRI military expenditure figures are presented on a calendar-year basis with a few exceptions. The exceptions are Canada, the UK and the USA, for which NATO statistics report data on a fiscal-year basis. Calendar-year data are calculated on the assumption of an even rate of expenditure throughout the fiscal year.

The deflator used for conversion from current to constant prices is the consumer price index (CPI) of the country concerned. This choice of deflator is connected to the purpose of the SIPRI data—that they should be an indicator of resource use on an opportunity cost basis.[2]

For most countries the conversion to dollars is done by use of the average market exchange rates (MERs). The exceptions are countries in transition whose economies are still so closed that MERs, which are based on price ratios in foreign transactions only, do not accurately reflect the price ratios of the economy in general. For these countries conversion to dollars is made by use of purchasing power parity (PPP) rates.

The ratio of military expenditure to GDP is calculated in domestic currency at current prices and for calendar years.

---

[2] A military-specific deflator would be the more appropriate choice if the objective were to measure the purchasing power in terms of military personnel, goods and services.

Appendix 5D. Military expenditure in Africa

WUYI OMITOOGUN

I. Introduction

Military expenditure in Africa has been increasing since 1997 after a relatively long period of decline. In 1999, the total calculable expenditure on military activities was about 22 per cent higher in real terms than at the low point of 1996. However, this new increase does not fully reflect the total amount spent on military activities in the region. For instance, because of great distortions in the economy and inconsistencies in the official figures (probably due to the ongoing war), Angola's military expenditure is not included in the regional total. If it were added the 1999 figure would be almost 50 per cent higher.

Over the seven-year period 1990–96 military expenditure in Africa fell by about 25 per cent in real terms. The main factors behind the decline were poor economic conditions, budget constraints and the demilitarization process in Southern Africa generally, and more specifically South Africa, the continent's major military spender. The decline was, however, not evenly distributed. Military spending in North Africa, for instance, rose throughout the 1990s, mainly because of increased military spending in Algeria. The reasons for the change in trend since 1997 are: (*a*) the persistence of many of the continent's conflicts and the involvement of several states in them;[1] and (*b*) the steady increase over the years in the military spending of some of Africa's major spenders, notably Nigeria, Algeria and Ethiopia.

In *Nigeria* the abolition in early 1999 of the dual exchange rate, which gave the military and some special arms of the government—mainly the presidency—access to much cheaper foreign exchange than the rest of the economy, led to an almost 100 per cent increase, albeit fictitious, in the country's official military expenditure for 1999. The special naira : dollar exchange rate, at 22 : 1 for imports and other purchases in dollar terms, was far below the market exchange rate of 85 : 1. The practice meant that the actual cost of the military budget (especially the capital vote) could be four times the officially reported defence budget figures, the remaining costs being hidden in the exchange rate subsidy. In *Algeria* the continued violence still ensures that the country's military expenditure remains one of the highest in the region. In *Ethiopia* the continuation of hostilities with neighbouring Eritrea means increased military spending; in 1999 it was more than three times the pre-war level. The involvement of *Zimbabwe*, *Namibia*, *Rwanda* and *Uganda* in the war in the Democratic Republic of Congo (DRC) also led to significant increases in their officially reported military expenditure. *South Africa*, whose reduction in military spending earlier in the 1990s was a major factor in the overall decline of the continent's military expenditure, is set to have another round of increases beginning from 1999. In September 1999 its cabinet approved an arms procurement programme worth about $5 billion (29.9 billion rand) over the next eight years[2] which will lead to significantly increased military expenditure over the next three years.[3]

---

[1] On the current conflicts in Africa, see chapters 1 and 2, and appendix 1B in this volume.

[2] Heitman, H., 'South Africa signs orders for $5 billion', *Jane's Defence Weekly*, 8 Dec. 1999, p. 3.

[3] Engelbrecht, L., 'South Africa boosts defence spending', *Defence Systems Daily*, 29 Oct. 1999, URL <http://defence-data.com/current/page5646.htm>.

Table 5D. African military expenditure, 1990–99

Figures are in US $b., at constant 1995 prices and exchange rates. Figures in italics are percentages. Figures do not always add up to totals because of the conventions of rounding.

Region[a]	1990	1991	1992	1993	1994	1995	1996	1997	1998	1999	% change 1990–99
Africa[b]	11.9	11.1	9.9	9.9	10.0	9.4	8.9	9.3	[9.5]	[10.6]	*– 11*
North	2.4	2.5	2.7	2.9	3.4	3.1	3.2	[3.5]	[3.7]	..	*+ 54[c]*
Sub-Saharan	9.5	8.7	7.2	7.0	6.6	6.3	5.8	5.8	5.8	[6.6]	*– 30[b]*
World	**1 007**	..	**818**	**787**	**763**	**724**	**708**	**718**	**[704]**	**[719]**	**– 28.6**

[a] For the country coverage of the regions, see appendix 5A, table 5A.1.

[b] Total military expenditure in Africa and Sub-Saharan Africa is much higher than indicated in this table because of the exclusion of Angola from these totals. Because of the effect of war on the Angolan economy, it is impossible to make a time series in constant dollars for Angola. Its official military expenditure may be as high as $5–6 billion in 1996–97, which would mean that total Sub-Saharan military expenditure was twice the figure in the table above.

[c] Change over the period 1990–98.

Source: Appendix 5A, table 5A.1.

However, SIPRI figures, which are based on officially reported data, do not fully represent the total resources committed to military activities in Africa because of the hidden cost of armed conflict that is pervasive in the region. Continuing conflicts in different parts of Africa in 1999 have involved the diversion of vital resources to military purposes in far more countries than at any other time in the recent past. The magnitude of expenditures and costs related to armed conflicts, although important and probably increasing, is difficult to estimate as they are not reflected in official budgets, partly because of the emerging pattern of financing many of the wars on the continent. What is certain, however, is that the costs of war to the belligerents have been considerable and, in view of the stark poverty on the continent, a diversion of scarce resources. With little prospect of an early end to many of the conflicts and the involvement of some African states in distant conflicts for reasons that range from the logic of the regional security complex[4] to economic motivations, this new increase is set to continue for some time.

This appendix describes some of the costs involved in armed conflicts on the African continent, for three categories of countries: (*a*) those on whose territory conflict is taking place; (*b*) those siding with factions in a conflict; and (*c*) those involved in regional peacekeeping missions. It begins with a general description of the new mechanisms involved in the financing of armed conflict.

II. The financing of armed conflict

In conditions of war and armed conflict, the financing of military activities takes extraordinary forms. This is particularly the case in many developing countries endowed with valuable natural resources such as diamonds, emeralds, oil and copper. During war these resources are exploited by whoever can provide protection. Those

[4] Buzan, B., *People, States and Fear: An Agenda for International Security Studies in the Post-Cold War Era* (Harvester Wheatsheaf: Hemel Hempstead, 1991), pp. 190–93.

who are able to provide protection, especially in the new types of war,[5] are the different fighting units, public and private, state and non-state, including regular armed forces, remnants of paramilitary groups, self-defence units, foreign mercenaries and regular foreign troops. Mary Kaldor has categorized the sources of funding these new wars into four types. These are: (a) 'asset transfer'—the redistribution of existing assets to benefit the fighting units (e.g., looting, robbery, hostage-taking and deriving profits from control over market prices); (b) 'war taxes' or 'protection' money from the production of primary commodities and various forms of illegal trading; (c) external assistance, in particular for imports, such as remittances from abroad to individual families, direct assistance from the diaspora living abroad or assistance from foreign governments; and (d) the diversion of humanitarian assistance for governments' or warring factions' own use. For countries involved in this type of war, data on government military expenditure are irrelevant for measuring military expenditure. This is illustrated by the current scenarios of armed conflict in Africa.

Even more important is the set of social relationships formed by these systems for financing wars—a factor that works strongly against ending wars.

III. Countries on whose territory conflict is taking place

The costs of war to those actually in conflict are for obvious reasons difficult to determine or estimate. This section provides examples which serve to illustrate the magnitude of these costs and the mechanisms for financing these wars.

The *DRC*, with the most intractable of the wars, cannot offer any reasonable figure for its military expenditure because of the continuing conflict, but nearly all government receipts are diverted to the prosecution of the war with the rebels, even as those receipts continue to decline as a result of rebel activities.[6] The cost to the DRC of hired mercenaries—mainly from Russia and Ukraine—is also unknown, but they are constantly engaged in flying the DRC's fighter aircraft.[7] In addition there is the cost of arms imports. The DRC Government owes the Government of Zimbabwe about 100 million Zimbabwean dollars (ZD) (US$2.6 million) for arms imports and recently stopped paying the monthly instalments of the agreed phased repayment scheme on these supplies (arms and munitions) from Zimbabwean Arms Industries (ZDI).[8]

A major problem of the government is that it is not effectively in control of the country, particularly in some of the mineral mining centres. This has opened up sources of financing for other armed factions. The main diamond mining area at Mbuji-Mayi in central DRC is virtually surrounded by the Rwandan-backed Rassemblement Congolais pour la Démocratie (Congolese Rally for Democracy, RCD) rebels, while the Ugandan-backed faction of the RCD collects customs duties on the north-east border of the country. The continued presence of different countries in the DRC is not unconnected with the vast resources the country possesses. To many of the belligerents and their supporters war will remain attractive as long as the profits of violence outweigh the gains of peace.

---

[5] Kaldor, M., *New and Old Wars: Organized Violence in a Global Era* (Polity Press: Cambridge, 1999). chapter on financing wars. pp. 101–107.

[6] 'War stifles economy', *Africa Research Bulletin*, 16 Mar.–15 Apr. 1999, pp. 13835–36, and 'Investment: a hostage to Kabila's capriciousness', *Africa Research Bulletin*, 16 Aug.–15 Sep. 1999, p. 14021.

[7] 'The DRC air force loses another "bomber"', *Defence Systems Daily (South Africa and Southern Africa)*, 18 Nov. 1999, URL <http://defence-data.com/current>.

[8] Mutsakani, A., 'Arms firm in desperate bid to get Kabila to pay up', *Financial Gazette* (Harare), 29 July 1999, URL <http://www.africaonline.co.zwfingaz/99/stage/archive/990729/national4213.html>.

In *Sudan*, with Africa's most enduring civil war, according to some sources the government spends over half of the state budget every year[9] on the civil war it has waged since 1989 with the Sudan People's Liberation Army (SPLA) and other rebel factions. If this is true the military expenditure of Sudan will be four times higher than officially reported annually since 1989. Estimated government expenditure for 1999 is $1.09 billion.[10] This diversion of budget resources, according to President Omar Hassan al-Bashir, makes it impossible for the government to 'provide the minimum limits for survival for the Sudanese' and 'puts even ministers and government officials below the poverty line'.[11]

The *Angolan* Government has been engaged in armed conflict with different groups in the country since independence in 1975. The most resilient of the groups is the União Nacional para a Independência Total de Angola (National Union for the Total Independence of Angola, UNITA). It has engaged the government in several bitter wars, the most recent being from 1998. The government is also involved in the wars in the DRC and the Republic of Congo (Congo-Brazzaville), primarily with the aim of closing all channels of supplies to UNITA. Faced with an external debt burden of $11 billion and depressed world oil prices from 1998, in 1999 the country resorted to mortgaging its future oil sales to pay for military equipment.[12] This became necessary because of the increased and successful UNITA attacks on the outskirts of the capital, Luanda, towards the end of 1998 and in the early part of 1999. This put the government in a desperate situation, forcing it to withdraw its forces from the DRC to support the war effort at home. It is difficult to estimate how much the government is committing to the war effort, but given its open declaration in April 1999 that it had exhausted its savings (apparently on the war) this may well be over three-quarters of the annual state budget.[13] Angola derives four-fifths of its government income from oil exports[14] and the diversion of resources to war in 1999 has had a severe impact on social provision for its citizens. The rise in oil prices since June 1999, the military successes recorded by the government since late 1999 against UNITA and the effect of UN sanctions against UNITA have, however, recently provided the needed relief to the government.

In *Algeria* conflict which started in 1992 when the election that the Front Islamique du Salut (Islamic Salvation Front, FIS) was poised to win was cancelled is still continuing, if at a reduced rate. The normality promised by the election of Abdelaziz Bouteflika as President, in April 1999, was in jeopardy by the close of the year, with increased violence around the capital, Algiers, culminating in the killing of Abdelkader Hachani, a senior leader of the FIS. Bouteflika's promised amnesty for jailed Islamic militants who renounced violence by 15 January 2000 appeared not enough to prevent a spiral of violence in the country. This was probably behind his inclusion of persons who had committed other offences in the new general amnesty

[9] Economist Intelligence Unit, *Country Report, Sudan,* 2nd quarter 1999, p. 20.
[10] Clayton, A., 'Sudanese government counts cost of war', *Jane's Defence Weekly*, vol. 31, no. 6 (10 Feb. 1999), p. 6.
[11] Clayton (note 10).
[12] United Nations Office for the Coordination of Humanitarian Affairs (OCHA), Integrated Regional Information Network–Southern Africa (IRIN-SA), 'Government mortgages oil sales for military equipment', 11 May 1999, URL <http://www.reliefweb.int/IRIN/sa/countrystories/angola/19990511a.htm>.
[13] Gordon, C., 'Angola's debt burden', *Daily Mail and Guardian*, 1 July 1999, URL <http://www.mg.co.za/mg/news/99jul1/1jul-angola2.html>.
[14] US Energy Information Administration, 'Angola', URL <http://www.eia.doe.gov/emeu/cabs/angola.html>.

announced on 12 January. The new announcement resulted in the immediate disbanding of the armed wing of the FIS but the other armed faction, the Groupe Islamique Armé (Armed Islamic Group, GIA) vowed to continue with violence. As a result of the continued insecurity, Algeria's military expenditure has been increasing. The 1999 defence budget of 122 billion Algerian dinars (AD) ($1.9 billion) was 8.3 per cent higher in nominal terms than that in 1998. In the proposed budget for the year 2000 defence is the largest single item, exceeding the education vote for the first time. It is also 16.4 per cent higher than the allocation for fiscal year (FY) 1999 and 26 per cent more than the amount for 1998.[15] Algerian military expenditure continues to be one of the highest in Africa and the security situation does not suggest a likely change of trend in the near future.

The costs of the border war between *Ethiopia* and *Eritrea* have been considerable to these two aid-dependent states. Ethiopia has reportedly spent over $300 million and Eritrea close to the same amount on armaments and other military-related activities since the beginning of the war in 1998.[16] To support their war efforts both have had to resort to extra-budgetary measures. *Ethiopia* diverted the proceeds of the privatization of state companies while cutting the allocations to other sectors of the economy, such as road repair.[17] It has also imposed a surtax of 10 per cent on some imported commodities, purportedly to cover the budget deficit.[18] The war has been aggravating the worsening food situation in Ethiopia by depriving the country of able-bodied peasants in the north, who have been enticed to enlist for the war as a result of the relatively high wages, about $30–50 per month.[19] Ethiopia's official military expenditure, which dropped sharply at the beginning of the 1990s, has been rising slowly again since 1994. With an estimated $1 million currently being spent on the war per day, the government's target ceiling of 1.3 billion birr (about $174 million) for military expenditure for FY 1998/99 was probably exceeded.[20] Although military spending was 3.2 per cent and 3.5 per cent of GDP in 1997 and 1998, respectively, the amount spent on arms will push that share in 1999 close to 12 per cent. *Eritrea* hopes to raise about $400 million from donations from its citizens abroad in addition to revenues from increased taxes and treasury bonds to further finance the war.[21]

IV. Countries siding with a faction in war

A number of African states have had significant increases in their official military expenditure as a result of their involvement in conflicts other than their own. There

[15] Daoud, A., 'Parliament begins FY00 budget in difficult conditions', North Africa Journal, issue 69, week ending 18 Nov. 1999, URL <http://www.north-africa.com/archives/docs/111899A.htm>. See also *SIPRI Yearbook 1999: Armaments, Disarmament and International Security* (Oxford University Press: Oxford, 1999), p. 302.

[16] 'Futile war in Africa', *International Herald Tribune*, 8 Feb. 1999, p. 8. See also 'The Ethiopian offensive: where does it end?', *Defence Systems Daily*, 9 Feb. 1999, URL <http://defence-data.com/current/page3734.htm>.

[17] 'Ceasefire under threat', *Africa Confidential*, vol. 40, no. 22 (5 Nov. 1999), p. 2.

[18] 'Surtax imposed to make up for budget deficit', *Addis Tribune*, 21 Jan. 2000, URL <http://Addis TribuneOnline.Net/Archives/2000/01/21-01-00/Surt.htm>.

[19] Integrated Regional Information Network–Central and East Africa (IRIN-CEA), 'Ethiopia: separating humanitarian needs and political issues', 20 July 1999, URL http://www.reliefweb.int/IRIN/cea/countrystories/ethiopia/19990710.htm>.

[20] Economist Intelligence Unit, *Country Report Ethiopia*, 2nd quarter 1999. p. 9.

[21] 'Carnage on the plain', *The Economist*, 17–23 Apr. 1999, p. 35.

has been external involvement mainly in the war in the DRC but also in Guinea-Bissau and the Republic of Congo.

Of the countries involved in the DRC conflict, *Zimbabwe*'s involvement has generated much controversy over the costs and objectives of intervention. Part of the initial reasons for President Robert Mugabe's sending troops to the DRC was the expected economic gains from the enterprise.[22] The initial deal between presidents Kabila of the DRC and Mugabe, signed on 4 September 1998, providing for Zimbabwe's support was to pave the way for a self-financing involvement that would also benefit Zimbabwe economically. Under the agreement ZDI was to supply arms and munitions to the DRC troops and a Zimbabwean mining company, Ridgepointe, would get a minority share (37.5 per cent) and take over the management of Gécamines, the DRC state mining company which controls the country's copper and cobalt mines. The profit from the enterprise would be shared according to an agreed formula whereby the DRC Government put 20–30 per cent of its 62.5 per cent share into financing Zimbabwe's support in the war.[23]

It is doubtful whether these revenues will cover the costs of maintaining 11 000 troops in the DRC, given recent revelations about the costs to the Zimbabwean Exchequer of staying in the DRC: the cost of lost equipment is estimated at 7.7 billion ZD or over $200 million.[24] This is in addition to the money expected to be paid to the families of those who died in the war and the cost of providing succour to the injured. The Zimbabwean Government's estimate of the cost of this enterprise ($3 million per month) was disputed by the International Monetary Fund (IMF) and the World Bank[25] who put on hold aid promised to Zimbabwe, amounting to $340 million, which the government desperately needed.[26] The donors claimed that the total monthly cost of Zimbabwe's involvement was probably about $27 million.[27] If this is true, then the official defence budget of Zimbabwe has been greatly understated since 1998 when the country entered the DRC war. The official defence budget has increased steadily over the past few years. The original budget for FY 1999, of 5.4 billion ZD, was supplemented by an allocation of 1.8 billion ZD later in the year, raising the total to 7.2 billion ZD ($190 million)—an increase of close to 100 per cent over 1998. In the FY 2000 budget the government has allocated 9 billion ZD ($237 million) to defence. This is at the expense of more pressing social issues such as health, especially the Aids epidemic in the country.

The increase in *Namibia's* military expenditure in the past two years has also been due primarily to its involvement in the DRC conflict. Its military expenditure rose from the original allocation of 443 million Namibian dollars (ND) in 1998 to 559 million ND ($91 million) in 1999 and a contingency fund of ND 104 million from the Ministry of Finance is likely to be devoted to the additional cost related to the DRC war.[28] In January 2000, the government also announced a supplementary

[22] 'Rhodies to the rescue', *Africa Confidential*, vol. 40, no. 22 (5 Nov. 1999), pp. 5–6.

[23] 'Rhodies to the rescue' (note 22). See also Mutsakani (note 8).

[24] Peta, B., 'Zim loses $7b arms in DRC war', *Financial Gazette* (Harare), 25 Nov. 1999, URL <http://www.fingaz.co.zw/fingaz/99/99/stage/archive/991124/national19163.html.>.

[25] Morris, H. and Fidler, S., 'Zimbabwe misled IMF over spending on war', *Financial Times*, 4 Oct. 1999, p. 1; and Hawkins, T., 'Zimbabwe's reform programme unwinds', *Financial Times*, 8 Oct. 1999, p. 9.

[26] Mutume, G., 'The economics of financing war in Africa', *Daily Mail and Guardian* (Johannesburg), 20 Oct. 1999, URL <http://www.mg.co.za/mg/news/99oct2/20oct-war.html>.

[27] 'World Bank suspends aid to Zimbabwe', *Financial Times*, 6 Oct. 1999, p. 6.

[28] Maletsky, C., 'DRC war to draw on contingency funding', *The Namibian*, 6 Aug. 1999, URL <http://www.namibian.com.na/Focus/DRCcrisis/funding.html>.

defence budget of ND 173 million.[29] The war is believed to be costing Namibia about $150 000 per day[30] in addition to compensation worth about ND 250 000 ($41 000) each to the families of those who lost their lives in the war.

The continued involvement of *Rwanda* and *Uganda* in military activities in neighbouring countries, especially in the DRC, is becoming a source of concern for donors, on whom both countries depend for the financing of part of their annual budgets. While their defence budgets appear to show some stability or modest increases over the last couple of years, their continued involvement in military activities is believed to be eating deep into their social budgets. The IMF decided to postpone the release of part of the agreed loan to *Uganda* in 1999 because of overspending of the defence budget in the first half of FY 1998/99.[31] The *Rwandan* Government has had to use extra-budgetary funding, including reallocating civilian budgets such as teachers' salaries to defence purposes.[32] The IMF disputed the official figure, reported by the Rwandan Government in 1998, of military expenditure accounting for 4.3 per cent of GDP.[33] It is estimated that the share of GDP taken by defence in 1998 is about 8 per cent, taking into account extra resources derived from incomes from semi-public companies and illegal trading in diamonds from the DRC.[34]

Similarly, in Uganda funds ostensibly meant for the police in the state budget were diverted to the military to hide the expenditure from the aid donors and lending organizations, who insist on modest military expenditure.[35] In the draft state budget for FY 2000 the Rwandan Government has proposed a reduction of 62 million francs[36] ($96 000) in defence spending. This is more symbolic than real since it is a mere 0.2 per cent reduction on the 1999 budget. However, the Speaker of the Parliament asked for financial support from all Rwandans, home and abroad, for the country's peacekeeping and security operations in view of the fact that 'our involvement in the Democratic Republic of Congo has caused a budgetary gap to be filled if this is not going to be an obstacle to our army's performance'.[37]

Both Rwanda and Uganda claim that, in spite of these obvious gaps and their military activities, their government budgets are not unusually affected. This may be true, since both are reported to have shown up on the list of diamond exporters because of illegal mining in the DRC; they are not known as diamond producers.[38]

---

[29] 'The NDF gets the lion's share of the additional budget', *Defence Systems Daily (South Africa and Southern Africa)*, 31 Jan. 2000, URL <http://defence-data.com/com/current/pages6370.htm>.

[30] IRIN-SA, 'Namibia will withdraw troops once UN peacekeepers in place', 25 Nov. 1999, URL <http://www.irin.org.za/sa/countrystories/namibia/19991125.htm>.

[31] Andrew M. Mwenda and Agencies, 'Domestic debt record shs 100bn, IMF suspends aid to Uganda', *The Monitor* (Kampala), 13 Mar. 1999, URL <http://www.africanews.com/monitor/freeissues/13mar99/front.html#anchor1>.

[32] *Libre Beligique*, 2 Nov. 1999, p. 10, in 'Military spending stalls Rwandan economy', Foreign Broadcast Information Service, *Daily Report-Western Europe (FBIS-WEU)*, FBIS-WEU-1999-1102, 3 Nov. 1999.

[33] 'Military spending stalls Rwandan economy' (note 32).

[34] 'Military spending stalls Rwandan economy' (note 32); and Mutume, G., 'The economics of financing war in Africa', *Daily Mail and Guardian* (Johannesburg), 20 Oct. 1999, URL <http://www.mg.co.za/mg/news/99oct2/20oct-war.html>.

[35] This was revealed by a Ugandan police officer at a public inquiry into police corruption in the country. 'Creative accounting in Africa: hidden skills', *The Economist*, 9 Oct. 1999, p. 64.

[36] IRIN-CEA, 'Rwanda: defence cuts in new budget', 11 Nov. 1999, URL <http://www.reliefweb.int/IRIN/cea/countrystories/rwanda/19991111.htm>.

[37] Panafrican News Agency (PANA), 'Rwanda calls on citizens to make peace contributions', 11 Nov. 1999, URL <tttp://www.africanews.org/east/rwanda/stories/1999111_feat3.html>.

[38] Mutume (note 34).

Senegal, which is still grappling with its own internal rebellion in the Casamance region,[39] announced an increase in its annual budget as a result of the prohibitive cost of its intervention in the crisis in Guinea-Bissau in April 1998. The government estimated the cost of its support for the now ousted regime of President João Bernardo Vieira at 2.5 billion CFA francs ($38 million).[40] This costly enterprise was financed from the proceeds of privatizing state-owned companies, especially the national telecommunications company.[41]

IV. Countries involved in peacekeeping operations

A third group of countries has had increased expenditures as a result of involvement in regional peacekeeping missions. *Guinea* and *Nigeria* in the last quarter of 1999 provided cost estimates of their involvement in the peacekeeping operations of the Economic Community of West African States Monitoring Group (ECOMOG) in Liberia and Sierra Leone. The cost of intervention in Lesotho by South Africa and Botswana to support Prime Minister Pakalitha Mosisili is also gradually coming to light.

Guinea officially estimates the cost of its involvement in ECOMOG at $500 million.[42] This is in addition to the effect of a large influx of refugees from Sierra Leone and Liberia, two countries bordering it and recently at war. The new democratic government in Nigeria estimated the cost of its leadership of ECOMOG in the period 1989–99 at over $8 billion.[43] This is close to one-third of the country's foreign debt (estimated at over $30 billion) and a big burden on the economy. How it was financed is not clear because the total official defence budget for the country during this period was just a little above the estimated expenditure for the cost of peacekeeping. The most likely explanation is that it was financed through the mechanism of the dual exchange rate. The near-100 per cent increase in Nigeria's military expenditure in 1999, the first year of a new civilian government, was to a great extent the result of the abolition of this practice. The defence budget for FY 2000 also reflects this harmonization of exchange rates, so that the budgeted total of 34 billion naira ($340 million) represents a 47 per cent rise in nominal terms over the 1998 figure.

The cost of the seven-month (September 1998–March 1999) intervention of *South Africa* and *Botswana* in Lesotho has been estimated at about $140 million, or $4.9 million per week.[44] Although this does not appear to have had any adverse effect on the overall budget of either country, the question remains whether the Lesotho Government, which suffered severe economic reverses as a result of the crisis, will reimburse them.

---

[39] The government and the rebels agreed to put a halt to fighting in Dec. 1999 at peace talks in Banjul, Gambia, within the framework of a ceasefire signed in July 1993 but which never held.

[40] 'Neighbourly intervention does not come cheap', *Africa Research Bulletin*, 16 May–15 June 1999, p. 13908.

[41] 'Neighbourly intervention' (note 40), p. 13908.

[42] IRIN, 'Guinea: counting the cost of Sierra Leone's war', 15 Nov. 1999, URL <http://www.irin.org.za/wa/countrystories/guinea/19991015.htm>.

[43] 'A survey of Nigeria', *The Economist*, 15 Jan. 2000, p. 4.

[44] Economist Intelligence Unit, *Country Report Lesotho*, 3rd quarter 1999, p. 22.

6. Arms production

ELISABETH SKÖNS and REINHILDE WEIDACHER

I. Introduction

The profound changes in the system of arms production which characterized the whole of the 1990s were still continuing in 1999, although at a slower pace. By the end of the decade the reduction in the level of arms production, which had been significant during the first half of the decade, had ceased and arms production seemed rather to have begun to increase in most of the major centres of arms production, but the processes of reorganization, concentration and internationalization continued during 1999.

This chapter summarizes the trend in arms sales in the 100 largest arms-producing companies in the Organisation for Economic Co-operation and Development (OECD) and developing countries except China during 1998 (section II, based on data in appendix 6A). Section III provides an overview of the continued process of concentration in the arms industry during 1999 in these countries. Developments in arms production over the decade of the 1990s are examined in section IV. This section also aims to assess the trends in the volume of arms production, government military research and development (R&D) expenditure, concentration, diversification and dependence on arms exports over the 1990s in the major arms-producing countries. It is based on data for the 100 largest companies and on the scarce data that are available giving national coverage. Section V describes developments in Russia in 1999. Appendix 6A provides financial and employment data for the 100 largest companies and appendix 6B lists the major national and international acquisitions of arms-producing activities by US and West European companies in the period since 1998.

The main findings are as follows.

1. The combined arms sales of the 100 largest arms-producing companies in the OECD and developing countries except China amounted to $154.5 billion in 1998.

2. During 1999 the main developments in the concentration of arms production were:

(*a*) The process of rapid concentration in the USA, which began around 1995 and included a number of 'mega-mergers' among leading US arms-producing companies, had largely come to an end. During 1999 the newly formed giants experienced sharp falls in profits and share prices and were preoccupied with consolidation. On the subcontractor level concentration continued, primarily in the military electronics and information technology sectors.

(*b*) The creation of the first major international arms-producing company in Europe was agreed—the tri-national (France, Germany and Spain) European Aeronautics, Defence and Space Company (EADS). This decision was followed by the setting up of a series of cross-border joint ventures which combined entire sectors of military production of the companies involved.

(*c*) In several countries in other regions a greater acceptance of foreign ownership in their domestic arms industries is emerging. The rationale for this change, which in some countries has involved a major shift in defence industrial policy, appears to be the difficulty of maintaining a national military industrial capability in an environment of increasing costs and international competition in arms production.

3. Russia began to assign greater priority to arms production by increased funding, greater efforts to increase military exports, and a more focused defence industrial policy aimed at strengthening and consolidating the remaining core of the arms industry. Official data on the military output of the Russian defence complex show an increase of 5 per cent in real terms in 1998 and 37 per cent in 1999. However, this increase comes after a long period of rapid reductions. Russian military output in 1999 remained at only 14 per cent of the level in the Soviet Union at the time of its disintegration in 1991. In the longer-term perspective this is therefore a rather modest recovery.

4. The 1990s were a decade of profound change and restructuring in the arms industry in most parts of the world. The main features were: (*a*) a significant downsizing of the industry in the main arms-producing countries; (*b*) faster concentration in the very top layer of the arms industry, although not notably in the lower layers; (*c*) a significant degree of diversification from military to civilian production among arms-producing companies in general, while at the same time a small number of (mostly large) companies have increased their dependence on arms sales considerably; and (*d*) efforts to use arms exports as a strategy to compensate for the loss of domestic sales, most notably in France and the UK. Russia also assigns increasing importance to arms exports as a strategy to maintain capacity in its arms industry.

As a result of the trends in downsizing and restructuring during the 1990s, the character and structure of the world arms production system were rather different at the end of the decade from what they were at the beginning. The structure had become smaller but more concentrated and polarized system. The US arms industry had assumed a more dominant leading role, followed by the two or three major European producers. Arms production was also concentrated on a small number of large companies, while average arms sales had fallen over the decade.

Simultaneously with the process of concentration, which has widened the gaps between countries and companies, there are the trends of military industrial cooperation, internationalization and increasing arms exports. These, together with the trend for civilian technology to gain an increasing lead over military technology in some areas and increasing globalization in civilian technology, have increased the difficulty of monitoring and controlling the flows of military and military-relevant technologies.

There is a risk that the increasing leverage of the arms industry will reduce political influence over the development of military technology and thus over government arms procurement. There is a need for more monitoring of the internationalization of the system of arms production and for greater transparency in arms production and arms exports, in particular in the large corporations. Arms-producing companies should be made more accountable to their customers, which means governments and the broader public.

II. The SIPRI 'top 100'

The combined arms sales of the 100 largest arms-producing companies in the OECD and developing countries in 1998 amounted to $154.5 billion (table 6.1). Compared with the arms sales of the same 100 companies in 1997 ($151.7 billion), this represents an increase of 1.8 per cent in nominal terms, or roughly 1 per cent in real terms.[1] To a great extent the increase reflects the continued rapid concentration in the top layers of the arms industry during 1998.[2]

While US and West European companies increased their share of the total slightly—to 92 per cent—companies in other regions saw their shares fall. This was the result of real increases in the arms sales of the US and West European companies; of slower increases or actual reductions in the arms sales of companies in other regions; and of exchange rate fluctuations reducing the dollar values of the arms sales of companies in these other regions.

The rapid concentration in the US arms industry culminated in 1997–98, as can be seen in the arms sales of the US companies among the top 100. The 39 US companies in 1998 increased their arms sales by around 15 per cent in real terms in 1997, but only by around 1 per cent in 1998. Thus, during 1998 their share in the total arms sales of the top 100 increased only slightly (from 55.5 per cent in 1997 to 56.0 per cent in 1998).

The same slight increase is seen in the share of the 38 West European companies. There was, however, some important variation between the European countries. While the 13 British companies increased their share by almost 1 percentage point, which is a significant increase, the share of the 11 French companies fell by 0.7 percentage points. The six German companies among the top 100 increased their share in the total to 3.8 per cent in 1998 as a result of a strong increase in their combined arms sales (by 11 per cent in 1998).

---

[1] If instead the comparison is made with the 100 companies which were the largest in 1997, with combined arms sales of $155.0 billion in 1997, the level is about the same in nominal terms and 1.6% down in real terms. The factors behind this slight decrease are difficult to identify since two different sets of companies are being compared.

[2] The comparison excludes those companies which were in the 1997 list but have since been acquired by other companies. Their disappearance has resulted in space for new companies to be included, while their arms sales in 1998 are included in those of the acquiring companies. Some of the increase in 1998 reflects this fact: a larger share of the total arms industry is included among the top 100 as a result of concentration.

Table 6.1. Regional/national shares of arms sales[a] for the top 100 arms-producing companies in the OECD and developing countries in 1998[b]

Number of companies 1998	Region/ country	Percentage of total arms sales		Arms sales 1998 (US $b.)
		1997[c]	1998	
39	USA	55.5	56.0	86.6
38	*West European OECD*	*35.6*	*36.0*	*55.4*
13	UK	15.4	16.2	25.0
11	France	11.6	10.9	16.9
6	Germany	3.5	3.8	5.9
2	Italy	2.3	2.3	3.5
3	Sweden	1.3	1.4	2.1
1	Spain	0.7	0.7	1.0
2	Switzerland	0.8	0.7	1.0
12	*Other OECD*	*5.1*	*4.5*	*6.9*
7	Japan[d]	4.2	3.5	5.4
2	Australia	0.4	0.4	0.6
2	Canada	0.3	0.3	0.5
1	Turkey	0.2	0.3	0.4
11	*Non-OECD countries*	*3.8*	*3.5*	*5.6*
6	Israel	2.0	2.1	3.3
3	India	1.0	0.8	1.3
1	Singapore	0.5	0.4	0.6
1	South Africa	0.3	0.2	0.4
		100.0	*100.0*	**154.5**

[a] Arms sales include both domestic procurement and exports.

[b] For a list of member countries in the OECD, see appendix 7A.1. The category of developing countries covers all countries other than the OECD and the former and current centrally planned economies, for which there is a lack of comparable data on the enterprise level. Companies in South Korea and Taiwan are not included because of lack of data on their arms sales.

[c] Data for 1997 are for the same companies that were the top 100 companies in 1998.

[d] For Japanese companies data are for new military contracts rather than arms sales.

Source: Appendix 6A.

This was not the result of a general increase in German arms sales, but almost entirely due to the increase in one company, Rheinmetall, following its acquisitions of other arms-producing companies (see section III).

Twelve companies in four other OECD countries (Australia, Canada, Japan and Turkey) accounted for 4.5 per cent of the combined arms sales of the top 100 companies in 1998—a reduced share compared with 1997. The decline is due to the fall in Japanese arms sales,[3] which partly reflects the depreciation of

[3] The combined arms sales of arms-producing companies in Japan fell by *c.* 9% in real terms, or *c.* 15% in current US dollars.

the yen but primarily the decline in new contracts from the Japan Defense Agency—by about 7 per cent in real terms between 1997 and 1998.[4]

Eleven companies in four developing countries—India, Israel, Singapore and South Africa—had combined arms sales of $5.6 billion in 1998 and accounted for 3.5 per cent of the total top 100 arms sales.

There are other companies that would belong in the top 100 if sufficient data were available. Apart from Chinese enterprises, for which no data at all are available, the main absentees from table 6.1 are companies in South Korea and Taiwan. While these companies do not report any data to SIPRI or release sufficient time-series data on their arms sales to make it possible to include them in the top 100 list, some data have been provided for 1998. In South Korea, the major aerospace companies were merged in 1999 into a new company, Korea Aerospace Industries (KAI), with expected total sales of $700 million, an estimated $530 million in arms sales, and around 3200 employees.[5] The largest arms-producing company in Taiwan, the Aviation Industry Development Center (AIDC), reported total sales of roughly $1 billion in 1998–99[6] and around 4300 employees, but no figure for its arms sales.[7]

III. The concentration of arms production

The process of concentration among arms-producing companies continued during 1999 but with a shift in geographical loci and intensity. During the period up to and including 1998 the most rapid concentration took place in the USA. During 1999, however, there was only one major acquisition among US arms-producing companies on the prime contractor level.[8] Instead, concentration increased on the subcontractor level, and the focus of the concentration process appeared to have shifted to Western Europe. There concentration has increasingly resulted in cross-border joint ventures and, in 1999, the first major international merger. The decision in January 1999 to combine the two largest British arms-producing companies into one company, BAE Systems— the largest European arms-producing company by far—put an end to British Aerospace (BAe)'s discussions on merging with German DaimlerChrysler Aerospace (DASA). However, it did not, as many analysts initially speculated, constitute a major impediment to the process of internationalization in Western Europe. Instead, it took only a few months before the announcement in September of the EADS, merging three national aerospace companies.[9]

[4] New contract awards by the Japan Defense Agency (JDA) declined from 1.32 trillion yen in fiscal year (FY) 1997 to 1.24 trillion yen in 1998 (current prices). 'JDA reveals its top 10 contractors', *Defense News*, 26 Apr. 1999, p. 10; and 'Japanese vendors face smaller defence pie', *Defense News*, 20–26 July 1998, p. 14.

[5] KAI will include Samsung Aerospace, Hyundai Space and Aircraft and the aerospace division of Daewoo Heavy Industries. 'Korean consolidation scheduled for August', *Aviation Week & Space Technology*, 21 June 1999, p. 31.

[6] Finnegan, P., 'Taipei seeks to tighten offset regulations', *Defense News*, 23 Aug. 1999.

[7] *Jane's All the World's Aircraft 1999/2000* (Butler & Tanner: London, 1999), p. 490.

[8] The acquisition of Avondale Industries by Litton.

[9] Intra-European arms-producing companies established earlier, such as Eurocopter and Matra BAe Dynamics, are joint venture companies merging the activities of single sectors of their parent companies but not full-scale mergers.

Concentration is also crossing other international borders, both across the Atlantic and with other parts of the world, although the scope of this process is still rather limited. In particular, the largest arms-producing companies are striving to expand their networks and ownership to other regions. While in 1998 interest in transatlantic ownership deals was relatively high, both in industry and on the political agendas on both sides of the Atlantic, in 1999 efforts to develop a framework for closer transatlantic military industrial links were postponed to the future. The development of transatlantic military industrial relations will depend on progress in the modification of the US regulatory framework in the years to come.

The major arms-producing companies in the Western centres of arms production (France, Germany, the UK and the USA) are also acquiring companies in other parts of the world. During 1999 such acquisitions took place in Australia, Brazil, South Korea, South Africa and Switzerland. A number of smaller arms-producing countries appear increasingly to be accepting foreign ownership in their defence industrial bases. These developments are described in the following sections.

The USA

The restructuring of the US arms industry appears to have reached its peak in 1998, at least at the prime contractor level. It was followed, beginning in 1999, by efforts to consolidate and evaluate the resulting new structures. A large number of mega-mergers among major US military prime contractor companies, culminating in 1997–98, resulted in the concentration of a great many firms into a few huge arms-producing companies, many of them conglomerates involved in different types of military production. Since 1998 this process has been halted among prime contractor companies, but the process of concentration continued during 1999 at the level of subcontractors, primarily in the sectors of electronics and information technology.[10]

Several negative consequences of the rapid concentration in the US arms industry are slowly being recognized: (*a*) for companies, the fall in profitability and in share prices of several major companies, believed to be the result of the burden of debt from acquisitions and difficulties in integrating company cultures and activities; (*b*) for the government, reduced competition and reduced government control over arms production in general and over the process of downsizing in particular; and (*c*) for the economy at large, the focus on concentration of arms production at the expense of diversification into civilian production.

These consequences are largely related to the way in which concentration took place, driven as it eventually became by financial-market interests[11]

---

[10] See, e.g., James, A. D., 'Medium sized defence electronics companies and US defence industry restructuring', draft, 16 Feb. 2000, forthcoming in 2000 in the research report series of the Swedish National Defence Research Establishment (FOA), Division of Defence Analysis (in English).

[11] See, e.g., American Forces Press Service, 'DOD concerned about defence industrial base', 8 Nov. 1999, URL <http://www.defenselink.mil/news>.

rather than national interests. The first stage of concentration in the US arms industry was driven primarily by the need for capacity reductions against the background of forecast major cuts in future arms procurement. It was reinforced by the government policy initiated in 1993 of supporting arms industry consolidation by reimbursing merger costs, which led to net savings for the government. However, the expected results have not been achieved. While there has been a wave of financial mergers in the US arms industry, this has not led to much rationalization at plant level or to capacity reduction. One explanation provided for this failure is that government policy was too narrow. It did not provide sufficient compensation to workers and communities affected by plant closures, so it was undermined by political resistance. As a result, the number of major weapon platform lines has not in fact declined in the United States. Rationalization has been meagre.[12]

Four large conglomerates emerged from the wave of mergers and acquisitions in the US arms industry after the mid-1990s—Boeing, Lockheed Martin, Northrop Grumman and Raytheon. All but Boeing are highly dependent on military sales[13] and reported sharp falls in profits or even losses in the aftermath of their acquisitions: Northrop Grumman in 1998, and Lockheed Martin and Raytheon in 1999.[14] Repeated profit warnings by the two latter companies were followed by dramatic falls in their share prices.[15] The poor financial performance of large defence firms led the Department of Defense (DOD) in November 1999 to commission a task force of the Defense Science Board to study the financial health of the arms industry. For the same reason, company size in achieving competitive advantage in arms production has been questioned: the competitiveness of a company in specific market segments may instead be the key to success.[16]

Anti-trust concerns and the issue of excessive downsizing have led to a more cautious approach by the US Government since 1998. To ensure some degree of competition the DOD has taken a series of decisions to oppose proposed mergers and acquisitions—in 1997 the acquisition by General Dynamics of the military vehicle company United Defense; in 1998 the merger of the aerospace companies Northrop Grumman and Lockheed Martin; and in 1999 the proposed acquisition of Newport News Shipbuilding, first by General

---

[12] Gholz, E. and Sapolsky, H. M., 'Restructuring of the US defense industry', *International Security*, vol. 24, no. 3 (Winter 1999/2000), pp. 5–51.

[13] Boeing also experienced severe problems in 1997, but these were largely related to its civilian production.

[14] Lockheed Martin had net earnings for the first 9 months of 1999 of $89 million ($876 million in 1998) and had accumulated around $11 billion in debt. *International Herald Tribune*, 9 Nov. 1999, p. 16. Raytheon registered a net loss in the 3rd quarter of 1999 of $169 million (profits of $11 million in 1998). Both companies have announced comprehensive reorganization plans aimed at consolidating and streamlining core business areas.

[15] The price of Lockheed Martin shares fell from c. $55 in Nov. 1998 to below $20 in Nov. 1999 and Raytheon shares even more sharply, from $75 to c. $27. Wall, R., 'Industry woes worry Pentagon', *Aviation Week & Space Technology*, 8 Nov. 1999, pp. 30–31. The DOD stepped in in Oct. 1999, declaring that Raytheon was not a troubled contractor despite reports that it was behind schedule and over budget on several weapon programmes. *Air Letter*, 15 Oct. 1999, p. 5.

[16] James (note 10).

Dynamics and subsequently by Litton Industries.[17] More recently, in late 1999, the US Government has expressed concern that downsizing through concentration could lead to the loss of important engineering and technological skills and capabilities.[18]

Concentration may also have resulted in a slowing down in diversification from military to civilian production. As was foreseen early on,[19] by encouraging mergers of arms-producing activities, government subsidies in combination with financial-market interests may actually have contributed to impede diversification and conversion because they led to the creation of military specialized companies and to splitting civilian from military activities. The government, which initially had encouraged concentration in order to help industry adjust to lower levels of procurement and at the same time reduce government procurement costs (a policy symbolized by the 'Last Supper' at the DOD in 1993), was by late 1999 trying to regain some influence over those developments in the arms industry which have consequences for both it and the industry and giving increased attention to the role of the financial markets as one of the driving forces behind the process.

Further mergers and acquisitions among arms-producing companies in the USA are still likely, although at the second- and third-tier levels, because there is still scope for further concentration among these.[20] Consolidation within mega-conglomerates is resulting in strategic divestitures of subsidiary companies and units, which is facilitating mergers and acquisitions at lower levels. Raytheon has already completed several sales of non-core operations in deals which amounted to around $760 million by August 1999.[21] Lockheed Martin plans to sell off a number of units with combined annual sales of $1.8 billion.[22] During 1999 mergers and acquisitions in the US arms industry involved to an overwhelming degree companies in the field of military electronics and information technology (appendix 6B, table 6B.1).

Western Europe

The structure of the West European arms industry underwent profound change during 1999, resulting in a rather different defence industrial landscape. Inter-

---

[17] 'Pentagon determined to fight monopolies', *Air Letter,* 19 Apr. 1999, p. 4. The 2 failed hostile takeover bids were followed by the acquisition of Avondale Industries by Litton. Previously Newport News had agreed to and received government approval for the takeover of Avondale.

[18] John Hamre, Deputy Secretary of Defense, at the Strategic Responsiveness Conference on 3 Nov. 1999, stated: 'We loaded a lot of downsizing on the back of acquisition practices. There comes a point where you can't lose the design and engineering expertise we have invested in through our private sector'. US DOD, 8 Nov. 1999 in defence-aerospace.com, URL <http://www.defense-aerospace.com/data/communiques/index.htm>.

[19] Markusen, A., 'The economics of defense industry mergers and divestitures', Project on Regional and Industrial Economics, Rutgers University: New Brunswick, N.J., 1997; and Oden, M., 'Cashing-in, cashing-out and converting: Restructuring in the defense industrial base in the 1990s', eds A. Markusen and S. Costigan, *Arming the Future: A Defense Industry for the 21st Century* (Council on Foreign Relations Press: New York, 1999), chapter 3, pp. 74–105.

[20] Wall (note 15).

[21] Pettibone, R., 'Raytheon performing best among US giants', *World Aerospace & Defense Intelligence*, 6 Aug. 1999, p. 9.

[22] 'The defense company that bombed', *Washington Post*, 8 Nov. 1999, pp. 21–22.

nationalization of arms production took a big leap forward in two ways: the first major international company was formed; and the network of joint ventures was expanded to include the military activities of most of the major arms-producing companies in Europe, increasingly encompassing entire industrial sectors rather than single product categories. Increased internationalization will require more government cooperation and focused policies if governments are to maintain control over developments in the increasingly interconnected West European defence industrial base.

Two major decisions in 1999 served to ignite the process. The first was the agreement in January 1999 by the British GEC to sell its arms-producing subsidiary, Marconi Electronic Systems, to BAe, rather than making a transatlantic deal, as had been discussed in 1998. The second, largely provoked by this national concentration event in the UK, and facilitated by the partial privatization and consolidation of the military aerospace and electronics industry in France, was the decision in September 1999 to create the first major intra-European aerospace and defence company, the EADS, by combining the arms-producing activities of Aérospatiale Matra,[23] DASA and, subsequently, as announced in November, Spanish CASA.

The formation of these two large corporate structures created the ground for the reorganization of the missile, radar systems and space activities of the companies involved into three large West European joint ventures, linking the two new conglomerates to one another and to other major West European arms-producing companies. The three joint ventures are: (*a*) 'New Matra BAe Dynamics', which will integrate the missile activities of the British–Italian Alenia Marconi Systems into the 'old' Franco-British Matra BAe Dynamics; (*b*) Astrium, which will combine the satellite activities of DASA with those of the Franco-British joint venture Matra Marconi Space; and (*c*) 'New Alenia Marconi Systems', which will add the radar activities of 'old' BAe to those of the 'old' Alenia Marconi Systems. These joint ventures involve the activities of the parent companies in entire industrial sectors rather than being limited to specific armaments programmes, as was formerly usual for cross-border joint ventures. They also include a major part of West European production in the respective sectors. A number of companies remaining outside these joint ventures are either linked up to them through minority shares[24] or planning to join later.[25]

Other sectors, such as land systems and shipbuilding,[26] which had been rather insulated from the process of restructuring in arms production, were

---

[23] This decision was preceded by the merger of French state-owned Aérospatiale with the private Matra Haute Technologies of Lagardère, which had been completed only in July 1999.

[24] Matra BAe Dynamics also holds a 30% share of the missile business of Daimler-Chrysler Aerospace, LFK. The share may be increased to 49%. BAe holds a 35% share in Swedish Saab, which in 1999 decided to merge its missile activities with those of the partly state-owned company Celsius.

[25] Alenia Spazio, the space subsidiary of the Italian Finmeccanica (IRI), is also expected to join the new joint venture company.

[26] For a summary of developments in the US and West European naval shipbuilding industry, see Barrie, D. and Holzer, R., 'Shipbuilders determine survival strategy', *Defence News,* 11 Oct. 1999, pp. 8, 12.

Table 6.2. The structure of the West European arms industry in early 2000[a]

Companies are ranked according to their arms sales within each sector.

Sector	Company (parent company or owner) (subsidiaries and joint ventures in italics)	Sector sales 1998 ($ m.)	
		Total sales	Arms sales
Aircraft	BAE Systems	(13 000)	(8 700)
	EADS	(11 500)	(1 500)
	Dassault Aviation (Aérospatiale 45.8%)	3 830	1 870
	Alenia Aeronautica (Finmeccanica)	1 200	(600)
	'New Saab' (BAE Systems 35%)	(410)	(410)
	Aermacchi[b]	200	180
Helicopters	*Eurocopter* (EADS)	1 890	830
	GKN Westland (GKN)	. .	. .
	Agusta (Finmeccanica)	590	400
Missiles	*Matra BAe Dynamics* (BAE Systems 37.5%; EADS 37.5%; Finmeccanica 25%)	(2 700)	(2 700)
	Airsys and *Shorts Missiles Systems* (Thomson-CSF)	. .	. .
	'New Saab' (BAE Systems 35%)	(590)	(590)
	LFK (DASA 70%, Matra BAe Dynamics 30%)	390	390
	Bodenseewerke Gerätetechnik (Diehl)	220	180
Space	*Astrium* (EADS 75%; BAE Systems 25%)	(2 450)	. .
	Alcatel Space (Alcatel Alsthom 51%; Thomson-CSF 49%)	1 420	240
	Alenia Spazio (Finmeccanica)	590	. .
Electronics	Thomson-CSF (incl. missiles)	(8 500)	(4 900)
	BAE Systems (partly within AMS)	. .	. .
	EADS	. .	(1 200)
	New AMS (BAE Systems 50%; Finmeccanica 50%)	(1 200)	(1 200)
	Sagem	3 180	570
	Smiths Industries	1 990	460
	'New Saab' (BAE Systems 35%)	. .	(370)
	Ericsson	23 200	260
Land systems	*Rheinmetall DeTec* (Rheinmetall)	(2 000)	(2 000)
	GIAT Industries	1 200	1 200
	Royal Ordnance[b] (BAE Systems)	(800)	(800)
	Krauss Maffei Wegmann	(740)	(740)
	Swiss Amm. E. and *Swiss Ordnance E.* (RUAG SUISSE)	. .	. .
	Vickers (Rolls Royce)	1 480	570
	Alvis Vehicle	440	410
	Alenia Difesa (Finmeccanica)	. .	(300)
Shipbuilding	DCN	1 900	1 840
	HDW (Babcock 50%; Preussag 25%; Celsius 25%)	(1 100)	(500)
	VSEL and *Yarrow Shipbuilders* (BAE Systems)	. .	. .
	Bazan	490	420
	Fincantieri	2 460	260
	Vosper Thornycroft	400	250
	Blohm & Voss and *Thyssen Nordseewerke* (Thyssen-Krupp)	370	(200)

( ) = SIPRI estimates.

[a] Based on agreements reached by Jan. 2000.

[b] Data are for 1997.

Source: SIPRI arms industry files.

also affected during 1999. Concentration in the production of land systems is centred around the German company Rheinmetall, which has made a series of both national and international acquisitions.[27] In 1999 it acquired the military activities (artillery, small arms and ordnance) of the Swiss Oerlikon Contraves from Oerlikon-Bührle and the military activities of the German company sIWKA—Kuka Wehrtechnik and Henschel Wehrtechnik. It also increased its stake in the Dutch ammunition company Eurometaal. The acquisition of the British Vickers by the engine company Rolls Royce created expectations of further concentration in the European military vehicles sector, since Rolls Royce is expected to divest the military vehicle unit, Vickers Defence Systems, in the near future.

In naval shipbuilding the German HDW and the Swedish Kockums Naval Systems decided to merge in September 1999. This was the first intra-European merger of two major shipbuilding companies. HDW had been expected to participate in the consolidation of German shipbuilding on a national level by merging with the two shipyards of Thyssen Industrie—Blohm & Voss and Thyssen Nordseewerke.[28]

This series of national and international acquisitions during 1999 (listed in appendix 6B) has resulted in a rather significant reshaping of the West European arms industry. A small number of increasingly international companies dominate the various arms industry sectors and are linked, through share holdings, joint ventures and armaments cooperation programmes, to one another and to other minor companies within their respective fields. However, by early 2000 there was still a considerable degree of fragmentation in the West European arms industry, as is seen in table 6.2. In aircraft the major company remaining outside the two large combinations in early 2000 was Finmeccanica's Alenia Aeronautica, and both EADS and BAE Systems were competing for an alliance with the Italian company.[29] Military electronics capabilities are spread over a number of companies, although with Thomson-CSF in a dominant position. The most fragmented sectors are still those of land systems and shipbuilding.

Attention is being given in Western Europe to the US experience of the consequences of increased concentration for company performance, competition and diversification.[30] The premises for the restructuring of arms production are, however, somewhat different in Western Europe. First, one factor behind the low degree of political involvement in the process of concentration in the

---

[27] For an analysis of the restructuring of German production of land systems, and in particular of the company strategy of Rheinmetall, see Lock, P., 'Rheinmetall: a paradigm of restructuring of the defence sector in Germany', discussion paper for CREDIT/METDAC under the European Commission's Targeted Socio-Economic Research Programme (TSER), [1999], URL <http://www.Peter-Lock.de/Neuer%20Ordner/rheinmetall.html>.

[28] 'Kommt bald die grosse Werftenfusion?' [Will the major shipbuilding merger come soon?], *Frankfurter Allgemeine Zeitung*, 28 Jan. 1998, p. 21.

[29] Finmeccanica holds a 19% stake in Eurofighter. An alliance with the company is therefore decisive for the role of EADS and BAE Systems within the programme.

[30] 'Companies see limits to size advantage', *Defense News*, 26 July 1999, pp. 1, 58.

US arms industry is the high degree of privatization in the industry.[31] By contrast, several West European governments are directly involved in the process of concentration through their ownership in the industry (even though concentration has been largely industry-led in Western Europe as well). Second, concern for national interests and export control has been central in the European concentration process from an early stage, since it was clear that, because national markets in Europe were smaller, further concentration had to involve the internationalization of arms production.

The demands from the industry for intergovernmental decisions to create an economic and legal framework for consolidation across European borders and develop a common market for military equipment were not met by any significant developments during 1999. On the contrary, on the unilateral level, two governments decided to withdraw from important multinational cooperation programmes in favour of national programmes. The British Government decided to exit from the Horizon naval shipbuilding programme, and France to withdraw from the international multi-role armoured vehicle (MRAV) programme, preferring national programmes of their own.

Transatlantic military industrial links

The new military industrial environment which is emerging has led to increased interest during the past three years in transatlantic military industrial links of different kinds. The determining factor has been the effort to achieve increased competitiveness through size and access to foreign markets in a global market consisting of a small number of large orders. The need for interoperability between US and European equipment and infrastructure used in joint military action has reinforced this interest, in particular after the experience of NATO forces in the Kosovo province of the Federal Republic of Yugoslavia (FRY).

The future development of transatlantic military industrial alignments depends largely on the outcome of the ongoing policy review within the US Government under the rubric of globalization. While there is a growing realization in the US Government that the forces of globalization have an impact on arms production as well as civilian production, it is having difficulty in reaching consensus on what policy conclusions to draw from this.

The expectations in late 1998 of future transatlantic mega-mergers following the acquisition in 1998 by a British company (GEC) of a large US military contractor (Tracor) came to nought, at least for the time being, as a result of (a) the decision by GEC in January 1999 to sell most of its military activities to BAe rather than link up with a US company, which had been under consideration, and (b) the presentation of the US Government position on transatlantic links by Deputy Defense Secretary John Hamre in his 'dinner' speech on 25 October 1999 to a group of European and US defence industry and

---

[31] The issue of private ownership in US arms production and the military sector in general is discussed in Markusen, A., 'The case against privatizing national security', draft paper, Council on Foreign Relations, New York, 24 Sep. 1999.

government representatives. The message was that while there was still 'plenty of room for more transatlantic cooperation', including partnerships, joint ventures and financing agreements, 'we need a little more time before we get to the mega-merger category'.[32] By this he meant that the regulatory frameworks on both sides of the Atlantic did not allow the management of 'the technology and industrial security challenges of a transnational corporation'.[33] While there was intense activity during 1999 in the DOD to streamline the licensing system for US arms exports, a similar process within the Department of State— the ultimate decision-making authority—started only in late 1999.[34]

In the long run, current trends point to a relaxation of export controls on defence-related technology coupled with US efforts to maintain a lead in as many critical defence-related technologies as possible.[35] A policy of selective security clearances is emerging, manifested in the decision to give BAE Systems a privileged position on the US market.[36] In the meantime US restrictions continue to create obstacles to transatlantic cooperation. This was exemplified in 1999 by the decision of DASA to engineer US components out of its systems because of the difficulty of getting US licences approved, the German refusal to accept 'black boxes' of US sensitive technology, and German reluctance for this reason to buy the Patriot Advanced Capability 3 (PAC-3) surface-to-air missile system from the USA.[37]

Foreign acquisitions in other regions

Companies in the Western centres of arms production (France, Germany, the UK and the USA) made a number of important acquisitions in smaller arms-producing countries in 1999 which will serve to improve their position on foreign arms markets.[38] Such acquisitions are likely to continue or even increase in number, since smaller arms-producing countries often have the choice only between accepting foreign ownership in their arms industries and giving up production entirely. Ownership by major Western companies of arms-producing companies in smaller and less advanced countries commonly

[32] 'Pentagon dampens hopes for arms mergers', *Air Letter*, 28 Oct. 1999, p. 5; and Fitchett, J., 'Trans-Atlantic deals in defense don't fly', *International Herald Tribune*, 2 Nov. 1999, pp. 13–14.

[33] 'Fletcher Conference on Strategic Responsiveness', 3 Nov. 1999, URL <http://www.defenselink.mil/speeches/1999/s19991103-depsecdef.html>. The quotation is from Hamre's remarks to this conference.

[34] 'State Dept. calls for arms export control review', *Defense News*, 8 Nov. 1999, pp. 1–26.

[35] See also Reinsch, W. A. (Under-Secretary for Export Administration, US Department of Commerce), 'Export controls in the age of globalization', *The Monitor* (University of Georgia, Athens, Ga.), vol. 5, no. 3 (summer 1999), pp. 3–6.

[36] Nicoll, A., 'America in its sights', *Financial Times*, 14 Dec. 1999. Similarly, security restrictions were relaxed for a British subsidiary in the USA (Allison Engine of Rolls Royce). Nicoll, A., 'US set to relax military rules for UK aero engine arm', *Financial Times*, 11 Jan. 2000, p. 5.

[37] Black boxes are physical or software barriers to prevent classified technology from being copied. 'Germans balk at US control over PAC-3', *Defense News*, 22 Nov. 1999, pp. 3, 28.

[38] During 1999 the French Thomson-CSF, which was not involved in the major concentration events in the West European arms industry, was among the most active in acquiring companies or shares of companies in other regions. *Le Monde*, 2 Nov. 1999, in 'Subject to head winds: Thomson-CSF increases local alliances at the international level', Foreign Broadcast Information Service, *Daily Report–Western Europe (FBIS-WEU)*, FBIS-WEU-1999-1101, 2 Nov. 1999.

involves the provision of capital and, more importantly, input of advanced technology. The overall development is similar to and preceded by developments in the civilian market, but raises different and important questions for national security. It may limit a smaller country's autonomy in its arms procurement decisions, and complicates control of the international transfer of military technology by supplier governments.

Acquisitions in smaller countries by large foreign arms producers are not new to 1999.[39] Nevertheless, the recent increase in Western acquisitions in other regions deserves special attention, in particular in the current context when a small group of large US and West European companies are assuming an increasingly dominant position in the world arms industry.

The determinants of this development are multi-fold. Companies in smaller and developing countries need investment by foreign companies in order to secure the capital necessary for restructuring and to obtain access to advanced weapon technology. Foreign ownership, partial or complete, may support the survival of local production capacities when domestic procurement contracts for advanced and expensive weapons are won by foreign competitors. Direct investment in the domestic arms industry is therefore often demanded by the importing country as one form of military offset arrangement. These offset requirements compel seller companies to invest in foreign arms-producing companies in order to increase their access to foreign and potentially dynamic military markets. Only marginally do seller companies seem to be motivated by the possibility of moving production to locations where labour is cheap.

Australia since the mid-1990s has sold significant assets of its arms industry to foreign companies as part of the policy of corporatization and privatization of arms production on which it embarked in 1985. In 1999 one of the largest arms-producing companies in Australia, ADI, was sold to a Franco-Australian joint venture between Thomson-CSF and Transfield Holding. The government still has to decide whether to sell its 48.5 per cent share in the Australian Submarine Corporation. In Brazil and South Africa agreed or imminent equipment procurement programmes stimulated the establishment of alliances between domestic companies and major foreign military contractors in 1999. In South Korea the overall industrial restructuring process which was initiated in the aftermath of the Asian financial crisis has opened up both new possibilities and needs for investment by foreign companies in the domestic arms industry. Similar developments are likely to follow in a number of other smaller arms-producing countries, including Indonesia and Malaysia, which are embarking on arms procurement and arms industry restructuring programmes.

The largest arms-producing company in Brazil, the aerospace company Embraer, has for some time been seeking a foreign partner to improve its competitiveness in the military aircraft sector. Privatized in 1994, it has since been able to increase its sales significantly, mainly on the civilian market. The Brazilian Air Force plans to procure between 70 and 150 fighter aircraft in the

---

[39] Nor is the process unique to regions outside Europe and North America: e.g., Belgium, the Netherlands and Switzerland have sold major assets of their defence industrial bases to foreign companies and most Canadian arms-producing companies are subsidiaries of US military contractors.

near future and Embraer wishes to increase the share of military sales in its total sales from the current 12 per cent to around 30 per cent within a few years.[40] In October 1999 a French consortium led by Dassault Aviation, and including also Thomson-CSF, Aérospatiale Matra and SNECMA, agreed to acquire a 20 per cent share in Embraer. In December 1999, however, the Brazilian Air Force made public its opposition to the deal, as it is seen as limiting its options when selecting the new fighter aircraft.[41]

The South African arms industry is undergoing a process of privatization, which also involves a substantial degree of foreign ownership. After a sharp decline in national arms production in the early 1990s,[42] in 1999 the South African National Defence Force (SANDF) decided on a comprehensive equipment modernization programme. The possibility for domestic companies to participate in the programme will be closely related to their establishing partnerships with foreign arms-producing companies.[43] Such alliances have been stimulated by offset requirements stipulating that around 35 per cent of total offsets should take the form of foreign investment in South Africa.[44] Around $2.4 billion of total offsets of 104 billion rand (around $17 billion) envisaged in the modernization programme have reportedly been earmarked for direct investment in the South African arms industry.[45]

In 1998 the government announced the privatization of Denel, the largest South African arms-producing company. BAE Systems, which has won contracts to sell its Hawk trainer aircraft and, together with Saab, the Gripen fighter aircraft to the SANDF, is expected to acquire around 20 per cent of Denel Aviation.[46] Other West European companies have acquired shares and subsidiaries of the largest private South African arms-producing companies, Reunert, Grintek and Altron (see table 6.3).[47]

The South Korean announcement in April 1998 that it would accept foreign ownership in its arms industry meant a change in its defence industrial policy. When in October 1999 the country's aerospace companies were merged into KAI as part of the government-supported industry restructuring programme, a major problem was the high level of debt in the merging companies and units. The aim is therefore to raise around 30 per cent of its capital requirements

[40] *World Aerospace & Defense Intelligence*, 29 Oct. 1999, pp. 13–14.

[41] The air force asked the government's anti-trust board to investigate the deal. The government owns a 'golden share' minority stake in Embraer. The balance between government and company interests is discussed in 'Is Embraer flying too high? French link-up plan draws flak from the military', *Latin American Weekly Report,* 14 Dec. 1999, WR-99-4914, p. 585.

[42] Domestic arms production (including exports) dropped by *c.* 40% in real terms in the period 1989–95. Batchelor, P. and Willett, S., SIPRI, *Disarmament and Defence Industrial Adjustment in South Africa* (Oxford University Press: Oxford, 1998), p. 220.

[43] Heitman, H.-R., 'Industry waits on the edge', *Jane's Defence Weekly,* 11 Nov. 1998, p. 42.

[44] Engelbrecht, L., 'South Africa to get R104 billion for R21.3 billions arms', *Defence Systems Daily,* 17 Sep. 1999, URL <http://defence-data.com/>.

[45] 'South Africa spending spree defended', *World Aerospace & Defense Intelligence*, 10 Dec. 1999, p. 11.

[46] Ferguson, G., 'British Aerospace to boost Denel', *Defense News*, 25 Jan. 1999, p. 20.

[47] 'South Africa firms reap benefits of defence', *Air Letter*, 2 Aug. 1999, p. 4.

Table 6.3. Major arms-producing companies and foreign ownership in Australia and South Africa, 1999

Company name (parent company)	Sector^a	Foreign ownership
Australia		
ADI	El SA/A Sh	100% Transfield Thomson-CSF (50% Transfield Holdings, Australia 50% Thomson-CSF, France)
Australian Submarine Corporation (ASC)	Sh	49% Australian Industry Development Australia, 48.5% Kockums Naval Systems (HDW), Sweden
BAe Australia	Comp (Ac)	100% BAE Systems, UK
Boeing Australia	Comp (Ac)	100% Boeing, USA
South Africa		
African Defence Systems (Altron)	El	100% Thomson-CSF, France
ATE	El	20% BAE Systems, UK
Denel Aviation (Denel)	Ac	Planned acq. of 20% by BAE Systems, UK
Grintek Avitronics (Grintek)	El	49% Celsius, Sweden
Reutech Radar Systems (Reunert)	El	33% DASA, Germany
Reumech OMC, Astral and Gear Ratio (Reunert)	MV	100% Vickers, UK

^a For sector codes, see appendix 6A.

Source: SIPRI arms industry files.

through investment by major Western aerospace companies.[48] Another foreign acquisition took place in October 1999 in the context of the formation of a joint venture between Thomson-CSF and Samsung Electronics in optronics, military communications, naval combat systems and air defence systems: Thomson-CSF acquired 50 per cent of the military electronics activities of Samsung Electronics, with military electronics sales of around $140 million.[49]

IV. Trends in arms production during the 1990s

The world arms industry has undergone profound changes in the past decade, most importantly a significant reduction in output and employment. This was most distinct in the members of the cold war military alliances, NATO and the Warsaw Treaty Organization (WTO). The general reduction followed a period of intense military build-up in the first half of the 1980s. Company strategies

[48] In Dec. 1999 Boeing, BAe Systems and a US–French consortium (Lockheed Martin, Aérospatiale and the investment company Carlyle Group) were selected for a short list of candidate foreign partners for KAI. 'Two US–European alliances compete for ROK aerospace deal', *Korea Times,* 24 Dec. 1999, in Foreign Broadcast Information Service, *Daily Report–East Asia (FBIS-EAS),* FBIS-EAS-1999-1224, 24 Dec. 1999.

[49] 'Samsung, Thomson-CSF form joint-venture', *Defence Systems Daily,* 1 Nov. 1999, URL <http://defence-data.com.htm>.

Table 6.4. Trends in national arms production, 1987–98

1990 = 100, at constant 1995 prices and exchange rates (except Russia).

Country	1987	1988	1989	1990	1991	1992	1993	1994	1995	1996	1997	1998	1997 curr. US $b.
USA	115	106	108	100	94	85	83	72	67	61	64	..	100.7
UK	102	109	103	100	88	87	79	77	82	91	92	90	22.1
France	94	100	100	100	90	86	77	71	63	69	73	71	19.0
Sub-total	**111**	**106**	**106**	**100**	**93**	**86**	**82**	**73**	**68**	**65**	**68**	..	**141.8**
Japan	88	95	99	100	102	95	91	81	73	77	80	76	8.5
Germany	..	..	..	100	..	..	..	..	59	..	..	..	(7.0)
Russia	..	..	..	..	100	50	33	20	17	13	9	10	..

Sources and definitions:

USA: DOD equipment expenditure plus military exports minus military imports—US Office of Management and Budget, *The Budget of the United States Government: Historical Tables* (annual), URL<http://w3.access.gpo.gov/usbudget/index.html>; and US Department of Defense Security Assistance Agency, *Foreign Military Sales, Foreign Military Construction Sales and Military Assistance Facts*, annual (various editions).

UK: Ministry of Defence expenditure on equipment in the UK plus military exports—Ministry of Defence (later Government Statistical Service), *UK Defence Statistics*, annual (various editions); and Society of British Aerospace Companies, *UK Aerospace Statistics*, annual (various editions).

France: Military sales—Assemblée Nationale, *Rapport fait au Nom de la Commission des Finances, de l'Économie Générale et du Plan sur le Projet de Loi de Finances* [Report for the Commission on Finance, the Economy and Planning on the draft budget bill], annexe 40 (Défense), annual, various editions; and Direction Générale d'Armements in *Air Letter*, 1 Apr. 1999, p. 7.

Japan: Japan Defense Agency equipment expenditure minus US Foreign Military Sales (FMS)—Japan Defense Agency, *Defense of Japan*, annual (various editions); and *Foreign Military Sales, Foreign Military Construction Sales and Military Assistance Facts*, see above.

Germany: Information received from Bundesverband der Deutschen Industrie (German Industry Association) e.V., 7 Apr. 1997.

Russia: table 6.11.

of adjustment to the new military industrial environment include exiting from arms production entirely or partly, diversification into civilian production, mergers and acquisitions, rationalization and increased military exports.

Statistical information on arms production is generally weak and fragmented.[50] Within the limits of the available data, this section discusses general trends in arms production since 1987—the peak year of military expenditure. It is based on official data on national arms production and exports (tables 6.4 and 6.8), on OECD data on government military R&D expenditure (table 6.5), and on company data for the arms-producing companies in the SIPRI top 100 list (tables 6.6, 6.7 and 6.9).

[50] Sköns, E. and Weidacher, R., 'Arms production', *SIPRI Yearbook 1999: Armaments, Disarmament and International Security* (Oxford University Press: Oxford, 1999), pp. 407–409; and URL <http://projects.sipri.se/milex/aprod/data.html>.

Table 6.5. Trends in government expenditure on military R&D, 1990–98
1990 = 100, constant 1995 prices and exchange rates.

Country	1990	1991	1992	1993	1994	1995	1996	1997	1998	1998 curr. US $b.
USA	100	95	93	93	83	80	79	81	80	39.8
UK	100	82	76	84	73	72	73	77	75	3.9
France	100	82	78	79	77	67	64	59	52	3.6
Sub-total	**100**	**92**	**90**	**91**	**82**	**78**	**76**	**78**	**76**	**47.3**
Japan	100	123	143	169	172	188	201	207	172	1.1
Germany	100	87	81	75	73	78	85	79	71	1.6
Total	**100**	**92**	**90**	**91**	**83**	**79**	**79**	**79**	**77**	**49.9**

Notes: Government expenditure on military R&D does not represent total expenditure on military R&D, as it does not include company-funded military R&D. Data on government R&D vary considerably between sources (the OECD, the UN and national governments). Arnett, E., 'Military research and development', *SIPRI Yearbook 1999: Armaments, Disarmament and International Security* (Oxford University Press: Oxford, 1999), pp. 351–70.

Sources: OECD, *Main Science and Technology Indicators*, no. 2 (1999).

Quantitative trends

Most indicators show that the value of global arms production fell by one-third in real terms during the period 1990–97. The combined value of arms production in the three main centres of production (the USA, the UK and France) declined by around 40 per in real terms over the 11-year period 1987–97.

The period of decline varied widely between the six largest arms-producing countries and there was great variation in the scale of the reduction (table 6.4). The sharpest reduction took place in Russia—by 90 per cent over the period 1991–98 according to official national data. In the USA and Germany the reductions have also been substantial, amounting to almost 50 per cent over the period 1987–96 in the USA and 1990–95 in Germany. Japan and the UK have seen the smallest reductions in arms production.

In the USA and the UK the reduction began in the late 1980s; in France and Japan it started in 1991 and 1992, respectively. For Germany no time series is available, which makes it impossible to establish the trend in any detail. In Russia arms production began to decline in the country's first year of existence, 1992. The decline ended in most countries in the mid-1990s. Since then arms production has increased in the UK, France and Japan, while the trend in Germany after 1995 is impossible to assess because of lack of data. In Russia arms production began to increase in 1998 from its low of 1997 (table 6.10). The decline in US arms production seems also to have levelled off. While the exact trend after 1997 is unknown, the strong increase in the US budget for arms procurement since 1999[51] is an indication that US arms production has begun to increase significantly.

[51] See chapter 5, section IX in this volume.

Table 6.6. Trends in the value of combined arms sales and in average company size of the top 100, top 50, top 10 and top five arms-producing companies, 1990–98

Unit	1990	1991	1992	1993	1994	1995	1996	1997	1998	1998 (curr. US $b.)
Index 1990 = 100, at constant 1995 prices and exchange rates										
SIPRI top 100	100	93	84	79	74	71	70	70	69	154.5
SIPRI top 50	100	93	84	80	74	73	72	73	73	136.6
SIPRI top 10	100	92	79	80	87	83	87	96	101	86.3
SIPRI top 5	100	92	78	87	93	92	101	115	123	63.8
Average company arms sales, US$ billion at constant 1995 prices and exchange rates[a]										
SIPRI top 100	2.2	2.0	1.8	1.7	1.6	1.6	1.5	1.5	1.5	1.5
SIPRI top 50	3.7	3.4	3.1	2.9	2.7	2.7	2.6	2.7	2.7	2.7
SIPRI top 10	8.0	7.4	6.3	6.4	7.0	6.6	7.0	7.7	8.0	8.6
SIPRI top 5	9.5	8.8	7.4	8.3	8.8	8.7	9.6	10.9	11.7	12.8

Note: This table is based on the companies which were the 100 largest, 50 largest, etc., in each year, i.e., a changing set of companies.

[a] Except final column.

Source: SIPRI arms industry database, 1999.

Government expenditure on military R&D has fallen at a slower rate than overall arms production. The combined expenditures of the USA, the UK and France fell by 24 per cent between 1990 and 1998. The aggregate reduction in the military R&D expenditure over the same period in these three countries plus Germany and Japan was 23 per cent (table 6.5). The decline in US, British and German military R&D ceased in the mid-1990s. However, US defence plans show a continued decline in military R&D for the period 2000–2005 (table 5.11). Expenditure on military R&D in Germany and the UK has been increasing since the mid-1990s but in both countries preliminary data for 1998 show a drop. In France the decline continued up to and including 1998, the last year for which data are available. Japan's expenditure on military R&D increased until 1997 but fell significantly in 1998.

In sum, the quantitative trends in military production and R&D during the 1990s show a significant drop during the first half of the decade, although smaller than the fall in arms production. Production was scaled down as a result of the deep cuts in arms procurement following the end of the cold war, but military R&D activities were less affected. During the second half of the 1990s the decline slowed and towards the end of the decade it had ceased in most of the major arms-producing countries. It is not clear whether this is a temporary halt or whether the main arms-producing countries have resumed the previous long-term increase in arms production.

Table 6.7. Companies which had the largest increase in the share of military sales in total sales, 1990–98

Company	Country	Military share of total sales (%)		Change 1990–98 (percentage points)
		1990	1998	
Elbit Systems	Israel	45	100	55
Saab	Sweden	9	63	54
Celsius	Sweden	14	67	53
British Aerospace (BAe)	UK	44	74	30
GEC	UK	25	55	30
Racal Electronics	UK	13	38	25
Hunting	UK	28	50	22
Babcock International	UK	22	44	22
ITT Industries	USA	8	29	21
Bharat Electronics	India	57	75	18
Vickers	UK	23	39	16
Litton	USA	58	73	15
GKN	UK	4	19	15
MKEK	Turkey	63	77	14
Boeing	USA	18	28	10

Source: SIPRI arms industry database, 1999.

Concentration

A dominant feature of the restructuring has been the process of concentration in ownership and production, which has involved large-scale mergers and acquisitions and huge joint ventures for special types or broad categories of weapon systems. Through mergers and acquisitions, 24 of the 100 companies that were the largest in 1990 had left the military market as independent companies by the end of 1998. Of these, 12 sold off their military specialized business in the period 1990–98, while the rest where absorbed as a whole by, or merged into, larger military contractors. Subsequently another 10 companies ceased to be independent as a result of merger and acquisition agreements reached during 1999.

As a result of this rapid concentration, the five largest companies accounted for an increasing share of the combined arms sales of the top 100—22 per cent in 1990 but around 41 per cent in 1998. The effect of concentration can also be seen in the differences in arms sales trends between the largest arms-producing companies and the top 100 generally. While the overall trend for the top 100 was downwards over the period, the decline was less sharp among the top 50; the arms sales of the top five companies even showed a significant increase—of 23 per cent over the period, to $63.8 billion in 1998 (table 6.6). Another effect is that company size in the top layer of the arms industry has increased considerably, in spite of the overall trend of decline in the industry. This change in industrial structure is likely to increase the leverage of a few companies.

Table 6.8. Trends in arms exports in the USA, the UK and France, 1990–98

Country	1987	1988	1989	1990	1991	1992	1993	1994	1995	1996	1997	1998
Share of exports in total arms sales (%):												
USA	13	11	12	11	11	11	13	12	15	13	21	..
UK	32	34	36	38	32	28	28	29	41	48	50	48
France	32	33	31	31	25	26	20	17	22	30	41	40

Sources and definitions: see table 6.4.

Diversification

It is difficult to use aggregate statistics to identify diversification from military to civilian production. However, some conclusions can be drawn. Of the arms-producing companies which were the 100 largest in 1990, 15 have left arms production altogether, either by selling off their arms-producing activities or by spinning them off into independent companies. Another 12 have been acquired or merged with other companies and for 8 there were no comparable data or no data at all.

Of these 100 companies, 65 were still independent arms-producing companies at the end of 1998. Of these 53 (more than 80 per cent) were directly affected by the decline of the market in that they saw a reduction of their arms sales during the period 1990–98. It is the behaviour of this group of companies which is interesting to study. Data on the trend in their civilian sales provide some indication. The great majority (36 companies, or 68 per cent) managed to increase their civilian sales during the period, and as many as 45 per cent were able to increase civilian sales to more than compensate for their loss of arms sales. This is a fairly positive record for the adjustment process. How far this has also involved conversion—the reuse of economic, physical or labour resources for civilian production—is impossible to say on the basis of aggregate statistics.

While most companies have been able to reduce their dependence on military sales during the period of drawdown in arms procurement, some have increased it. Table 6.7 lists the 15 companies among the 100 largest in 1998 which increased their dependence on arms sales by 10 percentage points or more during the period 1990–98.

Exports

Cuts in domestic arms procurement have been met in some countries and companies by increased arms exports. In both France and the UK there has been a sharp increase in arms exports since the mid-1990s—in fact the resumed increase in arms sales in these two countries since the mid-1990s is the result entirely of increased arms exports. Domestic arms sales continued to decline after 1995 in both. The share of exports in their total arms sales is therefore very high—by 1998 an estimated 48 per cent in the UK and 40 per cent in

Table 6.9. Changes in the share of exports in total arms sales in major arms-producing companies, 1989–91 and 1996–98

Figures are percentages.

Company	1989–91	1996–98
Lockheed/Lockheed Martin, USA[a]	8	24
Boeing, USA	16	25
Raytheon, USA	8	11
BAe, UK[b]	(30)	(65)
Thomson-CSF, France	66	65

[a] Figures are for total sales to foreign governments, primarily to military customers.

[b] No comparable data are available for BAe. The arms sales share is estimated on the assumption that the export share is the same for arms sales as for commercial sales, which probably leads to an underestimate.

Source: SIPRI arms industry database, 1999.

France (table 6.8). In the United States the share has been roughly constant throughout the period on the national level, except for 1997, while individual US arms-producing companies, primarily the larger ones, have increased their export share as well.[52]

Data on arms exports are available for only a few companies. Data for some of the major companies in 1998 confirm that the dependence on arms exports has increased in these companies over the decade (table 6.9).

V. Russia[53]

Efforts to put an end to almost a decade's decline in arms production in the Russian Federation intensified during 1999. Economic factors have been the major determinant of this decline. Russian arms procurement expenditure has been radically cut since 1991 and since 1995 the government has not been able to pay the arms industry for goods delivered. This has resulted in a large accumulated government debt to the industry since 1995, while the industry has accumulated a debt to the federal government largely as a result of the government's failure to pay it.

During 1998 and 1999, the institutional framework was subject to several significant changes and, unlike in previous years, the federal government took concrete measures to fulfil its promise to pay some of its debt to the arms industry. Since the financial crisis of August 1998 successive Russian governments have emphasized the need to restore some of the capacity lost in arms production during the 1990s, and even seen arms production as a vehicle of economic growth.[54] During 1999 it became clear that the arms industry will

[52] For a discussion of different types of arms export statistics, see appendix 7E in this volume.

[53] Professor Julian Cooper, University of Birmingham, provided invaluable help in the preparation of this section.

[54] Former Prime Minister Yevgeniy Primakov has emphasized the importance of working out a defence industrial policy: 'In order to maintain our position on the world scene, we need a locomotive to

receive higher priority in Russian economic and technology policy and that this will have an impact on the allocation of resources to the industry. There was broad consensus in Russian politics on this strategy. It has evolved as a result of two factors: the changing international security climate, as manifested primarily by the military intervention by NATO forces in the FRY, which resulted in a profound change in Russian threat perceptions;[55] and the deterioration in Russian industrial production and economic development. The implementation of this policy will depend not only on political support but also on the robustness of the federal budget, the financial strength of the enterprises and possibly also the state–enterprise relationship in Russia.

Trends in Russian arms production

The dramatic decline in Russian arms production after 1991 was halted in 1998, and in 1999 there was a significant increase for the first time since the Soviet Union broke up in 1991. In a longer-term perspective, however, this represented a rather modest recovery, bringing the level of arms production roughly back to that of 1996 but still significantly less than that of 1991 or even 1992. Table 6.10 presents official data on the trends in military and civilian output of the group of arms-producing enterprises which constitute the core of the Russian arms industry—the *voyenno-promyshlenny kompleks* (VPK), literally the 'military–industrial complex'.[56] According to these data, which reflect about 90 per cent of the value of Russian arms production, total production of the VPK increased by 33 per cent in 1999 but, while the growth in civilian output amounted to 29 per cent, that of military output was 37 per cent in real terms. While these data are difficult to interpret because of the lack of information about how they are calculated, they are widely used within Russia and are at least a rough guide to trends. What they show is a definite change in trend in 1999, albeit from a sharply reduced level. They also show a much higher rate of growth in arms production than in total industrial production in Russia, which increased by around 8 per cent in real terms in 1999.

pull us forward . . . The defence industry may and must be that locomotive'. ITAR-TASS (Moscow), 7 Oct. 1999, in 'Primakov: Defence industry Russia's locomotive', Foreign Broadcast Information Service, *Daily Report–Central Eurasia (FBIS-SOV)*, FBIS-SOV-1999-1007, 11 Oct. 1999. According to former Prime Minister Sergey Stepashin, 'the defence industry complex has to become an engine of the revival of our industry'. According to the current Prime Minister, Vladimir Putin, 'the military industrial complex and the weapons trade will be a priority of the country's economic policy'. *Rossiyskaya Gazeta*, 11 Nov. 1999, pp. 1–2, in 'Putin sees defence sector as economic "priority"', FBIS-SOV-1999-1111, 12 Nov. 1999.

[55] The change was reflected in the new military doctrine. A draft of the new doctrine was published by *Krasnaya Zvezda* on 9 Oct. 1999, pp. 3–4. The final version, as approved by President Putin on 21 Apr. 2000, was published in *Nezavisimaya Gazeta*, 22 Apr. 2000. An unofficial translation into English was released by BBC Monitoring on 22 Apr. 2000.

[56] The term 'military–industrial complex' is used in Russia to mean that part of the defence industry which is overseen by specialized government oversight agencies—reportedly accounting for over 90% of total military output. This usage is followed in the discussion of the Russian arms industry in this chapter. In accepted Western usage, the term MIC denotes the pooling of the vested interests of the military establishment and the arms industry, and originated in US President Dwight Eisenhower's farewell address in Jan. 1961, in which he warned against the 'unwarranted influence, whether sought or unsought, by the military–industrial complex'.

Table 6.10. Russia: output and employment in the defence complex (VPK), 1991–99[a]
1991 = 100 (constant prices).

	1991	1992	1993	1994	1995	1996	1997	1998	1999
Military output	100	49.5	32.5	19.9	16.6	12.8	9.4	9.9	13.5
Civilian output	100	99.6	85.6	52.6	41.3	29.1	28.7	26.5	34.1
Total output	100	80.4	64.6	39.2	31.2	22.7	19.7	19.2	25.5
Total employment	100	90.3	79.9	78.2	67.1	58.6	52.7	47.3	44.4[b]
Output by branch:									
Aviation	100	84	68	36	31	22	17	18	24
Missiles and space[c]	100	94	88	63	53	39	43	45	65
RKA[d]						100	101	115	146
Electronics	100	72	48	26	22	15	15	15	21
Communications	100	74	58	32	21	15	13	11	15
Radio	100	84	78	49	34	27	23	27	28
Shipbuilding	100	89	78	58	55	41	31	31	44
Armaments	100	84	69	43	32	26	25	22	29
Munitions	100	70	57	37	29	21	18	16	23
For comparison:									
Total ind. output	100	82	70	55	54	52	53	50	54

Note: Figures are available only in index form or as annual percentage changes. These are based on data on production (not sales), expressed in constant roubles, which have been deflated by the use of specific price indices for military and civilian products.

[a] On the definition of the VPK, see note 56. The table excludes enterprises under the Ministry of Atomic Energy, responsible for the development and production of nuclear weapons.

[b] Jan.–Nov.

[c] Missiles and space refers to output of the Missile–Space Department of the Ministry of the Economy, although during 1999 all missile–space activity was transferred to Rossiyskoye Aviatsionno-Kosmicheskoye Agentsvo (the Russian Aerospace Agency, RAKA).

[d] Rossiyskoye Kosmicheskoye Agentsvo (Russian Space Agency, RKA); since 1999 the space activities of RAKA.

Sources: Data provided by Prof. Julian Cooper, University of Birmingham, based on the following. **Output and employment data 1991–98**: URL <http://i.vpk.ru/fin/eko>; **for 1999**: URL <http://t.vpk.ru/forecasts/results/2_3_99_12.htm>. **Output by branch for 1991–96**: Tsentr ekonomicheskoy konyunktury pri pravitelstve Rossiyskoy Federatsii', *Rossiya,* various issues, 1993–no. 2 (1997). **Total industrial production**: Bank of Finland, *Russian Economy: The Month in Review,* no. 5 (1998); and Goskomstat, URL <http://www.gks.ru>.

Employment in the Russian arms industry has continued to decline in spite of the increase in production in 1998 and 1999. However, during the period of decline employment cuts have lagged considerably behind production cuts. While the aggregate reduction in total output of the VPK during the period 1991–99 was 74 per cent, the cut in employment was only 56 per cent, which indicates that there is significant scope for rationalization (table 6.10). The reduction in employment is therefore most likely to continue, in particular since rationalization is one of the important aims of the evolving Russian defence industrial policy.

The actual size of Russian arms production is difficult to estimate because official data are mostly expressed in index terms and absolute numbers are seldom provided. Theoretically, an approximate magnitude can be estimated indirectly, either on the basis of the size of the state defence order, or by adding together federal expenditure for arms procurement from national production and military R&D with arms exports.

The state defence order is the combined government order for military and non-military equipment for the Ministry of Defence (MOD), for other forces such as the Ministry of Interior troops, and for arms exports under government-to-government agreements. To take it as a guide would probably produce an overestimate of arms production as it includes several major items unrelated to military production but excludes a smaller part of Russian arms exports—those by enterprises which have independent export rights.[57] Since there are no data available on the component parts of the state defence order nor on independently granted arms exports for 1999, it is impossible to derive an estimate of Russian arms production by this method.

The use of federal expenditure data is also problematic but provides a tentative estimate. Expenditure on arms procurement, military R&D and construction amounted to 32.6 billion roubles in 1999.[58] Deducting an estimated 4.4 billion roubles for construction,[59] this leaves approximately 28 billion roubles for procurement and military R&D for the MOD only—approximately $1.2 billion at the official exchange rate, or $3.5 billion in purchasing-power parity terms (PPP) terms.[60] Assuming that arms imports are negligible and adding the value of Russian arms exports from new production, estimated at roughly $2.2 billion in 1999,[61] the provisional estimate derived for Russian arms production in 1999 is about $3.4 billion ($5.7 billion in PPP terms).

Defence industrial policy

The new Russian defence industrial policy, which began to emerge with decisions taken in December 1997,[62] became increasingly assertive in 1999. It has three main elements: increased funding, consolidation and increased competitiveness in arms exports. To further review defence industrial policy and recommend government measures to assist it, the government announced on

[57] Total Russian arms exports for 1999 amounted to $3.5 billion, of which $2.8 billion was accounted for by the state agency Rosvooruzheniye. 'Rosvooruzheniye planning to top 1999 export level', ITAR-TASS (Moscow), 11 Apr. 2000, 1458 GMT, in FBIS-SOV-2000-0411, 13 Apr. 2000. This total includes all revenues from what is called 'military–technical cooperation', including not only exports of military equipment from new production but also new equipment from stocks, second-hand equipment, upgrading work, military training and other activities. Most exports of newly-produced military equipment are managed by Rosvooruzheniye, while the enterprises granted independent export rights account for a smaller share. However, some of Rosvooruzheniye's export revenues are for other activities. The assumption here is that 80% of its total sales, or $2.2 billion, are for military hardware from new production.

[58] See chapter 5, table 5.9 in this volume.

[59] This estimate is based on previous trends. See chapter 5, table 5.9 in this volume.

[60] The PPP rate for 1999 is estimated at c. 8 roubles : 1USD, by applying the deviation index for 1998 between the market exchange rate and the PPP rate—3.03—to the 1999 market exchange rate of 24.625 roubles : 1USD. On the use of PPPs, see 'Sources and methods for military expenditure data', *SIPRI Yearbook 1999* (note 49), appendix 7C, pp. 330–33.

[61] See note 57.

[62] Sköns and Weidacher (note 50), pp. 393–94.

22 June 1999 the appointment of a committee (the Komissiya Pravitelstva Rossiyskoy Federatsii po Voyenno-promyshlennym Voprosam, or Commission of the Russian Federation for Military–Industrial Questions), chaired by the Prime Minister and managed by Deputy Prime Minister Ilya Klebanov.

Planned consolidation according to the Federal Programme for Restructuring and Conversion of the Defence Industry for the years 1998–2000 involves concentration of the industry, aiming to reduce the number of enterprises from around 1700 in 1997 to 670 by 2000. This has, however, been difficult to achieve and by the end of 1999 the number of enterprises officially constituting the VPK was virtually unchanged. The goal for the aircraft industry is to form a maximum of 10 technologically integrated concerns out of the existing 350 enterprises.[63] While a merger between the two major aircraft companies, MiG and Sukhoi, has been on the agenda since 1998, it did not materialize during 1999. However, MiG has undergone a major reorganization and a similar plan is being implemented for Sukhoi. There has also been some reorganization of the two major producers of air defence equipment, Almaz and Antei, and the feasibility of integration of the air defence industry was under study during 1999.[64]

To promote arms production, manage the restructuring and increase oversight over the arms industry, a reorganization of the management of the arms-producing enterprises was decided and implemented during 1999. Five new government agencies for the defence industry were created, specialized by sector and responsible for research, development, production, modernization and use of weapon systems in their respective fields. In February the government decided to transfer the responsibility for the aviation industry from the Ministry of the Economy to Rossiyskoye Kosmicheskoye Agentsvo (Russian Space Agency), which was then renamed Rossiyskoye Aviatsionnoye-Kosmicheskoye Agentsvo (Russian Aerospace Agency).[65] This was followed by a presidential decree on 28 May creating four new agencies for the remaining sectors of arms production, to be operational in August.[66] These five agencies have control and licensing authority over all state-owned facilities (enterprises and organizations) in their respective sectors and also oversee some aspects of the activities of joint stock companies, with and without state share-

[63] 'New Russian industry chief tries again to force reforms', *Defense News,* 12 July 1999, p. 17.

[64] See, e.g., 'Two firms to control Russian air defense sector', *Defense News,* 31 Jan. 2000, p. 17.

[65] 'Aircraft industry takeover examined', *Rossiyskaya Gazeta* (electronic version), 25 May 1999, p. 2, in FBIS-SOV-1999-0526, 1 June 1999.

[66] 'Critics say Moscow's shift in industry oversight needs stability, money to prevail', *Defense News,* 21 June 1999, p. 30. The 4 new bodies were the Agencies for (*a*) Ammunition (Rossiyskoye Agentstvo po Boyepripasam, RAB), (*b*) Conventional Weapons (Rossiyskoye Agentstvo po Obychnym Vooruzheniyam, RAOV), (*c*) Control Systems (Rossiyskoye Agentstvo po Sistemam Upravleniya (RASU) and (*d*) Shipbuilding (Rossiyskoye Agentstvo po Sudostroyeniya, RAS). The RAOV has responsibility for oversight of the manufacture of armoured vehicles, artillery systems, missile systems, high-precision weapons, firearms and cartridges for firearms, and optical and electronic devices for weapons and for civilian equipment. ITAR-TASS (Moscow), 2 Feb. 2000, in 'Putin approves statute of Conventional Weapons Agency', FBIS-SOV-2000-0202, 3 Feb. 2000. The RASU has responsibility for oversight of the entire radio, communications equipment and electronics industries. The RAS' responsibilities include both military and civilian shipbuilding.

holdings. The new organization included a total of 1674 enterprises and organizations (table 6.11).

In 1999 there were several government decisions and actual measures to improve the financial conditions in the arms industry: (*a*) by repaying its debt to the enterprises and by forgiving the industry part of its debt to the federal budget; (*b*) by faster implementation of the adopted budget (so that new debts would not be incurred); and (*c*) by increasing orders to the arms industry.

The size of the accumulated government debt to the arms-producing enterprises was reported as 25.6 billion roubles in August 1999.[67] The government reiterated its aim to pay some of this debt during the course of the year but the repayment targets shifted somewhat. In early 2000 the targets were to pay by the end of the first quarter 2000 all debts incurred on arms contracts during 1999; to pay by the end of April all arrears incurred for 1997–98; and to pay the entire accumulated debt within two or three years.[68] In December 1999 Prime Minister Vladimir Putin instructed the Ministry of Finance to study the possibility of also writing off part of the industry's debt to the federal budget,[69] debts which to a great extent have been caused by government failure to pay for goods delivered and which have resulted in bankruptcies and unplanned closures in the arms industry.

The target for 1999 was to not incur new debts to the industry. In previous years the defence budget adopted and in particular the procurement budget have been far from implemented in actual expenditure, and thus in payments to the arms industry. In 1999, however, the rate of implementation was significantly higher than in previous years. By late December 1999 the government reported that over 90 per cent of state defence contracts in that year had been paid for in 1999, as against 20 per cent in 1998.[70] However, in early 2000 the reported rate of implementation was only 50–60 per cent, the failure being attributed by the government to the Chechnya war.[71]

The third element has been the decision to increase domestic orders to the arms industry. In October 1999 a supplementary procurement budget for 1999 was announced, amounting to 4 billion roubles, to be used to buy additional equipment needed for the war in Chechnya, including aircraft, helicopters and communication equipment.[72] The proposed defence budget for 2000 does not include detailed figures for arms procurement: these are lumped together with allocations for R&D and construction.[73] According to Prime Minister Putin the allocation for arms procurement in 2000 represents an increase of around

[67] Interfax (Moscow), 6 Aug. 1999, in 'Russian Government to clear military industrial debts', FBIS-SOV-1999-0806, 8 Aug. 1999.

[68] Deputy Prime Minister Ilya Klebanov at a press conference. Interfax (Moscow), 27 Jan. 2000, 1117 GMT, in 'Russian Government approves 2000 defense order', FBIS-SOV-2000-0127, 28 Jan. 2000.

[69] Radio Rossii Network, 18 Aug. 1999, in 'Putin emphasizes funding of the military–industrial complex', FBIS-SOV-1999-0818, 19 Aug. 1999.

[70] According to Prime Minister Putin. Interfax (Moscow), 24 Dec. 1999, in 'Putin: Russian defense bill to be endorsed in Jan', FBIS-SOV-1999-1224, 24 Dec. 1999.

[71] 'Russian Government approves 2000 defense order' (note 68).

[72] 'Russia to boost weapons spending', *Air Letter*, 11 Oct. 1999, p. 4.

[73] See chapter 5 in this volume.

Table 6.11. The agencies of the Russian arms industry, autumn 1999

Agency	Number of enterprises and organizations		
	Total	State-owned	JSCs
Russian Aerospace Agency (RAKA)	430	n.a.	n.a.
Russian Agency for Conventional Weapons (RAOV)	137	62	75
Russian Agency for Ammunition (RAB)	138	106	32
Russian Agency for Shipbuilding (RAS)	170	76	94
Russian Agency for Control Systems (RASU)	769	276	493
Total	**1 644**	**n.a.**	**n.a.**

Note: JSCs = Joint stock companies.

Source: Information provided by Julian Cooper from: *Sobraniye Zakonodatelstva Rossiyskoy Federatsii* [Collection of legislation of the Russian Federation], no. 33 (1999), articles 4113, 4114, 4115 and 4122; and (for RAKA) URL <http://i.vpk.ru/cgi-bin/>, accessed 10 Feb. 2000.

50 per cent. However, the sources of finance for this increase were not elaborated.

Exports are significant for the VPK since they account for a great part of arms production. Russian arms-producing enterprises have become increasingly dependent on arms exports but have had great difficulty in competing on the international arms market.[74] In some sectors the share is extremely high.[75] The sharp devaluation of the rouble in August 1998 contributed to make Russian weapons more competitive on the international market. It is also clear that Russian defence industrial policy will continue to give high priority to arms exports, both as a source of revenue for investment in the industry and for the maintenance and development of the technological capability of the industry.

[74] See chapter 7, section IV in this volume.

[75] According to Alexander Nozdrachev, Director General of the Russian Agency for Conventional Weapons, the export share for armoured vehicles, artillery and guns for the first 8 months of 1999 was 84%. 'Russian defence industry shows short-term rebound', *Defense News,* 18 Oct. 1999.

Appendix 6A. The 100 largest arms-producing companies, 1998

REINHILDE WEIDACHER and the SIPRI ARMS INDUSTRY NETWORK*

Table 6A contains information on the 100 largest arms-producing companies in the OECD and the developing countries ranked by their arms sales in 1998.[1] Companies with the designation *S* in the column for rank in 1997 are subsidiaries; their arms sales are included in the figure in column 6 for the holding company. Subsidiaries are listed in the position in which they would appear if they were independent companies. In order to facilitate comparison with data for the previous year, the rank order and arms sales figures for 1997 are also given. Where new data for 1997 have become available, this information is included in the table; thus the 1997 rank order and the arms sales figures for some companies which appeared in table 10A in the *SIPRI Yearbook 1999* have been revised.

Sources and methods

Sources of data. The data in the table are based on the following sources: company reports, a questionnaire sent to over 400 companies, and corporation news published in the business sections of newspapers, military journals and on the Internet. Company archives, marketing reports, government publication of prime contracts and country surveys were also consulted. In many cases exact figures on arms sales were not available, mainly because companies often do not report their arms sales or lump them together with other activities. Estimates were therefore made.

Definitions. Data on total sales, profits and employment are for the entire company, not for the arms-producing sector alone. Profit data are after taxes in all cases when the company provides such data. Employment data are either a year-end or a yearly average figure as reported by the company. Data are reported on the fiscal year basis reported by the company in its annual report.

Key to abbreviations in column 5. A = artillery, Ac = aircraft, El = electronics, Eng = engines, Mi = missiles, MV = military vehicles, SA/A = small arms/ammunition, Sh = ships, and Oth = other. Comp ( ) = components of the product within the parentheses. It is used only for companies which do not produce any final systems.

---

[1] For the membership of the Organisation for Economic Co-operation and Development, see the glossary in this volume. The category of developing countries covers all countries other than the OECD and the former and current centrally planned economies, for which there is a lack of comparable data on the enterprise level since 1989.

* Participants in the SIPRI Arms Industry Network: Dipankar Banerjee, Institute for Peace and Conflict Studies (New Delhi); Peter Batchelor, Centre for Conflict Resolution (Cape Town); Paul Dunne, Middlesex Business University (London); Ken Epps, Project Ploughshares Canada (Ontario); Jean-Paul Hébert, CIRPES (Paris); Peter Hug (Bern); Christos Kollias, School of Business and Economics (Larissa); Luc Mampaey, Groupe de Recherche et d'Information sur la Paix et la Sécurité, GRIP (Brussels); Lesley McCulloch, Australia National University (Canberra); Arcadi Oliveres, Centre d'Estudis sobre la Pau i el Desarmament (Barcelona); Ton van Oosterhout, TNO (The Hague); and Reuven Pedatzur, The Galili Center for Strategy and National Security (Ramat Efal).

Table 6A. The 100 largest arms-producing companies in the OECD and developing countries, 1998

Figures in columns 6, 7, 8 and 10 are in US $m.[a] Figures in italics are percentages.

1	2	3	4	5	6	7	8	9	10	11
Rank[b]					Arms sales					
1998	1997	Company[c]	Country	Sector[d]	1998	1997	Total sales 1998	Col. 6 as % of col. 8	Profit 1998	Employment 1998
1	1	Lockheed Martin	USA	Ac El Mi	17 880	18 500	26 266	68	1 001	165 000
2	2	Boeing	USA	Ac El Mi	15 900	14 500	56 154	28	1 120	231 000
3	7	Raytheon	USA	El Mi	12 480	5 070	19 530	64	864	108 200
4	3	British Aerospace, BAe	UK	A Ac El Mi SA/A	10 520	10 410	14 264	74	1 146	47 900
5	6	GEC[e]	UK	El Sh	7 010	6 030	12 630	55	1 746	74 250
6	5	Northrop Grumman	USA	Ac El Mi SA/A	6 720	7 210	8 902	75	194	49 600
7	8	Thomson	France	El Mi SA/A	4 310	4 220	..	..	..	..
S	S	Thomson-CSF (Thomson)	France	El Mi SA/A	4 310	4 220	6 866	63	–258	48 850
8	9	General Dynamics, GD	USA	MV Sh	4 160	3 650	4 970	84	364	30 700
9	11	TRW	USA	Comp (El MV) Oth	4 100	3 420	11 886	34	477	78 000
10	12	United Technologies	USA	El Eng	3 260	3 310	25 715	13	1 255	178 800
11	10	Litton	USA	El Sh	3 230	3 470	4 400	73	181	34 900
12	13	DaimlerChrysler, DC	FRG	Ac El Eng MV Mi	3 050	2 840	146 470	2	5 358	441 500
S	S	DaimlerChrysler Aerospace, DASA (DC)	FRG	Ac El Eng Mi	3 020	2 820	9 748	31	608	45 860
13	14	IRI	Italy	A Ac El MV Mi SA/A Sh	2 690	2 680	17 812	15	1 832	112 650
14	15	Mitsubishi Heavy Industries	Japan	Ac MV Mi Sh	2 540	2 250	22 212	11	138	..
S	S	Finmeccanica (IRI)	Italy	A Ac El MV Mi SA/A	2 420	2 410	6 543	37	–279	47 780
15	16	DCN[f]	France	Sh	2 150	2 180	2 217	97	..	17 580
16	17	Rolls Royce	UK	Eng	2 150	2 130	7 447	29	431	42 000

		Company	Country	Sector						
17	18	Aérospatiale Groupe	France	Ac Mi	2 000	1 980	9 301	22	195	36 650
S	S	Matra BAe Dynamics (Matra HT/BAe, UK)	France	Mi	1 970	1 540	1 970	100	..	..
18	19	Dassault Aviation Groupe	France	Ac	1 870	1 870	3 826	49	314	11 630
19	20	Newport News	USA	Sh	1 720	1 600	1 862	92	66	18 000
20	22	General Electric	USA	Eng	1 600	1 500	100 469	2	9 296	293 000
21	24	Lagardère	France	El Mi Oth	1 470	1 320	11 889	12	311	49 960
S	S	Matra Haute Technologies, Matra HT (Lagardère)	France	El Mi Oth	1 470	1 320	3 555	41	381	17 750
22	23	Allied Signal	USA	Ac El	1 370	1 340	15 128	9	1 331	70 400
23	30	ITT Industries	USA	El	1 290	1 100	4 493	29	146	..
24	36	Rheinmetall	FRG	A El MV SA/A	1 280	990	4 589	28	155	30 240
25	29	Israel Aircraft Industries, IAI	Israel	Ac El Mi	1 220	1 100	1 874	65	41	14 050
26	28	GIAT Industries	France	A MV SA/A	1 200	1 120	1 223	98	−148	10 270
27	34	Celsius	Sweden	A El SA/A Sh	1 200	1 000	1 798	67	64	10 900
28	25	CEA	France	Oth	1 190	1 250	3 094	38	−30	16 150
29	27	GKN	UK	Ac MV	1 160	1 150	6 139	19	944	35 520
S	–	Thomson-CSF Detexis (Thomson-CSF)	France	El	1 110	0	1 390	80	..	7 200
30	35	Textron	USA	Ac El Eng MV	1 100	1 000	9 683	11	608	64 000
31	31	United Defense	USA	MV	1 100	1 070	1 218	90	−120	5 130
32	33	SEPI	Spain	Ac El Oth	1 020	1 010				
33	38	SNECMA Groupe	France	Eng	970	910	4 825	20	276	23 110
S	S	Matra BAe Dynamics France (Matra BAe Dynamics, France/UK)	France	Mi	930	930	930	100	..	2 770
34	21	Alcatel Alsthom[g]	France	El	920	1 590	23 638	4	2 602	118 270
35	39	Alliant Tech Systems	USA	SA/A	850	910	1 090	78	51	6 110
S	S	Eurocopter Group (Aérospatiale/DASA, FRG)	France	Ac	830	770	1 892	44	56	9 510
36	47	Hunting	UK	Oth	810	720	1 627	50	36	11 170

1	2	3	4	5	6	7	8	9	10	11
Rank[b]					Arms sales			Col. 6 as	Profit	Employment
1998	1997	Company[c]	Country	Sector[d]	1998	1997	Total sales 1998	% of col. 8	1998	1998
37	41	FIAT	Italy	Eng MV SA/A	790	810	50 999	2	692	220 550
38	32	Mitsubishi Electric[h]	Japan	El Mi	790	1 060	28 982	3	−340	116 480
39	44	GTE	USA	El	740	730	25 473	3	2	120 000
40	59	L-3 Communications	USA	El	720	550	1 037	69	33	8 000
41	43	Harris	USA	El	700	760	3 890	18	133	28 500
42	26	Kawasaki Heavy Industries[h]	Japan	Ac Eng Mi Sh	670	1 210	9 183	7	−47	26 490
43	48	Saab	Sweden	Ac El Mi	650	670	1 037	63	115	7 890
44	45	Ordnance Factories[i]	India	A SA/A	640	720	737	86	..	155 000
45	46	Singapore Technologies	Singap.	A El Eng MV Mi SA/A	620	720	..	..	..	..
46	53	Racal Electronics	UK	El	620	590	1 628	38	108	11 280
S	S	Rheinmetall Ind. (Rheinmetall)	FRG	A El MV SA/A	610	600	610	100	41	3 490
47	49	Eidgenössische Rüstungsb.[j]	Switzerl.	A Ac Eng SA/A	600	640	692	87	14	4 170
48	62	Gencorp	USA	El Eng	600	520	1 737	34	84	10 770
49	60	Rockwell International	USA	El Mi	600	540	6 752	9	−427	41 000
50	50	SAGEM Groupe	France	El	570	630	3 179	18	135	13 980
51	56	Vickers	UK	Eng MV SA/A	570	560	1 478	39	204	8 000
52	63	Diehl	FRG	Mi SA/A	550	510	1 741	31	..	12 610
53	64	Avondale Industries	USA	Sh	550	510	749	74	37	5 550
54	82	Israel Military Industries	Israel	A MV SA/A	530	360	550	96	13	4 080
55	65	Rafael	Israel	SA/A Oth	510	500	510	100	85	4 100
56	58	Ishikawajima-Harima[h]	Japan	Eng Sh	490	550	8 051	6	44	..
S	S	ST Engineering, STE (ST)	Singap.	Ac El Eng Sh	490	550	993	49	92	7 790
S	S	FIAT Aviazione (FIAT)	Italy	Eng SA/A	470	450	1 368	34	..	5 830
57	70	Smiths Industries	UK	El	460	410	1 985	23	245	14 100
58	73	Stewart & Stevenson	USA	MV	460	400	1 207	38	−73	4 240

		Company	Country	Activity						
S	S	MTU (DASA)	FRG	Eng	460	500	1 845	25	124	6 630
59	83	MKEK	Turkey	SA/A	440	360	570	77	91	9 120
60	61	Oerlikon-Bührle	Switzerl.	A Ac El Mi SA/A	430	520	2 504	17	-117	13 740
61	69	Mannesmann	FRG	MV	420	420	21 335	2	705	116 250
S	S	Bazan (SEPI)^k	Spain	El Eng Sh	420	420	486	87	-40	7 270
62	67	Hindustan Aeronautics^i	India	Ac Mi	410	470	439	94	27	33 970
63	78	Elbit Systems	Israel	El	410	370	410	100	28	1 910
64	–	Alvis	UK	MV Oth	410	120	443	94	22	1 550
65	71	Koor Industries	Israel	A El	400	400	3 322	12	12	..
S	S	Tadiran (Koor Industries)	Israel	El	400	400	1 136	35	67	7 680
S	S	Agusta (Finmeccanica)	Italy	Ac	400	370	593	67	..	5 170
66	–	Cordant Technologies	USA	Eng SA/A	390	200	2 427	16	142	18 000
67	4	General Motors, GM	USA	El Eng Mi	390	7 450	161 315	..	2 956	594 000
68	77	Mitre	USA	Oth	390	380	527	75	8	..
S	S	LFK (DASA)	FRG	Mi	390	410	390	100	-20	1 230
69	68	Denel^l	S. Africa	A Ac El MV Mi SA/A	380	460	575	66	-69	..
70	84	Allegheny Teledyne	USA	El Eng Mi	380	340	3 923	10	241	21 500
S	S	SAGEM (SAGEM Groupe)	France	El	380	540	3 050	13	131	15 840
S	S	Hollandse Signaalapparaten (Thomson-CSF, France)	Netherl.	El	370	350	370	100	22	3 110
71	74	Babcock International Group, BI	UK	Sh	360	390	820	44	42	6 980
72	79	Dyncorp	USA	Comp (Ac)	360	370	1 234	29	15	15 040
73	76	EDS	USA	El	360	380	16 891	2	743	120 000
74	80	EG&G	USA	Comp (El Oth)	360	370	1 408	25	2	13 000
S	S	Babcock Rosyth Defence (BI)	UK	Sh Oth	360	390	360	100	-7	3 490
75	87	Cobham	UK	Comp (Ac El) Oth	350	320	636	55	72	5 270
76	90	Devonport Management	UK	Sh	350	290	436	80	19	3 700
77	66	Honeywell	USA	El Mi	350	490	8 427	4	572	57 000
78	52	NEC^h	Japan	El	340	620	36 356	1	-1 207	157 770
S	S	CASA (SEPI)	Spain	Ac	340	350	1 123	30	52	7 440
79	96	Sundstrand	USA	Ac Oth	330	270	2 005	17	226	10 900

1	2	3	4	5	6	7	8	9	10	11
Rank[b]					Arms sales			Col. 6 as	Profit	Employment
1998	1997	Company[c]	Country	Sector[d]	1998	1997	Total sales 1998	% of col. 8	1998	1998
80	86	Wegmann Group	FRG	MV	320	320	320	100	..	1 090
81	75	AM General Corporation	USA	MV	320	390	393	83	–8	1 290
S	S	Matra Marconi Space (Matra HT/GEC,UK)	France	Oth	320	360	1 412	23	46	4 660
82	85	Tenix	Australia	Sh Comp (MV)	300	320	327	90	..	4 000
83	72	Toshiba[h]	Japan	El Mi	290	400	41 471	1	–109	198 000
84	92	Preussag	FRG	Sh	280	280	19 976	1	306	66 560
S	S	HDW (Preussag)	FRG	Sh	280	280	571	48	..	3 260
85	55	Lucent Technologies	USA	El	280	570	30 147	1	2 287	141 600
86	94	Motorola	USA	El	280	280	29 398	1	–962	133 000
87	95	Primex Technologies	USA	SA/A	280	280	495	57	16	3 000
S	S	Sextant Avionique (Thomson-CSF)	France	El	280	320	690	40	..	..
88	81	ADI	Australia	El SA/A Sh	270	360	342	78	–18	3 110
89	57	Dassault Electronique[m]	France	El	270	550	..	..	..	..
90	93	Komatsu[i]	Japan	MV SA/A	270	280	8 109	3	–95	..
91	89	Ericsson	Sweden	El	260	310	23 200	1	1 640	103 670
S	S	Fincantieri Gruppo (IRI)	Italy	Sh	260	280	2 463	11	–172	9 450
92	–	CAE	Canada	Oth	250	240	721	34	52	6 900
93	–	Vosper Thornycroft	UK	Sh	250	230	399	63	38	3 470
94	–	BFGoodrich	USA	Comp (Ac) MV	250	220	3 951	6	227	18 410
95	–	DRS Technologies	USA	El	250	170	273	93	3	2 180
96	91	Oshkosh Truck	USA	MV	250	290	903	28	15	..
S	S	GM Canada (GM, USA)	Canada	Eng MV	250	350	21 436	1	..	..
97	–	Nichols Research Corporation	USA	El	240	200	427	55	14	..

S	S	Computing Devices Canada (GD, USA)	Canada	El	240	260	277	85	..	1 200
S	–	Alcatel Space (Alcatel Alsthom)	France	Oth	240	0	1 424	17	..	..
S	S	IVECO (FIAT)	Italy	MV	240	260	4 845	5	..	17 990
S	S	Singapore Aerospace (STE)	Singap.	Ac El Eng	240	270	496	49	61	3 970
98	100	Bombardier	Canada	El Mi	230	250	7 752	3	373	53 000
99	97	Bharat Electronics[i]	India	El	230	260	306	75	13	15 740
100	–	Federman	Israel	El	220	250	..	..	..	..
S	S	El-Op (Federman)	Israel	El	220	250	320	68	..	2 000

a The period average of market exchange rates of the International Monetary Fund's *International Financial Statistics* is used for conversion to US dollars.

b Rank designations in the column for 1997 may not correspond to those given in table 10A in the *SIPRI Yearbook 1999* because of subsequent revision. A dash (–) in this column indicates either that the company did not produce arms in 1997, or that it did not exist as it was structured in 1997, in which case there is a zero (0) in column 7, or that it did not rank among the 100 top companies in 1997. Companies with the designation S in the column for rank are subsidiaries.

c Names in brackets are names of parent companies.

d A key to abbreviations in column 5 is provided on p. 327.

e The figure for GEC arms sales in 1998 is a SIPRI estimate, because data in the GEC Annual Report for fiscal year (FY) 1999 (1 Apr. 1998–31 Mar. 1999) are not comparable to data for previous years. The SIPRI estimate for 1998 (£4230 million) is based on GEC arms sales for 1997 (£3683 million), adding to this the amount of increase in the sales of Marconi Electronic Systems and the increase in the arms sales of Marconi Communications.

f All figures for DCN are for 1997.

g The figure for Alcatel Alsthom arms sales in 1998 includes (in addition to the arms sales of Alcatel Space) only a six-month estimate for the arms sales of Alcatel Alsthom, since their military electronics activities were transferred to Thomson-CSF in June 1998.

h For Japanese companies figures in the arms sales column represent new military contracts rather than arms sales.

i For Indian companies (Ordnance Factories, Hindustan Aeronautics, Bharat Electronics) all figures are for 1997, because the Indian Government no longer reports arms sales (or financial and employment) data in the *Ministry of Defence Annual Report.*

j Eidgenössische Rüstungsbetriebe has been renamed RUAG SUISSE since Jan. 1999.

k The figure for Bazan arms sales in 1998 is an estimate based on the share of arms sales in their total sales in 1997.

l All figures for Denel are for 1997.

m The figures for Dassault Electronique are estimates for only six months, because the company was transferred to Thomson-CSF in June 1998.

Appendix 6B. Major acquisitions by West European and US arms-producing companies, 1998–January 2000

Table 6B.1. Major acquisitions among US arms-producing companies, 1998–January 2000

Acquisitions and agreements on acquisitions as of end-January 2000.

Sector	Buyer company	Acquired company	Seller company	Price (US $m.)	Comments	Year of acquisit.
El	Allied Signal	Honeywell		14 000	Total sales $8400 m.; arms sales $350 m.	1999
Ac (Comp)	BFGoodrich	ACES II	Boeing	. .	Ejection seat company	1999
Eng (Comp)	BFGoodrich	Rohr Industries		1 300	Arms sales $60 m.	1998
Space	Boeing	Hughes Electronics space and communications activities	General Motors	3 750	Minor military satellite prod.	Agreed
El	Condor Systems	ARGOSystems	Boeing	. .		1999
El	Condor Systems	Applied Tech. div.	Litton	120	Total sales $130 m.	1999
El	DRS Technologies	Second Generation Ground Electro-Optical Systems and Focal Plane Array (part)	Raytheon	45	Sale required by Dept. of Justice	1998
El	Engineered Support Systems	Systems & Electronics, Inc. (SEI)	ESCO	85	Total sales $175 m.	1999
El	General Dynamics	Communication Systems Division, Worldwide Tele-communications Services, and Electronic Systems Division	GTE	1 050	Total sales c. $1200 m.	1999
El	General Dynamics	Computing Devices	Ceridian	600	Total sales $600 m.	1998

Sh	General Dynamics	NASSCO Holdings, Inc.		415	Total sales $485 m.	1998
El	ITT Industries	Space and Defense Communications division	Stanford Telecommunications	190		1999
El	L-3 Communications	Aydin Corp.		72	Total sales $130 m.	1999
El	L-3 Communications	Interstate Electronic Corporation	Scott Technologies	60	Total sales est. $95 m.	1999
El	L-3 Communications	Ocean Systems	Allied Signal	67	Total sales $100 m.	1998
El	L-3 Communications	Electrodynamics	Carpenter Technol. Corp.	..		1998
El	L-3 Communications	Microdyne		90	Total sales $73 m.	1998
El	L-3 Communications	Space&Navigation Systems	Allied Signal	55	Sale required by Dept. of Justice	1999
El	L-3 Communications	Storm Control Systems		..		1998
El	L-3 Communications	SPD Technologies		230	Total sales $170 m.	1998
El	L-3 Communications	ILEX Systems		53	Total sales $63 m.	1998
El	L-3 Communications	LNX TrexCom	Trex Communications Corp.	..		1999
El	L-3 Communications	EMP TrexCom	Trex Communications Corp.	..		1999
Sh	Litton	Avondale Industries		529	Total sales $750 m.; arms sales $550 m.	1999
El	Northrop Grumman	Ryan Aeronautical	Allegheny Teledyne	140	Arms sales est. $100 m.	1999
El	Northrop Grumman	Information Syst. Division	California Microwave	93	Total sales $121 m.	1999
El	Northrop Grumman	International Research Inst.		55	Total sales $60 m.	1998
El	Raytheon	Communications Systems	Allied Signal	63	Total sales $122 m.	1998
El	Science Applic. Internat.	Information Services	Boeing	..	Total sales est. $300 m.	1999
El	TriQuint Semiconductor	Monolithic Microwave	Raytheon	39	Sale required by Dept. of Justice	1998
Ac (Comp)	United Technologies	Sundstrand		4 300	Total sales $2010 m.; arms sales $330 m.	1999

Table 6B.2. Major international acquisitions among West European arms producing companies, 1998–January 2000

Acquisitions and agreements on acquisitions as of end-January 2000.

Sector	Buyer company	Acquired company	Seller company	Price (US $m.)	Comments	Year of acquisit.
Ac Mi	British Aerospace, UK	35% Saab, Sweden	Investor, Sweden	c. 450	Approved by CEC in July 1998	1998
Mi	Matra BAe Dynamics, France/UK	30% LFK, Germany	DASA, Germany	45	Total sales DM884 m.; option to increase share to 49%	1998
SA/A	Rheinmetall, Germany	33% Eurometaal, Netherlands	Dynamit Nobel (Metall-gesellschaft), Germany	..	Total sales DM240 m.; share increased to 67%	1998
A SA/A	Rheinmetall, Germany	Oerlikon Contraves, Switzerland	Oerlikon Bührle, Switzerland	..	Total sales CHF504 m.; subsid. in Italy, Germany, Canada, Singapore, Malaysia	1999
Ac (Comp)	SNECMA, France	50% Messier Dowty, UK	TI Group, UK	345	Total sales £247 m.; share increased to 100%	1998
EI	Thomson-CSF, France	Siemens Forsvarssystem, Norway	Siemens, Germany	..	Total sales NOK 140 m.	1998
EI	Thomson-CSF, France	DI Electro-Optic, Netherl.	Delft Instruments, Netherlands	..		1999
EI	Thomson-CSF, France	Odelft Electronic Instruments, Italy	Delft Instruments, Netherlands	..		1999
EI	Thomson-CSF, France	Racal Electronics, UK		2 170	Total sales $1630 m.; arms sales $620 m.	Agreed
Mi	Thomson-CSF, France	50% Shorts Missile Systems, UK	Bombardier, Canada	..	Total sales $102 m.; share increased to 100%	Agreed

Note: CEC = Commission of the European Communities.

Table 6B.3. Major transatlantic acquisitions among arms-producing companies, 1998–January 2000

Acquisitions and agreements on acquisitions as of end-January 2000.

Sector	Buyer company	Acquired company	Seller company	Price (US $m.)	Comments	Year of acquisit.
EI	Cobham, UK	Conax, USA		66		1998
EI	DRS Technologies	European Data Systems, UK		..		1999
EI	GEC, UK	Tracor, USA		1 400	Total sales $1265 m.; arms sales $950 m.	1998
MV	General Motors, USA	Mowag, Switzerland		..		1999
Ac (Comp)	GKN, UK	Interlake Corp., USA		560	450 employees	1999
SA/A	Primex Technologies, USA	CMS Group, USA	DASA, Germany	123		1998
Eng	Rolls Royce, UK	National Airmotive, USA	First Aviation Services, USA	73	380 employees	1999
EI	Thomson-CSF, France	Electro-optical activities of Allied Signal Aerospace, Canada	Allied Signal, USA	..	Total sales $14.2 m.	1999
Ac (Comp)	TRW, USA	LucasVarity, UK		6 610		1999
EI	Ultra Electronics, UK	Sonobuoy div.	Raytheon, USA	22		1998

Table 6B.4. Acquisitions by Western arms-producing companies in other regions, 1998–January 2000

Acquisitions and agreements on acquisitions as of end-January 2000.

Sector	Buyer company	Acquired company	Seller company	Price (US $m.)	Comments	Year of acquisit.
Ac	Consortium led by Dassault Aviation, France	20% Embraer, Brazil		208	Total sales $1300 m.; arms sales $160 m.; Brazilian Government holds a golden share in Embraer	Agreed
Ac	Boeing–Czech Airlines, USA/Czech Republic	34% Aero Vodochody, Czech Republic	Czech Government	33	Boeing holds 90% of the joint venture with CSA Czech Airlines	1998
El	Celsius, Sweden	49% Grintek Avitronics, South Africa	Grinaker, South Africa	..		1999
El	DASA, Germany	33% Reutech Radar Systems, South Africa	Reunert, South Africa	..		1999
El	Thomson-CSF, France	50% of military activities of Samsung Electronics, South Korea	Samsung Electronics, South Korea	120	Total sales $137 m.	1999
El	Thomson-CSF, France	100% African Defence Systems, South Africa	Altron, South Africa	..	50% acq. in 1998, 50% in 1999	1998–99
El	Transfield, Australia/ Thomson-CSF, France	ADI, Australia	Australian Government	347	Total sales A$543 m., arms sales A$422 m.	1999
El SA/A Sh						
MV	Vickers, UK	Reumech OMC, Astral and Gear Ratio, South Africa	Reunert, South Africa	c. 15+6	(Price contingent on performance)	1999

7. Transfers of major conventional weapons

BJÖRN HAGELIN, PIETER D. WEZEMAN and
SIEMON T. WEZEMAN

I. Introduction

Transparency in information and data on arms transfers is necessary to inform the current debate on the impact of arms transfers on war and peace. The SIPRI arms transfer project identifies trends in global transfers of major conventional weapons using the SIPRI trend indicator.[1] The project provides estimates of the military value of weapon transfers as well as of military technology involved in the licensed manufacture of conventional weapons.

On the basis of the trend indicator, global arms transfers increased over the 30-year period from 1950. However, after 1987 they declined rapidly. The five-year moving averages shown in figure 7.1 show fairly stable levels of global arms transfers from 1995, at about one-half of the 1982 peak value.[2]

The dominant trends of the major suppliers and recipients are presented in section II. Select arms transfers to recipients in regions characterized by military–political tension or armed conflict are discussed in section III. These examples illustrate that, in spite of official calls for restraint in the transfer of arms to countries in regions of conflict, such transfers continue to be made.

Two important considerations behind the decisions to supply major conventional weapons are discussed in sections IV and V. Although many different considerations are taken into account in each such decision, two general types—the economic considerations of the supplier and the resulting buyer's market, and foreign and military policy considerations—are identified in these sections.

The available government and industry information on arms exports presented in appendix 7E is examined in section VI. Governments also take part in unilateral or multilateral decisions not to supply weapons. Information on arms embargoes decided collectively by international organizations or by groups of nations and in force during 1995–99 are presented in section VII.

---

[1] SIPRI data on arms transfers refer to actual deliveries of major conventional weapons. To permit comparison between the data on such deliveries of different weapons and identification of general trends, SIPRI uses a *trend-indicator value*. The SIPRI values are therefore only an indicator of the volume of international arms transfers and not of the actual financial values of such transfers. Thus they are not comparable to economic statistics such as gross domestic product or export/import figures. The method used in calculating the trend-indicator value is described in appendix 7D. A more extensive description of the methodology used, including a list of sources, is available on the SIPRI Internet site, URL <http://www.sipri.se/projects/armstrade/atmethods.html>. The figures may differ from those given in previous SIPRI Yearbooks. The SIPRI arms transfers database is constantly updated as new data become available, and the trend-indicator values are revised each year.

[2] Five-year moving averages are calculated as a more stable measure of the trend in arms transfers than the often erratic year-to-year figures.

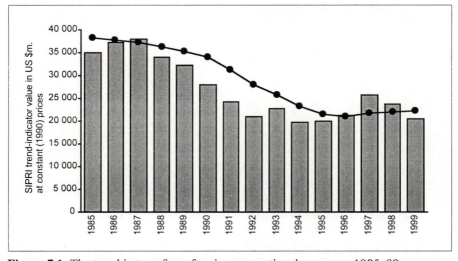

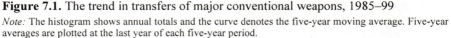

Figure 7.1. The trend in transfers of major conventional weapons, 1985–99

Note: The histogram shows annual totals and the curve denotes the five-year moving average. Five-year averages are plotted at the last year of each five-year period.

SIPRI's first estimate of the total financial value of the global arms trade is presented in section IV. The estimate is based on the available government and industry information on arms exports, as presented in appendix 7E, since the SIPRI trend-indicator value is unsuitable for this purpose—it does not represent actual financial flows (payments). Although the number of countries that submit detailed information about their arms exports on a regular basis is low, there is sufficient information on which to base a rough estimate.

Section VIII summarizes the main findings.

II. The major suppliers and recipients

Appendix 7A presents the volume of transfers of major conventional weapons for the period 1995–99. The *USA* remained by far the largest supplier—delivering almost as much as all other suppliers combined—for the period as well as for each year (table 7A.2). The USA was also the country with most recipients, some 35 customers in 1999. Its major recipients in 1995–99 were Taiwan, Saudi Arabia, South Korea, Egypt and Japan (table 7.1). Expected deliveries as reflected in new orders indicate that the USA will retain its dominant position for at least the next 10 years.

Russia is one of the two major suppliers whose arms transfers for 1999 were greater than those for 1998. It was the second largest supplier in 1999 as well as for the period 1995–99. However, its deliveries for this period amounted to only 27 per cent of those of the USA. That Russia's main recipients are China and India, countries on which the USA has imposed unilateral arms export restrictions, suggests that there is no major competition between Russia and the USA in arms exports.

Table 7.1. Transfers of major conventional weapons to the leading recipients, 1995–99

The list includes countries/non-state actors with aggregate imports of $500 million or more for 1995–99 from at least one of the seven major suppliers. Figures are trend-indicator values expressed in US $m. at constant 1990 prices.

Recipients	Seven major suppliers							Other	Total
	USA	Russia	France	UK	FRG	Neths	China		
Africa	176	899	272	42	26	1	80	982	**2 478**
Americas	1 540	612	518	1 297	528	213	–	3 088	**7 796**
Brazil	175	–	68	834	266	1	–	220	**1 564**
Others	1 365	612	450	463	262	212	–	2 861	**6 232**
Asia	20 996	9 888	6 362	1 822	1 161	574	1 566	5 003	**47 372**
China	–	3 346	197	16	–	–	..	435	**3 994**
India	–	3 469	80	217	136	369	–	366	**4 637**
Indonesia	6	–	35	682	539	14	–	55	**1 331**
Japan	4 250	–	–	45	8	–	–	40	**4 343**
Kazakhstan	–	816	–	–	–	–	–	–	**816**
Korea, South	4 904	203	267	76	454	51	–	56	**6 011**
Malaysia	523	690	43	686	–	19	–	613	**2 574**
Myanmar	–	86	–	–	–	–	621	–	**707**
Pakistan	360	122	527	3	–	40	345	1 476	**2 873**
Singapore	1 122	28	49	17	–	58	–	466	**1 740**
Taiwan	8 716	–	5 154	–	–	–	–	86	**13 936**
Thailand	1 042	–	13	8	22	25	448	836	**2 394**
Viet Nam	–	858	–	–	–	–	–	62	**920**
Others	73	270	–	72	–	–	152	528	**1 096**
Europe	10 648	1 829	984	657	1 888	607	19	2 192	**18 824**
Greece	2 491	248	118	16	722	366	–	130	**4 091**
Finland	2 244	206	30	3	–	1	–	29	**2 513**
Italy	569	–	4	368	43	–	–	–	**984**
Spain	900	–	149	82	135	10	–	112	**1 388**
Switzerland	1 672	–	–	–	–	–	–	–	**1 672**
UK	532	–	37	..	25	–	–	332	**926**
Others	2 240	1 375	646	188	963	230	19	1 507	**7 250**
Middle East	19 570	1 396	3 589	3 520	2 339	842	548	1 453	**33 257**
Egypt	4 379	143	2	–	10	196	–	11	**4 741**
Israel	2 348	–	47	–	510	–	–	–	**2 903**
Kuwait	1 588	207	314	538	–	–	–	75	**2 722**
Qatar	–	–	828	270	–	35	–	1	**1 134**
Saudi Arabia	6 659	–	96	1 988	–	–	–	550	**9 231**
Turkey	3 533	142	491	74	1 815	33	–	373	**6 461**
UAE	234	542	1 679	193	4	525	–	91	**3 268**
Others	829	362	132	457	–	53	548	496	**2 798**
Oceania	511	–	4	4	90	–	–	905	**1 514**
Other[a]	1	–	1	–	52	–	–	18	**72**
Total	53 443	14 628	11 731	7 343	6 085	2 239	2 212	13 633	**111 314**

[a] Includes the UN and NATO (as non-state actors, not as combinations of all member states) and unknown recipients.

Note: The SIPRI data on arms transfers refer to actual deliveries of major conventional weapons. To permit comparison between the data on such deliveries of different weapons and identification of general trends, SIPRI uses a *trend-indicator value*. The SIPRI values are therefore only an indicator of the volume of international arms transfers and not of the actual financial values of such transfers. Thus they are not comparable to economic statistics such as gross domestic product or export/import figures. Figures may not add up because of rounding.

Source: SIPRI arms transfers database.

Table 7.2. Shares of new equipment in transfers of major conventional weapons by the seven major suppliers, 1995–99

Figures are percentages. Those in brackets show the share of new weapons in total transfers in each category.

Equipment category	USA	Russia	France	UK	FRG	Neths	China
Aircraft	80 (92)	53 (82)	44 (92)	60 (89)	5 (47)	5 (92)	23 (100)
Artillery	2 (84)	1 (52)	0 (85)	1 (66)	8 (83)	– (–)	1 (82)
Armoured vehicles	7 (67)	19 (90)	19 (97)	13 (94)	8 (28)	– (–)	15 (100)
Guidance and radar	7 (84)	7 (98)	7 (100)	6 (84)	2 (58)	92 (94)	8 (100)
Ships	4 (38)	20 (100)	29 (92)	21 (63)	77 (80)	2 (3)	53 (100)
% of new equipment	85	87	94	82	66	39	100

Note: Shares are calculated using the SIPRI trend-indicator value and may not add up to totals because of rounding. Missiles are excluded since several suppliers transfer missiles from old stock—such transfers do not truly reflect industrial activity. 0 = < 0.5 per cent; – = none.

Source: SIPRI arms transfers database.

The major European suppliers were France, the UK and Germany. Arms deliveries by *France* increased between 1995 and 1998 but dropped back to below the 1996 level in 1999 and accounted for about 10 per cent of global deliveries of major arms in 1995–99. This was still only 20 per cent below the level of Russian transfers for that period. The major recipients of French weapons in 1995–99 were Taiwan and the United Arab Emirates (UAE).

The *UK* was ranked as the world's fourth largest supplier for the period 1995–99, accounting for close to 7 per cent of global arms transfers. The level of British major arms transfers has more than halved since 1997, with the decline spread over most equipment categories. One important explanation for the decline is the absence of new orders for combat aircraft after the last deliveries in 1998 of Tornado aircraft to Saudi Arabia, Britain's major recipient during the past five-year period.

Germany, the fifth largest supplier during 1995–99, accounted for roughly 5 per cent of the global market. An increase in Germany's arms exports from 1998 meant that its share of the export market was slightly higher than that of the UK in 1999. The major recipient of arms from Germany in 1995–99 was Turkey. In contrast to the early 1990s, when Germany was a major supplier because it transferred second-hand weapons, its transfers in 1999 were mainly of new weapons.

SIPRI's arms transfer statistics cover six categories of military equipment. To indicate the importance of major arms transfers for the arms industry, table 7.2 lists the shares of new major conventional weapons in five of these categories from the seven major suppliers for 1995–99. Most of the transfers from all but one of the major suppliers (the Netherlands) were of new equipment. A single category accounted for the majority of new deliveries for all these suppliers except France: aircraft (including helicopters) for the USA, the UK and Russia; ships for China and Germany; and guidance and radar equipment for the Netherlands. Although the transfers involved a variety of aircraft types, the table suggests that there is strong competition in the aircraft industry in particular. Furthermore, without a variety of customers, reduced demand will have important consequences for the companies involved.

In addition, all ships, aircraft, armoured vehicles and guidance and radar equipment in China's arms exports were new, as were transfers of guidance and radar equipment from France and of ships from Russia. Even if a particular category accounted for a small share of new equipment transfers, such as artillery pieces for most of these suppliers, over 50 per cent of all such artillery pieces transferred from these suppliers were new. The reason is the small volume of some of the transfers. It may thus be suggested that strong industrial interests—and therefore also strong pressure on the respective government—will continue to support foreign sales in many of these categories of equipment. The economic considerations are discussed further in section IV.

Appendix 7A shows that the five major recipients in the period 1995–99, as in 1994–98, were Taiwan, Saudi Arabia, Turkey, South Korea and Egypt (table 7A.1). Since World War II the location of the main export markets has changed from Europe (1950s–70s) to the Middle East (mainly in the 1980s) and Asia (1990s, especially since 1995).[3] The importance of the Middle Eastern market may again increase in the future as a result of a Middle East peace agreement and a possible increase in oil revenues that may lead to military modernization and new arms transfers.

One factor which will influence the suppliers' future share of sales of modern weapons is investment in advanced military research and development (R&D). Without such investment, suppliers can only compete in the less advanced systems. Alternatively, they have to specialize in narrow technological niches, leading to greater product dependency with related risks of export vulnerability. Four of the five major suppliers show reductions of around 20 per cent in government support for military R&D from 1990 to 1997.[4] Although some defence companies may be willing and able to support R&D projects from their own funds, cost problems will restrain military R&D in most producer countries, leading, for instance, to more R&D cooperation between countries in Europe. Although it is difficult to find reliable and comparable figures for Russian military R&D, it seems likely that long-term R&D allocations will remain a serious problem for Russia.[5] Arms exports are

---

[3] For a discussion of the major recipients, see section III below and appendix 7B in this volume.

[4] See chapter 6 in this volume (table 6.5). Regarding military R&D in the USA, see also 'Securing America's industrial strength', report by the National Research Council (National Academy of Sciences), summarized by Mann, P., 'Dollar trends crisscross in research expenditures', *Aviation Week & Space Technology*, 14 Feb. 2000, p. 72.

[5] See table 5.9 in chapter 5 in this volume. Combining the 2 R&D items puts the reduction in Russia's military R&D budget at 34% in constant prices over the period 1994–98. This figure refers to the change in the total official Russian military R&D budget under the heading of Ministry of Defence and additional military R&D items under the science budget. Budget data in current roubles have been deflated by using the Russian consumer price index, which increased by 435% during this period. Note that these data are for budgeted allocations—actual expenditures for these years were often considerably lower. See also Khripunov, I., 'Moscow reacts', *Bulletin of the Atomic Scientists*, July–Aug. 1999, pp. 32–35.

unlikely to generate the necessary revenues, although they are a major source of foreign currency. Moreover, Russian companies do not have the same possibilities as the US or European companies for advanced military technology and R&D cooperation.[6] As a result, Russia may be a less important major supplier in the future.

The USA will remain by far the major investor in military R&D, keeping national control over all major programmes. Following NATO operations against Serbia there was renewed interest in US 'smart' weapons and requests to replenish the arsenals of the participants in the NATO forces. Also, if proposals by the recent US Defense Science Board's Task Force on Globalization and Security are made official policy, the US position as the major arms exporter may be further strengthened and the gap in the most advanced technologies vis-à-vis other suppliers sustained.[7]

III. Major arms transfers and conflict

One of the main motivations for national arms procurement—some of which is through arms imports—is to increase national security by enabling a country to deter or defend against external aggression or an internal challenge to the government. However, it is generally acknowledged that some arms transfers do not increase national or regional security since neighbouring countries often regard the deliveries as threatening to their security.[8] In particular, major arms transfers to recipients in areas of conflict, that is, regions marked by military–political tension (including shooting incidents) or armed conflict, have long been an issue in the discussion about arms transfers, specifically in the Western world, where most of the main supplier countries are to be found.

The result is widely stated policy guidelines by the major arms-exporting nations that caution should be exercised when considering transfers to recipients in areas of tension and conflict.[9] However, several considerations

[6] Mann, P., 'Russia's defense facing 25-year rehabilitation', *Aviation Week & Space Technology*, 8 Nov. 1999, p. 68. This also throws doubt on the Defence Ministry's goal of fully upgrading Russia's forces by 2025, if this is to be understood as meaning basically new equipment.

[7] The task force proposed that the USA should not worry about protecting technological capabilities in general since they will eventually be available elsewhere, which may support US–European military interdependence. Controls should, however, be tightened for unique US technologies. 'US ponders defense globalization', *Arms Sales Monitor*, no. 42 (Jan. 2000), p. 1; and *The Monitor* (University of Georgia, Athens, Ga.), vol. 6, no. 2 (2000), pp. 3–5.

[8] A number of attempts have therefore been made to control destabilizing acquisitions. E.g., the 1990 Treaty on Conventional Armed Forces in Europe (the CFE Treaty) limits numbers of the most offensive weapons, the Missile Technology Control Regime (MTCR) was set up to prevent missile proliferation, and the specific purpose of the UN Register of Conventional Arms (UNROCA) is to make visible, through greater transparency, destabilizing build-ups of weapons. On conventional arms control see chapter 10 and on missile proliferation see chapter 11 in this volume.

[9] In the early 1990s the 5 permanent members of the UN Security Council (the P5, also the main exporters), the participating states of the Conference on Security and Co-operation in Europe (CSCE, now the Organization for Security and Co-operation in Europe—OCSE) and the EU concluded policy documents on this matter. For discussions of the criteria involved, see Anthony, I. *et al.*, 'The trade in major conventional weapons', *SIPRI Yearbook 1992: World Armaments and Disarmament* (Oxford University Press: Oxford, 1992), pp. 295–97; Anthony, I. *et al.*, 'Arms production and arms trade', *SIPRI Yearbook 1993: World Armaments and Disarmament* (Oxford University Press: Oxford, 1993), pp. 461–62; and Hagelin, B., Wezeman, P. D. and Wezeman. S. T., 'Transfers of major conventional

affect a decision to supply, or not to supply, major weapons. Policy guidelines or related political statements are not legally binding or specific as to how these general ambitions are to be achieved. Since 1947 Japan has banned virtually all weapon exports,[10] while most governments keep their options open on a case-by-case basis, reserving the right to define themselves when a recipient is at war.[11]

This section presents some examples of arms deals that show how restrictive guidelines are, in reality, not always imposed on recipients in areas of conflict. In fact, at least six of the major recipients listed in table 7.1 are in conflict regions.[12] This does not mean, however, that these recipients were directly involved in intense armed conflict in 1999, and some are presented below under areas of tension rather than areas of war.

Areas of tension

Greece and Turkey

Greece and Turkey are engaged in bilateral controversies over the Aegean Sea and Cyprus.[13] Although both are members of NATO, they appear to compete with each other in their arms acquisitions, mainly through imports. Each has major acquisition plans that seem closely related to those of the other country. Turkey ranked third and Greece eighth among the major arms importers in 1995–99 (table 7A.1). It is noteworthy that, apart from the USA, the main suppliers to both countries are European governments, although Turkey has developed an important military relationship with Israel (see section V). Among the new orders, both ordered German submarines in 1998–99. Greece decided to purchase airborne early-warning (AEW) radars from Sweden mounted on Brazilian aircraft, after which Turkey decided to acquire new AEW aircraft. Greece has decided to participate in the multinational Eurofighter project as well as acquire several other systems, while Turkey will not acquire more combat aircraft for the time being because of its AEW priority.

The Middle East

Tensions remain high between Israel, on the one hand, and Syria, Iraq and Iran, on the other. Israel was the fifth largest importer of major weapons in 1999, importing mainly from the USA. Israel's threat perceptions for the future include missile attacks from Iran and Iraq, possibly with nuclear, biolo-

weapons', *SIPRI Yearbook 1999: Armaments, Disarmament and International Security* (Oxford University Press: Oxford, 1999), pp 439–42. Texts of these documents are reproduced on the SIPRI Internet site at URL <http://projects.sipri.se/expcon/atcontrol_menu.htm>. In their national regulations many countries have stipulations which restrict arms deliveries to countries at war or in a region of conflict.

[10] Japan considers certain dual-use items, such as transport aircraft, offshore patrol vessels and light all-terrain vehicles, not to be weapons, and it has exported such items to foreign armed forces.

[11] See the SIPRI Internet site, URL <http://projects.sipri.se/expcon/expcon.htm>, for details of arms export control regimes.

[12] India, Indonesia, Israel, Myanmar, Pakistan and Turkey. For the definition of armed conflict used by SIPRI and a presentation of major armed conflicts during 1999, see chapter 1 in this volume.

[13] Hagelin, Wezeman and Wezeman (note 9), pp. 431–36.

gical or chemical warheads, and some Israeli acquisitions seem directed at deterring or even pre-empting such attacks. Iran and Iraq are within the range of the F-15 and F-16 combat aircraft imported or ordered by Israel in 1999.[14] The first of three conventional Dolphin submarines, built in Germany to Israeli specifications, was delivered to Israel in 1999. Several sources claim that these submarines may be equipped with US Harpoon missiles modified for attacking land targets, armed with Israeli-developed nuclear warheads and guidance kits, giving Israel a nuclear second-strike capability.[15]

The peace process may reduce the intensity of the Arab–Israeli conflict in the future, specifically that between Israel and Syria. Paradoxically, as has been the case in previous peace agreements, this may result in Israel acquiring more weapons, a possibility that has been strongly criticized by Arab states. For instance, in return for leaving the Golan Heights, Israel has requested equipment and new weapons from the USA worth at least $10 billion.[16]

The South China Sea

Because of its claims on all the islands in the South China Sea and its acquisition of modern weapons, China is regarded as the main threat by other states in the region. China ranked second among the major recipients in 1999 because of continued deliveries of major weapons from Russia—including the first of two Sovremenny Class destroyers, giving the Chinese Navy a major leap in power-projection capability[17]—and it placed new orders for Russian Su-30 combat aircraft.

Many of the equipment programmes in the region are maritime-oriented, as illustrated by Italian and British deliveries to Malaysia as well as by the force modernization plans of the Malaysian armed forces.[18] Viet Nam, involved over the years in several shooting incidents with Chinese forces in the South China Sea, is also modernizing its small navy with Russian ships and missiles.

However, arms imports by countries in the region do not only reflect their rivalry with China. In response to Malaysia's 1997 order for Russian AA-12 air-to-air missiles for its MiG-29 combat aircraft, Singapore wants to buy the US equivalent, the AIM-120, for its F-16 combat aircraft. In 1999 the USA seemed prepared to consider this transfer because of the introduction of the AA-12 to the region.[19] Singapore, while not a claimant to any South China Sea

---

[14] See interview with Major General Eitan Ben-Eliahu (Commander-in-Chief, Israel Defence Force-Air Force), *Jane's Defence Weekly*, vol. 33, no. 6 (9 Feb. 2000), p. 32.

[15] Blanche, E., 'German subs give Israel heftier punch', *Jane's Intelligence Review*, Sep. 1999, p. 6; and 'First Dolphins move in on Israeli Navy', *International Defense Review*, Sep. 1999, p. 8. See also appendix 8A, table 8A.8 in this volume.

[16] Rodan, S., 'Israel seeks more than $10b to leave the Golan Heights', *Jane's Defence Weekly*, vol. 32, no. 25 (22 Dec. 1999), p. 2.

[17] 'Chinese naval CNC inspects destroyer', *Defence Systems Daily*, 26 Oct. 1999, URL <http://defence-data.com/current/page5622.htm>. However, it will be many years before the ship can be used effectively. Gill, B., 'China's newest warships', *Far Eastern Economic Review*, 27 Jan. 2000, p. 14.

[18] Sengupta, P. K., 'Malaysia's force modernisation plans back on stream', *Asian Defence Journal*, Dec. 1999, pp. 14–17.

[19] *Asia Pacific Defence Reporter*, 1 Dec. 1999, p. 17. Together with the French MICA, these missiles are the only long-range 'fire-and-forget' air-to-air missiles (AAMs). The USA has previously refused

islands, seems determined to increase the reach of its armed forces, taking delivery of the first of four KC-135R tanker aircraft in 1999. While a number of smaller tanker aircraft have already been delivered to the region, these are the first of the kind that can be regarded as 'force multipliers'.[20]

North-East Asia

Two bilateral relationships in particular—between China and Taiwan and between North and South Korea—have caused high tensions in North-East Asia, also involving shooting incidents. Both have created concern in other countries and have led to actual and planned arms imports in addition to indigenous production. China's acquisition of Russian weapons and technology since 1990 has been regarded by Taiwan as a threat. Taiwan has been the largest recipient of major conventional weapons, mainly from the USA, since 1997. Chinese acquisition since 1992 of Russian Su-27 combat aircraft was countered by US deliveries of 150 F-16 combat aircraft to Taiwan, completed in 1999. The proposed Taiwan Security Enhancement Act, if enacted, will imply closer US–Taiwanese relations.[21]

Tension on the Korean Peninsula and, more specifically, the development of ballistic missiles in North Korea were a major stimulus for South Korean arms acquisitions in 1999. South Korea was the third-largest arms importer in 1999. The North Korean missile test in August 1998[22] also became a factor in Japan's decision in 1999 to participate in US surface-to-air missile R&D.

Areas of armed conflict

This section presents examples of transfers of major weapons to countries in Africa and South Asia involved in armed conflict or located in an area of armed conflict. The widely accepted policy guidelines referred to above that restraint should be exercised when considering transfers to recipients in areas of conflict are of particular relevance to countries actually involved in armed conflict. Nevertheless, such transfers take place.

Many of the ongoing wars are fought with small arms and small quantities of major weapons. Transfers of small arms are not registered by SIPRI. Transfers of major weapons to these wars are sometimes so obscure or small in volume that open sources do not permit SIPRI to confirm deliveries; they are therefore not included in appendix 7C.

---

delivery to most regions, considering that it would introduce new and possibly destabilizing technology. In recent years, however, Russia and France have accepted orders for the AA-12 and MICA, respectively.

[20] The few tanker aircraft delivered earlier had neither the range nor the fuel-carrying capacity to be effective in supporting combat missions.

[21] Fidler, S., 'House likely to look at closer Taiwan ties', *Financial Times*, 28 Oct. 1999, p. 6. The US Congress seems more prepared to back Taiwan than the Administration. References to specific advanced weapons were deleted in the latest version considered by Congress.

[22] See chapters 8 and 11 in this volume.

Africa

Africa is the world's most conflict-ridden region, and in 1999 the majority of the most intense major armed conflicts were located there. Many African states were involved in the war in the Democratic Republic of the Congo (DRC).[23] Major weapons supplied to parties involved in that war came mainly in small quantities from China and former Soviet republics. However, many of the major weapons in the DRC were supplied before the war, at a time when the delivery may not have been controversial. If recipients become involved in armed conflict after deliveries have begun, the supplier may still feel obliged to honour the contract. In January 2000 the British Government seemed willing to permit the supply of spare parts for British-made Hawk light-attack aircraft delivered to Zimbabwe in 1982 and 1992. This type of aircraft was reportedly used to back the DRC Government against rebel forces.[24]

In addition to the DRC, the region about which the participants in the Wassenaar Arrangement expressed most concern in late 1998 was the Horn of Africa.[25] The war between Eritrea and Ethiopia illustrates that arms deliveries do not always provide a reliable indicator of armed conflict. Deliveries immediately before the 1998 fighting did not indicate that there were plans for war. During the 1998 border war Ethiopia reportedly used MiG-21 and MiG-23 combat aircraft delivered during the 1970s and 1980s, while Eritrea used MB-339 combat aircraft delivered in 1997.[26]

However, when heavy fighting broke out again in February 1999 both countries had been or were being supplied with additional combat aircraft and other weapons, reflecting their preparedness to continue the conflict at that time. Ethiopia was provided with armoured vehicles and Russian military helicopters in addition to second-hand Su-27 combat aircraft which were used in combat against new MiG-29 combat aircraft delivered to Eritrea, all supplied by Russia in 1998 and 1999. Unlike most deliveries to other African countries, these are advanced aircraft.[27]

---

[23] See chapter 1 and appendix 1B in this volume.

[24] Reuters, 'UK rejects reported split over Zimbabwe arms sales', 21 Jan. 2000, in *Daily Mail & Guardian* (Internet edn), URL <http://www.mg.co.za/mg/news/2000jan21jan-zim-arms.html>; and Claude, P., 'Tony Blair finds it hard to reconcile "diplomatic ethics" with arms sales', *Le Monde*, 22 Jan. 2000, p. 2, in '*Le Monde* decries UK arms sales policy', in Foreign Broadcast Information Service, *Daily Report–West Europe (FBIS-WEU)*, FBIS-WEU-2000-0124, 27 Jan. 2000. It is not clear, however, if the deliveries have taken place.

[25] Bonner, R., 'Porous accord on arms', *International Herald Tribune*, 7 Dec. 1998, p. 5. See URL <http://projects.sipri.se/expcon/Wassenaar-documents.html> for a presentation of the Wassenaar Arrangement. The arrangement is also discussed in appendix 11B in this volume.

[26] 'Ethiopia–Eritrea hostilities', *AirForces Monthly*, Aug. 1998, p. 10.

[27] As the rapid deliveries outpaced the supply of trained local pilots, mercenaries were used to fly at least some of these aircraft in both countries. The presence of Russian mercenaries was confirmed by a former representative of the Russian export agency Rosvooruzheniye in Ethiopia. 'MiGs & Sukhois in air combat over Ethiopia', *AirForces Monthly*, May 1999, p. 14. There are also examples showing that weapon deliveries make no difference to a conflict. They may be old, worn and badly serviced, as seems to have been the case with deliveries in 1999 from Central and East European countries to Uganda of tanks and MiG-21 aircraft. Harris, P., 'Uganda pays over the odds for tanks that will not work', *Jane's Intelligence Review*, Apr. 1999, p. 3; and 'Ugandan MiG-21 controversy', *AirForces Monthly*, Dec. 1999, p. 20.

South Asia

Renewed fighting broke out between India and Pakistan over Kashmir in May 1999, followed in September by a military coup in Pakistan. Nevertheless, several European and other countries went ahead with deliveries of previously ordered major arms, although some (e.g., the UK) agreed to subject licence applications to greater scrutiny.[28] An arms transfer denial is considered to be a strong negative political act and it is clear that supplier governments are anxious to maintain their credibility by not stopping the flow of arms, ammunition and spare parts once an arms deal has been signed. Both India and Pakistan received military equipment in 1999, some from the same supplier. France delivered refurbished Mirage-5 combat aircraft to Pakistan. France is also supplying the avionics for Russian aircraft being delivered to India.[29] Pakistan is assembling Swedish RBS-70 anti-aircraft missiles,[30] and after the fighting in 1999 India placed its first order in 10 years for Bofors spare parts and ammunition for the FH-77B howitzer,[31] which was one of India's most important weapons during the conflict. The Swedish Government agreed to transfer a more modern version of the howitzer to India for trials in 2000.[32]

IV. Economic considerations

The importance of foreign policy considerations in arms export decisions has decreased substantially for the two major suppliers, Russia and the USA, since the end of the cold war.[33] For the other major arms suppliers such considerations were already less important.[34] Commercial considerations for arms exports have instead gained in importance in the 1990s.[35] The dissolution of the Soviet Union resulted in a contraction in the arms market; there was reduced procurement in countries with the largest arms industries[36] and a political and industrial push for exports to compensate for reduced domestic markets. For the recipients, this created leverage and opportunities for obtaining both weapons and military technology at lower costs—in effect a buyer's market.

Global economic data on arms transfers provide some insights into these issues. The SIPRI trend indicator was designed to estimate the military value of major arms transfers, not to assess the financial flows from the international

---

[28] Wighton, D., 'Departments at odds over arms', *Financial Times*, 13 Jan. 2000, p. 8.

[29] *Jane's All the World's Aircraft 1999–2000* (Jane's Information Group: Coulsdon, 1999), pp. 434–35.

[30] *Jane's Land-based Air Defence Systems 2000* (Jane's Information Group: Coulsdon, 1999), p. 28.

[31] Försvarsindustriföreningen (FIF) [Defence Industry Association], Stockholm, 5 Feb. 2000, URL <http://www.defind.se/news.htm>.

[32] '[Celsius] offer SP FH77 B to India', *Defence Systems Daily*, 21 Oct. 1999.

[33] Anthony, I., 'The conventional arms trade', ed. A. J. Pierre, *Cascade of Arms: Managing Conventional Weapons Proliferation* (Brookings Institution Press: Washington, DC, 1997), p. 15.

[34] On pre-1990 arms export motives of France, the UK and Germany, see Brzoska, M. and Ohlson, T., SIPRI, *Arms Transfers to the Third World 1971–85* (Oxford University Press: Oxford, 1987).

[35] Keller, W. W. and Nolan, J. E., 'The arms trade: business as usual?', *Foreign Policy*, no. 109 (winter 1997/98), pp. 113–25.

[36] See chapter 6 in this volume.

arms trade. However, it is the arms *trade*—that is, transfers of all weapons for which money or economic goods are expected in return—as opposed to arms *transfers* that reveals the economic scale of the global arms market. The total financial value of the arms trade can be estimated by aggregating all reported government data on arms exports (appendix 7E). Because most of the major supplier governments today report details of their arms trade, SIPRI is able to estimate this value for the first time in this Yearbook.[37] However, in the absence of reliable data over a longer period, no trend can be estimated; the data only permit a single-year estimate for 1998. The global financial value of the legal international arms trade in 1998 is estimated to be $35–$49 billion.[38] This is a rough estimate as the available data still lack reliability and comparability, as explained in appendix 7E.

This estimated value of the international arms trade is roughly 0.6–0.9 per cent of total world trade,[39] suggesting that the global economic impact of the arms trade is low. Its impact on the economy of individual countries, organizations, companies and individuals, however, may be important. This section gives national examples of economic factors which have influenced recent arms transfers.

The sellers

In spite of the restrictive national regulations, government actors support arms exports for at least two perceived economic reasons.[40] First, arms exports support the national economy by preserving jobs and providing foreign currency. Exports of surplus equipment also provide revenues. Second, arms exports support the armed forces of the exporting country as they reduce discontinuity in national R&D and arms production. An extension of the production run often results in economies of scale, which means a lower acquisition cost per item for the national armed forces.

[37] See section VI for more on developments in arms export transparency. Government data on arms exports are unavailable for only 1 significant country, China. However, available open information on Chinese deliveries and weapon prices indicates that Chinese arms exports are insignificant compared to the estimated global total volume of arms exports. Problems of reliability and comparability are described in appendix 7E.

[38] The lower estimate is the aggregation of reported minimum values and the higher estimate the aggregation of reported maximum values of delivered arms. For some smaller countries only data on arms licences are available. When this is the case, these values have been used. A maximum value for the USA for 1998 was not available from the source which reported the data for years up to 1997, the US Arms Control and Disarmament Agency (ACDA). However, the ACDA value is based on data from other sources which were available. It was therefore possible to reconstruct what can be assumed to be close to the ACDA estimate of the value of US arms deliveries in 1998, i.e. $25.6 billion.

[39] Total world exports for 1998 amounted to $5405 billion. *International Financial Statistics* (International Monetary Fund: Washington, DC, Jan. 2000), p. 62.

[40] In addition, personal economic gain—through corruption or commissions—may also be a consideration that supports arms exports. E.g., in 1999 it was alleged that revenues from Rosvooruzheniye were used to support electoral campaigns for Russian President Boris Yeltsin. In Germany the Christian Democrat Party became involved in a scandal when it was alleged that it received part of *c.* $500 000 paid by an arms-producing company in 1991. A parliamentary committee of enquiry is investigating whether the political decision to sell 36 armoured vehicles to Saudi Arabia for $261 million, which included about 50% for brokers, was influenced by the payment. Saradzhyan, S., 'Yeltsin shakes up Russian export agency', *Defense News*, 16 Aug. 1999, p. 18; and 'Goldgräber in Kriegszeiten' [Gold-diggers in wartime], *Der Spiegel*, 11 Dec. 1999, pp. 32–37.

The USA

The USA is the largest exporter of arms in both military and financial terms. Arms exports make up about 2.3–3.7 per cent of total US exports for 1998.[41] The importance of economic incentives in US arms export policy was illustrated by a 1999 US General Accounting Office report, which stated that one of the government's goals in exporting defence items is to reduce the costs of weapon procurement by the Department of Defense (DOD). The report concluded that export sales of five reviewed major weapon systems saved the DOD at least $342 million, but that the DOD has not developed guidelines for maximizing savings from export sales.[42] Other actors in the arms trade, such as companies, are basically interested in keeping production going and maximizing their profits. For instance, in early 1999 Lockheed Martin faced a potential gap in 2001 in its F-16 combat aircraft production, but in late 1999 it managed to secure new export orders for 74 F-16s to bridge this gap.[43]

Russia

The continued low level of Russian arms procurement increases the importance of its arms exports. Arms export revenues are an important source of foreign currency for Russia, and exports are important, if not decisive, in keeping production lines open.[44] Then Russian Prime Minister Sergey Stepashin was quoted as saying that arms exports were vital because additional sources for financing defence were not available.[45] Russian arms exports in 1998 are estimated at $2.7 billion, which is about 3.7 per cent of total Russian exports.[46] While remaining optimistic about future arms exports, Russian government officials do not expect this figure to increase significantly in the years ahead.[47] Known foreign orders for Russian major conventional weapons confirm this expectation. However, it is unclear how this translates into total profits, partly because the terms for Russian arms exports often involve barter, repayments for debt, dumped prices and/or payment in other than hard currency. Moreover, attempts to enter new markets, that is, countries mainly supplied by the USA and Western Europe, have had only limited success.[48]

[41] Total US exports amounted to $683 billion in 1998. International Monetary Fund (note 39), p. 796. Some of the weapons included in the US arms export figures were supplied as aid and paid for by the US Government. These exports will therefore not result in any export revenues for the US economy.
[42] United States General Accounting Office, *Defense Trade, Department of Defense Savings From Export Sales are Difficult to Capture*, GAO/NSIAD-99-191, Sep. 1999.
[43] 'Lockheed to increase F-16 production', *Air Letter*, 27 Jan. 2000, p. 5.
[44] See chapter 6, section V in this volume.
[45] Kemp, D., 'Russia pushes defence sales as exports hit highest for years', *Jane's Defence Weekly*, vol. 32, no. 2 (14 July 1999), p. 17.
[46] See appendix 7E in this volume.
[47] 'Russian export agency healthy, says chief', *Defense News*, 13 Dec. 1999; and Interfax (Moscow), 'Rosvooruzheniye: no plans for huge increase in arms exports', 26 Jan. 1999, Foreign Broadcast Information Service, *Daily Report–Central Eurasia (FBIS-SOV)*, FBIS-SOV-1999-0126, 26 Jan. 1999.
[48] The only sizeable Russian market expansion in 1999 was the sale and first delivery of new air defence systems to NATO member Greece, valued at $519 million, and the Greek decision to buy 2 military hovercraft from Russia.

Russia appears to be increasingly prepared to sell weapons at very low prices, as illustrated by sales to Malaysia and Bangladesh.[49] It sold 18 MiG-29 combat aircraft to Malaysia for $600 million, or $33 million each, in 1994. Bangladesh purchased eight MiG-29s in 1999 for $124 million, or $15.5 million each.[50] Even allowing for the likelihood that the Malaysian deal involves more spares and related weapons, for example, this comparison shows a clear deflation. The sale to Bangladesh can be compared with orders placed in 1999 for eight much lighter AMX-T aircraft by Venezuela from a Brazilian/Italian consortium for $150 million[51] and for nine roughly similar Swedish JAS-39 Gripen aircraft by South Africa for more than $50 million each.[52]

By far the most important buyers of Russian arms are India, since the 1960s, and China, since the early 1990s. Although India has received weapons from West European suppliers it is dependent on Russia for many of its major weapons. In November 1999 India expressed its intention to procure a wide range of weapons from Russia. However, payment is a problem. While current Indian procurements are paid for with hard currency, India wants to pay for the new weapons in rupees.[53]

Russia has provided China with weaponry to modernize its armed forces substantially. China's major order in 1999 was for about 40 Su-30K combat aircraft, the most advanced in the Russian Air Force, worth $2 billion. The Chinese Navy received the first of two Russian Sovremenny Class destroyers in 1999.

Europe

European arms-producing companies compete in all but a few available markets. Although intra-European exports normally give rise to little controversy, exports to other regions may be controversial. In both Germany and the UK, sharp differences exist between government ministries regarding permits or support for arms export deals. A ban on the use of British Government export credits for arms exports to the world's poorest nations was announced in early 2000—after the ministries of defence and trade and industry had warned that there would be a heavy cost to Britain's arms industry if exports to certain countries were not supported with such credits. They also pressed for an end to

[49] Even lower prices have been reported in other deals. Makienko, K., 'Russia on the world arms market: 1998 and early 1999 assessment', *The Monitor* (University of Georgia, Athens, Ga.), vol. 5, no. 3 (summer 1999), p. 21. Attractive low prices are outweighed by political, economic and technological doubts on the part of potential clients. See, e.g., Zarzecki, T. W., 'Are arms transfers from the former Soviet Union a security threat? The case of combat aircraft', *Journal of Slavic Military Studies*, vol. 12, no. 1 (Mar. 1999), pp. 124–48.

[50] 'Bangladesh court halts MiG-29 payments', *International Air Letter,* 30 Sep. 1999, p. 1.

[51] *AirForces Monthly*, Nov. 1999, p. 14.

[52] Heitman, H., 'South Africa signs order for $5 billion', *Jane's Defence Weekly*, vol. 32, no. 23 (8 Dec. 1999), p. 3.

[53] India intended to buy: 1 aircraft-carrier, 60 combat aircraft, 6 long-range air defence systems, 2 submarines, 3 frigates, c. 300 tanks, 6 long-range maritime bombers, 2 AEW aircraft and licensed production of 40 advanced combat aircraft. Raghuvanshi, V. and Saradzhyan, S., 'Agreement sets stage for arms technology flow to New Delhi', *Defense News*, 22 Nov. 1999, p. 13.

the freeze on arms exports to Pakistan after the 1999 coup. The Department for International Development and the Foreign Office opposed this, and remained committed to the principle of an 'ethical foreign policy'.[54]

In Germany the Ministry of Defence stressed the need for arms exports to support the arms industry, and criticized the reluctance of the Green Party in the government coalition to support permits for arms exports.[55] Still, in the autumn of 1999 the German Government permitted a German consortium to enter a competition to supply up to 1000 tanks to Turkey. Of the five ministers involved in the decision, the two ministers from the Green Party argued against the deal because of human rights abuses by the Turkish Government and the ongoing war in Kurdistan. German Chancellor Gerhard Schröder focused on Turkey's NATO membership and European Union candidacy as reasons why a permit should not be denied.[56] However, the main company involved stressed that the prospective order could create a turnover of billions of dollars and observers assumed that this was an important element in the government's decision to grant the licence.[57]

Second-hand weapon sales

Sales of second-hand weapons at low prices are of a different economic magnitude from sales of major weapons. The economic gain in such transactions is very small compared to the overall economy of developed states, but may be high for states in need of foreign currency, as well as for the armed forces. The military value, and thus also the possible impact on peace and security, may therefore in certain cases be much higher than the financial value seems to indicate.

Russia and Eastern Europe

Russian surplus equipment is sold through Promexport, which reported signing contracts worth $400 million and making a profit of over $120 million in 1998, the latter being transferred to the Ministry of Defence for use in its budget.[58] Promexport's deliveries in 1999 included combat aircraft to Ethiopia and combat helicopters to Sri Lanka, both countries involved in wars.

Other former Soviet republics and East European countries also sold batches of surplus weapons to warring countries with little restraint. Belarus, for which export revenues of only some tens of millions of dollars still matter, sold

---

[54] Elliott, L., 'Ban on arms export credits', *The Guardian*, 12 Jan. 2000, p. 11; and MacAskill, E., 'Cabinet battle rages over ethical foreign policy', *The Guardian*, 12 Jan. 2000, p. 1.

[55] Stoltenberg, J., 'Scharping attackiert Fischer: Waffenexporte sind notwendig' [Scharping attacks Fischer: arms exports are necessary], *Berliner Morgenpost,* 23 Oct. 1999, URL <http://www.berliner-morgenpost.de/bin/bm/search/suche_archiv.cgi>.

[56] 'Schroeder defends Ankara tank delivery', *International Herald Tribune*, 24 Oct. 1999, p. 2. On Turkey's EU candidacy see also chapter 4 in this volume.

[57] Sommer, T., 'Heuchler der SPD' [SPD hypocrites], *Die Zeit*, 28 Oct. 1999, URL <http://www.Zeit.de/tag/aktuell/199944.1_leiter_.html>; and Michalsky, O., 'Spaltpilz' [Wedge], *Berliner Morgenpost*, 21 Oct. 1999, p. 4.

[58] Timergaliyeva, D., 'Promexport boosts sales of axed weapons', ITAR-TASS (Moscow), 29 June 1999, FBIS-SOV-1999-0629, 29 June 1999.

around 30 MiG-29 combat aircraft to Algeria for an unknown sum in 1999.[59] Poland sold seven MiG-21s to Uganda in 1999, reportedly for $1.5 million each.[60] Poland also sold 50 surplus T-55 tanks, reportedly for $1.2 million, destined for Yemen, but stopped deliveries when it was discovered that the first 20 had ended up in Sudan.[61]

The USA and Europe

US stocks of second-hand weapons are enormous and sales have been planned to support military modernization.[62] In Europe large stocks of second-hand weapons are still available and sizeable transfers still take place. During the 1990s Germany was the major European exporter of second-hand weapons, but such exports have now dropped to a low level. One example of the low prices charged for second-hand weapons was a $120 million deal in which France continued to deliver 40 second-hand Mirage-5 and Mirage-3 combat aircraft to Pakistan in 1999. The price is largely to cover the costs of an extensive refurbishment of the aircraft's ground-attack capability.[63]

The Netherlands announced a target revenue of 640 million Dutch guilders (c. $320 million) from its sales of second-hand weapons,[64] most of the proceeds of which would go to its procurement budget. The Ministry of Defence therefore has a strong incentive to actively pursue such sales. Dutch exports to Chile in 1999 of 200 upgraded surplus Leopard-1 tanks gave Chile the chance to considerably upgrade its main battle tank inventory.[65]

The buyer's market

The examples in table 7.3 illustrate that most of the arms producers that are able to compete do so for potentially large export deals. The table is limited to aircraft, tanks and surface-to-air missile (SAM) systems, but the competition for supplies of other weapons is similar. In order to compete, suppliers have to offer compensation to offset the buyers' costs. This permits increasing recipient leverage; that is, recipients can play off potential suppliers against each other, thereby obtaining weapons on more favourable financial terms than would otherwise be possible. In 1999 South Africa signed contracts

---

[59] Saradzhyan, S., 'Russia will send MiG-29 fighters to Belarus for delivery to Algiers', *Defense News*, 11 Oct. 1999, p. 25.

[60] 'Ugandan MiG-21 controversy', *AirForces Monthly*, 11 Dec. 1999, p. 20.

[61] Blanche, E., 'Czech Republic to sell upgraded MBTs to Yemen', *Jane's Defence Weekly*, vol. 32, no. 13 (29 Sep. 1999), p. 18. The Czech Republic, however, decided to sell T-55s to Yemen and was not put off by the risk that they would end up in Sudan.

[62] E.g., in 1996 up to 400 surplus F-16 combat aircraft were ready to be sold off, which would provide funds for the US Air Force to procure newer versions of the F-16. 'US slashes surplus equipment prices', *Military Technology,* Oct. 1996. Despite low prices and interest from several countries only 36 had been sold by the end of 1999 (see entries for Thailand and Portugal in appendix 7C).

[63] *Air Forces Monthly*, Aug. 1999, p. 14.

[64] Dutch Ministry of Defence, Defensienota 2000, 29 Nov. 1999, URL <http://WWW.MINDEF.NL/defensienota/index.html>.

[65] $250 000 for a 30-year old but upgraded Leopard-1 main battle tank is a fraction of the price of an equally or less capable new light tank.

valued at up to 29.99 billion rand ($5 billion) for the supply of weapons by foreign companies. In return these companies have committed themselves to create business for a total of 104 billion rand ($17.3 billion) in South Africa by counter-purchases and investment,[66] but such compensation plans may cover a period of 10–15 years and may never be realized. Despite the large compensations offered to South Africa, it decided to postpone the decision on two-thirds of its planned combat aircraft acquisitions to a future date.[67]

The delivery of certain weapons and technologies is regarded by some suppliers as destabilizing for the military balance in some regions. However, strong competition not only leads to offers of compensation, but may in some cases push suppliers to give up such nationally imposed export limitations. For instance, the UAE used the competition between US and French companies to optimize procurement of new combat aircraft. In 1999 the UAE announced a preference for the latest version of the F-16 combat aircraft with advanced air-to-air missiles, claiming that it was unwilling to accept a less advanced version as it could otherwise buy a package of advanced aircraft and missiles from France. The US Government was reluctant to allow transfer of the desired F-16 package. However, the order enabled Lockheed Martin, the F-16 producer, to maintain its production line and secure a first export order for this version. The UAE demands for offsets were economically unfavourable for Lockheed Martin in burdening the company with investment commitments. In a reciprocal agreement the UAE received the package while Lockheed Martin seems to have avoided the offsets.[68]

It can also be concluded from table 7.3 that in a number of cases suppliers chose not to enter competitions for potentially large and lucrative arms procurements. In some cases, such as sales to Israel and Egypt, the lack of international competition is explained by the fact that the USA pays or has paid for most of the US weapons delivered through grant aid. Also, China's dependence on Russia for arms stems from the fact that most other potential suppliers imposed arms export embargoes on China.[69] However, despite China's dependence on Russia as the sole supplier of most of its advanced major weapons, and despite doubts within Russia on the military strategic wisdom of such sales, the poor state of the Russian arms industry still gives China leverage over Russian export decisions.[70] The prime example in 1999 was the sale of Su-30 combat aircraft.

---

[66] Heitman (note 52).

[67] 'Idag skrev Sydafrika under Gripenkontraktet' [Today South Africa signed the Gripen contract], Försvarsindustriföreningen (note 31) 3 Dec. 1999. South Africa can opt out of the order for 19 of the 28 Gripens ('reversed option') until 2004, meaning the supplier accepts greater uncertainty than in a normal contract with an option on a possible future additional purchase.

[68] Kemp, D., 'UAE seals deal for 80 Desert Falcons', *Jane's Defence Weekly,* vol. 33, no. 11 (15 Mar. 2000), p. 4. For more information about the negotiations see 'US–UAE close to making F-16 deal', *World Aerospace & Defense Intelligence,* 21 May 1999, p. 5; 'US and UAE close to deal', *Financial Times,* 22 Oct. 1999, p. 8; and Allen, R., 'Spread of weapons of mass destruction concentrates minds', *Financial Times,* 28 Oct. 1999, p. 5.

[69] The EU has imposed an arms embargo on China since 1989 (see section VII of this chapter) and the USA has a nationally imposed arms embargo.

[70] Chufrin, G., SIPRI, *Russia and Asia: the Emerging Security Agenda* (Oxford University Press: Oxford, 1999), p. 310.

Table 7.3. Examples of supplier competition for sales of aircraft, tanks and surface-to-air missile (SAM) systems in 1999

The arms procurement plans listed are all in an advanced state.

Recipient country	Planned procurement	Approx. no.	Country of competing companies
Australia	Combat helicopter	25–30	France/Germany, Italy, USA (2), South Africa
Brazil	Combat aircraft	50	Germany, Germany/Italy/UK/Spain, France, USA (2), Russia, Sweden/UK
Chile	Combat aircraft	20	France, Sweden, USA(2+surplus), (Russia)
China	Combat aircraft	40	Russia (W)
Czech Rep.	Combat aircraft	36	France, Sweden, USA (2)
Egypt	Combat aircraft	24	USA
Egypt	Trainer aircraft	80	Brazil, China (W), Czech Republic, Italy, France/Germany
Eritrea	Combat aircraft	10	Russia
India	Combat aircraft	18	Russia, France
India	Tanks	315	Russia (W), India
Israel	Combat aircraft	110	USA (2)
Greece	Long-range SAMS	4	USA (W), Russia
Greece	Combat aircraft	115–45	Germany/Italy/UK/Spain, France (W), USA (2), (Russia)
Greece	Tanks	500	France, Germany, Russia UK, Ukraine, USA
Korea, South	Long-range SAMS	14	France/Italy, Russia, USA
Korea, South	Combat aircraft	40	France, Germany/Italy/UK/Spain, Russia, USA
Norway	Combat aircraft	30	Germany/Italy/UK/Spain, USA
Pakistan	Combat aircraft	100	China
Saudi Arabia	Tanks	450	France, UK, USA
South Africa	Combat aircraft	30	Germany, France, Sweden/UK (W), Russia
Turkey	Combat helicopter	145	France/Germany, Italy, USA (2), Russia/Israel
Turkey	Tanks	1 000	France, Germany, Pakistan, Russia, Ukraine, UK, USA, (Italy), (Israel)
UAE	Combat aircraft	80+30	USA (W), France (W), (Russia)

Notes: (W) = competition won (includes also part of a total order) by company in country; (country) = company entered but offer no longer under consideration; country/country = international consortium; (2) = 2 companies in one country submitted entries.

Source: SIPRI arms transfers database.

V. Foreign and military policy considerations

Arms transfers may be used by a supplier to show or gain support, while a refusal to supply arms may be used to reflect criticism or punish a foreign government. Support may involve rewards for good behaviour or for approval of the supplier's foreign and military policies. This is most clearly evident, first, among formal military alliance members and, second, between non-allied governments that share foreign and military policy interests. Transfers between the USA and other NATO states, as well as transfers within NATO Europe, are used to illustrate the first type of relation.[71] Since the dissolution

---

[71] The policy relevance of arms transfers is strongly reflected in military aid. However, since the late 1950s, military aid has been a diminishing part of US transfers to Europe, continuing mainly to Greece, Portugal and Turkey. However, even for deliveries to these allies, commercial considerations now seem to be of increasing importance in US arms transfers.

of the Warsaw Treaty Organization, Russia no longer has major alliance relations in Europe. The second type of support is illustrated by US relations with countries in the Middle East and military relations between Israel and Turkey.

NATO Europe

European NATO allies receive weapons and technologies not yet transferred from the USA to other countries, and some deliveries are clearly unique. For instance, the UK is the only foreign country receiving Tomahawk cruise missiles. The UK has often chosen US equipment in the past, such as the AH-64D Apache helicopter, the first of which was delivered in 1999.

Today there are European ambitions to achieve greater regional self-reliance in military R&D and acquisition as well as greater operational independence. These ambitions, reflected in the 1994 concept of a NATO European Security and Defence Identity (ESDI) and the 1999 NATO Defence Capabilities Initiative (DCI),[72] may increase intra-European military–technological cooperation and arms acquisitions, and thus have consequences for transatlantic arms transfers. A representative of the Délégation Générale des Armaments (DGA, the French General Armaments Delegation) has stated that: 'The accession to NATO of Poland, Hungary, and the Czech Republic must not be accompanied by a US monopoly on arms supplies'.[73] In fact, transatlantic military trade has long been a political stumbling block within NATO because of the disproportionate US advantage and US unwillingness to share advanced technology—as seen from Europe. This led, for instance, to Germany's refusal in 1999 to accept 'black boxes' of US sensitive technology[74] and its reluctance to buy the latest version of the Patriot surface-to-air missile from the USA.[75]

Creating a balance in transatlantic military trade that is seen as politically, economically and militarily acceptable on both sides of the Atlantic is not easily done. It is becoming a more complicated balancing act not least for the UK, which wants to maintain its 'special relationship' with the USA while at the same time supporting the European ambition. In 1999 the Meteor air-to-air missile project, in which the UK collaborates with other European countries, became a test of British priorities. It is planned to arm European-made combat aircraft with the missile. During 1999 Raytheon invited the UK to participate in a new advanced medium-range air-to-air missile (AMRAAM) project. In Europe this offer was seen as an attempt to block the Meteor, thereby com-

[72] The documents from the meeting of the North Atlantic Council in Washington, DC, on 23–24 Apr. 1999 at which the DCI was launched and the EDSI suggested are published in *NATO Review*, vol. 47, no. 2 (summer 1999). See also chapter 4 in this volume.

[73] Jakubyszyn, C., 'In France, a tool available at government's discretion', *Le Monde*, 22 Jan. 2000, in 'French arms export policy reviewed', FBIS-WEU-2000-012, 27 Jan. 2000. The first major weapon contract between an old NATO member and one of the new members was the 1999 Polish order for British AS-90 howitzer artillery turrets. 'Poland in UK gun deal', *Financial Times*, 27 July 1999, p. 6.

[74] The term 'black box' refers to a unit in a military system where the technological content is unknown to the customer.

[75] 'Germans balk at US control over PAC-3', *Defense News*, 22 Nov. 1999, pp. 3 and 28.

plicating future exports of European combat aircraft if armed with the US missile because of US military technology transfer restrictions. The dilemma has become an opportunity for the UK to show its support for a European alternative after having withdrawn from the multinational European Horizon frigate project in 1999. In January 2000 it seemed as if the UK would choose the Meteor.[76] The companies involved in the project have also countered by suggesting that the Meteor be made to fit Boeing-produced combat aircraft such as the F-15 and F/A-18.[77]

Since Europe is an important military market for US weapons, increasing arms transfers within Europe do not always meet with US approval. Strong US interests will continue to favour European acquisitions of US equipment, making use of the military–political argument. One of the most obvious examples of US irritation was the official DOD reaction to Greece's choice of four Swedish Ericsson airborne early-warning systems. In 1999 the DOD Director of Defense Procurement wrote to her Greek counterpart questioning the decision on political and technological grounds[78]—some claim she even urged the Greek Government to reconsider.[79]

The Middle East

In 1999 the USA and Israel drafted a new bilateral defence agreement to replace a 1988 accord. This was deemed necessary because of the new international security situation in general and the perceived and potential Iranian and Iraqi missile threats to Israel in particular.[80] The USA, for instance, supports the Israeli Arrow-2 anti-ballistic missile project.[81]

This missile threat is perceived by more nations in the Middle East and could result in the USA being willing to supply previously restricted technologies to non-allied but friendly nations. Such technologies do not have to be directly related to the missile threat as such, but could increase the recipient's military capabilities in other ways. Some of the most restricted technologies are the 'source' or 'software codes' without which aircraft are limited to

[76] Gow, D., 'European consortium wins £1bn RAF contract', *The Guardian,* 20 Jan. 2000, p. 11.

[77] Nicoll, A., 'European missile companies lobby US', *Financial Times*, 18 Feb. 2000, p. 7. Boeing is already involved in cooperation with BAE Systems. A similar but much larger dilemma is the future European acquisition of a new combat aircraft. One alternative is the US Joint Strike Fighter programme, in which the UK is a full collaborative partner while several other European countries have only made minor commitments. Another alternative is the European Eurofighter combat aircraft. Norway seems to have been subject to certain pressures from the USA because of its interest in the Eurofighter. Fyhn, M., 'USA presser Norge i drama om kampfly' [USA pushes Norway in the combat aircraft drama], *Aftenposten*, 4 Sep. 1999.

[78] Barrie, D. and Clark, C., 'Pentagon rebuffs Greek AEW pick', *Defense News*, 1 Feb. 1999, p. 3.

[79] Kemp, I. and Hoyle, C., 'Greeks announce intent to buy Eurofighter', *Jane's Defence Weekly*, vol. 31, no. 7 (17 Feb. 1999), p. 3. The US Government was also accused of delaying certain arms deliveries to Greece. Dhimakas, L., 'Delaying tactics by United States', *Ta Nea* (Athens), 18 Oct. 1999, in 'Greek daily views US "blockade" of arms deliveries', FBIS-WEU-1999-1019, 18 Oct. 1999.

[80] Rodan, S., 'Israel, USA draft new strategic agreement', *Jane's Defence Weekly*, vol. 32, no. 18 (3 Nov. 1999), p. 16. The focus of the new agreement is said to be on missile defence, intelligence exchange and cooperation as well as ways to maintain Israel's regional qualitative edge.

[81] Orme, W. A., Jr, 'Missile defenses test succeeds in Israel', *International Herald Tribune*, 2 Nov. 1999, p. 1.

the missions and using the weapons for which they are programmed by the manufacturer in line with US Government policy.[82] The UAE requested access to such technology for buying new F-16 combat aircraft. The USA finally decided to supply the aircraft despite its initial reluctance because of the risk of upsetting the military balance in the region.[83]

Strategic cooperation or strategic partnership between two countries may be regarded as a way of supporting military and foreign policy relationships short of entering into alliances. Such partnerships need not involve major suppliers. One illustration of a different relationship is the establishment of Israeli–Turkish military cooperation,[84] which has already raised concerns in Greece as well as among Arab states.[85] The breakthrough came with the Israeli–Palestine Liberation Organisation (PLO) Declaration of Principles in September 1993. Turkey and Israel have not supplied each other with major weapons in the past. The agreements include arms transfers as well as defence industrial cooperation, such as the sale of Popeye long-range air-to-surface missiles and a major $600 million programme to upgrade 54 F-4 Phantom aircraft.[86] Again, because of the possible regional ballistic missile threat to both Israel and Turkey, defence against such missiles is said to have been one of the issues discussed as well as cooperation on other advanced military systems.[87]

[82] 'UAE set to tie up F-16 deal next week', *Air Letter*, 10 Nov. 1999, p. 4.

[83] 'UAE to be first F-16 buyer to get codes', *Air Letter*, 8 Dec. 1999, p. 4; 'US–UAE close to making F-16 deal', *World Aerospace & Defense Intelligence*, 21 May 1999, p. 5; 'US and UAE close to deal', *Financial Times*, 22 Oct. 1999, p. 8; 'UAE F-16 deal—much ado about nothing?', *Defence Systems Daily/Defence Analysis*, Dec. 1999, URL <http://defence-data.com/current/page6041.htm>; and Allen, R., 'Spread of weapons of mass destruction concentrates minds', *Financial Times*, 28 Oct. 1999, pp. 5 and 8. See also Kemp (note 68).

[84] Bekdil, E. and Opall-Rome, B., 'Turkey fears new Israeli Government may dilute ties', *Defense News*, 14 June 1999, p. 56. There is information that Israel may also contemplate a similar agreement with Greece. 'Israel plays both sides in the Greek–Turkish dispute', Global Intelligence Update, *Defense Systems Daily*, 10 Aug. 1999; Waxman, D., 'Turkey and Israel: A new balance of power in the Middle East', *Washington Quarterly*, winter 1999, pp. 27–32; and Eisenstadt, M., 'Turkish–Israeli military cooperation: an assessment', ed. E. Aronson and M. Neal, *Peace Watch/Policy Watch. Anthology* (Washington Institute for Near East Policy: Washington, DC, 1997).

[85] Dimakos, S. L., 'Israeli assault on Greek armaments', *Ta Nea* (Athens), 13 Aug. 1999, in 'Israeli companies said vying for Greek armament market', FBIS-WEU-1999-0816, 13 Aug. 1999. Some security concerns are mentioned by Koknar, M., 'Rough neighborhood', *Armed Forces Journal International*, Sep. 1999, pp. 20–26. An Iranian daily also commented critically on Turkish–Israeli military cooperation. 'Secularists, allies of the Zionists', *Jomhuri-ye Eslami* (Tehran), 26 Oct. 1999, in 'Iran paper on Turkey–Israel military ties', Foreign Broadcast Information Service, *Daily Report–Near East and South Asia (FBIS-NES)*, FBIS-NES-1999-1203, 26 Oct. 1999. Even if it was not in direct response to Israeli–Turkish cooperation, in Oct. Greece and Armenia signed a defence cooperation pact involving military training, research, information exchange and defence industrial cooperation. Athens News Agency, 'Greece, Armenia sign defense cooperation pact', in FBIS-WEU-1999-1018, 18 Oct. 1999.

[86] The first 2 upgraded Phantoms were delivered in Jan. 2000. The upgrading work will take place in both Israel and Turkey. 'First two Turkish F-4 aircraft upgraded by IAI delivered', *Defence Systems Daily*, 27 Jan. 2000. In 1999 it was reported that Israeli Military Industries was also prepared to upgrade Turkish M-60A1 tanks. 'Israel faces pressure over planned Turkish M60 upgrade', *World Aerospace & Defense Intelligence*, 18 Dec. 1998, p. 10.

[87] 'Threats from above', *Armed Forces Journal*, Jan. 2000, p. 18.

VI. Arms transfer reporting and transparency

The UN Register of Conventional Arms

On 13 August 1999 the UN Secretary-General released the seventh annual report of information received from governments on their arms imports and/or exports for calendar year 1998. By that time, 64 countries plus the Cook Islands and Niue had responded in some way to the request for information.[88] As of March 2000, this number had increased to 80 countries.[89] China was the only major supplier that did not report. As in 1998 this was probably in protest against the inclusion of Taiwan as a recipient in the US report.[90] Among the most useful reports from the point of view of transparency were those from several former Soviet republics—specifically from Russia, which supplied information on transfers, mainly to Africa, that was not yet publicly available.

The geographical pattern of participation in 1999 was similar to that of previous years. Participation is high among states that are members of international organizations in which confidence-building measures are high on their agenda. Nearly all members of the Organization for Security and Co-operation in Europe (OSCE), the Organization of American States (OAS), the Association of South-East Asian Nations (ASEAN) and the ASEAN Regional Forum (ARF) reported. In the Middle East and Africa participation was still low. Israel was the only Middle Eastern country that had responded by the time the Secretary-General's report was released. As of May 2000, only one other Middle Eastern country, Iran, submitted data after the publication of the annual report.

In 2000 a group of governmental experts is to convene to study, for the third time, possibilities for expanding the scope of the register and for developing transparency regarding weapons of mass destruction and related technology transfers.[91] In response to an appeal for views on these matters the EU, together with the members of the European Free Trade Association (EFTA) and other European countries 'associated with' the EU,[92] noted the importance of increased transparency on conventional weapons. The Arab League reaffirmed its demand for the inclusion of weapons of mass destruction while

---

[88] This does not include the 18 countries and Palestine for which, as members of the Arab League, Saudi Arabia submitted a *note verbale* reaffirming the Arab League's *note verbale* in 1997, expressing support for the idea of the UNROCA but at the same time disagreeing with its present structure. The Arab League members (listed in the Glossary in this volume) were therefore unwilling to provide the information requested. Reply by Saudi Arabia dated 28 Apr. 1999, in UN document A/54/226, 13 Aug. 1999, pp. 98. See also the original Arab League's reply by Mauritania dated 2 Sep. 1997, in UN document A/52/312, 28 Aug. 1997, pp. 71–72. While 3 Arab League members, Jordan, Libya and Qatar, reported in 1998 on actual arms imports and/or exports for 1997, they did not respond in 1999.

[89] UN document A/54/226 (note 88). This document and its addenda and corrigenda are available at URL <http://www.un.org/Depts/dda/CAB/rep542261.pdf. Earlier UNROCA reports can be found at URL <http://domino.un.org/REGISTER:NSF>.

[90] In 1998 China declared that it would not report because the USA reported exports to 'Taiwan'. The US report in 1999 still included exports to Taiwan, as exports to the 'Taiwan Province of China', but by Mar. 2000 this still seemed not to have mollified China.

[91] UN General Assembly Resolution 53/77, 4 Dec. 1998, section V.

[92] Bulgaria, Czech Republic, Estonia, Hungary, Latvia, Lithuania, Poland, Romania, Slovakia, Slovenia and Cyprus.

another view, supported by Japan and the USA, was that these weapons should be reported in a separate forum.[93] As in 1994 and 1997, there seems little hope that a consensus on how to improve and/or expand the UN Register of Conventional Arms (UNROCA) will be reached.

EU transparency

While this was not its original intention, in October 1999 the EU published the aggregate values of arms exports as submitted by its members in the framework of the 1998 EU Code of Conduct for Arms Exports.[94] While the report is of political importance in showing an intention to achieve greater transparency and in supporting public debate, the published data give only aggregate totals with no explanation of definition and methodology. Other than for Luxembourg and Ireland the report does not add much new information to that already available in public reports by the individual governments.[95]

The EU arms export report illustrates the problem of national data comparability. The data are presented under the general heading of arms exports implying comparability, but the sources from which they seem to be derived (see appendix 7E) indicate that for each country the value of total 'arms exports' is based on a different definition (see more below).

National transparency

It is still the exception rather than the rule for countries regularly to make available detailed information (i.e., revealing more than the aggregate arms export totals presented in table 7E). In recent years, however, arms export transparency has received increased attention. This has led to improved reporting in a number of countries.

The government and industrial statistics on the value of arms exports presented in appendix 7E show aggregate arms exports only. Twelve of the countries listed published more comprehensive data showing the value of arms exports to individual countries (Norway doing so for the first time).[96] The German and French governments announced in 1998 and 1999, respectively, that they would publish annual reports on national arms exports, but in both cases this was delayed until 2000.[97]

---

[93] These views are published as annexes to UN document A/54/226 (note 88).

[94] Council of the European Union, Annual Report in Conformity with Operative Provision 8 of the European Union Code of Conduct for Arms Exports, Brussels, 28 Sep. 1999. The Code of Conduct is discussed in Hagelin, Wezeman and Wezeman (note 9), pp. 439–42, and the text is reproduced in the same volume, pp. 503–505.

[95] See Hagelin, Wezeman and Wezeman (note 9), p. 440 for a discussion on the usefulness of arms export data as provided by EU members.

[96] Australia, Canada, Finland, Italy, the Netherlands, Norway, Spain, Sweden, Switzerland, the UK and the USA.

[97] Information received from the German Ministry of Economics, Bonn, 14 Dec. 1999 and from Observatoire des transferts d'armements, Lyon, 17 Feb. 2000. The French Government published its first annual report on arms exports in March 2000.

As described in appendix 7E, the values of arms exports given in table 7E are not characterized by transparency, reliability or comparability. Some of these problems are illustrated below by the examples of the UK, the USA and Italy for data published in 1999.

There are two *British* Government sources on arms exports, each reporting different figures. First, an annual report on arms exports is published by the Foreign and Commonwealth Office, the Department of Trade and Industry, and the Ministry of Defence as part of the British Government's commitment to increasing transparency and accountability on arms exports. The most recent (second) edition gives the value of deliveries of defence equipment at £1968.3 million.[98]

Second, the *UK Defence Statistics*, published by the Government Statistical Service for the British Ministry of Defence, reports deliveries of defence equipment valued at £3527 million, almost double the previous figure.[99] Data from this publication are often used to show the success of British arms producers on the global market.[100] According to the Ministry of Defence both figures are derived from data supplied by Customs and Excise (C&E). They vary because of slightly different definitions and significant revisions to C&E data which occurred after publication of the *UK Defence Statistics* and before publication of the annual report on arms exports.[101] It is difficult to understand how the original data could be so different from the revised data, however.

As in previous years, the *US* Government report on arms exports remains by far the most comprehensive and detailed,[102] but it contains data inexplicably different from those reported in other public sources. This puts its reliability in doubt. For example, it reports deliveries to Kuwait of LAV-25 armoured vehicles and orders for Pandur armoured vehicles.[103] Other reported arms exports cannot be supported from other sources, such as the US licence for the export of 2451 Sidewinder air-to-air missiles to the UK. Further, a

---

[98] British Foreign and Commonwealth Office, Department of Trade and Industry and Ministry of Defence, *Annual Report on Strategic Export Controls*, 3 Nov. 1999. Available on the Internet site of the British Foreign and Commonwealth Office, URL <http://www.fco.gov.uk/news/newstext.asp?2956>.

[99] British Government Statistical Service, *UK Defence Statistics* (Stationary Office: London, 1999). This publication also gives an even higher arms export figure adjusted with information from the Society of British Aerospace Companies (SBAC) on items where the official commodity classifications do not distinguish between military and civil aerospace equipment. Thus for 1997 the highest estimate in *UK Defence Statistics* (£6685 million) was double that in the *Annual Report on Strategic Export Controls* (£3359.6 million). For 1998 the SBAC gives a total for military exports of £5.72 billion by its members, indicating that the adjusted *UK Defence Statistics* figure would be up to 3 times higher than the figure in *Annual Report on Strategic Export Controls* (note 98). *UK Aerospace Statistics 1998* (Society of British Aerospace Companies: London, 1999).

[100] See, e.g., 'UK in second place behind USA in arms sales race', *Jane's Defence Weekly*, vol. 31, no. 11 (17 Mar. 1999), p. 5, in which the Head of the British Defence Export Services Organisation explains the arms export success of 1998, i.e., $10 billion in orders.

[101] Personal communication with A. J. Tranham, British Ministry of Defence, Directorate of Export Services Policy 2, London, 22 Feb. 2000. It is also reported that a British Ministry of Defence spokesman admitted that the *UK Defence Statistics* figure is wrong. 'Addicted to the arms trade', *The Economist*, 18 Sep. 1999, p. 42.

[102] US Department of State, *US Arms Exports: Direct Commercial Sales Authorizations for Fiscal Year 98*, Washington, DC, 1999. This is also known as the '655 Report'.

[103] For a detailed summary of the Pandur delivery to Kuwait see Foss, F. (ed.), *Jane's Armour and Artillery, 1999–2000* (Jane's Information Group Limited: Coulsdon, 1999), p. 525.

considerable number of countries are reported to have ordered spare parts for weapons not elsewhere reported to be in use by these countries.

In 1999 the *Italian* Government admitted that it had made a mistake in its export data for 1997. A miscalculation resulted in reported arms exports of 2065 billion lire instead of 1487 billion lire.[104]

VII. International arms embargoes

Table 7.4 lists the 25 countries subject to a partial or complete embargo on arms transfers, military services or other military-related transfers at any time during 1995–99, as decided and stated collectively by an international organization or group of nations (e.g., the embargo against Burundi by eight African states).[105] At the end of 1999 there were 16 countries and 3 rebel groups under international arms embargoes. Of these 7 were under mandatory, legally binding embargoes decided by the UN Security Council, while the others were only under politically binding voluntary embargoes.[106] Actions taken during 1999 are described below, with examples of the problems encountered in enforcing international embargoes.[107]

On 12 February 1999 the UN Security Council implemented a voluntary embargo on arms transfers to both *Ethiopia* and *Eritrea*, then involved in an armed conflict. The EU followed with a voluntary embargo on 15 March.[108] These had little effect. Since the beginning of the conflict in 1998 most arms deliveries to these states had originated from former Soviet republics and East European countries. During the embargo deliveries continued from several of these countries, including Russia, a permanent member of the Security Council.

On 17 September 1999 the EU imposed a four-month moratorium on arms sales to *Indonesia* following harsh Indonesian action in East Timor and in preparation for the UN-supervised referendum on the future status of East Timor. The moratorium covered deliveries of arms under existing contracts.[109] The sanctions were related to the situation in East Timor only, which improved dramatically with the introduction of a UN-sanctioned multinational peace-keeping force and the subsequent withdrawal of Indonesian troops.

[104] Information from Chiara Bonaiuti, Italian Observatory on Arms Trade (Oscar), Firenze, 21 Oct. 1999.

[105] Tobias Etzold, an intern at SIPRI in 1999, assisted in compiling this information.

[106] Since 1945 only the UN Security Council has imposed mandatory embargoes. All other embargoes have been of a voluntary nature.

[107] Regarding the EU embargoes see URL <http://projects.sipri.se/expcon/euframe/euembargo.html>.

[108] CFSP, Common Position of 15 March 1999 defined by the Council on the basis of Article J.2 of the Treaty on European Union, concerning Ethiopia and Eritrea, European Union, *Official Journal*, no. L072 (18 Mar. 1999), p. 0001–0001, URL <http://europa.eu.int/eur-lex/en/lif/dat/1999/en_499X0206.html>.

[109] CFSP, Council Common Position of 16 September 1999 concerning restrictive measures against the Republic of Indonesia, 1999/624/CFSP, European Union, *Official Journal* L 245 (17 Sep. 1999), p. 33, URL <http://europa.eu.int/abc/doc/off/bull/en/9909/p104071.htm>.

Table 7.4. International arms embargoes

Target	Entry into force	Lifted	Legal basis	Organization
Mandatory UN embargoes				
Angola (UNITA)	15 Sep. 1993	–	UNSCR 864	UN
Iraq	6 Aug. 1990	–	UNSCR 661	UN
Liberia[a]	19 Nov. 192	–	UNSCR 788	UN
Libya	31 Mar. 1992	5 Apr. 1999	UNSCR 748	UN
Rwanda	17 May 1994	16 Aug. 1995[b]	UNSCR 918	UN
Rwanda (rebels)[c]	16 Aug. 1998	–	UNSCR 1011	UN
Sierra Leone	8 Oct. 1997	5 June 1998	UNSCR 1132	UN
Sierra Leone (rebels)[d]	5 June 1998	–	UNSCR 1171	UN
Somalia	23 Jan. 1992	–	UNSCR 733	UN
Yugoslavia	25 Sep. 1991	1 Oct. 1996	UNSCR 713	UN
Yugoslavia (FRY)	31 Mar. 1998	–	UNSCR 1160	UN
Non-mandatory UN embargoes				
Afghanistan	22 Oct. 1996	–	UNSCR 1076	UN
Eritrea	12 Feb. 1999	–	UNSCR 1227	UN
Ethiopia	12 Feb. 1999	–	UNSCR 1227	UN
EU embargoes (non-mandatory)				
Afghanistan[e]	17 Dec. 1996	–	96/746/CFSP	EU
Bosnia and Herzegovina[f]	5 July 1991	–	–	EU
China	27 June 1989	–	–	EU
Croatia[f]	5 July 1991	–	–	EU
DRC[e]	7 Apr. 1993	–	–	EU
Ethiopia[e,f]	15 Mar. 1999	–	–	EU
Eritrea[e,f]	15 Mar. 1999	–	–	EU
Indonesia[f]	17 Sep. 1999	17 Jan. 2000	–	EU
Iraq	4 Aug. 1990	–	–	EU
Libya	27 Jan. 1986	–	–	EU
Macedonia[g]	5 July 1991	26 Feb. 1996		EU
Myanmar (Burma)[e]	29 July 1991[h]	–	–	EU
Nigeria[e]	20 Nov. 1995	1 June 1999	95/515/CFSP	EU
Sierra Leone[f]	8 Dec. 1997	–	98/409/CFSP	EU
Slovenia[g]	5 July 1991	26 Feb. 1996[i]		EU
Sudan[e]	15 Mar. 1994	–	94/165/CFSP	EU
Yugoslavia[g]	5 July 1991	–	–	EU
Other international embargoes (non-mandatory)				
Azerbaijan[j]	28 Feb. 1992	–	–	OSCE
Burundi	6 Aug. 1996	23 Jan. 1999	–	8 African countries[k]
Nigeria	24 Apr. 1996	Nov. 1999	–	Commonwealth

Notes: FRY = Federal Republic of Yugoslavia; CFSP = Common Foreign and Security Policy; EU = European Union; OSCE = Organization for Security and Co-operation in Europe; UNITA = National Union for the Total Independence of Angola; UNSCR = UN Security Council Resolution.

[a] Does not apply to deliveries to ECOMOG forces in Liberia.

[b] The arms embargo was suspended on this date and formally ended on 1 Sep. 1996.

[c] Does not apply to deliveries to government forces in Rwanda. The embargo is also on equipment for persons in neighbouring states if the equipment is for use in Rwanda.

[d] Does not apply to deliveries to government or ECOMOG forces in Sierra Leone.

[e] Does not apply to deliveries under existing contracts.

[f] The Central and East European countries associated with the EU, the associated country Cyprus and the EFTA countries (Iceland, Liechtenstein, Norway and Switzerland), members of the European Economic Area, have declared that they share the objectives of these embargoes.

[g] Imposed as an embargo against the territory of the former Yugoslavia.

[h] A 'decision to refuse the sale of any military equipment' was made by the EU General Affairs Council on 29 July 1991. On 28 Oct. 1996 a decision confirming the embargo (96/635/CFSP) was made by the EU Council of Ministers for Foreign Affairs.

[i] On this date the embargo was changed to a case-by-case evaluation governed by the EU common criteria on arms exports adopted in 1991. The embargo was officially lifted on 10 Aug. 1998.

[j] Only on deliveries to forces engaged in combat in the Nagorno-Karabakh area (these would include Azerbaijani, Armenian and local forces).

[k] DRC, Eritrea, Ethiopia, Kenya, Rwanda, Tanzania, Uganda and Zambia.

Source: SIPRI arms transfers archives.

However, new conflicts involving the Indonesian armed forces soon erupted in other parts of Indonesia. Some EU countries wanted the embargo extended to signal disapproval of the new actions, while others preferred to give Indonesia a sign of approval of its concessions on East Timor. In the absence of unanimity to maintain it, the EU embargo was not prolonged after 17 January 2000.[110] Even members of the Indonesian Government questioned the decision, fearing efforts by the armed forces to gain political control.[111]

The UN mandatory arms embargo on *Libya* was imposed in 1992 in response to Libya's refusal to cooperate in the investigation of the bombing of Pan Am flight 103 in 1988. It was lifted on 5 April 1999 after Libya handed over two suspects to an international court.[112] As there were additional reasons for the 1986 EU embargo against Libya it was maintained.[113]

Many media reports in 1999 claimed breaches of the UN arms embargo on the *Federal Republic of Yugoslavia (FRY)*, but only those related to the transfer of small quantities of small arms, mainly from or via Albania, to the Kosovo Liberation Army (KLA) could be verified.[114] Reports of deliveries of sophisticated air defence systems from Russia before and during the NATO air strikes in Yugoslavia were denied by Russia and have proved impossible to verify.[115]

[110] Among those in favour of an extension was the Netherlands. Frank Slijper, AMOK-Noord, Groningen, Private communication to the authors on questions to the Dutch Foreign Minister from Parliament, 14 Jan. 2000. Among the most vocal in favour of not extending was the UK (the largest EU exporter of military equipment to Indonesia in recent years). *Financial Times*, 14 Jan. 2000, p. 12.

[111] Indonesian Environment Minister Sarwano Kusumaatmadja in *The Independent*, 18 Jan. 2000.

[112] UN document S/PRST/1999/10, 8 Apr. 1999.

[113] Common Position of 16 April 1999 defined by the Council on the basis of Article J.2 of the Treaty on European Union concerning Libya, 1999/261/CFSP, European Union, *Official Journal*, no. L103 (20 Apr. 1999), p. 1; and Council Common Position of 13 September 1999 amending Common Position 1999/261/CFSP concerning Libya, 1999/611/CFSP, European Union, *Official Journal*, no. L242 (14 Sep. 1999), p. 31. See also chapter 2 in this volume.

[114] Supplies of weapons to the KLA were also reported from or via Macedonia, Greece and Italy. Smith, C., 'Small arms trafficking may export Albania's anarchy', *Jane's Intelligence Review*, Jan. 1999, pp. 24–28; and 'Kosovo rebels get flood of arms', *International Herald Tribune*, 13 July 1998, p. 5.

[115] Xinhua, 'Russia denies violation of arms embargo on Kosovo', 20 July 1999.

The situation was the same with regard to other reports of breaches of international embargoes. Reports claiming that deliveries of MiG-23 and Su-24 combat aircraft and Mi-24 combat helicopters had been made to the União Nacional Para a Independência Total de Angola (UNITA, National Union for the Total Independence of Angola) cannot be verified and seem, certainly in the case of the MiG-23s and Su-24s, outlandish. There was, however, evidence that weapons and other military equipment were delivered to UNITA, mostly from East European countries and former Soviet republics (Ukraine is often mentioned).[116] A report from the chairman of the UN Sanctions Committee on Angola stated that weapons had been delivered from East European sources via neighbours of Angola and other African countries. According to the report 5–10 aircraft flew into UNITA-held territory every evening. While not all carried weapons, this underlines the ease with which weapons could be smuggled in.[117] A second report was published in early 2000 which actually names a number of countries involved over the past five years: Burkina Faso, the Republic of Congo, Rwanda, Togo and Zaire.[118]

The above-mentioned reports suggest that a number of African countries lack the will to enforce the embargo on UNITA or, for that matter, other embargoes in Africa. Some countries seem to be involved in actively breaching embargoes by allowing arms-transporting aircraft to transit or even to unload cargoes that are then transported further by land. At the same time, many African countries that want to observe embargoes lack the means to enforce them. The UN reports on Angola recommended improved sanctions monitoring, including a small number of monitors in neighbouring and even more distant African states (e.g., Togo and Côte d'Ivoire) as well as in Ukraine. The reports also noted that one of the problems was that UNITA was able to pay for weapons from the profits made by selling diamonds mined in areas under UNITA control. Another problem was the sheer size of the area to be monitored.[119]

VIII. Conclusions

Since 1995 the transfer of major conventional weapons has been fairly stable, at about half of the peak cold war level. The USA is by far the largest supplier, responsible for almost as many deliveries as all other suppliers combined. Russia was the second largest supplier in 1995–99 as well as in 1999, but it accounted for only 27 per cent of the US level. The other major suppliers were France, the UK and Germany.

---

[116] Human Rights Watch, 'Angola unravels: The rise and fall of the Lusaka Peace Process', Washington, DC, Sep. 1999.

[117] UN, Report of the Security Council Committee established pursuant to resolution 864 (1993) concerning the situation in Angola, UN document S/1999/147, 12 Feb. 1999; and UN, Security Council Committee established pursuant to resolution 864 (1993) concerning the situation in Angola, Report on the Chairman's visit to Central and Southern Africa, May 1999, UN document S/1999/644, 4 June 1999.

[118] UN document S/2000/203, 10 Mar. 2000.

[119] UN document S/1999/147 (note 116); and UN document S/1999/644 (note 116).

The major recipients in 1995–99 were Taiwan, Saudi Arabia, Turkey, South Korea and Egypt. In 1999 Taiwan was the largest recipient for the third year running. One of the five major recipients, and five more of the countries importing weapons from the major suppliers, were involved in major armed conflicts. International arms embargoes seem successful in limiting, but not stopping, transfers of major weapons.

The USA is expected to remain by far the major supplier and major military R&D investor in the future, retaining national control over all major programmes. The European countries may overcome major financial restrictions through regional cooperation. Russia's long-term position in advanced military R&D, and therefore as a major competitor in production of advanced weapons, is unclear. In 1997–98 France delivered more weapons than Russia, and French deliveries were only 20 per cent below the level of Russian transfers for the period 1995–99.

There seems little hope that the UNROCA will be significantly improved or expanded in 2000. Nevertheless, in recent years transparency has received increased attention, which has led to improved national arms transfer reporting. This has enabled SIPRI to make its first estimate of the global turnover of the international arms trade—$35–49 billion for 1998.

Both the Middle East and North-East Asia are regions in which new threat perceptions may influence future military acquisition plans. Israel's scenarios include missile attacks from Iran and Iraq, possibly with nuclear, biological or chemical warheads, and Israeli acquisitions of missiles, aircraft and submarines already seem to be directed at deterring or even pre-empting such attacks. Chinese acquisitions of Russian combat aircraft were countered by US deliveries of large numbers of F-16s to Taiwan. Since 1997 Taiwan has been the largest recipient of major conventional weapons, supplied mainly by the USA. Tension on the Korean Peninsula, and more particularly the August 1998 North Korean missile test, was a major stimulus for South Korean arms acquisitions in 1999, and also a factor in Japan's decision to participate in US surface-to-air missile R&D.

Appendix 7A. The volume of transfers of major conventional weapons: by recipients and suppliers, 1995–99

BJÖRN HAGELIN, PIETER D. WEZEMAN and
SIEMON T. WEZEMAN

Table 7A.1. The recipients of major conventional weapons

The list includes all countries/non-state actors with imports of major conventional weapons for 1995–99. The countries are ranked according to the 1995–99 aggregate imports. Figures are trend-indicator values expressed in US $m. at constant (1990) prices.

Rank order								
1995–99	1994–98[a]	Recipient	1995	1996	1997	1998	1999	1995–99
1	1	Taiwan	1 223	1 391	5 201	4 415	1 706	13 936
2	2	Saudi Arabia	973	1 728	2 770	2 529	1 231	9 231
3	3	Turkey	1 370	1 146	968	1 843	1 134	6 461
4	5	Korea, South	1 562	1 574	738	892	1 245	6 011
5	4	Egypt	1 688	941	903	461	748	4 741
6	7	India	945	1 021	1 565	540	566	4 637
7	8	Japan	847	533	594	1 280	1 089	4 343
8	6	Greece	869	270	829	1 490	633	4 091
9	14	China	437	1 095	609	165	1 688	3 994
10	9	UAE	448	558	772	895	595	3 268
11	13	Israel	281	73	46	1 298	1 205	2 903
12	11	Pakistan	278	552	640	564	839	2 873
13	12	Kuwait	684	1 254	437	221	126	2 722
14	16	Malaysia	1 015	51	567	25	916	2 574
15	17	Finland	162	566	396	568	821	2 513
16	10	Thailand	611	615	924	59	185	2 394
17	18	Singapore	244	548	132	653	163	1 740
18	22	Switzerland	106	199	400	459	508	1 672
19	15	USA	384	356	621	138	111	1 610
20	21	Brazil	235	483	445	180	221	1 564
21	19	Spain	363	434	211	91	289	1 388
22	20	Indonesia	359	541	113	105	213	1 331
23	24	Chile	546	215	123	127	177	1 188
24	26	Qatar	15	58	553	391	117	1 134
25	25	Italy	187	241	552	4	–	984
26	23	Iran	248	505	48	91	67	959
27	32	UK	93	216	92	370	155	926
28	34	Viet Nam	270	242	92	162	154	920
29	40	Kazakhstan	162	229	166	–	259	816
30	35	Norway	99	195	182	164	170	810
31	36	Netherlands	42	215	119	174	225	775
32	37	Australia	115	149	19	141	341	765
33	33	Peru	35	147	435	15	108	740
34	49	New Zealand	4	18	343	13	337	715
35	39	Myanmar	223	93	231	133	27	707
36	31	Mexico	43	58	194	396	14	705

Rank order

1995–99	1994–98[a]	Recipient	1995	1996	1997	1998	1999	1995–99
37	27	Oman	171	333	158	27	–	689
38	29	Sweden	83	47	257	222	79	688
39	42	Denmark	129	53	74	195	137	588
40	48	Cyprus	33	180	110	21	242	586
41	43	Argentina	70	51	78	112	223	534
42	38	Algeria	341	46	35	101	–	523
43	30	Germany	145	110	5	115	126	501
44	41	Austria	44	14	192	197	48	495
45	28	Canada	165	157	104	25	33	484
46	51	France	41	30	160	138	105	474
47	46	Colombia	79	39	162	116	40	436
48	50	Jordan	19	53	108	202	44	426
49	57	Hungary	54	119	62	39	56	330
50	53	Bahrain	26	222	74	8	–	330
51	52	Sri Lanka	60	163	1	64	26	314
52	54	Slovakia	252	35	–	–	–	287
53	60	Bangladesh	128	4	25	–	130	287
54	47	Morocco	40	91	146	–	–	277
55	59	Poland	154	114	–	–	1	269
56	56	Eritrea	3	31	33	202	–	269
57	61	Ethiopia	–	–	53	179	8	240
58	75	Venezuela	–	36	33	23	142	234
59	55	Angola	1	10	3	189	–	203
60	87	North Korea	35	2	2	1	156	196
61	69	Yemen	129	–	–	–	53	182
62	63	Tunisia	72	73	23	1	–	169
63	65	Bulgaria	–	123	40	–	6	169
64	58	Philippines	32	30	54	51	–	167
65	45	Armenia	49	104	–	–	–	153
66	68	Bosnia and Herzegovina	–	51	77	2	16	146
67	67	Romania	–	37	15	50	35	137
68	66	Belgium	20	–	36	43	37	136
69	73	Botswana	6	23	67	4	34	134
70	64	Croatia	86	2	41	–	–	129
71	76	Ecuador	12	23	50	7	24	116
72	79	Uganda	33	–	–	46	32	111
73	74	Sudan	3	29	66	–	10	108
74	70	Syria	43	21	–	20	20	104
75	92	Macedonia	–	–	–	9	95	104
76	72	South Africa	38	38	9	–	14	99
77	80	Uruguay	7	4	31	24	13	79
78	77	Lebanon	40	27	6	5	–	78
79	108	Georgia	–	–	8	7	60	75
80	81	Belarus	–	–	–	66	–	66
81	82	Congo (DRC)	1	46	18	–	–	65
82	84	Slovenia	18	13	8	4	19	62
83	83	Brunei	–	17	31	7	–	55
84	85	Kenya	–	–	54	–	–	54
85	149	Bahamas	–	–	–	–	54	54
86	71	Cambodia	–	29	16	4	2	51
87	88	NATO[c]	–	–	–	49	–	49
88	91	Lithuania	7	18	–	18	4	47
89	44	Portugal	15	2	14	7	1	39

Table 7A.1, *contd*

Rank order

1995–99	1994–98[a]	Recipient	1995	1996	1997	1998	1999	1995–99
90	86	Estonia	22	1	14	2	–	39
91	124	Rwanda	–	1	2	2	29	34
92	90	Ireland	–	–	–	2	30	32
93	94	Mauritius	–	30	1	–	–	31
94	98	Sierra Leone	16	–	8	–	6	30
95	95	Czech Republic	2	23	5	–	–	30
96	96	Laos	–	–	14	14	–	28
97	97	Yugoslavia (FRY)	18	–	8	–	–	26
98	101	Latvia	19	1	1	–	4	25
99	104	Congo (Rep. of)	–	–	18	1	–	19
100	105	Albania	19	–	–	–	–	19
101	103	Papua New Guinea	–	–	18	–	–	18
102	89	United Nations[c]	8	–	–	1	8	17
103	78	Nigeria	–	14	–	–	–	14
104	109	Cameroon	–	4	4	6	–	14
105	106	Togo	3	–	10	–	–	13
106	110	Palestinian A[d]	1	12	–	–	–	13
107	147	Suriname	–	–	–	–	12	12
108	111	Panama	–	–	12	–	–	12
109	107	Namibia	3	–	2	7	–	12
110	102	Ghana	–	7	4	–	–	11
111	125	Jamaica	–	–	–	5	5	10
112	114	El Salvador	3	3	–	3	–	9
113	116	Cape Verde	–	–	–	9	–	9
114	112	Fiji	8	–	–	–	–	8
115	118	Chad	1	–	–	7	–	8
116	119	Malta	–	1	6	–	–	7
117	93	Mauritania	1	1	5	–	–	7
118	115	Moldova	7	–	–	–	–	7
119	120	Mali	–	–	7	–	–	7
120	134	Dominican Republic	–	4	–	–	3	7
121	122	Lebanon/SLA[b]	–	6	–	–	–	6
122	117	Unknown[e]	4	–	–	1	1	6
123	113	Israel/PLO[b]	–	5	–	–	–	5
124	123	Lebanon/Hezbollah[b]	2	1	1	–	–	4
125	126	Zimbabwe	–	3	–	1	–	4
126	129	Palau	–	4	–	–	–	4
127	130	Luxembourg	–	4	–	–	–	4
128	132	Guinea	–	–	–	4	–	4
129	133	Micronesia	–	–	4	–	–	4
130	136	Djibouti	3	–	–	–	–	3
131	137	Belize	–	3	–	–	–	3
132	127	Zambia	–	2	–	–	–	2
133	135	Senegal	2	–	–	–	–	2
134	139	Paraguay	–	2	–	–	–	2
135	140	Niger	–	–	2	–	–	2
136	141	Côte d'Ivoire	2	–	–	–	–	2
137	143	Guatemala	–	–	–	1	–	1
138	62	Yemen/Southern rebels[b]	–	–	–	–	–	< 0.5
139	144	Turkey/PKK[b]	–	–	–	–	–	< 0.5
140	145	Sri Lanka/LTTE[b]	–	–	–	–	–	< 0.5

Rank order

1995–99	1994–98[a]	Recipient	1995	1996	1997	1998	1999	1995–99
141	128	Tuvalu	–	–	–	–	–	< 0.5
142	146	Tonga	–	–	–	–	–	< 0.5
143	138	Tanzania	–	–	–	–	–	< 0.5
144	99	Tajikistan	–	–	–	–	–	< 0.5
145	142	Malawi	–	–	–	–	–	< 0.5
146	148	Maldives	–	–	–	–	–	< 0.5
147	131	Kiribati	–	–	–	–	–	< 0.5
148	121	Bolivia	–	–	–	–	–	< 0.5
149	100	Azerbaijan	–	–	–	–	–	< 0.5
		Total	**19 994**	**21 292**	**25 715**	**23 718**	**20 606**	**111 325**

[a] The rank order for recipients in 1994–98 differs from that published in the *SIPRI Yearbook 1999* (pp. 428–29) because of the subsequent revision of figures for these years.

[b] Non-state actor: rebel group. SLA = South Lebanese Army; PLO = Palestine Liberation Organization; PKK = Kurdish Workers' Party; LTTE = Liberation Tigers of Tamil Eelam.

[c] Non-state actor: international organization.

[d] Non-state actor: Palestinian Authority

[e] One or more unknown recipient(s).

Notes: '–' = between 0 and 0.5. Totals and figures for 1995–99 may not add up because of rounding.

The SIPRI data on arms transfers refer to actual deliveries of major conventional weapons. To permit comparison between the data on such deliveries of different weapons and identification of general trends, SIPRI uses a *trend-indicator value*. The SIPRI values are therefore only an indicator of the volume of international arms transfers and not of the actual financial values of such transfers. Thus they are not comparable to economic statistics such as gross domestic product or export/import figures.

Source: SIPRI arms transfers database.

Table 7A.2. The suppliers of major conventional weapons

The list includes all countries with exports of major conventional weapons for 1995–99. The countries are ranked according to the 1995–99 aggregate exports. Figures are trend-indicator values expressed in US $m. at constant (1990) prices.

Rank order								
1995–99	1994–98[a]	Supplier	1995	1996	1997	1998	1999	1995–99
1	1	USA	9 188	9 307	11 433	13 073	10 442	53 443
2	2	Russia	3 339	3 581	2 831	1 752	3 125	14 628
3	3	France	812	1 989	3 389	3 840	1 701	11 731
4	4	UK	1 206	1 520	2 460	1 079	1 078	7 343
5	5	Germany	1 465	1 413	682	1 191	1 334	6 085
6	7	Netherlands	365	397	559	589	329	2 239
7	6	China	837	730	347	219	79	2 212
8	8	Ukraine	176	218	618	607	429	2 048
9	9	Italy	305	384	408	335	533	1 965
10	11	Canada	426	189	172	140	168	1 095
11	12	Israel	212	274	266	162	144	1 058
12	10	Spain	96	83	624	185	43	1 031
13	14	Belarus	24	129	508	58	38	757
14	15	Sweden	186	150	42	117	157	652
15	19	Australia	20	14	317	3	298	652
16	16	Belgium	298	145	89	23	28	583
17	13	Czech Republic	187	161	28	21	124	521
18	17	Moldova	–	–	378	–	–	378
19	20	Switzerland	76	125	65	31	58	355
20	18	Poland	187	49	20	1	51	308
21	23	Slovakia	85	48	49	8	–	190
22	46	Kazakhstan	24	9	–	2	155	190
23	31	Bulgaria	2	17	3	40	89	151
24	21	Norway	54	9	58	2	–	123
25	25	Singapore	2	–	76	42	1	121
26	38	Indonesia	32	–	11	–	66	109
27	29	South Africa	18	33	9	31	14	105
28	26	Greece	–	30	52	21	1	104
29	28	Korea, South	25	20	27	30	–	102
30	24	Brazil	40	28	28	3	–	99
31	33	Hungary	6	57	24	–	–	87
32	34	Georgia	86	–	–	–	–	86
33	35	Kuwait	–	–	–	84	–	84
34	41	Austria	5	14	5	12	37	73
35	27	Korea, North	48	22	–	–	–	70
36	37	UAE	27	4	38	–	–	69
37	39	Kyrgyzstan	61	–	–	–	–	61
38	56	Turkey	–	–	–	3	46	49
39	43	Finland	22	2	1	7	16	48
40	45	Cyprus	–	43	–	–	–	43
41	44	Romania	7	4	8	2	19	40
42	32	Qatar	–	–	37	–	–	37
43	47	Chile	–	30	–	2	3	35
44	30	Unknown[b]	1	14	16	–	–	31
45	42	Japan	16	11	3	–	–	30
46	40	Egypt	16	9	5	–	–	30
47	49	Estonia	–	14	–	–	–	14
48	48	New Zealand	–	–	13	–	–	13

Rank order

1995 –99	1994[a] –98	Supplier	1995	1996	1997	1998	1999	1995–99
49	52	Taiwan	–	2	5	–	–	7
50	53	Nicaragua	6	–	–	–	–	6
51	36	Jordan	–	–	5	–	–	5
52	54	Iran	2	1	1	–	–	4
53	55	India	3	–	–	–	–	3
54	22	Denmark	–	3	–	–	–	3
55	51	Argentina	3	–	–	–	–	3
56	57	Yugoslavia (FRY)	–	–	2	–	–	2
57	58	Saudi Arabia	–	2	–	–	–	2
58	60	Libya	–	–	2	–	–	2
59	59	Pakistan	–	1	–	–	–	1
60	62	Syria	–	–	–	–	–	< 0.5
61	61	Oman	–	–	–	–	–	< 0.5
62	63	Malaysia	–	–	–	–	–	< 0.5
63	50	Latvia	–	–	–	–	–	< 0.5
64	64	Cambodia	–	–	–	–	–	< 0.5
		Total	**19 994**	**21 292**	**25 715**	**23 718**	**20 606**	**111 325**

[a] The rank order for suppliers in 1994–98 differs from that published in the *SIPRI Yearbook 1999* (p. 424) because of the subsequent revision of figures for these years.

[b] One or more unknown supplier(s).

Notes: '–' = between 0 and 0.5. Totals and figures for 1995–99 may not add up because of rounding.

The SIPRI data on arms transfers refer to actual deliveries of major conventional weapons. To permit comparison between the data on such deliveries of different weapons and identification of general trends, SIPRI uses a *trend-indicator value*. The SIPRI values are therefore only an indicator of the volume of international arms transfers and not of the actual financial values of such transfers. Thus they are not comparable to economic statistics such as gross domestic product or export/import figures.

Source: SIPRI arms transfers database.

Appendix 7B. The volume of transfers of major conventional weapons: by regions and other groups of recipients and suppliers, 1990–99

BJÖRN HAGELIN, PIETER D. WEZEMAN and
SIEMON T. WEZEMAN

Table 7B.1. Volume of imports of major conventional weapons

Figures are SIPRI trend-indicator values expressed in US $m. at constant (1990) prices. Regional and group figures include transfers between countries/non-state actors in the same region or organization, unless otherwise noted.

	1990	1991	1992	1993	1994	1995	1996	1997	1998	1999
World total	28 097	24 336	21 128	22 684	19 693	19 994	21 292	25 715	23 718	20 606
Internat. organizations	–	–	–	4	37	8	–	–	50	8
Unknown	–	–	–	1	63	2	14	15	–	–
Africa	1 359	1 308	393	311	564	570	449	569	759	133
Sub-Saharan	570	233	301	184	253	116	239	366	656	133
Americas	1 425	2 089	1 171	1 245	1 969	1 578	1 579	2 287	1 171	1 180
North	369	1 020	567	775	1 108	548	513	725	162	144
Central	325	165	6	16	–	3	10	12	9	62
South	700	883	577	331	735	983	999	1 357	604	961
Asia	9 931	7 392	5 517	6 037	5 671	8 430	8 727	11 718	9 132	9 365
Central Asia	. .	. .	–	–	24	162	229	166	–	259
North-East Asia	3 349	3 100	3 473	3 672	2 118	4 104	4 595	7 144	6 753	5 884
South-East Asia	1 190	996	717	987	2 187	2 754	2 166	2 174	1 213	1 660
South Asia	3 211	1 920	1 329	1 378	1 341	1 411	1 740	2 231	1 168	1 561
Europe	7 616	6 458	6 797	5 432	4 526	3 137	3 417	3 910	4 456	3 904
Middle East	7 408	6 862	6 832	9 171	6 624	6 138	6 943	6 845	7 992	5 340
Oceania	357	190	377	443	301	127	171	384	154	678
Rebel groups	19	29	1	1	197	2	7	1	. .	. .
ASEAN	862	822	662	685	2 123	2 530	2 043	2 159	1 208	1 658
CSCE/OSCE	8 884	8 256	8 715	8 217	6 960	5 217	5 253	5 692	6 460	5 425
CIS	. .	. .	100	60	360	218	333	174	73	319
CIS Europe	. .	. .	100	60	336	56	104	8	73	60
EU	3 127	4 700	5 309	3 067	3 203	2 192	2 202	2 936	3 615	2 686
EU from non-EU	2 599	3 444	4 174	1 943	1 921	1 348	1 498	1 911	2 522	2 017
GCC	3 611	2 133	2 421	3 953	1 864	2 317	4 153	4 764	4 071	2 069
NATO	4 796	6 815	7 493	6 029	5 679	3 921	3 427	3 966	4 797	3 156
NATO Europe	4 428	5 794	6 925	5 253	4 572	3 373	2 916	3 242	4 634	3 069
OECD	6 960	8 935	10 064	8 471	7 243	5 325	6 727	7 165	9 005	7 724
P5	1 408	2 563	3 018	1 716	846	955	1 697	1 482	811	2 059
WEU	3 008	4 575	5 272	3 036	3 096	1 775	1 522	2 018	2 432	1 571

Note: Tables 7B.1 and 7B.2 show the volume of arms transfers for different geographical regions and subregions, selected groups of countries, rebel groups and international organizations. Countries/rebel groups can belong to only one region. As many countries are included in more than one group or organization, totals cannot be derived from these figures. Countries are included in the values for the different international organizations from the year of joining. Figures may not necessarily add up to totals because of rounding. The following countries/rebel groups are included in each region or group.

Table 7B.2. Volume of exports of major conventional weapons

Figures are SIPRI trend-indicator values expressed in US $m. at constant (1990) prices. Regional and group figures include transfers between countries/non-state actors in the same region or organization, unless otherwise noted.

	1990	1991	1992	1993	1994	1995	1996	1997	1998	1999
World total	28 097	24 336	21 128	22 684	19 693	19 994	21 292	25 715	23 718	20 606
Internat. organizations	–	–	–	–	–	–	–	–	–	–
Unknown	–	38	38	41	3	4	–	–	1	1
Africa	43	51	94	54	10	18	33	11	31	14
Sub-Saharan	8	51	94	54	10	18	33	9	31	14
Americas	8 694	10 416	12 681	11 991	9 962	9 662	9 553	11 632	13 218	10 613
North	8 619	10 325	12 533	11 927	9 919	9 614	9 495	11 604	13 214	10 610
Central	6	1	85	23	–	6	–	–	–	–
South	69	90	62	41	43	43	58	28	5	3
Asia	1 184	1 126	854	1 388	846	1 048	794	470	293	302
Central Asia	. .	. .	–	–	–	85	9	–	2	155
North-East Asia	1 087	1 124	845	1 361	810	926	785	382	249	79
South-East Asia	4	1	8	23	32	34	–	87	42	1
South Asia	93	2	–	3	3	3	1	–	–	–
Europe	17 939	12 545	7 336	8 961	8 530	8 987	10 586	12 901	9 921	9 192
Middle East	95	119	154	265	261	256	290	352	248	190
Oceania	141	81	7	24	23	20	14	330	3	298
Rebel groups	–	1	1	–	–	–	–	–	–	–
ASEAN	4	1	8	23	32	34	–	87	42	67
CSCE/OSCE	26 558	22 792	19 870	20 888	18 449	18 686	20 090	24 506	23 140	20 003
CIS	. .	. .	2 785	3 559	1 602	3 710	3 937	4 335	2 419	3 747
CIS Europe	. .	. .	2 785	3 559	1 602	3 625	3 928	4 335	2 417	3 592
EU	5 724	5 333	3 739	4 584	5 928	4 759	6 131	8 310	7 400	5 257
EU to non-EU	5 196	4 077	2 604	3 460	4 646	3 915	5 427	7 285	6 307	4 588
GCC	2	28	–	62	52	27	6	75	84	–
NATO	14 369	15 806	16 277	16 609	16 033	14 214	15 468	19 925	20 482	15 878
NATO Europe	5 749	5 483	3 744	4 681	6 114	4 601	5 973	8 321	7 268	5 268
OECD	15 122	16 423	16 787	16 900	16 285	14 538	16 023	20 449	20 702	16 393
P5	22 395	18 854	17 308	18 463	13 687	15 382	17 127	20 460	19 963	16 425
WEU	5 620	5 324	3 739	4 435	5 698	4 547	5 961	8 263	7 263	5 047

International organizations: NATO and the United Nations as non-state actors—not as combinations of all member states.

Africa: Algeria, Angola, Benin, Botswana, Burkina Faso, Burundi, Cameroon, Cape Verde, Central African Republic, Chad, Comoros, Congo (Rep. of), Congo (DRC), Côte d'Ivoire, Djibouti, Equatorial Guinea, Eritrea, Ethiopia, Gabon, Gambia, Ghana, Guinea, Guinea-Bissau, Kenya, Lesotho, Liberia, Libya, Madagascar, Malawi, Mali, Mauritania, Mauritius, Morocco, Mozambique, Namibia, Niger,

Nigeria, Rwanda, Sao Tomé and Principe, Senegal, Seychelles, Sierra Leone, Somalia, South Africa, Sudan, Swaziland, Tanzania, Togo, Tunisia, Uganda, Zambia, Zimbabwe, Union for the Total Independence of Angola (UNITA, Angola)

Sub-Saharan Africa: Angola, Benin, Botswana, Burkina Faso, Burundi, Cameroon, Cape Verde, Central African Republic, Chad, Comoros, Congo (Rep. of), Congo (DRC), Côte d'Ivoire, Djibouti, Equatorial Guinea, Eritrea, Ethiopia, Gabon, Gambia, Ghana, Guinea, Guinea-Bissau, Kenya, Lesotho, Liberia, Madagascar, Malawi, Mali, Mauritania, Mauritius, Mozambique, Namibia, Niger, Nigeria, Rwanda, Sao Tomé and Principe, Senegal, Seychelles, Sierra Leone, Somalia, South Africa, Sudan, Swaziland, Tanzania, Togo, Uganda, Zambia, Zimbabwe, Union for the Total Independence of Angola (UNITA, Angola)

Americas: Argentina, Bahamas, Barbados, Belize, Bolivia, Brazil, Canada, Chile, Colombia, Costa Rica, Cuba, Dominica, Dominican Republic, Ecuador, El Salvador, Grenada, Guatemala, Guyana, Haiti, Honduras, Jamaica, Mexico, Nicaragua, Panama, Paraguay, Peru, St Vincent & the Grenadines, Suriname, Trinidad & Tobago, Uruguay, USA, Venezuela, Farabundo Marti National Liberation Front (FMLN, El Salvador)

North America: Canada, USA

Central America: Bahamas, Barbados, Belize, Costa Rica, Cuba, Dominica, Dominican Republic, El Salvador, Grenada, Guatemala, Haiti, Honduras, Jamaica, Mexico, Nicaragua, Panama, St Vincent & the Grenadines, Trinidad & Tobago, Farabundo Marti National Liberation Front (FMLN, El Salvador)

South America: Argentina, Bolivia, Brazil, Chile, Colombia, Ecuador, Guyana, Paraguay, Peru, Suriname, Uruguay, Venezuela

Asia: Afghanistan, Bangladesh, Bhutan, Brunei, Cambodia, China, India, Indonesia, Japan, Kazakhstan (1992–), North Korea, South Korea, Kyrgyzstan (1992–), Laos, Malaysia, Maldives, Mongolia, Myanmar (Burma), Nepal, Pakistan, Philippines, Singapore, Sri Lanka, Taiwan, Tajikistan (1992–), Thailand, Turkmenistan (1992–), Uzbekistan (1992–), Viet Nam, Khmer Rouge (Cambodia), Liberation Tigers of Tamil Eelam (LTTE, Sri Lanka), Mujahideen (Afghanistan)

Central Asia: Kazakhstan (1992–), Kyrgyzstan (1992–), Tajikistan (1992–), Turkmenistan (1992–), Uzbekistan (1992–)

North-East Asia: China, Japan, North Korea, South Korea, Taiwan

South-East Asia: Brunei, Cambodia, Indonesia, Laos, Malaysia, Myanmar, Philippines, Singapore, Thailand, Viet Nam, Khmer Rouge (Cambodia)

South Asia: Bangladesh, Bhutan, India, Maldives, Nepal, Pakistan, Sri Lanka, Liberation Tigers of Tamil Eelam (LTTE, Sri Lanka)

Europe: Albania, Armenia (1992–), Austria, Azerbaijan (1992–), Belarus (1992–), Belgium, Bosnia and Herzegovina (1992–), Bulgaria, Croatia (1992–), Cyprus, Czechoslovakia (–1992), Czech Republic (1993–), Denmark, Estonia (1991–), Finland, France, Georgia (1992–), German DR (–1990), Germany, Greece, Hungary, Iceland, Ireland, Italy, Latvia (1991–), Liechtenstein, Lithuania (1991–), Luxembourg, Macedonia (1992–), Malta, Moldova (1992–), Monaco, Netherlands, Norway, Poland, Portugal, Romania, Russia (1992–), Slovakia (1993–), Slovenia (1992–), Spain, Sweden, Switzerland, UK, Ukraine (1992–), USSR (–1991), Yugoslavia (Former, –1991), Yugoslavia (FRY, 1992–)

Middle East: Bahrain, Egypt, Iran, Iraq, Israel, Jordan, Kuwait, Lebanon, Oman, Palestinian Authority), Qatar, Saudi Arabia, Syria, United Arab Emirates, North Yemen (–1990), Turkey, South Yemen (–1990), Yemen (1991–), Hizbollah (Lebanon), Kurdish Workers' Party (PKK, Turkey), Lebanese Forces (LF, Lebanon), South Lebanese Army (SLA, Lebanon), Southern Rebels (Yemen)

Oceania: Australia, Fiji, Kiribati, Marshall Islands, Micronesia, New Zealand, Palau, Papua New Guinea, Samoa, Solomon Islands, Tonga, Tuvalu, Vanuatu

Rebel groups (only those rebel groups which had imports/exports in the period 1990–99 are listed): Farabundo Marti National Liberation Front (FMLN, El Salvador), Hizbollah (Lebanon), Khmer Rouge (Cambodia), Kurdish Workers' Party (PKK, Turkey), Lebanese Forces (LF, Lebanon), Liberation Tigers of Tamil Eelam (LTTE, Sri Lanka), Mujahideen (Afghanistan), South Lebanese Army (SLA, Lebanon), Southern Rebels (Yemen), Union for the Total Independence of Angola (UNITA, Angola)

Association of South-East Asian Nations (ASEAN): Brunei, Indonesia, Laos (1997–), Malaysia, Myanmar (Burma, 1997–), Philippines, Singapore, Thailand, Viet Nam (1995–)

Conference on Security and Co-operation in Europe (CSCE)/Organization for Security and Co-operation in Europe (OSCE): Albania (1991–), Andorra, Armenia (1992–), Austria, Azerbaijan (1992–), Belarus (1992–), Belgium, Bosnia and Herzegovina (1992–), Bulgaria, Canada, Croatia (1992–), Cyprus, Czechoslovakia (–1992), Czech Republic (1993–), Denmark, Estonia (1991–), Finland, France, Georgia (1992–), German DR (–1990), Germany, Greece, Holy See, Hungary, Iceland, Ireland, Italy, Kazakhstan (1992–), Kyrgyzstan (1992–), Latvia (1991–), Liechtenstein, Lithuania (1991–), Luxembourg, Macedonia (1995–), Malta, Moldova (1992–), Monaco, Netherlands, Norway, Poland, Portugal, Romania, Russia (1992–), San Marino, Slovakia (1992–), Slovenia (1992–), Spain, Sweden, Switzerland, Tajikistan (1992–), Turkey, Turkmenistan (1992–), UK, Ukraine (1992–), USA, USSR (–1992), Uzbekistan (1992–), Yugoslavia (Former, –1991), Yugoslavia (FRY, suspended since 1992)

Commonwealth of Independent States (CIS): Armenia, Azerbaijan, Belarus, Georgia (1993–), Kazakhstan, Kyrgyzstan, Moldova, Russia, Tajikistan, Turkmenistan, Ukraine, Uzbekistan

Commonwealth of Independent States (CIS) Europe: Armenia, Azerbaijan, Belarus, Georgia (1993–), Moldova, Russia, Ukraine

European Union (EU): Austria (1995–), Belgium, Denmark, Finland (1995–), France, Germany, Greece, Ireland, Italy, Luxembourg, Netherlands, Portugal, Spain, Sweden (1995–), UK

GCC (Gulf Co-operation Council): Bahrain, Kuwait, Oman, Qatar, Saudi Arabia, United Arab Emirates

NATO: Belgium, Canada, Czech Republic (1999–), Denmark, France, Germany, Greece, Hungary (1999–), Iceland, Italy, Luxembourg, Netherlands, Norway, Poland (1999–), Portugal, Spain, Turkey, UK, USA

NATO Europe: Belgium, Czech Republic (1999–), Denmark, France, Germany, Greece, Hungary (1999–), Iceland, Italy, Luxembourg, Netherlands, Norway, Poland (1999–), Portugal, Spain, Turkey, UK

P5 (5 Permanent members of the UN Security Council): China, France, Russia (1992–)/USSR (–1992), UK, USA

Organisation for Economic Co-operation and Development (OECD): Australia, Austria, Belgium, Canada, Czech Rep. (1995–), Denmark, Finland, France, Germany, Greece, Hungary (1996–), Iceland, Ireland, Italy, Japan, South Korea (1996–), Luxembourg, Mexico (1994–), Netherlands, New Zealand, Norway, Poland (1996–), Portugal, Spain, Sweden, Switzerland, Turkey, UK, USA

Western European Union (WEU): Belgium, France, Germany, Greece, Italy, Luxembourg, Netherlands, Portugal, Spain, UK

Appendix 7C. Register of the transfers and licensed production of major conventional weapons, 1999

BJÖRN HAGELIN, PIETER D. WEZEMAN and SIEMON T. WEZEMAN

The register in table 7C.1 lists major weapons on order or under delivery, or for which the licence was bought and production was under way or completed during 1999. Sources and methods for the data collection are explained in appendix 7D. Entries in table 7C.1 are alphabetical, by recipient, supplier and licenser. 'Year(s) of deliveries' includes aggregates of all deliveries and licensed production since the beginning of the contract. 'Deal worth' values in the comments refer to real monetary values as reported in sources and not to SIPRI trend-indicator values. Conventions, abbreviations and acronyms are explained at the end of the table. For cross-reference, an index of recipients and licensees for each supplier can be found in table 7C.2.

Table 7C.1. Register of transfers and licenced production of major conventional weapons, 1999, by recipients

Recipient/ supplier (S) or licenser (L)	No. ordered	Weapon designation	Weapon description	Year of order/ licence	Year(s) of deliveries	No. delivered/ produced	Comments
Algeria							
S: Belarus	(36)	MiG-29 Fulcrum-A	Fighter aircraft	(1998)		..	Ex-Belorussian Air Force; no. ordered could be 28 from Belarus and 8 MiG-29UB trainer version from Russia via Belarus
Russia	3	Su-24 Fencer	Bomber aircraft	(1999)		..	Ex-Russian Air Force; probably refurbished before delivery
	6	SS-N-25 ShShMS	ShShM system	1998		..	Probably for refit of 3 Koni Class frigates and 3 Nanuchka Class corvettes
	(96)	SS-N-25/X-35 Uran	ShShM	1998		..	Probably for 3 refitted Koni Class frigates and 3 refitted Nanuchka Class corvettes
L: UK	3	Kebir Class	Patrol craft	(1990)	1997–98	2	Algerian designation El Yadekh Class

Argentina

No.	Weapon designation	Weapon description	Year of order	Year of delivery	No. delivered	Comments
S: France						
1	Durance Class	Support ship	1999	1999	1	Ex-French Navy; Argentine designation Patagonia Class
Italy						
20	Palmaria 155mm turret	Artillery turret	(1985)	1996–99	(18)	Turret for Argentine TAMSE VCA-155 self-propelled gun; turrets delivered 1986–87 but production of VCA-155 delayed
(16)	RAT-31S/L	Surveillance radar	1999		..	Part of $185 m deal with US company for civilian and military air surveillance system
Netherlands						
6	DA-05	Surveillance radar	(1979)	1985–90	(4)	For 6 MEKO-140 Type (Espora Class) frigates; status of last 2 uncertain
6	WM-28	Fire control radar	(1979)	1985–90	(4)	For 6 MEKO-140 Type (Espora Class) frigates; status of last 2 uncertain
USA						
36	A-4M Skyhawk-2	FGA aircraft	1994	1997–99	(36)	Ex-US Marines; deal worth $282 m; incl 8 refurbished before delivery and 28 refurbished in Argentina with US-supplied kits; Argentine designation A-4AR Fightinghawk; incl 4 refurbished to TA-4AR trainer version
16	Bell-205/UH-1H	Helicopter	1996	1997–99	(10)	Ex-US Army; EDA aid; incl 8 for Navy; delivery 1997–2000
6	P-3B Orion	ASW/MP aircraft	1996	1998–99	6	Ex-US Navy; EDA aid; for Navy; 1 or 2 more delivered for spares only
L: Germany (FRG)						
6	MEKO-140 Type	Frigate	1979	1985–90	4	Argentine designation Espora Class; last 2 delayed for financial reasons, their status uncertain

Australia

No.	Weapon designation	Weapon description	Year of order	Year of delivery	No. delivered	Comments
S: Canada						
2	DHC-8 Dash-8-200	Transport aircraft	1999		..	Deal worth $25 m; for Coast Guard; delivery 2000
63	Piranha 8x8	APC	1998		..	Incl 5 ambulance, 16 APC/CP, 18 radar reconnaissance and 11 repair version; Australian designation ASLAV-PC/A/C/S/F; assembled in Australia; delivery 2001–2005
5	Piranha/LAV(R)	ARV	1998		..	Australian designation ASLAV-R; assembled in Australia; delivery 2001–2005

Recipient/ supplier (S) or licenser (L)	No. ordered	Weapon designation	Weapon description	Year of order/ licence	Year(s) of deliveries	No. delivered/ produced	Comments
	82	Piranha/LAV-25	IFV	1998		..	Australian designation ASLAV-25; assembled in Australia; delivery 2001–2005
Norway	(60)	Penguin Mk-2-7	Air-to-ship missile	1998		..	Deal worth $46–49 m; for Navy SH-2G helicopters; delivery 2001–2002
	..	Penguin Mk-2-7	Air-to-ship missile	1999		..	Deal worth $49 m; for Navy SH-2G helicopters; delivery after 2001/2002
Sweden	8	9LV	Fire control radar	(1991)	1996–98	(2)	For 8 MEKO-200ANZ Type (Anzac Class) frigates
	8	Sea Giraffe-150	Surveillance radar	1991	1996–98	(2)	For 8 MEKO-200ANZ Type (Anzac Class) frigates
UK	12	Hawk-100	FGA/trainer aircraft	1997		..	Deal worth $640 m incl 21 licensed production; UK export designation Hawk-127; delivery 2000
	6	MSTAR	Battlefield radar	1999		..	Deal worth $32 m incl licensed production of 55; Australian designation Amstar
	(420)	ASRAAM	Air-to-air missile	1998	1999	(2)	For F/A-18 FGA aircraft; deal worth A$100 m; delivery 1999–2002
USA	(7)	Boeing-737 AEW	AEW&C aircraft	1999		..	Deal worth $1.32 b; contract not yet signed; delivery from 2004/2005; Australian project name Wedgetail
	12	C-130J-30 Hercules	Transport aircraft	1995	1999	(7)	Deal worth $670 m; option on 12 more
	2	CH-47D Chinook	Helicopter	1998	1999	(1)	Deal worth $45 m; delivery 1999/2000
	3	P-3B Orion	ASW/MP aircraft	1994	1995–99	3	Ex-US Navy; modified in Australia to TAP-3 for training; 1 more delivered for spares only
	11	SH-2G Super Seasprite	ASW helicopter	1997		..	Ex-US Navy SH-2Fs rebuilt to SH-2G; for Navy; US export designation SH-2G(A); deal worth $550 m; incl some assembly in Australia; delivery 2001–2002
	8	Mk-45 127mm/54	Naval gun	(1989)	1994–99	(5)	For 8 MEKO-200ANZ Type (Anzac Class) frigates
	8	AN/SPS-49	Surveillance radar	1993	1996–98	(2)	For 8 MEKO-200ANZ Type (Anzac Class) frigates
	4	AN/TPS-117	Surveillance radar	1998		..	Deal worth $68–90 m; assembled in Australia; delivery from 2000
	8	Mk-41	ShAM system	(1991)	1996–98	(2)	For 8 MEKO-200ANZ Type (Anzac Class) frigates

No. ordered	Weapon designation	Weapon description	Year of order	Year(s) of deliveries	No. delivered	Comments
. .	RGM-84 ShShMS	ShShM system	(1999)			For MEKO-200ANZ Type (Anzac Class) frigates
. .	RGM-84A/C Harpoon	ShShM	(1999)			For 8 MEKO-200ANZ Type (Anzac Class) frigates
(48)	RIM-7P Seasparrow	ShAM	(1991)	1996–99	(34)	For 4 MEKO-200ANZ Type (Anzac Class) frigates
(192)	RIM-7PTC ESSM	ShAM	(1998)		. .	For 4 MEKO-200ANZ Type (Anzac Class) frigates; contract not yet signed
6	Mk-41	ShAM system	1999		. .	For refit of 6 Adelaide (Perry) Class frigates; deal worth $37.7 m; delivery 2002–2005
(288)	RIM-7PTC ESSM	ShAM	(1999)		. .	For 6 refitted Adelaide (Perry) Class frigates; contract not yet signed
. .	AIM-120B AMRAAM	Air-to-air missile	(1998)		. .	Final contract not yet signed
51	Popeye-1	ASM	1998		. .	For F-111C/G bomber aircraft; deal worth $90 m; delivery from 2000
L: Germany (FRG)						
8	MEKO-200ANZ Type	Frigate	1989	1996–98	2	Australian designation Anzac Class; delivery 1996–2004; more produced for export
Italy						
6	Gaeta Class	MCM ship	1994	1999	2	Deal worth $636 m; Australian designation Huon Class; delivery 1999–2002
Sweden						
6	Type-471	Submarine	1987	1996–99	3	Deal worth $2.8 b; Australian designation Collins Class; delivery 1996–2001
UK						
21	Hawk-100	FGA/trainer aircraft	1997		. .	Deal worth $640 m incl 12 delivered direct; UK export designation Hawk-127; delivery 2000–2006
55	MSTAR	Battlefield radar	1999		. .	Deal worth $32 m including direct delivery of 6; Australian designation Amstar
Austria						
S: France						
22	RAC	Surveillance radar	1995	1997–99	(22)	Deal worth $129 m (offsets $344 m) incl Mistral missiles
Sweden						
(1 700)	RBS-56 Bill-2	Anti-tank missile	1996	1998–99	(600)	Austrian designation PAL-2000
Bahamas						
S: USA						
2	Bahamas Class	Patrol craft	1997	1999	2	

Recipient/ supplier (S) or licenser (L)	No. ordered	Weapon designation	Weapon description	Year of order/ licence	Year(s) of deliveries	No. delivered/ produced	Comments
Bahrain							
S: USA	10	F-16C/D	FGA aircraft	1998		..	'Peace Crown-2' deal; incl F-16D trainer version; option on more; delivery 2000
	..	AGM-65D Maverick	ASM	1999		..	
	26	AIM-120A AMRAAM	Air-to-air missile	1999		..	Deal worth $110 m
Bangladesh							
S: China	4	FT-7	Fighter/trainer ac	(1996)	1999	3	
Korea, South	1	Daewoo 2300t Type	Frigate	1998	1999	..	Deal worth $100 m; delivery 2001
Russia	3	Mi-17 Hip-H	Helicopter	(1998)	1999	3	Deal worth $4 m and trade-in of 7 ex-Bangladeshi Mi-8 helicopters
	8	MiG-29S Fulcrum-C	FGA aircraft	1999	1999	(2)	Deal worth $124 m; incl 2 MiG-29UB trainer version; delivery 1999–2000
	(48)	AA-10a/b Alamo/R-27	Air-to-air missile	1999	1999	(12)	For 8 MiG-29S FGA aircraft
	(96)	AA-11 Archer/R-73	Air-to-air missile	1999	1999	(24)	For 8 MiG-29S FGA aircraft
Belgium							
S: USA	(10)	AGM-65G Maverick	ASM	1999	1999	(10)	For use against Yugoslavia in 1999 war over Kosovo; loan
	72	AIM-120B AMRAAM	Air-to-air missile	1995	1998–99	(72)	For F-16AM/BM FGA aircraft
L: Austria	54	Pandur	APC	1997	1998–99	(54)	Incl 5 APC/CP, 4 ARV and 4 ambulance version; deal worth $42 m (offsets 100%)
Bosnia and Herzegovina							
S: USA	15	Bell-205/UH-1H	Helicopter	1996	1999	15	Ex-US Army; 'Train and Equip Program' aid; incl 2 UH-1V version

Botswana

No. ordered	Designation	Description	Year of order	Year of deliveries	No. delivered/produced	Comments
S: Austria (20)	SK-105A1 Kurassier	Tank destroyer (G)	1997	1999	20	Option on 30 more
UK (18)	L-118 105mm	Towed gun	(1997)	1999	(18)	Ex-UK Army

Brazil

No. ordered	Designation	Description	Year of order	Year of deliveries	No. delivered/produced	Comments
S: Belgium 87	Leopard-1A1	Main battle tank	1995	1997–99	(87)	Ex-Belgian Army
France 8	AS-532U2/AS-332L2	Helicopter	1999	1999	..	Deal worth $90.5 m; for Army; delivery 2000–2001
5	F-406 Caravan-2	Light transport ac	1998	1999	(2)	Deal worth $25.6 m; incl 1 for maritime patrol; delivery 1999–2000
(4)	Mirage-3E	Fighter aircraft	1996	1997–99	(4)	Probably ex-French Air Force aircraft sold back to producer, refurbished and sold to Brazil; probably incl 2 Mirage-3D trainer version
Germany (FRG) 2	Grajau Class	Patrol craft	1998	1999	(1)	Delivery 1999–2000
Italy 6	Albatros Mk-2	ShAM system	1995	1999	(1)	For refit of 6 Niteroi Class frigates; deal worth $111.5 m incl 13 RTN-30X and 7 RAN-20S radars; delivery 1999–2001
(144)	Aspide Mk-1	ShAM	1996	1999	(24)	For 6 refitted Niteroi Class frigates; deal worth $48.5 m; delivery 1999–2001
13	Orion RTN-30X	Fire control radar	1995	1999	(3)	For refit of 6 Niteroi Class frigates; deal worth $111.5 m incl 7 RAN-20S radars and 6 Albatros ShAM systems; probably 1 for training; delivery 1999–2001
7	RAN-20S	Surveillance radar	1995	1999	(1)	For refit of 6 Niteroi Class frigates; deal worth $111.5 m incl 13 RTN-30X radars and 6 Albatros ShAM systems; delivery 1999–2001
Sweden 5	Erieye	AEW radar	(1994)	1999	(1)	Deal worth $143 m; for 5 ERJ-145SA/R-99A AEW aircraft; delivery 1999–2002
USA 9	P-3A Orion	ASW/MP aircraft	1999		..	Ex-US Navy; refurbished before delivery; 3 more ordered for spares only; delivery 2002
6	AN/TPS-34	Surveillance radar	1997	1999	(1)	For SIVAM air surveillance network; US export designation TPS-B-34
20	RGM-84A/C Harpoon	ShShM	(1999)		..	FMS deal worth $39 m; could be AGM-84 version

Recipient/ supplier (S) or licenser (L)	No. ordered	Weapon designation	Weapon description	Year of order/ licence	Year(s) of deliveries	No. delivered/ produced	Comments
L: Germany (FRG)	1	SNAC-1	Submarine	1995		..	Brazilian designation Tikuna Class; delivery 2004
	3	Type-209/1400	Submarine	1984	1994–99	3	Brazilian designation Tupi Class
Singapore	2	Grajau Class	Patrol craft	1996	1999	(2)	
Brunei							
S: France	3	MM-38/40 ShShMS	ShShM system	(1998)		..	For 3 Yarrow-95m Type frigates
	(48)	MM-40 Exocet	ShShM	(1998)		..	For 3 Yarrow-95m Type frigates
	..	Mistral	Portable SAM	1998		..	Deal worth $30 m
Indonesia	3	CN-235MPA	MP aircraft	(1995)		..	For 3 Yarrow-95m Type frigates
Netherlands	3	Goalkeeper	CIWS	(1997)		..	For 3 Yarrow-95m Type frigates
UK	3	Yarrow-95m Type	Frigate	1998		..	Delivery from 2002
	3	AWS-9	Surveillance radar	(1998)		..	On 3 Yarrow-95m Type frigates
	3	Seawolf GWS-26	ShAM system	(1998)		..	On 3 Yarrow-95m Type frigates
	6	ST-1802SW	Fire control radar	(1998)		..	On 3 Yarrow-95m Type frigates; part of Seawolf ShAM system
	(72)	Seawolf VL	ShAM	(1998)		..	For 3 Yarrow-95m Type frigates
Bulgaria							
S: Canada	6	Bell-206B JetRanger-3	Helicopter	1999	1999	6	Deal worth $8.4 m
Italy	30	M-113A1	APC	(1998)	1999	(30)	Ex-Italian Army; aid
Cambodia							
S: Czech Republic	6	L-39Z Albatros	Jet trainer aircraft	(1994)	1997–99	(6)	Ex-Czech Air Force; deal worth $3.6 m incl refurbishment and training in Israel
Canada							
S: France	1 600	Eryx	Anti-tank missile	1996	1998–99	(1 600)	Deal worth $17 m

	No.	Weapon designation	Weapon description	Year of order	Year of delivery	No. delivered	Comments
Germany (FRG)	121	Leopard-1A5 turret	Tank turret	1996	1999	(20)	Ex-FRG Army; deal worth $105 m; refurbished before delivery; for refurbishment of 114 Canadian Leopard-1 tanks; 2 more delivered for spares only; turrets delivered 1997–98
Italy	15	EH-101-500	Helicopter	1998		..	Deal worth $404 m (offsets 110%); for SAR; Canadian designation AW-520 Cormorant; delivery 2001–2002
South Africa	2	RG-31 Nyala	APC	1999	1999	2	For use in Kosovo
UK	18	Hawk-100	FGA/trainer aircraft	1997		..	Deal worth $574 m; for civilian company for training of pilots from Canadian and other NATO air forces under NATO Flying Training in Canada (NFTC) programme; option on 5 or 6 more; UK export designation Hawk Mk-115; delivery 2000/2001
	4	Upholder class	Submarine	1998		..	Lease worth $504 m; in exchange for UK use of Canadian bases for training for 8 years; Canadian designation Victoria Class; delivery 2000–2001
USA	24	PC-9/T-6A Texan-2	Trainer aircraft	1997		..	For civilian company for training of pilots from Canadian and other NATO air forces under NFTC programme; US export designation T-6A-1; delivery 2000
	..	AGM-65G Maverick	ASM	(1999)		..	FMS deal
	12	AGM-84A/C Harpoon	Air-to-ship missile	1998	1998–99	(12)	Deal worth $20 m
L: Switzerland	240	Piranha-3 8x8	IFV	1997	1998–99	(160)	Deal worth $358 m; Canadian designation Kodiak; delivery 1998–2000
	120	Piranha-3 8x8	IFV	1998		..	Deal worth $163 m; Canadian designation Kodiak; delivery 2000
	120	Piranha-3 8x8	IFV	1999		..	Canadian designation Kodiak; deal worth $169 m; delivery probably 2001
	171	Piranha-3 8x8	IFV	(1999)		..	Canadian designation Kodiak; incl 71 tank-destroyer, 39 AEV and 47 artillery fire control version; delivery probably 2001–2002

Recipient/ supplier (S) or licenser (L)	No. ordered	Weapon designation	Weapon description	Year of order/ licence	Year(s) of deliveries	No. delivered/ produced	Comments
Chile							
S: France	(29)	AMX-30B2	Main battle tank	1998	1998–99	(29)	Ex-French Army
	1	Scorpene Class	Submarine	1997		..	Deal worth $400 m incl 1 from Spain; Chilean designation Hyatt Class; delivery of both 2004–2006/7
Israel	(2)	Phalcon	AEW&C aircraft	(1989)	1995	1	Chilean designation Condor; status of second uncertain
Italy	128	M-113A2	APC	(1996)	1998–99	(128)	Ex-Italian Army
Netherlands	200	Leopard-1V	Main battle tank	1998	1998–99	(114)	Ex-Dutch Army; refurbished before delivery; deal worth $46 m; delivery 1999–2000
	8	M-113C&R	Recce vehicle	1998		..	Ex-Dutch Army
Spain	1	Scorpene Class	Submarine	1997		..	Deal worth $400 m incl 1 from France; Chilean designation Hyatt Class; delivery of both 2004–2006/7
UK	..	Rayo	MRL	1995	1998	1	Assembled in Chile; rockets produced in Chile
L: Switzerland	(120)	Piranha 8x8D	APC	(1991)	1994–99	(90)	No. ordered could be 100
China							
S: France	(11)	Castor-2B	Fire control radar	(1986)	1994–99	(11)	For 2 Luhu Class (Type-052) and 2 Luhai Class, and refit of 2 Luda-1 Class (Type-051) destroyers and 5 Jiangwei-2 Class frigates; probably assembled in China
	(6)	DRBV-15 Sea Tiger	Surveillance radar	1986	1987–99	(6)	For 2 Luhu Class (Type-052) and 2 Luhai Class, and refit of 2 Luda-1 Class (Type-051) destroyers; probably assembled in China
	(15)	Crotale Naval EDIR	ShAM system	1986	1994–99	(11)	For 2 Luhu Class (Type-052) and up to 4 Luhai Class, and refit of 2 Luda-1 Class (Type-051) destroyers and for up to 7 Jiangwei-2 Class frigates;

probably assembled in China; Chinese designation HQ-7

Supplier	No.	Weapon designation	Weapon description	Year of order	Year(s) of deliveries	No. delivered/produced	Comments
	(360)	R-440N Crotale	ShAM	1986	1990–99	(264)	For 2 Luhu Class (Type-052) and up to 4 Luhai Class, and refit of 2 Luda-1 Class (Type-051) destroyers and for up to 7 Jiangwei-2 Class frigates; possibly assembled or produced in China; US/NATO designation of Chinese Crotale CSA-4
Israel	(2)	EL/M-2075 Phalcon	AEW radar	(1997)		..	For modification of 1 Il-76 transport aircraft delivered from Russia or Uzbekistan to A-50I AEW&C aircraft; option on 3–6 more; delivery 2000
Russia	(1)	Il-76M Candid-B	Transport aircraft	(1997)		..	Possibly newly produced aircraft from Uzbekistan sold via Russia; possibly refurbished in Russia before delivery; for modification to A-50I AEW&C aircraft in Israel; option on more; delivery 2000
	(8)	Ka-27PL Helix-A	ASW helicopter	1998	1999	(8)	Incl 4 Ka-28PS SAR version
	(30)	Su-30K Flanker	FGA aircraft	1999	1999	..	Deal worth $2 b; no. ordered could be up to 45; delivery from 2000
	(15)	SA-15/Tor-M1	Mobile SAM system	(1997)	1999	15	For 15 SA-15/TOR-M1 SAM systems
	(240)	SA-15 Gauntlet/9M330	SAM	(1997)	1999	(240)	Delivery 1999–2000
	20	SA-15/Tor-M1	Mobile SAM system	1998	1999	(5)	For 20 SA-15/TOR-M1 SAM systems
	(320)	SA-15 Gauntlet/9M330	SAM	1998	1999	(80)	
	2	Sovremenny Class	Destroyer	1996	1999	1	Originally ordered for Soviet/Russian Navy but cancelled before completion and sold to China; delivery 1999–2000
	2	Top Plate	Surveillance radar	1996	1999	1	On 2 Sovremenny Class destroyers
	4	Bass Tilt	Fire control radar	1996	1999	2	On 2 Sovremenny Class destroyers; for use with AK-630 30mm guns
	2	Kite Screech	Fire control radar	1996	1999	1	On 2 Sovremenny Class destroyers; for use with AK-130 130mm guns
	6	Palm Frond	Surveillance radar	1996	1999	3	On 2 Sovremenny Class destroyers
	4	SA-N-7 ShAMS/Shtil	ShAM system	1996	1999	2	On 2 Sovremenny Class destroyers
	12	Front Dome	Fire control radar	1996	1999	3	On 2 Sovremenny Class destroyers; for use with SA-N-7 ShAMs

Recipient/ supplier (S) or licenser (L)	No. ordered	Weapon designation	Weapon description	Year of order/ licence	Year(s) of deliveries	No. delivered/ produced	Comments
	(132)	SA-N-7 Gadfly/Smerch	ShAM	1996	1999	(66)	For 2 Sovremenny Class destroyers; could be SA-N-12/17
	2	SS-N-22 ShShMS	ShShM system	1996	1999	1	On 2 Sovremenny Class destroyers
	(50)	SS-N-22 Sunburn/P-80	ShShM	1998	1999	(25)	For 2 Sovremenny Class destroyers
	4	AK-130 130mm	Naval gun	1996	1999	2	On 2 Sovremenny Class destroyers
	2	Kilo Class/Type-636E	Submarine	1993	1997–99	2	
UK	(6)	Searchwater	AEW radar	1996		..	Deal worth $62 m; for use on Y-8 MP aircraft or possibly SA-341/Z-8 helicopter; status uncertain
L: France	..	AS-350B Ecureuil	Helicopter	(1992)	1994–99	(6)	Chinese designation Z-11
	..	AS-365N Dauphin-2	Helicopter	1988	1992–99	(13)	Chinese designation Z-9A-100 Haitun and Z-9G; more produced for civilian customers
Israel	..	Python-3	Air-to-air missile	1990	1990–99	(8 000)	Chinese designation PL-8; no. delivered could be much lower or higher
Russia	(200)	Su-27SK Flanker-B	FGA aircraft	1996	1998–99	(8)	Incl some only assembled in China; Chinese designation J-11; delivery 1998–2007/8
Colombia S: USA	6	S-70A/UH-60L	Helicopter	1998	1999	(6)	For Police anti-narcotics operations; aid
	(14)	S-70A/UH-60L	Helicopter	1999		..	FMS deal worth $221 m; contract not yet signed
Croatia S: USA	5	AN/FPS-117	Surveillance radar	1999		..	Deal worth $94 m; delivery 2000
Cyprus S: Russia	1	SA-10d/S-300PMU-1	SAM system	1997	1999	1	Deal worth $420 m incl missiles; originally for use on Cyprus but after international pressure based in Greece (on Crete) under Greek control

No. ordered	Weapon designation	Weapon description	Year of order	Year(s) of deliveries	No. delivered	Comments
(96)	SA-10 Grumble/5V55R	SAM	1997	1999	(96)	Deal worth $420 m incl 1 SA-10d/S-300PMU-1 SAM system; to be based in Greece (on Crete)
6	SA-15/Tor-M1	Mobile SAM system	1999	1999	(6)	Originally ordered by Greece but delivered to Cyprus as replacement for Cypriot SA-10 SAM system stationed in Greece
(102)	SA-15 Gauntlet/9M330	SAM	1999	1999	(102)	For 6 SA-15/Tor-M1 SAM systems

Denmark

S: Canada						
(3)	Challenger-604	Transport aircraft	1998	1999	(3)	For MP, SAR and VIP transport; option on 2 more
Germany (FRG)						
51	Leopard-2A4	Main battle tank	1997	1998–99	(51)	Ex-FRG Army; deal worth $91 m
Norway						
8	Arthur	Tracking radar	1997		..	Deal worth $40 m; delivery from 2000
Switzerland						
22	Piranha-3 8x8	APC	1997	1999	(2)	Incl 18 APC, 2 CP and 2 ARV versions; incl assembly of 20 in Denmark; delivery 1999–2000
USA						
12	M-270 MLRS 227mm	MRL	1996	1998–99	12	Deal worth $146 m
3	Mk-48	ShAM system	(1995)	1998–99	(3)	For refit of 3 Niels Juel Class corvettes

Dominican Republic

S: Chile						
(8)	T-35 Pillan	Trainer aircraft	1998	1999	(8)	Option on 1 more
Spain						
2	C-212-400 Aviocar	Transport aircraft	1999		..	

Ecuador

S: Israel						
2	Kfir C2	FGA aircraft	1998	1999	2	Ex-Israeli Air Force; refurbished before delivery; deal worth $60 m incl refurbishment of some 10 Kfir C2 in Ecuadorean service
(48)	Python-4	Air-to-air missile	(1996)	1999	(24)	Designation uncertain; for 8 Kfir C2 modified to Kfir CE FGA aircraft
USA						
2	Bell-412EP Sentinel	ASW helicopter	(1996)	1998–99	2	For Navy

Egypt

S: China						
80	K-8 Karakorum-8	Jet trainer aircraft	(1999)		..	Deal worth $345 m; Chinese export designation K-8E; contract not yet signed
Finland						
..	155-GH-52-APU	Towed gun	1999		..	Deal worth $21 m; incl assembly in Egypt; final contract not yet signed

Recipient/ supplier (S) or licenser (L)	No. ordered	Weapon designation	Weapon description	Year of order/ licence	Year(s) of deliveries	No. delivered/ produced	Comments
USA	4	CH-47D Chinook	Helicopter	1998	1999	(4)	FMS deal worth $104 m
	21	F-16C/D	FGA aircraft	1996	1999	(11)	'Peace Vector-5' FMS deal; aid; delivery 1999–2000
	24	F-16C/D	FGA aircraft	1999	..	..	Deal worth $1.2 b; incl 12 F-16D version; delivery 2001–2002
	10	SH-2G Super Seasprite	ASW helicopter	1994	1998–99	(10)	FMS deal; ex-US Navy SH-2F rebuilt to SH-2G; US export designation SH-2G(E); option on 10 more
	24	M-109/SP-122 122mm	Self-propelled gun	1999		..	Deal worth $27 m; delivery 2000
	50	M-88A2 Hercules	ARV	1998		..	FMS deal worth $197.9 m; assembled in Egypt
	5	AN/APS-145	AEW radar	(1999)		..	FMS deal worth $138 m; for upgrade of existing Egyptian E-2C AEW&C aircraft; delivery from 2002
	1	Perry Class	Frigate	1998	1999	1	Ex-US Navy; Egyptian designation Mubarak Class
	1	AN/SPS-49	Surveillance radar	1998	1999	1	On 1 ex-US Perry Class frigate
	1	AN/SPS-55	Surveillance radar	1998	1999	1	On 1 ex-US Perry Class frigate
	1	WM-28	Fire control radar	1998	1999	(1)	On 1 ex-US Perry Class frigate; for use with 76mm gun
	1	Mk-13	ShAM system	1998	1999	1	On 1 ex-US Perry Class frigate
	1	AN/SPG-60 STIR	Fire control radar	1998	1999	1	On 1 ex-US Perry Class frigate; for use with Standard ShAM
	(54)	RIM-66B Standard-1MR	ShAM	(1998)	1999	(54)	For 1 Perry (Mubarak) Class frigate
	1	Phalanx Mk-15	CIWS	1998	1999	1	On 1 ex-US Perry Class frigate
	8	I-HAWK SAMS	SAM system	(1996)	1998–99	(3)	Ex-US Army; EDA aid; refurbished for $206 m before delivery
	180	MIM-23B HAWK	SAM	1996	1998–99	(60)	Ex-US Army
	927	AGM-114K Hellfire	Anti-tank missile	1996	1998–99	(927)	Deal worth $45 m; for AH-64A helicopters
	(2 372)	BGM-71D TOW-2	Anti-tank missile	1996	1998–99	(1 500)	Deal worth $59 m
	1 058	FIM-92A Stinger	Portable SAM	1998		..	For 50 Avenger AAV(G/M)s
	42	RGM-84A/C Harpoon	ShShM	1998	1999	(21)	

No. ordered	Weapon designation	Weapon description	Year of order	Year(s) of deliveries	No. delivered	Comments
L: Germany (FRG)						
..	Fahd	APC	1978	1986–99	(680)	Developed for production in Egypt; more produced for export
USA						
100	M-1A1 Abrams	Main battle tank	1999			FMS deal worth $564 m; option on 100 more
..	AIM-9P Sidewinder	Air-to-air missile	(1988)	1989–99	(4 600)	
Estonia						
S: France						
(21)	Rasit	Battlefield radar	1996	1998–99	(21)	
Germany (FRG) 1	Lindau Class	Minesweeper	1999	1999	..	Ex-FRG Navy; gift; delivery 2000
Poland 10	T-55AM-1	Main battle tank	1999	1999	..	Ex-Polish Army; gift; delivery 2000
Ethiopia						
S: Czech Republic						
(4)	L-39C Albatros	Jet trainer aircraft	(1997)			
Russia (2)	Mi-24V/Mi-35 Hind-E	Combat helicopter	1998	1999	(2)	Ex-Russian Air Force; deal worth $150–160 m incl Su-27 fighter aircraft and Mi-8 helicopters
Finland						
S: France						
(510)	Mistral	Portable SAM	(1989)	1990–98	(510)	For Navy; for Sako (modified SADRAL) SAM system on 1 Hamina, and 4 refitted Helsinki and 4 Rauma Class FAC, and 2 Hameenma and 1 refitted Pohjanmaa Class minelayers
Norway 1	Hughes-500/OH-6A	Helicopter	1998	1999	1	Second-hand
Sweden 2	Hughes-500/OH-6A	Helicopter	1998	1999	2	Second-hand
USA 64	F/A-18C/D Hornet	FGA aircraft	1992	1995–99	(55)	Incl 57 assembled in Finland; incl 7 F/A-18D trainer version; delivery 1995–2000
(384)	AIM-120A AMRAAM	Air-to-air missile	1992	1998–99	(214)	For 64 F/A-18C/D FGA aircraft
480	AIM-9S Sidewinder	Air-to-air missile	1992	1996–99	(450)	For 64 F/A-18C/D FGA aircraft
France						
S: Spain						
7	CN-235-100	Transport aircraft	1996	1998–99	(6)	Deal worth $90 m (offsets 100%, incl Spanish order for 15 AS-552UL helicopters); delivery 1998–2000/2001

Recipient/ supplier (S) or licenser (L)	No. ordered	Weapon designation	Weapon description	Year of order/ licence	Year(s) of deliveries	No. delivered/ produced	Comments
Sweden	12	Bv-206S	APC	1999		..	Mainly for use by French peacekeeping forces; deal worth $5.87 m; delivery 2000
USA	2	E-2C Hawkeye	AEW&C aircraft	1995	1998–99	2	For Navy (offsets incl French production of components)
	1	E-2C Hawkeye	AEW&C aircraft	1999		..	For Navy
Georgia							
S: Czech Republic	(120)	T-55AM-1	Main battle tank	1998	1999	(120)	Ex-Czech Army; incl some as payment for repair of Czech Su-25 aircraft in Georgia; incl some T-54 tanks
USA	6	Bell-205/UH-1H	Helicopter	1999		..	Ex-US Army; aid; 4 more for spares only; delivery 2000
Germany (FRG)							
S: France	13	AS-365N Dauphin-2	Helicopter	1997	1999	(3)	For Border Guard; option on 2 more; delivery 1999–2001
Netherlands	3	APAR	Surveillance radar	(1997)		..	For 3 Sachsen Class (Type-124) frigates; delivery 2002–2005
	3	SMART-L	Surveillance radar	(1997)		..	For 3 Sachsen Class (Type-124) frigates; delivery 2002–2005
Sweden	(30)	Bv-206S	APC	(1999)		..	Incl APC/CP and ambulance version; order not yet signed
UK	10	HARD	Surveillance radar	1998		..	For ASRAD SAM systems; delivery 2000–2003
	7	Super Lynx	ASW helicopter	1996	1999	(3)	Deal worth $154 m; UK export designation Lynx Mk-88A; for Navy; delivery 1999–2000
USA	3	Mk-41	ShAM system	1997		..	Deal worth $87 m; for 3 Sachsen Class (F-124 Type) frigates; delivery 2002–2005
	(78)	AGM-88A HARM	Anti-radar missile	(1995)	1998–99	(78)	Deal worth $87 m; for 3 Sachsen Class (F-124 Type) frigates; delivery 2002–2005

Supplier	No. ordered	Weapon designation	Weapon description	Year of order	Year(s) of deliveries	No. delivered	Comments
L: USA	320	AIM-120B AMRAAM	Air-to-air missile	1995	1999	(100)	For refurbished F-4F FGA aircraft; deal worth $170 m
	(1 400)	FIM-92C Stinger	Portable SAM	1986	1998–99	(550)	FRG designation Fliegerfaust-2; part of European Stinger Production Programme involving production of components in FRG, Greece, Netherlands and Turkey and final assembly in FRG; delivery 1998–2001/2
Greece **S: Brazil**	4	EMB-145	Transport aircraft	1999		..	For modification to AEW&C aircraft in Sweden with Erieye radars; option on 2 more; delivery to Greece from 2002
France	4	AS-532UL/AS-332L1	Helicopter	1999		..	For combat SAR; option on 2 more
	15	Mirage-2000-5	FGA aircraft	1999		..	Contract not yet signed
	..	MICA-EM	Air-to-air missile	(1999)		..	For Mirage-2000-5 FGA aircraft; contract not yet signed
	28	VBL	Recce vehicle	1997	1997–99	(28)	Incl for use with Greek forces in Albania
	25	VBL	Recce vehicle	1999		..	
	11	Crotale NG SAMS	SAM system	1999		..	Incl 9 for Air Force and 2 for Navy; deal worth $266 m (incl offsets)
	(176)	VT-1	SAM	1998		..	For 11 Crotale NG SAM systems
	(39)	AM-39 Exocet	Air-to-ship missile	(1997)	1998–99	(39)	For Mirage-2000 FGA aircraft
	170	Leopard-1A5	Main battle tank	1997	1998–99	(170)	Ex-FRG Army; offsets for Greek order for modernization of F-4E FGA aircraft in FRG
Germany (FRG)	5	TRS-3050 Triton-G	Surveillance radar	(1986)	1994–99	(4)	For 5 Jason Class landing ships; probably ex-FRG Navy; refurbished before delivery
	5	TRS-3220 Pollux	Fire control radar	(1986)	1994–99	(4)	For 5 Jason Class landing ships; probably ex-FRG Navy; refurbished before delivery
	(350)	FIM-92C Stinger	Portable SAM	1986	1998–99	(130)	Part of European Stinger Production Programme involving production of components in FRG, Greece, Netherlands and Turkey and final assembly in FRG; delivery 1998–2001/2

Recipient/ supplier (S) or licenser (L)	No. ordered	Weapon designation	Weapon description	Year of order/ licence	Year(s) of deliveries	No. delivered/ produced	Comments
	1	Type-214	Submarine	(1999)		..	Deal worth $919 m incl 2 licensed production; contract not yet signed; delivery 2005; option on 1 more
Italy	1	Etna Class	Support ship	(1999)		..	Deal worth $128 m; may be licensed production
Netherlands	3	LIROD	Fire control radar	(1999)		..	For 3 Super Vita Class FAC
	3	Variant	Surveillance radar	(1999)		..	For 3 Super Vita Class FAC
Russia	2	Pomornik Class	ACV/landing craft	(1999)		..	Deal worth $197 m incl 2 from Ukraine; contract not yet signed; delivery 2001
	2	Bass Tilt	Fire control radar	(1999)		..	On 2 Pomornik Class landing craft; for use with 30mm guns
	2	Cross Dome	Surveillance radar	(1999)		..	On 2 Pomornik Class landing craft
	15	SA-15/Tor-M1	Mobile SAM system	1999	1999	4	Deal worth $519 m (offsets 100%) incl missiles; original order for 21, but 6 diverted from Greece to Cyprus as compensation for Cypriot SA-10 SAM system stationed in Greece; option on 29 more; delivery 1999–2000
	(240)	SA-15 Gauntlet/9M330	SAM	1999	1999	(68)	Deal worth $519 m (offsets 100%) incl 15 SA-15/Tor M-1 SAM systems
Sweden	4	Erieye	AEW radar	1999	1999	..	For modification of 4 EMB-145 transport aircraft delivered from Brazil to AEW&C aircraft; deal worth $476 m; option on 2 more; delivery from 2002
UK	2	Hunt Class	MCM ship	1999		..	Ex-UK Navy; part of order for 3 Super Vita Class FAC
USA	7	CH-47D Chinook	Helicopter	1999		..	FMS deal worth $376 m; for delivery 2001
	40	F-16C/D	FGA aircraft	1993	1997–99	(40)	'Peace Xenia' programme worth $1.8 b; incl 8 F-16D trainer version
	45	PC-9/T-6A Texan-2	Trainer aircraft	1999		..	Deal worth $223 m (offsets 120% in Greek production of parts for 300 PC-9/T-6A); option on 5 more; delivery 2000–2003

Supplier	No.	Weapon designation	Weapon description	Year of order	Year(s) of deliveries	No. delivered	Comments
	12	M-109A5 155mm	Self-propelled gun	1997	1999	(12)	Option on 12 more
	18	M-270 MLRS 227mm	MRL	1998		..	FMS deal worth $54.9 m ($245 m incl 81 MGM-140A ATACMS SSMs, 11 M-577 APC/CPs, ammunition, trucks and radios); delivery 2000
	(2)	AN/TPQ-37	Tracking radar	1996	1999	(2)	Ex-US Army; loan till delivery of new Patriot SAM systems
	3	Patriot SAMS	SAM system	(1998)	1999	(3)	For 3 ex-US Army Patriot SAM systems on loan till delivery of new Patriot SAM systems
	(192)	MIM-104 PAC-2	SAM	(1998)	1999	192	Deal worth $887 m ($1.13 b incl option on 2 more; offsets 120%); delivery 2001–2002
	4	Patriot SAMS	SAM system	1999		..	For 4 Patriot SAM systems
	..	MIM-104 PAC-2	SAM	(1998)		..	
	248	AGM-114K Hellfire	Anti-tank missile	1998		..	FMS deal worth $24 m; for AH-64A helicopters
	100	AIM-120A AMRAAM	Air-to-air missile	(1995)	1998–99	(100)	Deal worth $70 m
	50	AIM-120B AMRAAM	Air-to-air missile	1996		..	For F-16C/D FGA aircraft; deal worth $90 m incl 84 AGM-88B missiles
	40	MGM-140A ATACMS	SSM	1997	1998–99	40	FMS deal
	(30)	MGM-140A ATACMS	SSM	1998		..	FMS deal worth $245 m incl 18 M-270 MRLS MRLs, 11 M-577 APC/CPs, ammunition, trucks and radios; delivery probably 2000
	(51)	MGM-140A ATACMS	SSM	1999		..	FMS deal
Ukraine	(32)	UGM-84A Sub Harpoon	SuShM	(1989)	1993–99	(32)	For 4 refitted Type-209 (Glavkos Class) submarines
	2	Pomornik Class	ACV/landing craft	(1999)		..	Deal worth $197 m incl 2 from Russia; contract not yet signed; delivery 2001
	2	Bass Tilt	Fire control radar	(1999)		..	On 2 Pomornik Class landing craft; for use with 30mm guns
	2	Cross Dome	Surveillance radar	(1999)		..	On 2 Pomornik Class landing craft
L: Denmark							
	4	Osprey-55 Type	Patrol craft	1998		..	Greek designation Pirpolitis Class or Hellenic-56 Type
Germany (FRG)	2	Type-214	Submarine	(1999)		..	Deal worth $919 m incl 1 delivered direct; contract not yet signed; delivery 2005; option on 1 more

Recipient/ supplier (S) or licenser (L)	No. ordered	Weapon designation	Weapon description	Year of order/ licence	Year(s) of deliveries	No. delivered/ produced	Comments
UK	3	Super Vita type	FAC(M)	1999		..	Deal worth $324 m; option on 4 more
Hungary							
S: France	180	Mistral	Portable SAM	1997	1998–99	180	Deal worth $100 m incl 9 SHORAR-2D radars, 45 ATLAS launchers and 54 UNIMOG trucks
Italy	9	SHORAR-2D	Surveillance radar	1997	1999	(9)	Deal worth $100 m incl 180 Mistral missiles, 45 ATLAS launchers and 54 UNIMOG trucks; sold through France
Russia	555	BTR-80	APC	1994	1996–99	(508)	Deal worth $320 m; payment for Russian debt to Hungary; incl 68 for Border Guard; delivery 1996–2000
India							
S: Israel	(56)	EL/M-2129	Artillery radar	1999		..	
	(200)	EL/M-2140	Battlefield radar	1999		..	
	(40)	Harpy	Anti-radar UAV	1997	1999	(20)	
Italy	(6)	Seaguard TMX	Fire control radar	1993	1998	(2)	For 3 Brahmaputra Class (Project-16A Type) frigates; for use with AK-630 30mm CIWS
Netherlands	3	LW-08	Surveillance radar	(1989)	1998	(1)	For 3 Brahmaputra Class (Project-16A Type) frigates; incl assembly in India; Indian designation RALW
	3	LW-08	Surveillance radar	(1996)	1997–99	(2)	For 3 Delhi Class (Project-15 Type) destroyers; incl assembly in India; Indian designation RALW or RAWL-2
	6	ZW-06	Surveillance radar	1990	1997–99	(4)	For 3 Delhi Class (Project-15 Type) destroyers; incl assembly in India; Indian designation Rashmi
	6	ZW-06	Surveillance radar	(1989)	1998	(2)	For 3 Brahmaputra Class (Project-16A Type) frigates
Poland	12	TS-11 Iskra	Jet trainer aircraft	1999	1999	12	Ex-Polish Air Force; deal worth $5.1 m
	43	WZT-3	ARV	1999		..	Deal worth $31.1 m

	No.	Weapon designation	Weapon description	Year of order	Year(s) of deliveries	No. delivered	Comments
Russia	(2)	A-50 Mainstay	AEW&C aircraft	(1999)		...	Lease; possibly ex-Russian Air Force; contract not yet signed
	4	Ka-31 Helix	AEW helicopter	1999		...	For Navy; deal worth $92 m; delivery 2000
	40	Su-30MKI Flanker	FGA aircraft	1996	1997	8	Deal worth $1.55 b; incl 8 Su-30MK version to be modified to Su-30MKI after delivery; delivery 1997–2002
	(360)	AA-10c/d Alamo/R-27E	Air-to-air missile	1996	1997–99	(180)	For Su-30MK/MKI FGA aircraft
	(720)	AA-11 Archer/R-73	Air-to-air missile	(1996)	1997	(144)	For Su-30MK/MKI FGA aircraft
	10	Su-30MK Flanker	FGA aircraft	1998	1999	(4)	Delivery 1999–2000
	(6)	BM-9A52/BM-23	MRL	(1998)		...	Status uncertain
	(24)	2S6M Tunguska	AAV(G/M)	(1996)	1997–99	(24)	No. ordered could be up to 50
	(384)	SA-19 Grison	SAM	(1996)	1997–99	(384)	For 24 2S6 AAV(G/M)s
	(45)	2S6M Tunguska	AAV(G/M)	1998		...	Status uncertain
	(720)	SA-19 Grison	SAM	(1998)		...	For 45 2S6 AAV(G/M)s
	(100)	T-90	Main battle tank	(1999)		...	No. ordered could be up to 315; may incl assembly or licensed production in India; reaction to Pakistani acquisition of 320 T-80UB tanks; status uncertain
	3	Garpun	Fire control radar	(1993)	1998	(1)	For 3 Brahmaputra Class (Project-16A Type) frigates; for use with SS-N-25 ShShM system
	3	SS-N-25 ShShMS	ShShM system	1993	1998	(1)	For 3 Brahmaputra Class (Project-16A Type) frigates
	3	Garpun	Fire control radar	(1993)	1997–99	(2)	For 3 Delhi Class (Project-15 Type) destroyers; for use with SS-N-25 ShShMS
	3	SS-N-25 ShShMS	ShShM system	1992	1997–99	(2)	For 3 Delhi Class (Project-15 Type) destroyers
	3	Krivak-4 Class	Frigate	1997		...	Deal worth Rs35.4 b; delivery possibly delayed from 2001/2002 to 2002/2003 because of financial problems of producer; ordered due to problems with indigenous production of major warships
	3	AK-100 100mm L/59	Naval gun	(1997)		...	On 3 Krivak-4 Class frigates
	3	Cross Sword	Fire control radar	(1997)		...	For 3 Krivak-4 Class frigates; for use with SA-N-9 ShAM system; status uncertain
	3	Garpun	Fire control radar	1997		...	On 3 Krivak-4 Class frigates; for use with SS-N-25 ShShM system
	3	Kite Screech	Fire control radar	1997		...	On 3 Krivak-4 Class frigates; for use with AK-100 100mm gun

Recipient/ supplier (S) or licenser (L)	No. ordered	Weapon designation	Weapon description	Year of order/ licence	Year(s) of deliveries	No. delivered/ produced	Comments
	3	SA-N-9 ShAMS	ShAM system	(1997)		..	On 3 Krivak-4 Class frigates; status uncertain
	..	SA-N-9 Tor-M	ShAM	(1997)		..	For 3 Krivak-4 Class frigates; status uncertain
	3	SS-N-25 ShShMS	ShShM system	(1997)		..	On 3 Krivak-4 Class frigatesfrigates
	3	Top Plate	Surveillance radar	1997		..	On 3 Krivak-4 Class frigates; designation uncertain
	4	SS-N-25 ShShMS	ShShM system	(1996)	1998	(1)	For last 4 Khukri Class (Project-25A Type) corvettes
	96	SS-N-25/X-35 Uran	ShShM	(1996)	1998	(24)	For last 4 Khukri Class (Project-25A Type) corvettes
	72	Alfa/3M-54	ShShM	(1998)		..	For 2 or 3 Kilo Class submarines and 3 Krivak-4 Class frigates; designation uncertain
	750	AA-12 Adder/R-77	Air-to-air missile	(1996)		..	For 125 MiG-21bis fighter aircraft upgraded to MiG-21-93 and possibly also for MiG-29 fighter aircraft
	800	AT-6 Spiral/9M114	Anti-tank missile	(1995)	1998–99	(800)	For Mi-24 (Mi-25 and Mi-35) helicopters
	216	SA-N-7 Gadfly/Smerch	ShAM	(1986)	1997	(72)	For 3 Delhi Class (Project-15 Type) destroyers
	98	SS-N-25/X-35 Uran	ShShM	1992	1997–99	(64)	For 3 Delhi Class (Project-15 Type) destroyers
	2	Kilo Class/Type-877E	Submarine	1997	1997	1	Incl 1 originally built for Russian Navy, but sold to India before completion; Indian designation Sindhughosh Class; for delivery 1997–2000
	3	AK-100 100mm L/59	Naval gun	(1986)	1997	(1)	For 3 Delhi Class (Project-15 Type) destroyers
	6	Bass Tilt	Fire control radar	(1986)	1997	(2)	For 3 Delhi Class (Project-15 Type) destroyers; for use with AK-650 30mm guns
	6	SA-N-7 ShAMS/Shtil	ShAM system	(1986)	1997	(2)	For 3 Delhi Class (Project-15 Type) destroyers
	18	Front Dome	Fire control radar	(1986)	1997	(6)	For 3 Delhi Class (Project-15 Type) destroyers; for use with SA-N-7 ShAM system
	3	Kite Screech	Fire control radar	(1986)	1997	(1)	For 3 Delhi Class (Project-15 Type) destroyers; for use with AK-100 100mm gun
	3	Head Net-C	Surveillance radar	1989	1998	(1)	For 3 Brahmaputra Class (Project-16A Type) frigates
	3	SA-N-4/ZIF-22	ShAM system	(1989)	1998	(1)	For 3 Brahmaputra Class (Project-16A Type) frigates
	90	SA-N-4 Gecko/Osa-M	ShAM	(1989)	1998	(20)	For 3 Brahmaputra Class (Project-16A Type) frigates
	8	Plank Shave	Surveillance radar	(1983)	1989–98	(5)	For 8 Khukri Class (Project-25/25A Type) corvettes
	8	Bass Tilt	Fire control radar	1983	1989–98	(5)	For 8 Khukri Class (Project-25/25A Type) corvettes; for use with 76mm gun and AK-630 30mm CIWS

	No.	Weapon designation	Weapon description	Year of order	Year of delivery	No. delivered	Comments
	8	Cross Dome	Surveillance radar	(1983)	1989–98	(5)	For 8 Khukri Class (Project-25/25A Type) corvettes
	(320)	SA-N-5 Grail/Strela-2M	ShAM	(1983)	1989–98	(200)	For 8 Khukri Class (Project-25/25A Type) corvettes
Slovakia	42	VT-72B	ARV	1999	1999	..	Deal worth $30.4 m
South Africa	90	Casspir	APC	1998	1999	90	Deal worth $12 m; ex-South African Police; refurbished before delivery; for army and police units in Kashmir
UK	2	Harrier T-4	FGA/trainer aircraft	1996	1999	(2)	Ex-UK Navy; deal worth £16.5 m incl refurbishment to Harrier T-60; for Navy
Ukraine	(360)	AA-10a/b Alamo/R-27	Air-to-air missile	(1996)	1997–99	(204)	For Su-30MK/MKI FGA aircraft; designation uncertain
Uzbekistan	(2)	Il-78M Midas	Tanker aircraft	1997		..	Sold via Russia; no. could be up to 6; possibly incl ex-Russian Air Force
L: France	..	SA-315B Lama	Helicopter	1971	1973–99	(154)	First 40 assembly only; also for civilian use; Indian designation Cheetah
	..	SA-316B Alouette-3	Helicopter	1962	1965–99	(211)	Also produced for civil use and export; incl some assembled from kits; Indian designation Chetak
Germany (FRG)	..	Milan-2	Anti-tank missile	1992	1993–99	(12 000)	
	33	Do-228-200MP	MP aircraft	1983	1988–99	(22)	For Coast Guard
	14	Do-228-200MP	MP aircraft	(1989)	1994–99	(14)	For Navy
	1	Aditya Class	Support ship	1987	1999	1	Designed for production in India; option on 1 more not used
Netherlands	212	Flycatcher	Fire control radar	(1987)	1988–99	(212)	Indian designation PIW-519; for use with L/70 40mm AA guns
	(20)	Reporter	Surveillance radar	(1997)	1998–99	(10)	
Russia	120	Su-30MKI Flanker	FGA aircraft	(1999)		..	Contract not yet signed; for delivery from 2002
UK	15	Jaguar International	FGA aircraft	1993	1995–99	(15)	Indian designation Shamsher
	17	Jaguar International	FGA aircraft	1999		..	Indian designation Shamsher; delivery 2001
USSR	1	Magar Class	Landing ship	(1996)		..	
	(375)	T-72M1	Main battle tank	(1980)	1991–99	(374)	Indian designation Ajeya; no. could be considerably higher
	..	AT-5a Spandrel/9M113	Anti-tank missile	(1988)	1989–99	(9 500)	For BMP-2 IFVs

Recipient/ supplier (S) or licenser (L)	No. ordered	Weapon designation	Weapon description	Year of order/ licence	Year(s) of deliveries	No. delivered/ produced	Comments
Indonesia							
S: France	(14)	AS-332B Super Puma	Helicopter	1997		..	No. ordered could be 16; delivery from 2000
Netherlands	4	LIROD	Fire control radar	(1994)	1999	2	For 4 PB-57 Type (Singa Class) patrol craft; deal worth HFL81 m incl 4 Variant radars; delivery 1999–2000
	4	Variant	Surveillance radar	(1999)	1999	2	For 4 PB-57 Type (Singa Class) patrol craft; deal worth HFL81 m incl LIROD radars; delivery 1999–2000
UK	16	Hawk-200	FGA aircraft	1996	1999	10	Deal worth $266 m; UK export designation Hawk Mk-209; delivery 1999–2000
	(45)	Scorpion-90	Light tank	1997	1998–99	(45)	Deal worth $134 m
	(91)	Stormer	APC	1995	1996–99	(35)	Incl APC/CP, ARV, bridgelayer and ambulance version
USA	2	TA-4J Skyhawk	Jet trainer ac	(1996)	1999	2	Ex-US Navy; refurbished in New Zealand before delivery
L: Germany (FRG)	..	Bo-105C	Helicopter	1976	1978–91	(45)	Incl for Army, Navy and Police
	4	PB-57 Type	Patrol craft	1993		..	Indonesian designation Singa Class; delivery probably from 2000
Spain	(10)	C-212-200 Aviocar	Transport aircraft	1997	1999	2	Incl some for Navy and possibly some for Army and Police
USA	6	C-212-200MPA Aviocar	MP aircraft	1996		..	For Navy; delivery 2000–2001
	1	Bell-412	Helicopter	1996		..	Deal worth $4.2 m; for Navy; no. ordered could be 2
Iran							
S: China	14	Y-7	Transport aircraft	1996	1998	(2)	Delivery 1998–2006
	(10)	C-801/802 ShShMS	ShShM system	(1995)	1996–99	(10)	For refit of 10 Kaman Class (Combattante-2 Type) FAC
	(80)	C-802/CSS-N-8 Saccade	ShShM	(1995)	1996–99	(80)	For 10 refitted Kaman Class (Combattante-2 Type) FAC; Iranian designation Tondar

	No.	Weapon designation	Weapon description	Year of order/ licence	Year(s) of deliveries	No. produced/ delivered	Comments
Russia	..	BMP-2	IFV	(1995)	1996–98	(5)	
Ukraine	(12)	An-74TK Coaler-C	Transport aircraft	(1997)	1997–99	..	Possibly assembly or licensed production in Iran
L: Russia	..	T-72S1	Main battle tank	(1996)	1997–99	(50)	
Ireland							
S: Switzerland	40	Piranha-3 8x8	APC	1999		..	Deal worth $50.8 m; incl 4 APC/CP, 1 ARV and 1 ambulance version; delivery 2000–2002
UK	1	Mod. Guardian Class	OPV	1997	1999	1	Irish designation Roisin Class; option on 1 more; financed by EU for fishery protection
Israel							
S: Germany (FRG)	2	Dolphin Class	Submarine	1991	1999	2	Deal worth $570 m; financed by FRG
	1	Dolphin Class	Submarine	1994		..	Deal worth $300 m; 50% financed by FRG; delivery 2000
USA	21	F-15I Strike Eagle	Fighter/bomber ac	1994	1998–99	(21)	Deal worth $1.76 b (offsets $1 b); financed by USA; Israeli designation Ra'am
	4	F-15I Strike Eagle	Fighter/bomber ac	1995	1999	4	Israeli designation Ra'am
	50	F-16I	FGA aircraft	1999		..	Deal worth $2.5 b (offsets 25%); option on 60 more; financed by USA; delivery 2003–2005
	(8)	Super King Air-200	Light transport ac	1997	1999	(4)	Israeli designation Zufut; incl for EW and ELINT
	(64)	AIM-120B AMRAAM	Air-to-air missile	(1998)	1998–99	(64)	FMS deal worth $28 m
Italy							
S: UK	(200)	Storm Shadow	ASM	1999		..	Delivery from 2003
USA	18	C-130J Hercules-2	Transport aircraft	1997		..	Delivery from 2000
	2	C-130J-30 Hercules	Transport aircraft	(1999)		..	Option on 4 more; contract not yet signed
	38	LVTP-7A1/AAV-7A1	APC	(1998)		..	FMS deal worth $126 m; delivery 2000–2001
	233	AIM-120B AMRAAM	Air-to-air missile	1997		..	Deal worth $116 m; for Navy AV-8B+ FGA aircraft
	735	FIM-92A Stinger	Portable SAM	1998		..	FMS deal worth $110 m
L: Germany (FRG)	2	Type-212	Submarine	1997		..	Option on 2 more; delivery 2004–2005

Recipient/ supplier (S) or licenser (L)	No. ordered	Weapon designation	Weapon description	Year of order/ licence	Year(s) of deliveries	No. delivered/ produced	Comments
Jamaica							
S: France	4	AS-355 Twin Ecureuil	Helicopter		1999	4	
Japan							
S: USA	13	BAe-125/RH-800	Transport aircraft	1995	1997–99	(6)	For SAR; 'H-X' programme; Japanese designation U-125A
	(10)	Beechjet-400T	Light transport ac	1992	1994–99	(10)	For training; Japanese designation T-400; 'TC-X' programme
	2	Boeing-767/AWACS	AEW&C aircraft	1994	1999	2	Deal worth $773 m; Japanese designation E-767
	(9)	Gulfstream-4	Transport aircraft	1994	1996–99	(5)	Japanese designation U-4
	(20)	Super King Air-350	Light transport ac	1997	1999	(1)	For Army; Japanese designation LR-2
	(72)	M-270 MLRS 227mm	MRL	1993	1995–99	(45)	Assembled in Japan
	9	Mk-48	ShAM system	(1993)	1996–99	(4)	For 9 Murasame Class frigates
	2	Mk-41	ShAM system	(1999)		:	For 2 Murasame Class frigates
	22	Phalanx Mk-15	CIWS	(1993)	1996–98	(8)	For 11 Murasame Class frigates
	6	Phalanx Mk-15	CIWS	(1993)	1998	(2)	For 3 Osumi Class AALS
	40	AIM-120B AMRAAM	Air-to-air missile	(1998)		:	Deal worth $22 m
	(16)	RIM-66M Standard-2	ShAM	1999		:	FMS deal
	5	RIM-66M Standard-2	ShAM	1998		:	FMS deal
	(216)	RIM-7M Seasparrow	ShAM	1993	1996–99	(96)	Deal worth $13.4 m; probably for Murasame Class frigates
L: France	(297)	MO-120-RT-61 120mm	Mortar	1992	1993–99	(272)	Incl for use with Type-96 APC/mortar carrier
Germany (FRG)	(460)	FH-70 155mm	Towed gun	(1982)	1984–99	(460)	For Army
USA	(89)	Bell-209/AH-1S	Combat helicopter	1982	1984–99	(88)	For Army
	60	CH-47D Chinook	Helicopter	1986	1988–99	(52)	Incl for Army; Japanese designation CH-47J and CH-47JA
	193	F-15C/D Eagle	FGA/trainer aircraft	1978	1982–99	(193)	US export designation F-15J; incl 38 F-15DJ trainer version; originally a total of 201 was planned, but only 193 ordered

No. ordered	Weapon designation	Weapon description	Year of order	Year(s) of deliveries	No. delivered/ produced	Comments
210	Hughes-500M/OH-6D	Helicopter	1977	1978–99	(209)	Incl 193 for Army and 17 for Navy, incl for training
(64)	S-70/UH-60J Blackhawk	Helicopter	1988	1991–99	(35)	Incl 18 for Navy
(80)	S-70/UH-60J Blackhawk	Helicopter	1995	1998–99	(10)	For Army; Japanese designation UH-60JA; deal worth $2.67 b
98	S-70B/SH-60J Seahawk	ASW helicopter	1988	1991–99	(70)	For Navy; total requirement about 100
3	UP-3D Orion	EW aircraft	1994	1997–99	3	For Navy

Jordan
S: Turkey

2	CN-235-100	Transport aircraft	1998	1999	2	Lease

UK

2	Aardvark	AEV	1999	1999	2	Aid
288	Challenger	Main battle tank	1995	1999	(14)	Ex-UK Army; Jordanian designation Al Hussein

USA

(96)	AIM-7M Sparrow	Air-to-air missile	1998	1998–99	(96)	Aid; for 16 F-16A/B FGA aircraft

Kazakhstan
S: Russia

(38)	Su-27SK Flanker-B	FGA aircraft	(1995)	1996–99	(26)	Ex-Russian Air Force; payment for Russian debt to Kazakhstan
1	SA-10c/S-300PMU	SAM system	1998		..	Probably ex-Russian Air Army
(36)	SA-10 Grumble/5V55R	SAM	(1998)		..	For 1 SA-10c/S-300PMU SAM system

Korea, North
S: Kazakhstan

(34)	MiG-21bis Fishbed-N	Fighter aircraft	(1998)	1999	(34)	Ex-Kazakh Air Force; 6 more confiscated in Azerbaijan while being delivered; illegal deal worth $8 m

Korea, South
S: France

5	F-406 Caravan-2	Light transport ac	1997	1999	(5)	Deal worth $24 m; for Navy; for use as target tugs
(48)	Crotale NG SAMS	SAM system	(1999)		..	Korean designation Pegasus; for use with Korean developed missiles; mounted on Korean K-200 APC

Germany (FRG)

(1 294)	Mistral	Portable SAM	(1997)	1998–99	(1 178)	Deal worth $300 m
12	Bo-105C	Helicopter	1997	1999	(4)	Assembled in South Korea; for Army; delivery 1999–2000

Recipient/ supplier (S) or licenser (L)	No. ordered	Weapon designation	Weapon description	Year of order/ licence	Year(s) of deliveries	No. delivered/ produced	Comments
Indonesia	8	CN-235-220	Transport aircraft	1997		..	Deal worth $143 m (offsets incl Korean deliveries of vehicles and other military equipment to Indonesia); delivery 2000
Israel	100	Harpy	Anti-radar UAV	1997	1998–99	(100)	
Netherlands	4	Goalkeeper	CIWS	1995	1999	(4)	For 2 Okpo Class (KDX-2000 or KDX-1 Type) frigates
	3	Goalkeeper	CIWS	1999		..	For 3 KDX-2 Type frigates; delivery from 2002
UK	13	Super Lynx	ASW helicopter	1997	1999	(5)	For Navy; deal worth $328 m incl Sea Skua missiles and upgrade of 11 South Korean Navy Super Lynx helicopters, delivery 1999–2000
USA	8	RH-800XP	Reconnaissance ac	1996		..	'Peace Pioneer' deal worth $461 m; incl 4 RH-800RA and RH-800SIG SIGINT aircraft; deal temporary suspended in 1998 after corruption charges; delivery 2000–2001
	30	T-38 Talon	Jet trainer aircraft	1996	1999	30	Ex-US Air Force; lease; deal worth $86 m
	29	M-270 MLRS 227mm	MRL	1996	1998–99	29	Deal worth $624 m incl 1626 rockets, 111 ATACMS SSMs, 14 M-577A2 APC/CPs, 4 M-88A1 ARVs and 54 light trucks
	111	MGM-140A ATACMS	SSM	1997	1999	(111)	Deal worth $624 m incl 29 MLRS MRLs, 1626 MLRS rockets, 14 M-577A2 APC/CPs, 4 M-88A1 ARVs and 54 light trucks
	14	M-113A2	APC	1996	1999	(14)	All M-577A2 APC/CP version; deal worth $624 m incl 29 MLRS MRLs, 1626 MLRS rockets, 111 ATACMS SSMs, 4 M-88A1 ARVs and 54 trucks
	3	AN/SPS-49	Surveillance radar	1994	1998–99	(3)	For 3 Okpo Class (KDX-2000 or KDX-1 Type) frigates
	1	Mk-48	ShAM system	1997	1999	(1)	For 1 Okpo Class (KDX-2000 or KDX-1 Type) frigate
	(45)	RIM-7P Seasparrow	ShAM	1992	1998–99	(45)	For Okpo Class (KDX-2000 or KDX-1 Type) frigates; FMS deal worth $19 m

No. ordered	Weapon designation	Weapon description	Year of order	Year(s) of deliveries	No. delivered	Comments
3	RGM-84 ShShMS	ShShM system	(1992)	1998–99	(3)	For 3 Okpo Class (KDX-2000 or KDX-1 Type) frigates
3	Mk-41	ShAM system	(1999)	1998–99	..	For 3 KDX-2 Class destroyers
(300)	AIM-9S Sidewinder	Air-to-air missile	1994	1998–99	(300)	FMS deal worth $34 m
100	Popeye-1	ASM	(1997)		..	Deal worth $125 m incl modification of 30 F-4E FGA aircraft; US designation AGM-142; delivery 2000–2003
..	UGM-84A Sub Harpoon	SuShM	(1994)	1998–99	(16)	For Type-209 (Chang Bogo Class) submarines
L: Russia/USSR						
..	AT-4 Spigot/9M111	Anti-tank missile	(1987)	1991–99	(900)	More possibly produced for export
..	SA-16 Gimlet/Igla-1	Portable SAM	(1989)	1992–99	(160)	
Kuwait						
S: China						
18	PZL-45 155mm	Self-propelled gun	1998		..	Deal worth $186.5 m
France						
8	MRR-3D	Surveillance radar	1995	1998–99	(6)	On 8 P-37BRL Type FAC
8	P-37BRL Type	FAC(M)	1995	1998–99	(6)	'Garoh' deal worth $475 m; Kuwaiti designation Um Almaradim Class; also designated Combattante-1 Type
UK						
(80)	Sea Skua SL	ShShM	1997	1999	(40)	For 8 PB-37BRL Type FAC; deal worth $89 m
USA						
48	M-109A6 Paladin	Self-propelled gun	(1999)		..	Contract not yet signed
70	Pandur	APC	1996	1998–99	(70)	Incl IFV, APC/CP, APC/mortar carrier, ARV, ambulance and armoured car versions; option on 200 more
Latvia						
S: Germany (FRG)						
1	Lindau Class	Minesweeper	1999	1999	1	Ex-FRG Navy; gift; Latvian designation Nemejs Class
Lebanon						
S: USA						
8	Bell-205/UH-1H	Helicopter	1998		..	Ex-US Army; aid; option on 8 more; delivery 2000

Recipient/ supplier (S) or licenser (L)	No. ordered	Weapon designation	Weapon description	Year of order/ licence	Year(s) of deliveries	No. delivered/ produced	Comments
Lithuania							
S: Germany (FRG)	1	Lindau Class	Minesweeper	1999	1999	1	Ex-FRG Navy; gift
Macedonia							
S: Bulgaria	(8)	D-20 152mm	Towed gun	1999	1999	(8)	Ex-Bulgarian Army; gift; no. delivered could be 10
	(108)	D-30 122mm	Towed gun	1999	1999	(108)	Ex-Bulgarian Army; gift; no. delivered could be up to 142
	(114)	T-55	Main battle tank	1999	1999	(114)	Ex-Bulgarian Army; no. delivered could be 94; gift
	36	T-55M	Main battle tank	1999	1999	36	Ex-Bulgarian Army; gift
France	20	RATAC	Battlefield radar	(1998)	1999	(20)	Ex-French Army; gift; designation uncertain
Greece	10	4K-7FA-G-127	APC	1999	1999	10	Ex-Greek Army; gift; Greek designation Leonidas-1
Italy	(30)	M-113A1	APC	1998	1999	(30)	Ex-Italian Army; aid
Turkey	20	F-5A/B Freedom Fighter	FGA aircraft	1998		..	Ex-Turkish Air Force; possibly refurbished before delivery; gift
USA	(36)	M-101A1 105mm	Towed gun	1998	1998–99	(36)	Ex-US Army; incl 18 aid
Malaysia							
S: France	2	MM-38/40 ShShMS	ShShM system	(1992)	1999	2	For 2 Lekiu Class frigates
Indonesia	6	CN-235-220	Transport aircraft	1995	1999	6	Option on 12 more; deal worth $101 m; deal incl barter/offsets (Malaysia delivering 20 MD-3-160 trainer aircraft and 500 cars to Indonesia; delivery delayed from 1997 to 1999
Italy	2	Assad Class	Corvette	1997	1999	2	Originally built for Iraq but embargoed; Malaysian designation Laksamana Class; deal worth $253 m incl 2 ordered 1997
	2	RAN-12L/X	Surveillance radar	1997	1999	2	On 2 Assad Class corvettes
	4	RTN-10X	Fire control radar	1997	1999	4	On 2 Assad Class corvettes; for use with Albatros ShAM system and 76mm and 40mm guns
	2	Albatros Mk-2	ShAM system	1997	1999	2	On 2 Assad Class corvettes
	(18)	Aspide Mk-1	ShAM	(1997)	1999	(18)	For 2 Assad Class corvettes

	No.	Weapon designation	Weapon description	Year of order	Year of delivery	No. delivered	Comments
	2	Otomat/Teseo	ShShM system	1997	1999	2	On 2 Assad Class corvettes
	(24)	Otomat Mk-2	ShShM	(1997)	1999	(24)	For 2 Assad Class corvettes
	(24)	Otomat Mk-2	ShShM	1995	1998–99	(24)	For 2 Assad Class corvettes
Netherlands	2	DA-08	Surveillance radar	1992	1999	2	For 2 Lekiu Class frigates
Russia	2	Mi-17 Hip-H	Helicopter	(1999)	1999	2	
	(96)	AA-12 Adder/R-77	Air-to-air missile	(1997)		:	For 16 MiG-29S FGA aircraft
Sweden	2	Sea Giraffe-150	Surveillance radar	1992	1999	2	For 2 Lekiu Class frigates
UK	6	Super Lynx	ASW helicopter	1999		:	Deal worth $158 m; for Navy; delivery 2003
	2	Lekiu Class	Frigate	1992	1999	2	Deal worth $600 m; delivery delayed from 1996 after problems with software for combat system
	4	ST-1802SW	Fire control radar	1992	1999	4	On 2 Lekiu Class frigates; for use with Seawolf ShAM system
	2	Seawolf GWS-26	ShAM system	1992	1999	2	On 2 Lekiu Class frigates
	32	Seawolf VL	ShAM	1993	1999	(32)	For 2 Lekiu Class frigates
L: Germany (FRG)	6	MEKO-A-100 Type	OPV	1998		:	Deal worth $1.34 b; 'New Generation Patrol Vessel (NGPV)' programme; delivery 2003–2005/2006
Switzerland	20	MD-3-160 AeroTiga	Trainer aircraft	1993	1995–99	(20)	More produced for export and civil customers
Mexico							
S: Italy	30	SF-260M	Trainer aircraft	1999	1999	:	
USA	73	Cessna-182	Light aircraft	(1999)	1999	50	For anti-narcotics operations; delivery 1999–2000
	8	MD Explorer	Helicopter	(1998)	1999	(2)	
Morocco							
S: France	2	Floreal Class	Frigate	1998		:	Deal worth $130–140 m; delivery 2000–2001
Myanmar							
S: China	10	F-7M Airguard	Fighter aircraft	(1993)		:	Status uncertain
	2	FT-7	Fighter/trainer ac	(1993)		:	Status uncertain
	(72)	PL-2B	Air-to-air missile	1993		:	
	12	K-8 Karakorum-8	Jet trainer aircraft	(1997)	1998–99	(12)	For 12 F-7M/FT-7 fighter aircraft; status uncertain

Recipient/ supplier (S) or licenser (L)	No. ordered	Weapon designation	Weapon description	Year of order/ licence	Year(s) of deliveries	No. delivered/ produced	Comments
Netherlands S: Finland	90	XA-188	APC	1997	1998–99	90	Deal worth $82 m (offsets 100%); incl 20 for Marines; incl for use with peacekeeping forces
Germany (FRG)	874	FIM-92C Stinger	Portable SAM	(1992)	1998–99	(300)	Part of European Stinger Production Programme involving production of components in FRG, Greece, Netherlands and Turkey and final assembly in FRG; delivery 1998–2001/2
Italy	2	127mm/54	Naval gun	1996		..	For 2 LCF Type frigates; option on 2 more; ex-Canadian Navy guns sold back to producer and refurbished before delivery
Romania	4	LCU Mk-9	Landing craft	(1996)	1999	4	Designed in Netherlands for Dutch Navy; produced in Romania and assembled in Netherlands
USA	30	AH-64D Apache	Combat helicopter	1995	1998–99	(9)	Deal worth $686 m (offsets $873 m)
	605	AGM-114K Hellfire	Anti-tank missile	1995	1996–99	(150)	For AH-64D helicopters; deal worth $127 m
	6	CH-47D Chinook	Helicopter	1993	1998–99	6	Deal worth $54 m; for 2 LCF Type frigates
	2	Mk-41	ShAM system	(1996)		..	FMS deal worth $24 m incl 8 training missiles; for LCF type frigates
	16	RIM-66M Standard-2	ShAM	(1998)		..	
	36	AGM-65G Maverick	ASM	1997	1999	(36)	Deal worth $6 m; not incl some as short-term lease from USA before delivery started
	200	AIM-120A AMRAAM	Air-to-air missile	1995	1998–99	200	For F-16A/B-MLU FGA aircraft
New Zealand S: Australia	2	MEKO-200ANZ Type	Frigate	1989	1997–99	2	Deal worth $554.7 m; New Zealand designation Te Kaha Class; option on 2 more not used
Sweden	2	9LV	Fire control radar	1991	1997–99	2	For 2 MEKO-200ANZ Type (Te Kaha Class) frigates; for use with Seasparrow ShAM system and 127mm gun
	2	Sea Giraffe-150	Surveillance radar	1991	1997–99	2	For 2 MEKO-200ANZ Type (Te Kaha Class) frigates

No. ordered	Weapon designation	Weapon description	Year of order	Year(s) of deliveries	No. delivered	Comments
4	SH-2G Super Seasprite	ASW helicopter	1997		..	For Navy; deal worth $185 m (offsets 36%); option on 2 more; US export designation SH-2G(NZ); delivery 2000–2001
1	SH-2G Super Seasprite	ASW helicopter	1999		..	For Navy; deal worth $23 m; US export designation SH-2G (NZ)
2	Mk-45 127mm/54	Naval gun	(1989)	1997–99	2	For 2 MEKO-200ANZ Type (Te Kaha Class) frigates
2	AN/SPS-49	Surveillance radar	(1993)	1997–99	2	For 2 MEKO-200ANZ Type (Te Kaha Class) frigates
2	Mk-41	ShAM system	1992	1997–99	2	For 2 MEKO-200ANZ Type (Te Kaha Class) frigates
(24)	RIM-7P Seasparrow	ShAM	(1991)	1997–99	(24)	For 2 MEKO-200ANZ Type (Te Kaha Class) frigates

Norway

S: Finland

No. ordered	Weapon designation	Weapon description	Year of order	Year(s) of deliveries	No. delivered	Comments
22	XA-200	APC	1999		..	Deal worth $10.1 m; delivery 2000
Germany (FRG)						
9	Leopard-1/BL	ABL	1995		(9)	Ex-FRG Army Leopard-1 tanks modified to ABL before delivery
Sweden						
104	CV-9030	IFV	1994	1998–99	64	Deal worth $241 m (offsets $184 m); option on more; delivery 1998–2000
USA						
12	Arthur	Tracking radar	1997	1999	(1)	Deal worth $85 m; delivery 1999–2002
(304)	AGM-114A Hellfire	Anti-tank missile	1996	1996–99	(304)	For coast defence; deal worth $36 m (offsets 100%); assembled in Sweden; Norwegian designation N-HSDS
500	AIM-120A AMRAAM	Air-to-air missile	1996	1998–99	(234)	For F-16A/B-MLU FGA aircraft; deal worth $150 m (offsets incl assembly in Norway)
..	BGM-71F TOW-2A	Anti-tank missile	1996		..	Deal worth $46 m (offsets 100%); status uncertain

Oman

S: Switzerland

No. ordered	Weapon designation	Weapon description	Year of order	Year(s) of deliveries	No. delivered	Comments
12	PC-9	Trainer aircraft	1999		..	Delivery probably 2000
UK						
20	Challenger-2	Main battle tank	1997		..	Deal worth $172 m; delivery 2000/2001
..	Martello S-743D	Surveillance radar	1999		..	Delivery 2002

Pakistan

S: Belarus

No. ordered	Weapon designation	Weapon description	Year of order	Year(s) of deliveries	No. delivered	Comments
(5 760)	AT-11 Sniper/9M119	Anti-tank missile	1996	1997–99	(5 760)	For 320 T-80UD tanks; status uncertain
China						
(100)	F-7MG	Fighter aircraft	1999		..	Delivery probably from 2000
..	FC-1	FGA aircraft	1999		..	Being developed for Pakistan; status uncertain

Recipient/ supplier (S) or licenser (L)	No. ordered	Weapon designation	Weapon description	Year of order/ licence	Year(s) of deliveries	No. delivered/ produced	Comments
	(3)	C-801/802 ShShMS	ShShM system	(1996)	1997	(1)	For 3 Jalalat-2 Class FAC
	(24)	C-802/CSS-N-8 Saccade	ShShM	(1996)	1997	8	For 3 Jalalat-2 Class FAC
	(3)	Type-347G	Fire control radar	(1996)	1997	(1)	For 3 Jalalat-2 Class FAC; for use with Type-76A 37mm guns
France	34	Mirage-5	FGA aircraft	1996	1998–99	(22)	Ex-French Air Force; refurbished before delivery; 'Blue Flash-6' deal worth $120 m incl 6 Mirage-3D fighter/trainer aircraft; for delivery 1998–2000
	2	Agosta-90B Type	Submarine	1994	1999	1	Incl 1 assembled in Pakistan; deal worth $750 m incl 1 licensed production; deal also incl additional $200 m modernization of Karachi Shipyard to built submarines; Pakistani designation Khalid Class; for delivery 1999–2002
	(24)	SM-39 Exocet	SuShM	1994	1999	(8)	Deal worth $100 m; for 3 Agosta-90B Type submarines
Sweden	..	RBS-70	Portable SAM	(1985)	1988–99	(300)	Assembled in Pakistan
Ukraine	320	T-80UD	Main battle tank	1996	1997–99	320	Deal worth $550 m; incl 50 taken from Ukrainian Army inventory
L: China	..	Hongjian-8	Anti-tank missile	1989	1990–99	(1 500)	Pakistani designation Baktar Shikan
	..	QW-1 Vanguard/Anza-2	Portable SAM	(1993)	1994–99	(550)	Pakistani designation Anza-2
France	1	Agosta-90B Type	Submarine	1994		..	Deal worth $750 m incl 2 delivered direct; Pakistani designation Khalid Class; for delivery 2002
Sweden	..	Supporter	Trainer aircraft	1974	1981–99	(141)	Pakistani designation Mushshak; for Army and Air Force; more produced for export
USA	755	M-113A2	APC	1989	1991–99	(755)	Assembled in Pakistan from kits delivered between 1989 and 1991
Paraguay							
S: Taiwan (ROC)	12	F-5E/F Tiger-2	FGA aircraft	1997		..	Ex-Taiwanese Air Force; incl 2 F-5F trainer version; gift; status uncertain

	No.	Weapon designation	Weapon description	Year of order	Year(s) of deliveries	No. delivered	Comments
Peru							
S: Russia	6	Il-103	Light aircraft	1999	1999	6	
	3	MiG-29S Fulcrum-C	FGA aircraft	1998	1999	(3)	Deal worth $117.4 m incl spare parts and support for 18 MiG-29s delivered from Belarus
Philippines							
S: Australia	(2)	Transfield-56m Type	Patrol craft	(1997)		..	For Coast Guard
Poland							
S: UK	6	AS-90 155mm turret	Artillery turret	1999		..	Prior to licensed production; to be fitted on Polish chassis; Polish designation Chrobry
USA	2	Perry Class	Frigate	1999		..	Ex-US Navy; gift; delivery 2000–2001
	2	Mk-13	ShAM system	1999		..	On 2 ex-US Perry Class frigates
	2	AN/SPG-60 STIR	Fire control radar	1999		..	On 2 ex-US Perry Class frigates; part of Standard ShAM system
	(108)	RIM-66B Standard-1MR	ShAM	(1999)		..	For 2 Perry Class frigates
	2	AN/SPS-49	Surveillance radar	1999		..	On 2 ex-US Perry Class frigates
	2	AN/SPS-55	Surveillance radar	1999		..	On 2 ex-US Perry Class frigates
	2	Phalanx Mk-15	CIWS	1999		..	On 2 ex-US Perry Class frigates
	2	WM-28	Fire control radar	1999		..	On 2 ex-US Perry Class frigates; for use with 76mm gun
L: Russia	3	An-28RM Bryza-1RM	MP aircraft	(1998)	1999	3	For Navy
UK	(72)	AS-90 155mm turret	Artillery turret	1999		..	To be fitted on Polish chassis; Polish designation Chrobry
Portugal							
S: Germany (FRG)	9	EC-135/EC-635	Helicopter	1999		..	Deal worth $38 m; for Army; delivery in 2001
UK	21	L-119 105mm	Towed gun	1997	1998–99	(21)	
USA	20	F-16A/B	FGA aircraft	1998		..	Ex-US Air Force; refurbished to F-16AM/BM before delivery; incl 4 F-16B trainer version; 5 more delivered for spares only; 'Peace Atlantis-2' programme worth $268 m; delivery 2001–2003

Recipient/ supplier (S) or licenser (L)	No. ordered	Weapon designation	Weapon description	Year of order/ licence	Year(s) of deliveries	No. delivered/ produced	Comments
Qatar							
S: France	12	Mirage-2000-5	FGA aircraft	1994	1997–99	12	Deal worth $1.25 b; French export designation Mirage-2000-5EDA; incl 3 Mirage-2000DDA trainer version
	(144)	MICA-EM	Air-to-air missile	1994	1997–99	(144)	Deal worth $280 m incl R-550 missiles; for 12 Mirage 2000-5 FGA aircraft
	(144)	R-550 Magic-2	Air-to-air missile	1994	1997–99	(144)	Deal worth $280 m incl MICA-EM missiles; for 12 Mirage 2000-5 FGA aircraft
	..	Apache-A	ASM	1994		..	For Mirage-2000-5 FGA aircraft; French export designation Black Pearl
UK	36	Piranha 8x8 AGV-90	Armoured car	1996	1998–99	(36)	Option on more
Romania							
S: France	(200)	R-550 Magic-2	Air-to-air missile	1996		..	For MiG-21, MiG-23 and MiG-29 fighter aircraft; may incl assembly or licensed production in Romania; status uncertain
Germany (FRG)	(32)	Gepard	AAV(G)	(1997)	1999	2	Ex-FRG Army; probably refurbished before delivery; gift worth $37 m; 11 more for spares only; delivery 1999–2000
Israel	(960)	NT-D Spike/NT-G Gill	Anti-tank missile	(1998)	1999	(50)	For 24 modified SA-330 (IAR-330) helicopters; designation uncertain
	(1 000)	Python-3	Air-to-air missile	(1997)	1998–99	(120)	For 110 MiG-21 fighter aircraft modified to MiG-21 Lancer and for IAR-99 trainer aircraft
USA	5	AN/FPS-117	Surveillance radar	1995	1998–99	5	Deal worth $82 m
L: Russia/USSR	..	SA-7b Grail/Strela-2M	Portable SAM	(1978)	1978–99	(2 280)	Romanian designation A-94 or CA-94; incl for Navy (SA-N-5); incl modified CA-94M version

No.	Designation	Description	(5)	1998	1999	(4)	Comments
Rwanda							
S: Russia							
16	Mi-17 Hip-H	Helicopter	(5)				Status uncertain; possibly incl some ex-Russian Air Force
Saudi Arabia							
S: Canada							
	Bell-412	Helicopter		1999			Delivery from 2000
425	Piranha 8x8	APC		1990	1994–99	(352)	Incl 71 ambulance, 18 ALV, 182 APC/CP and 34 engineer version and 73 fitted with UK AMS 120mm mortar turret; ordered via USA as FMS deal worth $700 m incl 765 other version; for National Guard; delivery 1994–2000
111	Piranha/LAV(AT)	Tank destroyer (M)		1990	1994–99	(111)	Ordered via USA as FMS deal worth $700 m incl 1006 other version; for National Guard
67	Piranha/LAV(R)	ARV		1990	1994–99	(67)	Ordered via USA as FMS deal worth $700 m incl 1050 other version; for National Guard
384	Piranha/LAV-25	IFV		1990	1994–99	(384)	Ordered via USA as FMS deal worth $700 m incl 733 other version; for National Guard
130	Piranha/LAV-90	Armoured car		(1999)		..	Ordered via USA as part of 1990 FMS deal worth $700 m incl 987 other version; for National Guard; delivery from 2000
France							
12	AS-532U2/AS-332L2	Helicopter		1996	1998–99	(8)	Armed with 20mm gun; for combat SAR; deal worth $508 m
2	La Fayette Class	Frigate		1994		..	'Sawari-2' deal worth $3.42 b incl other weapons, construction of a naval base and training (offsets 35%); French export designation F-3000S Type; Saudi designation Arriyad Class; delivery from 2001 or 2002
2	100mm Compact	Naval gun		1994		..	On 2 La Fayette Class frigates
2	Arabel	Fire control radar		(1994)		..	On 2 La Fayette Class frigates
2	DRBV-26C Jupiter-2	Surveillance radar		1994		..	On 2 La Fayette Class frigates
2	Castor-2J	Fire control radar		1994		..	On 2 La Fayette Class frigates
2	Crotale Naval EDIR	ShAM system		1994		..	On 2 La Fayette Class frigates

Recipient/ supplier (S) or licenser (L)	No. ordered	Weapon designation	Weapon description	Year of order/ licence	Year(s) of deliveries	No. delivered/ produced	Comments
	(72)	VT-1	ShAM	(1994)		..	For 2 La Fayette Class frigates; for use with Crotale ShAM system
	2	EuroSAAM VLS	ShAM system	(1994)		..	On 2 La Fayette Class frigates
	2	MM-38/40 ShShMS	ShShM system	1994		..	On 2 La Fayette Class frigates
	(32)	MM-40 Exocet	ShShM	1994		..	For 2 La Fayette Class frigates
	1	La Fayette Class	Frigate	1997		..	'Sawari-2' deal worth $3.42 b incl other weapons, construction of a naval base and training (offsets 35%); French export designation F-3000S Type; Saudi designation Arriyad Class; delivery 2005
	1	100mm Compact	Naval gun	(1997)		..	On 1 La Fayette Class frigate
	1	Arabel	Fire control radar	1997		..	On 1 La Fayette Class frigate
	1	DRBV-26C Jupiter-2	Surveillance radar	(1997)		..	On 1 La Fayette Class frigate
	1	Castor-2J	Fire control radar	(1997)		..	On 1 La Fayette Class frigate
	1	Crotale Naval EDIR	ShAM system	(1997)		..	On 1 La Fayette Class frigate
	(36)	VT-1	ShAM	(1997)		..	For 1 La Fayette Class frigate; for use with Crotale ShAM system
	1	EuroSAAM VLS	ShAM system	1997		..	On 1 La Fayette Class frigate
	1	MM-38/40 ShShMS	ShShM system	(1997)		..	On 1 La Fayette Class frigate
	(16)	MM-40 Exocet	ShShM	(1997)		..	For 1 La Fayette Class frigate
	48	ASTER-15	ShAM	(1997)		..	For 3 La Fayette Class frigates
UK	73	AMS 120mm	Mortar turret	1996		..	Deal worth $57 m incl ammunition; for 73 Piranha/LAV APC/mortar carriers; delivery 2000
USA	72	F-15S Strike Eagle	Fighter/bomber ac	1992	1995–99	72	Deal worth $9 b incl AGM-65D/G, AIM-7M and AIM-9S missiles
	900	AGM-65D Maverick	ASM	1992	1995–99	(900)	For 72 F-15S fighter/bomber aircraft; incl AGM-65G version
	300	AIM-7M Sparrow	Air-to-air missile	1992	1995–98	(300)	For 72 F-15S fighter/bomber aircraft
L: UK	..	MSTAR	Battlefield radar	(1997)	1998–99	(20)	

	No.	Weapon designation	Weapon description	(Year order)	Year deliveries	No. delivered	Comments
Sierra Leone							
S: Ukraine	2	Mi-17 Hip-H	Helicopter	(1997)	1999	2	Ex-Ukrainian Air Force; designation uncertain
Singapore							
S: Israel	12	EL/M-2228	Fire control radar	(1993)	1996–99	(12)	For 12 Fearless Class patrol craft/FAC
Russia	..	Python-4	Air-to-air missile	(1997)	1997–99	(160)	For F-5S and F-16 FGA aircraft
	(350)	SA-16 Gimlet/Igla-1	Portable SAM	1997	1998–99	(350)	Deal incl also 30 launchers; no. delivered could be 440
Sweden	3	Sjöormen Class	Submarine	1997		..	Ex-Swedish Navy; refitted before delivery; Singaporean designation Challenger Class; 1 more for spares only; delivery from 2000
USA	8	AH-64D Apache	Combat helicopter	1999		..	FMS deal worth $647 m incl $25.9 m for Longbow radars and incl 192 AGM-114K missiles; delivery from 2002; contract not yet signed
	192	AGM-114K Hellfire	Anti-tank missile	1999	1999	..	FMS deal worth $620 m incl 8 AH-64D helicopters
	(4)	CH-47D Chinook	Helicopter	(1997)		..	No. ordered could be up to 10
	12	F-16C/D	FGA aircraft	1997	1999	(3)	'Peace Carvin-3' deal worth $350 m; incl 6 F-16D trainer version; delivery 1999–2000
	4	KC-135A Stratotanker	Tanker aircraft	1997	1999	(1)	Ex-US Air Force; FMS deal worth $280 m incl refurbishment to KC-135R before delivery; delivery 1999/2000
	50	AIM-7M Sparrow	Air-to-air missile	1994	1997–99	(50)	Deal worth $890 m incl 18 F-16C/D FGA aircraft and 36 AIM-9S missiles
Slovakia							
S: France	2	AS-350B Ecureuil	Helicopter	1997		..	Assembled in Slovakia; status uncertain
	(5)	AS-532U2/AS-332L2	Helicopter	(1997)		..	Assembled in Slovakia; status uncertain
Slovenia							
S: Switzerland	9	PC-9	Trainer aircraft	1997	1998–99	9	Upgraded for ground attack in Israel shortly after delivery

Recipient/ supplier (S) or licenser (L)	No. ordered	Weapon designation	Weapon description	Year of order/ licence	Year(s) of deliveries	No. delivered/ produced	Comments
L: Austria	(70)	Pandur	APC	1998	1999	(35)	Slovenian designation Valuk
South Africa							
S: France	..	Mistral	Portable SAM	(1999)		..	For Rooivalk combat helicopter; contract not yet signed
Germany (FRG)	4	MEKO-A200 Type	Frigate	1999		..	Deal worth $1.115 b (offsets 335%); for delivery 2004–2005
	3	Type-209/1400	Submarine	1999		..	Deal worth $862 m (offsets 375%); delivery 2004/5–2007
Italy	30	A-109 Hirundo	Helicopter	1999		..	Option on 10 more; deal worth $240 m; delivery 2002–2005
Sweden	9	JAS-39 Gripen	FGA aircraft	1999		..	Deal worth $1.16 b incl 12 Hawk-100 from UK; all JAS-39B trainer version; for delivery 2006–2009; option on 19 more
UK	12	Hawk-100	FGA/trainer aircraft	1999		..	Deal worth $1.16 b incl 9 JAS-39 from Sweden; delivery 2005; option on 12 more
USA	2	C-130B Hercules	Transport aircraft	1995	1999	2	Ex-US Air Force; gift; refurbished in UK before delivery
L: Germany (FRG)	3	Type-209/1200	Submarine	1994	1999	1	Deal worth $510 m; Korean designation Chang Bogo Class; delivery 1999–2000
Netherlands	3	MW-08	Surveillance radar	1994	1998–99	(3)	For 3 Okpo Class (KDX-2000 or KDX-1 Type) frigates
	6	STIR	Fire control radar	(1992)	1998–99	(6)	For 3 Okpo Class (KDX-2000 or KDX-1 Type) frigates; for use with Seasparrow and 127mm gun
	3	MW-08	Surveillance radar	1999		..	For 3 KDX-2 Type frigates
	6	STIR	Fire control radar	1999		..	For 3 KDX-2 Type frigates
USA	72	F-16C/D	FGA aircraft	1991	1997–99	(70)	Deal worth $2.52 b 48 delivered direct; incl some F-16D trainer version; for delivery 1997–2000

No.	Designation	Description	Year of order	Year(s) of deliveries	No. delivered	Comments
20	F-16C/D	FGA aircraft	(1999)		..	Deal worth $663 m; contract not yet signed; delivery from 2000
57	S-70A/UH-60P	Helicopter	(1994)	1995–99	(57)	
3	Mk-45 127mm/54	Naval gun	1999	1999	..	For 3 KDX-2 Type frigates; deal worth $22 m; delivery 2001–2003
(1 125)	K-1 ROKIT/Type-88	Main battle tank	1981	1984–99	(1 125)	Developed for Korean production; incl 5 prototypes
..	K-1A1/Type-88	Main battle tank	(1994)	1996–97	(2)	Incl 2 or 3 prototypes
57	LVTP-7A1/AAV-7A1	APC	1995	1997–99	(39)	Incl 5 LVTR-7/AAVR-7 ARV and 4 LVTC-7/AAVC-7 APC/CP version; deal worth $91 m; for Marines; Korean designation Korean Amphibious Vehicle (KAAV); delivery 1997–2001
67	LVTP-7A1/AAV-7A1	APC	1999		..	Deal worth $99–120 m; Korean designation Korean Armoured Amphibious Vehicle (KAAV); for Marines; delivery 2001/2–2006
(300)	M-992 FDCV/CP	APC/CP	1995	1998–99	(118)	
..	M-167 Vulcan	AAA system	(1986)	1986–99	(215)	Incl some fitted on KIFV APC chassis
Spain						
S: Canada						
4	AN/VPS-2 Modified	Fire control radar	(1994)	1998	(2)	For 4 Meroka CIWS on 2 Galicia Class AALS
France						
15	AS-532U2/AS-332L2	Helicopter	1997	1998–99	(6)	Deal worth $205 m (offsets 100%); delivery 1998–2003
Germany (FRG)						
15	EC-120B Colibri	Helicopter	1999	1999	..	Deal worth $16 m, for training; delivery 2000–2001
4	Buffel	ARV	1998	1998	..	Deal worth $2.26 b (offsets 80%) incl 12 licensed production and 219 Leopard-2A5+ tanks
Italy						
22	B-1 Centauro	Tank destroyer (G)	1999	1999	..	Deal worth $70 m (offsets 100%); delivery 2000–2001
2	RAN-30X	Surveillance radar	(1993)	1998	(1)	For use with Meroka CIWS on 2 Galicia Class AALS
2	Spada-2000	SAM system	(1996)	1998–99	2	For Air Force
(51)	Aspide-2000	SAM	(1996)	1997–99	(51)	For 2 Spada-2000 SAM systems
Netherlands						
2	DA-08	Surveillance radar	(1994)	1998	(1)	For 2 Galicia Class AALS
UK						
56	L-118 105mm	Towed gun	1995	1996–99	(56)	Deal worth $63 m incl ammunition
(50)	MSTAR	Battlefield radar	(1996)	1996–99	(40)	

Recipient/ supplier (S) or licenser (L)	No. ordered	Weapon designation	Weapon description	Year of order/ licence	Year(s) of deliveries	No. delivered/ produced	Comments
USA	24	F/A-18A/B Hornet	FGA aircraft	1995	1995–99	18	Ex-US Navy; option on 6 more; deal worth $288 m; refurbished before delivery; Spanish designation C-15; delivery 1995–2000
	4	Mk-45 127mm/54	Naval gun	1999		..	Ex-US Navy; refurbished before delivery; for 4 F-100 Class frigates
	4	AN/SPY-1F	Surveillance radar	1996		..	Deal worth $750 m; part of AEGIS air defence system for 4 F-100 Class frigates
	4	Mk-41	ShAM system	(1997)		..	For 4 F-100 Class frigates
	(384)	RIM-7PTC ESSM	ShAM	(1997)		..	For 4 F-100 Class frigates
	44	AGM-65F Maverick	Air-to-ship missile	1999		..	For Navy AV-8B FGA aircraft
	(200)	AIM-120A AMRAAM	Air-to-air missile	(1996)	1999	(100)	
	100	AIM-120B AMRAAM	Air-to-air missile	(1998)		..	FMS deal worth $52 m
	100	AIM-7P Sparrow	Air-to-air missile	1997	1999	(50)	For F-18A/B FGA aircraft; delivery 1999/2000
	226	Javelin	Anti-tank missile	1999		..	Deal worth $25 m incl 12 launchers; contract not yet signed
L: Germany (FRG)	12	Buffel	ARV	1998		..	Deal worth $2.26 b (offsets 80%) incl 4 direct delivered and 219 Leopard-2A5+ tanks
	219	Leopard-2A5+	Main battle tank	1998		..	Spanish designation Leopard-2A5E; deal worth $2.26 b (offsets 80%) incl 16 Buffel ARVs; delivery from 2002
UK	4	Sandown/CME Type	MCM ship	1993	1999	2	Deal worth $381 m; Spanish designation Segura Class; delivery 1999–2000
Sri Lanka **S:** Russia	6	Mi-24P/Mi-35P Hind-F	Combat helicopter	(1998)	1998–99	(6)	Ex-Russian Army; refurbished before delivery; bought for use against LTTE rebels
UK	(2)	C-130K Hercules	Transport aircraft	(1998)		..	Ex-UK Air Force; refurbished before delivery; delivery 2000

No.	Weapon designation	Weapon description	Year of order	Year(s) of delivery	No. delivered	Comments
(3)	Mi-24V/Mi-35 Hind-E	Combat helicopter	(1998)	1999	(2)	Ex-Ukrainian Air Force; bought for use against LTTE rebels

Sri Lanka/LTTE
S: Unknown

(10)	AT-4 Spigot/9M111	Anti-tank missile	(1999)	1999	(10)	

Sudan
S: Poland

20	T-55AM-1	Main battle tank	(1998)	1999	20	Ex-Polish Army; export licence for 50 given for delivery to Yemen but after first 20 illegally diverted to Sudan the rest were kept in Poland

Suriname
S: Spain

1	C-212-400 Aviocar	Transport aircraft	1997	1999	1	
1	C-212-400 Patrullero	MP aircraft	1997	1999	1	

Sweden
S: France

..	TRS-2620 Gerfaut	Surveillance radar	1993	1997–99	(50)	Deal worth $17.7 m; for CV-90 AAV(G)s
(31)	BLG-60	ABL	(1994)	1998–99	(31)	Former GDR equipment; possibly refurbished in FRG or in other country before delivery
10	Buffel	ARV	1999		..	Option on 4 more; deal worth SEK59 m; delivery 2002–2003
5	Piranha-3 10x10	APC	1998	1998–99	(5)	Option on more; all APC/CP version

Germany (FRG) *(for BLG-60 row)*; Switzerland *(for Piranha-3 row)*

L: Germany (FRG)

91	Leopard-2A5+	Main battle tank	1994	1998–99	(48)	Deal worth $770 m incl 160 ex-FRG Army Leopard-2 tanks (offsets 120%); option on 90 more; Swedish designation Strv-122; delivery 1998–2001

Switzerland
S: France

12	AS-532UC/AS-332	Helicopter	1998		..	Deal worth $208 m; incl 10 assembled in Switzerland; delivery 2000–2002

Recipient/ supplier (S) or licenser (L)	No. ordered	Weapon designation	Weapon description	Year of order/ licence	Year(s) of deliveries	No. delivered/ produced	Comments
Sweden	2	Master-A	Surveillance radar	1998		..	Part of Florako air surveillance network
	186	CV-9030	IFV	(1999)		..	Deal worth $482 m; contract not yet signed; delivery from 2002
USA	34	F/A-18C/D Hornet	FGA aircraft	1993	1996–99	(34)	Deal worth $2.3 b (offsets worth $1.35 b); incl 8 F/A-18D trainer version; incl assembly of 32 in Switzerland
	12 000	BGM-71D TOW-2	Anti-tank missile	(1985)	1988–99	(12 000)	Deal worth $209 m incl 400 launchers and night vision sights; assembled in Switzerland
Syria							
S: Russia	(1 000)	AT-14/Kornet	Anti-tank missile	(1998)	1998–99	(1 000)	
Taiwan (ROC)							
S: Canada	30	Bell-206B JetRanger-3	Helicopter	(1997)	1998–99	(30)	For training; also designated TH-67 Creek
USA	13	Bell-206/OH-58D(I)	Combat helicopter	1999	1999	(1)	FMS deal worth $172 m incl ammunition; assembled in Taiwan; delivery 1999–2001
	(21)	Bell-209/AH-1W	Combat helicopter	1997	1999	(9)	FMS deal worth $479 m; delivery 1999/2000
	9	CH-47D Chinook	Helicopter	1999		..	FMS deal worth $300–486 m; for delivery 2001–2002
	2	E-2C Hawkeye	AEW&C aircraft	1999		..	Deal worth $400 m; US export designation E-2T; contract not yet signed; delivery 2002
	150	F-16AM/BM	FGA aircraft	1992	1997–99	(150)	Deal worth $5.8 b incl 600 AIM-7M and 900 AIM-9S missiles; incl 30 F-16BM trainer version
	11	S-70B/SH-60B Seahawk	ASW helicopter	1997		..	For Navy; US export designation S-70C(M)-2 Thunderhawk
	300	M-60A3 Patton-2	Main battle tank	1996	1998–99	(300)	Ex-US Army; deal worth $223 m
	(1)	AN/FPS-117	Surveillance radar	1992	1999	(1)	US export designation GE-592; part of Sky Net air defence system
	8	AN/SPG-60 STIR	Fire control radar	(1989)	1993–98	(7)	For 8 Perry (Cheng Kung) Class frigates; for use with Standard ShAM system

No. ordered	Weapon designation	Weapon description	Year of order	Year(s) of deliveries	No. delivered/produced	Comments
8	AN/SPS-49	Surveillance radar	(1989)	1993–98	(7)	For 8 Perry (Cheng Kung) Class frigates
8	Mk-13	ShAM system	1989	1993–98	(7)	For 8 Perry (Cheng Kung) Class frigates
(383)	RIM-66B Standard-1MR	ShAM	(1994)	1994–98	(323)	For Perry (Cheng Kung) Class frigates
8	Phalanx Mk-15	CIWS	1991	1993–98	(7)	For 8 Perry (Cheng Kung) Class frigates
8	WM-28	Fire control radar	(1989)	1993–98	(7)	For 8 Perry (Cheng Kung) Class frigates
2	Knox Class	Frigate	1998	1999	2	Ex-US Navy; 1 or 2 more delivered for spares only; Taiwanese designation Chin Yang Class
2	Mk-42/9 127mm/54	Naval gun	1998	1999	2	On 2 ex-US Knox Class frigates
2	AN/SPG-53	Fire control radar	1998	1999	2	On 2 ex-US Knox Class frigates
2	AN/SPS-10	Surveillance radar	1998	1999	2	On 2 ex-US Knox Class frigates
2	AN/SPS-40B	Surveillance radar	1998	1999	2	On 2 ex-US Knox Class frigates
2	Mk-16	ASW missile system	1998	1999	2	On 2 ex-US Knox Class frigates
2	Phalanx Mk-15	CIWS	1998	1999	2	On 2 ex-US Knox Class frigates
2	RGM-84 ShShMS	ShShM system	1998	1999	2	On 2 Knox Class frigates
58	AGM-84A/C Harpoon	Air-to-ship missile	1998		..	FMS deal worth $101 m; for F-16AM/BM FGA aircraft
600	AIM-7M Sparrow	Air-to-air missile	1992	1997–99	(600)	Deal worth $5.8 b incl 150 F-16AM/BM aircraft and 900 AIM-9S missiles
900	AIM-9S Sidewinder	Air-to-air missile	1992	1997–99	(900)	Deal worth $5.8 b incl 150 F-16AM/BM FGA aircraft and 600 AIM-7M missiles
1 786	BGM-71D TOW-2	Anti-tank missile	1997		..	Deal worth $80 m
(1 299)	FIM-92A Stinger	Portable SAM	1997		..	Deal worth $200 m incl 79 Avenger AAV(M)s, 50 man-portable launchers and training; number ordered could be up to 1599
728	FIM-92A Stinger	Portable SAM	1998	1998–99	..	FMS deal worth $180 m incl 61 launchers
52	RGM-84A/C Harpoon	ShShM	1997	1998–99	(26)	FMS deal worth $95 m
L: USA						
8	Perry Class	Frigate	1989	1993–98	7	Taiwanese designation Cheng Kung Class; 'Kwang Hua-1' project; last 1 delayed for financial reasons; delivery 1993–2002/3
Thailand						
S: Canada						
20	Bell-212	Helicopter	1993	1997–99	(15)	Deal worth $130 m

Recipient/ supplier (S) or licenser (L)	No. ordered	Weapon designation	Weapon description	Year of order/ licence	Year(s) of deliveries	No. delivered/ produced	Comments
Germany (FRG)	20	Alpha Jet	Jet trainer aircraft	1999		..	Ex-FRG Air Force; refurbished before delivery; 5 more delivered for spares only; deal worth $34.5 m; for ground attack; delivery 2000–2001
Italy	2	Gaeta Class	MCM ship	1996	1999	(2)	Deal worth $120 m; Thai designation Lat Ya Class
Switzerland	16	PC-9	Trainer aircraft	(1997)	1998–99	(16)	
	(36)	GHN-45 155mm	Towed gun	1997	1999	(18)	
USA	(16)	F-16A/B	FGA aircraft	(1999)		..	Ex-US Air Force; contract not yet signed; deal worth $157 m incl 2 more for spares only
	3	AN/FPS-130X	Surveillance radar	1995	1998–99	(3)	Part of RTADS air defence system
L: Australia	3	LCU-50m Type	Landing craft	1997		..	Thai designation Man Nok Class; delivery 2000/2001
UK	3	Khamronsin Class	OPV	1997		..	Supplier uncertain; Thai designation Hua Hin Class
Turkey							
S: France	2	AS-532UL/AS-332L1	Helicopter	1997		..	'Phoenix-2' deal worth $430 m incl 28 licensed production; for SAR; incl 1 for armed SAR; delivery 2000
	5	Circe Class	MCM ship	1997	1998–99	5	Ex-French Navy; refitted before delivery; deal worth $50 m; Turkish designation Edinçik Class
	1	Tenace Class	Tug	1999	1999	1	Ex-French Navy
Germany (FRG)	197	RATAC-S	Battlefield radar	1992	1995–99	(197)	Incl assembly in Turkey; Turkish designation Askarad
	(1 500)	FIM-92C Stinger	Portable SAM	1986	1998–99	(600)	Part of European Stinger Production Programme involving production of components in FRG, Greece, Netherlands and Turkey and final assembly in FRG; delivery 1998–2001/2
	1	Frankenthal Class	MCM ship	1999		..	Deal worth $625 m incl 5 licensed production; delivery 2003/2004
	4	Type-209/1400	Submarine	1998		..	Turkish designation Preveze Class; deal worth $556 m; delivery 2003–2006

	No.	Weapon designation	Weapon description	Year of order	Year(s) of deliveries	No. delivered	Comments
Israel	(46)	Popeye-1	ASM	(1998)			For F-4E-2000 FGA aircraft
Italy	1	A-109 Hirundo	Helicopter	(1999)	1999	1	For Coast Guard; for training and VIP transport
	5	Bell-412EP/AB-412EP	Helicopter	1998			Deal worth $52 m; for SAR; for Coast Guard; for delivery 2000
	4	Bell-412EP/AB-412EP	Helicopter	1999			For SAR; for Coast Guard; deal worth $35 m
	4	Seaguard	CIWS	(1994)	1998	2	For 2 MEKO-200T-2 Type (Barbaros Class) frigates; for use with Sea Zenith 25mm CIWS
Netherlands	3	MW-08	Surveillance radar	1995	1998–99	(2)	For 3 Kılıç Class FAC
	3	STING	Fire control radar	1995	1998–99	(2)	For 3 Kılıç Class FAC; for use with 76mm and 35mm guns
	4	STIR	Fire control radar	(1994)	1998	2	For 2 MEKO-200T-2 Type (Barbaros Class) frigates; for use with Seasparrow VLS ShAM system and 127mm gun
Norway	16	Penguin Mk-2-7	Air-to-ship missile	1999			Deal worth up to $40 m; for Navy S-70/SH-60B helicopters
UK	2	AWS-6 Dolphin	Surveillance radar	(1994)	1998	1	For 2 MEKO-200T-2 Type (Barbaros Class) frigates
	2	AWS-9	Surveillance radar	(1994)	1998	1	For 2 MEKO-200T-2 Type (Barbaros Class) frigates
	41	Rapier Mk-2	SAM	1999	1999	(20)	Ex-UK Air Force; on loan till delivery of new Rapier-2B missiles; delivery 1999–2000
USA	8	CH-53E Super Stallion	Helicopter	(1999)			Deal worth $345 m; contract not yet signed
	50	S-70A/UH-60L	Helicopter	1999	1999	20	Originally ordered 1992, but deal suspended in 1994 until 1999 because of financial reasons and as reaction to US policy towards Turkish actions against Kurds; deal worth $561 m (offsets worth $110 m); US export designation S-70A-28; Turkish designation Karaku; for delivery 1999–2001
	8	S-70B/SH-60B Seahawk	ASW helicopter	1998			For Navy; US export designation S-70B-28; delivery 2000–2001
	84	AGM-114B Hellfire-2	ASM	1999			Deal worth $6.7 m; for Navy S-70B/SH-60B helicopters; delivery from 2001
	2	Mk-45 127mm/54	Naval gun	(1994)	1998	1	For 2 MEKO-200T-2 Type (Barbaros Class) frigates
	2	RGM-84 ShShMS	ShShM system	(1992)	1998	1	For 2 MEKO-200T-2 Type (Barbaros Class) frigates
	16	RGM-84A/C Harpoon	ShShM	1995			Deal worth $15.3 m; for 1 MEKO-200T-2 Type (Barbaros Class) frigate

Recipient/ supplier (S) or licenser (L)	No. ordered	Weapon designation	Weapon description	Year of order/ licence	Year(s) of deliveries	No. delivered/ produced	Comments
	(40)	RIM-7P Seasparrow	ShAM	(1994)	1996–98	(25)	For 2 MEKO-200T-2 Type (Barbaros Class) frigates
	3	RGM-84 ShShMS	ShShM system	1993	1998–99	(2)	For 3 Kiliç Class FAC
	(48)	RGM-84A/C Harpoon	ShShM	1993	1998–99	(32)	For 3 Kiliç Class FAC
	2	Perry Class	Frigate	1998	1999	2	Ex-US Navy; Turkish designation Gaziantep Class; 1 more delivered for spares only
	2	AN/SPG-60 STIR	Fire control radar	1998	1999	2	On 2 ex-US Perry Class frigates
	2	AN/SPS-49	Surveillance radar	1998	1999	2	On 2 ex-US Perry Class frigates
	2	AN/SPS-55	Surveillance radar	1998	1999	2	On 2 ex-US Perry Class frigates
	2	Mk-13	ShAM system	1998	1999	2	On 2 ex-US Perry Class frigates
	2	Phalanx Mk-15	CIWS	1998	1999	2	On 2 ex-US Perry Class frigates
	2	WM-28	Fire control radar	1998	1999	2	On 2 ex-US Perry Class frigates
	138	AIM-120A AMRAAM	Air-to-air missile	(1993)	1997–99	(138)	FMS deal; for F-16C/D FGA aircraft
	500	AIM-9S Sidewinder	Air-to-air missile	1994	1998–99	(500)	Deal worth $55 m incl 30 training missiles
	(48)	UGM-84A Sub Harpoon	SuShM	(1993)	1997–99	(23)	For 4 Type-209/1400 (Preveze Class) submarines
L: France	28	AS-532UL/AS-332L1	Helicopter	1997		..	'Phoenix-2' deal worth $430 m incl 2 delivered direct; incl 18 for SAR and 10 for Army; incl 5 for armed SAR; delivery 2000–2003
Germany (FRG)	10 000	Eryx	Anti-tank missile	1998		..	Deal worth $487 m; delivery 2000–2009
	5	Frankenthal Class	MCM ship	1999		..	Deal worth $625 m incl 1 direct delivery; delivery 2004–2007
	2	Kiliç Class	FAC(M)	1993	1999	1	Deal worth $250 m incl 1 delivered direct; delivery 1999–2000
	1	MEKO-200T-2 Type	Frigate	1994		..	Deal worth $525 m incl 1 delivered direct (incl DM 150 m financed by FRG aid); Turkish designation Barbaros Class; delivery 2000
Spain	2	Type-209/1400	Submarine	1993	1998–99	2	Turkish designation Preveze Class
	9	CN-235MP	MP aircraft	(1998)		..	Incl 6 for Navy and 3 for Coast Guard; deal worth $108–120 m
UK	..	Shorland S-55	APC	(1990)	1994–99	(60)	For Gendarmerie

	No.	Weapon designation	Weapon description	Year of order	Year of delivery	No. delivered	Comments
USA	840	Rapier Mk-2B	SAM	1999		..	Deal worth $130–150 m; for use with Rapier SAM systems refurbished to Rapier B1X; delivery 2001–2010
	40	F-16C/D	FGA aircraft	1994	1998–99	40	Second part of $2.8 b 'Peace Onyx-2' deal; financed by Turkish Defence Fund with aid from USA, UAE, Saudi Arabia and Kuwait as reward for Turkish participation in 1990–91 Persian Gulf War
	650	AIFV	IFV	1988	1990–99	(456)	Deal worth $1.08 b incl 830 APC, 48 tank destroyer and 170 APC/mortar carrier version (offsets $705 m)
	665	AIFV	IFV	(1999)		..	Deal worth $450 m; incl APC and mortar carrier versions
UAE							
S: France	14	AS-350B Ecureuil	Helicopter	1999		..	For Dubai; deal worth $27 m; incl for training
	(7)	AS-565SA Panther	ASW helicopter	1995	1999	(1)	For Abu Dhabi; deal worth $230 m incl AS-15TT missiles; no. ordered could be 6; delivery 1999–2000
	2	AS-565SA Panther	ASW helicopter	1997		..	For Dubai; deal worth $30 m incl 5 SA-342K helicopters
	30	Mirage-2000-5 Mk-2	FGA aircraft	1998		..	Deal worth $3.4 b incl upgrade of 33 UAE Air Force Mirage-2000 to Mirage-2000-5 Mk-2; incl 11 Mirage-2000DAD trainer version; incl 12 ex-French Air Force Mirage-2000 rebuilt to Mirage-2000-5 Mk-2; delivery from 2003
	5	SA-342K/L Gazelle	Helicopter	1997		..	For Dubai; deal worth $30 m incl 2 AS-565SA helicopters
	390	Leclerc	Main battle tank	1993	1994–99	(279)	Deal worth $4.6 b incl 46 Leclerc ARVs (offsets 60%); incl 2 Leclerc Driver Training Tank version; delivery 1994–2000
	46	Leclerc DNG	ARV	1993	1997–99	(45)	Deal worth $4.6 b incl 390 Leclerc tanks (offsets 60%)
	(56)	AS-15TT	Air-to-ship missile	(1997)	1999	(10)	Deal worth $230 m incl 7 AS-565SA helicopters

Recipient/ supplier (S) or licenser (L)	No. ordered	Weapon designation	Weapon description	Year of order/ licence	Year(s) of deliveries	No. delivered/ produced	Comments
	(756)	MICA-EM	Air-to-air missile	1998		..	For 30 new Mirage-2000-5 Mk-2 and 33 Mirage-2000 modified to Mirage-2000-5 Mk-2
Netherlands	87	M-109A3 155mm	Self-propelled gun	1995	1997–99	(87)	Ex-Dutch Army; refurbished before delivery for $32.4 m; for Abu Dhabi
	10	Scout	Surveillance radar	1996	1997–99	(6)	For refit of 2 Kortenaer Class frigates, 6 TNC-45 Type FAC and 2 other ships
Russia	(400)	BMP-3	IFV	(1994)	1994–99	(400)	For Dubai
Turkey	128	AIFV-APC	APC	1997	1999	(72)	For Dubai; incl 75 artillery support/logistic and 53 ACV-ENG engineer version; deal worth $75 m incl 8 ARV version; delivery 1999–2000
	8	AIFV-ARV	ARV	1997	1999	(4)	For Dubai; deal worth $75 m incl 128 AIFV-APC version; delivery 1999–2000
UK	..	Black Shahine	ASM	1998		..	For 30 new Mirage-2000-5 Mk-2 and 33 Mirage-2000 modified to Mirage-2000-5 Mk-2
USA	80	F-16C/D Block-60	FGA aircraft	(1999)		..	Incl 40 F-16D Block-60 trainer version; deal worth $5 b; contract not yet signed
	24	RGM-84A/C Harpoon	ShShM	1998	1998–99	(24)	For 2 Kortenaer (Abu Dhabi) Class frigates; FMS deal
	72	RIM-7M Seasparrow	ShAM	1997	1998–99	(72)	Deal worth $27 m; for 2 Kortenaer (Abu Dhabi) Class frigates
UK							
S: Canada	5	BD-700 Global Express	Transport aircraft	1999		..	Deal worth $1.3 b incl ASTOR radars (offsets 100%); for modification to AGS aircraft with ASTOR radars
Germany (FRG)	(7)	Alpha Jet	Jet trainer aircraft	1999	1999	(6)	Ex-FRG Air Force; 6 more delivered for spares only; for use as training and test aircraft by DERA
	(99)	G-115D	Trainer aircraft	1998	1999	(4)	Deal worth $28 m; for civilian company for training of UK pilots; UK designation G-115E Tutor

	No.	Weapon designation	Weapon description	Year of order	Year of delivery	No. delivered	Comments
Netherlands	2	Goalkeeper	CIWS	(1996)		..	For 2 Albion Class AALS
Norway	4	FBRV	ARV	(1999)		..	Deal worth £7.5 m ($12.4 m); for Marines; delivery 2002/2003 or 2004
Sweden	(127)	BvS-10	APC	(1999)		..	For Marines; incl APC/CP and ARV version; contract not yet signed
USA	8	AH-64D Apache	Combat helicopter	1995	1999	(1)	Deal worth $3.95 b (offsets 100%) incl 59 licensed production and 980 AGM-114 missiles; UK designation WAH-64D; delivery 2000
	980	AGM-114 Longbow	Anti-tank missile	1995		..	Deal worth $3.95 m incl 67 AH-64D helicopters; assembled in UK; delivery 2000–2003
	(1 600)	AGM-114K Hellfire	Anti-tank missile	(1996)		..	Assembled in UK; delivery from 2000
	5	ASTOR	AGS radar	1999		..	Deal worth $1.3 b (offsets 100%) incl 5 BD-700 aircraft; for modification of 5 BD-700 transport aircraft delivered from Canada to AGS aircraft
	10	C-130J Hercules-2	Transport aircraft	1994		..	Deal worth $1.56 b (offsets 100%) incl 10 C-130J-30; UK designation Hercules C-5; delivery 2000–2001
	15	C-130J-30 Hercules	Transport aircraft	1994	1998–99	(3)	Deal worth $1.56 b (offsets 100%) incl 10 C-130J; UK designation Hercules C-4; option on 5 more; delivery 1999–2000
	8	MH-47E Chinook	Helicopter	1995		..	Deal worth $365 m incl 6 CH-47D version; UK designation Chinook HC-Mk-3; delivery from 2000
	65	BGM-109 T-LAM	SLCM	1995	1998–99	(65)	Deal worth $316 m; for 10 Swiftsure and Trafalgar Class submarines
	20	BGM-109 T-LAM	SLCM	1999		..	Deal worth $50 m
L: USA	59	AH-64D Apache	Combat helicopter	1995		..	Deal worth $3.95 b (offsets 100%) incl 8 delivered direct and 980 AGM-114 missiles; UK designation WAH-64D; delivery 2001–2003
USA							
S: Germany (FRG)	1	Boeing-707-320C	Transport aircraft	(1998)	1999	1	Ex-FRG Air Force; modified in USA to E-8C J-STARS airborne command aircraft

Recipient/ supplier (S) or licenser (L)	No. ordered	Weapon designation	Weapon description	Year of order/ licence	Year(s) of deliveries	No. delivered/ produced	Comments
Israel	1 700	Popeye-1/AGM-142	ASM	1998		..	US designation AGM-142A Raptor or Have Nap
UK	8	UFH 155mm	Towed gun	1997		..	US designation XM-777; prior to licensed production; delivery from 2000
L: Austria	(50)	Pandur	APC	1999		..	Deal worth $51 m; US designation Armored Ground Mobility System (AGMS); more produced for export
Italy	12	Osprey Class	MCM ship	1986	1993–99	12	
Switzerland	(711)	PC-9/T-6A Texan-2	Trainer aircraft	1995	1999	(12)	Incl 339 for Navy; 'JPATS' programme worth $7 b; US designation Beech Mk-2 or T-6A Texan-2
UK	234	Hawk/T-45A Goshawk	Jet trainer aircraft	1981	1988–99	(113)	For Navy; US designation T-45A or T-45C Goshawk; 'VTXTS' or 'T-45TS' programme; incl 2 prototypes; delivery 1988–2004
	(723)	UFH 155mm	Towed gun	(1997)		..	Incl 450 for Marines; US designation M-777; delivery 2000–2003
	1	Cyclone Class	Patrol craft	1997		..	Deal worth $23.2 m; delivery 2000
Uganda **S: Poland**	7	MiG-21bis Fishbed-N	Fighter aircraft	(1999)	1999	(7)	Ex-Polish Air Force; incl 1 MiG-21UM trainer; possibly non-flyable
United Nations **S: South Africa**	27	RG-32 Scout	APC	1998	1998–99	(27)	For UN peacekeeping, monitoring and humanitarian operations
	23	RG-32 Scout	APC	1998	1999	(23)	For UN peacekeeping, monitoring and humanitarian operations
	75	RG-32 Scout	APC	1999	1999	(35)	Deal worth $9 m; for use with UN in Kosovo

Uruguay

Supplier	No.	Weapon designation	Weapon description	Year of order	Year(s) of deliveries	No. delivered	Comments
S: Czech Republic	(30)	BMP-1	IFV	(1996)	1998-99	(30)	Ex-Czech Army
Italy	13	SF-260M	Trainer aircraft	(1998)	1999	(6)	
UK	2	Jetstream-31	Light transport ac	1998	1999	2	Ex-UK Navy

Venezuela

Supplier	No.	Weapon designation	Weapon description	Year of order	Year(s) of deliveries	No. delivered	Comments
S: Brazil	8	AMX-T	FGA/trainer aircraft	1999		..	Deal worth $150 m; delivery from 2001
Canada	4	Bell-412EP	Helicopter	1997	1999	4	For SAR
France	(10)	AS-532U2/AS-332L2	Helicopter	(1997)	1999	(10)	For Air Force; delivery 2001–2002
Israel	3	Barak ADAMS	SAM system	1999		..	For Air Force
Israel	..	Barak	SAM/ShAM	1999		..	Deal worth $110 m; option on 16 more; delivery from 2000
Italy	8	MB-339FD	Jet trainer aircraft	1999		..	Deal worth $12 m
	12	SF-260M	Trainer aircraft	1998		..	Designation uncertain
Korea, South	1	Endeavour Class	Support ship	1999		..	For use with 3 Barak SAM systems; for Air Force; delivery 2001–2002
Netherlands	3	Flycatcher Mk-2	Fire control radar	1999		..	
Poland	2	Reporter	Surveillance radar	1997	1999	(2)	For use with Guardian 40mm guns
	(6)	M-28 Skytruck	Light transport ac	(1997)		..	For National Guard; deal worth $20 m
Sweden	4	Giraffe-AD	Surveillance radar	1998		..	For use with RBS-70 SAMs
	..	RBS-70	Portable SAM	1999		..	Deal worth $42 m incl anti-tank rockets

Viet Nam

Supplier	No.	Weapon designation	Weapon description	Year of order	Year(s) of deliveries	No. delivered	Comments
S: Russia	(6)	Bass Tilt	Fire control radar	1996		..	For 6 BPS-500 Type FAC; for use with 76mm and AK-630 30mm guns
	(6)	Cross Dome	Surveillance radar	1996		..	For 6 BPS-500 Type FAC
	(6)	SS-N-25 ShShMS	ShShM system	1996		..	For 6 BPS-500 Type FAC
	96	SS-N-25/X-35 Uran	ShShM	1996		..	For 6 BPS-500 Type FAC
	(144)	SA-N-5 Grail/Strela-2M	ShAM	(1996)		..	For 6 BPS-500 Type FAC; designation uncertain
	2	Tarantul-2 Class	FAC(M)	(1998)	1999	2	
	2	Bass Tilt	Fire control radar	1998	1999	2	On 2 Tarantul-2 Class FAC; for use with 76mm and 30mm guns
	2	Plank Shave	Surveillance radar	1998	1999	2	On 2 Tarantul-2 Class FAC

Recipient/ supplier (S) or licenser (L)	No. ordered	Weapon designation	Weapon description	Year of order/ licence	Year(s) of deliveries	No. delivered/ produced	Comments
L: Russia	2	SS-N-2 ShShMS	ShShM system	1998	1999	2	On 2 Tarantul-2 Class FAC
	(16)	SS-N-2d Styx/P-21	ShShM	(1998)	1999	(16)	For 2 Tarantul-2 Class FAC
	(24)	SA-N-5 Grail/Strela-2M	ShAM	(1998)	1999	(24)	For 2 Tarantul-2 Class FAC
L: Russia	(6)	BPS-500 Type	FAC(M)	1996		..	Vietnamese designation Ho-A Class
Yemen							
S: Czech Republic	12	L-39C Albatros	Jet trainer aircraft	1999	1999	(12)	
	97	T-55	Main battle tank	1999	1999	..	Ex-Czech Army; incl some T-54 tanks; refurbished before delivery
Yugoslavia							
L: Russia/USSR	..	AT-3 Sagger/9M14M	Anti-tank missile	(1974)	1976–99	(15 100)	Incl for Mi-8 helicopters and M-80 IFVs
	..	SA-7b Grail/Strela-2M	Portable SAM	(1980)	1981–99	(2 745)	Yugoslavian designation Strela-2M and Strela-2M/A
Unknown							
S: France	..	Eryx	Anti-tank missile	1999	1999	(100)	Recipient is an undisclosed Gulf Cooperation Council (GCC) member state

Abbreviations and acronyms

ac	Aircraft	LTTE	Liberation Tigers of Tamil Eelam
AAA	Anti-aircraft artillery	(M)	Missile-armed
AALS	Amphibious assault landing ship	MCM	Mine countermeasures
AAV	Anti-aircraft vehicle	MP	Maritime patrol
ABL	Armoured bridge-layer	MRL	Multiple rocket launcher
ACRV	Armoured command and reconnaissance vehicle	no.	Number
ACV	Air-cushion vessel (hovercraft)	OPV	Offshore patrol vessel
AEV	Armoured engineer vehicle	Recce	Reconnaissance
AEW	Airborne early-warning	SAM	Surface-to-air missile
AEW&C	Airborne early-warning and control	SAR	Search and rescue
AGS	Airborne ground-surveillance	ShAM	Ship-to-air missile
AIFV	Armoured infantry fighting vehicle	ShShM	Ship-to-ship missile
ALV	Armoured logistic vehicle	SIGINT	Signals intelligence
AMV	Anti-mine vehicle	SLCM	Submarine-launched cruise missile
APC	Armoured personnel carrier	SSM	Surface-to surface missile
APC/CP	Armoured personnel carrier/command post	SuShM	Submarine-to-ship missile
ARV	Armoured recovery vehicle	UAV	Unmanned aerial vehicle (drone)
ASM	Air-to-surface missile	VIP	Very important person
ASW	Anti-submarine warfare	VLS	Vertical-launch system
CIWS	Close-in weapon system		
EDA	Excess Defense Articles (US)		
ELINT	Electronic intelligence		
EW	Electronic warfare	**Conventions**	
FAC	Fast attack craft		
FGA	Fighter/ground attack	. .	Data not available or not applicable
FMF	Foreign Military Funding (US)	( )	Uncertain data or SIPRI estimate
FMS	Foreign Military Sales (US)	m	million (10^6)
(G)	Gun-armed	b	billion (10^9)
IFV	Infantry fighting vehicle		
incl	Including/includes		

'Status uncertain' is used in the comments field when sources are contradictory about the (continued) existence of the reported deal.

'Unknown' is used in cases where it has not been possible to identify a supplier or recipient with an acceptable degree of certainty.

Table 7C.2. Index of suppliers of major conventional weapons and their recipients and licencees, 1999

This index lists recipients and licensees by suppliers of major weapons on order or under delivery, or for which the licence was bought and production was under way or completed during 1999. The types of weapon involved in the transfers can be found by cross-referencing with the register of the transfers and licensed production of major conventional weapons in 1999 in table 7C.2. Entries are alphabetical, by supplier, recipient and licensee.

Supplier	Recipients (**R**) and licensees (**L**)
Australia	**R:** New Zealand, Philippines; **L:** Thailand
Austria	**R:** Botswana; **L:** Belgium, Slovenia, USA
Belarus	**R:** Algeria, Pakistan
Belgium	**R:** Brazil
Brazil	**R:** Greece, Venezuela
Bulgaria	**R:** Macedonia
Canada	**R:** Australia, Bulgaria, Denmark, Saudi Arabia, Spain, Taiwan, Thailand, UK, Venezuela
Chile	**R:** Dominican Republic
China	**R:** Bangladesh, Egypt, Iran, Kuwait, Myanmar, Pakistan; **L:** Pakistan
Czech Republic	**R:** Cambodia, Ethiopia, Georgia, Uruguay, Yemen
Denmark	**L:** Greece
Finland	**R:** Egypt, Netherlands, Norway
France	**R:** Argentina, Austria, Brazil, Brunei, Canada, Chile, China, Estonia, Finland, Germany, Greece, Hungary, Indonesia, Jamaica, South Korea, Kuwait, Macedonia, Malaysia, Morocco, Pakistan, Qatar, Romania, Saudi Arabia, Slovakia, South Africa, Spain, Sweden, Switzerland, Turkey, UAE, Venezuela, Unknown;[a] **L:** China, India, Japan, Pakistan, Turkey
Germany	**R:** Brazil, Canada, Denmark, Estonia, Greece, Israel, South Korea, Latvia, Lithuania, Netherlands, Norway, Portugal, Romania, South Africa, Spain, Sweden, Thailand, Turkey, UK, USA; **L:** Argentina, Australia, Brazil, Egypt, Greece, India, Indonesia, Italy, Japan, South Korea, Malaysia, Spain, Sweden, Turkey
Greece	**R:** Macedonia
Indonesia	**R:** Brunei; South Korea, Malaysia
Israel	**R:** Chile, China, Ecuador, India, South Korea, Romania, Singapore, Turkey, USA, Venezuela; **L:** China
Italy	**R:** Argentina, Brazil, Bulgaria, Canada, Chile, Greece, Hungary, India, Macedonia, Malaysia, Mexico, Netherlands, South Africa, Spain, Thailand, Turkey, Uruguay, Venezuela; **L:** Australia, USA
Kazakhstan	**R:** North Korea

Korea, South	**R:** Bangladesh, Venezuela
Netherlands	**R:** Argentina, Brunei, Chile, Germany, Greece, India, Indonesia, South Korea, Malaysia, Spain, Turkey, UAE, UK, Venezuela; **L:** India, South Korea
Norway	**R:** Australia, Denmark, Finland, Turkey, UK
Poland	**R:** Estonia, India, Sudan, Uganda, Venezuela
Romania	**R:** Netherlands
Russia	**R:** Algeria, Bangladesh, China, Cyprus, Ethiopia, Greece, Hungary, India, Iran, Kazakhstan, Malaysia, Peru, Rwanda, Singapore, Sri Lanka, Syria, UAE, Viet Nam; **L:** China, India, Iran, North Korea, Poland, Romania, Viet Nam, Yugoslavia
Singapore	**L:** Brazil
Slovakia	**R:** India
South Africa	**R:** Canada, India, United Nations
Spain	**R:** Chile, Dominican Republic, France, Suriname; **L:** Indonesia, Turkey
Sweden	**R:** Australia, Austria, Brazil, Finland, France, Germany, Greece, Malaysia, New Zealand, Norway, Pakistan, Singapore, South Africa, Switzerland, UK, Venezuela; **L:** Australia, Pakistan
Switzerland	**R:** Denmark, Ireland, Oman, Slovenia, Sweden, Thailand; **L:** Canada, Chile, Malaysia, USA
Taiwan	**R:** Paraguay
Turkey	**R:** Jordan, Macedonia, UAE
UK	**R:** Australia, Botswana, Brunei, Canada, Chile, China, Germany, Greece, India, Indonesia, Ireland, Italy, Jordan, Kuwait, South Korea, Malaysia, Oman, Poland, Portugal, Qatar, Saudi Arabia, South Africa, Spain, Sri Lanka, Turkey, UAE, USA, Uruguay; **L:** Algeria, Australia, Greece, India, Poland, Saudi Arabia, Spain, Thailand, Turkey, USA
USA	**R:** Argentina, Australia, Bahamas, Bahrain, Belgium, Bosnia and Herzegovina, Brazil, Canada, Colombia, Croatia, Denmark, Ecuador, Egypt, Finland, France, Georgia, Germany, Greece, Indonesia, Israel, Italy, Japan, Jordan, South Korea, Kuwait, Lebanon, Macedonia, Mexico, Netherlands, New Zealand, Norway, Poland, Portugal, Romania, Saudi Arabia, Singapore, South Africa, Spain, Switzerland, Taiwan, Thailand, Turkey, UAE, UK; **L:** Egypt, Germany, Indonesia, Japan, South Korea, Pakistan, Taiwan, Turkey, UK
Ukraine	**R:** Greece, India, Iran, Pakistan, Sierra Leone, Sri Lanka
Unknown[a]	**R:** Sri Lanka/LTTE[b]
Uzbekistan	**R:** India

[a] 'Unknown' is used in cases where it has not been possible to identify a supplier or recipient with an acceptable degree of certainty.
[b] Liberation Tigers of Tamil Eelam.

Appendix 7D. Sources and methods[1]

I. The SIPRI sources

The sources for the data presented in the arms transfer registers are of a wide variety: newspapers; periodicals and journals; books, monographs and annual reference works; and official national and international documents. The common criterion for all these sources is that they are open—published and available to the general public.

Published information cannot provide a comprehensive picture because not all arms transfers are fully reported in the open literature. Published reports provide partial information, and substantial disagreement among reports is common. Order and delivery dates and exact numbers of weapons ordered and delivered may not always be clear from the sources. Therefore, the exercise of judgement and the making of estimates are important elements in compiling the SIPRI arms transfers database. Estimates are kept at conservatively low levels and may very well be underestimates.

II. Selection criteria

SIPRI arms transfer data cover six categories of major conventional weapons or systems. The statistics presented refer to the transfer of systems in these six categories only. The categories are defined as:

1. Aircraft: all fixed-wing aircraft and helicopters, with the exception of micro-light aircraft and powered and unpowered gliders.
2. Armoured vehicles: all vehicles with integral armour protection, including all types of tank, tank destroyer, armoured car, armoured personnel carrier, armoured support vehicle and infantry combat vehicle.
3. Artillery: multiple rocket launchers; naval, fixed and towed guns, howitzers and mortars, with a calibre equal to or above 100-mm; as well as all armoured self-propelled guns, regardless of calibre.
4. Guidance and radar systems: all land- and ship-based surveillance and fire-control radars, and all non-portable land- and ship-based launch and guidance systems for missiles covered in the SIPRI 'missile' category.
5. Missiles: all powered, guided missiles with conventional warheads. Unguided rockets, guided but unpowered shells and bombs, free-fall aerial munitions, anti-submarine rockets, drones and unmanned air vehicles (UAV) and torpedoes are excluded.
6. Ships: all ships with a standard tonnage of 100 tonnes or more, and all ships armed with artillery of 100-mm calibre or more, torpedoes or guided missiles.

The registers and statistics do not include transfers of small arms, trucks, towed or naval artillery under 100-mm calibre, ammunition, support items, services and components or component technology. Publicly available information is inadequate to track these items satisfactorily on a global scale.

---

[1] A more extensive description of the SIPRI Arms Transfers Project methodology, including a list of the sources used, is available on the SIPRI Internet site, URL <http://www.sipri.se/projects/armstrade/atmethods.html>.

To be included in the SIPRI arms transfers registers, items must be destined for the armed forces, paramilitary forces or intelligence agencies of another country and they must be transferred voluntarily by the supplier. This excludes captured weapons and weapons obtained through defectors. It does include weapons delivered (illegally) without proper authorization by the government of the supplier or recipient country. The weapons must have a military purpose. Systems such as VIP (very important person) aircraft used mainly for other government branches but registered with and operated by the armed forces are excluded. Arms supplied for technical or arms procurement evaluation purposes only, or to companies, are not included.

Arms supplied to rebel forces in an armed conflict are included as deliveries to the individual rebel forces.

In cases where it has not been possible to identify a supplier or recipient with an acceptable degree of certainty, deliveries are identified as coming from 'unknown' suppliers or going to 'unknown' recipients.

III. The SIPRI trend-indicator value

The SIPRI system for valuation of arms transfers is designed as a *trend-measuring device*, to permit the measurement of changes in the total flow of major weapons and its geographical pattern. Expressing the valuation in trend-indicator values, in which similar weapons have similar prices, reflects both the quantity and quality of the weapons transferred. Values are based only on *actual deliveries* during the year/ years covered in the relevant tables and figures.

Production under licence is included in the arms transfers statistics in such a way as to reflect the average import share from the licenser embodied in the weapon. In reality, this share is normally high in the beginning, gradually decreasing over time.

The SIPRI valuation system is not comparable to official economic statistics such as gross domestic product, public expenditure and export/import figures. The monetary values assigned do not correspond to the actual prices paid, which vary considerably depending on different pricing methods, the length of production runs and the terms involved in individual transactions. For instance, a deal may or may not cover spare parts, training, support equipment, compensation, offset arrangements for the local industries in the buying country, and so on. Furthermore, using only actual sales prices—even assuming that the information were available for all deals, which it is not—would exclude military aid and grants, and the total flow of arms would therefore not be measured. In the SIPRI register of the transfers and licensed production of major conventional weapons (appendix 7C), however, actual contract values are given when available and verifiable. These values are included in order to give an indication of the financial scope of the deal concerned.

IV. Continuity

As new data become available the SIPRI database on arms transfers is constantly updated for all years included in the database (from 1950). Thus data from two SIPRI Yearbooks or other SIPRI publications cannot be combined. It is therefore advisable for readers who require time-series data for periods before the years covered in this Yearbook to contact SIPRI.

Appendix 7E. Government and industry statistics on national arms exports

PIETER D. WEZEMAN

Publicly available government and industry statistics on the value of national arms exports are listed in table 7E. These data are included here for four reasons: (*a*) to make them more accessible; (*b*) to illustrate the current state of government transparency on arms export data; (*c*) to underline the fact that arms export data from different countries are only comparable to a limited extent; and (*d*) to provide a rough indication of the financial scale of arms exports.

Caution should be exercised when using the data in table 7E for detailed analysis. Only some of the statistics are fully explained, definitions are not consistent from country to country and the reports give different definitions of what is included in the category 'arms'. Some countries release figures only on arms exports, others aggregate exports of arms and dual-use equipment. Some release data on the value of items *delivered*, others on the value of items *approved* for export, some on both. In some countries different reports present different national arms export data. To underline this last type of inconsistency, all relevant data are included in the table. No attempt has been made to compensate for any of these comparability problems or possible lack of reliability.

Despite these methodological reservations, in the absence of good alternatives the values are considered useful as a rough indication of the financial scale of arms exports. Such an indication cannot be derived from the SIPRI arms transfer trend-indicator values as these indicate the volume of international arms transfers and not actual financial values (see appendix 7D).

The table is not comprehensive and there are other countries, such as China, whose exports would be larger than those of some of the countries listed in the table. However, SIPRI estimates that the countries in the table together account for 93 per cent of the total volume of deliveries of major conventional weapons in 1999 and it can be assumed that these countries together account for a similar high percentage of total arms exports in financial terms.

Table 7E is based on publications of governments and arms industry associations, well-documented reports on government statements, and government and arms industry association replies to SIPRI's requests for information. Comments are worded as closely as possible to details in the documents cited. If the comment does not specify whether the values refer to permits or deliveries, this distinction is not specified in the original source. Sources refer to the last year reported for each country. Sources for previous years are given in earlier SIPRI Yearbooks. The 1998 US dollar series is calculated on the basis of average 1998 exchange rates. SIPRI collects hyperlinks to Internet sites containing official arms export data, which in several cases include data disaggregated by recipients and category.[1]

---

[1] These are listed at URL <http://www.sipri.se/projects/armstrade/atlinks.html>.

Table 7E. Government and industry data on national arms exports, 1994–98

Country	Currency unit (current prices)	1994	1995	1996	1997	1998	1998 (US $m.)	Explanation of data
Australia	m. A. dollars[a]	28.4	39.2	435.2	19	..	..	Value of shipments of military goods (fiscal years)
Belgium	m. B. francs[b]	11 403	8 230	8 180	7 460	12 537	345	Value of arms exports
	m. euros	..	..	..	..	649.7	729	Value of licences for arms exports
Brazil	m. US dollars[c]	2.6	12.4	8.7	26	70	70	Value of arms exports
Canada	m. C. dollars[d]	497.4	447.3	464.8	304.3	421.4	284	Shipments of military goods, excluding exports to the USA
Industry	m. C. dollars[e]	..	..	798	..	851	574	Defence revenues from markets outside Canada and USA
Industry	m. C. dollars[e]	..	..	996	..	1 010	681	Defence revenues from US market
Czech Rep.	m. US dollars[f]	194	154	117	182	104.1	104.1	Value of arms exports
Finland	m. F. markkaa[g]	61	132	69	81.5	184	34	Value of exports of defence matériel
France	m. francs[h]	11 600	10 900	18 600	..	..	..	Value of exports of defence equipment
	m. francs[i]	16 774	18 991	29 430	43 294	41 178	6 978	Value of deliveries of defence equipment and associated services
	m. francs[i]	31 741	33 537	19 392	30 184	49 627	8 412	Value of export orders for defence equipment and associated services
Germany	m. D. marks[j]	2 131	1 982	1 006	1 384	1 338	760	Value of exports of weapons of war
	m. euros	..	..	..	..	2 829	3 175	Value of licences for arms exports
India	m. rupees[k]	..	960	1 430	1 860	760	18	Value of exports by defence public-sector undertakings and ordnance factories (fiscal years)
Ireland	m. euros	..	..	..	..	20	22	Value of licences for arms exports
Israel	m. US dollars[l]	1 419	1 369	1 466	1 654	1 879	1 879	Value of the shipment of military goods
Italy	b. lire[m]	915	1 228	1 196	2 065	1 944	1 120	Value of deliveries of military equipment
	b. lire[m]	2 952	1 559	2 165	1 726	1 838	1 059	Value of export licences for military equipment
Korea, South	m. US dollars[n]	59.9	67.9	31.9	69.4	..	..	Value of defence industrial products exports
	m. US dollars[o]	..	..	45	58	147	147	Value of arms exports
Netherlands	m. guilders[p]	1 006	1 029	922	2 438	952	480	Value of export licences for military goods
Industry	m. guilders[q]	1 200	900	1 600	1 900	..	..	Value of exports as reported by the defence industry

Table 7E, *contd*

Country	Currency unit (current prices)	1994	1995	1996	1997	1998	1998 (US $m.)	Explanation of data
Norway	m. kroner[r]	..	..	985	1 060	1 135	150	Value of actual deliveries of defence *matériel*
Portugal	m. escudos[s]	3 430	6 803	4 157	3 205	3 806	21	Value of exports of defence materials, equipment, technology
	m. euros	..	..	..	..	14.7	16	Value of licences for arms exports
Romania	m. US dollars[t]	122	168	77	56	56	56	Value of arms exports
Russia	m. US dollars[u]	1 700	..	3 900	3 600	2 700	2 700	Value of exports of military equipment
Slovakia	m. koruny[v]	3 320	2 452	2 214	1 273	..	..	Value of exports of military production
Slovenia	m. tolars[w]	2 730	966	2 290	726	..	..	Value of exports of defence equipment
South Africa	m. rand[x]	..	855	517	1 324.9	646	117	Value of export permits issued
Spain	m. pesetas[v]	9 478	16 400	19 473	95 128	..	..	Value of exports of defence *matériel* (excl. dual-use equipment)
	m. euros	..	..	..	..	164	184	Value of licences for arms exports
	m. pesetas[z]	..	..	63 000	..	..	..	Foreign sales of defence *matériel* by major companies
Sweden	m. kronor[aa]	3 181	3 313	3 087	3 101	3 514	442	Value of actual deliveries of military equipment
	m. kronor[aa]	4 268	6 543	2 859	5 061	3 273	412	Value of export permits granted for sales of military equipment
Industry	m. kronor[bb]	4 075	3 514	4 289	3 667	4 434	558	Foreign sales of military and civil products to military customers
Switzerland	m. S. francs[cc]	221	141.2	232.9	294.3	212.7	147	Value of exports of war *matériel*
Taiwan	m. NT dollars[dd]	..	..	..	25 500	..	..	Value of military sales in 2-year periods
Turkey ind.	m. US dollars[ee]	..	..	236	..	..	..	Export turnover of defence industries
UK	m. pounds[ff]	..	..	..	3 359.6	1 968.3	3 260	Value of deliveries of defence equipment
	m. pounds[gg]	1 798	2 076	3 402	4 598	3 527	5 842	Value of deliveries of defence equipment
	m. pounds[gg]	2 946	4 723	6 177	6 685	..	..	Value of deliveries of defence equipment and items where the official commodity classifications do not distinguish between military and civil aerospace equipment
	m. pounds[gg]	4 608	4 970	5 080	5 540	6 049	10 020	Value of export orders for defence equipment
Ukraine	m. US dollars[hh]	..	..	..	600	..	..	Value of arms exports

USA							
m. dollars[ii]	9 468	11 940	11 574	19 233	13 522	13 522	Value of deliveries of defence articles and services through the US Government (foreign military sales) in fiscal years
m. dollars[ii]	3 339	3 173	1 563	1 818	2 045	2 045	Value of deliveries of munitions-controlled items directly from US manufacturers
m. dollars[ii]	13 292	8 950	10 300	8 782	8 231	8 231	Value of agreements on sales of defence articles and services through US Government (foreign military sales) in fiscal years
m. dollars[jj]	22 200	22 900	23 000	31 800	..	..	Value of arms transfer deliveries
m. dollars[jj]	39 200	28 500	38 300	34 000	..	..	Value of arms transfers agreements

.. = no data available or received

a Australian Department of Defence, Industry and Procurement Infrastructure Division, *Annual Report: Exports of Defence and Strategic Goods from Australia, 1997/98*, June 1999.

b Belgian Ministry of Foreign Affairs, *Rapport van de regering aan het parlement over de toepassing van de wet van 5 augustus 1991 betreffende de in-, de uit-, en de doorvoer van wapens, munitie, en speciaal voor militair gebruik dienstig materieel en de daaraan verbonden technologie, 1 januari 1997 tot 31 december 1997* [Government report to parliament on the implementation of the law of 5 Aug. 1991 on the import, export and passage of weapons, ammunition and *matériel* for military use and related technology, 1 Jan.–31 Dec. 1997], 1998.

c Information received from the Brazilian Embassy, Stockholm, 21 Mar. 2000.

d Canadian Department of Foreign Affairs and International Trade, Exports Controls Division, Export and Import Controls Bureau, *Annual Report: Export of Military Goods from Canada, 1998*, Nov. 1999.

e Grover, B., Canadian Defence Industries Association, 'Canadian Defence Industry 1999: a statistical overview of the Canadian defence industry', Dec. 1999, URL <http://www.cdia/fullreport.htm>.

f Information received from the Embassy of the Czech Republic, Stockholm, 26 Oct. 1999.

g Internet site of the Finnish Ministry of Defence, URL <http://www.vn.fi/plm/ekvas.htm>.

h Information from La Délégation Générale pour l'Armement, URL <http://www.defense.gouv.fr/dga/fr/activites/rapport_d_activite_1998/l_armement_en_1998>.

i Ministère de la Défense, *Rapport au Parlement sur les exportations d'armement de la France, Résultats 1998* [Report to Parliament on French arms exports, results 1998], Mar. 2000.

j Information received from the German Ministry of Economics, Bonn, 14 Dec. 1999.

k Indian Ministry of Defence, *Annual Report 1998/99*, p. 42.

l Information received from the Foreign Defence Assistance and Defence Exports organization (SIBAT), Ministry of Defence, Israel.

m Camera dei Deputati, *Relazione sulle operazioni autorizzate e svolte per il controllo dell'esportazione, importazione e transito dei materiali di armamento nonchè dell'esportazione e del transito dei prodotti ad alta tecnologia (anno 1997)* [Chamber of Deputies, Report on operations authorized and carried out concerning the control of export, import and transit of weapons material as well as the export and transit of high-technology products (1997)], 30 Mar. 1998.

n Ministry of National Defense, South Korean Defence White Paper 1998, 1999, p. 370.

o Quoted from a report for the National Assembly's investigation on government affairs submitted by the Defense Ministry. *JoongAng Ilbo* (Seoul), 29 Sep. 1999, URL <http://english.joongang.co.kr/jnews/jnews.asp?n_id=1990929001>.

p Netherlands Ministry of Economic Affairs, *Jaarrapport Nederlands wapenexportbeleid 1998* [The Netherlands arms export policy in 1998], URL <http://info.minez.nl/-nieuwskiosk/kamerbrieven/1999/fs_kamer.htm>.

q Information received from Commissariat for Military Production of the Netherlands Ministry of Economic Affairs.

r Norwegian Ministry of Foreign Affairs, *Eksport av forsvarsmateriell fra Norge i 1998* [Arms exports from Norway in 1998], St meld nr 45 (1998/99), 18 June 1999.

s Portuguese Ministry of Defence, *Anuario Estatistico da Defesa Nacional 1998* [Annual national defence statistics, 1998], Sep. 1999, p. 101.

t Information received from the Embassy of Romania, Stockholm, 16 Feb. 2000.

u The Russian data on arms exports consist of the official data of the state arms export companies Rosvooruzheniye and Promexport and estimates for other enterprises that have been granted licences to engage in foreign military–technical cooperation. Rosvooruzheniye was the prime exporter with an export revenue in 1998 of $2.3 billion. See Teleinformatsionnaya Sem (TS-VPK), URL < http://ia.vpk.ru/cgi-bin/ia/fin/rep.pl>; and Makienko, K., 'Russia and the world arms market: 1998 and early 1999 assessment', *The Monitor*, vol. 5, no. 3 (summer 1999), pp. 20–22. On enterprises known to have been granted licences to engage in foreign military–technical cooperation see SIPRI Export Control Project, URL <http://projects.sipri.se/expcon/natexpcon/Russia/Russian_enterprise_docs/enterprise_exports.htm>.

v Information received from the Ministry of the Economy, Republic of Slovakia.

w Information received from the Ministry of Foreign Affairs, Republic of Slovenia.

x Internet site of the National Conventional Arms Control Committee, Republic of South Africa, URL <http://www.mil.za/SANDF/DRO/NCACC/ncacc.htm>.

y Spanish Ministry of Economy and Agriculture, *Exportaciones realizadas de material de defensa y de material de defensa y de doble uso en 1997, por países de destino* [Exports of military and dual-use equipment in 1997, by country of destination], 30 July 1998.

z Figures are an aggregate of relevant data on the Internet site of the Spanish Ministry of Defence, URL <http://www.mde.es/mde/infoes/industria/texto13.htm>.

aa Swedish Ministry for Foreign Affairs, *Redogörelse för den svenska krigsmaterielexporten år 1998* [Swedish exports of military equipment in 1998], Regeringens skrivelse 1998/99:128, 29 Apr. 1999.

bb Figures are an aggregate of relevant data on the Internet site of the Association of Swedish Defence Industries, URL <http://www.defind.se/statistik.htm>.

cc Bundesamt für Aussenwirtschaft, 'Ausfuhr von Kriegsmaterial 1998' [Exports of defence *matériel* 1998], Pressemitteilung, 5 Feb. 1999.

dd Ministry of National Defense, Republic of China, *1998 National Defense Report*, Taipei, Apr. 1998.

ee Information received from the Defense Industry Manufacturers Association, Turkey, 16 Apr. 1997.

ff British Foreign and Commonwealth Office, *Annual Report on Arms Exports*, 2 Nov. 1999, URL <http://www.fco.gov.uk/news/newstext.asp?2956>.

gg British Government Statistical Service, *UK Defence Statistics 1999*. The 2 British Government sources used in this table give different figures under the same heading 'Value of deliveries of defence equipment'.

hh 'Ukraine increased military equipment exports last year 2.3 fold', Interfax (Moscow), 23 Apr. 1998, in Foreign Broadcast Information Service, *Daily Report–Central Eurasia* (FBIS-SOV), FBIS-SOV-98-113, 23 Apr. 1998.

ii *Foreign Military Sales, Foreign Military Construction Sales and Military Assistance Facts, as of September 30, 1998*, Deputy for Financial Management Comptroller, Department of Defense Security Cooperation Agency, Washington, DC, URL <http://web.deskbook.osd.mil/appfiles/RLIB0536.XLS>.

jj US Bureau of Arms Control, *World Military Expenditures and Arms Transfers 1998*, URL <http://www.state.gov/www/global/arms/bureau_ac/wmeat98/wmeat98.html>.

Sources: All data in euros: Council of the European Union, Annual Report in Conformity with Operative Provision 8 of the European Union Code of Conduct on Arms Exports, Brussels, 28 Sep. 1999, p. 7.

Part III. Non-proliferation, arms control and disarmament, 1999

8. Nuclear arms control and non-proliferation

SHANNON KILE

I. Introduction

Developments in 1999 gave rise to growing concern that progress in nuclear arms control and disarmament had stagnated or was even in danger of being reversed. The US Senate voted to reject ratification of the 1996 Comprehensive Nuclear Test-Ban Treaty (CTBT), thereby at least temporarily blocking the treaty's entry into force. The Conference on Disarmament (CD) failed to open negotiations on a global Fissile Material Treaty (FMT). The meagre results of the third meeting of the Preparatory Committee for the year 2000 Review Conference of the 1968 Treaty on the Non-Proliferation of Nuclear Weapons (Non-Proliferation Treaty, NPT) reflected the continuing division between the nuclear weapon states and the non-nuclear weapon states over non-proliferation and disarmament goals and reinforced the pessimistic assessments of the Review Conference's prospects for success. The centrepiece of Russian–US nuclear arms reduction endeavours, the 1993 Treaty on Further Reductions and Limitation of Strategic Offensive Arms (START II Treaty), was not ratified by the Russian Federal Assembly (Parliament) in 1999. The controversy over ballistic missile defences and the future of the 1972 Treaty on the Limitation of Anti-Ballistic Missile Systems (ABM Treaty) became more intense during the year and threatened to halt further reductions in strategic nuclear forces and reverse the progress made to date.

This chapter reviews the principal developments in nuclear arms control and non-proliferation in 1999. Section II examines the discussions between Russia and the USA over US proposals to amend the ABM Treaty to permit the development and deployment of a limited national missile defence (NMD) system. Section III describes the main developments related to the START Treaty regime and assesses the prospects for further negotiated nuclear arms reductions. Section IV reviews the principal Russian–US cooperative nuclear security activities under way in 1999. Section V assesses the implications of the US Senate's decision not to ratify the CTBT for the four decade-long effort to bring about a permanent halt to nuclear testing. Section VI describes the procedural impasse in the CD that blocked the opening of negotiations on an FMT, while section VII summarizes the results of the 1999 Preparatory Committee meeting for the 2000 NPT Review Conference. Section VIII examines progress in implementation of the 1994 US–North Korean Agreed Framework, and section IX describes recent changes in nuclear doctrines. Section X presents the conclusions.

Appendix 8A provides data on the nuclear forces of the five NPT-defined nuclear weapon states and on the nuclear arsenals of India, Israel and Pakistan.

Appendix 8B describes the origins of the International Atomic Energy Agency's (IAEA) strengthened safeguards system and the main problems hindering the implementation of that programme.

II. The ABM Treaty and ballistic missile defence

In 1999 the debate over ballistic missile defence (BMD) and the future of the ABM Treaty continued to complicate Russian–US nuclear arms reduction efforts and to generate partisan controversy in Washington.[1] Proposals from the US Administration for amending the ABM Treaty to permit the eventual deployment of a limited national missile defence system were rejected by Russia, which warned that such changes would effectively eviscerate the treaty and undermine the basis for Russian–US nuclear arms control cooperation. At the same time, Republican leaders in the US Congress intensified their calls for the ABM Treaty to be scrapped altogether in the light of perceived new missile threats.

Developments in US national missile defence

On 22 July US President Bill Clinton signed into law the National Missile Defense Act of 1999. The legislation, which had been overwhelmingly approved by Congress, committed the USA 'to deploy as soon as is technologically possible an effective National Missile Defense system capable of defending the territory of the United States against limited ballistic missile attack (whether accidental, unauthorized, or deliberate)'.[2] It stipulated that the NMD programme would be part of the regular budget process and that the USA remained committed to negotiating with Russia further reductions in their nuclear forces.[3] In signing the bill into law, Clinton emphasized that no decision to deploy an NMD system had been made. He stated that a decision would be based on the following considerations: (*a*) a determination that a new long-range ballistic missile threat to the USA is emerging; (*b*) an assessment of the technological feasibility and operational effectiveness of a proposed NMD system; (*c*) overall system cost; and (*d*) the progress made in achieving US arms control objectives, 'including any amendments to the ABM Treaty that may be required to accommodate a possible NMD deployment'.[4]

---

[1] The ABM Treaty was signed by the USA and the USSR in May 1972, entered into force in Oct. 1972, and was amended in the 1974 Protocol. For a brief summary of the provisions, see annexe A in this volume. For the text of the ABM Treaty; the Agreed Statements, Common Understandings and Unilateral Statements; and the 1974 Protocol see Stützle, W., Jasani, B. and Cowen, R., SIPRI, *The ABM Treaty: To Defend or Not to Defend?* (Oxford University Press: Oxford, 1987), pp. 207–13.

[2] National Missile Defense Act of 1999, Public Law 106-38, 22 July 1999.

[3] Mann, P., 'Support gathers steam for national missile defense', *Aviation Week & Space Technology*, vol. 150, no. 12 (22 Mar. 1999), p. 29; and Knowlton, B., 'US Senate approves missile-shield plan', *International Herald Tribune*, 18 Mar. 1999, pp. 1, 3.

[4] United States Information Service (USIS), 'Text: President Clinton signs Missile Defense Act', The White House, Office of the Press Secretary, 23 July 1999, *European Washington File* (US Embassy: Stockholm, 23 July 1999).

The law marked an important change in US missile defence policy as well as a reversal of the Clinton Administration's opposition to similar NMD legislation proposed since 1995. Under the '3 +3' formula adopted in 1997, the USA had undertaken to pursue a 'technology readiness' programme for a limited NMD system which could be deployed within three years of a decision to do so, with an initial Deployment Readiness Review to take place three years later, in June 2000.[5] The National Missile Defense Act of 1999—a law supported by both the legislative and executive branches and by both political parties—committed the USA to deploying a limited NMD system once available technologies are judged to be sufficiently proven or promising. Its enactment was part of the broader shift in the US missile defence debate that occurred in 1999: the main point of contention was no longer whether a limited NMD system would be deployed but in what form.[6]

This shift reflected the emergent consensus in the USA in favour of developing and deploying a limited or 'thin' NMD system designed to protect US territory against an attack by a small number of long-range missiles—possibly armed with nuclear or other weapons of mass destruction—launched by so-called 'rogue states', such as North Korea and Iraq. Political support for an NMD system was galvanized by North Korea's unannounced launch on 31 August 1998 of a three-stage Taepo Dong I ballistic missile. The launch was widely seen as lending credence to concerns expressed by proponents of missile defence that the USA would face such a threat in the foreseeable future. North Korea had already come under intense international scrutiny because of suspicions that it had a clandestine programme to develop nuclear weapons (see section VIII). Its missile launch also underscored the findings of the influential Rumsfeld Commission Report, published earlier in 1998. The report had warned that the threat to US troops deployed overseas and potentially to US territory posed by emerging ballistic missile capabilities in countries such as Iran and North Korea was 'broader, more mature and evolving more rapidly than has been reported in estimates and reports by the Intelligence Community'.[7] In September 1999 an unclassified version of the National Intelligence Estimate (NIE) was released which assessed the ballistic missile threat to the USA until the year 2015. The NIE concluded that 'during the next 15 years the United States most likely will face ICBM threats from Russia, China, and North Korea, probably from Iran and possibly from Iraq'.[8] It noted, however, that the development of long-range missiles by North Korea, Iran and Iraq was not a certainty and would depend on a variety of

---

[5] Kile, S., 'Nuclear arms control', *SIPRI Yearbook 1999: Armaments, Disarmament and International Security* (Oxford University Press: Oxford, 1999), pp. 541–42.

[6] Daalder, I. *et al*, 'Deploying NMD: not whether but how', *Survival*, vol. 42, no. 1 (spring 2000), pp. 6–28.

[7] Executive Summary of the Report of the Commission to Assess the Ballistic Missile Threat to the United States, 15 July 1998, URL <http://www.house.gov/hasc/testimony/105thcongress/BMThreat.htm>.

[8] National Intelligence Council, 'Foreign Missile Developments and the Ballistic Missile Threat to the United States through 2015', Sep. 1999, available at URL <http://www.fas.org/irp/threat/missile/nie99msl.htm#rtoc2>.

factors, including political and economic and relations with the West and developments in each country's region.

NMD programme problems

In January 1999 Secretary of Defense William Cohen announced that the administration would ask Congress for a significant increase in Department of Defense (DOD) funding for preparing the groundwork for an NMD system.[9] Congress subsequently authorized an additional $2.2 billion for NMD for fiscal year (FY) 2000; this amount came on top of the nearly $10.5 billion already authorized for NMD research and development (R&D) programmes for the period FY 1999–2005.

In order to reduce the technical risks associated with meeting an early deployment deadline, the NMD programme was restructured in 1999 into a series of phased deployment-readiness decisions so that the target date for deploying an NMD system was delayed from 2003 (as envisioned in the '3+3' formula) to 2005.[10] However, in November 1999 a report prepared by an independent panel of experts appointed by the DOD (the Welch Committee) warned that the NMD programme continued to be at a 'high risk' of failure.[11] The panel recommended that, in the light of likely delays in crucial tests, the Deployment Readiness Review scheduled to take place in the summer of 2000 should be changed to a 'deployment feasibility' assessment in order 'to avoid regressing to a very high risk schedule'.[12]

The panel's concerns were underscored by the technical problems plaguing the Pentagon's NMD testing programme.[13] In October 1999 the US Ballistic Missile Defense Organization (BMDO) announced that a prototype NMD interceptor had successfully destroyed a target vehicle over the central Pacific Ocean carried by a modified Minuteman intercontinental ballistic missile (ICBM).[14] However, DOD officials later acknowledged that the interceptor

[9] 'Cohen announces plan to augment missile defense programs', US Department of Defense News Release no. 018-99, Office of the Assistant Secretary of Defense (Public Affairs), 20 Jan. 1999, URL <http://www.defenselink.mil/news/Jan1999/b01201999_bt018-99.html>.

[10] Wall, R., 'US missile defense system delayed', *Aviation Week & Space Technology*, vol. 150, no. 4 (25 Jan. 1999), pp. 40–41.

[11] Report of the National Missile Defense Review Committee, 16 Nov. 1999, reproduced by the Ballistic Missile Defense Organization, URL http://www.acq.osd.mil/bmdo/bmdolink/html/docs.html>.; and Mann, P., 'Missile defense still troubled', *Aviation Week & Space Technology*, vol. 151, no. 21 (22 Nov. 1999), pp. 31–32. The panel noted that among other technical and organizational problems, the NMD programme was plagued by inadequate testing, spare parts shortages and lapses in management oversight.

[12] Report of the National Missile Defense Review Committee (note 11). The Ballistic Missile Defense Organization (BMDO) plans to conduct 19 intercept tests involving the different elements of the NMD system architecture through the year 2005. Critics point out that the initial NMD deployment decision is scheduled to be made after only 3 intercept tests have been completed. O'Hanlon, M., 'Star Wars strikes back', *Foreign Affairs*, vol. 78, no. 6 (Nov./Dec. 1999), p. 74.

[13] Graham, B., 'Pentagon's antimissile program needs defense', *Washington Post*, 14 Nov. 1999, pp. A1, 6; and Mann, P., 'Missile defense still "troubled"', *Aviation Week & Space Technology*, vol. 151, no. 21 (22 Nov. 1999), pp. 31–32.

[14] National missile defense conducts successful intercept test', News release no. 459-99, Office of Assistant Secretary of Defense (Public Affairs), 2 Oct. 1999, URL <http://www.defenselink.mil/news/Oct1999/b10031999_bt-459.html>. The purpose of the test was to demonstrate the ability of the inter-

had suffered a number of guidance and target discrimination problems during the test. In a second flight test, conducted in January 2000, the interceptor failed to hit the target.[15]

The proposed NMD system

The US Administration has chosen the basic architecture for a limited NMD system, although there remains considerable uncertainty about the timing and size of an eventual deployment. The proposed system is designed to defend the 50 US states against 'the most immediate' missile threat, that is, the 'launch of a few tens of warheads accompanied by simple penetration aids' by North Korea; it is also intended to provide a defence against a similar attack launched from the Middle East.[16] According to the revised planning guidelines adopted by the administration in late 1999, the system—which is to be ready for possible deployment beginning in 2005—would consist of 100 missile interceptors based in central Alaska.[17] An associated ground-based tracking radar would be built in the western Aleutian Islands.[18] The system could be expanded later to include 100–150 interceptor missiles based at a second site (likely to be situated in North Dakota), along with additional tracking radars, in order to meet greater threats from more sophisticated missiles launched from North Korea or the Middle East.[19]

Other elements of the planned NMD architecture include a set of launch-detection satellites scheduled to be placed in geosynchronous orbit after 2004, called the Space-Based Infra-Red System (SBIRS)–High system, which would establish a target missile's launch corridor. The five existing ballistic missile early-warning radars—located in the USA and at Thule, Greenland, and Fylingdales, UK—would be upgraded to provide tracking information and estimates of missile flight trajectories.[20] In addition, a missile defence battle-management and command, control and communications system would be built at the North American Aerospace Defense headquarters at Cheyenne Mountain, Wyoming. The system also envisions the use of the SBIRS–Low satellite system, which is scheduled for deployment in low-earth orbit after

ceptor's exo-atmospheric kill vehicle (EKV) to intercept and destroy a ballistic missile target using only the kinetic energy of the collision

[15] Becker, E., 'Missile fails in setback for US defense plan', *International Herald Tribune*, 20 Jan. 2000, p. 1.

[16] Testimony of Walter B. Slocombe, Under Secretary of Defense for Policy, to the Armed Services Committee, US House of Representatives, 13 Oct. 1999.

[17] The USSR chose to deploy (and Russia continues to maintain) an ABM system around Moscow. The USA deployed an ABM system known as Safeguard at an ICBM silo complex at Grand Forks, North Dakota; it achieved an initial operating capability in 1975 but was deactivated in 1976. The USA must obtain Russia's consent in order to move its designated ABM site to Alaska.

[18] The ABM Treaty would have to be amended to permit the USA to deploy an X-band tracking radar at Shemya Island, which is located more than 150 km from a proposed ABM site in central Alaska and hence prohibited under Article III.

[19] Slocombe (note 16).

[20] Wilkening, D., 'Amending the ABM Treaty', *Survival*, vol. 42, no. 1 (spring 2000), pp. 31–32. Articles III and VI of the ABM Treaty would have to be amended to permit the early-warning radars to perform the function of ABM radars. In the case of the radars at Thule and Fylingdales, Article IX (under which each of the parties undertakes not to deploy ABM systems or their components outside its territory) would have to be amended.

2006, to provide significantly improved target tracking information and discrimination capabilities (i.e., the ability to distinguish incoming warheads from decoys and penetration aids).[21]

The size and scope of the proposed NMD system have been criticized by some missile defence advocates, who argue that the current plans will lead to a fragile defence capability that will be inadequate to meet emerging ballistic missile threats.[22] They have complained that the administration's plans are driven more by concerns with preserving intact the ABM Treaty than by considerations of operational effectiveness. Proponents of a more robust US NMD system have called for expanded plans that involve a sea-based as well as a land-based component—to be supplemented later by space- and air-based components—to form a layered missile defence.[23] Such a defence would require wholesale changes to the ABM Treaty or its outright abandonment.

Russian–US discussions on the ABM Treaty

In announcing the decision to seek significantly increased funding for national missile defence, Defense Secretary Cohen acknowledged that the deployment of a limited NMD system would require modifications to the ABM Treaty, to be the subject of negotiations with Russia.[24] Senior administration officials rejected subsequent press accounts that the USA had threatened to withdraw from the treaty. Following talks in late January 1999 with Russian Foreign Minister Igor Ivanov, US Secretary of State Madeleine Albright reaffirmed the USA's commitment to preserving the ABM Treaty as the 'cornerstone of strategic stability' and noted that further discussions would be held in the recently established Russian–US Strategic Stability Working Group.[25]

On 20 June 1999, at the conclusion of a Group of Eight (G8) summit meeting in Cologne, Germany, Clinton and Russian President Boris Yeltsin issued a Joint Statement Concerning Strategic Offensive and Defensive Arms and Further Strengthening of Stability. The Joint Statement marked the first step towards the resumption of the Russian–US discussions of strategic issues which had been interrupted by the acrimonious political dispute over NATO's air strikes in the former Yugoslavia. Among other points, the two leaders recognized the 'fundamental importance' of the ABM Treaty for efforts to strengthen strategic stability and to further reduce strategic offensive nuclear

[21] Slocombe (note 16); and Wilkening (note 20). This would require amending the treaty's prohibition (in Article V) on developing and deploying space-based ABM systems or components.

[22] See, e.g., Gompert, D. and Isaacson, J., *Planning a Ballistic Missile Defense System of Systems: An Adaptive Strategy* (RAND: Santa Monica, Calif., 1999); and Spence, F., Office of the Chairman of the Armed Services Committee, US House of Representatives, 'Nuclear deterrence: the cornerstone of US national security', *National Security Report*, vol. 3, no. 2 (Aug. 1999), pp. 1, 4.

[23] Heritage Foundation Commission on Missile Defence, *Defending America: A Plan to Meet the Urgent Missile Threat* (Heritage Foundation: Washington, DC, 1999).

[24] 'Cohen announces plan to augment missile defense programs' (note 9); and Hoffman, D., 'US plans threaten Moscow arms pact', *International Herald Tribune*, 22 Jan. 1999, pp. 1, 5.

[25] USIS, Transcript of press conference remarks of Secretary of State Madeleine Albright and Foreign Minister Igor Ivanov, Moscow, 26 Jan. 1999, Office of the Spokesman, US Department of State, *European Washington File* (US Embassy: Stockholm, 26 Jan. 1999).

arms.[26] They called for discussions on the treaty to be held later in the summer in the light of 'possible changes in the strategic situation' that have a bearing on 'its viability and effectiveness'.[27]

The subsequent discussions made little headway. Following preliminary talks between US and Russian experts held in August, Russian Deputy Foreign Minister Grigoriy Berdennikov told reporters that Russia saw 'no reasons or practical needs or possibilities for changing any key aspects and restrictions of the ABM Treaty'.[28] At further talks in the autumn, senior US officials put forward a set of specific proposals for amending the ABM Treaty, but the confidential discussions reportedly made no progress towards reaching an agreement.[29]

US proposals for amending the ABM Treaty

The Clinton Administration has proposed a series of 'modest' changes to the ABM Treaty that would permit the USA to proceed with the phased deployment of a limited NMD system.[30] The changes primarily involve adjustments in the number of ABM interceptors and the location of interceptor launcher sites permitted by the treaty.[31] According to Under Secretary of State John Holum, the USA would seek to permit the deployment of a system designed to respond to the threat of a few warheads but which 'would not interfere with the basic purpose of the treaty'.[32]

US officials emphasized that this would not undermine the stability of the strategic balance between Russia and the USA or jeopardize further reductions in US and Russian strategic offensive arms. They argued that it would enable the USA to defend its territory against a limited attack involving relatively unsophisticated missiles and that, since it could be easily overwhelmed by Russia's large arsenal of long-range missiles, it would not threaten Russia's second-strike nuclear retaliatory capability.

[26] Joint Statement Between the United States and the Russian Federation Concerning Strategic Offensive and Defensive Arms and Further Strengthening of Stability, The White House, Office of the Press Secretary, Cologne, Germany, 20 June 1999.

[27] Joint Statement (note 26).

[28] Quoted by Interfax (Moscow), 19 Aug. 1999, in 'Russian official confirms opposition to ABM revision', Foreign Broadcast Information Service, *Daily Report–Central Eurasia* (FBIS-SOV), FBIS-SOV-1999-0819, 20 Aug. 1999.

[29] ITAR-TASS (Moscow), 18 Sep. 1999, in 'Envoy: Russia refuses to consider revising ABM Treaty', FBIS-SOV-1999-0918, 21 Sep. 1999; Gordon, M., 'Russians firmly reject US plan to reopen ABM Treaty', *New York Times* (Internet edn), 21 Oct. 1999, URL <http://www.nytimes.com/library/world/global/102199us-russia-abm.html>; and Jones, G., 'Russia, US in thorny arms control talks', Reuters, 21 Oct. 1999, URL <http://dailynews.yahoo.com/index/html>.

[30] Graham, B., 'US to seek modest shift in arms pact', *International Herald Tribune*, 9 Sep. 1999, p. 7.

[31] The 1974 Protocol to the ABM Treaty limits the parties to a single deployment area—either around the national capital or at an ICBM launch complex—containing no more than 100 ABM launchers and 100 single-warhead missile interceptors; associated engagement radars within the deployment area cannot exceed specified numbers and are subject to qualitative restrictions.

[32] USIS, Transcript of press conference remarks of John Holum, Under Secretary of State for Arms Control and International Security Affairs, at the Conference on Disarmament, Geneva, 21 Jan. 1999, Office of the Spokesman, US Department of State, *European Washington File* (US Embassy: Stockholm, 22 Jan. 1999).

In an effort to convince their Russian counterparts that any eventual NMD system would not be directed against Russia, US officials also proposed a number of cooperative measures aimed at increasing transparency and building confidence in the area of missile defence. These reportedly included US offers to assist Russia with the completion of its early-warning radar at Mishelvka, near Irkutsk, in Siberia; the radar is oriented towards the south-east, covering North Korea and other countries in Asia.[33] They also included a proposal to expand the Russian–US agreement in the 1998 Joint Statement on the Exchange of Information on Missile Launches and Early Warning. Under the proposal the USA would share radar data not only on the origin point and expected destination of launched missiles but also on the entire flight trajectories.[34] Other ideas reportedly under consideration were joint computer simulations of anti-missile systems and collaboration in developing missile launch-detection satellites.[35] However, in November 1999 a US Administration official denied newspaper reports that the USA was seeking Russia's acquiescence to amending the ABM Treaty by offering it compensation on other issues.[36]

Russian objections to amending the ABM Treaty

US proposals to amend the ABM Treaty to permit the deployment of a limited NMD system generated intense opposition in Russia. Deputy Foreign Minister Berdennikov declared that 'Russia is not bargaining over the ABM Treaty' and ruled out any amendments to the treaty.[37] On 3 November 1999 Russia announced that it had tested a short-range SH-08 Gazelle interceptor rocket for the Moscow ABM system in what was seen as a symbolic warning to the USA not to unilaterally proceed with plans to build an NMD system.[38]

Russian officials tended to view missile defences primarily from the perspective of maintaining the Russian–US strategic nuclear balance; there were concerns in Moscow that even a limited NMD system consisting of a single ABM site in Alaska would be capable of intercepting Russian missiles launched in a retaliatory strike against the USA. The USA's claims about the

[33] Mufson, S. and Graham, B., 'US offers aid to Russia on radar site', *Washington Post* (Internet edn), 17 Oct. 1999, URL <http://www.washingtonpost.com/wp-srv/WPlate/1999-10/17/1951-101799-idx.html>.

[34] For a description of the 1998 US–Russian Joint Statement on the Exchange of Information on Missile Launches and Early Warning, see Kile (note 5), p. 540.

[35] Mufson and Graham (note 33). In addition, 2 prominent US missile defence experts put forward a controversial proposal for a joint US–Russian boost-phase interceptor to counter a specific North Korean or Iranian missile threat to US cities; the programme was offered as a substitute for deployment of a wider US NMD system. Ratnam, G., 'US–Russian missile plan stirs controversy', *Defense News,* vol. 14, no. 48 (22 Nov. 1999), p. 26.

[36] John Holum, Under Secretary of State for Arms Control and International Security Affairs, cited by Interfax (Moscow), 9 Nov. 1999, in 'US official says no pressure on ABM Treaty', FBIS-SOV-1999-1109, 10 Nov. 1999.

[37] Quoted by ITAR-Tass (Moscow), 20 Oct. 1999, in 'Spokesman: Russia "not bargaining" over ABM Treaty', FBIS-SOV-1999-1020, 21 Oct. 1999. Some Russian officials and analysts argued that Russia's acceptance of a set of modest amendments to the ABM Treaty would encourage the USA to later demand more far-reaching changes to accommodate its missile defence plans.

[38] Hoffman, D., 'Russia tests an ABM amid warnings to US', *International Herald Tribune,* 4 Nov. 1999, p. 5.

emerging ballistic missile threat posed by states such as Iran, Iraq and North Korea were dismissed by Russia as being exaggerated.[39] Russian officials emphasized that the ABM Treaty was the cornerstone of the entire Russian–US nuclear arms control framework and warned that the deployment of any national missile defences—the prohibition of which is the 'basic purpose' of the ABM Treaty—would lead to the collapse of that framework.[40]

Russian Ministry of Defence officials warned that an abrogation of the ABM Treaty by the USA would lead to a Russian withdrawal from existing arms reduction treaties, including the 1987 Treaty on the Elimination of Intermediate-Range and Shorter-Range Missiles (INF Treaty), the START I Treaty and the unratified START II Treaty. This would mean that 'all mutual exchanges of information will be ended, and hundreds of verification missions that both sides carry out on a reciprocal basis will be discontinued'.[41] The result, according to Colonel General Vladimir Yakovlev, commander of the Russian Strategic Rocket Forces, would be a reversal of the arms control achievements of the past two decades, with the Russian and US strategic forces becoming less transparent and more unpredictable to one another.[42]

Russian military planners at the same time also derided the likely effectiveness of the NMD system envisioned by the Pentagon in countering even a limited ballistic missile attack.[43] They repeatedly warned that Russia would respond to any unilateral US decision to deploy an NMD system with a variety of technical countermeasures, some of which were designed in the 1980s as a response to the USA's Strategic Defense Initiative (SDI). One widely mentioned response was Russian development of a multiple-warhead version of its new single-warhead Topol-M (SS-27) ICBM. This step would be a violation of the ban on multiple-warhead ICBMs, which is the central provision of the unratified START II Treaty.

International reactions

Concerns about US missile defence plans were not confined to Russia. A senior Chinese Foreign Ministry official warned that a US decision to deploy an NMD system would have an adverse impact on regional and global stability

[39] Babakin, A., 'Where the antimissile missiles in Alaska are targeted', *Rossiyskaya Gazeta*, 10 Nov. 1999, p. 7, in 'Experts on "collapse" of ABM Treaty, Russian response', FBIS-SOV-1999-1109, 10 Nov. 1999; and Nesirsky, M., 'Russian general sees US corporate push on Star Wars', Reuters, 1 Dec. 1999, URL <http://dailynews.yahoo.com/index.html>.

[40] One unnamed Foreign Ministry spokesman pointed out that amending the ABM Treaty to permit national missile defences would 'mean turning the ABM Treaty inside out, that is, the treaty would begin to allow what it was developed and signed to ban'. Quoted by ITAR-TASS (Moscow), 28 Oct. 1999, in 'Russia not negotiating ABM Treaty changes', FBIS-SOV-1999-1028, 29 Oct. 1999.

[41] Maj. Gen. Vladimir Dvorkin, Director of the Central Research Institute of the Russian Ministry of Defence, quoted in Hoffman, D., 'Russians scoff at missile defenses', *International Herald Tribune*, 24 Nov. 1999, p. 6.

[42] Cited in Interfax (Moscow), 20 Oct. 1999, in 'Moscow can respond to US ABM withdrawal', FBIS-SOV-1999-1020, 21 Oct. 1999.

[43] Hoffman (note 41). Some prominent missile defence critics in the USA have argued that an attacker could defeat the NMD system envisioned by the Pentagon by using relatively simple countermeasures. See Lewis, G., Postol, T. and Pike, J., 'Why national missile defense won't work', *Scientific American*, vol. 281, no. 2 (Aug. 1999), pp. 22–28.

and could trigger a new nuclear arms race, adding that 'the nuclear disarmament process would grind to a halt or even be reversed'.[44] In the autumn of 1999, Chinese and Russian officials held consultations to discuss a common approach to ABM Treaty-related issues.[45] On 5 November the United Nations First Committee approved a draft resolution sponsored by Belarus, China and Russia (and supported by France) which called on the parties to the ABM Treaty 'to limit the deployment of anti-ballistic missile systems and to refrain from the deployment of such systems for a defence of the territory of its country'.[46]

A number of NATO allies expressed concern about the ramifications of the US missile defence plans for alliance cohesion and for the international security environment. European defence officials disputed US claims about the severity of the missile threat posed by 'rogue states'.[47] They expressed particular concern that the abandonment or evisceration of the ABM Treaty by the USA would complicate relations with Russia and might spark a renewed nuclear arms competition. They were also concerned that a US NMD shield would contribute over the long term to 'decoupling' transatlantic security by creating a situation in which Europe would be vulnerable to ballistic missile attack emanating from a regional trouble spot such as the Middle East while the USA would not be.[48]

Other ABM Treaty controversies

In 1999 two other agreements related to the ABM Treaty continued to generate debate in the USA. Republican leaders in Congress remained opposed to ratifying the 1997 theatre missile defence (TMD) demarcation agreement.[49] They also vowed to defeat the 1997 Memorandum of Understanding on Suc-

---

[44] Sha Zukang, Director of the Department of Disarmament Affairs, Ministry for Foreign Affairs of China, quoted by Lim, B., 'China rejects US anti-missile defense plans', Reuters, 24 Nov. 1999, URL <http://dailynews.yahoo.com/index.html>.

[45] ITAR-TASS (Moscow), 27 Nov. 1999, in 'Russia, China reiterate commitment to ABM Treaty', FBIS-SOV-1999-1127, 29 Nov. 1999.

[46] 'Draft resolution calling for compliance with 1972 ABM Treaty approved in Disarmament Committee by vote 54–4–73', United Nations Press Release GA/DIS/3161, 5 Nov. 1999.

[47] Clark, C. and Hill, L., 'Europe disputes need for ballistic missile defense', *Defense News*, vol. 14, no. 49 (13 Dec. 1999), pp. 3, 28.

[48] Becker, E., 'Allies fear US project may renew arms race', *New York Times* (Internet edn), 20 Nov. 1999, URL <http://www.nytimes.com/library/world/europe/112099summit-missile.html>; and Boese, W., 'NATO ministers skeptical of US NMD plans', *Arms Control Today*, vol. 29, no. 8 (Dec. 1999), p. 21.

[49] TMD systems occupy a 'grey zone' and are not formally subject to the restrictions of the ABM Treaty, which limits only strategic ABM systems. However, the demarcation between strategic and theatre ballistic missiles is not clearly defined and the technical characteristics of defences against them overlap considerably. In Sep. 1997, as part of a package of agreements related to TMD and the ABM Treaty, the foreign ministers of Belarus, Kazakhstan, Russia, Ukraine and the USA signed 2 Agreed Statements setting out technical parameters to clarify the demarcation line between strategic and theatre (non-strategic) missile defences, thereby resolving a protracted dispute between Russia and the USA over the issue. For a description of the Agreed Statements, see Kile, S., 'Nuclear arms control', *SIPRI Yearbook 1998: Armaments, Disarmament and International Security* (Oxford University Press: Oxford, 1998), pp. 420–23.

cession (MOUS), which would make the ABM Treaty a multilateral accord.[50] Republican leaders have claimed that the ABM Treaty has lapsed and is 'of no force and effect' unless the Senate ratifies the MOUS. The TMD Demarcation Agreement and the MOUS have been at the centre of a wider doctrinal dispute between the White House and Capitol Hill over whether the ABM Treaty should remain the 'cornerstone of strategic stability' in the post-cold war world. By the end of 1999 the Clinton Administration had still not submitted the agreements to the Senate for its advice and consent, ignoring a 1 June 1999 'deadline' to do so imposed by the Republican chairman of the Senate Foreign Relations Committee.[51]

TMD cooperation in East Asia

Following lengthy negotiations, US and Japanese officials signed an agreement in August 1999 to cooperate on TMD R&D efforts.[52] The five-year programme will focus on improving the Standard Missile SM-3, the interceptor used in the US Navy's Theater Wide (formerly known as Upper Tier) missile defence system.[53] A Pentagon analysis of options for missile defence in East Asia had determined that a BMD architecture using the Navy Theater Wide system would require fewer elements for defending Japan against a ballistic missile attack launched from North Korea than one based on other systems.[54] The impetus for the Japanese Government to move forward on TMD cooperation had come from the 1998 launch by North Korea of a Taepo Dong I missile that flew over Japan.

The announcement of the US–Japanese agreement on collaboration on a TMD R&D programme provoked criticism in China. Senior Chinese officials expressed concern that the advanced-capability US TMD systems currently under development would have considerable 'inherent capabilities' against China's relatively small arsenal of long-range ballistic missiles. Moreover, they expressed concern about the political implications of US–Japanese cooperation in developing regional missile defences that would eventually include Taiwan.[55]

[50] In Sep. 1997 the foreign ministers of Belarus, Kazakhstan, Russia, Ukraine and the USA signed the MOUS, pursuant to which the 4 former Soviet republics collectively assumed the rights and obligations of the USSR under the ABM Treaty. Kile (note 5), p. 544.

[51] 'Helms sets June deadline for ABM agreements', Arms Control Today, vol. 29, no. 1 (Jan./Feb. 1999), p. 28.

[52] Aldinger, C., 'US, Japan to begin missile defense effort', Reuters, 16 Aug. 1999, URL <http://dailynews.yahoo.com/index.html>.

[53] Wall, R., 'US, Japan agree on cooperative missile defense', Aviation Week & Space Technology, vol. 151, no. 8 (23 Aug. 1999), p. 46.

[54] Wall, R., 'Asia examines missile defense', Aviation Week & Space Technology, vol. 150, no. 24 (14 June 1999), p. 203.

[55] Zhang, M., China's Changing Nuclear Posture (Carnegie Endowment for International Peace: Washington, DC, 1999), pp. 48–49; and Diamond, H., 'China warns US on East Asian missile defense cooperation', Arms Control Today, vol. 29, no. 1 (Jan./Feb. 1999), p. 27.

III. The START treaties

Implementation of the START I Treaty

The Treaty on the Reduction and Limitation of Strategic Offensive Arms (START I Treaty) was signed by the Soviet Union and the USA in 1991 and entered into force for Russia and the USA in 1994. The Soviet Union's obligations under the treaty had been assumed by Russia as its legal successor state; the treaty was later joined by Belarus, Kazakhstan and Ukraine, the other former Soviet republics with strategic nuclear weapons based on their territories.[56] In 1999 the parties continued to implement the reductions in strategic nuclear delivery vehicles (SNDVs) and accountable warheads mandated by the treaty (see table 8.1). The progress made towards reaching the START I force limits was accompanied by a relative lack of controversy over the parties' compliance in the Joint Compliance and Inspection Commission (JCIC).[57] In April 1999, at a meeting of senior US and Russian foreign ministry officials in Geneva, a number of compliance disputes were discussed.[58] Throughout the year, some critics of the START I Treaty in Russia complained that the USA was not strictly complying with its provisions, in particular those related to inspection and transparency measures.[59]

The START II Treaty

The START II Treaty was signed by Russia and the USA on 3 January 1993.[60] It was ratified by the US Senate in January 1996 but at the end of 1999 remained unratified by the Russian Parliament,[61] where the treaty has been criticized in the Duma for its allegedly inequitable impact on Russia's strategic nuclear force structure and defence budget.[62] Russia's ratification has also become linked to the state of political relations between Russia and the USA. On several occasions in recent years ratification of the treaty seemed set to

[56] Belarus, Kazakhstan and Ukraine committed themselves as parties to the treaty to eliminate all the nuclear weapons based on their territories, leaving Russia as the sole nuclear weapon successor state of the USSR. The transfers of nuclear warheads to Russia were completed in 1996.

[57] The JCIC is the forum established by the START I Treaty in which the parties can resolve compliance questions, clarify ambiguities and discuss ways to facilitate its implementation.

[58] ITAR-TASS (Moscow), 29 Apr. 1999, in 'Russian, US officials discuss implementing START I', FBIS-SOV-1999-0429, 29 Apr. 1999.

[59] Ruban, O., 'Nuclear cheating: sleight of hand over US military secrets', *Moskovskiy Komsomlets*, 27 May 1999, in 'US disarmament "cheating" assailed', FBIS-SOV-1999-0528, 1 June 1999; and Interfax (Moscow), 28 July 1999, in 'Popkovich: Duma may ratify START II Treaty in Oct/Nov', FBIS-SOV-1999-0728, 29 July 1999.

[60] For a description of the provisions of the START II Treaty see Lockwood, D., 'Nuclear arms control', *SIPRI Yearbook 1993: World Armaments and Disarmament* (Oxford University Press: Oxford, 1993), pp. 554–59. In 1997 Russia and the USA signed a Protocol to the START II Treaty extending the final reduction deadline by 5 years to 31 Dec. 2007. For a description of the START II Protocol, see Kile (note 47), pp. 410–11. See also the brief descriptions in annexe A in this volume.

[61] According to the 1993 Russian Constitution, treaty ratification requires a simple majority vote in both the lower (Duma) and the upper (Federation Council) chambers of parliament.

[62] For a discussion of Russian concerns about START II, see Kile, S., 'Nuclear arms control', *SIPRI Yearbook 1997: Armaments, Disarmament and International Security* (Oxford University Press: Oxford, 1997), pp. 371, 374–77.

win the Duma's reluctant consent, only to be side-tracked by international developments unrelated to its provisions that strained their relations.

In March 1999, following a lobbying campaign by the government of then Prime Minister Yevgeniy Primakov, leaders of the main parliamentary factions agreed to put START II ratification on the Duma's legislative agenda.[63] On 22 March President Yeltsin submitted a draft ratification bill containing a number of conditions and reservations.[64] A key condition in the draft bill was that Russia would exchange the START II instruments of ratification only after the US Senate had ratified the 1997 TMD Demarcation Agreement and the MOUS, making the ABM Treaty a multilateral accord. This raised the possibility that the START II Treaty would fail to enter into force even if it is ratified by the Duma, since both the TMD agreement and the MOUS face strong opposition in the US Senate. The draft bill also stated that Russia would consider withdrawing from START II if the USA abrogated the ABM Treaty.[65] The Duma's deliberations were scheduled to begin in early April. However, the NATO bombing attacks on the Federal Republic of Yugoslavia, which began on 24 March, prompted parliamentary leaders to halt action on the treaty and to request Yeltsin to recall the ratification bill. In the view of one Russian observer, the intense anti-Western sentiment unleashed by the NATO air strikes effectively closed a 'window of opportunity' for START II ratification.[66]

Despite the sharp deterioration of Russia's relations with NATO and with the USA in particular, senior officials in Moscow—including President Yeltsin—reaffirmed that START II ratification remained a 'top priority' for the government.[67] The prospects for ratification received a boost on 23 June 1999, when the Duma passed legislation setting out investment priorities and 'inviolable' funding levels for Russia's strategic nuclear forces until 2010.[68] However, against the background of the growing controversy over US missile defence plans and the future of the ABM Treaty, START II supporters subsequently failed to bring the treaty to a vote in the Duma. In the light of the par-

[63] Interfax (Moscow), 16 Mar. 1999, in 'Duma may debate START II before Primakov visit to US', FBIS-SOV-1999-0316, 17 Mar. 1999; and Hoffman, D., 'Russia moves towards ratifying START II', *Washington Post*, 17 Mar. 1999, p. A24.

[64] Federal bill on ratification of the Treaty between the Russian Federation and the United States of America on Further Reduction and Limitation of Strategic Offensive Arms, Dec. 1998, full version of draft text reproduced by the Center for Policy Studies in Russia (PIR), Moscow, URL <http://www.pircenter.org/acl/messages/55.htm>.

[65] Federal bill on the ratification of [START II] (note 64). The draft law also stated that Russia would consider the deployment of nuclear weapons on the territory of new NATO member states to be grounds for withdrawing from the treaty.

[66] Pikayev, A., *The Rise and Fall of START II: The Russian View*, Working Papers no. 6 (Non-proliferation Project, Carnegie Endowment for International Peace: Washington, DC, Sep. 1999), pp. 30–32.

[67] Foreign Minister Igor Ivanov, quoted by ITAR-TASS (Moscow), 22 June 1999, in 'START II Russia's top priority', FBIS-SOV-1999-0622, 23 June 1999; and Interfax (Moscow), 2 July 1999, in 'Yeltsin calls for early START II ratification', FBIS-SOV-1999-0702, 6 July 1999.

[68] 'On funding the state defense order for strategic nuclear forces of the Russian Federation', *Rossiyskaya Gazeta*, in 'Strategic nuclear forces funding law', in FBIS-SOV-1999-0723, 27 July 1999. The approval of a funding plan for the strategic forces had been one of the conditions set out in the draft ratification bill.

Table 8.1. START I aggregate numbers of strategic nuclear delivery vehicles and accountable warheads, 1 January 2000[a]

Category[b]	Russia	Ukraine[c]	Ex-Soviet total[d]	USA	Final limits 5 Dec. 2001[e]
Strategic nuclear delivery vehicles	1 338	59	1 397	1 451	1 600
Total treaty-accountable warheads	6 472	526	6 998	7 763	6 000
ICBM and SLBM warheads	5 876	270	6 146	6 185	4 900

ICBM = intercontinental ballistic missile; SLBM = submarine-launched ballistic missile

[a] The numbers in this table are in accordance with the START I Treaty counting rules and include delivery vehicles which have been deactivated; the estimates of the number of operational systems in appendix 8A are smaller.

[b] The START I Treaty also places limits on inventories of mobile and heavy ICBMs and on aggregate ballistic missile throw-weight.

[c] The transfer of strategic nuclear warheads from Ukraine to Russia was completed in May 1996. The warheads remain START-accountable until their associated delivery vehicles have been eliminated or converted in accordance with procedures specified in the treaty.

[d] Belarus and Kazakhstan completed the elimination of the former Soviet ICBMs and associated launchers based on their territories in 1996.

[e] These ceilings applied equally to the USA and the Soviet Union as the signatories of the START I Treaty. Of the former Soviet parties (Belarus, Kazakhstan, Russia and Ukraine), only Russia will retain strategic nuclear forces at the end of the START I implementation period.

Source: START I Treaty Memorandum of Understanding, 1 Jan. 2000.

liamentary elections in December, some deputies expressed concern that a vote in favour of START II might be seen as a 'lack of patriotism'.[69] The outgoing Duma refused to take action on the treaty, despite appeals from Prime Minister Vladimir Putin for it to approve the accord.[70]

Towards a START III treaty

In 1999 Russia and the USA continued to discuss elements of a START III treaty—for which Clinton and Yeltsin had agreed an outline at their 1997 summit meeting in Helsinki—that would mandate deeper bilateral cuts in their strategic nuclear forces.[71] In the Joint Statement issued at the June 1999 G8 summit meeting in Cologne, the two governments reaffirmed their readiness to 'conduct new negotiations on strategic offensive arms aimed at further redu-

[69] Nikolai Stolyarov, Deputy Chairman of the Duma International Affairs Committee, quoted by ITAR-TASS (Moscow), 30 July 1999, in 'NATO action in FRY delays START-2 ratification', FBIS-SOV-1999-0730, 2 Aug. 1999.

[70] Reuters, 'Russian Duma refuses to mull START-2 ratification, 13 Dec. 1999, URL <http://dailynews.yahoo.com/index.html>; and Wines, M., 'Russia calls for action on arms treaty', *New York Times* (Internet edn), 22 Dec. 1999, URL <http://www.nytimes.com/library/world/europe/122299russia-arms-treaty.html>. The START II Treaty was ratified by the Duma on 14 Apr. 2000 and by the Federation Council on 19 Apr. 2000.

[71] For a description of the 1997 Helsinki framework agreement on START III, see Kile (note 49), pp. 414–16.

cing for each side the level of strategic nuclear warheads, elaborating measures of transparency concerning existing strategic nuclear warheads and their
elimination' as well as other measures contributing to the 'irreversibility of
deep reductions'.[72] Following preliminary talks in August between US and
Russian experts on missile defences and other strategic issues, the two sides
issued a communiqué in which they 'confirmed their readiness to begin talks
on the START III treaty immediately after the START II Treaty has been ratified'.[73] This statement accommodated the US Administration's insistence that
it would not open formal talks on START III until Russia had ratified
START II.

In these talks, Russia reportedly suggested lowering the START III warhead
ceiling from 2000–2500 each, as agreed in 1997, to 1500 or less.[74] The proposal for deeper reductions has become an increasingly attractive one in the
Duma, even among some arms control sceptics, since it holds out the prospect
of requiring the USA to make reductions to force levels that Russia could
afford to sustain as it eliminates ICBMs, ballistic-missile submarines and
heavy bombers reaching the end of their service lives. There has been a
growing realization among deputies that a rapid downsizing of the Russian
strategic nuclear forces is nearly unavoidable because of chronic investment
shortfalls; Russian nuclear force levels are set to decline well below the
START II limits by 2010, regardless of whether or not the treaty enters into
force.[75] The USA has resisted proposals for lowering the 2000–2500 warhead
ceiling, since cuts below this level would require a revision of the US targeting
doctrine and a restructuring of its 'triad' of strategic nuclear forces.

IV. Russian–US cooperative nuclear security activities

The Cooperative Threat Reduction programme

Despite the downturn in their political relations in 1999, Russia and the USA
continued to make progress in implementing a variety of nuclear weapon-
related dismantlement and security initiatives under the Cooperative Threat
Reduction (CTR) programme (also called the Nunn–Lugar programme after
the two senators who co-sponsored the original authorizing legislation). The
programme began in 1991 under the administrative auspices of the US DOD.
Its immediate aim was to provide bilateral financial and technical assistance to

[72] Joint Statement (note 26).

[73] Interfax (Moscow), 19 Aug. 1999, in 'US, Russian negotiators agree on ABM's importance', FBIS-
SOV-1999-0819, 20 Aug. 1999.

[74] Moscow also reportedly raised the idea of banning both nuclear and conventionally armed sea-
launched cruise missiles. Interfax (Moscow), 19 Aug. 1999, in 'Russia proposes 50% cut in warheads in
START III, FBIS-SOV-1999-0819, 20 Aug. 1999. US officials have opposed placing limits on SLCMs,
which generated considerable controversy during the START I negotiations.

[75] According to Roman Popkovich, Chairman of the Duma Defence Committee, the rapid obsoles-
cence of Russia's strategic nuclear forces means that if Russia does not 'achieve a simultaneous reduction of the maximum number of nuclear warheads', the USA's nuclear strength 'will be 4–6 times
greater' than Russia's by 2008–10. Quoted by Interfax (Moscow), 23 Aug. 1999, in 'US "not interested"
in Russia's ratifying START II', FBIS-SOV-1999-0823, 24 Aug. 1999.

Belarus, Kazakhstan, Russia and Ukraine for consolidating the former Soviet nuclear arsenal and ensuring its custodial safety. Since 1993 the CTR programme has evolved to encompass a wide range of nuclear non-proliferation and demilitarization activities across the former Soviet Union aimed at reducing the danger of 'loose nukes' or bomb-making materials and expertise finding their way into the hands of terrorist organizations or states harbouring nuclear weapon ambitions.[76] The programme also provides assistance for the storage and destruction of chemical weapons in Russia,[77] and funds have been authorized for dismantling biological weapons research and production facilities in Kazakhstan and Russia.

CTR projects fall into three general categories of activity: weapon destruction and dismantlement; chain of custody (i.e., the safe and secure transport and storage of nuclear weapons and weapon-usable fissile material); and demilitarization and defence conversion. The largest share of CTR funds has been obligated under the Strategic Offensive Arms Elimination (SOAE) programme for dismantling and destroying former Soviet strategic nuclear weapons in Belarus, Kazakhstan, Russia and Ukraine. The DOD has provided training, logistics, facility construction and US-made equipment which, among other activities, has been used for eliminating ICBMs and associated launch silos, SLBMs and their submarine launchers, and heavy bombers as well as for transporting and disposing of toxic liquid fuel for rocket engines. This programme has been credited with helping Belarus, Kazakhstan and Ukraine to fulfil their pledges to become non-nuclear weapon states. For fiscal year (FY) 1999, the US Congress approved $142.4 million for SOAE programme assistance, primarily to expedite Russia's elimination of strategic nuclear forces pursuant to the START I Treaty.[78]

In the summer of 1999 the USA signed protocols with Russia and Ukraine extending the original bilateral umbrella agreements by seven years, until 2006, to continue CTR activities in these countries.[79] Overall, for FYs 1992–99 the USA had obligated $2.7 billion to cooperative nuclear security initiatives across the former Soviet Union; of this amount, $1.7 billion had been earmarked for efforts in Russia. In January 1999 President Clinton announced that he would request an additional $2.8 billion—an increase of nearly 70 per cent over planned spending—to support these activities through

---

[76] For a detailed description of CTR programme activities, see Kile, S. and Arnett, E., 'Nuclear arms control', *SIPRI Yearbook 1996: Armaments, Disarmament and International Security* (Oxford University Press: Oxford, 1996), pp. 640–47. A number of programme activities in the former Soviet Union, in particular those connected with implementing export controls regulations and strengthening nuclear material accounting and control regimes, are now funded and administered by the US Departments of State and Energy.

[77] See chapter 9 in this volume.

[78] US Department of Defense, Office of the Secretary of Defense, Cooperative Threat Reduction program funding, 31 Jan. 1999, URL <http://www.ctr.osd.mil/07frame.htm>.

[79] 'United States and Russia extend Nunn–Lugar Cooperative Threat Reduction agreement', Office of the Assistant Secretary of Defense (Public Affairs), News release no. 307-99, 24 June 1999; and 'United States and Ukraine extend Nunn–Lugar Cooperative Threat Reduction agreement', Office of the Assistant Secretary of Defense (Public Affairs), News release no. 365-99, 5 Aug. 1999. These umbrella agreements define the general rights and obligations of each of the parties and set out the legal and customs frameworks for the provision of aid.

FY 2005 as part of the Expanded Threat Reduction Initiative aimed at countering the threat of terrorism involving chemical or biological weapons.[80]

Fissile material storage facility

An important CTR-funded activity under way in 1999 was the construction of a facility at the Mayak Production Association in Russia for the secure and environmentally safe storage of fissile material. The facility is intended to alleviate Russia's acute shortage of secure storage space for fissile material, thereby allowing it to proceed with nuclear warhead dismantlement. It may also be used to store spent reactor fuel from Russian nuclear-powered submarines, pending disposition of the material. The start of work at Mayak was considerably delayed by Russian–US disagreements over the new facility's financing arrangements and design. The first of two storage wings is scheduled to be completed in the autumn of 2002; its 25 000-container capacity will store the plutonium extracted from an estimated 6250 nuclear warheads.[81]

Aspects of the project were criticized in a report published in April 1999 by the US General Accounting Office (GAO), particularly the adequacy of transparency arrangements at the Russian facility, which had been the subject of lengthy Russian–US negotiations.[82] The report noted that US and Russian officials had not reached agreement on measures that could assure the USA that the plutonium at Mayak was securely stored and would not be used for weapons.[83] It also warned that the USA's share of the construction costs, which had already risen by nearly one-third to a total of $413 million, might rise further because of Russia's financial problems.

Material physical control and accounting

The creation of an effective fissile material physical control and accounting (MPC&A) regime has become one of the highest priorities in nuclear cooperation between the USA and Russia and other states of the former Soviet Union. The security shortcomings identified at many nuclear facilities (e.g., research reactors and laboratories, fuel fabrication facilities, uranium enrichment plants, nuclear material storage sites and nuclear weapon production plants)

[80] Miller, J. and Broad, W., 'Clinton sees threat of germ terrorism', *International Herald Tribune*, 23–24 Jan. 1999, pp. 1, 6; and 'US, Russia extend CTR program until 2006', *Arms Control Today*, vol. 29, no. 4 (June 1999), p. 23.

[81] US Department of Defense, Office of the Secretary of Defense, 'Cooperative Threat Reduction program funding, 31 Jan. 1999', URL <http://www.ctr.osd.mil/funding/fundrus.htm>; and Russian–American Nuclear Security Advisory Council (RANSAC), Congressional Appropriations/Authorization Committees: Wrap-up of FY99 US–Russian Cooperative Nuclear Security Activities, URL <http:www.princeton.edu/~ransac/congress/99wrapup.html>.

[82] In 1999 US officials also complained that they were increasingly being denied access to the site by the Russian security service. Gordon, M., 'Russians balk at opening nuclear sites to US eyes', *New York Times* (Internet edn), 3 Nov. 1999, URL <http://www.nytimes.com/library/world/global/ 110399russia-us-nuke.html>.

[83] US General Accounting Office (GAO), *Weapons of Mass Destruction: Efforts to Reduce Russia's Arsenal May Cost More, Achieve Less than Planned*, GAO/NSIAD-99-76, 13 Apr. 1999. It also noted that Russian negotiators had not agreed to US proposals aimed at confirming that the plutonium stored at the facility originated solely from dismantled warheads.

have spurred a variety of cooperative measures aimed at preventing the theft or unauthorized diversion of highly enriched uranium (HEU), plutonium and other weapon-usable nuclear material. A key objective of these efforts is to foster the development of an 'indigenous safeguards culture' in the newly independent states.

As of the autumn of 1999, the MPC&A programme of the US Department of Energy (DOE) had undertaken joint projects to improve the security of nuclear weapon-usable material at 55 facilities in Belarus, Georgia, Kazakhstan, Latvia, Lithuania, Russia, Ukraine and Uzbekistan.[84] In Russia, cooperative MPC&A programmes have been initiated at more than 40 sites, typically involving scientists and technicians from the USA's national laboratories working directly with their counterparts in Russian laboratories and scientific institutes; security upgrades were expected to be completed for more than 50 tonnes of weapon-usable nuclear materials by the end of 1999.[85] On 2 October Russian Minister of Atomic Energy Yevgeniy Adamov and US Secretary of Energy Bill Richardson signed a new agreement aimed at expanding bilateral MPC&A cooperation. The agreement provided for the establishment of a Joint Coordinating Committee (JCC), which would be responsible for developing joint action plans, recommendations and appropriate implementing agreements. It would also serve as the forum for resolving disputes between the parties. Russia agreed to 'take all necessary measures to permit access' by US officials at the facilities where joint MPC&A activities are being conducted.[86]

The Nuclear Cities Initiative

The Nuclear Cities Initiative (NCI) was established in 1998 by a Russian–US agreement under which the USA undertook to assist Russia in reducing and restructuring the large nuclear weapon production complex it inherited from the Soviet Union.[87] The purpose of the NCI is to create a framework for cooperation in providing civilian jobs for workers displaced from nuclear weapon-related enterprises at 10 closed 'nuclear cities' managed by the Ministry of Atomic Energy (Minatom) (see table 8.2). The US DOE will provide business training and support for commercial enterprise development in these cities whose workers face difficult living conditions and the prospect of mass redundancies. The overarching aim of the NCI is to prevent a 'brain drain' from the

[84] US Department of Energy, Material Protection, Control and Accounting Program, 'The agreement between the United States and the Russian Federation on nuclear materials protection, control and accounting (MPC&A) is signed', Sep./Oct. 1999 News, URL <http://www.dp.doe.gov/nn/mpca/news.htm#1>.

[85] Speech by US Energy Secretary Bill Richardson to the National Press Club, Washington, DC, 3 Mar. 1999, in 'Non-proliferation policy: speech by Energy Secretary', *Disarmament Diplomacy*, no. 35 (Mar. 1999), URL <http://www.acronym.org.uk/35doe.htm>.

[86] US–Russian Agreement Regarding Cooperation in the Area of Material Physical Protection, Control and Accounting, 2 Oct. 1999, text reproduced by US Department of Energy, URL <http://www.dp.doe.gov/ nn/mpca/pubs/mpca-agrmnt/eng_text.htm>.

[87] US–Russian Agreement on the Nuclear Cities Initiative, 22 Sep. 1998, text reproduced by RANSAC (note 81), URL <http://www.princeton.edu/~ransac/initiatives/formalcooperation.html>.

Table 8.2. Summary of the principal activities in Russia's 'nuclear cities'

City	Former name of city	Nuclear weapon and related activities
Lesnoy	Sverdlovsk-45	Warhead assembly and disassembly; plutonium pit and secondary storage
Novouralsk	Sverdlovsk-44	HEU production and storage;[a] LEU production for nuclear power reactors; blending down of HEU from dismantled warheads into LEU
Ozersk	Chelyabinsk-65	Tritium production;[b] MOX fuel production; reprocessing of naval and civil reactor fuel; warhead component fabrication and disassembly; storage of plutonium and HEU recovered from dismantled nuclear weapons
Sarov	Arzamas-16	Warhead research and development; assembly and disassembly; plutonium and HEU storage
Seversk	Tomsk-7	Plutonium production;[c] spent fuel reprocessing; uranium enrichment; blending down of HEU from dismantled warheads into LEU; storage of plutonium and HEU recovered from dismantled nuclear weapons
Snezhinsk	Chelyabinsk-70	Warhead design; plutonium and HEU storage
Trekhgorniy	Zlatoust-36	Warhead assembly and dismantlement; plutonium and HEU uranium storage
Zarechniy	Penza-19	Warhead component fabrication; warhead assembly and dismantlement; plutonium and HEU storage
Zelenogorsk	Krasnoyarsk-45	Uranium enrichment; blending down of HEU from dismantled warheads into LEU
Zheleznogorsk	Krasnoyarsk-26	Plutonium production;[c] spent fuel reprocessing; nuclear waste storage

HEU = highly enriched uranium; LEU = low-enriched uranium; MOX = mixed-oxide.
[a] Production of weapon-usable material was halted in 1989.
[b] Plutonium production was halted in 1992.
[c] In 1997 Russia agreed to convert (with US financial assistance) the cores of the ADE-4 and ADE-5 reactors at Seversk and the ADE-2 reactor at Zheleznogorsk so that they no longer produce weapon-usable plutonium. In early 2000 Russia proposed shutting down the reactors entirely.

Sources: United States Department of Energy (DOE), Office of Nonproliferation and National Security, *Report to the Congress on the Nuclear Cities Initiative* (DOE: Washington, DC, 22 Sep. 1998; and Carnegie Endowment for International Peace and the Monterey Institute of International Studies, *The Nuclear Successor States of the Soviet Union: Nuclear Weapons and Sensitive Exports Status Report*, no. 5 (Mar. 1998).

former Soviet Union to third countries of scientists and technicians with expertise in developing and manufacturing nuclear weapons while at the same time allowing the Russian authorities to close nuclear facilities and eliminate excess weapon production capacity in an orderly way. According to Russian estimates, there is a need to create 30 000–50 000 new jobs for workers in these cities; the DOE calculated that the NCI would cost approximately $550 million over a period of about five to seven years.[88]

In 1999 the Nuclear Cities Initiative came under critical scrutiny in the US Congress following the publication of a GAO report casting doubt on the likely effectiveness of the programme.[89] The report noted that numerous uncertainties and questions surrounded plans to create jobs in the 'nuclear cities', which the Russian authorities still consider to be sensitive areas. Given the inhospitable investment climate in Russia and the limited commercial success evidenced in similar joint conversion programmes, it concluded that the NCI 'is likely to be a subsidy program for Russia for many years rather than a stimulus for economic development'.[90] Congress subsequently appropriated $7.5 million for the NCI in FY 2000, which was one-half of the amount requested by the DOE; as a result, DOE officials said that NCI activities initially would focus on one nuclear city (Sarov, formerly Arzamas-16) instead of three.[91] In a related move, Congress reduced funding for the Initiatives for Proliferation Prevention (IPP) programme, which is also intended to address the 'brain drain' problem, primarily because of concern raised in the GAO report that US funds appeared to be going to some Russian scientists still working on weapon projects.[92]

Implementation of the HEU Agreement

On 26 March 1999 Richardson and Adamov signed an accord on financing arrangements aimed at reviving the faltering 1993 Highly Enriched Uranium Agreement (HEU Agreement).[93] Under the agreement, the USA had agreed to purchase from Russia over 20 years up to 500 tonnes of HEU extracted from dismantled nuclear warheads for use as civilian reactor fuel.[94] The deal was originally valued at $12 billion. However, the international market price of uranium subsequently collapsed, leading to a prolonged dispute between Russia and the USA over price and compensation arrangements.[95] In 1998 Russian officials threatened to withdraw from the HEU deal altogether and to

---

[88] United States Department of Energy (DOE), Office of Nonproliferation and National Security, *Report to the Congress on the Nuclear Cities Initiative* (DOE: Washington, DC, 22 Sep. 1998).

[89] United States General Accounting Office (GAO), *DOE's New Initiative Will Focus More Aid on Russia's Nuclear Cities*, GAO/RCED-99-54, Feb. 1999.

[90] GAO (note 89), p. 6.

[91] Pincus, W., 'US to cut hiring of Russian scientists', *International Herald Tribune*, 13–14 Nov. 1999, p. 2.

[92] GAO (note 89), pp. 36–49; and Pincus (note 91). The IPP programme attempts to utilize R&D projects involving the US national laboratories, US industry and scientific institutes in the former Soviet Union as the basis for self-sustaining business ventures that will attract investments by US companies. The ultimate goal is to create jobs for former Soviet weapon scientists in non-military commercial enterprises.

[93] Miller, J., 'Russia and US sign a nuclear deal', *International Herald Tribune*, 29 Mar. 1999, p. 5. The text of the HEU Agreement is reproduced in *SIPRI Yearbook 1994* (Oxford University Press: Oxford, 1994), p. 673–75.

[94] The agreement specifies that Russia will blend down the HEU extracted from warheads with LEU to make LEU enriched to approximately 4.4%; not less than 10 t of HEU per year will be purchased in the first 5 years and not less than 30 t per year thereafter.

[95] See Kile (note 62), pp. 382–83.

begin selling natural uranium on the world market because Russia had not been compensated for the natural uranium content of the low-enriched uranium (LEU) it delivered to the USA in 1997 and 1998.[96] Under the 1999 agreement, Russia will receive $325 million from the USA as compensation for the LEU shipments.[97]

V. The Comprehensive Nuclear Test-Ban Treaty

The future of the CTBT was complicated in 1999 when the US Senate voted in October to reject ratification of the treaty. The vote set back international efforts to bring the CTBT into force since the USA is one of the 44 members of the CD with nuclear power or research reactors on their territories, listed in Annexe 2 of the treaty, which must ratify the CTBT in order for it to enter into force.[98] It also marked a break in the trend in which a growing number of states had either joined the treaty or expressed their intention to do so. The prospects for the test ban's entry into force had been brightened earlier in the year by indications that India was prepared to unconditionally sign the treaty.[99] India's opposition to the CTBT had been a key stumbling block to concluding the treaty negotiations in the CD.[100]

As of 31 December 1999, 155 states had signed the CTBT and 51 had deposited the instruments of ratification, including two of the NPT-defined nuclear weapon states, France and the UK.[101] Of the 44 states listed in Annexe 2 of the treaty, 41 had signed the treaty and 27 had ratified it.

The Conference on Facilitating Entry into Force

On 6–8 October 1999 a Conference on Facilitating the Entry into Force of the Comprehensive Nuclear Test-Ban Treaty was convened in Vienna. The meeting was attended by 92 states. As specified in Article XIV of the CTBT, its

[96] 'US hopes for quick end to Russian uranium feud', *Moscow Times*, 14 Jan. 1999, reproduced by RANSAC (note 81), URL <http://www.princeton.edu/~ransac/nuclearnews/03.31.99.html>; and Interfax (Moscow), 24 July 1998, in 'Russia, US to sign statement on nuclear towns', FBIS-SOV-98-205, 24 July 1998.

[97] The US Congress had made the appropriation of the funds for the payment contingent on Minatom's commercial arm finalizing a deal with a group of Canadian, French and German energy companies in which they agreed to purchase the blended-down LEU output from Russia for the next 10 years. Pincus, W., '$525 million for Russian nonproliferation deals added to bill', *Washington Post*, 1 Nov. 1998, p. A12; and Miller (note 93).

[98] This requirement, which was the source of considerable controversy during the closing stages of the CTBT negotiations in the CD, reflected the view that the treaty must capture a certain minimum set of nuclear weapon-capable states to be effective in promoting non-proliferation objectives. Arnett, E., 'The Comprehensive Nuclear Test-Ban Treaty', *SIPRI Yearbook 1997* (note 62), p. 405. See annexe A in this volume for a list of the 44 states.

[99] Chellaney, B., 'Covert diplomacy', *Hindustan Times* (Internet edn), 10 Feb. 1999, URL <http://www.hindustantimes.com/ht/nonfram/100299/detopi01.htm>; Mukarji, A., 'Govt. has "committed" itself to signing the CTBT', *Hindustan Times* (Internet edn), 6 May 1999, URL <http://www.hindustantimes.com/ht/nonfram/060599/detfor03.htm>; and 'CTBTO hopes for Indian signature after elections', *Times of India* (Internet edn), 27 Aug. 1999, URL <http://www.timesofindia.com/270899/27worl8.htm>.

[100] Arnett, E., 'The Comprehensive Nuclear Test-Ban Treaty', *SIPRI Yearbook 1996* (note 76), pp. 404–407; and Kile (note 5), pp. 526–28.

[101] See annexe A in this volume.

purpose was to consider 'what measures consistent with international law may be undertaken to accelerate the ratification process in order to facilitate the early entry into force of the treaty'.[102] One measure not under consideration was to waive the provision requiring that the 44 states listed in Annexe 2 join the treaty before it can enter into force. The negotiating record in the CD made clear that the drafters had ruled out waiving the entry into force provision or otherwise amending the treaty to authorize such changes.[103] This situation contributed to limiting the meeting to a largely admonitory role. The Conference issued a 12-point Final Declaration that *inter alia* reaffirmed the importance of universal adherence to the CTBT for nuclear non-proliferation and disarmament efforts. It called on all states, in particular those whose ratification was needed for the treaty's entry into force, to join it as soon as possible.[104]

The US Senate's rejection of the CTBT

On 13 October 1999 the US Senate decided by a vote of 51–48 not to ratify the CTBT.[105] The vote culminated a long partisan battle between the White House and Republican leaders in the Senate. President Clinton was the first world leader to sign the CTBT when it was opened for signature in 1996 and he described its entry into force as his administration's highest arms control priority. The treaty subsequently stalled in the Senate Foreign Relations Committee, whose Republican chairman, Senator Jesse Helms, a longstanding opponent of the test ban, had given it a low priority for legislative action. In early October 1999 Senate Majority Leader Trent Lott unexpectedly scheduled a ratification vote following increasingly vocal calls from Democrats to bring the treaty before the full Senate.[106] Lott was criticized both inside the Senate and elsewhere for setting a date for the vote that left little time for holding hearings. At the same time, the White House and Democratic congressional leaders came under criticism from treaty proponents for forcing an advice-and-consent vote before having secured the support of the two-thirds majority of senators needed to win ratification.[107] As it became increas-

---

[102] Article XIV provides for the convening of an annual entry-into-force conference by the states which have deposited their instruments of ratification (other states may participate as observers) if the treaty has not entered into force 3 years after the date of the anniversary of its opening for signature. The text of the CTBT is reproduced in *SIPRI Yearbook 1997* (note 62), appendix 12A, pp. 414–31.

[103] Bunn, G., Johnson, R. and Kimball, D., 'Accelerating the entry into force of the Comprehensive Nuclear Test-Ban Treaty: the Article XIV Special Conference', Coalition to Reduce Nuclear Dangers, May 1999, URL <http://www.clw.org/pub/clw/coalition/rpteif99.htm>.

[104] 'Final Declaration unanimously adopted at CTBT conference', Press release, Public Information Section, Preparatory Commission for the Comprehensive Nuclear Test-Ban Treaty Organization, Vienna, 8 Oct. 1999.

[105] Wilson, C., 'Senate rejects global nuclear test-ban treaty', Reuters, 14 Oct. 1999, URL <http://dailynews.yahoo.com/index.html>.

[106] Cerniello, C., 'Senators call on Helms to allow vote on CTB Treaty', *Arms Control Today*, vol. 29, no. 4 (June 1999), p. 20; and Ellis, S., 'Senators urge immediate CTBT ratification', *European Washington File* (United States Information Service, US Embassy: Stockholm, 20 July 1999), URL <http://www.usis.usemb.se/wireless/200/eur004.htm>.

[107] Schmitt, E., 'Senate will debate treaty banning nuclear testing', *New York Times* (Internet edn), 2 Oct. 1999, URL <http://www12.nytimes.com/library/world/global/100299treaty-nuke.html>; and

ingly clear that the Senate would reject the CTBT, White House officials and congressional leaders struggled to forge a compromise that would involve withdrawing the treaty from consideration until after a new president took office in January 2001. The idea of postponing the vote was backed by a majority of senators.[108] However, efforts to reach a compromise deal failed, reportedly because of opposition from a small number of Republican senators intent on defeating the treaty and delivering a personal rebuff to Clinton.[109]

In assessing the vote, Clinton denounced the 'reckless partisanship' that had led to the defeat of the treaty and warned of the risk of a 'new isolationism' emerging in the USA; his complaints were echoed by many political leaders and journalists.[110] Senate opponents of the CTBT responded that the vote to reject the treaty reflected serious substantive concerns about its provisions and aims.[111]

The US Senate's objections

Aside from partisan political considerations, opposition to the CTBT centred largely on two issues. The first was whether compliance with the treaty's 'zero-yield' test ban could be adequately verified. This issue had gained increased salience in the light of the allegedly poor performance of the International Monitoring System (IMS), which is being built under the auspices of the Provisional Technical Secretariat of the Preparatory Committee of the Comprehensive Nuclear Test-Ban Organization (CTBTO), in detecting some of the nuclear explosions conducted by India in 1998.[112] Treaty opponents argued that the IMS—which is designed to guarantee the detection and location of explosions having yields as low as 1 kt—would not be able to detect with high confidence low-yield nuclear explosive tests, particularly those conducted using evasive techniques such as cavity 'decoupling' (i.e., conducting a nuclear explosion in an underground cavern so as to attenuate the seismic sig-

Hoagland, J., 'Blame the Clinton team, too, for this giant fiasco', *International Herald Tribune*, 16–17 Oct. 1999, p. 6.

[108] Knowlton, B., 'Republicans suggest deal on avoiding treaty vote', *International Herald Tribune*, 11 Oct. 1999, pp. 1, 3; and Reuters, 'Clinton officials press for delayed treaty vote', 11 Oct. 1999, URL <http://dailynews.yahoo.com/index.html>.

[109] Elliot, M., Hirsh, M. and Barry, J., 'The lost leader', *Newsweek*, 25 Oct. 1999, p. 27.

[110] Sanger, D., 'Clinton says "new isolationism" imperils US security', *New York Times* (Internet edn), 15 Oct. 1999, URL <http://www12.nytimes.com/library/global/101599treaty-nuke.html>; Judt, T., 'An errant superpower flaunts its ignorance', *International Herald Tribune*, 18 Oct. 1999, p. 8; and 'A damaging decision', *International Herald Tribune*, 16–17 Oct. 1999, p. 6

[111] Excerpts from news conference remarks of Senator Trent Lott, in 'Lott's view: "it was not about politics, it was about substance"', *New York Times* (Internet edn), 15 Oct. 1999, URL <http://www12. nytimes.com/library/world/global/101599treaty-lott-text.htm>; and Helms, J., 'This treaty was dangerously irresponsible', *Wall Street Journal*, 18. Oct. 1999.

[112] The IMS, which was only partially complete at the time of the Indian nuclear tests, will have a network of 50 primary and 120 auxiliary seismological stations equipped to detect seismic activity and to distinguish between natural events, such as earthquakes, and nuclear explosions. It will also include 80 radionuclide, 60 infrasound and 11 hydroacoustic stations. These monitoring stations will transmit data from the IMS to the International Data Centre (IDC) at Vienna, which will then make both the raw and processed data available to all states parties.

nals produced by the blast).[113] Treaty critics also pointed to press reports that the Central Intelligence Agency (CIA) had concluded that US national technical means (NTM) of verification—the use of which is explicitly provided for in the treaty—would not be able to detect in all circumstances very-low-yield nuclear tests conducted by Russia.[114] These uncertainties led some CTBT opponents to conclude that a determined cheater would be able to carry out 'militarily significant' nuclear tests under the treaty with little risk of detection.[115] Treaty proponents argued that the array of monitoring measures provided for under the CTBT could effectively verify compliance with the test ban.[116]

The second issue was concern about the potentially negative long-term impact of a permanent halt to nuclear testing of the US nuclear arsenal. Treaty opponents questioned whether the centrepiece of the Clinton Administration's plans for US nuclear weapon custodianship—the Stockpile Stewardship Program (SSP)—could replace nuclear testing over the long term in ensuring a high level of confidence in the safety and reliability of nuclear weapons as they reached the end of their service lives.[117] The directors of three national laboratories (Sandia, Lawrence Livermore and Los Alamos) testified before the Senate that there was no guarantee that the SSP would succeed and that it would take 5–10 years for its effectiveness to be properly assessed.[118] Clinton Administration officials pointed out, however, that under the CTBT Safeguards Programme the USA was committed to maintaining the basic capability to resume nuclear test activities if the safety or reliability of a nuclear weapon type deemed vital to its nuclear deterrent could no longer be certified during the annual review process.[119]

---

[113] Many analysts have argued, however, that the synergistic relationship between the different monitoring technologies (seismic, radionuclide, hydroacoustic and infrasound) used in the IMS will enable it to detect and identify explosions having yields well below 1 kt, permitting effective verification of the treaty. See, e.g., Findlay, T., 'US security benefits from test ban monitoring & on site inspections', Coalition to Reduce Nuclear Dangers, *Issue Brief*, vol. 3, no. 4 (27 Sep. 1999), URL <http://www.clw.org/pub/clw/coalition/briefv3n14.htm>. A 1998 test explosion conducted in Kazakhstan using 0.1 kt of conventional explosives was detected by IMS stations in Africa, Asia, Australia, Europe and North America. Meier, O., 'Verifying the CTBT: responses to Republican criticism', *Disarmament Diplomacy*, no. 40 (Sep./Oct. 1999), pp. 19–21.

[114] Macilwain, 'US Senate ignores scientific advice in failing to ratify test ban treaty', *Nature*, vol. 401 (21 Oct. 1999), p. 735; and Broad, W., 'Washington in war of words on policing nuclear test ban treaty', *International Herald Tribune*, 11 Oct. 1999, p. 3.

[115] Bailey, K., 'The Comprehensive Test Ban Treaty: the costs outweigh the benefits', *Policy Analysis* (CATO Institute), no. 330 (15 Jan. 1999), pp. 11–14.

[116] See, e.g., Paine, C., 'Facing reality: a test ban will benefit US and international security', Natural Resources Defense Council, Feb. 1999, URL <http://www.clw.org/coalition/ nrdc0299.htm>.

[117] The Stockpile Stewardship Program, which is being designed and implemented by the DOE's National Laboratories at an annual cost of $4.5 billion, involves using a set of computational and experimental simulations as part of a programme of intensive surveillance, non-nuclear testing and rebuilding of nuclear warheads to maintain their safety and reliability.

[118] Ellis, S., 'Stockpile Stewardship tests weapons by computer, not explosions', *European Washington File* (United States Information Service, US Embassy: Stockholm, 7 Oct. 1999), URL <http://www.usis.usemb.se/wireless/400/ eur004.htm>; and Schmidt, E., 'In test ban debate, echo of the cold war', *International Herald Tribune*, 11 Oct. 1999, pp. 1, 3. The directors' testimony was criticized, however, as having more to do with budgetary politics than with concerns about the likely effectiveness of the SSP. Macilwain (note 114).

[119] USIS, Testimony of the Honorable William H. Cohen to the Senate Armed Services Committee Hearing on the Comprehensive Nuclear Test-Ban Treaty, 6 Oct. 1999, *European Washington File* (US

Some treaty critics expressed more fundamental doubts about the wisdom of the USA joining a legally binding ban on nuclear testing. They questioned its likely effectiveness in curbing the spread of nuclear weapons to additional states.[120] They also argued that the test ban was a dubious means to an ultimately undesirable end: the promotion of global nuclear disarmament through the nuclear weapon states' gradual loss of confidence in the reliability of their nuclear arsenals. In this regard they judged the CTBT to be qualitatively different from arms limitation agreements such as the START treaties. Sceptics expressed misgivings about joining a ban on nuclear testing when nuclear deterrence remained the foundation of US national security policy and defence planning.[121]

The positions of other countries

In the wake of the Senate vote there were no indications that any state with nuclear weapon capabilities intended to reconsider its position vis-à-vis the CTBT or abandon its moratorium on nuclear testing. The Chinese Government expressed its 'deep regrets' at the Senate's decision to reject the CTBT and stated that it would maintain its moratorium on testing; it also pledged to accelerate its process of ratifying the treaty.[122] The Russian Government reiterated its commitment to ratifying the test ban treaty and also vowed to speed up the ratification process.[123]

In India, where the Bharatiya Janata Party (BJP)-led government had reversed its strident opposition to the CTBT, the US Senate's vote complicated the domestic debate about whether to sign the treaty but did not deflect the course of government policy. Newly re-elected Prime Minister Atal Bihari Vajpayee promised that India would continue to refrain from further nuclear testing and said that his coalition government was 'in the process of securing a national consensus' in favour of signing the CTBT.[124] External Affairs Minister Jaswant Singh similarly declared that India would continue to observe its voluntary moratorium on nuclear testing, which he noted was a 'de facto

Embassy: Stockholm, 6 Oct. 1999); and USIS, White House Fact Sheet: Reasons for Ratifying the CTBT, *European Washington File* (US Embassy: Stockholm, 7 Oct. 1999).

[120] Senator Richard Lugar stated that the CTBT's 'usefulness to the goal of non-proliferation is highly questionable. Its likely ineffectuality will risk undermining support and confidence in the concept of multilateral arms control'. Quoted in Bolton, J. 'CTBT: clear thinking', *Jerusalem Post* (Internet edn), 18 Oct. 1999, URL <http://www. jpost.com/com/Archive/ 18. Oct. 1999/Opinion/Article-2.html>.

[121] Krauthammer, C., 'Arms control: the end of an illusion', *Weekly Standard* (Internet edn), vol. 5, no. 7 (1 Nov. 1999), URL <http://www.weeklystandard.com/magazine/mag_5_7_99/kraut_feat_5_7_99. html>; and Barry, J., 'The myths of the test ban treaty', *Newsweek*, 25 Oct. 1999, p. 31.

[122] Browne, A., 'China vows full speed ahead on nuclear pact', Reuters, 14 Oct. 1999, URL <http://dailynews.yahoo.com/index.html>.

[123] Nesirky, M., 'Russia concerned by US Senate nuclear vote', Reuters, 14 Oct. 1999, URL <http://dailynews.yahoo.com/index.html>.

[124] Mazumdar, S., 'The dominant pole: an interview with Indian Prime Minister Atal Bihari Vajpayee', *Newsweek*, 18 Oct. 1999, p. 49; Guruswamy, K., 'US pleased by India's nuclear stance', Associated Press, 25 Oct. 1999, URL <http://www.newsday.com/ap/rnmpin03.htm>; and Nanda, P., 'CTBT: a wide enough consensus', *Times of India*, 30 Oct. 1999, URL <http://www.timesofindia. com/301099/30worl9.htm>.

acceptance of the CTBT'.[125] Singh also said that Indian scientists were 'confident of conducting subcritical tests permitted by the CTBT' in order to ensure the credibility of India's nuclear deterrent.[126] By the end of the year the Vajpayee Government had cautiously begun consultations on the CTBT with both opposition parties and coalition allies, while linking India's signature to making substantive progress on sanctions-related issues in its ongoing 'nuclear dialogue' with the USA.[127]

In Pakistan, the government of then Prime Minister Mohamed Nowaz Sharif had linked its signature of the test ban treaty to a lifting of the economic and trade sanctions imposed by the USA in 1998 following Pakistan's nuclear tests. It had moved away from its earlier demand that India sign the accord first.[128] The Pakistani observer attending the October 1999 Conference on Facilitating the Entry into Force of the Comprehensive Nuclear Test-Ban Treaty confirmed that Pakistan remained committed to signing the CTBT, albeit only under circumstances 'free from coercion'.[129] Following the military-led *coup d'état* that deposed Sharif on 12 October, Foreign Minister Abdul Sattar reiterated that Pakistan supported the CTBT despite the US Senate's vote. He noted, however, that if India conducted another nuclear explosion before the CTBT enters into force, Pakistan retained the right to do the same regardless of whether or not it had signed the treaty.[130] In late December 1999, some observers speculated that Pakistan's military government might be willing to sign the CTBT before India in order to secure concessions from the USA and to avoid deepening its international isolation.[131]

[125] 'India's moratorium is de-facto acceptance of CTBT: Jaswant', *Hindustan Times* (Internet edn), 26 Nov. 1999, URL <http://www2.hindustantimes.com/ht/nonfram/261199/detfro02.htm>.

[126] Quoted by Raja Mohan, C., 'Jaswant Singh for consensus on CTBT', *The Hindu* (Internet edn), 29 Nov. 1999, URL <http://www.indiaserver.com/thehindu/1999/11/29/stories/01290001.htm>. Subcritical experiments release no nuclear energy; the configuration and quantities of explosives and nuclear materials used do not produce a critical mass (i.e., a self-sustaining nuclear fission chain reaction).

[127] 'No consensus yet', *Hindustan Times* (Internet edn), 25 Dec. 1999, URL <http://www2.hindustantimes.com/ht/nonfram/251299/detedi01.htm>; and Subrahmanyam, K., 'CTBT consensus: work towards converting rejectionists', *Times of India* (Internet edn), 27 Dec. 1999, URL <http://www.timesofindia.com/271299/27edit4.htm>.

[128] 'Decision on CTBT linked to removal of sanctions: FM', *Dawn* (Internet edn), 9 Sep. 1999, URL <http://www.dawn.com/daily/19990909/top4.htm>. For a description of these sanctions and export restrictions, see Anthony, I. and French, E., 'Non-cooperative responses to proliferation', *SIPRI Yearbook 1999* (note 5), pp. 677–90.

[129] 'Delhi still threatening "nuclear arms race", says Islamabad', *Dawn* (Internet edn), 9 Oct. 1999, URL <http://www.dawn.com/daily/19991009/top2.htm>. On 27 Oct. 1999, President Clinton exercised his authority to waive economic sanctions imposed on India after the May 1998 nuclear tests but retained most of them on Pakistan under Section 508 of the Foreign Assistance Act, which prohibits aid to countries where elected governments are toppled by military coups. Presidential Determination No. 2000–04, The White House, Office of the Press Secretary, 27 Oct. 1999; and 'US lifts 2 sanctions on Pakistan', *Dawn* (Internet edn), 29 Oct. 1999, URL <http://www.dawn.com/daily/ 19991029/top4.htm>.

[130] Quoted by Akhtar, H., 'Sattar's address at ISS: Pakistan to reply if India tests nuclear device', *Dawn* (Internet edn), 26 Nov. 1999, URL <http://www.dawn.com/daily/19991126/top3.htm>.

[131] Baruah, A., 'No benefits in not signing CTBT: Pak', *The Hindu* (Internet edn), 5 Jan. 2000, URL <http://www.indiaserver.com/thehindu//2000/01/05/stories/0305000e.htm>; and Hoodbhoy, P., 'Why the CTBT is controversial', *Dawn* (Internet edn), 13 Jan. 2000, URL <http://www.dawn.com2000/ 01/13/op.htm#1>. >

Implications of the US Senate vote

The US Senate's decision did not mean that the test ban has been permanently rejected by the USA, since the CTBT can be brought up for a new ratification vote when circumstances are more favourable for its approval.[132] Secretary of State Albright assured foreign leaders that the USA 'will continue to act in accordance with its obligations as signatory under international law, and will seek reconsideration of the treaty at a later date'.[133] However, she later conceded that the substantive concerns expressed by treaty sceptics highlighted the need for proponents of the accord to engage in a sustained dialogue on issues connected with the test ban. Accordingly, the Clinton Administration would establish a high-level bipartisan task force to work closely with the Senate on addressing these issues.[134]

The Senate vote heightened international concern about the health of the nuclear non-proliferation regime. In many countries the CTBT had been seen as a litmus test of the willingness of the nuclear weapon states to fulfil their obligations under Article VI of the NPT to end the nuclear arms race. Jayantha Dhanapala, the UN Under Secretary-General for Disarmament Affairs, pointed out that many countries had agreed in 1995 to indefinitely extend the NPT only on the basis of a written pledge by the nuclear weapon states to negotiate and ratify a test ban treaty and to take other steps towards nuclear disarmament.[135]

In addition, the treaty's defeat in the Senate cast doubt on the USA's crucially important leadership role in that regime. The Senate action undermined Washington's moral authority in leading efforts to draw states such as India and Pakistan into legally binding arrangements aimed at promoting important nuclear non-proliferation objectives and reducing nuclear weapon-related dangers. More broadly, the Senate's willingness to sacrifice an important arms control treaty for what seemed to many observers to be partisan political reasons called into question Washington's reliability in implementing international agreements.[136]

The CTBT's defeat did not in itself undermine the no-testing norm codified in the treaty.[137] The Senate's decision provoked an outpouring of international

---

[132] USIS, Transcript of President's statement on the rejection of the test ban treaty, The White House, Office of the Press Secretary, 13 Oct. 1999, *European Washington File* (US Embassy: Stockholm, 13 Oct. 1999).

[133] Quoted in 'US remains committed to a non-nuclear testing policy', Coalition to Reduce Nuclear Dangers, Press release, 3 Nov. 1999, URL <http://www.clw.org/pub/clw/coalition/rel110399.htm>. Senate Majority Leader Trent Lott has claimed, however, that the vote to reject the treaty 'serves to release the United States from any possible obligations as a signatory of the negotiated text of the treaty'. Quoted in Gertz, B., 'Lott hits Clinton's stance on nuke pact', *Washington Times*, 3 Nov. 1999.

[134] '"High-level task force" on test ban treaty to be established', Coalition to Reduce Nuclear Dangers, *Issue Brief*, vol. 3, no. 19 (12 Nov. 1999), URL <http://www.clw.org/coalition/index.html>.

[135] Cited in Drozdiak, W., 'US warned of dangers in rejecting test ban', *International Herald Tribune*, 8 Oct. 1999, pp. 1, 6.

[136] Storey, D., 'Defeat of treaty a blow to US prestige', Reuters, 14 Oct. 1999, URL <http://dailynews.yahoo.com/index.html>.

[137] Bunn, G., 'The status of norms against nuclear testing', *Nonproliferation Review*, vol. 6, no. 2 (winter 1999), pp. 20–32.

condemnation which reflected the widespread support that this norm enjoys.[138] Despite its lack of legal standing, the no-testing norm is already having important effects. It has served to constrain the nuclear testing plans of all the declared nuclear weapon states over the past five years. In some cases these tests would have allowed nuclear force modernization based on new warhead designs.[139] In particular, they would have permitted the development of very-low-yield warheads ('micro-nukes') and third-generation nuclear weapons that are envisioned in some nuclear war-fighting doctrines.[140] One analyst has argued that, in preventing these tests, the ban is having an effect on nuclear doctrines and modernization programmes that is practically independent of the CTBT's legal status.[141]

VI. Negotiations on a Fissile Material Treaty

The Conference on Disarmament concluded its 1999 session without opening negotiations on a treaty to ban the production of fissile material for military purposes, despite having established an ad hoc negotiating committee.[142] Negotiations were blocked by a procedural impasse arising from the failure of the CD to reach agreement on a programme of work for the year, which is a prerequisite for convening the negotiating committee. This impasse resulted in the CD not conducting any negotiations during its 1999 session and led to renewed calls for changes in the CD's structure and procedures.

Two principal issues prevented the CD, which operates on the basis of consensus, from agreeing on a work programme.[143] The first was connected with the long-standing demand from the Group of 21 (G-21) non-aligned states in the CD for the establishment of an ad hoc committee on nuclear disarmament.[144] This demand has been consistently rejected by four of the nuclear weapon states—France, Russia, the UK and the USA. In 1999 some progress was made towards forging a compromise approach, with most of the delegations appearing to accept—albeit in some cases with great reluctance—the idea of informal discussions for exchanging views on nuclear disarmament

---

[138] Crossette, B., 'World leaders react with dismay to rejection of treaty', *New York Times* (Internet edn), 15 Oct. 1999, URL <http://www12.nytimes.com/library/world/global/101599treaty-react.htm>; and Johnson, M., 'Nations upset by US treaty vote', Associated Press, 14 Oct. 1999, URL <http://dailynews.yahoo.com/index.html>.

[139] Some treaty opponents have argued that an important reason for rejecting the test ban treaty is because it would effectively prevent the USA from modernizing its nuclear weapon arsenal for new roles and missions. Bailey (note 115), pp. 4–6.

[140] Arnett, E., 'Implications of nuclear weapons modernization programmes', in Arnett, E. (ed.), SIPRI, *Nuclear Weapons after the Comprehensive Test Ban* (Oxford University Press: Oxford, 1996), pp. 135–41.

[141] Arnett (note 100), pp. 409–12.

[142] A mandate had been agreed in Mar. 1995 for a committee to 'negotiate a non-discriminatory, multilateral and effectively verifiable treaty banning the production of fissile material for nuclear weapons or other nuclear explosive devices'. Conference on Disarmament document CD/1299, 24 Mar. 1995.

[143] During the third part of its 1999 session the CD admitted 5 new members—Ecuador, Ireland, Kazakhstan, Malaysia and Tunisia—thereby bringing total membership in the body to 66 states; see the glossary in this volume. 'Decision on the expansion of the membership of the Conference on Disarmament', Conference on Disarmament document CD/1588, 5 Aug. 1999.

[144] See the glossary in this volume for the over 30 (originally 21) member states of the Group of 21.

within an ad hoc working group.[145] The second issue was connected with Chinese-led calls for the re-establishment of an ad hoc negotiating committee under item three of the CD agenda, 'Prevention of an arms race in outer space' (PAROS).[146] China, along with Russia and some other member states, has argued that the 'weaponization' of outer space has become an urgent topic for the CD to address in the light of the USA's plans to move ahead with preparations for developing an NMD system. For its part, the USA has been unwilling to go along with proposals to initiate negotiations in the CD on the military uses of outer space.[147]

Statements by a number of delegations during the 1999 session suggested that political support for a convention banning the production of fissile material for military purposes is gaining momentum in the CD. No member states actively opposed opening negotiations on the ban, and several representatives stressed the importance of the ban in promoting nuclear disarmament and urged the CD to promptly convene the ad hoc committee. A working paper put forward by France, the UK and the USA proposed revising the 1995 mandate to include a provision that the committee be reconvened each year until negotiations are concluded, without the need for annual reauthorization.[148] This proposal was rejected by India and Pakistan on the grounds that the creation of permanent committees was without precedent and contrary to the CD's rules of procedure.[149]

VII. The NPT Preparatory Committee

The third meeting of the Preparatory Committee for the 2000 NPT Review Conference was held at UN Headquarters in New York on 10–21 April 1999.[150] Delegations from 119 states parties to the NPT participated under the

[145] The mandate for such a working group has yet to be determined. It is likely to resemble the 'NATO-5' proposal put forward by Belgium, Germany, Italy, the Netherlands and Norway calling on the CD to 'study ways and means of exchanging information and views . . . on endeavours towards nuclear disarmament'. 'Proposal on nuclear disarmament', Conference on Disarmament document CD/1565, 2 Feb. 1999.

[146] China proposed the establishment of an ad hoc committee 'to negotiate the conclusion of an international legal instrument banning the testing, deployment and use of any weapons, weapon systems or components thereof in outer space'. 'Re-establishment of an ad hoc committee on the prevention of an arms race in outer space and its mandate', Conference on Disarmament document CD/1576, 18 Mar. 1999. An ad hoc committee established in 1994 failed to reach agreement on a set of proposed confidence-building measures in outer space.

[147] However, in Mar. 1998 the CD did appoint a special coordinator to seek members' views on practical ways to prevent an arms race in outer space.

[148] 'Working paper on the programme of the conference', Conference on Disarmament document CD/1586, 20 May 1999.

[149] Johnson, R., 'Geneva Update No. 47: update on the CD impasse', *Disarmament Diplomacy*, no. 37 (June 1999), p. 21.

[150] The 1995 NPT Review and Extension Conference had sought to strengthen the review process by requiring that Preparatory Committee meetings be held in each of the 3 years leading up to the 5-yearly Review Conferences. The purpose of the Preparatory Committee meetings is to 'consider principles, objectives and ways in order to promote the full implementation of the Treaty, as well as its universality, and to make recommendations thereon to the Review Conference'. 'Strengthening the review process for the treaty', New York, 11 May 1995, NPT/CONF.1995/32 (Part I), reproduced in *SIPRI Yearbook 1996* (note 76), appendix 13A, pp. 590–91.

chairmanship of Ambassador Camilio Reyes Rodriguez of Colombia.[151] It took place against the background of growing concern about the future of the strengthened NPT review process arising from the failure of the 1998 Preparatory Committee meeting to reach agreement on any substantive or procedural issues.[152]

The third Preparatory Committee meeting adopted a final report containing organizational and procedural decisions for the 2000 NPT Review Conference, scheduled to take place at UN on 24 April–19 May 2000, thereby obviating the need to call an extraordinary committee session. These decisions included an agreement on the rules of procedure, the adoption of a provisional agenda and the allocation of agenda items to the three Main Committees;[153] consideration of proposals to establish subsidiary bodies under the Main Committees was deferred to the Review Conference. The committee also agreed to commission background documentation related to the implementation of various provisions of the NPT and to the decisions taken at the 1995 NPT Review and Extension Conference.[154] However, it was unable to agree on a recommendation for what should be the 'products' or 'outcomes' of the conference. The main question was whether it should produce two documents—a Final Declaration reviewing implementation of the treaty and an updated version of the programme of action outlined 1995 Principles and Objectives setting out new objectives—or a single document containing elements of both. The decision was deferred to the Review Conference. Finally, as in the two preceding years, the committee failed to reach agreement on recommendations to the Review Conference on a host of important substantive issues, such as the implementation of the IAEA's strengthened safeguards system, the scope of a Fissile Material Treaty and the de-alerting of strategic nuclear forces, related to the NPT regime.[155]

---

[151] 'Preparatory Committee for 2000 Review Conference of Non-proliferation Treaty concludes final session at headquarters', United Nations Press Release DC/2645, 26 May 1999.

[152] Some observers warned that a similar failure at the 1999 PrepCom meeting would mean that the states parties would go into the 2000 Review Conference with little to show for their involvement in the strengthened review process and thereby would discredit that process and contribute to undermining the credibility of the NPT itself. Rauf, T. and Simpson, J., 'The 1999 NPT PrepCom', *Nonproliferation Review*, vol. 6, no. 2 (winter 1999), pp. 118–19.

[153] Review conferences have adopted the practice of allocating 'clusters' of issues to three Main Committees (MCs), addressing nuclear disarmament (MC.1), safeguards and nuclear weapon-free zones (MC.2) and nuclear energy (MC.3). Some parties have argued that this structure is inefficient and should be replaced by an article-by-article review of the treaty.

[154] Johnson, R., 'The Third PrepCom: what happened and why', *Disarmament Diplomacy*, no. 37 (May 1999), URL <http://www.acronym.org.uk/37npt.htm>. The Committee specifically included the Resolution on the Middle East among the latter set of decisions. The dispute over allowing background documentation related to the implementation of this resolution had been one of the principal obstacles contributing to the stalemate that arose in the 1998 PrepCom meeting. See Kile (note 5), p. 531.

[155] At the insistence of many delegations that the results of the 1999 PrepCom should not reflect purely procedural issues, it was decided to append both versions of the Chairman's unadopted working papers to the Final Report, along with a list of proposed amendments to the papers. These documents are likely to form the basis for substantive discussions at the upcoming Review Conference. See Johnson (note 154). For a discussion of the IAEA strengthened safeguards system, see appendix 8B.

Assessment of the results of the meetings

The meagre results of the Preparatory Committee meetings held since 1995 have disappointed proponents of the notion of 'permanence through accountability' that underlies the strengthened NPT review process. The meetings have been largely paralysed by disagreements between the states parties over the principles and procedures governing the committee's activities, its role in the strengthened review process, and over the meaning and aims of that process. Many non-nuclear weapon states parties have favoured giving the committee a more substantive role in promoting implementation of the nuclear disarmament commitments contained in the NPT and the 1995 Principles and Objectives.[156] At the 1999 Preparatory Committee meeting, the New Agenda Coalition, which emerged out of a 1998 initiative launched by the foreign ministers of eight non-nuclear weapon states, presented a working paper that outlined specific steps for promoting progress towards nuclear disarmament.[157] By contrast, the nuclear weapon states parties generally have sought to limit the role of the committee to compiling a list of proposals to be taken up at the 2000 Review Conference and to deciding on the procedural arrangements for that conference. They have shown little interest in allowing the Preparatory Committees to move in the direction of becoming 'mini-review conferences'. The nuclear weapon states have also acted increasingly *en bloc* in resisting efforts to use the strengthened review process to mandate concrete action on nuclear disarmament.[158]

The disagreements on procedural and substantive issues do not bode well for the prospects of a successful 2000 Review Conference, if success is judged in terms of the conference adopting by consensus a Final Declaration based on the working reports of the three Main Committees. A host of contentious issues will make it difficult for the states parties to work out compromise language for a set of conclusions about NPT implementation in the period 1995–2000. At the same time, the conference will have to address fundamental questions about the modalities of the strengthened review process, including the role of the Principles and Objectives document in that process. While a failure to reach agreement on a Final Declaration would by no means fatally undermine the NPT, it could weaken international support for the treaty at a time when the non-proliferation regime is confronting serious challenges.

---

[156] The document on Principles and Objectives for Nuclear Non-Proliferation and Disarmament was adopted by the 1995 NPT Review and Extension Conference; it is reproduced in *SIPRI Yearbook 1996* (note 76), pp. 591–93.

[157] Concern that the international community was lapsing into complacency with regard to its previous commitments to work towards nuclear disarmament prompted 8 nations to issue a Joint Declaration, which was subsequently adopted by the UN First Committee, urging a 'clear commitment to the speedy, final and total elimination' of nuclear weapons by the states possessing them. 'A nuclear-weapons-free world: the need for a new agenda', Joint Declaration by the Ministers for Foreign Affairs of Brazil, Egypt, Ireland, Mexico, New Zealand, Slovenia, South Africa and Sweden, 9 June 1998.

[158] Rauf, T., 'The 1998 NPT PrepCom: farewell to the strengthened review process?', *Disarmament Diplomacy*, no. 26 (May 1998), p. 3.

VIII. The US–North Korean Agreed Framework

In early 1999, the 1994 US–North Korean Agreed Framework appeared to be on the brink of collapse because of a series of disputes between North Korea and the USA related to the implementation of the accord.[159] It had also been jeopardized by international concern over North Korea's ballistic missile programme.[160] The importance of the Agreed Framework in halting North Korea's alleged nuclear weapon programme was emphasized by a report issued in October 1999 reviewing US policy on the Korean Peninsula. Authored by former Secretary of Defense William Perry, the report argued that the 'Agreed Framework's limitations, such as the fact that it does not cover ballistic missiles, are best addressed by supplementing rather than replacing' the accord.[161]

The dispute between the USA and North Korea in 1998 over US allegations that North Korea was building an underground nuclear weapon-related facility at Kumchang-ni, approximately 50 kilometres north-west of its nuclear plant at Yongbyon, was resolved in 1999. US officials had pressed North Korea for access to the complex in order to 'clarify the nature of the suspect construction'.[162] They subsequently warned that failure to resolve suspicions about the site, which was revealed in satellite surveillance photographs, could jeopardize the Agreed Framework. North Korea denied allegations that it was building a nuclear weapon-related facility. After difficult negotiations, a US inspection team was granted access to the site in May 1999. The US inspectors concluded that the site did not appear to be configured to support any nuclear functions and did not otherwise violate the Agreed Framework.[163] A second inspection visit is scheduled to take place in May 2000.

By the end of 1999 implementation of the Agreed Framework appeared to be back on track as political tensions over North Korea's ballistic missile programme began to abate and problems with the project's financial arrangements were addressed. In December the Korean Peninsula Energy Development Organization (KEDO)—a 12-nation international consortium organized by the USA in cooperation with Japan and South Korea—announced a $4.6 billion turn-key contract with South Korea's state utility company for construction of two 1000-MW(e) (megawatts electric) light-water reactors (LWRs) at Kumho, North Korea.[164] The funding shortfall that had delayed the start of construction

[159] For a description of the Agreed Framework, see Kile (note 5), pp. 532–33.

[160] See chapter 11 in this volume.

[161] 'Review of United States policy towards North Korea: findings and recommendations', Unclassified report by Dr William J. Perry, North Korea Policy Coordinator and Special Advisor to the President and the Secretary of State, 12 Oct. 1999.

[162] 'US–DPRK talks', Press statement, US Department of State, 10 Sep. 1998, reproduced in 'US statement on North Korea talks', *Disarmament Diplomacy*, no. 30 (Sep. 1998), pp. 45–46.

[163] 'Report on the US visit to the site at Kumchang-ni, Democratic People's Republic of Korea', Statement by James Rubin, Office of the Spokesman, US State Department, 25 June 1999. The site was not found not to contain a plutonium production reactor or reprocessing plant, either completed or under construction.

[164] Rice, M., 'KEDO signs contract to begin work on North Korean reactors', *Arms Control Today*, vol. 29, no. 8 (Dec. 1999), p. 22. The lion's share of the estimated $4.6 billion cost of the LWR project is

work was partially resolved earlier in the year when KEDO reached interim financing agreements with the governments of Japan and South Korea. The first of the reactors is scheduled to be completed in 2007, four years behind the original schedule. The second reactor is to be completed by the end of 2008.[165]

IX. Nuclear doctrines

In 1999 a number of developments related to nuclear doctrines served to highlight the continued salience of nuclear weapons in military planning. In October the Russian Defence Ministry published a long-delayed draft military doctrine in which nuclear weapons were accorded a relatively greater role in Russian defence planning than in the previous military doctrine, adopted in 1993.[166] Among other provisions, the draft doctrine described in general terms the purposes that Russia's nuclear weapons serve and the scenarios in which they might be used. As in the 1993 military doctrine, the new document did not include a pledge that Russia would not use nuclear weapons first in a conflict. However, it modified the previous doctrine's provision related to negative security assurances in order to allow Russia to use nuclear weapons in response to a chemical or biological weapon attack initiated by a non-nuclear weapon state.[167] In addition, the draft doctrine stated that Russia reserved the right to use nuclear weapons 'in response to large-scale aggression involving conventional weapons situations that are critical for the security of the Russian Federation and its allies'. This vaguely worded provision has been widely seen as being an acknowledgement that the country's conventional military strength might not be sufficient to prevail in regional conflicts with non-nuclear weapon states or entities.[168]

In India, a proposal for a national nuclear doctrine attracted considerable international notoriety when it was published on 17 August 1999 by a non-official National Security Advisory Board. Among other provisions, the draft doctrine envisioned the long-term development by India of substantial nuclear forces. It reaffirmed previous official statements that India would pursue a

to be covered by a $3.2 billion contribution from South Korea, with Japan contributing $1 billion; the European Union has also agreed to contribute to the project. The USA has assumed the main responsibility for underwriting the costs of compensatory oil supplies (500 000 tonnes of heavy fuel oil per annum) to North Korea until the new reactors are in operation.

[165] Choe, S., 'Nuke reactors to be built in North Korea', Associated Press, 15 Dec. 1999, URL <http://www.newsday.com/ap/rnmpin0s.htm>. Construction work will be halted upon completion of the containment building for the first reactor pending the satisfactory conclusion of an IAEA special inspection to verify that North Korea has not diverted spent reactor fuels for weapon purposes and is in compliance with its full-scope IAEA safeguards agreement.

[166] A draft of the new Military Doctrine was published in *Krasnaya Zvezda*, 9 Oct. 1999, pp. 3–4. The final version, as approved by President Vladimir Putin on 21 Apr. 2000, was published in *Nezavisimaya Gazeta*, 22 Apr. 2000. An unofficial English translation was released by BBC Monitoring on 22 Apr. 2000.

[167] This new provision is similar to one reportedly adopted by the USA. See Kile (note 49), p. 418.

[168] Sokov, N., *Overview: An Assessment of the Draft Russian Military Doctrine*, CNS Report (Center for Nonproliferation Studies (CNS), Monterey Institute of International Studies: Monterey, Calif., Oct. 1999), URL <http://cns.miis.edu/pubs/reports/sokov.htm>.

policy of 'credible minimum nuclear deterrence' in which the 'fundamental purpose of Indian nuclear weapons is to deter the use and threat to use of nuclear weapons by any State or entity against India and its forces'; while India would not be the first to use nuclear weapons in a conflict, it would respond to any nuclear attack with nuclear weapons 'to inflict damage unacceptable to the aggressor'.[169] In order to ensure the credibility of the country's deterrence posture, the draft doctrine indicated that India would develop a 'triad' of air-, sea- and land-based nuclear forces; survivability would be 'enhanced by a combination of multiple redundant systems, mobility, dispersion and deception'.[170] India would also invest in an 'effective and survivable' command and control and early-warning infrastructure.[171] The draft doctrine was criticized by some analysts in India for its allegedly provocative tone and for seeming to pave the way for an open-ended nuclear weapon programme.[172] External Affairs Minister Singh subsequently sought to distance the government from the recommendations contained in the draft doctrine, emphasizing its provisional and non-official nature. He noted that while India is committed to maintaining a 'minimum but credible nuclear deterrent', a 'traditional triad' of nuclear forces (i.e., one with land, sea and air forces) is not a 'pre-requisite for credibility'.[173]

In its new Strategic Concept unveiled in April 1999, NATO affirmed its intention to maintain nuclear forces in Europe for the indefinite future. The NATO document stressed that these forces would be 'at the minimum level consistent with the prevailing security environment' and that circumstances in which their use might have to be contemplated were 'extremely remote'.[174] The alliance's reaffirmation of its commitment to a nuclear posture disappointed some arms control advocates, who saw it as undermining efforts to marginalize the role of nuclear weapons in military planning.

X. Conclusions

In 1999 the Russian–US nuclear arms control framework came under increasing strain as political pressure mounted within the USA to adjust one of the

---

[169] 'Draft report of the National Security Advisory Board on Indian nuclear doctrine', 17 Aug. 1999, URL <http://www.meadev.gov.in/govt/indnucld.htm>. Pakistan has consistently rejected Indian calls to declare a similar policy of 'no first-use' of nuclear weapons.

[170] According to one of the participants on the 27-member National Security Advisory Board which prepared the draft doctrine, India's nuclear force is likely to include no more than a few dozen weapons over the next 5 years. Chellaney, B., 'India, too, has a right to credible nuclear deterrence', *International Herald Tribune*, 1 Sep. 1999, p. 6.

[171] Draft report of the National Security Advisory Board on Indian nuclear doctrine' (note 169).

[172] Constable, P., 'India vows to fire nuclear weapons only if attacked', *International Herald Tribune*, 18 Aug. 1999, p. 3. Other critics suggested that the release of the document shortly before national elections was part of the Indian nuclear establishment's strategy to commit the new government to an ambitious nuclear forces development programme.

[173] Quoted in Raja Mohan, C., 'Jaswant Singh for consensus on CTBT', *The Hindu*, 29 Nov. 1999, URL <http://www.indiaserver.com/thehindu/1999/11/29/stories/01290001.htm>.

[174] 'The Alliance's Strategic Concept approved by the Heads of State and Government participating in the meeting of the North Atlantic Council in Washington DC on 23rd and 24th April 1999', NATO Press Release NAC–S(99)65, 24 Apr. 1999.

key pillars of that framework to take into account the emergence of perceived new threats in the post-cold war world and new technological possibilities for countering those threats. The US Administration's proposal to amend the ABM Treaty to permit the deployment of limited national missile defences designed to counter putative ballistic missile threats posed by 'rogue states' led to an intensifying doctrinal dispute between Washington and Moscow over the future of that treaty as the cornerstone of the Russian–US strategic nuclear relationship. The dispute contributed to further souring their already difficult political relations and led to blunt warnings from Russia that the achievements made in recent years in building smaller, more transparent nuclear arsenals were in jeopardy. It also complicated the fate of the START II Treaty in Russia and fuelled doubts about whether that long-stalled treaty would enter into force even if it were ratified by the Parliament.

In 1999 there was also renewed concern about the vitality of the NPT and the broader nuclear non-proliferation regime stemming from the US Senate's decision not to ratify the CTBT. The Senate's vote weakened the USA's crucially important leadership role within that regime and eroded its credibility in leading efforts to draw states such as India and Pakistan into legally binding arrangements aimed at promoting important nuclear non-proliferation objectives and reducing nuclear weapon-related dangers. In addition, the test ban treaty had been widely seen by non-nuclear weapon states parties to the NPT as a litmus test of the willingness of the nuclear weapon states to fulfil their disarmament commitment under Article VI of the treaty. The Senate's vote not to ratify the CTBT did little to dispel the impression that the nuclear weapon states had become complacent in upholding their end of the NPT 'bargain'; this complacency threatened to erode international support for the treaty regime and for wider nuclear non-proliferation efforts.

While the overall post-cold war nuclear arms control framework was not in immediate danger of collapse at the end of 1999, it was increasingly clear that serious problems need to be addressed. This in turn underscored that there is an urgent need to conceptualize a new arms control and disarmament agenda that will be able to address the risks and challenges likely to emerge in the future international security system.[175]

---

[175] See SIPRI, *The Stockholm Agenda for Arms Control*, Report based on the Rapporteur's Statement at the Nobel Symposium on A Future Arms Control Agenda, 1–2 Oct. 1999 (SIPRI: Stockholm, 1999).

Appendix 8A. Tables of nuclear forces

ROBERT S. NORRIS and WILLIAM M. ARKIN

Although Russia and the United States have made significant reductions in their deployed strategic nuclear delivery vehicles within the framework of the 1991 Treaty on the Reduction and Limitation of Strategic Offensive Arms (START I Treaty), they continue to maintain large stockpiles of strategic and non-strategic (or tactical) nuclear weapons. Tables 8A.1 and 8A.2 show the composition of the US and Russian operational strategic nuclear forces and present estimates of their non-strategic nuclear weapon holdings. The size of Russia's inventory of non-strategic nuclear weapons is believed to considerably exceed that of the USA but is difficult to estimate on the basis of public information.

The nuclear arsenals of the three other NPT-defined nuclear weapon states—the United Kingdom, France and China—are considerably smaller than those of Russia and the USA; data on their delivery vehicles and nuclear warhead stockpiles are presented in tables 8A.3, 8A.4, and 8A.5, respectively. China is the only one of the five NPT-defined nuclear weapon states which is currently undertaking a significant strategic nuclear force modernization programme, but its plans for the size and composition of its strategic forces are unknown.

It is particularly difficult to obtain public information about the nuclear arsenals of the three de facto nuclear weapon states—India, Pakistan and Israel. Tables 8A.6, 8A.7 and 8A.8, respectively, present estimates of the size of their nuclear weapon stockpiles and provide information about potential nuclear weapon delivery means.

The figures contained in the tables are estimates based on public information but contain some uncertainties, as reflected in the notes.

The following acronyms appear in the tables and notes below; other acronyms are defined in the notes.

AB	Air base
ACM	Advanced cruise missile
ADM	Atomic demolition mine
AFB	Air force base
ALCM	Air-launched cruise missile
ASW	Anti-submarine warfare
CALCM	Conventional air-launched cruise missile
ICBM	Intercontinental ballistic missile
IRBM	Intermediate-range ballistic missile
MIRV	Multiple independently targetable re-entry vehicle
MRV	Multiple re-entry vehicle
MOU	Memorandum of Understanding
RV	Re-entry vehicle
SAM	Surface-to-air missile
SLBM	Submarine-launched ballistic missile
SLCM	Sea-launched cruise missile
SRAM	Short-range attack missile
SRBM	Short-range ballistic missile
SSBN	Nuclear-powered, ballistic-missile submarine
SSN	Nuclear-powered submarine
TEL	Transporter–erector–launcher

Table 8A.1. US nuclear forces, January 2000

Type	Designation	No. deployed	Year first deployed	Range (km)[a]	Warheads x yield	Warheads
Strategic forces						
Bombers						
B-52H[b]	Stratofortress	76/56	1961	16 000	ALCM 5–150 kt	400
					ACM 5–150 kt	400
B-2[c]	Spirit	21/16	1994	11 000	Bombs, various	950
Total		**97/72**				**1 750**
ICBMs						
LGM-30G[d]	Minuteman III					
	Mk-12	200	1970	13 000	3 x 170 kt	600
	Mk-12A	300	1979	13 000	3 x 335 kt	900
LGM-118A	MX/Peacekeeper	50	1986	11 000	10 x 300 kt	500
Total		**550**				**2 000**
SLBMs						
UGM-96A[e]	Trident I C-4	192	1979	7 400	8 x 100 kt	1 536
UGM-133A[f]	Trident II D-5					
	Mk-4	192	1992	7 400	8 x 100 kt	1 536
	Mk-5	48	1990	7 400	8 x 475 kt	384
Total		**432**				**3 456**
Total strategic						**7 206**
Non-strategic forces						
Tomahawk SLCM[g]		325	1984	2 500	1 x 5–150 kt	320
B61-3, -4, -10 bombs[h]		n.a.	1979	n.a.	0.3–170 kt	1 350
Total non-strategic						**1 670**

[a] Range for aircraft indicates combat radius, without in-flight refuelling.

[b] B-52Hs can carry up to 20 ALCMs/ACMs each. Because the US bomber force is shrinking, only about 400 ALCMs and 400 ACMs are deployed, with several hundred other ALCMs in reserve. In 1999 the US Air Force ordered conversion of another 322 ALCMs to conventional cruise missiles, as CALCM Block I and Block IA configurations. The last 50 will be fitted with a deep-penetration warhead to strike hardened targets. The missiles will be delivered from late 1999 through early 2001. The Nuclear Posture Review (NPR) released on 22 Sep. 1994 recommended eventually retaining 66 B-52Hs, but the air force decided on a higher number. The B-52Hs have been consolidated at 2 bases: the 2nd Bomb Wing at Barksdale AFB, Louisiana, and the 5th Bomb Wing at Minot AFB, North Dakota. The first figure in the *No. deployed* column is the total number of B-52Hs in the inventory, including those for training, test and backup. The second figure is the 'primary aircraft inventory', i.e., the number of operational aircraft available for nuclear and conventional missions.

Under the START II Treaty the B-1Bs will not be counted as nuclear weapon carriers. The USA has completed a reorientation of its B-1Bs to conventional missions. By the end of 1997 all the B-1Bs were out of the strategic war plan altogether and are not included in the table. Of the original 100 B-1Bs, 6 have crashed: 1 in 1987, 2 in 1988, 1 in 1992, 1 in 1997 and the most recent 1 on 18 Feb. 1998.

[c] The first B-2 bomber was delivered to the 509th Bombardment Wing at Whiteman AFB, Missouri, on 17 Dec. 1993. The wing has 2 squadrons: the 393rd squadron was declared operational on 1 Apr. 1997; and the 325th was activated on 8 Jan. 1998. By the end of 1995, 8 more B-2s had arrived at Whiteman AFB; 5 were delivered in 1996, 4 in 1997, 2 in 1998

Table 8A.1 *Notes, contd*

and 1 in 1999. All 6 aircraft from the test programme are being modified to achieve an operational capability, which brings the total number to 21.

The B-2 is configured to carry various combinations of nuclear and conventional munitions. The first 16 aircraft were produced as Block 10 versions, able to carry the B83 nuclear bomb (and the Mk 84 conventional bomb). These were followed by 3 production Block 20 versions, able to carry the B61 nuclear bomb. Finally, the last 2 aircraft were production Block 30 versions, able to carry both types of nuclear bomb and an assortment of conventional bombs, munitions and missiles. Earlier Block 10 and 20 aircraft are being upgraded to Block 30 standards. Originally scheduled to be completed in 2000, the upgrades will stretch to 2002 as a result of work being added. At completion there will be 21 Block 30 B-2s. The first figure in the *No. deployed* column is the total number of B-2s delivered to Whiteman AFB; the second figure is an approximate number of those available for nuclear and conventional missions.

d The 500 Minuteman IIIs have been consolidated from 4 bases to 3. The last Minuteman III missile was removed from its silo on 3 June 1998 for transfer to Malmstrom AFB, Montana, or to Hill AFB, Utah. Currently, the 200 Minuteman IIIs at Malmstrom are deployed in 4 missile squadrons (10th, 12th, 490th and 564th) of 50 missiles each as part of the 341st Space Wing. There are 150 Minuteman IIIs at Minot AFB, North Dakota, in 3 missile squadrons (740th, 741st and 742nd) as part of the 91st Space Wing. The 150 Minuteman IIIs at F.E. Warren AFB, Wyoming, in 3 missile squadrons (319th, 320th and 321st) and the 1 missile squadron of 50 MX ICBMs (400th) are part of the 90th Space Wing.

To comply with the ban on MIRVs when the START II Treaty enters into force, the number of warheads on each of the 500 Minuteman III missiles will have to be reduced from 3 to 1, and the MX will be retired. Some Minuteman missiles have already been downloaded to carry only 1 re-entry vehicle. Currently, 300 Minuteman III missiles have the higher-yield W78 warhead and 200 have the W62 warhead. While several de-MIRVing options are possible, the Air Force has begun to place the Mark 21/W87 warhead on some Minuteman missiles at F.E. Warren AFB. Up to 500 W87s will be removed from the 50 MX missiles when they are retired. The W87 warhead has the preferred safety features, including the insensitive high explosive (IHE), fire resistant pit (FRP) and enhanced nuclear detonation system (ENDS), whereas the W78 has only ENDS. A drawback is the difficulty of putting multiple warheads back on the missiles if the force is reconstituted. A second option would be to place a single W78 on each missile. The third would be to put W78s on a portion of the force, e.g., 150 of the 500 missiles, and W87s on the rest, using the newer warhead to permit easier re-MIRVing. Previously, the downloading was to have been accomplished within 7 years of the entry into force of the START I Treaty, i.e., by 5 Dec. 2001. Under the 1997 START II Protocol it does not have to be completed until the end of 2007. (In Mar. 1997 Presidents Clinton and Yeltsin, at a summit meeting in Helsinki, agreed to adjust some of the START II timetables regarding elimination and deactivation. On 26 Sep. 1997 Russia and the USA signed a Protocol extending the implementation period by 5 years, from the beginning of 2003 to the end of 2007. However, all delivery vehicles which would be eliminated to meet the START II limits will still have to be deactivated by the end of 2003 through the removal of warheads or through some other jointly agreed method.)

US silo destruction has been completed in accordance with the START I Treaty at Ellsworth AFB, South Dakota, and Whiteman AFB, 2 bases that once deployed Minuteman II ICBMs. Destruction of the 150 silos that once housed the Minuteman IIIs and the 15 missile alert facilities (with their underground launch control centres, LCCs) at Grand Forks AFB, North Dakota, began during 1999. The first silo was blown up on 6 Oct. near Langdon, North Dakota; 14 were destroyed by mid-Dec. The entire process is scheduled to be completed by 1 Dec. 2001.

A 3-part programme to upgrade the Minuteman missiles continues. The missile alert facilities (i.e., LCCs) have been updated with Rapid Execution and Combat Targeting (REACT) consoles. The second part is the Guidance Replacement Program, which is designed to extend the life of the guidance system to beyond 2020. The improvements include new electronics and software and are being carried out by Boeing. Full-rate production began in 1999. The measures will eventually increase the accuracy of the Minuteman III to near that of the current MX—a circular error probable (CEP) of 100 metres. The third part is the Propulsion Replacement Program, which involves 'repouring' the first and second stages, incorporating the latest solid-propellant and bonding technologies, and replacing obsolete or environmentally unsafe materials and components. On 13 Nov. the first re-manufactured Minuteman III missile was successfully launched from Vandenberg AFB, California, to the Kwajalein Missile Range in the Pacific Ocean. As a cost-saving measure, the US Air Force has transferred responsibility for maintaining the readiness of the 550 ICBMs to TRW, Inc., a private contractor. The $3.4 billion contract was awarded on 22 Dec. 1997 and runs until the end of 2012.

e The W76 warheads from the Trident I missiles have been fitted on Trident II submarines home-ported at Kings Bay, Georgia, and are supplemented by 400 W88 warheads, the number of warheads built before production ceased in 1990.

f Eighteen Ohio Class submarines constitute the current SSBN fleet. The earlier SSBNs included 5 George Washington Class (SSBN-598), 5 Ethan Allen Class (SSBN-608) and 31 Lafayette Class (SSBN-616) submarines. Since the first patrol, in Nov. 1960, these 59 submarines have made over 3500 patrols.

The 1994 NPR recommended completing construction of 18 Ohio Class SSBNs and then retiring 4 older SSBNs. The navy has chosen the submarines that will be upgraded and those that will be retired. The 4 newest Trident I-equipped SSBNs based in the Pacific at Bangor, Washington, will be backfitted to be able to fire Trident II missiles. In order of their upgrade they are the *Alaska* (732) and *Nevada* (733) (during 2000 and 2001) followed by the *Jackson* (730) and *Alabama* (731) (during 2004 and 2005). The *Alaska* is scheduled to enter the Puget Sound Naval Shipyard for overhaul and conversion in Apr. or May 2000. The 4 older submarines (*Ohio, Michigan, Florida* and *Georgia*) will be retired as SSBNs, 2 each in 2002 and 2003. One possibility is to convert 2 or all 4 submarines to carry cruise missiles and to be used for special operations forces (SOF). Twenty-two of the launch tubes would be converted to carry up to 154 land-attack cruise missiles and the 2 remaining launch tubes modified for SOF delivery vehicles. Initially, the missiles would be Tomahawks but later they could be the Land Attack Standard Missile or the Navy Tactical Missile. Conversion is permitted but is a more costly and extensive process since it involves removing the submarine's missile tubes. Modification leaves the tubes empty but must be agreed by Russia and the USA. START I contained an Agreed Statement allowing for 2 US special-purpose Poseidon submarines. If the navy wanted to replace those 2 Poseidons with 2 Trident submarines, this would have to be agreed in a future treaty. A US Navy study completed in early 1999 concluded that the conversions presented no technical challenges, but the substantial cost and the difficult treaty implications may nonetheless prevent them from going forward. The navy has extended the service life of the Ohio Class Trident SSBN to 42 years.

The US Navy continues to purchase Trident II SLBMs. Twelve missiles were requested in the FY 2000 Pentagon budget and 12 in the FY 2001 budget. The NPR called for backfitting 4 Trident I-equipped SSBNs with Trident IIs, increasing the number of missiles to be procured from 390 to 425, at an extra cost of $2.2 billion. Twenty-eight additional missiles were bought for the research and development programme. The total cost of the programme is now $27.355 billion, or $60 million per missile. Through to the end of FY 2000, $24.378 billion has been authorized. Some have questioned the need to continue to buy more missiles if the future force under a START III accord is going to be fewer than 14 SSBNs. A force of 10 submarines, e.g., requires 347 missiles and would result in significant savings. The 85th consecutive successful Trident II missile test flight was conducted in 1999.

The Bangor base will undergo some adaptation to support the Trident II and a 10-year, $5 billion programme is scheduled to begin in 2000. The backfitting of the 4 SSBNs will take place from FY 2000 to FY 2005. Beginning in 2002, 3 submarines will be moved from Kings

Table 8A.1 *Notes, contd*

Bay to Bangor to balance the 14-submarine fleet. To comply with START II warhead limits the navy will have to either download its SLBMs, retire additional SSBNs or do both. Under the new START II timetable, SLBMs can have no more than 2160 warheads by the end of 2004 and no more than 1750 warheads by the end of 2007. If there is a START III accord with limits of 2000–2500 deployed strategic warheads, the SSBN portion would probably account for *c.* one-half. This would mean a fleet of 10–12 submarines, depending on the number of warheads per SLBM. Some speculate that with an SSBN fleet of a dozen or less the Bangor base could be closed, although war planners object because targets in China would not be adequately covered.

While much has changed, some things have not. The practice of each SSBN having 2 crews remains unchanged. Currently, the SSBN force operates on a 112-day cycle that consists of a 77-day patrol followed by a 35-day refit period. In 2000, at any given time, 9 or 10 US SSBNs will be on patrol, a rate equal to that at the height of the cold war. Roughly one-half of the number of those on patrol (2 or 3 in each of the Atlantic and Pacific oceans) will be on 'hard' alert, i.e., within range of their targets. The remaining patrolling SSBNs are in transit to or from their launch-point areas and could be generated up to hard alert within a matter of hours or days. Although the START counting rules attribute 8 warheads per Trident missile as the counting rule, the actual loading of a submarine will normally be less than the full complement of 192 per vessel. A missile's range can be extended by carrying fewer warheads. Some SLBMs may have 5 or 6 warheads while others have 7 or 8. It is the Single Integrated Operational Plan (SIOP) that ultimately determines how an SSBN will be loaded, where the SLBMs will be launched from, and at which targets the warheads are aimed.

g Approximately one-half of the US Navy's stock of nuclear-armed Tomahawk SLCMs, with W80 warheads, are presumed to be stored ashore at Naval Submarine Base, Bangor, Washington, after being transferred from Naval Air Station North Island in San Diego, California, in 1998. The other half are presumably stored ashore at the Naval Weapons Station, Yorktown, Virginia. As a result of the 1994 NPR surface vessels no longer carry nuclear-armed Tomahawk missiles, but the option was retained to redeploy them on attack submarines, although none is currently deployed.

h An ample supply of B61 tactical nuclear bombs exists for various US and European NATO aircraft. US aircraft include the F-16A/B/C/D Fighting Falcon, F-15E Strike Eagle and F-117A Nighthawk. Aircraft for NATO allied air forces include F-16s and Tornado fighter bombers. It is estimated that *c.* 150 bombs are deployed at 10 air bases in 7 European NATO nations. The air bases include: Kleine Brogel, Belgium; Buechel AB, Germany; Ramstein AB, Germany; Spangdahlem AB, Germany; Araxos, Greece; Aviano, Italy; Ghedi-Torre, Italy; Volkel, Netherlands; Incirlik, Turkey; and RAF Lakenheath, UK. In the USA, significant numbers of B-61s are stored at AFBs in Nevada and New Mexico.

Sources: Cohen, W., Secretary of Defense, *Annual Report to the President and the Congress* (US Department of Defense: Washington, DC, 2000), pp. 69–77, D-1; START I Treaty Memoranda of Understanding, Sep. 1990, 5 Dec. 1994, 1 July 1995, 1 Jan. 1996, 1 July 1996, 1 Jan. 1997, 1 July 1997, 1 July 1998, 1 Jan. 1999, 1 July 1999; US Senate Committee on Foreign Relations, START II Treaty, Executive Report 104-10, 15 Dec. 1995; US Air Force Public Affairs, Personal communications; International Institute for Strategic Studies, *The Military Balance 1999/2000* (Oxford University Press: Oxford, 1999); Natural Resources Defense Council (NRDC); and 'NRDC Nuclear Notebook', *Bulletin of the Atomic Scientists*, various issues.

Table 8A.2. Russian nuclear forces, January 2000

Type	NATO designation	No. deployed	Year first deployed	Range (km)[a]	Warheads x yield	Warheads
Strategic offensive forces						
Bombers						
Tu-95MS6[b]	Bear-H6	29	1984	12 800	6 x AS-15A ALCMs, bombs	174
Tu-95MS16[b]	Bear-H16	34	1984	12 800	16 x AS-15A ALCMs, bombs	544
Tu-160[c]	Blackjack	6	1987	11 000	12 x AS-15B ALCMs or AS-16 SRAMs, bombs	72
Total		69				790
ICBMs[d]						
SS-18[e]	Satan	180	1979	11 000	10 x 550/750 kt	1 800
SS-19[f]	Stiletto	150	1980	10 000	6 x 750 kt	900
SS-24 M1/M2[g]	Scalpel	36/10	1987	10 000	10 x 550 kt	460
SS-25[h]	Sickle	360	1985	10 500	1 x 550 kt	360
SS-27[i]	. .	20	1997	10 500	1 x 550 kt	20
Total		756				3 540
SLBMs[j]						
SS-N-18 M1	Stingray	176	1978	6 500	3 x 500 kt (MIRV)	528
SS-N-20	Sturgeon	60	1983	8 300	10 x 200 kt (MIRV)	600
SS-N-23	Skiff	112	1986	9 000	4 x 100 kt (MIRV)	448
Total		348				1 576
Total strategic offensive						~ 6 000
Strategic defensive forces						
SAMs						
SA-5B Gammon, SA-10 Grumble		1 200				1 200
Non-strategic forces[k]						
Land-based non-strategic						
Bombers and fighters:						
Tu-22M Backfire (120), Su-24 Fencer (280)		400			AS-4 ASM, AS-16 SRAM, bombs	1 600
Naval non-strategic						
Attack aircraft:						
Tu-22M Backfire (70), Su-24 Fencer (70)		140			AS-4 ASM, bombs	400
SLCMs						
SS-N-9, SS-N-12, SS-N-19, SS-N-21, SS-N-22						500
ASW weapons						
SS-N-15, SS-N-16, torpedoes	n.a.					300
Total defensive and non-strategic						**4 000[l]**

[a] Range for aircraft indicates combat radius, without in-flight refuelling.

[b] According to the 1 July 1999 START I MOU, the Bear bombers are deployed at the following air bases: Bear-H16—21 at Ukrainka (79th Heavy Guard Bomber Regiment), 13 at Engels and 20 at Uzin (Ukraine); Bear-H6—27 at Ukrainka, 2 at Engels and 4 at Uzin

Table 8A.2 *Notes, contd*

(Ukraine). The 40 Bear-H bombers (27 Bear-H6s and 13 Bear-H16s) that were based in Kazakhstan were withdrawn to Russia, including some 370 AS-15 ALCM warheads. The 24 Bear bombers in Ukraine are poorly maintained and are not considered operational. On 25 June 1999, 2 Tu-95 Bear bombers flew within 96 km of Iceland as part of an extensive Russian exercise that took place outside St Petersburg called Zapad '99 (West '99). They were intercepted by 4 US F-15 fighters and a P-3 training aircraft, according to US officials. West '99 involved up to 50 000 troops from 5 military districts and 3 naval fleets as well as over 30 ships, 4 submarines, including the nuclear-powered Kirov, and Russian Air Force and Navy aircraft capable of launching air-to-air and air-to-ground cruise missiles.

[c] According to the 1 July 1999 START I MOU, 17 Blackjacks are based in Ukraine at Priluki, and 6 are in Russia at Engels AFB near Saratov with the 200th Heavy Guard Bomber Regiment. The Blackjacks at Priluki are poorly maintained and are not considered operational. An agreement announced on 24 Nov. 1995 that called for Ukraine to eventually return the Blackjacks, Bears and more than 300 cruise missiles to Russia collapsed during the spring and summer of 1997. In Oct. 1999 it was announced that a deal had been struck to return 3 Bear bombers, 8 Blackjack bombers and 500 cruise missiles, worth some $291 million, from Ukraine as partial payment for Kiev's debt to Russia for natural gas. According to press reports some of these aircraft may have been transferred from Ukraine to Russia. They are not included in the table. Some time ago the Russian Ministry of Defence ordered 6 new Blackjacks from the Kazan aircraft company, which belongs to the Tupolev group. Five of those have been completed and are at the Zhukovskiy Test Centre. With some effort and resources there could soon be as many as 20 Russian Blackjack bombers.

[d] Deactivation and retirement of ICBMs and their launchers proceed through at least 4 stages. In stage 1, an ICBM is removed from alert status by electrical and mechanical procedures. Next, warheads are removed from the missile. In stage 3 the missile is withdrawn from the silo. Finally, to comply with START-specified elimination procedures the silo is blown up and eventually filled in. The number of missiles and warheads will vary depending on which step the analyst chooses to feature.

[e] In the Sep. 1990 START I Treaty MOU, the Soviet Union declared 104 SS-18s in Kazakhstan (at Derzhavinsk and Zhangiz-Tobe) and 204 in Russia (30 at Aleysk, 64 at Dombarosvkiy, 46 at Kartaly and 64 at Uzhur). All of the SS-18s in Kazakhstan and 24 in Russia (12 at Dombarosvkiy and 12 at Uzhur) are non-operational, leaving 180 in Russia. Beginning in Apr. 1995 the first SS-18 silos in Kazakhstan were blown up; by mid-1997 all 104 had been destroyed. Under the START I Treaty Russia is permitted to retain 154 SS-18s. If the START II Treaty is fully implemented, all SS-18 missiles will be destroyed, but Russia may convert up to 90 SS-18 silos for deployment of single-warhead ICBMs.

[f] In the Sep. 1990 START I Treaty MOU, the Soviet Union declared 130 SS-19s in Ukraine and 170 in Russia. A Nov. 1995 agreement included the sale of 32 SS-19s, once deployed in Ukraine, back to Russia. Some SS-19s in Russia are being withdrawn from service. Under START II Russia may keep up to 105 SS-19s downloaded to a single warhead.

[g] Of the original 56 silo-based SS-24 M2s, 46 were in Ukraine at Pervomaysk and 10 are in Russia at Tatishchevo. By the beginning of 2000 only the 10 in Russia were considered operational. All 36 rail-based SS-24 M1s are in Russia—at Bershet, Kostroma and Krasnoyarsk.

[h] By 27 Nov. 1996 the last remaining SS-25 missiles in Belarus and their warheads were shipped back to Russia. These may be redeployed. The new variant of the SS-25 is called the Topol-M by Russia and designated the SS-27 by the US Government (see note [i]). It is assembled at Votkinsk in Russia and, along with the Tu-160 Blackjack, is the only Russian strategic weapon system still in production. Flight testing began on 20 Dec. 1994. On 22 Oct. 1998 a Topol-M ICBM exploded after being launched from the Plesetsk test site. This was the fifth test launch and the missile was intended to fly across Russia to a target on the Kamchatka Peninsula. The sixth test, on 8 Dec. 1998, was successful. Four flight tests were conducted in

1999: on 3 June, 16 Sep., 1 Oct. and 14 Dec. Two silo-based SS-27s were put on 'trial service' in Dec. 1997 in Tatishchevo, in the south-western Russian Saratov region. On 27 Dec. 1998, according to the Russian Government, the 104th Regiment, under the Taman Missile Division, had 10 missiles that were operational. Another 10 Topol-Ms were declared operational in Dec. 1999. The silos formerly housed SS-19 missiles.

[i] An ambitious Topol-M (SS-27) production schedule was announced in 1998 by General Vladimir Yakovlev, Commander-in-Chief of the Strategic Rocket Forces; he said that 20–30 SS-27s a year were planned to be made operational over the next 3 years and 30–40 a year for the 3 years after that. If this schedule is adhered to, by the end of 2001 there will be 70–100 missiles and by the end of 2004 there would be 160–220. It is obvious that these schedules are not being met. A more realistic rate, given the limited resources, would be 10–15 missiles per year, with perhaps some 60–80 fielded by the end of 2005.

[j] Nearly two-thirds of the SSBN fleet has been withdrawn from operational service. The table assumes that all the Yankee Is, Delta Is, Delta IIs, 3 Delta IIIs and 3 Typhoons have been withdrawn from operational service, leaving 21 SSBNs of 3 classes (11 Delta III, 7 Delta IV and 3 Typhoon). According to a Russian Navy vice-admiral, 2 Typhoons are 'unfit for combat'. A third Typhoon was withdrawn in 1998 and the entire class is likely to be retired. Operational SSBNs are based on the Kola Peninsula (at Nerpichya and Yagelnaya) and at Rybachi (15 km south-west of Petropavlovsk) on the Kamchatka Peninsula. The operational tempo of the Russian SSBNs has been reduced significantly since the end of the cold war. It was reported that 1 submarine is currently on patrol in the Atlantic and 1 in the Pacific, with at least another in each fleet on pier-side alert. Reportedly, for a 3-month period from May to July 1998 there were no SSBNs on patrol because of concerns over safety. The keel of the new Borey Class SSBN was laid in Nov. 1996. Construction has been intermittent and was suspended altogether in 1998. Commander-in-Chief of the Navy Admiral Vladimir Kuroyedov announced that the submarine was being redesigned to accommodate a new missile. It is unlikely that any Borey Class SSBNs will join the fleet over the next 6 or 7 years. Despite the rhetoric about maintaining a sea-based leg of the triad, the future of the Russian SSBN force remains very much in doubt. On 17 Nov. 1999 the Russian Navy fired 2 SS-N-20 missiles from a Typhoon Class submarine in the Barents Sea. The missiles hit targets 4900 km away on Kamchatka Peninsula and 'demonstrated top combat readiness', according to Admiral Kuroyedov.

[k] Assessing the composition and number of Russian non-strategic forces is very difficult. The estimates provided are derived from the initiatives announced by President Gorbachev in Oct. 1991 and President Yeltsin in Jan. 1992, and from various updates regarding dismantlement since then. Many warheads from ships, submarines and aircraft have been removed and consolidated at central storage sites, with a portion removed and dismantled.

[l] It is estimated that an additional 10 000 non-deployed warheads have an indeterminate status: they have been retained as either spares or a reserve for redeployment, or have been retired and are awaiting dismantlement.

Sources: START I Treaty Memoranda of Understanding, 1 Sep. 1990, 5 Dec. 1994, 1 July 1995, 1 Jan. 1996, 1 July 1996, 1 Jan. 1997, 1 July 1997, 1 Jan. 1998, 1 July 1998, 1 Jan. 1999, 1 July 1999; 'NRDC Nuclear Notebook', *Bulletin of the Atomic Scientists*, various issues; International Institute for Strategic Studies, *The Military Balance 1999/2000* (Oxford University Press: Oxford, 1999); Podvig, P. L. (ed.), *Strategicheskoye Yadernoye Vooruzheniye Rossii* [Russian strategic nuclear weapons] (IzdAT: Moscow, 1998); Wilkening, D. A., *The Evolution of Russia's Strategic Nuclear Force* (Stanford University, Center for International Security and Cooperation: Stanford, Calif., 1998); and Natural Resources Defense Council (NRDC).

Table 8A.3. British nuclear forces, January 2000[a]

Type	Designation	No. deployed	Year first deployed	Range (km)	Warheads x yield	Warheads in stockpile
SSBNs/SLBMs[b]						
D-5	Trident II	48	1994	7 400	1–3 x 100 kt	185[c]

[a] In July 1998 the results of the Strategic Defence Review (SDR), undertaken by the Labour Government, were announced. The decisions with regard to the British nuclear forces were:

1. Only 1 submarine will be on patrol at any time, carrying a reduced load of 48 warheads—half the Conservative Government's announced ceiling of 96.

2. The submarine on patrol will be at a reduced alert state and will carry out a range of secondary tasks; its missiles will be detargeted, and after notice the SSBN will be capable of firing its missiles within several days rather than within several minutes, as during the cold war.

3. There will be fewer than 200 operationally available warheads, a one-third reduction from the Conservative Government's plans.

4. The number of Trident II (D-5) missiles already purchased or ordered was reduced from 65 to 58.

As a result of these decisions the total explosive power of the operationally available weapons will be reduced by over 70% compared to the eventual future force. The explosive power of each Trident submarine will be one-third less than that of the 4 Chevaline-armed Polaris submarines, the last of which was retired in 1996.

The Atomic Weapons Establishment (AWE) will be managed by an industrial consortium consisting of Lockheed Martin, Serco Limited and British Nuclear Fuels starting on 1 Apr. 2000. The 10-year contract is for £2.2 billion. On 1 Apr. 1999 the Chief of Defence Logistics assumed overall responsibility for the routine movement of nuclear weapons within the UK. Day-to-day duties are being transferred, in phases, from Royal Air Force (RAF) personnel to the Ministry of Defence (MOD) Police, with support from AWE civilians and the Royal Marines. The process will occur gradually and be completed by 31 Mar. 2002.

The RAF operated 8 squadrons of dual-capable Tornado GR.1/1A aircraft. At the end of Mar. 1998, with the withdrawal of the last remaining WE177 bombs from operational service, the Tornadoes' nuclear role was terminated, bringing to an end a 4-decade long history of RAF aircraft carrying nuclear weapons. By the end of Aug. 1998 the remaining WE177 bombs had been dismantled. The *c.* 40 Tornadoes currently at RAF Bruggen in Germany will be reassigned to RAF Lossiemouth and RAF Marham in the UK by the end of 2001, and the base at Bruggen will be closed.

[b] The first submarine of the new Trident Class, the HMS *Vanguard*, went on its first patrol in Dec. 1994. The second submarine, *Victorious*, entered service in Dec. 1995. The third, *Vigilant*, was launched in Oct. 1995 and entered service in the autumn of 1998. The fourth and final submarine of the class, *Vengeance*, was launched on 19 Sep. 1998 and commissioned on 27 Nov. 1999 at the Marconi-Marine Shipyard in Barrow-in-Furness. It will enter service as part of the First Submarine Squadron and go on patrol in late 2000 or early 2001. The submarine has a total complement of 205 to provide a Ship's Company of 130 for a patrol. The current estimated cost of the programme is $18.8 billion.

Each Vanguard Class SSBN carries 16 US-produced Trident II (D-5) SLBMs. There are no specifically US or British Trident II missiles but a pool of SLBMs at Strategic Weapons Facility Atlantic at the Kings Bay Submarine Base, Georgia. The UK has title to 58 SLBMs but does not actually own them. A missile that is deployed on a US SSBN may at a later date deploy on a British one, or vice versa.

[c] Several factors enter into the calculation of the number of warheads that will be in the future British stockpile. It is assumed that the UK will produce only enough warheads for

3 boatloads of missiles, a practice it followed with the Polaris. As stated in the SDR, there will be 'fewer than 200 operationally available warheads' in the stockpile and no more than 48 warheads per SSBN. If all 4 SSBNs were fully loaded (MIRV x 3) that would total 192 warheads. The government also stated that it will be the practice that normally only 1 SSBN will be on patrol, with the other 3 in various states of readiness.

A further consideration is the 'sub-strategic mission'. An MOD official described it as follows: 'A sub-strategic strike would be the limited and highly selective use of nuclear weapons in a manner that fell demonstrably short of a strategic strike, but with a sufficient level of violence to convince an aggressor who had already miscalculated our resolve and attacked us that he should halt his aggression and withdraw or face the prospect of a devastating strategic strike' (*RUSI Journal*, 1996). The sub-strategic mission has begun with *Victorious* and 'will become fully robust when *Vigilant* enters service', according to the 1996 White Paper. If this has remained the policy then some Trident II SLBMs already have a single warhead and are assigned targets once covered by WE177 gravity bombs. E.g., when the *Vigilant* is on patrol, 10, 12 or 14 of its SLBMs may carry up to 3 warheads per missile, while the other 2, 4 or 6 missiles may be armed with just 1 warhead. There is some flexibility in the choice of yield of the Trident warhead. (Choosing to only detonate the unboosted primary could produce a yield of 1 kt or less. Choosing to detonate the boosted primary could produce a yield of a few kilotons.) With these 2 missions an SSBN would have *c.* 36–44 warheads on board during its patrol.

The table assumes that the future British stockpile for the SSBN fleet will be *c.* 160 warheads. With an additional 15% for spares, the total stockpile is estimated to be *c.* 185 warheads. At any given time the sole SSBN on patrol would carry *c.* 40 warheads. The second and third SSBNs could put to sea fairly rapidly, with similar loadings, while the fourth might take longer because of its cycle of overhaul and maintenance.

Sources: Norris, R. S., Burrows, A. S. and Fieldhouse, R. W., *Nuclear Weapons Databook Vol. V: British, French, and Chinese Nuclear Weapons* (Westview: Boulder, Colo., 1994), p. 9; British Ministry of Defence (MOD), *Strategic Defence Review* (MOD: London, July 1998); MOD, *Statement on the Defence Estimates 1996,* Cm 3223 (Her Majesty's Stationery Office: London, 1996); MOD, *Defence White Paper 1999*, Cm 4446 (Stationery Office: London, 1999); MOD press releases and Web site URL <http://www.mod.uk/policy/wp99/press.htm>; British House of Commons, *Parliamentary Debates (Hansard)*; Ormond, D., 'Nuclear deterrence in a changing world: the view from a UK perspective', *RUSI Journal*, June 1996, pp. 15–22; and 'NRDC Nuclear Notebook', *Bulletin of the Atomic Scientists*, vol. 55, no. 4 (July/Aug. 1999), pp. 78–79.

Table 8A.4. French nuclear forces, January 2000[a]

Type	No. deployed	Year first deployed	Range (km)[b]	Warheads x yield	Warheads in stockpile
Land-based aircraft[c]					
Mirage 2000N	45	1988	2 750	1 x 300 kt ASMP	60
Carrier-based aircraft[d]					
Super Étendard	24	1978	650	1 x 300 kt ASMP	20
SLBMs[e]					
M4A/B	32	1985	6 000	6 x 150 kt	192
M45	32	1996	6 000	6 x 100 kt	192
Total					**464**

[a] On 22 and 23 Feb. 1996 President Jacques Chirac announced several reforms for the French armed forces for the period 1997–2002. The decisions in the nuclear area were a com-

Table 8A.4 *Notes, contd*

bination of the withdrawal of several obsolete systems and a commitment to modernize those that remain.

After officials considered numerous plans to replace the silo-based S3D IRBM during President François Mitterrand's tenure, President Chirac announced that the missile would be retired and that there would be no replacement. On 16 Sep. 1996 all 18 missiles on the Plateau d'Albion were deactivated. It took 2 years and cost $77.5 million to fully dismantle the silos and complex.

Other recent actions include completion of the dismantlement of the South Pacific test facilities at Mururoa and Fangataufa. France ceased producing plutonium for weapons in 1992 and highly enriched uranium in 1996. It has pledged to close down and dismantle the Marcoule reprocessing plant and the Pierrelatte enrichment plant, actions it began in 1998.

In July 1996, after 32 years of service, the Mirage IVP was converted from its nuclear role and retired. Five Mirage IVPs will be retained for reconnaissance missions and are in the 1/91 Gascogne squadron at Mont-de-Marsan. The other aircraft were put into storage at Châteaudun.

b Range for aircraft assumes combat radius, without in-flight refuelling, and does not include the 90- to 350-km range of the Air-Sol Moyenne Portée (ASMP) air-to-surface missile.

c Three squadrons of Mirage 2000Ns have now assumed a 'strategic' role, in addition to their 'pre-strategic' one. A fourth Mirage 2000N squadron at Nancy—now conventional—is scheduled to be replaced with Mirage 2000Ds. Those aircraft may be modified to carry the ASMP and be distributed to the 3 Mirage 2000N squadrons at Luxeuil and Istres, along with the Mirage IVP's ASMP missiles. It is estimated that *c*. 80 were produced for ASMP missiles. The number of missiles built was probably closer to 100. In a Feb. 1996 speech, President Chirac said that a longer-range ASMP (500 km as opposed to 300 km, sometimes called the 'ASMP Plus') will be developed for service entry in about a decade.

The Rafale is planned to be the multi-purpose navy and air force fighter/bomber for the 21st century. Its roles include conventional ground attack, air defence, air superiority and nuclear delivery of the ASMP and/or ASMP Plus. The carrier-based navy version will be introduced first, with the air force Rafale D attaining a nuclear strike role in *c*. 2005. The air force still plans to buy a total of 234 Rafales.

d France built 2 aircraft-carriers, 1 of which entered service in 1961 (*Clemenceau*) and the other in 1963 (*Foch*). Both were modified to handle the AN 52 nuclear gravity bomb with Super Étendard aircraft. The *Clemenceau* was modified in 1979 and the *Foch* in 1981. The AN 52 was retired in July 1991. Only the *Foch* was modified to 'handle and store' the replacement ASMP, and *c*. 20 were allocated for 2 squadrons—*c*. 24 Super Étendard aircraft.

The *Clemenceau* was never modified to 'handle and store' the ASMP. The 32 780-ton aircraft-carrier was decommissioned in Sep. 1997. The new aircraft-carrier, *Charles de Gaulle*, was to enter service at the end of 1999, 3 years behind schedule, but has been further delayed to 1 July 2000 because of various problems encountered during trials. At that time the *Foch* will be laid up. The *Charles de Gaulle* will have a single squadron of Super Étendards (presumably with *c*. 10 ASMPs) until the Rafale M is introduced in 2002, when a second carrier may be ordered. The navy plans to purchase a total of 60 Rafale Ms, of which the first 16 will perform an air-to-air role. Missions for subsequent aircraft may include the ASMP and/or the ASMP Plus.

e The lead SSBN, *Le Triomphant*, was rolled out from its construction shed in Cherbourg on 13 July 1993. It entered service in Sep. 1996 armed with the M45 SLBM and new TN 75 warheads. The second SSBN, *Le Téméraire*, entered service in 1999. The schedule for the third, *Le Vigilant*, has slipped and it will not be ready until 2001. The service date for the fourth SSBN is *c*. 2005. It is estimated that there will eventually be 288 warheads for the fleet of 4 new Triomphant Class SSBNs because only enough missiles and warheads will be purchased for 3 submarines. This loading is the case today, with 5 submarines in the fleet—only 4 sets of M4 SLBMs were procured. President Chirac announced on 23 Feb. 1996 that the fourth submarine would be built and that a new SLBM, known as the M51, will replace the M45. The service entry date has been advanced to 2008 instead of 2010. Under a reorganization plan, the French Navy will base its SSBNs (formerly at Île-Longue) and its SSNs (formerly at Toulon) at Brest. Under this reform the Navy will shut down its SSBN command installations at Houilles (Yvelines) and transfer their activities to Brest. The infrastructure for communication with the submarines will remain at Rosnay (Indre).

Sources: Norris, R. S., Burrows, A. S. and Fieldhouse, R. W., *Nuclear Weapons Databook Vol. V: British, French, and Chinese Nuclear Weapons* (Westview: Boulder, Colo., 1994), p. 10; *Air Actualités*, various issues; Address by M. Jacques Chirac, President of the Republic, at the École Militaire, Paris, 23 Feb. 1996; International Institute for Strategic Studies, *The Military Balance 1999/2000* (Oxford University Press: Oxford, 1999), pp. 52–55; and 'NRDC Nuclear Notebook', *Bulletin of the Atomic Scientists*, vol. 55, no. 4 (July/Aug. 1999), pp. 77–78.

Table 8A.5. Chinese nuclear forces, January 2000

Type	NATO designation	No. deployed	Year first deployed	Range (km)[a]	Warheads x yield	Warheads in stockpile
Aircraft[b]						
H-6	B-6	120	1965	3 100	1–3 bombs	120
Q-5	A-5	30	1970	400	1 x bomb	30
Land-based missiles[c]						
DF-3A	CSS-2	40	1971	2 800	1 x 3.3 Mt	40
DF-4	CSS-3	20	1980	5 500	1 x 3.3 Mt	20
DF-5A	CSS-4	20	1981	13 000	1 x 4–5 Mt	20
DF-21A	CSS-5	48	1985–86	1 800	1 x 200–300 kt	48
SLBMs[d]						
Julang I	CSS-N-3	12	1986	1 700	1 x 200–300 kt	12
Non-strategic weapons[e]						
Artillery/ADMs, Short-range missiles					Low kt	120
Total						**~ 410**

[a] Range for aircraft indicates combat radius, without in-flight refuelling.

[b] The Chinese bomber force is antiquated, based on Chinese-produced versions of 1950s-vintage Soviet aircraft. With the retirement of the Hong-5, a redesign of the Soviet Il-28 Beagle medium bomber, the main bomber is the Hong-6. This aircraft is based on the Soviet Tu-16 Badger medium-range bomber, which entered service with Soviet forces in 1955. China began producing the H-6 in the 1960s under a licensing agreement. It was used to drop live weapons in 2 nuclear tests, a fission bomb in May 1965 and a multi-megaton bomb in June 1967. For more than a decade China has been developing a supersonic fighter-bomber, the Hong-7 (or FB-7), at the Xian Aircraft Company. The aircraft is not believed to have a nuclear mission.

Modernization of the Chinese bomber force could occur through adaptation of aircraft purchased from abroad. China purchased 24 Su-27SK and 2 Su-27UBK Russian Flanker fighters beginning in 1992 at a cost of $1 billion. These aircraft are currently with the 3rd Air Division at Wuhu airfield, 250 km west of Shanghai. Under a separate agreement Russia sold production rights to China to assemble and produce Su-27s in China at the Shenyang plant, with Russian engineers ensuring quality control. The first 2 aircraft flew in Dec. 1998. The People's Liberation Army Air Force (PLAAF) has a requirement for 200 Su-27s, which will

Table 8A.5 *Notes, contd*

take until at least 2015 to acquire under existing schedules. The Su-27 has an air-to-ground capability, but there is no evidence at this time that the PLAAF is modifying it for a nuclear role.

All figures for bomber aircraft are for nuclear-configured versions only. Hundreds of aircraft are also deployed in non-nuclear versions. The table assumes 150 bombs for the force, with yields estimated between 10 kt and 3 Mt.

  c China defines missile ranges as follows: short-range, < 1000 km; medium-range, 1000–3000 km; long-range, 3000–8000 km; and intercontinental range, > 8000 km.

The DF-3/CSS-2 missile has been deployed for more than 25 years and is being gradually retired. The 2-stage, liquid-fuelled DF-4/CSS-3 is deployed in a silo and transportable mode. The DF-21/CSS-5 is a 2-stage solid-propellant missile carried in a canister on a TEL. The improved Mod 2 version is not yet deployed. The first flight test of the 3-stage DF-31 mobile ICBM was conducted from Wuzhai, 400 km south-west of Beijing, on 2 Aug. 1999 in which a dummy warhead and several decoys were fired. Other flight tests are planned but it is unclear when the missile will be deployed or what the size of the force will be. The DF-41 has been cancelled, although a new road-mobile, solid-propellant ICBM is in development. The nuclear capability of the 600-km range M-9 (CSS-6) and the 300-km range M-11 (CSS-7) is unconfirmed. An improved M-11 Mod 2 was displayed in a military parade on 1 Oct. in Beijing. There is also a 150-km range road-mobile CSS-8 with a solid-fuel first stage and a liquid-fuel second stage.

The Taiwanese Defence Minister has specifically referred to the M-9 and M-11 as nuclear-capable. Taiwanese officials report that the number of M-type missiles in China's 3 southern provinces has risen from 30–50 to 160–200 since 1997.

China has had the technical capability to develop MRV payloads for 20 years. An MRV system releases 2 or more RVs along the missile's flight path at a single target, landing in a confined area at approximately the same time. The more sophisticated and flexible MIRV system releases 2 or more RVs to independent targets over a wider area over a longer span of time.

  d China has had great difficulty in developing SLBMs and SSNs. It has only 1 operational Xia Class SSBN. The programme was intended to be larger, but technical difficulties with solid fuel for the SLBMs and with nuclear reactors for the submarines curtailed full development of this 'leg' of its triad. The single existing submarine was built at Huludao Naval Base and Shipyard in the northern Bohai Gulf and was launched in Apr. 1981. It was finally deployed in Jan. 1989 at the Jianggezhuang Submarine Base, where the nuclear warheads for its Julang I missile are believed to be stored. The Xia Class SSBN, and the 5 Han Class SSNs, have never sailed beyond China's regional waters. A second Xia Class submarine was begun but never finished. A new SSBN, designated Type 094, is reported to be about to begin construction. It is expected to carry the 3-stage Julang II SLBM, a variant of the DF-31. Deployment of this system is many years away. Julang means 'Giant Wave'.

  e Information on Chinese non-strategic nuclear weapons is limited and contradictory, and there is no confirmation of their existence from official sources. China's initial interest in such weapons may have been spurred by worsening relations with the Soviet Union in the 1960s and 1970s. Several low-yield nuclear tests in the late 1970s, and a large military exercise in June 1982 simulating the use of non-strategic nuclear weapons, suggest that they may have been developed.

Sources: Norris, R. S., Burrows, A. S. and Fieldhouse, R. W., *Nuclear Weapons Databook Vol. V: British, French, and Chinese Nuclear Weapons* (Westview: Boulder, Colo., 1994); US Department of Defense, National Air Intelligence Center (NAIC), *Ballistic and Cruise Missile Threat* (NAIC: Wright-Patterson Air Force Base, Ohio, Apr. 1999); US Central Intelligence Agency, National Intelligence Council, *Foreign Missile Developments and the Ballistic Missile Threat to the United States Through 2015,* Sep. 1999, URL <http://www.cia.gov/cia/

publications/nie/nie99msl.html>; Lewis, J. W. and Hua, D., 'China's ballistic missile programs: technologies, strategies, goals', *International Security*, vol. 17, no. 2 (fall 1992), pp. 5–40; Allen, K. W., Krumel, G. and Pollack, J. D., *China's Air Force Enters the 21st Century* (Rand: Santa Monica, Calif., 1995); International Institute for Strategic Studies, *The Military Balance 1999/2000* (Oxford University Press: Oxford, 1999); and 'NRDC Nuclear Notebook', *Bulletin of the Atomic Scientists*, vol. 55, no. 3 (May/June 1999), pp. 79–80.

Table 8A.6. Indian nuclear forces, January 2000[a]

Type/Designation	Range (km)[b]	Payload (kg)	Comment
Aircraft[c]			
MiG-27 Flogger/Bahadhur	800	3 000	At Hindan Air Base
Jaguar IS/IB/Shamsher	1 600	4 775	At Ambala Air Base
Missiles[d]			
Agni I	1 500	1 000	Tested but status unclear
Agni II	2 000	1 000	First flight test on 11 Apr. 1999

[a] It is very difficult to estimate the size and composition of India's nuclear arsenal. An estimate is made here of a stockpile of 25–40 nuclear warheads although there are indications of more ambitious plans. On 17 Aug. 1999 a widely publicized draft document on Indian nuclear doctrine, prepared by a 27-member National Security Advisory Board, called for the creation of a 'credible minimum deterrent' to be based 'on a triad of aircraft, mobile land-based missiles and sea-based assets' ('Draft report of the National Security Advisory Board on Indian nuclear doctrine'). However, the Board's recommendations had no official standing.

[b] Range for aircraft indicates combat radius, without in-flight refuelling.

[c] India has several types of aircraft that could be used to deliver a nuclear weapon, although considerations of range, payload and speed narrow its choice to 1 or 2 types. The most likely Indian aircraft for nuclear weapon delivery are the MiG-27 and the Jaguar. The MiG-27 Flogger is a nuclear-capable Soviet aircraft produced in the 1970s and 1980s. Hindustan Aeronautics assembled, under licence, 165 aircraft which India calls the Bahadhur (Valiant or Brave). The single-seat aircraft weighs almost 18 000 kg when fully equipped and can fly to a range of c. 800 km. It can carry up to 3000 kg of bombs on external hardpoints. There are 9 operational squadrons. It is not known which of the bases may host nuclear-capable aircraft but 1 likely candidate where there could be some dedicated aircraft for a nuclear mission is Hindan, north of New Delhi. Some 50 MiG-27MLs are deployed there, less than 640 km from Lahore. A few aircraft from Squadrons 9 (Wolf Pack), 10 (Winged Daggers) or 18 (Flying Bullets) may be specially modified to carry 1 or more nuclear bombs.

The second type of Indian aircraft is the Jaguar IS/IB, known as the Shamsher (Lion). The Jaguar was nuclear-capable with the British Royal Air Force from 1975 to 1985 and with the French Air Force from 1974 to 1991. Originally a joint Anglo-French aircraft, the first 40 were supplied by British Aerospace, with the remaining 91 assembled or manufactured by Hindustan Aeronautics. With a gross weight of 15 450 kg the aircraft has a range of 1600 km with a maximum external load of 4775 kg. There are 4 operational squadrons. Which of the Indian bases may host nuclear-capable aircraft is not known but 1 likely candidate where there could be some dedicated aircraft for a nuclear mission is Ambala, 525 km from Islamabad. A few aircraft from Squadrons 5 (Tuskers), 14 (Bulls) and 20 (Lightnings) may be specially modified to carry 1 or more nuclear bombs. In Indian Air Force organization, Hindan and Ambala are part of Western Command, located at Palam and reporting to headquarters in New Delhi.

[d] India is developing and may deploy 1 or more types of ballistic missile for nuclear weapon delivery. The Indian 2-stage Agni (Fire) IRBM has been tested to a range of 1500 km,

Table 8A.6 *Notes, contd*

and a longer-range (2500 km) version is under development. The first stage uses a solid propellant taken from the satellite launch vehicle based on the US Scout missile. The liquid-fuelled second stage is a shortened version of the Prithvi. The warhead section separates from the second stage during flight. India conducted 3 flight tests between 1989 and early 1994. In 1996 the Indian Government claimed that the project was a technology demonstration and shelved the missile but could resume it at any time.

On 11 Apr. 1999 India conducted the initial flight test of the Agni II IRBM. It was fired from a rail launcher on Inner Wheeler Island, a new part of the Chadipur-on-sea missile test range in the eastern state of Orissa. The missile flew 2000 km in 11 minutes. The missile is 20 metres long, weighs *c.* 16 tons and has a 1000-kg payload. Road- and rail-mobile versions are under development. A new IRBM is also under development.

The Prithvi (Earth) is a single-stage, dual-engine, liquid-fuel, road-mobile SRBM which began development in 1983 and was first tested in 1988. There have been 15 tests since 1988. It is 9 metres long and 1.1 metres in diameter and weighs 4000 kg. The 2 versions of the Prithvi are not considered to have a nuclear role at this time.

One version is a battlefield support version now being delivered to the army with a range of 150 km and a warhead weight of 1000 kg. By Oct. 1995, 20 pre-production Prithvi SS-150s had been delivered to the army to form the 333rd Missile Regiment, under the 40th Artillery Division, based in Secunderabad. The army has a requirement for 75 Prithvis, ordered in May 1994. An unspecified number of Prithvi SS-150s are reportedly based near Jalandhar, northern Punjab, for use as a non-strategic battlefield missile against Pakistan.

The second variant is the air force version that may enter service in 2001 with a range of 250 km and a warhead weight of 500–750 kg. Five successful technical tests of the SS-250 version have been carried out. If the Prithvi SRBM is deployed in states such as Kashmir, Punjab and Gujarat, which border Pakistan, this would place the cities of Islamabad, Lahore, Karachi and Hyderabad and many of Pakistan's strategic military installations within its range. A third version is in development for the navy with a range of 350 km and a payload of 750–1000 kg.

Sources: US Air Force, National Air Intelligence Center, *Ballistic and Cruise Missile Threat*, (Wright-Patterson Air Force Base, Ohio, Apr. 1999); US Central Intelligence Agency, National Intelligence Office for Strategic and Nuclear Programs, *Foreign Missile Developments and the Ballistic Missile Threat to the United States Through 2015*, Sep. 1999; Burrows, W. E. and Windrem, R., *Critical Mass* (Simon & Schuster: New York, 1994); 'Draft report of the National Security Advisory Board on Indian nuclear doctrine', 17 Aug. 1999, URL <http://www.meadev.gov.in/govt/indnucld.htm>; and Bharat Rakshak: A Consortium of Indian Military Websites, URL <http://216.10.0.133>; and Albright, D., Berkhout, F. and Walker, W., SIPRI, *Plutonium and Highly Enriched Uranium 1996: World Inventories, Capabilities and Policies* (Oxford University Press: Oxford, 1997).

Table 8A.7. Pakistani nuclear forces, January 2000[a]

Type/Designation	Range (km)	Payload (kg)	Comment
Aircraft[b]			
F-16A/B	1 600	5 450	At Sargodha AB
Missiles[c]			
Ghauri I (Hatf-5)	1 300–1 500	500–750	Basically North Korean Nodong missiles
Ghauri II (Hatf-6)	2 000–2 300	750–1 000	Test fired on 14 Apr. 1999

[a] It is very difficult to estimate the size and composition of Pakistan's nuclear arsenal. Over a 20-year period Pakistan pursued a gas centrifuge uranium-enrichment method to produce material for its nuclear weapons. There is some uncertainty about how many centrifuges Pakistan has and thus how much weapon-grade uranium has been produced. It is estimated that It may have a stockpile of 15–20 nuclear weapons, assuming a solid-core implosion design using *c.* 15–20 kg per warhead. With the announcement of ambitious plans by India and the generally worsening relations between the 2 countries, Pakistan may increase its nuclear forces significantly in the coming years.

[b] Range for aircraft indicates combat radius, without in-flight refuelling. The aircraft in the Pakistani Air Force that is most likely to be used in the nuclear weapon delivery role is the US-manufactured F-16, although other aircraft, such as the Mirage V or the Chinese-produced A5, could also be used. Twenty-eight F-16A (single-seat) and 12 F-16B (2-seat) trainers were delivered to the Pakistani Air Force between 1983 and 1987. At least 8 of the original order are no longer in service. In Dec. 1988 Pakistan ordered 11 additional F-16A/Bs as attrition replacements but to date they have not been delivered because of the Pressler Amendment, which forbids military aid to suspected nuclear weapon states. The US Government announced on 6 Oct. 1990 that it had embargoed any further arms deliveries to Pakistan. The 11 embargoed aircraft are being stored in the Arizona desert near Davis-Monthan AFB. In Sep. 1989 plans were announced for Pakistan to acquire 60 more F-16s. Of that order 17 were built by the end of 1994, but because of the embargo they joined the others at Davis-Monthan and have not been delivered.

Some of the F-16s most likely to have been modified to carry nuclear weapons are deployed with Squadrons 9 and 11 at Sargodha AB, 160 km north-west of Lahore. There are also F-16s with Squadron 14 at Kamra AB. The F-16 has a range of over 1600 km, or more if drop tanks are used. It can carry up to 5450 kg externally on 1 under-fuselage and 6 underwing stations.

[c] According to Pakistani bomb designer Abdul Qadeer Khan, the Ghauri missile is currently the only nuclear-capable missile, although other missiles in the Pakistani armed forces could be configured to carry a nuclear warhead. The Ghauri was first flight-tested on 6 Apr. 1998 to a distance of 1100 km, probably with a payload of up to 700 kg. The single-stage, liquid-fuelled Ghauri is basically a North Korean Nodong missile. A Ghauri II was tested on 14 Apr. 1999, 3 days after the Indian Agni II test flight. It was launched from a mobile launcher at Dina, *c.* 60 km east of the Pakistani capital of Islamabad, and landed in Jiwani, in the south-western Baluchistan province.

Pakistan has obtained M-11 missiles and technology from China and has reverse-engineered a Chinese M-9 missile; the missile has a range of 700 km, can carry a payload of 1000 kg and is called the Shaheen (Eagle). Pakistan conducted the initial flight test of the Shaheen from the coastal town of Sominani on 15 Apr. 1999. Neither missile is believed to have a nuclear capability at this time.

Sources: Burrows, W. E. and Windrem, R., *Critical Mass* (Simon & Schuster: New York, 1994); Three-Four-Nine: The Ultimate F-16 Site, URL <http://www.f-16.net/reference/users/f16_pk.html>; Albright, D., Berkhout, F. and Walker, W., SIPRI, *Plutonium and Highly Enriched Uranium 1996: World Inventories, Capabilities and Policies* (Oxford University Press: Oxford, 1997); and *Jane's Intelligence Review,* various issues.

Table 8A.8. Israeli nuclear forces, January 2000[a]

Type	Year first deployed	Range (km)	Comment
Aircraft[b]			
F-16A/B/C/D/I Fighting Falcon	1980	1 600	260 purchased or received, 50 more on order
F-15I Thunder	1998	3 500	25 delivered Jan. 1998 to May 1999
Land-based missiles[c]			
Jericho I	1972	1 200	Possibly 50 at Zekharyeh
Jericho II	1984–85	1 800	Possibly 50 at Zekharyeh, on TELs in caves
Submarine[d]			
Dolphin	2000		Possible future SLCM platform
Non-strategic/battlefield[e]			
Artillery and landmines			

[a] Estimating the size and composition of the Israeli nuclear stockpile is extremely difficult. It is estimated that Israel may have as many as 200 warheads consisting of aircraft bombs, missile warheads and non-strategic/battlefield types. Israel has been a nuclear weapon power since late 1966, when its first bombs were manufactured. Although small in size and population, Israel has created an extensive and modern nuclear infrastructure. The weapons are assembled at the design laboratory at Rafael, outside Haifa, known as Division 20. Dimona, in the Negev desert, is the location of a plutonium–tritium production reactor and underground chemical separation and nuclear component fabrication facilities. A facility in the town of Yavne, south of Tel Aviv near the coast, controls and monitors missile test flights launched into the Mediterranean Sea. According to some sources, there are nuclear weapon bunkers for aircraft and missiles at Tel Nof AB, in the Negev desert. A second set of bunkers near the village of Tirosh is believed to be a nuclear storage site.

[b] Range for aircraft indicates combat radius, without in-flight refuelling. Over the past 30 years Israel has had many different types of aircraft capable of carrying nuclear bombs. These include the F-4 Phantom, the A-4 Skyhawk, and more recently the F-16 and F-15E. In 1999 the Israeli Government announced that it would purchase 50 F-16Is worth *c.* $2.5 billion. Israel will begin to receive the aircraft at the beginning of 2003, and the last aircraft will be supplied 2 years later. Under the terms of the contract Israel has an option to purchase 60 more aircraft but must decide by Sep. 2001. If the government exercises the option, delivery of the extra aircraft will continue until 2008. In 4 previous orders Israel has purchased or received 260 F-16s from 1980 to 1995. These include 103 F-16A, 22 F-16B, 81 F-16C and 54 F-16D models. Some number of nuclear bombs may be allocated to specific dedicated, certified aircraft, probably at the Tel Nof AB.

In Jan. 1994 Israel selected the Boeing F-15E Strike Eagle for the long-range strike and air-superiority roles. Called the F-15I Ra'am (Thunder) in Israel, 25 aircraft were delivered to the Israeli Air Force from Jan. 1998 to May 1999.

A second, but less likely, air base where nuclear bombs may be stored is Ramat David, in northern Israel, home to the 109, 110 and 117 Squadrons, flying the F-16C/D. Aircraft from Squadrons 110 and 117 attacked and destroyed the Iraqi Osirak nuclear reactor outside Baghdad on 7 June 1981.

[c] Israel's quest for a missile capability began simultaneously with its quest for nuclear weapons. In Apr. 1963—several months before the Dimona reactor began operating—Israel signed an agreement with the French company Dassault to produce a surface-to-surface ballis-

tic missile. Israeli specifications called for a 2-stage missile capable of delivering a 750-kg warhead to 235–500 km with a circular error probable (CEP) of less than 1 km. The missile system, known as the Jericho (or MD-620), should take less than 2 hours to prepare, be launched from fixed or mobile bases, and be capable of firing at a rate of 4–8 per hour. In early 1966 *The New York Times* reported that Israel had purchased the first instalment of 30 missiles, but soon after the June 1967 Six-Day War France imposed an embargo on new military equipment. Because of the embargo Israel began to produce the Jericho missile on its own. In 1974 the US Central Intelligence Agency (CIA) cited the Jericho as evidence that Israel had made nuclear weapons—the CIA said that the Jericho made little sense as a conventional missile and was 'designed to accommodate nuclear warheads'.

Israel subsequently developed the Jericho II, a missile with similarities to the US Pershing II. In May 1987 Israel tested an improved version of the Jericho II that flew 800 km. A second test was conducted in Sep. 1988 and a third in Sep. 1989, which reportedly flew 1300 km. A document published in 1989 by the US Arms Control and Disarmament Agency gave the maximum range of the improved Jericho as 1450 km, long enough to reach the southern border of the Soviet Union. Israel vigorously pursued certain technologies in the USA and elsewhere for the missile, including a terminal guidance system using radar imaging. It is thought that the range has been increased to 1800 km. According to an article published in 1997 in *Jane's Intelligence Review*, there were *c.* 50 Jericho II missiles at the Zekharyeh missile base, some 45 km south-east of Tel Aviv in the Judean Hills. According to an analysis of satellite images of the base, the missiles appear to be stored in caves. Upon warning they would be dispersed on their TELs so as not to be destroyed. The shorter-range Jericho I is deployed nearby in approximately equal numbers.

d Israel contracted with the German company Howaldtswerke-Deutsche Werft in Kiel to build 3 diesel-powered submarines for the Israeli Defense Force Navy (IDF/N). Designated the Dolphin Class, they are 57.3 metres long, displace 1900 tons, can reach a speed of 20 knots, and have a crew of 35. The first submarine, the *Dolphin*, arrived in Haifa on 27 July 1999. The second, the *Leviathan,* joined the fleet by the end of the year, and delivery of the third, the *Tekuma,* is to take place in mid-2000. It is possible that the IDF/N may plan to equip the Dolphin submarines with a nuclear land-attack capability by modifying US-supplied Sub Harpoon anti-ship missiles (130-km range) with an indigenously developed nuclear warhead and guidance kit.

e An explosion high in the atmosphere on 22 Sep. 1979 off the coast of South Africa in the South Indian Ocean is believed by some to have been a clandestine Israeli test, possibly of a neutron weapon. There are also reports that Israel has developed nuclear artillery shells and possibly ADMs.

Sources: Burrows, W. E. and Windrem, R., *Critical Mass* (Simon & Schuster: New York, 1994), pp. 275–313; Hersh, S. M., *The Samson Option* (Random House: New York, 1991); and Albright, D., Berkhout, F. and Walker, W., SIPRI, *Plutonium and Highly Enriched Uranium 1996: World Inventories, Capabilities and Policies* (Oxford University Press: Oxford, 1997); and Hough, H., 'Could Israel's nuclear assets survive a first strike?', *Jane's Intelligence Review*, vol. 9, no. 9 (1997), pp. 407–10.

Appendix 8B. Nuclear verification: the IAEA strengthened safeguards system

NICHOLAS ZARIMPAS

I. Introduction

The international nuclear safeguards system, which has been administered by the International Atomic Energy Agency (IAEA) for over three decades,[1] was in the 1990s confronted with new challenges—a growing list of responsibilities combined with limited resources, the ambitions of some states to acquire nuclear weapons, exemplified by the case of Iraq, and a longer agenda resulting from the nuclear disarmament process. The IAEA's adoption in 1997 of a Model Additional Protocol for strengthening safeguards measures was an important milestone in the process of establishing a more extensive and effective universal verification regime, but progress towards acceptance of the new measures by the IAEA member states has been disappointingly slow.

International safeguards are one of the principal mechanisms employed to ensure compliance with the terms and objectives of the 1968 Treaty on the Non-Proliferation of Nuclear Weapons (the Non-Proliferation Treaty, NPT).[2] In Article III of the treaty, non-nuclear weapon states (NNWS) parties undertake to accept safeguards in agreements concluded with the IAEA 'with a view to preventing diversion of nuclear energy from peaceful uses to nuclear weapons or other nuclear explosive devices'. The safeguards are applied on all source or special fissionable material in their peaceful nuclear activities.

This appendix reviews IAEA safeguards, which are aimed at providing increased assurance of the absence of undeclared nuclear activities and material, with the ultimate goal of reinforcing the global nuclear non-proliferation regime. The existing safeguards arrangements are outlined in section II. Section III discusses the reasons why strengthened safeguards were needed, and their evolution is described in section IV. Section V focuses on the prospects for and concerns regarding the new safeguards system, and section VI presents the conclusions.

II. Classical safeguards

During the 1950s nuclear technology transfers were subject to unilateral safeguards and inspection by the supplier country.[3] As early as 1961, despite opposition from

---

[1] The IAEA Statute, which established the Agency as an autonomous intergovernmental UN body, entered into force in July 1957. It endows the Agency with the twin purposes of promoting the peaceful uses of nuclear energy and ensuring that nuclear activities with which the IAEA is associated are not used to further any military purpose.

[2] The NPT is reproduced in Kokoski, R., SIPRI, *Technology and the Proliferation of Nuclear Weapons* (Oxford University Press: Oxford, 1995), pp. 255–58. For the list of states which have ratified, acceded to or succeeded to the NPT as of Jan. 2000, see annexe A in this volume.

[3] For a detailed discussion of the historical evolution of IAEA safeguards, see Fischer, D. and Szasz, P., ed. J. Goldblat, SIPRI, *Safeguarding the Atom: A Critical Appraisal* (Taylor & Francis: London, 1985).

India, the Soviet Union and several other developing countries, the IAEA established its first international safeguards on research reactors with a capacity of up to 100 MWth (megawatts thermal). They were extended in 1964 to cover also large reactor facilities of over 100 MWth.[4]

The 'item-specific' or 'facility-specific' safeguards regime was adopted in 1965.[5] INFCIRC/66, which covered only agreed installations, was a reasonably flexible scheme since it permitted inspection at all times, provided for continuous inspections of large nuclear power reactors and did not limit the access of inspectors within a nuclear plant.[6]

After the entry into force of the NPT, the current 'full-scope' or Comprehensive Safeguards Agreements were established in 1971.[7] INFCIRC/153 contains a detailed NPT Model Safeguards Agreement to serve as the basis for safeguards on all peaceful nuclear activities and material in the NNWS parties to the NPT. The technical objective of full-scope safeguards, as stated in paragraph 28 of the Model Safeguards Agreement, is 'the timely detection of diversion of significant quantities of *nuclear material* from peaceful nuclear activities to the manufacture of nuclear weapons or of other nuclear explosive devices or for purposes unknown, and deterrence of such diversion by the risk of early detection'. In a broader sense, the political goal of safeguards is to promote transparency and build confidence by providing assurances that states are complying with their non-proliferation obligations and that they are not using their safeguarded facilities for military purposes.

At the time when INFCIRC/153 was adopted, it was thought that clandestine, undeclared activities would be discovered predominantly by national intelligence-gathering organizations. Inspectors were not permitted free access throughout a state to look for undeclared activities. In essence, INFCIRC/153 safeguards efforts have concentrated on nuclear material in declared nuclear facilities, primarily through meticulous material accountancy.[8] International inspectors regularly visit, under agreed rights of access, strategic parts of declared nuclear installations to verify their accounting records and confirm their inventories of nuclear material, thereby ensuring the correctness of submitted declarations.[9] To complement material accountancy, continuous surveillance (by cameras and other electronic techniques) and containment (use of specially designed seals, containers, physical barriers, etc.) are applied at key

---

[4] IAEA, The Agency's Safeguards, IAEA document INFCIRC/26, 30 Mar. 1961; and INFCIRC/26/Add.1, 9 Apr. 1964. IAEA INFCIRC documents are available on the IAEA Internet site at URL <http://www.iaea.org/worldatom/infcircs>.

[5] IAEA, The Agency's Safeguards System (1965), IAEA document INFCIRC/66, 3 Dec. 1965; INFCIRC/66/Rev.1, 12 Sep. 1967; and INFCIRC/66/Rev.2, 16 Sep. 1968. INFCIRC/66-type measures are still in force for those states that have not entered into NPT-type agreements with the IAEA (i.e., Cuba, India, Israel and Pakistan).

[6] Fischer, D., 'Safeguards: past, present & future', *IAEA Bulletin*, Dec. 1997, p. 32.

[7] IAEA, The Structure and Content of Agreements Between the Agency and States Required in Connection with the Treaty on the Non-Proliferation of Nuclear Weapons (NPT Model Safeguards Agreement), IAEA document INFCIRC/153, 10 Mar. 1971, INFCIRC/153 (Corrected), June 1972 and INFCIRC/153 (Corrected), 1983. By Jan. 2000, the IAEA had 224 safeguards agreements in force with 140 states; for the list of states with safeguards agreements under the NPT, see annexe A in this volume. The majority of these agreements are of the INFCIRC/153-type. Goldschmidt, P., IAEA Deputy Director General for Safeguards, Private communication with the author, 5 May 2000.

[8] INFCIRC/153 did provide for 'special' inspections to deal with inconsistencies and suspected sites. Special inspections, however, were politically sensitive and were not carried out until the early 1990s, when a failed attempt was made to conduct them in North Korea. Fischer, W. and Stein, G., 'On-site inspections: experience from nuclear safeguarding', *Disarmament Forum*, no. 3 (1999), p. 46.

[9] These declarations are drawn up by facility operators under the supervision of the national safeguards authority—the State System of Accounting and Control of nuclear material (SSAC).

points in many installations. Because inspection activities are proportional to the quantities of nuclear material and thus the size of the nuclear programmes, the majority of the IAEA safeguards efforts have in recent years focused largely on NNWS such as Canada, Germany and Japan, which have significant nuclear infrastructures, large numbers of power reactors and sophisticated fuel cycle facilities.

Since the late 1970s there has been considerable debate about the IAEA's capability to safeguard processes that handle bulk amounts of nuclear material that is not in solid form and thus more difficult to monitor. In that regard, concerns were expressed whether a large reprocessing or uranium enrichment plant in the Western world could be safeguarded effectively. At the same time, Iraq progressed with its clandestine programme, and the three states then called the 'nuclear threshold' states (India, Israel and Pakistan) more openly acquired weapon-usable material and built up their nuclear capability.[10]

The five nuclear weapon states (NWS) recognized under the NPT,[11] although they are not obliged to do so by the terms of the treaty, have entered into Voluntary Offer Agreements with the IAEA which allow the Agency to apply selective safeguards on all or on certain facilities within their territory or under their jurisdiction or control. In this way, the NWS have demonstrated their good will by sharing some of the costs and burdens, for example, by accepting the risk that commercially sensitive information might be disclosed during the inspection and verification processes. It is, in fact, under such agreements that material declared excess to military needs is, at least partly and for the time being, safeguarded by the IAEA.

All nuclear facilities in the European Union (EU) member states are also subject to regional full-scope safeguards administered by the European Atomic Energy Community (Euratom).[12] Under existing agreements, the IAEA cooperates and interacts with the Euratom Inspectorate with a view to avoiding duplication of work and lowering costs. While Euratom has taken the lead for the EU states, the IAEA is always in a position to derive its own independent conclusions about the absence of diversion of nuclear material. Notably, the New Partnership Approach, agreed between the IAEA and Euratom in 1992, led to a clear reduction of the IAEA's on-site inspection efforts in Europe.[13] It also facilitated closer and more efficient cooperation between the two bodies through the use of common equipment, exchange of information, joint inspections, research and development (R&D) efforts, and inspector training. Similarly, under the 1994 Quadripartite Safeguards Agreement and the 1997 Co-operation Agreement,[14] the IAEA is improving and strengthening its joint efforts with the

---

[10] Fischer (note 6), p. 33.

[11] As defined in Article IX of the NPT, only those states which manufactured and exploded a nuclear weapon or other nuclear explosive device prior to 1 Jan. 1967—China, France, Russia, the United Kingdom and the United States—are recognized as nuclear weapon states.

[12] The 1957 Treaty establishing the European Atomic Energy Community (Euratom Treaty) entered into force on 1 Jan. 1958. Euratom was established to promote common efforts between the then member states of the European Community, now between the 15 EU member states, in the development of nuclear energy for peaceful purposes.

[13] Information on the New Partnership Approach is available on the IAEA Internet site at URL <http://www.iaea.org/worldatom/inforesource/bulletin/bull371/chitumbo.html>.

[14] The 1991 Quadripartite Safeguards Agreement, in force since 4 Mar. 1994, is a comprehensive safeguards agreement between Argentina, Brazil, the ABACC and the IAEA covering all nuclear materials in all activities carried out in Argentina and Brazil. IAEA document INFCIRC/435, Mar. 1994. The 1997 IAEA–ABACC Co-operation Agreement is in IAEA document GC(41)/26, 29 Sep. 1997.

Brazilian–Argentine Agency for Accounting and Control of Nuclear Materials (ABACC).[15]

III. The need to strengthen safeguards

While safeguards cannot be seen in isolation from other political, diplomatic, economic and technological confidence-building initiatives aimed at reinforcing the nuclear non-proliferation regime, effective implementation of safeguards is essential for maintaining the peaceful application of nuclear technology for sustainable development and for limiting the spread of nuclear weapons, thus enhancing international security.[16]

A number of important events, developments and considerations in the 1990s affected the global nuclear non-proliferation and verification regimes. It became evident that the classical safeguards approach, the centrepiece of the IAEA verification system for more than 20 years, needed in-depth, radical changes.

Challenges to classical safeguards

After the 1991 Persian Gulf War, several IAEA inspections carried out under special mandates established in UN Security Council resolutions revealed the full scope and magnitude of the Iraqi clandestine nuclear weapon programme.[17] Iraq, in violation of its obligations under the NPT, had pursued almost every conceivable method of obtaining fissile material.[18] Moreover, a vast array of equipment and expertise had been acquired in spite of the multilateral export control mechanisms that were in force. The discovery of this elaborate and extensive programme surprised the international community and triggered calls for improvement of the effectiveness of IAEA verification. In particular, the traditional role of safeguards administered under INFCIRC/153 with regard to detection of illicit undeclared activities was questioned. The case of Iraq laid the foundation for strengthening the safeguards regime. Importantly, the lessons learned clearly showed that more intrusive inspections and better access to enhanced information were needed.

Since 1993 the IAEA has also been confronted with another challenge—the nuclear ambitions of the Democratic People's Republic of Korea (North Korea). IAEA verification efforts unveiled inconsistencies in North Korea's submitted declarations, which together with intelligence information received from member states established that North Korea was not in compliance with its NPT safeguards obligations.[19] With the precedent of Iraq, the IAEA swiftly drew attention to North Korea's non-

---

[15] ABACC was set up to apply the Common System of Accounting and Control of Nuclear Materials (SCCC), a bilateral full-scope safeguards system established under the 1991 Agreement between Argentina and Brazil for the Exclusively Peaceful Use of Nuclear Energy. IAEA document INFCIRC/395, 15 Nov. 1995.

[16] IAEA, 'Non-proliferation and safeguards aspects', *Nuclear Fuel Cycle and Reactor Strategy: Adjusting to New Realities*, Key Issue Papers from a symposium held in co-operation with the European Commission, the OECD Nuclear Energy Agency and the Uranium Institute, 3–6 June 1997, Key issue paper no. 5 (IAEA: Vienna, 1997), p. 227.

[17] Iraq is a party to the NPT and has had an INFCIRC/153-type Comprehensive Safeguards Agreement with the IAEA since 1973.

[18] For a detailed description of the Iraqi nuclear programme, see Kokoski (note 2), pp. 97–145.

[19] North Korea became a party to the NPT in 1985. Its safeguards agreement with the IAEA entered into force in 1992.

compliance after its request for a special inspection was rejected. At the request of the UN Security Council the Agency has since 1994 continuously monitored the freeze on the North Korean graphite-moderated reactor programme.[20] Nevertheless, the North Korean authorities are reluctant to cooperate and comply fully with such safeguards requirements as the provision of assurances about preserving crucial information relevant to their nuclear activities. In spite of its intense efforts, the Agency is still not in a position to verify North Korea's initial inventory declarations.

Monitoring the voluntary dismantlement of the South African nuclear weapon programme and safeguarding the resulting fissile material, in remarkably good and close cooperation with the South African authorities, were a positive experience.[21] Although the IAEA was not in a position to detect the South African activities in time to alert the international community, once the Agency became involved it demonstrated through appropriate measures, including inspections, that a South African nuclear weapon programme no longer existed or posed a threat.[22]

The volume of IAEA verification activities and the complexity of the resulting inspection workload have increased continuously since the late 1980s, while the Agency's financial and human resources have remained virtually unchanged.[23] The total number of nuclear facilities under safeguards has grown drastically; in 1999, 900 nuclear facilities and other locations were under IAEA safeguards.[24] Large reprocessing and mixed-oxide (MOX) fuel fabrication plants have come into operation in Europe.[25] MOX fabrication is expected to grow, as well as the use of MOX fuel in commercial light water reactors. Flows and stocks of safeguarded nuclear material have also been rising steadily. Notably, the imbalance between separation and utilization of plutonium has resulted in large inventories of separated plutonium in the civilian fuel cycle, the bulk of which is currently stored at the major British, French and Russian reprocessing sites.[26] The IAEA's limited resources are further stretched by the involvement of its inspectorate force in activities related to preventing the illicit traffic in nuclear material, examining aspects of safeguarding final waste repositories and setting international standards for the protection of nuclear material.

Fifteen new states emerged from the collapse of the Soviet Union. All the newly independent states (NIS) are parties to the NPT, and the majority of them have safeguards agreements in force with the IAEA. A number of these states (e.g., Armenia, Kazakhstan, Lithuania and Ukraine) have significant nuclear energy activities involving a wide variety of installations, while three of them (Belarus, Kazakhstan and

[20] For a discussion of North Korea's 1994 agreement to freeze its nuclear programme, see Kokoski (note 2), pp. 229–31.

[21] South Africa has been a party to the NPT since 1991.

[22] Kokoski (note 2), p. 244.

[23] The IAEA has operated under near zero-real-growth budget conditions since the mid-1980s. In 1999 total safeguards expenditure was less than $100 million ($78.9 million from the regular budget and $13.5 million from extra-budgetary contributions). Goldschmidt (note 7).

[24] Goldschmidt (note 7).

[25] MOX fuel contains both uranium and plutonium. These European plants are the BNFL (British Nuclear Fuels plc) THORP (Thermal Oxide Reprocessing Plant), COGEMA (Compagnie Générale des Matières Nucléaires, France) UP2-800, UP3 and MELOX plants; for a discussion on safeguarding reprocessing and MOX fuel fabrication plants, see Howsley, R. *et al.*, 'Safeguarding of large scale reprocessing and MOX plants', Paper presented at the IAEA symposium on Nuclear Fuel Cycle and Reactor Strategy: Adjusting to New Realities, held in cooperation with the European Commission, the OECD Nuclear Energy Agency and the Uranium Institute, 3–6 June 1997, Vienna.

[26] OECD Nuclear Energy Agency, *Management of Separated Plutonium: The Technical Options* (OECD: Paris, 1997), pp. 14–16; and Albright, D., Berkhout, F. and Walker, W., SIPRI, *Plutonium and Highly Enriched Uranium 1996: World Inventories, Capabilities and Policies* (Oxford University Press: Oxford, 1997), pp. 191–37.

Ukraine) previously hosted Soviet nuclear weapons on their territory. The application of IAEA safeguards required intensive efforts aimed at verifying initially declared inventories, installing and testing surveillance, monitoring and communication devices, as well as providing the necessary training.[27] Substantial progress has been achieved since the early 1990s and the IAEA continues its efforts.

The 1995 NPT Review and Extension Conference expressed strong support for further strengthening the effectiveness and the efficiency of IAEA safeguards, while recognizing the central role of the Agency as the competent authority responsible for verifying and assuring compliance with the NPT.[28] Since then, additional states have adhered to the treaty and entered into safeguards agreements with the IAEA.[29]

New tasks for the IAEA

Apart from dealing with the challenges outlined above, the Agency may also be called upon to undertake new, demanding tasks in the future. Pursuant to Article VI of the NPT, there is an obligation for the NWS to end the arms race and pursue negotiations, in good faith, leading to general and complete nuclear disarmament, under strict and effective international control. With the end of the cold war and the implementation of disarmament treaties between Russia and the USA, significant quantities of fissile material which are no longer needed for defence purposes are becoming redundant. A relatively small quantity of excess weapon-grade plutonium (2 tonnes) and highly enriched uranium (10 tonnes) at three sites in the United States is, at present, placed under IAEA safeguards.[30] In 1996 discussions were initiated between the IAEA, Russia and the USA (the Trilateral Initiative) to define an appropriate future role for the Agency in verification of excess fissile material and examine the associated technical, legal and financial implications.[31] These deliberations have continued, and substantial progress has been recorded in developing and testing verification provisions. Discussions are being held on the verification methods to be applied at the K-Area Material Storage Facility, located at the Savannah River site in the United States and at the Mayak Fissile Material Storage Facility at Ozersk in Russia.[32] Within this framework, the other NWS may in the future participate and submit their excess fissile material to IAEA control. It is foreseen that Agency involvement in verifying compliance with the arms reduction processes will eventually shift more of its inspection efforts to the NWS. Such an expanded role may involve financial and management difficulties.

Although negotiations on the long-proposed Fissile Material Treaty (FMT) for a ban on the production of fissile material for nuclear weapons have not yet opened because of a procedural impasse in the Geneva-based Conference on Disarmament (CD), the conclusion and implementation of such a treaty would be an important step

---

[27] Murakami, K., 'Verification in newly independent states', *IAEA Bulletin*, Dec. 1997, pp. 9–12.

[28] Principles and Objectives for Nuclear Non-Proliferation and Disarmament, NPT/CONF.1995/32/ DEC.2, 11 May 1995. The Principles and Objectives are 'yardsticks' for measuring the implementation of the NPT in the strengthened review process.

[29] In this connection it is important to note that, as of Jan. 2000, 54 NNWS parties to the NPT did not have comprehensive safeguards agreements in force with the IAEA, as required under the treaty.

[30] Highly enriched uranium (HEU) is uranium containing 20% or more of the isotope ^{235}U.

[31] Blix, H., 'Future directions of nuclear verification', *IAEA Bulletin*, Dec. 1997, p. 39.

[32] 'Talks on future IAEA verification of ex-weapon material', *IAEA News Briefs*, Oct./Nov. 1999, p. 4.

towards advancing nuclear disarmament.[33] Given the accumulated knowledge of the IAEA, its demonstrated expertise and the maturity of its system, it is widely assumed that the Agency is the best-equipped international body to readily undertake verification of compliance with an FMT. The IAEA Director General offered to the CD President the Agency's assistance in developing the technical verification arrangements for this treaty.[34] Depending on the scope and terms of an FMT, different levels of additional burden to the IAEA Inspectorate can be envisaged. Although it seems very unlikely that all the nuclear power reactors in the NWS will be safeguarded, measures will certainly need to be applied to monitor facilities involved in the production of material used in nuclear weapons as well as to all civilian fuel reprocessing and uranium enrichment plants.[35] Such additional tasks can be expected to considerably increase the IAEA's workload.

IV. The evolution of the IAEA strengthened safeguards system

An effective, efficient and reliable global safeguards regime is necessary to support the goals of arms control agreements, the nuclear-weapon-free zone treaties and the ongoing disarmament process.[36] There has been a constant evolution of safeguards over the past three decades in parallel with major political and diplomatic developments and technology advances. Novel monitoring and verification techniques have been systematically integrated into the established approaches, more powerful tools employed, and enhanced training curricula offered to inspectors. Despite the progress that has been made, however, the detection of diversion, or of anomalies, of nuclear material (predominantly through material accountancy) in declared plants and facilities remains at the heart of the classical safeguards scheme. Notably, as discussed above, the lessons learned from the Iraqi experience as well as the cases of North Korea and South Africa, coupled with the strict IAEA budgetary constraints and increasing workload, clearly revealed the limitations of classical safeguards. Thus a shift in focus became justified and a new momentum emerged towards more intrusive and streamlined safeguards to also ensure the absence of undeclared nuclear material and clandestine facilities and to permit a more efficient use of resources.

In 1992 the IAEA Board of Governors affirmed that the scope of comprehensive safeguards is not limited to nuclear material declared to the Agency by a state but also includes nuclear material subject to safeguards which has not been declared.[37] It subsequently adopted a number of decisions confirming the right of the IAEA to carry out special inspections, approving the requirement for the early provision to the Agency of facility design information, and endorsing a voluntary, expanded reporting

---

[33] For a discussion of safeguards and nuclear verification related to disarmament and an FMT, see Blix, H., Development of International Law Relating to Disarmament and Arms Control since the First Hague Peace Conference in 1899, Especially the Rules and Practices regarding Verification and Compliance, revised report prepared for the Centennial of the First International Peace Conference, pursuant to United Nations General Assembly Resolutions A/RES/52/154 and A/RES/53/99, May 1999.

[34] ElBaradei, M., 'Safeguarding the atom: the IAEA & international nuclear affairs', *IAEA Bulletin*, Dec. 1999, p. 4.

[35] Fischer (note 6), p. 35.

[36] Full-scope safeguards are also applied pursuant to nuclear-weapon-free zone treaties: the 1967 Treaty of Tlatelolco, the 1985 Treaty of Rarotonga, the 1996 Treaty of Pelindaba and the 1995 Treaty of Bangkok. For summaries of and the parties to these treaties, see annexe A in this volume. See also Prawitz, J., 'NWFZs: their added value in a strengthened international safeguards system', Draft paper prepared for Forschungsinstitut der Deutschen Gesellschaft für Auswärtige Politik, 11 Jan. 2000.

[37] Hooper, R., 'The IAEA's Additional Protocol', *Disarmament Forum*, no. 3 (1999), p. 10.

scheme for imports and exports of nuclear material and exports of specified equipment and non-nuclear material.[38]

Programme 93 + 2

In December 1993 the IAEA Secretariat, responding to a request from the Board of Governors, presented the so-called Programme 93 + 2, a major and ambitious undertaking to strengthen the existing safeguards regime.[39] The operational, technical, legal, financial and resource requirements of Programme 93 + 2 were thoroughly evaluated by the IAEA Secretariat, the IAEA Standing Advisory Group on Safeguards Implementation (SAGSI) and several member states, and in March 1995 the Board of Governors endorsed the main directions of the programme.

The first significant development took place in June 1995. The IAEA Board of Governors endorsed a new, comprehensive set of measures to be implemented under existing IAEA legal authority provided by the Comprehensive Safeguards Agreements in force with member states. Such measures formed what is known as Part-I of Programme 93 + 2 and included the following:[40] (a) access to information concerning the status of the State System of Accounting and Control of nuclear material (SSAC), information on certain closed-down or decommissioned nuclear facilities and locations outside facilities, and information which is obtained by performing environmental sampling within declared nuclear facilities; (b) unannounced routine inspections at declared facilities and other locations; (c) use of a wide variety of advanced technologies for remote monitoring and unattended measurements with remote data transmission; and (d) increased cooperation with single-state SSACs and regional organizations such as Euratom and ABACC.

Nevertheless, the evolution and the eventual adoption of Programme 93 + 2 were neither smooth nor easy. As Bruno Pellaud, then IAEA Deputy Director General for Safeguards, maintained in 1996 in an address to the annual meeting of the Uranium Institute, the nuclear fuel industry was sceptical about complying with the new regime, mainly because of the implementation burdens and the demands on the operator.[41] Fears were also expressed that the necessary guarantees of confidentiality of commercially sensitive information would not be forthcoming and about the handling of potential inconsistencies that would come to light through additional information and access. The IAEA argued that the improved transparency and non-proliferation assurances resulting from the application of the strengthened safeguards may lead to simpler, less frequent inspections in a large number of nuclear facilities of lesser proliferation concern, such as light-water reactor power plants.

In May 1997, after lengthy and difficult negotiations involving some 70 member states and the two regional inspectorates, the IAEA Board of Governors adopted Part-II of Programme 93 + 2, a reinforced control and verification scheme of nuclear

---

[38] IAEA (note 16), p. 236; and Goldschmidt, P., 'The IAEA safeguards system moves into the 21st century', *IAEA Bulletin*, Dec. 1999, p. S-20.

[39] Programme 93 + 2, to strengthen the effectiveness and improve the efficiency of safeguards, was launched in 1993 and was to make recommendations within 2 years. While consultations between governments and the IAEA were not completed in 2 years, the programme was supported in 1995 at the NPT Review and Extension Conference.

[40] IAEA (note 16), pp. 236–37.

[41] Pellaud, B., 'The strengthening of safeguards and the nuclear industry', Paper presented at the Uranium Institute, London, 4 Sep. 1996.

activities which is detailed in INFCIRC/540.[42] This document contains a Model Additional Protocol, designed for states with a (INFCIRC/153-type) Comprehensive Safeguards Agreement in force, in order to strengthen the effectiveness and improve the efficiency of the safeguards system, as a contribution to global nuclear non-proliferation objectives. The strengthened features primarily address the completeness of states' declarations, that is, ensuring the absence of undeclared nuclear material and activities. It is worth noting that the IAEA Board of Governors requested the IAEA Director General to also negotiate Additional Protocols with the NWS, which would lead to the implementation of selective measures in their civilian facilities. Such negotiations were also requested, in part, for other states not having NPT-type agreements with the Agency.[43]

The adoption of INFCIRC/540, which is a totally new instrument, was a major step forward after the entry into force of the NPT in 1970. Its principal provisions, which constitute the legally binding obligations for implementing the IAEA strengthened safeguards system, can be summarized as follows:[44]

1. Additional information,[45] not supplied under the Comprehensive Safeguards Agreement, which is relevant to:

(*a*) nuclear fuel cycle-related R&D activities, not involving nuclear material, including general plans related to the future development of such activities;

(*b*) all the buildings on a nuclear site;

(*c*) uranium mines and concentration plants, and thorium concentration plants;

(*d*) locations where nuclear material intended for non-nuclear purposes is present;

(*e*) locations engaged in the manufacture of sensitive nuclear-related technologies;[46]

(*f*) exports and imports of specific sensitive equipment and non-nuclear material;

2. Complementary physical access to:

(*a*) any place on a nuclear site;

---

[42] IAEA, Model Protocol Additional to the Agreement(s) between State(s) and the International Atomic Energy Agency for the Application of Safeguards, IAEA document INFCIRC/540, Sep. 1997. INFCIRC/540 was corrected twice in 1998: in INFCIRC/540/Corr.1 (12 Oct.) and INFCIRC/540 (Corrected) (Dec.).

[43] 'The Board of Governors has also requested the Director General to negotiate additional protocols or other legally binding agreements with nuclear-weapon States incorporating those measures provided for in the Model Protocol that each nuclear-weapon State has identified as capable of contributing to the non-proliferation and efficiency aims of the Protocol, when implemented with regard to that State, and as consistent with that State's obligations under Article I of the NPT. The Board of Governors has further requested the Director General to negotiate additional protocols with other States that are prepared to accept measures provided for in the Model Protocol in pursuance of safeguards effectiveness and efficiency objectives.' IAEA (note 42), Foreword.

[44] IAEA (note 16), p. 237; IAEA (note 42); and Hooper, R., 'The system of strengthened safeguards', *IAEA Bulletin*, Dec. 1997, p. 28.

[45] Such information is to be provided in what are commonly called 'expanded declarations'.

[46] These include: the manufacture of centrifuge rotor tubes or the assembly of gas centrifuges; the manufacture of diffusion barriers; the manufacture or assembly of laser-based systems; the manufacture or assembly of electromagnetic isotope separators; the manufacture or assembly of columns or extraction equipment; the manufacture of aerodynamic separation nozzles or vortex tubes; the manufacture or assembly of uranium plasma generation systems; the manufacture of zirconium tubes; the manufacture or upgrading of heavy water or deuterium; the manufacture of nuclear grade graphite; the manufacture of flasks for irradiated fuel; the manufacture of reactor control rods; the manufacture of criticality safe tanks and vessels; the manufacture of irradiated fuel element chopping machines; and the construction of hot cells.

(*b*) any location related to the nuclear fuel cycle (from uranium mines to nuclear waste facilities), including fuel cycle-related R&D, manufacturing and import locations;

(*c*) any decommissioned facility, or decommissioned location outside facilities where nuclear material was customarily used;

(*d*) additional locations specified by the IAEA, beyond declared ones, to carry out wide-area environmental sampling.

3. Various administrative arrangements targeted at streamlining the processes of designating IAEA safeguards inspectors and obtaining their visas, as well as the use of internationally established direct communications systems.

According to the IAEA Statute, Additional Protocols must be individually negotiated with the states concerned, be subsequently approved by the IAEA Board of Governors, and meet each state's statutory and/or constitutional requirements for entry into force.

As of January 2000, 37 states have signed and 8 states (Australia, the Holy See, Indonesia, Japan, Jordan, Monaco, New Zealand and Uzbekistan) have ratified Protocols Additional to their IAEA Safeguards Agreements.[47]

Integrated safeguards

Following the adoption of the Additional Protocol and in close cooperation with its member states, the IAEA has embarked on a high-priority programme aimed at facilitating the operational implementation of the new provisions and optimizing the overall safeguards system.

This optimal combination of classical safeguards with the strengthened measures is intended gradually to lead to an integrated verification system aimed at providing credible assurances about both the absence of undeclared activities and material and the non-diversion of declared material.[48] A holistic, more qualitative approach would thus encompass the fuel cycle of an entire state rather than only its declared facilities. The IAEA, employing its additional powers under its enlarged verification rights, would be in a position to draw a comprehensive picture of all nuclear activities in a state and, therefore, better guarantee not only the correctness but also the completeness of states' declarations. Closely linked are the expected improvements in the cost-effectiveness of safeguards. Classical measures, however, such as material accountancy, will continue to be of vital importance, in particular as regards unirradiated direct-use material[49] and fuel processing facilities (reprocessing, enrichment and MOX fabrication).

Since early 1998, IAEA consultations regarding the implementation of integrated safeguards have emphasized improved cooperation with the SSACs and regional inspectorates, environmental sampling, and use of unannounced routine inspections and remote surveillance techniques. In addition, efforts are targeted towards realigning internal procedures as well as negotiating and concluding Additional Protocols with member states.

---

[47] In addition, the Protocol of Peru was approved by the IAEA Board of Governors in Dec. 1999. The Additional Protocol of Ghana is provisionally applied. URL <http://www.iaea.org/worldatom/updates/safeguards.html>.

[48] Carlson, J. *et al.*, 'Nuclear safeguards as an evolutionary system', *Nonproliferation Review*, winter 1999, pp. 109–17.

[49] Direct-use material is plutonium containing less than 80% ^{238}Pu, HEU and ^{233}U.

A dialogue has been established between the IAEA, state authorities and nuclear operators on guidelines for the application of, and reporting under, the Additional Protocol. An information campaign is also under way, while field trials to determine the feasibility and test the sensitivity of the new sampling techniques have been performed.[50] To this end, a global network would be utilized in the future, consisting of the IAEA's Safeguards Analytical Laboratory at Seibersdorf, Austria, and other selected specialized national analytical laboratories. Particular attention is also paid to enhanced information retrieval, analysis and evaluation. In this regard, access to reliable and diverse information obtained from open sources and the sharing of information with technologically advanced member states are contemplated.[51]

V. Prospects and concerns

Despite the problems encountered with the Iraqi clandestine nuclear weapon programme and the continued non-compliance of North Korea, there is no doubt that much has been accomplished in recent years by the IAEA and the international safeguards community. The Part-I measures of Programme 93 + 2 have begun to be applied. Verification of ex-military fissile material has been initiated, albeit on a very modest scale, and considerable progress has been made in the NIS following the implementation of safeguards-relevant measures. A wealth of expertise has been accumulated from devising techniques for safeguarding large, fully automated fuel processing facilities in operation in Europe.[52] Regional inspectorates have improved their cooperation with the IAEA and have concluded new agreements towards this end.

Although the strengthened safeguards system was adopted by the IAEA in a timely fashion, formidable challenges lie ahead. Negotiating and concluding Additional Protocols with the IAEA member states and, more importantly, their final acceptance and entry into force without undue delay remain the most decisive factors for the future of the system and, arguably, also for the future of the IAEA. Universal adherence to the Additional Protocol was a key consideration that was widely addressed by states during the contentious consultations which led to its adoption by the IAEA Board of Governors.[53] Some two and a half years after the adoption of INFCIRC/540, the number of states with Additional Protocols in force is very small.[54] Although it is difficult to comment on the underlying causes, procedures connected with ratification are time-consuming and lengthy. Given the intrusive nature of the new provisions, however, ratification in some states may well involve assessment of the overall ratification process or even taking into account the prospect that certain other states will or will not ratify the Additional Protocol. It is encouraging that the 13 NNWS and

---

[50] Dahlin, G., Eiborn, M. and Larsson M., Swedish Nuclear Power Inspectorate, Private communication with the author, 1 Dec. 1999. See also Goldschmidt (note 38), p. S-10.

[51] Intelligence information supplied to the IAEA by certain member states played an important role in pointing to the undeclared activities in Iraq and North Korea.

[52] See note 25.

[53] Schaper, A., 'The case for universal full-scope safeguards on nuclear material', *Nonproliferation Review*, winter 1998, p. 73.

[54] The total number of concluded Additional Protocols 'falls short of expectations', according to the IAEA Director General. Statement by the IAEA Director General to the 54th session of the United Nations General Assembly, United Nations, New York, 4 Nov. 1999. See also IAEA Board of Governors, Excerpts from the Introductory Statement by the IAEA Director General, 9 Dec. 1999, URL <http://www.iaea.org/worldatom/Press/Statements/1999/ebsp1999n017.shtml>.

2 NWS of the European Union, as well as China and the USA, have concluded and signed Additional Protocols with the IAEA.[55] The aim of the EU was for all member states to have ratified their protocols before mid-2000, when the 2000 NPT Review Conference will be held. Indeed, the adherence of key states with sizeable civilian nuclear power programmes may set in motion a much needed new momentum.

The delays involved in bringing Additional Protocols into force may be seen from a wider non-proliferation perspective. In the late 1990s, the prevailing international climate concerning nuclear disarmament was unfavourable.[56] Therefore, the number of Additional Protocols adopted before the 2000 NPT Review Conference can contribute to the success of the conference and would not only have a purely symbolic value. The Principles and Objectives that were agreed during the 1995 NPT Review and Extension Conference[57] would be reinforced if a majority of states were to ratify the new measures before the spring of 2000, although this is unlikely.

Acceptance of Additional Protocols alone would not be sufficient for establishing a concrete basis for the strengthened system. Full and true implementation of the provisions, which would open up a new dimension in international nuclear verification, is another major challenge. In this regard, egalitarian and transparent application would be a prerequisite. It remains to be seen how the IAEA will finally codify and administer the new measures—whether it will gradually focus its attention on more proliferation-sensitive activities, such as fuel cycle processing and R&D, or continue, at least for some time to come, to cover all types of installation. More importantly, it can be argued that the effectiveness of the new regime will be truly tested in a very limited number of states with questionable proliferation credentials or with high proliferation motivations. Assuming that the Agency will continue to be constrained in the future by its limited resources, a streamlined approach is expected to evolve. In this respect, nuclear operators may in the longer term benefit from a more rationalized and cost-effective approach which places less emphasis on routine safeguards activities.

In the near term, the Agency will have the laborious and complex task of applying classical (INFCIRC/153- and INFCIRC/66-type) safeguards and Voluntary Offer Agreements, in parallel with Programme 93 + 2 Part-I and INFCIRC/540 measures. Additionally, the initial expanded declarations of states should be established and evaluated. As the complete integration of the two approaches and the elimination of obsolete procedures and inevitable redundancies will most likely take some time to materialize, this may put further strain on the Agency's resources. Prioritization and diligent planning of resource allocation, both human and financial, are critical factors for a fully operational IAEA integrated safeguards system. This is closely connected with developments that could potentially increase the role of the IAEA in the disarmament process. As discussed above, such expanded responsibilities would undoubtedly require that substantially increased resources are made available to the IAEA and would lead to a redistribution of its inspection efforts worldwide.

Concerning implementation, it should be recognized that personnel in large commercial facilities are generally accustomed to providing information and are adequately trained to cooperate with inspectors. Smaller R&D establishments, however,

---

[55] It should be noted, however, that the measures accepted by individual NWS vary widely. Russia signed its Additional Protocol on 22 Mar. 2000.

[56] Dhanapala, J., 'Reinforcing the NPT regime: international challenges & opportunities', *IAEA Bulletin*, Dec. 1999, pp. 5–8.

[57] See note 28.

may not possess such expertise. In this regard, setting up and maintaining good communication links between state authorities and less safeguards-experienced operators would be central for the smooth operation of an integrated system. Enhanced training would also be provided to IAEA inspectors in order to familiarize them with the application of the new sophisticated techniques.

Environmental sampling, which is foreseen in INFCIRC/540, could well unveil—in certain cases—largely unknown activities in member states, some of which may have been carried out several decades ago. It is expected that processing of such information would be handled with great care, under the Additional Protocol's stringent provisions for confidentiality. Similarly, potential false alarms owing to complementary access and environmental sampling and analysis would have to be treated with equal discretion.

VI. Conclusions

The international safeguards community reacted swiftly to a number of challenges that confronted the global nuclear verification regime. The adoption of the Model Additional Protocol by the IAEA Board of Governors in 1997 to strengthen the safeguards system was a fundamental step towards limiting the spread of nuclear weapons and enhancing international security. Universal acceptance and full implementation of the new system are imperative for guaranteeing the political assurances necessary for advancing the non-proliferation and disarmament agenda.

In the short term, administering and harmonizing the existing safeguards arrangements for detection of diversion of nuclear material with the new, more comprehensive measures for detection of possible undeclared activities will be critically influenced by many interrelated factors, including the costs of implementation, availability of resources and infrastructure, cooperation with state authorities and operators, and, more importantly, determined support from the IAEA member states. Such support could best be expressed by promptly bringing the Additional Protocols into force and by granting adequate financial resources to the Agency.

Once the evolving integrated safeguards system has been fully implemented and confidence in it has been gained, the IAEA will have a very powerful instrument in its hands to provide better assurances about the peaceful applications of nuclear energy and facilitate progress in the disarmament process.

9. Chemical and biological weapon developments and arms control

JEAN PASCAL ZANDERS and MARIA WAHLBERG*

I. Introduction

Progress on the implementation of the 1993 Chemical Weapons Convention (CWC)[1] continued in 1999. Three of the four declared possessors of chemical weapons (CW) continued or began destruction operations and some previously outstanding issues were resolved. Nevertheless, problems relating to the timely execution of certain treaty obligations by some states continue to generate tension between parties to the CWC.

The negotiation on a protocol to the 1972 Biological and Toxin Weapon Convention (BTWC)[2] made progress on several technical issues. The industrialized and developing countries took initiatives to bridge their differences on non-proliferation and technical cooperation. The issue of monitoring compliance with the future regime remained the main stumbling block.

Despite progress in implementing the CWC and strengthening the BTWC proliferation remained a cause for concern. In 1999 more information became available about past chemical and biological weapon (CBW) programmes in Russia, Serbia and South Africa, and the use of or inadvertent exposure to CBW in a regional war, such as the one in Kosovo, appeared to have become a more realistic threat.

Section II of the chapter deals with the implementation of the CWC, CW destruction in the USA, the reasons why CW destruction has not yet begun in Russia and abandoned CW in China. The negotiations to strengthen the BTWC are discussed in section III and CBW proliferation concerns in section IV. Section V presents the conclusions. Appendix 9A investigates the likelihood of a terrorist organization setting up its own CBW production capability and assesses the potential consequences of terrorists using chemical and biological warfare agents against population centres on the basis of computer simulations. Appendix 9B describes the future prospects of CBW disarmament in Iraq against the background of the experiences of the United Nations Special Commission on Iraq (UNSCOM).

---

[1] A brief summary of the convention and a list of parties are given in annexe A in this volume. The full text is available on the SIPRI CBW Project Internet site, URL <http://projects.sipri.se/cbw/cbw-main page.html>.

[2] A brief summary of the convention and a list of parties are given in annexe A in this volume. The full text is available on the SIPRI CBW Project Internet site, URL <http://projects.sipri.se/cbw/cbw-main page.html>.

* Melissa Hersh, Jacqueline Simon and Maria Andersson assisted with the collection of data for this chapter.

II. Chemical weapon disarmament

Implementing the CWC

The CWC entered into force on 29 April 1997. By 31 December 1999, 129 states had ratified or acceded to the convention and an additional 41 states had signed it.[3] Twenty-two UN members have neither signed nor ratified the CWC.[4] None of the countries of greatest concern in Asia and the Middle East—Egypt, Israel, North Korea, Libya and Syria—joined the convention in 1999. Although Nigeria and Sudan became parties to the CWC in 1999, Africa remains the most under-represented continent.[5] As of 6 December 1999, inspectors from the Organisation for the Prohibition of Chemical Weapons (OPCW) had completed 620 inspections at 312 sites in 35 countries since the entry into force of the CWC.[6] The Fourth Conference of States Parties (CSP) was held in The Hague on 28 June–3 July 1999.[7]

As of 17 November, 32 of the 129 parties had not yet submitted their initial industry declarations to the OPCW, and several others had only submitted partial declarations. Such submissions are required within 30 days after the CWC enters into force for the party and are essential to establish the verification requirements for the party. By 20 November the Technical Secretariat (TS) had received 96 per cent of the total assessed contributions of 108.1 million guilders (c. $47 million) for 1999. Just over one-half of the number of parties at that time (64 of 126) had paid their assessment in full, and a further 13 parties had made a partial payment or received a credit on the basis of their 1997 cash surplus.[8] Many of the parties that had not paid are small states with low assessed contributions.

Complaints were made by some parties about the unequal distribution of industry inspections. The majority of these inspections have been carried out

---

[3] Estonia, the Holy See, Liechtenstein, Micronesia, Nicaragua, Nigeria, San Marino and Sudan became parties in 1999.

[4] Those states are Angola, Andorra, Antigua and Barbuda, Barbados, Belize, Egypt, Eritrea, Iraq, Kiribati, Korea (North), Lebanon, Libya, Mozambique, Palau, Sao Tome and Principe, the Federal Republic of Yugoslavia (FRY), Solomon Islands, Somalia, Syria, Tonga, Tuvalu and Vanuatu.

[5] Sudan joined the CWC in reaction to the US bombing in Aug. 1998 of a pharmaceutical plant allegedly producing CW. Zanders, J. P., French, E. M. and Pauwels, N., 'Chemical and biological weapon developments and arms control', *SIPRI Yearbook 1999: Armaments, Disarmament and International Security* (Oxford University Press: Oxford, 1999), pp. 581–82.

[6] These comprise 14 inspections of abandoned CW sites, 138 inspections of CW destruction facilities, 150 inspections of CW production facilities, 91 inspections of CW storage facilities, 25 inspections of old CW facilities, 54 inspections of Schedule 1 facilities, 110 inspections of Schedule 2 facilities, and 37 inspections of Schedule 3 facilities and 1 other facility. Feakes, D., 'Developments in the Organisation for the Prohibition of Chemical Weapons', *CBW Conventions Bulletin*, no. 46 (Dec. 1999), p. 17.

[7] Report of the Fourth Session of the Conference of States Parties, OPCW document C-IV/6, 2 July 1999.

[8] OPCW, *Secretariat Brief*, no. 20 (9 Dec. 1999). Concern was also expressed that some parties still had to meet their financial obligations for previous financial years. E.g., 34 of the then 121 parties had not paid their 1998 assessment. According to Article VIII, para. 8 of the CWC, a party which is in arrears to an amount equal to or in excess of the amount owed for the previous 2 full years will lose its vote in the OPCW. Some parties to the CWC are also slow to reimburse the verification costs under Article IV and Article V: out of a total of 12.51 million guilders (c. $5.5 million) just over 2.3 million guilders (c. $1 million) had been reimbursed by 20 Nov. 1999.

at Schedule 2 facilities,[9] which only relatively few states possess. (Of the 126 inspectable Schedule 2 plant sites that had been declared in 1999, 90 were located in five states that are parties to the CWC.) In 1998, 79 per cent of the industry inspections took place in eight states; no such inspections were carried out in 101 of the then 121 parties. In 1999 a larger number of Schedule 3 inspections were conducted than in 1998, and 27 states parties received at least one industry inspection.[10] In September 1999 a new selection methodology to achieve a more equitable geographic distribution of inspections of Schedule 3 plant sites was adopted by the Executive Council of the OPCW.[11]

The continuing delays with respect to the US initial industry declarations also affected the OPCW inspections and the budget planning for 2000. The US Government was unable to collect the industry declarations required by the CWC because the necessary national regulations had not been issued. This put the USA in technical non-compliance with the CWC and caused certain other industrialized parties to express irritation with the USA. German Ambassador Klaus Neubert, for instance, addressing the Fourth CSP on behalf of the European Union (EU), stated that the situation had 'led in 1998 to 64 per cent of Schedule 2 inspections and 54 per cent of Schedule 3 inspections being carried out in Member States of the European Union'.[12] Several parties, including some EU members, attempted through the budget planning procedure to limit the burden of inspections on their industries, arguing that their US competitors were not similarly affected. Following difficult discussions, the Fourth CSP adopted the budget for 2000; it proposes 252 inspections (120 inspections of CW and CW-related facilities and 132 chemical industry inspections). A quota of industry inspections is reserved for the USA, but they contain complex adjustment mechanisms to take into account the date of submission of the US initial industry declarations. On 30 December the Bureau of Export Administration of the Department of Commerce and the Bureau of Arms Control of the Department of State published an 'interim rule' and request for comments (by 31 January 2000); the US initial industry declarations are expected to be

---

[9] According to the CWC Verification Annex, part VII, para. 16, each Schedule 2 facility 'shall receive an initial inspection as soon as possible but preferably not later than three years after entry into force of this Convention'.

[10] Mathews, R. J., 'Verifying chemical disarmament: advent and performance of the OPCW', *Verification 2000* (Verification Research, Training & Information Centre (VERTIC): London, 2000).

[11] Australia and the Republic of Korea, Methodology for selecting Schedule 3 and discrete organic chemical (DOC) plant sites for inspection, Executive Council document EC-XVI/NAT.5, 16 Sep. 1999.

[12] Neubert, K., Statement made on behalf of the European Union to the Fourth Conference of States Parties to the Organisation for the Prohibition of Chemical Weapons, The Hague, 28 June 1999. The nature of an industrial facility's obligations depends on the types and quantities of chemicals it produces, processes, transfers and consumes. The CWC categorizes chemical compounds of particular concern in schedules depending on their importance for the production of chemical warfare agents or for legitimate civilian manufacturing processes. Each list has different reporting requirements. Schedule 1 contains compounds that can be used as CW and that have few uses for permitted purposes. They are subject to the most stringent controls. Schedule 2 includes chemicals that are key precursors to CW but which generally have greater commercial application. Schedule 3 chemicals can be used to produce CW but are also used in large quantities for non-prohibited purposes. The CWC also places reporting requirements on firms which produce DOC that are not on any of the schedules and contains special requirements for firms that produce 'unscheduled' DOC with phosphorus, sulphur or fluorine.

submitted in the first half of 2000.[13] CW inspections of US storage facilities, destruction sites, and so on are proceeding without procedural problems.

A revised notification procedure for the transfer of saxitoxin, a Schedule 1 chemical, was adopted.[14] On 31 October 1999, a new paragraph reflecting this change was added to Part VI of the Verification Annex of the CWC using the simplified amendment procedure for administrative or technical purposes.[15] However, the problem of retransfer of saxitoxin has not been solved. Canada and the United Kingdom withdrew their joint proposal to allow the retransfer of saxitoxin under certain conditions following both an evaluation by the TS that the proposal is not a simple administrative or technical change but rather an amendment to the CWC under Article XV, and the failure of the 14th session of the Executive Council (on 2–5 February 1999) to reach consensus on the issue of retransfer.[16]

As part of the implementation of Article X on assistance and protection against CW the OPCW established a CW protection network (comprised of experts from states parties) so that parties to the CWC seeking advice or assistance can have rapid access to experts and expertise.[17] Other measures, including internal training courses for inspectors, were approved to increase the readiness of the OPCW to coordinate assistance and to investigate chemical warfare allegations. In October the OPCW conducted a successful full-scale 'investigation of alleged use' exercise in the Czech Republic in which chemical warfare agent simulants were used.[18] The OPCW still needs experts in specific technical areas and certain types of equipment for investigations of alleged use.[19] During a visit by OPCW Director-General José Bustani to Iran in January 1999, Iran offered to establish an international centre for the treatment of chemical warfare casualties and for training medical personnel in the treatment of such casualties.[20]

Since the entry into force of the CWC no party has called for a challenge inspection—the most intrusive verification mechanism available in the event of a serious compliance concern. Any location on the territory of a party, whether declared to the OPCW or not, can be the subject of a short-notice challenge inspection. In order to test the complex procedures outlined in the CWC for such an inspection and to evaluate the possible political ramifica-

[13] *Federal Register*, vol. 64, no. 250 (30 Dec. 1999), pp. 73744–811.

[14] Saxitoxin is a powerful neurotoxin used in small quantities for medical and diagnostic purposes. As a Schedule 1 chemical it was impossible to transfer it to non-parties or to retransfer it between parties for such purposes. The issue is discussed in Zanders, French and Pauwels (note 5), pp. 567–68.

[15] The amended Part VI of the Verification Annex is available at the SIPRI CBW Project Internet site, URL <http://projects.sipri.se/cbw/docs/cw-cwc-verannex5bis.html>.

[16] Feakes, D., 'Developments in the Organisation for the Prohibition of Chemical Weapons', *CBW Conventions Bulletin*, no. 43 (Mar. 1999), p. 5.

[17] Bustani, J., Statement to the First Committee of the United Nations General Assembly, 19 Oct. 1999, URL <http://www.opcw.nl>.

[18] Pelly, G., 'The investigation of alleged use exercise in the Czech Republic', *OPCW Synthesis*, no. 5 (Nov./Dec. 1999), pp. 2–3.

[19] OPCW, *Secretariat Brief*, no. 20 (9 Dec. 1999). At the 15th session of the Executive Council, Bustani had identified the areas for which expertise was needed: biomedicine, explosives, forensic science and autopsy. OPCW, *Secretariat Brief*, no. 15 (5 May 1999).

[20] OPCW, *Secretariat Brief*, no. 14 (18 Feb. 1999).

tions, the OPCW organized a full-scale mock challenge inspection in a Brazilian chemical plant in October 1999. The inspection was carried out in a manner that took account of politically sensitive issues. This apparently did not compromise its effectiveness, and an initial evaluation indicated that the TS will be able to improve its procedures and that valuable experience was obtained in the mock inspection.

The issue of determining the usability of CW produced between 1925 and 1946 was not resolved in 1999. Consequently, the TS is unable to close the files of 24 inspections involving such chemical weapons.[21] Another major unresolved question relates to determining thresholds for the declaration of mixtures containing low concentrations of either Schedule 2 or Schedule 3 chemicals. This question is important for determining the cut-off point for providing notification of transfers. As of 29 April 2000, three years after the entry into force of the CWC, Schedule 2 chemicals may no longer be exported from parties to the CWC to non-parties. The matter of low concentrations of Schedule 2 chemicals in mixtures therefore requires urgent resolution.[22]

Destruction of chemical weapons and related facilities

By the end of January 2000 the destruction of approximately 4000 tonnes of chemical agents and more than 1 million munitions had been monitored by OPCW inspectors. All of the 60 declared CW production facilities throughout the world had been inspected and sealed. The OPCW has certified the destruction of 20 of them and approved the conversion of an additional 5 facilities.[23] In 1999 three of the four states parties that have declared CW stockpiles to the OPCW—India, South Korea and the USA—began destroying these weapons. Russia has not begun the destruction of its CW stockpiles largely owing to a lack of sufficient funding. The details of the Indian and South Korean CW stockpiles and the plans for their destruction have not been made public.

The United States

The US CW destruction programme consists of two major components: assembled CW and non-stockpiled chemical *matériel*. Incineration is the US Army's baseline destruction technology,[24] but for each of the two components Congress has directed the US Department of Defense (DOD) to explore alternative destruction technologies in response to strong public and political opposition to incineration. With respect to stockpiled items,[25] the US Army

---

[21] Bustani, J., Opening statement to the 17th session of the Executive Council, 30 Nov. 1999, URL <http://www.opcw.nl>. If CW produced between 1925 and 1946 are deemed usable they must be destroyed under OPCW supervision in the same manner as CW produced after 1946.

[22] Bustani (note 21).

[23] OPCW, 'The OPCW completes its first 1000 days', Press Release no. 2/2000, 25 Jan. 2000.

[24] In this disposal method the stockpiled items are disassembled into agents, metal parts and the 'energetic' (e.g., explosives and/or propellants) and each component is subsequently incinerated separately.

[25] The stockpile is stored at 9 locations: Edgewood Chemical Activity, Aberdeen Proving Ground, Md.; Anniston Chemical Activity, Anniston, Ala.; Blue Grass Chemical Activity, Richmond, Ky.; Newport Chemical Depot, Newport, Ind.; Pine Bluff Chemical Activity, Pine Bluff, Ark.; Pueblo Chemical

has launched two projects. The Alternative Technologies and Approaches Program (ATAP) investigates ways to neutralize the chemical warfare agents stored in 'ton containers' at Aberdeen Proving Ground and Newport. Both are low-volume stockpile sites.[26] The Assembled Chemical Weapons Assessment (ACWA) programme, which explores CW disposal options for the Blue Grass and Pueblo storage sites, is discussed below.

Non-stockpiled chemical *matériel* might be recovered from as many as 100 locations.[27] Existing technologies are being used to destroy the unfilled components of the binary CW and former production facilities. The other elements of the non-stockpiled chemical *matériel* pose a variety of technological challenges as a consequence of the different physical configurations and conditions, agent fill types (of buried CW and in chemical agent identification sets), quantities and locations. Current technologies are being used to meet transfer, storage, handling and transport requirements. New processes are being developed for munition identification and characterization and the destruction of the agent and the energetic through neutralization.[28]

The current estimate of the cost for the elimination of the US CW stockpile has risen sharply largely because the DOD must explore, develop and test alternative technologies while still meeting the CWC-imposed deadlines. The current cost estimate for the destruction of stockpiled items ($15.6 billion) is just under $500 000 per ton. (For comparison, a common benchmark for hazardous waste treatment cost is $300 per ton.) According to a 1998 independent audit, the budget could rise by another 8.6 per cent or $1.3 billion.[29]

Destruction of the CW stockpile proceeded according to plan in 1999. As of 13 February 2000, a total of 5686 agent tons had been destroyed at the two currently operational facilities, the Johnston Atoll Chemical Agent Disposal System (JACADS) and the Tooele Chemical Agent Disposal Facility (TOCDF). Of the 31 496 agent tons originally declared to the OPCW, 25 810 tons still await destruction.

All munitions containing mustard agent at JACADS were destroyed in 1999. In 1998 the stockpile of the nerve agent sarin was eliminated, and the nerve agent VX is the only compound awaiting complete destruction.[30] As of 13 February 2000, 1754 agent tons or 86.3 per cent of the original tonnage

Depot, Pueblo, Colo.; Deseret Chemical Depot, Tooele, Utah; Umatilla Chemical Depot, Hermiston, Ore.; and Johnston Atoll Chemical Activity, Johnston Atoll (south-west of Hawaii).

[26]An overview of the alternative destruction technologies is provided in Zanders, French and Pauwels (note 5), p. 572. One US ton is equal to 0.907 metric tonne.

[27] The Non-Stockpile Chemical Materiel Project deals with 5 categories of chemical warfare *matériel*: (*a*) binary CW; (*b*) miscellaneous chemical warfare items, including unfilled munitions, support equipment and devices to be employed in conjunction with the use of CW; (*c*) recovered CW; (*d*) former production facilities; and (*e*) buried chemical warfare *matériel*. All categories of non-stockpiled chemical *matériel*, except buried items, must be destroyed according to the CWC-mandated time lines.

[28] US Army Project Manager for Non-Stockpile Chemical Materiel, Program Manager for Chemical Demilitarization, 'Overarching research plan: non-stockpile chemical materiel program', 9 June 1999, pp. 8–9, URL <http://pmcdtech.stoneweb.com/ORP.htm>.

[29] Wright, A. G., 'Chemical independence', *Engineering News-Record*, 15 Feb. 1999, URL <http://www.enr.com/new/c0215.asp>. The 1984 budget estimate for the total CW destruction programme was $1.7 billion.

[30] *Reach*, vol. 1, no. 3 (1999), p. 2.

(2031 tons) had been destroyed, as well as 88.9 per cent of the original amount of munitions.[31] Commencement of the closure proceedings for JACADS is planned for 2000.[32]

At the TOCDF, 3932 tons or 28.8 per cent of the original tonnage (13 616 tons) were destroyed as of 13 February 2000, as well as 33.2 per cent of the original amount of munitions. All of the munitions destroyed thus far were filled with sarin.[33] The programme is currently running slightly behind schedule, but it is believed that the delay can be overcome. Completion of the destruction activities and closure of the facility are still anticipated for the end of fiscal year (FY) 2003.[34]

Construction work on the facilities in Anniston and Umatilla is about half completed. Both plants are slated to commence destruction operations in 2002. Work on construction of the facility in Pine Bluff started in 1999, and it should become operational in 2003. Construction at Aberdeen began in June 1999, and the facility should become operational in 2004. Construction of the Newport, Pueblo and Blue Grass facilities has not yet started. In the latter two cases, work is on hold pending the completion and submission of a report to Congress on the relative effectiveness of three different technologies other than incineration and the final selection of the destruction technology.[35]

On 30 September the US Department of the Army submitted to Congress its ACWA report on technologies other than incineration. One of the three alternatives (plasma waste convertor) was considered immature and rejected. The second alternative—neutralization of mustard agent followed by treatment in an immobilized cell bioreactor—was considered suitable for assembled mustard munitions, and the third alternative—neutralization plus supercritical-water-oxidation—was deemed applicable for all assembled chemical weapons.[36] All technologies are able to destroy agents with at least 99.9999 per cent effectiveness.

In accordance with Public Law 104-201, the US National Academy of Sciences performed an independent technical review and evaluation of the seven technology packages that had passed the initial screening by the DOD as part of the ACWA programme. The report criticized the alternative destruction methods as being less mature for the elimination of the parts of the munitions other than the warfare agent. In addition, the primary chemical decomposition process in all the technology packages produces environmentally unacceptable

[31] 'Processing status as of 13 February 2000 for the Johnston Atoll Chemical Agent Disposal System (JACADS)', URL <http://www-pmcd.apgea.army.mil/print/aag_jacads.html>.

[32] US Army Program Manager for Chemical Demilitarization, 'JACADS public information and involvement closure strategy', Working draft, Feb. 1999, p. 1, URL <http://www-pmcd.apgea.army.mil>.

[33] 'Processing status as of 13 February 2000 . . .' (note 31).

[34] Office of the Under Secretary of Defense (Comptroller), 'Chemical Demilitarization program: program funding execution assessment', Washington, DC, 26 July 1999, p. 3, URL <http://www_pmcd.apgea.army.mil>; and 'Incinerator faltering in race to destroy chemical weapons', *Environment News Service*, 1 Dec. 1999, URL <http://ens.lycos.com/corpus/ens/dec99/19991%2D12%2D01%D06.html>.

[35] Office of the Under Secretary of Defense (note 34), pp. 3–5; and Military Construction Appropriations Act, 2000, Public Law 106-52, section 131.

[36] '30 September', *CBW Conventions Bulletin*, no. 46 (Dec. 1999), p. 32. The ACWA programme was initiated in accordance with Public Laws 104-201 and 104-208 (1996).

reaction products. The report therefore recommended substantial additional testing, operational verification and integration prior to full-scale implementation. It also noted that none of the ACWA technology packages can meet the CWC-imposed deadlines unless there is 'an extraordinary commitment of resources' in 'a concerted national effort'.[37] Such a concerted national effort was not forthcoming in 1999. The Military Construction Appropriations Act, 2000 (Public Law 106-52) provided $93 million less than the amount requested by the Clinton Administration for the CW demilitarization programme, although Congress appropriated $301 million for projects not related to CW that the DOD did not consider as priorities.[38]

The Russian Federation

In 1999 Russia was unable to begin the destruction of its large CW stockpile (totalling 40 000 agent tonnes at seven storage sites[39]) as a consequence of its internal political, social and budgetary difficulties. The Russian Government has reaffirmed that it is politically and legally committed to destroy its CW stockpile and to destroy or convert its former production facilities and other CW-related sites. By presidential decree the functions of the abolished Russian Federation President's Committee for the Convention Problems of Chemical and Biological Weapons were transferred to the Russian Agency for Munitions in May 1999.[40]

Opposition to CW disarmament continues in some quarters. In June the State Duma passed a resolution on the unsatisfactory implementation of the CWC which noted among other things that Russia could not destroy its CW in a safe manner.[41] CW disarmament is opposed by two groups: ecologists, whose chief concern is the lack of environmentally safe CW destruction technologies, and extreme nationalists. The ecologists hold the view that, at present, destruction is more dangerous than continued stockpiling, and the extreme

---

[37] US National Research Council, Committee on Review and Evaluation of Alternative Technologies for Demilitarization of Assembled Chemical Weapons, *Review and Evaluation of Alternative Technologies for Demilitarization of Assembled Chemical Weapons* (National Academy Press: Washington, DC, 1999), Executive Summary, pp. 1–8, URL <http://books.nap.edu/books/0309066395/html/>.

[38] *Statement by the President* (White House, Office of the Press Secretary: Washington, DC, 17 Aug. 1999), URL <http://www.pub.whitehouse.gov/uri-res/I2R?urn:pdi://oma.eop.gov.us/1999/8/18/8.text.1>.

[39] Russian CW are stored at Kambarka, Udmurt Republic; Gorny, Saratov *oblast*; Kizner, Udmurt Republic; Maradikovsky, Kirov *oblast*; Pochep, Bryansk *oblast*; Leonidovka, Penza *oblast*; and Shchuchye, Kurgan *oblast*. In July 1999 a Norwegian newspaper, reportedly on the basis of information from the Norwegian ecological organization Bellona, alleged that CW components were also stored near Severomorsk on the Kola Peninsula, but the Russian authorities and Bellona denied this. Stormark, K., 'Tikkende bombe' [Ticking bomb], *Verdens Gang* (Internet edn, Oslo), 15 July 1999, URL <http://www.vg.no/pub/skrivervennlig.hbs?artid=2812917>; Interfax (Moscow), 19 July 1999, in 'Russian general: no chemical weapons in Kola Peninsula', Foreign Broadcast Information Service, *Daily Report–Central Eurasia (FBIS-SOV)*, FBIS-SOV-1999-0719, 20 July 1999; and Interfax (Moscow), 20 July 1999, in 'Environmentalists not aware of CW parts at Severomorsk', FBIS-SOV-1999-0720, 20 July 1999.

[40] Russian Federation Presidential Edict no. 651, signed by President Boris Yeltsin, dated 25 May 1999, 'On the structure of federal executive organs', in 'Edict lists new Russian federal organs', FBIS-SOV-1999-0601, 29 May 1999.

[41] ITAR-TASS (Moscow), 11 June 1999, in 'Russia urges compliance with chemical arms convention', FBIS-SOV-1999-0612, 14 June 1999; and Scorobogatko, T., 'Arsenic for dessert?', *Moscow News*, no. 29 (4 Aug. 1999).

nationalists argue that the elimination of its chemical weapons will reduce Russia's military stature. The latter group claims that CW are needed to counter the proliferation of non-conventional weapons along the southern border. (Some advocates of CW disarmament reject this argument by pointing to the availability of tactical nuclear weapons.[42])

According to its own assessment, the Russian CW destruction programme is between three and five years behind schedule.[43] Some US estimates are more pessimistic. In the autumn of 1999 Russia submitted a request to the Executive Council of the OPCW for a delay in the implementation of the first intermediate destruction deadline for Category 1 CW, citing lack of financial resources as the principal reason.[44] If CW destruction is carried out as planned,[45] it is estimated that the Russian CW destruction programme will cost approximately $5.7 billion. The figure must be viewed in the light of Russia's budget deficit and debt burden: the projected repayments on Russia's international debts for 1999 are approximately $17.5 billion.[46] Consequently, CW destruction is low on Russia's list of priorities. In recent years, funding of the federal destruction programme has been cut to about 1–2 per cent of the annual amount needed.[47] By the end of 1998 the debt to organizations involved in the CW destruction programme exceeded 100 million roubles ($4 million at early 1999 exchange rates). In the 1999 budget only 5.4 per cent of the necessary expenditure was allocated.[48] Nevertheless, there is a need for urgency.[49] Around some storage and former production sites the concentration

---

[42] In the spring of 1999 Russia reportedly cancelled several high-level negotiations with the USA to complete plans for a CW demilitarization plant because of the war in Kosovo (although several US officials and contractors denied the direct link between these events). Lifland, J., 'NATO's airstrikes chill Russia's plans to destroy chemical weapons', *Anniston Star* (Internet edn), 5 Apr. 1999, URL <http://www.annistonstar.com/news/news_19990405_6083.html>.

[43] ITAR-TASS (Moscow), 25 Jan. 1999, in 'Bad financing delays destruction of chemical weapons', FBIS-SOV-99-025, 26 Jan. 1999; and Nogov, M., 'Arsenal is a windfall for a spy', *Rossiyskaya Gazeta*, 26 Mar. 1999, p. 13, in 'Gorny CW destruction plant gets go-ahead', FBIS-SOV-1999-0331, 1 Apr. 1999.

[44] A state party must have destroyed 1% of its Category 1 CW (CW based on Schedule 1 chemicals) by the third year after entry into force of the CWC. It can make a request for postponement under Part IV(A), para. 22 of the Verification Annex to the CWC. Pending a request for further written information, the OPCW Executive Council's 17th session (30 Nov.–3 Dec.) deferred the matter to its 18th session before making a recommendation to the 5th CSP (May 2000). OPCW, *Secretariat Brief*, no. 20 (9 Dec. 1999).

[45] The plans for destruction of the Russian CW stockpile are discussed in Zanders, J. P. and Hart, J., 'Chemical and biological weapon developments and arms control', *SIPRI Yearbook 1998: Armaments, Disarmament and International Security* (Oxford University Press: Oxford, 1998), pp. 463–66; and Hart, J. and Miller, C. (eds), *Chemical Weapon Destruction in Russia: Political, Legal and Technical Aspects*, SIPRI Chemical & Biological Warfare Studies no. 17 (Oxford University Press: Oxford, 1998).

[46] Perera, J., 'Russia finally faces up to its CW legacy', *Jane's Intelligence Review*, vol. 11, no. 4 (Apr. 1999), p. 23.

[47] Babakin, A., 'Dual-purpose troops; they protect Russians from man-made accidents and are prepared to eliminate chemical weapons stocks and even to destroy locusts', *Rossiyskaya Gazeta*, 4 Mar. 1999, p. 13, in 'CW destruction methods viewed', FBIS-SOV-1999-0304, 5 Mar. 1999; and Livotkin, D., 'Stanislav Petrov: "We'll fulfill our commitments to the international community"' (Interview with Col.-Gen. Stanislav Petrov, Head of the Radiological, Chemical and Biological Defence Forces), *Yaderny Kontrol*, no. 9 (winter 1998/99), pp. 29–30.

[48] Scorobogatko (note 41).

[49] E.g., the walls of the large steel tanks in which most of the mustard and lewisite agent is stored are being consumed at an annual rate of 0.1–0.12 millimetres (mm). After 50 years of storage, their original thickness of 11 mm has been reduced by 5–6 mm, posing serious risks of structural weakness and leak-

of toxic pollutants is extremely high (in many cases several thousand times the permitted level), which has serious health implications.[50]

In order to meet the health and social needs of the local population, a part of the budget is slated for the development of regional infrastructure near the stockpile sites. On 22 September Prime Minister Vladimir Putin issued a government resolution establishing polyclinical consultative–diagnostic centres which will examine the health of citizens who live and work near CW storage and destruction sites. The financing of the project is to start in 2000, and its cost must be covered by the programme for the elimination of CW.[51]

In March the plan for the first CW destruction plant, to be located in Gorny, was approved by the State Commission of Environmental Experts, which appears to signal the possibility of compromise between the military and environmentalists.[52] Shchuchye and Kambarka were identified as the next two sites for plant construction.[53] In an effort to speed up the destruction process it was proposed that a mobile complex (the complex for the destruction of faulty chemical munitions, KUASI), operated by the Radiation, Chemical and Biological Defence Troops, be used for the destruction of malfunctioning special munitions.[54]

Russia has declared to the OPCW 24 former production facilities located in five regions: Berezniki, Perm region (1 facility); Chapayevsk (3 facilities); Dzerzhinsk, Nizhegorodskaya region (7 facilities); Novocheboksarsk, Chuvash Republic (5 facilities); and Volgograd (8 facilities).[55] The OPCW issued destruction certificates for 3 facilities: the pilot production plant for sarin, soman and VX and the corresponding filling facilities in Volgograd; a mustard production facility in Dzerzhinsk; and a lewisite plant in Chapayevsk. Destruction certificates for other installations are pending. Russia currently

---

age. (Artillery shells and tactical missile warheads, in contrast, are reportedly thick-walled and therefore better suited for long-term storage.) Belous, V. S. (Maj. Gen.) and Podberezkin, A. I., 'There is no alternative to chemical disarmament', *Nezavisimoye Voyennoye Obozreniye* (Moscow), 4–10 June 1999, p. 4, in 'Chemical weapons disarmament viewed', FBIS-SOV-1999-0626, 30 June 1999; and Perera (note 46), p. 24.

[50] Scorobogatko (note 41); Blackwood, Jr., M. E., 'Arsenic and old weapons: chemical weapons disposal in Russia', *Nonproliferation Review*, vol. 6, no. 3 (spring/summer 1999), p. 90; and Perera (note 46), pp. 24–27.

[51] Resolution of the Government of the Russian Federation, no. 1082, 22 Sep. 1999, *Rossiyskaya Gazeta*, 5 Oct. 1999, in 'New clinics for CW destruction, storage sites', FBIS-SOV-1999-1012, 19 Oct. 1999. Construction of housing, high-voltage power lines, water pipelines, purification systems and water pumping facilities (where not previously present) began in 1998 and continued in 1999. Livotkin (note 47), p. 30.

[52] Nogov (note 43).

[53] ITAR-TASS (Moscow), 25 Jan. 1999, in 'Bad financing delays destruction of chemical weapons', FBIS-SOV-99-025, 26 Jan. 1999. Gorny and Kambarka are the sites with the largest bulk holdings of mustard and lewisite agents, and there is growing fear of leakage of these agents.

[54] Babakin (note 47). The KUASI has already destroyed *c.* 400 tonnes of nerve agent from damaged munitions. It was demonstrated to international experts visiting Shikhany in 1987 and is described as an environmentally safe, closed technological cycle. It appears, however, that the proposal is part of a lobbying effort by the Russian NBC (nuclear, biological and chemical) Protection Troops to enhance its own role and to have the CW destruction plant in Chapayevsk (designed to utilize this technology) reopened. The facility was closed in 1989 before it was operational because of strong local opposition but was maintained and later used by OPCW inspector trainees.

[55] Utkina, S., Gorbovsky, A. and Zhuchkov, A., 'Russian views on conversion of former chemical weapons production facilities', *OPCW Synthesis*, no. 5 (Nov./Dec. 1999), pp. 1, 13–14.

uses 18 facilities for purposes not prohibited under the CWC and hopes to obtain permission from the OPCW to convert other facilities for such use, arguing that destruction would be economically and socially disadvantageous.

Russia has sought massive foreign aid in order to meet its CW destruction obligations. A growing list of Western countries provide such assistance, although the funding levels fall far short of the amount Russia requires.[56] Following discussions between German and Russian officials in Gorny in August 1999, it was announced that Germany will provide 44 million Deutschmarks ($23 million) for the destruction of CW at Gorny—in addition to the 21 million Deutschmarks ($11 million) contributed earlier to the project.[57] On 21 January 2000 it was announced that Italy would provide $8.3 million towards construction of the necessary infrastructure to destroy CW in the Udmurt Republic in 2000–2002.[58]

The USA, in the framework of the Cooperative Threat Reduction (CTR) programme,[59] has thus far been the major contributor. Destruction assistance, however, received a major setback in 1999: as of FY 2000 no CTR funds may be obligated or expended for planning, design or construction of a CW destruction facility in Russia. A maximum of $20 million may be obligated for security enhancements at CW storage sites. No CTR funds may be used for housing, environmental restoration or retraining.[60] This drastic reduction in funds—the Clinton Administration had requested $130.4 million, an increase of $44 million over the FY 1999 appropriation[61]—is largely because of a critical report by the US General Accounting Office (GAO) questioning Russia's ability to meet the CW destruction targets in Shchuchye. The GAO noted, among other things, that the project has fallen approximately 18 months behind schedule and will not begin operation until 2006. At the planned annual destruction rate of 500 tonnes, the goal of eliminating 95 per cent of the depot's 5600 tonnes of nerve agent would not be achieved before 2017. (The formal destruction deadline in the CWC is 2007 and can be extended until 2012 in special circumstances.) The GAO report also expressed doubt that, in the light of its economic difficulties, Russia will be able or willing to

[56] Zanders, French and Pauwels (note 5), pp. 573–75. Russia has sought foreign financial assistance for infrastructure improvements to better the lives of the people living near the CW destruction sites. Such measures would include hospitals, roads, water and sewage systems, retraining, etc. The view is that improvements would help overcome local resistance to CW destruction by providing benefits resulting from disarmament and new jobs to replace those lost by the closing of the CW facility. However, foreign donors have been reluctant to invest in programmes that are not directly related to destruction.

[57] Agence France Presse (AFP), (Moscow) via Lexis Nexis, 'Germany to finance Russian plant to destroy chemical weapons', 28 Aug. 1999.

[58] Federal News Service, 'Joint press briefing by Russian Foreign Minister Igor Ivanov and Italian Foreign Minister Lamberto Dini', Official Kremlin International News Broadcast, 21 Jan. 2000.

[59] The CTR programme is discussed in chapter 8 in this volume.

[60] National Defense Authorization Act for Fiscal Year 2000, Public Law 106-65, 5 Oct. 1999, Title XIII, Cooperative Threat Reduction with States of the Former Soviet Union, sections 1302, 1303 and 1305.

[61] National Defense Authorization Act for Fiscal Year 2000, Report of the Committee on Armed Services, House of Representatives on H.R. 1401, House of Representatives, 106th Congress, 1st Session, Report 106-162, 24 May 1999, p. 415.

invest the funds needed to destroy the CW at the other storage sites.[62] Other motivations for the reductions offered by members of the US Congress included the opinion that the Russian CW pose more of a local environmental hazard than a security threat to the USA; the conviction that the enhancement of security at the existing CW depots will contribute more to US security and non-proliferation goals than continued investment in destruction processes; and, most fundamentally, the belief that the assistance cannot meet the original CTR goals (i.e., assisting Russia to meet the CWC deadlines, encouraging other countries to provide assistance and advancing US non-proliferation goals).[63] The cut in US assistance led to publication of information on former Soviet CW production facilities and an appeal for international help in the OPCW publication *OPCW Synthesis*.[64]

Abandoned chemical weapons in China

According to the Japanese Ministry of Foreign Affairs, Japanese Army troops abandoned approximately 700 000 chemical munitions in China during their retreat at the end of World War II.[65] In July 1999 Japan and China signed a Memorandum of Understanding (MOU) on the destruction of abandoned chemical weapons in China. Both governments agreed to jointly select a mature destruction technology that is reliable in terms of destruction efficiency, safety and the environment. The location of the various destruction facilities has not been decided, but it is anticipated that destruction will be completed in accordance with the CWC time lines.[66] In order to meet its obligations under the CWC, Japan established the Office for Abandoned Chemical Weapons in the Prime Minister's Office on 1 April 1999. Its duties include study of the destruction technology and development of a destruction plan. Following the creation of this body the Japanese Government appropriated 809 million yen (*c.* $8 million) in the supplementary budget for FY 1999 and included 2.826 billion yen (*c.* $27 million) in the draft FY 2000 budget.[67]

III. Biological weapon disarmament

The Ad Hoc Group (AHG) of states parties to the BTWC continued to discuss a protocol with verification mechanisms and other legally binding measures to strengthen the convention. The AHG was established by the BTWC Special

---

[62] US General Accounting Office, *Weapons of Mass Destruction: Effort to Reduce Russian Arsenals May Cost More, Achieve Less Than Planned*, GAO/NSIAD-99-76, Apr. 1999, pp. 11–16.

[63] National Defense Authorization Act for Fiscal Year 2000 (note 61), pp. 415–17.

[64] Utkina, Gorbovsky and Zhuchkov (note 55).

[65] Ministry of Foreign Affairs of Japan, 'Budget for the destruction of abandoned chemical weapons in China', 24 Dec. 1999, URL <http://www.mofa.go.jp/announce/announce/1999/12/1224.html>. China maintains that the actual figure is almost 3 times as high. Zanders, French and Pauwels (note 5), p. 576.

[66] Ministry of Foreign Affairs of Japan, 'Signing of the Memorandum of Understanding between Japan and China on the Destruction of Abandoned Chemical Weapons in China', 30 July 1999, URL <http://www.mofa.go.jp/announce/announce/1999/7/730.html>.

[67] Ministry of Foreign Affairs of Japan (note 65).

Conference in 1994 and began its work in January 1995. It met five times in 1999.[68] The negotiations were assisted by the Friends of the Chair (FoC), who facilitate the discussions on specific issues.[69] Although the discussions moved towards establishing a final framework for the protocol and key elements of it were negotiated in detail, there was a growing sense of stagnation at the end of 1999.

The delegations have expressed their positions and preferences on the various outstanding issues (these are enclosed in brackets in the rolling text of the draft protocol). Without true negotiations that will lead to compromises and so-called 'package deals' progress appears impossible. Some states—most of which belong to the non-aligned movement (NAM)[70]—seek acceptance of their positions before they are willing to enter endgame negotiations. So far this has only led to reiteration of previously stated positions. In contrast, the EU adopted a position in May that endorsed strong and effective compliance measures.[71] However, the USA's non-committal stance on the future protocol, evidenced by its reservations regarding verification of the biotechnology industry, created a deepening division in the Western Group (the regional group which has the largest share of relevant industries and research institutes). The members of the North Atlantic Treaty Organization (NATO) formally endorsed the negotiations at NATO's 50th anniversary summit meeting in Washington in April and called for completion of the negotiations before the Fifth Review Conference of the BTWC to be held in 2001.[72]

The draft protocol envisages the creation of an international body: the Organization for the Prohibition of Bacteriological (Biological) and Toxin Weapons (OPBTW).[73] It is modelled on the OPCW and the Comprehensive Nuclear Test-Ban Treaty Organization (CTBTO). The OPBTW would consist of a Conference of States Parties, an Executive Council and a Technical Secre-

---

[68] The 13th session was held on 4–22 Jan., the 14th on 29 Mar.–9 Apr., the 15th on 28 June–23 July, the 16th on 13 Sep.–8 Oct., and the 17th on 22 Nov.–10 Dec.

[69] Following the 15th session FoC papers with proposals for further consideration (which have been included as Part II of the Procedural Report since Oct. 1998) were for the first time structured according to the draft protocol, with strike-through text indicating deletions and bold text denoting additions. Pearson, G. S., 'Strengthening the Biological and Toxin Weapons Convention', *CBW Conventions Bulletin*, no. 46 (Dec. 1999), p. 5.

[70] A list of the NAM members is given in the glossary in this volume.

[71] European Union, Common Position of 17 May 1999 adopted by the Council on the basis of Article 15 of the Treaty on European Union, relating to progress towards a legally binding Protocol to strengthen compliance with the Biological and Toxin Weapons Convention (BTWC), and with a view to the successful completion of substantive work in the Ad Hoc Group by the end of 1999, *Official Journal*, L 133 (28 May 1999), pp. 3–4. The document was also endorsed by an additional 13 states, including the states associated to the EU and other states. Pearson, G. S., 'Strengthening the Biological and Toxin Weapons Convention', *CBW Conventions Bulletin*, no. 45 (Sep. 1999), p. 14. Despite the joint declaration some EU members which have a large biotechnology industry (e.g., Germany) hold positions similar to that of the USA with respect to a strong compliance regime.

[72] NATO, Washington Summit Communiqué, 'An alliance for the 21st century', Press Release NAC-S(99)64, 24 Apr. 1999, para. 35; and NATO Press Release M-NAC2(99)166, 15 Dec. 1999, para. 43. Excerpts from the Washington Summit Communiqué are reproduced in appendix 4A in this volume.

[73] Procedural Report of the Ad Hoc Group of the States Parties to the Convention on the Prohibition of the Development, Production and Stockpiling of Bacteriological (Biological) and Toxin Weapons and on Their Destruction, Ad Hoc Group document BWC/AD HOC GROUP/47 (Part I), 15 Oct. 1999, Article IX.

tariat. The Netherlands and Switzerland have made formal offers to host the organization.

As in 1998 Article II of the draft protocol, dealing with definitions and criteria, Article III on compliance measures (which will establish the future verification regime) and Article VII on scientific and technological exchanges continued to be politically contentious. At the end of 1999 the title of Article II of the draft protocol remained in brackets because there is considerable disagreement regarding its content. Most AHG participants are concerned that explicit definition of biological and toxin weapons is tantamount to amendment of Article I of the BTWC and not in accordance with the procedures of Article XI of the convention, which specifies the amendment procedure. They also fear that defining the terms too exactly may restrict the scope of the protocol too much. Other participants claim that defining the terms is essential for unambiguous implementation of the protocol and would not have the effect of amending the BTWC.[74]

Compliance mechanisms

The draft Article III envisages three compliance mechanisms: declarations, visits and investigations. The declarations to be submitted by the parties to the OPBTW would contain information on past offensive and defensive biological weapon (BW) programmes, current activities and relevant facilities. The on-site visits are intended to ensure the completeness and correctness of the submitted declarations and to generate confidence in the compliance of other states parties. In contrast, investigations would address cases of suspected non-compliance. Following the 13th AHG session, in January 1999, visits and investigations were treated separately; this is important as the former activities are non-confrontational and intended to generate transparency and build confidence, whereas the latter are accusatory.[75] Like similar provisions of the CWC, draft Article III also contains language that encourages or compels parties to submit timely declarations.[76]

The discussions on the declaration formats have made steady progress. The formats are designed so that parties will not have to reveal commercial secrets or national security information.[77] However, there are divisions of opinion with respect to the 'declaration triggers' (i.e., the minimum level of production or consumption of certain treaty-relevant commodities that requires declaration) as these are directly linked to the definition of facilities that have legit-

[74] Procedural Report . . . (note 73), Article II, fn 4.

[75] Procedural Report of the Ad Hoc Group of the States Parties to the Convention on the Prohibition of the Development, Production and Stockpiling of Bacteriological (Biological) and Toxin Weapons and on Their Destruction, Ad Hoc Group document BWC/AD HOC GROUP/44 (Part I), 29 Jan. 1999, Article III, D, Part II and Article III, G.

[76] Procedural Report of the Ad Hoc Group of the States Parties to the Convention on the Prohibition of the Development, Production and Stockpiling of Bacteriological (Biological) and Toxin Weapons and on Their Destruction, Ad Hoc Group document BWC/AD HOC GROUP/46 (Part I), 30 July 1999, Article III, D, III.

[77] Pearson, G. S., 'The BTWC protocol enters the endgame', *Disarmament Diplomacy*, no. 39 (July/Aug. 1999), p. 8.

imate purposes under the BTWC. It is often difficult to distinguish between permitted and prohibited purposes on the basis of the technologies (goods, equipment, tools, skills, knowledge, and so on) used in a particular facility because most have a dual-use potential. However, there is broad agreement on the inclusion of certain categories such as facilities operating at the highest biosafety level,[78] facilities involved in biological defence programmes or activities, vaccine production facilities, and facilities working with biological agents and toxins that are listed in an annexe to the protocol. The exact definitions of the categories are still under discussion; agreement has not been achieved on the category 'other production facilities'.[79]

Visits to provide confidence that declarations are accurate are arguably one of the most controversial aspects of the draft protocol. Not only are there differences of opinion between the regional groups in the AHG, but the Western Group has also been unable to present a unified position. The latest draft protocol outlines three types of visit: (a) visits to clarify declarations; (b) mandatory visits, with annual quota ceilings, to randomly selected facilities in order to follow up on declarations; and (c) voluntary visits to assist in compiling individual facility or national declarations, to resolve ambiguities in declarations, to encourage further assistance and cooperation or to resolve a particular concern.[80]

The protocol would benefit greatly from a strong compliance regime. This implies a central role for the randomly selected visits, which must be intrusive to be effective. Differences about the degree of intrusiveness have split the Western Group; the three countries with the highest number of relevant facilities—Germany, Japan and the USA—oppose strong measures.[81] The USA (which faces strong opposition to the proposed verification mechanisms from its pharmaceutical industry, but which also has extensive BW defence programmes) is the least willing to accept randomly selected visits, even to the point of opposing a British alternative proposal of 'transparency visits' which was put forward in the Western Group during preparation for the 16th session of the AHG.[82] When the USA signalled that it might accept the proposal if

---

[78] Biosafety levels (BL1–BL4) classify health and safety controls for work with different types of biological material. BL4 is the highest containment level and BL1 the lowest. They have been adopted by the World Health Organization (WHO). WHO, *Laboratory Biosafety Manual* (WHO: Geneva, 1983), pp. 3–5.

[79] Wilson, H., 'Strengthening the BWC: issues for the Ad Hoc Group', *Disarmament Diplomacy*, no. 42 (Dec. 1999), p. 31.

[80] Procedural Report . . . (note 73), Article III, D, II. No new rolling text was produced after the 17th session and the discussion papers were produced separately. 'Ad Hoc Group 17th session', Biological and Toxin Weapons Convention (BTWC) Database, Department of Peace Studies, University of Bradford, URL <http://www.brad.ac.uk/acad/sbtwc/ahg49/ahg49.htm>. In the Ad Hoc Group document BWC/AD HOC GROUP/44 (Part I), 29 Jan. 1999, and in subsequent documents, 'randomly-selected' visits replaces the previously used term 'random' visits.

[81] Germany, however, also subscribed to the EU common position with respect to randomly selected visits. European Union (note 71).

[82] In a letter dated 24 May 1999, US Secretary of Commerce William Daley wrote to Secretary of State Madeleine Albright: 'I still believe that we should continue to oppose random and routine visits, including "transparency visits". . . . Our best experts, including the intelligence community and many of those who participated in the Iraq inspections, continue to tell us that, regardless of how intrusive we make an inspection regime, there is virtually no chance of discovering biological weapons activities.

there were unanimous approval for it in the group, there was strong pressure to adopt it as a common Western Group proposal.[83] However, several members of the group remained dissatisfied with the compromise.

When the NAM Group submitted a working paper on visits, which included stronger measures than the British transparency visits,[84] some Western states (e.g., Australia, the Netherlands, New Zealand and Norway) publicly welcomed the document as providing a helpful contribution to stimulating negotiations on this issue. (Other Western countries objected to this public display of internal division in the Western Group.) Some other elements of the NAM proposal were unacceptable to the entire Western Group.[85] However, the greatest relevance of the NAM working paper may be that it prepared the way for the possibility of compromise in the final stage of the negotiations between compliance measures, which are important to the West, and technical cooperation, in which developing countries have strong interest. The NAM working document also showed that under South Africa's coordination a degree of unanimity in the negotiation group on the issue of compliance had been achieved, although some members, including China, have reportedly not accepted every aspect of the proposal.

The draft protocol distinguishes between two types of investigation. Facility investigations can be initiated in the case of suspicion of illicit activities inside an installation. Field investigations can be launched if BW use is suspected. At the end of 1999 two major issues remained unresolved. First, agreement was not reached on whether the Executive Council of the OPBTW would decide on launching an investigation using the 'red light' or the 'green light' procedure.[86] The opposing views reflect the concern that the procedure may be abused. Second, there is concern that under the currently proposed mechanisms a field investigation might turn into a facility investigation if, during the field investigation, an unnatural outbreak of disease were to occur that might

They are simply too easy to move, conceal, or even sanitize within hours—without leaving a trace. . . . I seriously question a negotiating strategy of attempting to mollify the most hard-line members of the Western Group. . . . We have repeatedly assured US industry that we oppose random and routine on-site activities.' Quoted in Hatch Rosenberg, B., 'Bioterrorism or prevention?', *ASA Newsletter*, no. 74 (27 Aug. 1999), p. 12. This letter was written shortly after the EU Common Position was announced. European Union (note 71).

[83] Wilson (note 79), p. 33.

[84] Proposed text for visits, Working paper submitted by the NAM and other states, Ad Hoc Group document BWC/AD HOC GROUP/WP.402, 22 Sep. 1999.

[85] E.g., the NAM proposed that all types of visit, including voluntary visits and invitations for voluntary assistance, be included in an annual quota of visits. If the quota is exceeded, then the Director-General of the OPBTW 'shall reduce the provision for randomly-selected visits in order to accommodate the extra voluntary assistance and/or voluntary clarification visits correspondingly'. This proposal would weaken the whole compliance regime as the provisions for voluntary visits are weaker than those for clarification visits. Proposed text for visits (note 84), paras 5, 7; and Wilson (note 79), p. 33.

[86] The CWC contains the so-called red-light and the Comprehensive Nuclear Test-Ban Treaty (CTBT) the green-light procedure. Under the red-light procedure an inspection would go ahead unless a majority voted against it; under the green-light procedure initiation of a challenge inspection would require a majority vote. For further discussion, see Klotz, L. C. and Sims, M. C., 'The BWC: challenge investigation voting procedures', *CBW Conventions Bulletin*, no. 41 (Sep. 1998), pp. 1, 3.

plausibly be linked to the facility.[87] In particular, there is concern that a field investigation might facilitate access that would have been harder to obtain if the request had been for a facility investigation.

Technical cooperation and development

The question of the right to technical cooperation and development as part of arms control or disarmament treaties has been a politically sensitive issue since the entry into force of the 1968 Treaty on the Non-Proliferation of Nuclear Weapons (Non-Proliferation Treaty, NPT). Article X of the BTWC deals with opportunities for technology transfers and technical cooperation for peaceful purposes among parties and requests them to implement the convention in a manner so as not to hamper the economic development of other parties. Article VII of the draft protocol attempts to implement the commitment. However, the discussions remain closely tied to the debate on the role of export controls, and of the Australia Group (AG) in particular, under the future BTWC regime.[88] The experience of implementation of the CWC has somewhat reinforced the convictions of the opposing sides in the debate: certain developing countries argue that the AG participants have not changed their export control regulations since the entry into force of the CWC despite a treaty obligation to review them,[89] while many industrialized states note that numerous parties have not yet enacted national legislation to implement the CWC, so that it is impossible to track transactions in accordance with the transfer mechanisms in the CWC.

In 1999 considerably more attention was paid to Article VII of the draft protocol than in the past. The argument that transparency with respect to technology transactions enhances confidence in the compliance of states parties gained wider currency. As a result, some progress was made. The idea of a Cooperation Committee as a subsidiary body of the OPBTW to oversee the implementation of Article X of the BTWC and Article VII of the draft protocol was introduced by the NAM at the 13th session[90] and subsequently endorsed by the Netherlands and New Zealand at the 14th session.[91] By the

[87] An example is a case similar to the accidental release of anthrax from Sverdlovsk (now Yekaterinburg) in the former Soviet Union in 1979, when more than 60 people downwind of a military installation died.

[88] This debate originates with the tension between the generic non-proliferation obligation in Article III and the cooperation commitments in Article X of the BTWC. Some 30 states coordinate their national export control regulations within the AG, an informal consultative arrangement set up in 1985 in the wake of the confirmation of Iraq's use of CW in the 1980–88 Iraq–Iran War. In the late 1980s the commonly agreed export control lists were gradually expanded to include biological warfare agents and dual-use technologies of relevance to the manufacture of BW. These issues are discussed in Anthony, I. and Zanders, J. P., 'Multilateral security-related export controls', *SIPRI Yearbook 1998* (note 45), pp. 386–94.

[89] Several AG participants have, in fact, reviewed their national export control regulations and concluded that they conform to their CWC obligations.

[90] Establishment of a Cooperation Committee, Working paper submitted by the NAM and other states, Ad Hoc Group document BWC/AD HOC GROUP/WP.349, Jan. 1999.

[91] BWC Article X/Protocol Article VII, Working paper submitted by the Netherlands and New Zealand, Ad Hoc Group document BWC/AD HOC GROUP/WP.362, 6 Apr. 1999, para. I.

end of the 17th session the AHG (with the exception of the USA) had accepted the idea, but agreement was not reached on the committee's structure and mandate. Australia, France, Germany, Sweden, Switzerland and the UK circulated a 'non-paper' outlining the position of a Cooperation Committee within the OPBTW and its powers with respect to making recommendations.[92] The NAM members preferred a stronger mandate for the new body than the one suggested in the non-paper, but they nevertheless welcomed the document as a useful first step in the concrete implementation of Article X of the BTWC.[93]

The increasingly cooperative atmosphere on the issue of non-proliferation and technical cooperation was further encouraged at the end of the 16th session of the AHG, when the NAM submitted a working paper on measures to strengthen Article III of the BTWC (which contains the generic non-proliferation obligation).[94] This explicit recognition of the relevance of Article III and the attempt to strike a balance between the non-proliferation obligations and the avoidance of 'measures that hamper the peaceful economic and technological development of States Parties'[95] were welcomed by the Western Group. Although the document was a NAM paper distributed as a contribution to assist further negotiation, it reportedly does not reflect the national positions of all the NAM members.[96] Nevertheless, as with the working paper on visits, it may prove to be an important building block once the endgame negotiations begin.

IV. Proliferation concerns

In 1999 several statements were made with respect to CBW proliferation. According to the Russian Federation's Foreign Intelligence Service (Sluzhba Vneshney Razvedki, SVR) 25 countries, many of which are located close to Russia's borders, have or are developing various types of non-conventional weaponry.[97] The US Central Intelligence Agency (CIA) and Arms Control and Disarmament Agency (ACDA) claim that at least 16 states currently have active CW programmes and as many as 12 countries are claimed to be pursuing offensive BW programmes.[98] The following states are alleged to have an offensive BW capability or to be in the process of seeking such a capability: China, Egypt, Iran, Iraq, Libya, Russia and Syria. North Korea may

---

[92] A non-paper is a note circulated to delegations that has not been formally introduced as a working document or country position.

[93] Wilson (note 79), p. 30.

[94] Measures to strengthen the implementation of Article III of the Convention, Working paper submitted by the NAM and other States, Ad Hoc Group document BWC/AD HOC GROUP/WP.407, 8 Oct. 1999.

[95] Measures to strengthen the implementation of Article III of the Convention (note 94).

[96] Wilson (note 79), p. 30.

[97] Belous and Podberezkin (note 49).

[98] Lauder, J. A., Special Assistant to the Director of Central Intelligence for Nonproliferation, 'Unclassified statement for the record on the worldwide WMD threat to the Commission to Assess the Organization of the Federal Government to Combat the Proliferation of Weapons of Mass Destruction', 29 Apr. 1999, URL <http://www.odci.gov/cia/public_affairs/speeches/archives/1999/lauder_speech_042999.html>.

be able to wage biological warfare. Sudan may be interested in acquiring BW, and there is insufficient evidence to determine whether Taiwan is conducting activities prohibited under the BTWC. Iran, Iraq, North Korea, Libya, Sudan and Syria are also alleged to be acquiring chemical weapons.[99] This section highlights the CBW proliferation debate.[100]

The NATO Weapons of Mass Destruction Initiative

NATO views the proliferation of non-conventional weapons as a major security concern. At the Washington summit meeting celebrating its 50th anniversary, the alliance launched its Weapons of Mass Destruction (WMD) Initiative to respond to the security threats posed by nuclear, biological and chemical weapons (NBC) and their means of delivery. The WMD Initiative will integrate the political and military aspects of the NATO response to proliferation. It will also create a WMD Centre within the International Staff at NATO Headquarters in Brussels to coordinate activities related to non-conventional weapons, including political consultations and efforts to improve defence preparedness. The centre is expected to be established in early 2000, but its tasks had not yet been fully defined at the end of 1999. The creation of an intelligence and information database on non-conventional weapons in order to improve the quality and increase the quantity of intelligence and information-sharing among NATO members was also considered.[101] The WMD Initiative is the concretization of the NATO ministerial guidance and force goals adopted in 1996 and 1997.[102]

The Washington summit meeting statement stressed that 'the principal non-proliferation goal of the alliance and its members is to prevent proliferation from occurring, or, should it occur, to reverse it through diplomatic means'.[103] The position does not preclude military preparedness: NATO's new Strategic Concept calls for a balanced mix of forces, response capabilities and strengthened defences 'to address appropriately and effectively' the proliferation risks.[104] The Strategic Concept explicitly excludes a biological or chemical warfare capability for NATO, but stresses that 'defensive precautions will

---

[99] US Arms Control and Disarmament Agency, 'Adherence to and compliance with arms control agreements', 1998 report submitted to the Congress, Washington, DC, 1999, URL <http://state.gov/www/global/arms/reports/annual/comp98.html>; and US Central Intelligence Agency, Nonproliferation Center, 'Unclassified report to Congress on the acquisition of technology relating to weapons of mass destruction and advanced conventional munitions, 1 January through 30 June 1999', Washington, DC, Feb. 2000, URL <http://www.odci.gov/cia/publications/bian/bian_feb_2000.html>.

[100] CBW terrorism and the future of the disarmament of Iraq are discussed in appendices 9A and 9B.

[101] NATO, Washington Summit Communiqué (note 72), para. 31; and NATO, 'Final Communiqué of the Meeting of the North Atlantic Council in Defence Ministers Session held in Brussels', Press Release, M-NAC-D(99)156 (2 Dec. 1999), para. 20.

[102] Zanders, J. P. and Hart, J., 'Chemical and biological weapon developments and arms control', *SIPRI Yearbook 1998* (note 45), pp. 476–77.

[103] NATO, Washington Summit Communiqué (note 72), para. 30.

[104] NATO, 'The Alliance's Strategic Concept', Press Release NAC-S(99)65, 24 Apr. 1999, para. 53, h.

remain essential' even if further progress with respect to banning CBW can be achieved.[105]

BW concerns regarding Russia

Doubts about the termination of Russia's BW programme, as decreed by then President Boris Yeltsin in April 1992, persisted in 1999. An analysis based on multiple political and economic parameters published by the Swedish Defence Research Establishment (FOA) in December concluded that the retention of a biological warfare capability appears to be the current policy choice. Factors that may contribute to a continuation of the offensive BW programme include the enduring social and economic crisis, a further deterioration of relations with the West and with Russia's neighbours, a continuing focus on the re-establishment of Russia's status as a superpower, and the prospect of an inefficient protocol to the BTWC.[106] A former high-ranking official of the Soviet BW programme, Dr Ken Alibek, who now lives in the USA, has claimed that the military stockpiles of biological warfare agents have been destroyed but that research into (genetically modified) pathogens for offensive military use continues.[107] He has revealed many details of the Soviet BW programme and its underlying motives.[108]

Of particular concern is the dominance of former military personnel in key positions in microbiological research and development (R&D) establishments and the biopharmaceutical industry. Despite the transfer of the State Concern Biopreparat to the Ministry of Health in 1992 and later to the Ministry of the Economy (previously the Ministry of Industry), the organization apparently retained its Soviet-era director and most of its military personnel.[109] Biopreparat personnel also occupy a prominent position in the civilian biopharmaceutical sector.[110] The conversion of the organization—which employs some 40 000 personnel, including 9000 scientists and engineers—to legitimate civilian purposes appears problematic and, according to the FOA report, thus far to have been essentially cosmetic.[111]

---

[105] NATO (note 104), para. 57.
[106] Lilja, P., Roffey, R. and Westerdahl, K. S., *Disarmament or Retention: Is the Soviet Biological Weapons Programme Continuing in Russia?* (Swedish Defence Research Establishment (FOA): Umeå, Dec. 1999), p. 10; and Tucker, J. B., 'Biological weapons in the former Soviet Union: an interview with Dr Kenneth Alibek', *Nonproliferation Review*, vol. 6, no. 3 (spring/summer 1999), p. 9.
[107] Tucker (note 106), pp. 6, 8.
[108] Alibek, K., *Biohazard* (Hutchinson: London, 1999).
[109] The Biopreparat organization was established in 1973—1 year after the opening for signature of the BTWC—by the Communist Party Central Committee. It was funded by the Ministry of Defence but placed under the civilian Main Administration of the Microbiological Industry (Glavmikrobioprom). Tucker, J. B., 'Biological weapons proliferation from Russia: how great a threat?', Remarks to the 7th Carnegie International Non-Proliferation Conference, 11–12 Jan. 1999, Carnegie Endowment for International Peace, Washington, DC, URL <http://www.ceip.org/programs/npp/tucker.htm>. The entire Soviet BW programme reportedly involved 60 000–70 000 people. Tucker (note 106), p. 5.
[110] Rimmington, A., 'Fragmentation and proliferation? The fate of the Soviet Union's offensive biological weapons programme', *Contemporary Security Policy*, vol. 20, no. 1 (Apr. 1999), p. 93. Rosmedprom, which represents over 70 pharmaceutical companies and acts as interlocutor with government agencies, apparently shares the same headquarters.
[111] Lilja, Roffey and Westerdahl (note 106), p. 44.

The dire social and professional conditions in which the former BW specialists currently live significantly increase the risk of a 'brain drain' to countries that may be interested in acquiring BW. Since Yeltsin's 1992 decree the BW-related establishments have laid off large numbers of personnel, while the remaining staff work under Spartan conditions and often go without pay for long periods.[112] The feared mass exodus of BW scientists and technicians does not appear to have materialized, although some BW specialists are known to have sought contracts abroad.[113] Furthermore, because the former Soviet BW-relevant research installations continue to be largely controlled by the military, they may still be engaged in the development of an offensive capability in violation of the BTWC.

International assistance for BW conversion in Russia

In order to employ these experts in R&D programmes permitted under the BTWC, a number of programmes were launched in the 1990s. Several countries (the EU states, Japan, South Korea, Norway and the USA) provide money to support such programmes through the International Science and Technology Centre (ISTC) in Moscow.[114] In a separate initiative, the US National Academy of Sciences runs a cooperative research programme on dangerous pathogens, which is funded through the CTR programme, in order to identify further opportunities for the conversion of BW-related facilities and equipment and to create opportunities for the US biotechnology industry to invest in Russia.[115] The US Department of Energy (DOE) also manages the Initiatives for Proliferation Prevention (IPP) programme, which involves collaborative activities among the DOE national laboratories, US industry partners and institutes in the former Soviet Union.[116]

However, investment in these initiatives remains modest, especially as they seek to address clear violations of a major disarmament treaty. The four US-sponsored programmes spent a total of $310.3 million on 1733 collaborative research projects between 1994 and 1998. Of that sum only $26 million went to biotechnology (178 projects) and $11.3 million to chemistry grants (69 projects). The remaining funds are targeted at experts who previously developed nuclear and missile technology.[117] By the end of 1998 only 9.8 per cent of the total funds of the ISTC programme ($18.5 million) had been approved for projects related to biotechnology.[118] Thirty per cent of the IPP programme funds ($22.5 million for FY 1999) are earmarked for chemical and

---

[112] Smithson, A. E., *Toxic Archipelago: Preventing Proliferation from the Former Soviet Chemical and Biological Weapons Complexes*, Report no. 32 (Henry L. Stimson Center: Washington, DC, Dec. 1999), p. 16.

[113] Tucker (note 106), p. 6.

[114] The initiative dates from Nov. 1992, but the State Duma did not consider the agreement until late 1993 so the Board of Governors first met in Mar. 1994. Smithson (note 112), p. 22, fn. 68.

[115] Lilja, Roffey and Westerdahl (note 106), p. 38.

[116] US General Accounting Office, *Nuclear Nonproliferation: Concerns with DOE's Efforts to Reduce the Risks Posed by Russia's Unemployed Weapons Scientists*, Report GAO/RCED-99-54, Feb. 1999, pp. 15, 19, 34. See also chapter 8 in this volume.

[117] Smithson (note 112), p. x.

[118] Lilja, Roffey and Westerdahl (note 106), p. 37.

biological projects.[119] From the perspective of the Russian institutes the funds appear minimal. For example, although the Vektor Centre for Virology and Biotechnology accounts for a high proportion of the ISTC funds allocated, the amount is only 1 per cent of the centre's total income.[120] Several analysts have therefore called for significant increases in support for research projects that would engage the skills of BW specialists for purposes permitted under the BTWC as a highly cost-effective way to prevent BW proliferation.[121]

Despite the modest sums involved, the programmes have been criticized. In 1998 funding for US cooperative initiatives on BW-related projects was halved to $7 million because of doubts about Russian compliance with the BTWC and in response to Russian nuclear and missile technology sales to Iran.[122] Funding levels may be expected to decrease significantly in 2000. In a critical note on the IPP programme, the US GAO noted that the programme 'has not achieved its broader nonproliferation goal of long-term employment [for Russian scientists] through the commercialization of projects' and that some scientists currently working on Russia's non-conventional weapons are receiving IPP funds.[123] The FOA report also noted that none of the six facilities under the Russian Ministry of Defence that are known to the West has applied for international conversion funds and that thus far no Western experts have been allowed to visit them.[124]

The past South African CBW programme

The trial of Dr Wouter Basson, the principal figure in South Africa's CBW programme, Project Coast, began on 4 October 1999.[125] In response to the CBW threats believed to have been posed by the war in Angola in the late 1980s Basson was tasked with collecting information on foreign CBW programmes. His initial investigation revealed that the existing international norms against these weapons were totally inadequate, had not kept abreast of scientific developments and lacked effective control measures.[126] Basson faces multiple charges of fraud, murder and conspiracy to murder, and possession of drugs (ecstasy, mandrax and cocaine). With respect to Project Coast, Basson is

[119] US General Accounting Office (note 116).

[120] Lilja, Roffey and Westerdahl (note 106), p. 38. Vektor used to be 90% financed by the Ministry of Defence but now generates 80% of its income through commercial contracts, which involve pre-packing and quality control of drugs. However, the institute has serious problems in funding basic research.

[121] Lilja, Roffey and Westerdahl (note 106), pp. 36–40; Rimmington (note 110), p. 100; and Smithson (note 112).

[122] Miller, J. and Broad, W. J., 'Germ weapons: in Soviet past or in the new Russia's future?', *New York Times* (Internet edn), 28 Dec. 1998, URL <http://www.nytimes.com/library/world/europe/122898 germ-warfare.html>.

[123] US General Accounting Office (note 116), pp. 5–6.

[124] Lilja, Roffey and Westerdahl (note 106), p. 39. The institutes are: Institute of Microbiology, Kirov; Institute of Military Medicine, St Petersburg; Institute of Technical Military Problems, Yekaterinburg (formerly Sverdlovsk); Strizhi, Kirov *oblast*; Virology Institute, Sergiyev Posad (formerly Zagorsk); and Vozrazhdenie Island, Aralsk, Kazakhstan.

[125] For more details about Project Coast see Zanders, French and Pauwels (note 5), pp. 583–85.

[126] The then existing international norms against CBW were the 1925 Geneva Protocol, which prohibits the (first) use of chemical and biological warfare agents in war among the contracting parties, and the BTWC, which currently has no verification mechanisms.

accused of having posed as a prosperous businessman as part of a scheme to enrich himself rather than having acted in the interest of the South African National Defence Forces (SANDF).[127] In November the court heard testimony by former Surgeon General and manager of Project Coast General Niel Knobel on the origins of South Africa's CBW programme. The court also heard testimony that, on 7 January 1993, a ministerial decision was taken to transfer all of the technology and research to CD-ROM and to destroy all paper documents. However, in January 1997, following Basson's arrest, it emerged that he had kept highly classified technological and scientific documents related to Project Coast in two steel trunks.[128] More details about the organization of the CBW programme are expected to be learned with the continuation of the trial in 2000.

CBW proliferation concerns in North Korea

In 1999 the uncertainties about North Korea's security policies deepened and increased the concern about its non-conventional weapon capabilities, including CBW. A November 1999 US congressional report on North Korea criticized the Clinton Administration's programmes for aid to North Korea and highlighted the North Korean armament programmes; it noted with respect to CW that 'it is not the types of agents or stockpile levels that have attracted the most attention, but rather the assumed efforts to develop CW warheads for its Nodong and Taepo Dong ballistic missiles'.[129] The report assessed the evolving BW threat in similar terms: the new generation of long-range missiles is able to reach Japan and US military installations in the western Pacific and is alleged to be able to reach the US mainland in the near future.[130]

North Korea is believed to have stockpiled a broad range of chemical and biological warfare agents and to have many types of delivery systems, including artillery shells, multiple rocket launchers, rockets (Free Rocket Over Ground, FROG) and ballistic missiles (Scud and Rodong I), aerial bombs and spray tanks. Although the report noted that there is no public evidence that North Korea has undertaken the development of genetically engineered biological warfare agents, it stated that it is 'reasonable to assume that [it] will explore this avenue to the extent possible', because the US DOD 'was openly discussing interest in such agents 30 years ago'.[131]

According to a 1999 White Paper by the South Korean Ministry of National Defense, North Korea maintains eight CW production factories, four research and six storage facilities for CW, as well as 'many facilities' for producing BW. It also alleged that North Korea will attempt to maintain its CBW pro-

---

[127] Basson trial, week 3 report, 29 Oct. 1999, prepared and distributed by Chandré Gould and Marlene Burger, Centre for Conflict Resolution, University of Cape Town.

[128] Basson trial, week 7 report, 25 Nov. 1999, prepared and distributed by Chandré Gould and Marlene Burger, Centre for Conflict Resolution, University of Cape Town.

[129] North Korea Advisory Group, 'Report to the Speaker US House of Representatives', Nov. 1999, chapter 1, B, URL <http://www.house.gov/international_relations/nkag/report.htm>.

[130] See also chapters 8 and 11 in this volume.

[131] North Korea Advisory Group (note 129).

duction capabilities in spite of the serious economic difficulties and the strengthening global norms against such weapons because of, among other reasons, their low production cost.[132] The paper referred to the figure cited in the April 1997 CBW threat re-evaluation which indicated that the amount of chemical munitions has increased from 1000 tons to 2500–5000 tons and that North Korea possesses more than 10 types of BW, including anthrax.[133]

Other proliferation concerns

Iraq remains a major source of concern.[134] The United States continues to view Iran as a major CBW proliferation threat. The CIA claims that Iran remains one of the most active countries seeking technologies for non-conventional weapons abroad. Iran allegedly began a BW programme during the 1980–88 Iraq–Iran War and may now have a limited capability for BW deployment. A 1999 CIA report noted that, although Iran is a party to the CWC, it has manufactured and stockpiled chemical weapons—including blister, blood and choking agents and the bombs and artillery shells for delivering them—and continues to seek the technology to create a more advanced and self-sufficient CW infrastructure.[135] In January 2000 the US House of Representatives passed the Iran Nonproliferation Act, which is aimed at deterring states, particularly Russia, from providing assistance to Iran's non-conventional weapon programmes.[136] According to a London newsletter, the Israeli intelligence organization Mossad has reportedly estimated that as many as 10 000 Russian scientists may be working on covert non-conventional weapon programmes in Iran following a dedicated recruitment effort.[137] The Iranian Government has denied all such allegations.

In Sudan, the Sudan People's Liberation Army (SPLA) accused the government of using CW to bomb Lanya and Kaya on 23 July. The UN sent a team of doctors to aid the victims of the attack, and the Norwegian People's Aid agency reportedly confirmed that an attack had occurred.[138] The government denied the allegation and refused to accept an international investigation of the charges unless the United States accepted an investigation into the 1998 US

[132] South Korea, Ministry of National Defense, *Defense White Paper 1999* (Ministry of National Defense: Seoul, 1999), p. 57.
[133] South Korea (note 132), p. 84. The document does not indicate whether the CW weight estimates refer to the agent filling or the complete munition. Press reports, however, presented the estimates of the increase as a new development. E.g., 'Pulling out the stops: N. Korea beefs up its military', *Newsreview*, vol. 28, no. 42 (16 Oct. 1999), p. 8. The North Korea Advisory Group also quotes the 1997 South Korean CW estimate of 5000 tonnes. North Korea Advisory Group (note 129).
[134] The status of the dismantlement of its CBW programme under UN supervision is discussed in appendix 9B in this volume.
[135] US Central Intelligence Agency, Nonproliferation Center, 'Unclassified report to Congress on the acquisition of technology relating to weapons of mass destruction and advanced conventional munitions, 1 January through 30 June 1999', URL <http://www.odci.gov/cia/publications/bian/bian_feb_2000.html>.
[136] Iran Nonproliferation Act of 2000, H.R. 1883, 24 Jan. 2000. It is reproduced at URL <http://thomas.loc.gov/cgi-bin/query/C?c106:./temp/~c106NHJK5t>.
[137] The newsletter is cited in '21 January', *CBW Conventions Bulletin*, no. 43 (Mar. 1999), p. 43.
[138] Achieng, J., 'UN doctors sent to treat victims of "chemical-bombs" in Sudan', CNN, 17 Aug. 1999, URL <http://www.cnn.com>.

bombing of the Al Shifa pharmaceutical plant.[139] Investigators retained by the owner of the plant, Saleh Idris, found no evidence of CW compounds in soil samples and he sued the USA for damages. The US Administration defended its decision despite questions about whether or not chemical warfare agents had been present in the soil samples that were clandestinely obtained by the CIA and which prompted the attack.[140]

According to Alibek, Cuba established a BW programme in the early 1980s. He alleged that Soviet assistance enabled Cuba to set up a sophisticated R&D base for biotechnology that was also used for the covert development of BW.[141] US officials were sceptical of these claims and indicated that they had no evidence that such a programme existed.[142]

The war in Kosovo led to concern in April 1999 that Serbia might use CW against NATO forces or to terrorize the Albanian population in Kosovo. US President Bill Clinton threatened a 'swift and overwhelming' response to any use of chemical warfare agents or any other non-conventional weapons.[143] Serbia presumably had taken over the Yugoslavian chemical warfare capability. Several facilities involved in the research, production and storage of CW were reported to be located on Serbian territory: Prva Iskra in Baric, Miloje Blagojevic in Lucani (near Casak), and Miloje Zakic and Merima in Krusevic. A facility at the Military Technical Institute of the former Yugoslavia in Potoci (near Mostar, Bosnia and Herzegovina) was disassembled by Serbian troops in February 1992 and moved to Lucani. All of the facilities were part of the Yugoslavian chemical warfare programme, which reportedly began in the late 1960s and became overtly offensive in the late 1970s. The programme produced the following CW agents: the neurotoxicants sarin, soman, tabun and VX; the vesicant sulphur mustard; and the incapacitants BZ and CS. A wide range of delivery systems were also produced, including rockets, bombs, landmines and artillery shells of various calibres.[144]

Chechen President Aslan Maskhadov accused Russia of using CW during the shelling of the Chechen capital Grozny on 5–6 December 1999, in which 31 people were killed. It was claimed that an additional 200 people suffered burns. Maskhadov appealed to the OPCW to investigate. The Russian military leadership categorically denied the allegation and claimed that Chechnya was misinformed. Deputy Chief of the Russian General Staff Valeriy Manilov and

---

[139] AFP (Paris), 7 Aug. 1999, in 'Sudan not to accept UN inquiry on chemical weapons', Foreign Broadcast Information Service, *Daily Report–Sub-Saharan Africa* (FBIS-AFR), FBIS-AFR-1999-0807, 9 Aug. 1999; and '12 October', *CBW Conventions Bulletin*, no. 46 (Dec. 1999), p. 37.

[140] Risen, J. and Johnston, D., 'Experts find no arms chemicals at bombed Sudan plant', *New York Times* (Internet edn), 9 Feb. 1999, URL <www.nytimes.com/library/world/africa/020999sudan-plant. html>.

[141] Alibek (note 108), pp. 273–75.

[142] Tamayo, J. O., 'US skeptical of report on Cuban biological weapons', *Miami Herald* (Internet edn), 23 June 1999, URL <http://www.herald.com/content/today/news/americas/carib/cuba/digdocs/ 038648.htm>.

[143] Miller, J., 'US officials suspect deadly chemical weapons in Yugoslav army arsenal', *New York Times* (Internet edn), 16 Apr. 1999. URL <http://www.nytimes.com/library/world/europe/041699 kosovo-chemwar.html>.

[144] Federation of American Scientists, 'Chemical agents in the former Yugoslavia', 8 Apr. 1999, URL <http://www.fas.org/nuke/guide/serbia/index.html>.

Colonel-General Stanislav Petrov, commander of the Russian NBC Protection Troops, in turn accused Chechnyan rebels of planting chemicals (chlorine, ammonia and combustibles such as liquid nitrogen) in containers and railway tanks, which could be exploded by remote control, along routes likely to be used by Russian troops.[145] Reciprocal accusations of chemical warfare continued to be made in early 2000.

In June, during fighting in Kashmir, Pakistan investigated claims by Kashmiri politicians and militant groups that India was using chemical shells.[146] This was the first time that a party to the CWC had accused another party to the convention of waging chemical warfare. India denied the charges, and Pakistan did not request an investigation of alleged use by the OPCW or emergency assistance under Article X of the CWC.

On 10 November 1999, former Prime Minister of Kazakhstan Akezhan Kazhegeldin told the Western media that his country may begin producing CBW. Two days later a speaker for the Kazakh National Security Committee, Kenzhebulat Beknazarov, refuted the claim.[147]

After years of intense debate, the World Health Organization (WHO) decided to delay destruction of the last samples of variola (smallpox) virus. Since the disease was eradicated in 1980 samples of the virus have been kept in two laboratories in Atlanta and Moscow, respectively. In 1993 the WHO recommended the simultaneous destruction of both samples. However, the decision to do so was postponed several times for scientific reasons and also because of growing concern that some states may have retained undisclosed stocks. In 1999 the dominant arguments opposed destruction. A study published in January by the Washington-based Institute of Medicine concluded that 'the most compelling need for long-term retention of live variola virus is for the development of antiviral agents or novel vaccines to protect against a reemergence of smallpox due to accidental or intentional release of variola virus'. It stressed that 'continuing investigation of variola virus could lead to new and important discoveries with real potential for improving human health'.[148] In April it became clear that the USA would retain its sample of smallpox virus. Russia has also opposed destruction of the sample it possesses. The WHO subsequently decided to delay destruction of the smallpox samples until at least 2002 because of doubts about whether all stocks have been

---

[145] AFP (Paris), 7 Dec. 1999, in 'Chechens charge Russians with using chemical weapons', FBIS-SOV-1999-1207, 8 Dec. 1999; ITAR-TASS, 9 Dec. 1999, in 'Russia denies using chemical weapons in Chechnya', FBIS-SOV-1999-1209, 9 Dec. 1999; Interfax, 10 Dec. 1999, in 'Russia denies using chemical warfare in Chechnya', FBIS-SOV-1999-1210, 10 Dec. 1999; and ITAR-TASS, 10 Dec. 1999, in 'General: chemical blasts targeted against civilians', FBIS-SOV-1999-1210, 10 Dec. 1999.

[146] AFP (Hong Kong), 14 June 1999, in 'Kashmiri groups condemn alleged use of chemical weapons', Foreign Broadcast Information Service, Daily Report–Near East and South Asia (FBIS-NES), FBIS-NES-1999-0614, 15 June 1999; AFP via Lexis Nexis, 'Pakistan investigates India's reported use of chemical weapons', 14 June 1999; and Rawalpindi Jang, 15 June 1999, p. 10, in 'Daily urges probe into use of chemical weapons by India', FBIS-NES-1999-0617, 18 June 1999.

[147] Interfax (Moscow), 12 Nov. 1999, in 'Kazakhstan: no plans to develop CBW weaponry', FBIS-SOV-1999-1112, 20 Nov. 1999.

[148] Institute of Medicine, Assessment of Future Scientific Needs for Live Variola Virus (National Academy Press: Washington, DC, 1999), p. 85.

destroyed. A US intelligence report suggested that Iraq, North Korea and Russia are all probably concealing stocks for future military use.[149]

V. Conclusions

Political will appears to be the key to both the successful implementation of the CWC and the achievement of a meaningful protocol to the BTWC. In 1999 agreement on a range of technical matters ensured the steady advancement of the CWC treaty-building process and the negotiation of the BTWC protocol in the Ad Hoc Group. However, the obstructionist policies or the apparent lack of political commitment to CBW disarmament of some key players caused tension in the OPCW and the AHG.

Russia's internal political, social and economic problems raised questions about its ability to meet its treaty obligations. In 1999 Russia was the only declared possessor which had not started the destruction of its CW stockpile, and there is serious international concern that it still has illegal BW programmes. In some quarters the USA is perceived as not fully committed to multilateral disarmament. Its technical non-compliance with the CWC regarding initial industry declarations and its opposition to strong compliance mechanisms for the future BTWC protocol are widely attributed to lack of guidance from the Clinton Administration and some serious doubts in certain quarters about the verifiability of the future BTWC regime. The US Congress is furthermore reducing appropriations for assistance programmes to eliminate or prevent the proliferation of CBW in Russia or to engage scientists and specialists in activities permitted under the BTWC and the CWC.

The negotiation of the protocol to the BTWC reached a crucial point at the end of 1999 when the participants in the Ad Hoc Group outlined their national positions on various technical matters. Initiatives were undertaken by both the industrialized and the developing countries in an effort to narrow the gap between the diverging views on non-proliferation and technical cooperation, which may form the basis of package deals in the final stage of the negotiations. However, measures for monitoring compliance with the future protocol continued to hamper progress. Other important differences remained between the Western Group and the NAM, and there were diverging views within both groups. There was a deep internal division regarding verification measures in the Western Group (whose industry would be most affected by the future BW disarmament regime), which prevented it from taking the lead in this crucial

---

[149] Altman, L. K., 'Killer smallpox gets a new lease on life', *New York Times* (Internet edn), 25 May 1999, URL <http://www.nytimes.com/library/national/science/052599hth-doctors.html>; Broad, W. J., 'Government report says 3 nations hide stocks of smallpox', *New York Times* (Internet edn), 13 June 1999, URL <http://www.nytimes.com/library/world/global/061399intel-report.html>; and Altman, L. K., Broad, W. J. and Miller, J., 'Smallpox: the once and future scourge?', *New York Times* (Internet edn), 15 June 1999, URL <http://www.nytimes.com/library/national/science/061599sci-smallpox.html>; Miller, J. and Broad, W. J., 'Clinton to announce that US will keep sample of lethal smallpox virus, aides say', *New York Times* (Internet edn), 22 Mar. 1999, URL <http://www.nytimes.com/library/national/science/042299sci-smallpox.html>; and Miller, J. and Altman, L. K., 'Health panel recommends a reprieve for smallpox', *New York Times* (Internet edn), 22 May 1999, URL <http://www.nytimes.com/library/world/global/052299smallpox.html>.

area. There is a significant risk that the USA may become isolated (and consequently will not join a strong protocol) or that a weak protocol will be achieved, which will affect its long-term viability. In addition, several developing countries have sought concessions from the West with respect to technical cooperation before they are willing to enter the endgame negotiations; a continuation of the AHG discussions in 2000 and beyond is therefore another possible outcome.

Proliferation of CBW remained a major concern in 1999. Some states remain unwilling to join the CWC regime despite the effect on their national economies in terms of reduced access to certain key commodities. This may indicate a determination to maintain major CBW armament programmes in the face of strengthening international norms.

Appendix 9A. Risk assessment of terrorism with chemical and biological weapons

JEAN PASCAL ZANDERS, EDVARD KARLSSON,
LENA MELIN, ERIK NÄSLUND and LENNART THANING

I. Introduction

In the 1990s terrorism became a major security concern and several international cooperative efforts to combat it were launched.[1] With the 1994 and 1995 releases of the nerve agent sarin by the Japanese religious cult Aum Shinrikyo terrorism made a qualitative leap: for the first time a terrorist organization had discharged a so-called weapon of mass destruction.[2] While some analysts had predicted this development, the reasons why terrorist organizations should resort to chemical and biological weapons (CBW) remain unclear. Most studies focus on the potential consequences of such an attack. Relatively small amounts of chemical or biological (CB) warfare agents are claimed to be able to produce huge numbers of casualties—according to some estimates, hundreds of thousands. Because of the immensity of the envisaged consequences the political motives for such terrorist attacks appear inexplicable. Nevertheless, many studies do not view the terrorist interest in CBW as abnormal because it corresponds with increases in the lethality of individual terrorist attacks, the emergence of new terrorist organizations with vague or non-existent ideologies, and the diffusion of scientific knowledge and technological skills. The reasons why the Aum Shinrikyo sarin attacks produced relatively few casualties, why the cult was unable to produce a viable biological warfare agent or why such events did not occur earlier are currently not or only unsatisfactorily explained.

This appendix offers a multidisciplinary analysis of the factors that contribute to or inhibit the acquisition of CBW by terrorist organizations and the way these factors may influence the consequences of an attack with such agents. There are many possible scenarios—with varying degrees of plausibility—involving the release of toxic substances or pathogens by terrorists. They include tampering with food using commercially available poisons, sabotage of storage facilities for harmful chemicals, economic terrorism such as the release of pathogens with the aim to destroy crops or kill or injure livestock (rather than people), the release of lethal agents in order to cause indiscriminate casualties, and so on. In a climate of fear even hoaxes or the threat of the use of toxicants or pathogens may achieve the terrorists' goals. This analysis focuses on one scenario: the domestic development, manufacture and use of highly

---

[1] The United Nations General Assembly adopted the International Convention for the Suppression of Terrorist Bombings on 9 Jan. 1998. A proposal to create a NATO Centre for Weapons of Mass Destruction was also made in 1998. These and other international initiatives are discussed in Zanders, J. P., French, E. M. and Pauwels, N., 'Chemical and biological weapon developments and arms control', *SIPRI Yearbook 1999: Armaments, Disarmament and International Security* (Oxford University Press: Oxford, 1999), pp. 593–95; and in chapter 9 in this volume.

[2] Stock, T., Haug, M. and Radler, P., 'Chemical and biological weapon developments and arms control', *SIPRI Yearbook 1996: Armaments, Disarmament and International Security* (Oxford University Press: Oxford, 1996), pp. 701–704; and Zanders, J. P., Eckstein, S. and Hart, J., 'Chemical and biological weapon developments and arms control', *SIPRI Yearbook 1997: Armaments, Disarmament and International Security* (Oxford University Press: Oxford, 1997), p. 467.

lethal chemical or biological agents (such as sarin or anthrax) by a terrorist organization, which has the potential to cause mass casualties. (It does not address scenarios of states transferring CBW to such groups.) Section II defines CB terrorism and provides a historical overview of the phenomenon. Section III investigates the types of terrorist organizations that are most often associated with CB terrorism and criminality and assesses the likelihood of their developing such weapons. The processes involved in the sub-state proliferation of CBW and the prerequisites for initiating and sustaining a significant CBW programme are examined in section IV. Section V models the release of anthrax and sarin in realistic terrorist scenarios and assesses the consequences. Section VI presents the conclusions.

II. Understanding chemical and biological terrorism

In September 1984 the Rajneesh religious cult poured a solution containing *Salmonella typhimurium*, a common cause of food poisoning, in the salad bars of several restaurants in The Dalles, Oregon, causing 751 people to become ill. The attack was part of a plot to prevent the re-election in November of two Wasco County Court Commissioners, who were hostile to the cult. The Wasco County Court was blocking the cult's plan to expand the village it had founded three years earlier. It is believed that the cult carried out the trial food poisoning to determine whether it was possible to keep Wasco County voters at home on election day owing to illness. In October, however, the cult realized that the attempt to take over the county would fail and no additional attacks were conducted.[3]

On 20 March 1995 Aum Shinrikyo released sarin in the Tokyo underground system. Thirteen people died, and there were more than 5500 other casualties. Although it ostensibly was preparing CB warfare agents for 'Armageddon', the cult used the sarin to prevent police raids on its premises. On 27 June 1994, Aum Shinrikyo had conducted a less publicized sarin attack in the town of Matsumoto, resulting in 7 deaths and injuries to 600 people. That attack was directed against a dormitory housing judges who were expected to rule against the cult in a land dispute.[4]

Defining chemical and biological terrorism

The above cases are instances of the indiscriminate release of pathogens and toxic chemicals for terrorist purposes. Terrorism is a complex social phenomenon because its causative factors, nature and goals and the identity of the perpetrators vary depending on the epoch or society under consideration.[5] Generally, terrorism is an

[3] Carus, W. S., 'Bioterrorism and biocrimes: the illicit use of biological agents in the 20th century', Working Paper, Center for Counterproliferation Research, National Defense University, Washington, DC, Aug. 1998 (Mar. 1999 revision), pp. 57–66; Carter, L. F., *Charisma and Control in Rajneeshpuram: the Role of Shared Values in the Creation of a Community* (Cambridge University Press: Cambridge, 1990), pp. 201–27; and Török, T. J. *et al.*, 'A large community outbreak of salmonellosis caused by intentional contamination of restaurant salad bars', *Journal of the American Medical Association*, vol. 278, no. 5 (Aug. 1997), pp. 389–95.

[4] Stock, Haug and Radler (note 2); and Tu, A. T., Untitled paper delivered at Chem-Bio '98: Combating the Terrorist Threat, organized by Jane's Information Group, Washington, DC, 6–7 Oct. 1998.

[5] Clutterbuck, R., *Terrorism in an Unstable World* (Routledge: London, 1994); Jervas, G. (ed.), *FOA Report on Terrorism* (Swedish Defence Research Establishment (FOA): Stockholm, June 1998); Jervas, G. (ed.), *NBC-Weapons and Terrorism: Two Foreign Contributions and Four Swedish Views* (Swedish Defence Research Establishment: Stockholm, Oct. 1998); Roberts, B. (ed.), *Terrorism with Chemical and Biological Weapons: Calibrating Risks and Responses* (Chemical and Biological Arms Control

extra-legal activity that uses or threatens to use premeditated violence to instil chronic fear in a victim in pursuit of strategic goals specified by the perpetrator. The types of terrorism vary depending on motive, function, effect, nature of the violence and mode of combat or strategy. On the surface, it appears that both the Rajneesh and Aum Shinrikyo cults resorted to CB terrorism to thwart attempts by law enforcement officials to interfere with their activities. However, the deeper motivations and intended outcomes were fundamentally dissimilar, which contributed to important differences in their preparations for CB terrorism and agent selection. Such differences are significant when assessing the threat and consequences of CB terrorism.

Terrorism with CB materials involves the use of a toxic substance or pathogen. Despite the fact that the nature and goals of the terrorist activity may differ considerably between two periods, terrorism with CB materials has been practised throughout history and in all types of civilization.[6] Its use has always been limited, however, because only a few people have had access to such substances and possessed the knowledge to use them. Chemicals and pathogens were used in both world wars for assassinations and sabotage.[7] Since World War II 'poison weapons' have been mostly associated with the intelligence services of certain countries.[8] Common to most attacks with CB materials is the clear mission-oriented purpose of the attacks and the discriminate use of the poisonous agents. This direct goal–instrument relationship may explain, in part, why no 'mass destruction' has resulted from such attacks.

Since the sarin attacks in the Tokyo underground system, much attention has been paid to a subset of CB materials: the chemical and biological warfare agents. These weapons are toxic chemicals or pathogens designed, developed and selected by the military to support certain missions established in the military doctrine of a state. Chemical warfare agents represent a compromise in terms of military utility:

1. A presumptive agent must not only be highly toxic, but also 'suitably highly toxic' so that it is not too difficult to handle.

2. It must be possible to store the substance in containers for long periods without degradation and without corroding the packaging material.

3. Such an agent must be relatively resistant to atmospheric water and oxygen so that it does not lose its effect when dispersed.

4. It must also withstand the shearing forces created by the explosion and heat when it is dispersed.[9]

Institute: Alexandria, Va., 1997); Stern, J., *The Ultimate Terrorists* (Harvard University Press: Cambridge, Mass., 1999); and Laqueur, W., *The New Terrorism* (Oxford University Press: New York, 1999).

[6] Lewin, L., *Die Gifte in der Weltgeschichte* [Poisons in world history] (Verlag von Julius Springer: Berlin, 1920) details many examples of poisoning for political purposes.

[7] E.g., Wheelis, M., 'Biological sabotage in World War I', eds E. Geissler and J. E. van Courtland Moon, *Biological and Toxin Weapons: Research, Development and Use from the Middle Ages to 1945*, SIPRI Chemical & Biological Warfare Studies no. 18 (Oxford University Press: Oxford, 1999), pp. 35–62; and Bojtzov, V. and Geissler, E., 'Military biology in the USSR, 1920–45', eds Geissler and van Courtland Moon (note 7), p. 163.

[8] Some recent cases are described in Zanders, J. P. and Hart, J., 'Chemical and biological weapon developments and arms control', *SIPRI Yearbook 1998: Armaments, Disarmament and International Security* (Oxford University Press: Oxford, 1998), p. 481; and Zanders, French and Pauwels (note 1), pp. 583–85.

[9] *Chemical Weapons: Threat, Effects and Protection*, FOA Briefing Book no. 16 (Swedish Defence Research Establishment: Sundbyberg, Sweden, 1992), p. 20.

In the past the military have had several types of chemical warfare agent at their disposal and an agent appropriate to the mission has been selected on the basis of volatility versus persistency, and lethality versus incapacitation. Candidate biological warfare agents have similarly been selected on the basis of a compromise between pathogenicity, survivability of the agent after release and controllability. Military biological warfare programmes have included lethal, incapacitating and anti-crop agents. This mission-oriented selection process has shaped the direct goal–instrument relationship. The compromise with respect to the selection of the agents in terms of their military utility may have made CB warfare agents less attractive to terrorists.

Some potential CB warfare agents (sarin, VX, anthrax, botulinum toxin, and so on) are among the most lethal substances that exist. Central to the catastrophic CB terrorism scenarios resulting in mass casualties is the focus on toxicity or pathogenicity. However, the manufacture of large batches of such agents poses technological and organizational problems. Terrorists would also have to overcome difficulties in the weaponization (i.e., preparing the agent to be delivered as a weapon) and dissemination of these agents. Aum Shinrikyo managed to overcome several of these hurdles, but the impediments are such that few other terrorist organizations would be able to replicate its armament programme in future.

III. Profiles of terrorist organizations with interest in CBW

Especially since the late 1960s several individuals or non-state groupings—autonomous organizations without formal connection to a government—have shown interest in CB materials.[10] According to the Swedish Defence Research Establishment (FOA) database of such incidents, most of the known actors behind CB-related incidents cannot be linked to a state sponsor of terrorism or to a more 'established' terrorist organization. Instead, they are what are called the 'new terrorists'.[11] The only cases of large-scale terrorist use of CB agents have involved the two religious cults discussed above. Right-wing extremists, animal rights activists and single individuals are responsible for a considerable number of the remaining incidents.

General aims

Proselytization is a major aim of all religious cults, and they often attract a large following of members and sympathizers who contribute to the material wealth of the

[10] A 1995 survey of CB terrorism lists over 24 instances of terrorist use or threat of use of biological materials and a considerable number of threats and incidents involving poisonous substances. The cases range from apparently empty threats to reports of acquisition and actual discovery of possession. Nevertheless, many of the listed cases could arguably be classified as attempts at homicide, suicide or criminal extortion motivated by financial rather than political gain. Purver, R., 'Chemical and biological terrorism: the threat according to the open literature', Canadian Security Intelligence Service (CSIS), Ottawa, June 1995, URL <http://www.csis-scrs.gc.ca/eng/miscdocs/tabintre.html#preface>, esp. sections 'Biological terrorism' and 'Chemical terrorism'. The recent spate of hoaxes in the USA has significantly increased the number of cases. For an overview, see Carus (note 3). These events should not be counted as incidents of CB terrorism because live CB agents were not involved.

[11] The FOA database places such incidents into 1 of 6 categories: (a) threats of use of CB agents or hoaxes without actual possession; (b) manufacture or purchase of CB agents but no actual use; (c) claimed, but not confirmed, possession; (d) confirmed possession; (e) attempt but failure to use CB agents (no casualties for different reasons); and (f) successful use (verified casualties). It contains approximately 350 incidents from 1969 to 1999 as well as a few earlier ones and is currently supported by approximately 1000 documents, reports, newspaper articles, etc.

cult and its leadership.[12] Some cults attempt to convert their financial strength into political power in order to consolidate their position and acquire formal legitimacy or to have some of the cult's principles adopted by the broader society. Expansion may also bring some cults into conflict with the local population and authorities, and via the electoral process they may try to influence decisions in their favour.

Many cults use physical and psychological violence within the cult, which in some cases has led to collective suicide. Cults that have a tendency to use violence internally may also use physical violence against outsiders if they feel threatened. As demonstrated by the Rajneesh and Aum Shinrikyo cults, the greater the perceived existential threat, the greater the chance that the cult will resort to extreme measures. Isolation from society also produces paranoid projections of the external threat to the cult. Destructive cults, such as Aum Shinrikyo, particularly tend to become more closed, guarded and isolated from the outside world when the perceived threat increases.[13] A cult that is interested in acquiring CB agents is likely to be violent.

The 'patriot organizations' consist of Christian identity movements,[14] branches of the Ku Klux Klan, militia groups and neo-Nazis. They are mostly based in the United States, but several are also active in Europe. They became prominent in the 1990s as the left-wing terrorist organizations declined in strength. Most of them are anti-Semitic, anti-government and xenophobic and wish to preserve the national and cultural values of their nation. There may be major ideological and social differences among the members of these organizations and the issues which they perceive as important may vary. Such differences are particularly noticeable between European and US groups.[15] There is also a strong resentment of state organs, politicians, the police force and other 'opponents', although it is expressed less clearly outside the USA. Right-wing violence is on the increase.

Animal rights activists wish to influence behaviour towards animals in captivity. In pursuit of their goals they may conduct acts of sabotage against research institutes or companies that trade products based on animal experiments with the intent of damaging them or their reputation. Since the mid-1980s some animal rights activists have threatened to use toxic substances or have claimed that they have used such substances. Some instances of tainted foodstuffs in shops have been confirmed. Animal rights activists are most prominent in North America and Western Europe.[16]

The loner often appears to be an ordinary citizen with an extraordinary idea of how to achieve his goal. In some cases the motive for his attack may be hate or revenge directed towards an individual, a person in authority or a company. Attacks on com-

---

[12] A cult is a religious grouping with a deviated doctrine of faith, which usually comprises a mixture of elements from different religions. A sect, in contrast, is a side branch of an established religion.

[13] Melin, L., *Kulter: Religiösa kulter och deras ledare, en beskrivning av sex kulter* [Religious cults and their leaders, a description of six cults], (Swedish Defence Research Establishment: Umeå, Sweden, 1997), p. 13 (in Swedish). Destructive cults are characterized by: (*a*) an authoritarian pyramid structure, (*b*) a charismatic or messianic leader, (*c*) deception in recruitment and/or fund-raising, (*d*) physical or psychological isolation from society, and (*e*) use of mind control techniques.

[14] This race-based theology, one of the far right's fastest growing segments, claims that white Christians are the true biblical Israelites. Flynn, K. and Gerhardt, G., *The Silent Brotherhood: Inside America's Racist Underground* (Macmillan: New York, 1989), p. xi.

[15] A detailed comparative description is presented in Laqueur (note 5), pp. 105–26.

[16] The most active groups are the Animal Rights Militia (ARM) and Animal Aid Association (AAA) in Canada and the Animal Liberation Front (ALF) in the UK and Belgium. In 1992–95 there were 5 incidents in Canada. In 1984–97, 8 incidents of alleged food poisoning occurred in the UK. Purver (note 10), pp. 37, 86; 'Thanksgiving turkeys recalled', *The Sun* (Kuala Lumpur), 14 Oct. 1996, URL <http://prn.usm.my/headline/poison/oct96.html#w310>; and Animal Liberation Frontline Information Service, 'Animal rights militia fact sheet', URL <http://www.enviroweb.org/ALFIS/index2.shtml>.

panies are often made by disgruntled employees. In several European cases the motive has been economic extortion directed at a specific company.[17] Other incidents do not appear to have a clear motive.

Structure

Religious cults often have similar structures despite varying religious views. There is always a strict hierarchic organization, and successful cults almost invariably have a strong and charismatic leader who is surrounded by an inner core of loyal followers.[18] Cults are often financially stable because most of them force their followers to donate all their assets when they join. Via the Internet they are able to market themselves, advertise their activities, sell goods and solicit donations. They recruit mostly from the middle or upper classes and often focus their efforts on well-educated young people. Aum Shinrikyo, for instance, recruited many students and researchers from university campuses. The majority of those who joined the Rajneesh cult had graduated from high school or a university.[19]

Patriot organizations are able to draw on broadly based support and sympathy for a variety of issues but are generally less tightly structured than the religious cults, smaller in size (to the point of consisting of one individual) and only loosely connected to each other. They nevertheless share certain traits with religious cults. A strong charismatic figure plays the central role, and some form of the Christian religion is important to most of the patriot associations. In some cases the centrality of religion makes them virtually indistinguishable from some religious cults. They regard the Book of Revelation as a key part of the Bible, and Identity theology, for example, claims that Armageddon is approaching, possibly in the form of a nuclear war.[20] Unlike the cults where the followers, freely or as the result of the use of force, remain with one organization, the members of patriot organizations move between different groups with the same set of values. New groups are formed as a result of internal disagreement or by splitting up established groups and changing the name. Despite the often weak institutionalized connections, right-wing extremists in the USA and several West European countries are linked to each other via computer networks, through which they share and disseminate information. They also use the Internet to solicit funds and sell merchandise. Currently, there is a trend towards the establishment of smaller leaderless cells, organized around an ideology instead of a

[17] Especially in Germany and the UK, the food industry has become a popular target for blackmailing threats. There have been several incidents in which products were poisoned with cyanide and insecticides. The food industry suffered huge losses as it had to recall tonnes of products from the supermarkets. 'German food industries targets of blackmailers', *The Sun* (Kuala Lumpur), 20 Feb. 1998, URL <http://prn.usm.my/headline/poison/feb98.html#w34>; Parkes, C., 'HP responds to the new terrorism: public management of food tampering cases', *Financial Times*, 25 July 1989; and Elliott, C., Langton, J. and Blundy, D., 'How to fight the supermarket terrorists', *Sunday Telegraph*, 30 Apr. 1989.

[18] Some well-known examples are Bhagwan Rajneesh of the Rajneesh cult, Shoko Asahara of Aum Shinrikyo, Jim Jones of the People's Temple, Sun Myung Moon of the Unification Church, Marshall Herff Applewhite of Heaven's Gate and David Koresh of the Branch Davidians.

[19] Latkin, C. A. *et al.*, 'Who lives in Utopia? A brief report on the Rajneeshpuram research project', *Sociological Analysis*, vol. 48, no. 1 (1987), p. 76.

[20] E.g., the now dissolved Covenant, the Sword, and Arm of the Lord (CSA) was a violence-prone purveyor of anti-Semitism and racism under the guise of being a church; it soon also became a military encampment of survivalists waiting for Armageddon. Many active organizations are also convinced that a holy racial war is coming, which is, in part, described in the literature popular in these circles. Some of the most popular books are *The Turner Diaries* and the sequel, *Hunter*, by William Pierce; *A Candidate for the Order* by Michael A. Hoffman; and *The March Up Country* by Harold Covington.

leader. These cells are able to plot terrorist attacks with reduced risk of infiltration by law enforcement officials. Like the cults, most patriot organizations are closed to the outside world and have a great sense of external threat.

Animal rights movements also have a weak structural make-up. Actions such as releasing animals from their cages can be carried out by a few people. The animal rights movement asserts that it is leaderless and against a hierarchical order, but it is difficult to verify this claim. In the United Kingdom, at least, some prominent figures seem to broadly direct the movement and, presumably, control a variety of activities. Well-established Internet networks offer instructions on propaganda initiatives or the organization of demonstrations and blockades, advertise future actions, describe the results and often glorify the participating 'warriors'. Although the groups raise money by selling merchandise and soliciting donations, it seems unlikely that they can accumulate significant sums.

A loner is an individual without formal connection to an organization or a person who works without instructions and logistical or financial support from an organization. Nevertheless, according to the FOA database such individuals are responsible for approximately 25 per cent of all incidents involving CB materials; arguably, they pose the greatest challenge to law enforcement officials. If a loner is caught, it is usually because someone has informed the authorities, the loner himself has talked too much or he was caught in the act.[21]

The interest in CB materials

Materially and structurally many cults are capable of undertaking CB programmes, although whether or not they do so will depend on their characteristics and goals. Aum Shinrikyo's failure to win seats in the Lower House of Japan's Parliament in 1990 fuelled its leader's apocalyptic visions, hate towards the government and paranoia. Shortly after the election failure the cult made its first attempts to manufacture biological agents. Aum Shinrikyo set up a complex of chemical factories and biological laboratories over a period of almost five years.[22] Its leader, Shoko Asahara, had long been fascinated by non-conventional weapons, and they played a central role

[21] In 1998 Larry Wayne Harris and an accomplice attempted to buy equipment to test anthrax (which later proved to be a harmless vaccine strain) for $20 million from a businessman who contacted the Federal Bureau of Investigation (FBI). Claiborne, W., 'Two men charged with possessing anthrax', *Washington Post*, 20 Feb. 1998, URL <http://www.washingtonpost.com/wp-srv/digest/nat1.htm>. In 1995 Harris had ordered plague germs from the American Type Culture Collection (ATCC). However, when he called the ATCC because the shipment was delayed he revealed that he was unfamiliar with its procedures. The sales representative contacted the Centers for Disease Control and Prevention (CDC) in Atlanta, Georgia, which in turn informed the FBI. Windrem, R., 'The man who talks too much', MSNBC, 20 Feb. 1998, URL <http://www.msnbc.som/news/145425.asp>.
In 1998, Valeriy Borzov manufactured mustard gas in his Moscow flat but was revealed by a person who knew that offers to sell the gas had been made to various mafia groups by Borzov. Kartsev, A., 'Rysk kemist tillverkade senapsgas i lägenheten', [Russian chemist manufactured mustard gas in his apartment], *Göteborgs-Posten*, 17 Sep. 1998 (in Swedish).
In 1998 Kathryn Schoonover was arrested outside a post office in Marina del Rey, Calif., when she was about to mail more than 100 envelopes containing sodium cyanide in plastic bags and brochures for nutritional and dietary supplements. Apparently, she did not attempt to conceal her activities in the post office. Hastings, D., 'Authorities seek answers on cyanide letter', *Boston Globe*, 25 Aug. 1998, URL <http://www.boston.com/dailynews/wirehtm...thorities_seek_answers_on_cyanide.shtm>.
[22] In addition to the 2 sarin attacks in Matsumoto (1994) and Tokyo (1995), the cult made several unsuccessful attempts to spray botulinum toxin and anthrax from the roofs of trucks and was apparently interested in other pathogens, such as the Ebola virus and Q fever. WuDunn, S., Miller, J. and Broad, W. J., 'How Japan germ terror alerted world', *New York Times*, 26 May 1998, pp. A1, A10.

in his predictions of approaching Armageddon. Ultimately, the cult did not use its chemical weapons in pursuit of its grand visions but to counter direct threats posed by law enforcement officials. Bhagwan Rajneesh, the leader of the Rajneesh cult, did not make apocalyptic statements, but anticipated defeat in an election important to the future of the cult apparently was deemed to justify extreme measures. The cult bought a relatively harmless organism, whose cultivation was not technically difficult, from a medical laboratory.[23] The attack was not planned far in advance as cultivation of the organism reportedly started in late summer 1984 and its dissemination took place in September.[24]

Although the patriot organizations have not yet used non-conventional weapons, there are many indications of a growing interest in such weapons. On several occasions poisons, toxins or infective agents (including cyanide, ricin and typhoid bacteria) have been found in the possession of right-wing extremists.[25] In some instances there have been plans to release the toxicants in the water reservoirs of large cities. If successful, the attacks would have indiscriminately affected the whole population, not just the designated enemies of these groups. Other reports detail attacks or planned attacks with toxic substances against specific targets such as politicians or other individuals, although such operations would be far easier to carry out with firearms (which most right-wing groups possess). So far, most of the patriot organizations that have either manufactured or purchased CB materials have limited themselves to agents that are relatively safe to handle without special precautions such as protective clothing. Most of the reported incidents have only involved plans to use CB agents.

The animal rights activists have acted similarly and have utilized CB materials such as cyanide, rat poison, oven cleaner and mercury. Generally, they have not used these agents against people.[26] Given their structure and limited financial assets, it is difficult to envisage how they could finance the purchase or manufacture of chemical or biological warfare agents. Furthermore, their members are mainly teenagers, who usually lack the knowledge and skill to set up and run a CBW production programme or to carry out a large-scale attack with CBW. There have been no cases of verified possession of chemical or biological warfare agents, but a threat with CBW or an allegation of use can terrorize individuals and negatively affect a targeted company.

Loners have experimented with biological and chemical warfare agents, which could cause large numbers of casualties if employed in sufficient amounts utilizing efficient dissemination technique. Some of the loners who have been involved in terrorist activities have had a university degree in microbiology or chemistry[27] and have experimented with potentially more dangerous agents. A loner can be a threat if he possesses the intellectual, technical and operational skills to select and disperse CB

[23] Carter (note 3), p. 204.

[24] Callister, S. and Zaitz, L. L., 'Sheela, once a roaring, snarling tigress, docile, tamed by court', *The Oregonian*, 23 July 1986.

[25] Campbell, J. K., *Weapons of Mass Destruction Terrorism* (Interpact Press: Seminole, Fla., 1997), pp. 113–15; and Purver (note 10), p. 37.

[26] One incident occurred on 11 Jan. 1999 when 4 animal rights activists threw a corrosive agent at a guard at the Swedish Institute for Infection and Disease Control (SMI) with the obvious intent of injuring him. He was not injured and no motive for the attack has been established. 'Djurrättsaktivister anhållna' [Animal rights activists arrested], *Svenska Dagbladet*, 12 Jan. 1999 (in Swedish).

[27] There are several examples of well-educated loners. Larry Wayne Harris was taking courses in advanced microbiology at Ohio State University. Harris, L. W., 'Bacteriological warfare: a major threat to North America. What you and your family can do defensively before and after. A civil defense manual', 1998, URL <http://norden1.com/~hawkins/civil.htm>. Schoonover claims that she has a background in chemistry. Hastings (note 21). Borzov studied chemistry at Moscow University. Kartsev (note 21).

materials. The likelihood of conducting a 'successful' large-scale release resulting in mass casualties is slim, but a smaller attack can be sufficiently difficult for authorities to handle. Most loners will probably continue to experiment with the less harmful CB materials that are described in underground literature and on the Internet.

CBW hoaxes are another type of terrorist threat. A series of such hoaxes were apparently inspired by the highly publicized 24 April 1997 incident in which a Petri dish supposedly containing anthrax and plague was delivered to the Washington headquarters of the Jewish organization B'nai B'rith.[28] In the latter part of 1998 and throughout 1999 various US organizations and authorities received letters and parcels containing anthrax threats. The fear of terrorist attacks with CB materials has taken on such enormous proportions in the USA that hoaxes are almost as potent a terrorist tool as actual use of the agents. Hoaxes are currently able to close down entire facilities or installations.[29]

IV. Sub-state proliferation: the process of acquiring CBW

In order to judge the likelihood of terrorist attacks with CBW it is necessary to have a clear understanding of the weapon acquisition process from the perspective of the demand side: the terrorist organization. Using the assimilation model, a heuristic device designed for studying CBW armament programmes in countries for which limited information is available on decision-making processes and the structure of armament programmes, it is possible to identify and assess the key parameters in a CBW programme set up by a terrorist organization.[30] There are three main sets of parameters to consider: the material base of the terrorist organization, the tension between norms and threats, and the group strategy and structure.

The material base of the terrorist organization

The material base of a terrorist organization is a key determinant of whether or not it will be able to develop and produce CBW domestically. The material base consists of the organization's physical base and its internal characteristics.

The physical base comprises elements that determine whether the organization will be able to acquire chemical and biological weapons. A terrorist organization has little

---

[28] United States Fire Administration, *Fire Department Response to Biological Threat at B'nai B'rith Headquarters, Washington, DC*, Report no. 114 of the major fires investigation project, Technical Report Series (United States Fire Administration: Emmitsburg, Md., Apr. 1997), p. 2.

[29] E.g., in Jan. 2000 some 20 letters alleged to contain anthrax were sent to abortion clinics across the USA, forcing them to close certain areas or be wholly evacuated. Associated Press (AP) via Yahoo News, 'Anthrax threat closes Ala. clinic', 3 Jan. 2000, URL <http://dailynews.yahoo.com/h/ap/20000103/us/clinic_threats_2.html>; Seewer, J., AP via Yahoo News, 'More threats to abortion clinics', 4 Jan. 2000, URL <http://dailynews.yahoo.com/h/ap/20000104/us/clinic_threats_4.html>; AP via Yahoo News, 'Anthrax threat closes Ohio clinic', 4 Jan. 2000, URL <http://dailynews.yahoo.com/h/ap/20000104/us/clinic_threats_3.html>; and Jones, T. F. *et al.*, 'Mass psychogenic illness attributed to toxic exposure at a high school', *New England Journal of Medicine*, 13 Jan. 2000, pp. 96–100.

[30] Zanders, J. P., 'Tackling the demand side of chemical and biological weapon proliferation', ed. D. Schroeer, *Technology Transfer* (Ashgate Publishing: London, 1999), forthcoming. Regarding the adaptation of the assimilation model for the study of terrorist organizations, see Zanders, J. P., 'Assessing the risk of chemical and biological weapons proliferation to terrorists', *Nonproliferation Review*, vol. 6, no. 4 (fall 1999), pp. 17–34. The model is also explained with graphics in the Internet Educational Module on CBW Non-proliferation, created by the SIPRI CBW Project, the Centre for Peace and Security Studies of the Free University of Brussels and the International Relations and Security Network (ISN), Zurich, URL <http://cbw.sipri.se>.

influence over certain elements. For example, the organization's geographical location and the type of culture in which it is embedded will have a direct bearing on the nature of the organization and its appeal. Aum Shinrikyo enjoyed its greatest success in Japan, where alienated members of the intellectual stratum of society were receptive to mysticism, and in Russia, where many victims of the social disintegration following the collapse of the Soviet Union were similarly seeking solace in various kinds of mysticism.[31] In contrast, the cult was unsuccessful in Germany and the USA despite its efforts (the lack of a strong and charismatic regional leader may have been a contributing factor). Other important components of geographical location for Aum Shinrikyo included the overall level of scientific, technological and industrial development of the Japanese society, the tax exemptions granted to recognized religious organizations (which enabled Aum to amass its considerable assets) and the general hands-off attitude of the Japanese authorities towards religious organizations as a consequence of the religious persecutions before 1945. Some elements of the physical base (e.g., number of members, financial assets, property owned and infrastructure) can be altered by a terrorist organization through targeted policies with great investment of time and resources. Aum Shinrikyo constantly attempted to expand its membership and to extract the largest possible amount of wealth from its members, their families and its sympathizers. The transfer of property rights, including those of companies, was part of the initiation rites of new members of the cult.

The second component of the material base consists of the internal characteristics of the terrorist organization. The organization can relatively easily exploit, manipulate or develop certain of these characteristics to achieve its goals. Its culture may be based on social ideology, apocalyptic or millenarian visions, racial superiority, ethnic nationalism, religious fanaticism, and so on. In the quest to acquire CBW the level of education and training of the members, as well as the science and technology base that they are able to establish, become important factors. Aum Shinrikyo launched repeated recruitment drives to attract promising young scientists and people with needed skills from Japan's leading institutes. These individuals were able to set up the programmes and build the necessary installations. However, in the CBW programmes the reliance on relatively unskilled cult members for the operation and maintenance of the installations contributed to many leaks and accidents. Internal secrecy and dedication to the cause of Aum Shinrikyo in the selection of members to work on the CBW programmes were negative factors, as was Aum Shinrikyo's limited functional specialization. For example, the people in charge of developing the agents were also responsible for developing the dissemination devices. They also executed the attacks, and their lack of experience in operational planning contributed to many mistakes and failures. In an organization the accumulated finances and skills must be transformed into significant levels of economic and industrial development. Success depends on how the organization as a whole is able to optimize its (always limited) resources and prioritize their allocation to meet its goals.

Norms and threats

Norms influence the willingness of the terrorist organization to pursue CBW. However, they form a complex aspect of social interaction and often do not manifest them-

---

[31] References to Aum Shinrikyo in this section are based on the analysis by Kaplan, D. E. and Marshall, A., *The Cult at the End of the World: The Incredible Story of Aum* (Arrow Books: London, 1996).

selves in an absolute form. The application of a norm hinges on the recognition of the other party as an equal partner. However, for political entities based on religion this may be problematic as authority and sovereignty are derived directly from God. The rules, norms and values which apply to members of the faith do not apply to non-members. Historical analysis reveals that regulations such as the prohibition of the use of poisoned weapons governed the conduct of belligerents of the same faith, but the use of such weapons was permitted against infidels.[32] As evidenced by Nazi Germany and the Japanese biological weapon (BW) experiments in World War II, sentiments of racial and cultural superiority can affect the formulation and application of norms. Several of the terrorist organizations profiled here display similar traits.

This has a double implication for terrorist organizations. First, the norms maintained by the group may differ significantly from those of the broader society. Internal or external constraints that could raise the threshold for acquiring CBW may therefore be non-existent, and the success of the armament dynamic may depend entirely on factors in the material base. Second, because of their convictions the group members may differentiate themselves from the rest of society to such an extent that the elimination of non-members—even on a large scale—can be easily justified. This world view may remove any moral objection against CBW use.

The strength of norms is also directly linked to the nature of the threat. This raises the question of whether an existential threat to a terrorist organization (e.g., a threat which is gradually building and which the group feels it cannot manage) contributes to the erosion of the group's norms. As noted above, the Rajneesh cult and Aum Shinrikyo resorted to the indiscriminate use of biological and chemical agents in response to what they perceived to be an existential threat.

Group strategy and structure

If the leadership of a terrorist organization decides to initiate a CBW armament programmes it must make decisions regarding the allocation of its resources. These decisions, and the nature of the programme, will depend on the organization's goals and the way it is structured. A loosely structured, amorphous group with little central guidance or an organization structured in small cells for maximum security (e.g., patriot organizations, animal rights groups and loners) will find it harder to set up a CBW armament programme than a vertically structured, highly integrated and ideologically uniform group, such as Aum Shinrikyo or the Rajneesh cult. On the other hand, any organization will be constrained by its material base and will have to import many of the components and technologies necessary for a CBW armament programme. For a terrorist organization this can be a formidable challenge. A state actor enjoys freedom from prosecution, can buy technologies abroad and hire foreign

---

[32] E.g., in his work published in the late Middle Ages, *Von allerlei Kriegsgewehr und Geschütz* [On types of gun and cannon], Wulff von Senftenberg expressed reservations about his own proposals for 'poisonous fumes' if used against Christians, but had fewer misgivings regarding use against the 'godless Turks' or other infidels. Meyer, J., *Der Gaskampf und die chemischen Kampfstoffe* [Gas warfare and chemical warfare agents] (Verlag S. Hirzel: Leipzig, 1925), p. 277; and Jones, D. P., 'The role of chemists in research on war gases in the United States during World War I', PhD diss., University of Wisconsin, 1969, p. 40. International norms and laws emerged in the Westphalian state system because the sovereign territorial states recognized each other as equal systemic units that could enforce an international agreement within the territory of their jurisdiction. E.g., the first known international agreement on the prohibition of the use of poison weapons was concluded in Strasbourg between France and the German Empire in 1675, 27 years after the Peace of Westphalia. Officers were to exemplarily punish the person who possessed or used such implements. Lewin (note 6), p. 563.

specialists. In contrast, a terrorist organization must work in secrecy because of the threat that law enforcement officials may raid its facilities. This makes it impossible for the organization to hire an outside specialist or technician for a limited time to solve a particular problem. Instead the organization must recruit and convince such an individual of the justness of its cause. The degree of dependency on external skills and technologies is also a function of the complexity of the weapon system which the leaders of the group have decided to acquire.

The influence of the various parameters can be illustrated by comparing the activities of the Aum Shinrikyo and the Rajneesh cults. The Rajneesh cult was responding to a rapidly evolving crisis that threatened its continued existence in Oregon. The cult therefore had no time to develop its material base. Because its goal was limited in scope and time (i.e., influencing the outcome of local elections) it could opt for an incapacitating rather than a lethal agent, thereby decreasing the technical demands on the laboratory. The choice of a salmonella strain also simplified the dissemination as a liquid solution could be poured on food in public places. In addition, this reduced the need for functional specialization in the cult. The straightforward goal–instrument relationship also meant that as soon as the cult realized that it would not attain the desired outcome it terminated its programme.

Aum Shinrikyo's plans were more ambitious: it sought to destabilize Japan and to eventually take over all governmental functions. To this end, the cult pursued a broad set of instruments, including conventional weapons, an earthquake machine, a laser gun and a nuclear device as well as CBW. While many accounts of Aum Shinrikyo's activities have focused narrowly on the CBW programmes, the important point is that the cult actively sought a broad range of weaponry. This had two major implications.

First, the element of priority resource allocation by the cult leadership became an important element of the CBW armament dynamic. The cult spread its huge financial assets and other resources over several weapon programmes as it tried to become self-sufficient in every area. Each programme placed increasing demands on manpower, the ability of the offices outside Japan to purchase the required technologies, and so on. Had the cult concentrated its resources on CBW it might have achieved greater success in terms of creating a viable biological weapon or larger production batches of higher-quality chemical warfare agents. Ultimately, the cult had some success in a few of its weapon programmes. Second, there was no rationale for the CBW programmes without the other weapon programmes. Chemical and biological weapons could conceivably have played a role in destabilizing Japan, but they would have been insufficient to establish the cult's own form of governance. A large-scale release of chemical or biological warfare agents in isolation would have been met by a massive response from the law enforcement authorities (as happened after the Tokyo underground attack), possibly leading to the demise of the organization. In other words, it was impossible in practice for Aum Shinrikyo to concentrate its resources on CBW alone. Because of its grand strategy the leadership had to spread its large, but limited, resources over various programmes. Together, the various constraints and conflicting imperatives led to a reduction of the quality and quantity of the chemical agents and to failure with respect to the biological agents. In summary, the factors that contributed to the establishment of the CBW programmes were also responsible for Aum Shinrikyo's limited success.

V. Assessing the consequences of the release of CBW

The dissemination patterns for chemical and biological warfare agents in a terrorist attack differ in many respects from those in military operations. Utilizing FOA models for the dispersion of the chemical and biological warfare agents used, two realistic scenarios have been developed.[33]

The first scenario assumes that, at a shopping centre, a cult like Aum Shinrikyo has disseminated a type and quantity of anthrax similar to that which was accidentally released from a military microbiology facility in Sverdlovsk in 1979.[34] The scenario demonstrates that, given realistic conditions, several hundred people concentrated in a relatively narrow area would be infected but not necessarily killed. This contrasts with the many predictions that such use would result in mass casualties over large areas.

The second scenario is modelled on the 1994 Matsumoto attack by Aum Shinrikyo, but some parameters have been optimized (e.g., the quality of the sarin and the single point of release). Nonetheless, the casualty patterns observed at Matsumoto and Tokyo—few fatalities, a high proportion of other casualties and a significant number of exposed individuals who displayed no physiological symptoms—may, in fact, be typical of a terrorist release of sarin.

The scenario of a terrorist attack with a biological warfare agent

The dissemination of biological warfare agents into the air can cause numerous casualties even far from the release point. However, virulent strains of the relevant micro-organisms would need to be used, and technical skills and equipment for culturing and storing the organisms as well as the appropriate technology to release the agent efficiently would also be required. In order for the aerosol particles to be able to reach the non-ciliated alveolar region in the lungs, the particle size has to be less then 10 μm and preferably around 5 μm.[35] In theory, terrorists can cause massive casualties with rather limited means. However, in practice, they may experience great difficulty in acquiring and growing virulent strains of the pathogens because of a lack of technical skills and equipment. Aum Shinrikyo, for instance, sprayed botulinum toxin over Tokyo several times in 1990 and conducted similar activities with anthrax spores in 1993 without any known effects. Japanese authorities later disclosed that the cult had used a relatively harmless anthrax vaccine strain and that the aerosolizer was not sufficiently efficient.

The following scenario assumes that a terrorist organization comparable to Aum Shinrikyo has overcome any technical hurdles and is able to aerosolize an amount of respirable anthrax spores comparable to that accidentally released in Sverdlovsk. In the scenario, the 4 billion respirable anthrax spores are released over a 15-minute interval from a road 15 metres above street level. The south-westerly wind has a

---

[33] In order not to provide potential terrorists with precise predictions, the scenarios utilize published data about past events. Certain modelling parameters have been wholly or partially excluded. The results nevertheless present a true picture of the potential consequences of the release of chemical or biological warfare agents.

[34] In that incident in the former Soviet Union an estimated 4 billion respirable spores became airborne and approximately 65 people died. Meselson, M. *et al.*, 'The Sverdlovsk anthrax outbreak of 1979', *Science*, vol. 266 (Nov. 1994).

[35] The aerosol particles may consist of different amounts of spores: the more spores, the larger the aerosol particle.

speed of approximately 4.5 metres per second at a height of 10 metres. The target is a large shopping mall in central Tokyo.

Even with relatively advanced spray equipment the diameter of most of the released aerosol particles would be larger than 10 μm. It is therefore reasonable to assume that about 5 per cent of the spores released by a terrorist group would be of respirable size. In order to generate 4 billion respirable spores, a total of approximately 80 billion respirable spores would have to be released. Such an amount can easily be suspended in a few litres of solution. With optimal distribution and inhalation this number could infect approximately 4–5 million people (the infective dose ID_{50} is assumed to be 8000–10 000 inhaled spores).[36] However, the estimate is of limited value since only a small fraction of the released spores would reach people because of the dispersion in the atmosphere. An even smaller fraction of the amount would be respirable.

The dispersion, inhalation and deposition patterns have been calculated using a stochastic particle dispersion model.[37] In figures 9A.1–9A.3 the course of the dispersion of the calculated aerosol cloud is shown at 2, 6 and 18 minutes after the release of the anthrax spores. The figures illustrate typical dispersion patterns and show relative concentrations (the darker the shading, the higher the concentration). The irregularities (i.e., the isolated pockets) are patterns that change rapidly during the passage of the aerosol cloud.

It is likely that individuals would spend more time than the 15 minutes of the agent release in the shopping mall, and as many as 20 000–30 000 persons could be exposed to the cloud of spores. Figure 9A.4 shows the dose (i.e., the number of spores that a person standing still at one point during the entire passage of the aerosol cloud would receive and retain in the lungs). The respiration rate was set at 25 litres per minute, a typical value for moderate physical exercise. Although most people would not remain in the same place for 15 minutes, figure 9A.4 nonetheless depicts a conceivable result of the release. In their study of the anthrax release at Sverdlovsk, Meselson and his co-authors suggest a dose–response relation for inhalation of anthrax spores based on an LD_{50} value of 8000 and a geometric standard deviation of 27.[38] For anthrax it is possible to assume that an infective dose (ID) can be substituted for the lethal dose (LD). Using this relation, a rough estimate of the probability of infection at the different doses can be calculated (table 9A.1).[39] The curve of the estimated dose–response relation is illustrated in figure 9A.4.

[36] ID_{50} represents the number of spores which, if inhaled, yields a 50% risk of infection.

[37] Schönfeldt, F., *A Langevin Equation Dispersion Model for the Stably Stratified Planetary Boundary Layer*, FOA-report FOA-R--97-00523-862--SE (Swedish Defence Research Establishment: Umeå, Sweden, 1997). In a particle dispersion model, a certain amount of mass is represented by a tracer 'particle'. A large number of particles are released and move in the wind and turbulence fields. By collecting the particles in boxes estimates of the concentration can be made. E.g., 10 particles/m³ equal 100 mg/m³ if each particle represents 10 mg. In the current scenario each particle stands for a certain number of micro-organisms.

[38] Meselson *et al.* (note 34). LD_{50} represents the number of spores which, if inhaled, yields a 50% risk of death.

[39] This estimate is based on a small amount of data from experiments on monkeys.

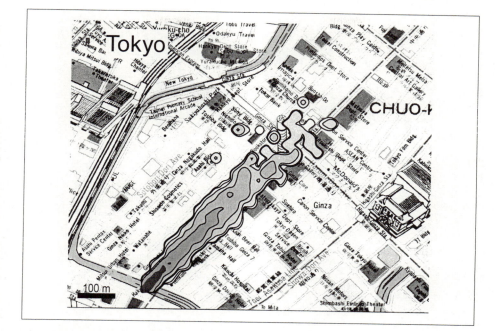

Figure 9A.1. Relative concentration pattern 2 minutes after release
Source: Swedish Defence Research Laboratory (FOA), Umeå, Sweden.

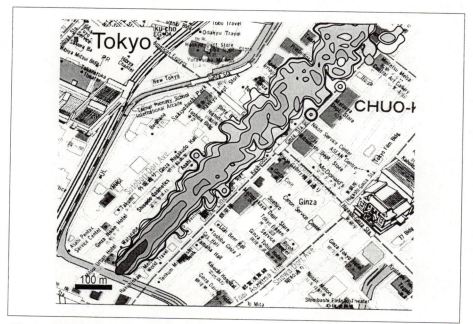

Figure 9A.2. Relative concentration pattern 6 minutes after release
Source: Swedish Defence Research Laboratory (FOA), Umeå, Sweden.

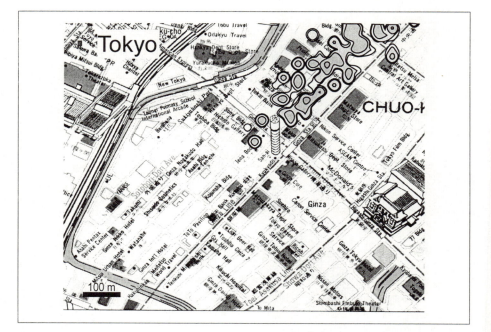

Figure 9A.3. Relative concentration pattern 18 minutes after start and 3 minutes after end of release

Source: Swedish Defence Research Laboratory (FOA), Umeå, Sweden.

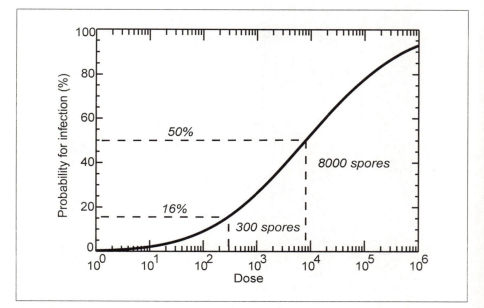

Figure 9A.4. Dose–response relationship for anthrax

Source: Swedish Defence Research Laboratory (FOA), Umeå, Sweden.

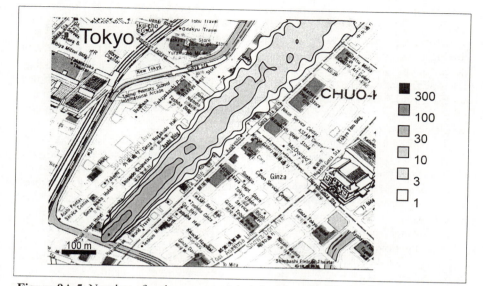

Figure 9A.5. Number of anthrax spores inhaled and retained in the lungs
Source: Swedish Defence Research Laboratory (FOA), Umeå, Sweden.

Table 9A.1. Estimated dose–response relation (infection) for inhaled anthrax spores

Dose (number of spores inhaled by 1 person)	Probability of infection of 1 person (%)
8000	50.0
300	16.0
100	9.2
30	4.5
10	2.1
3	0.8
1	0.3

Source: Swedish Defence Research Laboratory (FOA), Umeå, Sweden.

The probability of infection for each of the areas inside the dose contours in figure 9A.5 can be calculated based on table 9A.1. If the concentration of people in the street were 0.2 person/m², the total number of infected individuals would be approximately 300 people. This number is indicative of the magnitude of expected casualties as certain factors, such as the movement of people and the spread of the aerosol cloud into the buildings, are ignored. Furthermore, a relatively large fraction of the spores would be deposited on the streets, roofs, walls, and other surfaces. If they became airborne again the dose would increase, but it is uncertain to what extent this would occur. At the outset of the scenario it was accepted that only 5 per cent of the mass of the released aerosol had a respirable particle size of less than 10μm. It is also possible that mechanical stress from people walking or vehicles passing could disintegrate the non-respirable particles. In the process, some of these particles could become of respirable size and contribute to the dose if they again became airborne. In any case, the authorities would face a huge decontamination problem.

Without medical treatment most of the infected people would die. However, if treatment with wide spectrum antibiotics were started within 24 hours after the first symptoms appeared this would decrease the number of fatalities considerably. If, following a warning, the authorities were prepared to treat the approximately 30 000 people in the scenario with antibiotics within a few days after their exposure (incubation time for anthrax is 1–7 days) the consequences would be limited. If there were no warning, however, it would take too long to make a correct diagnosis and begin massive prophylactic treatment. Effective medical treatment of the people with symptoms would nevertheless save many lives.

The consequences of an anthrax release at, for example, a large sporting event, where there would be a greater concentration of people, can be estimated by applying the pattern of the spread of contamination illustrated in figure 9A.5. If 30 000 spectators were seated in an area that was 150 metres long (a density of approximately three people/square metre), roughly 1500 people would be infected. Anthrax is not very infectious (i.e., only those exposed to the agent cloud would be infected). Dissemination of a more contagious biological warfare agent could, however, significantly increase the burden on the medical services. A biological warfare agent in dry powder form might be easier to disseminate, but there would be substantial technical problems and a significant risk of infection during preparation of the agent.

The scenario of a terrorist attack with a chemical warfare agent

Terrorists operating in secrecy cannot manufacture or transport large amounts of toxic agents into populated areas. For the 1995 attack in the Tokyo underground Aum Shinrikyo manufactured 6–7 litres of 30 per cent pure sarin (1 litre of solution weighed approximately 1 kilogram), which were transferred to 11 nylon-polyethylene bags. The bags were placed on the floor of five railway carriages on different trains and punctured with the sharpened tips of umbrellas.[40] Most injuries were caused by inhalation of the toxic vapour, but some may also have been the consequence of direct skin contamination from the sarin that was spilled on the floor. The low purity of the sarin solution reduced evaporation significantly (compared to pure sarin). For the Matsumoto attack in 1994 the cult manufactured 5–10 litres of purer sarin.[41] In that attack evaporation was accelerated because the agent was dropped on to an electric heater and released outdoors. However, the process may also partially have decomposed the agent into less toxic compounds. In both attacks the amount of pure sarin that was actually airborne was less than the liquid amount.

Evaporation is a slow process that is further influenced by the surface area of the liquid, agent purity, temperature and air turbulence.[42] Sarin is a liquid that evaporates

---

[40] Tu, A. T., 'Overview of sarin terrorist incidents in Japan in 1994 and 1995', *Proceedings of the Sixth International Symposium on Protection Against Chemical and Biological Warfare Agents*, Stockholm, Sweden, 10–15 May 1998 (Swedish Defence Research Establishment: Umeå, Sweden, May 1998), pp. 13–18.

[41] For a detailed description of the Matsumoto attack, see Kaplan and Marshall (note 31), chapters 19 and 20; and Croddy, E., 'Urban terrorism . . . chemical warfare in Japan', *Jane's Intelligence Review*, vol. 7, no. 11 (Nov. 1995), pp. 520–23. Additional details are from documents, notes and press reports stored in the Harvard Sussex Information Bank on CB warfare, armament and arms limitation at SPRU (Science and Technology Policy Research), University of Sussex, Brighton, UK.

[42] Karlsson, E. *et al.*, 'Consequences of release of the nerve agent sarin in restricted spaces: some calculations in order to illustrate the terrorist attack in the Tokyo underground', *Supplement to the Proceedings of the Fifth International Symposium on Protection Against Chemical and Biological*

at a rate similar to that of water. The total evaporation time for sarin spilled indoors is estimated to be several hours. This low evaporation rate can produce a high agent concentration because the limited volume of the room prevents the agent from mixing with larger volumes of clean air. Normally, ventilation is also too low for rapid dilution. Outdoors a much larger amount of agent is needed because of the dispersive effects of wind and air turbulence. If there is little wind and low turbulence, high agent concentration can be achieved outdoors. The effect indoors of an outdoor release depends on the ventilation and on the amount of adsorption by indoor surfaces. A low level of ventilation will reduce the effect, and increased ventilation after the agent has dissipated outdoors will also reduce the effect indoors.

The following simulation is based on the outdoor sarin attack in Matsumoto. In that attack the Aum Shinrikyo members vaporized the sarin by dropping it on an electric heater in the back of a lorry. The resulting toxic cloud dispersed over a densely populated residential area at night. An estimated 3 kg of pure sarin were airborne over a 25-minute period. However, the attack did not proceed as planned because the person in charge overslept, and the release point had to be changed at the last moment because the judges who were the target of the attack had already left the courthouse. The sarin, while purer than that used in Tokyo in March 1995, had too high a proportion of isopropyl alcohol, giving it a cobalt blue colour. Furthermore, the heat generated by the heater created a white hydrogen chloride or hydrogen fluoride mist inside and around the lorry. Fear of discovery led to hasty abandonment of the operation, and the lorry left the site with the valves for releasing the sarin still open, which caused further casualties.

In order to assess the potential of a terrorist attack with vaporized sarin, the simulation uses the setting and conditions of the Matsumoto attack, but assumes a single point of release and the use of pure sarin. As in the actual attack, the wind direction shifts from west to south-south-east and back during the period of release and the subsequent formation of the sarin vapour. The wind speed is low and varies between 1.8 and 0.5 metres per second.

In the simulation the continuous release forms a narrow plume that moves with the wind (figure 9A.6). The low wind speed and air turbulence at night produce low horizontal dispersion and contribute to formation of the narrow plume. The concentration of sarin is highest close to the release point, but at greater distances the plume becomes wider and the concentration lower. However, because the direction of the wind varies over time (which is normal at low wind speeds), the agent is swept over a wider area than that of the narrow plume itself. Consequently, the sarin cloud strikes certain objects that are some distance downwind for only a limited time while some objects may be missed completely. The vertical dispersion is also low, resulting in lower agent concentration on the higher floors of the buildings. The indoor concentration is lower than the outside concentration, but the agent remains inside the rooms for a period that is longer than that of the passage of the cloud. Buildings with open windows acquire a high indoor concentration that relatively quickly fades away after the cloud passes.

Warfare Agents, Stockholm, Sweden, 11–16 June 1995 (Swedish Defence Research Establishment, Department of NBC Defence: Umeå, Sweden, 1995), pp. 173–180.

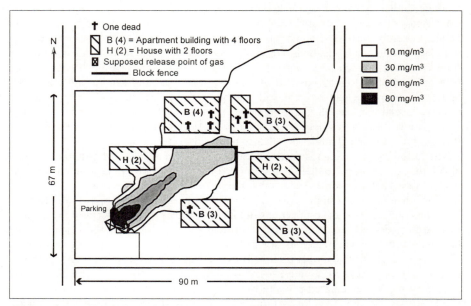

Figure 9A.6. Simulation of the plume dispersion in Matsumoto

Source: Swedish Defence Research Laboratory (FOA), Umeå, Sweden.

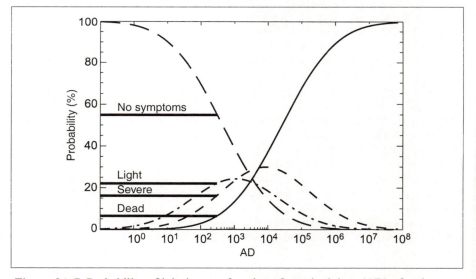

Figure 9A.7. Probability of injuries as a function of acquired dose (AD) of sarin

The calculations are based on the probit function $Pr = a + b \ln (AD)$ where $b = 0.34$ and a is -0.94 for light injuries, -1.56 for severe injuries and -2.33 for lethal injuries. The values of the regression coefficients are obtained from animal experiments and converted to human values.

Source: Koch, B., Swedish Defence Research Establishment (FOA), Umeå, Sweden, private communication with Lennart Thaning.

The effect on people depends on agent concentration, respiration, transfer rate from the lungs to the blood, and exposure time. The concept 'acquired dose' (AD) is used to model casualties as a result of exposure to a toxic agent. The AD is defined as:

$$AD = [(concentration) \times (respiratory\ rate) \times (transfer\ factor)]^n \times (time)$$

where $n = 1.65$ for sarin, the transfer factor is 0.5, and the respiratory rate is 15 litres/min for people at rest.

Figure 9A.7 indicates the effect of an AD of 800, which would be obtained in a room 75 metres from the point of release after 50 minutes. The outcome of such a dose is that 12 per cent of those exposed would die, 22 per cent would suffer severe injuries, and 25 per cent would sustain light injuries. The remaining 41 per cent would not display any symptoms. This wide range of responses was observed in the Matsumoto attack. Individuals who had all been in the same room during the attack arrived at hospital in varying conditions: some were unconscious while others exhibited minor symptoms. However, some of those who did not complain of any symptoms nonetheless had a tremendous decrease in their acetylcholinesterase level.[43]

It is difficult to compare the release patterns and effects of such terrorist use of a chemical warfare agent with those of similar military use. The amounts of highly pure agent delivered by the military may range from tens of kilograms to several tonnes per hour depending on the mission and the target size. Bombs, artillery shells or missiles may be used to disseminate the agent over an area of the order of one square kilometre. The large amounts of agent and the dissemination method produce an immediate high concentration. There are two effects of such a release. First, a primary cloud, which may have an immediate high agent concentration, is formed and drifts away on the wind. A substantial part of the agent will consist of droplets that are deposited in the immediate vicinity of the target. Second, evaporation from the ground produces a secondary cloud that, depending on the type of agent and the weather conditions, may persist for many days.

The effects of the release by terrorists of a chemical warfare agent will vary depending on the circumstances. As a consequence of the probable method of release, there will be only a single cloud of agent and its vertical dispersion will be limited (unless it is released from an elevated point). If people are outside or indoors with the windows open when the sarin cloud passes, the severity of the injuries and the number of fatalities will increase. However, those outdoors may escape the vapour, which would reduce its effect. Because of low vertical dispersion the people on the lower floors of a building are normally at greater risk than those on the higher floors. A larger volume of agent or a more efficient method of dissemination would also increase the number of casualties. If the agent were less pure the evaporation rate would be reduced as would the amount of airborne agent. Some first-generation chemical warfare agents such as phosgene and chlorine are far more volatile than nerve agents and would dissipate more quickly. Although less toxic than nerve agents, such agents can cause severe casualties, especially if released indoors. Hydrogen cyanide and industrial chemicals like sulphur dioxide and ammonia have similar properties. A terrorist could obtain and use such chemicals in or near a populated area.

---

[43] Acetylcholinesterase is an enzyme found in some nerve endings that controls the functioning of the neurotransmitter acetylcholine. Nerve agents reduce the levels of acetylcholinesterase, so that the transmission of nerve impulses via the acetylcholine becomes uncontrolled, leading to the malfunctioning of many bodily organs and ultimately resulting in death.

Most chemical warfare agents act more rapidly than biological warfare agents, and prompt identification of the agent and immediate medical treatment is required to prevent severe poisoning. The treatment will vary from agent to agent.[44] If the antidote to a nerve agent is injected shortly after exposure to it the effect of the nerve agent will be considerably reduced. Detoxification of hydrogen cyanide can be accelerated by immediate treatment with antidotes that bind cyanide ions in the blood. Exposure to phosgene, chlorine, sulphur dioxide and ammonia may cause pulmonary oedema (i.e., abnormal accumulation of liquid in the lung tissues), and treatment with oxygen together with substances to widen the bronchi and cortisone is required.

As is the case with a BW attack, prompt identification of the agent, the availability of antidotes (in the case of nerve agents) and quick medical treatment may considerably reduce the consequences of exposure.

VI. Conclusions

This appendix focuses on chemical and biological weapons because they represent a new qualitative element of the terrorist threat. Toxicants and pathogens have often been used in assassinations and sabotage in the past. Currently, a large number of people may have access to the knowledge and technologies required to manipulate these agents, which can increase the quantitative dimension of the threat, but the use of these agents generally will not cause mass casualties. In contrast, chemical and biological warfare agents are indiscriminate by nature; theoretically, some military-grade agents can produce large numbers of fatalities and casualties. Their insidiousness makes them ideal instruments of terror and chaos. The processes for manufacturing and disseminating the most lethal and complex CB warfare agents in sufficient quantities to obtain such effects are more complex than those for other chemical and biological materials. Despite large investments, Aum Shinrikyo's CBW programme experienced considerable problems. In addition, such a programme is dependent on external sources of supply, and the programme must be conducted in secrecy because of its illegality. This considerably complicates the acquisition of such weaponry.

The likelihood of the recurrence of events like the 1994 and 1995 releases of sarin in Japan must be judged on the basis of realistic, testable parameters. This appendix utilizes a multidisciplinary approach to profile the new terrorist organizations and analyse the prerequisites for large-scale CBW programmes. Only vertically organized, highly integrated and ideologically uniform groups (such as a religious cult) are able to carry out large-scale CBW production in secrecy. The material base (number of members, financial assets, property owned and infrastructure) on which a terrorist group can draw plays a critical role. Variations in the composition of a group have a direct impact on its ability to sustain a CBW programme. This reduces the number of potential CBW terrorists. Aum Shinrikyo's material base was substantial, and few other terrorist organizations will be able to match it. The cult's difficulties and ultimate failure are therefore significant in the risk assessment of terrorism with chemical and biological weapons.

Technical hurdles affected the range and quality of the warfare agents that Aum Shinrikyo was able to develop. Military-grade warfare agents are therefore unlikely to constitute the primary threat from such a group. The sarin attacks in Japan demonstrated that a terrorist CBW attack may result in few fatalities while numerous victims

[44] *Chemical Weapons* (note 9), pp. 29–30, 38, 47.

will probably suffer short or low-level exposure to the chemical or biological warfare agents. The simulations in this appendix suggest that even if agents of a high quality are employed the casualty patterns observed at Matsumoto and Tokyo may be typical.

If the material base of a terrorist group is restricted it may only be able to produce a limited quantity of high-quality chemical or biological warfare agents. Loosely structured and cell-based terrorist groups or loners can manufacture small quantities of such agents. While this increases the possibility of the use of these agents in terrorist attacks, small quantities are unlikely to cause mass casualties, although high-quality agents would be effective for targeting individuals or small groups. Such discriminate use of warfare agents does not differ fundamentally from the more 'traditional' use of chemical or biological materials. In recent decades various terrorist organizations and individuals have possessed extremely toxic substances, but until recently this did not affect the risk assessment of terrorism.

First-generation chemical warfare agents such as phosgene or hydrogen cyanide are not difficult to produce in large quantities, and various terrorist organizations could manufacture them. Because of their chemical properties they are less lethal than nerve agents and are therefore unlikely to produce large numbers of casualties. Some persistent first-generation warfare agents could be employed to interrupt critical services rather than to cause bodily harm. Other types of agent, such as animal or plant pathogens, would be better suited for economic terrorism: and could cause widespread damage to the targeted society without necessarily killing or injuring individuals.

Governments face a multitude of CB terrorism threats, but the most catastrophic scenarios involving mass casualties, though possible, are not likely to occur. (Catastrophic scenarios involving non-conventional weapons, which feature in many policy debates, are often made plausible by insistence on the existence of a threat posed by state-sponsored terrorism.) Nevertheless, because of the potential consequences for the targeted society of a terrorist attack with CBW, governments must be prepared for such an attack. The key issue is thus to devise and execute balanced policies. Over-reaction can lead to country-wide anxiety and paranoia. In such an atmosphere, hoaxes may become as efficient—especially in terms of economic terrorism—as actual attacks with CBW.

Appendix 9B. The future of chemical and biological weapon disarmament in Iraq: from UNSCOM to UNMOVIC

MARIA WAHLBERG, MILTON LEITENBERG and
JEAN PASCAL ZANDERS

I. Introduction

After the 1991 Persian Gulf War the United Nations Security Council adopted
Resolution 687, which among other things required Iraq unconditionally to destroy
and 'undertake not to use, develop, construct or acquire' non-conventional weapons
or ballistic missiles with a range greater than 150 kilometres.[1] In order to monitor
Iraq's implementation of this obligation the ceasefire resolution created the United
Nations Special Commission on Iraq (UNSCOM). It had two basic functions: to
inspect and oversee the destruction or elimination of Iraq's chemical and biological
weapon (CBW) and ballistic missile capabilities and its CBW and ballistic missile
production and storage facilities; and to monitor Iraq over the longer term to ensure
its continued compliance with the obligations of Resolution 687.

In 1999 UNSCOM was disbanded following a period in which Iraq systematically
obstructed UNSCOM inspections and exploited the political disagreement among the
permanent members of the UN Security Council to its advantage. At the end of 1999
the Security Council adopted Resolution 1284 which replaced UNSCOM with the
United Nations Monitoring, Verification and Inspection Commission (UNMOVIC).[2]
It is uncertain whether UNMOVIC will be more successful than UNSCOM.

Section II of this appendix analyses the process which led to the creation of
UNMOVIC and examines the provisions of Resolution 1284. Section III investigates
the reasons for the failure of UNSCOM that may also hamper UNMOVIC. Section IV
provides an overview of Iraq's declarations with respect to its chemical and biological
weapons, UNSCOM's findings and the discrepancies between them. Section V presents the conclusions.

II. Developments in 1999

Iraq suspended all cooperation with UNSCOM in 1998. Consequently, no inspections
were carried out in 1999. The UN Security Council remained deeply divided as
regards the future disarmament regime for Iraq and the conditions for lifting the sanc-

---

[1] UN Security Council Resolution 687, 3 Apr. 1991. The task of inspecting, destroying and removing
all of Iraq's nuclear weapon capabilities was assigned to the International Atomic Energy Agency
(IAEA). UNSCOM's mandate also included the obligation to assist and cooperate with the IAEA in its
work in Iraq. The activities of UNSCOM are described in the 1991–99 SIPRI Yearbooks and in SIPRI,
'Iraq: the UNSCOM experience', *Fact Sheet*, Oct. 1998, reproduced at URL <http://www.sipri.se/pubs/
Factsheet/unscom.html>.

[2] UN Security Council Resolution 1284, 17 Dec. 1999.

tions that have been imposed on Iraq.[3] In 1999 the UNSCOM findings were reviewed by independent panels, and the five permanent members of the Security Council began exploring alternatives to UNSCOM in order to break the deadlock on the issue of inspections.

The review panels

On 30 January 1999 the Security Council adopted a Canadian proposal to establish three independent review panels, which were chaired by Security Council President Ambassador Celso Amorim of Brazil. The first panel worked on disarmament and issues related to the future monitoring and verification of Iraqi compliance with the UN resolutions. The second and third panels dealt with humanitarian matters and the return of prisoners of war and Kuwaiti property, respectively.[4]

The disarmament panel was asked to recommend measures to re-establish an effective disarmament and monitoring and verification regime in Iraq. Its report noted that some disarmament issues had not yet been satisfactorily resolved, and proposals were made for integrating the remaining disarmament tasks into a reinforced Ongoing Monitoring and Verification (OMV) system whose mechanisms for disarmament, monitoring and verification could reinforce each other.[5] The report stated that, although these mechanisms 'address different dimensions of the broader problematic', they could be implemented using the same or similar tools, including 'on-site inspections with full access, including no-notice inspections, sample analysis, aerial surveillance, evaluation of documentation, interviews [and] installed monitoring equipment'.[6] Because the relevant Security Council resolutions already permitted the use of such measures there was no need to rewrite the UNSCOM mandate. However, the intensity, frequency, intrusiveness and methods of the preparatory work had to be altered. The report noted that the implementation of the reinforced OMV was dependent on the firm and active support of the Security Council and on Iraqi acceptance of the OMV and cooperation. Iraq was required to provide access to all locations, documents and information and not to interfere with monitoring equipment or to conceal, remove or destroy relevant evidence.[7]

The end of UNSCOM

UNSCOM Executive Chairman Richard Butler stepped down from his post when his contract expired on 30 June. He subsequently expressed his frustration with the

[3] The Security Council imposed economic sanctions prohibiting all exports and imports to and from Iraq following Iraq's invasion of Kuwait in 1990. Resolution 687 continued the sanctions in order to compel Iraq to meet the various ceasefire conditions. The sanctions were not absolute. Iraq was allowed to import certain goods for humanitarian purposes and to export fixed quantities of oil under UN supervision. Iraq viewed the sanctions and the food-for-oil arrangement as an infringement of its national sovereignty.

[4] Note by the President of the Security Council, UN document S/1999/100, 30 Jan. 1999.

[5] Letters dated 27 and 30 March 1999, respectively, from the Chairman of the panels established pursuant to the note by the President of the Security Council of 30 January 1999 (S/1999/100) addressed to the President of the Security Council, UN document S/1999/356, 30 Mar. 1999. The 20-member panel included officials from UNSCOM, the IAEA, the Organisation for the Prohibition of Chemical Weapons (OPCW) and the United Nations.

[6] Letters dated 27 and 30 March 1999 . . . (note 5), p. 15. The original OMV proposal was based on the assumption that all disarmament issues would have been resolved.

[7] Letters dated 27 and 30 March 1999 . . . (note 5).

inability of the Security Council to uphold its own resolutions and questioned its ability 'to function as the guardian of international peace and security.' Butler called Russia Iraq's 'chief advocate' in the Security Council and alleged that Russia had pressured UNSCOM to accept Iraq's claim that it had fully met its disarmament requirements. Butler also harshly criticized UN Secretary-General Kofi Annan for what he regarded as misguided attempts to deal with Iraq through diplomacy.[8]

The expulsion of the UNSCOM inspectors from Iraq in 1998 was a major contributing factor to the US and British air strikes against Iraq in December.[9] The attacks caused deep divisions in the Security Council, and later events, such as the NATO air campaign in Kosovo in the spring of 1999, exacerbated the tensions. Furthermore, press reports in January and March claimed that the US intelligence services had used UNSCOM to spy on Iraq without UNSCOM's knowledge. UNSCOM was susceptible to such accusations because it utilized intelligence, weapon and other types of experts, who had been seconded to UNSCOM by UN member states, in order to obtain information which Iraq was attempting to conceal. Although Butler insisted that UNSCOM had not accepted or used such assistance from UN member states except for the purpose of disarming Iraq, UNSCOM's credibility with some Security Council members was severely damaged.[10] The claims reinforced Russia's view that UNSCOM was a US tool and Russia's UN Ambassador Sergey Lavrov even refused to attend a Security Council briefing by Butler in April.[11]

When UNSCOM withdrew from Baghdad in December 1998 some reference standards of chemical warfare agents (i.e., small amounts of chemicals used to calibrate equipment) and samples of mustard gas were left behind. When this became public in June 1999 Russia misrepresented the implications of the action and called for an emergency session of the Security Council. The amounts were too small to pose any danger, but Butler recommended that an expert team be dispatched to Baghdad to dispose of the chemicals.[12] Because Iraq refused to allow UNSCOM personnel to enter the country, four experts from the Organisation for the Prohibition of Chemical Weapons (OPCW), who did not have any previous connection to UNSCOM, were sent to Iraq. They destroyed the chemicals and closed the UNSCOM laboratory in the Baghdad Monitoring and Verification Centre in July.[13]

---

[8] Butler, R., *Talk*, Sep. 1999, URL <http://www.talkmagazine.com>; and Butler, R., 'Bewitched, bothered, and bewildered: repairing the Security Council', *Foreign Affairs*, vol. 78, no. 5 (Sep./Oct. 1999), pp. 9–12. Butler also reiterated claims based on intelligence reports that a senior Russian official had received personal payments from Iraq.

[9] Zanders, J. P., French, E. M. and Pauwels, N., 'Chemical and biological weapon developments and arms control', *SIPRI Yearbook 1999: Aramaments, Disarmament and International Security* (Oxford University Press: Oxford, 1999), pp. 586–92.

[10] Gellman, B., 'Annan suspicious of UNSCOM role', *Washington Post*, 6 Jan. 1999, pp. A1, A22; Weiner, T., 'US admits spies worked as inspectors of Iraqi arms', *International Herald Tribune*, 8 Jan. 1999, pp. 1, 10; Weiner, T., 'US explains how spy put eavesdropping device in Iraq', *International Herald Tribune*, 9–10 Jan. 1999, pp. 1, 5; United States Information Service, 'UNSCOM's Butler says inspectors were not used for spying (UN Security Council will soon decide UNSCOM's future role)', *Washington File*, 11 Jan. 1999, URL <http://pdqtest1.env?CQ_SESSION_KEY=AFTCNVBJRHBM& CQ_QUERY_HANDLE=124008&CQ_CUR_DOCUMENT=3&>; and Gellman, B., 'US spied on Iraqi military via UN', *Washington Post*, 2 Mar. 1999, p. A1.

[11] Xinhua News Agency via CNN Custom News, 'Security Council meets on Iraq', 15 Apr. 1999, URL <http://www.cnn.com>.

[12] 'UN tentatively considers Iraq policy options amidst new UNSCOM controversy, from UNSCOM to UNCIM?', *Disarmament Diplomacy*, no. 38 (June 1999), p. 55.

[13] United Nations, 'Agreement reached between UN and Government of Iraq on composition of technical mission to inspect and clean up UNSCOM's Baghdad Laboratories', Press Release, no. SG/SM/7044 IK/277, 24 June 1999; OPCW, 'Statement by the Director-General, OPCW experts mission to Iraq: an update', Press Release, no. 017/99, 20 July 1999; United States Information Service, 'Security

The reference standards for the nerve agent VX were at the centre of the controversy. While Iraq had admitted that it had produced VX, it had always denied that it had weaponized VX (i.e., prepared the agent to be delivered as a weapon). However, in 1998 UNSCOM announced that it had found the degradation products of VX on some remnants of missile warheads. Russia demanded additional analysis of the VX reference standards, implying that the UNSCOM inspectors had deliberately contaminated the warheads. As part of the agreement in the Security Council to destroy the VX standards, UNSCOM had to answer questions from China and France about the VX standards and provide sensitive information about its laboratory methods. The Security Council finally agreed to drop the issue in early September.[14]

At the same time US resolve about the disarmament of Iraq seemed to be waning.[15] The Clinton Administration appeared rather to pursue a policy of containment and a strong commitment to sanctions. This contributed to the almost continuous US bombing of military targets in northern and southern Iraq where Coalition aircraft enforced no-fly zones for Iraqi aircraft in order to protect the Kurdish and Shi'ite population. The USA shifted its focus to the removal of President Saddam Hussein from power and supported Iraqi opposition groups in exile. Under the 1998 Iraq Liberation Act President Bill Clinton was authorized to spend up to $97 million in support of Iraqi opposition groups.[16] Iraq remained focused on denying UNSCOM inspectors access to its territory and on the abolition of the sanctions against it.

The search for a new verification regime

Despite deep divisions between the five permanent members of the Security Council, diplomatic efforts to return inspectors to Iraq continued. By early 1999 it was clear that UNSCOM would have to be replaced by a new body. Although the Security Council members accepted the conclusion of the disarmament panel that unresolved disarmament issues should be addressed by a reinforced OMV system, disagreement on the future of the sanctions complicated the discussions. China, France and Russia held the view that concessions on the sanctions would induce Iraq to comply with its disarmament obligations. The United Kingdom and the United States, in contrast, maintained that Iraq must demonstrate full cooperation and compliance with the existing Security Council resolutions before the sanctions could be lifted. Several proposals for a new disarmament arrangement were circulated in the Security Council, including two draft resolutions, one by Russia and one by the UK and the Netherlands.[17]

Council allows destruction of VX samples in Iraq', *Washington File*, 27 July 1999, URL <http://www. usia.gov/cgi-bin/washfile/display.pl?p=/products/washfile/latest&f=99072701.nlt&t=/products/washfile/ newsitem.shtml>; and OPCW, 'OPCW mission in Baghdad successfully completed', Press Release, no. 018/99, 29 July 1999.

[14] 'UN Council gets secret data on chemical weapons', Reuters via CNN News, 25 Aug. 1999, URL <http://www.cnn.com>; and 'Security Council drops Iraq laboratory controversy', Reuters via CNN News, 3 Sep. 1999, URL <http://www.cnn.com>.

[15] Hoagland, J., 'The Iraq mess', *Washington Post*, 6 Aug. 1999, p. A21; Crossette, B., 'America moves apart from the UN on Iraq', *New York Times* (Internet edn), 26 Dec. 1999, URL <http://www. nytimes.com/library/.review/122699us-un-iraq-reviewhtml>; and Byman, D., 'All talk, no action may be best with Iraq', *Washington Post*, 2 Jan. 2000, p. B04.

[16] Written Statement of Martin S. Indyk, Assistant Secretary for Near Eastern Affairs, Department of State, House International Relations Committee, 8 June 1999, reproduced at URL <http://www.erols. com>.

[17] Russian Federation, Draft Resolution on Iraq, 15 Apr. 1999, photocopied; and Britain and the Netherlands, Draft Resolution, 15 Apr. 1999, photocopied.

According to the Russian draft, the Security Council would approve a plan for the reinforcement of the OMV system to be submitted to the UN Secretary-General. Once the new OMV system had become fully operational, the UN sanctions would be lifted. In contrast, the British–Netherlands draft did not set any new conditions for the end of the sanctions but instead reaffirmed the provisions of Resolution 687. However, it proposed to replace UNSCOM with a Commission on Investigation, Inspection and Monitoring (UNCIIM), which would take over all assets, liabilities, staff and archives from UNSCOM and implement a reinforced OMV system based on the report of the disarmament panel.

Negotiations in the Security Council gradually brought the positions closer. A second draft resolution, submitted by Russia together with China and France, contained stricter disarmament requirements for Iraq. The sanctions would be suspended for a renewable period of 100 days rather than being lifted.[18] A 9 September draft resolution by China and Russia proposed replacing UNSCOM with a UN Monitoring and Inspection Commission (UNMIC). The sanctions would be suspended only after the new OMV system had been effectively and efficiently operational, with cooperation from the Government of Iraq, for 60 days.[19]

Meanwhile, the British–Netherlands draft was further refined and presented to the Security Council in June, this time co-sponsored by Argentina and Slovenia and supported by the USA. The draft resolution suggested replacing UNSCOM with a Special Commission on Inspection and Monitoring (UNCIM). The draft proposed to suspend the sanctions after Iraq had demonstrated full cooperation with UNCIM and the International Atomic Energy Agency (IAEA) for two consecutive periods of 120 days each and had completed the remaining disarmament tasks in accordance with a list prepared by UNCIM.[20]

Iraq continued to insist that it had already fully complied with its disarmament obligations and maintained that the inspectors could not return as long as sanctions remained in place. It rejected the proposals put forward by the disarmament panel, stating that it had not participated in the panel and that it would not comply unless its opinion was taken into account.[21] Iraq also declared that the efforts in the Security Council to devise a new disarmament regime were tactics to further delay lifting of the sanctions and vowed not to accept any resolution that only provided for a time-limited suspension of the sanctions.[22]

Security Council Resolution 1284

At the end of 1999 pressure to reach consensus on a resolution for a new Iraqi disarmament and inspection system increased in the Security Council. The negotiations

[18] Center for Nonproliferation Studies, Monterey Institute of International Studies, Iraq Special Collection, 'Draft proposals for new UN Iraq monitoring body: China/France/Russia proposal', URL <http://cns.miis.edu/research/iraq/uncim/draft1.htm>.
[19] Working Paper by China and Russia, 9 Sep. 1999, photocopied.
[20] Center for Nonproliferation Studies, Monterey Institute of International Studies, Iraq Special Collection, 'Draft proposals for new UN Iraq monitoring body: UK/Netherlands/Argentina/Slovenia proposal', URL <http://cns.miis.edu/research/iraq/uncim/draft2.htm>.
[21] 'Iraq rejects UN inquiries on weapons, sanctions', Reuters via CNN Custom News, 9 Apr. 1999, URL <http://www.cnn.com>; and 'Ramadan rejects UNSC proposals', Baghdad Republic of Iraq Network in Arabic, Foreign Broadcast Information Service (FBIS) translated text, 1600 GMT 14 Apr. 1999, reproduced at URL <http://www.erols.com>.
[22] Olson, E., 'Iraqi bars compromise on lifting of UN sanctions', *International Herald Tribune*, 5 Nov. 1999, p. 5.

concentrated more and more on further development of the British–Netherlands draft resolution, which had the support of 11 of the 15 Security Council members: the UK, the USA and 9 non-permanent members. In November it also became clear that China, France and Russia would not veto the resolution. Resolution 1284 was adopted on 17 December by 11 votes and 4 abstentions. China, France and Russia as well as Malaysia criticized the resolution as too strict and ambiguous as regards the criteria for suspending the sanctions.[23]

Resolution 1284 created the United Nations Monitoring, Verification and Inspection Commission, which replaces UNSCOM and assumes the responsibilities previously mandated to it. Like UNSCOM, UNMOVIC is a subsidiary body of the Security Council; unlike UNSCOM, the Executive Chairman will not report directly to the Security Council, but via the UN Secretary-General. The role of the IAEA is reaffirmed in the resolution: it will continue its work with the cooperation and assistance of UNMOVIC. The resolution requested the Secretary-General to appoint an Executive Chairman of UNMOVIC who is to submit to the Security Council for its approval an organizational plan for UNMOVIC within 45 days of his appointment. Iraq is required to cooperate with UNMOVIC by giving it 'immediate, unconditional and unrestricted access to any and all areas, facilities, equipment, records and means of transport which they wish to inspect in accordance with the mandate of UNMOVIC, as well as to all officials and other persons under the authority of the Iraqi Government whom UNMOVIC wishes to interview'.[24] Within 60 days after starting work in Iraq, UNMOVIC and the IAEA are each to draw up a work programme for approval by the Security Council. These work programmes should include the implementation of a reinforced OMV based on the recommendations of the disarmament panel and identify the key remaining disarmament tasks to be completed by Iraq. The resolution states that 'what is required of Iraq for the implementation of each task shall be clearly defined and precise'.[25]

Resolution 1284 also addresses the sanctions against Iraq. The Security Council expressed its intention to suspend the sanctions for a period of 120 days upon receipt of reports from the Executive Chairman of UNMOVIC and from the Director General of the IAEA that Iraq has cooperated in all respects in fulfilling the work programmes and that the reinforced system of ongoing monitoring and verification is fully operational. The suspension is also subject 'to the elaboration of effective financial and other operational measures to ensure that Iraq does not acquire prohibited items' and other import and export restrictions elaborated in earlier Security Council resolutions. The sanctions will be automatically reimposed five days after UNMOVIC or the IAEA reports to the Security Council that Iraq is not in full cooperation or is in violation of any of the other conditions for suspension of the sanctions, unless the Security Council decides otherwise.[26] The 120-day suspension period is renewable if Iraq continues to cooperate. There will no longer be a limit on the amount of oil that Iraq can export. The revenues from oil exports will, in accordance with the food-for-oil programme, be put in an escrow account and used to purchase food and medicine.

The resolution is unclear about whether the sanctions can be suspended following completion of the key remaining disarmament tasks or whether progress in achieving

[23] Press release: Security Council establishes new monitoring commission for Iraq adopting resolution 1284 (1999) by vote of 11-0-4, UN document SC/6775, 17 Dec. 1999.
[24] UN Security Council Resolution 1284 (note 2), para. 4.
[25] UN Security Council Resolution 1284 (note 2), para. 7.
[26] UN Security Council Resolution 1284 (note 2), paras 33, 35.

these goals suffices. Paragraph 34 of the resolution states that, in reporting to the Security Council, the Executive Chairman of UNMOVIC should take into account the progress made in completing the key remaining disarmament tasks as the basis for his assessment.[27] The UK and the USA stressed that the suspension of the sanctions depended on Iraqi cooperation and compliance with its disarmament obligations.[28]

Earlier drafts of the British–Netherlands proposal included a passage stating that the new inspection organization was to take over all of UNSCOM's assets, liabilities, staff and archives. Resolution 1284 omits the word 'staff' and instead specifies that UNMOVIC staff should be drawn from the broadest possible geographical base.

A short time after Resolution 1284 was adopted it was rejected by Iraq. Iraqi Deputy Prime Minister Tariq Aziz reiterated the long-standing Iraqi position that Iraq has fulfilled its disarmament requirements in accordance with previous Security Council resolutions and that therefore the sanctions should be lifted unconditionally.[29] At the time of writing, the Security Council had reached consensus on the nomination of Hans Blix of Sweden, former Director General of the IAEA, as Executive Chairman of UNMOVIC after rejecting the nomination by Kofi Annan of UNSCOM's first Executive Chairman Rolf Ekéus.[30] It remained unclear whether Iraq would allow the new inspections.[31] Earlier, the Russian representative to the Security Council, Sergey Lavrov, had pointed out that Iraq's acceptance of renewed inspections depended not only on the choice of Executive Chairman, 'but also [on] the composition of the inspection and monitoring staff and the list of issues that President Saddam Hussein's government would have to address'.[32] It remains to be seen whether Iraq will be able to exercise a de facto veto in the Security Council through one of the permanent members that abstained from the vote on Resolution 1284.

III. The legacy of UNSCOM

Although UNMOVIC represents a new beginning, its potential effectiveness may be hampered by the legacy of UNSCOM. Some of the practices that emerged during the stand-offs between Iraq and the UN Security Council, such as the intervention of the UN Secretary-General, have been formalized in Resolution 1284. In addition, UNMOVIC will start out with mostly new, and thus inexperienced, personnel, giving

---

[27] UN Security Council Resolution 1284 (note 2), para. 34.

[28] Foreign and Commonwealth Office, 'Edited transcript of interview given by the Foreign Secretary, Robin Cook, for BBC Radio 4, London', 18 Dec. 1999, URL <http://www.fco.gov.uk/news/ newstext. asp?3138>; and Department of State, 'Ambassador A. Peter Burleigh, US Deputy Permanent Representative to the United Nations, Statement on Iraq, UN Security Council', 17 Dec. 1999', URL <http:// www.usia.gov/topical/pol/ usandun/burl1217.htm>.

[29] Permanent Mission of Iraq to the United Nations, 'Commenting on the resolution which the Security Council adopted yesterday, Mr Tariq Aziz, the Deputy Prime Minister said', Press Release, 18 Dec. 1999, URL <http://www.Iraqi-Mission.org/pr121899.htm>.

[30] Crossette, B., 'UN straining to appoint top inspector of Iraqi arms', *New York Times* (Internet edn), 17 Jan. 2000, URL <http://www.nytimes.com>; 'Russia nixes UN chief's choice of Ekéus for Iraq', Reuters via Fox News, 17 Jan. 2000, URL <http://www.foxnews.com/ world/0117/i_rt_0117_60.sml>; 'Iraq nomination hits trouble', BBC News, 18 Jan. 2000, URL <http://news.bbc.co.uk/hi/english/world/ middle_east/newsid_607000/607502.stm>; and Press release: Secretary-General appoints Hans Blix of Sweden Executive Chairman of UN Monitoring, Verification and Inspection Commission, UN document SG/A/721, 27 Jan. 2000.

[31] Crossette, B., 'Iraqis seem less hostile to new weapons inspector', *New York Times* (Internet edn), 28 Jan. 2000, URL <http://www.nytimes.com>.

[32] Crossette, B., 'Annan faces growing split over arms inspector for Iraq', *New York Times* (Internet edn), 19 Jan. 2000, <http://www.nytimes.com>.

Iraq a significant edge if it attempts to conceal CBW operations during the first phases of UNMOVIC's operations. Consequently, if UNMOVIC were to report early this would meet with suspicion from some Security Council members. If it were to report late other Security Council members might accuse it of wilful procrastination in order to hamper lifting of the sanctions. The following discussion describes the confrontations between Iraq and UNSCOM, which, if repeated, may result in renewed paralysis of the inspection and monitoring activities.

The disarmament regime defined in UN Security Council resolutions 687, 707 and 715 required Iraq to declare all of its chemical and biological weapons, and UNSCOM inspectors were given access unprecedented in the history of arms control to all suspected Iraqi CBW sites.[33] Nevertheless, it soon became clear that Iraq was systematically concealing as much as possible of its prohibited weapon programmes. The Security Council repeatedly determined that Iraq was in 'material breach' of its obligations under Resolution 687 after Ekéus had presented evidence to that effect. As early as February 1992 Iraq began to argue that it had fully disclosed its weapon programmes and that the sanctions should be lifted.[34] It consistently maintained this position for the next seven years irrespective of unequivocal evidence demonstrating the falsehood of the claim. The defection of Lieutenant General Hussein Kamal in August 1995 forced the Iraqi Government to admit that 'it had been engaged in a dedicated concealment effort to hide proscribed items and documents from the Commission' and that 'its full, final and complete disclosures over a number of years have been deliberately misleading'.[35]

However, support for UNSCOM in the Security Council was on the decline in the mid-1990s. As the consequence of the lack of consensus in the Security Council, Ekéus could no longer obtain a determination by the Security Council that Iraq was in material breach of Security Council resolutions in response to specific Iraqi violations. In June 1996, in order to be able to continue UNSCOM's work in the face of Security Council inaction, Ekéus compromised for the first time on the authority of UNSCOM as established by Security Council resolutions when he agreed on the 'modalities' of visits to sites to be inspected. The compromises were minor, but Iraq used them as a precedent to appeal for special conditions and to negotiate. The unwillingness of the Security Council to make an issue of each Iraqi obstruction hardened Iraq's resolve. On 23 October 1997 China, France and Russia abstained rather than supported UNSCOM's determination that Iraq had not fulfilled the terms of UN Security Council Resolution 1115.[36] Iraq immediately exploited this support from three of the five permanent members of the Security Council. Within days it demanded that all US personnel be withdrawn from UNSCOM, which precipitated another crisis.

---

[33] Resolution 687 (note 1); UN Security Council Resolution 707, 15 Aug. 1991; and UN Security Council Resolution 715, 11 Oct. 1991.

[34] Trevan, T., *Saddam's Secrets: The Hunt for Iraq's Hidden Weapons* (Harper Collins: London, 1999), pp. 158–59.

[35] Report of the Secretary-General on the Activities of the Special Commission Established by the Secretary-General Pursuant to paragraph 9(b)(1) of Resolution 687 (1991), UN document S/1996/258, 11 Apr. 1996.

[36] UN Security Council Resolution 1115, 21 June 1997, demanded that Iraq give UNSCOM inspectors immediate, unconditional and unrestricted access to all sites and records which UNSCOM wished to inspect.

The interventions by Kofi Annan following the departure of Ekéus as Executive Chairman were far more significant.[37] This development offered an opportunity for Iraq to undercut UNSCOM and the role of new Executive Chairman Butler. Iraq had succeeded in bypassing UNSCOM. Annan and his senior envoys in effect became interlocutors for Iraqi claims that the Security Council resolutions placed an unfair burden on Iraq. The fact that Iraq remained in non-compliance with Security Council Resolution 687 became irrelevant. The Memorandum of Understanding (MOU) which was negotiated and signed by Annan with Iraq on 23 February 1998 compromised UNSCOM's basic authority and the Security Council resolutions.[38] It was only a matter of months before Iraq violated the MOU, and by the end of 1998 Annan was reluctantly forced to admit that this had happened. In short order, Iraq expelled UNSCOM entirely from the country. With crucial assistance from members of the Security Council Iraq had successfully faced down the United Nations.

These developments could not have occurred without the split in the Security Council. Although all of the relevant Security Council resolutions were mandated under Chapter VII of the UN Charter, recourse to the use of force depended always and almost entirely on the willingness of the UK and the USA to conduct military activities. Even in those instances when China, France and Russia voted to condemn Iraq's non-compliance, they did not support the use of force. As long as Iraq perceived that it had support for its non-compliance in the Security Council, it had no reason to comply. Iraq's central administration was clearly able to withstand the sanctions. It had also evaded the sanctions for a number of years and exported oil products by land and sea routes.[39] Nonetheless, Iraq had forfeited six or seven years of oil export earnings, commonly estimated at $100 billion,[40] as the trade-off for its decision not to comply with Security Council resolutions. The disaffection in 1997 and 1998 of US allies in the Persian Gulf and the support for Iraq in the Security Council caused US political decision makers to become increasingly reluctant to bear the cost and face the criticism of upholding the disarmament regime that the Security Council resolutions had imposed on Iraq.

China, France and Russia were no longer primarily concerned with the elimination and the future acquisition of non-conventional weapons by Iraq, which undermined the integrity of the Security Council and its resolutions. In the case of the chemical reference samples Russia established a context in which evidence provided by UNSCOM was questioned and rejected. There are numerous references to the economic motives of China, France and Russia.[41] France and Russia have sought the repayment by Iraq of outstanding debts from the 1980s, and companies in all three

---

[37] Zanders, French and Pauwels (note 9), pp. 586–92; and SIPRI, 'Iraq: the UNSCOM experience' (note 1).

[38] Memorandum of Understanding between the United Nations and the Republic of Iraq, 23 Feb. 1998, URL <http://www.un.org/NewLinks/uniraq.htm>. According to the MOU, UNSCOM inspectors were to have immediate, unconditional and unrestricted access in conformity with UN resolutions. UNSCOM pledged to respect the legitimate concerns of Iraq relating to national security, sovereignty and dignity. At the presidential sites the inspectors were to be accompanied by diplomats 'friendly' to Iraq and experts who would ensure that Iraq's national sovereignty and dignity were respected. The MOU is discussed in Zanders, French and Pauwels (note 9), p. 587.

[39] US Department of State, 'Palaces and oil smuggling', *Saddam Hussein's Iraq*, 13 Sep. 1999, URL <http://usinfo.state.gov/regional/nea/iraq/iraq99.htm>.

[40] Oxford Institute for Energy Studies (OIES), Rosser, K., 'Suspending sanctions on Iraq: make haste, slowly', *OIES Monthly Comment*, Nov. 1999, URL <http://associnst.ox.ac.uk/energy/>.

[41] Black, I., 'The impasse of Iraq', *The Guardian*, 1 July 1999, p. 7; Whitney, C. R., 'France heads for UN clash over US-led Iraq bombing', *International Herald Tribune*, 20 Aug. 1999, p. 5; and Crossette, B., 'Oppose arms monitors, Baghdad warns Paris', *International Herald Tribune*, 6 Dec. 1999, p. 1.

countries have already made new contractual relationships pending the termination of sanctions. It is likely, however, that political and economic considerations have played an equally important role. Changes in Russian domestic politics since 1994 have led to a sharp deterioration in US–Russian international political collaboration, and a similar development has taken place in US–Chinese relations. In addition, both China and Russia have opposed Security Council operations carried out under the provisions of Chapter VII of the UN Charter. Finally, it seems to have become more important for China, France and Russia to oppose international policies driven by US political objectives than to act on the basis of the substantive issues involved. In addition, irritation developed in the UN bureaucracy regarding UNSCOM's privileges and power.

IV. Summary of the UNSCOM findings

On 25 January 1999 the Security Council received two comprehensive and detailed UNSCOM reports.[42] The first dealt with Iraq's declarations regarding missiles and CBW and presented UNSCOM's assessment of the declarations. The second report was on the current situation as regards monitoring and verification.

Iraq's uncooperative behaviour and refusal to comply with its disarmament obligations is a recurrent theme in the first report, which also contains an annexe on Iraq's actions to obstruct the disarmament process. UNSCOM deemed all eight 'full, final and complete' disclosure statements submitted by Iraq (as well as eight additional drafts) to be inaccurate and incomplete. Various special expert commissions, which were set up in response to the demands of Iraq, France and Russia, assessed UNSCOM's findings; all of them concluded that UNSCOM's assessments were correct. The Chinese and Russian experts who served with UNSCOM agreed that Iraq had not fully disclosed its CBW programmes or turned over all of the relevant materials related to those programmes. However, these analyses did not affect the positions taken by the governments of China, France and Russia.

Tables 9B.1 and 9B.2 present an overview of Iraq's CBW declarations and UNSCOM's findings and estimates of weaponry and equipment that are still unaccounted for based on UNSCOM's January 1999 report. By the end of 1999 the accounting of Iraq's BW-related activities was still incomplete. Many questions also remain with respect to Iraq's chemical weapon programme.

V. Conclusions

It is highly uncertain whether UNMOVIC will be able to complete UNSCOM's tasks. The three permanent members of the Security Council that criticized UNSCOM most—China, France and Russia—abstained in the vote on Resolution 1284 establishing the new body, and it is unclear whether they will refrain from interfering in its work. Russia, for instance, blocked the appointment of one nominee for the position of Executive Chairman on grounds that the person was unacceptable to Iraq. Iraq has so far rejected UNMOVIC and it remains to be seen whether the Security Council

---

[42] Both reports are contained in Letter dated 27 January 1999 from the Permanent Representatives of the Netherlands and Slovenia to the United Nations addressed to the President of the Security Council, UN document S/1999/94, 29 Jan. 1999.

Table 9B.1. Chemical weapons in Iraq, as of January 1999

A. Type of weapon or equipment	Iraqi declarations			UNSCOM findings				
	B. Holdings as of Jan. 1991	C. Amount destroyed in 1991 Persian Gulf War	D. Unilateral destruction	E. Amount of C accounted for	F. Amount of D accounted for	G. Destruction under UNSCOM supervision	H. Other	I. Discrepancy
Special munitions[a]	127 941[b]	41 998	29 662	±34 000	13 660	40 048	16 263[c]	±23 970
Bulk CW agent (tonnes)								
Mustard	295.0	..	..	..	..	295.0	..	..
Tabun	76.0	..	..	..	..	76.0	..	..
Sarin and its mixtures	40.0	..	..	..	..	40.0	..	..
VX	1.5	..	1.5	..	–	..	..	1.5
Total	**412.5**	**..**	**1.5**	**..**	**–**	**411.0**	**..**	**1.5**
CW precursor chemicals (tonnes)[d]	3915 (5 650)[e]	823	242	823[f]	153[g]	2 610[h]	200 + 40[i]	129 − 40[j] (1 864 − 40)[k]
CW production equipment	553	152[l]	..	75	..	405[m]	–[n]	73[o]

[a] Includes aerial bombs, artillery shells, rockets and missile warheads for both chemical and biological warfare agents.

[b] Including 28 615 munitions filled with chemical or biological warfare agents.

[c] The UNSCOM report states '16 263 munitions were not destroyed, but nevertheless accounted for by UNSCOM. These include 15 616 unfilled munitions which were converted by Iraq for conventional weapons purposes in 1993–94. These also include 438 filled munitions destroyed, according to Iraq, during a fire accident.' A further 2 munitions were removed for analysis outside Iraq. The report gives no explanation for the remaining 207 munitions. However, it adds that the 'numerical discrepancy of several hundred munitions in the overall accounting can be attributed to minor deviations in physical counting of large piles of weapons'. Letter dated 27 January 1999 from the Permanent Representatives of the Netherlands and Slovenia to the United Nations addressed to the President of the Security Council, UN document S/1999/94, 29 Jan. 1999, appendix 2, 'Status of the verification of Iraq's chemical weapons programme', para. 10 (a) and table 1, col. 3, rows 5, 12.

^d Comprises unused chemicals for chemical weapon production, which require separate accounting.

^e Iraq declared that it had produced or procured a total of 20 150 tonnes of precursor chemicals and consumed 14 500 tonnes in the production of chemical warfare agents, leaving 5650 tonnes to be accounted for. UN document S/1999/94, 29 Jan. 1999, appendix 2, para. 18. According to Iraq, this variance with the officially declared amount of 3915 tonnes can be attributed to the lack of sufficient information on the actual deliveries by former suppliers, the consumption of precursors in the production of chemical warfare agents and losses as a consequence of unsuitable storage, spillage, leakage, and so on. UN document S/1999/94, 29 Jan. 1999, appendix 2, para. 20.

^f UNSCOM confirmed the destruction qualitatively but was not able to make a quantitative verification. UN document S/1999/94, 29 Jan. 1999, appendix 2, para. 21.

^g UNSCOM found evidence of destruction of additional amounts of precursor chemicals but was unable to verify the quantities.

^h 2814 tonnes according to the addition of the figures related to the destruction under UNSCOM supervision in UN document S/1999/94, 29 Jan. 1999, appendix 2, table 3, col. 6.

ⁱ UNSCOM released 200 tonnes of precursor chemicals for civilian use under its supervision. Furthermore, UNSCOM reports that 'tens of tonnes were consumed by Iraq in the 1990s for civilian purposes under UNSCOM supervision'. UN document S/1999/94, 29 Jan. 1999, appendix 2, table 3, col. 6, row 11. As UNSCOM was able to fully account for 2850 tonnes, of which 2610 tonnes were destroyed and 200 tonnes released under its supervision, this Iraqi consumption of precursors is 40 tonnes. UN document S/1999/94, 29 Jan. 1999, appendix 2, para. 21.

^j Calculation based on available figures as exact quantitative accounting of the precursor chemicals destroyed during the Persian Gulf War and unilaterally by Iraq is impossible. The origin of the amount of 40 tonnes is explained in note i.

^k Calculation based on amounts accounted for by UNSCOM. The origin of the amount of 40 tonnes is explained in note i.

^l Calculation based on Iraq's total declarations minus pieces of equipment destroyed under UNSCOM supervision. UN document S/1999/94, 29 Jan. 1999, appendix 2, table 4, cols 2, 3.

^m According to the present authors' calculations the figure should be 401. UN document S/1999/94, 29 Jan. 1999, appendix 2, table 4, col. 3.

ⁿ Several tens of pieces of equipment were buried under the debris of production buildings destroyed in the Gulf War.

^o The discrepancy may be explained in part or whole by the destruction of the equipment during the Gulf War. The amount would be 76 if based on the figure in note m.

Source: Letter dated 27 January 1999 from the Permanent Representatives of the Netherlands and Slovenia to the United Nations addressed to the President of the Security Council, UN document S/1999/94, 29 Jan. 1999.

Table 9B.2. Biological weapons in Iraq, as of January 1999

| Iraqi declarations | | | UNSCOM findings[a] |
Type of weapon or equipment	Amount declared in 'full, final and complete disclosures' (FFCDs)	Material balances	Assessment of Iraqi declarations
Al-Hussein missile warheads (BW)	25	All destroyed unilaterally	Not supported by conclusive evidence
Warhead fillings[b]			Analysis of samples from excavated remnants of warhead containers does not support FFCDs; locations of remnants are inconsistent with FFCDs; consequently, there are major doubts about the accounts of weapon fillings, deployment and subsequent destruction
Botulinum toxin	16	..	
Anthrax spores	5	..	
Aflatoxin	4	..	
R-400 aerial bombs (BW)	200	157 filled and 43 unfilled bombs destroyed unilaterally	R-400 declaration changed several times; account in the 1997 FFCD was incomplete and inaccurate according to review by international experts
Bomb fillings			Only partial verification of destruction of bombs
Botulinum toxin	100	..	
Anthrax spores	50	..	
Aflatoxin	7	..	
Aircraft drop tanks[c]	4	1 destroyed in the 1991 air campaign; 3 destroyed unilaterally by Iraq	No validation of data in Iraq's declarations; 12 more drop tanks may have been modified for BW use; there was verification of destruction of 3 drop tanks by Iraq but no physical evidence to support Iraq's claim that 1 drop tank was destroyed in the war
Aerosol generators	June 1996 FFCD includes description of devices but does not state number produced; production of 12 aerosol generators acknowledged in interviews with Iraqi personnel	No Iraqi declaration about disposal	Aerosol generators have not been accounted for

Iraqi declarations Type of weapon or equipment	Amount declared in 'full, final and complete disclosures' (FFCDs)	Material balances	UNSCOM findings[a] Assessment of Iraqi declarations
Mobile storage tanks for agents	47	Unknown number destroyed, but not specified whether unilaterally or in Persian Gulf War[d]	Remnants of c. 22 destroyed tanks turned over to UNSCOM; remnants of 2 more tanks found; rest unaccounted for
Bulk botulinum toxin[e]	19 180 l.	10 820 l. filled in missile warheads and bombs; 499–569 l. used in field trials; 1181 l. wasted in handling; 7665–7735 l. destroyed unilaterally	Iraq's statements unsupported; unable to verify amount of botulinum toxin produced; unable to verify Iraq's material balance
Bulk anthrax spores	8 445 l.[f]	4975 l. filled in missile warheads and bombs; 52.2 l. wasted in handling; 3412 l. destroyed unilaterally	Statements in 1997 FFCDs unsupported: unable to verify amount of anthrax produced; unable to verify Iraq's material balance
Bulk aflatoxin	2 200 l.	1120 l. filled in missile warheads and bombs; 231–301 l. used in field trials; 30.5 l. wasted in handling; 900–970 l. destroyed unilaterally	Statements in 1997 FFCDs unsupported: unable to verify amount of aflatoxin produced; unable to verify Iraq's material balance
Bulk *Clostridium perfringens*	340 l.	338 l. unilaterally destroyed	Neither figure verified
Bulk ricin	10 l. (produced from 100 kg castor beans)	All used in field trials	Neither figure verified
Bulk wheat cover smut	Not quantifiable	All unilaterally destroyed	Neither declaration verified
Growth media Casein	17 554 kg	7074 kg used in botulinum toxin production; 145 kg lost or wasted; 10 335 kg destroyed under UNSCOM supervision	Generally unable to verify the figures[g] Minimum of 460 kg unaccounted for based on UNSCOM importation data
Thioglycollate broth	6 036 kg	4130 kg used in botulinum toxin production; 58 kg lost or wasted; 1848 kg destroyed under UNSCOM supervision	Minimum of 80 kg unaccounted for based on UNSCOM importation data

Iraqi declarations			UNSCOM findings[a]
Type of weapon or equipment	Amount declared in 'full, final and complete disclosures' (FFCDs)	Material balances	Assessment of Iraqi declarations
Yeast extract	7 070 kg	1964 kg used in botulinum toxin, anthrax and *Clostridium perfringens* production; 15 kg lost or wasted; 4942 kg destroyed under UNSCOM supervision	Minimum of 520 kg unaccounted for based on UNSCOM importation data
Peptone	1 500 kg	45 kg used in *Clostridium perfringens* production; 705 kg lost or wasted; 625 kg destroyed under UNSCOM supervision	Minimum of 1100 kg unaccounted for based on UNSCOM importation data

[a] All declarations by Iraq in the FFCDs were repeatedly rejected by UNSCOM and panels of international experts in Sep. 1997, Mar. 1998 and July 1998.

[b] UNSCOM found 7 missile warheads with traces of anthrax as opposed to the 5 declared. Confronted with this evidence, Iraqi officials claimed that they had confused the numbers of BW warheads. In July 1998 Iraq stated to an UNSCOM team that, instead of the declared numbers, there had, in fact, been 16 anthrax missile warheads and 5 botulinum toxin missile warheads. Interview with UNSCOM official, Munich, 25 Oct. 1999; and Letter dated 27 January 1999 from the Permanent Representatives of the Netherlands and Slovenia to the United Nations addressed to the President of the Security Council, UN document S/1999/94, 29 Jan. 1999, appendix 3, section 'Al-Hussein missile warheads'.

[c] Iraq was also developing a pilotless aircraft to carry the drop tanks.

[d] The UNSCOM report does not state whether the Iraqi declaration specified how destruction took place—unilaterally or in the Persian Gulf War.

[e] UNSCOM data only give the volume of bulk agents but not the concentration of the agent in the mix; it is therefore impossible to give the approximate weight of the biological warfare agents.

[f] Based on statements by Iraqi officials, UNSCOM inspectors calculated the following conversion equation for the anthrax bombs: 100 l. of filling = 140 kg (density = ±1.4), containing 1.2% dried anthrax spores. Per 100 l. there would thus be 1.68 kg of agent. Trevan, T., *Saddam's Secrets: The Hunt for Iraq's Hidden Weapons* (Harper Collins: London, 1999), p. 318. Based on this equation, Iraq may have produced approximately 141.9 kg of anthrax spores.

[g] Iraq did not report all the growth media that UNSCOM knows it imported. The figures on growth media used in the production of biological warfare agents are derived from estimates of how much agent was produced. According to the Jan. 1999 UNSCOM report, these figures are the result of a theoretical calculation and have little supporting evidence. There are also substantial uncertainties about the amounts declared as lost or wasted.

Source: Letter dated 27 January 1999 from the Permanent Representatives of the Netherlands and Slovenia to the United Nations addressed to the President of the Security Council, UN document S/1999/94, 29 Jan. 1999.

members will act in unison if and when Iraq refuses to cooperate with UNMOVIC or to allow inspectors inside the country or otherwise constrains their activities.

Resolution 1284 contains ambiguities as a consequence of the need to secure as broad a consensus as possible. It makes the UN Secretary-General a gatekeeper between the Executive Chairman of UNMOVIC and the Security Council. The diplomatic compromises between Iraq and UNSCOM that were worked out by Kofi Annan signalled that the basic provisions of Resolution 687 were negotiable and emboldened the Iraqi leadership in its policies of resistance and concealment. Iraq took advantage of the internal divisions in the Security Council when it violated the agreed compromises and ultimately expelled the UNSCOM inspectors. Iraq will now be able to lodge its complaints with the Secretary-General over the head of the Executive Chairman of UNMOVIC. As demonstrated by the 1998 MOU regarding the presidential sites, the interposition of the Secretary-General between the Security Council and the Executive Chairman opens the door for diplomatic compromises on Iraq's basic obligations under international law.

No inspections or monitoring have been conducted in Iraq since December 1998. UNMOVIC will have to redo the work done by UNSCOM—including the highly confrontational no-notice inspections of sensitive sites—because Iraq has moved relevant materials, equipment and files. In contrast to 1991, Iraq has since perfected its concealment operations while UNMOVIC will have to start out with inexperienced personnel.

Between 1991 and 1999 the Security Council, succumbing to the short-term interests of some members, was unable to deal with Iraq's blatant and determined violation of its rules and of the generally accepted norms against the acquisition, possession or use of chemical, biological or nuclear weapons. For major disarmament treaties, such as the 1993 Chemical Weapons Convention or the 1972 Biological and Toxin Weapons Convention, the Security Council is the ultimate arbiter in the case of material breaches. The UNSCOM experience raises serious doubts about the ability or willingness of the Security Council to uphold fundamental norms in the name of the international community when confronted by a determined and persistent violator. Few cases will be as clear-cut as that of Iraq.

10. Conventional arms control

ZDZISLAW LACHOWSKI

I. Introduction

A long-awaited breakthrough in the European arms control regime took place in 1999. Work on the Agreement on Adaptation of the Treaty on Conventional Armed Forces in Europe (the Agreement on Adaptation) and the Vienna Document 1999 of the Negotiations on Confidence- and Security-Building Measures in Europe reached fruition, and both documents were signed at the Summit Meeting of the Organization for Security and Co-operation in Europe (OSCE) in Istanbul in November. This was in striking contrast to the general political mood in Europe, marked by sustained Russian opposition to NATO enlargement, worsening NATO–Russian relations as a result of the inter-vention in the Kosovo province of the Federal Republic of Yugoslavia (FRY) and international concern about the conflict in Chechnya, on the one hand, and the rather lacklustre condition of other areas of arms control, on the other. As in previous years, the entry into force of the 1992 Open Skies Treaty remained deadlocked.

The NATO intervention in the FRY in the spring of 1999 marred regional arms control efforts in the Balkans, but some small progress was reported in the latter half of the year.

Other than in Latin America there was little progress in conventional arms control outside Europe, which reflected the general stalemate in this field.

The 1997 Convention on the Prohibition of the Use, Stockpiling, Production and Transfer of Anti-Personnel Mines and on their Destruction entered into force on 1 March 1999.

This chapter describes the major issues and developments relating to con-ventional arms control in 1999. Section II deals with critical aspects of the implementation of the 1990 Treaty on Conventional Armed Forces in Europe (the CFE Treaty) and the CFE Treaty adaptation talks. The Agreement on Adaptation is discussed in section III. Section IV covers regional arms control efforts in Europe, and the status of the Open Skies Treaty is briefly reviewed in section V. Section VI reviews conventional arms control-related develop-ments outside Europe, and section VII addresses the issue of anti-personnel mines. The conclusions are presented in section VIII. Appendix 10A examines developments in the field of European confidence- and security-building measures (CSBMs). Appendix 10B provides the texts of Chapter X of the Vienna Document 1999, on regional measures; a consolidated text showing the adaptation of the 1990 CFE Treaty in accordance with the 1999 Agreement on Adaptation; and the 1999 Final Act of the Conference of the States Parties to the Treaty on Conventional Armed Forces in Europe.

Table 10.1. CFE ceilings and holdings, as of 1 January 1999

State[a]	Tanks		ACVs		Artillery		Aircraft		Helicopters	
	Ceilings	Holdings	Ceilings	Holdings	Ceilings	Holdings	Ceilings	Holdings	Ceilings	Holdings
Armenia	220	102	220	204	285	225	100	6	50	7
Azerbaijan	220	262	220	331	285	303	100	48	50	15
Belarus	1 800	1 778	2 600	2 513	1 615	1 515	294	252	80	62
Belgium	334	155	1 099	526	320	243	232	137	4	46
Bulgaria	1 475	1 475	2 000	1 986	1 750	1 744	235	233	67	43
Canada	77	0	263	0	32	0	90	0	12	0
Czech Republic	957	938	1 367	1 219	767	754	230	114	50	34
Denmark	353	337	336	286	503	503	106	76	18	12
France	1 306	1 207	3 820	3 653	1 292	1 050	800	596	390	314
Georgia	220	79	220	113	285	106	100	7	50	3
Germany	4 069	3 096	3 281	2 480	2 445	2 056	900	534	293	204
Greece	1 735	1 735	2 498	2 364	1 920	1 886	650	522	30	20
Hungary	835	807	1 700	1 332	840	839	180	138	108	59
Italy	1 348	1 256	3 339	2 917	1 955	1 595	650	535	142	134
Moldova	210	0	210	209	250	153	50	27	50	0
Netherlands	743	359	1 080	640	607	398	230	164	50	10
Norway	170	170	275	180	491	189	100	73	24	0
Poland	1 730	1 675	2 150	1 437	1 610	1 580	460	298	130	104
Portugal	300	187	430	355	450	359	160	101	26	0
Romania	1 375	1 373	2 100	2 100	1 475	1 441	430	360	120	16
Russia[b]	6 400	5 510	11 480	10 064	6 415	6 299	3 416	2 870	890	761
Slovakia	478	478	683	683	383	383	100	94	40	19
Spain	891	676	2 047	1 181	1 370	1 150	310	201	90	28
Turkey	2 795	2 554	3 120	2 515	3 523	2 811	750	346	103	26
Ukraine[b]	4 080	4 014	5 050	4 902	4 040	3 739	1 090	964	330	265
UK	1 015	542	3 176	2 396	636	429	900	533	384	249
USA	4 006	846	5 152	1 704	2 742	558	784	223	404	136

[a] Iceland, Kazakhstan and Luxembourg have no TLE in the application zone. [b] TLE belonging to the Black Sea Fleet is not included.

Source: Joint Consultative Group, Group on Treaty Operation and Implementation, JCG.TOI/9/99, Vienna, 13 July 1999.

Table 10.2. Reductions of TLE belonging to naval infantry and coastal defence forces required by the legally binding Soviet pledge of 14 June 1991, as of May 1999

Numbers in parentheses indicate the percentage of liabilities reduced.

State/area	Tanks	ACVs[a]	Artillery	Total
Liabilities of Russia				
Outside ATTU zone	331	488	436	**1 255**
Inside ATTU zone	331	488	436	**1 255**
Ukraine/Russia	158/113	369/380	152/56	**679/549**
Sub-total in ATTU zone	602	1 237	644	**2 483**
Total	**933**	**1 725**	**1 080**	**3 738**
Reductions by Russia				
Outside ATTU zone	331	488	436	**1 255**
Inside ATTU zone	331	488	436	**1 255**
Ukraine[b]/Russia	113[c]	380[c]	56[d]	**549**[c, d]
Sub-total in ATTU zone	331 (*55.0*)	488 (*39.5*)	436 (*67.7*)	**1 255** (*50.5*)
Total	**662** (*71.0*)	**976** (*56.6*)	**872** (*80.7*)	**2 510** (*67.2*)

[a] Armoured combat vehicles.

[b] Because the numbers of Ukrainian naval infantry and coastal defence TLE items are covered by the national overall holdings not exceeding its maximum national level for holdings, the reduction norms for Ukraine amount to zero.

[c] To be reduced not later than 25 May 1999.

[d] To be reduced not later than 13 Aug. 1999.

Source: Consolidated matrix on the basis of data available as of 1 January and updated in May 1999, JCG document JCG.TOI/9/99, Joint Consultative Group, Vienna, 13 June 1999.

II. Conventional arms control in Europe: the CFE Treaty

The 1990 CFE Treaty set equal ceilings within its Atlantic-to-the-Urals (ATTU) application zone on the major categories of heavy conventional armaments and equipment of the groups of states parties, originally the NATO and the Warsaw Treaty Organization (WTO) states. There are now 30 states parties.[1] The main reduction of excess treaty-limited equipment (TLE) was carried out in three phases from 1993 to 1995. By 1 January 1999 some 51 700 TLE items within the ATTU zone had been scrapped or converted to civilian use by the parties, with many parties reducing their holdings to lower levels than required. Data on CFE ceilings and holdings in the treaty application zone as of 1 January 1999 are presented in table 10.1. Regarding its outstanding implementation issues, Russia stated that it would complete

[1] A list of states parties to the CFE Treaty is given in annexe A in this volume. For discussion of conventional arms control in Europe before 1999, see the relevant chapters in previous SIPRI Yearbooks. The texts of the 1990 CFE Treaty and Protocols are available on the OSCE Internet site at URL <http://www.osce.org/docs/english/1990-1999/cfe/cfetreate.htm>.

Table 10.3. Destruction or conversion of Russian conventional armaments and equipment beyond the Urals to civilian use, as of May 1999

Numbers in parentheses are percentages of liabilities reduced.

Area	Tanks	ACVs[a]	Artillery	Total
Liabilities				
Beyond the Urals	6 000	1 500	7 000	**14 500**
Naval infantry/ coastal defence	331	488	436	**1 255**
Reductions				
Beyond the Urals	3 741[b] *(64.2)*	2 677 *(178.5)*	6 424 *(91.8)*	**12 842** *(88.6)*
Naval infantry/ coastal defence	331 *(100.0)*	488 *(100.0)*	436 *(100.0)*	**1 255** *(100.0)*

[a] Armoured combat vehicles.

[b] Under para. 3 of Annex E to the Final Document of the 1996 CFE Review Conference, an additional 1177 battle tanks in excess of these 3741 should be deemed destroyed or rendered militarily unusable as a result of applying methods referred to in para. 1 of Annex E to 1177 ACVs in excess of the quota of 1500. CFE, Final Document of the First Conference to Review the Operation of the Treaty on Conventional Armed Forces in Europe and the Concluding Act of the Negotiation on Personnel Strength, Vienna, 15–31 May 1996, CFE-TRC/DG.2 Rev. 5, 31 May 1996, Annex E: Statement of the representative of the Russian Federation to the Review Conference of the Treaty on Conventional Armed Forces in Europe. The annex is reproduced in *SIPRI Yearbook 1997: Armaments, Disarmament and International Security* (Oxford University Press: Oxford, 1997), pp. 515–17.

Source: Consolidated matrix on the basis of data available as of 1 January and updated on May 1999, JCG document JCG.TOI/9/99, Joint Consultative Group, Vienna, 13 June 1999.

by August 1999 the destruction or conversion of its naval infantry and coastal defence forces in accordance with the legally binding Soviet pledge of 14 June 1991 (table 10.2) and, under its political commitment of the same day, reported the reduction of almost 14 100 items (*c.* 90 per cent of its total liability of 15 755 items—see table 10.3) inherited from the former USSR outside the ATTU zone (the deadline is 2000). More than 3000 intrusive on-site inspections had taken place by the end of 1999.

On 19 November 1999, after nearly three years of negotiation, the Agreement on Adaptation of the CFE Treaty was signed by the states parties at the Istanbul OSCE Summit Meeting, introducing a new regime of arms control based on national and territorial ceilings, both codified as binding limits.

Treaty operation and implementation issues

The Joint Consultative Group (JCG), established to monitor implementation, resolve issues arising from implementation, and consider measures to enhance the viability and effectiveness of the CFE Treaty, focused on the challenge of adapting the treaty to the new security environment in Europe. At the same time it continued to scrutinize the operation and implementation of the treaty in 1999.

Russia has been in breach of the 1996 Flank Document since 31 May 1999.[2] Its holdings of TLE in the flank zone exceeded the allowed limits, especially in ACVs. In the interest of finalizing the Agreement on Adaptation of the CFE Treaty, NATO decided to tolerate this case of non-compliance—but did not recognize it as lawful.

In September Russia transferred part of its TLE quota of battle tanks, ACVs, artillery pieces, combat aircraft and attack helicopters to Kazakhstan.[3] This was in accordance with the JCG decision on treaty adaptation of 30 March 1999[4] which, inter alia, allowed Kazakhstan, whose previous entitlements were zero, to have national ceilings of 50 battle tanks, 200 ACVs, 100 artillery pieces, 15 combat aircraft and 20 combat helicopters at the northern end of the Caspian Sea, within the ATTU zone. The rationale was Kazakhstan's desire to have a limited number of heavy weapons to protect its oil facilities.

In 1999 one issue still outstanding was that of the discrepancy of 1970 TLE items between actual levels and the aggregate amount of TLE that the eight former Soviet republics were committed to scrap or convert based on Soviet data at the signature of the treaty in 1990. Most of the unaccounted-for TLE is believed to be derelict or not under government control (in the hands of rebels) in the Caucasian states.

During the NATO bombing of the FRY, Russia requested challenge inspections of NATO airbases in Aviano, Italy, and Tazar, Hungary, in accordance with CFE Treaty provisions. The base at Aviano was the primary facility used for the air operation. In spite of the ongoing offensive, NATO accepted the request and the inspections were carried out, confirming compliance with the terms of the treaty.

The conflict in Chechnya

A major issue of non-compliance arose in the autumn of 1999. In a diplomatic note of 6 October, Moscow informed NATO and the other parties that it had been forced to exceed its flank limits for TLE and send more ground forces to the North Caucasus in the ongoing struggle with Chechen rebels. The forces had moved into the territory several days earlier. In the OSCE Forum for Security Co-operation (FSC), Russia invoked a 'supreme national interest' clause, not envisaged explicitly for such a situation in the treaty itself,[5] in

[2] Final Document of the First Conference to Review the Operation of the Treaty on Conventional Armed Forces in Europe and the Concluding Act of the Negotiation on Personnel Strength, Vienna, 31 May 1996, Annex A: Document agreed among the States Parties to the Treaty on Conventional Armed Forces in Europe of 19 November 1990 (the Flank Document) is reproduced in *SIPRI Yearbook 1997: Armaments, Disarmament and International Security* (Oxford University Press: Oxford, 1997).
[3] 'Russia transferring some CFE arms quotas to Kazakhstan', Interfax (Moscow), in Foreign Broadcast Information Service, *Daily Report–Central Eurasia (FBIS–SOV)*, FBIS-SOV-1999-0927, 27 Sep. 1999.
[4] JCG, Decision of the Joint Consultative Group on CFE Treaty Adaptation, Joint Consultative Group document JCG no. 3/99, 30 Mar. 1999.
[5] Article XIX of the 1990 CFE Treaty provides for supreme interests to be invoked only when a state decides to withdraw from the treaty. Article VII allows changes in the maximum levels for

notifying the other 29 parties of the action. It expected understanding from the other states parties in the face of the seriousness of the situation.[6]

US Republican senators severely criticized the Russian move, which cast doubts on compliance with its arms control obligations, using it as an additional argument against ratification of the Comprehensive Nuclear Test-Ban Treaty. The Clinton Administration, however, took a pragmatic view, recognizing Russian transparency about exceeding treaty limits in Chechnya and asking Russian leaders to 'demonstrate their intent' to return to compliance.[7] At the OSCE Permanent Council in early October German Foreign Minister Joschka Fischer called on the parties to 'concentrate their energies' and to conclude the adaptation of the CFE Treaty,[8] but in early November several NATO foreign ministries considered postponing the summit meeting.[9]

The NATO countries sought a high-level political declaration from Russia regarding its compliance with the CFE Treaty. During his visit to Oslo on 1–2 November, then Russian Prime Minister Vladimir Putin gave assurances that his country would reduce its military presence in Chechnya to levels envisaged in the treaty as soon as 'necessary conditions' are created; he failed, however, to mention any deadline for the withdrawal or for coming into compliance with the adapted treaty. Putin promised that Russia would provide more information about its forces through additional transparency measures and allowing more inspections in the North Caucasus. At the same time, he said, this could only happen when it 'becomes possible to give them [the inspectors] necessary security guarantees'.[10] This reservation was not satisfactory to other parties. Some questioned the value of attending a summit meeting as long as the breach of the treaty and other OSCE provisions continued, and proposed that the meeting be postponed. Norway, however, holding the OSCE Chairmanship-in-Office, announced on 4 November that the OSCE Summit Meeting would take place.

No figures on the excess Russian troops in Chechnya were made public. First it was said that they were 'way, way beyond the limits'.[11] Some Western sources estimated that the limits on heavy ground equipment were exceeded by

holdings of a state party (to be notified at least 90 days in advance), provided these changes are preceded or accompanied by a corresponding reduction of TLE by one or more states 'belonging to the same group of states parties'.

[6] 'Russia tells US it will violate arms pact', *Washington Times*, 7 Oct. 1999, URL <http://washtimes.com/news/news3.html>. At the FSC the Russian delegates sought unofficially to draw a parallel between their conduct in Chechnya and NATO's earlier conduct in the case of Kosovo.

[7] United States Information Service (USIS), 'Text: Address to OSCE Council by State's Ron Asmus in Vienna Oct. 18', *Washington File* (US Embassy: Stockholm, 18 Oct. 1999).

[8] Speech by Joschka Fischer, Federal Minister for Foreign Affairs for Germany, OSCE Permanent Council, Vienna, 6 Oct. 1999, URL <http://www.osceprag.cz/e/docs/speech/j_fischer-en.htm>.

[9] 'Der russische Krieg in Tschetschenien gefährdet den OSZE-Gipfel in Istanbul' [The Russian war in Chechnya threatens the OSCE summit in Istanbul], *Frankfurter Allgemeine Zeitung*, 2 Nov. 1999, pp. 1–2.

[10] For excerpts from Putin's statement see 'Russia: Putin notes significance of OSCE summit', ITAR–TASS (Moscow), in FBIS-SOV-1999-1101, 1 Nov. 1999; and Eggleston, R., 'Russia: Chechen operation threatens arms treaty', Radio Free Europe/Radio Liberty, *RFE/RL Research Report*, 4 Nov. 1999, URL <http://www.rferl.org/nca/features/1999/11/F.RU.991104133628.htm>.

[11] Eggleston (note 10).

some 60 per cent. At the end of the year Russia stated that it fielded 1493 tanks, 3534 ACVs and 1985 artillery pieces in and around Chechnya, which was nearly 200 tanks, 2150 ACVs and 300 artillery pieces in excess of the sub-ceilings in the Flank Document.[12]

In the last week before the OSCE Summit Meeting, 12 prominent Republican senators sent two letters to President Clinton, demanding that he call on Russia to halt the hostilities in Chechnya immediately, withdraw Russian troops and open negotiations with Chechen President Aslan Maskhadov. Their criticism notwithstanding, the senators raised no objections in principle to the Agreement on Adaptation itself, asking President Clinton to slow down rather than speed up the negotiations.[13]

Assuming that the Russian Government would sign the Agreement on Adaptation, Germany and other European states chose not to isolate Russia at the OSCE Summit Meeting. On 10 November Germany decided to sign the agreement in the belief that its failure would undermine security and stability in many regions.[14] The European states assumed that the time between the signing and ratification of the Agreement on Adaptation would enable Russia to return to compliance with the new parameters.[15]

In their communiqué at the end of the year NATO foreign ministers, while stressing their concern about continued Russian non-compliance with flank limitations, noted Russia's pledge to comply with all the provisions and commitments of the CFE Treaty 'as soon as possible', to provide maximum transparency regarding its forces in the North Caucasus in accordance with both the CFE Treaty and the Vienna Document 1999, and its assurances that Russian non-compliance with flank limits would be temporary.[16]

The Armenian–Azerbaijani dispute

Armenia and Azerbaijan remain locked in the dispute over Nagorno-Karabakh. This self-proclaimed republic, which is not recognized by the international community, possesses armed forces not accounted for under the CFE Treaty. In February 1999 Azerbaijan reiterated its claims that Armenia's military cooperation with Russia had led to the growing instability in the region and resulted in 'aggressive' supplies of modern equipment, including TLE, to Armenia, exceeding CFE Treaty limits. Claiming that the combination of Armenia's armed forces with those of Nagorno-Karabakh plus Russian

[12] Hagemann, G.-H., 'Konventionelle Rüstungskontrolle' [Conventional arms control], *Europäische Sicherheit*, no. 2, vol. 49 (Feb. 2000), p. 43.

[13] 'Führende amerikanische Senatoren sind gegen die Unterzeichnung des KSE-Vertrags in Istanbul' [Leading US senators are against the signing of the CFE Treaty in Istanbul], *Frankfurter Allgemeine Zeitung*, 13 Nov. 1999, p. 2.

[14] 'Zuversicht in Berlin über Istanbuler OSCE-Treffen' [Confidence in Berlin in the OSCE Istanbul meeting], *Frankfurter Allgemeine Zeitung*, 11 Nov. 1999, p. 2. Another concern of the German Government was the anti-arms control mood of the US Senate.

[15] 'Russland mahnen, nicht vorführen' [Admonish not reproach Russia], *Frankfurter Allgemeine Zeitung*, 17 Nov. 1999, p. 2.

[16] NATO Press Release M-NAC2(99)166, Final Communiqué, Ministerial Meeting of the North Atlantic Council held at NATO Headquarters, Brussels, on 15 Dec. 1999, URL <http://www.nato.int/docu/pr/1999/p99-166e.htm>.

military bases in Armenia upset the balance of forces in the region, Azerbaijan demanded higher TLE ceilings. Consequently, at the time of the JCG decision of 30 March 1999, Azerbaijan had refused to declare its projected national and territorial limits for inclusion in the appended chart.

An international group of inspectors from Belgium, Turkey and the UK carried out an inspection of the Russian military base at Gyumri, Armenia, on 17 April and found it to be in compliance with the information provided under the treaty's Protocol on Notification and Exchange of Information. On 11–14 May another international team of Belgian, French and Turkish inspectors visited an army unit at an unidentified place 'near Yerevan' and declared it, too, to be in full compliance with the treaty.[17]

Withdrawals of Russian TLE from Georgia and Moldova

The issue of Russian armed forces stationed in Georgia and Moldova came to the fore once again in early 1999. For several years both countries have demanded full respect for their sovereignty regarding temporary deployments on their territory or reallocation of equipment quotas under the 1992 Tashkent Agreement.[18] The JCG decision of 30 March 1999 stressed the 'desirability of early mutually acceptable results to bilateral discussions on the withdrawal and consequent reduction of Russian forces in Georgia and of the withdrawal of Russian forces from Moldova'.[19] In was in the context of the conflict in Chechnya in late 1999 that Russia found itself under strong political pressure to show, albeit reluctantly, a measure of flexibility and good will with regard to these two cases.

The four bases on *Georgia's* territory have existed by virtue of its unratified agreement of 1994 with Russia. In 1999 Georgia insisted on closing down two Russian military bases—the Vaziani airbase near the Georgian capital, Tbilisi, and the Gudauta base in the separatist province of Abkhazia. The other two bases, at Akhalkalaki and Batumi, are likely to be used by Russia for some time. The Georgian authorities are afraid that closing the latter bases in the near future would have an adverse impact on Georgia's economy and on ethnic relations within the country. As the OSCE Summit Meeting in Istanbul drew near, Russian–Georgian relations worsened. Meanwhile President Eduard Shevardnadze announced Georgia's willingness to join NATO by 2005, the Russian–Chechen hostilities affected neighbouring Georgia (Georgian villages near the border with Chechnya were shelled) and agreements signed by Azerbaijan, Georgia and Turkey to constitute the legal framework for the construction of an oil pipeline from the Caspian Sea to Ceyhan on the

---

[17] RFE/RL Armenian Service, Armenia Report Archive, News Briefs, 26 Feb. 1999 and 15 May 1999, URL <http://www.rferl.org/bd/ar/reports/archives/index.html>; *RFE/RL Newsline*, 19 Apr. 1999, URL <http://www.rferl.org/newsline>; and 'Full compliance with CFE treaty requirements', Snark (Yerevan), in FBIS-SOV-1999-0519, 15 May 1999.

[18] The 1992 Tashkent Agreement, signed by the former Soviet republics, with the exception of the Baltic states, with territories in the ATTU zone, set out the division of the former Soviet CFE Treaty obligations and entitlements.

[19] JCG (note 4).

Mediterranean coast of Turkey, bypassing Russian territory, also fuelled Russia's anger.[20]

The difficult Georgian–Russian negotiations lasted until the last days before the summit meeting. On 17 November the two states signed a joint statement to the effect that Russia would reduce the levels of its heavy ground weapons on Georgian territory to the equivalent of a brigade, meeting the requirements of the Agreement on Adaptation by the end of 2000.[21] By that time the Russian TLE located at Vaziani and Gudauta and the repair facilities in Tbilisi would be withdrawn, and the bases themselves would be disbanded and closed down by mid-2001. Georgia undertook to grant Russia the right to temporary deployment of its TLE at the Batumi and Akhalkalaki bases. It was also agreed that negotiations on how long and under what conditions these bases would function and on the Russian military facilities in Georgia would be completed during 2000.[22]

The situation in *Moldova* was different. A residual 2500-strong contingent of the former 14th Russian Army is present in the Trans-Dniester region.[23] In July 1994 Moldova proclaimed permanent neutrality under its new constitution, and since then it has refused to host foreign forces on its territory. The October 1994 agreement with Russia on the withdrawal of Russian troops, however, has not entered into force. In December 1998 the OSCE Ministerial Council in Oslo recommended a number of steps, including: (*a*) assistance relating to the removal and/or destruction of Russian armaments, military equipment, ammunition and other ordnance; (*b*) the elaboration, within a period of six months of the Oslo meeting, of a schedule for the withdrawal of these items; (*c*) completion of the remaining protocols of the October 1994 Moldovan–Russian agreement on the withdrawal of Russian troops; and (*d*) resumption of the activities of the Mixed Moldovan–Russian Commission on military issues.[24]

In early 1999 the Moldovan Government called first for the problem of removing huge quantities of Russian armaments and munitions to be tackled. In the spring Moldova was promised increased US assistance to help the Russian troops withdraw from the country. In September the Chief of the Russian General Staff, Anatoliy Kvashnin, reportedly suggested that a permanent military base be established for the group of Russian troops.[25] Moldova rejected the proposal on constitutional grounds, reiterating that it cannot allow even

[20] *RFE/RL Newsline*, 19 Nov. 1999.

[21] The most significant reduction will be that of ACVs, from 481 to 241.

[22] OSCE, Final Act of the Conference of the States Parties to the Treaty on Conventional Armed Forces in Europe, Istanbul, 17 Nov. 1999, Annex 14, Joint Statement of the Russian Federation and Georgia. The text of the Final Act is reproduced in appendix 10B in this volume.

[23] According to official information, in early 1999 Russia had 119 tanks and 129 ACVs, 129 artillery pieces, 7 helicopters, 2800 railway carriages of ammunition and almost 50 000 light weapons in the Trans-Dniester region. 'Russian military pullout reportedly beginning in Dniestr', Radio Romania Network (Bucharest), in FBIS-SOV-1999-1116, 16 Nov. 1999.

[24] OSCE, Oslo Ministerial Council, Decision on Moldova, OSCE document MC(7).DEC/2, Oslo, 2–3 Dec. 1998, URL <http://www.osce.org/e/minf-l-e-htm>.

[25] 'Less than a week after Lucinschi–Yeltsin meeting, Russian suggests that Moscow create permanent military bases in the Dniester region', *Ziua* (Bucharest, Internet edn), 7 Sep. 1999, in 'Russian chief of staff wants permanent troops in Dniester', FBIS-SOV-1999-0908, 7 Sep. 1999.

temporary deployments of foreign conventional armaments on its territory. On the eve of the Istanbul OSCE Summit Meeting, the Moldovan authorities asked a number of Western countries and European organizations to support the withdrawal of Russian troops and evacuation of munitions. It is expected that financial assistance will be rendered to Russian servicemen being withdrawn from the region. In early 2000, however, Russia was once more reported to be making the settlement of the Trans-Dniester conflict a condition for the withdrawal of its troops and armaments from Moldova.[26]

At the Istanbul meeting, Moldova once again renounced the right to receive a temporary deployment on its territory,[27] while Russia pledged to withdraw and/or destroy Russian TLE by the end of 2001 and pull out its troops by the end of 2002.[28] The OSCE welcomed the progress in the removal and destruction of the Russian military equipment and decided to instruct the Permanent Council to consider the expansion of the mandate of the OSCE Mission to Moldova to help facilitate withdrawal and destruction of armaments, and to consider the establishment of an OSCE-administered fund for voluntary international financial assistance.[29]

Progress at the negotiations in 1999

After a year of stalemate, at the end of 1998 consensus was reached on accelerating the CFE adaptation talks in Vienna in the first months of 1999. On 8 December 1998 NATO, joined by the three states then about to become members, issued the Statement on CFE,[30] setting a framework for its negotiating position in the run-up to the signature of an adaptation agreement at the Istanbul Summit Meeting. The next round of negotiations began on 21 January 1999, with the aim of intensifying efforts towards prompt and tangible progress, especially with regard to the issues of the flank zone, special status for Central Europe and the levels of temporary deployments.

On 25 January an understanding was reached between Russia and Turkey with respect to the Russian military presence in the southern flank. With the flank problem eased, another major Russian demand was an interim agreement on the status of Central Europe before the formal enlargement of NATO by three new members. This issue took more than two months of intensive negotiations in both Vienna and other capitals of the CFE Treaty parties. Among the three prospective NATO members, the special case was Poland where, in view of concessions demanded by Moscow, the political elites and

---

[26] 'The OSCE opposes Russia's stance on Dniester withdrawal', ITAR-TASS (Moscow), in FBIS-SOV-2000-0117, 17 Jan. 2000.

[27] OSCE (note 22), Annex 13, Statement on behalf of the Republic of Moldova, 19 Nov. 1999.

[28] OSCE (note 22); and OSCE, Istanbul Summit Declaration, OSCE document SUM.DOC/2/99, Istanbul, 19 Nov. 1999, URL <http://www.osce.org/e/docs/summits/istadec/99e.htm>.

[29] OSCE, Summit Declaration (note 28), para. 19.

[30] The text of the Statement on CFE issued at the Ministerial Meeting of the North Atlantic Council with the Three Invited Countries held in Brussels, 8 December 1998, Adaptation of the Treaty on Conventional Armed Forces in Europe (CFE): Restraint and Flexibility, NAC Press Release M-NAC-D-2 (98) 141, 8 Dec. 1998, is reproduced in *SIPRI Yearbook 1999: Armaments, Disarmament and International Security* (Oxford University Press: Oxford, 1999), pp. 663–65.

the military were seriously concerned about the prospect of the country being a 'second-class' party to an adapted CFE Treaty and an unequal member of the alliance. The Czech Republic and Hungary demonstrated no particular interest in securing higher levels of holdings for themselves. In early March 1999 the Polish Government was pressured by the Parliament not to reduce its armed forces excessively. The situation was complicated by the fact that the USA and major European powers, such as France and Germany, had insisted that Poland accommodate the Russian concerns. Polish–US consultations in the winter of 1998/99 reportedly brought about stronger US support for the Polish position.[31]

As it approached NATO membership, Poland was aggressively seeking to protect its perceived national security and defence interests. It claimed that it could not accept a discriminatory status that would obstruct its alliance obligations and compromise NATO's further enlargement, while Russia (and Belarus) would not reciprocate with similar pledges. It therefore demanded appropriate weapon cuts from both countries and that CFE Treaty adaptation should not be linked to NATO enlargement.[32]

Another bone of contention was the exceeding of territorial ceilings for brief periods of time by major temporary deployments. Russia had long sought to curtail deployments of armed forces for special reasons, for example, in the case of joint military manoeuvres or in crisis situations (the so-called exceptional temporary deployments).

In early March Russia and NATO made mutual concessions which later facilitated compromises by states parties on several critical issues: lower national and territorial ceilings on armed forces, flank arrangements and stronger verification measures, as specified in the JCG decision of 30 March on CFE Treaty adaptation.[33] This also set the stage for finalizing the Agreement on Adaptation. With the main differences concerning the parameters of the agreement settled, the negotiations continued in the JCG.[34]

The NATO air intervention in the FRY, which started on 24 March 1999, led to an angry response from the Russian Defence Ministry and top military officials. In May Defence Minister Igor Sergeyev threatened to reconsider or even withdraw Moscow's endorsement of the newly reached CFE agreement,

---

[31] *Rzeczpospolita*, 10 Dec. 1998, p. 6; and Interview with Bronislaw Geremek, 'Polityka na miare realnej sily Polski' [A policy matching Poland's real strength], *Rzeczpospolita*, 16 Feb. 1999, p. 6.

[32] The bone of contention was a linkage created by Russia between the TLE reductions of new NATO members (chiefly the Polish reductions) and Russia's acceptance of exceptional temporary deployments. Russia had demanded that the new members freeze their territorial ceilings and reduce their national limits, so that NATO did not exceed its aggregate ceilings under the original treaty. The solution found during Polish–Russian negotiations was that Russia would accept TLE deployments in excess of territorial ceilings, while Poland, albeit not reducing its limits, would agree to gradually adjust its levels of holdings in accordance with its national programme for the restructuring of the armed forces.

[33] JCG (note 4).

[34] For more detailed discussion of the developments in the first 3 months of 1999, see Lachowski, Z., 'Conventional arms control', *SIPRI Yearbook 1999* (note 30), pp. 613–33.

along with other arms control agreements.[35] Russia's militant anti-NATO rhetoric notwithstanding, Russian experts and officials admitted that in the light of headway made in the negotiations, especially with regard to constraints preventing strong concentrations of armaments, there was little sense in proposing a balance of forces between Russia and NATO.[36] One leading Russian expert's conclusion from the March 1999 accord was that 'in the north and south of the country and in the region of Central Europe, Russian interests are sufficiently well secured'.[37]

From the spring of 1999 the negotiations in the JCG concentrated on details of the Agreement on Adaptation. It was not until the Russian deployments in late September–early October in the southern flank in and around Chechnya that public attention was drawn to CFE Treaty adaptation. France and the UK were the most critical in their condemnation of the war in Chechnya, with France contemplating not signing the OSCE Charter for European Security and the Agreement on Adaptation unless Russia was more cooperative on the Chechen issue.[38] Eventually, the NATO states decided to sign the agreement, along with other OSCE documents, but it was clear that they would probably withhold ratification until Russia met its arms control obligations.[39]

On 19 November 1999 at Istanbul the 30 states parties to the CFE Treaty signed the Agreement on Adaptation of the Treaty on Conventional Armed Forces in Europe, subject to ratification, and the political declaration entitled the Final Act of the Conference of the States Parties to the Treaty on Conventional Armed Forces in Europe (the CFE Final Act).[40] Although satisfaction over the new agreement was clouded by Russian non-compliance in Chechnya, the parties saw it largely as a success for European peace, security and stability. NATO, however, pointed out that entry into force of the

---

[35] *Kosovo Situation Reports: May 1999*, CBS Report for Congress, Congressional Research Service, Library of Congress, CRS-6, 24 May 1999, pp. 1, 8.

[36] 'Although experts talk about NATO's predominance over Russia in all arms categories, it is practically impossible for the "present-day NATOists" to realize it; similarly, the adapted CFE Treaty will not allow the transfer of considerable numbers of TLE items within European territory.' Oznobishchev, S. K., 'Problemy ogranicheniya obychnykh vooruzheniev' [Problems of conventional arms limitations], *Rossiya i Zapad: Krizis Otnoshenii v Sfere Bezopasnosti i Problema Kontrola nad Vooruzheniyami* [Russia and the West: the crisis of relations in the sphere of security and the problem of arms control], (IMEMO, Russian Academy of Sciences: Moscow, 1999), p. 66.

[37] Chernov, V. L., 'Osnovnye elementy adaptirovannogo Dogovora ob obychnykh vooruzhennykh silakh v Evrope' [The principal elements of the adapted treaty on conventional armed forces in Europe], *Rossiya i Zapad* (note 36), p. 68.

[38] 'Le conflict en Tchétchénie au centre du sommet de l'OSCE' [The conflict in Chechnya at the centre of the OSCE summit], *Le Monde*, 19 Nov. 1999, p. 4; and 'Fudge pervades the menu in Istanbul', *Financial Times*, 19 Nov. 1999, p. 2. For excerpts from the Charter for European Security see appendix 4A in this volume.

[39] 'OSCE summit: stage set for Russian clash with West', *Financial Times*, 17 Nov. 1999, p. 2.

[40] Agreement on Adaptation of the Treaty on Conventional Armed Forces in Europe, CFE.DOC/1/99, Istanbul, 19 Nov. 1999, available on the OSCE Internet site at URL <http://www.osce.org/docs/english/1990-1999/cfe/cfeagree.htm>; and OSCE (note 22). A consolidated text showing the amended CFE Treaty as adapted in accordance with the 1999 Agreement on Adaptation is given in appendix 10B.

Agreement on Adaptation can only be 'envisaged in the context of compliance by all States Parties with the Treaty's limitations'.[41]

In Russia the signing of the agreement had a mixed reception. Strong differences of opinion and arguments between Russian military delegates and diplomats as to the scope of the compromises with NATO had already been seen during the course of the adaptation talks. The Chairman of the Duma Foreign Affairs Committee, Vladimir Lukin, saw the agreement as 'a compromise, but a winning one'.[42] In turn, the Deputy Chairman of the Duma Defence Committee, Alexei Arbatov, found it insufficiently radical and 'not fully meeting Russia's interests' because it failed to secure deep cuts in the arsenals of the parties. He doubted whether the Duma would ratify it soon.[43] Nevertheless, in its resolution of 30 November, the Duma approved the results of the OSCE Summit Meeting 'as important steps towards a comprehensive, indivisible and equal for all system of security in Europe'.[44]

III. The adapted CFE Treaty regime

The Agreement on Adaptation introduces numerous amendments to the original CFE Treaty, deleting articles wholly or in part and in many cases replacing them with new provisions,[45] in order to adapt it to the new security situation in Europe. It builds on a number of proposals submitted and JCG documents agreed during the nearly three-year negotiating effort by the 30 states parties, including the crucial JCG decision of 30 March 1999, which determined the core of the future agreement.

[41] NATO Final Communiqué (note 16), para. 40. President Clinton stated on 19 Nov. that he would not submit the Agreement on Adaptation to the US Senate for advice and consent to ratification until Russian forces in the North Caucasus 'have in fact been reduced to the flank levels set forth in the adapted Treaty'. United States Information Service (USIS), 'Clinton statement on conventional armed forces in Europe treaty', *Washington File* (US Embassy: Stockholm, 19 Nov. 1999).

[42] ITAR-TASS (Moscow), 22 Nov. 1999, in 'Russia: Lukin says CFE treaty main gain at OSCE summit', FBIS-SOV-1999-1122, 22 Nov. 1999.

[43] Interfax (Moscow), 18 Nov. 1999, in 'Russia: Duma's Arbatov sees CFE treaty as unequal', FBIS-SOV-1999-1122, 18 Nov. 1999. A harsh view of the logic of bloc confrontation was presented by Sergey Rogov, Director of the Institute of US and Canada Studies in Moscow. In an article written before the Istanbul meeting, entitled 'The West revives a cold war', he offered a catalogue of alleged deficiencies of the European arms control regime: the alleged failure of the CFE regime to stave off the 'aggressive war' in the FRY; NATO's operation in the FRY with no UN or OSCE mandate; the CFE regime lacking a pan-European character; alleged huge deployments by NATO of heavy equipment outside the ATTU area (in Albania, Bosnia and Herzegovina, and the former Yugoslav Republic of Macedonia, FYROM); disproportion in TLE ceilings among various states; discrimination against Russia in the Central European and flank regions; and a great imbalance of forces between the Atlantic Alliance and Russia in comparison with the former NATO–Soviet ratio. Consequently he advised against speeding up the signing of the Agreement on Adaptation. 'Zapad vozrozhdaet kholodnuyu voynu' [The West revives the cold war], *Nezavisimaya Gazeta*, 17 Nov. 1999, pp. 1, 6.

[44] Interfax (Moscow), 30 Nov. 1999, in 'Russia: Duma approves results of OSCE summit', FBIS-SOV-1999-1130, 30 Nov. 1999. See also Vladykin, O., 'Breakthrough on the flanks', *Obshchaya Gazeta* (Moscow, Internet edn), 23 Dec. 1999, in 'Ministries' glee over Istanbul CFE reported', FBIS-SOV-199-1223, 23 Dec. 1999.

[45] Hereafter in this chapter, as in the documents concerned, Arabic numerals refer to the articles of the 1999 Agreement on Adaptation and Roman numerals to those of the 1990 CFE Treaty.

Table 10.4. National ceilings and sub-ceilings for TLE categories in active units

State	Battle tanks	ACVs[a] Total	of which AIFVs+HACVs	of which HACVs	Artillery	Aircraft	Heli-copters
Armenia	220	220	135	11	285	100	50
Azerbaijan	220	220	135	11	285	100	50
Belarus (1)	1 800	2 600	1 590	130	1 615	294	80
Belgium[b]	300	989	600	237	288	209	46
Bulgaria	1 475	2 000	1 100	100	1 750	235	67
Canada	77	263	263	0	32	90	13
Czech Rep. (2)	957	1 367	954	69	767	230	50
Denmark[b]	335	336	210	17	446	82	18
France[b]	1 226	3 700	1 983	535	1 192	800	390
Georgia	220	220	135	11	285	100	50
Germany[b]	3 444	3 281	3 281	80	2 255	765	280
Greece	1 735	2 498	1 599	70	1 920	650	30
Hungary (3)	835	1 700	1 020	85	840	180	108
Iceland	0	0	0	0	0	0	0
Italy	1 267	3 127	1 970	0	1 818	618	142
Kazakhstan	50	200	0	0	100	15	20
Luxembourg	0	0	0	0	0	0	0
Moldova	210	210	130	10	250	50	50
Netherlands[b]	520	864	718	0	485	230	50
Norway	170	275	181	0	491	100	24
Poland (4)	1 730	2 150	1 700	107	1 610	460	130
Portugal	300	430	267	77	450	160	26
Romania	1 375	2 100	552	72	1 475	430	120
Russia[b] (5)	6 350	11 280	7 030	574	6 315	3 416	855
Slovakia (6)	478	683	476	34	383	100	40
Spain[b]	750	1 588	1 228	191	1 276	310	90
Turkey	2 795	3 120	1 993	93	3 523	750	103
Ukraine (7)	4 080	5 050	3 095	253	4 040	1 090	330
UK[b]	843	3 017	1 335	200	583	855	365
United States[b]	1 812	3 037	2 372	0	1 553	784	404

[a] Armoured combat vehicles.

[b] States parties whose agreed national ceilings (NCs), as shown here, are lower in 2 or more equipment categories than their MNLHs as of 1 Jan. 1997.
  (1) Of which no more than 1525 tanks, 2175 ACVs and 1375 artillery pieces in active units.
  (2) Of which no more than 754 tanks, 1223 ACVs and 629 artillery pieces in active units.
  (3) Of which no more than 658 tanks, 1522 ACVs and 688 artillery pieces in active units.
  (4) Of which no more than 1362 tanks, 1924 ACVs and 1319 artillery pieces in active units.
  (5) Of which no more than 5575 tanks and 5505 artillery pieces in active units.
  (6) Of which no more than 376 tanks, 611 ACVs and 314 artillery pieces in active units.
  (7) Of which no more than 3130 tanks, 4350 ACVs and 3240 artillery pieces in active units.

Source: Protocol on National Ceilings for Conventional Armaments and Equipment limited by the Treaty on Conventional Armed Forces in Europe, Agreement on Adaptation of the Treaty on Conventional Armed Forces in Europe, 19 Nov. 1999. The text is available on the OSCE Internet site at URL <http://www.osce.org/docs/english/1990-1999/cfe/cfeagree.htm>.

Table 10.5. Territorial ceilings and sub-ceilings for ground TLE categories

State	Tanks	ACVs	Artillery
Armenia (3)(4)	220	220	285
Azerbaijan (3)(4)	220	220	285
Belarus (5)	1 800	2 600	1 615
Belgium	544	1 505	497
Bulgaria (3)(4)	1 475	2 000	1 750
Czech Republic (5)	957	1 367	767
Denmark (5)	353	336	503
France	1 306	3 820	1 292
Georgia (3)(4)	220	220	285
Germany (5)	4 704	6 772	3 407
Greece	1 735	2 498	1 920
Hungary (3)(4)	835	1 700	840
Iceland (3)(4)	0	0	0
Italy (5)	642	3 805	2 062
Kazakhstan (5)	50	200	100
Luxembourg (5)	143	174	47
Moldova (3)(4)	210	210	250
Netherlands (5)	809	1 220	651
Norway (3)(4)	170	282	557
Poland (5)	1 730	2 150	1 610
Portugal (5)	300	430	450
Romania (3)(4)	1 375	2 100	1 475
Russia (5)	6 350	11 280	6 315
of which (1)(3)(4)	1 300	2 140	1 680
Slovakia (5)	478	683	383
Spain (5)	891	2 047	1 370
Turkey (3)(4)	2 795	3 120	3 523
Ukraine (5)	4 080	5 050	4 040
of which (2)(3)(4)	400	400	350
United Kingdom (5)	843	3 029	583

(1) In the Leningrad MD, excluding the Pskov *oblast*; and in the North Caucasus MD, excluding: the Volgograd *oblast*; the Astrakhan *oblast*; that part of the Rostov *oblast* east of the line extending from Kushchevskaya to the Volgodonsk *oblast* border, including Volgodonsk; and Kushchevskaya and a narrow corridor in Krasnodar *kray* leading to Kushchevskaya. This territorial sub-ceiling shall not be exceeded pursuant to Article VII for military exercises and temporary deployments in the category of ACVs.

(2) In the Odessa *oblast*.

(3) States parties which shall not increase their TCs or territorial sub-ceilings pursuant to Article V (5), only in conjunction with a corresponding decrease, pursuant to Article V(4) (A), in the TCs or territorial sub-ceilings of other states parties, as identified by this footnote.

(4) States parties which shall not exceed their TCs or territorial sub-ceilings pursuant to Article VII by more than 153 tanks, 241 ACVs and 140 artillery pieces.

(5) States parties which shall not exceed their TCs or territorial sub-ceilings pursuant to Article VII by more than 459 tanks, 723 ACVs and 420 artillery pieces.

Source: Protocol on Territorial Ceilings for Conventional Armaments and Equipment limited by the Treaty on Conventional Armed Forces in Europe, Agreement on Adaptation of the Treaty on Conventional Armed Forces in Europe, 19 Nov. 1999. The text is available on the OSCE Internet site at URL < http://www.osce.org/docs/english/1990-1999/cfe/cfeagree.htm>.

Table 10.6. National TLE limits under the 1990 CFE Treaty and the 1999 Agreement on Adaptation

State	Year	Tanks	ACVs^c	Artillery	Aircraft	Helicopters
NATO	1990	19 142	29 822	18 286	6 662	2 000
	1999^a	19 096	31 787	19 529	7 273	2 282
WTO/f.WTO	1990	20 000	30 000	20 000	6 800	2 000
	1999^b	16 478	24 783	16 783	5 930	1 712
Total	**1990**	**39 142**	**59 822**	**38 286**	**13 462**	**4 000**
	1999	**35 574**	**56 570**	**36 312**	**13 203**	**3 994**
Difference		− 3 568	− 3 252	− 1 974	− 259	− 6

^{a} Enlarged NATO '16+3'.
^{b} 'Former WTO − 3'.

Source: Protocol on National Ceilings for Conventional Armaments and Equipment limited by the Treaty on Conventional Armed Forces in Europe, Agreement on Adaptation of the Treaty on Conventional Armed Forces in Europe, 19 Nov. 1999. The text is available on the OSCE Internet site at URL <http://www.osce.org/docs/english/1990-1999/cfe/cfeagree.htm>.

The Agreement on Adaptation will enter into force when all 30 signatory states have ratified it, after which the CFE Treaty will only exist in its amended form.

The basic tenets of the agreement stand in contrast to the original treaty. Instead of rivalry and division, the principle of a common and indivisible security space underlies politico-military relations in the new Europe. A system of individual state-to-state limits is to replace the balance-of-forces symmetry between two blocs (NATO and the WTO). Finally, the exclusive bloc-related character of the treaty is to be changed: the European conventional arms regime is declared open to all the other European countries following the entry into force of the Agreement on Adaptation.[46]

Under the Agreement on Adaptation two nation-related types of ceiling replace the now obsolete group (bloc) structure: national ceilings (NC) and territorial ceilings (TC), as shown in tables 10.4 and 10.5. The Agreement on Adaptation reduces the aggregate levels of heavy armaments by more than 9000 TLE items compared with the original CFE Treaty aggregate ceilings (table 10.6), although the total number of holdings in 1999 was even lower (see table 10.7). Among states that proposed significant reductions of their current entitlements, the USA offered a 42 per cent cut (by 7590 TLE) from its current maximum national levels for holdings (MNLH) of 13 088 items, and its holdings are still less than half its national limit—3467 vs 7186 TLE items—

[46] Any European state may submit to the depositary (the Netherlands Government) a written request to accede to the treaty including: (*a*) the designation of its existing TLE; (*b*) its proposed national and territorial ceilings and the related subceilings for TLE; and (*c*) any other information deemed relevant by the requesting state. Any decision by the states parties regarding the request is subject to consensus. The agreed terms for accession will be laid down in an Agreement on Accession between the parties and the requesting state. Agreement on Adaptation (note 40), Article 18, amending Article XVIII.

Table 10.7. CFE Treaty limits and holdings, 1990–99

	Holdings, Nov. 1990	CFE limit, 1990	Holdings, Nov. 1995	Holdings, Jan. 1999	Adapted CFE limit, 1999
Total	201 005	154 712	130 813	124 226	145 653

and Germany declared an almost 9 per cent cut (by 963 TLE items). Russia proposed a reduction of 385 TLE items[47] from its entitlement of 28 601. The four Visegrad countries (the Czech Republic, Hungary, Poland and Slovakia) offered to lower their aggregate holdings by 1700 TLE items by 2003.

The new structure of limitations

States parties set their initial national limits with the understanding that they would take 'a restrained approach, maintaining only such military capabilities . . . as are commensurate with individual or legitimate security interests'.[48] The national limits are for each state party, covering all five categories of equipment. The ceilings do not exceed the up-to-date MNLH, which have been notified under the CFE Treaty. The national ceilings also retain two sub-ceilings: for active units and for sub-categories of armaments (armoured infantry fighting vehicles—AIFVs—and heavy armoured combat vehicles—HACVs). Since the NATO states parties that signed the original treaty have decided to remove all their stored equipment, the sub-ceilings for active units of member states are equal to their NCs; the three new NATO member states and Belarus, Russia, Slovakia and Ukraine have decided to retain part of their equipment in their designated permanent storage sites (DPSS). Only states with territory in the ATTU zone have territorial ceilings: thus the USA and Canada do not possess TCs. Twenty parties have set their territorial ceilings at the same level as their national ground weapon limits. Russia and Ukraine have additional territorial sub-ceilings for their flank areas. TCs enable parties to host or receive foreign ground forces. Aircraft and helicopters are excluded from this type of limit, despite Russian pressure for their inclusion. The main rule is that TCs will be either equal to or higher than NCs.

Upward revisions of national and territorial ceilings

The future system of national and territorial ceilings will be more rigid than the original CFE Treaty's structure of limits on the TLE that might be located in and moved within large zonal areas. The Agreement on Adaptation specifies that any upward revision of the national ceiling of one state party should be

---

[47] This part of its entitlement was given to Kazakhstan.
[48] Decision of the JCG concerning certain basic elements for treaty adaptation, 23 July 1997, reproduced in *SIPRI Yearbook 1998: Armaments, Disarmament and International Security* (Oxford University Press: Oxford, 1998), pp. 541–43.

compensated by a corresponding decrease in the NC on the same TLE category of one or more other parties. Prior notification should be made 90 days before the revision becomes effective and it should be notified to all other parties. Between five-yearly review conferences (the first was held in 1996; the second will be held in May 2001) national ceilings/sub-ceilings for active units may be increased by no more than 40 tanks, 60 ACVs and 20 artillery pieces or 20 per cent of the established national ceilings, whichever is greater, but in no case exceeding 150 tanks, 250 ACVs and 100 artillery pieces.[49] For combat aircraft and attack helicopters, the upward revision numbers are 30 and 25, respectively. Upward increases of national ceilings/sub-ceilings for active units in excess of the permitted levels will be subject to a consensus decision by all parties.[50] Moreover, any party with a sub-ceiling for active units may increase it provided that this is accompanied by a decrease in its NC by four in this same category of ground TLE (i.e., for each TLE item added, four items of the same category must be eliminated).[51]

An NC may also be decreased unilaterally by a party in any category of TLE, but this confers no right on any other party to increase its NC.

A party's territorial ceiling/sub-ceiling can be increased. The rule and parameters for upward revisions of TCs are similar to those for NCs: an increase will be accompanied by a corresponding decrease by another party/parties; the same parameters apply for exceeding TCs; an increase in territorial ceiling/sub-ceiling in any category in excess of these levels will be subject to the consent of all other parties.

Exemptions for peace operations and forces in transit

UN/OSCE-mandated peace missions are exempt from the territorial ceilings/sub-ceilings of a party on whose territory TLE necessary for the given mission is present. Parameters for force levels and the duration of UN/OSCE-mandated missions will be guided by a resolution or decision of either body. Such missions must be duly notified.

In addition to the exemption from counting rules under Article III, 1(G) of the CFE Treaty ('external constraints'), Article V.3 of the adapted treaty also makes armaments and equipment in transit within the ATTU zone exempt from the territorial ceilings/sub-ceilings of transited parties. Several specific conditions will be met: (*a*) territorial ceilings will not be exceeded, except as otherwise provided for in Article VII of the adapted treaty (military exercises and temporary deployments); (*b*) there is no numerical limit for TLE in transit to a destination outside the ATTU area; (*c*) the entire transit takes no longer than 42 days; and (*d*) the TLE in transit does not remain on the territory of

---

[49] The rationale is to avoid the smaller countries feeling discriminated against. While any party may, e.g., increase its arsenals by a maximum of 40 tanks, even if this exceeds 20% of its NC, no party may exceed the ceiling of 150 tanks.

[50] Agreement on Adaptation (note 40), Article 5, amending Article IV.

[51] This was not applied to Russia's flank zone.

any single transited state party, or on a territory with a territorial sub-ceiling, longer than 21 days.[52]

Military exercises and temporary deployments

The disadvantage of upward revisions of territorial ceilings/sub-ceilings is that they require the consent of or compensation by one or more other states, resulting in a cumbersome procedure. Temporary deployments are a more expedient alternative, especially in various security contingencies. Similarly, more convenient provisions for military exercises must be provided. The agreement ensures that neither military exercises nor temporary deployments have a destabilizing effect.

Each state party has the right to host exercises on its territory or on a territory with a territorial sub-ceiling in accordance with the Protocol on Territorial Ceilings. The number of ground TLE items in excess of its territorial ceiling/sub-ceiling for a military exercise, alone or in combination with any other manoeuvre or any temporary deployment on that territory, cannot exceed the number of tanks, ACVs and artillery pieces specified for temporary deployments for each state (see below). A military exercise or successive exercises that will result in a territorial ceiling/sub-ceiling being exceeded for more than 42 days will thereafter be considered a temporary deployment.

The Agreement on Adaptation provides for two kinds of temporary deployment in excess of TCs: (a) a 'basic' deployment up to the equivalent of a brigade (up to 153 tanks, 241 ACVs and 140 artillery pieces); and (b) for 'exceptional circumstances', a deployment in each party outside the former flank area of up to three brigades (459 tanks, 723 ACVs and 420 artillery pieces). Explanatory reports to the JCG and regular updates are envisaged.[53]

If a temporary deployment exceeds 153 tanks, 241 ACVs and 140 artillery pieces, a conference of parties will be convened to explain the nature of the circumstances which have given rise to the temporary deployment, in accordance with Article XXI,1bis of the adapted treaty. If a military exercise in conjunction with a temporary deployment causes the TC to be exceeded by more than the basic temporary deployment levels, any party may also request the convening of a conference of states parties.[54]

The duration of temporary deployments is not limited. If a military exercise exceeding a territorial ceiling/sub-ceiling is to last more than 42 days, on the 43rd day, at the latest, all relevant information will be provided by the party whose ceiling has been exceeded (purpose and duration, TLE involved, the total number in excess and the area of deployment) and by the parties that participate in the territorial ceiling/sub-ceiling (the total number of TLE and the area of deployment). In the case of temporary deployments, within 21 days of its territorial ceiling/sub-ceiling being exceeded, a party must provide relevant

---

[52] Agreement on Adaptation (note 40), Article 6, amending Article V.
[53] Agreement on Adaptation (note 40), Article 8, amending Article VII.
[54] Agreement on Adaptation (note 40), Article 19, amending Article XXI.

detailed information, including the anticipated duration of the deployment. Afterwards it will provide subsequent updates every 90 days.

Each party will provide notification when a cumulative increase of 30 tanks, 30 ACVs or 10 artillery pieces in excess of the number previously notified occurs.

The party whose territorial ceiling/sub-ceiling has been exceeded will inform all other parties whenever the numbers of TLE no longer exceed its ceilings.

The flank issue

One of the major rationales behind the adaptation of the CFE Treaty was the redistribution of Russian armed forces after the end of the cold war. Because of its separate special status (specific limitations on ground forces, territorial constraints and additional verification measures) and divergent views about how it should be accommodated in the new conventional arms control regime, the flank issue had remained most controversial between Russia and NATO and other states concerned since 1993. Russia considered itself to have been treated unfairly because of the number and rigidity of the additional limitations applied to its territory, and therefore demanded equal treatment.

NATO argued that the reconciliation of the flank regime with the structure of the adapted treaty should form an integral part of the adaptation; retain the legally binding character of the flank obligations; not compromise the security interests of any state party or lead to less stability and predictability than in the rest of the ATTU area; ensure that the flank countries enjoy a political status equal to that of other parties; and enable the opening of the adapted treaty to accession by other states.[55]

Three former Soviet republics (Azerbaijan, Georgia and Moldova) had also taken issue with Russia over the implementation of CFE flank provisions, as discussed in section II above. Another problem compounding the situation was that two other countries (Bulgaria and Romania) were seeking to leave the flank regime in their efforts to join NATO. Both countries were afraid that flank limitations on temporary deployments might adversely affect their chances of joining NATO. Among the NATO countries, Greece remained most opposed to maintaining flank limitations.

On 25 January 1999, following Russian–Turkish talks and intra-NATO consultations, an agreement was reached with respect to the southern flank. Turkey, a firm opponent of relaxation of flank limits, agreed to allow 2140 ACVs in Russia's revised flank areas.[56] Moreover, all the Russian weapons in the flank areas could be deployed in active units. In return, Russia reportedly agreed to reduce its holdings in Georgia and Moldova.[57] Although Bulgaria and

---

[55] Lachowski (note 34), pp. 628–31.

[56] The text of the agreement was not made public. Russia provided information on the agreement on 11 Feb. ITAR-TASS (Moscow), 11 Feb. 1999, in 'Russia, Turkey reach accord on CFE Treaty flank problems', FBIS-SOV-1999-0212, 12 Feb. 1999.

[57] Institute for Defense and Disarmament Studies, *Arms Control Reporter* (IDDS: Brookline, Mass.), sheet 407.B.597, 1999.

Table 10.8. Russian and Ukrainian entitlements in the former flank zone and the redefined flank zone

	Tanks	ACVs	Artillery
Russia			
Flank zone entitlements[a] (1990 CFE Treaty)	700	580	1 280
plus those in storage	(600)	(800)	(400)
Temporary deployments (1996 Final Document)	1 897	4 397	2 422
in original flank zone (31 May 1996–31 May 1999)			
Sub-limits in original flank zone (May 1999)	1 800	3 700[b]	2 400
Territorial sub-limits for revised flank[c]	1 300	2 140	1680
(1999 Agreement on Adaptation)			
Ukraine			
Flank zone entitlements[d] (1990 CFE Treaty)	280	350	390
plus those in storage	(400)	(–)	(500)
Territorial sub-limits for the Odessa *oblast*	400	400	350
(1996 Final Document; 1999 Agreement on Adaptation)			

[a] The Leningrad and North Caucasus MDs.

[b] No more than 552 located within the Astrakhan and Volgograd *oblasts* (regions) respectively; no more than 310 within the eastern part of the Rostov *oblast* (as described in note *c*); and no more than 600 within the Pskov *oblast*.

[c] In the Leningrad MD, excluding the Pskov *oblast*; and in the North Caucasus MD, excluding: the Volgograd *oblast*; the Astrakhan *oblast*; that part of the Rostov *oblast* east of the line extending from Kushchevskaya to the Volgodonsk *oblast* border, including Volgodonsk; and Kushchevskaya and a narrow corridor in Krasnodar *kray* leading to Kushchevskaya.

[d] The Odessa MD.

Romania opposed the Russian–Turkish deal, the accord paved the way for the settlement of the overall flank issue.

The 30 March 1999 JCG decision set out a number of 'principles and modalities' to guide the 'maintenance and reconciliation' of the substance of the modified flank provisions in the adapted treaty. The principles included: (*a*) the legally binding character of the provisions; (*b*) preventing a build-up of forces; (*c*) equal initial TCs and initial NCs/up-to-date maximum national levels for holdings; (*d*) upward revision of the relevant TCs and sub-limits only through transfers among the flank states; (*e*) brigade-level temporary deployment limits; and (*f*) an enhanced regime of verification and information exchange. The modalities prescribed: (*a*) single sub-limits for Russia and Ukraine; (*b*) subordination of Russian forces in other countries to general rules regarding NCs, TCs and temporary deployments; and (*c*) the desirability of an early solution to the reduction of Russian forces in Georgia and of the withdrawal of Russian forces from Moldova. With the exception of the issue of the Russian presence in Georgia and Moldova, all these arrangements found their way into the Agreement on Adaptation.

Although the flank zone's functions are retained, there is no explicit reference to a flank zone in the Agreement on Adaptation. The 12 parties with territory in the former flank zone[58] will have the right to increase their territorial ceilings/sub-ceilings only in conjunction with a corresponding decrease in the territorial sub-ceilings of other parties in that area. In addition to national and territorial ceilings for the 12 flank states, Russia and Ukraine will have one territorial sub-ceiling each, applied to the Leningrad and North Caucasus MDs excluding some administrative areas (Russia) and the Odessa *oblast* (Ukraine). In no case may a territorial ceiling/sub-ceiling be exceeded temporarily by more than 153 tanks, 241 ACVs or 140 artillery pieces by these states. Outside their flank areas, Russia and Ukraine may temporarily deploy up to three brigades each.

The issues of Russian armaments and equipment abroad within the flank zone were settled in the politically binding CFE Final Act and the OSCE Summit Declaration adopted at the Istanbul Summit Meeting.[59]

Accommodation in Central Europe

NATO has pledged that it will refrain from additional permanent stationing of substantial ground and air combat forces on the territory of the three new member states. It has also promised increased transparency with regard to its defence plans and programmes in the context of any future stationing.[60] Earlier plans for the establishment of an enhanced stability zone were not formalized in treaty form because of the strong opposition of the Central European countries, particularly Poland, to having quasi-flank limitations imposed on them. Instead, in a series of political declarations, first appended to the March 1999 JCG decision and later to the CFE Final Act, the states concerned made concessions aimed at alleviating fears arising from the enlargement of NATO.

Accordingly, Belarus, the Czech Republic, Hungary, Poland and Slovakia stated that their national and territorial ceilings would equal their MNLH.[61] Together with Germany and Ukraine they undertook not to use the mechanism for upward revisions of the territorial ceilings. Moreover, the Visegrad countries pledged to reduce their respective territorial ceilings in ground armaments and equipment through either full or partial conversion of storage entitlements over the next several years.[62] At the same time, they all firmly reserved their right to host temporary deployments up to an equivalent of three brigades.[63]

---

[58] Armenia, Azerbaijan, Bulgaria, Georgia, Greece, Iceland, Moldova, Norway, Romania, Russia, Turkey and Ukraine.

[59] Regarding Georgia and Moldova, see section II above.

[60] See note 30.

[61] Belarus gave up its earlier insistence on letting its holdings exceed the current MNLH by 20%.

[62] Under the 30 Mar. 1999 JCG decision on treaty adaptation, as reaffirmed by the CFE Final Act, the Czech Republic, Hungary, Poland and Slovakia agreed to lower their territorial limits by a total of 1700 TLE items by 2002/2003, thus limiting the number of foreign troops deployed on their territories.

[63] The wording of the individual declarations varies slightly. Poland's declaration is the firmest, subjecting its reductions to 'reciprocal will and restraint in the immediate neighbourhood', especially the force levels in Kaliningrad and Belarus. CFE Final Act (note 22), Annexes 3 and 10.

In response, Russia promised to show 'due restraint' regarding ground TLE and deployments in the Kaliningrad and Pskov *oblasts* and not to increase its air and ground combat forces on a permanent basis; it also reserved the option for operational reinforcements, including temporary deployments.

Host nation consent

Throughout the negotiations a long-standing argument was that there should be no unwanted foreign military presence on the territory of a state party, meaning especially Georgia and Moldova. Along with these countries' bilateral agreements with Russia on force withdrawals, as reached in the CFE Final Act and confirmed in the OSCE Summit Declaration, the Agreement on Adaptation provides in the amended Article I that the TLE of a party 'shall only be present on the territory of another State Party in conformity with international law, the explicit consent of the host State Party, or a relevant resolution of the United Nations Security Council'.[64] Consent of the host state must be given in advance and be reflected through the appropriate notifications under the Protocol on Information Exchange.[65] As a result, the adapted treaty enhances regional stability and the sovereignty of Russia's neighbours.[66] The significance of this clause was reaffirmed in the NATO foreign ministers' communiqué issued one month later.[67]

Enhanced transparency

The Agreement on Adaptation builds upon the CFE Treaty information-exchange and verification regime. Most major changes with regard to information provision and verification were introduced as a result of the new structure of limitations. Some changes stem from the experience of CFE Treaty implementation and the need to provide more detailed information. Other changes concern the issues on which parties were seeking greater restrictions and transparency (combat aircraft and attack helicopters).

Consequently, large sections are added to or amended in the Protocol on Notifications and Exchange of Information with regard to such issues as the overall holdings of TLE and other equipment subject to the treaty, transit of armaments and equipment through or within the area of application, quarterly information on the total numbers of and changes in ground and air TLE actually present in the area of application and within the territory of a party, use of the headroom between national holdings and TCs by another party,

---

[64] Agreement on Adaptation (note 40), Article 2, amending Article I.
[65] Agreement on Adaptation (note 40), Article 14, amending Article XIII.
[66] On 28 May 1999 Russia reportedly alleged that NATO's deployments around Kosovo violated the CFE Treaty by hindering inspections of NATO forces in the FYROM and Albania. Since none of these countries is a party to the CFE Treaty, such charges would have been irrelevant. 'Russia complains of CFE violation by NATO', *Disarmament Diplomacy*, no. 38 (June 1999). However, the Vienna Document CSBM provisions were breached—see appendix 10A.
[67] NATO (note 16).

information on military exercises and temporary deployments exceeding TCs, and information on operations in support of peace.

Information is to be furnished on the actual location of ground armaments deployed outside the territory of the party that is declared as the peacetime location. Aggregated information is also to be provided on the numbers and types of TLE items entering into or being removed from service as well as the types and numbers of TLE items having been withdrawn from the 'decommissioned and awaiting disposal' category.

In line with the 1996 Flank Document,[68] more detailed and frequent information is demanded from Russia and Ukraine on their flank zones.

Because of past disputes over armoured ambulances (not subject to treaty limitations), information is required on overall holdings of armoured personnel carrier ambulances and on locations housing more than 18 such items.

Under the Protocol on Inspections, the number of annual inspections that a party must permit on its territory was increased from 15 to 20 per cent of its objects of verification (OOV). This is warranted by the significant reduction in the number of OOVs that has resulted from large cuts in armaments and equipment carried out since 1992. An addition was made for inspections in the so-called designated areas (areas within which territorial ceilings/sub-ceilings are exceeded as a result of military exercises or temporary deployments).

The matter of dividing costs of inspections between inspected and inspecting states is regulated in the agreement. Cases of *force majeure* delaying the conduct of inspections are addressed. More detailed descriptions of the area of the OOV subject to inspection or a declared site or data with regard to equipment are to be provided during a pre-inspection briefing.

Russia and Ukraine are obliged to accept more inspections with regard to their respective (flank) areas covered by territorial sub-ceilings. Each year Russia will accept in addition to its passive declared site inspection quota up to 10 supplementary inspections.[69] Ukraine will additionally accept one supplementary declared site inspection in the Odessa *oblast*.

With regard to disposal of TLE in excess of reduction liabilities through destruction/modification, a special section XII is added to the Protocol on Reductions to make the procedures more transparent, including notification, observation visits (immediate or postponed visits to cover two or more disposals and inspections) and cooperative measures for the provision of evidence of destruction (displaying each item two weeks before its disposal and its dismantled parts two weeks after its destruction).

IV. Regional arms control in Europe

The 1996 Florence Agreement on Sub-Regional Arms Control (negotiated under Article IV of Annex 1-B of the 1995 General Framework Agreement for

---

[68] Flank Document (note 2), pp. 512–14.
[69] Up to 4 inspections in the areas excluded from the original flank zone (the Pskov *oblast* of the Leningrad MD plus the *oblasts* removed from the North Caucasus MD) and up to 6 inspections in the redefined zone.

Peace in Bosnia and Herzegovina, the Dayton Agreement) signed by Bosnia and Herzegovina and its two entities (the Federation of Bosnia and Herzegovina and the Republika Srpska), Croatia and the FRY[70] is the only 'hard' regional arms control arrangement now in force below the pan-European level. The main characteristic feature of this arms control agreement is that it was imposed from outside on the former parties to a conflict, and compliance with its terms must be both monitored and assisted by the international community.

Implementation of the Florence Agreement

The Chairmanship of the Sub-Regional Consultative Commission (SRCC) was transferred from the Personal Representative of the Chairman-in-Office (Carlo Jean) to be held in rotation by the parties. The parties adopted a protocol governing the procedures for chairmanship and establishing a rotational procedure for it.

The first months of 1999 were overshadowed by the worsening situation in Kosovo. As a result of the start of NATO's intervention on 24 March 1999, the FRY 'suspended'[71] on 31 March the implementation of the Florence Agreement on FRY territory, and the authorities of the Republika Srpska curtailed their contacts with the NATO states participating in the air campaign against the Belgrade regime. These events affected the activities planned earlier, especially the schedule of inspections.

Nevertheless, in late April and mid-June two informal meetings of the SRCC were held in Zagreb under the Croatian chairmanship. The parties agreed to continue the implementation of the agreement and convene a formal SRCC meeting once the FRY retracted its decision on suspension. An invitation to the FRY to carry out inspections on the territory of the other parties without obligations of reciprocity was accepted on the condition that the FRY participated in informal meetings of the SRCC (the end of the bombing campaign against the FRY on 10 June made the offer redundant). The parties also decided to continue to evaluate various issues, especially the updating of the Protocol on Existing Types of Armaments[72] and limiting the exceptions to the

---

[70] For the purpose of this section, 'regional' in the OSCE context refers to areas beneath the continental/OSCE level. Regional CSBMs, including the 1996 Agreement on Confidence- and Security-Building Measures in Bosnia and Herzegovina, are discussed in appendix 10A in this volume. The Florence Agreement was negotiated in accordance with the General Framework Agreement for Peace in Bosnia and Herzegovina, Dayton, Ohio, 21 Nov. 1995, Annex 1-B: Agreement on Regional Stabilization, Article IV: Measures for sub-regional arms control. The Agreement on Regional Stabilization is reproduced in *SIPRI Yearbook 1996: Armaments, Disarmament and International Security* (Oxford University Press: Oxford, 1996), pp. 241–43. The text of the Florence Agreement is reproduced in *SIPRI Yearbook 1997* (note 2), pp. 517–24.

[71] Suspension is not envisaged in the Florence Agreement. Article XII provides for withdrawal from the agreement 42 months after its entry into force (i.e., 14 Dec. 1999). The notice of the decision to withdraw should be made at least 150 days prior to the withdrawal.

[72] A new, improved version of this protocol was agreed at the First Conference to Review the Implementation of the Agreement on Sub-Regional Arms Control (Vienna, 15–19 June 1998) and attached to the Final Document of the Conference as an Annex.

ceilings provided by the Florence Agreement.[73] The proposal of France and Germany to carry out inspections of undeclared sites in October 1999 was accepted. Finally, the modalities for notification of the equipment limited by the agreement, destroyed or damaged, and the modification of military postures (such as a new list of objects of inspection) were to be defined.

On 19 July the FRY Government pledged to resume its implementation of the Florence Agreement and on 28 August it notified termination of the suspension of its participation in the implementation of the agreement and agreed to fully resume its participation in the SRCC in September 1999. The arrest on 25 August of General Momir Talic, Chief of Staff of the Armed Forces of the Republika Srpska, based on the warrant issued by the International Criminal Tribunal for the Former Yugoslavia, was a potential set-back, but it did not block the activities of the Consultative Commission; the Republika Srpska only postponed an inspection due in this period.

After the NATO intervention, the issue arose of the FRY making up for its weapon losses to the limits envisaged in the agreement. There were, however, differences in the NATO and FRY reports on the numbers of agreement-limited armaments destroyed.

On 16 September the FRY provided the SRCC with completely new information; a new inspection plan was approved and all the inspections planned for the year were completed by mid-December 1999. The inspections were conducted in an efficient and cooperative way, and all the parties requested OSCE assistance for the inspection and escort teams.

There are a few immediate tasks for the continued implementation of the Florence Agreement. First, inspections of undeclared sites ('challenge inspections') are to be improved to further enhance transparency and confidence. France and Germany will provide a specific training course for such inspections. Second, the parties will be encouraged to adopt voluntary limitations on the exemptions to the armament ceilings, and to make voluntary reductions of these ceilings. Defence budgets and military manpower should also be reduced and aligned with the average levels of the neighbouring countries.[74]

The participants in the international summit meeting on the Stability Pact for South Eastern Europe, initiated by the European Union in Cologne and placed under OSCE auspices in 1999, issued on 30 July the Sarajevo Summit Declaration in which they committed themselves to full implementation of existing arms control and confidence-building measures (CBMs) and to efforts for their improvement.[75] They also welcomed the recommitment of the sig-

---

[73] E.g., the Republika Srpska has a limit of 113 ACVs and because of exceptions its holdings number 286 ACVs. It is proposed that the exceptions be either eliminated or reduced.

[74] Jean, C. (Lt-Gen.), Personal Representative of the OSCE Chairman-in-Office, Implementation of Article II (Confidence- and Security-building Measures in Bosnia and Herzegovina) and Article IV (Sub-Regional Arms Control), Annex 1-B, Dayton Peace Agreement Accords in 1999, Istanbul, 1999.

[75] Sarajevo Summit Declaration of the Heads of State and Government of the participating and facilitating countries of the Stability Pact and the Principals of participating and facilitating International Organizations and Agencies and regional initiatives, Sarajevo, 30 July 1999, URL <http://www.stabilitypact.org/summit.htm>. See also chapter 4 in this volume.

natories present (the FRY was not invited) to fulfilling their arms control obligations under the Dayton Agreement.

In April, the USA suspended the Train and Equip programme for Bosnia and Herzegovina on the grounds of the failure of the Army of the Federation of Bosnia and Herzegovina to fully integrate its forces.[76] In late October both entities of Bosnia and Herzegovina announced that they would reduce their armies by 15 per cent, under a decision taken by the country's collective presidency. The Federation Army would reduce its size by 20 battalions, of which 15 would come from the Muslim forces and five from the Bosnian–Croatian forces. The Republika Srpska would cut back 10 battalions. A number of other units would also be reduced. This decision was warranted by the lack of funds to support the existing manpower.[77]

Negotiations under Article V of the Agreement on Regional Stabilization

The objective of the talks under Article V of Annex 1-B of the Dayton Agreement,[78] which deal with broader regional arms control, is to find lasting solutions for the stabilization of South-Eastern Europe. Work on the mandate of the Article V negotiations was concluded on 27 November 1998. The talks were to begin in mid-January 1999, but were postponed until March because of the discovery of a massacre in the Kosovo village of Racak on 15 January. After the meeting of the 20 participating countries on 8 March the talks were temporarily suspended because of the NATO air campaign. They were not resumed until 6 September. At the end of the year, the negotiations were reported to be at a very early stage—several potential CSBMs and transparency measures had been put forward and examined.[79] The OSCE Summit Meeting in Istanbul welcomed the entry of the negotiations into their sub-

---

[76] Boese, W., 'Belgrade suspends implementation of sub-regional arms accord', *Arms Control Today*, vol. 29, no. 3 (Apr./May 1999), p. 43. The first suspension took place on 1–17 June 1998 because of the failure of the 2 armed forces to stop using separate rank insignia and flags. In Sep. 1999, it was reported that the USA had renewed military aid under the Train and Equip programme. 'US company renews Bosnia military aid deal', *New Europe*, no. 329 (13–19 Sep. 1999), p. 33.

[77] *Jane's Defence Weekly*, vol. 32, no. 17 (27 Oct. 1999), p. 5.

[78] General Framework Agreement for Peace in Bosnia and Herzegovina, Dayton, Ohio, 21 Nov. 1995, Annex 1-B: Agreement on Regional Stabilization, Article V, Regional Arms Control Agreement. The Agreement on Regional Stabilization is reproduced in *SIPRI Yearbook 1996* (note 70), pp. 241–43.

[79] Germany has proposed a system of 'cross-information and verification', aimed at a closer alignment of the Florence Agreement with the CFE Treaty regime. Under this system, information provided by the parties to the Article IV Agreement would be made available to the states parties to the CFE Treaty who are Article V parties, and vice versa. Similarly, participation in inspections would be settled, without changing the passive quotas system. Albania, Austria, the FYROM and Slovenia, which do not belong to any of these arms control regimes, could be included in this information and verification system on the basis of their declared holdings. Jopp, H. D., 'Regionale Rüstungskontrolle in Europa: Die Rüstungskontrollvereinbarungen nach dem Abkommen von Dayton (Mitte 1997 bis Mitte 1999), [Arms control in Europe: the arms control accords after the Dayton Agreement (mid-1997 to mid-1999)], Institut für Friedensforschung und Sicherheitspolitik an der Universität Hamburg/IFSH (Hrsg.), *OSZE-Jahrbuch 1999* (Nomos Verlagsgesellschaft: Baden-Baden, 1999), p. 394. The participating countries are the 5 former Yugoslav republics plus Albania, Austria, Bulgaria, France, Germany, Greece, Hungary, Italy, the Netherlands, Romania, Russia, Spain, Turkey, the UK and the USA.

stantive phase and urged the participants to complete their work by the end of 2000.[80]

V. The Open Skies Treaty

The entry into force of the 1992 Open Skies Treaty remained deadlocked by the failure of Belarus, Russia and Ukraine to ratify this international confidence-building instrument. No progress had been made towards ratification by these three countries by the end of 1999. The OSCE Summit Meeting reaffirmed the significance of the treaty and urged early completion of the process of its ratification and entry into force. As in previous years, signatories continued reciprocal voluntary overflights in 1999. The OSCE participants underlined that trial flights are in no way a substitute for the regime of observation flights as set forth in the treaty.[81] On 2 March 2000 the Ukrainian Parliament ratified the treaty.[82]

VI. Conventional arms control-related endeavours outside Europe

In contrast to the steady progress in Europe in the field of conventional arms control, there was little or no progress in other regions. Conventional arms control outside Europe remains on a rudimentary level of evolution, and for the most part is confined to first-generation CBMs.

Asia

The ASEAN Regional Forum

South-East Asia sustains a regular confidence-building dialogue which aspires to combine talks on political- and security-related developments in the region, defence policies, non-proliferation and arms control, including various voluntary confidence-building measures.

The political and security dialogue conducted within the Association of South-East Asian Nations (ASEAN) Regional Forum (ARF) covers both military and defence-related measures and non-military issues that have a significant impact on regional security.[83] Non-mandatory CBMs discussed and implemented within the ARF differ from European CSBMs in character and scope, the degree of institutionalization and enforcement, the nature of the

---

[80] OSCE, Istanbul Summit Declaration (note 28), para. 41.

[81] OSCE, Istanbul Summit Declaration (note 28), para. 42.

[82] This leaves Belarus and Russia as the only states whose ratification is necessary for the treaty to enter into force. The ratification discussion in the State Duma Defence Committee in the end of Mar. 2000 was inconclusive. It was agreed that the Duma would submit the treaty for ratification after the issues of the 1993 Treaty on Further Reduction and Limitation of Strategic Offensive Arms (the START II Treaty), the 1972 Treaty on the Limitation of Anti-Ballistic Missile systems (the ABM Treaty) and the 1996 Comprehensive Nuclear Test-Ban Treaty (the CTBT) have been resolved. 'Russian Duma discusses ratification of Open Skies Treaty', ITAR-TASS (Moscow), 30 Mar. 2000, in FBIS-SOV-2000-0330, 30 Mar. 2000.

[83] For the members of ASEAN and the ARF see the glossary in this volume.

challenges they address and the variety of participants. It is a flexible, step-by-step process characterized by a host of different types of annual meeting and with a steadily growing record of accomplishments. It is intended that the ARF should develop from incremental confidence building through preventive diplomacy to playing an active role in resolving conflicts, which may create the premises for an agreement. Two meetings of the Intersessional Support Group on CBMs (ISG on CBMs) are usually held between the annual meetings of the ARF. The ASEAN foreign ministers annually review recommendations made by the ISG and ARF senior officials. In the language of ARF documents, the process continues to develop 'at a pace that is comfortable to all participants', and decisions are made by consensus.[84] Pursuing consensus at all costs, often resulting in agreement on the lowest common denominator, and avoiding interfering in one another's affairs to address critical problems have long been criticized as ASEAN's main weaknesses. In 1999 there was continued scepticism as to whether ASEAN can make significant progress towards preventive diplomacy and conflict resolution.[85]

In the intersessional year 1998–99 the ISG, co-chaired by Thailand and the USA, met in Honolulu (4–6 November 1998) and Bangkok (3–5 March 1999). In accordance with the ARF's broadly conceived notion of comprehensive security, the participants sought to focus on defence-related CBMs, while also addressing a wide spectrum of non-military measures. The topic of the overlap between CBMs and preventive diplomacy was discussed in Honolulu (with a focus on CBMs and maritime cooperation) and Bangkok (emphasizing CBMs/preventive diplomacy).

As instructed by the ASEAN foreign ministers, the participants of the ISG on CBMs considered the two 'baskets' of proposed CBMs.[86] They recommended that ARF members be encouraged to exchange visits by their naval vessels in order to enhance transparency and confidence, to exchange visits to military establishments, and to compile and circulate to other ARF members national lists of publications and experts on CBMs. In the context of the overlap between CBMs and preventive diplomacy, the participants discussed extensively the four proposals tabled: (*a*) an enhanced role for the ARF Chairman, including the concept of a good offices role, enhanced liaison with external parties, interaction between (official) Track I and (non-official) Track II dialogues, and a stronger coordinating role for the Chairman between ARF meetings; (*b*) the development of a register of experts or 'eminent persons' among ARF participants to serve as a pool of resources in CBMs and preventive diplomacy; (*c*) an Annual Security Outlook provided by the individual participants as a basis for discussions in the ARF Senior Officials Meetings and ministerial meetings; and (*d*) voluntary background briefings on issues affecting regional security. Moreover, in the context of maritime cooperation,

---

[84] Chairman's Statement, The Sixth Meeting of the ASEAN Regional Forum, Singapore, 26 July 1999, URL <http://www.dfat.gov.au/arf/990799_arf_chairman.html>.

[85] 'ASEAN: organisation ponders a modest role', *Financial Times*, 27 July 1999, p. 4.

[86] Basket 1 CBMs are earmarked for the near future and those of Basket 2 are to be considered in the medium term. See Lachowski (note 34), p. 639.

the ISG on CBMs recommended that this cooperation be included in future ISG agendas.[87]

The ASEAN ministers gathered at the sixth ARF meeting, in July 1999, extended the mandate of the ISG on CBMs to further explore the overlap between CBMs and preventive diplomacy for the next intersessional year.

Arms control-related endeavours in Asia

In late May 1999, experts from 16 Asian countries meeting in Almaty, Kazakhstan, agreed on a draft declaration of principles for a planned Asian security system, to be operated by the Conference on Interaction and Confidence-Building Measures in Asia (CICA). The planned conference was based on the initiative put forward by Kazakh President Nursultan Nazarbayev in 1992. The experts recommended that the text of the declaration be signed at the meeting of foreign ministers scheduled for September.

On 14 September the Declaration on the Principles Guiding Relations among the CICA Member States was signed by 16 foreign ministers.[88] Along with the principles guiding relations among the signatories, the declaration addressed, in very general terms, the issue of disarmament and arms control. In addition to the support for zones free of nuclear weapons and other weapons of mass destruction in Asia, the states 'reaffirm[ed] their belief' in the need to ensure security at the lowest level of armaments and military forces and 'recognize[d] the necessity' to curb excessive and destabilizing accumulations of conventional armaments.[89]

On 25 August, the heads of states of China, Kazakhstan, Kyrgyzstan, Russia and Tajikistan (the 'Shanghai Five') held a summit meeting in Bishkek, Kyrgyzstan. The main issue discussed at the summit meeting—attended by Presidents Jiang Zemin, Nursultan Nazarbayev, Askar Akayev, Boris Yeltsin and Imomali Rakhmonov—was the demarcation of the former Chinese–Soviet border and reduction of the number of troops stationed along it.[90] Under the 1997 Treaty on Mutual Reduction of Military Forces in Border Areas between China, Kazakhstan, Kyrgyzstan, Russia and Tajikistan the first Russian–Chinese trial inspection was carried out in October 1999.[91]

---

[87] For these and other CBM initiatives see Co-Chairmen's Summary Report of the Meetings of the ARF Intersessional Support Group on Confidence Building Measures held in Honolulu, USA, 4–6 Nov. 1998, and in Bangkok, Thailand, 3–5 Mar. 1999, URL <http://www.aseansec.org/politics/arf6a.htm>.

[88] 'Kazakhstan hosts regional security conference', *RFE/RL Newsline*, 15 Sep. 1999; and RFE/RL Kazakh Service, Kazakh Report Archive, 14 Sep. 1999, URL <http://www.rferl.org/bd/ka/reports/archives/index.html>. For a list of the members of CICA see the glossary in this volume.

[89] *Note Verbale* dated 16 September 1999 from the Permanent Mission of the Republic of Kazakhstan addressed to the Secretariat of the Conference on Disarmament transmitting the text of the Declaration on the principles guiding relations among member states of the Conference on Interaction and Confidence-building Measures in Asia. Conference on Disarmament document CD/1596, 29 Sep. 1999.

[90] RFE/RL Kazakh Service, Kazakh Report, 27 Aug. 1999, URL<http://www.rferl.org/bd/ka/reports/archives/1999/08/270899.html>.

[91] OSCE document FSC.JOUR/273, 27 Oct. 1999.

The four-party talks on Korea

The four-party talks between China, North Korea, South Korea and the USA on reducing tensions and putting a formal end to the Korean War have made some headway, according to reports in the middle of the year. Set up in January 1999, the sub-committee on tension reduction produced a set of proposals which included some simple military-related CBMs, such as communications channels and exchange of observers. A seminar to study confidence building in the light of some third-country experiences, as proposed by the Swiss Government, has also been tabled. In the view of a US State Department senior official, the talks 'have begun to move into more substantive areas'.[92]

Latin America

After two years of intense consultations by Brazil and the United States on a regional transparency regime, on 26 May 1999 the Organization of American States (OAS) approved the Inter-American Convention on Transparency in Conventional Weapons Acquisitions. The convention was opened for signature in Guatemala on 7 June. As an important arms control arrangement, the new OAS convention is a further step in building confidence, security and transparency to help decrease rivalries and tensions in the western hemisphere.

Africa

At the end of 1999 there were more major armed conflicts in Africa than in any other continent.[93] Since the early 1990s, in addition to a number of large-scale wars, low-intensity conflicts have plagued several countries in Africa. At the same time the continent has the least developed institutional framework for controlling arms. Efforts by the international community to limit the flow of armaments to and within Africa have had little effect. There is primarily a demand for light weapons, although several states also import considerable amounts of heavy weapons. Monitoring and enforcement mechanisms are inadequate to support various UN steps aimed at curbing arms trafficking to African countries.

The 1998 Economic Community of West African States (ECOWAS) moratorium on the import, export and manufacture of light weapons has for the most part been ineffective because of the lack of resources to establish a policing and enforcement system to combat arms trafficking. Consequently, in 1999 arms transfers continued unabated throughout much of West Africa.[94] Nevertheless ECOWAS took a number of steps at its Lomé summit meeting in December, aimed at reducing armed conflict in the region and supporting the

[92] USIS, 'Transcript: August 9 background briefing on Korea four-party talks', *Washington File* (US Embassy: Stockholm, 11 Aug. 1999).
[93] See chapter 1 in this volume.
[94] USIS, 'State Department on arms and conflict in Africa', *Washington File* (US Embassy: Stockholm, 14 July 1999).

community's light weapons moratorium. These measures include a code of conduct which obliges ECOWAS members to seek prior authorization before importing light weapons into West Africa. The summit meeting also approved the implementation of the prototype of a regional arms register and database on the categories of light weapons and ammunition covered by the moratorium.[95]

VII. Anti-personnel mines

The 1997 Convention on the Prohibition of the Use, Stockpiling, Production and Transfer of Anti-Personnel Mines and on their Destruction (the APM Convention) entered into force on 1 March 1999.[96] Crowning the first stage of the 'Ottawa Process' of 1996–97,[97] the APM Convention is a hybrid agreement combining disarmament with humanitarian law. It aims at the elimination of all anti-personnel mines (APMs).[98]

The parties to the amended (landmine) Protocol II of the 1981 Convention on Prohibitions or Restrictions on the Use of Certain Conventional Weapons which may be deemed to be Excessively Injurious or to have Indiscriminate Effects (CCW Convention, or 'Inhumane Weapons' Convention)[99] held their first annual conference on 15–17 December 1999 in Geneva.

Efforts in the Conference on Disarmament (CD) to highlight the issue of landmines, and especially to negotiate a permanent ban on their transfer, continued to produce a stalemate in 1999, underscoring the crisis of this body.

The APM Convention

The APM Convention entered into force on 1 March 1999. By that date 133 states had signed and 65 had ratified the convention. According to new estimates by the civil society-based monitoring network, the Landmine Monitor, there are more than 250 million APMs stored in the arsenals of at least 104 countries; between 225 million and 250 million landmines are stockpiled by countries that have not signed the convention. It is estimated that more than 19 million stockpiled landmines have been destroyed from the

---

[95] 'ECOWAS summit takes fresh steps to support small arms moratorium', *Disarmament Diplomacy*, no. 42 (Dec. 1999), URL<http://www.acronym.org.uk/42ecowas.htm>.

[96] The text of the convention is reproduced in *SIPRI Yearbook 1998* (note 48), pp. 567–74. For a brief summary of the convention and a list of parties and signatories, see annexe A in this volume.

[97] The Ottawa Process is the initiative launched by the Canadian Government in 1996, led by the International Campaign to Ban Landmines. Lachowski, Z., 'Conventional arms control', *SIPRI Yearbook 1997* (note 2), pp. 498–99.

[98] 'Landmine' is the broad term commonly used for this type of weapon. The convention defines a mine as 'a munition designed to be . . . exploded by the presence, proximity or contact of a person or vehicle' (Article 2), and an APM as 'a mine designed to be exploded by the presence, proximity or contact of a person and that will incapacitate, injure or kill one or more persons'. Only APMs are prohibited by the convention, which does not cover anti-tank mines, other anti-vehicle mines or anti-ship mines at sea or in inland waterways.

[99] For states parties to Protocol II of the CCW Convention see annexe A in this volume.

Table 10.9. The status of the APM Convention, as of 14 March 2000

Region	Signed but not ratified	Ratified/ acceded/ approved	Unable to sign/ opposed	Unknown/ undecided	Total
Africa	20	23	2	8	53
Americas	8	25	2	0	35
Asia–Pacific	8	16	6	28	58
Europe	7	30	2	5	44
Total	**43**	**94**	**12**	**41**	**190**

Source: Based on International Campaign to Ban Landmines, 'Ratification updates', 14 Mar. 2000, URL <http://www.icbl.org>.

arsenals of at least 50 countries in recent years.[100] The main producers and exporters of landmines—China, India, Pakistan, Russia and the USA—as well as many user countries involved in conflicts around the world have not signed the convention, however. It is also weakened by the absence of strong monitoring and enforcement provisions.

As of 14 March 2000, 94 states had ratified, approved or acceded to the convention, and 43 had signed but not ratified it. The signatories included all the states of the Western Hemisphere except the USA and Cuba, all the NATO nations except the USA and Turkey, all the EU member states except Finland, 43 African countries and 24 states in the Asia–Pacific region (table 10.9). Belarus, China, Cuba, Egypt, India, Iran, Libya, Pakistan, Russia, Sri Lanka, Syria and the USA either are opposed to or claim to be unable to accede to the convention.

To compensate, among other things, for the absence of a traditional verification mechanism in the APM Convention, the International Campaign to Ban Landmines (ICBL) established the Landmine Monitor to assess implementation and progress of and compliance with the APM Convention and more generally monitor other aspects of the 'global landmine crisis' in all countries of the world. The first annual Landmine Monitor Report was presented to the first conference of states parties, in Maputo, Mozambique, on 3–7 May 1999.[101]

In the course of the year the USA repeatedly reaffirmed its commitment to cease using landmines outside South Korea by 2003 and to sign the APM Convention by 2006 if alternatives to APMs and mixed anti-tank systems are developed. Russia, having welcomed the entry into force of the

---

[100] For more information see *Anti-Personnel Landmine Stockpiles and Their Destruction*, Landmine Monitor Fact Sheet prepared by Mary Wareham, Human Rights Watch, Geneva, Switzerland, 9–10 Dec. 1999 (revised 14 Dec. 1999), URL <http://www.icbl.org/lm/1999/stockdestr.htm>.
[101] International Campaign to Ban Landmines, Landmine Monitor, *Landmine Monitor Report 1999: Towards a Mine-Free World*, 1999.

APM Convention, indicated during the June meeting of the Group of Eight (G8) industrialized states in Cologne that it would sign the treaty.[102]

During the year a number of countries completed the destruction of their APM stockpiles: Australia, Bosnia and Herzegovina, France, Hungary, Mali, South Africa and the UK.[103]

Amended Protocol II of the CCW Convention

The 1996 amended Protocol II of the CCW Convention, restricting or prohibiting the use of 'mines, booby traps and other devices', entered into force on 3 December 1998.[104] The amended Protocol II supplemented the original protocol of 1981 with a number of provisions concerning its applicability, the detectability of all APMs, a ban on the transfer of prohibited mines, responsibility for mine clearance, and so on.

The US Senate approved the amended Protocol II on 20 May 1999, and on 24 May President Clinton signed the instrument of ratification. At the first annual conference of the parties to the protocol the USA proposed strengthening the protocol restrictions on the use of landmines, particularly anti-vehicle mines (making them detectable, providing self-destructing and self-deactivating mechanisms on remotely delivered anti-vehicle mines and enhancing the reliability of these mechanisms), adopting procedures similar to those of the APM Convention for handling non-compliance cases and allegations (allowing questions of compliance to be raised with the UN Secretary-General, who can call a meeting of parties which can authorize a fact-finding mission). The US proposals did not receive much support at the conference, but the USA hopes to build support for its initiatives in the run-up to the CCW Review Conference scheduled for 2001.[105]

Altogether, 47 states had ratified the amended Protocol II by the end of 1999, including India, Pakistan, the UK and the USA, which did so during the year.

VIII. Conclusions

The documents signed at the OSCE Summit Meeting in Istanbul are important and substantial. By the end of 1999 the conventional arms control regime, which was low on the security agenda immediately after the cold war, had become a political instrument that will strengthen stability and confidence across Europe in the decades ahead.

In spite of some potentially adverse events during the late 1990s, and particularly in 1999, the almost three-year negotiating effort initiated at the OSCE

---

[102] 'Russia plans to sign agreement banning land mines', ITAR-TASS (Moscow), in FBIS-SOV-1999-0609, 9 June 1999.

[103] Landmine Monitor Fact Sheet (note 100), pp. 5–6.

[104] The text of the amended Protocol II is reproduced in *SIPRI Yearbook 1998* (note 48), pp. 559–67. The amended Protocol II is reviewed in Lachowski (note 97), pp. 496–97.

[105] Boese, W., 'U.S. wants strengthened CCW landmines protocol', *Arms Control Today*, Jan./Feb. 2000, p. 26.

Summit Meeting in Lisbon in 1996 reached a successful conclusion. Under the Agreement on Adaptation, military stability in Europe is no longer based on the concept of a balance of forces. Despite their uneven course, the CFE adaptation talks stood a good chance of success because the obsolete cold war regime had long been in need of adjustment to the political and security environment in Europe, underlain by the principles of mutual reassurance, partnership and cooperative security. By the same token, the Agreement on Adaptation stands to bring about a broader change in security policy.

For all the militant rhetoric and threats (including threats of retaliatory deployment of tactical nuclear weapons close to NATO borders) sometimes heard from the Russian military authorities, neither the formal admission of the three Central European states to NATO, nor the NATO intervention in the FRY in the spring of 1999, nor the severe Western criticism of the Russian Army's conduct in Chechnya in the autumn affected Russia's strategic interest in a successful conclusion to the CFE adaptation talks. The Agreement on Adaptation allays two major Russian concerns—regarding Central Europe and the southern flank—by a combination of politically and legally binding instruments. It helps dispel many of the fears stemming from international developments since the early 1990s, particularly recent events in Europe. With its sense of inferiority in conventional armaments largely abated, Russia may have become more inclined to engage actively in nuclear arms control.

Despite its concern over the military and humanitarian aspects of Russia's conduct in Chechnya, NATO was also anxious to conclude the CFE adaptation talks provided its own military capabilities and operational flexibility were not impaired. NATO sees Russia as an important, if difficult, partner in building a cooperative security system—a partner whose interests and concerns should be considered and accommodated. The security concerns of Central European parties to the treaty were also appropriately considered and assuaged, both in the agreement and through the set of politically binding statements by the states concerned.

The immediate challenge is ratification of the Agreement on Adaptation. Here, the main obstacle is Russia: as long as Russia is in breach of the CFE Treaty, the chances of other states ratifying the Agreement on Adaptation are virtually non-existent. Another problem is the domestic ratification process in the Duma. At the beginning of 2000 it was an open question whether the new parliament would speedily endorse the new conventional arms control regime in Europe. Certainly the outcome of the Russian parliamentary elections in December 1999, the new composition of the Duma, and the ratifications of the 1996 Comprehensive Nuclear Test-Ban Treaty (the CTBT) and the 1993 Treaty on Further Reduction and Limitation of Strategic Offensive Arms (the START II Treaty) by the Russian Parliament in April 2000[106] suggest that

---

[106] See also chapter 8 in this volume.

Russia's approach to arms control is becoming less passive, less entrenched and more collaborative.[107]

If the Agreement on Adaptation is ratified, it will stand a chance of being extended to cover other European states and gradually becoming a pan-European system. While the absence of bloc divisions makes ratification possible for the non-aligned European countries, entering into the CFE Treaty regime remains a difficult decision for the Baltic states. With their insignificant armed forces still under formation they are in a military–security no man's land, but within the adapted CFE regime they would have more influence on the politico-military conduct of their neighbour, Russia. However, entering the CFE regime is seen by the Baltic states as potentially weakening their case for early NATO membership.

Some of the Balkan states are subject to a similar conventional arms control regime, imposed by the international community in the aftermath of the 1991–95 war in Bosnia and Herzegovina. Some are parties to the CFE Treaty, and others are outside any 'hard' conventional arms control framework. The ongoing negotiation on regional stability for the entire Balkan region (under the Dayton Agreement), is at an early stage. Unlike the subregional arms control framework of the Florence Agreement it is based on broad political–military rather than technical–military premises. The complex situation in the Balkans means that the course of the negotiation is likely to be tortuous, and rapid progress can hardly be expected until the status of Kosovo is clarified, or indeed solved.

Entry into force of the Agreement on Adaptation would meet the main goals and premises of the framework for arms control as envisaged by the 1996 OSCE Summit Meeting in Lisbon. This would pave the way for the remaining parts of the OSCE agenda for arms control to be put into effect, especially with regard to reducing regional instability, stabilizing crisis situations and ensuring transparency.

[107] During his visit to Grozny on 20 Mar. 2000, then Acting Russian President Vladimir Putin said that the campaign in Chechnya was not over but that Russia would withdraw some troops to comply with CFE limits. *RFE/RLE Newsline*, 22 Mar. 2000.

Appendix 10A. Confidence- and security-building measures in Europe

ZDZISLAW LACHOWSKI

I. Introduction

The Organization for Security and Co-operation in Europe (OSCE) continued its efforts to implement and further develop confidence- and security-building measures (CSBMs) at the pan-European and regional levels in 1999. The Annual Implementation Assessment Meeting (AIAM) focused on improving the Vienna Document 1994 and adapting it to the new security environment in Europe. The negotiations were crowned with the adoption of the Vienna Document 1999 of the Negotiations on Confidence- and Security-Building Measures. At the same time Vienna Document CSBMs faced challenges in the light of events in 1999. These efforts and challenges are reported in section II. The 1996 Agreement on Confidence- and Security-Building Measures in Bosnia and Herzegovina continued to operate successfully in 1999; its implementation is examined in section III. The conclusions are presented in section IV.

II. Vienna Document CSBMs

The Annual Implementation Assessment Meeting

At its ninth Annual Implementation Assessment Meeting, held in Vienna on 1–3 March 1999, the OSCE Forum for Security Co-operation (FSC) assessed the record of implementation of the existing CSBMs and other norm- and standard-setting measures, and discussed their operation and application in accordance with Chapter X of the Vienna Document 1994.[1] No substantial improvement in the implementation of CSBMs was noted for 1998/99.[2]

Six ad hoc working groups met to modernize the Vienna Document, answer questions put by OSCE participating states and facilitate information exchange among them. They made proposals within the framework set by the FSC in previous years to adapt the document to the European security situation and addressed eight broad topics.[3]

1. *Annual exchange of military information.* Participating states were generally in compliance with the requirements for exchange of military information. While some

---

[1] The Vienna Document 1994 of the Negotiations on Confidence- and Security-Building Measures is reproduced in *SIPRI Yearbook 1995: Armaments, Disarmament and International Security* (Oxford University Press: Oxford, 1995), pp. 799–820.

[2] At the AIAM opening plenary the Swedish representative stated that by and large the same states remained in non-compliance, and even states with a good implementation record had not distributed information on defence planning for 1998. He warned against the erosion of the CSBM regime and the OSCE *acquis* in general, but was encouraged by the generally smooth operation of inspections and evaluation. OSCE document FSC.AIAM/16/99, 1 Mar. 1999.

[3] OSCE Forum for Security Co-operation, 1999 Annual Implementation Assessment Meeting, Summary, Chairman's Report. Reports of the Working Group Co-ordinators, Vienna, 1–3 Mar. 1999, OSCE document FSC.AIAM/41/99, 11 Mar. 1999.

shortcomings were noted, improvement was considered possible. An increase in automated data exchange was seen as a welcome addition to the traditional provision of hard copy. Refinement of existing measures was discussed, reflecting the work of modernizing the Vienna Document.

2. *Defence planning.* There was broad agreement as to the uniqueness of information exchange in this area, but several delegations regretted that only about half the OSCE participating states had taken part. There were proposals to enhance the dialogue on defence planning, for example through regular defence planning/military seminars to enable more substantive discussions (AIAM discussions are seen as too formal), exchange of information indicating changes in defence planning, better use of requests for clarification, and regional and bilateral sharing of defence planning information.

3. *Military activities.* The working group discussed the voluntary nature of many current notifications, the implications of the trend towards multinational military activities, the notification of activities below the thresholds or in certain specific zones, the failure to fulfil commitments in submitting annual calendars, and using the AIAM to clarify non-compliance with certain provisions of the Vienna Document.

4. *Compliance and verification.* The discussion focused on the long-standing problems of the quota regime: the rapid exhaustion of the quotas of inspections and evaluation visits, the concentration of visits in the first quarter of the year and instances of early requests to book a visit. Suggested improvements included increasing the quotas, with the cost to be borne by the inspecting state, and better distribution throughout the year, as well as the prevention of unduly early requests. Hungary repeated its offer to accept four additional inspections over and above its yearly quota. It was suggested that changes should be made in the areas of reporting, definition of auxiliary personnel, size of the specified areas, permissible auxiliary means, helicopter overflights for inspection purposes, and giving the verification groups a multinational character.

5. *Risk reduction.* While the absence of any registered recourse to risk reduction in 1998 was taken as a sign of a stable security situation in the OSCE area, some room for improvement was indicated. For example, the consultation and cooperation mechanism for unusual military activities lacks a strong and effective follow-up procedure. The absence of a clearly defined role for the OSCE Permanent Council in risk reduction may make states reluctant to use these provisions in conflict prevention. Combining the risk reduction mechanism with stabilizing measures for localized crisis situations was also noted as a way for the OSCE to respond to crisis situations.

6. *Contacts.* Since the adoption of a five-year period for air base visits in January 1997, visits have been scheduled more intensively. However, several states have yet to meet these obligations. It was noted that too much importance is given to demonstrations of infrastructure and too little to explaining air base routines. With regard to military cooperation, it was noted that only 18 participating states had enabled others to visit a military facility during the first five-year period. Synchronization of the periods of implementation of the various measures providing for visits and observation of military activities was proposed. Improvements in demonstrations of new types of major weapon and equipment system were also pointed out.

7. *Communications.* In early 1999, 41 OSCE participating states[4] were actively linked to the OSCE Communications Network. Increased participation requires cheaper and more readily available technical connections. The obstacles are partly

[4] For a list of the OSCE participating states see the glossary in this volume.

technical and partly political in nature. The Internet was suggested as a substitute for more costly means of communication, but the risk of interception and unauthorized access remained the main reservation to this solution.

8. *Other agreed measures.* The participants reported on their implementation of and discussed the norm- and standard-setting measures—the Code of Conduct on Politico-Military Aspects of Security,[5] the Global Exchange of Military Information (GEMI), the principles governing conventional arms transfers, and the principles governing non-proliferation—stabilizing measures for localized crisis situations, and CSBMs stemming from regional and subregional arrangements.

An all-weather tool? The challenges of Kosovo and Chechnya

The question of whether the CSBMs are of relevance in 'all-weather' conditions was thrown into stark relief in 1999. The Kosovo crisis and the war in Chechnya were litmus tests for the viability of CSBMs *'inter arma'*.

On 19 May the Russian delegation made a statement in the FSC about the inspection carried out in the Former Yugoslav Republic of Macedonia (FYROM) on 7–9 May, complaining that the Russian inspection team had been denied access to all areas and facilities where NATO formations and units were stationed in contravention of the Vienna Document provisions. On 2 June Russia stated that it had encountered similar obstacles during its inspection visit to Albania on 17–19 May, claiming that: (*a*) the flight of Russian inspectors to the specified area was unduly delayed and directed to a point of entry other than that designated (in contravention of Vienna Document 1994, paras 84 and 86); (*b*) their inspection teams were denied inspection from the air (paras 81 and 83.6); (*c*) their inspection teams were not allowed into areas where US armed forces and equipment were concentrated (para. 80); and (*d*) their inspection teams were refused access to briefings by US commanders of formations in Albania and the FYROM (para. 96).

Russia also claimed that there were more than 13 000 NATO troops in the FYROM. Thus they were subject to observation (para. 45.4). The USA had allegedly failed to notify the concentration in advance, and observers were invited only after the Russian inspection team had informed the participating states about its work in the area.

NATO, Albania and the FYROM responded that the 'hostile environment' justified denial of access on the basis of exceptions for 'areas or sensitive points' (para. 79) for

---

[5] CSCE, Budapest Document 1994, Budapest Decisions IV, Code of Conduct on Politico-Military Aspects of Security, URL <http://www.osce.org/docs/english/1990-1999/summits/buda94e.htm>. The Second OSCE Follow-up Conference on the Code of Conduct on Politico-Military Aspects of Security and its implementation was held in Vienna on 29–30 June 1999. The delegations put forward numerous proposals concerning the implementation, assessment and further development of the code. The absence of clarity regarding some areas of the code and the requirements for their implementation was noted. The Kosovo crisis also had an impact on the debates. The proposals included a joint session of the OSCE Permanent Council and the FSC in 2000 on the provisions of the code and the application of lessons learned from the events in the Balkans; the inclusion of paramilitary forces in the information exchange; revision of the questionnaire on the code regarding further differentiation between armed forces and internal security forces; provision of additional documents on legislation regarding parliamentary control of armed forces; a special meeting in Jan. 2000 for parliamentarians to discuss parliamentary control of armed forces; monthly discussion of code topics in FSC Working Group B; assessment of the applicability of the code for peacekeeping; and a code of conduct on combating terrorism. See Chairman's perception, OSCE document FSC.DEL/235/99, 1 July 1999; and Summary of suggestions tabled during the Second Follow-up Conference on the Code of Conduct, OSCE document FSC.GAL/84/99/Rev.1, 19 July 1999.

safety, security and force protection reasons.[6] Both Albania and the FYROM pleaded technical reasons for not providing a helicopter for inspection purposes (those available allegedly fell short of the required safety standards). Changing the entry points for inspectors (from Tirana to Gajder in Albania, and from Skopje to Ohrid in the FYROM) was said to have been to accommodate ongoing humanitarian airlift operations. Concerning non-compliance with the observation threshold, the FYROM said it would issue invitations at a later date.[7] The Russian observation visit took place well after the end of the NATO campaign in Yugoslavia (5–7 July 1999).

According to observers, the FYROM incident occurred because the US command perceived the implementation of CSBMs during the 1999 Kosovo crisis as a threat to NATO 'operational security'. Other NATO states, such as Germany and the UK, had allowed their commanders in the FYROM to provide information to the Russian inspectors. Germany, in particular, found US arguments about the sensitive equipment in the FYROM rather unconvincing, since the operation there served clearly humanitarian needs.[8] The sophisticated Apache helicopters stationed in Albania created different circumstances.

Another challenge to compliance with the Vienna Document 1994 arose in the autumn. On 8 October Russia confirmed that its concentration of forces in the North Caucasus had exceeded some of the thresholds (para. 38.3.1) and it provided additional information on 27 October and on 25 February 2000. Unlike the NATO concentrations in Albania and the FYROM, the Russian presence in Chechnya comprised forces engaged in war. Russia claimed that it has demonstrated exceptional good will and transparency in providing updated information on the conditions of military operations against the Chechen 'terrorists'. The NATO states demanded that Russia provide not only numbers, but also details on the purpose, level of command, time frame and envisaged area of the operation (paras 41 and 43), and other relevant information. Western countries repeatedly urged Russia to update its October information and allow an observation visit in accordance with the Vienna Document 1999 (paras 47.3 and 47.4).[9]

Events in 1999 showed that CSBMs and related mechanisms can play a limited 'foul-weather' role in dealing with crises and conflicts. The main problem is not so much a lack of measures as the unwillingness to use them in a full or timely manner or to activate them for risk reduction.

[6] A NATO representative claimed that the main function of NATO in the FYROM was to provide humanitarian assistance. NATO had hoped the Russian team would inspect the work at refugee centres, but as they were interested in areas where 'difficult and potentially dangerous' conditions existed they were shown a training exercise involving NATO forces. OSCE document FSC.DEL/145/99, 2 June 1999.

[7] See e.g., OSCE documents FSC.DEL/142/99, 2 June 1999; FSC.DEL/145/99, 2 June 1999; FSC.DEL/146/99, 2 June 1999; and FSC.DEL/157/99, 9 June 1999.

[8] The USA alleged that, because Russia could hand over sensitive information on NATO military equipment in the vicinity of the Federal Republic of Yugoslavia (FRY), the USA had postponed the inspection request until the FYROM, without NATO endorsement, authorized the Russian inspection just before the deadline envisaged by the Vienna Document 1994 during the air campaign in the spring of 1999. 'Der Kosovo-Konflikt belastet die europäische Rüstungskontrolle' [The Kosovo conflict weighs against European arms control], *Frankfurter Allgemeine Zeitung*, 19 May 1999, p. 9.

[9] Vienna Document 1999 of the Negotiations on Confidence- and Security-Building Measures, FSC.DOC/1/99, Vienna, 16 Nov. 1999. The text is available on the OSCE website, URL <http://www.osce.org>. The feasibility and security of conducting an observation inside Chechnya during the war are questionable. Russia allowed a German team to inspect areas adjacent to Chechnya in Feb. 2000. NATO and EU countries have pointed out that, apart from its CSBM non-compliance, Russia has probably violated the provisions of Chapters VI, VII and VIII, in particular paras 30, 31, 34 and 36 of the Code of Conduct on Politico-Military Aspects of Security, especially in respect of taking due care to avoid injury to civilians and their property and to avoid the indiscriminate and disproportionate use of force.

The Vienna Document 1999

Since 1989 the OSCE participating states have continued the CSBM negotiations under the mandate established for the negotiations that led to the Vienna Documents of 1990, 1992 and 1994. In the wake of the 1994 OSCE Budapest Decisions, in which the participating states undertook to devote more attention to improving the implementation and adoption of new CSBMs to meet new challenges, since 1995 the states have discussed and agreed successive amendments to the Vienna Document 1994.[10] In October 1997, in line with the decisions of the 1996 OSCE summit meeting in Lisbon to expand and add to agreed measures,[11] the FSC launched a review of the Vienna Document 1994, with the aim of completing the review during 1998. As the negotiations had to accommodate other essential changes in the field of European security (such as NATO enlargement) and arms control (adaptation of the 1990 Treaty on Conventional Armed Forces in Europe, the CFE Treaty), they were completed only in 1999.

On 16 November 1999 the Vienna Document 1999 was adopted at Istanbul by the FSC. The document entered into force as of 1 January 2000, containing 'a significant number of changes and additions to the preceding document'.[12] However, on closer inspection, the new document hardly reflects the more than 100 proposals put forward during the negotiations.

The most important addition is Chapter X, which envisages complementing OSCE-wide CSBMs with voluntary political and legally binding measures tailored to regional needs. The chapter sets criteria (principles) according to which such measures should be created. The measures should: (*a*) be in accordance with basic OSCE principles; (*b*) contribute to strengthening security and stability in the OSCE area; (*c*) add to existing transparency and confidence; (*d*) complement existing CSBMs; (*e*) comply with international laws and obligations; (*f*) be consistent with the Vienna Document; and (*g*) not endanger the security of third parties in the region.

It is proposed that the FSC be the repository of regional CSBM agreements, as well as assist in developing, negotiating and implementing regional measures. Chapter X also presents a range of possible measures for regions and border areas. A list of proposals and a compilation of bilateral and regional measures prepared by the Conflict Prevention Centre (CPC) is to serve as a 'source of inspiration and reference' for participating states.

Other major additions and changes included in the Vienna Document 1999 include:

1. *Annual exchange of military information.* The lower limits for reporting planned increases in personnel strength for more than 21 days now refer to 1000 (formerly 1500) troops for each active combat unit and 3000 (formerly 3500) troops for each active formation. Proposals concerning major weapons and equipment systems 'operated either outside the command organization of the military forces or of the

---

[10] These efforts are documented in Lachowski, Z., 'Confidence- and security-building measures in Europe', *SIPRI Yearbook 1997: Armaments, Disarmament and International Security* (Oxford University Press: Oxford, 1997), pp. 503–504; Lachowski, Z. and Henrichon, P., 'Confidence- and security-building measures in Europe', *SIPRI Yearbook 1998: Armaments, Disarmament and International Security* (Oxford University Press: Oxford, 1998), pp. 532–33; and Lachowski, Z. and Kronestedt, P., 'Confidence- and security-building measures in Europe', *SIPRI Yearbook 1999: Armaments, Disarmament and International Security* (Oxford University Press: Oxford, 1999), pp. 646–49.

[11] Lisbon Declaration 1996: Framework for Arms Control, OSCE document FSC.DEC/8/96; and Development of the Agenda of the Forum for Security Cooperation, OSCE document FSC.DEC/9/96.

[12] 'OSCE adopts Vienna Document 1999 on confidence- and security-building measures', OSCE Secretariat Press Release, 16 Nov. 1999.

military forces as a whole' and provision of information on transport, tanker and/or airborne early-warning and control aircraft, and/or helicopters in air formations and air units of the air forces, air defence aviation and naval aviation permanently based on land (para 10.2) were not included in the Vienna Document 1999.[13]

2. *Defence planning.* A separate chapter on defence planning has been added. The annual information will also include the date on which the defence budget for the year ahead was approved by the national authorities and details of the identity of these authorities. The information will be provided not later than three (formerly two) months after approval of the defence budget. States are obliged to notify and explain any inability to meet this deadline and to give an envisaged date for submission. States with no armed forces will provide their 'NIL reports' with their annual military information (para. 15). If necessary, discrepancies between expenditures and previously reported budgets should be clarified and states should also provide information on the relation of the military budget to gross national product (para. 15.3). Another clarification concerns information on budgets (para. 15.4). The chapter also encourages states to hold periodic high-level OSCE military doctrine seminars.

3. *Risk reduction.* Under the unusual military activities mechanism, new provisions entitle both requesting and responding states to ask other states that have expressed concern to participate in meetings to discuss such activities (para. 16.2.1.2). The meetings will be chaired by the Chairman-in-Office (CIO) or his representative, who will prepare a report of the meeting for all participating states. The requesting or the responding state or both may ask for meetings of all participating states. The CIO or his representative will convene such meetings, during which both the requesting and responding states will present their viewpoints. The Permanent Council and the FSC will provide a joint forum for such meetings, and they will jointly assess the situation. Appropriate measures may be recommended to the states involved (para. 16.3.1.2). A proposal for OSCE inspections to clarify military activities giving rise to concern was not included in the Vienna Document 1999.

4. *Contacts.* Each state will now arrange at least one visit to an air base in any five-year period (para. 20) and provide annual information on its plans for contacts (paras 36 and 37). Russian proposals for naval base visits were not included.

5. *Notification and observation.* Military activities, 'including those where forces of other participating States are participants' (para. 40), shall be notified. The parameters for notifications and observation are retained.[14] There was no consensus on requiring notification of transfers of formations of land forces of one or more participating states through another participating state's territory into or within the zone of application in order to participate in a notifiable military activity or to be concentrated.[15]

---

[13] Unless otherwise indicated, the references to proposals and suggestions that have not been included are based on Coordinator of the Ad Hoc Working Group, 'Chairman's perception' of the text of the draft Document. OSCE document FSC.VD/29/99, Vienna, 7 July 1999.

[14] The 1997 French–German–Polish proposal provided for a lowering of the notification threshold to 5000 troops or 150 tanks or 250 ACVs or 150 pieces of artillery. In mid-1999, lower thresholds for at least ACVs (from 500 to 350) and artillery (from 250 to 200) were considered.

[15] Another 2 amendments discussed in 1998 failed to be introduced: (*a*) notification of the largest military activity, when no activity reaches the notification thresholds; and (*b*) notification of non-routine concentrations of at least 5000 troops or 150 tanks, 250 ACVs or 150 pieces of artillery. Neither was there agreement on the Ukrainian proposal to lower the observation thresholds. See Lachowski and Kronestedt (note 10), p. 647.

6. *Constraints.* The new parameters and the time frame for activities subject to notification are introduced in line with the FSC decisions of 1996 and 1997.[16]

7. *Compliance and verification.* There are a number of changes under the heading 'Inspection'. Failure to carry out or accept an inspection due to *force majeure* is addressed in detail (para. 78). Representatives of forces of states other than the receiving state are obliged to cooperate in relevant phases of the inspection (para. 82). Requests for an inspection are to be submitted at least 36 hours but no more than five days before the estimated entry into the territory of the receiving states (para. 85).[17] The inspection team, consisting of up to four inspectors, may include nationals from up to three participating states (there is no longer mention of an interpreter, para. 91). Aircraft will be provided by the receiving country unless otherwise agreed (para. 99).

There are also changes under 'Evaluation'. No participating state will be obliged to accept more than two visits per calendar month.[18] Requests for evaluation visits should be submitted no earlier than seven (and no later than five) days before the estimated entry into the territory. Cases of *force majeure* are dealt with as under inspections. The teams should consist of no more than three (formerly two) persons unless otherwise agreed. More detailed provisions are included on the size of the team, nationalities and the content of the request (para. 124).

The inspecting/evaluating teams may use additional equipment for the inspection, to be specified in the request and subject to the specific consent of the receiving state (paras 95 and 85.8; and 131 and 113.5).[19] The report of the inspection/evaluation must be communicated to all states within 14 days (paras 105 and 135).

8. *The OSCE Communications Network.* Unlike the Vienna Document 1994, the Vienna Document 1999 states that the use and arrangements of the communications network will be governed by the relevant OSCE documents. On 6 October the FSC adopted a separate OSCE Communications Network Document which superseded, among other things, Chapter IX of the Vienna Document 1994.[20]

Despite high expectations connected with the Vienna Document negotiations, the outcome was fairly modest. Along with numerous other specific proposals, some parts failed to gain consensus: for example, those regarding naval measures and activities (Russia) and new aircraft (the USA), transparency in the field of military infrastructure, e.g., airfields (NATO), notification of non-routine concentrations of forces (the USA), regular dialogue on defence planning and defence policy/military strategy, and further lowering of thresholds or paramilitary forces (France–Germany–Poland). Thus the adaptation of the CSBM regime is still not complete.

---

[16] OSCE document FSC.DEC/7/96, 13 Nov. 1996; and OSCE document FSC.DEC/7/97, 9 Apr. 1997.

[17] An attempt to set parameters for the size and shape of the 'specified area' has failed.

[18] This is intended to better distribute the quota of visits throughout the year.

[19] Proposals regarding use of the Global Positioning System and mobile telephones by inspectors/evaluators were not accepted.

[20] Decision no. 5/99, OSCE document FSC.DEC/5/99, 6 Oct. 1999. The OSCE Communications Network is broader in scope than the Vienna Documents 1994 and 1999 and is also used for information exchange under the 1990 CFE Treaty, the 1992 Open Skies Treaty and in OSCE correspondence.

Table 10A. Notified military activities planned for 2000 and information on additional activities held in 1999

States	Dates/Start window	Type/Name of activity	Area	Level of command	No. of troops	Type of forces or equipment	No./type of div.	Comments
1. Czech Rep., Denmark, France, Germany, Italy, Netherlands, Norway, Poland, UK, USA	1 Feb.–20 Mar.; FTX 13–17 Mar.	Joint combined live exercise: Joint Winter 2000	North Norway	DEFCOMNON with 6 divs and German, US forces subordinated ('Northland'), DEFCOMNON with AMF (land) ('Southland')	11 120	Air, land and maritime forces	Div. level; 2 light divs	Joint combined live exercise under 1 single command, national troops and multinational staff. Phase I: deployment; Phase II: pre-FTX operations, combat enhancement training and force integration training; Phase III: live FTX; Phase IV: redeployment
2. Germany, USA	8–12 Apr.	Corps BCTP WFX	Grafenwoehr, Germany	Corps	9 500	Land forces	Arm. div.	Corps Battle Command Training Program warfighter exercise
3. Austria	10–15 Apr.	..	Allentsteig, Heidenreichstein, Horn, Grossgerungs, Weitra	Corps and brig.	c. 12 000	Land and air forces	Arm. div.	Attack and defence operations; air missions
5. Germany, Hungary, Italy, Netherlands, Portugal, Turkey, UK, USA	20 May–10 June	Dynamic Mix 2000	Central Mediterranean, Capo Teulada, Italy, northern Greece	COMSTRIKEFORSOUTH, COMNAVSOUTH, COMAIRSOUTH, COMLANDSOUTH, COMLANDSOUTHEAST	6 500, incl. 4 500 land forces, 2 000 amphib. assault marine forces	Land and amphibious forces	..	Large-scale exercise, NATO Southern Region. Total no. of personnel may exceed notification threshold
6. Finland	5–22 June	Ahmavaara 2000	Southern and central Finland	Army units, Air Force Command, Naval Command	12 500	Land, air and naval forces	..	Staff training exercise for army, air force and naval units. Invitations to voluntary observation visits will be extended to Denmark, Estonia, Germany, Latvia, Lithuania, Norway, Poland, Russia

							Div. level; ground forces	
7. France, Italy, Portugal, Spain	16–28 June	Livex FTX	Spain	CJTF (Command South Task Force), CHOD Spain	c. 9 000	Ground, naval and air forces		Training interoperability of peace-keeping and evacuation forces
Additional activities held in 1999[a]								
1. Macedonia	2 Mar.–indefinite	Concentration of forces	Northern part of Macedonia		12 230	Ground forces	..	Prepare for executing a peace implementation mission in Kosovo and support humanitarian operations
2. Russia	8 Oct.–indefinite	Concentration of forces	Russian border area to Chechnya		>9 000 troops; >250 MBT; c. 500 APCs	Ground forces	..	..
3. Russia	15 Oct.–indefinite	Concentration of forces; anti-terrorist activities	Russian border area to Chechnya, territory of Chechnya and adjacent areas of Dagestan, Ingushetia, North Ossetia and Stavropolskiy krai	Gen. Staff, land forces; Staff, North Caucasus MD	46 863 troops;	Ground forces	..	Observers will be invited as soon as their safety can be guaranteed

Notes: AMF = Allied Mobile Force; Arm. = armoured; BCTP = Battle Command Training Program; CINCNW = Commander-in-Chief Allied Forces North Western Europe; CJTF = Combined Joint Task Force; COMJTFNON = Commander Joint Task Force Northern Norway; COMAIRSOUTH = Commander Allied Air Forces Southern Europe; COMLANDSOUTH = Commander Allied Land Forces Southern Europe; COMLANDSOUTHEAST = Commander Allied Land Forces South-East; COMNAVSOUTH = Commander Allied Naval Forces Southern Europe; COMSTRIKEFORSOUTH = Commander Allied Striking and Support Forces Southern Europe; DEFCOMNON = Defence Command North Norway; div. = division; FTX = field training exercise; Livex = live exercise; WFX = warfighter exercise.

[a] Supplementary information on military activities held in 1999.

The implementation record for 1999[21]

Since 1994, numerous states have presented either no information or incomplete or irregular information on defence planning and/or military budgets. Others began to provide information in 1998 or 1999, and only Bosnia and Herzegovina and Kyrgyzstan failed to participate in the annual exchange of military information for 1999 (as of 15 December 1998). For 2000, Bosnia and Herzegovina was the sole state in noncompliance in this and other respects. The provision of information under voluntary CSBMs is proceeding quite well. There were eight requests for explanations of unusual military activities, all concerning the Kosovo crisis in the spring of 1999, and one request for clarification (para. 135) on the Russian Zapad '99 (West '99) exercise in June 1999.

Seven military activities were notified in 1999, of which three were planned.[22] The total number of troops for the 'Battle Griffin 99' field training exercise (FTX) was increased from 22 070 to 24 089. 'Destined Glory 99' was cancelled because of the NATO operation in Kosovo, and 'Dynamic Mix 99' was also cancelled. Two military activities (concentrations of forces in the FYROM and in the border area near Chechnya, Russia, the latter being notified twice) were conducted outside the annual calendars submitted by 15 November 1998. Only one notifiable observation of a military activity, the deployment of NATO forces in the FYROM, was carried out. Greece invited observers to its corps-level exercise 'Filippos 99' in western FYROM on 13–17 September 1999, in accordance with paragraph 136.2 of the Vienna Document 1994. Russia notified an increase in the threshold in Chechnya in October, but stated that observers would be invited only when their safety could be guaranteed.

By the end of 1999, 45 states had submitted their annual calendars (only 27 had done so by the 15 November 1999 deadline).

By the end of 1999 a total of 73 inspections had been requested in 33 countries and 70 had been conducted. Several were carried out on the basis of bilateral agreements (e.g., the 1998 Hungarian–Romanian CSBM agreement) or initiatives (Swedish–Finnish, 1998), including the Slovakian inspection in Hungary, according to their bilateral agreement, which entered into force on 11 January 1999.

Of the 75 evaluation visits requested, 72 were conducted—10 of them under bilateral agreements between or initiatives by participating states.

III. Regional CSBMs

Implementation of the Agreement on CSBMs in Bosnia and Herzegovina

The Agreement on Confidence- and Security-Building Measures in Bosnia and Herzegovina of 26 January 1996 (negotiated under Article II of Annex 1-B of the 1995 General Framework Agreement for Peace in Bosnia and Herzegovina, the Dayton Agreement) outlines a set of measures to enhance mutual confidence and reduce the risk of conflict in the country. The parties to the agreement are Bosnia and Herzegovina and its two entities: the Federation of Bosnia and Herzegovina and the Republika Srpska.

---

[21] OSCE, Conflict Prevention Centre, Quarterly CPC Survey on CSBM information exchanged 1/00 in preparation of the Annual Implementation Assessment Meeting 2000, OSCE document FSC.GAL/19/00, 25 Feb. 2000.
[22] Lachowski and Kronestedt (note 10), p. 648.

Stability and peace in Bosnia and Herzegovina remain dependent on strong international engagement and presence. Several major domestic factors also determine the level of military security. Formally, two separate armed forces exist, but in reality there are three. The two components of the Federation of Bosnia and Herzegovina are not integrated at all. There is a lack of transparency in the military budgets. The joint institutions are extremely weak. In 1999, Bosnia and Herzegovina was unable to either receive Vienna Document inspections or to conduct the Article IV inspections scheduled to Croatia and Yugoslavia.

The second conference to review the implementation of the CSBM agreement was held in Vienna on 15–19 March 1999.[23] Delegations from Bosnia and Herzegovina and its two entities took part under the chairmanship of the Personal Representative of the OSCE Chairman-in-Office, Carlo Jean. The parties noted that 'certain progress' had been made since the first review conference and reaffirmed their commitment to implement the agreement together with voluntary measures to enhance confidence and security. It was noted that the annual exchange of information had improved. Military liaison missions had been established and had worked efficiently. The Joint Consultative Commission (JCC), with the active involvement of all the parties, had been able to resolve most of the issues submitted to it. Successful seminars had been conducted and the network of security and strategic experts was developing.

The parties adopted a number of decisions on enhancing the agreement and with regard to the need for further consideration of implementation issues. They agreed, inter alia, on a new notification format to cover all changes in conventional armaments and equipment and another format regarding information on defence-related matters (military budgets). The latter will be used to notify all kinds of foreign military support. Exchanges of information on defence-related matters will be accompanied by joint assessments of the parties' annual information. Later during the year the parties exchanged information on matters related to defence, to some extent replicating the format of the Vienna Document 1994. Moreover, they agreed on definitions of 'object of inspection', 'single activity' and 'historical collection'—to facilitate compliance with the inspection regime. A JCC working group is seeking agreement on common interpretation of further terms in the agreement.

Definitions of 'weapons-manufacturing facility' and various types of forces are among the issues yet to be resolved. The parties adopted a new protocol regulating visits to weapons-manufacturing facilities and agreed on the number of annual visits. Such visits began in 1999 and no major discrepancies were discovered. The parties will also discuss notification and verification of mobilization exercises, support exchanges of military publications and field manuals, and organize joint workshops for their armed forces.

The implementation of CSBMs continued during the year. Developments in the spring of 1999 (the NATO intervention in Kosovo) did not substantially interrupt the conduct of scheduled inspections or the transmission of all required notifications. The decision of the Republika Srpska not to participate in voluntary activities (visits, seminars, workshops, etc.) organized by or in NATO countries taking part in the air campaign required some rescheduling of events, with Austria, Sweden and Switzerland taking over the tasks. Some activities took place, others were postponed and there were some modifications regarding inspections and visits to weapons-

---

[23] Final Document of the Second Conference to Review the Implementation of the Agreement on Confidence- and Security-building Measures in Bosnia and Herzegovina, Vienna, 15–19 Mar. 1999. The first review conference was held on 16–20 Feb. 1998.

manufacturing facilities. A total of 64 inspections (under Articles II and IV) and 10 visits were carried out in 1999.[24]

Notable progress was achieved in the field of transparency in military spending. For the first time, all three parties had notified their defence outlays for 1998 and exchanged data on authorizations of their military budgets for 1999. They also exchanged data about their respective foreign military assistance for the first time.

The operation of the Military Liaison Missions between the Defence Staffs is governed by Standard Operating Procedures agreed in 1999 by the Chiefs of the Defence Staffs of the Federation of Bosnia and Herzegovina and the Republika Srpska.

At the JCC meeting in June the parties conducted a new information exchange and agreed to a new format for quarterly notification of any changes to the annual information exchange. A yearly programme of voluntary activities was also approved. Numerous seminars were held during the year with a view to consolidating the contacts and cooperation between the entity armed forces, reducing military budgets and postures, and establishing a state dimension of security and defence.

The goals for 2000 are twofold: (*a*) to implement the postponed activities and consolidate what was achieved in 1999 (defence budget transparency, reduction of military postures, reinforcement of the joint institutions of Bosnia and Herzegovina, and cooperation between the entity armed forces); and (*b*) to increase cooperation by Bosnia and Herzegovina with the OSCE and with other international organizations with a view to future integration.

IV. Conclusions

The 1999 OSCE Review Conference, held on 20 September–1 October, reviewed the implementation of the Vienna Document 1994.[25] All the participating states found the CSBM regime to be useful and unique, and it was suggested that the new and emerging risks and challenges might even increase its significance. The regime still copes with various compliance issues: submission of timely information; implementation shortcomings; a need for international assistance to some participating states in technical and other aspects of implementation; and better responses to 'foul-weather' contingencies, such as the use of force in internal conflicts. Improvements should be made to allow for better reporting and discussion of military potential, evaluation quotas, spreading verification throughout the year, allowing for modern communications/positioning equipment, and so on. Events in 1999 demonstrated that the 'foul-weather' qualities of the Vienna Document 1994, that is, its relevance in times of tension, should be enhanced. Regional CSBMs are gaining in importance and, by the same token, the Vienna Document 1999 is becoming a cornerstone of regional and bilateral efforts to develop a sense of mutual confidence and security.

Efforts by the OSCE participating states to modernize the European CSBM regime—the adaptation of the Vienna Document 1994—were concluded in 1999. The outcome is modest, at least in comparison with the hopes pinned on the review begun

[24] Status of Implementation of Article II (Confidence- and Security-Building Measures in Bosnia and Herzegovina) and Article IV (Sub-Regional Arms Control), Annex 1-B, Dayton Peace Accords in 1999), Lt-Gen. Carlo Jean, Personal Representative of the OSCE Chairman-in-Office, Istanbul, 17–18 Nov. 1999.

[25] Review of the implementation of all OSCE principles and commitments, Politico-military aspects of security, Report of the Rapporteur, OSCE Review Conference, OSCE document RC(99).JOUR/10, Annex 3, 1 Oct. 1999.

in 1997 and the host of proposals submitted to improve the accord. Nevertheless, the process of assessing and recommending improvements in CSBM implementation continues, thus ensuring the continuous monitoring of developments in the new European security situation. Regional approaches, perhaps the most promising addition in the Vienna Document 1999, should help better handle contingencies below the pan-European level. 'Regionalization' of CSBMs is by no means new: regional arrangements can be seen in the Baltic Sea region, the Black Sea region (maritime operations), the South Eastern Defence Ministers' meetings (coordination of regional politico-military problems) and numerous bilateral CSBM agreements among participating states. These and other arrangements can now refer to a new framework, criteria and directions.

The regional CSBM experiment in the volatile environment of the Balkan state of Bosnia and Herzegovina is proceeding fairly well, albeit still under the umbrella of international institutions and military forces. It is to be hoped that, apart from political and civilian arrangements, the network of various arms control-related agreements (under Articles II, IV and V of Annex 1-B of the 1995 Dayton Agreement) and the arms control and CSBM parts of the Stability Pact for South Eastern Europe,[26] will inject enough stability and security into the Balkans to help make the peace process in the region irreversible.

[26] Stability Pact for South Eastern Europe, Cologne, 10 June 1999, URL <http://europa.eu.int/comm/external_relations/see/stapact/10_june_99.htm>. See also chapter 4 in this volume. The Stability Pact is reproduced (without the Annex) in appendix 4A.

Appendix 10B. Documents on conventional arms control

VIENNA DOCUMENT 1999

Istanbul, 16 November 1999

Excerpt

. . .

X. Regional measures

(138) The participating States are encouraged to undertake, including on the basis of separate agreements, in a bilateral, multilateral or regional context, measures to increase transparency and confidence.

(139) Taking into account the regional dimension of security, participating States, on a voluntary basis, may therefore complement OSCE-wide confidence- and security-building measures through additional politically or legally binding measures, tailored to specific regional needs.

(140) On a voluntary basis, numerous measures provided for in the Vienna Document, in particular, could be adapted and applied in a regional context. Participating States may also negotiate additional regional CSBMs, in accordance with the principles set out in paragraph (142).

(141) The framework for the negotiation of measures relating to regional military confidence-building and co-operation should be determined by the preferences of the States involved and the nature of the measures to be agreed upon.

(142) Such measures should:

(142.1) – be in accordance with the basic OSCE principles, as enshrined in its documents;

(142.2) – contribute to strengthening the security and stability of the OSCE area, including the concept of the indivisibility of security;

(142.3) – add to existing transparency and confidence;

(142.4) – complement, not duplicate nor replace, existing OSCE-wide CSBMs or arms control agreements;

(142.5) – be in accordance with international laws and obligations;

(142.6) – be consistent with the Vienna Document;

(142.7) – not be detrimental to the security of third parties in the region.

(143) Agreed regional CSBMs form part of the OSCE-wide web of interlocking and mutually reinforcing agreements. Negotiation and implementation within the OSCE area of regional or other agreements not binding on all OSCE participating States are a matter of direct interest to all participating States. Participating States are therefore encouraged to inform the Forum for Security Co-operation (FSC) of the regional CSBM initiatives undertaken and agreements reached, as well as of their implementation, when appropriate. The FSC could be the repository of regional CSBM agreements.

(144) There are a wide range of possible measures which could serve regional needs, such as:

(144.1) – exchange of information on defence planning, military strategy and doctrine as far as they refer to a particular regional context;

(144.2) – further development of the provisions with regard to risk reduction;

(144.3) – enhancement of the existing mechanism for consultation and co-operation as regards unusual military activities conducted by participating States;

(144.4) – joint training courses and manoeuvres;

(144.5) – intensification of military contacts and co-operation, particularly in border areas;

(144.6) – establishment of cross-border communications networks;

(144.7) – reduction of the thresholds for military activities, in particular with regard to border areas;

(144.8) – reduction of the thresholds for notifications and observations of certain military activities that a State is allowed to carry out in a given period, particularly in border areas;

(144.9) – agreement on additional inspection and evaluation visits by neighbouring States, especially in border areas;

(144.10) – increase in the size of evaluation teams and agreement to multinational evaluation teams;

(144.11) – creation of bi-national or regional verification agencies to co-ordinate 'out of the region' verification activities.

(145) A list of proposals, as well as a com-

pilation of bilateral and regional measures prepared by the CPC will serve as a source of inspiration and reference for participating States.

(146) Participating States are encouraged to provide the CPC with appropriate information on such measures. The CPC is tasked with continuously updating the above-mentioned document, and making it available to the participating States.

(147) If requested by the parties directly involved, the FSC may assist in the development, negotiation and implementation of regional measures. It may also, if asked by those parties, direct the CPC to provide technical assistance, facilitate the process of information exchange or assist in any agreed verification activities relating to regional CSBMs.

Source: Vienna Document 1999 of the Negotiations on Confidence- and Security-Building Measures, FSC.DOC/1/99, 16 Nov. 1999. The text is available on the OSCE Internet site, URL <http://www.osce.org>.

THE AMENDED CFE TREATY

Unofficial text

Note: The Agreement on Adaptation of the Treaty on Conventional Armed Forces in Europe, signed on 19 November 1999, introduces amendments to the 1990 Treaty on Conventional Armed Forces in Europe. This consolidated text prepared at SIPRI shows the amended CFE Treaty as adapted in accordance with the provisions of the Agreement on Adaptation; the protocols are not included. The reader is referred to the OSCE Internet site for the full original texts. For the 1990 CFE Treaty see URL <http://www.osce.org/docs/english/1990-1999/cfe/cfetreate.htm>, and for the 1999 Agreement on Adaptation see <http://www.osce.org/docs/english/1990-1999/cfe/cfeagree.htm>.

The preamble of the Agreement on Adaptation and its two concluding provisions, Articles 30 and 31, are reproduced here in italic text.

The Republic of Armenia, the Republic of Azerbaijan, the Republic of Belarus, the Kingdom of Belgium, the Republic of Bulgaria, Canada, the Czech Republic, the Kingdom of Denmark, the French Republic, Georgia, the Federal Republic of Germany, the Hellenic Republic, the Republic of Hungary, the Republic of Iceland, the Italian Republic, the Republic of Kazakhstan, the Grand Duchy of Luxembourg, the Repub-

lic of Moldova, the Kingdom of the Netherlands, the Kingdom of Norway, the Republic of Poland, the Portuguese Republic, Romania, the Russian Federation, the Slovak Republic, the Kingdom of Spain, the Republic of Turkey, Ukraine, the United Kingdom of Great Britain and Northern Ireland, and the United States of America, hereinafter referred to as the States Parties,

Conscious of the fundamental changes that have occurred in Europe since the Treaty on Conventional Armed Forces in Europe was signed in Paris on 19 November 1990, hereinafter referred to as the Treaty,

Determined to sustain the key role of the Treaty as the cornerstone of European security,

Noting the fulfilment of the objective of the original Treaty of ensuring that the numbers of conventional armaments and equipment limited by the Treaty within the area of application of the Treaty would not exceed 40,000 battle tanks, 60,000 armoured combat vehicles, 40,000 pieces of artillery, 13,600 combat aircraft and 4,000 attack helicopters,

Have agreed as follows:

The Republic of Armenia, the Republic of Azerbaijan, the Republic of Belarus, the Kingdom of Belgium, the Republic of Bulgaria, Canada, the Czech Republic, the Kingdom of Denmark, the French Republic, Georgia, the Federal Republic of Germany, the Hellenic Republic, the Republic of Hungary, the Republic of Iceland, the Italian Republic, the Republic of Kazakhstan, the Grand Duchy of Luxembourg, the Republic of Moldova, the Kingdom of the Netherlands, the Kingdom of Norway, the Republic of Poland, the Portuguese Republic, Romania, the Russian Federation, the Slovak Republic, the Kingdom of Spain, the Republic of Turkey, Ukraine, the United Kingdom of Great Britain and Northern Ireland, and the United States of America, hereinafter referred to as the States Parties,

Guided by the Mandate for Negotiation on Conventional Armed Forces in Europe of 10 January 1989,

Guided by the objectives and the purposes of the Organization for (formerly Conference on) Security and Co-operation in Europe, within the framework of which the negotiation of this Treaty was conducted in Vienna,

Recalling their obligation to refrain in their mutual relations, as well as in their international relations in general, from the threat or use of force against the territorial integrity or political independence of any State, or in any other manner inconsistent with the purposes and principles of the Charter of the United Nations,

Conscious of the need to prevent any military conflict in Europe,

Conscious of the common responsibility which they all have for seeking to achieve greater stability and security in Europe, and bearing in mind their right to be or not to be a party to treaties of alliance,

Striving to develop further and consolidate a new pattern of security relations among all the States Parties based on peaceful cooperation and thereby to contribute to establishing a common and indivisible security space in Europe,

Committed to the objectives of maintaining a secure, stable and balanced overall level of conventional armed forces in Europe lower than heretofore, of eliminating disparities prejudicial to stability and security and of eliminating the capability for launching surprise attack and for initiating large-scale offensive action in Europe,

Affirming that this Treaty is not intended to affect adversely the security interests of any State,

Having taken note of the Final Act of the Conference of the States Parties to the Treaty on Conventional Armed Forces in Europe held in Istanbul from 17 to 19 November 1999, as well as of the statements made by certain States Parties concerning their political commitments referred to therein,

Affirming their commitment to continue the conventional arms control process including negotiations, taking into account the opening of the Treaty for accession by other participating States of the Organization for Security and Co-operation in Europe with territory in the geographic area between the Atlantic Ocean and the Ural Mountains as well as future requirements for European stability and security in the light of political developments in Europe,

Have agreed as follows:

Article I

1. Each State Party shall carry out the obligations set forth in this Treaty in accordance with its provisions, including those obligations relating to the following five categories of conventional armed forces: battle tanks, armoured combat vehicles, artillery, combat aircraft and combat helicopters.

2. Each State Party shall also carry out the other measures set forth in this Treaty designed to ensure security and stability.

3. Conventional armaments and equipment of a State Party in the categories limited by the Treaty shall only be present on the territory of another State Party in conformity with international law, the explicit consent of the host State Party, or a relevant resolution of the United Nations Security Council. Explicit consent must be provided in advance, and must continue to be in effect as provided for in Article XIII, paragraph 1 *bis*.

4. This Treaty incorporates the Protocol on Existing Types of Conventional Armaments and Equipment, hereinafter referred to as the Protocol on Existing Types, with an Annex thereto; the Protocol on National Ceilings for Conventional Armaments and Equipment Limited by the Treaty on Conventional Armed Forces in Europe, hereinafter referred to as the Protocol on National Ceilings; the Protocol on Territorial Ceilings for Conventional Armaments and Equipment Limited by the Treaty on Conventional Armed Forces in Europe, hereinafter referred to as the Protocol on Territorial Ceilings; the Protocol on Procedures Governing the Reclassification of Specific Models or Versions of Combat-Capable Trainer Aircraft into Unarmed Trainer Aircraft, hereinafter referred to as the Protocol on Aircraft Reclassification; the Protocol on Procedures Governing the Reduction of Conventional Armaments and Equipment Limited by the Treaty on Conventional Armed Forces in Europe, hereinafter referred to as the Protocol on Reduction; the Protocol on Procedures Governing the Categorisation of Combat Helicopters and the Recategorisation of Multi-purpose Attack Helicopters, hereinafter referred to as the Protocol on Helicopter Recategorisation; the Protocol on Notification and Exchange of Information, hereinafter referred to as the Protocol on Information Exchange, with an Annex on the Format for the Exchange of Information, hereinafter referred to as the Annex on Format; the Protocol on Inspection; and the Protocol on the Joint Consultative Group.

Each of these documents constitutes an integral part of this Treaty.

Article II

1. For the purposes of this Treaty:

(A) [deleted]

(B) The term 'area of application' means the entire land territory of the States Parties in Europe from the Atlantic Ocean to the Ural Mountains, which includes all the European island territories of the States Parties, including the Faroe Islands of the Kingdom of Denmark, Svalbard including Bear Island of the Kingdom of Norway, the islands of Azores and Madeira of the Portuguese Republic, the Canary Islands of the Kingdom of Spain and Franz Josef Land and Novaya Zemlya of the Russian Federation.

In the case of the Republic of Kazakhstan and the Russian Federation, the area of application includes all territory lying west of the Ural River and the Caspian Sea.

In the case of the Republic of Turkey, the area of application includes the territory of the Republic of Turkey north and west of a line extending from the point of intersection of the Turkish border with the 39th parallel to Muradiye, Patnos, Karayazi, Tekman, Kemaliye, Feke, Ceyhan, Dogankent, Gözne and thence to the sea.

(C) The term 'battle tank' means a self-propelled armoured fighting vehicle, capable of heavy firepower, primarily of a high muzzle velocity direct fire main gun necessary to engage armoured and other targets, with high cross-country mobility, with a high level of self-protection, and which is not designed and equipped primarily to transport combat troops. Such armoured vehicles serve as the principal weapon system of ground-force tank and other armoured formations.

Battle tanks are tracked armoured fighting vehicles which weigh at least 16.5 metric tonnes unladen weight and which are armed with a 360-degree traverse gun of at least 75-millimetres calibre. In addition, any wheeled armoured fighting vehicles entering into service which meet all the other criteria stated above shall be deemed battle tanks.

(D) The term 'armoured combat vehicle' means a self-propelled vehicle with armoured protection and cross-country capability. Armoured combat vehicles include armoured personnel carriers, armoured infantry fighting vehicles and heavy armament combat vehicles.

The term 'armoured personnel carrier' means an armoured combat vehicle which is designed and equipped to transport a combat infantry squad and which, as a rule, is armed with an integral or organic weapon of less than 20-millimetres calibre.

The term 'armoured infantry fighting vehicle' means an armoured combat vehicle which is designed and equipped primarily to transport a combat infantry squad, which normally provides the capability for the troops to deliver fire from inside the vehicle under armoured protection, and which is armed with an integral or organic cannon of at least 20 millimetres calibre and sometimes an anti-tank missile launcher. Armoured infantry fighting vehicles serve as the principal weapon system of armoured infantry or mechanised infantry or motorised infantry formations and units of ground forces.

The term 'heavy armament combat vehicle' means an armoured combat vehicle with an integral or organic direct fire gun of at least 75 millimetres calibre, weighing at least 6.0 metric tonnes unladen weight, which does not fall within the definitions of an armoured personnel carrier, or an armoured infantry fighting vehicle or a battle tank.

(E) The term 'unladen weight' means the weight of a vehicle excluding the weight of ammunition; fuel, oil and lubricants; removable reactive armour; spare parts, tools and accessories; removable snorkelling equipment; and crew and their personal kit.

(F) The term 'artillery' means large calibre systems capable of engaging ground targets by delivering primarily indirect fire. Such artillery systems provide the essential indirect fire support to combined arms formations.

Large calibre artillery systems are guns, howitzers, artillery pieces combining the characteristics of guns and howitzers, mortars and multiple launch rocket systems with a calibre of 100 millimetres and above. In addition, any future large calibre direct fire system which has a secondary effective indirect fire capability shall be counted against the artillery ceilings.

(G) [deleted]

(H) The term 'designated permanent storage site' means a place with a clearly defined physical boundary containing conventional armaments and equipment limited by the Treaty which are counted within national ceilings but which are not subject to limitations on conventional armaments and equipment limited by the Treaty in active units.

(I) The term 'armoured vehicle launched bridge' means a self-propelled armoured transporter-launcher vehicle capable of carrying and, through built-in mechanisms, of emplacing and retrieving a bridge structure. Such a vehicle with a bridge structure operates as an integrated system.

(J) The term 'conventional armaments and equipment limited by the Treaty' means battle tanks, armoured combat vehicles, artillery, combat aircraft and attack helicopters subject to the numerical limitations set forth in

Articles IV, V, VII, the Protocol on National Ceilings and the Protocol on Territorial Ceilings.

(K) The term 'combat aircraft' means a fixed-wing or variable-geometry wing aircraft armed and equipped to engage targets by employing guided missiles, unguided rockets, bombs, guns, cannons, or other weapons of destruction, as well as any model or version of such an aircraft which performs other military functions such as reconnaissance or electronic warfare. The term 'combat aircraft' does not include primary trainer aircraft.

(L) The term 'combat helicopter' means a rotary wing aircraft armed and equipped to engage targets or equipped to perform other military functions. The term 'combat helicopter' comprises attack helicopters and combat support helicopters. The term 'combat helicopter' does not include unarmed transport helicopters.

(M) The term 'attack helicopter' means a combat helicopter equipped to employ anti-armour, air-to-ground, or air-to-air guided weapons and equipped with an integrated fire control and aiming system for these weapons. The term 'attack helicopter' comprises specialised attack helicopters and multi-purpose attack helicopters.

(N) The term 'specialised attack helicopter' means an attack helicopter that is designed primarily to employ guided weapons.

(O) The term 'multi-purpose attack helicopter' means an attack helicopter designed to perform multiple military functions and equipped to employ guided weapons.

(P) The term 'combat support helicopter' means a combat helicopter which does not fulfill the requirements to qualify as an attack helicopter and which may be equipped with a variety of self-defence and area suppression weapons, such as guns, cannons and unguided rockets, bombs or cluster bombs, or which may be equipped to perform other military functions.

(Q) The term 'conventional armaments and equipment subject to the Treaty' means battle tanks, armoured combat vehicles, artillery, combat aircraft, primary trainer aircraft, unarmed trainer aircraft, combat helicopters, unarmed transport helicopters, armoured vehicle launched bridges, armoured personnel carrier look-alikes and armoured infantry fighting vehicle look-alikes subject to information exchange in accordance with the Protocol on Information Exchange.

(R) The term 'in service', as it applies to conventional armed forces and conventional armaments and equipment, means battle tanks, armoured combat vehicles, artillery, combat aircraft, primary trainer aircraft, unarmed trainer aircraft, combat helicopters, unarmed transport helicopters, armoured vehicle launched bridges, armoured personnel carrier look-alikes and armoured infantry fighting vehicle look-alikes that are within the area of application, except for those that are held by organisations designed and structured to perform in peacetime internal security functions or that meet any of the exceptions set forth in Article III.

(S) The terms 'armoured personnel carrier look-alike' and 'armoured infantry fighting vehicle look-alike' mean an armoured vehicle based on the same chassis as, and externally similar to, an armoured personnel carrier or armoured infantry fighting vehicle, respectively, which does not have a cannon or gun of 20 millimetres calibre or greater and which has been constructed or modified in such a way as not to permit the transportation of a combat infantry squad. Taking into account the provisions of the Geneva Convention 'For the Amelioration of the Conditions of the Wounded and Sick in Armed Forces in the Field' of 12 August 1949 that confer a special status on ambulances, armoured personnel carrier ambulances shall not be deemed armoured combat vehicles or armoured personnel carrier look-alikes.

(T) The term 'reduction site' means a clearly designated location where the reduction of conventional armaments and equipment limited by the Treaty in accordance with Article VIII takes place.

(U) The term 'reduction liability' means the number in each category of conventional armaments and equipment limited by the Treaty that a State Party commits itself to reduce pursuant to the provisions of the Treaty, in order to ensure compliance with Article IV.

2. Existing types of conventional armaments and equipment subject to the Treaty are listed in the Protocol on Existing Types. The lists of existing types shall be periodically updated in accordance with Article XVI, paragraph 2, subparagraph (D) and Section IV of the Protocol on Existing Types. Such updates to the existing types lists shall not be deemed amendments to this Treaty.

3. The existing types of combat helicopters listed in the Protocol on Existing Types shall be categorised in accordance with Section I of the Protocol on Helicopter Recategorisation.

Article III

1. For the purposes of this Treaty, the States Parties shall apply the following counting rules:

All battle tanks, armoured combat vehicles, artillery, combat aircraft and attack helicopters, as defined in Article II, within the area of application shall be subject to the numerical limitations and other provisions set forth in Articles IV, V, VII, the Protocol on National Ceilings and the Protocol on Territorial Ceilings, with the exception of those which in a manner consistent with a State Party's normal practices:

(A) Are in the process of manufacture, including manufacturing-related testing;

(B) Are used exclusively for the purposes of research and development;

(C) Belong to historical collections;

(D) Are awaiting disposal, having been decommissioned from service in accordance with the provisions of Article IX;

(E) Are awaiting, or being refurbished for, export or re-export and are temporarily retained within the area of application. Such battle tanks, armoured combat vehicles, artillery, combat aircraft and attack helicopters shall be located elsewhere than at sites declared under the terms of Section V of the Protocol on Information Exchange or at no more than 10 such declared sites which shall have been notified in the previous year's annual information exchange. In the latter case, they shall be separately distinguishable from conventional armaments and equipment limited by the Treaty;

(F) Are, in the case of armoured personnel carriers, armoured infantry fighting vehicles (AIFVs), heavy armament combat vehicles (HACVs) or multi-purpose attack helicopters, held by organisations designed and structured to perform in peacetime internal security functions; or

(G) Are in transit through the area of application from a location outside the area of application to a final destination outside the area of application, and are in the area of application for no longer than a total of seven days.

Article IV

1. Within the area of application, each State Party shall limit and, as necessary, reduce its battle tanks, armoured combat vehicles, artillery, combat aircraft and attack helicopters so that the numbers do not exceed the national ceiling, the subceiling for active units and the subceiling for sub-categories established in accordance with this Article and the Protocol on National Ceilings for that State Party. The subceiling for active units shall establish the maximum number of battle tanks, armoured combat vehicles and pieces of artillery that a State Party may hold in active units within the area of application. The subceiling for active units shall be equal to the national ceiling unless otherwise specified by the Protocol on National Ceilings. Any battle tanks, armoured combat vehicles and pieces of artillery under a national ceiling in any category in excess of the corresponding subceiling for active units shall be located in designated permanent storage sites. The subceiling for sub-categories shall establish the maximum aggregate number of armoured infantry fighting vehicles and heavy armament combat vehicles and the maximum number of heavy armament combat vehicles that a State Party may hold within the area of application in the category of armoured combat vehicles.

2. Within the area of application all conventional armaments and equipment in the categories limited by the Treaty: shall be accounted for and controlled by a State Party; shall, in accordance with the provisions in Article III, be counted against the national ceiling of a State Party; shall in the area of application be transferred only to other States Parties as provided for in this Treaty; and shall be subject to the provisions of the Protocol on Information Exchange. In the case that a State Party is unable to exercise its authority in this respect, any State Party can raise the matter in accordance with the provisions in Article XVI and Article XXI with a view to addressing the situation and ensuring full observance of Treaty provisions with respect to such conventional armaments and equipment in the categories limited by the Treaty. The inability of a State Party to exercise its authority in respect of the above mentioned conventional armaments and equipment in the categories limited by the Treaty shall not in itself release a State Party from any Treaty obligations.

3. Each State Party shall have the right to change its national ceiling, its subceiling for active units and its subceiling for subcategories as follows:

(A) Each State Party shall have the right, in accordance with paragraphs 4 and 6 of this Article, to increase its national ceiling, its subceiling for active units and its subceiling for sub-categories in any category or sub-category of conventional armaments and equipment limited by the Treaty. Any such increase shall be preceded or accompanied by a corresponding decrease in the national ceiling, the subceiling for active units or the subceiling for sub-categories of one or more other States Parties in the same category or sub-category, except as provided for in paragraph 6 of this Article. The State Party or States Parties undertaking the corresponding decrease in their national ceiling, subceiling for active units or subceiling for sub-categories shall notify all States Parties of their consent to the corresponding increase in the national ceiling, subceiling for active units or subceiling for sub-categories of another State Party. No national ceiling for a State Party with territory in the area of application shall exceed that State Party's territorial ceiling in the same category of conventional armaments and equipment limited by the Treaty.

(B) Each State Party shall have the right to decrease unilaterally its national ceiling, subceiling for active units or subceiling for sub-categories in any category or sub-category of conventional armaments and equipment limited by the Treaty. A unilateral decrease in the national ceiling, subceiling for active units or subceiling for sub-categories of a State Party shall by itself confer no right on any other State Party to increase its national ceiling, subceiling for active units or subceiling for sub-categories.

4. Within each five-year period between conferences of States Parties held in accordance with Article XXI, paragraph 1, each State Party shall have the right to increase its national ceiling or subceiling for active units:

(A) In the categories of battle tanks, armoured combat vehicles and artillery by no more than 40 battle tanks, 60 armoured combat vehicles and 20 pieces of artillery or 20 percent of the national ceiling established for that State Party in the Protocol on National Ceilings for battle tanks, armoured combat vehicles and artillery, whichever is greater, but in no case exceeding 150 battle tanks, 250 armoured combat vehicles and 100 pieces of artillery;

(B) In the categories of combat aircraft and attack helicopters by no more than 30 combat aircraft and 25 attack helicopters.

Each State Party shall have the right to increase its national ceiling or subceiling for active units in excess of the levels set forth in paragraph 4, subparagraphs (A) and (B) above, subject to the consent of all other States Parties.

5. A State Party intending to change its national ceiling, subceiling for active units or subceiling for sub-categories shall provide notification to all other States Parties at least 90 days in advance of the date, specified in the notification, on which such a change is to take effect. For increases subject to the consent of all other States Parties, the change shall take effect on the date specified in the notification provided that no State Party, within 60 days of the notification, objects to the change and notifies its objection to all other States Parties. A national ceiling, a subceiling for active units or a subceiling for sub-categories shall remain in effect until a change to that ceiling or subceiling takes effect.

6. In addition to the provisions of paragraph 4, any State Party with a subceiling for active units lower than its national ceiling in the categories of battle tanks, armoured combat vehicles and artillery shall have the right to increase that subceiling, provided that:

(A) The increase in the subceiling for active units is accompanied by a decrease in its national ceiling in the same category of conventional armaments and equipment limited by the Treaty;

(B) For each battle tank, armoured combat vehicle or piece of artillery by which a State Party increases its subceiling for active units, that State Party will decrease its national ceiling by four in the same category of conventional armaments and equipment limited by the Treaty;

(C) The resultant subceiling for active units does not exceed the new national ceiling achieved through the decrease mandated by subparagraph (B) above.

Article V

1. Within the area of application, as defined in Article II, each State Party shall limit the total number of its battle tanks, armoured combat vehicles and artillery on its territory and of battle tanks, armoured combat vehicles and artillery of other States Parties that it permits to be present on its territory and each State Party shall limit its battle tanks, armoured combat vehicles and pieces of artillery present on the territory of other States Parties so that the overall numbers do not exceed the territorial ceilings and the territorial subceilings established in accord-

ance with this Article and the Protocol on Territorial Ceilings, except as otherwise provided for in Article VII.

2. Battle tanks, armoured combat vehicles and artillery present on the territory of a State Party for an operation in support of peace conducted under and consistent with a resolution or a decision of the United Nations Security Council or the Organization for Security and Co-operation in Europe shall be exempt from that State Party's territorial ceiling or territorial subceiling. The duration of the presence of these battle tanks, armoured combat vehicles and artillery on the territory of a State Party shall be consistent with such a resolution or decision.

Battle tanks, armoured combat vehicles and artillery present on the territory of a State Party for an operation in support of peace pursuant to this paragraph shall be subject to notification in accordance with the Protocol on Information Exchange.

3. Battle tanks, armoured combat vehicles and artillery in transit shall be exempt from the territorial ceilings of transited States Parties and from territorial subceilings without prejudice to the exemption from counting rules under Article III, paragraph 1, sub-paragraph (G), provided that:

(A) Battle tanks, armoured combat vehicles and artillery in transit to a location within the area of application do not cause the territorial ceiling of the State Party of final destination to be exceeded, except as otherwise provided for in Article VII. For battle tanks, armoured combat vehicles and artillery in transit to a location outside the area of application there shall be no numerical limit;

(B) Battle tanks, armoured combat vehicles and artillery in transit do not remain on the territory of the transited States Parties in the area of application longer than a total of 42 days; and

(C) Battle tanks, armoured combat vehicles and artillery in transit do not remain on the territory of any single transited State Party, or on a territory with a territorial subceiling, in the area of application longer than 21 days.

Battle tanks, armoured combat vehicles and artillery in transit under this paragraph shall be subject to notification in accordance with Section XII of the Protocol on Information Exchange. Any State Party may request clarification in the Joint Consultative Group with regard to a notified transit. The States Parties involved shall respond within seven days of the request.

4. Each State Party shall have the right to change its territorial ceiling or territorial subceiling as follows:

(A) Each State Party shall have the right, in accordance with paragraph 5 of this Article, to increase its territorial ceiling or territorial subceiling for battle tanks, armoured combat vehicles and artillery in any category. Any such increase shall be preceded or accompanied by a corresponding decrease in the same category in the territorial ceiling or territorial subceiling of one or more other States Parties, subject to the provisions of the Protocol on Territorial Ceilings regarding relevant territorial ceilings and territorial subceilings. The State Party or States Parties undertaking the corresponding decrease in their territorial ceiling or territorial subceiling shall notify all States Parties of their consent to the corresponding increase in the territorial ceiling or territorial subceiling of another State Party.

(B) Each State Party shall have the right to decrease unilaterally its territorial ceiling or territorial subceiling for battle tanks, armoured combat vehicles and artillery in any category; however, no territorial ceiling in any category shall be at any time lower than the corresponding national ceiling. A unilateral decrease in the territorial ceiling or territorial subceiling of a State Party shall by itself confer no right on any other State Party to increase its territorial ceiling or territorial subceiling. Any decrease in a national ceiling under the provisions of Article IV, paragraph 6, shall result in a decrease of the corresponding territorial ceiling by an amount equal to the decrease in the national ceiling.

5. Subject to the provisions above, within each five-year period between conferences of States Parties held in accordance with Article XXI, paragraph 1, each State Party shall have the right to increase its territorial ceiling or territorial subceiling by no more than 40 battle tanks, 60 armoured combat vehicles and 20 pieces of artillery or 20 percent of the territorial ceiling or territorial subceiling established for that State Party in the Protocol on Territorial Ceilings for battle tanks, armoured combat vehicles and artillery, whichever is greater, but in no case exceeding 150 battle tanks, 250 armoured combat vehicles and 100 pieces of artillery.

Each State Party shall have the right to increase its territorial ceiling or territorial subceiling in excess of the levels set forth in this paragraph, subject to the consent of all other States Parties.

6. A State Party intending to change its territorial ceiling or territorial subceiling in any category shall provide notification to all other States Parties at least 90 days in advance of the date, specified in the notification, on which such a change is to take effect. For increases subject to the consent of all other States Parties, the change shall take effect on the date specified in the notification provided that no State Party, within 60 days of the notification, objects to the change and notifies its objection to all other States Parties. A territorial ceiling or a territorial subceiling shall remain in effect until a change to that ceiling or subceiling takes effect.

Article VI [deleted]

Article VII

1. Each State Party shall have the right to exceed on a temporary basis, for military exercises and temporary deployments, the territorial ceilings and territorial subceilings established in the Protocol on Territorial Ceilings, subject to the provisions of this Article.

(A) Military exercises:

(1) Each State Party shall have the right to host on its territory military exercises which cause its territorial ceiling to be exceeded, and, for States Parties with a territorial subceiling, to conduct or host exercises which cause its territorial subceiling to be exceeded in accordance with the Protocol on Territorial Ceilings;

(2) The number of battle tanks, armoured combat vehicles and pieces of artillery present on the territory of a State Party in excess of its territorial ceiling or territorial subceiling for a military exercise, alone or in combination with any other military exercise or any temporary deployment on that territory, shall not exceed the number of battle tanks, armoured combat vehicles and pieces of artillery specified for each State Party in sub-paragraph (B), sub-subparagraph (1), of this paragraph and in the Protocol on Territorial Ceilings;

(3) A military exercise or successive military exercises notified in accordance with the Protocol on Information Exchange, that result in a territorial ceiling or a territorial subceiling being exceeded for more than 42 days shall thereafter be considered a temporary deployment as long as the territorial ceiling or territorial subceiling continues to be exceeded.

(B) Temporary deployments:

(1) Each State Party shall have the right to host on its territory temporary deployments in excess of its territorial ceiling, and, for States Parties with a territorial subceiling, to conduct or host temporary deployments in excess of their territorial subceiling. For this purpose, territorial ceilings and territorial subceilings may be exceeded, on a temporary basis, by no more than 153 battle tanks, 241 armoured combat vehicles and 140 pieces of artillery, unless otherwise set forth in the relevant provisions of the Protocol on Territorial Ceilings. In exceptional circumstances and unless otherwise set forth in the relevant provisions of the Protocol on Territorial Ceilings, a territorial ceiling may be exceeded, on a temporary basis, by no more than 459 battle tanks, 723 armoured combat vehicles and 420 pieces of artillery.

(2) Upon notification of a temporary deployment exceeding a territorial ceiling by more than 153 battle tanks, 241 armoured combat vehicles, and 140 pieces of artillery, the Depositary shall convene a conference of the States Parties in accordance with Article XXI, paragraph 1 *bis*.

2. Should a military exercise, in conjunction with a temporary deployment taking place simultaneously on the territory of the same State Party, cause the territorial ceiling to be exceeded by more than 153 battle tanks, 241 armoured combat vehicles or 140 pieces of artillery, any State Party shall have the right to request the Depositary to convene a conference of the States Parties in accordance with Article XXI, paragraph 1 *bis*.

For exercises and temporary deployments pursuant to paragraph 1, subparagraphs (A) and (B), of this Article, an explanatory report shall be provided to the Joint Consultative Group by the States Parties involved. In the case of temporary deployments, the report shall be submitted as soon as possible and in any case no later than the notification foreseen in Section XVIII, paragraph 4, subparagraph (A), sub-subparagraph (2), and subparagraph (B), sub-subparagraph (2), of the Protocol on Information Exchange. Subsequent updates shall be provided every two months until the territorial ceiling or the territorial subceiling is no longer exceeded.

Article VIII

1. Any battle tanks, armoured combat vehicles, artillery, combat aircraft and attack helicopters in excess of the numerical limitations set forth in Article IV and in the Proto-

col on National Ceilings shall be eliminated only by means of reduction in accordance with the Protocol on Reduction, the Protocol on Helicopter Recategorisation, the Protocol on Aircraft Reclassification, the footnote to Section I, paragraph 2, subparagraph (A), of the Protocol on Existing Types and the Protocol on Inspection. In the case of accession, any reductions by the acceding State as well as the time limit within which they shall be carried out shall be specified in accordance with the provisions of the Agreement on Accession.

2. The categories of conventional armaments and equipment subject to reductions are battle tanks, armoured combat vehicles, artillery, combat aircraft and attack helicopters. The specific types are listed in the Protocol on Existing Types.

(A) Battle tanks and armoured combat vehicles shall be reduced by destruction, conversion for non-military purposes, placement on static display, use as ground targets, or, in the case of armoured personnel carriers, modification in accordance with the footnote to Section 1, paragraph 2, subparagraph (A), of the Protocol on Existing Types.

(B) Artillery shall be reduced by destruction or placement on static display, or, in the case of self-propelled artillery, by use as ground targets.

(C) Combat aircraft shall be reduced by destruction, placement on static display, use for ground instructional purposes, or, in the case of specific models or versions of combat-capable trainer aircraft, reclassification into unarmed trainer aircraft.

(D) Specialised attack helicopters shall be reduced by destruction, placement on static display, or use for ground instructional purposes.

(E) Multi-purpose attack helicopters shall be reduced by destruction, placement on static display, use for ground instructional purposes, or recategorisation.

3. Conventional armaments and equipment limited by the Treaty shall be deemed to be reduced upon execution of the procedures set forth in the Protocols listed in paragraph 1 of this Article and upon notification as required by these Protocols. Armaments and equipment so reduced shall no longer be counted against the numerical limitations set forth in Articles IV, V, the Protocol on National Ceilings and the Protocol on Territorial Ceilings.

4. Reduction of conventional armaments and equipment limited by the Treaty shall be carried out at reduction sites, unless otherwise specified in the Protocols listed in paragraph 1 of this Article, within the area of application. Each State Party shall have the right to designate as many reduction sites as it wishes, to revise without restriction its designation of such sites and to carry out reduction and final conversion simultaneously at a maximum of 20 sites. States Parties shall have the right to share or co-locate reduction sites by mutual agreement.

5. Any reductions, including the results of the conversion of conventional armaments and equipment limited by the Treaty for non-military purposes, shall be subject to inspection, without right of refusal, in accordance with the Protocol on Inspection.

Article IX

1. In the case of removal from service by decommissioning of battle tanks, armoured combat vehicles, artillery, combat aircraft and attack helicopters, within the area of application:

(A) Such conventional armaments and equipment limited by the Treaty shall be decommissioned and awaiting disposal at no more than eight sites which shall be notified as declared sites in accordance with the Protocol on Information Exchange and shall be identified in such notifications as holding areas for decommissioned conventional armaments and equipment limited by the Treaty. If sites containing conventional armaments and equipment limited by the Treaty decommissioned from service also contain any other conventional armaments and equipment subject to the Treaty, the decommissioned conventional armaments and equipment limited by the Treaty shall be separately distinguishable; and

(B) The numbers of such decommissioned conventional armaments and equipment limited by the Treaty shall not exceed, in the case of any individual State Party, one percent of its notified holdings of conventional armaments and equipment limited by the Treaty, or a total of 250, whichever is greater, of which no more than 200 shall be battle tanks, armoured combat vehicles and pieces of artillery, and no more than 50 shall be attack helicopters and combat aircraft.

2. Notification of decommissioning shall include the number and type of conventional armaments and equipment limited by the Treaty decommissioned and the location of decommissioning and shall be provided to all other States Parties in accordance with Section X, paragraph 1, subparagraph (B), of

the Protocol on Information Exchange.

Article X

1. Designated permanent storage sites shall be notified in accordance with the Protocol on Information Exchange to all other States Parties by the State Party to which the conventional armaments and equipment limited by the Treaty contained at designated permanent storage sites belong. The notification shall include the designation and location, including geographic coordinates, of designated permanent storage sites and the numbers by type of each category of its conventional armaments and equipment limited by the Treaty at each such storage site.

2. Designated permanent storage sites shall contain only facilities appropriate for the storage and maintenance of armaments and equipment (e.g., warehouses, garages, workshops and associated stores as well as other support accommodation). Designated permanent storage sites shall not contain firing ranges or training areas associated with conventional armaments and equipment limited by the Treaty. Designated permanent storage sites shall contain only armaments and equipment belonging to the conventional armed forces of a State Party.

3. Each designated permanent storage site shall have a clearly defined physical boundary that shall consist of a continuous perimeter fence at least 1.5 metres in height. The perimeter fence shall have no more than three gates providing the sole means of entrance and exit for armaments and equipment.

4. Conventional armaments and equipment limited by the Treaty located within designated permanent storage sites shall be counted as conventional armaments and equipment limited by the Treaty not in active units, including when they are temporarily removed in accordance with paragraphs 7, 8 and 10 of this Article.

Conventional armaments and equipment limited by the Treaty in storage other than in designated permanent storage sites shall be counted as conventional armaments and equipment limited by the Treaty in active units.

5. Active units or formations shall not be located within designated permanent storage sites, except as provided for in paragraph 6 of this Article.

6. Only personnel associated with the security or operation of designated permanent storage sites, or the maintenance of the armaments and equipment stored therein, shall be located within the designated permanent storage sites.

7. For the purpose of maintenance, repair or modification of conventional armaments and equipment limited by the Treaty located within designated permanent storage sites, each State Party shall have the right, without prior notification, to remove from and retain outside designated permanent storage sites simultaneously up to 10 percent, rounded up to the nearest even whole number, of the notified holdings of each category of conventional armaments and equipment limited by the Treaty in each designated permanent storage site, or 10 items of the conventional armaments and equipment limited by the Treaty in each category in each designated permanent storage site, whichever is less.

8. Except as provided for in paragraph 7 of this Article, no State Party shall remove conventional armaments and equipment limited by the Treaty from designated permanent storage sites unless notification has been provided to all other States Parties at least 42 days in advance of such removal. Notification shall be given by the State Party to which the conventional armaments and equipment limited by the Treaty belong. Such notification shall specify:

(A) the location of the designated permanent storage site from which conventional armaments and equipment limited by the Treaty are to be removed and the numbers by type of conventional armaments and equipment limited by the Treaty of each category to be removed;

(B) the dates of removal and return of conventional armaments and equipment limited by the Treaty; and

(C) the intended location and use of conventional armaments and equipment limited by the Treaty while outside the designated permanent storage site.

9. [deleted]

10. Conventional armaments and equipment limited by the Treaty removed from designated permanent storage sites pursuant to paragraph 8 of this Article shall be returned to designated permanent storage sites no later than 42 days after their removal, except for those items of conventional armaments and equipment limited by the Treaty removed for industrial rebuild.

Such items shall be returned to designated permanent storage sites immediately on completion of the rebuild.

11. Each State Party shall have the right to replace conventional armaments and equip-

ment limited by the Treaty located in designated permanent storage sites. Each State Party shall notify all other States Parties, at the beginning of replacement, of the number, location, type and disposition of conventional armaments and equipment limited by the Treaty being replaced.

Article XI [deleted]

Article XII

1. Armoured infantry fighting vehicles held by organisations of a State Party designed and structured to perform in peacetime internal security functions are not limited by this Treaty.

2. The foregoing notwithstanding, in order to enhance the implementation of this Treaty and to provide assurance that the number of such armaments held by such organisations of a State Party shall not be used to circumvent the provisions of this Treaty, any such armaments in excess of the levels set forth in subparagraphs (A), (B) or (C) of this paragraph, whichever is greater, shall constitute a portion of the permitted levels in the category of armoured combat vehicles, as established in Articles IV and V and in the Protocol on National Ceilings and the Protocol on Territorial Ceilings, and changed in accordance with Articles IV and V:

(A) Holdings of armoured infantry fighting vehicles held, within the area of application, by organisations designed and structured to perform in peacetime internal security functions, present on the territory of the State Party as notified pursuant to the information exchange effective as of 19 November 1990; or

(B) Five percent of the national ceiling established for the State Party in the Protocol on National Ceilings in the category of armoured combat vehicles, as changed in accordance with Article IV; or

(C) 100 such armoured infantry fighting vehicles.

In the case of acceding States, the numbers shall be established in the Agreement on Accession.

3. Each State Party shall further ensure that organisations designed and structured to perform in peacetime internal security functions refrain from the acquisition of combat capabilities in excess of those necessary for meeting internal security requirements.

4. A State Party that intends to reassign battle tanks, artillery, armoured infantry fighting vehicles, combat aircraft and attack helicopters in service with its conventional armed forces to any organisation of that State Party not a part of its conventional armed forces shall notify all other States Parties no later than the date such reassignment takes effect.

Such notification shall specify the effective date of the reassignment, the date such equipment is physically transferred, as well as the numbers, by type, of the conventional armaments and equipment limited by the Treaty being reassigned.

Article XIII

1. For the purpose of ensuring verification of compliance with the provisions of this Treaty, each State Party shall provide notifications and exchange information pertaining to its conventional armaments and equipment and to the conventional armaments and equipment of other States Parties that it permits to be present on its territory, in accordance with the Protocol on Information Exchange.

1. *bis* The presence of conventional armaments and equipment of a State Party on the territory of another State Party as set forth in Article V, paragraph 1, for transit as set forth in Article V, paragraph 3, for military exercises as set forth in Article VII, paragraph 1, subparagraph (A), and for temporary deployment as set forth in Article VII, paragraph 1, subparagraph (B), shall be in accordance with Article I, paragraph 3. Consent of the host State Party shall be reflected through the appropriate notifications in accordance with the Protocol on Information Exchange.

2. Such notifications and exchange of information shall be provided in accordance with Article XVII.

3. Each State Party shall be responsible for its own information; receipt of such information and of notifications shall not imply validation or acceptance of the information provided.

Article XIV

1. For the purpose of ensuring verification of compliance with the provisions of this Treaty, each State Party shall have the right to conduct, and the obligation to accept, within the area of application, inspections in accordance with the provisions of the Protocol on Inspection.

2. The purpose of such inspections shall be:

(A) To verify, on the basis of the information provided pursuant to the Protocol on Information Exchange, the compliance of States Parties with the numerical limitations set forth in Articles IV, V, VII, the Protocol on National Ceilings and the Protocol on Territorial Ceilings;

(B) To monitor any reductions of battle tanks, armoured combat vehicles, artillery, combat aircraft and attack helicopters carried out at reduction sites in accordance with Article VIII and the Protocol on Reduction;

(C) To monitor the certification of recategorised multi-purpose attack helicopters and reclassified combat-capable trainer aircraft carried out in accordance with the Protocol on Helicopter Recategorisation and the Protocol on Aircraft Reclassification, respectively.

3. No State Party shall exercise the rights set forth in paragraphs 1 and 2 of this Article in order to elude the objectives of the verification regime.

4. In the case of an inspection conducted jointly by more than one State Party, one of them shall be responsible for the execution of the provisions of this Treaty.

5. The number of inspections pursuant to Sections VII and VIII of the Protocol on Inspection which each State Party shall have the right to conduct and the obligation to accept during each specified time period shall be determined in accordance with the provisions of Section II of that Protocol.

6. The number of inspections, pursuant to Section IX of the Protocol on Inspection, that each State Party shall have the right to conduct and the State Party whose territorial ceiling or territorial subceiling is temporarily exceeded shall have the obligation to accept shall be determined in accordance with the provisions of that Section.

7. Each State Party which carries out disposal of conventional armaments and equipment limited by the Treaty in excess of reduction liabilities shall provide for confirmation of the results of the disposal either by inviting an observation team or through the use of cooperative measures, in accordance with the provisions of Section XII of the Protocol on Inspection.

Article XV

1. For the purpose of ensuring verification of compliance with the provisions of this Treaty, a State Party shall have the right to use, in addition to the procedures referred to in Article XIV, national or multinational technical means of verification at its disposal in a manner consistent with generally recognised principles of international law.

2. A State Party shall not interfere with national or multinational technical means of verification of another State Party operating in accordance with paragraph 1 of this Article.

3. A State Party shall not use concealment measures that impede verification of compliance with the provisions of this Treaty by national or multinational technical means of verification of another State Party operating in accordance with paragraph 1 of this Article. This obligation does not apply to cover or concealment practices associated with normal personnel training, maintenance or operations involving conventional armaments and equipment limited by the Treaty.

Article XVI

1. To promote the objectives and implementation of the provisions of this Treaty, the States Parties hereby establish a Joint Consultative Group.

2. Within the framework of the Joint Consultative Group, the States Parties shall:

(A) Address questions relating to compliance with or possible circumvention of the provisions of this Treaty;

(B) Seek to resolve ambiguities and differences of interpretation that may become apparent in the way this Treaty is implemented;

(C) Consider and, if possible, agree on measures to enhance the viability and effectiveness of this Treaty;

(D) Address, upon the request of any State Party, questions concerning the intention of any State Party to revise its national ceiling upwards under Article IV, paragraph 4, or its territorial ceiling under Article V, paragraph 5;

(E) Receive and consider the explanatory report, and any subsequent updates, provided in accordance with Article VII, paragraph 2;

(F) Update the lists contained in the Protocol on Existing Types, as required by Article II, paragraph 2;

(G) Consider measures of cooperation to enhance the verification regime of the Treaty, including through the appropriate utilisation of results of aerial inspections;

(H) Resolve technical questions in order to seek common practices among the States Parties in the way this Treaty is implemented;

(I) Work out or revise, as necessary, rules of procedure, working methods, the scale of distribution of expenses of the Joint Consultative Group and of conferences convened under this Treaty and the distribution of costs of inspections between or among States Parties;

(J) Consider and work out appropriate measures to ensure that information obtained through exchanges of information among the States Parties or as a result of inspections pursuant to this Treaty is used solely for the purposes of this Treaty, taking into account the particular requirements of each State Party in respect of safeguarding information which that State Party specifies as being sensitive;

(K) Consider, upon the request of any State Party, any matter that a State Party wishes to propose for examination by any conference to be convened in accordance with Article XXI; such consideration shall not prejudice the right of any State Party to resort to the procedures set forth in Article XXI;

(L) Consider any request to accede to this Treaty, pursuant to Article XVIII, by acting as the body through which the States Parties may establish, and recommend approval of, the terms under which a requesting State accedes to the Treaty;

(M) Conduct any future negotiations, if the States Parties so decide; and

(N) Consider matters of dispute arising out of the implementation of this Treaty.

3. Each State Party shall have the right to raise before the Joint Consultative Group, and have placed on its agenda, any issue relating to this Treaty.

4. The Joint Consultative Group shall take decisions or make recommendations by consensus. Consensus shall be understood to mean the absence of any objection by any representative of a State Party to the taking of a decision or the making of a recommendation.

5. The Joint Consultative Group may propose amendments to this Treaty for consideration and confirmation in accordance with Article XX. The Joint Consultative Group may also agree on improvements to the viability and effectiveness of this Treaty, consistent with its provisions. Unless such improvements relate only to minor matters of an administrative or technical nature, they shall be subject to consideration and confirmation in accordance with Article XX before they can take effect.

6. Nothing in this Article shall be deemed to prohibit or restrict any State Party from requesting information from or undertaking consultations with other States Parties on matters relating to this Treaty and its implementation in channels or fora other than the Joint Consultative Group.

7. The Joint Consultative Group shall follow the procedures set forth in the Protocol on the Joint Consultative Group.

Article XVII

The States Parties shall transmit information and notifications required by this Treaty in written form.

They shall use diplomatic channels or other official channels designated by them, including and in particular, the OSCE Communications Network.

Article XVIII

1. Any participating State of the Organization for Security and Co-operation in Europe whose land territory lies in Europe within the geographic area between the Atlantic Ocean and the Ural Mountains may submit to the Depositary a written request to accede to this Treaty.

2. The requesting State shall include in its request the following information:

(A) The designation of its existing types of conventional armaments and equipment;

(B) Its proposed national and territorial ceilings and the related subceilings for each category of armaments and equipment limited by the Treaty; and

(C) Any other information deemed relevant by the requesting State.

3. The Depositary shall notify all States Parties of the request and of the information provided by the requesting State.

4. The requesting State may modify or supplement this information. Any State Party may request additional information.

5. States Parties shall, beginning no later than 21 days after the notification pursuant to paragraph 3 of this Article, hold meetings of the Joint Consultative Group at which the States Parties shall address the request, conduct negotiations and establish the terms for accession. The requesting State may be invited to attend meetings of the Joint Consultative Group if the States Parties so decide.

6. Each request shall be considered individually by the States Parties in an expeditious manner. Any decision shall be taken by consensus.

7. The agreed terms for accession shall be

enshrined in an Agreement on Accession between the States Parties and the requesting State, which shall be circulated to all States Parties and the requesting State by the Depositary and deposited in the archives of the Depositary.

8. Upon the receipt of confirmation of approval of the Agreement on Accession by all States Parties, the Depositary shall so inform all States Parties and the requesting State. The requesting State may then, subject to ratification in accordance with its constitutional procedures, submit an instrument of accession to the Treaty that shall acknowledge the terms and conditions of the Agreement on Accession.

9. This Treaty shall enter into force for the requesting State 10 days after the deposit of its instrument of accession to the Treaty with the Depositary, at which time the requesting State shall become a State Party to the Treaty.

Article XIX

1. This Treaty shall be of unlimited duration. It may be supplemented by a further treaty.

2. Each State Party shall, in exercising its national sovereignty, have the right to withdraw from this Treaty if it decides that extraordinary events related to the subject matter of this Treaty have jeopardised its supreme interests. A State Party intending to withdraw shall give notice of its decision to do so to the Depositary and to all other States Parties. Such notice shall be given at least 150 days prior to the intended withdrawal from this Treaty. It shall include a statement of the extraordinary events the State Party regards as having jeopardised its supreme interests.

3. Each State Party shall, in particular, in exercising its national sovereignty, have the right to withdraw from this Treaty if another State Party increases its holdings in battle tanks, armoured combat vehicles, artillery, combat aircraft or attack helicopters, as defined in Article II, which are outside the scope of the limitations of this Treaty, in such proportions as to pose an obvious threat to the balance of forces within the area of application.

Article XX

1. Any State Party may propose amendments to this Treaty. The text of a proposed amendment shall be submitted to the Depositary, which shall circulate it to all the States Parties.

2. If an amendment is approved by all States Parties, it shall enter into force in accordance with the procedures set forth in Article XXII governing the entry into force of this Treaty.

Article XXI

1. Forty-six months after entry into force of this Treaty, and at five-year intervals thereafter, the Depositary shall convene a conference of the States Parties to conduct a review of the operation of this Treaty, to include, *inter alia*, a review of the operation and the levels of national ceilings, territorial ceilings and territorial subceilings, and related commitments, together with other Treaty elements, taking into account the need to ensure that the security of no State Party is diminished.

1. *bis* Upon notification of a temporary deployment exceeding a territorial ceiling by more than 153 battle tanks, 241 armoured combat vehicles or 140 pieces of artillery, or upon request by a State Party pursuant to Article VII, paragraph 2, the Depositary shall convene a conference of the States Parties at which the hosting and deploying States Parties shall explain the nature of the circumstances which have given rise to the temporary deployment. The conference shall be convened without delay but no later than seven days after the notification and shall continue for up to 48 hours unless otherwise agreed by all States Parties. The Chairman of the Joint Consultative Group shall inform the Permanent Council and the Forum for Security Co-operation of the Organization for Security and Co-operation in Europe of the situation.

2. The Depositary shall convene an extraordinary conference of the States Parties if requested to do so by any State Party which considers that exceptional circumstances relating to this Treaty have arisen. In order to enable the other States Parties to prepare for this conference, the request shall include the reason why that State Party deems an extraordinary conference to be necessary. The conference shall consider the circumstances set forth in the request and their effect on the operation of this Treaty. The conference shall open no later than 15 days after receipt of the request and, unless it decides otherwise, shall last no longer than three weeks.

3. The Depositary shall convene a conference of the States Parties to consider an amendment proposed pursuant to Article XX,

if requested to do so by three or more States Parties. Such a conference shall open no later than 21 days after receipt of the necessary requests.

4. In the event that a State Party gives notice of its decision to withdraw from this Treaty pursuant to Article XIX, the Depositary shall convene a conference of the States Parties which shall open no later than 21 days after receipt of the notice of withdrawal in order to consider questions relating to the withdrawal from this Treaty.

Article XXII

1. This Treaty shall be subject to ratification by each State Party in accordance with its constitutional procedures; it shall be open for accession by States pursuant to Article XVIII. Instruments of ratification and, in the case of accession, instruments of accession shall be deposited with the Government of the Kingdom of the Netherlands, hereby designated the Depositary.

2. This Treaty shall enter into force 10 days after instruments of ratification have been deposited by all States Parties listed in the Preamble.

3. The Depositary shall promptly inform all States Parties of:

(A) The deposit of each instrument of ratification or accession;

(B) The entry into force of this Treaty;

(C) Any withdrawal in accordance with Article XIX and its effective date;

(D) The text of any amendment proposed in accordance with Article XX;

(E) The entry into force of any amendment to this Treaty;

(F) Any request to accede to the Treaty pursuant to Article XVIII;

(G) Any request to convene a conference in accordance with Article XXI;

(H) The convening of a conference pursuant to Article XXI; and

(I) Any other matter of which the Depositary is required by this Treaty to inform the States Parties.

4. This Treaty shall be registered by the Depositary pursuant to Article 102 of the Charter of the United Nations.

Article XXIII

The original of this Treaty, of which the English, French, German, Italian, Russian and Spanish texts are equally authentic, shall be deposited in the archives of the Depositary. Duly certified copies of this Treaty shall be transmitted by the Depositary to all States Parties.

. . .

Article 30

1. Changes to maximum levels for holdings, notified under the provisions of the Treaty during the period between signature and entry into force of the Agreement on Adaptation of the Treaty on Conventional Armed Forces in Europe, hereinafter referred to as the Agreement on Adaptation, shall also be considered changes to the levels specified in the Protocol on National Ceilings and, if the State Party concerned so requests, to the Protocol on Territorial Ceilings, provided that:

(A) Such changes are consistent with the limitations set forth in Article IV, paragraphs 3 and 4, and Article V, paragraphs 4 and 5, of the Treaty, and

(B) The numerical limits set forth in Article IV, paragraph 4, and Article V, paragraph 5, of the Treaty are applied in proportion to the time that has elapsed between signature and entry into force of the Agreement on Adaptation.

2. In the case where such changes would require the consent of all other States Parties as set forth in Article IV, paragraph 4, and Article V, paragraph 5, of the Treaty, such changes shall be considered changes to the levels specified in the Protocol on National Ceilings, provided that no State Party provides a written objection to such changes within 60 days of entry into force of the Agreement on Adaptation.

3. Notwithstanding the provisions of paragraph 1 and 2 of this Article, notified changes shall not be considered changes to the Protocol on National Ceilings and the Protocol on Territorial Ceilings where a State Party is notifying a unilateral decrease in its maximum levels for holdings, unless that State Party so requests.

Article 31

1. This Agreement on Adaptation shall be subject to ratification by each State Party in accordance with its constitutional procedures.

2. Instruments of ratification shall be deposited with the Depositary.

3. This Agreement on Adaptation shall enter into force 10 days after instruments of ratification have been deposited by all States Parties listed in the Preamble, after which time the Treaty shall exist only in its amended form.

4. Upon entry into force of this Agreement on Adaptation, the numerical levels set forth in Article IV, paragraph 4, and Article V, paragraph 5, of the Treaty shall be reduced in proportion to the time remaining between the date of entry into force and the next review conference pursuant to Article XXI, paragraph 1.

5. The original of this Agreement on Adaptation, of which the English, French, German, Italian, Russian and Spanish texts are equally authentic, shall be deposited in the archives of the Depositary. Duly certified copies of this Agreement on Adaptation shall be transmitted by the Depositary to all States Parties.

6. This Agreement on Adaptation shall be registered by the Depositary pursuant to Article 102 of the Charter of the United Nations.

In witness thereof, the undersigned duly authorised have signed this Agreement on Adaptation.

Done at Istanbul, this nineteenth day of November nineteen hundred and ninety-nine, in the English, French, German, Italian, Russian and Spanish languages.

FINAL ACT OF THE CONFERENCE OF THE STATES PARTIES TO THE TREATY ON CONVENTIONAL ARMED FORCES IN EUROPE

Istanbul, 19 November 1999

The Republic of Armenia, the Republic of Azerbaijan, the Republic of Belarus, the Kingdom of Belgium, the Republic of Bulgaria, Canada, the Czech Republic, the Kingdom of Denmark, the French Republic, Georgia, the Federal Republic of Germany, the Hellenic Republic, the Republic of Hungary, the Republic of Iceland, the Italian Republic, the Republic of Kazakhstan, the Grand Duchy of Luxembourg, the Republic of Moldova, the Kingdom of the Netherlands, the Kingdom of Norway, the Republic of Poland, the Portuguese Republic, Romania, the Russian Federation, the Slovak Republic, the Kingdom of Spain, the Republic of Turkey, Ukraine, the United Kingdom of Great Britain and Northern Ireland, and the United States of America, the States Parties to the Treaty on

Conventional Armed Forces in Europe of 19 November 1990, hereinafter referred to as the Treaty,

Having met in Istanbul from 17 to 19 November 1999,

Guided by Section III of the Final Document of the First Conference to Review the Operation of the Treaty on Conventional Armed Forces in Europe and the Concluding Act of the Negotiation on Personnel Strength, of May 1996,

Guided by the Document on the Scope and Parameters of the Process Commissioned in Paragraph 19 of the Final Document of the First CFE Treaty Review Conference adopted in Lisbon on 1 December 1996,

Taking into account the Decision of the Joint Consultative Group No. 8/97 of 23 July 1997, concerning Certain Basic Elements for Treaty Adaptation,

Recalling their commitment at the OSCE Oslo Ministerial Meeting in December 1998 to complete the process of adaptation of the Treaty by the time of the OSCE Summit in 1999,

Taking into account the Decision of the Joint Consultative Group No. 3/99 of 30 March 1999,

Recalling the Decision of the Joint Consultative Group No. 8/99 of 11 November 1999 on the Agreement on Adaptation of the Treaty on Conventional Armed Forces in Europe, hereinafter referred to as the Agreement on Adaptation,

Have taken note of the Statement on Adaptation of the Treaty on Conventional Armed Forces in Europe issued by the North Atlantic Council and the Representatives of the Czech Republic, the Republic of Hungary and the Republic of Poland at the Ministerial Meeting held in Brussels on 8 December 1998, and have taken note of the commitments contained therein;

Have taken note of the statement by the Russian Federation, which is attached to this Final Act, concerning its commitments on restraint and the use of Treaty flexibilities in the region which includes the Kaliningrad oblast and the Pskov oblast;

Have noted with appreciation that in the course of the adaptation negotiations several States Parties have committed themselves to reducing their permitted levels of armaments and equipment limited by the Treaty, thus reflecting the fundamental changes in the European security environment since the signing of the Treaty in November 1990;

Have further taken note of the statements

by the Czech Republic, the Republic of Hungary, the Republic of Poland and the Slovak Republic, which are attached to this Final Act, concerning their commitments regarding the future adjustment of their territorial ceilings, and the relevant conditions;

Have taken note of the statements by the Republic of Belarus, the Czech Republic, the Federal Republic of Germany, the Republic of Hungary, the Republic of Poland, the Slovak Republic and Ukraine, which are attached to this Final Act, concerning their commitments regarding their future use of the provisions on increasing territorial ceilings set forth in the Agreement on Adaptation, and the relevant conditions;

Have undertaken to move forward expeditiously to facilitate completion of national ratification procedures, so that the Agreement on Adaptation can enter into force as soon as possible, taking into account their common commitment to, and the central importance of, full and continued implementation of the Treaty and its associated documents until and following entry into force of the Agreement on Adaptation; and, in this context, have taken note of the statement by the Government of the Russian Federation on 1 November 1999, including its commitment, contained therein, to all obligations under the Treaty and, in particular, to agreed levels of armaments and equipment;

Have welcomed the joint statement by Georgia and the Russian Federation of 17 November 1999, which is attached to this Final Act;

Have taken note of the statement by the Republic of Moldova, which is attached to this Final Act, concerning its renunciation of the right to receive a temporary deployment on its territory and have welcomed the commitment of the Russian Federation to withdraw and/or destroy Russian conventional armaments and equipment limited by the Treaty by the end of 2001, in the context of its commitment referred to in paragraph 19 of the Istanbul Summit Declaration;

Have expressed their intention to review the above elements, as appropriate, at the Second Conference to Review the Operation of the Treaty, which will take place in May 2001;

Have noted that, following entry into force of the Agreement on Adaptation, other participating States of the Organization for Security and Co-operation in Europe with territory in the geographic area between the Atlantic Ocean and the Ural Mountains will have the possibility to apply for accession to the Treaty;

Have noted that a consolidated version of the Treaty as amended by the Agreement on Adaptation is being produced for information and to facilitate implementation;

Have adopted this Final Act at the time of signature of the Agreement on Adaptation.

This Final Act, in all six official languages of the Treaty, shall be deposited with the Government of the Kingdom of the Netherlands, as the designated Depositary for the Treaty, which shall circulate copies of this Final Act to all States Parties.

Annex 1

Statement on behalf of the Czech Republic
Upon the signature of the Agreement on Adaptation of the CFE Treaty the Czech Republic establishes its territorial and national ceiling at the level of its currently notified maximum national levels for holdings.

The Czech Republic will reduce its territorial ceiling in all three ground categories of TLE by conversion of its DPSS entitlements not later than by the year 2002. This means that the Czech territorial and national ceiling will then be:
- battle tanks   795
- armoured combat vehicles   1,252
- artillery pieces   657

The reduced TC and NC in the three ground categories of TLE, will only take effect upon successful and satisfactory conclusion of the adaptation process. In deciding to exercise the above unilateral restraint, the Czech Republic reserves the right to receive on its territory exceptional temporary deployments up to 459 battle tanks, 723 armoured combat vehicles and 420 artillery pieces in excess of the country's territorial ceiling.

Annex 2

Statement on behalf of the Republic of Hungary
Upon signature of the Agreement on Adaptation of the Treaty on Conventional Armed Forces in Europe, the Republic of Hungary intends to establish its national and territorial ceiling at the level of its present Maximum National Levels for Holdings.

However, in the current and foreseeable

security environment, defence plans of the country make possible significant reductions in Treaty-Limited Equipment. The Republic of Hungary is ready to reduce its territorial ceiling in the three ground categories of TLE by conversion of the country's DPSS entitlements by no later than the end of the year 2002. This means that the Hungarian national and territorial ceiling will be at that time:

– battle tanks 710
– armoured combat vehicles 1,560
– artillery pieces 750

The reduced Hungarian NC and TC will take effect only upon successful and satisfactory conclusion of the adaptation process. In undertaking the above unilateral restraint, the Republic of Hungary reserves the right to receive on its territory exceptional temporary deployments up to 459 battle tanks, 723 armoured combat vehicles and 420 artillery pieces in excess of the country's territorial ceiling.

Annex 3

Statement on behalf of the Republic of Poland
The Republic of Poland commits herself politically to the following:

At signature of the adapted CFE Treaty, Polish territorial ceilings equal our currently notified maximum national levels for holdings.

In light of the on-going restructurization of the Polish armed forces, Polish actual holdings in the Treaty-limited ground categories of armament and equipment not later than the end of 2001 will not exceed:

– battle tanks 1,577
– armoured combat vehicles 1,780

and not later than the end of 2002 will not exceed:

– artillery pieces 1,370

Subject to reciprocal good will and restraint in the immediate neighbourhood of Poland, Polish territorial ceilings not later than the end of 2003 will be adjusted to match the above numbers for actual holdings, through the partial conversion of the DPSS, in accordance with the mechanisms envisaged in the adapted CFE Treaty.

It is understood that during this period of time, Poland in accordance with her immediate and full access to Exceptional Temporary Deployments rights may host on its territory up to:

– battle tanks 459
– armoured combat vehicles 723
– artillery pieces 430

Annex 4

Statement on behalf of the Slovak Republic
Upon the signature of the Agreement on Adaptation of the Treaty on Conventional Armed Forces in Europe the Slovak Republic establishes its Territorial and National Ceilings at the level of its currently notified Maximum National Levels for Holdings.

The Slovak Republic undertakes a political commitment to reduce its territorial ceiling in the ground categories of the armament and equipment limited by the Treaty on Conventional Armed Forces in Europe, through the partial conversion of the Designated Permanent Storage Site entitlements, in accordance with the mechanism provided for in the adapted Treaty on Conventional Armed Forces in Europe. Not later than by the end of the year 2003, the Territorial Ceiling of the Slovak Republic will be:

– battle tanks 323
– armoured combat vehicles 643
– artillery pieces 383

The Slovak Republic reserves the right to host on its territory Temporary Deployments in excess of the Territorial Ceiling established in the Protocol on Territorial Ceilings up to 459 battle tanks, 723 armoured combat vehicles and 420 artillery pieces.

Annex 5

Statement on behalf of the Russian Federation
In the context of the political commitments and efforts of other States Parties to the Treaty on Conventional Armed Forces in Europe (CFE Treaty), in particular those aimed at further strengthening stability in Central Europe, the Russian Federation will show due restraint with regard to ground TLE levels and deployments in the region which includes the Kaliningrad oblast and the Pskov oblast. In the present politico-military situation, it has no reasons, plans or intentions to station substantial additional combat forces, whether air or ground forces, in that region on a permanent basis.

If necessary, the Russian Federation will rely on the possibilities for operational reinforcement, including temporary deployments, in a manner compatible with the CFE Treaty mechanisms.

Annex 6

Statement on behalf of the Republic of Belarus
The Republic of Belarus undertakes the following political commitments:

Taking into account the statements of other States Parties with regard to the reduction of their territorial ceilings (TCs), the Republic of Belarus will be prepared, upon signing of the adapted CFE Treaty, to make its national ceilings (NCs) equal to the existing maximum national levels for holdings (MNLHs) of Treaty-limited conventional armaments and equipment (TLE).

The TCs of the Republic of Belarus for ground categories of TLE will thus be equal to its NCs.

In addition, in current and foreseeable security circumstances and in the context of similar restraint by other States Parties, including those in the immediate vicinity of its borders, the Republic of Belarus will not make use of the general mechanism foreseen in the adapted Treaty for upward revision of its TCs.

Annex 7

Statement on behalf of the Czech Republic
In the current and foreseeable security circumstances, and in the context of comparable commitments by other States Parties, the Czech Republic undertakes not to make use of the general mechanisms of the adapted CFE Treaty for upward revision of the territorial ceilings.

Annex 8

Statement on behalf of the Federal Republic of Germany
Mr. Chairman,
Under the agenda item 'Statements on unilateral political commitments' I am authorized on behalf of the Federal Republic of Germany to state the following:

The Federal Republic of Germany commits itself, in the current and foreseeable security circumstances and in the context of comparable commitments by other States Parties, not to make use of the general mechanisms provided for in an adapted CFE Treaty for upward revision of territorial ceilings.

Annex 9

Statement on behalf of the Republic of Hungary
The Republic of Hungary declares that, in the current and foreseeable security circumstances and in the context of comparable commitments by other States Parties, the Republic of Hungary undertakes not to make use of the general mechanism provided in the adapted CFE Treaty for upward revision of territorial ceilings.

Annex 10

Statement on behalf of the Republic of Poland
The Republic of Poland commits herself politically to the following:

Under current and foreseeable security circumstances and depending on reciprocal measures of restraint in her immediate vicinity, including, in particular, the Russian Federation with regard to its current force levels in Kaliningrad, and Belarus with regard to its territorial ceilings at least not exceeding current MNLHs, Poland will not make use of her right for upward revision of her both current and future territorial ceilings, as envisaged in the adapted CFE Treaty.

Annex 11

Statement on behalf of the Slovak Republic
In the current and foreseeable security circumstances and in the context of similar restraints by other States Parties, the Slovak Republic undertakes a political commitment not to make use of general mechanism provided for in the adapted Treaty on Conventional Armed Forces in Europe for upward revision of Territorial Ceilings.

Annex 12

Statement on behalf of Ukraine
Ukraine commits itself, in the current and foreseeable security circumstances and in the context of comparable commitments by other States Parties, not to make use of the general mechanism provided for in the adapted CFE Treaty for upward revision of territorial ceilings.

Annex 13

Statement on behalf of the Republic of Moldova
The Republic of Moldova renounces the right to receive a temporary deployment on its territory due to its Constitutional provisions which control and prohibit any presence of foreign military forces on the territory of Moldova.

Annex 14

Joint Statement of the Russian Federation and Georgia
Istanbul, 17 November 1999
The Russian Federation and Georgia, guided by paragraphs 14.2.3 and 14.2.7 of the Decision of the Joint Consultative Group of 30 March 1999 concerning adaptation of the CFE Treaty,

confirming their intention to properly implement the adapted CFE Treaty as adopted,

wishing to promote the development and strengthening of co-operative relations between the Russian Federation and Georgia, have agreed as follows.

1. The Russian Side undertakes to reduce, by no later than 31 December 2000, the levels of its TLE located within the territory of Georgia in such a way that they will not exceed 153 tanks, 241 ACVs and 140 artillery systems.

2. No later than 31 December 2000, the Russian Side will withdraw (dispose of) the TLE located at the Russian military bases at Vaziani and Gudauta and at the repair facilities in Tbilisi.

The Russian military bases at Gudauta and Vaziani will be disbanded and withdrawn by 1 July 2001.

The issue of the utilization, including the joint utilization, of the military facilities and infrastructure of the disbanded Russian military bases remaining at those locations will be resolved within the same time-frame.

3. The Georgian Side undertakes to grant to the Russian Side the right to basic temporary deployment of its TLE at facilities of the Russian military bases at Batumi and Akhalkalaki.

4. The Georgian Side will facilitate the creation of the conditions necessary for reducing and withdrawing the Russian forces. In this connection, the two Sides note the readiness of OSCE participating States to provide financial support for this process.

5. During the year 2000 the two Sides will complete negotiations regarding the duration and modalities of the functioning of the Russian military bases at Batumi and Akhalkalaki and the Russian military facilities within the territory of Georgia.

Source: OSCE document CFE.DOC/2/99, 19 Nov. 1999, URL <http://www.osce.org/docs/english/1990-1999/cfe/cfefinact99e.htm>

11. Responses to proliferation: the North Korean ballistic missile programme

IAN ANTHONY

I. Introduction

Many governments believe that the spread of ballistic missiles to states and regions where they did not previously exist poses a serious threat to international security. However, there are no strong legal or political norms against the development and production of ballistic missiles. Governments concerned by the implications of missile proliferation must decide how to respond to the development of capabilities that are not illegal. Under these conditions defining a practical response to ballistic missile proliferation has become a difficult and pressing problem for a significant number of governments.

Developments on the Korean peninsula in the 1990s have provided one example of how different types of response—legal, political and military—have been combined in an effort to manage the emergence of a new missile force in the Democratic People's Republic of Korea (North Korea).[1]

In spite of the absence of legal and political norms that focus explicitly on ballistic missile delivery systems, the impact of missile proliferation can be discussed in relation to two other questions.[2]

First, it can be addressed in relation to the use of ballistic missiles to deliver weapons against which there are strong legal and political norms. These norms have been expressed in treaties to which many states have acceded. They are either treaties aimed specifically at the proliferation of weapons, such as the 1968 Treaty on the Non-Proliferation of Nuclear Weapons (Non-Proliferation Treaty, NPT), or comprehensive disarmament treaties, such as the 1972 Biological and Toxin Weapons Convention (BTWC) and the 1993 Chemical Weapons Convention (CWC).

Second, the nature of ballistic missiles can be argued to create a particular kind of security problem that merits attention. According to this argument, regional missile forces are likely to be part of a strategy of deterrence by punishment. Within regional force structures missiles are likely to be relatively

---

[1] In different locations the approaches taken by affected states and by the international community in general have been different. For a discussion of regional and international responses to missile and other forces in India, Iraq and Pakistan see Anthony, I. and French, E., 'Non-cooperative responses to proliferation: multilateral dimensions', *SIPRI Yearbook 1999: Armaments, Disarmament and International Security* (Oxford University Press: Oxford, 1999), pp. 667–91.

[2] Discussions of ballistic missile proliferation include Carus, W. S., *Ballistic Missiles in Modern Conflict*, Washington Paper 146 (Center for Strategic and International Studies: Washington, DC, 1991); Nolan, J. E., *Trappings of Power: Ballistic Missiles in the Third World* (Brookings Institution: Washington, DC, 1991); and Karp, A., SIPRI, *Ballistic Missile Proliferation: The Politics and Technics* (Oxford University Press: Oxford, 1996).

scarce. Unlike manned aircraft, missiles are not reusable; missiles can there-fore generate a limited number of missions. Initially, regional missile forces are also expected to be relatively inaccurate. Used with high-explosive war-heads, inaccurate missiles are unlikely to disrupt the military operations of an adversary. Even when armed with warheads containing biological weapons or chemical agent such missiles would have a limited direct impact on the mili-tary operations of an adversary.

For these reasons, missile forces may be concentrated on targets that are large, stationary and of high value to the society of the adversary. Centres of economic activity (such as ports and airfields) as well as population centres are considered likely targets.

The traditional response to threats of this kind has been to deploy counter-vailing capabilities to provide deterrence against the emerging threat. There may be a strong incentive for a state that feels itself threatened by an adversary missile force to develop a symmetrical capability. The incentive to try to elim-inate the risk posed by missiles by attacking them prior to launch may also be high for an adversary that feels itself likely to be subject to attack. This height-ens crisis instability by giving both sides in a confrontation an incentive to be the first to use their weapons.[3]

At present there is no effective defence against missile attacks other than pre-emption—although several countries are examining the feasibility of national and theatre missile defence systems. Moreover, the question of whether the further development of missile defences by Russia and the United States can be reconciled with their legal commitments under the 1972 Anti-Ballistic Missile (ABM) Treaty has emerged as a highly controversial and pol-itically charged issue.[4]

After the end of the cold war traditional responses based on deterrence and arms control have been supplemented by a political response that cannot be defined as arms control in the traditional meaning. This new arms control includes the application of sanctions and the offering of incentives that, taken together, are intended to change the behaviour of a proliferator. These meas-ures are not reciprocal, reflecting the asymmetric relationships between the parties involved.

The accelerated development of a family of long-range rocket engines by North Korea in the 1990s has had a significant impact on the threat percep-tions of countries in North-East Asia.[5] These rocket engines give North Korea the potential to develop medium-range or even intercontinental ballistic mis-siles. The rockets may also be used to place payloads (such as satellites) into

[3] The argument that ballistic and cruise missiles represent a particular kind of challenge is outlined in Roche, J., 'Proliferation of tactical aircraft and ballistic and cruise missiles in the developing world', ed. E. Arnett, *The Diffusion of Advanced Weaponry: Technologies, Regional Implications and Responses* (American Association for the Advancement of Science: Washington, DC, 1994).

[4] This issue is discussed in chapter 8 in this volume.

[5] In this chapter North-East Asia includes China (the People's Republic of China and the 'Republic of China' on Taiwan), Japan, the Democratic People's Republic of Korea (North Korea), the Republic of Korea (South Korea) and Russia. These definitions are based on Gill, B., 'North-East Asia and multi-lateral security institutions', *SIPRI Yearbook 1994* (Oxford University Press: Oxford, 1994), pp. 149–68.

space. International concern about the North Korean ballistic missile programme is linked to a residual suspicion that North Korea has a clandestine programme to assemble the material base, production technology and know-how needed to make a nuclear weapon.

In 1985 North Korea joined the NPT. In the context of NPT participation, North Korea committed itself not to develop a nuclear weapon and concluded a bilateral full-scope safeguards agreement with the International Atomic Energy Agency (IAEA). On 1 April 1993 the IAEA Board of Governors reported that North Korea was in non-compliance with its safeguards obligations.[6]

North Korea's refusal to comply with its safeguards agreement, strong circumstantial evidence of an earlier nuclear weapon programme and the ongoing ballistic missile development programme create a serious challenge to regional security in North-East Asia. In response, several states—most notably Japan, the Republic of Korea (South Korea) and the United States—have had to consider what mix of diplomacy, deterrence and defence will best serve their national security interests.

While concerns about the direction of North Korean arms acquisition programmes are long-standing, the North Korean missile development programme has been the focus of much activity since 31 August 1998, when North Korea fired a Taepo Dong I three-stage rocket along a flight path that passed over Japan.[7] In 1999 efforts to freeze or roll back North Korean ballistic missile programmes were undertaken with new urgency.

II. The North Korean ballistic missile programme

As North Korea is a closed and secretive society authoritative information about the origins (including the motives and intentions of the leadership), scope and scale of its military programmes is in short supply.

One source that examines regional security from a North Korean perspective identifies five primary background elements for military programmes: (a) the increasing diplomatic isolation of North Korea as China and Russia have improved their relations with South Korea; (b) the loss of the strategic guarantee provided by the Soviet Union in conditions where the US–South Korean alliance remains in place; (c) a progressive deterioration in the conventional military balance between North Korea and South Korea; (d) a progressive deterioration in the balance of economic and technological factors that provides the basis for military power; and (e) a combination of domestic economic crisis and external pressure for greater openness and a market economy

[6] IAEA Board of Governors Resolution GOV/2645, 1 Apr. 1993. The effort to prevent North Korea from producing fissile materials that could form a core component of a nuclear weapon is undertaken in the 1994 Agreed Framework. The Agreed Framework is discussed in Kile, S., 'Nuclear arms control and non-proliferation', *SIPRI Yearbook 1999* (note 1), pp. 532–35. The developments in 1999 are discussed in chapter 8 in this volume.

[7] Madeiros, E., 'Report on the Second US–China Conference on Arms Control, Disarmament and Nonproliferation', Center for Nonproliferation Studies, Monterey Institute of International Studies, URL <http://cns.miis.edu/cns/projects/eanp/conf/uschina2/report.htm>.

that challenges the socialist system (and with it the position of the current government).[8]

Together, these elements have led North Korea to conclude that a long transition period will be needed before a reunification of Korea could be brought about on terms acceptable to North Korea. Under these conditions the strategy of North Korea has two main elements. First, there is the progressive exclusion of any possible Japanese influence over affairs on the Korean peninsula. Second, the strategy is designed to bring about a military environment on the Korean peninsula that eliminates nuclear, biological and chemical (NBC) weapons and removes the foreign (i.e., US) troop presence.[9]

Within this broad strategic framework the North Korean ballistic missile programme has both a political and a military rationale.

From a political perspective, the medium- and long-range missile programme provides an instrument with which North Korea can try to break the progressive isolation that has resulted from the changes in its relations with its former allies China and Russia. Some analysts believe that this political rationale provides the most important argument in favour of missile development in North Korea.[10]

Given the progressive decay of North Korean conventional armed forces, the ballistic missile programme also provides a bargaining chip that can be included in political discussions. In the absence of a missile programme (and related programmes for NBC weapons) there would be little for other states to discuss with North Korea apart from humanitarian assistance.

From a military perspective, the missile programme has been described as 'the bite of the cornered dog'. The modernization of South Korean air defences and the assistance rendered by the United States in surveillance and target acquisition mean that North Korea can have little confidence in the value of manned aircraft in any conflict.[11] Ballistic missiles represent the only delivery vehicle that North Korea could confidently expect to penetrate existing air defences.

Assuming that South Korean and/or US forces establish air superiority during a conflict, the vulnerability of missile launch sites to air attack suggests a strong incentive for North Korea to use its missile forces in the early stages of any conflict. Meanwhile, since missile forces are unlikely to be available in quantities large enough to disrupt the military operations of South Korean and US forces if armed with conventional warheads, they may be used in a

[8] Pae Sang Hak, 'The Democratic People's Republic of Korea', ed. E. Arnett, SIPRI, *Nuclear Weapons After the Comprehensive Test Ban: Implications for Modernization and Proliferation* (Oxford University Press: Oxford, 1997).

[9] North Korean approaches to arms control are discussed in Joo-Hong Nam, 'How much is enough? The politics of arms control in Korea', *Korean Journal of International Studies*, vol. 21, no. 2 (1990); and Man Won Jee, 'Controlling demand: insecurities, budgets and domestic political factors', *Korean Journal of International Studies*, vol. 24, no. 4 (1993), pp. 431–57.

[10] E.g., Stanley Foundation, *US Relations with North Korea: Prospects for Engagement*, Report of the Thirty-Ninth Strategy for Peace Conference, Warrenton, Va., 29–31 Oct. 1998, URL <http://www.stanleyfdn.org/CONFRPTS/USFP/SPC98/Nkorea98/report.html>.

[11] Although North Korea has a small number of modern MiG-29 and MiG-23 combat aircraft, most of its inventory is of earlier generations.

countervalue deterrence strategy armed with non-conventional warheads. If projections that North Korean missiles will soon be able to reach the US mainland prove to be correct, a countervalue strategy may also be applied to the United States as well as South Korea.

The South Korean characterization of the threat posed by North Korean missiles follows this line. According to a recent Ministry of National Defense White Paper:

North Korea's purpose in producing and stockpiling CB weapons and mid- and long-range guided missiles is not only that they conserve resources; they can also be used as a means of strategic threat and negotiation. They can also play a decisive role in military strategy and operations. In using these weapons to attack major cities and strategic targets simultaneously in the South, Pyongyang could maximize the military and psychological effects it has aimed for as well as devastate strategic targets.[12]

Missiles under development

Open source information about North Korean missile programmes comes mainly from Japan, South Korea and the United States. The data on these programmes in the public domain seem to be a mixture of observed information combined with estimates or projections used to fill gaps in knowledge. Observed information—such as measurements derived from the satellite image of a rocket—has been combined with assumptions about, for example, the weight of the payload, the nature of the fuel used and the efficiency of the rocket engine to produce an estimated firing range. As a result, different estimates can be produced for a given missile depending on the assumptions made.

Reflecting the lack of reliable information, the descriptions of the characteristics of North Korean missiles that are in the public domain have given different specifications for the same engine at different times. The names for North Korean missiles have been assigned to them by Western analysts.

The public information suggests that North Korea began its missile production and development programme in the early 1980s in cooperation with Egypt and Iran.[13] The initial focus was on production of the Scud-B missile (with a range of approximately 300 kilometres). In the late 1980s North Korea is believed to have initiated a new programme to extend the range of the Scud-B to 500–600 km. This missile was designated the Scud-C, which is believed to have entered production in 1991. Both the Scud-B and Scud-C are single-stage missiles. In 1993 another single-stage missile with an estimated range of 1000 km was tested. This missile was designated the Nodong I and may be in

[12] Republic of Korea, Ministry of National Defense, *White Paper, 1998*, URL <http://www.mnd.go.kr/mndweb/mnden/mnd/m_2index.htm>.

[13] Gerardi, G. J. and Plotts, J. A., 'An annotated chronology of DPRK missile trade and developments', *Nonproliferation Review*, vol. 2, no. 1 (fall 1994), pp. 65–98; and Wright, D., 'Will North Korea negotiate away its missiles?', *Breakthroughs: MIT Security Studies Program*, vol. 7 no. 1 (spring 1998), pp. 29–36. The Federation of American Scientists provides an overview of North Korean ballistic missile development at URL < http://www.fas.org/nuke/guide/dprk/missile/index.html>.

production—although sources differ on exactly when this production began and on its scale.[14] Subsequently, resources seem to have been provided to develop an additional engine with a longer range than that of the Nodong I.[15]

As an element of its missile development programme North Korea seems to be planning to test various combinations of these rocket engines. The range estimates for missiles partly reflect different assumptions about potential alternative configurations of the rocket stages that North Korea has developed. For example, range estimates could be altered depending on whether a missile combined two large rocket stages or one large rocket stage supplemented by several smaller rockets.

The identified missiles are the Taepo Dong I (which combines the Nodong I, Scud-C and a small third stage into a three-stage missile) and the Taepo Dong II (which is believed to combine two of the new long-range rocket stages into a two-stage missile).[16] The main significance of the Taepo Dong I test conducted in August 1998 was that it demonstrated a capacity to build multiple-stage missiles as opposed to the single-stage Scud and Nodong missiles. Successful stage separation had been considered to be one of the more difficult barriers to the development of long-range missiles by the developing countries.[17]

The Nodong I is believed to have a range of 1000–1300 km. The Taepo Dong I is believed to have a range of 1500–2000 km. The estimated range of the Taepo Dong II has been reported at 4000–6000 km. The North Korean Advisory Group (comprising nine members of the US Congress) produced a report in November 1999 that suggested a potential range of 10 000 km for the Taepo Dong II missile if it flew with a reduced payload or incorporated a smaller third stage.[18]

While pointing out its legal right to develop, produce and export missiles of any type, North Korea has claimed that its long-range rocket stages are space launch vehicles (SLVs). The stated purpose of the launch that took place in August 1998 was to place a satellite (the Kwangmyungsun or Bright Star I)

[14] *Defense of Japan, 1998*, White Paper of the Japan Defense Agency, June 1998, p. 43. In testimony to the Japanese Parliament Foreign Minister Masahiko Komura stated that North Korea has 10 Nodong I missiles ready for launch. 'Report: N. Korea deploys missiles', *Newsday*, 30 June 1999, URL <http://newsday.com/ap/rnmpin11.htm>. Other sources suggest that the Nodong I is being produced and tested in Iran under the name Shahab III and in Pakistan under the name Ghauri II. US Central Intelligence Agency, National Intelligence Council, *Foreign Missile Developments and the Ballistic Missile Threat to the United States Through 2015*, Sep. 1999, URL <http://www.cia.gov/cia/publications/nie/nie99msl.html>.

[15] Vick, C. P., *North Korea Special Weapons Guide: Taep'o-dong 2 (TD-2)*, Federation of American Scientists, URL <http://www.fas.org/nuke/guide/dprk/missile/td-2.htm>.

[16] National Intelligence Council (note 14). Some reports also refer to a missile designated Nodong II, which may be an additional missile type or may be an alternative designation for the Taepo Dong I.

[17] Karp (note 2), pp. 132–37. Other design and production problems that a country would need to solve in developing long-range ballistic missiles would be re-entry, guidance and control systems as well as warhead design.

[18] In this way a Taepo Dong II would be able to reach the west coast of the USA. *Does North Korea Pose a Greater Threat to US National Security Than It Did Five Years Ago?*, North Korea Advisory Group, Report to the Speaker presented on 29 Oct. 1999, reproduced in United States Information Service, 'Text: Congressional report on North Korean threat', *Washington File*, 3 Nov. 1999, URL <http://www.usia.gov/cgi-bin/washfile/display.pl?p=/products/washfile/topic/intrel&f=99110304.epo&t=/products/wasshfile/newsitem.shtml>.

into orbit. Moreover, the North Korean space programme is said to include two more Bright Star satellites—suggesting that at least two additional launches can be anticipated.[19]

North Korea claimed that the satellite was launched successfully and began transmitting as anticipated. However, South Korea and the USA have stated that no satellite can be found in the orbit where North Korea claims it has been placed and no transmissions have been intercepted on the frequency on which it is said to transmit.[20]

Analysis of telemetry from the rocket launch has subsequently led South Korea and the USA to conclude that the rocket launch was an attempt to launch a satellite but that the launch failed.[21]

III. Responses to North Korea's ballistic missile programme

At present there is no regional or subregional forum or organization able to address security issues in a comprehensive manner.[22] Responses to North Korea's ballistic missile programme can be divided into three types: actions by the United Nations, other multilateral political responses and unilateral actions by states.

The IAEA–North Korean safeguards agreement and the work of the IAEA to implement it provided the basis for UN Security Council intervention in the North Korean nuclear programme. In Resolution 825 the Security Council encouraged UN member states to facilitate a solution to the problem of North Korean safeguards non-compliance. In this way the United States could engage in a bilateral dialogue with North Korea that has been expanded to include the issue of ballistic missile proliferation while remaining within a multilateral framework created by Resolution 825.[23]

[19] Kim Ji-ho, 'North Korea brags epochal change on anniversary of missile launch', *Digital Korea Herald*, 2 Sep. 1999, URL <http://www.koreaherald.co.kr>.

[20] Lee Sung-yul, 'Missile or satellite, Seoul still worried', *Digital Korea Herald*, 10 Sep. 1998, URL <http://www.koreaherald.co.kr>; 'Missile or satellite?', *Korea Newsreview*, 12 Sep. 1998, pp. 4–5, 16; and Volkov, I., 'Beep beep or boom boom?', *Moskovskiye Novosti*, 14 Feb. 1999, in Foreign Broadcast Information Service, *Daily Report–Central Eurasia (FBIS-SOV)*, FBIS SOV-1999-0224, 26 Feb. 1999.

[21] Republic of Korea (note 12), p. 57.

[22] The Association of South-East Asian Nations (ASEAN) Regional Forum (ARF) has apparently played no direct role in addressing the issue of weapon proliferation on the Korean peninsula. North Korea has refused invitations to participate in the ARF. So far, the proposal of a North-East Asian sub-group within the ARF made by South Korea has not been adopted. ASEAN foreign ministers, meeting in Singapore in July 1999, issued a statement that pointed to the risk that missile testing and development could have 'serious consequences for stability in the Korean peninsula and the region'. Richardson, M., 'Forum in Asia raises the heat on North Korea over missiles', *International Herald Tribune*, 27 July 1999, p. 1. Lists of the members of ASEAN and ARF are given in the glossary in this volume.

[23] UN Security Council Resolution 825, 11 May 1993. North Korea is a party to the BTWC, under which 'weapons, equipment or means of delivery' designed to use biological or toxin weapons for hostile purposes are subject to a comprehensive disarmament obligation. North Korea is strongly suspected of having developed biological weapons. A state party could request assistance from the UN Security Council if it had been harmed, was likely to be harmed or was exposed to danger as a consequence of a North Korean violation of the BTWC. While this provision of the treaty has never been used, discussions are currently under way to try to develop a strengthened enforcement system for the BTWC. See also chapter 9 in this volume. The definition of a chemical weapon in the CWC includes delivery systems. However, although North Korea is strongly suspected of having chemical weapons, it has not signed the CWC.

654 NON-PROLIFERATION, ARMS CONTROL, DISARMAMENT, 1999

In practice, however, North Korean ballistic missile programmes have been addressed outside the framework of treaties by those states that feel most threatened by the emerging military capacities. The responses have been based on several elements: diplomacy, denying North Korea the material and technology base to develop missiles, deterrence, developing defensive systems and economic sanctions.

Multilateral political responses

Officials from China, North Korea, South Korea and the USA attend Four-Party Talks. These talks stem from a 1996 proposal put forward by the USA and South Korea and have been under way since 1997. Their objective is to bring a formal end to the hostilities of the Korean War and so help to bring 'lasting peace and stability to the Korean Peninsula and contribute greatly to the peace and stability of the entire region'.[24] These discussions do not directly address 'hard' security issues or arms control.

The United States, because of its system of military alliances, is accustomed to discussing issues of mutual concern with Japan and South Korea. Officials from Japan, South Korea and the USA meet regularly in a Trilateral Coordination and Oversight Group. At these meetings the United States can brief the other states on developments in the US–North Korean channel while all of the countries can inform about and coordinate their policies regarding North Korea. In addition, there are regular meetings at the political level between these three countries.[25] However, these countries do not pursue a harmonized strategy towards North Korea, and there are important differences between their respective national approaches.

Concern about the implications of North Korean weapon proliferation has stimulated a variety of less customary ad hoc contacts and discussions among countries in North-East Asia.

In August 1999 defence ministers from South Korea and China held their first ever talks with the specific intention of discussing security and stability on the Korean peninsula.[26] In June 1999 the South Korean Minister of Defense proposed closer cooperation between the armed forces of South Korea and Japan.[27] China and Japan have held regular bilateral discussions for a number of years, including on issues related to security. In July 1999 Japanese Prime Minister Keizo Obuchi and Minister for Foreign Affairs Masahiko Koumura met their Chinese counterparts in Beijing. The discussions included an

---

[24] Described at US State Department, 'Four-Party Talks on the Korean peninsula, 1997–98', URL <http://www.state.gov/www/regions/eap/korea_4party_talks_1997.html>.

[25] The foreign ministers met in Sep. 1998, after the North Korean rocket launch, and met again in Singapore on 27 July 1999. The heads of state and government met during the Auckland Asia–Pacific Economic Cooperation (APEC) leaders meeting in Sep. 1999.

[26] 'South Korea, China to hold first-ever defense ministers talks', *Inside China Today*, 19 Aug. 1999, URL <http://www.insidechina.com/features.php3?id=86461>.

[27] 'Defense Minister urges cooperation between ROK, Japan armed forces', *Digital Korea Herald*, 3 June 1999, URL <http://www.koreaherald.co.kr/t_news/1999/03/__01/19990306_0128.html>.

exchange of views on the Korean peninsula, with the question of possible additional missile tests by North Korea raised specifically.[28]

The Group of Eight (G8) heads of state and government discussed the question of how to respond to the development of ballistic missiles by North Korea at their summit meeting in Cologne in June 1999. While undertaking to examine 'further individual and collective means of addressing this problem', the summit meeting did not elaborate any specific strategy.[29]

National responses

The United States

The United States has been the primary actor seeking to address the negative consequences of North Korean weapon development and production programmes. Issues related to weapon proliferation are discussed by the USA and North Korea bilaterally rather than in the framework of the Four-Party Talks.

One important objective of the USA is to curtail North Korea's efforts to develop, deploy and sell long-range missiles. The United States has mixed coercive and cooperative elements in an effort to achieve this objective. It has made clear to North Korea that normalization of relations and a peace agreement cannot be concluded without resolving the question of North Korean nuclear and missile capabilities.[30]

Since 1996 North Korea and the USA have discussed both 'vertical' ballistic missile proliferation (i.e., the development of missiles by North Korea) and 'horizontal' proliferation (i.e., the transfer of missiles or related technologies to other countries by North Korea).

In September 1999 North Korea and the USA reached an agreement by which North Korea would suspend the development and testing of its long-range ballistic missile programme. The agreement, which is not public, is discussed below.

In exchange for the suspension the United States agreed to ease unilateral sanctions maintained against North Korea in the framework of US national law—specifically, the Trading with the Enemy Act (TEA) of 1917. The USA and North Korea are technically still at war and under the TEA the US president may, during time of war, investigate, regulate or prohibit a wide range of financial transactions.[31] Under this authority an embargo was established in 1950 on financial transactions between North Korea and any US citizen or permanent resident, wherever they live in the world, all people and organiza-

---

[28] Ministry of Foreign Affairs of Japan, 'Results of the visit to the People's Republic of China and Mongolia by Prime Minister Keizo Obuchi', Press Conference by the Press Secretary, 13 July 1999, URL <http://www.mofa.go.jp/announce/press/1999/7/713.html#2>.

[29] 'G8 Communiqué Köln 1999: Final', 20 June 1999. Documentation on the G8 is available at G8 Information Centre, University of Toronto, Canada, URL <http://www.g7.utoronto.ca/>. A list of the G8 members is given in the glossary in this volume.

[30] Lee Hun-kyung, 'Inter-Korean relations in aftermath of Perry Report', *Korea Focus*, vol. 7, no. 4 (July/Aug. 1999).

[31] United States Code Title 50. War and National Defense, Trading With The Enemy Act of 1917, Act 6 Oct. 1917, ch. 106, 40 stat. 411.

tions physically located in the USA and all branches, subsidiaries and controlled affiliates of any US organization throughout the world.[32]

The United States maintained comprehensive sanctions against North Korea from 1950 to 1989, when a ban against academic, cultural and sporting contacts was relaxed. Sanctions were modified in 1989 to permit the transfer of US humanitarian assistance to North Korea. In 1994 there was a further easing of sanctions to permit the implementation of the 1994 US–North Korean Agreed Framework.[33]

In September 1999 the sanctions regime was modified again to remove the ban on exports and imports of US and North Korean consumer goods and to ease restrictions on US investment in North Korea. In addition, direct and personal commercial transactions between US and North Korean legal persons (including companies) were permitted and US commercial carriers were no longer prohibited from calling at North Korean ports and airports under the TEA.[34]

The decision to ease sanctions was taken in the overall context of the comprehensive review of US policy towards North Korea that was completed in 1999.[35] This review, undertaken by former Secretary of Defense William J. Perry at the request of the president, concluded that there was a need to revise the US approach towards North Korea. Having concluded that the status quo was not acceptable from the US perspective, the review evaluated alternative approaches to managing bilateral relations with North Korea.

The Perry Report recommended against undermining the Government of North Korea and determined that accelerated democratic reform in North Korea was desirable but unlikely in the short term. In discussions with Perry and his team North Korea offered to cease missile exports in exchange for compensation for earnings that could have been anticipated from missile sales. The report recommended against 'buying' changes in North Korean policy as this path was felt to create an incentive for North Korea to engage in provocative behaviour in pursuit of financial rewards.

The main recommendation of the report was that 'the U.S. should be prepared to establish more normal diplomatic relations with the DPRK and join in the ROK's policy of engagement and peaceful coexistence'. The United States would maintain its existing policy of deterrence and the existing size and structure of forces in the region and on the Korean peninsula.

The practical effect of easing sanctions under the TEA is mitigated by the fact that North Korea is subject to several US laws with overlapping authority.

[32] Office of Foreign Assets Control, *An Overview of the Foreign Assets Control Regulations as they Relate to North Korea: Title 31 Part 500 of the US Code of Federal Regulations* (US Department of the Treasury: Washington, DC, 23 Feb. 1999).

[33] Agreed Framework of 21 October 1994 between the United States of America and the Democratic People's Republic of Korea, IAEA document INFCIRC/457, 2 Nov. 1994.

[34] US State Department, 'Further easing of sanctions against North Korea', *Fact Sheet*, 17 Sep. 1999, URL <http://www.state.gov/www/regions/eap/fs-nkorea_sancs_990917.html>.

[35] 'Review of United States policy toward North Korea: findings and recommendations', Unclassified Report by Dr William J. Perry, US North Korea Policy Coordinator and Special Advisor to the President and the Secretary of State, Washington, DC, 12 Oct. 1999, URL <http://www.state.gov/www/regions/eap/991012_northkorea_rpt.html>.

Many transactions no longer prohibited under the TEA after September 1999 remained prohibited by other US legislation. In particular, US laws related to terrorism and missile proliferation have a bearing on North Korea. The Antiterrorism and Effective Death Penalty Act of 1996 prohibits all financial transactions by US legal persons with any state designated a terrorism-supporting nation in the 1979 Export Administration Act (a list that includes North Korea).[36]

Although the Perry Report recommended changes in US policy, the responsibility for translating this recommendation into specific decisions rested primarily with the State Department. While Perry was given to understand that a change in US policy would lead to the suspension of missile testing, his report also recommended against a policy of offering direct economic incentives.

The US decision to ease sanctions was made after a meeting between officials in Berlin on 7–12 September 1999. It is not clear from public reports exactly what was said at this meeting, but it appears that North Korea agreed to suspend missile launches while US–North Korean normalization talks are under way.[37]

It is also not clear whether a direct link was made between the suspension of missile launches and the modification of US sanctions that was announced shortly afterwards or whether these developments should be seen as indirectly linked—part of the overall progress towards normalization.

US Secretary of State Madeleine Albright and Perry addressed the issue of North Korean missile development in a joint press briefing shortly after the Berlin meeting. Albright described the outcome of the agreement as 'the first positive step towards the suspension of testing'. Perry referred to 'an agreement for suspension of testing'.[38]

US National Security Adviser Sandy Berger stated that the agreement was for 'a temporary ban' on North Korea's missile programme while talks continue about a permanent end to the programme.[39] Berger presented the agreement as part of a process of normalization of relations between North Korea, and Japan, South Korea and the USA.

After being briefed on the outcome of the talks Japanese Prime Minister Keizo Obuchi suggested that North Korea had not made precise commitments related to a particular missile type or range or a particular type of activity. Instead, a commitment had been made not to take actions that would interfere

---

[36] Department of the Treasury, 'Testimony of Richard Newcomb, Director, Treasury Office of Foreign Assets Control before the House of Representatives Judiciary Sub-Committee on Crime', Press Release, no. RR-1742 (10 June 1997), URL <http://www.treas.gov/press/release/pr1742.htm>.

[37] Ministry of Foreign Affairs of Japan, 'Press Conference by the Press Secretary, 28 Sep. 1999', URL <http://www.mofa.go.jp/announce/press/1999/9/928.html>.

[38] US State Department, Secretary of State Madeleine K. Albright and Dr William Perry, 'Press briefing on US relations with North Korea', Washington, DC, 17 Sep. 1999, URL <http://secretary.state.gov/www/statements/1999/990917a.html>.

[39] Reuters, 'Berger says US gave little to Korea for missile ban', 20 Sep. 1999, URL <http://www.cnn.com>. The Sep. Berlin meeting was one of the regular series of meetings between US officials and officials from North Korea. The US delegation was led by Ambassador Charles Kartman, who is the Special Envoy for the Korean Peace Talks as well as the US representative to the Korean Peninsula Energy Development Organization (KEDO).

with the positive atmosphere in US–North Korean talks. Obuchi described this as 'a step toward North Korea freezing a missile launch' not 'as a sign that the North has abandoned a launch completely'.[40]

This ambiguity led to some criticism of the agreement. First, it was unclear, perhaps even in Pyongyang, what kinds of space research North Korea could undertake without being considered by the United States to be in breach of its undertaking.[41] As noted above, the logic of the North Korean space programme as described in official statements would suggest that additional rocket launches are likely. Second, how would the USA and other concerned countries respond in the event of additional rocket launches presented as satellite launch attempts?[42]

In parallel with its diplomatic efforts to freeze and then roll back North Korean missile programmes, the United States has also continued to advocate the development of theatre missile defences (TMD) and exploration of the feasibility of a limited national missile defence (NMD) system.[43] Advocates of an NMD system for the USA tend to refer to the North Korean Taepo Dong II programme as the primary justification for the development of such a system.[44]

Japan

The deployment of the Nodong I missile from the mid-1990s already placed targets in Japan within reach of North Korean missiles. However, when North Korea launched a longer range multiple-stage Taepo Dong I missile over Japan in August 1998 without prior warning, the reaction was severe. The Japanese Government had earlier made an official communication to North Korea that a missile test with a range that could reach targets in Japan would have a serious negative impact on their bilateral relations. Although the rocket landed in international waters, the fact that an explicit statement had been ignored contributed to the shock expressed by the Japanese Government that a

[40] Holland, S., 'N. Korea appears to agree to missile freeze', Reuters, 13 Sep. 1999, URL <http://dailynews.yahoo.com/h/nm/19990913/ts/korea_usa_4.html>.

[41] Gertz, B., 'North Korea continues to develop missiles', *Washington Times* (Internet edn), 28 Oct. 1999, URL <http://www.washtimes.com/investiga/investiga1.html>. Some also criticized the overall approach of economic incentives to modify North Korean behaviour. The former head of the State Department office responsible for counter-terrorism observed: 'they threaten us and we keep paying them off'. Associated Press, 'Easing of sanctions against North Korea called extortion', 19 Sep. 1999, URL <http://www.spokane.net/stories/1999/Sep/19/S636713.asp>.

[42] US officials have not specified the steps that they would take in the event of a resumption of testing. US Secretary of Defense William Cohen has referred to the 'serious implications' such a step would entail. Whitesides, J., 'Cohen: N. Korea missile to have serious implications', Reuters, Yahoo News, 26 July 1999, URL <http://dailynews.yahoo.com/headlines/ts/story.html?s=v/nm/19990726/ts>.

[43] The background to the US debate on missile defence is described in Arnett, E., 'Military research and development', *SIPRI Yearbook 1998: Armaments, Disarmament and International Security* (Oxford University Press: Oxford, 1998), pp. 275–88. For additional information on recent developments in the US debate see chapter 8 in this volume.

[44] E.g., the presentation of Senator Thad Cochran to the Twelfth Multinational Conference on Theater Missile Defense, Edinburgh, Scotland, 1 June 1999, reproduced as 'Responding to an escalating threat', *Comparative Strategy*, vol. 18, no. 4 (1999). Cochran was the sponsor of the National Missile Defense Act that was approved by the Congress in May 1999 and subsequently signed into law by President Bill Clinton.

launch would be conducted without prior notice into an area where commercial shipping and aircraft were operating.[45]

The reactions outlined by Japanese officials stressed diplomatic responses to the launch as well as certain measures that could be considered sanctions.[46] Although Japan had already suspended both normalization talks and humanitarian assistance to North Korea before August 1998, it was announced that possible modifications to these policies would be postponed. In addition, Japanese members of the Korean Peninsula Energy Development Organization (KEDO) suspended their participation in the organization, effectively suspending its activities.[47]

The suspension of Japanese support for KEDO seemed to threaten the implementation of the 1994 US–North Korean Agreed Framework, intended to eliminate the risk that North Korea would develop and deploy nuclear weapons. The collapse of the Agreed Framework would in turn increase the risk of a crisis involving North Korea and the United States.[48]

Public reaction in Japanese newspapers and from some parliamentarians made reference to military responses, including the need for Japan to develop an effective independent deterrent to a North Korean missile attack.[49]

Japan has consistently referred to the August 1998 launch of the Taepo Dong I missile as a missile test, rejecting the idea that it might have been the launch of an SLV. The presence of North Korean fishing boats in the area where the missile landed was considered to undermine North Korea's assertion that the rocket firing was a satellite launch as these boats were assumed to be equipped with instruments to monitor the test.[50]

Although aware in general terms that a launch was being prepared, Japan did not have the technical means to monitor North Korean launch sites. The USA provided Japan with information about the time, date and trajectory of the missile launch.[51]

Japanese officials referred to the need to continue technical studies of a ballistic missile defence (BMD) system, to expedite the development of a

[45] Ministry of Foreign Affairs of Japan, 'Comment by Chief Cabinet Secretary Hiromu Nonaka on North Korea's test missile launch', 31 Aug. 1998, URL <http://www.mofa.go.jp/announce/announce/1998/8/831.htm>. The rocket launch was one of several events that led to deteriorating relations between Japan and North Korea. Others included incursions by North Korean ships into Japanese territorial waters and flights by North Korean combat aircraft close to Japanese airspace.
[46] The Japanese Defense Agency apparently stated that if a North Korean missile attack on Japan were known to be imminent, there was no legal barrier to a pre-emptive attack on the launch facility. Agence France Presse, 'North Korea warns of "thousand-fold retaliation"', 9 Mar. 1999, URL <http://www.defense-aerospace.com/afp/defense/990309054207.4zq83omd.html>.
[47] Ministry of Foreign Affairs of Japan, 'Announcement by the Chief Cabinet Secretary on Japan's immediate response to North Korea's missile launch', 1 Sep. 1998, URL <http://www.mofa.go.jp/announce/announce/1998/9/901-2.html>.
[48] In 1994 the USA began to prepare for a military operation on the Korean peninsula prior to the negotiation of the Agreed Framework.
[49] A summary of public Japanese responses is contained in United States Information Agency, 'North Korea's missile test: foreign media reaction', Daily Digest, Washington, DC, 3 Sep. 1998.
[50] Ministry of Foreign Affairs of Japan, 'Press conference by the Press Secretary', 4 Sep. 1999, URL <http://www.mofa.go.jp/announce/press/1998/9/904.htm>.
[51] Ministry of Foreign Affairs of Japan, 'Press conference by the Press Secretary', 1 Sep. 1998, URL <http://www.mofa.go.jp/announce/press/1998/9/901.html>.

Japanese satellite surveillance capability and to explore the use of non-military satellite images by government agencies.[52] In March 1999 the Japanese Government diverted 960 million yen from the defence budget into a fund to support participation in BMD research along with partners in the USA. In August 1999 Japan and the United States agreed the programme outline for cooperative research on ballistic missile technologies.[53] The Japan Defense Agency earmarked 11.3 billion yen in 1999 to develop a military satellite that is planned to be launched in 2002.[54]

In 1999 Japanese officials continued to discuss North Korea's missile programmes with counterparts in South Korea and the USA.

In November 1999 the Japanese Government restored civil charter flights to Pyongyang that had been suspended after the missile launch in August 1998—citing the risk to civil aviation from unannounced launches.[55] In December 1999, in the light of the statements made by North Korea about the suspension of missile launch activities during the US–North Korean talks, the Japanese Government decided to consider the question of whether normalization talks and humanitarian assistance, including food aid, would be restored with North Korea.[56]

South Korea

The North Korean long-range ballistic missile development programme does not add to the defence dilemma of South Korea directly. North Korea has produced Scud-C missiles with a range sufficient to reach targets throughout South Korea since the early 1990s.

In 1999 the possibility that North Korea was continuing to develop facilities that could contribute to a covert nuclear weapon programme in spite of the Agreed Framework was of greater concern in South Korea than the development of additional ballistic missile delivery systems.[57] However, external responses to the North Korean missile programmes are of concern to South Korea because they have the potential to disturb current policy initiatives supported by Seoul and to complicate relations between Japan, South Korea and the USA. Therefore, ballistic missile proliferation and how to respond to it are

---

[52] Ministry of Foreign Affairs of Japan (note 47).

[53] Ministry of Foreign Affairs of Japan, 'Exchange of notes concerning a program for cooperative research on ballistic missile technologies based on the Mutual Defense Assistance Agreement between Japan and the United States of America', Press Release, 16 Aug. 1999, URL <http://www.infojapan. org/announce/announce/1999/8/816.html>.

[54] Jun Kwan-woo, 'Pyongyang inadvertently helps Tokyo's military build-up', *Digital Korea Herald*, 3 Apr. 1999, URL <http://www.koreaherald.co.kr>.

[55] Ministry of Foreign Affairs of Japan, 'Announcement by Chief Cabinet Secretary Mikio Aoki on the resumption of chartered flights between Japan and North Korea', 2 Nov. 1999, URL <http://www. mofa.go.jp/announce/announce/1999/11/1102-2.html>.

[56] Ministry of Foreign Affairs of Japan, 'Announcement by Chief Cabinet Secretary Mikio Aoki on policies vis-à-vis North Korea', 14 Dec. 1999, URL <http://www.mofa.go.jp/announce/announce/1999/ 12/1214.html>.

[57] Suspicions about continued covert North Korean nuclear weapon development activity in 1999 are discussed in chapter 8 in this volume.

both controversial and important in the internal political process in South Korea.

South Korea has supported the diplomatic initiatives of the USA that are themselves to a degree stimulated by the 'sunshine policy' of the government of President Kim Dae-Jung.[58] The logic of the sunshine policy is that engagement of North Korea based on non-interference in domestic political affairs and economic assistance will, over time, produce greater benefits than a policy of confrontation.[59] While South Korea has invested in modernizing its air defences, it has not initiated an NMD programme. Nor has South Korea shown any interest in bilateral cooperation with the United States in the TMD area.[60]

In the interim, the policy of South Korea is based on deterrence by denial as well as diplomacy. Together with the active assistance of US forces stationed in South Korea the South Korean armed forces are tasked with defeating any military action that might be launched from North Korea. The modernization of the South Korean armed forces includes reductions in active service manpower and the introduction of advanced weapon systems.

In the 1990s an internal debate continued in South Korea about the utility of developing a ballistic missile that would give the option of responding in kind to a North Korean missile attack and so strengthen deterrence. At present South Korea is constrained by a bilateral agreement with the USA not to develop missiles with a range longer than 180 km.[61]

South Korea is already developing a significant lead in air power through modernization plans based on manned combat aircraft. The modernization of the South Korean Air Force, together with the difficulty that North Korea is experiencing with its own air defence modernization, is likely to provide South Korea with both air superiority and ground-attack options without a new missile programme. The United States has argued that a South Korean missile programme could stimulate further missile proliferation and introduce an irritant into relations with the USA without any meaningful gain in military capability. A missile force could also undermine public support for the current South Korean defence policy if it appeared that a strategy of denial was changing to a strategy based on punishment through countervalue strikes.

An element that is present in the discussion in China and South Korea is concern that Japanese reactions to North Korea's missile programme may undermine the foundations of regional security in North-East Asia.

---

[58] The basic elements of the programme are described in an article by the president: Kim Dae-Jung, 'Seeking to prevent a North Korean missile test', *International Herald Tribune*, 30 Aug. 1999. See also the discussion in the Republic of Korea, Ministry of National Defense, *White Paper, 1999*, URL <http://www.mnd.go.kr/mnden/sub_menu/w_book/1999/index.html>.

[59] A similar logic underpins the approach suggested in the Perry Report (note 35).

[60] 'Seoul reaffirms no plan to join US-led theater missile defense plan', *Digital Korea Herald*, 4 May 1999, URL <http://www.koreaherald.co.kr>; and 'Kim calls for military cooperation with Moscow', *Digital Korea Herald*, 6 Sep. 1999, URL <http://www.koreaherald.co.kr>.

[61] Originally, the 1979 bilateral agreement restricted the range of South Korean missiles to 180 km. South Korea and the USA have agreed in principle that South Korea may develop missiles with a range of up to 300 km, but this agreement has never been operationalized. President Kim Dae-Jung has asked the USA to revise the agreement to permit the development of missiles with a range of up to 500 km. Kim Tae-woo, 'The North's missile threat calls for reinforced defense capability', *Korea Focus*, vol. 7, no. 4 (July/Aug. 1999), pp. 105–108.

China

The security situation on the Korean peninsula has created a series of dilemmas for China, whose main interest is stability. The August 1998 North Korean missile test and the prospect of additional tests in 1999 had significant negative potential from a Chinese perspective.

A crisis between North Korea and the United States would raise the question of what steps China could be expected to take in the framework of its 1961 Treaty of Friendship, Cooperation and Mutual Assistance with North Korea.[62] Such a crisis could have a negative impact on US–Chinese relations.

China has supported the denuclearization of the Korean peninsula since the early 1990s, including the elimination of nuclear-weapon delivery systems.[63] The development by North Korea of missile systems with a long enough range to reach targets in Japan and, potentially, the USA stimulates the discussion and development of missile defence capabilities. Most Chinese analysts believe that the TMD systems under discussion in North-East Asia are in real-ity aimed at Chinese missile forces, with North Korean missile programmes providing no more than a pretext.[64]

The existence of programmes of concern in North Korea adds substance to the arguments advanced by the USA that missile defences are legitimate and necessary.[65] North Korean programmes have also created public pressure in Japan to proceed with wider defence modernization, including BMD cooper-ation, which China does not welcome.

Of particular concern to China is the possibility that these developments could converge to lead to the development of a US–Japanese TMD architec-ture that would be extended (albeit not explicitly) over the airspace of Taiwan. China has used ballistic missile test firings as one element of its overall policy aimed at bringing Taiwan under a single political authority.

At the same time, the recent developments have underlined that China has limited influence in North Korea. Apart from a general resistance to initiatives that can be interpreted as interference in the domestic affairs of other states, China has seen a reduction in bilateral trade with North Korea.[66]

China also has limited interest in multilateral engagement in conflict resolu-tion or arms control on the Korean peninsula. During the nuclear crisis of 1993–94 China saw a risk that multilateral engagement would provide an

[62] 'Chronological review, 1945–1998', *A Handbook on North Korea* (Naewoe Press: Seoul, 1998), p. 138.

[63] In addition, the domestic economic crisis in North Korea has contributed to a steady increase in cross-border refugees as well as an increase in smuggling. China has a stronger interest in economic development in North Korea than in diversion of resources into military programmes.

[64] Ding, A. S., 'China's attitude towards missile defense', Paper presented to the Sixteenth Sino-European Conference, Queens' College, Cambridge, 1–3 Sep. 1999.

[65] From a Chinese perspective the 'worst case' would be the extension of a TMD system to include the airspace over Taiwan. The Taiwanese Minister of Defence has identified missile defence as the first priority for future procurement. CNN Custom News, 'Defence Minister Tang talks about threat from China', 30 Aug. 1999, URL <http://www.cnn.com>.

[66] Bilateral trade is said to have declined by over 37% from 1997 to 1998 with a further decline of over 50% predicted for 1998 and 1999. CNN Custom News, 'Analysis: Chinese influence over North Korea wanes', 8 Mar. 1999, URL <http://www.cnn.com>.

additional legitimate legal basis for a long-term US regional military presence.[67]

The current arrangements, by which the United States takes the main responsibility for managing the security implications of North Korean ballistic missile development under the umbrella of a general authorization from the United Nations, are probably the best available from the Chinese perspective.

Russia

The revision of first Soviet and then Russian policy towards North Korea to a large extent created the conditions under which the North Korean leadership accelerated the ballistic missile programme.[68] In conditions where the Soviet Union offered a credible security guarantee and provided the material means for continuous force modernization, ballistic missiles played a much less central role in North Korean military planning.

After 1995 Russia indicated a willingness to enter into limited cooperation with North Korea. In August 1995 Russia offered North Korea a draft Treaty of Friendship to replace that of 1961, but without a clause on mutual military assistance.[69]

Although questions have periodically been raised about whether or not Russia, a participating state in the Missile Technology Control Regime (MTCR),[70] supports ballistic missile programmes in states such as Iran, there have been no public reports of Russian involvement in North Korean ballistic missile programmes.

Russian statements have underlined three elements of Russia's regional security policy. First, the statements emphasize the importance of normalization of relations on the Korean peninsula.

Second, Russia stresses the need for a broader security system in North-East Asia to replace the existing architecture based on alliances. Russian Minister of Defence Igor Sergeyev, while visiting South Korea in September 1999, noted the lack of political integration in North-East Asia and pointed out that alliances always cause concern in third states.[71]

Third, Russia has supported the good-faith participation of all states in existing arms control and disarmament treaties. In particular, Minister of Defence Sergeyev stressed the need to respect the provisions of the ABM Treaty. In

---

[67] The crisis is discussed in Kile (note 6).

[68] The evolving Soviet/Russian policy is described in Ivanov, V., 'Russia in Northeast Asia: is it making a comeback?', *Peace Forum* (Seoul), no. 25 (winter 1997/98); Ko Jae-nam, 'Russia's role in regional cooperation in Northeast Asia', *Korea Focus*, vol. 7, no. 4 (1999); and Fedorovsky, A. N., 'Russian policy and interests on the Korean peninsula', ed. G. Chufrin, SIPRI, *Russia and Asia–Pacific Security: Proceedings of the Conference on Russia and Asia–Pacific Security, Tokyo, 19–21 Feb. 1999* (Stockholm International Peace Research Institute: Solna, Sweden, Oct. 1999).

[69] The Treaty of Friendship was signed in Pyongyang on 9 Feb. 2000 and subsequently ratified in the Russian and North Korean parliaments on 9 and 12 Apr. 2000, respectively. Interfax, 12 Apr. 2000, in 'Moscow welcomes ratification of treaty with North Korea', FBIS-SOV-2000-0412, 13 Apr. 2000.

[70] The MTCR is discussed in appendix 11A in this volume.

[71] 'Stability in Northeast Asia meets Russia's interests: minister', ITAR-TASS, 2 Sep. 1999, reproduced at URL <http://www.cnn.com>.

addition, he supported the idea of developing 'a global system of control over non-proliferation of missiles and missile technologies'.

The European Union

France and the United Kingdom have been engaged in issues related to the non-compliance of North Korea with its IAEA safeguards agreement because of their status as UN Security Council permanent members. However, individual member states of the European Union (EU) have not been closely engaged in developments on the Korean peninsula. Ten of the 15 EU member states do not recognize North Korea and have no diplomatic links with it.

Following the August 1998 rocket launch from North Korea the EU Presidency issued a statement on behalf of the EU that expressed 'grave concern at this test which undermines the efforts to enhance peace and security on the Korean Peninsula' and called on North Korea 'to refrain from any further testing and to exercise utmost restraint in its missile development and export activities. The European Union urges North Korea to join international non-proliferation efforts'.[72]

The EU opened an informal political dialogue with North Korea in December 1998 by which officials from the EU troika have conducted meetings with officials from North Korea.[73] The EU has donated humanitarian aid (consisting of medical supplies and technical assistance in the agricultural sector) and the European Atomic Energy Community (Euratom) is part of KEDO.[74]

IV. Conclusions

The absence of a global legal and normative framework within which to address the perceived threat posed by the long-range ballistic missile programmes of North Korea did not mean that no remedial political action could be taken by concerned states. It is an open question whether the developments in 1999 have contributed to a political norm against ballistic missile proliferation.

Existing talks between North Korea and the USA taking place under the umbrella of a UN Security Council resolution were expanded in 1996 to include ballistic missile proliferation. This flexible approach mirrors that elsewhere in the post-cold war international system with the USA playing a leadership role, coordinating its policies with concerned states through informal arrangements.

---

[72] European Union, 'Common foreign and security policy (11/23)', *Bulletin EU*, no. 9-1998, URL <http://europa.eu.int/abc/doc/off/bull/en/9809/p103011.htm>.

[73] The troika consists of the state holding the presidency of the EU together with the immediate past president and the succeeding president. The political dialogue was initiated to demonstrate support for the Four-Party Talks and after consultation with South Korea. The EU has defined a new policy to govern relations with South Korea. European Union, Directorate of Trade, URL <http://europa.eu.int/comm/dg01/korea1a.htm>.

[74] The EU provides KEDO with ECU 15 million each year through Euratom (which is a member of the Executive Board of KEDO).

In spite of the fact that all of the major powers that have an active interest in developments on the Korean peninsula favour stability, it has not been possible to eliminate the risk that North Korea will acquire NBC weapons along with ballistic missile delivery systems.[75] While none of the approaches tried has succeeded completely in this regard, a temporary freeze on missile testing appears to have been achieved in September 1999.

In spite of their agreement on the overall objective of preventing further development and, if possible, rolling-back North Korean ballistic missile programmes, there are differences in emphasis among these major powers on the specific approach.

Only the United States strongly favours the development of defensive systems to counter a North Korean missile force. Japan has offered lukewarm support in the form of a limited financial commitment to the further development of advanced air defence systems (such as the shipborne AEGIS/Standard system) that were already under way. South Korea has not supported the development of defensive systems while China and Russia have strongly opposed this approach.

Only South Korea strongly favours the development of broadly symmetrical capabilities to counter North Korean missiles in kind. However, Japan already has a highly developed capacity to design and produce SLVs. This would provide a platform from which ballistic missiles could be developed should a political decision be taken to do so. Recently, Japan has heavily increased its investment in space programmes. China, Russia and the USA all oppose the development of new and additional regional missile forces.

Japan and South Korea have both indicated that they are interested in increasing their investment in airborne and space-based surveillance and monitoring systems. This would reduce the dependence on the United States for basic information about developments in North Korea. In Japan in particular the public shock at the unexpected and undetected North Korean missile launch in August 1998 has created a political momentum behind increased funding of an independent satellite surveillance capability.

None of the major powers in the region believes that the North Korean Government is likely to collapse or be replaced in the short term. In their general approach to managing political relations with North Korea, these powers have de-emphasized the role of sanctions and coercion. South Korea has adopted a policy of engagement and patient diplomacy that has been supported by the USA. Neither China nor Russia employs sanctions against North Korea— except in so far as both support the application of export controls to prevent transfers of missiles or missile-related technologies to North Korea. At the same time, the United States maintains a very strong, if no longer total, sanctions regime against North Korea. The recent US decisions offer the prospect of future relaxation but this is both reversible and highly conditional. Japan

---

[75] Since the policy of the EU is essentially declaratory (and to some extent economic) it is excluded from consideration here.

has applied sanctions in 1999 and, although they were lifted in December, it is highly likely that they would be imposed again in case of further missile tests.

Given that all of the states have decided to work with the existing government in Pyongyang, they have similar views about the desirability of normalizing relations to facilitate communication and dialogue. However, North Korea has resisted joining any multilateral forum other than the Four-Party Talks.[76]

The temporary freeze on missile testing notwithstanding, it is likely that North Korea will launch missiles in future as part of its SLV programme. The international response to such launches—in particular in Japan—is not known. Therefore, it seems very likely that enhancing stability and security on the Korean peninsula will remain an important issue in the foreseeable future.

---

[76] North Korea has participated sporadically in the non-governmental Council for Security Cooperation in the Asia Pacific (CSCAP) meetings as well as participating in the initial meeting of the non-governmental Northeast Asia Cooperation Dialogue (NEACD). A list of the CSCAP members is given in the glossary in this volume.

Appendix 11A. Multilateral weapon and technology export controls

IAN ANTHONY

I. Introduction

This appendix describes identified changes in the guidelines and procedures of five multilateral export control regimes: the Nuclear Suppliers Group (NSG), the Zangger Committee, the Australia Group (AG), the Missile Technology Control Regime (MTCR), and the Wassenaar Arrangement on Export Controls for Conventional Arms and Dual-Use Goods and Technologies (WA). In 1999 Turkey joined the Zangger Committee, the only identified change in the membership of any of the identified regimes. Table 11A lists the members of these regimes.

In December 1999 the participating states in the Wassenaar Arrangement conducted an assessment of the need for changes or refinements in the arrangement's approach and operation. This appendix describes and discusses the main issues raised during the assessment. In addition, it outlines the main issues confronting the European Union (EU) in considering the further development of the dual-use export control system established in 1995.

II. The Zangger Committee, the Nuclear Suppliers Group and the Australia Group

The Zangger Committee

The Zangger Committee was established in 1974 after four years of discussions among a group of states parties about how to interpret their obligations under Article 3.2 of the 1968 Treaty on the Non-Proliferation of Nuclear Weapons (Non-Proliferation Treaty, NPT). The committee is not part of the NPT but is an informal arrangement.

Under Article 3.2 each state party 'undertakes not to provide: (*a*) source or special fissionable material, or (*b*) equipment or material especially designed or prepared for the processing, use or production of special fissionable material, to any non-nuclear-weapon State for peaceful purposes' unless the source or special fissionable material is subject to safeguards.

The NPT does not explicitly control nuclear technology and the committee undertook to define what was meant by 'especially designed or prepared equipment or material for the processing, use or production of special fissionable material'.

The Zangger Committee agreed a Trigger List that participating states implement through national export control systems. An item on this list must not be exported unless the end-user accepts full-scope International Atomic Energy Agency (IAEA) safeguards.[1]

---

[1] The Trigger List is published by the IAEA in Communications received from members regarding the export of nuclear material and of certain categories of equipment and other material, INFCIRC/209/Rev., Nov. 1990, URL <http://www.iaea.or.at/worldatom/infcircs/inf209r1.html>.

Table 11A. Membership of multilateral weapon and technology export control regimes, as of 1 January 2000

State	Zangger Committee[a] 1974	NSG[b] 1978	Australia Group[a] 1985	MTCR[c] 1987	Wassenaar Arrangement 1996
Argentina	x	x	x	x	x
Australia	x	x	x	x	x
Austria	x	x	x	x	x
Belgium	x	x	x	x	x
Brazil		x		x	
Bulgaria	x	x			x
Canada	x	x	x	x	x
China	x				
Czech Republic	x	x	x	x	x
Denmark	x	x	x	x	x
Finland	x	x	x	x	x
France	x	x	x	x	x
Germany	x	x	x	x	x
Greece	x	x	x	x	x
Hungary	x	x	x	x	x
Iceland			x	x	
Ireland	x	x	x	x	x
Italy	x	x	x	x	x
Japan	x	x	x	x	x
Korea, South	x	x	x		x
Latvia		x			
Luxembourg	x	x	x	x	x
Netherlands	x	x	x	x	x
New Zealand		x	x	x	x
Norway	x	x	x	x	x
Poland	x	x	x	x	x
Portugal	x	x	x	x	x
Romania	x	x	x		x
Russia	x	x		x	x
Slovakia	x	x	x		x
South Africa	x	x		x	
Spain	x	x	x	x	x
Sweden	x	x	x	x	x
Switzerland	x	x	x	x	x
Turkey	x[d]			x	x
UK	x	x	x	x	x
Ukraine	x	x		x	x
USA	x	x	x	x	x
Total	**34**	**35**	**30**	**32**	**33**

Note: The years in the column headings indicate when the export control regime was formally established, although the groups may have met on an informal basis before then.

[a] The European Commission is represented in this regime as an observer.

[b] The Nuclear Suppliers Group. The European Commission is represented in this regime as an observer.

[c] The Missile Technology Control Regime.

[d] This state became a member of the regime in 1999.

In November 1999, 32 of the 34 states that participate in the Zangger Committee sent a communication to the Director General of the IAEA informing of a modification to the Trigger List.[2]

The Nuclear Suppliers Group

The Nuclear Suppliers Group was established in 1978 following three years of discussion among seven nuclear supplier countries (Canada, France, the Federal Republic of Germany, Japan, the Soviet Union, the United Kingdom and the United States). It is an informal arrangement of nuclear supplier states that seek to prevent the acquisition of nuclear weapons by states other than those recognized as nuclear weapon states in the framework of the NPT.

The NSG has developed guidelines for nuclear transfers and for nuclear-related dual-use equipment, material and related technology that participating states apply in making national decisions about what kinds of exports to authorize. The NSG has also drawn up lists of items to which these guidelines apply. These guidelines and lists are published by the IAEA.[3]

The NSG participating states held informal consultations in May 1999. In light of the NPT Review Conference to be held in the year 2000 the participating states agreed to undertake transparency and outreach exercises that would clarify the role of the NSG in the overall nuclear non-proliferation regime.[4] In addition, a working group was established to clarify the appropriate control of components.[5]

The decision to undertake transparency and outreach programmes reflected the discussions at an international seminar on the role of export controls in nuclear non-proliferation organized by the Nuclear Suppliers Group in April 1999.[6] This seminar was a response to the call for transparency in nuclear-related export controls to be promoted 'within the framework of dialogue and cooperation' made at the 1995 NPT Extension and Review Conference.[7] The seminar brought together representatives from NSG participating states, non-participating states, the nuclear industry and the research and non-governmental sector for a wide-ranging and open discussion of all aspects of the NSG.[8]

The reciprocal nature of the seminar allowed NSG participating states to describe and explain their activities, and non-participating states were able to state their views

---

[2] The 2 states that did not send such communications to the Diretor General were China and Russia. The communications were published by the IAEA as Communication of 15 November 1999 received from member states regarding the export of nuclear material and of certain categories of equipment and other material, INFCIRC/209/Rev.2, 9 Mar. 1000, URL <http://www.iaea.org/worldatom/infcircs/2000index.html>.

[3] Communication received from certain member states regarding the guidelines for the export of nuclear material, equipment and technology: nuclear transfers, INFCIRC/254/Rev.3/Part 1, 16 Sep. 1997; and Communication received from certain member states regarding the guidelines for the export of nuclear material, equipment and technology: nuclear-related dual-use transfers, INFCIRC/254/Rev.2/Part 2/Mod.1, 19 Mar. 1996.

[4] Background information about the conference is presented in chapter 8 in this volume.

[5] Nuclear Suppliers Group Plenary Meeting, Press Statement, Florence, Italy, 5–6 May 1999, reproduced at URL <http://projects.sipri.se/expcon/nsg_plenary99.htm>.

[6] This was the second such seminar organized by the NSG. The first was held in 1997.

[7] Principles and objective for nuclear non-proliferation and disarmament, 11 May 1995, NPT/CONF/1995/32/DEC.2, reproduced in *SIPRI Yearbook 1996: Armaments, Disarmament and International Security* (Oxford University Press: Oxford, 1996), pp. 591–93.

[8] The papers and presentations from the seminar will be published by the NSG as *2nd International Seminar on the Role of Export Controls in Nuclear Non-Proliferation* (forthcoming).

on perceived negative effects from NSG activities. The view was expressed that more focused activities could supplement general exchanges. For example, the NSG could facilitate dialogue and explore the possibility of cooperation with specific states that do not participate in the NSG but which share a commitment to nuclear non-proliferation.

The Australia Group

The Australia Group was established in 1985 following international concern at the use of chemical weapons (CW) in the 1980–88 Iraq–Iran War. The participating states in this informal grouping cooperate to maintain and develop their national export controls to prevent the further spread of chemical exports that may be used for, or diverted to, CW programmes.

The AG has agreed a series of lists that define dual-use precursor chemicals, biological agents, chemical and biological equipment and related technology. The participating states are politically bound to ensure that these items are subject to national export controls.

Australia Group participants held informal consultations in October 1999 on CW and biological weapon (BW) proliferation. Participants exchanged information about national export licensing measures and procedures and chemical and biological programmes of concern. In addition, the participants discussed how the AG could support the 1993 Chemical Weapons Convention (CWC) and the 1972 Biological and Toxin Weapons Convention (BTWC).[9]

The AG seeks to do this in two ways: first, through attempts 'to prevent the intentional or inadvertent supply by their nationals of materials or equipment to chemical or biological weapons programmes';[10] and second, by assisting the Ad Hoc Group of States Parties to strengthen the effectiveness of the BTWC.

III. The Missile Technology Control Regime

The MTCR is an informal, voluntary association of countries that share the goals of non-proliferation of unmanned delivery systems for weapons of mass destruction and coordination of national export licensing efforts aimed at preventing their proliferation. Initially established in 1987, MTCR membership had increased to 32 states by 1999.

The efforts of the MTCR notwithstanding, in the 1990s a number of countries continued with programmes to acquire ballistic and cruise missile inventories. These programmes have evolved in two ways. First, the missiles under development have been of increasingly long range. Second, the programmes have become increasingly indigenous in nature. In a number of cases the countries with long-range indigenous missile development programmes also have nuclear weapon programmes of concern.

---

[9] A brief summary of both conventions and lists of parties are given in annexe A in this volume. Full texts are available at the SIPRI CBW Project Internet site, URL <http://projects.sipri.se/cbw/cbw-main page.html>.

[10] Media Release: Australia Group Meeting, 4–8 Oct. 1999, Paris, Australia Group document AG/Oct99/Press/Chair/22.

In December 1998 India confirmed the further development and testing of the Agni II missile.[11] The missile was tested to a range of 2000 kilometres in April 1999.[12]

There is some evidence that the missile acquisition programmes of some of these countries are interconnected. Iran and Syria are believed to have acquired the Scud-C missile as a result of trilateral cooperation between themselves and North Korea. Iran, North Korea and Pakistan are believed to cooperate in the development of a longer-range missile. The Shahab IV in Iran and the Ghauri II in Pakistan are both believed to be derivations of the Nodong I developed in North Korea or possibly export versions of this missile.[13]

These trends mean that a growing number of countries are within range of these emerging missile forces. Moreover, because of their indigenous nature, these programmes create new challenges to export controls.

During the 1990s these programmes stimulated a new interest in the issue of ballistic missile defences (BMD). The feasibility and desirability of developing a range of different BMD programmes is now being investigated, in particular in the United States.[14] The programmes under evaluation range from limited-area defence of troops in the field to wide-area defence systems capable of providing protection to territories as large as the continental United States.

Countries that are engaged in developing long-range ballistic missiles include India, Iran, North Korea and Pakistan. In addition, there are concerns that Iraq will re-establish its long-range ballistic missile programme in the absence of effective enforcement of United Nations decisions prohibiting such a development.[15] In their discussions in 1999 the MTCR members examined recent developments in South Asia, North-East Asia and in the Middle East, in particular.

The MTCR members conducted 'an in-depth discussion on possible new, qualitative responses' to the problem of ballistic missile proliferation.[16] The main programmes of concern are indigenous or depend on technology transfers between states that are not members of the MTCR. In these conditions members will continue to encourage other states to apply the MTCR guidelines to exports of relevant equipment and technology. In addition, one suggestion is that export controls will need to be supplemented with other types of countermeasures. Under consideration are strengthened international norms against missile proliferation, confidence-building measures addressed to reducing demand for missiles, and economic and diplomatic pressure on states with programmes of concern. In the longer term the development of regional or global legal restrictions on missile forces is also under consideration.

---

[11] Nicholson, M., 'India: Long-range nuclear missile approved', *Financial Times* (Internet edn), 10 Dec. 1998, URL <http://www.ft.com/hippocampus/qe506e.htm>.

[12] Singh, M., 'Agni-II adds fire power to N-deterrence', *Indian Express* (Internet edn), 12 Apr. 1999, URL <http://www.expressindia.com/ie/daily/19990412/ige12018.html>.

[13] Kak, K., 'Missile proliferation and international security', *Strategic Analysis* (New Delhi), vol. 23, no. 3 (June 1999).

[14] These BMD systems, if developed and fielded, are seen by many outside the United States as a direct challenge to the existing arrangement of strategic stability based on deterrence by punishment See chapter 8 in this volume.

[15] See also appendix 9B in this volume.

[16] Plenary Meeting of the Missile Technology Control Regime, Press Release, Noordwijk, 11–15 Oct. 1999. It is reproduced at URL <http://projects.sipri.se/expcon/mtcr99.htm>.

IV. The Wassenaar Arrangement

The Wassenaar Arrangement on Export Controls for Conventional Arms and Dual-Use Goods and Technologies began operations in September 1996. The objectives of the WA are to promote transparency, exchange of information and exchange of views on transfers of an agreed range of items with a view to promoting responsibility in transfers of conventional arms and dual-use goods and technologies.

At the time it was established the participating states recognized that the procedures and objectives of the WA should evolve over time in line with changing conditions and reflecting the discussions among the group. In the original Initial Elements,[17] one of the founding documents of the WA, the participating states agreed to assess the overall functioning of this arrangement regularly, for the first time in 1999.

In 1999 participating states submitted many observations and proposals to the General Working Group conducting the assessment. During the plenary meeting on 1–3 December the WA participating states considered more than 50 specific proposals for regime changes. The number of submissions in itself suggested that participating states see value in the WA as a forum for discussion and that many of them would like to see more rapid progress towards building on the Initial Elements. Apart from its existing procedures for information exchange, the WA has provided a forum in which to discuss information contained in voluntary reports or special studies conducted by individual participating states.

However, the plenary meeting that took place in December 1999 did not agree on many changes to the way in which the WA functions. The participating states agreed to improve the efficiency and effectiveness of the general information exchange. Limited changes in the reporting requirements for deliveries of conventional arms were elaborated. The failure to adopt other proposals reflected the fact that decision making within the WA is by consensus. It is sufficient for one participating state to withhold consent in order for a proposal to fail.

The proposals made during the assessment can be grouped under five general headings: general information exchange, specific information exchange, licensing procedures and practices, expansion of participation, and the relationship between the WA and other multilateral initiatives.[18]

General information exchange

During Wassenaar Arrangement meetings an opportunity is provided for general exchange of information and views on issues that participating states believe to be important and relevant to the purposes of the WA. In recent years this kind of discussion has been considered by participating states to be valuable in addressing specific concerns.[19]

During the assessment it was proposed that this element of the WA activities could be made more productive if discussions were more focused and better prepared. The

[17] Initial Elements, as adopted by the Plenary of 11–12 July 1996. The document is reproduced at URL <http://www.wassenaar.org/docs/IE96.html> and URL <http://projects.sipri.se/expcon/wass_elements.htm>.

[18] In addition the administrative routines for the WA, including the development of a system for electronic information exchange among participating states, have consumed a lot of time in discussion.

[19] E.g., in 1996 the participating states were able to use the information exchange to determine national policies towards transfers of arms and ammunition to parties to the conflict in Afghanistan.

participating states could determine regions on which exchange of information could best serve the purposes of the WA. The chairman of the General Working Group could, it was proposed, facilitate discussion within the WA by preparing a paper that would form the basis for an exchange of views. The document would consider information and views presented by participating states along with reliable public information in compiling such a paper. The chairman would focus on the 1998 'elements for objective analysis and advice concerning potentially destabilising accumulations of conventional weapons' to provide a framework for the discussion paper.[20]

A series of such regional evaluations could, over time, lead to the development of a single global view of destabilizing accumulations of conventional arms and dual-use technologies that could be updated on a rolling basis in the light of new discussions among participating states.

Specific information exchange

In addition to the general information exchange, participating states also provide one another with more specific kinds of information.

Conventional arms

For conventional arms the participating states exchange information every six months on deliveries to non-participating states of conventional arms as defined in an annexe to the Initial Elements. The definition of conventional arms is identical with the seven categories identified as part of the UN Register of Conventional Arms.[21] (The seven WA categories agreed in 1996 as part of the Initial Elements were battle tanks, armoured combat vehicles, large-calibre artillery systems, combat aircraft, attack helicopters, warships, and missiles or missile systems.) During the initial years of reporting information to the UN Register many WA participating states chose not to report details such as the model and type of weapon.

When the Initial Elements were agreed, it was expected that this procedure would be adapted to permit steadily increasing transparency over transfers to non-participating states as the WA evolved. In recent years a growing number of states have reported the details of model and type as part of their annual submission to the UN Register. This has raised expectations within the WA that modifications are needed if the WA information exchange is to add to transparency. During 1999 proposals were made to revise the scope of existing categories for conventional arms and to add new categories.

The proposals aimed at modifying the existing categories had two objectives. The first was to clarify what kinds of item fall within each category in an attempt to harmonize the interpretation of what equipment should be reported. Without additional clarity there was a risk that different states would take a different decision on whether or not to report transfers of essentially the same item. The second objective was to bring new types of equipment into the exchange.

---

[20] Elements for objective analysis and advice concerning potentially destabilising accumulations of conventional weapons, non-binding paper approved by the Wassenaar Arrangement, 3 Dec. 1998. It is reproduced at URL <http://www.wassenaar.org> and URL <http://www.sipri.se/projects/expcon/expcon.htm>.

[21] The UN Register of Conventional Arms is discussed in chapter 7 in this volume.

In order to clarify the reporting requirement the category 'attack helicopter' was changed to 'military and attack helicopter'. It is clear from the new definition that helicopters designed, equipped or modified for reconnaissance, target acquisition (including anti-submarine warfare), communications, command of troops, electronic warfare or mine-laying should be reported.

In order to bring additional systems within the scope of one category 'combat aircraft' was replaced with 'military aircraft/unmanned aerial vehicles'. In future, deliveries of unmanned aerial vehicles (UAVs) specially designed, modified or equipped for military use to non-participating states should be included in the information exchange.[22]

While the proposals to modify the categories for attack helicopters and combat aircraft were accepted, others were not. For example, it was proposed to change the category 'missiles or missile systems' to distinguish between the missiles themselves and their launchers, to lower the calibre threshold for the reporting of transfers of 'large-calibre artillery systems' and to lower the tonnage threshold for the reporting of 'warships'. None of these changes was accepted.

Apart from modifying existing categories of equipment, there were also proposals to add new categories. Proposals included categories for small arms, man-portable air defence systems (MANPADS), logistics equipment and troop transport equipment. While none of these categories was added to the information exchange, the participating states agreed to discuss the development of guidelines for exports of MANPADS as part of their future programme.

Many of these proposals had widespread support among the WA participating states. However, they were consistently opposed by Russia and Ukraine. Along with other states opposing one or more of the proposals this was sufficient to block any progress in the further development of the general information exchange for conventional arms.

To summarize, the reporting arrangements for conventional arms still include seven categories: battle tanks, armoured combat vehicles, large-calibre artillery systems, military aircraft/unmanned air vehicles, military and attack helicopters, warships, and missiles or missile systems.

Dual-use items

Under the Initial Elements participating states notify licences denied to non-participants with respect to items on the List of Dual-Use Goods and Technologies, where the reasons for denial are relevant to the purposes of the arrangement.

The dual-use list is divided into two tiers. Items in Tier 1 are considered less sensitive than items in Tier 2. Tier 2 is itself divided into two parts, one of which is for items considered very sensitive.

For Tier 1 items participating states notify all licences denied on an aggregate basis twice per year. For Tier 2 items denials are notified individually on 'an early and timely basis, that is preferably within 30 days but no later than within 60 days, of the date of the denial'. For Tier 2 items participating states also notify licences granted and transfers made on an aggregate basis twice a year as well as denials. For the identified extremely sensitive items participating states are expected to 'exert extreme

---

[22] This includes UAVs for electronic warfare, suppression of air defence systems, reconnaissance missions, as well as systems for the control and receiving of information from unmanned aerial vehicles.

vigilance' in applying national conditions and criteria while considering the licence application, although there is no presumption to deny a licence.

During the assessment it was proposed to enhance the information exchange within the dual-use pillar by requiring participating states to consult before approving a similar or identical licence denied to the same end-user by another member. This so-called 'no undercut' provision is used in some of the other non-proliferation arrangements to prevent an end-user of concern from 'licence shopping'.[23] The provision is believed to reassure states that they are not being placed at a commercial disadvantage by denying a licence on non-proliferation grounds.

A second proposal was to include additional information in denial notifications related to items in Tier 1 of the dual-use list. In the Initial Elements different specific elements are included in the indicative content suggested for denial notifications for items in Tier 1 and Tier 2 of the dual-use list. For Tier 2 items the indicative list suggests that a denial notification will include information on the end-user and end-use of the item. It is suggested that this information be broken down into intermediate and ultimate end-users to give the fullest picture of the path the item would have passed en route to the final destination.

Given that the reporting procedures for dual-use items are already far in advance of those for conventional arms, many participating states expressed the view that the main emphasis in the WA should be enhancing transparency in the arms pillar rather than devoting additional attention to dual-use items. Some went as far as to suggest a formal linkage—that progress on the dual-use pillar should be suspended pending a meaningful expansion of transparency measures in the conventional arms pillar.

However, neither of the proposals described above was accepted and the dual-use information exchange was not amended—although the decision not to make amendments may not have been a result of any direct linkage.

Licensing procedures and practices

The Wassenaar Arrangement established a specific Licensing and Enforcement Officers Meeting (LEOM) as one of its sub-groups. The LEOM meets between plenary sessions. At LEOM meetings experts confronted with similar problems can exchange views on specific subjects in detail.

Many of the participating states have identified this as one of the most valuable elements of the WA activities. However, the question of how to establish priorities and conduct discussions on these issues has proved to be extremely complicated. The issues that appear to be the most persistent and challenging ones on the agenda in the area of licensing and enforcement include: (a) combating illegal arms transfers, (b) legal controls on arms brokers, (c) effective enforcement of end-user provisions of national export control systems, (d) controlling intangible technology transfers, and (e) implementation of 'catch-all' controls.

Measures to combat illegal arms transfers

All participating states agree that responding to the risk or fact of circumvention of export controls is one of the main goals of the WA. However, the diversity of national export control laws and regulations means that there is no single definition of what is

---

[23] E.g., similar provisions are an element of the NSG, the EU dual-use export control system and as an element in the EU Code of Conduct on arms transfers.

legal or illegal. An action that is a circumvention of export controls in one state may be a legal act in others.

During the assessment some WA participating states proposed further harmonization of national control systems to reduce the extent of this problem. Others regard this as inappropriate for the WA. Since the WA is a forum for information exchange and each state is responsible for its own laws and regulations, the argument runs, harmonization might be the outcome of WA activities but it should not be an objective. During the assessment process Russia consistently opposed any proposal that suggested harmonization of national control systems.

The Russian position has been that exports approved by a state authority cannot be considered illegal. In granting authorization for an export the national authorities have already determined that the export will not contribute to excessive and destabilizing arms accumulations. Therefore, Russia is not prepared to discuss what it considers legitimate exports in the framework of the WA. Many other participating states reject the Russian position, arguing that only by pooling their information on all transfers can the WA identify patterns and trends that may be of concern and come to a considered judgement on the overall effect of any single export.

Some WA participating states are suspicious of any proposal for harmonization that appears to be extraterritorial in its impact—that is, a measure that requires one state to enforce the national laws of another state.

In addition to legal issues, enforcement issues are also an important part of the activities of the LEOM and the WA generally. One outcome of the assessment was an affirmation that states should have 'strong, effective, transparent and national law-based enforcement of export controls'.[24] Moreover, four basic elements of enforcement were listed: (*a*) a preventive programme, (*b*) a process for investigation, (*c*) penalties for violations, and (*d*) international cooperation. In the area of enforcement there are also inconsistencies and unresolved questions among the WA participating states in each of these basic elements.

In the area of prevention the balance of responsibilities between the exporter (e.g., a public entity or an entity under private ownership) is different in different states. The legal authority and resources (human, technical and financial) available to those responsible for investigating a possible evasion of export controls differ from state to state. In addition to varying views on what represent meaningful and appropriate penalties for violations of export control laws, the probability of being able to secure a conviction also differs widely across the WA because of dissimilarities in the criminal justice systems of different states. These factors shape attitudes and approaches to international cooperation. For example, the question has been raised how such a heterogeneous group of states can share intelligence information in a manner that enhances prevention, investigation and prosecution of illegal exports while safeguarding other important interests such as the integrity of sources.

Legal controls on arms brokers

An issue that has begun to receive prominence in discussions both within the WA and elsewhere is whether and how the activities of arms brokers should be controlled. A

---

[24] Wassenaar Arrangement on Export Controls for Conventional Arms and Dual-Use Goods and Technologies, 'Public statement for 1999 plenary', 3 Dec. 1999. It is reproduced in appendix 11B in this volume.

broker is an intermediary that brings together two parties (the buyer and the seller). The broker could be an individual or a specialized company.

The principle underlying most current export control laws is based on the movement of specified items. An item that is subject to control may not legally leave the jurisdiction of the exporting state without the appropriate authorization.

The responsibility for ensuring that the appropriate authorization is gained lies with the exporter. A broker (who may be a citizen of one state but conducting business in another) never takes ownership or physical possession of any of the goods that are involved in the deal that he mediates. He gains an income (usually paid by the seller) for providing a service. The broker is not an exporter but a mediator. If the broker takes ownership or physical possession of the items then he becomes the exporter and so is subject to existing controls.

While the act of brokering is subject to legal controls in a few countries, it is not in many others. However, it has been agreed in the framework of the WA that the participating states will examine the feasibility and value of extending national controls into this area.

Effective enforcement of end-user provisions

An important problem in export control is how to ensure that controlled items authorized for export are received by the stated end-user rather than being diverted to another, unauthorized, recipient. Currently, different WA participating states have different approaches to end-user verification. Moreover, the character of the problem is different for conventional arms as compared with dual-use items.

States that maintain close security ties with arms recipients—for example, in the framework of alliances or other government-to-government agreements—can make verification of conventional arms end-user provisions a fairly routine element of military-to-military contacts. Verification can also be combined with customer service provisions carried out by industry in cases where government and industry work closely together.

Where exports are more commercial and industry-led in their orientation governments may not be able to make such arrangements. These governments may rely on documentary assurances provided by an end-user (either an official procurement authority of the importing state or a legitimate agent acting on behalf of such an authority). End-user provisions of this kind are vulnerable where exporters provide licensing officers with false documentation that appears authentic.

During the assessment of the WA it was proposed that participating states introduce a requirement for an International Import Certificate. A standard document might ease the problems for enforcement officers in authenticating end-user provisions. However, this proposal was not adopted.

For dual-use items the problem of verification is made more difficult by the fact that the items may well have a civilian end-user or end-use. Where the end-user is not a part of government (e.g., because it is a manufacturer buying intermediate goods for incorporation into a final product or because it is the civilian user of a dual-use product) additional problems may arise. These problems are mainly practical—the sheer volume of items that would need to be monitored. However, there may also be legal problems—for example, there may not be legal authority for intrusive end-user monitoring in the importing state.

Controlling intangible technology transfers

The principle guiding export controls is usually based on the movement of defined items. Historically, these have mainly been manufactured goods—end products, components and sub-assemblies needed to operate those end products and machinery dedicated to the production, testing, maintenance and use of those end products.

Over time the nature of the items that need to be controlled to achieve the objectives of export controls has expanded for two main reasons: first, because design and production capabilities have gradually spread to a wider circle of states; and second, because of changes in the technology of products used in the military sector.[25]

The effective control over the distribution of military products has become more and more dependent on controlling so-called intangible technologies—computer software being the prime example. The development of the Internet and the anticipated future growth of 'e-commerce' is creating a new challenge for export controls.

There is a difference between the transfer of a technology that is itself intangible and the transfer of a technology by intangible means. For example, a software code that is stored on a computer disk and transferred across a customs boundary may be subject to control via a requirement for a licence for the disk. The same software code may not be subject to control if transferred over the Internet since the code itself is not then stored in a physical medium.

An additional intractable problem in the management of intangible technology transfer is the regulation of contacts between individuals in multinational project teams. Where knowledge and information are transferred in discussions between colleagues of different nationalities working on a common project there may be a legal licensing requirement. How to manage this problem is the subject of discussion in all export control regimes, including the WA.

The implementation of 'catch-all' controls

Changes in technology and in the global defence market have challenged the traditional approach to export controls based on the physical movement of listed items. Since the early 1990s a growing number of states have adopted an alternative approach to export controls for transactions that could contribute to illegal nuclear, biological or chemical (NBC) weapon programmes. The new approach does not depend on control lists.

This 'catch-all' approach created a legal obligation on exporters to seek authorization before transferring any item (whether or not on a control list) to an end-user if there was reason to believe that the transfer would contribute to an NBC weapon programme. The legal scope and practical application of this catch-all provision have been the subject of much discussion within export control regimes aimed at preventing the proliferation of NBC weapons.

The differentiation between many civil and military goods is becoming more difficult as a result of changes in the defence manufacturing process. The use of so-called commercial 'off-the-shelf' technology (i.e., the incorporation of components built to civil standards into defence products) is expected to challenge the current practice of maintaining separate control lists for dual-use items and military items. It may not be

---

[25] Recently, a third change has occurred with the application of export controls to non-military security problems. While this change will also have an impact on the nature of control lists, it is not relevant here.

possible to maintain a comprehensive munitions list that is confined to items specially designed, equipped or modified for military use.

In those conditions a choice will need to be made whether items should be listed on both a military and a dual-use list. In that case exporters may need to go through two licensing processes for the same export transaction in countries where different legislation controls dual-use exports and arms exports. Alternatively, items may be placed on only one list. If these items are placed on the dual-use list then many items destined for a military end-user may be subject to a decision process designed to avoid the proliferation of NBC weapons. If the same items are placed on the military list then many purely civilian transactions will be evaluated against criteria intended to control transfers to the military. This has the potential to act as an unnecessary restriction on legitimate trade.

During the WA assessment the question was raised whether a military end-user catch-all provision might be an alternative to traditional list-based approaches to export control. Under such an arrangement any item transferred to a military end-user would require authorization prior to export. However, this proposal was not adopted.

Expansion of participation

A number of states have either applied to participate in the WA or have made preliminary contacts as part of their process of deciding whether to apply. These countries include Belarus, Chile, China, Estonia, Kazakhstan and South Africa. However, the participation in the WA was not extended in 1999.

Extending participation in the WA depends on the consent of all participating states. In evaluating the extension states take into account three conditions: (a) whether the state is a producer/exporter of items listed on the WA control lists (i.e., arms or 'high technology' industrial equipment); (b) the non-proliferation standing of the state concerned—in particular adherence to the NPT, the BTWC, the CWC and (if applicable) START I, including the Lisbon Protocol;[26] and (c) the status of national export controls in the state.

The application of Estonia has been supported by many states. However, the decision to block Estonian participation was taken on the grounds that Estonia is not a significant supplier of items controlled in the WA munitions and dual-use lists.

China, which had expressed an interest in evaluating WA participation, withdrew this interest as one element of its wider protest about the conduct of the war in Kosovo—in particular the accidental destruction of the Chinese embassy in Belgrade.

In the cases of Kazakhstan and South Africa concerns were expressed about the effectiveness of current export control systems or the way in which export policies were implemented. In Kazakhstan the case of an illegal export of MiG-21 fighter aircraft to North Korea has received much public attention. Although the export was authorized, it was on the basis of false documentation. The listed buyer was a Czech company that had in turn listed India as the final end-user of the aircraft. In fact, the aircraft were transported to Azerbaijan, where they were impounded, and were en route to North Korea. In the case of South Africa there are residual concerns in some states about whether it fully respected the UN embargo on arms supplies to Rwanda.

---

[26] The 1991 US–Russian Treaty on the Reduction and Limitation of Strategic Offensive Arms (START I); and the 1992 Protocol to Facilitate the Implementation of the START Treaty (the Lisbon Protocol). See also chapter 8 in this volume.

The relationship between the WA and other multilateral initiatives

In 1998 the WA participating states welcomed the Declaration of a Moratorium on the Importation, Exportation and Manufacture of Light Weapons[27] by the Economic Community of West African States (ECOWAS) member states. The WA states agreed to collaborate with ECOWAS to respect the provisions of the moratorium as well as providing advice and technical assistance to implement it.

This was in many ways an interesting and novel development in that a group of states agreed to cooperate with one another through an informal arrangement rather than bilaterally or through an international organization. It was thought that this type of pragmatic arrangement might offer a flexible new instrument to address the problem of inhibiting destabilizing arms acquisitions in West Africa. The WA reiterated its support for the moratorium in 1999 without providing details of specific actions undertaken.

V. Adaptation of the European Union dual-use export control system

In 1994 the European Union established an export control system for dual-use goods through two enactments. First, the EC Dual-Use Goods Regulation (Council Regulation no. 3381/94) established the control system within European Community law. Second, the EU Council Decision (Council Decision 94/942/CFSP) established those elements of the control system considered to fall under the national jurisdiction of EU member states (because of their direct bearing on foreign policy and national security) under the intergovernmental Common Foreign and Security Policy.[28] This system entered into force in 1995.

At the time the EU dual-use export control system was established, it was recognized to be the first step in a process that would lead to future adaptation of the system. The Commission of the European Communities monitored the implementation of the dual-use export control system during the initial period of its operation and, in May 1998, reported findings and recommendations to the European Parliament and to the European Council.[29] Based on these findings and recommendations the Commission drafted a proposal for a new regulation that would, if adopted, replace the two founding documents agreed in 1994.[30]

---

[27] The 3-year arms production and transfer moratorium was signed on 31 Oct. 1998 and entered into force on 1 Nov. 1998. It is discussed in Adam, B., 'Efforts to control the international trade in light weapons', *SIPRI Yearbook 1999: Armaments, Disarmament and International Security* (Oxford University Press: Oxford, 1999), p. 514; and Lachowski, Z., 'Conventional arms control', *SIPRI Yearbook 1999* (note 27), p. 637.

[28] The EU dual-use export control system is described in Anthony, I., Eckstein, S. and Zanders, J. P., 'Multilateral military-related export control measures', *SIPRI Yearbook 1997: Armaments, Disarmament and International Security* (Oxford University Press: Oxford, 1997), pp. 345–63.

[29] Report COM(1998)257 final of 15 May 1998 for a Council Regulation (EC) setting up a Community regime for the control of exports of dual-use goods and technology, Brussels, May 1998. Article 18 of the original regulation requires the Commission to carry out this monitoring and reporting. The Commission has a general right to propose new Community legislation.

[30] Proposal for a Council Regulation (EC) setting up a Community regime for the control of exports of dual-use goods and technologies, COM(1998)257 final, Brussels, Aug. 1998.

After receiving the proposal in August 1998 EU member states began to evaluate whether and how the existing dual-use control system might be modified. At the end of 1999 no decision had been taken about changes to existing legislation.

The main proposals in the Commission draft were for changes in six areas.[31]

The first proposal was to bring the system entirely within Community law rather than dividing the legal base of the system between Community law and an inter-governmental agreement.[32]

The European Court of Justice has ruled that, in the application of the EC common commercial policy, 'neither the particular nature of the goods nor the fact that the control measures are taken in light of foreign policy or security consideration has any bearing on Article 113 being applicable'.[33] This reference is to Article 113 of the Treaty of Rome that established a common commercial policy as an element of EC law.[34] The common commercial policy 'shall be based on uniform principles, particularly in regard to changes in tariff rates, the conclusion of tariff and trade agreements, *the achievement of uniformity in measures of liberalization, export policy* and measures to protect trade such as those to be taken in case of dumping or subsidies'.[35]

As a result of this ruling it is likely that member states will have to accept that only those items specifically exempted from the common commercial policy (under Article 296EC) can be kept outside Community law.

EU member states are sensitive about ceding authority in areas that directly affect their security policy and their treaty-based non-proliferation and disarmament commitments. The Court of Justice rulings observed, however, that in policy fields for which the Community has exclusive competence, such as commercial policy, national measures are permissible only if they are specifically authorized by the Community.

Export authorizations would, under the proposal, be issued by the competent authorities of member states 'except for those exports covered by the Community General Export Authorization' (discussed below). Under the proposal authority to update the list of goods to which the dual-use export controls apply would also be delegated to a List Group composed of a representative from each member state as well as the Commission.

The second important change proposed was the introduction of new licensing procedures, namely, the development of a Community General Export Authorization. This licence would grant general authorization to EU exporters to export dual-use items in specific named parts of the EU dual-use list to 10 countries.[36] Exporters would have to keep records of all such transactions according to specifications laid

---

[31] Directorate General I External Relations: Commercial policy and Relations with North America, the Far East, Australia and New Zealand, 'Proposal for a new regulation regarding the export of dual-use goods: main issues', Press Release, Mar. 1999.

[32] To some degree this proposal was motivated by the rulings of the European Court of Justice in the cases Werner v. Germany—Case C-70/94, Judgement of October 17, 1995-[1995] ECR I-3189—and Leifer and Others—Case C-83/94, Judgement of October 17, 1995-[1995] ECR I-3231.

[33] Proposal for a Council Regulation . . . (note 30), p. 4

[34] Following the entry into force of the 1997 Treaty of Amsterdam on 1 May 1999, Article 113 became Article 133EC of the consolidated treaty. Excerpts from the treaty are reproduced in 'Documents on European security', *SIPRI Yearbook 1998: Armaments, Disarmament and International Security* (Oxford University Press: Oxford, 1998), pp. 177–81.

[35] Article 133(1)EC, emphasis added.

[36] The 10 countries are Australia, Canada, the Czech Republic, Hungary, Japan, New Zealand, Norway, Poland, Switzerland and the USA. These countries are legally bound by all relevant non-proliferation treaties, cooperate in informal multilateral export control via participation in the various regimes and are considered to have national export control systems of a high standard.

out for national general licences. However, exporters would not have to apply for individual authorizations prior to export.

The third proposed change was the introduction of a 'catch-all' military end-use control (described in section IV) for goods exported to a country subject to a UN arms embargo. In most cases where a state has been subject to a UN arms embargo it has not been subject to a general trade embargo. In such conditions civilian trade and trade in dual-use products for civilian end-users may continue, subject to national export control restrictions. The military end-use requirement would create a legal obligation on EU exporters to seek authorization from their national authorities before they exported any item (whether or not on a control list) to a military end-user in the state in question.

The fourth change proposed is the introduction of Community-level controls on intangible technology transfers. As noted above, the issue of intangible technology transfers has been much discussed among export control officials in different forums. The Commission proposal would extend the authorization requirement for items on the dual-use list to 'transmission of technologies via electronic media, telephone and fax'.

It has been difficult to define an intangible technology transfer in a way that can be incorporated into export controls without paralysing all human contact between nationals of different countries. The regulation excludes the supply of services or the transmission of technology requiring cross-border movement of natural persons from the authorization requirement. Dual-use items exported by EU governments or via legal and natural persons acting on behalf of governments are also exempted from the authorization requirement.

The fifth change proposed is the progressive abolition of licensing procedures for intra-Community trade of virtually all dual-use products currently subject to national exceptions on security grounds. For example, most encryption technology 'cannot be traded without authorisation' within the EC. Under the export control system proposed in the regulation the only dual-use items for which national authorization would be required prior to intra-Community transfers would be separated plutonium and enriched uranium.

The Commission also envisages that the restrictions on intra-Community transfers of military goods would be phased out over time to create a single market for military goods within the EC. This free market (which would also include binding rules on non-discrimination in respect of arms procurement by EU member states) would mean that exports were subject to restriction at the point where an item was exported beyond the Community customs boundary. For transfers within the EU simplified procedures would apply.

Through this proposal the Commission is anticipating the trajectory of government responses to European defence industry restructuring. In November 1997 the Commission published the document Implementing European Union Strategy on Defence-Related Industries.[37] One element of the communication was a draft Common Position on Framing a European Armaments Policy. Article 5 of the draft included 'a sim-

---

[37] Communication to the Council, the European Parliament, the Economic and Social Committee and the Committee of the Regions on Implementing European Union Strategy on Defence-Related Industries, COM(97)583 final, Brussels, 12 Nov. 1997. After Nov. 1997 the Commission began preparing a White Paper on arms export policy formulating various options that could lead to a common EU arms export policy. The objective would be to eliminate limits to defence industrial cooperation among EU member states. Action Plan for the Defence-Related Industries, COM(97)583, final/annex II, Brussels, 12 Nov. 1997.

plified system applicable to intra-community transfers including export and re-export guarantees, and monitoring and surveillance mechanisms'.

The Commission proposal was not accepted by the EU member states. However, in July 1998 defence ministers from six EU member states (France, Germany, Italy, Spain, Sweden and the UK) expressed their intention to establish a cooperative framework for future defence industrial development.[38] These six countries—each of which has significant arms production capacity and has historically exported significant quantities of conventional arms—all regard a strong, competitive and efficient defence industry as a key element of European security and identity as well as of the European scientific and technological base.

The negotiations may result in legally binding commitments that significantly reduce the requirement for licences for trade in defence articles and services among these six states. Moreover, where transfers of cooperatively produced defence articles and services to third countries are concerned there could also be significant changes in present licensing practices.

These six states intend to 'promote convergence in the field of conventional arms exports. They will take the necessary measures to develop common rules about defence exports, including the harmonisation of their control policies'. Common rules and, if possible, standard procedures for exports to third parties would permit the introduction of simplified procedures for transfers of items among the six states—either for their own use or for re-export within the European Union.

Among the six states there are substantive differences on, for example, arms exports to the Arab states on the southern littoral of the Persian Gulf and to countries in South Asia. Consequently, harmonization of control policies will require a revision to the foreign policy of some or all of these six states towards, for example, India, Pakistan and Saudi Arabia.

The logic of the Commission proposal is that this kind of development could not be confined to six EU member states within the framework of an evolving European Union security and defence policy. At some point this kind of arrangement, if concluded, would have to be placed in the framework of EU law.

The sixth proposal for change is to enhance the administrative cooperation between member states in cases where a sensitive export is under consideration. Under the proposal member states would be legally obliged to share additional information with other member states and the Commission in cases where authorization to carry out an export was denied.[39]

Under the existing dual-use system a member state is obliged to consult with a member state that had previously denied authorization for an essentially identical export before authorizing that export. Under the proposal a member state that authorizes an export essentially identical to one that has previously been denied by another member state would be obliged to explain the reason why authorization was granted.

At the time of writing the Commission proposal was still being considered by member states.

---

[38] Letter of intent between 6 defence ministers on measures to facilitate the restructuring of the European defence industry, 6 July 1998, reproduced at URL <http://projects.sipri.se/expcon/loi/lointent.htm>.

[39] One complaint of the Commission is that member states exchange information with one another without informing the Commission. This makes it impossible for the Commission to make a comprehensive evaluation of the working of the dual-use control system.

VI. Conclusions

After a period in which new states joined the multilateral forums in which export controls are discussed each year, the pace of expansion in membership and participation has slowed down.

The participating states conducted an assessment of the functioning of the Wassenaar Arrangement. By adding to the knowledge and information available to participating states the WA can increase the effectiveness of national efforts to control international transfers of conventional arms and dual-use items. The assessment underlined that the objectives of the WA as laid down in 1996 remained valid and that the arrangement was playing a useful role in helping to prevent circumvention of national export controls.

While creating greater transparency is one key objective of the WA, the 1999 assessment led to minor improvements in the efficiency of the information exchange. Although the evolutionary nature of the WA means that additional changes can be expected in future, the procedures adopted in the arrangement—in particular the consensus principle—have led to disappointment in some states about the extent and pace of progress towards greater harmonization and effectiveness. At the same time, the broadened discussion among the participating states of arms transfers to regions of concern has increased understanding of the international arms trade.

A deterioration in the political relations between key states may have had a negative impact on the overall progress. It is also likely that changes in the domestic political environment of some states have slowed the pace of development. In particular, a change in Russia's attitude towards enhanced international cooperation has been detected in various organizations and forums. The Wassenaar Arrangement is not excepted from this Russian change of position. Ukraine, after following a policy of enhanced cooperation with international regimes over the past few years, is also ambivalent about further transparency measures in the area of conventional arms transfers.

The Nuclear Suppliers Group emphasized the role of transparency in generating confidence that exports of controlled items did not contribute to nuclear programmes of concern. After expanding the level of public information about the collective activities and the national export controls of participating state, the NSG began to explore how to incorporate non-participating states into informal transparency mechanisms.

In 1999 the member states of the European Union carried out an evaluation of the first five years of the EU dual-use export control system based on reports prepared by the Commission. This evaluation may lead to changes in the system.

Nevertheless, developments in 1999 illustrate that the international cooperation in developing national export controls that evolved in the 1990s is still seen as an important instrument of policy by many of the participating governments.

In the European Union the discussion of export controls for conventional arms and dual-use goods has become an important element in the overall institutional and political development of the organization.

Appendix 11B. The Wassenaar Arrangement 1999 plenary meeting statement

WASSENAAR ARRANGEMENT ON EXPORT CONTROLS FOR CONVENTIONAL ARMS AND DUAL-USE GOODS AND TECHNOLOGIES

PUBLIC STATEMENT FOR 1999 PLENARY

Vienna, 3 December 1999

The fifth Plenary meeting of the Wassenaar Arrangement (WA) was held December 1–3, 1999 under the chairmanship of Ambassador Staffan Sohlman (Sweden).

The Plenary discussed the work carried out in 1999 on a number of issues relevant to the WA's purposes, including: information sharing on arms and sensitive technology flows to regions in conflict or otherwise of concern; issues related to specific projects, programmes and end-users of concern; and on diversions and unauthorised transhipments. Participating States also examined global arms import trends and sensitive emerging technologies.

Participating States reaffirmed their commitment to maintain responsible national policies consistent with the purposes and objectives of the Wassenaar Arrangement; and to maximum restraint as a matter of national policy when considering licensing for the export of arms and sensitive dual-use items to all destinations, where the risks are judged greatest, in particular to regions where conflict is occurring. They noted with concern continuing illicit arms flows to zones of conflict, including to states and parties subject to mandatory UNSC arms embargoes. They also noted with concern licit transfers to zones of conflict from states not participating in the Wassenaar Arrangement. They decided to continue, on the basis of information exchanged, their discussion of regions where the risks are judged greatest with a view to enhancing the effectiveness of the Wassenaar Arrangement, taking into account the right to self defence of legitimate governments.

The Plenary reiterated its encouragement that Participating States undertake an appropriate collaborative role with ECOWAS Member States to respect the provisions of the ECOWAS Moratorium, and consider providing advisory and/or technical assistance in the implementation of the Moratorium.

Participating States confirmed that they share the concerns regarding the threat to civil aviation, peace-keeping, crisis management, and anti-terrorist operations posed by the illicit possession of Man Portable Air-Defence Systems (MANPADS) and recognised the need for appropriate measures to prevent such possession. In this connection, Participating States agreed to continue discussion of this issue, in particular, with a view to possible development of guidelines.

In addition to its regular annual review, the Plenary concluded the first overall Assessment of the functioning of the Arrangement, which was carried out over the past year in accordance with the 1996 decision by Participating States. The Plenary drew a number of conclusions from this assessment.

Participating States agreed that Wassenaar Arrangement objectives remain valid as laid down in the Initial Elements. It was also agreed that, in line with these goals, the WA should continue to contribute to preventing circumvention of export controls, inter alia, by terrorist or organised criminal groups that seek to acquire armaments and dual-use items.

Participating States agreed to improve the efficiency and effectiveness of the General Information Exchange.

Participating States, while deciding not to revise the WA Initial Elements at this point, reaffirmed again the evolutionary nature of the WA, noting the provisions in the Initial Elements for review of particular issues outside an overall assessment.

Participating States, having analysed the agreed criteria for assessing destabilising accumulations of weapons and proposals to improve arms transparency, agreed to elaborate reporting requirements for the exchange of information on arms deliveries. (An amended version of Appendix 3 to the Initial Elements is attached).

Participating States continued to consider and discuss the question of small arms and light weapons transfers, and their illicit trafficking. They reaffirmed the importance of implementing responsible export policies and maintaining effective export controls with respect to small arms and light weapons, and decided to study the issue further as a matter of urgency.

Whilst acknowledging the current practice of voluntary reporting on arms transfer denials on an individual basis and undercuts of such denials, Participating States agreed to study the value of reporting such transfers and denials.

Recognising that the level of transparency in the dual-use pillar is already advanced, Participating States decided to study the possible inclusion of end-user data in denial notifications of Tier One items on the list of dual-use goods and technologies, and of items on Tier Two and its subset of Very Sensitive items.

Participating States agreed to certain control list amendments. They also agreed that the lists should continue to be updated in a timely manner and in accordance with Wassenaar procedures to keep them relevant to security, technological and commercial developments.

Participating States recognised it is important to have comprehensive controls of listed "software" and "technology", including controls on intangible transfers. Participating States also recognised that it is important to continue deepening WA understanding of how and how much to control those transfers. In this context, Participating States agreed that the possibility of taking national measures should be considered.

Participating States affirmed that there should be strong, effective, transparent and national law-based enforcement of export controls. The elements of export control enforcement include a preventive programme, an investigatory process, penalties for violations and international cooperation.

Participating States reaffirmed that the Wassenaar Arrangement is open, on a global and non-discriminatory basis, to prospective adherents that comply with the agreed criteria for participation.

Participating States agreed to work actively with non-Participating States with a view to contributing to the ability of non-participants to implement responsible national export control policies in line with WA purposes, to establish and enforce effective national export control systems, and to provide support, as appropriate, in meeting criteria for membership by non-Participating States.

It was also agreed that an information exchange at the political/institutional level with other international fora dealing with issues similar to the WA's may be developed not only concerning the areas and nature of each other's activities to avoid duplication of work, or to facilitate complementarity, but also concerning parallel or even joint actions, after comprehensive coordination and preparation.

Members of the Plenary expressed their sincere thanks to Ambassador Staffan Sohlman for his major contributions to the work of the Wassenaar Arrangement during his term in office as Chairman.

The next WA Plenary regular meeting is to be held in Bratislava in November/December 2000. Ambassador Alojz Némethy (Slovakia) will assume the chairmanship as of 1 January 2000.

Appendix 3: Specific Information Exchange on Arms

Content by category

1. Battle tanks

Tracked or wheeled self-propelled armoured fighting vehicles with high cross-country mobility and a high level of self-protection, weighing at least 16.5 metric tonnes unladen weight, with a high muzzle velocity direct fire main gun of at least 75 mm calibre.

2. Armoured combat vehicles

2.1 Tracked, semi-tracked or wheeled self-propelled vehicles, with armoured protection and cross-country capability designed, or modified and equipped:

2.1.1 to transport a squad of four or more infantrymen, or

2.1.2 with an integral or organic weapon of at least 12.5 mm calibre, or

2.1.3 with a missile launcher.

2.2 Tracked, semi-tracked or wheeled self-propelled vehicles, with armoured protection and cross-country capability specially designed, or modified and equipped:

2.2.1 with organic technical means for observation, reconnaissance, target indication, and designed to perform reconnaissance missions, or

2.2.2 with integral organic technical means for command of troops, or

2.2.3 with integral organic electronic and technical means designed for electronic warfare.

3. Large calibre artillery systems

3.1 Guns, howitzers, mortars, and artillery pieces combining the characteristics of a gun or a howitzer capable of engaging surface targets by delivering primarily indirect fire, with a calibre of 100 to 155 mm, inclusive.

3.2 Guns, howitzers, mortars, and artillery pieces combining the characteristics of a gun or a howitzer capable of engaging surface targets by delivering primarily indirect fire, with a calibre above 155 mm.

3.3 Multiple-launch rocket systems capable of engaging surface targets, including armour, by delivering primarily indirect fire with the calibre of 100 mm and above.

4. Military aircraft/unmanned aerial vehicles

4.1 Military aircraft:

Fixed-wing or variable-geometry wing aircraft which are designed, equipped or modified:

4.1.1 to engage targets by employing guided missiles, unguided rockets, bombs, guns, machine guns, cannons or other weapons of destruction.

4.1.2 to perform reconnaissance, command of troops, electronic warfare, electronic and fire suppression of air defence systems, refuelling or airdrop missions.

4.2 Unmanned aerial vehicles:

Unmanned aerial vehicles, specially designed, modified, or equipped for military use including electronic warfare, suppression of air defence systems, or reconnaissance missions, as well as systems for the control and receiving of information from the unmanned aerial vehicles.

'Military aircraft' does not include primary trainer aircraft, unless designed, equipped or modified as described above.

5. Military and attack helicopters

Rotary-wing aircraft which are designed, equipped or modified to:

5.1 engage targets by employing guided or unguided, air-to-surface, anti-armour weapons, air to sub-surface or air-to-air weapons, and equipped with an integrated fire-control and aiming system for these weapons.

5.2 perform reconnaissance, target acquisition (including anti-submarine warfare), communications, command of troops, or electronic warfare, or mine laying missions.

6. Warships

Vessel or submarines armed and equipped for military use with a standard displacement of 750 metric tonnes or above, and those with a standard displacement of less than 750 metric tonnes equipped for launching missiles with a range of at least 25 km or torpedoes with a similar range.

7. Missiles or missile systems

Guided or unguided rockets, ballistic or cruise missiles capable of delivering a warhead or weapon of destruction to a range of at least 25 km, and means designed or modified specifically for launching such missiles or rockets, if not covered by categories 1 to 6.

This category:

7.1 also includes remotely piloted vehicles with the characteristics for missiles as defined above;

7.2 does not include ground-to-air missiles.

Source: Wassenaar Arrangement on Export Controls for Conventional Arms and Dual-Use Goods and Technologies, 'Public statement: December 3, 1999', URL <http://www.wassenaar.org>.

Annexes

Annexe A. Arms control and disarmament agreements

Annexe B. Chronology 1999

Annexe A. Arms control and disarmament agreements

RAGNHILD FERM

Notes

1. The agreements are listed in the order of the date on which they were opened for signature (multilateral agreements) or signed (bilateral agreements); the date on which they entered into force and the depositary for multilateral treaties are also given. Information is as of 1 January 2000 unless otherwise indicated. Where confirmed information on entry into force or new parties became available in early 2000, this information is given in notes.

2. The main source of information is the lists of signatories and parties provided by the depositaries of the treaties.

3. States listed as parties have ratified, acceded or succeeded to the agreements. Former non-self-governing territories, upon attaining independence, sometimes make general statements of continuity to all agreements concluded by the former colonial power. This annexe lists as parties only those former colonies which have made an uncontested declaration on continuity or have notified the depositary about its succession.

4. For a few major treaties, the substantive parts of the most important reservations, declarations and/or interpretive statements made in connection with a state's signature, ratification, accession or succession are given in footnotes below the list of parties.

5. The Russian Federation, constituted in 1991 as an independent state, has confirmed the continuity of international obligations assumed by the Soviet Union. In order to become signatories/parties, the other former Soviet republics which were constituted in 1991 as independent sovereign states subsequently signed, ratified or acceded to agreements.

6. Czechoslovakia split into two states, the Czech Republic and Slovakia, in 1993. Both states have succeeded to all the agreements listed in this annexe to which Czechoslovakia was a party.

7. The Socialist Federal Republic of Yugoslavia (SFRY) split into several states in 1991–92. The international legal status of what remains of the former Yugoslavia—the Federal Republic of Yugoslavia (FRY)—is ambiguous but, since the FRY considers that it is the same entity as the former SFRY, 'Yugoslavia' is listed for those agreements which the SFRY signed or ratified. (The former Yugoslav republics of Bosnia and Herzegovina, Croatia, Macedonia and Slovenia have succeeded, as independent states, to several agreements.)

8. Taiwan, while not recognized as a sovereign state by some nations, is given as a party to those agreements which it has ratified.

9. Unless otherwise stated, the multilateral agreements listed in this annexe are open to all states for signature, ratification, accession or succession.

10. A complete list of UN member states, with the year in which they became members, appears in the glossary at the front of this volume. Not all the states listed in this annexe are UN members.

Protocol for the Prohibition of the Use in War of Asphyxiating, Poisonous or Other Gases, and of Bacteriological Methods of Warfare (Geneva Protocol)

Opened for signature at Geneva on 17 June 1925; entered into force on 8 February 1928; depositary French Government

The protocol declares that the parties agree to be bound by the prohibition on the use in war of these weapons.

Parties (133): Afghanistan, Albania, Algeria,[1] Angola,[1] Antigua and Barbuda, Argentina, Australia, Austria, Bahrain,[1] Bangladesh,[1] Barbados, Belarus, Belgium, Benin, Bhutan, Bolivia, Brazil, Bulgaria, Burkina Faso, Cambodia, Cameroon, Canada, Cape Verde, Central African Republic, Chile, China,[1] Côte d'Ivoire, Cuba, Cyprus, Czech Republic, Denmark, Dominican Republic, Ecuador, Egypt, Equatorial Guinea, Estonia, Ethiopia, Fiji,[1] Finland, France, Gambia, Germany, Ghana, Greece, Grenada, Guatemala, Guinea-Bissau, Holy See, Hungary, Iceland, India,[1] Indonesia, Iran, Iraq,[1] Ireland, Israel,[2] Italy, Jamaica, Japan, Jordan,[3] Kenya, Korea (North),[1] Korea (South),[1] Kuwait,[1] Laos, Latvia, Lebanon, Lesotho, Liberia, Libya,[1] Liechtenstein, Lithuania, Luxembourg, Madagascar, Malawi, Malaysia, Maldives, Malta, Mauritius, Mexico, Monaco, Mongolia, Morocco, Nepal, Netherlands, New Zealand, Nicaragua, Niger, Nigeria,[1] Norway, Pakistan, Panama, Papua New Guinea,[1] Paraguay, Peru, Philippines, Poland, Portugal,[1] Qatar, Romania, Russia, Rwanda, Saint Kitts and Nevis, Saint Lucia, Saint Vincent and the Grenadines, Saudi Arabia, Senegal, Sierra Leone, Slovakia, Solomon Islands, South Africa, Spain, Sri Lanka, Sudan, Swaziland, Sweden, Switzerland, Syria, Tanzania, Thailand, Togo, Tonga, Trinidad and Tobago, Tunisia, Turkey, Uganda, UK,[4] Uruguay, USA,[4] Venezuela, Viet Nam,[1] Yemen, Yugoslavia[1]

[1] The protocol is binding on this state only as regards states which have signed and ratified or acceded to it. The protocol will cease to be binding on this state in regard to any enemy state whose armed forces or whose allies fail to respect the prohibitions laid down in it.

[2] The protocol is binding on Israel only as regards states which have signed and ratified or acceded to it. The protocol shall cease to be binding on Israel in regard to any enemy state whose armed forces, or the armed forces of whose allies, or the regular or irregular forces, or groups or individuals operating from its territory, fail to respect the prohibitions which are the object of the protocol.

[3] Jordan undertakes to respect the obligations contained in the protocol with regard to states which have undertaken similar commitments. It is not bound by the protocol as regards states whose armed forces, regular or irregular, do not respect the provisions of the protocol.

[4] The protocol shall cease to be binding on this state with respect to use in war of asphyxiating, poisonous or other gases, and of all analogous liquids, materials or devices, in regard to any enemy state if such state or any of its allies fails to respect the prohibitions laid down in the protocol.

Signed but not ratified: El Salvador

Treaty for Collaboration in Economic, Social and Cultural Matters and for Collective Self-defence among Western European states (Brussels Treaty)

Opened for signature at Brussels on 17 March 1948; entered into force on 25 August 1948; depositary Belgian Government

The treaty provides for close cooperation of the parties in the military, economic and political fields.

Parties (7): *Original parties:* Belgium, France, Luxembourg, Netherlands, UK

Germany and Italy acceded through the 1954 Protocols.

See also the Protocols of 1954.

Convention on the Prevention and Punishment of the Crime of Genocide (Genocide Convention)

Adopted at Paris by the UN General Assembly on 9 December 1948; entered into force on 12 January 1951; depositary UN Secretary-General

Under the convention any commission of acts intended to destroy, in whole or in part, a national, ethnic, racial or religious group as such is declared to be a crime punishable under international law.

Parties (130): Afghanistan, Albania,* Algeria,* Antigua and Barbuda, Argentina,* Armenia, Australia, Austria, Azerbaijan, Bahamas, Bahrain,* Bangladesh,* Barbados, Belarus,* Belgium, Belize, Bosnia and Herzegovina, Brazil, Bulgaria,* Burkina Faso, Burundi, Cambodia, Canada, Chile, China,* Colombia, Congo (Democratic Republic of), Costa Rica, Côte d'Ivoire, Croatia, Cuba, Cyprus, Czech Republic, Denmark, Ecuador, Egypt, El Salvador, Estonia, Ethiopia, Fiji, Finland,* France, Gabon, Gambia, Georgia, Germany, Ghana, Greece, Guatemala, Haiti, Honduras, Hungary,* Iceland, India,* Iran, Iraq, Ireland, Israel, Italy, Jamaica, Jordan, Kazakhstan, Korea (North), Korea (South), Kuwait, Kyrgyzstan, Laos, Latvia, Lebanon, Lesotho, Liberia, Libya, Liechtenstein, Lithuania, Luxembourg, Macedonia (Former Yugoslav Republic of), Malaysia,* Maldives, Mali, Mexico, Moldova, Monaco, Mongolia,* Morocco,* Mozambique, Myanmar (Burma),* Namibia, Nepal, Netherlands, New Zealand, Nicaragua, Norway, Pakistan, Panama, Papua New Guinea, Peru, Philippines,* Poland,* Portugal,* Romania,* Russia,* Rwanda,* Saint Vincent and the Grenadines, Saudi Arabia, Senegal, Seychelles, Singapore,* Slovakia, Slovenia, South Africa, Spain,* Sri Lanka, Sweden, Syria, Tanzania, Togo, Tonga, Tunisia, Turkey, Uganda, UK, Ukraine,* Uruguay, USA,* Venezuela,* Uzbekistan, Viet Nam,* Yemen,* Yugoslavia, Zimbabwe

*With reservation and/or declaration upon ratification, accession or succession.

Signed but not ratified: Bolivia, Dominican Republic, Paraguay

Geneva Convention IV Relative to the Protection of Civilian Persons in Time of War

Opened for signature at Geneva on 12 August 1949; entered into force on 21 October 1950; depositary Swiss Federal Council

The convention establishes rules for the protection of civilians in areas covered by war and on occupied territories.

Parties (188): Afghanistan, Albania,* Algeria, Andorra, Angola,* Antigua and Barbuda, Argentina, Armenia, Australia,* Austria, Azerbaijan, Bahamas, Bahrain, Bangladesh, Barbados,* Belarus,* Belgium, Belize, Benin, Bhutan, Bolivia, Bosnia and Herzegovina, Botswana, Brazil, Brunei, Bulgaria,* Burkina Faso, Burundi, Cambodia, Cameroon, Canada, Cape Verde, Central African Republic, Chad, Chile, China,* Colombia, Comoros, Congo (Democratic Republic of), Congo (Republic of), Costa Rica, Côte d'Ivoire, Croatia, Cuba, Cyprus, Czech Republic,* Denmark, Djibouti, Dominica, Dominican Republic, Ecuador, Egypt, El Salvador, Equatorial Guinea, Estonia, Ethiopia, Fiji, Finland, France, Gabon, Gambia, Georgia, Germany,* Ghana, Greece, Grenada, Guatemala, Guinea, Guinea-Bissau,* Guyana, Haiti, Holy See, Honduras, Hungary,* Iceland, India, Indonesia, Iran,* Iraq, Ireland, Israel,* Italy, Jamaica, Japan, Jordan, Kazakhstan, Kenya, Kiribati, Korea (North),* Korea (South),* Kuwait,* Kyrgyzstan, Laos, Latvia, Lebanon, Lesotho, Liberia, Libya, Liechtenstein, Lithuania, Luxembourg, Macedonia (Former Yugoslav Republic of),* Madagascar, Malawi, Malaysia, Maldives, Mali, Malta, Mauritania, Mauritius, Mexico, Micronesia, Moldova, Monaco, Mongolia, Morocco, Mozambique, Myanmar (Burma), Namibia, Nepal, Netherlands, New Zealand, Nicaragua, Niger, Nigeria, Norway, Oman, Pakistan,* Palau, Panama, Papua

New Guinea, Paraguay, Peru, Philippines, Poland,* Portugal,* Qatar, Romania,* Russia,* Rwanda, Saint Kitts and Nevis, Saint Lucia, Saint Vincent and the Grenadines, Samoa (Western), San Marino, Sao Tome and Principe, Saudi Arabia, Senegal, Seychelles, Sierra Leone, Singapore,* Slovakia,* Slovenia, Solomon Islands, Somalia, South Africa, Spain, Sri Lanka, Sudan, Suriname,* Swaziland, Sweden, Switzerland, Syria, Tajikistan, Tanzania, Thailand, Togo, Tonga, Trinidad and Tobago, Tunisia, Turkey, Turkmenistan, Tuvalu, Uganda, UK, Ukraine,* United Arab Emirates, Uruguay,* USA,* Uzbekistan, Vanuatu, Venezuela, Viet Nam,* Yemen,* Yugoslavia,* Zambia, Zimbabwe

* With reservation and/or declaration upon ratification, accession or succession.

In 1989 the Palestine Liberation Organization (PLO) informed the depositary that it had decided to adhere to the four Geneva Conventions and the two Protocols of 1977.

See also Protocols I and II of 1977.

Protocols to the 1948 Brussels Treaty (Paris Agreements on the Western European Union)

Opened for signature at Paris on 23 October 1954; entered into force on 6 May 1955; depositary Belgian Government

The three protocols modify the 1948 Brussels Treaty, allowing the Federal Republic of Germany and Italy to become parties in return for controls over German armaments and force levels (annulled, except for weapons of mass destruction, in 1984). The Protocols to the Brussels Treaty are regarded as having created the Western European Union (WEU).

Members of the WEU: Belgium, France, Germany, Greece, Italy, Luxembourg, Netherlands, Portugal, Spain, UK

Antarctic Treaty

Opened for signature at Washington, DC, on 1 December 1959; entered into force on 23 June 1961; depositary US Government

Declares the Antarctic an area to be used exclusively for peaceful purposes. Prohibits any measure of a military nature in the Antarctic, such as the establishment of military bases and fortifications, and the carrying out of military manoeuvres or the testing of any type of weapon. The treaty bans any nuclear explosion as well as the disposal of radioactive waste material in Antarctica.

In accordance with Article IX, consultative meetings are convened at regular intervals to exchange information and hold consultations on matters pertaining to Antarctica, as well as to recommend to the governments measures in furtherance of the principles and objectives of the treaty.

The treaty is subject to ratification by the signatories and is open for accession by UN members or by other states invited to accede with the consent of all the parties entitled to participate in the consultative meetings provided for in Article IX.

Parties (43): Argentina,[†] Australia,[†] Austria, Belgium,[†] Brazil,[†] Bulgaria, Canada, Chile,[†] China,[†] Colombia, Cuba, Czech Republic, Denmark, Ecuador,[†] Finland,[†] France,[†] Germany,[†] Greece, Guatemala, Hungary, India,[†] Italy,[†] Japan,[†] Korea (North), Korea (South),[†] Netherlands,[†] New Zealand,[†] Norway,[†] Papua New Guinea, Peru,[†] Poland,[†] Romania,* Russia,[†] Slovakia, South Africa,[†] Spain,[†] Sweden,[†] Switzerland, Turkey, UK,[†] Ukraine, Uruguay,*[†] USA[†]

* With reservation and/or declaration upon ratification, accession or succession.

† Party entitled to participate in the consultative meetings.

The Protocol on Environmental Protection to the Antarctic Treaty (**Madrid Protocol**) was signed on 4 October 1991 and entered into force on 14 January 1998.

Treaty Banning Nuclear Weapon Tests in the Atmosphere, in Outer Space and Under Water (Partial Test Ban Treaty, PTBT)

Opened for signature at Moscow on 5 August 1963; entered into force on 10 October 1963; depositaries British, US and Russian governments

The treaty prohibits the carrying out of any nuclear weapon test explosion or any other nuclear explosion: (*a*) in the atmosphere, beyond its limits, including outer space, or under water, including territorial waters or high seas; and (*b*) in any other environment if such explosion causes radioactive debris to be present outside the territorial limits of the state under whose jurisdiction or control the explosion is conducted.

Parties (125): Afghanistan, Antigua and Barbuda, Argentina, Armenia, Australia, Austria, Bahamas, Bangladesh, Belarus, Belgium, Benin, Bhutan, Bolivia, Bosnia and Herzegovina, Botswana, Brazil, Bulgaria, Canada, Cape Verde, Central African Republic, Chad, Chile, Colombia, Congo (Democratic Republic of), Costa Rica, Côte d'Ivoire, Croatia, Cyprus, Czech Republic, Denmark, Dominican Republic, Ecuador, Egypt, El Salvador, Equatorial Guinea, Fiji, Finland, Gabon, Gambia, Germany, Ghana, Greece, Guatemala, Guinea-Bissau, Honduras, Hungary, Iceland, India, Indonesia, Iran, Iraq, Ireland, Israel, Italy, Jamaica, Japan, Jordan, Kenya, Korea (South), Kuwait, Laos, Lebanon, Liberia, Libya, Luxembourg, Madagascar, Malawi, Malaysia, Malta, Mauritania, Mauritius, Mexico, Mongolia, Morocco, Myanmar (Burma), Nepal, Netherlands, New Zealand, Nicaragua, Niger, Nigeria, Norway, Pakistan, Panama, Papua New Guinea, Peru, Philippines, Poland, Romania, Russia, Rwanda, Samoa (Western), San Marino, Senegal, Seychelles, Sierra Leone, Singapore, Slovakia, Slovenia, South Africa, Spain, Sri Lanka, Sudan, Suriname, Swaziland, Sweden, Switzerland, Syria, Taiwan, Tanzania, Thailand, Togo, Tonga, Trinidad and Tobago, Tunisia, Turkey, Uganda, UK, Ukraine, Uruguay, USA, Venezuela, Yemen, Yugoslavia, Zambia

Signed but not ratified: Algeria, Burkina Faso, Burundi, Cameroon, Ethiopia, Haiti, Mali, Paraguay, Portugal, Somalia

Treaty on Principles Governing the Activities of States in the Exploration and Use of Outer Space, Including the Moon and Other Celestial Bodies (Outer Space Treaty)

Opened for signature at London, Moscow and Washington, DC, on 27 January 1967; entered into force on 10 October 1967; depositaries British, Russian and US governments

The treaty prohibits the placing into orbit around the earth of any objects carrying nuclear weapons or any other kinds of weapons of mass destruction, the installation of such weapons on celestial bodies, or the stationing of them in outer space in any other manner. The establishment of military bases, installations and fortifications, the testing of any type of weapons and the conduct of military manoeuvres on celestial bodies are also forbidden.

Parties (102): Afghanistan, Algeria, Antigua and Barbuda, Argentina, Australia, Austria, Bahamas, Bangladesh, Barbados, Belarus, Belgium, Benin, Brazil,* Brunei, Bulgaria, Burkina Faso, Canada, Chile, China, Cuba, Cyprus, Czech Republic, Denmark, Dominican Republic,

Ecuador, Egypt, El Salvador, Equatorial Guinea, Fiji, Finland, France, Germany, Greece, Guinea-Bissau, Hungary, Iceland, India, Iraq, Ireland, Israel, Italy, Jamaica, Japan, Kazakhstan, Kenya, Korea (South), Kuwait, Laos, Lebanon, Libya, Madagascar,* Mali, Mauritius, Mexico, Mongolia, Morocco, Myanmar (Burma), Nepal, Netherlands, New Zealand, Niger, Nigeria, Norway, Pakistan, Papua New Guinea, Peru, Poland, Portugal, Romania, Russia, Saint Kitts and Nevis, Saint Lucia, Saint Vincent and the Grenadines, San Marino, Saudi Arabia, Seychelles, Sierra Leone, Singapore, Slovakia, Solomon Islands, South Africa, Spain, Sri Lanka, Sweden, Swaziland, Switzerland, Syria, Taiwan, Thailand, Togo, Tonga, Tunisia, Turkey, Uganda, UK, Ukraine, Uruguay, USA, Venezuela, Viet Nam, Yemen, Zambia

* With reservation and/or declaration upon ratification, accession or succession.

Signed but not ratified: Bolivia, Botswana, Burundi, Cameroon, Central African Republic, Colombia, Congo (Democratic Republic of), Ethiopia, Gambia, Ghana, Guyana, Haiti, Holy See, Honduras, Indonesia, Iran, Jordan, Lesotho, Luxembourg, Malaysia, Nicaragua, Panama, Philippines, Rwanda, Somalia, Trinidad and Tobago, Yugoslavia

Treaty for the Prohibition of Nuclear Weapons in Latin America and the Caribbean (Treaty of Tlatelolco)

Opened for signature at Mexico, Distrito Federal, on 14 February 1967; entered into force on 22 April 1968. The treaty was amended in 1990, 1991 and 1992; amendments not in force as of 1 January 2000; depositary Mexican Government

The treaty prohibits the testing, use, manufacture, production or acquisition by any means, as well as the receipt, storage, installation, deployment and any form of possession of any nuclear weapons by Latin American and Caribbean countries.

The parties should conclude agreements with the IAEA for the application of safeguards to their nuclear activities. The IAEA has the exclusive power to carry out special inspections.

The treaty is open for signature by all the independent states of the region.

Under *Additional Protocol I* states with territories within the zone (France, the Netherlands, the UK and the USA) undertake to apply the statute of military denuclearization to these territories.

Under *Additional Protocol II* the recognized nuclear weapon states (China, France, Russia (at the time of signing, the USSR), the UK and the USA) undertake to respect the statute of military denuclearization of Latin America and not to contribute to acts involving a violation of the treaty, nor to use or threaten to use nuclear weapons against the parties to the treaty.

Parties to the original treaty (32): Antigua and Barbuda, Argentina, Bahamas, Barbados, Belize, Bolivia, Brazil, Chile, Colombia, Costa Rica, Dominica, Dominican Republic, Ecuador, El Salvador, Grenada, Guatemala, Guyana, Haiti, Honduras, Jamaica, Mexico, Nicaragua, Panama, Paraguay, Peru, Saint Kitts and Nevis, Saint Lucia, Saint Vincent and the Grenadines, Suriname, Trinidad and Tobago, Uruguay, Venezuela

Signed but not ratified: Cuba

Ratifications of the amended treaty deposited: Argentina, Barbados, Belize, Brazil, Chile, Colombia, Costa Rica, Ecuador, El Salvador, Grenada, Guatemala, Guyana, Jamaica, Mexico, Paraguay, Peru, Suriname, Uruguay, Venezuela (Note that some countries have ratified only certain amendments.)

Parties to Additional Protocol I: France,[1] Netherlands, UK,[2] USA[3]

Parties to Additional Protocol II: China,[4] France,[5] Russia,[6] UK,[2] USA[7]

[1] France declared that Protocol I shall not apply to transit across French territories situated within the zone of the treaty, and destined for other French territories. The protocol shall not limit the participation of the populations of the French territories in the activities mentioned in Article 1 of the treaty, and in efforts connected with the national defence of France. France does not consider the zone described in the treaty as established in accordance with international law; it cannot, therefore, agree that the treaty should apply to that zone.

[2] When signing and ratifying Protocols I and II, the UK made the following declarations of understanding: The signing and ratification by the UK could not be regarded as affecting in any way the legal status of any territory for the international relations of which the UK is responsible, lying within the limits of the geographical zone established by the treaty. Should any party to the treaty carry out any act of aggression with the support of a nuclear weapon state, the UK would be free to reconsider the extent to which it could be regarded as bound by the provisions of Protocol II.

[3] The USA ratified Protocol I with the following understandings: The provisions of the treaty do not affect the exclusive power and legal competence under international law of a state adhering to this Protocol to grant or deny transit and transport privileges to its own or any other vessels or aircraft irrespective of cargo or armaments; the provisions do not affect rights under international law of a state adhering to this protocol regarding the exercise of the freedom of the seas, or regarding passage through or over waters subject to the sovereignty of a state. The declarations attached by the USA to its ratification of Protocol II apply also to Protocol I.

[4] China declared that it will never send its means of transportation and delivery carrying nuclear weapons to cross the territory, territorial sea or airspace of Latin American countries.

[5] France stated that it interprets the undertaking contained in Article 3 of Protocol II to mean that it presents no obstacle to the full exercise of the right of self-defence enshrined in Article 51 of the UN Charter; it takes note of the interpretation by the Preparatory Commission for the Denuclearization of Latin America according to which the treaty does not apply to transit, the granting or denying of which lies within the exclusive competence of each state party in accordance with international law. In 1974, France made a supplementary statement to the effect that it was prepared to consider its obligations under Protocol II as applying not only to the signatories of the treaty, but also to the territories for which the statute of denuclearization was in force in conformity with Protocol I.

[6] On signing an ratifying Protocol II, the USSR stated that it assumed that the effect of Article 1 of the treaty extends to any nuclear explosive device and that, accordingly, the carrying out by any party of nuclear explosions for peaceful purposes would be a violation of its obligations under Article 1 and would be incompatible with its non-nuclear weapon status. For states parties to the treaty, a solution to the problem of peaceful nuclear explosions can be found in accordance with the provisions of Article V of the NPT and within the framework of the international procedures of the IAEA. It declared that authorizing the transit of nuclear weapons in any form would be contrary to the objectives of the treaty.

Any actions undertaken by a state or states parties to the treaty which are not compatible with their non-nuclear weapon status, and also the commission by one or more states parties to the treaty of an act of aggression with the support of a state which is in possession of nuclear weapons or together with such a state, will be regarded by the USSR as incompatible with the obligations of those countries under the treaty. In such cases it would reserve the right to reconsider its obligations under Protocol II. It further reserves the right to reconsider its attitude to this protocol in the event of any actions on the part of other states possessing nuclear weapons which are incompatible with their obligations under the said protocol.

[7] The USA signed and ratified Protocol II with the following declarations and understandings: Each of the parties retains exclusive power and legal competence, to grant or deny non-parties transit and transport privileges. As regards the undertaking not to use or threaten to use nuclear weapons against the parties, the USA would consider that an armed attack by a party, in which it was assisted by a nuclear weapon state, would be incompatible with the treaty.

Treaty on the Non-proliferation of Nuclear Weapons (Non-Proliferation Treaty, NPT)

Opened for signature at London, Moscow and Washington, DC, on 1 July 1968; entered into force on 5 March 1970; depositaries British, Russian and US governments

The treaty prohibits the transfer by nuclear weapon states (defined in the treaty as those which have manufactured and exploded a nuclear weapon or other nuclear explosive device prior to 1 January 1967) to any recipient whatsoever, of nuclear weapons or other nuclear explosive devices or of control over them, as well as the assistance, encouragement or inducement of any non-nuclear weapon state to manufacture or otherwise acquire such weapons or devices. It also prohibits the receipt by non-nuclear weapon states from any transferor whatsoever, as well as the manufacture or other acquisition by those states, of nuclear weapons or other nuclear explosive devices.

The parties undertake to facilitate the exchange of equipment, materials and scientific and technological information for the peaceful uses of nuclear energy and to ensure that potential benefits from peaceful applications of nuclear explosions will be made available to non-nuclear weapon parties to the treaty. They also undertake to pursue negotiations in good faith on effective measures relating to cessation of the nuclear arms race at an early date and to nuclear disarmament, and on a treaty on general and complete disarmament.

Non-nuclear weapon states undertake to conclude safeguard agreements with the International Atomic Energy Agency (IAEA) with a view to preventing diversion of nuclear energy from peaceful uses to nuclear weapons or other nuclear explosive devices. A Model Protocol, additional to the agreements and strengthening the measures, was approved in 1997; Additional Safeguards Protocols are signed by states individually with the IAEA.

A Review and Extension Conference, convened in 1995 in accordance with the treaty, decided that the treaty should remain in force indefinitely.

Parties (188): Afghanistan,[†] Albania, Algeria,[†] Andorra, Angola, Antigua and Barbuda,[†] Argentina,[†] Armenia,[†] Australia,[†] Austria,[†] Azerbaijan,[†] Bahamas,[†] Bahrain, Bangladesh,[†] Barbados,[†] Belarus,[†] Belgium,[†] Belize,[†] Benin, Bhutan,[†] Bolivia,[†] Bosnia and Herzegovina,[†] Botswana, Brazil, [†] Brunei,[†] Bulgaria,[†] Burkina Faso, Burundi, Cambodia, Cameroon, Canada,[†] Cape Verde, Central African Republic, Chad, Chile,[†] China,[†] Colombia, [†] Comoros, Congo (Democratic Republic of),[†] Congo (Republic of), Costa Rica,[†] Côte d'Ivoire,[†] Croatia,[†] Cyprus,[†] Czech Republic,[†] Denmark,[†] Djibouti, Dominica,[†] Dominican Republic,[†] Ecuador,[†] Egypt,[†] El Salvador,[†] Equatorial Guinea, Eritrea, Estonia,[†] Ethiopia,[†] Fiji,[†] Finland,[†] France,[†] Gabon, Gambia,[†] Georgia, Germany,[†] Ghana,[†] Greece,[†] Grenada,[†] Guatemala,[†] Guinea, Guinea-Bissau, Guyana,[†] Haiti, Holy See,[†] Honduras,[†] Hungary,[†] Iceland,[†] Indonesia,[†] Iran,[†] Iraq,[†] Ireland,[†] Italy,[†] Jamaica,[†] Japan,[†] Jordan,[†] Kazakhstan,[†] Kenya, Kiribati,[†] Korea (North),[†] Korea (South),[†] Kuwait, Kyrgyzstan, Laos, Latvia,[†] Lebanon,[†] Lesotho,[†] Liberia, Libya,[†] Liechtenstein,[†] Lithuania,[†] Luxembourg,[†] Macedonia (Former Yugoslav Republic of), Madagascar,[†] Malawi,[†] Malaysia,[†] Maldives,[†] Mali, Malta,[†] Marshall Islands, Mauritania, Mauritius,[†] Mexico,[†] Micronesia, Moldova, Monaco,[†] Mongolia,[†] Morocco,[†] Mozambique, Myanmar (Burma),[†] Namibia,[†] Nauru,[†] Nepal,[†] Netherlands,[†] New Zealand,[†] Nicaragua,[†] Niger, Nigeria,[†] Norway,[†] Oman, Palau, Panama, [†] Papua New Guinea,[†] Paraguay,[†] Peru,[†] Philippines,[†] Poland,[†] Portugal,[†] Qatar, Romania,[†] Russia,[†] Rwanda, Saint Kitts and Nevis,[†] Saint Lucia,[†] Saint Vincent and the Grenadines,[†] Samoa (Western),[†] San Marino,[†] Sao Tome and Principe, Saudi Arabia, Senegal,[†] Seychelles, Sierra Leone, Singapore,[†] Slovakia,[†] Slovenia,[†] Solomon Islands,[†] Somalia, South Africa,[†] Spain,[†] Sri Lanka,[†] Sudan,[†] Suriname,[†] Swaziland,[†] Sweden,[†] Switzerland,[†] Syria,[†] Taiwan, Tajikistan, Tanzania, Thailand,[†] Togo, Tonga,[†] Trinidad and Tobago,[†] Tunisia,[†] Turkey,[†] Turkmenistan, Tuvalu,[†] Uganda, UK,[†] Ukraine,[†] United Arab Emirates, Uruguay,[†] USA,[†] Uzbekistan, [†] Vanuatu, Venezuela,[†] Viet Nam,[†] Yemen, Yugoslavia,[†] Zambia,[†] Zimbabwe[†]

[†] Party with safeguards agreements in force with the International Atomic Energy Agency (IAEA), as required by the treaty, or concluded by a nuclear weapon state on a voluntary basis.

Additional Safeguards Protocols are in force for 8 states (Australia, the Holy See, Indonesia, Japan, Jordan, Monaco, New Zealand and Uzbekistan); 37 states have signed but not ratified Additional Protocols. Taiwan, although not an IAEA member, has agreed to the application of the measures contained in the protocols.

Treaty on the Prohibition of the Emplacement of Nuclear Weapons and other Weapons of Mass Destruction on the Seabed and the Ocean Floor and in the Subsoil thereof (Seabed Treaty)

Opened for signature at London, Moscow and Washington, DC, on 11 February 1971; entered into force on 18 May 1972; depositaries British, Russian and US governments

The treaty prohibits implanting or emplacing on the seabed and the ocean floor and in the subsoil thereof beyond the outer limit of a 12-mile seabed zone any nuclear weapons or any other types of weapons of mass destruction as well as structures, launching installations or any other facilities specifically designed for storing, testing or using such weapons.

Parties (95): Afghanistan, Algeria, Antigua and Barbuda, Argentina,[1] Australia, Austria, Bahamas, Belarus, Belgium, Benin, Bosnia and Herzegovina, Botswana, Brazil,[2] Bulgaria, Canada,[3] Cape Verde, Central African Republic, China, Congo (Republic of), Côte d'Ivoire, Croatia, Cuba, Cyprus, Czech Republic, Denmark, Dominican Republic, Equatorial Guinea, Ethiopia, Finland, Germany, Ghana, Greece, Guatemala, Guinea-Bissau, Hungary, Iceland, India,[4] Iran, Iraq, Ireland, Italy,[5] Jamaica, Japan, Jordan, Korea (South), Laos, Latvia, Lesotho, Libya, Liechtenstein, Luxembourg, Malaysia, Malta, Mauritius, Mexico,[6] Mongolia, Morocco, Nepal, Netherlands, New Zealand, Nicaragua, Niger, Norway, Panama, Philippines, Poland, Portugal, Qatar, Romania, Russia, Rwanda, Saint Vincent and the Grenadines, Sao Tome and Principe, Saudi Arabia, Seychelles, Singapore, Slovakia, Slovenia, Solomon Islands, South Africa, Spain, Swaziland, Sweden, Switzerland, Taiwan, Togo, Tunisia, Turkey,[7] UK, Ukraine, USA, Viet Nam,[8] Yemen, Yugoslavia,[9] Zambia

Signed but not ratified: Bolivia, Burundi, Cambodia, Cameroon, Colombia, Costa Rica, Gambia, Guinea, Honduras, Lebanon, Liberia, Madagascar, Mali, Myanmar (Burma), Paraguay, Senegal, Sierra Leone, Sudan, Tanzania, Uruguay

[1] Argentina precludes any possibility of strengthening, through this treaty, certain positions concerning continental shelves to the detriment of others based on different criteria.

[2] Brazil stated that nothing in the treaty shall be interpreted as prejudicing in any way the sovereign rights of Brazil in the area of the sea, the seabed and the subsoil thereof adjacent to its coasts. It is the understanding of Brazil that the word 'observation', as it appears in para. 1 of Article III of the treaty, refers only to observation that is incidental to the normal course of navigation in accordance with international law.

[3] Canada declared that Article I, para. 1, cannot be interpreted as indicating that any state has a right to implant or emplace any weapons not prohibited under Article I, para. 1, on the seabed and ocean floor, and in the subsoil thereof, beyond the limits of national jurisdiction, or as constituting any limitation on the principle that this area of the seabed and ocean floor and the subsoil thereof shall be reserved for exclusively peaceful purposes. Articles I, II and III cannot be interpreted as indicating that any state but the coastal state has any right to implant or emplace any weapon not prohibited under Article I, para. 1 on the continental shelf, or the subsoil thereof, appertaining to that coastal state, beyond the outer limit of the seabed zone referred to in Article I and defined in Article II. Article III cannot be interpreted as indicating any restrictions or limitation upon the rights of the coastal state, consistent with its exclusive sovereign rights with respect to the continental shelf, to verify, inspect or effect the removal of any weapon, structure, installation, facility or device implanted or emplaced on the continental shelf, or the subsoil thereof, appertaining to that coastal state, beyond the outer limit of the seabed zone referred to in Article I and defined in Article II.

[4] The accession by India is based on its position that it has full and exclusive rights over the continental shelf adjoining its territory and beyond its territorial waters and the subsoil thereof. There cannot, therefore, be any restriction on, or limitation of, the sovereign right of India as a coastal state to verify, inspect, remove or destroy any weapon, device, structure, installation or facility, which might be implanted or emplaced on or beneath its continental shelf by any other country, or to take such other steps as may be considered necessary to safeguard its security.

[5] Italy stated, *inter alia*, that in the case of agreements on further measures in the field of disarmament to prevent an arms race on the seabed and ocean floor and in their subsoil, the question of the delimita-

tion of the area within which these measures would find application shall have to be examined and solved in each instance in accordance with the nature of the measures to be adopted.

[6] Mexico declared that the treaty cannot be interpreted to mean that a state has the right to emplace weapons of mass destruction, or arms or military equipment of any type, on the continental shelf of Mexico. It reserves the right to verify, inspect, remove or destroy any weapon, structure, installation, device or equipment placed on its continental shelf, including nuclear weapons or other weapons of mass destruction.

[7] Turkey declared that the provisions of Article II cannot be used by a state party in support of claims other than those related to disarmament. Hence, Article II cannot be interpreted as establishing a link with the UN Convention on the Law of the Sea. Furthermore, no provision of the Seabed Treaty confers on parties the right to militarize zones which have been demilitarized by other international instruments. Nor can it be interpreted as conferring on either the coastal states or other states the right to emplace nuclear weapons or other weapons of mass destruction on the continental shelf of a demilitarized territory.

[8] Viet Nam stated that no provision of the treaty should be interpreted in a way that would contradict the rights of the coastal states with regard to their continental shelf, including the right to take measures to ensure their security.

[9] In 1974, the Ambassador of Yugoslavia transmitted to the US Secretary of State a note stating that in the view of the Yugoslav Government, Article III, para. 1, of the treaty should be interpreted in such a way that a state exercising its right under this article shall be obliged to notify in advance the coastal state, in so far as its observations are to be carried out 'within the stretch of the sea extending above the continental shelf of the said state'. The USA objected to the Yugoslav reservation, which it considers incompatible with the object and purpose of the treaty.

Convention on the Prohibition of the Development, Production and Stockpiling of Bacteriological (Biological) and Toxin Weapons and on their Destruction (Biological and Toxin Weapons Convention, BTWC)

Opened for signature at London, Moscow and Washington, DC, on 10 April 1972; entered into force on 26 March 1975; depositaries British, Russian and US governments

The convention prohibits the development, production, stockpiling or acquisition by other means or retention of microbial or other biological agents, or toxins whatever their origin or method of production, of types and in quantities that have no justification of prophylactic, protective or other peaceful purposes, as well as weapons, equipment or means of delivery designed to use such agents or toxins for hostile purposes or in armed conflict. The destruction of the agents, toxins, weapons, equipment and means of delivery in the possession of the parties, or their diversion to peaceful purposes, should be effected not later than nine months after the entry into force of the convention. According to a mandate from the 1996 BTWC Review Conference, verification and other measures to strengthen the convention are being discussed and considered in an Ad Hoc Group.

Parties (144): Afghanistan, Albania, Argentina, Armenia, Australia, Austria, Bahamas, Bahrain, Bangladesh, Barbados, Belarus, Belgium, Belize, Benin, Bhutan, Bolivia, Bosnia and Herzegovina, Botswana, Brazil, Brunei, Bulgaria, Burkina Faso, Cambodia, Canada, Cape Verde, Chile, China, Colombia, Congo (Democratic Republic of), Congo (Republic of), Costa Rica, Croatia, Cuba, Cyprus, Czech Republic, Denmark, Dominica, Dominican Republic, Ecuador, El Salvador, Equatorial Guinea, Estonia, Ethiopia, Fiji, Finland, France, Gambia, Georgia, Germany, Ghana, Greece, Grenada, Guatemala, Guinea-Bissau, Honduras, Hungary, Iceland, India,* Indonesia, Iran, Iraq, Ireland,* Italy, Jamaica, Japan, Jordan, Kenya, Korea (North), Korea (South), Kuwait, Laos, Latvia, Lebanon, Lesotho, Libya, Liechtenstein, Lithuania, Luxembourg, Macedonia (Former Yugoslav Republic of), Malaysia, Maldives, Malta, Mauritius, Mexico,* Monaco, Mongolia, Netherlands, New Zealand, Nicaragua, Niger, Nigeria, Norway, Oman, Pakistan, Panama, Papua New Guinea, Paraguay, Peru, Philippines, Poland, Portugal, Qatar, Romania, Russia, Rwanda, Saint Kitts and Nevis, Saint Lucia, Saint

Vincent and the Grenadines, San Marino, Sao Tome and Principe, Saudi Arabia, Senegal, Seychelles, Sierra Leone, Singapore, Slovakia, Slovenia, Solomon Islands, South Africa, Spain, Sri Lanka, Suriname, Swaziland, Sweden, Switzerland,* Taiwan, Thailand, Togo, Tonga, Tunisia, Turkey, Turkmenistan, Uganda, UK, Ukraine, Uruguay, USA, Uzbekistan, Vanuatu, Venezuela, Viet Nam, Yemen, Yugoslavia, Zimbabwe

* With reservation and/or declaration upon ratification, accession or succession.

Signed but not ratified: Burundi, Central African Republic, Côte d'Ivoire, Egypt, Gabon, Guyana, Haiti, Liberia, Madagascar, Malawi, Mali, Morocco, Myanmar (Burma), Nepal, Somalia, Syria, Tanzania, United Arab Emirates

Treaty on the Limitation of Anti-Ballistic Missile Systems (ABM Treaty)

Signed by the USA and the USSR at Moscow on 26 May 1972; entered into force on 3 October 1972

The parties undertake not to build nationwide defences against ballistic missile attack and limits the development and deployment of permitted strategic missile defences. The treaty prohibits the parties from giving air defence missiles, radars or launchers the technical ability to counter strategic ballistic missiles and from testing them in a strategic ABM mode.

A *Protocol* to the ABM Treaty, introducing further numerical restrictions on permitted ballistic missile defences, was signed in 1974.

In 1997 Belarus, Kazakhstan, Russia and Ukraine signed a **Memorandum of Understanding on Succession (MOUS)** in which they assumed the obligations of the former USSR regarding the treaty. Russia and the USA signed a set of Agreed Statements, including the **Demarcation Agreement,** specifying the demarcation line between strategic missile defences, which are not permitted under the treaty, and non-strategic or theatre missile defences (TMD), which are permitted under the treaty. The MOUS and Agreed Statements were ratified by Russia in April 2000.

Treaty on the Limitation of Underground Nuclear Weapon Tests (Threshold Test Ban Treaty, TTBT)

Signed by the USA and the USSR at Moscow on 3 July 1974; entered into force on 11 December 1990

The parties undertake not to carry out any individual underground nuclear weapon test having a yield exceeding 150 kilotons.

Treaty on Underground Nuclear Explosions for Peaceful Purposes (Peaceful Nuclear Explosions Treaty, PNET)

Signed by the USA and the USSR at Moscow and Washington, DC, on 28 May 1976; entered into force on 11 December 1990

The parties undertake not to carry out any underground nuclear explosion for peaceful purposes having a yield exceeding 150 kilotons or any group explosion having an aggregate yield exceeding 150 kilotons.

Convention on the Prohibition of Military or Any Other Hostile Use of Environmental Modification Techniques (Enmod Convention)

Opened for signature at Geneva on 18 May 1977; entered into force on 5 October 1978; depositary UN Secretary-General

The convention prohibits military or any other hostile use of environmental modification techniques having widespread, long-lasting or severe effects as the means of destruction, damage or injury to states party to the convention. The term 'environmental modification techniques' refers to any technique for changing— through the deliberate manipulation of natural processes—the dynamics, composition or structure of the earth, including its biota, lithosphere, hydrosphere and atmosphere, or of outer space. The understandings reached during the negotiations, but not written into the convention, define the terms 'widespread', 'long-lasting' and 'severe'.

Parties (66): Afghanistan, Algeria, Antigua and Barbuda, Argentina, Australia, Austria, Bangladesh, Belarus, Belgium, Benin, Brazil, Bulgaria, Canada, Cape Verde, Chile, Costa Rica, Cuba, Cyprus, Czech Republic, Denmark, Dominica, Egypt, Finland, Germany, Ghana, Greece, Guatemala, Hungary, India, Ireland, Italy, Japan, Korea (North), Korea (South),* Kuwait, Laos, Malawi, Mauritius, Mongolia, Netherlands,* New Zealand, Niger, Norway, Pakistan, Papua New Guinea, Poland, Romania, Russia, Saint Lucia, Saint Vincent and the Grenadines, Sao Tome and Principe, Slovakia, Solomon Islands, Spain, Sri Lanka, Sweden, Switzerland, Tajikistan, Tunisia, UK, Ukraine, Uruguay, USA, Uzbekistan, Viet Nam, Yemen

* With reservation and/or declaration upon ratification, accession or succession.

Signed but not ratified: Bolivia, Congo (Democratic Republic of), Ethiopia, Holy See, Iceland, Iran, Iraq, Lebanon, Liberia, Luxembourg, Morocco, Nicaragua, Portugal, Sierra Leone, Syria, Turkey, Uganda

Protocol I Additional to the 1949 Geneva Conventions, and Relating to the Protection of Victims of International Armed Conflicts, and

Protocol II Additional to the 1949 Geneva Conventions, and Relating to the Protection of Victims of Non-International Armed Conflicts

Opened for signature at Bern on 12 December 1977; entered into force on 7 December 1978; depositary Swiss Federal Council

The protocols confirm that the right of the parties to international or non-international armed conflicts to choose methods or means of warfare is not unlimited and that it is prohibited to use weapons or means of warfare which cause superfluous injury or unnecessary suffering.

Parties to Protocol I (155) and Protocol II (148): Albania, Algeria,* Angola,[1]* Antigua and Barbuda, Argentina,* Armenia, Australia,* Austria,* Bahamas, Bahrain, Bangladesh, Barbados, Belarus, Belgium,* Belize, Benin, Bolivia, Bosnia and Herzegovina, Botswana, Brazil, Brunei, Bulgaria, Burkina Faso, Burundi, Cambodia, Cameroon, Canada,* Cape Verde, Central African Republic, Chad, Chile, China,* Colombia, Comoros, Congo (Democratic Republic of),[1] Congo (Republic of), Costa Rica, Côte d'Ivoire, Croatia, Cuba, Cyprus, Czech Republic, Denmark,* Djibouti, Dominica, Dominican Republic, Ecuador, Egypt,* El Salvador, Equatorial Guinea, Estonia, Ethiopia, Finland,* France,[2] Gabon, Gambia, Georgia, Germany,* Ghana, Greece, Grenada, Guatemala, Guinea, Guinea-Bissau, Guyana, Holy See,* Honduras, Hungary, Iceland,* Ireland, Italy,* Jamaica, Jordan, Kazakhstan, Kenya, Korea (North),[1]

Korea (South),* Kuwait, Kyrgyzstan, Laos, Latvia, Lebanon, Lesotho, Liberia, Libya, Liechtenstein,* Luxembourg, Macedonia (Former Yugoslav Republic of), Madagascar, Malawi, Maldives, Mali, Malta,* Mauritania, Mauritius, Mexico,[1] Micronesia, Moldova, Mongolia, Mozambique,[1] Namibia, Netherlands,* New Zealand,* Nicaragua,[3] Niger, Nigeria, Norway, Oman,* Palau, Panama, Paraguay, Peru, Philippines,[2] Poland, Portugal, Qatar,*[1] Romania, Russia,* Rwanda, Saint Kitts and Nevis, Saint Lucia, Saint Vincent and the Grenadines, Samoa (Western), San Marino, Sao Tome and Principe, Saudi Arabia,[1]* Senegal, Seychelles, Sierra Leone, Slovakia, Slovenia, Solomon Islands, South Africa, Spain,* Suriname, Swaziland, Sweden,* Switzerland,* Syria,*[1] Tajikistan, Tanzania, Togo, Tunisia, Turkmenistan, Uganda, UK, Ukraine, United Arab Emirates,* Uruguay, Uzbekistan, Vanuatu, Venezuela, Viet Nam,[1] Yemen, Yugoslavia,* Zambia, Zimbabwe

Note: Monaco acceded to the protocols on 7 January 2000.

In 1989 the Palestine Liberation Organization (PLO) informed the depositary that it had decided to adhere to the four Geneva Conventions and the two Protocols.

* With reservation and/or declaration upon ratification, accession or succession.

[1] Party only to Protocol I.
[2] Party only to Protocol II.
[3] In accordance with the provisions of the protocols, they enter into force for a party 6 months after the deposit of its instrument of ratification or accession. This state ratified or acceded to the protocols in the second half of 1999 and the protocols entered into force for that state in 2000.

Convention on the Physical Protection of Nuclear Material

Opened for signature at Vienna and New York on 3 March 1980; entered into force on 8 February 1987; depositary IAEA Director General

The convention obligates the parties to protect nuclear material for peaceful purposes while in international transport.

Parties (64): Antigua and Barbuda, Argentina,* Armenia, Australia, Austria, Belarus, Belgium,† Bosnia and Herzegovina, Brazil, Bulgaria, Canada, Chile, China,* Croatia, Cuba, Cyprus, Czech Republic, Denmark,† Ecuador, Estonia, Euratom,*† Finland, France,*† Germany,† Greece,† Guatemala, Hungary, Indonesia,* Ireland,† Italy,*† Japan, Korea (South),* Lebanon, Liechtenstein, Lithuania, Luxembourg,† Macedonia (Former Yugoslav Republic of), Mexico, Moldova, Monaco, Mongolia,* Netherlands,*† Norway, Panama, Paraguay, Peru,* Philippines, Poland,* Portugal,† Romania, Russia,* Slovakia, Slovenia, Spain,*† Sweden, Switzerland, Tajikistan, Tunisia, Turkey,* UK,† Ukraine, USA, Uzbekistan, Yugoslavia

* With reservation and/or declaration upon ratification, accession or succession.

† Ratified as a Euratom member state.

Signed but not ratified: Dominican Republic, Haiti, Israel, Morocco, Niger, South Africa

Note: Sudan acceded to the convention on 18 May 2000.

Convention on Prohibitions or Restrictions on the Use of Certain Conventional Weapons which may be Deemed to be Excessively Injurious or to have Indiscriminate Effects (CCW Convention, or 'Inhumane Weapons' Convention)

The convention, with the original protocols I, II and III, was opened for signature at New York on 10 April 1981; entered into force on 2 December 1983; depositary UN Secretary-General

The convention is an 'umbrella treaty', under which specific agreements can be concluded in the form of protocols. To become a party a state must ratify a minimum of two of the original protocols.

Protocol I prohibits the use of weapons intended to injure by fragments which are not detectable in the human body by X-rays.

Protocol II prohibits or restricts the use of mines, booby-traps and other devices.

Amended Protocol II, reinforcing the constraints regarding landmines, entered into force on 3 December 1998.

Protocol III restricts the use of incendiary weapons.

Protocol IV, prohibiting the employment of laser weapons specifically designed to cause permanent blindness to unenhanced vision, entered into force on 30 July 1998.

Parties to the convention and original protocols (75): Argentina,* Australia, Austria, Belarus, Belgium, Benin,[1] Bosnia and Herzegovina, Brazil, Bulgaria, Cambodia, Canada, Cape Verde, China, Costa Rica, Croatia, Cuba, Cyprus,* Czech Republic, Denmark, Djibouti, Ecuador, Finland, France,*[2] Georgia, Germany, Greece, Guatemala, Holy See, Hungary, India, Ireland, Israel,[2] Italy, Japan, Jordan,[1] Laos, Latvia, Liechtenstein, Lithuania,[1] Luxembourg, Macedonia (Former Yugoslav Republic of), Malta, Mauritius, Mexico, Monaco,[3] Mongolia, Netherlands,* New Zealand, Niger, Norway, Pakistan, Panama, Peru,[1] Philippines, Poland, Portugal, Romania, Russia, Senegal, Slovakia, Slovenia, South Africa, Spain, Sweden, Switzerland, Tajikistan, Togo, Tunisia, Uganda, UK, Ukraine, Uruguay, USA,[2] Uzbekistan, Yugoslavia

* With reservation and/or declaration upon ratification, accession or succession.

[1] Party only to Protocols I and III.
[2] Party only to Protocols I and II.
[3] Party only to Protocol I.

Signed but not ratified the convention and original protocols: Afghanistan, Egypt, Iceland, Morocco, Nicaragua, Nigeria, Sierra Leone, Sudan, Turkey, Viet Nam

Parties to the amended Protocol II (47): Argentina, Australia, Austria, Belgium, Brazil, Bulgaria, Cambodia, Canada, Cape Verde, China, Costa Rica, Czech Republic, Denmark, Finland, France, Germany, Greece, Holy See, Hungary, India, Ireland, Italy, Japan, Liechtenstein, Lithuania, Luxembourg, Monaco, Netherlands, New Zealand, Norway, Pakistan, Panama, Peru, Philippines, Portugal, Senegal, Slovakia, South Africa, Spain, Sweden, Switzerland, UK, Ukraine, Uruguay, USA

Parties to Protocol IV (45): Argentina, Australia, Austria, Belgium, Brazil, Bulgaria, Cambodia, Canada, Cape Verde, China, Costa Rica, Czech Republic, Denmark, Finland, France, Germany, Greece, Holy See, Hungary, India, Ireland, Italy, Japan, Latvia, Liechtenstein, Lithuania, Luxembourg, Mexico, Netherlands, New Zealand, Norway, Panama, Peru, Philippines, Russia, Slovakia, South Africa, Spain, Sweden, Switzerland, Tajikistan, UK, Uruguay, Uzbekistan

South Pacific Nuclear Free Zone Treaty (Treaty of Rarotonga)

Opened for signature at Rarotonga, Cook Islands, on 6 August 1985; entered into force on 11 December 1986; depositary Director of the South Pacific Bureau for Economic Co-operation (from 1988, South Pacific Forum Secretariat)

The treaty prohibits the manufacture or acquisition by other means of any nuclear explosive device, as well as possession or control over such device by the parties anywhere inside or outside the zone area described in an annex. The parties also undertake not to supply nuclear material or equipment, unless subject to IAEA safeguards, and to prevent in their territories the stationing as well as the testing of any nuclear explosive device and undertake not to dump, and to prevent the dumping of, radioactive wastes and other radioactive matter at sea anywhere within the zone. Each party remains free to allow visits, as well as transit, by foreign ships and aircraft.

The treaty is open for signature by the members of the South Pacific Forum.

Under *Protocol 1* France, the UK and the USA undertake to apply the treaty prohibitions relating to the manufacture, stationing and testing of nuclear explosive devices in the territories situated within the zone, for which they are internationally responsible.

Under *Protocol 2* China, France, Russia, the UK and the USA undertake not to use or threaten to use a nuclear explosive device against the parties to the treaty or against any territory within the zone for which a party to Protocol 1 is internationally responsible.

Under *Protocol 3* China, France, the UK, the USA and Russia undertake not to test any nuclear explosive device anywhere within the zone.

Parties (12): Australia, Cook Islands, Fiji, Kiribati, Nauru, New Zealand, Niue, Papua New Guinea, Samoa (Western), Solomon Islands, Tuvalu, Vanuatu

Signed but not ratified: Tonga

Parties to Protocol 1: France, UK; **signed but not ratified:** USA

Parties to Protocol 2: China, France,[1] Russia, UK[2]; **signed but not ratified:** USA

Parties to Protocol 3: China, France, Russia, UK; **signed but not ratified:** USA

[1] France declared that the negative security guarantees set out in Protocol 2 are the same as the CD declaration of 6 Apr. 1995 referred to in UN Security Council Resolution 984 of 11 Apr. 1995.

[2] The UK declared that nothing in the treaty affects the rights under international law with regard to transit of the zone or visits to ports and airfields within the zone by ships and aircraft. The UK will not be bound by the undertakings in Protocol 2 in case of an invasion or any other attack on the UK, its territories, its armed forces or its allies, carried out or sustained by a party to the treaty in association or alliance with a nuclear weapon state or if a party violates its non-proliferation obligations under the treaty.

Treaty on the Elimination of Intermediate-Range and Shorter-Range Missiles (INF Treaty)

Signed by the USA and the USSR at Washington, DC, on 8 December 1987; entered into force on 1 June 1988

The treaty obligates the parties to destroy all land-based missiles with a range of 500–5500 km (intermediate-range, 1000–5500 km; and shorter-range, 500–1000 km) and their launchers by 1 June 1991. The treaty was implemented by the two parties before this date.

Treaty on Conventional Armed Forces in Europe (CFE Treaty)

*Opened for signature at Vienna on 19 November 1990; entered into force on
9 November 1992; depositary Netherlands Government*

The treaty sets ceilings on five categories of treaty-limited equipment (TLE)—battle
tanks, armoured combat vehicles, artillery of at least 100-mm calibre, combat aircraft
and attack helicopters—in an area stretching from the Atlantic Ocean to the Ural
Mountains (the Atlantic-to-the-Urals, ATTU, zone).

The treaty was negotiated and signed by the member states of the Warsaw Treaty
Organization (WTO) and NATO within the framework of the Conference on Security
and Co-operation in Europe (from 1995 the Organization for Security and Co-operation in Europe, OSCE).

The **1992 Tashkent Agreement** adopted by the former Soviet republics
(except the three Baltic states) with territories within the ATTU zone, and the
1992 Oslo Document (Final Document of the Extraordinary Conference of
the States Parties to the CFE Treaty), introduced modifications to the treaty
required because of the emergence of new states after the break-up of the
USSR.

Parties (30): Armenia, Azerbaijan, Belarus, Belgium, Bulgaria, Canada, Czech Republic,
Denmark, France, Georgia, Germany, Greece, Hungary, Iceland, Italy, Kazakhstan, Luxem-
bourg, Moldova, Netherlands, Norway, Poland, Portugal, Romania, Russia, Slovakia, Spain,
Turkey, UK, Ukraine, USA

The first Review Conference of the CFE Treaty adopted the **1996 Flank
Document**, which reorganized the flank areas geographically and numeri-
cally, allowing Russia and Ukraine to deploy more TLE along their borders.

On 19 November 1999 the CFE parties signed the **Agreement on Adaptation of the CFE Treaty**, which replaces the CFE Treaty bloc-to-bloc military
balance with individual state limits on TLE holdings and provides for a new
structure of limitations and new military flexibility mechanisms, flank sub-
limits and enhanced transparency; it opens the CFE regime to all the other
European states. It will enter into force when it has been ratified by all the
signatories. The **Final Act**, with annexes, contains politically binding
arrangements with regard to the North Caucasus, Central and Eastern Europe,
and withdrawals of armed forces from foreign territories.

Agreement on Adaptation: no ratifications

The Concluding Act of the Negotiation on Personnel Strength of Conventional Armed Forces in Europe (CFE-1A Agreement)

*Opened for signature by the parties to the CFE Treaty at Helsinki on
10 July 1992; entered into force simultaneously with the CFE Treaty;
depositary Netherlands Government*

The agreement limits the personnel of the conventional land-based armed
forces of the parties within the ATTU zone.

Vienna Documents 1990, 1992, 1994 and 1999 on Confidence- and Security-Building Measures

The Vienna Documents were adopted by the participating states of the Conference on Security and Co-operation in Europe (from 1995 the Organization for Security and Co-operation in Europe). The Vienna Document 1999 was adopted at Istanbul on 16 November 1999.

Vienna Document 1990 built on the 1986 Stockholm Document on Confidence- and Security-building Measures (CSBMs) and disarmament in Europe; subsequent Vienna documents introduced changes and additions to the provisions of the previous one.

The **Vienna Documents 1992 and 1994** introduced new mechanisms and parameters for military activities, defence planning and military contacts. The **Vienna Document 1999** introduces regional measures aimed at increasing transparency and confidence in a bilateral, multilateral and regional context and some improvements, in particular regarding the constraining measures.

Treaty on the Reduction and Limitation of Strategic Offensive Arms (START I Treaty)

Signed by the USA and the USSR at Moscow on 31 July 1991; entered into force on 5 December 1994

The treaty requires the USA and Russia to make phased reductions in their offensive strategic nuclear forces over a seven-year period. It sets numerical limits on deployed strategic nuclear delivery vehicles (SNDVs)—ICBMs, SLBMs and heavy bombers—and the nuclear warheads they carry. In the 1992 Protocol to Facilitate the Implementation of the START Treaty (**Lisbon Protocol**), Belarus, Kazakhstan and Ukraine also assumed the obligations of the former USSR under the treaty. They pledged to eliminate all the former Soviet strategic weapons on their territories within the seven-year reduction period and to join the NPT as non-nuclear weapon states in the shortest possible time.

Treaty on Open Skies

Opened for signature at Helsinki on 24 March 1992; not in force as of 1 January 2000; depositaries Canadian and Hungarian governments

The treaty obligates the parties to submit their territories to short-notice unarmed surveillance flights. The area of application stretches from Vancouver, Canada, eastward to Vladivostok, Russia.

The treaty was negotiated between the member states of the Warsaw Treaty Organization (WTO) and NATO. It is open for signature by the NATO states, the new states of the former WTO members, and the new states of the former Soviet Union except the three Baltic states. For six months after entry into force of the treaty, any other OSCE member state may apply for accession. The treaty will enter into force 60 days after the deposit of 20 instruments of ratification, including those of the depositaries (Canada and Hungary), and all the signatories with more than eight 'passive quotas' (i.e., flights which the state is obliged to accept); that is, Belarus, Canada, France, Germany, Italy, Russia, Turkey, the UK, Ukraine and the USA. After the treaty has entered into force, other OSCE states may apply for accession.

23 ratifications deposited: Belgium, Bulgaria, Canada, Czech Republic, Denmark, France, Georgia, Germany, Greece, Hungary, Iceland, Italy, Luxembourg, Netherlands, Norway, Poland, Portugal, Romania, Slovakia, Spain, Turkey, UK, USA

Signed but not ratified: Belarus, Kyrgyzstan, Russia

Note: Ukraine ratified the treaty on 2 March 2000.

Treaty on Further Reduction and Limitation of Strategic Offensive Arms (START II Treaty)

Signed by the USA and Russia at Moscow on 3 January 1993; not in force as of 1 January 2000

The treaty requires the USA and Russia to eliminate their MIRVed ICBMs and sharply reduce the number of their deployed strategic nuclear warheads to no more than 3000–3500 each (of which no more than 1750 may be deployed on SLBMs) by 1 January 2003 or no later than 31 December 2000 if the USA and Russia reach a formal agreement committing the USA to help finance the elimination of strategic nuclear weapons in Russia.

On 26 September 1997 the two parties signed a *Protocol* to the treaty providing for the extension until the end of 2007 of the period of implementation of the treaty.

Note: The US Senate ratified the treaty on 26 January 1996; the Russian Duma and Federation Council approved ratification on 14 and 19 April 2000, respectively.

Convention on the Prohibition of the Development, Production, Stockpiling and Use of Chemical Weapons and on their Destruction (Chemical Weapons Convention, CWC)

Opened for signature at Paris on 13 January 1993; entered into force on 29 April 1997; depositary UN Secretary-General

The convention prohibits both the use of chemical weapons (also prohibited by the 1925 Geneva Protocol) and the development, production, acquisition, transfer and stockpiling of chemical weapons. Each party undertakes to destroy its chemical weapons and production facilities within 10 years after the treaty enters into force.

Parties (129): Albania, Algeria, Argentina, Armenia, Australia, Austria, Bahrain, Bangladesh, Belarus, Belgium, Benin, Bolivia, Bosnia and Herzegovina, Botswana, Brazil, Brunei, Bulgaria, Burkina Faso, Burundi, Cameroon, Canada, Chile, China, Cook Islands, Costa Rica, Côte d'Ivoire, Croatia, Cuba, Cyprus, Czech Republic, Denmark, Ecuador, El Salvador, Equatorial Guinea, Estonia, Ethiopia, Fiji, Finland, France, Gambia, Georgia, Germany, Ghana, Greece, Guinea, Guyana, Holy See, Hungary, Iceland, India, Indonesia, Iran, Ireland, Italy, Japan, Jordan, Kenya, Korea (South), Kuwait, Laos, Latvia, Lesotho, Liechtenstein, Lithuania, Luxembourg, Macedonia (Former Yugoslav Republic of), Malawi, Maldives, Mali, Malta, Mauritania, Mauritius, Mexico, Micronesia, Moldova, Monaco, Mongolia, Morocco, Namibia, Nepal, Netherlands, New Zealand, Nicaragua, Niger, Nigeria, Norway, Oman, Pakistan, Panama, Papua New Guinea, Paraguay, Peru, Philippines, Poland, Portugal, Qatar, Romania, Russia, Saint Lucia, San Marino, Saudi Arabia, Senegal, Seychelles, Singapore, Slovakia, Slovenia, South Africa, Spain, Sri Lanka, Sudan, Suriname, Swaziland, Sweden, Switzerland, Tajikistan, Tanzania, Togo, Trinidad and Tobago, Tunisia, Turkey, Turkmenistan, UK, Ukraine, Uruguay, USA, Uzbekistan, Venezuela, Viet Nam, Zimbabwe

Signed but not ratified: Afghanistan, Azerbaijan, Bahamas, Bhutan, Cambodia, Cape Verde, Central African Republic, Chad, Colombia, Comoros, Congo (Democratic Republic of), Congo (Republic of), Djibouti, Dominica, Dominican Republic, Gabon, Grenada, Guatemala, Guinea-Bissau, Haiti, Honduras, Israel, Jamaica, Kazakhstan, Kyrgyzstan, Liberia, Madagascar, Malaysia, Marshall Islands, Myanmar (Burma), Nauru, Rwanda, Saint Kitts and Nevis, Saint Vincent and the Grenadines, Samoa (Western), Sierra Leone, Thailand, Uganda, United Arab Emirates, Yemen, Zambia

Note: Eritrea, Azerbaijan, Kazakhstan, Colombia, the Federal Republic of Yugoslavia and Malaysia ratified or acceded to the convention between 1 January and 1 May 2000.

Treaty on the Southeast Asia Nuclear Weapon-Free Zone (Treaty of Bangkok)

Opened for signature at Bangkok on 15 December 1995; entered into force on 27 March 1997; depositary Government of Thailand

The treaty prohibits the development, manufacture, acquisition or testing of nuclear weapons inside or outside the zone area as well as the stationing and transport of nuclear weapons in or through the zone. Each state party may decide for itself whether to allow visits and transit by foreign ships and aircraft. The parties undertake not to dump at sea or discharge into the atmosphere anywhere within the zone any radioactive material or wastes or dispose of radioactive material on land. The parties should conclude an agreement with the IAEA for the application of full-scope safeguards to their peaceful nuclear activities.

The zone includes not only the territories but also the continental shelves and exclusive economic zones of the states parties.

The treaty is open for signature by all the states in South-East Asia.

Under a *Protocol* to the treaty China, France, Russia, the UK and the USA are to undertake not to use or threaten to use nuclear weapons against any state party to the treaty. They should further undertake not to use nuclear weapons within the Southeast Asia nuclear weapon-free zone. The protocol will enter into force for each state party on the date of its deposit of the instrument of ratification.

Parties (9): Brunei, Cambodia, Indonesia, Laos, Malaysia, Myanmar (Burma), Singapore, Thailand, Viet Nam

Signed but not ratified: Philippines

Protocol: no signatures, no ratifications

Agreement on Confidence- and Security-Building Measures in Bosnia and Herzegovina

Signed at Vienna on 26 January 1996, entered into force on 26 January 1996

The agreement is largely based on the Vienna Document 1994 but includes additional restrictions and restraints measures on military movements, deployments and exercises and provides for exchange of information and data relating to major weapon systems.

Parties (3): Bosnia and Herzegovina and its two enetities—the Federation of Bosnia and Herzegovina and the Republika Srpska

African Nuclear-Weapon-Free Zone Treaty (Treaty of Pelindaba)

Opened for signature at Cairo on 11 April 1996; not in force as of 1 January 2000; depositary Secretary-General of the Organization of African Unity

The treaty prohibits the research, development, manufacture and acquisition of nuclear explosive devices and the testing or stationing of any nuclear explosive device. Each party remains free to allow visits, as well as transit by foreign ships and aircraft. The treaty also prohibits any attack against nuclear installations. The parties undertake not to dump or permit the dumping of radioactive wastes and other radioactive matter anywhere within the zone. The parties should conclude an agreement with the IAEA for the application of comprehensive safeguards to their peaceful nuclear activities.

The zone includes the territory of the continent of Africa, island states members of the OAU and all islands considered by the OAU to be part of Africa.

The treaty is open for signature by all the states of Africa. It will enter into force upon the 28th ratification.

Under *Protocol I* China, France, Russia, the UK and the USA are to undertake not to use or threaten to use a nuclear explosive device against the parties to the Treaty.

Under *Protocol II* China, France, Russia, the UK and the USA are to undertake not to test nuclear explosive devices anywhere within the zone.

Under *Protocol III* states with territories within the zone for which they are internationally responsible are to undertake to observe certain provisions of the treaty with respect to these territories. This protocol is open for signature by France and Spain.

The protocols will enter into force simultaneously with the treaty for those protocol signatories that have deposited their instruments of ratification.

11 ratifications deposited: Algeria, Botswana, Burkina Faso, Côte d'Ivoire, Gambia, Mali, Mauritania, Mauritius, South Africa, Tanzania, Zimbabwe

Signed but not ratified: Angola, Benin, Burundi, Cameroon, Cape Verde, Central African Republic, Chad, Comoros, Congo (Democratic Republic of), Congo (Republic of), Djibouti, Egypt, Eritrea, Ethiopia, Gabon, Ghana, Guinea, Guinea-Bissau, Kenya, Lesotho, Liberia, Libya, Malawi, Morocco, Mozambique, Namibia, Niger, Nigeria, Rwanda, Sao Tome and Principe, Senegal, Seychelles, Sierra Leone, Sudan, Swaziland, Togo, Tunisia, Uganda, Zambia

Protocol I ratification: China, France[1]; **signed but not ratified:** Russia,[2] UK,[3] USA[4]

Protocol II ratification: China, France; **signed but not ratified:** Russia,[2] UK,[3] USA[4]

Protocol III ratification: France

[1] France stated that the Protocols did not affect its right to self-defence, as stipulated in Article 51 of the UN Charter. It clarified that its commitment under Article 1 of Protocol I was equivalent to the negative security assurances given by France to non-nuclear weapon states parties to the NPT, as confirmed in its declaration made on 6 Apr. 1995 at the Conference on Disarmament, and as referred to in UN Security Council Resolution 984.

[2] Russia stated that as long as a military base of a nuclear state was located on the islands of the Chagos archipelago these islands could not be regarded as fulfilling the requirements put forward by the Treaty for nuclear-weapon-free territories. Moreover, since certain states declared that they would consider themselves free from the obligations under the Protocols with regard to the mentioned territories, Russia could not consider itself to be bound by the obligations under Protocol I in respect to the same territories. Russia interpreted its obligations under Article 1 of Protocol I as follows: It would not use nuclear weapons against a state party to the Treaty, except in the case of invasion or any other armed attack on Russia, its territory, its armed forces or other troops, its allies or a state towards which it had a

security commitment, carried out or sustained by a non-nuclear-weapon state party to the Treaty, in association or alliance with a nuclear-weapon state.

[3] The UK stated that it did not accept the inclusion of the British Indian Ocean Territory within the African nuclear weapon-free zone without its consent, and did not accept, by its adherence to Protocol I and III, any legal obligations in respect of that territory. Moreover, it would not be bound by its undertaking under Article 1 of Protocol I in case of an invasion or any other attack on the United Kingdom, its dependent territories, its armed forces or other troops, its allies or a state towards which it had security commitment, carried out or sustained by a party to the treaty in association or alliance with a nuclear-weapon state, or if any party to the treaty was in material breach of its own non-proliferation obligations under the treaty.

[4] The USA stated, with respect to Protocol I, that it would consider an invasion or any other attack on the USA, its territories, its armed forces or other troops, its allies or on a state toward which it had a security commitment, carried out or sustained by a party to the treaty in association or alliance with a nuclear-weapon state, to be incompatible with the treaty party's corresponding obligations. The USA also stated that neither the treaty nor Protocol III would apply to the activities of the UK, the USA or any other state not party to the treaty on the island of Diego Garcia or elsewhere in the British Indian Ocean Territories. No change was, therefore, required in US armed forces operations in Diego Garcia and elsewhere in these territories.

Agreement on Sub-Regional Arms Control (Florence Agreement)

Signed at Florence on 14 June 1996; entered into force upon signature

The agreement was negotiated under the auspices of the OSCE in accordance with the mandate in the 1995 General Framework Agreement for Peace in Bosnia and Herzegovina (Dayton Agreement). It sets numerical ceilings on armaments of the former warring parties: Bosnia and Herzegovina and its two entities, Croatia and the Federal Republic of Yugoslavia. Five categories of heavy conventional weapons are included: battle tanks, armoured combat vehicles, heavy artillery (75 mm and above), combat aircraft and attack helicopters. The reductions were completed by 31 October 1997. It is confirmed that 6580 weapon items were destroyed by that date.

Parties (5): Bosnia and Herzegovina and its two entities—the Federation of Bosnia and Herzegovina and the Republika Srpska—Croatia, Federal Republic of Yugoslavia

Comprehensive Nuclear Test-Ban Treaty (CTBT)

Opened for signature at New York on 24 September 1996; not in force as of 1 January 2000; depositary UN Secretary-General

The treaty prohibits the carrying out of any nuclear weapon test explosion or any other nuclear explosion, and urges each party to prevent any such nuclear explosion at any place under its jurisdiction or control and refrain from causing, encouraging, or in any way participating in the carrying out of any nuclear weapon test explosion or any other nuclear explosion.

The treaty will enter into force 180 days after the date of the deposit of the instrument of ratification of the 44 states listed in an annexe to the treaty but in no case earlier than two years after its opening for signature. All the 44 states possess nuclear power reactors and/or nuclear research reactors.

The 44 states whose ratification is required for entry into force are Algeria, Argentina, Australia, Austria, Bangladesh, Belgium, Brazil, Bulgaria, Canada, Chile, China, Colombia, Congo (Democratic Republic of), Egypt, Finland, France, Germany, Hungary, India, Indonesia, Iran, Israel, Italy, Japan, Korea (North), Korea (South), Mexico, Netherlands, Norway,

Pakistan, Peru, Poland, Romania, Russia, Slovakia, South Africa, Spain, Sweden, Switzerland, Turkey, UK, Ukraine, USA and Viet Nam.

51 ratifications deposited: Argentina, Australia, Austria, Azerbaijan, Belgium, Bolivia, Brazil, Bulgaria, Canada, Czech Republic, Denmark, El Salvador, Estonia, Fiji, Finland, France, Germany, Greece, Grenada, Hungary, Ireland, Italy, Japan, Jordan, Korea (South), Lesotho, Luxembourg, Mali, Mexico, Micronesia, Monaco, Mongolia, Netherlands, New Zealand, Norway, Panama, Peru, Poland, Qatar, Romania, Senegal, Slovakia, Slovenia, South Africa, Spain, Sweden, Switzerland, Tajikistan, Turkmenistan, UK, Uzbekistan

Signed but not ratified: Albania, Algeria, Andorra, Angola, Antigua and Barbuda, Armenia, Bahrain, Bangladesh, Belarus, Benin, Bosnia and Herzegovina, Brunei, Burkina Faso, Burundi, Cambodia, Cape Verde, Chad, Chile, China, Colombia, Comoros, Congo (Democratic Republic of), Congo (Republic of), Cook Islands, Costa Rica, Côte d'Ivoire, Croatia, Cyprus, Djibouti, Dominican Republic, Ecuador, Egypt, Equatorial Guinea, Ethiopia, Gabon, Georgia, Ghana, Guatemala, Guinea, Guinea-Bissau, Haiti, Holy See, Honduras, Iceland, Indonesia, Iran, Israel, Jamaica, Kazakhstan, Kenya, Kuwait, Kyrgyzstan, Laos, Latvia, Liberia, Liechtenstein, Lithuania, Macedonia (Former Yugoslav Republic of), Madagascar, Malawi, Malaysia, Maldives, Malta, Marshall Islands, Mauritania, Moldova, Morocco, Mozambique, Myanmar (Burma), Namibia, Nepal, Nicaragua, Niger, Oman, Papua New Guinea, Paraguay, Philippines, Portugal, Russia, Saint Lucia, Samoa (Western), San Marino, Sao Tome and Principe, Seychelles, Singapore, Solomon Islands, Sri Lanka, Suriname, Swaziland, Thailand, Togo, Tunisia, Turkey, Uganda, Ukraine, United Arab Emirates, Uruguay, USA, Vanuatu, Venezuela, Viet Nam, Yemen, Zambia, Zimbabwe

Note: Lithuania, Turkey, Bangladesh, Macedonia (Former Yugoslav Republic of) and Morocco ratified the treaty between 1 January and 1 May 2000.

Joint Statement on Parameters on Future Reductions in Nuclear Forces

Signed by the USA and Russia at Helsinki on 21 March 1997

In the Joint Statement the two sides agree that once the 1993 START II Treaty enters into force negotiations on a START III treaty will begin. START III will include lower aggregate levels of 2000–2500 nuclear warheads for each side.

Convention on the Prohibition of the Use, Stockpiling, Production and Transfer of Anti-Personnel Mines and on their Destruction (APM Convention)

Opened for signature at Ottawa on 3–4 December 1997 and at the UN Headquarters, New York, on 5 December 1997; entered into force on 1 March 1999; depositary UN Secretary-General

The convention prohibits anti-personnel mines, which are defined as mines designed to be exploded by the presence, proximity or contact of a person and which will incapacitate, injure or kill one or more persons.

Each party undertakes to destroy all its stockpiled anti-personnel mines as soon as possible but not later that four years after the entry into force of the convention for that state party. Each party also undertakes to destroy all anti-personnel mines in mined areas under its jurisdiction or control not later than 10 years after the entry into force of the convention for that state party.

Parties (90): Andorra, Antigua and Barbuda, Argentina, Australia, Austria, Bahamas, Barbados, Belgium, Belize, Benin, Bolivia, Bosnia and Herzegovina, Brazil, Bulgaria,

Burkina Faso, Cambodia, Canada, Chad, Costa Rica, Croatia, Czech Republic, Denmark, Djibouti, Dominica, Ecuador, El Salvador, Equatorial Guinea, Fiji, France, Germany, Grenada, Guatemala, Guinea, Holy See, Honduras, Hungary, Iceland, Ireland, Italy, Jamaica, Japan, Jordan, Lesotho, Liberia, Liechtenstein, Luxembourg, Macedonia (Former Yugoslav Republic of), Madagascar, Malawi, Malaysia, Mali, Mauritius, Mexico, Monaco, Mozambique, Namibia, Netherlands, New Zealand, Nicaragua, Niger, Niue, Norway, Panama, Paraguay, Peru, Portugal, Qatar, Saint Kitts and Nevis, Saint Lucia, Samoa (Western), San Marino, Senegal, Slovakia, Slovenia, Solomon Islands, South Africa, Spain, Swaziland, Sweden, Switzerland, Tajikistan, Thailand, Trinidad and Tobago, Tunisia, Turkmenistan, Uganda, UK, Venezuela, Yemen, Zimbabwe

Signed but not ratified: Albania, Algeria, Angola, Bangladesh, Botswana, Brunei, Burundi, Cameroon, Cape Verde, Chile, Colombia, Cook Island, Côte d'Ivoire, Cyprus, Dominican Republic, Ethiopia, Gabon, Gambia, Ghana, Greece, Guinea-Bissau, Guyana, Haiti, Indonesia, Kenya, Lithuania, Maldives, Malta, Marshall Islands, Mauritania, Moldova, Philippines, Poland, Romania, Rwanda, Saint Vincent and the Grenadines, Sao Tome and Principe, Seychelles, Sierra Leone, Sudan, Suriname, Tanzania, Togo, Ukraine, Uruguay, Vanuatu, Zambia

Note: The Philippines, Albania, Botswana and Togo ratified the convention between 1 January and 1 April 2000.

Inter-American Convention on Transparency in Conventional Weapons Acquisitions

Approved at the General Assembly of the Organization of American States in Guatemala on 7 June 1999; not in force as of 1 January 2000; depositary OAS General Secretariat

The convention provides for the exchange of information on the parties' acquisitions of conventional weapons, for the purpose of promoting regional transparency and confidence. Parties shall report annually to the depositary on their imports and exports of conventional weapons during the preceding calendar year.

The convention is open for signature by all OAS member states. It will enter into force on the 30th day following the date of deposit of the sixth instrument of ratification.

Ratification deposited: Canada

Signed but not ratified: Argentina, Bolivia, Brazil, Chile, Colombia, Costa Rica, Dominica, Ecuador, El Salvador, Guatemala, Haiti, Mexico, Nicaragua, Paraguay, Peru, Uruguay, USA, Venezuela

Annexe B. Chronology 1999

RAGNHILD FERM and CHRISTER BERGGREN

For the convenience of the reader, key words are given in the right-hand column, opposite each entry. The dates in the left-hand column are those applying at the location where the events occurred (time differences may mean that they were reported elsewhere as occurring on different dates). Definitions of the acronyms can be found on page xviii.

6 Feb.	Peace talks are held at Rambouillet, France, between the Republic of Serbia of the Federal Republic of Yugoslavia (FRY) and Kosovar Albanian separatists to resolve the conflict in the province of Kosovo. The talks are mediated by the six-country Contact Group—France, Germany, Italy, Russia, the UK and the USA. No agreement is reached. Further talks are held in Paris on 15–19 Mar.	FRY/Kosovo
10 Feb.	After serious fighting resumes between Ethiopia and Eritrea, the UN Security Council unanimously adopts Resolution 1227, demanding a halt to the hostilities and urging all states to immediately end all sales of arms and munitions to the two countries. On 27 Feb. the Security Council welcomes Eritrea's acceptance of the Framework Agreement for a peaceful settlement of the dispute, drawn up by the Organization of African Unity (OAU) in Dec. 1998. Two documents are later added to the agreement: the Modalities for the Implementation of the OAU Framework Agreement, and the Technical Arrangements. The latter document is not accepted by Ethiopia.	UN; Ethiopia/ Eritrea; OAU
21 Feb.	Indian Prime Minister Vajpayee and Pakistani Prime Minister Sharif, meeting in Lahore, Pakistan, sign the Lahore Declaration, stating that the two states will take immediate steps to reduce the risk of accidental or unauthorized use of nuclear weapons and develop measures for confidence building in the nuclear and conventional weapon fields, aimed at prevention of conflict. In a memorandum of understanding, signed by the foreign ministers, the two sides undertake to notify each other of ballistic missile flight tests and of any accidental, unauthorized or unexplained incident that could create the risk of a conflict or an outbreak of nuclear war between the two countries.	India/Pakistan; CBM; Nuclear weapons
1 Mar.	The 1997 Convention on the Prohibition of the Use, Stockpiling, Production and Transfer of Anti-Personnel Mines and on their Destruction (APM Convention) enters into force.	APM Convention

12 Mar.	The foreign ministers of the Czech Republic, Hungary and Poland submit to the US Secretary of State their countries' documents of accession to the 1949 North Atlantic Treaty (Washington Treaty), thereby becoming members of NATO.	NATO; Czech Rep.; Hungary; Poland
22 Mar.	President Yeltsin submits to the Duma the 1993 START II Treaty draft ratification bill, containing a number of conditions and reservations.	START II; Russia
24 Mar.	Following the failure of the negotiations on Kosovo (see *6 Feb.*) a NATO campaign is initiated to conduct air strikes against targets in the FRY. In reaction, Russia freezes its cooperation with NATO under the Partnership for Peace (PFP) programme and in the NATO–Russia Permanent Joint Council (PJC). Meetings of the PJC resume during the summer but are confined to issues related to Kosovo.	NATO/FRY; Russia; PFP; PJC
24–25 Mar.	At a meeting in Bamako, Mali, the foreign ministers of the Economic Community of West African States (ECOWAS) adopt a Plan of Action for the implementation of the Programme for Coordination and Assistance for Security and Development (PCASED). They also decide to submit to the ECOWAS heads of state a draft Code of Conduct for the implementation of the Moratorium on the Importation, Exportation and Manufacture of Light Weapons (adopted in Oct. 1998).	West Africa; ECOWAS; Small arms
26 Mar.	Russia and the USA sign an agreement resolving a dispute over price and compensation arrangements that have blocked implementation of the 1993 US–Russian Highly Enriched Uranium (HEU) Agreement.	Russia/USA; HEU
26 Mar.	The Second Protocol to the 1954 Convention for the Protection of Cultural Property in the Event of Armed Conflict is signed in The Hague.	Cultural Property Convention
31 Mar.	The FRY informs the Organization for Security and Co-operation in Europe (OSCE) that, because it is impossible to conduct inspections of FRY military forces in the light of the NATO air strikes (see *24 Mar.*), the FRY is 'temporarily suspending' implementation of the 1996 Agreement on Sub-Regional Arms Control (Florence Agreement). The suspension is terminated on 19 July.	Florence Agreement; FRY
2 Apr.	At a meeting of the Commonwealth of Independent States (CIS), held in Moscow, a protocol on extension of the 1992 Collective Security Treaty for five years is signed. Azerbaijan, Georgia and Uzbekistan do not attend the meeting and do not sign the protocol.	CIS; Azerbaijan, Georgia, Uzbekistan
8 Apr.	Following the fulfilment of the conditions set forth in paragraph 8 of UN Security Council Resolution 1192 (calling for the extradition of two Libyans accused of the 1988 bombing of Pan American flight 103 for the purpose of trial before court), the UN immediately suspends the arms embargo against Libya, in force since since 1992.	UN; Libya; Arms embargo

11 Apr.	India announces that it has successfully test-fired a two-stage ballistic missile, the Agni II, with a range in excess of 2000 km. On 14 Apr. Pakistan announces that it has successfully tested its Ghauri II (Hatf-6) intermediate-range ballistic missile.	India; Pakistan Nuclear weapons
13 Apr.	Russian President Yeltsin submits to the Duma the package of Russian–US strategic arms control agreements signed in New York on 26 Sep. 1997. It includes the START II Protocol and the Memorandum of Understanding on Succession (MOUS) to the 1972 ABM Treaty.	START II; ABM Treaty
23–25 Apr.	At the NATO 50th anniversary summit meeting, held in Washington, DC, the heads of state and government of the member states adopt the following documents: an updated Strategic Concept with a commitment to collective defence and the transatlantic link; the Washington Declaration, reaffirming NATO's collective defence commitments for the 21st century; the Membership Action Plan (MAP) for countries wishing to join the alliance; a decision to further enhance the effectiveness of the European Security and Defence Identity (ESDI); the Defence Capabilities Initiative; the Weapons of Mass Destruction Initiative to respond to the security threats posed by nuclear, biological and chemical weapons; and a statement declaring NATO's determination to resolve the Kosovo crisis.	NATO; ESDI; WMD; Kosovo
30 Apr.	The UN Disarmament Commission endorses the draft text of a treaty that would establish a nuclear weapon-free zone in Central Asia and adopts the Guidelines on Conventional Arms Control/Limitation and Disarmament.	UN; NWFZ; Central Asia; Conventional arms control
1 May	The 1997 Treaty of Amsterdam Amending the Treaty on European Union enters into force. It provides for the enhancement of the Common Foreign and Security Policy (CFSP), including a progressive framing of a common defence policy as provided in Article 17 of the 1992 Treaty on European Union (Maastricht Treaty). The Treaty of Amsterdam also provides for the possibility of integrating the Western European Union (WEU) into the European Union (EU), should the European Council so decide.	EU; WEU
5 May	The foreign ministers of Indonesia and Portugal sign, in New York, an agreement by which a popular consultation through direct ballot will be held in East Timor, in Aug. 1999, on the acceptance or rejection of a constitutional framework for autonomy within Indonesia. The agreement is endorsed by the UN Security Council on 7 May in Resolution 1236.	East Timor/ Indonesia; Portugal: UN
6 May	The foreign ministers of the Group of Eight (G8), meeting in Bonn, agree on General Principles for a peace plan for Kosovo, providing for withdrawal from Kosovo of all Serb military, police and paramilitary forces.	G8; Kosovo

7 May	The Government of Guinea-Bissau is overthrown by a rebel military junta. The coup leaders promise to hold elections in 1999. Presidential and legislative elections are held on 28–29 Nov.	Guinea-Bissau
10 May	The WEU starts a De-mining Assistance Mission (WEUDAM) in Croatia, the first operation conducted by the WEU at the request of the EU, according to the provisions of the 1992 Maastricht Treaty) and the 1997 Treaty of Amsterdam, stipulating that the WEU should implement EU decisions with defence implications.	Croatia; EU; WEU
11–15 May	Meeting in The Hague to issue the Hague Appeal for Peace, hundreds of organizations and individuals form the International Action Network on Small Arms (IANSA), aimed at facilitating action by non-governmental organizations (NGOs) to prevent the proliferation and misuse of small arms. The network is supported by the UN.	Small arms; UN
20 May	The US House of Representatives votes to approve the National Missile Defense Act of 1999, committing the USA to deploy as soon as is technologically possible an effective National Missile Defense (NMD) system capable of defending the territory of the USA against limited ballistic missile attack. President Clinton signs the act into law on 23 July. He emphasizes that no decision to deploy an NMD system has been taken.	ABM Treaty; USA; NMD
27 May	The International Criminal Tribunal for the Former Yugoslavia announces the indictment of President Milosevic and four other Serb leaders on charges of crimes against humanity. This is the first time a sitting head of state is indicted for human rights crimes.	UN; Former Yugoslavia; FRY
27 May	Kashmiri Mujahideen militants and Pakistani forces cross the Line of Control (LOC), the de facto border between India and Pakistan, near the town of Kargil. The fighting escalates and Indian aircraft violate Pakistani airspace. Aircraft are shot down on both sides.	India/Pakistan; Kashmir
3 June	The National Assembly of the Republic of Serbia and FRY President Milosevic approve the terms of the peace plan, based on the G8 General Principles (see *6 May*) and presented to the president by Russian Special Envoy Chernomyrdin and EU Envoy Ahtisaari. The plan includes the deployment in Kosovo, under UN auspices and with essential NATO participation, of effective international civil and security presences.	FRY; Kosovo; G8

3–4 June	The European Council, meeting in Cologne, Germany, adopts a Declaration on Strengthening the Common European Security and Defence Policy (CESDP, later also known as the European Security and Defence Policy, ESDP; see *10–11 Dec.*). The General Affairs Council is tasked with preparing the conditions and measures for including in the EU those functions of the WEU which will be necessary for the EU to fulfil its new responsibilities in the area of the Petersberg tasks. When final decisions are taken the WEU as an organization will have 'completed its purpose'.	EU; WEU; Petersberg tasks CESDP; ESDP
7 June	At the General Assembly of the Organization of American States (OAS), meeting in Guatemala, the Inter-American Convention on Transparency in Conventional Weapons is approved. It calls for openness and transparency in the acquisition of conventional weapons by the exchange of information among the states parties.	OAS; Conventional weapons
9 June	Military representatives of NATO and the FRY, meeting in Kumanovo (a Macedonian border town), sign a Military Technical Agreement for the cessation of hostilities in Kosovo and the phased pull-out from Kosovo of FRY forces (including all FRY and Serbian personnel and organizations with military capability) within 11 days. The NATO Kosovo Force (KFOR) will monitor and ensure compliance with the agreement.	NATO/FRY; Kosovo; UN; EU
10 June	The UN Security Council adopts, by a vote of 14 to 0 (China abstains), Resolution 1244, demanding that the FRY end the violence and repression in Kosovo and begin to complete the withdrawal from Kosovo of all military police and paramilitary forces. The Security Council decides on the deployment in Kosovo, under UN auspices, of an international civil and security presence, with substantial NATO participation, and calls for the demilitarization of the Kosovo Liberation Army (KLA). On 12 June KFOR forces enter Kosovo.	UN; Kosovo; NATO/FRY
10 June	At the Conference on South Eastern Europe, convened by the EU in Cologne, Germany, the facilitating states and institutions sign the Stability Pact for South Eastern Europe, aiming to promote lasting peace and stability in the region. The signatories request that the Pact be placed under the auspices of the OSCE. It came under OSCE auspices on 1 July.	SE Europe Stability Pact; EU; OSCE
11 June	The UN Security Council unanimously adopts Resolution 1246, establishing the UN Mission in East Timor (UNAMET) to organize and conduct the referendum (see *5 May*).	UN; East Timor
20 June	NATO and the Kosovo Liberation Army (KLA) sign an agreement on demilitarization of the KLA in accordance with UN Security Council Resolution 1244 (see *10 June*).	NATO/KLA; Kosovo

20 June	US President Clinton and Russian President Yeltsin, at the G8 meeting in Cologne, Germany, issue a Joint Statement Concerning Strategic Offensive and Defensive Arms and Further Strengthening of Stability. The two leaders stress the importance of making further reductions in nuclear strategic offensive arms and of preserving the 1972 ABM Treaty as a 'cornerstone of strategic stability'.	USA/Russia; ABM; Strategic weapons; G8
7 July	President Kabbah of Sierra Leone and the leader of the Revolutionary United Front (RUF), Sankoh, sign, in Lomé, Togo, the Lomé Peace Accord, allowing for power sharing by both parties. The agreement is brokered by Burkina Faso, Liberia, Nigeria and Togo.	Sierra Leone
10 July	The Government of the Democratic Republic of Congo (DRC) and Angola, Namibia, Rwanda, Uganda and Zimbabwe sign, in Lusaka, the Lusaka Ceasefire Agreement, providing for a ceasefire in the DRC conflict as of 12 July. The agreement is signed by the Mouvement de Libération Congolais (MLC) on 1 Aug. and by representatives of both factions of the Rassemblement Congolais pour la Démocratie (RCD) on 31 Aug.	DRC; Angola; Namibia; Rwanda; Uganda; Zimbabwe; MLC; RCD
30 July	The 36 facilitating states and 11 institutions of the Stability Pact for South Eastern Europe (see *10 June*), meeting in Sarajevo, issue the Sarajevo Summit Declaration, confirming their commitment to the Stability Pact.	SE Europe; Stability Pact; OSCE
30 July	China and Japan sign a memorandum of understanding on the destruction of Japanese abandoned chemical weapons in China. In accordance with the 1993 Chemical Weapons Convention, Japan will provide all necessary financial, technical, expert, facility and other resources for the purpose of destroying the chemical weapons.	China/Japan; CW; CWC
4 Aug.	The Tokyo Forum for Nuclear Non-Proliferation and Disarmament, a panel of nuclear disarmament experts, issues a report entitled *Facing Nuclear Dangers: An Action Plan for the 21st Century*. The report calls for steps to promote nuclear disarmament, including further transparency measures regarding the numbers and types of nuclear weapons, expansion of the scope of verification of nuclear disarmament to cover non-deployed weapons and the dismantling of nuclear weapons.	Nuclear disarmament
5 Aug.	The Conference on Disarmament (CD) decides to admit five new member states: Ecuador, Ireland, Kazakhstan, Malaysia and Tunisia.	CD
7 Aug.	Several hundred Islamic militants invade Dagestan from Chechnya. On 10 Aug. the self-proclaimed Islamic Shura (Council) of Dagestan declares the establishment of an independent Islamic state in the republic.	Chechnya; Dagestan

17 Aug.	In India, the 27-member National Security Advisory Board publishes an unofficial draft nuclear doctrine. It calls for India to build a nuclear arsenal based on the concept of 'credible minimum nuclear deterrence' and consisting of a 'triad of aircraft, mobile land-based missiles and sea-based assets'. The draft doctrine also reiterates India's pledge never to be the first to use nuclear weapons in an armed conflict. The draft is not approved by the Indian Government.	India; Nuclear weapons
25 Aug.	Referring to the agreements of Apr. 1996 and Apr. 1997, the heads of state of China, Kazakhstan, Kyrgyzstan, Russia and Tajikistan (the so-called Shanghai Five), meeting in Bishkek, Kyrgyzstan, call for enhanced regional security cooperation.	China; Kazakhstan; Kyrgyzstan; Russia; Tajikistan
30 Aug.	A referendum on autonomy within Indonesia or independence is held in East Timor (see *5 May* and *11 June*). 98.6 per cent of the eligible voters participate. The results of the referendum are announced simultaneously by UN Secretary-General Annan in New York and the Head of the UN Mission in East Timor (UNAMET) in Dili. 78.5 per cent of the voters vote in favour of independence and 21.5 per cent for autonomy within Indonesia. Violence breaks out after the announcement.	East Timor/ Indonesia; UN
14 Sep.	The foreign ministers of 16 Asian states, members of the Conference on Interaction and Confidence-building Measures in Asia (CICA), meeting in Almaty, Kazakhstan, agree on the Declaration on the Principles Guiding Relations among the CICA Member States.	CICA; CBM
15 Sep.	The UN Security Council unanimously adopts Resolution 1264, authorizing the International Force for East Timor (INTERFET) to protect and support the UN Mission in East Timor (UNAMET) (see *30 Aug.)* in carrying out its tasks.	UN; East Timor; Australia
17 Sep.	Following talks held in Berlin on 7–12 Sep. between representatives of North Korea and the USA, the US Government announces the easing of the sanctions against North Korea in force since the end of the Korean War in 1953. In return, on 24 Sep. North Korea suspends further ballistic missile tests while negotiations with the USA continue.	USA/N. Korea
23 Sep.	Russia attacks Grozny for the first time since 1996. Over a period of several weeks Russia also conducts air strikes against guerrilla bases in Chechnya to prevent incursions into Dagestan *(see 7 Aug.)*.	Russia/ Chechnya
5 Oct.	Chechen President Maskhadov declares martial law in Chechnya and calls for war against Russia.	Russia/ Chechnya

6 Oct.   Russia notifies other parties to the Treaty on Conventional   Russia; CFE;
Armed Forces in Europe (CFE Treaty) that it has been   Chechnya
forced to exceed its flank limits stipulated in the treaty, in
sending ground forces to the North Caucasus in the ongoing struggle with the Chechen rebels. It is thereby considered to be in violation of the treaty.

6–8 Oct.   A Special Conference on Facilitating the Entry into Force   CTBT
of the 1996 Comprehensive Nuclear Test-Ban Treaty
(CTBT) is held in Vienna, in accordance with Article 14.2
of the treaty. The Final Declaration calls on all states that
have not yet done so to sign and ratify the treaty.

9 Oct.   The Russian Ministry of Defence publishes a draft new   Russia; Nuclear
military doctrine in which the significance of nuclear   weapons
weapons in Russian security and defence policy is emphasized. The Russian Federation Security Council adopts the
doctrine on 4 Feb. 2000.

13 Oct.   The US Senate votes 51–48 not to approve US ratification   USA; CTBT
of the 1996 Comprehensive Nuclear Test-Ban Treaty.

22 Oct.   The UN Security Council unanimously adopts Resolu-   UN; Sierra
tion 1270, establishing the UN Mission in Sierra Leone   Leone
(UNAMSIL), to assist in the implementation of the Lomé
Peace Accord (see *7 July*) and a disarmament, demobiliza-
tion and integration plan. The mission replaces the UN
Observer Mission in Sierra Leone (UNOMSIL).

23 Oct.   The last troops of the ECOWAS Monitoring Group   ECOMOG;
(ECOMOG) withdraw from Liberia. (The first ECOMOG   Liberia
peacekeeping forces arrived in Liberia in Aug. 1990.)

25 Oct.   The UN Security Council unanimously adopts Resolu-   UN; East Timor
tion 1272, deciding to establish a UN Transitional Administration in East Timor (UNTAET), which will be given
overall responsibility for the administration of East Timor
and be empowered to exercise all legislative and executive
authority and the administration of justice.

4 Nov.   The Council of Europe adopts a resolution calling on   Council of
Russia to stop hostilities in Chechnya and open negotia-   Europe; Russia;
tions with Chechen President Maskhadov.   Chechnya

18–19 Nov.   The heads of state and governments of the OSCE, meeting   OSCE; Europe;
in Istanbul, endorse the Vienna Document 1999, adopted   CSBM; Russia;
by the OSCE Forum for Security Co-operation (FSC) on   Chechnya
16 Nov., introducing regional measures aimed at increasing transparency and confidence. They also adopt the
Istanbul Summit Declaration, reaffirming several elements
of a new European security system, and the Charter for
European Security for the 21st Century, including decisions on new mechanisms to enhance early warning, conflict prevention and crisis management. Russia agrees to
invite an OSCE fact-finding mission to visit the North
Caucasus.

19 Nov.	The parties to the 1990 Treaty on Conventional Armed Forces in Europe (CFE Treaty), meeting in the framework of the OSCE Summit Meeting in Istanbul, sign the Agreement on Adaptation of the CFE Treaty. The revised treaty replaces the CFE Treaty bloc-to-bloc military balance with individual state limits on treaty-limited equipment (TLE) holdings and provides for a new structure of limitations. It opens the CFE regime to all other European states. The parties also sign the Final Act of the Conference of the States Parties to the Treaty on Conventional Armed Forces in Europe (CFE Final Act).	CFE; OSCE
23 Nov.	The WEU Council, meeting in Luxembourg, adopts the Luxembourg Declaration, in which it reaffirms its readiness, in the framework of Article 17 of the 1992 Maastricht Treaty and if the EU so wishes, to continue to provide the EU with access to an operational capability and to elaborate and implement decisions and actions of the EU which have defence implications.	WEU; EU
25 Nov.	France and the UK adopt the Franco-British Declaration on European Defence, which confirms the intention of the two countries to support for at least one year the deployment within 60 days of a European rapid reaction force of 50 000–60 000 troops.	France; UK
28 Nov.	The Euzkadi Ta Askatasuna (ETA, Basque Homeland and Liberty) announces that it will break the ceasefire declared on 17 Sep. 1998 and resume its struggle for Basque independence.	ETA
29 Nov.	The Northern Ireland Assembly confirms the appointment of a 10-member power-sharing Cabinet to work under the leadership of First Minister Trimble and Deputy First Minister Mallon. After the first Cabinet meeting, on 2 Dec., Ireland removes from its constitution its territorial claim on Northern Ireland.	Northern Ireland; Ireland
30 Nov.	The UN Security Council unanimously adopts Resolution 1279, establishing the UN Observer Mission in the Democratic Republic of Congo (MONUC) to monitor implementation of the Lusaka Ceasefire Agreement (see *10 July*).	UN; DRC
8 Dec.	The Russia–Belarus Union State Treaty is signed in Moscow by Russian President Yeltsin and Belarussian President Lukashenko. The treaty commits the two countries to form a confederation governed by a Supreme State Council, with coordinated foreign, military and social policies as well as a joint economic system. The treaty is ratified by Russia on 13 Dec. and by Belarus on 14 Dec.	Russia/Belarus
10 Dec.	Russian President Yeltsin and Chinese President Jiang Zemin, meeting in Beijing, issue a Joint Statement stressing their determination to allow no country to interfere in another sovereign country's fight against domestic terrorism or to use the issue of human rights for that purpose.	China; Russia

10–11 Dec.	The European Council, meeting in Helsinki, decides to create the European Security and Defence Policy (ESDP, also called the Common European Security and Defence Policy, CESDP; see *3–4 June*). Several interim bodies, including a political and security committee, are set in place on 1 Mar. 2000. A capability to lead operations under the direction of the EU in cases where NATO is not engaged will be developed and a rapid deployment force of up to 60 000 troops, capable of sustaining for at least one year and being deployed within 60 days, will be established by the end of 2003. A decision is taken to invite Bulgaria, Latvia, Lithuania, Malta, Romania, Slovakia and Turkey to EU accession negotiations.	EU; NATO; ESDP, CESDP
16 Dec.	After two days of talks held in Washington, DC, under the mediation of US Secretary of State Albright, Israeli President Barak and Syrian Foreign Minister El Chareh agree to meet for peace talks on 3 Jan. 2000.	Israel/Syria; USA
17 Dec.	The UN Security Council adopts, by a vote of 11 to 0 (China, France, Malaysia and Russia abstain), Resolution 1284, establishing the UN Monitoring, Verification and Inspection Commission (UNMOVIC). The new commission will take over the responsibilities of the UN Special Commission on Iraq (UNSCOM), established in 1991 by UN Security Council Resolution 687, to monitor and verify the elimination of Iraq's chemical and biological weapons and all ballistic missiles with a range of over 150 km.	UN; Iraq
19 Dec.	Portugal hands over to China the sovereignty of Macao, the last European colony on mainland Asia.	Macao; China; Portugal
24–25 Dec.	President Bédié of Côte d'Ivoire is overthrown by General Guei in a military coup. The National Committee of Public Salvation is formed as the provisional government until general elections are held.	Côte d'Ivoire
29 Dec.	Indonesian military take control over Ambon Island in the province of Maluku (the Moluccas) to suppress violence between Muslims and Christians. The violence spreads to other Indonesian islands.	Indonesia
31 Dec.	Russian President Yeltsin resigns from his post six months before the expiry of his term. Prime Minister Putin is appointed acting head of state until elections are held on 26 Mar. 2000.	Russia
31 Dec.	After 96 years of US sovereignty the zone of the Panama Canal is handed over to Panama.	Panama; USA

About the contributors

Dr Ian Anthony (United Kingdom) is Leader of the SIPRI Internet Database on European Export Controls Project. In 1992–98 he was Leader of the SIPRI Arms Transfers Project. His most recent publication for SIPRI is *Russia and the Arms Trade* (1998), of which he is editor. He is also the editor of the SIPRI volume *Arms Export Regulations* (1991) and the SIPRI Research Report *The Future of Defence Industries in Central and Eastern Europe* (1994), and author of *The Naval Arms Trade* (SIPRI, 1990) and *The Arms Trade and Medium Powers: Case Studies of India and Pakistan 1947–90* (1991). He has written or co-authored chapters for the SIPRI Yearbook since 1988.

William M. Arkin (United States) is an independent expert on defence matters and a consultant to the Natural Resources Defense Council (NRDC). He is co-editor of the NRDC's *Nuclear Weapons Databook* series and co-author of several of the volumes in the series. He is a columnist for *The Bulletin of the Atomic Scientists* and *The Washington Post* Internet site. His recent publications include (with Robert S. Norris) *The Internet and the Bomb: A Research Guide to Policy and Information about Nuclear Weapons* (1997), *The US Military Online: A Directory for Online Access to the Department of Defense* (2nd edn, 1998) and *The Internet and Strategic Studies* (1998). He has contributed to the SIPRI Yearbook since 1985.

Christer Berggren (Sweden) is a librarian at SIPRI with special responsibilities for the Arms Control and Disarmament Documentary Survey Project.

Ylva Blondel (Sweden) is a PhD candidate at the Department of Peace and Conflict Research, Uppsala University.

Dr Gennady Chufrin (Russia) is the Leader of the SIPRI Project The Evolving Security Setting in the Caspian Sea Basin. In 1979–97 he was Head of the Department of South-East Asia and Deputy Director of the Institute of Oriental Studies of the Russian Academy of Sciences. In 1998–99 he was Leader of the SIPRI Project on Russia's Security Agenda. He is editor of *Russia and Asia: The Emerging Security Agenda* (SIPRI, 1999) and author of 'The Caspian Sea basin: the security dimensions' in the SIPRI Yearbook 1999.

Dr Renata Dwan (Ireland) is Leader of SIPRI's Project on Conflict Prevention, Management and Resolution. Previously she was Deputy Director of the East–West Institute's European Security Programme at the institute's Budapest Centre. She received her doctorate in International Relations from the University of Oxford, where she was Hedley Bull Junior Research Fellow in International Relations in 1994–97. In 1999 she was the editor of *Building Security in Europe's New Border-lands: Subregional Cooperation in the Wider Europe* (1999) and is co-editor (with Oleksandr Pavliuk) of *Building Security in the New States of Eurasia: Subregional Cooperation in the Former Soviet Space* (forthcoming, 2000).

Ragnhild Ferm (Sweden) is the Leader of the SIPRI Arms Control and Disarmament Documentary Survey Project. She has published chapters on nuclear explosions, the comprehensive nuclear test ban and other arms control agreements, and the annual chronologies of arms control and political events in the SIPRI Yearbook since 1982. She is the author of fact sheets in Swedish on SIPRI research topics.

Dr Björn Hagelin (Sweden) is Leader of the SIPRI Arms Transfers Project. Before joining SIPRI in 1998 he was a Researcher and Associate Professor at the Department of Peace and Conflict Research, Uppsala University. His recent publications include a chapter on Sweden's defence industry in Eriksson, A. and Hallenberg, J. (eds), *The Changing European Defence Industry Sector: Consequences for Sweden?* (2000), the article 'Saab, British Aerospace and the JAS 39 Gripen joint venture' in *European Security* (1998), and the monograph *One for All or All for One? Pentagon Tapping of Foreign Science and Technology* (1997).

Ann-Sofi Jakobsson Hatay (Sweden) is a PhD candidate at the Department of Peace and Conflict Research, Uppsala University. She has contributed to the SIPRI Yearbook since 1995.

Andrés Jato (Sweden) is a PhD student at the Department of Peace and Conflict Research, Uppsala University and is currently working in the Policy Planning Department of the Swedish Ministry for Foreign Affairs.

Dr Edvard Karlsson (Sweden) is Director of Research at the Swedish Defence Research Establishment (FOA) and Senior University Lecturer at Umeå University. He has conducted research on criminality and terrorism with chemical and biological agents since 1995 and on the nuclear, chemical and biological threat since 1977. Recent publications include (with Susanne Nyholm) 'Dry deposition and desorption of toxic gases to and from snow surfaces' in *Journal of Hazardous Materials* (1998) and (with Per Runn and Jan Sjöström) the FOA report *The Environmental Effects of Chemical Weapons* (1998, in Swedish).

Shannon Kile (USA) is a Researcher on the SIPRI Project on Military Technology and International Security. He is the author of a chapter in the SIPRI Research Report *The Future of the Defence Industries in Central and Eastern Europe* (1994) and a co-author (with Adam Daniel Rotfeld) of a chapter in the Organization for Security and Co-operation in Europe (OSCE) 1997 *OSCE Yearbook*. He has also contributed to two SIPRI books on Russian security policy: *Russia and Europe: The Emerging Security Agenda* (1997) and *Russia and Asia: The Emerging Security Agenda* (1999). He has contributed to the SIPRI Yearbook since 1995 on nuclear arms control.

Dr Zdzislaw Lachowski (Poland) is a Researcher on the SIPRI Project on Building a Cooperative Security System in and for Europe. He was previously a Researcher at the Polish Institute of International Affairs, where he studied problems of European security and issues concerning West European political integration. He has published extensively on these subjects. He is the author of *Between the Balance of Power and Conventional Arms Control in Europe: Adapting the CFE Regime to the New Security Environment* (1999, in Polish) and has contributed to the SIPRI Yearbook since 1992.

Milton Leitenberg (United States) is Senior Fellow at the Center for International and Security Studies, University of Maryland. In 1968–72 he was a researcher at SIPRI. He has conducted research at the Center for International Studies at Cornell University and at the Swedish Institute of International Affairs and has held a Visiting Chair in strategic studies at the Graduate School of International Affairs at Carleton University. He has also served as consultant to the Swedish foreign and defence ministries. He has published extensively on a wide range of topics in international security.

Evamaria Loose-Weintraub (Germany) is a Research Assistant on the SIPRI Military Expenditure and Arms Production Project. She is responsible for research on military expenditure in Europe (except for NATO members) and Central and South America. She is the author of chapters in the SIPRI volume *Arms Export Regulations* (1991) and co-author of a chapter in the SIPRI Research Report *The Future of the Defence Industries in Central and Eastern Europe* (1994) and has contributed to most editions of the SIPRI Yearbook since 1984.

Lena Melin (Sweden) is a Research Officer at the Department of Threat Assessment and Studies of Total Defence Systems at the Swedish National Defence Research Establishment. She has conducted research on criminality and terrorism with chemical and biological agents and the nuclear, chemical and biological threat since 1995. She has written the FOA report *Terrorism and Criminality: Incidents Involving Chemical Substances 1964–1999* (March 2000), *Terrorism and Criminality: Incidents Involving Biological Substances* (forthcoming, 2000) and *Illegal Manufacture of Mustard Gas* (forthcoming, 2000).

Dr Robert S. Norris (United States) is Senior Analyst with the Natural Resources Defense Council (NRDC) and Director of the *Nuclear Weapons Databook* series and co-author of several of the volumes in the series. He has contributed to the SIPRI Yearbook since 1985 and is a columnist for *The Bulletin of the Atomic Scientists*. One of his recent works (with William M. Arkin) is *Taking Stock: Worldwide Nuclear Deployments* (1998).

Dr Erik Näslund (Sweden) holds a PhD in theoretical physics and is Project Manager at Cap Gemini Ernst & Young. In 1989–2000 he was Senior Scientist at the Division of NBC Defence at the Swedish Defence Research Establishment specializing in dispersion modelling and atmospheric physics. He is the author of 'Simulation of a terrorist attack with chemical substances in a department store' in *Proceedings of the Sixth Topical Meeting on Emergency Preparedness and Response* (1997) and co-author (with Robert L. Lee) of 'Lagrangian stochastic particle model simulations of turbulent dispersion around buildings' in *Atmospheric Environment* (1998).

Dr Thomas Ohlson (Sweden) is Associate Professor at the Department of Peace and Conflict Research, Uppsala University. In 1982–87 he was leader of SIPRI's Arms Trade and Arms Production Project, and in 1987–90 he was senior researcher at the Centre for African Studies in Maputo, Mozambique. He is the author of five books and numerous book chapters and journal articles on armament and disarmament, North–South problems, regional security issues and conflict and conflict resolution (especially in Africa). His latest book is *Power Politics and Peace Policies: Intra-State Conflict Resolution in Southern Africa* (1998).

Wuyi Omitoogun (Nigeria) is a Research Assistant on SIPRI's Military Expenditure Project. Previously, he was a Research Assistant at the Centre for Trans-Saharan Studies, University of Maiduguri and at the Obafemi Awolowo University. He is co-author (with Elisabeth Sköns and Evamaria Loose-Weintraub) of 'Overview of world military expenditure' for the *UNESCO Encyclopaedia* (forthcoming, 2000).

Thomas Papworth (United Kingdom) holds a master's degree in international relations and is Research Assistant on the SIPRI projects Conflicts and Peace Enforcement, and Conflict Prevention, Management and Resolution. Before joining SIPRI he was an intern at the International Institute for Strategic Studies (IISS) in London and contributed to the IISS publication *The Military Balance 1999/2000* (1999).

Marta Reuter (Sweden) was a Research Assistant on the SIPRI projects Conflicts and Peace Enforcement, and Conflict Prevention, Management and Resolution in 1999.

Dr Adam Daniel Rotfeld (Poland) is Director of SIPRI and Leader of the SIPRI Project on Building a Cooperative Security System in and for Europe. He has participated in many multilateral negotiations and served as the Personal Representative of the Conference on Security and Co-operation in Europe (CSCE) Chairman-in-Office to examine the settlement of the conflict in the Trans-Dniester region (1992–93). He is the author or editor of over 20 books and more than 300 articles on the legal and political aspects of relations between Germany and the Central and East European states after World War II (recognition of borders, the Munich Agreement and the right of self-determination), human rights, confidence- and security-building measures (CSBMs), European security and the CSCE/OSCE process. He has written chapters on global and regional security systems and European and transatlantic security structures for the SIPRI Yearbook since 1991.

Dr Taylor B. Seybolt (United States) is the leader of the SIPRI Conflicts and Peace Enforcement Project. Prior to joining SIPRI he spent two years as research fellow at Harvard University. His research focuses on humanitarian military intervention. He contributed to 'Coordination in Rwanda: the humanitarian response to genocide and civil war', a Cambridge Conflict Management Group working paper, and has articles forthcoming on the effects of past interventions and US intervention policy.

Elisabeth Sköns (Sweden) is Leader of the SIPRI Military Expenditure and Arms Production Project. She is the author of chapters on the economics of arms production and the internationalization of arms production for SIPRI and other publications. She is also the author of chapters on military expenditure and their determinants and economic impact. She has contributed to most editions of the SIPRI Yearbook since 1983.

Margareta Sollenberg (Sweden) is a Research Assistant on the Uppsala Conflict Data Project at the Department of Peace and Conflict Research, Uppsala University. She has been editor of *States in Armed Conflict* since 1994 and has contributed to the SIPRI Yearbook since 1995.

Petter Stålenheim (Sweden) holds a master's degree in political science and public administration. He is a Research Assistant on the SIPRI Military Expenditure and Arms Production Project. He has contributed to the SIPRI Yearbook since 1998.

Dr Lennart Thaning (Sweden) holds a PhD in meteorology and is an expert on atmospheric dispersion at the Division of NBC Defence at the Swedish Defence Research Establishment. He is the co-author (with Alexander Bakalanov) of 'Simulation of the atmospheric transport and deposition on a local/meso- and regional scale after hypothetical accidents at the Kola nuclear power plant' in *The Science of Total Environment* (1997) and (with Edvard Karlson and Erik Näslund) of *Dispersion Models and Risk Assessment for Biological and Chemical Warfare Agents* (1997).

Maria Wahlberg (Sweden) is Research Assistant on SIPRI's Chemical and Biological Warfare Project. She holds a master's degree in political science from Stockholm University.

Professor Peter Wallensteen (Sweden) has held the Dag Hammarskjöld Chair in Peace and Conflict Research since 1985 and was Head of the Department of Peace and Conflict Research, Uppsala University in 1972–99. He has most recently edited *Preventing Violent Conflicts: Past Record and Future Challenges* (1998) and *International Intervention: New Norms in the Post-Cold War Era?* (1997). He is the author of *From War to Peace: On Conflict Resolution in the Global System* (1994) and has co-authored chapters in the SIPRI Yearbook since 1988.

Henry Wathen (United States) held a six-month internship at SIPRI in 1999–2000 on the SIPRI projects Conflicts and Peace Enforcement, and Conflict Prevention, Management and Resolution.

Reinhilde Weidacher (Italy) is a Researcher on the SIPRI Military Expenditure and Arms Production Project. She is the author of a report for the Swedish Defence Research Establishment on the Italian arms industry (1998) and co-author (with Elisabeth Sköns) of a chapter on the economics of arms production for the *Encyclopedia of Violence, Peace and Conflict* (1999) and of the forthcoming SIPRI Research Report *Arms Production in Western Europe in the 1990s*.

Pieter D. Wezeman (Netherlands) is a Researcher on the SIPRI Arms Transfers Project. He has co-authored (with Siemon T. Wezeman) several articles and papers on arms exports issues. He has contributed to the SIPRI Yearbook since 1995 and is responsible for the maintenance of the Arms Transfers Project's Internet pages. From 2000 he is concentrating on the issue of small arms transfers.

Siemon T. Wezeman (Netherlands) is a Researcher on the SIPRI Arms Transfers Project. He is co-author (with Edward J. Laurance and Herbert Wulf) of the SIPRI Research Report *Arms Watch: SIPRI Report on the First Year of the UN Register of Conventional Arms* (1993), (with Bates Gill and J. N. Mak) of *ASEAN Arms Acquisitions: Developing Transparency* (1995) and (with Pieter D. Wezeman) of a paper for the Bonn International Center for Conversion (BICC) on Dutch surplus weapon exports (1996). He has contributed to the SIPRI Research Report *Arms, Transparency and Security in South-East Asia* (1997) and to the SIPRI Yearbook since 1993.

Dr Jean Pascal Zanders (Belgium) is Leader of the SIPRI Chemical and Biological Warfare Project. He was previously Research Associate at the Centre for Peace and Security Studies at the Free University of Brussels. He has published extensively on chemical and biological weapon issues in English, Dutch and French since 1986 and has edited two books: *Chemical Weapons Proliferation* (1991, with Eric Remacle) and *The 2nd Gulf War and the CBW Threat* (1995). He has contributed to the SIPRI Yearbook since 1997 and to the SIPRI volume *The Challenge of Old Chemical Munitions and Toxic Armament Wastes* (1997). He was a co-author of the SIPRI Fact Sheets on the Chemical Weapons Convention (1997) and the United Nations Special Commission on Iraq (1998). He is the author of the article 'Assessing the risk of chemical and biological weapon proliferation to terrorists' in *Nonproliferation Review* (fall 1999) and co-author (with Elisabeth M. French) of the article 'Article XI of the Chemical Weapons Convention: between irrelevance and indispensability' in *Contemporary Security Policy* (1999).

Dr Nicholas Zarimpas (Greece) is Leader of SIPRI's Project on Military Technology and International Security. Previously, he worked on plutonium management and nuclear fuel cycle issues as a guest scientist at the Japan Nuclear Cycle Development Institute and as an administrator at the Nuclear Energy Agency of the Organisation for Economic Co-operation and Development (OECD). He has also held appointments with the Joint Research Centre Ispra and the Environment Directorate-General of the European Commission. During the past 10 years he has acted as scientific secretary to several international multidisciplinary research, technological and policy committees.

Staffan Ångman (Sweden) is a Research Assistant on the Uppsala Conflict Data Project at the Department of Peace and Conflict Research, Uppsala University. He contributed to the Yearbook in 1999.

SIPRI Yearbook 2000: Armaments, Disarmament and International Security

Oxford University Press, Oxford, 2000, 758 pp.
(Stockholm International Peace Research Institute)
ISBN 0-19-924162-7

ABSTRACTS

ROTFELD, A. D., 'Introduction: In search of a new security system for the 21st century', in *SIPRI Yearbook 2000*, pp. 1–12.

Today globalization generates interdependence and cooperation. The international security system should be inclusive, and security cooperation and mutual reassurance should replace mutual deterrence, associated with balance-of-power politics. Unlike the bipolarity and ideological clarity of the cold war era, the world today has no clear-cut dividing lines or overriding threat. A critical element of the shaping of a new international system is the ever growing recognition of democratic principles, respect for human rights and the rule of law, and market economy as the common values. International structures, organizations and institutions should be seen as forums in which national security interests can be addressed. This means that the new international system will function only when states find that it ensures their security more effectively than exclusive reliance on national strategies.

SEYBOLT, T. B., 'The war in the Democratic Republic of Congo', in *SIPRI Yearbook 2000*, pp. 59–75.

The Democratic Republic of Congo is the site of one of the world's most complicated wars. Since it began in August 1998, the armed forces of nine states and at least nine rebel groups have fought for control of the DRC Government; control of governments in Angola, Burundi, Rwanda and Uganda; and access to mineral wealth—all fuelled by ethnic hatred. The involvement of governments, insurgents and refugees from countries in central, western and southern Africa means that the course of the war and its outcome will influence political stability and economic development throughout central Africa for years to come.

SEYBOLT, T. B. in collaboration with the UPPSALA CONFLICT DATA PROJECT, 'Major armed conflicts', in *SIPRI Yearbook 2000*, pp. 15–49.

In 1999 there were 27 major armed conflicts in 25 countries, 2 of which were interstate conflicts. The number of major armed conflicts was unchanged from 1998 and continued the pattern of fewer major armed conflicts at the end than at the beginning of the decade. Most conflicts were in Africa: there were 11 in Africa, 9 in Asia, 3 in the Middle East, 2 in Europe and 2 in South America. More than 1000 people died in each of 14 of the conflicts, far fewer than 1000 people died in 11, and nearly 1000 died in 2 conflicts. There were five cases of foreign military intervention, three of which were authorized by an international organization, but only one by the United Nations.

DWAN, R., 'Armed conflict, prevention, management and resolution', in *SIPRI Yearbook 2000*, pp. 77–134.

In 1999 there was an increase in the number and type of international peace operations, notably in the Democratic Republic of Congo, Kosovo, Sierra Leone and East Timor. The changing nature of peacekeeping was demonstrated in Kosovo where, following NATO's non-authorized intervention, the UN leads a complex peace-building mission coordinating the activities of several regional and non-governmental organizations. The UN-tasked Australian-led multinational force in East Timor demonstrated a new and potentially efficient model for peace operations. International organizations began to give serious attention to conflict prevention in 1999, even as the limits of consensus on the rights and responsibilities of the international community in relation to sovereign states became more marked.

CHUFRIN, G., 'Russia: separatism and conflicts in the North Caucasus', in *SIPRI Yearbook 2000*, pp. 157–80.

Separatism is one of the most dangerous threats to Russian national security and territorial integrity today. It is particularly strong in the North Caucasus, where separatist forces often act under the guise of ethnic or religious movements. Although in most cases the Russian federal authorities tried to fight separatism by political means, in 1999 in Dagestan and Chechnya they had to resort to the use of force in order to defeat the Chechen-led armed rebellion. By the end of the year the federal forces had re-established control over most parts of Chechnya lost in the previous war, in 1994–96, but failed to achieve a decisive military victory over the separatists. Neither was there any political resolution of the conflict. As the conflict in Chechnya caused many casualties and a massive refugee problem among its civilian population, the Russian Government came under strong criticism from the West on humanitarian grounds and relations between Russia and the West soured.

ROTFELD, A. D., 'Europe: the new transatlantic agenda', in *SIPRI Yearbook 2000*, pp. 181–208.

The future of transatlantic relations is dependent on how the differing interests of the USA and Europe on three planes—economic, political and military—can be resolved. In essence, they are inseparable. The dilemma which the states of Europe face can be boiled down to the question how they are to secure the USA's politico-military commitment and leading role without acquiescing in US domination of and hegemony in Europe. The US dilemma concerns how the USA can help to consolidate the EU's independent capability to act in the field of security and defence policy without undermining NATO and its own role. At the Washington NATO summit meeting and the Cologne and Helsinki EU summit meetings, the EU gained recognition by NATO as a partner on defence matters. The OSCE Charter for European Security codified arrangements for closer cooperation between all security-related international institutions in Europe. The renationalization of security policies and too-slow progress in shaping a common European security and defence policy are much greater threats than too-rapid change.

SKÖNS, E., LOOSE-WEINTRAUB, E., OMITOOGUN, W. and STÅLENHEIM, P., 'Military expenditure', in *SIPRI Yearbook 2000*, pp. 231–59.

Military expenditure increased in many regions during 1999, after a long period of declining military spending, largely coinciding with the post-cold war period. Total world military expenditure increased by 2.1 per cent in real terms in 1999 and amounted to *c*. $780 billion in current terms. While this is almost one-third less than 10 years earlier, it represents a significant share of world economic resources—2.6 per cent of world gross national product. The rise is due primarily to increases in the major spender countries, including the USA, France, Russia and China, but military expenditure has also grown in Africa, Asia and other parts of Europe. The countries with the heaviest economic burden of military expenditure are generally poor countries involved in armed conflict and/or located in areas of tension. Furthermore, in many countries at war official military expenditure figures grossly understate the economic burden of military activities.

OMITOOGUN, W., 'Military expenditure in Africa', in *SIPRI Yearbook 2000*, pp. 281–98.

Military expenditure in Africa has been increasing since 1997, after a relatively long period of decline. The increase is due primarily to the involvement of many countries in the region in armed conflict, either directly or indirectly. The costs and methods of financing armed conflict vary but usually include resource absorption outside the official defence budget, making it difficult to accurately report on the amount of economic resources committed to military activities. While African military expenditure represents a small share of the world total, it constitutes a heavy economic burden in many African countries where social needs are competing for scarce economic resources.

SKÖNS, E. and WEIDACHER, R., 'Arms production', in *SIPRI Yearbook 2000*, pp. 299–326.

Restructuring of arms production continued during 1999, while the decline in the general level of arms production appears to have ceased towards the end of the 1990s. The aggregate arms sales of the SIPRI top 100 arms-producing companies in the OECD and developing countries, which account for roughly three-quarters of total world arms production, declined by 29 per cent during the first half of the 1990s, but by only 3 per cent during the period 1995–98. The decline in Russian arms production ceased in 1997: in 1999 it increased by 37 per cent, although it still amounted only to 13.5 per cent of Soviet arms production in 1991. The restructuring process in the OECD countries arms industries during the 1990s has resulted in greater concentration, particularly among the larger companies, and in diversification from military to civilian products in industry and in individual companies. A few companies have tended instead to specialize in military production, thereby increasing their dependence on arms sales and often on arms exports.

KILE, S., 'Nuclear arms control and non-proliferation', in *SIPRI Yearbook 2000*, pp. 443–77.

In 1999 nuclear arms control progress continued to stagnate. The controversy over the USA's plans for a limited national missile defence system and the future of the ABM Treaty complicated US–Russian efforts to negotiate further reductions in their nuclear arsenals and threatened to reverse previous achievements. The Russian Parliament again failed to vote on whether to ratify the START II Treaty. There was little progress made in advancing other important measures. Efforts to bring into force the Comprehensive Nuclear Test-Ban Treaty (CTBT) were set back by the US Senate's vote to reject ratification of the treaty. The opening of negotiations in the Conference on Disarmament on a Fissile Material Treaty (FMT) continued to be blocked by a procedural impasse.

HAGELIN, B., WEZEMAN, P. D. and WEZEMAN S. T., 'Transfers of major conventional weapons', in *SIPRI Yearbook 2000*, pp. 339–67.

Since 1995 the transfer of major conventional weapons, as measured by the five-year moving average of the SIPRI trend indicator, has been fairly stable, at about half of the peak level during the cold war. The USA was the dominant supplier, accounting in 1995–99 for almost as much as all other suppliers combined. Russia was the second largest supplier in 1995–99, as well as for 1999. The other major suppliers were France, the UK and Germany. The major recipients in 1995–99 were Taiwan, Saudi Arabia, Turkey, South Korea and Egypt. In 1999 Taiwan was the largest recipient for the third year in a row. Six of the leading recipients of weapons from the main suppliers were involved in major armed conflicts. Increased arms transfer reporting permitted SIPRI to estimate that in 1998 the value of the global arms *trade* was in the magnitude of $35–49 billion. For the future, the USA will remain the major supplier and the major military investor in research and development. Russia's long-term position as a major competitor in advanced weapons is uncertain.

ZARIMPAS, N., 'Nuclear verification: the IAEA strengthened safeguards system', in *SIPRI Yearbook 2000*, pp. 496–508.

International Atomic Energy Agency (IAEA) safeguards are aimed at providing increased assurance of the absence of undeclared nuclear activities and material, with the ultimate goal of reinforcing the global nuclear non-proliferation regime. Particular emphasis is given to the reasons for the development of strengthened safeguards, namely, the IAEA's growing list of responsibilities, its limited resources and the ambitions of some states to acquire nuclear weapons.

ZANDERS, J. P. and WAHLBERG, M., 'Chemical and biological weapon developments and arms control', in *SIPRI Yearbook 2000*, pp. 509–36.

Agreement on technical matters ensured the advancement of the Chemical Weapons Convention (CWC) and the negotiation of the protocol to the Biological and Toxin Weapons Convention (BTWC). Russia was the only declared possessor not to have started the destruction of its CW stockpile and serious international concern persisted that it still has illegal BW programmes. The USA was perceived as not fully committed to multilateral disarmament. It was in technical non-compliance with the CWC regarding initial industry declarations and it opposes strong compliance mechanisms for the future BTWC regime. The US Congress reduced the appropriations for assistance programmes that provide funding to eliminate or prevent the proliferation of chemical and biological weapons (CBW) in Russia. Proliferation of CBW is a major concern. Some states are unwilling to join the CWC despite the effect on their national economies in terms of reduced access to key commodities.

ZANDERS, J. P., KARLSSON, E., MELIN, L., NÄSLUND, E. and THANING, L., 'Risk assessment of terrorism with chemical and biological weapons', in *SIPRI Yearbook 2000*, pp. 537–59.

Chemical and biological weapons (CBW) represent the new qualitative element in the terrorist threat. The authors analyse the requirements for setting up CBW acquisition programmes, profile terrorist organizations and present computer models of the release of chemical or biological warfare agents. The processes for manufacturing and disseminating CBW in sufficiently large quantities are complex and there is little likelihood of the recurrence of an event like the 1995 release of sarin in the Tokyo underground. Governments face a threat that is possible but unlikely to occur. In the light of the potential consequences of a terrorist attack, no government can remain unprepared. The key issue is to devise and execute balanced policies. Overreaction can easily lead to country-wide anxiety and paranoia. In such an atmosphere, hoaxes may become as efficient as actual attacks.

WAHLBERG, M., LEITENBERG, M. and ZANDERS, J. P., 'The future of chemical and biological weapon disarmament in Iraq: from UNSCOM to UNMOVIC', in *SIPRI Yearbook 2000*, pp. 560–76.

Between 1991 and 1999 the United Nations Special Commission on Iraq (UNSCOM) was unable to complete the total elimination of Iraq's chemical and biological weapon capabilities and to set up a long-term monitoring mechanism to ensure that Iraq does not acquire these weapons in the future. The UN Security Council, succumbing to the short-term interests of some members, was unable to deal with Iraq's blatant and determined violation of the UN's own rules. Serious doubts therefore exist whether UNSCOM's successor organization, the UN Monitoring, Verification and Inspection Commission (UNMOVIC), will be able to complete UNSCOM's tasks.

LACHOWSKI, Z., 'Conventional arms control', in *SIPRI Yearbook 2000*, pp. 577–612.

A long-awaited breakthrough in the European arms control regime took place in 1999. The Agreement on Adaptation of the CFE Treaty and the Vienna Document 1999 were signed at the Istanbul OSCE summit in November. This stood in contrast to Russian opposition to NATO enlargement and worsened NATO–Russian relations in the wake of the intervention in Kosovo and the conflict in Chechnya. The intervention in Kosovo marred regional arms control endeavours in the Balkans, but some progress was reported later. Conventional arms control outside Europe was rather uneventful, except in Latin America, which reflected the general stalemate in this field.

LACHOWSKI, Z., 'Confidence- and security-building measures in Europe', *in SIPRI Yearbook 2000*, pp. 613–25.

The modernization of confidence- and security-building measures (CSBMs) was concluded in 1999. Regional approaches included in the Vienna Document 1999 should help better handle contingencies below the pan-European level. The Kosovo crisis and the war in Chechnya became the hard litmus test for the 'all weather' relevance of CSBMs. The regional CSBM experiment in the Balkans is proceeding fairly well, albeit still under the umbrella of international institutions and military forces. It is to be hoped that the network of various arms control related agreements will inject enough stability and security to help make the Balkan peace process irreversible.

ANTHONY, I., 'Responses to proliferation: the North Korean ballistic missile programme', in *SIPRI Yearbook 2000*, pp. 647–66.

In the 1990s North Korea has accelerated the development of large missiles, which have been tested in various configurations and could provide the capability to deliver a warhead over intercontinental ranges. North Korea has not met its obligations under bilateral safeguards agreements with the International Atomic Energy Agency, strengthening the suspicion that North Korea has a clandestine nuclear weapon programme. Given the continued state of high tension on the Korean peninsula, there is a widespread concern about the implications of weapon development in North Korea for regional and international security. In September 1999, the United States and North Korea reached an agreement, by which North Korea is expected to suspend the testing of its long-range ballistic missile programme. The chapter describes the international responses to the North Korean ballistic missile programme.

ANTHONY, I., 'Multilateral weapon and technology export controls', in *SIPRI Yearbook 2000*, pp. 667–87.

Recent developments in five multilateral weapon and technology export control regimes show how the pace of expansion in membership and participation has slowed down. The 35 states that participate in the Wassenaar Arrangement on Export Controls completed the first five-year review of the operation of the regime. The review led to agreement on expanded transparency measures for conventional arms transfers.

Errata

SIPRI Yearbook 1999: Armaments, Disarmament and International Security

Page 306, table 7A.2, figures for Estonia, 1992 and 1995–1997:	Should read: *1992,* 64.0; *1995,* 427; *1996,* 546; *1997,* 750.
Page 313, table 7A.3, figures for Estonia, 1992 and 1995–98:	Should read: *1992,* (20.1); *1995,* 37.2; *1996,* 38.7; *1997,* 48.1; *1998,* 50.6.
Page 316, table 7A.4, figure for Estonia, 1997:	Should read: *1997,* 1.2.
Page 634, last full paragraph, lines 2–3:	'Train and Equip Program to Croatia, accusing the latter of obstructing the Federation, not integrating some HVO (Croatian) military units into the' should read: 'Train and Equip Program to the Croatian Defence Council (HVO), accusing the latter of obstructing the Federation, not integrating some HVO military units into the'.

INDEX